AUTOMOTIVE ELECTRICAL AND ENGINE PERFORMANCE

EIGHTH EDITION

James D. Halderman

 Pearson

Vice President, Portfolio Management: Andrew Gilfillan
Executive Portfolio Manager: Jenifer Niles
Portfolio Management Assistant: Lara Dimmick
Senior Vice President, Marketing: David Gesell
Marketing Coordinator: Elizabeth MacKenzie-Lamb
Director, Digital Studio and Content Production: Brian Hyland
Digital Studio Producer: Allison Longley
Managing Producer: Cynthia Zonneveld
Managing Producer: Jennifer Sargunar
Content Producer: Holly Shufeldt
Content Producer: Faraz Sharique Ali
Manager, Rights Management: Johanna Burke
Operations Specialist: Deidra Smith
Cover Design: Pearson CSC
Cover Credit: Mevans/Getty Images
Full-Service Management and Composition: Integra Software Service Pvt. Ltd.
Printer/Binder: LSC Communications,Inc.
Cover Printer: Phoenix Color/Hagerstown
Text Font: Times LT Pro

Library of Congress Cataloging-in-Publication Data

Names: Halderman, James D., author.

Title: Automotive electrical and engine performance / James D. Halderman.

Description: Eigth edition. | Boston : Pearson, [2018]

Identifiers: LCCN 2018022216| ISBN 9780135224809 | ISBN 0135224802

Subjects: LCSH: Automobiles—Motors—Maintenance and repair. | Automobiles—Electric equipment—Maintenance and repair. | Automobiles—Performance.

Classification: LCC TL210 .H2885 2018 | DDC 629.2/72—dc23
    LC record available at https://lccn.loc.gov/2018022216

3 2021

ISBN 10:   0-13-522480-2
ISBN 13: 978-0-13-522480-9

BRIEF CONTENTS

CONTENTS

ABOUT THE AUTHOR

JIM HALDERMAN brings a world of experience, knowledge, and talent to his work. His automotive service experience includes working as a flat-rate technician, a business owner, and a professor of automotive technology at a leading U.S. community college.

He has a bachelor of science degree from Ohio Northern University and a master's degree from Miami University in Oxford, Ohio. Jim also holds a U.S. patent for an electronic transmission control device. He is an ASE-certified Master Automotive Technician and is also Advanced Engine Performance (L1) ASE certified. Jim is the author of many automotive textbooks, all published by Pearson Education. Jim has presented numerous technical seminars to national audiences, including the California Automotive Teachers (CAT) and the Illinois College Automotive Instructor Association (ICAIA). He is also a member and presenter at the North American Council of Automotive Teachers (NACAT). Jim was also named Regional Teacher of the Year by General Motors Corporation and a member of the advisory committee for the department of technology at Ohio Northern University. Jim and his wife, Michelle, live in Dayton, Ohio. They have two children. You can reach Jim at

jim@jameshalderman.com

SPECIAL THANKS   The author wishes to thank Chuck Taylor of Sinclair Community College in Dayton, Ohio, and Greg Pfahl who helped with many of the photos. A special thanks to Dick Krieger, Tom Birch. Curt Ward, and Jeff Rehkopf for their detailed and thorough review of the manuscript before publication. Most of all, I wish to thank Michelle Halderman for her assistance in all phases of manuscript preparation.

—James D. Halderman

ACKNOWLEDGMENTS

A large number of people and organizations have cooperated in providing the reference material and technical information used in this text. The author wishes to express sincere thanks to the following individuals for their special contributions:

Carl Borsani- Graphic Home
Randy Briggs, Car Quest Technical Institute
Randy Dillman
Rick Escalambre, Skyline College
Bill Fulton, Ohio Automotive Technology
Jim Linder, Linder Technical Services
Scot Manna
Dan Marinucci, Communique'
Albin Moore
Jim Morton, Automotive Training Center (ATC)
Dr. Norman Nall
Dave Scaler, Mechanic's Education Association
John Thornton, Autotrain
Mark Warren

PREFACE

Automotive Electrical and Engine Performance covers content and topics specified for both Electrical/Electronic System (A6) and Engine Performance (A8) by ASE/NATEF, as well as the practical skills that students must master to be successful in the industry. With this textbook, students preparing for the automotive profession get a firm background in the principles and practices of diagnosing and troubleshooting automotive electrical, electronic, and computer systems. The book is written in a clear, concise format at a level of detail that far exceeds most other texts. Well-known author, Jim Halderman, uses his helpful real-world tips and visuals to bring concepts to life and guide students through the procedures they'll use on the job.

UPDATES TO THE EIGHTH EDITION

The following changes and updates have been made to the new eighth edition based on requests from instructors and readers from throughout North America.

- Over 75 new full color line drawings and photos have been added to the new edition to help bring the subject to life.
- Updated throughout and correlated to the latest ASE/NATEF tasks.

- The number of chapters has increased from 43 to 46 chapters by splitting up larger chapters and placing the content into shorter more concise chapters.
- A new chapter on **Safety, Comfort and Convenience Accessories** (Chapter 23) has been added.
- A new chapter called **Air Management Systems** (Chapter 24) has been added.
- **Immobilizer Systems** (Chapter 25) has been added to the new edition.
- The ignition system chapter was split into two shorter chapters (Chapters 29 and 30) to make teaching and learning this topic easier.
- The new Tier 3 emission standards have been added (Chapter 41)

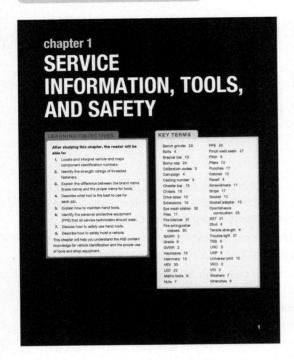

chapter 1
SERVICE INFORMATION, TOOLS, AND SAFETY

LEARNING OBJECTIVES AND KEY TERMS appear at the beginning of each chapter to help students and instructors focus on the most important material in each chapter. The chapter objectives are based on specific ASE tasks.

 **TECH TIP**

Right to Tighten

It is sometimes confusing which way to rotate a wrench or screwdriver, especially when the head of the fastener is pointing away from you. To help visualize while looking at the fastener, say "righty tighty, lefty loosey."

TECH TIP feature real-world advice and "tricks of the trade" from ASE-certified master technicians.

 **SAFETY TIP**

Shop Cloth Disposal

Always dispose of oily shop cloths in an enclosed container to prevent a fire. ● **SEE FIGURE 1–69.** Whenever oily cloths are thrown together on the floor or workbench, a chemical reaction can occur, which can ignite the cloth even without an open flame. This process of ignition without an open flame is called **spontaneous combustion**.

SAFETY TIPS alert students to possible hazards on the job and how to avoid them.

 CASE STUDY

Shocking Experience

A customer complained that after driving for a while, he got a static shock whenever he grabbed the door handle when exiting the vehicle. The customer thought that there must be an electrical fault and that the shock was coming from the vehicle itself. In a way, the shock was caused by the vehicle, but it was not a fault. The service technician sprayed the cloth seats with an anti-static spray and the problem did not reoccur. Obviously, a static charge was being created by the movement of the driver's clothing on the seats and discharged when the driver touched the metal door handle. ● **SEE FIGURE 9–39**.

Summary:

- **Complaint**—Vehicle owner complained that he got shocked when the door handle was touched.
- **Cause**—Static electricity was found to be the cause and not a fault with the vehicle.
- **Correction**—The seats and carpet were sprayed with an anti-static spray and this corrected the concern.

CASE STUDY present students with actual automotive scenarios and show how these common (and sometimes uncommon) problems were diagnosed and repaired.

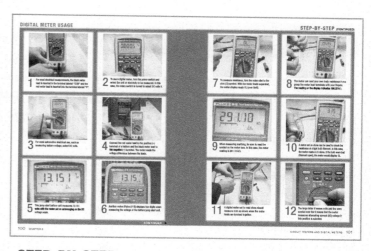

How Many Types of Screw Heads Are Used in Automotive Applications?

There are many, including Torx, hex (also called Allen), plus many others used in custom vans and motor homes. ● **SEE FIGURE 1–9.**

FREQUENTLY ASKED QUESTIONS are based on the author's own experience and provide answers to many of the most common questions asked by students and beginning service technicians.

NOTE: A parallel circuit drops the voltage from source voltage to zero (ground) across the resistance in each leg of the circuit.

NOTES provide students with additional technical information to give them a greater understanding of a specific task or procedure.

CAUTION: *Never* use hardware store (nongraded) bolts, studs, or nuts on any vehicle steering, suspension, or brake component. Always use the exact size and grade of hardware that is specified and used by the vehicle manufacturer.

CAUTIONS alert students about potential damage to the vehicle that can occur during a specific task or service procedure.

WARNING

Do not touch any orange wiring or component without following the vehicle manufacturer's procedures and wearing the specified personal protective equipment.

WARNINGS alert students to potential dangers to themselves during a specific task or service procedure.

STEP-BY-STEP photo sequences show, in detail, the steps involved in performing a specific task or service procedure.

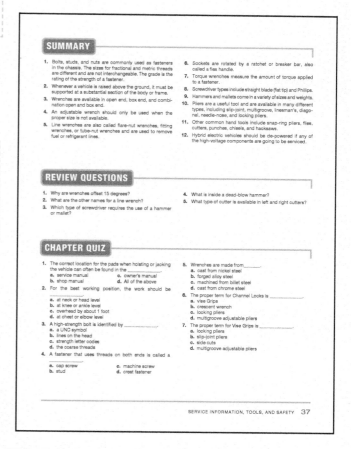

THE REVIEW QUESTIONS AND CHAPTER QUIZ at the end of each chapter help students review the material presented in the chapter and test themselves to see how much they've learned.

INSTRUCTOR RESOURCES

RESOURCES IN PRINT AND ONLINE
Automotive Technology

NAME OF SUPPLEMENT	PRINT	ONLINE	AUDIENCE	DESCRIPTION
Instructor Resource Manual 013525745X		✔	Instructors	NEW! The Ultimate teaching aid: Chapter summaries, key terms, chapter learning objectives, and lecture resources.
TestGen 0135257999		✔	Instructors	Test generation software and test bank for the text.
PowerPoint Presentation 0135257409		✔	Instructors	Slides include a lecture outline of the text to help instructors with in class instruction.
Image Bank 0135257433		✔	Instructors	All of the images from the textbook to create customized slides.
ASE Task Sheets – for instructors 0135257638		✔	Instructors	Downloadable ASE task sheets for easy customization.
ASE Task Sheets – for Students 0135257417	✔		Students	Student's can purchase a study activity manual that correlates ASE Automobile Standards to chapters and page numbers in the text.
VitalSource eBook 0135257492		✔	Students	An alternative to purchasing the print textbook, students can save up to 50% off the suggested list price of the print text. Visit **www.vitalsource.com**

All online resources can be downloaded from the Instructor's Resource Center: **www.pearsonhighered.com/ automotive** *Search for your specific title there and select the Resources.*

TECHNICAL AND CONTENT REVIEWERS

The following people reviewed the manuscript before production and checked it for technical accuracy and clarity of presentation. Their suggestions and recommendations were included in the final draft of the manuscript. Their input helped make this textbook clear and technically accurate while maintaining the easy-to-read style that has made other books from the same author so popular.

Jim Anderson
Greenville High School

Victor Bridges
Umpqua Community College

Dr. Roger Donovan
Illinois Central College

A. C. Durdin
Moraine Park Technical College

Al Engledahl
College of Dupage

Larry Hagelberger
Upper Valley Joint Vocational School

Oldrick Hajzler
Red River College

Betsy Hoffman
Vermont Technical College

Richard Krieger
Michigan Institute of Technology

Steven T. Lee
Lincoln Technical Institute

Carlton H. Mabe, Sr.
Virginia Western Community College

Roy Marks
Owens Community College

Tony Martin
University of Alaska Southeast

Kerry Meier
San Juan College

Fritz Peacock
Indiana Vocational Technical College

Dennis Peter
NAIT (Canada)

Greg Pfahl
Miami-Jacobs Career College

Kenneth Redick
Hudson Valley Community College

Jeff Rehkopf
Florida State College

Mitchell Walker
St. Louis Community College at Forest Park

Curt Ward
Joliet Junior College

Jennifer Wise
Sinclair Community College

chapter 1
SERVICE INFORMATION, TOOLS, AND SAFETY

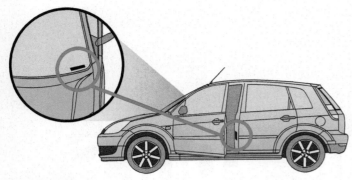

FIGURE 1–1 The vehicle identification number (VIN) is visible through the base of the windshield and on a decal inside the driver's door.

1 = United States	J = Japan	T = Czechoslovakia
2 = Canada	K = Korea	U = Romania
3 = Mexico	L = China	V = France
4 = United States	M = India	W = Germany
5 = United States	N = Turkey	X = Russia
6 = Australia	P = Philippines	Y = Sweden
8 = Argentina	R = Taiwan	Z = Italy
9 = Brazil	S = England	

CHART 1–1

The first number or letter in the VIN identifies the country where the vehicle was made.

VEHICLE IDENTIFICATION

MAKE, MODEL, AND YEAR All service work requires that the vehicle and its components be properly identified. The most common identification is the make, model, and year of the vehicle.

Make: e.g., Chevrolet

Model: e.g., Impala

Year: e.g., 2008

VEHICLE IDENTIFICATION NUMBER The year of the vehicle is often difficult to determine exactly. A model may be introduced as the next year's model as soon as January of the previous year. Typically, a new model year starts in September or October of the year prior to the actual new year, but not always. This is why the **vehicle identification number**, usually abbreviated **VIN**, is so important. ● **SEE FIGURE 1–1.**

Since 1981, all vehicle manufacturers have used a VIN that is 17 characters long. Although every vehicle manufacturer assigns various letters or numbers within these 17 characters, there are some constants, including:

- The first number or letter designates the country of origin. ● **SEE CHART 1–1.**
- The fourth or fifth character is the car line/series.
- The sixth character is the body style.
- The seventh character is the restraint system.
- The eighth character is often the engine code. (Some engines cannot be determined by the VIN number.)
- The tenth character represents the year on all vehicles. ● **SEE CHART 1–2.**

A = 1980/2010	L = 1990/2020	Y = 2000/2030
B = 1981/2011	M = 1991/2021	1 = 2001/2031
C = 1982/2012	N = 1992/2022	2 = 2002/2032
D = 1983/2013	P = 1993/2023	3 = 2003/2033
E = 1984/2014	R = 1994/2024	4 = 2004/2034
F = 1985/2015	S = 1995/2025	5 = 2005/2035
G = 1986/2016	T = 1996/2026	6 = 2006/2036
H = 1987/2017	V = 1997/2027	7 = 2007/2037
J = 1988/2018	W = 1998/2028	8 = 2008/2038
K = 1989/2019	X = 1999/2029	9 = 2009/2039

CHART 1–2

The pattern repeats every 30 years for the year of manufacture.

VEHICLE SAFETY CERTIFICATION LABEL A vehicle safety certification label is attached to the left side pillar post on the rearward-facing section of the left front door. This label indicates the month and year of manufacture, as well as, the **gross vehicle weight rating (GVWR)**, the **gross axle weight rating (GAWR)**, and the vehicle identification number.

VECI LABEL The **vehicle emissions control information (VECI)** label under the hood of the vehicle shows informative settings and emission hose routing information. ● **SEE FIGURE 1–2.**

The VECI label (sticker) can be located on the bottom side of the hood, the radiator fan shroud, the radiator core support, or on the strut towers. The VECI label usually includes the following information:

- Engine identification
- Emissions standard that the vehicle meets
- Vacuum hose routing diagram

FIGURE 1–2 The vehicle emissions control information (VECI) sticker is placed under the hood.

FIGURE 1–3 A typical calibration code sticker on the case of a controller. The information on the sticker is often needed when ordering parts or a replacement controller.

- Base ignition timing (if adjustable)
- Spark plug type and gap
- Valve lash
- Emission calibration code

CALIBRATION CODES **Calibration codes** are usually located on Powertrain Control Modules (PCMs) or other controllers. Whenever diagnosing an engine operating fault, it is often necessary to use the calibration code to be sure that the vehicle is the subject of a technical service bulletin or other service procedure. ● **SEE FIGURE 1–3.**

CASTING NUMBERS When an engine part, such as a block is cast, a number is put into the mold to identify the casting. ● **SEE FIGURE 1–4.** These **casting numbers** can be used to identify the part and check dimensions, such as the cubic inch displacement and other information, such as the year of manufacture. Sometimes changes are made to the mold, yet the casting number is not changed. Most

FIGURE 1–4 Casting numbers on major components can be either cast or stamped.

often the casting number is the best piece of identifying information that the service technician can use for identifying an engine.

SERVICE INFORMATION

SERVICE MANUALS Service information is used by the service technician to determine specifications and service procedures, and any needed special tools.

Factory and aftermarket service manuals contain specifications and service procedures. While factory service manuals cover just one year and one or more models of the same vehicle, most aftermarket service manufacturers cover multiple years and/or models in one manual. Included in most service manuals are the following:

- Capacities and recommended specifications for all fluids
- Specifications including engine and routine maintenance items
- Testing procedures
- Service procedures including the use of special tools when needed

ELECTRONIC SERVICE INFORMATION Electronic service information is available mostly by subscription and provides access to an Internet site where service manual–type information is available. ● **SEE FIGURE 1–5.** Most vehicle manufacturers also offer electronic service information to their dealers and to most schools and colleges that offer corporate training programs.

FIGURE 1–5 Electronic service information is available from aftermarket sources, such as ALLDATA and Mitchell On Demand, as well as, on websites hosted by vehicle manufacturers.

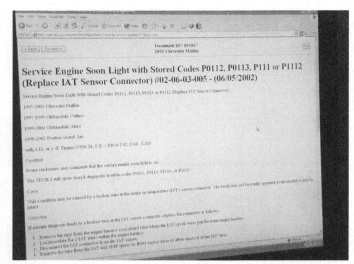

FIGURE 1–6 Technical service bulletins (TSBs) are issued by vehicle manufacturers when a fault occurs that affects many vehicles with the same problem. The TSB then provides the fix for the problem including any parts needed and detailed instructions.

TECHNICAL SERVICE BULLETINS **Technical service bulletins**, often abbreviated **TSBs**, sometimes called *technical service information bulletins* (*TSIBs*), are issued by the vehicle manufacturer to notify service technicians of a problem and include the necessary corrective action. Technical service bulletins are designed for dealership technicians but are republished by aftermarket companies, and made available along with other service information to shops and vehicle repair facilities. ● **SEE FIGURE 1–6.**

INTERNET The Internet has opened the field for information exchange and access to technical advice. One of the most useful websites is the International Automotive Technician's Network at **www.iatn.net**. This is a free site, but service technicians must register to join. If a small monthly sponsor fee is paid, the shop or service technician can gain access to the archives, which include thousands of successful repairs in the searchable database.

RECALLS AND CAMPAIGNS A **recall** or **campaign** is issued by a vehicle manufacturer and a notice is sent to all owners in the event of a safety-related fault or concern. While these faults may be repaired by shops, it is generally handled by a local dealer. Items that have created recalls in the past have included potential fuel system leakage problems, exhaust leakage, or electrical malfunctions that could cause a possible fire or the engine to stall. Unlike technical service bulletins whose cost is only covered when the vehicle is within the warranty period, a recall or campaign is always done at no cost to the vehicle owner.

? FREQUENTLY ASKED QUESTION

What Should Be Included on a Work Order?

A work order is a legal document that should include the following information:

1. Customer information
2. Identification of the vehicle including the VIN
3. Related service history information
4. The "three Cs":
   - Customer concern (complaint)
   - Cause of the concern
   - Correction or repairs that were required to return the vehicle to proper operation

THREADED FASTENERS

BOLTS AND THREADS Most of the threaded fasteners used on vehicles are **bolts**. Bolts are called *cap screws* when they are threaded into a casting. Automotive service technicians usually refer to these fasteners as *bolts*, regardless of how they are used. In this chapter, they are called bolts. Sometimes, studs are used for threaded fasteners. A **stud** is a short rod with threads on both ends. Often, a stud will have coarse threads on one end and fine threads on the other end. The end of the stud with coarse threads is screwed into the casting. A nut is used on the opposite end to hold the parts together.

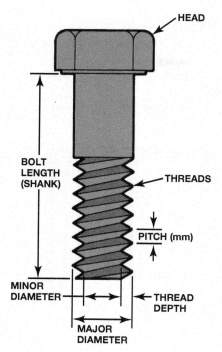

FIGURE 1–7 The dimensions of a typical bolt showing where sizes are measured.

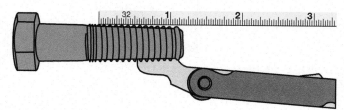

FIGURE 1–8 Thread pitch gauge used to measure the pitch of the thread. This bolt has 13 threads to the inch.

The fastener threads *must* match the threads in the casting or nut. The threads may be measured either in fractions of an inch (called fractional) or in metric units. The size is measured across the outside of the threads, called the *crest* of the thread. ● SEE FIGURE 1–7.

FRACTIONAL BOLTS
Fractional threads are either coarse or fine. The coarse threads are called **unified national coarse** (**UNC**), and the fine threads are called **unified national fine** (**UNF**). Standard combinations of sizes and number of threads per inch (called **pitch**) are used. Pitch can be measured with a thread pitch gauge as shown in ● SEE FIGURE 1–8. Bolts are identified by their diameter and length as measured from below the head, and not by the size of the head or the size of the wrench used to remove or install the bolt.

| | THREADS PER INCH | | OUTSIDE |
SIZE	NC UNC	NF UNF	DIAMETER INCHES
0	..	80	0.0600
1	64	..	0.0730
1	..	72	0.0730
2	56	..	0.0860
2	..	64	0.0860
3	48	..	0.0990
3	..	56	0.0990
4	40	..	0.1120
4	..	48	0.1120
5	40	..	0.1250
5	..	44	0.1250
6	32	..	0.1380
6	..	40	0.1380
8	32	..	0.1640
8	..	36	0.1640
10	24	..	0.1900
10	..	32	0.1900
12	24	..	0.2160
12	..	28	0.2160
1/4	20	..	0.2500
1/4	..	28	0.2500
5/16	18	..	0.3125
5/16	..	24	0.3125
3/8	16	..	0.3750
3/8	..	24	0.3750
7/16	14	..	0.4375
7/16	..	20	0.4375
1/2	13	..	0.5000
1/2	..	20	0.5000

CHART 1–3

American standard is one method of sizing fasteners.

Fractional thread sizes are specified by the diameter in fractions of an inch and the number of threads per inch. Typical UNC thread sizes would be 5/16–18 and 1/2–13. Similar UNF thread sizes would be 5/16–24 and 1/2–20. ● SEE CHART 1–3.

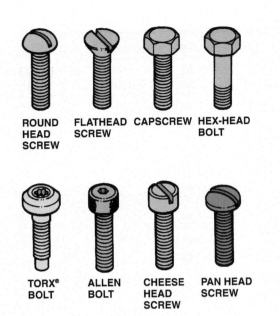

ROUND HEAD SCREW | FLATHEAD SCREW | CAPSCREW | HEX-HEAD BOLT

TORX® BOLT | ALLEN BOLT | CHEESE HEAD SCREW | PAN HEAD SCREW

FIGURE 1–9 Bolts and screws have many different heads that determine what tool is needed.

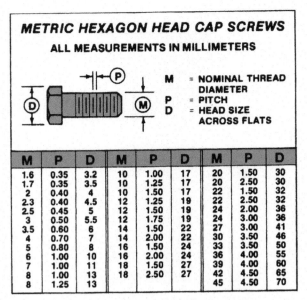

METRIC HEXAGON HEAD CAP SCREWS
ALL MEASUREMENTS IN MILLIMETERS

M = NOMINAL THREAD DIAMETER
P = PITCH
D = HEAD SIZE ACROSS FLATS

M	P	D	M	P	D	M	P	D
1.6	0.35	3.2	10	1.00	17	20	1.50	30
1.7	0.35	3.5	10	1.25	17	20	2.50	30
2	0.40	4	10	1.50	17	22	1.50	32
2.3	0.40	4.5	12	1.25	19	22	2.50	32
2.5	0.45	5	12	1.50	19	24	2.00	36
3	0.50	5.5	12	1.75	19	24	3.00	36
3.5	0.60	6	14	1.50	22	27	3.00	41
4	0.70	7	14	2.00	22	30	3.50	46
5	0.80	8	16	1.50	24	33	3.50	50
6	1.00	10	16	2.00	24	36	4.00	55
7	1.00	11	18	1.50	27	39	4.00	60
8	1.00	13	18	2.50	27	42	4.50	65
8	1.25	13				45	4.50	70

FIGURE 1–10 The metric system specifies fasteners by diameter, length, and pitch.

? FREQUENTLY ASKED QUESTION

How Many Types of Screw Heads Are Used in Automotive Applications?

There are many, including Torx, hex (also called Allen), plus many others used in custom vans and motor homes. ● SEE FIGURE 1–9.

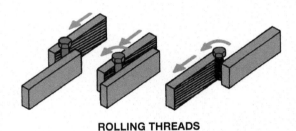

ROLLING THREADS

FIGURE 1–11 Stronger threads are created by cold-rolling a heat-treated bolt blank instead of cutting the threads, using a die.

METRIC BOLTS The size of a **metric bolt** is specified by the letter *M* followed by the diameter in millimeters (mm) across the outside (crest) of the threads. Typical metric sizes would be M8 and M12. Metric threads are specified by the thread diameter followed by X, and the distance between the threads measured in millimeters (M8 X 1.5). ● SEE FIGURE 1–10.

GRADES OF BOLTS Bolts are made from many different types of steel, and for this reason some are stronger than others. The strength or classification of a bolt is called the **grade**. The bolt heads are marked to indicate their grade strength.

The actual grade of bolts is two more than the number of lines on the bolt head. Metric bolts have a decimal number to indicate the grade. More lines or a higher grade number indicate a stronger bolt. In some cases, nuts and machine screws have similar grade markings. Higher grade bolts usually have threads that are rolled rather than cut, which also makes them stronger. ● SEE FIGURE 1–11.

CAUTION: *Never* use hardware store (nongraded) bolts, studs, or nuts on any vehicle steering, suspension, or brake component. Always use the exact size and grade of hardware that is specified and used by the vehicle manufacturer.

TENSILE STRENGTH OF FASTENERS Graded fasteners have a higher tensile strength than nongraded fasteners. **Tensile strength** is the maximum stress used under tension (lengthwise force) without causing failure of the fastener. Tensile strength is specified in pounds per square inch (PSI).

The strength and type of steel used in a bolt is supposed to be indicated by a raised mark on the head of the bolt. The type of mark depends on the standard to which the bolt was manufactured. Most often, bolts used in machinery are made to SAE Standard J429. ● SEE CHART 1–4 that shows the grade and specified tensile strength.

SAE BOLT DESIGNATIONS

SAE GRADE NO.	SIZE RANGE	TENSILE STRENGTH, PSI	MATERIAL	HEAD MARKING
1	1/4 through 1 1/2	60,000	Low or medium carbon steel	
2	1/4 through 3/4	74,000		
	7/8 through 1 1/2	60,000		
5	1/4 through 1	120,000	Medium carbon steel, quenched and tempered	
	1 1/8 through 1 1/2	105,000		
5.2	1/4 through 1	120,000	Low carbon martensite steel,* quenched and tempered	
7	1/4 through 1 1/2	133,000	Medium carbon alloy steel, quenched and tempered	
8	1/4 through 1 1/2	150,000	Medium carbon alloy steel, quenched and tempered	
8.2	1/4 through 1	150,000	Low carbon martensite steel,* quenched and tempered	

CHART 1-4

The tensile strength rating system as specified by the Society of Automotive Engineers (SAE).

*Martensite steel is a specific type of steel that can be cooled rapidly, thereby increasing its hardness. It is named after a German metallurgist, Adolf Martens.

Metric bolt tensile strength property class is shown on the head of the bolt as a number, such as 4.6, 8.8, 9.8, and 10.9; the higher the number, the stronger the bolt. ● **SEE FIGURE 1–12.**

NUTS Nuts are the female part of a threaded fastener. Most nuts used on cap screws have the same hex size as the cap screw head. Some inexpensive nuts use a hex size larger than the cap screw head. Metric nuts are often marked with dimples to show their strength. More dimples indicate stronger nuts. Some nuts and cap screws use interference fit threads to keep them from accidentally loosening. This means that the shape of the nut is slightly distorted or that a section of the threads is deformed. Nuts can also be kept from loosening with a nylon washer fastened in the nut or with a nylon patch or strip on the threads. ● **SEE FIGURE 1–13.**

NOTE: Most of these "locking nuts" are grouped together and are commonly referred to as *prevailing torque nuts.* This means that the nut will hold its tightness or torque and not loosen with movement or vibration. Most prevailing torque nuts should be replaced whenever removed to ensure that the nut will not loosen during service. Always follow the manufacturer's recommendations. Anaerobic sealers, such as Loctite, are used on the threads where the nut or cap screw must be both locked and sealed.

WASHERS Washers are often used under cap screw heads and under nuts. ● **SEE FIGURE 1–14.** Plain flat washers are used to provide an even clamping load around the fastener. Lock washers are added to prevent accidental loosening. In some accessories, the washers are locked onto the nut to provide easy assembly.

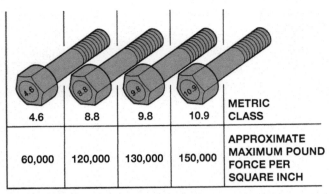

METRIC CLASS	4.6	8.8	9.8	10.9
APPROXIMATE MAXIMUM POUND FORCE PER SQUARE INCH	60,000	120,000	130,000	150,000

FIGURE 1–12 Metric bolt (cap screw) grade markings and approximate tensile strength.

HEX NUT **JAM NUT** **NYLON LOCK NUT** **CASTLE NUT** **ACORN NUT**

FIGURE 1–13 Nuts come in a variety of styles, including locking (prevailing torque) types, such as the distorted thread and nylon insert type.

FLAT WASHER **LOCK WASHER** **STAR WASHER** **STAR WASHER**

FIGURE 1–14 Washers come in a variety of styles, including flat and serrated used to help prevent a fastener from loosening.

 TECH TIP

A 1/2 Inch Wrench Does Not Fit a 1/2 Inch Bolt

A common mistake made by persons new to the automotive field is to think that the size of a bolt or nut is the size of the head. The size of the bolt or nut (outside diameter of the threads) is usually smaller than the size of the wrench or socket that fits the head of the bolt or nut. Examples are given in the following table:

Wrench Size	Thread Size
7/16 inch	1/4 inch
1/2 inch	5/16 inch
9/16 inch	3/8 inch
5/8 inch	7/16 inch
3/4 inch	1/2 inch
10 mm	6 mm
12 or 13 mm*	8 mm
14 or 17 mm*	10 mm

* European (Système International d'Unités-SI) metric.

 TECH TIP

It Just Takes a Second

Whenever removing any automotive component, it is wise to screw the bolts back into the holes a couple of threads by hand. This ensures that the right bolt will be used in its original location when the component or part is put back on the vehicle. Often, the same diameter of fastener is used on a component, but the length of the bolt may vary. Spending just a couple of seconds to put the bolts and nuts back where they belong when the part is removed can save a lot of time when the part is being reinstalled. Besides making certain that the right fastener is being installed in the right place, this method helps prevent bolts and nuts from getting lost or kicked away. How much time have you wasted looking for that lost bolt or nut?

HAND TOOLS

WRENCHES Wrenches are the most used hand tool by service technicians. **Wrenches** are used to grasp and rotate threaded fasteners. Most wrenches are constructed of forged alloy steel, usually chrome-vanadium steel. ● **SEE FIGURE 1–15.**

After the wrench is formed, it is hardened, and then tempered to reduce brittleness, and then chrome plated. There are several types of wrenches.

OPEN-END WRENCH. An open-end wrench is usually used to loosen or tighten bolts or nuts that do not require a lot of torque. Because of the *open* end, this type of wrench can be easily placed on a bolt or nut with an angle of 15 degrees, which allows the wrench to be flipped over and used again to continue to rotate the fastener. The major disadvantage of an open-end wrench is the lack of torque that can be applied due to the fact that the open jaws of the wrench only contact two flat surfaces of the fastener. An open-end wrench has two different sizes, one at each end. ● **SEE FIGURE 1–16.**

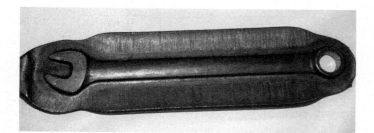

FIGURE 1–15 A wrench after it has been forged but before the flashing, extra material around the wrench, has been removed.

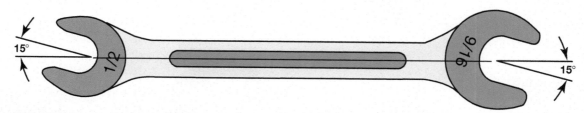

FIGURE 1–16 A typical open-end wrench. The size is different on each end; notice that the head is angled 15 degrees at the end.

BOX-END WRENCH. A *box-end wrench*, also called a *closed-end wrench*, is placed over the top of the fastener and grips the points of the fastener. A box-end wrench is angled 15 degrees to allow it to clear nearby objects.

Therefore, a box-end wrench should be used to loosen or to tighten fasteners because it grasps around the entire head of the fastener. A box-end wrench has two different sizes, one at each end. ● **SEE FIGURE 1–17.**

Most service technicians purchase *combination wrenches*, which have the open end at one end and the same size box end on the other end. ● **SEE FIGURE 1–18.**

A combination wrench allows the technician to loosen or tighten a fastener using the box end of the wrench, turn it around, and use the open end to increase the speed of rotating the fastener.

ADJUSTABLE WRENCH. An *adjustable wrench* is often used where the exact size wrench is not available or when a large nut, such as a wheel spindle nut, needs to be rotated, but not tightened. An adjustable wrench should not be used to loosen or tighten fasteners because the torque applied to the wrench can cause the movable jaws to loosen their grip on the fastener, causing it to become rounded. ● **SEE FIGURE 1–19.**

LINE WRENCHES. Line wrenches are also called *flare-nut wrenches*, *fitting wrenches*, or *tube-nut wrenches* and are designed to grip almost all the way around a nut used to retain a fuel or refrigerant line, and yet, be able to be installed over the line. ● **SEE FIGURE 1–20.**

TECH TIP

Hide Those from the Boss

An apprentice technician started working for a shop and put his top tool box on a workbench. Another technician observed that, along with a complete set of good-quality tools, the box contained several adjustable wrenches. The more experienced technician said, "Hide those from the boss." The boss does not want any service technician to use adjustable wrenches. If any adjustable wrench is used on a bolt or nut, the movable jaw often moves or loosens and starts to round the head of the fastener. If the head of the bolt or nut becomes rounded, it becomes that much more difficult to remove.

SAFE USE OF WRENCHES Wrenches should be inspected before use to be sure they are not cracked, bent, or damaged. All wrenches should be cleaned after use before being returned to the tool box. Always use the correct size of wrench for the fastener being loosened or tightened to help prevent the rounding of the flats of the fastener. When attempting to loosen a fastener, pull a wrench—do not push a wrench. If a wrench is pushed, your knuckles can be hurt when forced into another object if the fastener breaks loose

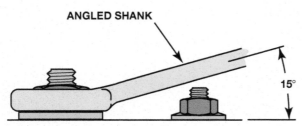

FIGURE 1–17 The end of a box-end wrench is angled 15 degrees to allow clearance for nearby objects or other fasteners.

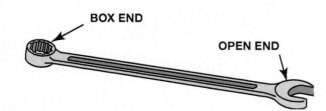

FIGURE 1–18 A combination wrench has an open end at one end and a box end at the other end.

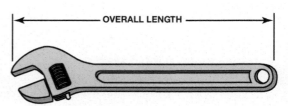

FIGURE 1–19 An adjustable wrench. Adjustable wrenches are sized by the overall length of the wrench and not by how far the jaws open. Common sizes of adjustable wrenches include 8, 10, and 12 inch.

FIGURE 1–20 The end of a typical line wrench, which shows that it is capable of grasping most of the head of the fitting.

or if the wrench slips. Always keep wrenches and all hand tools clean to help prevent rust and to allow for a better, firmer grip. Never expose any tool to excessive heat. High temperatures can reduce the strength ("draw the temper") of metal tools.

Never use a hammer on any wrench unless you are using a special "staking face" wrench designed to be used with a hammer. Replace any tools that are damaged or worn.

RATCHETS, SOCKETS, AND EXTENSIONS
A **socket** fits over the fastener and grips the points and/or flats of the bolt or nut. The socket is rotated (driven) using either a long bar called a **breaker bar** (flex handle) or a ratchet. ● **SEE FIGURES 1–21 AND 1–22.**

A **ratchet** is a tool that turns the socket in only one direction and allows the rotating of the ratchet handle back and forth in a narrow space. Socket **extensions** and **universal joints** are also used with sockets to allow access to fasteners in restricted locations.

DRIVE SIZE. Sockets are available in various **drive sizes**, including 1/4, 3/8, and 1/2 inch sizes for most automotive use. ● **SEE FIGURES 1–23 AND 1–24.**

Many heavy-duty truck and/or industrial applications use 3/4 and 1 inch sizes. The drive size is the distance of each side of the square drive. Sockets and ratchets of the same size are designed to work together.

TECH TIP

Right to Tighten

It is sometimes confusing which way to rotate a wrench or screwdriver, especially when the head of the fastener is pointing away from you. To help visualize while looking at the fastener, say "righty tighty, lefty loosey."

REGULAR AND DEEP WELL. Sockets are available in regular length for use in most applications or in a deep well design that allows for access to a fastener that uses a long stud or other similar conditions. ● **SEE FIGURE 1–25.**

TORQUE WRENCHES
Torque wrenches are socket turning handles that are designed to apply a known amount of force to the fastener. There are two basic types of torque wrenches:

1. **Clicker type.** This type of torque wrench is first set to the specified torque and then it "clicks" when the set torque value has been reached. When force is removed from the torque wrench handle, another click is heard. The setting on a clicker-type torque wrench should be

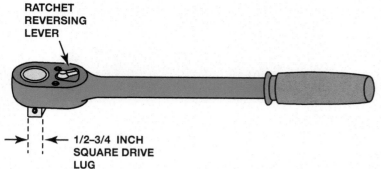

FIGURE 1–21 A typical ratchet used to rotate a socket. A ratchet makes a ratcheting noise when it is being rotated in the opposite direction from loosening or tightening. A knob or lever on the ratchet allows the user to switch directions.

RATCHET REVERSING LEVER

1/2-3/4 INCH SQUARE DRIVE LUG

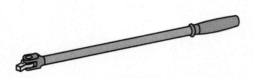

FIGURE 1–22 A typical flex handle used to rotate a socket, also called a breaker bar because it usually has a longer handle than a ratchet and, therefore, can be used to apply more torque to a fastener than a ratchet.

set back to zero after use and checked for proper calibration regularly. ● **SEE FIGURE 1–26.**

2. **Beam type.** This type of torque wrench is used to measure torque, but instead of presenting the value, the actual torque is displayed on the dial of the wrench as the fastener is being tightened. Beam-type torque wrenches are available in 1/4, 3/8, and 1/2 inch drives and both English and metric units. ● **SEE FIGURE 1–27.**

SAFE USE OF SOCKETS AND RATCHETS
Always use the proper size socket that correctly fits the bolt or nut. All sockets and ratchets should be cleaned after use before being placed back into the tool box. Sockets are available in short and deep well designs. Never expose any tool to excessive heat. High temperatures can reduce the strength ("draw the temper") of metal tools.

Never use a hammer on a socket handle unless you are using a special "staking face" wrench designed to be used with a hammer. Replace any tools that are damaged or worn.

Also select the appropriate drive size. For example, for small work, such as on the dash, select a 1/4 inch drive. For most general service work, use a 3/8 inch drive and for suspension and steering and other large fasteners, select

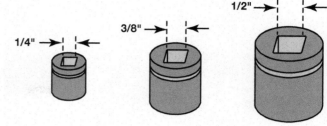

1/4"   3/8"   1/2"

FIGURE 1–23 The most commonly used socket drive sizes include 1/4, 3/8, and 1/2 inch drive.

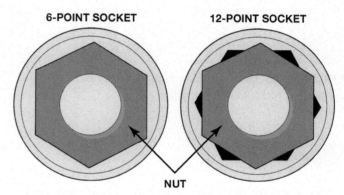

6-POINT SOCKET   12-POINT SOCKET

NUT

FIGURE 1–24 A 6-point socket fits the head of a bolt or nut on all sides. A 12-point socket can round off the head of a bolt or nut if a lot of force is applied.

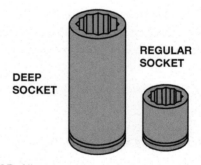

DEEP SOCKET   REGULAR SOCKET

FIGURE 1–25 Allows access to the nut that has a stud plus other locations needing great depth, such as spark plugs.

a 1/2 inch drive. When loosening a fastener, always pull the ratchet toward you rather than push it outward.

SCREWDRIVERS

STRAIGHT-BLADE SCREWDRIVER Many smaller fasteners are removed and installed by using a **screwdriver**. Screwdrivers are available in many sizes and tip shapes. The most commonly used screwdriver is called a *straight blade* or *flat tip*.

FIGURE 1-26 Using a clicker-type torque wrench to tighten connecting rod nuts on an engine.

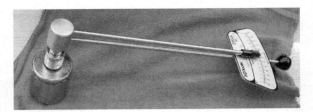

FIGURE 1-27 A beam-type torque wrench that displays the torque reading on the face of the dial. The beam display is read as the beam deflects, which is in proportion to the amount of torque applied to the fastener.

TECH TIP

Check Torque Wrench Calibration Regularly

Torque wrenches should be checked regularly. For example, Honda has a torque wrench calibration setup at each of its training centers. It is expected that a torque wrench be checked for accuracy before every use. Most experts recommend that torque wrenches be checked and adjusted as needed at least every year and more often if possible. ● SEE FIGURE 1-28.

FIGURE 1-28 Torque wrench calibration checker.

Flat-tip screwdrivers are sized by the width of the blade and this width should match the width of the slot in the screw. ● SEE FIGURE 1-29.

CAUTION: Do not use a screwdriver as a pry tool or as a chisel. Screwdrivers are hardened steel only at the tip and are not designed to be pounded on or used for prying because they could bend easily. Always use the proper tool for each application.

PHILLIPS SCREWDRIVER Another type of commonly used screwdriver is called a Phillips screwdriver, named for Henry F. Phillips, who invented the crosshead screw in 1934. Due to the shape of the crosshead screw and screwdriver, a Phillips screw can be driven with more torque than can be achieved with a slotted screw.

A Phillips head screwdriver is specified by the length of the handle and the size of the point at the tip. A #1 tip has a sharp point, a #2 tip is the most commonly used, and a #3 tip is blunt and is only used for larger sizes of Phillips head fasteners. For example, a #2 × 3 inch Phillips screwdriver would typically measure 6 inch from the tip of the blade to the end of the handle (3 inch long handle and 3 inch long blade) with a #2 tip.

Both straight-blade and Phillips screwdrivers are available with a short blade and handle for access to fasteners with limited room. ● SEE FIGURE 1-30.

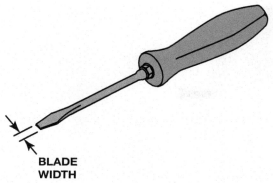

BLADE WIDTH

FIGURE 1–29 A flat-tip (straight-blade) screwdriver. The width of the blade should match the width of the slot in the fastener being loosened or tightened.

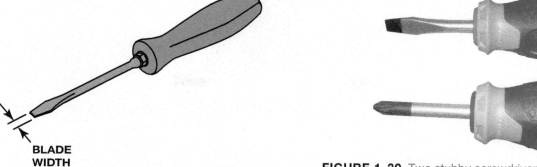

FIGURE 1–30 Two stubby screwdrivers that are used to access screws that have limited space above. A straight blade is on top and a #2 Phillips screwdriver is on the bottom.

TECH TIP

Use Socket Adapters with Caution

A **socket adapter** allows the use of one size of socket and another drive size ratchet or breaker bar. Socket adapters are available and can be used for different drive size sockets on a ratchet. Combinations include:

- 1/4 inch drive—3/8 inch sockets
- 3/8 inch drive—1/4 inch sockets
- 3/8 inch drive—1/2 inch sockets
- 1/2 inch drive—3/8 inch sockets

Using a larger drive ratchet or breaker bar on a smaller size socket can cause the application of too much force to the socket, which could crack or shatter. Using a smaller size drive tool on a larger socket will usually not cause any harm, but would greatly reduce the amount of torque that can be applied to the bolt or nut.

TECH TIP

Avoid Using "Cheater Bars"

Whenever a fastener is difficult to remove, some technicians will insert the handle of a ratchet or a breaker bar into a length of steel pipe sometimes called a **cheater bar**. The extra length of the pipe allows the technician to exert more torque than can be applied using the drive handle alone. However, the extra torque can easily overload the socket and ratchet, causing them to break or shatter, which could cause personal injury.

TORX A Torx is a six-pointed star-shaped tip that was developed by Camcar (formerly Textron) to offer higher loosening and tightening torque than is possible with a straight blade (flat tip) or Phillips. Torx is very commonly used in the automotive field for many components. Commonly used Torx sizes from small to large include T15, T20, T25, and T30. ● **SEE FIGURE 1–31.**

IMPACT SCREWDRIVER An *impact screwdriver* is used to break loose or tighten a screw. A hammer is used to strike the end after the screwdriver holder is placed in the head of the screw and rotated in the desired direction. The force from the hammer blow does two things: It applies a force downward holding the tip of the screwdriver in the slot and then applies a twisting force to loosen (or tighten) the screw. ● **SEE FIGURE 1–32.**

SAFE USE OF SCREWDRIVERS Always use the proper type and size screwdriver that matches the fastener. Try to avoid pressing down on a screwdriver because if it slips, the screwdriver tip could go into your hand, causing serious personal injury. All screwdrivers should be cleaned after use. Do not use a screwdriver as a prybar; always use the correct tool for the job.

HAMMERS AND MALLETS **Hammers** and mallets are used to force objects together or apart. The shape of the back part of the hammer head (called the *peen*) usually determines the name. For example, a ball-peen hammer has a rounded end like a ball and it is used to straighten oil pans and valve covers, using the hammer head, and for shaping metal, using the ball peen. ● **SEE FIGURE 1–33.**

NOTE: A claw hammer has a claw used to remove nails and is not used for automotive service.

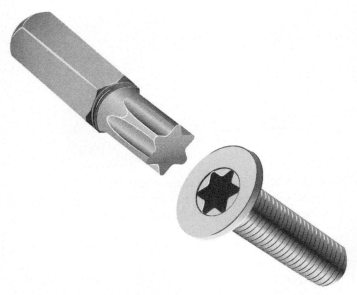

FIGURE 1–31 A Torx bit and fastener.

FIGURE 1–32 An impact screwdriver used to remove slotted or Phillips head fasteners that cannot be broken loose using a standard screwdriver.

A hammer is usually sized by the weight of the head of the hammer and the length of the handle. For example, a commonly used ball-peen hammer has an 8 ounce head with an 11 inch handle.

MALLETS. *Mallets* are a type of hammer with a large striking surface, which allows the technician to exert force over a larger area than a hammer, so as not to harm the part or component. Mallets are made from a variety of materials including rubber, plastic, or wood. ● **SEE FIGURE 1–34.**

DEAD-BLOW HAMMER. A shot-filled plastic hammer is called a *dead-blow hammer.* The small lead balls (shot) inside a plastic head prevent the hammer from bouncing off of the object when struck. ● **SEE FIGURE 1–35.**

SAFE USE OF HAMMERS AND MALLETS All mallets and hammers should be cleaned after use and not exposed to extreme temperatures. Never use a hammer or mallet that is damaged in any way and always use caution to avoid doing damage to the components and the surrounding area. Always follow the hammer manufacturer's recommended procedures and practices.

FIGURE 1–33 A typical ball-peen hammer.

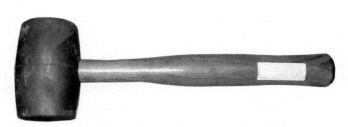

FIGURE 1–34 A rubber mallet used to deliver a force to an object without harming the surface.

TORX

A Torx is a six-pointed star shaped tip that was developed by Camcar (formerly Textron) to offer higher loosening and tightening torque than is possible with a straight (flat tip) or Phillips. Torx is very commonly used in the automotive field for many components. Commonly used Torx

sizes from small to large include: T15, T20, T25, and T30. ● **SEE FIGURE 1–31.**

Some Torx fasteners include a round projection in the center requiring that a special version of a Torx bit be used. These are called security Torx bits that have a hole in the center to be used on these fasteners. External Torx fasteners are also used mostly as engine fasteners and are labeled E instead of T plus the size, such as E45.

FIGURE 1–35 A dead-blow hammer that was left outside in freezing weather. The plastic covering was damaged, which destroyed this hammer. The lead shot is encased in the metal housing and then covered.

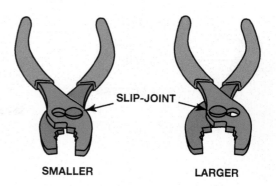

FIGURE 1–36 Typical slip-joint pliers are a common household pliers. The slip joint allows the jaws to be opened to two different settings.

PLIERS

SLIP-JOINT PLIERS A **pliers** is capable of holding, twisting, bending, and cutting objects and is an extremely useful classification of tools. The common household type of pliers is called the *slip-joint pliers*. There are two different positions where the junction of the handles meets to achieve a wide range of sizes of objects that can be gripped. ● **SEE FIGURE 1–36.**

MULTIGROOVE ADJUSTABLE PLIERS For gripping larger objects, a set of *multigroove adjustable pliers* is a commonly used tool of choice by many service technicians. Originally designed to remove the various size nuts holding rope seals used in water pumps, the name *water pump pliers* is

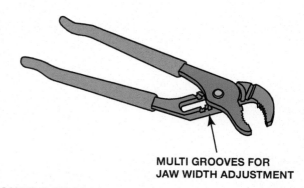

MULTI GROOVES FOR
JAW WIDTH ADJUSTMENT

FIGURE 1–37 Multigroove adjustable pliers are known by many names, including the trade name "Channel Locks®."

also used. These types of pliers are commonly called by their trade name *Channel Locks*®. ● **SEE FIGURE 1–37.**

LINESMAN'S PLIERS *Linesman's pliers* are a hand tool specifically designed for cutting, bending, and twisting wire. While commonly used by construction workers and electricians, linesman's pliers are a very useful tool for the service technician who deals with wiring. The center parts of the jaws are designed to grasp round objects, such as pipe or tubing without slipping. ● **SEE FIGURE 1–38.**

DIAGONAL PLIERS *Diagonal pliers* is designed to cut only. The cutting jaws are set at an angle to make it easier to cut wires. Diagonal pliers are also called *side cuts* or *dikes*. These pliers are constructed of hardened steel and they are used mostly for cutting wire. ● **SEE FIGURE 1–39.**

NEEDLE-NOSE PLIERS *Needle-nose pliers* are designed to grip small objects or objects in tight locations. Needle-nose pliers have long, pointed jaws, which allow the tips to reach into narrow openings or groups of small objects. ● **SEE FIGURE 1–40.**

TECH TIP

Pound with Something Softer

If you must pound on something, be sure to use a tool that is softer than what you are about to pound on to avoid damage. Examples are given in the following table.

The Material Being Pounded	What to Pound with
Steel or cast iron	Brass or aluminum hammer or punch
Aluminum	Plastic or rawhide mallet or plastic-covered dead-blow hammer
Plastic	Rawhide mallet or plastic dead-blow hammer

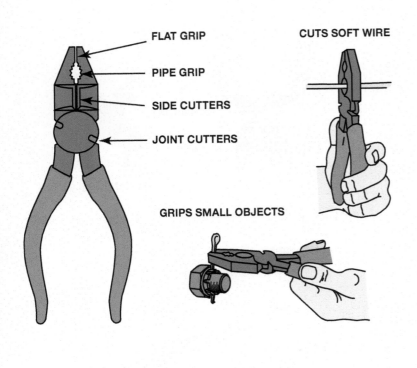

FLAT GRIP

PIPE GRIP

SIDE CUTTERS

JOINT CUTTERS

CUTS SOFT WIRE

FIGURE 1–38 Linesman's pliers are very useful because it helps perform many automotive service jobs.

GRIPS SMALL OBJECTS

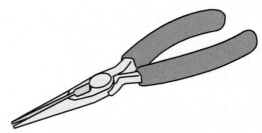

FIGURE 1–40 Needle-nose pliers are used where there is limited access to a wire or pin that needs to be installed or removed.

CUTTING WIRES CLOSE TO TERMINALS

PULLING OUT AND SPREADING COTTER PIN

FIGURE 1–39 Diagonal-cut pliers are another common tool that has many names.

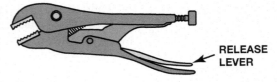

RELEASE LEVER

FIGURE 1–41 Locking pliers are best known by their trade name Vise Grips®.

Most needle-nose pliers have a wire cutter located at the base of the jaws near the pivot. There are several variations of needle-nose pliers, including right angle jaws or slightly angled to allow access to certain cramped areas.

LOCKING PLIERS *Locking pliers* are adjustable pliers that can be locked to hold objects from moving. Most locking pliers also have wire cutters built into the jaws near the pivot point. Locking pliers come in a variety of styles and sizes and are commonly referred to by the trade name *Vise Grips*®. The size is the length of the pliers, not how far the jaws open. ● **SEE FIGURE 1–41.**

SNAP-RING PLIERS *Snap-ring pliers* are used to remove and install snap-rings. Many snap-ring pliers are designed to be able to remove and install both and well as outward, expanding snap rings. Some snap-ring pliers can be equipped with serrated-tipped jaws for grasping the opening in the snap ring, while others are equipped with points, which are inserted into the holes in the snap ring. ● **SEE FIGURE 1–42.**

SAFE USE OF PLIERS Pliers should not be used to remove any bolt or other fastener. Pliers should only be used when specified for use by the vehicle manufacturer.

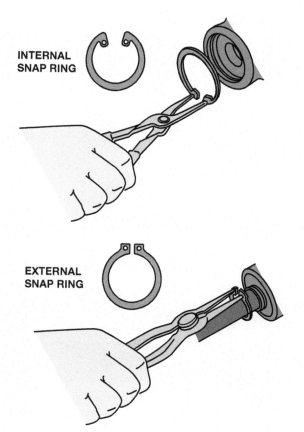

INTERNAL SNAP RING

EXTERNAL SNAP RING

FIGURE 1–42 Snap-ring pliers are also called lock ring pliers and most are designed to remove internal and external snap rings (lock rings).

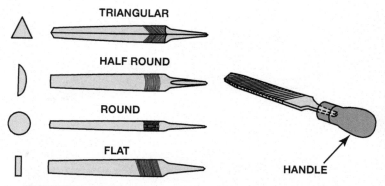

TRIANGULAR

HALF ROUND

ROUND

FLAT

HANDLE

FIGURE 1–43 Files come in many different shapes and sizes. Never use a file without a handle.

FILES

Files are used to smooth metal and are constructed of hardened steel with diagonal rows of teeth. Files are available with a single row of teeth called a *single cut file*, as well as two rows of teeth cut at an opposite angle called a *double cut file*. Files are available in a variety of shapes and sizes from small flat files, half-round files, and triangular files. ● **SEE FIGURE 1–43.**

SAFE USE OF FILES

Always use a file with a handle. Because files only cut when moved forward, a handle must be attached to prevent possible personal injury. After making a forward strike, lift the file and return the file to the starting position; avoid dragging the file backward.

SNIPS

Service technicians are often asked to fabricate sheet metal brackets or heat shields and need to use one or more types of cutters available called **snips**. *Tin snips* are the simplest and are designed to make straight cuts in a variety of materials, such as sheet steel, aluminum, or even fabric. A variation of the tin snips is called *aviation tin snips*. There are three designs of aviation snips including one designed to cut straight (called a *straight cut aviation snip*),

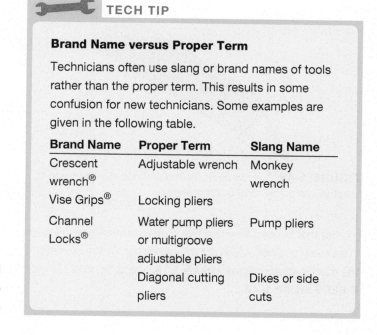

TECH TIP

Brand Name versus Proper Term

Technicians often use slang or brand names of tools rather than the proper term. This results in some confusion for new technicians. Some examples are given in the following table.

Brand Name	Proper Term	Slang Name
Crescent wrench®	Adjustable wrench	Monkey wrench
Vise Grips®	Locking pliers	
Channel Locks®	Water pump pliers or multigroove adjustable pliers	Pump pliers
	Diagonal cutting pliers	Dikes or side cuts

one designed to cut left (called an *offset left aviation snip*), and one designed to cut right (called an *offset right aviation snip*). ● **SEE FIGURE 1–44.**

UTILITY KNIFE

A *utility knife* uses a replaceable blade and is used to cut a variety of materials such as carpet, plastic, wood, and paper products, such as cardboard. ● **SEE FIGURE 1–45.**

SAFE USE OF CUTTERS

Whenever using cutters, always wear eye protection or a face shield to guard against the possibility of metal pieces being ejected during the cut. Always follow recommended procedures.

PUNCHES

A **punch** is a small diameter steel rod that has a smaller diameter ground at one end. A punch is used to drive a

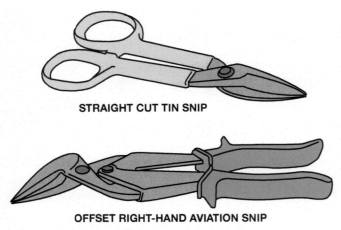

STRAIGHT CUT TIN SNIP

OFFSET RIGHT-HAND AVIATION SNIP

FIGURE 1–44 Tin snips are used to cut thin sheets of metal or carpet.

FIGURE 1–45 A utility knife uses replaceable blades and is used to cut carpet and other materials.

pin out that is used to retain two components. Punches come in a variety of sizes, which are measured across the diameter of the machined end. Sizes include 1/16, 1/8, 3/16, and 1/4 inch. ●**SEE FIGURE 1–46.**

CHISELS A **chisel** has a straight, sharp cutting end that is used for cutting off rivets or to separate two pieces of an assembly. The most common design of chisel used for automotive service work is called a *cold chisel*.

SAFE USE OF PUNCHES AND CHISELS Always wear eye protection when using a punch or a chisel because the hardened steel is brittle and parts of the punch could fly off and cause serious personal injury. See the warning stamped on the side of this automotive punch in ● **FIGURE 1–47.**

The tops of punches and chisels can become rounded off from use, which is called "mushroomed." This material must be ground off to help avoid the possibility of the overhanging material being loosened and becoming airborne during use. ●**SEE FIGURE 1–48.**

HACKSAWS A **hacksaw** is used to cut metals, such as steel, aluminum, brass, or copper. The cutting blade of

PIN

FIGURE 1–46 A punch used to drive pins from assembled components. This type of punch is also called a pin punch.

WEAR SAFETY GOGGLES

FIGURE 1–47 Warning stamped on the side of a punch warning that goggles should be worn when using this tool. Always follow safety warnings.

a hacksaw is replaceable and the sharpness and number of teeth can be varied to meet the needs of the job. Use 14 or 18 teeth per inch (TPI) for cutting plaster or soft metals, such as aluminum and copper. Use 24 or 32 teeth per inch for steel or pipe. Hacksaw blades should be installed with the teeth pointing away from the handle. This means that a hacksaw only cuts while the blade is pushed in the forward direction. ● **SEE FIGURE 1–49.**

SAFE USE OF HACKSAWS Check that the hacksaw is equipped with the correct blade for the job and that the teeth are pointed away from the handle. When using a hacksaw, move the hacksaw slowly away from you, then lift slightly and return for another cut.

BASIC HAND TOOL LIST

The following is a typical list of hand tools every automotive technician should possess. Specialty tools are not included.

Safety glasses

Tool chest

1/4 inch drive socket set (1/4 to 9/16 inch standard and deep sockets; 6 to 15 mm standard and deep sockets)

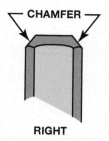

CHAMFER · MUSHROOM

RIGHT · WRONG

FIGURE 1–48 Use a grinder or a file to remove the mushroom material on the end of a punch or chisel.

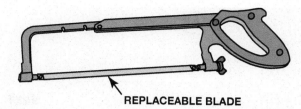

REPLACEABLE BLADE

FIGURE 1–49 A typical hacksaw that is used to cut metal. If cutting sheet metal or thin objects, a blade with more teeth should be used.

1/4 inch drive ratchet

1/4 inch drive 2 inch extension

1/4 inch drive 6 inch extension

1/4 inch drive handle

3/8 inch drive socket set (3/8 to 7/8 inch standard and deep sockets; 10 to 19 mm standard and deep sockets)

3/8 inch drive Torx set (T40, T45, T50, and T55)

3/8 inch drive 13/16 inch plug socket

3/8 inch drive 5/8 inch plug socket

3/8 inch drive ratchet

3/8 inch drive 1 1/2 inch extension

3/8 inch drive 3 inch extension

3/8 inch drive 6 inch extension

3/8 inch drive 18 inch extension

3/8 inch drive universal

1/2 inch drive socket set (1/2 to 1 inch standard and deep sockets)

1/2 inch drive ratchet

1/2 inch drive breaker bar

1/2 inch drive 5 inch extension

1/2 inch drive 10 inch extension

3/8 to 1/4 inch adapter

1/2 to 3/8 inch adapter

3/8 to 1/2 inch adapter

3/8" and 1/2" torque wrench

Torque angle gauge

Crowfoot set (fractional inch)

Crowfoot set (metric)

3/8 through 1 inch combination wrench set

10 through 19 mm combination wrench set

1/16 through 1/4 inch hex wrench set

2 through 12 mm hex wrench set

3/8 inch hex socket

13 to 14 mm flare-nut wrench

15 to 17 mm flare-nut wrench

5/16 to 3/8 inch flare-nut wrench

7/16 to 1/2 inch flare-nut wrench

1/2 to 9/16 inch flare-nut wrench

Diagonal pliers

Needle pliers

Adjustable-jaw pliers

Locking pliers

Snap-ring pliers

Stripping or crimping pliers

Ball-peen hammer

Rubber hammer

Dead-blow hammer

Five-piece standard screwdriver set

Four-piece Phillips screwdriver set

#15 Torx screwdriver

#20 Torx screwdriver

Center punch

Pin punches (assorted sizes)

Chisel

Utility knife

Valve core tool

Filter wrench (large filters)

Filter wrench (smaller filters)

Test light

Feeler gauge

Scraper

Pinch bar

Magnet

FIGURE 1–50 A typical beginning technician tool set that includes the basic tools to get started.

FIGURE 1–51 A typical 40 inch wide top and bottom professional tool box.

 **TECH TIP**

Need to Borrow a Tool More than Twice? Buy It!

Most service technicians agree that it is okay for a beginning technician to borrow a tool occasionally. However, if a tool has to be borrowed more than twice, be sure to purchase it as soon as possible. Also, whenever a tool is borrowed, be sure that you clean the tool and let the technician you borrowed the tool from know that you are returning the tool. These actions will help in any future dealings with other technicians.

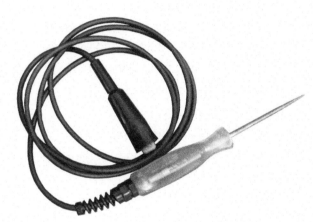

FIGURE 1–52 A typical 12 volt test light.

TOOL SETS AND ACCESSORIES

A beginning service technician may wish to start with a small set of tools before purchasing an expensive tool set. ● **SEE FIGURES 1–50 AND 1–51.**

ELECTRICAL HAND TOOLS

TEST LIGHT A test light is used to test for electricity. A typical automotive test light consists of a clear plastic screwdriver-like handle that contains a lightbulb. A wire is attached to one terminal of the bulb, which the technician connects to a clean metal part of the vehicle. The other end of the bulb is attached to a point that can be used to test for electricity at a connector or wire. When there is power at the point and a good connection at the other end, the lightbulb lights. ● **SEE FIGURE 1–52.**

SOLDERING GUNS

ELECTRIC SOLDERING GUN. This type of soldering gun is usually powered by 110-volt AC and often has two power settings expressed in watts. A typical electric soldering gun will produce from 85 to 300 watts of heat at the tip, which is more than adequate for soldering.

ELECTRIC SOLDERING PENCIL. This type of soldering iron is less expensive and creates less heat than an electric soldering gun. A typical electric soldering pencil (iron) creates 30 to 60 watts of heat and is suitable for soldering smaller wires and connections.

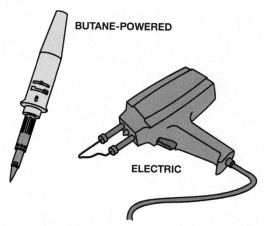

BUTANE-POWERED

ELECTRIC

FIGURE 1–53 Electric and butane-powered soldering guns used to make electrical repairs. Soldering guns are sold by the wattage rating. The higher the wattage, the greater the amount of heat created. Most solder guns used for automotive electrical work usually fall within the 60 to 160 watt range.

BUTANE-POWERED SOLDERING IRON. A butane-powered soldering iron is portable and very useful for automotive service work because an electrical cord is not needed. Most butane-powered soldering irons produce about 60 watts of heat, which is enough for most automotive soldering. ● **SEE FIGURE 1–53.**

ELECTRICAL WORK HAND TOOLS
In addition to a soldering iron, most service technicians who do electrical-related work should have the following:

- Wire cutters
- Wire strippers
- Wire crimpers
- Heat gun for heat shrink tubing

DIGITAL METER
A digital meter is a necessary tool for any electrical diagnosis and troubleshooting. A digital multimeter, abbreviated DMM, is usually capable of measuring the following units of electricity:

- DC volts
- AC volts
- Ohms
- Amperes

HAND TOOL MAINTENANCE

Most hand tools are constructed of rust-resistant metals, but they can still rust or corrode if not properly maintained. For best results and long tool life, the following steps should be taken:

 FREQUENTLY ASKED QUESTION

What Is an "SST"?

Vehicle manufacturers often specify a **special service tool (SST)** to properly disassemble and assemble components, such as transmissions and other components. These tools are also called special tools and are available from the vehicle manufacturer or their tool supplier, such as Kent-Moore and Miller tools. Many service technicians do not have access to special service tools so they use generic versions that are available from aftermarket sources.

- Clean each tool before placing it back into the tool box.
- Keep tools separated. Moisture on metal tools will start to rust more readily if the tools are in contact with another metal tool.
- Line the drawers of the tool box with a material that will prevent the tools from moving as the drawers are opened and closed. This helps to quickly locate the proper tool and size.
- Release the tension on all "clicker-type" torque wrenches.
- Keep the tool box secure.

TROUBLE LIGHTS

INCANDESCENT *Incandescent lights* use a filament that produces light when electric current flows through the bulb. This was the standard **trouble light**, also called a *work light* for many years until safety issues caused most shops to switch to safer fluorescent or LED lights. If incandescent lightbulbs are used, try to locate bulbs that are rated "rough service," which is designed to withstand shock and vibration more than conventional lightbulbs.

 WARNING

Do not use incandescent trouble lights around gasoline or other flammable liquids. The liquids can cause the bulb to break and the hot filament can ignite the flammable liquid, which can cause personal injury or even death.

FIGURE 1–54 A battery-powered LED trouble light.

FIGURE 1–55 A typical 1/2 inch drive air impact wrench. The direction of rotation can be changed to loosen or tighten a fastener.

FLUORESCENT A trouble light is an essential piece of shop equipment, and for safety, should be fluorescent rather than incandescent. Incandescent lightbulbs can scatter or break if gasoline were to be splashed onto the bulb creating a serious fire hazard. Fluorescent light tubes are not as likely to be broken and are usually protected by a clear plastic enclosure. Trouble lights are usually attached to a retractor, which can hold 20 to 50 feet of electrical cord.

LED TROUBLE LIGHT Light-emitting diode (LED) trouble lights are excellent to use because they are shock resistant, are long lasting, and do not represent a fire hazard. Some trouble lights are battery powered, and therefore, can be used in places where an attached electrical cord could present problems. ● **SEE FIGURE 1–54.**

FIGURE 1–56 A typical battery-powered 1/2 inch drive impact wrench.

AIR AND ELECTRICALLY OPERATED TOOLS

IMPACT WRENCH An impact wrench, either air or electrically powered, is a tool that is used to remove and install fasteners. The air-operated 1/2 inch drive impact wrench is the most commonly used unit. ● **SEE FIGURE 1–55.**

Electrically powered impact wrenches commonly include:

- Battery-powered units. ● **SEE FIGURE 1–56.**
- 110 volt AC-powered units. This type of impact is very useful, especially if compressed air is not readily available.

☠ WARNING

Always use impact sockets with impact wrenches, and always wear eye protection in case the socket or fastener shatters. Impact sockets are thicker walled and constructed with premium alloy steel. They are hardened with a black oxide finish to help prevent corrosion and distinguish them from regular sockets. ● SEE FIGURE 1–57.

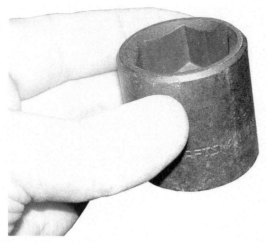

FIGURE 1–57 A black impact socket. Always use an impact-type socket whenever using an impact wrench to avoid the possibility of shattering the socket, which could cause personal injury. If a socket is chrome plated, it is not to be used with an impact wrench.

AIR RATCHET An air ratchet is used to remove and install fasteners that would normally be removed or installed using a ratchet and a socket. ● **SEE FIGURE 1–58.**

DIE GRINDER A die grinder is a commonly used air-powered tool that can also be used to sand or remove gaskets and rust. ● **SEE FIGURE 1–59.**

BENCH OR PEDESTAL-MOUNTED GRINDER These high-powered grinders can be equipped with a wire brush wheel and/or a stone wheel.

- **Wire brush wheel**—This type is used to clean threads of bolts, as well as, to remove gaskets from sheet metal engine parts.
- **Stone wheel**—This type is used to grind metal or to remove the mushroom from the top of punches or chisels. ● **SEE FIGURE 1–60.**

Most **bench grinders** are equipped with a grinder wheel (stone) on one end and a wire brush wheel on the other end. A bench grinder is a very useful piece of shop equipment and the wire wheel end can be used for the following:

- Cleaning threads of bolts
- Cleaning gaskets from sheet metal parts, such as steel valve covers

CAUTION: Only use a steel wire brush on steel or iron components. If a steel wire brush is used on aluminum or copper-based metal parts, it can remove metal from the part.

FIGURE 1–58 An air ratchet is a very useful tool that allows fast removal and installation of fasteners, especially in areas that are difficult to reach or do not have room enough to move a hand ratchet or wrench.

FIGURE 1–59 This typical die grinder surface preparation kit includes the air-operated die grinder, as well as, a variety of sanding disks for smoothing surfaces or removing rust.

FIGURE 1–60 A typical pedestal grinder with a wire wheel on the left side and a stone wheel on the right side. Even though this machine is equipped with guards, safety glasses, or a face shield should always be worn whenever using a grinder or wire wheel.

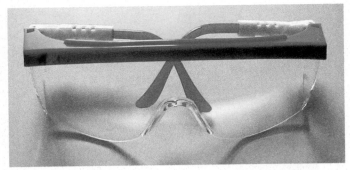

FIGURE 1–61 Safety glasses should be worn at all times when working on or around any vehicle or servicing any components.

The grinding stone end of the bench grinder can be used for the following:

- Sharpening blades and drill bits
- Grinding off the heads of rivets or parts
- Sharpening sheet metal parts for custom fitting

PERSONAL PROTECTIVE EQUIPMENT

Service technicians should wear **personal protective equipment (PPE)** to prevent personal injury. The personal protection devices include the following:

SAFETY GLASSES Wear safety glasses at all times while servicing any vehicle and be sure that they meet standard ANSI Z87.1. ● **SEE FIGURE 1–61.**

STEEL-TOED SAFETY SHOES ● **SEE FIGURE 1–62.** If steel-toed safety shoes are not available, then leather-topped shoes offer more protection than canvas or cloth-covered shoes.

BUMP CAP Service technicians working under a vehicle should wear a **bump cap** to protect the head against under-vehicle objects and the pads of the lift. ● **SEE FIGURE 1–63.**

HEARING PROTECTION Hearing protection should be worn if the sound around you requires that you raise your voice (sound level higher than 90 dB). For example, a typical

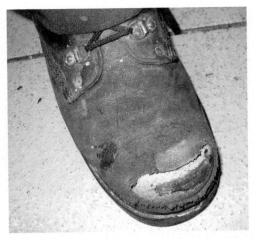

FIGURE 1–62 Steel-toed shoes are a worthwhile investment to help prevent foot injury due to falling objects. Even these well-worn shoes can protect the feet of this service technician.

FIGURE 1–63 One version of a bump cap is a molded plastic insert that is worn inside a regular cloth cap.

lawnmower produces noise at a level of about 110 dB. This means that everyone who uses a lawnmower or other lawn or garden equipment should wear ear protection.

GLOVES Many technicians wear gloves not only to help keep their hands clean, but also to help protect their skin from the effects of dirty engine oil and other possibly hazardous materials.

Several types of gloves and their characteristics include:

- **Latex surgical gloves.** These gloves are relatively inexpensive, but tend to stretch, swell, and weaken when exposed to gas, oil, or solvents.
- **Vinyl gloves.** These gloves are also inexpensive and are not affected by gas, oil, or solvents.
- **Polyurethane gloves.** These gloves are more expensive, yet very strong. Even though these gloves are also not affected by gas, oil, or solvents, they do tend to be slippery.

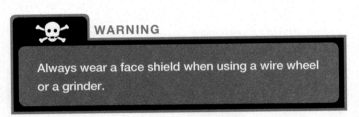

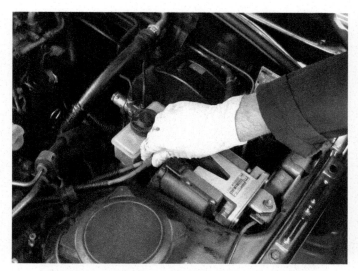

FIGURE 1–64 Protective gloves are available in several sizes and materials.

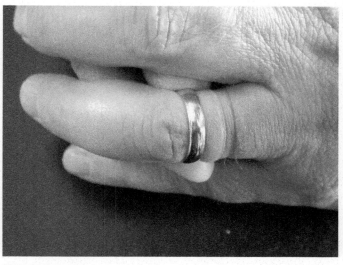

FIGURE 1–65 Remove all jewelry before performing service work on any vehicle.

- **Nitrile gloves.** These gloves are exactly like latex gloves, but are not affected by gas, oil, or solvents, yet they tend to be expensive.
- **Mechanic's gloves.** These gloves are usually made of synthetic leather and spandex and provide thermo protection, as well as protection from dirt and grime.
  ● **SEE FIGURE 1–64.**

SAFETY PRECAUTIONS

Besides wearing personal safety equipment, there are also many actions that should be performed to keep safe in the shop. These actions include:

- Remove jewelry that may get caught on something or act as a conductor to an exposed electrical circuit.
  ● **SEE FIGURE 1–65.**
- Take care of your hands. Keep your hands clean by washing with soap and hot water that is at least 110°F (43°C).
- Avoid loose or dangling clothing.
- When lifting any object, get a secure grip with solid footing. Keep the load close to your body to minimize the strain. Lift with your legs and arms, not your back.
- Do not twist your body when carrying a load. Instead, pivot your feet to help prevent strain on the spine.
- Ask for help when moving or lifting heavy objects.

FIGURE 1–66 Always connect an exhaust hose to the tailpipe of a vehicle to be run inside a building.

- Push a heavy object rather than pull it. (This is opposite to the way you should work with tools—never push a wrench! If you do and a bolt or nut loosens, your entire weight is used to propel your hand(s) forward. This usually results in cuts, bruises, or other painful injury.)
- Always connect an exhaust hose to the tailpipe of any running vehicle to help prevent the buildup of carbon monoxide inside a closed garage space.
  ● **SEE FIGURE 1–66.**
- When standing, keep objects, parts, and tools with which you are working between chest height and waist height. If seated, work at tasks that are at elbow height.
- Always be sure the hood is securely held open.

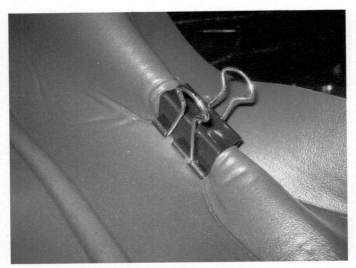

FIGURE 1–67 A binder clip being used to keep a fender cover from falling off.

FIGURE 1–68 Covering the interior as soon as the vehicle comes in for service helps improve customer satisfaction.

VEHICLE PROTECTION

FENDER COVERS Whenever working under the hood of any vehicle, be sure to use fender covers. They not only help protect the vehicle from possible damage but also provide a clean surface to place parts and tools. The major problem with using fender covers is that they tend to move and often fall off the vehicle. To help prevent the fender covers from falling off secure them to a lip of the fender using a *binder clip* available at most office supply stores. ● **SEE FIGURE 1–67.**

INTERIOR PROTECTION Always protect the interior of the vehicle from accidental damage or dirt and grease by covering the seat, steering wheel, and floor with a protective covering. ● **SEE FIGURE 1–68.**

✚ SAFETY TIP

Shop Cloth Disposal

Always dispose of oily shop cloths in an enclosed container to prevent a fire. ● **SEE FIGURE 1–69.** Whenever oily cloths are thrown together on the floor or workbench, a chemical reaction can occur, which can ignite the cloth even without an open flame. This process of ignition without an open flame is called **spontaneous combustion**.

SAFETY LIFTING (HOISTING) A VEHICLE

Many chassis and underbody service procedures require that the vehicle be hoisted or lifted off the ground. The simplest methods involve the use of drive-on ramps or a floor jack and safety (jack) stands, whereas in-ground or surface-mounted lifts provide greater access.

Setting the pads is a critical part of this hoisting procedure. All vehicle service information, including service, shop, and owner's manuals, include recommended locations to be used when hoisting (lifting) a vehicle. Newer vehicles have a triangle decal on the driver's door indicating the recommended lift points. The recommended standards for the lift points and lifting procedures are found in SAE Standard JRP-2184. ● **SEE FIGURE 1–70.**

FIGURE 1–69 All oily shop cloths should be stored in a metal container equipped with a lid to help prevent spontaneous combustion.

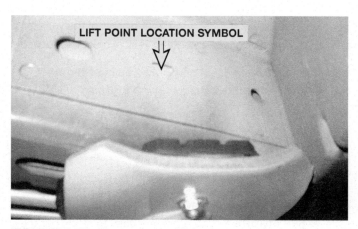

FIGURE 1–70 Most newer vehicles have a triangle symbol indicating the recommended hoisting lift location.

These recommendations typically include the following points:

1. The vehicle should be centered on the lift or hoist so as not to overload one side or put too much force either forward or rearward. ● SEE FIGURE 1–71.

2. The pads of the lift should be spread as far apart as possible to provide a stable platform.

3. Each pad should be placed under a portion of the vehicle that is strong and capable of supporting the weight of the vehicle.

    a. Pinch welds at the bottom edge of the body are generally considered to be strong.

CAUTION: Even though **pinch weld seams** are the recommended location for hoisting many vehicles with

(a)

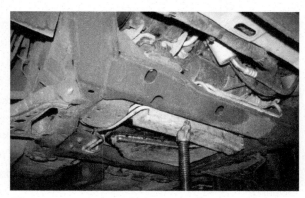

(b)

FIGURE 1–71 (a) Tall safety stands can be used to provide additional support for the vehicle while on the hoist. (b) A block of wood should be used to avoid the possibility of doing damage to components supported by the stand.

unitized bodies (unit-body), care should be taken not to place the pad(s) too far forward or rearward. Incorrect placement of the vehicle on the lift could cause the vehicle to be imbalanced, and the vehicle could fall. This is exactly what happened to the vehicle in ● FIGURE 1–72.

    b. Boxed areas of the body are the best places to position the pads on a vehicle without a frame. Be careful to note whether the arms of the lift might come into

FIGURE 1–72 This training vehicle fell from the hoist because the pads were not set correctly. No one was hurt but the vehicle was damaged.

contact with other parts of the vehicle before the pad touches the intended location. Commonly damaged areas include the following:

1. Rocker panel moldings

2. Exhaust system (including catalytic converter)

3. Tires or body panels (● **SEE FIGURES 1–73 AND 1–74.**)

4. The vehicle should be raised about a foot (30 centimeters [cm]) off the floor, then stopped and shaken to check for stability. If the vehicle seems to be stable when checked at a short distance from the floor, continue raising the vehicle and continue to view the vehicle until it has reached the desired height. The hoist should be lowered onto the mechanical locks, and then raised off of the locks before lowering.

CAUTION: Do not look away from the vehicle while it is being raised (or lowered) on a hoist. Often one side or one end of the hoist can stop or fail, resulting in the vehicle being slanted enough to slip or fall, creating physical damage not only to the vehicle and/or hoist, but also to the technician or others who may be nearby.

HINT: Most hoists can be safely placed at any desired height. For ease while working, the area in which you are working should be at chest level. When working on brakes or suspension components, it is not necessary to work on them down near the floor or over your head. Raise the hoist so that the components are at chest level.

5. Before lowering the hoist, the safety latch(es) must be released and the direction of the controls reversed. The speed downward is often adjusted to be as slow as possible for additional safety.

JACKS AND SAFETY STANDS

Floor jacks properly rated for the weight of the vehicle being raised are a common vehicle lifting tool. Floor jacks are portable and relatively inexpensive and must be used with safety (jack) stands. The floor jack is used to raise the vehicle off the ground and safety stands should be placed under the frame on the body of the vehicle. The weight of the vehicle should never be kept on the hydraulic floor jack because a failure of the jack could cause the vehicle to fall. ● **SEE FIGURE 1–75.** The jack is then slowly released to allow the vehicle weight to be supported on the safety stands. If the front or rear of the vehicle is being raised, the opposite end of the vehicle must be blocked.

CAUTION: Safety stands should be rated higher than the weight they support.

DRIVE-ON RAMPS

Ramps are an inexpensive way to raise the front or rear of a vehicle. ● **SEE FIGURE 1–76.** Ramps are easy to store, but they can be dangerous because they can "kick out" when driving the vehicle onto the ramps.

CAUTION: Professional repair shops do not use ramps because they are dangerous to use. Use only with extreme care.

ELECTRICAL CORD SAFETY

Use correctly grounded three-prong sockets and extension cords to operate power tools. Some tools use only two-prong plugs. Make sure these are double insulated and repair or replace any electrical cords that are cut or damaged to prevent the possibility of an electrical shock. When not in use, keep electrical cords off the floor to prevent tripping over them. Tape the cords down if they are placed in high foot traffic areas.

(a)

(b)

FIGURE 1–73 (a) An assortment of hoist pad adapters that are often needed to safely hoist many pickup trucks, vans, and sport utility vehicles (SUVs). (b) A view from underneath a Chevrolet pickup truck showing how the pad extensions are used to attach the hoist lifting pad to contact the frame.

(a)

(b)

FIGURE 1–74 (a) The pad arm is just contacting the rocker panel of the vehicle. (b) The pad arm has dented the rocker panel on this vehicle because the pad was set too far inward underneath the vehicle.

JUMP STARTING AND BATTERY SAFETY

To jump start another vehicle with a dead battery, connect good-quality copper jumper cables as indicated in ● **FIGURE 1–77** or a jump box. The last connection made should always be on the engine block or an engine bracket as far from the battery as possible. It is normal for a spark to be created when the jumper cables finally complete the jumper cable connections, and this spark could cause an explosion of the gases around the battery. Many newer vehicles have special ground connections built away from the battery just for the purpose of jump starting. Check the owner's manual or service information for the exact location.

Batteries contain acid and should be handled with care to avoid tipping them greater than a 45-degree angle. Always remove jewelry when working around a battery to avoid the possibility of electrical shock or burns, which can occur when the metal comes in contact with a 12-volt circuit and ground, such as the body of the vehicle.

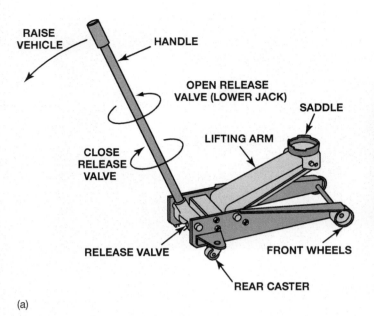

(a)

(b)

FIGURE 1–75 (a) A hydraulic hand-operated floor jack. (b) Whenever a vehicle is raised off the ground, a safety stand should be placed under the frame, axle, or body to support the weight of the vehicle.

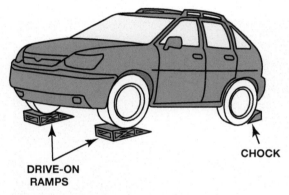

FIGURE 1–76 Drive-on-type ramps are dangerous to use. The wheels on the ground level must be chocked (blocked) to prevent accidental movement down the ramp.

SAFETY TIP

Air Hose Safety

Improper use of an air nozzle can cause blindness or deafness. Compressed air must be reduced to less than 30 PSI (206 kPa). ● **SEE FIGURE 1–78.** If an air nozzle is used to dry and clean parts, make sure the airstream is directed away from anyone else in the immediate area. Coil and store air hoses when they are not in use.

FIRE EXTINGUISHERS

There are four **fire extinguisher classes**. Each class should be used on specific fires only:

- Class A is designed for use on general combustibles, such as cloth, paper, and wood.
- Class B is designed for use on flammable liquids and greases, including gasoline, oil, thinners, and solvents.
- Class C is used only on electrical fires.
- Class D is effective only on combustible metals, such as powdered aluminum, sodium, or magnesium.

The class rating is clearly marked on the side of every fire extinguisher. Many extinguishers are good for multiple types of fires. ● **SEE FIGURE 1–79.**

When using a fire extinguisher, remember the word "PASS."

P = Pull the safety pin.

A = Aim the nozzle of the extinguisher at the base of the fire.

S = Squeeze the lever to actuate the extinguisher.

S = Sweep the nozzle from side to side.

● **SEE FIGURE 1–80.**

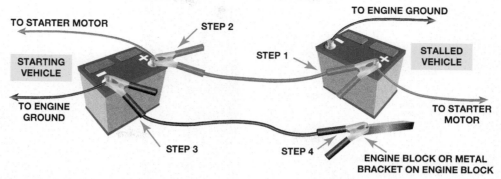

FIGURE 1–77 Jumper cable usage guide. Follow the same connections if using a portable jump box.

FIGURE 1–78 The air pressure going to the nozzle should be reduced to 30 PSI or less to help prevent personal injury.

TYPES OF FIRE EXTINGUISHERS
Types of fire extinguishers include the following:

- **Water.** A water fire extinguisher, usually in a pressurized container, is good to use on Class A fires by reducing the temperature to the point where a fire cannot be sustained.

- **Carbon dioxide (CO_2).** A carbon dioxide fire extinguisher is good for almost any type of fire, especially Class B and Class C materials. A CO_2 fire extinguisher works by removing the oxygen from the fire and the cold CO_2 also helps reduce the temperature of the fire.

- **Dry chemical (yellow).** A dry chemical fire extinguisher is good for Class A, B, and C fires. It acts by coating the flammable materials, which eliminates the oxygen from the fire. A dry chemical fire extinguisher tends to be very corrosive and will cause damage to electronic devices.

FIRE BLANKETS

Fire blankets are required to be available in the shop areas. If a person is on fire, a fire blanket should be removed from its storage bag and thrown over and around the victim to smother the fire. ● **SEE FIGURE 1–81** showing a typical fire blanket.

FIRST AID AND EYE WASH STATIONS

All shop areas must be equipped with a first aid kit and an eye wash station centrally located and kept stocked with emergency supplies. ● **SEE FIGURE 1–82.**

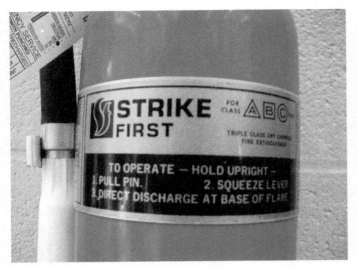

FIGURE 1–79 A typical fire extinguisher designed to be used on type A, B, or C fires.

FIGURE 1–81 A treated wool blanket is kept in an easy-to-open wall-mounted holder and should be placed in a central location in the shop.

FIGURE 1–80 A CO_2 fire extinguisher being used on a fire set in an open drum during a demonstration at a fire training center.

FIGURE 1–82 A first aid box should be centrally located in the shop and kept stocked with the recommended supplies.

FIRST AID KIT A first aid kit should include the following:

- Bandages (variety)
- Gauze pads
- Roll gauze
- Iodine swab sticks
- Antibiotic ointment
- Hydrocortisone cream
- Burn gel packets
- Eye wash solution
- Scissors
- Tweezers
- Gloves
- First aid guide

Every shop should have a person trained in first aid. If there is an accident, call for help immediately.

EYE WASH STATION An **eye wash station** should be centrally located and used whenever any liquid or chemical gets into the eyes. If such an emergency does occur, keep eyes in a constant stream of water and call for professional assistance. ● **SEE FIGURE 1–83.**

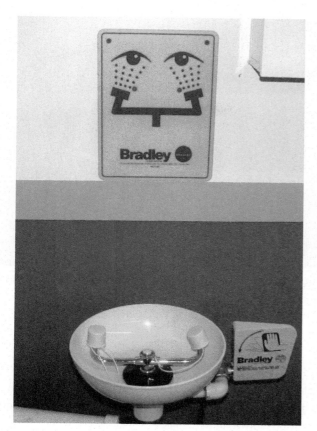

FIGURE 1–83 A typical eye wash station. Often a thorough flushing of the eyes with water is the first and often the best treatment in the event of eye contamination.

HYBRID ELECTRIC VEHICLE SAFETY ISSUES

Hybrid electric vehicles (HEVs) use a high-voltage battery pack and an electric motor(s) to help propel the vehicle. ● **SEE FIGURE 1–84** for an example of a typical warning label on a hybrid electric vehicle. The gasoline or diesel engine also is equipped with a generator or a combination starter and an integrated starter generator (ISG) or integrated starter alternator (ISA). To safely work around a hybrid electric vehicle, the high-voltage (HV) battery and circuits should be shut off following these steps:

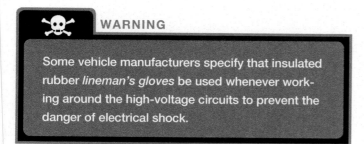

☠ **WARNING**

Some vehicle manufacturers specify that insulated rubber *lineman's gloves* be used whenever working around the high-voltage circuits to prevent the danger of electrical shock.

FIGURE 1–84 A warning label on a Honda hybrid warns that a person can be killed due to the high-voltage circuits under the cover.

➕ **SAFETY TIP**

Infection Control Precautions

Working on a vehicle can result in personal injury including the possibility of being cut or hurt enough to cause bleeding. Some infections such as hepatitis B, HIV (which can cause acquired immunodeficiency syndrome, or AIDS), and hepatitis C virus are transmitted through blood. These infections are commonly called blood-borne pathogens. Report any injury that involves blood to your supervisor and take the necessary precautions to avoid coming in contact with blood from another person.

STEP 1 Turn off the ignition key (if equipped) and remove the key from the ignition switch. (This will shut off all high-voltage circuits if the relay[s] is [are] working correctly.)

STEP 2 Disconnect the high-voltage circuits.

TOYOTA PRIUS The cutoff switch is located in the trunk. To gain access, remove three clips holding the upper left portion of the trunk side cover. To disconnect the high-voltage system, pull the orange-handled plug while wearing insulated rubber lineman's gloves. ● **SEE FIGURE 1–85.**

FORD ESCAPE/MERCURY MARINER Ford and Mercury specify that the following steps should be included when working with the high-voltage (HV) systems of a hybrid vehicle:

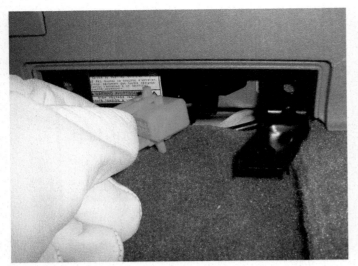

FIGURE 1–85 The high-voltage disconnect switch is in the trunk area on a Toyota Prius. Insulated rubber lineman's gloves should be worn when removing this plug.

FIGURE 1–87 The shut-off switch on a GM parallel hybrid truck is green because this system uses 42 volts instead of higher, and possibly fatal, voltages used in other hybrid vehicles.

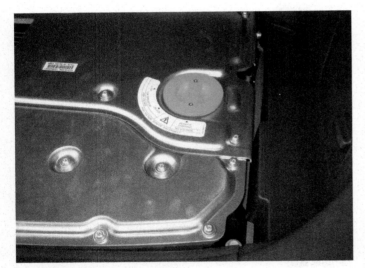

FIGURE 1–86 The high-voltage shut-off switch on a Ford Escape hybrid. The switch is located under the carpet at the rear of the vehicle.

- Four orange cones are to be placed at the four corners of the vehicle to create a buffer zone.

- High-voltage insulated gloves are to be worn with an outer leather glove to protect the inner rubber glove from possible damage.

- The service technician should also wear a face shield and a fiberglass hook should be in the area and used to move a technician in the event of electrocution.

The high-voltage shut-off switch is located in the rear of the vehicle under the right side carpet. ● **SEE FIGURE 1–86.**

Rotate the handle to the "service shipping" position, lift it out to disable the high-voltage circuit, and wait five minutes before removing high-voltage cables.

HONDA CIVIC   To totally disable the high-voltage system on a Honda Civic, remove the main fuse (labeled number 1) from the driver's side underhood fuse panel. This should be all that is necessary to shut off the high-voltage circuit. If this is not possible, then remove the rear seat cushion and seat back. Remove the metal switch cover labeled "up" and remove the red locking cover. Move the "battery module switch" down to disable the high-voltage system.

CHEVROLET SILVERADO/GMC SIERRA PICKUP TRUCK   The high-voltage shut-off switch is located under the rear passenger seat. Remove the cover marked "energy storage box" and turn the green service disconnect switch to the horizontal position to turn off the high-voltage circuits. ● **SEE FIGURE 1–87.**

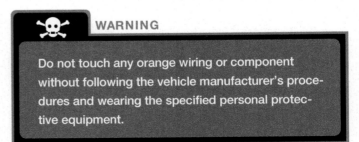

WARNING

Do not touch any orange wiring or component without following the vehicle manufacturer's procedures and wearing the specified personal protective equipment.

1 The first step in hoisting a vehicle is to properly align the vehicle in the center of the stall.

2 Most vehicles will be correctly positioned when the left front tire is centered on the tire pad.

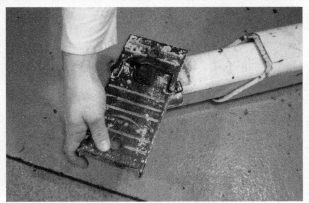

3 The arms can be moved in and out and most pads can be rotated to allow for many different types of vehicle construction.

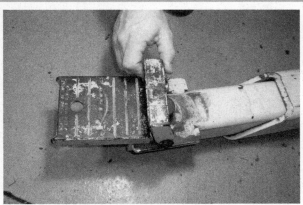

4 Most lifts are equipped with short pad extensions that are often necessary to use to allow the pad to contact the frame of a vehicle without causing the arm of the lift to hit and damage parts of the body.

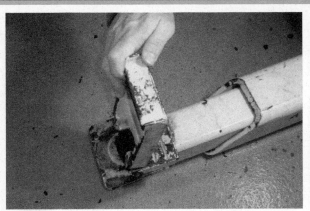

5 Tall pad extensions can also be used to gain access to the frame of a vehicle. This position is needed to safely hoist many pickup trucks, vans, and sport utility vehicles.

6 An additional extension may be necessary to hoist a truck or van equipped with running boards to give the necessary clearance.

CONTINUED ▶

STEP BY STEP

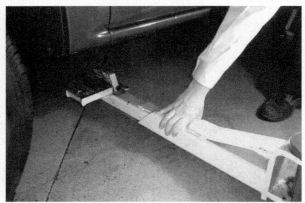

7 Position the pads under the vehicle under the recommended locations.

8 After being sure all pads are correctly positioned, use the electromechanical controls to raise the vehicle.

9 With the vehicle raised one foot (30 cm) off the ground, push down on the vehicle to check to see if it is stable on the pads. If the vehicle rocks, lower the vehicle and reset the pads. The vehicle can be raised to any desired working level. Be sure the safety is engaged before working on or under the vehicle.

10 If raising a vehicle without a frame, place the flat pads under the pinch weld seam to spread the load. If additional clearance is necessary, the pads can be raised as shown.

11 When the service work is completed, the hoist should be raised slightly and the safety released before using the hydraulic lever to lower the vehicle.

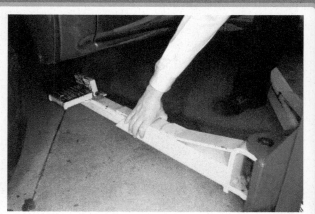

12 After lowering the vehicle, be sure all arms of the lift are moved out of the way before driving the vehicle out of the work stall.

1. Bolts, studs, and nuts are commonly used as fasteners in the chassis. The sizes for fractional and metric threads are different and are not interchangeable. The grade is the rating of the strength of a fastener.

2. Whenever a vehicle is raised above the ground, it must be supported at a substantial section of the body or frame.

3. Wrenches are available in open end, box end, and combination open and box end.

4. An adjustable wrench should only be used when the proper size is not available.

5. Line wrenches are also called flare-nut wrenches, fitting wrenches, or tube-nut wrenches and are used to remove fuel or refrigerant lines.

6. Sockets are rotated by a ratchet or breaker bar, also called a flex handle.

7. Torque wrenches measure the amount of torque applied to a fastener.

8. Screwdriver types include straight blade (flat tip) and Phillips.

9. Hammers and mallets come in a variety of sizes and weights.

10. Pliers are a useful tool and are available in many different types, including slip-joint, multigroove, linesman's, diagonal, needle-nose, and locking pliers.

11. Other common hand tools include snap-ring pliers, files, cutters, punches, chisels, and hacksaws.

12. Hybrid electric vehicles should be de-powered if any of the high-voltage components are going to be serviced.

REVIEW QUESTIONS

1. Why are wrenches offset 15 degrees?

2. What are the other names for a line wrench?

3. Which type of screwdriver requires the use of a hammer or mallet?

4. What is inside a dead-blow hammer?

5. What type of cutter is available in left and right cutters?

CHAPTER QUIZ

1. The correct location for the pads when hoisting or jacking the vehicle can often be found in the _____.
   a. service manual
   b. shop manual
   c. owner's manual
   d. All of the above

2. For the best working position, the work should be _____.
   a. at neck or head level
   b. at knee or ankle level
   c. overhead by about 1 foot
   d. at chest or elbow level

3. A high-strength bolt is identified by _____.
   a. a UNC symbol
   b. lines on the head
   c. strength letter codes
   d. the coarse threads

4. A fastener that uses threads on both ends is called a _____.
   a. cap screw
   b. stud
   c. machine screw
   d. crest fastener

5. Wrenches are made from_____.
   a. cast from nickel steel
   b. forged alloy steel
   c. machined from billet steel
   d. cast from chrome steel

6. The proper term for Channel Locks is _____.
   a. vise Grips
   b. crescent wrench
   c. locking pliers
   d. multigroove adjustable pliers

7. The proper term for Vise Grips is _____.
   a. locking pliers
   b. slip-joint pliers
   c. side cuts
   d. multigroove adjustable pliers

8. Two technicians are discussing torque wrenches. Technician A says that a torque wrench is capable of tightening a fastener with more torque than a conventional breaker bar or ratchet. Technician B says that a torque wrench should be calibrated regularly for the most accurate results. Which technician is correct?
   a. Technician A only
   b. Technician B only
   c. Both Technicians A and B
   d. Neither Technician A nor B

9. A yellow-handle snip is designed for_____.
   a. Straight cuts
   b. Left cuts
   c. Right cuts
   d. Cutting plastic only

10. What type of hammer is plastic coated, has a metal casing inside, and is filled with small lead balls?
    a. Dead-blow hammer
    b. Soft-blow hammer
    c. Sledgehammer
    d. Plastic hammer

chapter 2
ENVIRONMENTAL AND HAZARDOUS MATERIALS

HAZARDOUS WASTE

DEFINITION OF HAZARDOUS WASTE

Hazardous waste materials are chemicals, or components, that the shop no longer needs and that pose a danger to the environment and people if they are disposed of in ordinary garbage cans or sewers. However, no material is considered hazardous waste until the shop has finished using it and is ready to dispose of it.

PERSONAL PROTECTIVE EQUIPMENT (PPE)

When handling hazardous waste material, always wear the proper protective clothing and equipment detailed in the right-to-know laws. This includes respirator equipment. All recommended procedures must be followed accurately. Personal injury may result from improper clothing, equipment, and procedures when handling hazardous materials.

FEDERAL AND STATE LAWS

OCCUPATIONAL SAFETY AND HEALTH ACT

The U.S. Congress passed the **Occupational Safety and Health Act (OSHA)** in 1970. This legislation was designed to assist and encourage the citizens of the United States in their efforts to assure the following:

- Safe and healthful working conditions by providing research, information, education, and training in the field of occupational safety and health.
- Safe and healthful working conditions by authorizing enforcement of the standards developed under the act.

Because about 25% of workers are exposed to health and safety hazards on the job, OSHA standards are necessary to monitor, control, and educate workers regarding health and safety in the workplace.

EPA

The **Environmental Protection Agency (EPA)** publishes a list of hazardous materials that is included in the **Code of Federal Regulations (CFR)**. The EPA considers waste hazardous if it is included on the EPA list of hazardous materials, or it has one or more of the following characteristics:

- **Reactive**—Any material that reacts violently with water or other chemicals is considered hazardous.
- **Corrosive**—If a material burns the skin, or dissolves metals and other materials, a technician should consider it

hazardous. A pH scale is used, with number 7 indicating neutral. Pure water has a pH of 7. Lower numbers indicate an acidic solution and higher numbers indicates an alkaline (caustic) solution. If a material releases cyanide gas, hydrogen sulfide gas, or similar gases when exposed to low pH acid solutions, it is considered hazardous.

- **Toxic**—Materials are hazardous if they leak one or more of eight different heavy metals in concentrations greater than 100 times the primary drinking water standard.
- **Ignitable**—A liquid is hazardous if it has a flash point below 140°F (60°C), and a solid is hazardous if it ignites spontaneously.
- **Radioactive**—Any substance that emits measurable levels of radiation is radioactive. When individuals bring containers of a highly radioactive substance into the shop environment, qualified personnel with the appropriate equipment must test them.

WARNING

Hazardous waste disposal laws include serious penalties for anyone responsible for breaking these laws.

RIGHT-TO-KNOW LAWS

The **right-to-know laws** state that employees have a right to know when the materials they use at work are hazardous. The right-to-know laws started with the Hazard Communication Standard published by the Occupational Safety and Health Administration (OSHA) in 1983. Originally, this document was intended for chemical companies and manufacturers that required employees to handle hazardous materials in their work situation but the federal courts have decided to apply these laws to all companies, including automotive service shops. Under the right-to-know laws, the employer has responsibilities regarding the handling of hazardous materials by their employees. All employees must be trained about the types of hazardous materials they will encounter in the workplace. The employees must be informed about their rights under legislation regarding the handling of hazardous materials.

SAFETY DATA SHEETS (SDS).

All hazardous materials must be properly labeled, and information about each hazardous material must be posted on **safety data sheets (SDS)**, formally called *material safety data sheets* (MSDS), available from the manufacturer. In Canada, MSDS information is called **Workplace Hazardous Materials Information Systems (WHMIS)**.

FIGURE 2–1 Safety data sheets (SDS), formerly known as material safety data sheets (MSDS), should be readily available for use by anyone in the area who may come into contact with hazardous materials.

The employer has a responsibility to place MSDS information where it is easily accessible by all employees. The data sheets provide the following information about the hazardous material: chemical name, physical characteristics, protective handling equipment, explosion/fire hazards, incompatible materials, health hazards, medical conditions aggravated by exposure, emergency and first-aid procedures, safe handling, and spill/leak procedures.

The employer also has a responsibility to make sure that all hazardous materials are properly labeled. The label information must include health, fire, and reactivity hazards posed by the material, as well as the protective equipment necessary to handle the material. The manufacturer must supply all warning and precautionary information about hazardous materials. This information must be read and understood by the employee before handling the material. ● **SEE FIGURE 2–1.**

RESOURCE CONSERVATION AND RECOVERY ACT

Federal and state laws control the disposal of hazardous waste materials and every shop employee must be familiar with these laws. Hazardous waste disposal laws include the **Resource Conservation and Recovery Act (RCRA)**. This law states that hazardous material users are responsible for hazardous materials from the time they become a waste until the proper disposal is completed. Many shops hire an independent hazardous waste hauler to dispose of hazardous waste material. The shop owner, or manager, should have a written contract with the hazardous waste hauler. Rather than have hazardous waste material hauled to an approved hazardous

FIGURE 2–2 Tag that identifies the electrical power has been removed and service work is being done.

waste disposal site, a shop may choose to recycle the material in the shop. Therefore, the user must store hazardous waste material properly and safely, and be responsible for the transportation of this material until it arrives at an approved hazardous waste disposal site, where it can be processed according to the law. The RCRA controls the following types of automotive waste:

- Paint and body repair products waste
- Solvents for parts and equipment cleaning
- Batteries and battery acid
- Mild acids used for metal cleaning and preparation
- Waste oil and engine coolants or antifreeze
- Air-conditioning refrigerants and oils
- Engine oil filters

LOCKOUT/TAGOUT According to OSHA Title 29, code of Federal Regulations (CPR), part 1910.147, machinery must be locked out to prevent injury to employees when maintenance or repair work is being performed. Any piece of equipment that should not be used must be tagged and the electrical power disconnected to prevent it from being used. Always read, understand, and follow all safety warning tags. ● **SEE FIGURE 2–2.**

CLEAN AIR ACT Air-conditioning (A/C) systems and refrigerant are regulated by the **Clean Air Act (CAA)**, Title VI, Section 609. Technician certification and service equipment is also regulated. Any technician working on automotive A/C systems must be certified. A/C refrigerants must not be released or vented into the atmosphere, and used refrigerants must be recovered.

ASBESTOS HAZARDS

Friction materials, such as brake and clutch linings, often contain asbestos. While asbestos has been eliminated from most original equipment friction materials, the automotive service technician cannot know whether or not the vehicle being serviced is or is not equipped with friction materials containing asbestos. It is important that all friction materials be handled as if they do contain asbestos.

Asbestos exposure can cause scar tissue to form in the lungs. This condition is called **asbestosis**. It gradually causes increasing shortness of breath, and scarring to the lungs is permanent.

Even low exposures to asbestos can cause *mesothelioma*, a type of fatal cancer of the lining of the chest or abdominal cavity. Asbestos exposure can also increase the risk of *lung cancer*, as well as, cancer of the voice box, stomach, and large intestine. It usually takes 15 to 30 years or more for cancer or asbestos lung scarring to show up after exposure. Scientists call this the *latency period*.

Government agencies recommend that asbestos exposure should be eliminated or controlled to the lowest level possible. These agencies have developed recommendations and standards that the automotive service technician and equipment manufacturer should follow. These U.S. federal agencies include the National Institute for Occupational Safety and Health (NIOSH), Occupational Safety and Health Administration (OSHA), and Environmental Protection Agency (EPA).

ASBESTOS OSHA STANDARDS The Occupational Safety and Health Administration has established three levels of asbestos exposure. Any vehicle service establishment that does either brake or clutch work must limit employee exposure to asbestos to less than 0.2 fibers per cubic centimeter (cc) as determined by an air sample.

If the level of exposure to employees is greater than specified, corrective measures must be performed and a large fine may be imposed.

NOTE: Research has found that worn asbestos fibers, such as those from automotive brakes or clutches, may not be as hazardous as first believed. Worn asbestos fibers do not have sharp flared ends that can latch onto tissue, but rather are worn down to a dust form that resembles talc. Grinding or sawing operations on unworn brake shoes or clutch discs *will* contain *harmful* asbestos fibers. To limit health damage, always use proper handling procedures while working around any component that may contain asbestos.

FIGURE 2–3 All brakes should be moistened with water or solvent to help prevent brake dust from becoming airborne.

ASBESTOS EPA REGULATIONS The federal Environmental Protection Agency has established procedures for the removal and disposal of asbestos. The EPA procedures require that products containing asbestos be "wetted" to prevent the asbestos fibers from becoming airborne. According to the EPA, asbestos-containing materials can be disposed of as regular waste. Only when asbestos becomes airborne, is it considered to be hazardous.

ASBESTOS HANDLING GUIDELINES The air in the shop area can be tested by a testing laboratory, but this can be expensive. Tests have determined that asbestos levels can easily be kept below the recommended levels by using a liquid, like water, or a special vacuum.

NOTE: Even though asbestos is being removed from brake and clutch lining materials, the service technician cannot tell whether or not the old brake pads, shoes, or clutch discs contain asbestos. Therefore, to be safe, the technician should assume that all brake pads, shoes, or clutch discs contain asbestos.

HEPA VACUUM. A special **high-efficiency particulate air (HEPA) vacuum** system has been proven to be effective in keeping asbestos exposure levels below 0.1 fibers per cubic centimeter.

SOLVENT SPRAY. Many technicians use an aerosol can of brake cleaning solvent to wet the brake dust and prevent it from becoming airborne. A **solvent** is a liquid that is used to dissolve dirt, grime, or solid particles. Commercial brake cleaners are available that use a concentrated cleaner that is mixed with water. ● **SEE FIGURE 2–3.** The waste liquid is filtered, and when dry, the filter can be disposed of as solid waste.

DISPOSAL OF BRAKE DUST AND BRAKE SHOES. The hazard of asbestos occurs when asbestos fibers are airborne. Once the asbestos has been wetted down, it is then considered to be solid waste, rather than hazardous waste. Old brake shoes and pads should be enclosed, preferably in a plastic bag, to help prevent any of the brake material from becoming airborne. *Always follow current federal and local laws concerning disposal of all waste.*

USED BRAKE FLUID

Most brake fluid is made from polyglycol, is water soluble, and can be considered hazardous if it has absorbed metals from the brake system.

STORAGE AND DISPOSAL OF BRAKE FLUID

- Collect brake fluid in a container clearly marked to indicate that it is designated for that purpose.
- If the waste brake fluid is hazardous, be sure to manage it appropriately and use only an authorized waste receiver for its disposal.
- If the waste brake fluid is nonhazardous (such as old, but unused), determine from your local solid waste collection provider what should be done for its proper disposal.
- Do not mix brake fluid with used engine oil.
- Do not pour brake fluid down drains or onto the ground.
- Recycle brake fluid through a registered recycler.

USED OIL

Used oil is any petroleum-based or synthetic oil that has been used. During normal use, impurities such as dirt, metal scrapings, water, or chemicals can get mixed in with the oil. Eventually, this used oil must be replaced with virgin or re-refined oil. The EPA's used oil management standards include a three-pronged approach to determine if a substance meets the definition of *used oil*. To meet the EPA's definition of used oil, a substance must meet each of the following three criteria :

- **Origin.** The first criterion for identifying used oil is based on the oil's origin. Used oil must have been refined from crude oil or made from synthetic materials. Animal and vegetable oils are excluded from the EPA's definition of used oil.
- **Use.** The second criterion is based on whether and how the oil is used. Oils used as lubricants, hydraulic fluids, heat transfer fluids, and for other similar purposes are considered used oil. The EPA's definition also excludes products used as cleaning agents, as well as certain petroleum-derived products like antifreeze and kerosene.
- **Contaminants.** The third criterion is based on whether or not the oil is contaminated with either physical or chemical impurities. In other words, to meet the EPA's definition, used oil must become contaminated as a result of being used. This aspect of the EPA's definition includes residues and contaminants generated from handling, storing, and processing used oil.

NOTE: The release of only one gallon of used oil (a typical oil change) can make a million gallons of fresh water undrinkable.

If used oil is dumped down the drain and enters a sewage treatment plant, concentrations as small as 50 to 100 PPM (parts per million) in the waste water can foul sewage treatment processes. Never mix a listed hazardous waste, gasoline, waste water, halogenated solvent, antifreeze, or an unknown waste material with used oil. Adding any of these substances will cause the used oil to become contaminated, which classifies it as hazardous waste.

STORAGE AND DISPOSAL OF USED OIL Once oil has been used, it can be collected, recycled, and used over and over again. An estimated 380 million gallons of used oil are recycled each year. Recycled used oil can sometimes be used again for the same job or can take on a completely different task. For example, used engine oil can be re-refined and sold at some discount stores as engine oil or processed for furnace fuel oil. After collecting used oil in an appropriate container such as a 55-gallon steel drum, the material must be disposed of in one of two ways:

- Shipped offsite for recycling
- Burned in an onsite or offsite EPA-approved heater for energy recovery

Used (waste) oil must be stored in compliance with an existing **underground storage tank (UST)** or an **aboveground**

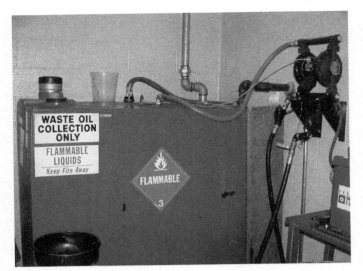

FIGURE 2–4 A typical aboveground oil storage tank.

storage tank (AGST) standard, or kept in separate containers.
● **SEE FIGURE 2–4.** Containers are portable receptacles, such as a 55-gallon steel drum.

KEEP USED OIL STORAGE DRUMS IN GOOD CONDITION. This means that they should be covered, secured from vandals, properly labeled, and maintained in compliance with local fire codes. Frequent inspections for leaks, corrosion, and spillage are an essential part of container maintenance.

NEVER STORE USED OIL IN ANYTHING OTHER THAN TANKS AND STORAGE CONTAINERS. Used oil may also be stored in units that are permitted to store regulated hazardous waste.

USED OIL FILTER DISPOSAL REGULATIONS. Used oil filters contain used engine oil that may be hazardous. Before an oil filter is placed into the trash or sent to be recycled, it must be drained using one of the following hot-draining methods approved by the EPA :

- Puncture the filter antidrainback valve or filter dome end and hot-drain for at least 12 hours
- Hot-drain and crushing
- Dismantling and hot draining
- Any other hot-draining method, which will remove all the used oil from the filter

After the oil has been drained from the oil filter, the filter housing can be disposed of in any of the following ways:

- Sent for recycling
- Picked up by a service contract company
- Disposed of in regular trash

SOLVENTS

The major sources of chemical danger are liquid and aerosol brake cleaning fluids that contain chlorinated hydrocarbon solvents. Several other chemicals that do not deplete the ozone, such as heptane, hexane, and xylene, are now being used in nonchlorinated brake cleaning solvents. Some manufacturers are also producing solvents they describe as environmentally responsible, which are biodegradable and noncarcinogenic (non-cancer-causing).

There is no specific standard for physical contact with chlorinated hydrocarbon solvents or the chemicals replacing them. All contact should be avoided whenever possible. The law requires an employer to provide appropriate protective equipment and ensure proper work practices by an employee handling these chemicals.

 **SAFETY TIP**

Hand Safety

Service technicians should wash their hands with soap and water after handling engine oil, differential oil, or transmission fluids or wear protective rubber gloves. Another safety tip is that the service technician should not wear watches, rings, or other jewelry that could come in contact with electrical or moving parts of a vehicle. ● **SEE FIGURE 2–5.**

EFFECTS OF CHEMICAL POISONING The effects of exposure to chlorinated hydrocarbon and other types of solvents can take many forms. Short-term exposure at low levels can cause symptoms, such as the following:

- Headache
- Nausea
- Drowsiness
- Dizziness
- Lack of coordination
- Unconsciousness

It may also cause irritation of the eyes, nose, and throat, and flushing of the face and neck. Short-term exposure to higher concentrations can cause liver damage with symptoms such as yellow jaundice or dark urine. Liver damage may not become evident until several weeks after the exposure.

FIGURE 2–5 Washing hands and removing jewelry are two important safety habits all service technicians should practice.

FIGURE 2–6 Typical fireproof flammable storage cabinet.

 FREQUENTLY ASKED QUESTION

How Can You Tell If a Solvent Is Hazardous?

If a solvent or any of the ingredients of a product contains "fluor" or "chlor," it is likely to be hazardous. Check the instructions on the label for proper use and disposal procedures.

HAZARDOUS SOLVENTS AND REGULATORY STATUS

Most solvents are classified as hazardous wastes. Other characteristics of solvents include the following:

- Solvents with flash points above 140°F (60°C) are considered flammable and, like gasoline, are federally regulated by the Department of Transportation (DOT).

- Solvents and oils with flash points above 140°F (60°C) are considered combustible and, like engine oil, are also regulated by the DOT. All flammable items must be stored in a fireproof container. ● **SEE FIGURE 2–6.**

It is the responsibility of the repair shop to determine if spent solvent is hazardous waste. Solvent reclaimers are available that clean and restore the solvent so it lasts indefinitely.

USED SOLVENTS Used or spent solvents are liquid materials that have been generated as waste and may contain xylene, methanol, ethyl ether, and methyl isobutyl ketone (MIBK). These materials must be stored in OSHA-approved safety containers with the lids or caps closed tightly. Additional requirements include the following:

- Containers should be clearly labeled "Hazardous Waste" and the date the material was first placed into the storage receptacle should be noted.

- Labeling is not required for solvents being used in a parts washer.

- Used solvents will not be counted toward a facility's monthly output of hazardous waste if the vendor under contract removes the material.

- Used solvents may be disposed of by recycling with a local vendor, like SafetyKleen®, to have the used solvent removed according to specific terms in the vendor agreement.

- Use aqueous-based (nonsolvent) cleaning systems to help avoid the problems associated with chemical solvents. ● **SEE FIGURE 2–7.**

COOLANT DISPOSAL

Coolant is a mixture of antifreeze and water. New antifreeze is not considered to be hazardous even though it can cause death if ingested. Used antifreeze may be hazardous due to dissolved metals from the engine and other components of the cooling system. These metals can include iron, steel, aluminum, copper, brass, and lead (from older radiators and

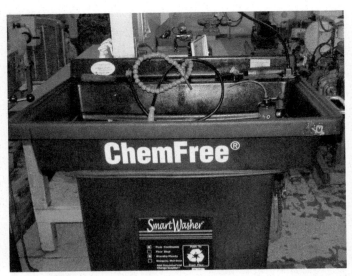

FIGURE 2–7 Using a water-based cleaning system helps reduce the hazards from using strong chemicals.

FIGURE 2–8 Used antifreeze coolant should be kept separate and stored in a leakproof container until it can be recycled or disposed of according to federal, state, and local laws. Note that the storage barrel is placed inside another container to catch any coolant that may spill out of the inside barrel.

heater cores). Coolant should be disposed of in one of the following ways:

- Coolant should be recycled either onsite or offsite.
- Used coolant should be stored in a sealed and labeled container. ● **SEE FIGURE 2–8.**
- Used coolant can often be disposed of into municipal sewers with a permit. Check with local authorities and obtain a permit before discharging used coolant into sanitary sewers.

LEAD-ACID BATTERY WASTE

About 70 million spent lead-acid batteries are generated each year in the United States alone. Lead is classified as a toxic metal, and the acid used in lead-acid batteries is highly corrosive. The vast majority (95% to 98%) of these batteries are recycled through lead reclamation operations and secondary lead smelters for use in the manufacture of new batteries.

BATTERY DISPOSAL Used lead-acid batteries must be reclaimed or recycled in order to be exempt from hazardous waste regulations. Leaking batteries must be stored and transported as hazardous waste. Some states have more strict regulations, which require special handling procedures and

transportation. According to the **Battery Council International (BCI)**, battery laws usually include the following rules:

1. Lead-acid battery disposal is prohibited in landfills or incinerators. Batteries are required to be delivered to a battery retailer, wholesaler, recycling center, or lead smelter.

2. All retailers of automotive batteries are required to post a sign that displays the universal recycling symbol and indicates the retailer's specific requirements for accepting used batteries.

3. Battery electrolyte contains sulfuric acid, which is a very corrosive substance capable of causing serious personal injury, such as skin burns and eye damage. In addition, the battery plates contain lead, which is highly poisonous. For this reason, disposing of batteries improperly can cause environmental contamination and lead to severe health problems.

BATTERY HANDLING AND STORAGE Batteries, whether new or used, should be kept indoors if possible. The storage location should be an area specifically designated for battery storage and must be well ventilated (to the outside). If outdoor storage is the only alternative, a sheltered and secured area with acid-resistant secondary containment is strongly recommended. It is also advisable that acid-resistant secondary containment be used for indoor storage. In addition, batteries should be placed on acid-resistant pallets and never stacked.

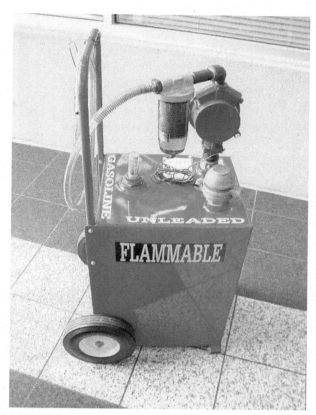

FIGURE 2–9 This red gasoline container holds about 30 gallons of gasoline and is used to fill vehicles used for training.

FUEL SAFETY AND STORAGE

Gasoline is a very explosive liquid. The expanding vapors that come from gasoline are extremely dangerous. These vapors are present even in cold temperatures. Vapors formed in gasoline tanks on many vehicles are controlled, but vapors from gasoline storage may escape from the can, resulting in a hazardous situation. Therefore, place gasoline storage containers in a well-ventilated space. Although diesel fuel is not as volatile as gasoline, the same basic rules apply to diesel fuel and gasoline storage. These rules include the following:

1. Use storage cans that have a flash-arresting screen at the outlet. These screens prevent external ignition sources from igniting the gasoline within the can when pouring the gasoline the gasoline or diesel fuel.

2. Use only a red approved gasoline container to allow for proper hazardous substance identification. ● **SEE FIGURE 2–9.**

3. Do not fill gasoline containers completely full. Always leave the level of gasoline at least one inch from the top of the container. This action allows expansion of the gasoline at higher temperatures. If gasoline containers are completely full, the gasoline will expand when the temperature increases. This expansion forces gasoline from the can and creates a dangerous spill. If gasoline or diesel fuel containers must be stored, place them in a designated storage locker or facility.

4. Never leave gasoline containers open, except while filling or pouring gasoline from the container.

5. Never use gasoline as a cleaning agent.

6. Always connect a ground strap to containers when filling or transferring fuel or other flammable products from one container to another to prevent static electricity that could result in explosion and fire. These ground wires prevent the buildup of a static electric charge, which could result in a spark and disastrous explosion.

AIRBAG HANDLING

Airbag modules are pyrotechnic devices that can be ignited if exposed to an electrical charge or if the body of the vehicle is subjected to a shock. Airbag safety should include the following precautions:

1. Disarm the airbag(s) if you will be working in the area where a discharged bag could make contact with any part of your body. Consult service information for the exact procedure to follow for the vehicle being serviced. The usual procedure is to deploy the airbag using a 12-volt power supply, such as a jump start box, using long wires to connect to the module to ensure a safe deployment.

2. Do not expose an airbag to extreme heat or fire.

3. Always carry an airbag pointing away from your body.

4. Place an airbag module facing upward.

5. Always follow the manufacturer's recommended procedure for airbag disposal or recycling, including the proper packaging to use during shipment.

6. Wear protective gloves if handling a deployed airbag.

7. Always wash your hands or body well if exposed to a deployed airbag. The chemicals involved can cause skin irritation and possible rash development.

FIGURE 2–10 Air-conditioning refrigerant oil must be kept separated from other oils because it contains traces of refrigerant and must be treated as hazardous waste.

This vehicle may include mercury-added devices installed by the manufacturer:

- **REAR SEAT VIDEO DISPLAY**
- **NAVIGATION DISPLAY**
- **H.I.D. HEADLAMPS**

Remove devices before vehicle disposal. Upon removal of devices please reuse, recycle or dispose as hazardous waste.

05020527AA

FIGURE 2–11 Placard near driver's door, including what devices in the vehicle contain mercury.

USED TIRE DISPOSAL

Used tires are an environmental concern because of several reasons, including the following:

1. In a landfill, they tend to "float" up through the other trash and rise to the surface.

2. The inside of tires traps and holds rainwater, which is a breeding ground for mosquitoes. Mosquito-borne diseases include encephalitis and dengue fever.

3. Used tires present a fire hazard and, when burned, create a large amount of black smoke that contaminates the air.

Used tires should be disposed of in one of the following ways:

1. Used tires can be reused until the end of their useful life.

2. Tires can be retreaded.

3. Tires can be recycled or shredded for use in asphalt.

4. Tires removed from the rims can be sent to a landfill (most landfill operators will shred the tires because it is illegal in many states to landfill whole tires).

5. Tires can be burned in cement kilns or other power plants where the smoke can be controlled.

6. A registered scrap tire handler should be used to transport tires for disposal or recycling.

AIR-CONDITIONING REFRIGERANT OIL DISPOSAL

Air-conditioning refrigerant oil contains dissolved refrigerant and is therefore considered to be hazardous waste. This oil must be kept separated from other waste oil or the entire amount of oil must be treated as hazardous. Used refrigerant oil must be sent to a licensed hazardous waste disposal company for recycling or disposal. ● **SEE FIGURE 2–10.**

WASTE CHART   All automotive service facilities create some waste and while most of it is handled properly, it is important that all hazardous and nonhazardous waste be accounted for and properly disposed. ● **SEE CHART 2–1** for a list of typical wastes generated at automotive shops, plus a checklist for keeping track of how these wastes are handled.

 TECH TIP

Remove Components That Contain Mercury

Some vehicles have a placard near the driver's side door that lists the components that contain the heavy metal, mercury. **Mercury** can be absorbed through the skin and is a heavy metal that once absorbed by the body does not leave. ● **SEE FIGURE 2–11.**

These components should be removed from the vehicle before the rest of the body is sent to be recycled to help prevent releasing mercury into the environment.

WASTE STREAM	TYPICAL CATEGORY IF NOT MIXED WITH OTHER HAZARDOUS WASTE	IF DISPOSED IN LANDFILL AND NOT MIXED WITH A HAZARDOUS WASTE	IF RECYCLED
Used oil	Used oil	Hazardous waste	Used oil
Used oil filters	Nonhazardous solid waste, if completely drained	Nonhazardous solid waste, if completely drained	Used oil, if not drained
Used transmission fluid	Used oil	Hazardous waste	Used oil
Used brake fluid	Used oil	Hazardous waste	Used oil
Used antifreeze	Depends on characterization	Depends on characterization	Depends on characterization
Used solvents	Hazardous waste	Hazardous waste	Hazardous waste
Used citric solvents	Nonhazardous solid waste	Nonhazardous solid waste	Hazardous waste
Lead-acid automotive batteries	Not a solid waste if returned to supplier	Hazardous waste	Hazardous waste
Shop rags used for oil	Used oil	Depends on used oil characterization	Used oil
Shop rags used for solvent or gasoline spills	Hazardous waste	Hazardous waste	Hazardous waste
Oil spill absorbent material	Used oil	Depends on used oil characterization	Used oil
Spill material for solvent and gasoline	Hazardous waste	Hazardous waste	Hazardous waste
Catalytic converter	Not a solid waste if returned to supplier	Nonhazardous solid waste	Nonhazardous solid waste
Spilled or unused fuels	Hazardous waste	Hazardous waste	Hazardous waste
Spilled or unusable paints and thinners	Hazardous waste	Hazardous waste	Hazardous waste
Used tires	Nonhazardous solid waste	Nonhazardous solid waste	Nonhazardous solid waste

CHART 2–1

Typical waste materials generated at auto repair shops and typical category (hazardous or nonhazardous) by disposal method.

 **TECH TIP**

What Every Technician Should Know

OSHA has adopted new hazardous chemical labeling requirements making it agree with global labeling standards established by the United Nations. As a result, workers will have better information available on the safe handling and use of hazardous chemicals, allowing them to avoid injuries and possible illnesses related to exposures to hazardous chemicals.
● **SEE FIGURE 2–12.**

HEALTH HAZARD	FLAME	EXCLAMATION MARK
• CARCINOGEN • MUTAGENICITY • REPRODUCTIVE TOXICITY • RESPIRATORY SENSITIZER • TARGET ORGAN TOXICITY • ASPIRATION TOXICITY	• FLAMMABLES • PYROPHORICS • SELF-HEATING • EMITS FLAMMABLE GAS • SELF-REACTIVES • ORGANIC PEROXIDES	• IRRITANT (SKIN AND EYE) • SKIN SENSITIZER • ACUTE TOXICITY • NARCOTIC EFFECTS • RESPIRATORY TRACT IRRITANT • HAZARDOUS TO OZONE LAYER (NON-MANDATORY)
GAS CYLINDER	CORROSION	EXPLODING BOMB
• GASES UNDER PRESSURE	• SKIN CORROSION/BURNS • EYE DAMAGE • CORROSIVE TO METALS	• EXPLOSIVES • SELF-REACTIVES • ORGANIC PEROXIDES
FLAME OVER CIRCLE	ENVIRONMENT (NON-MANDATORY)	SKULL AND CROSSBONES
• OXIDIZERS	• AQUATIC TOXICITY	• ACUTE TOXICITY (FATAL OR TOXIC)

FIGURE 2–12 The OSHA global hazardous materials labels.

SUMMARY

1. Hazardous materials include common automotive chemicals, liquids, and lubricants, especially those whose ingredients contain *chlor* or *fluor* in their name.

2. Right-to-know laws require that all workers have access to safety data sheets (SDS).

3. Asbestos fibers should be avoided and removed according to current laws and regulations.

4. Used engine oil contains metals worn from parts and should be handled and disposed of properly.

5. Solvents represent a serious health risk and should be avoided as much as possible.

6. Coolant should be disposed of properly or recycled.

7. Batteries are considered to be hazardous waste and should be discarded to a recycling facility.

REVIEW QUESTIONS

1. What are the five common automotive chemicals or products that may be considered hazardous?

2. Describe the labels used to identify flammables and explosive materials used by OSHA.

3. What is the proper disposal for used engine oil?

4. What is the correct disposal for used refrigerant oil?

5. What component(s) in a vehicle may contain the heavy metal mercury?

1. Hazardous materials include all of the following **except** _____.
   - a. engine oil
   - b. asbestos
   - c. water
   - d. brake cleaner

2. To determine if a product or substance being used is hazardous, consult _____.
   - a. a dictionary
   - b. an SDS
   - c. SAE standards
   - d. EPA guidelines

3. Exposure to asbestos dust can cause what condition?
   - a. Asbestosis
   - b. Mesothelioma
   - c. Lung cancer
   - d. All of the above

4. Wetted asbestos dust is considered to be _____.
   - a. solid waste
   - b. hazardous waste
   - c. toxic
   - d. poisonous

5. An oil filter should be hot-drained for how long before disposing of the filter?
   - a. 30 to 60 minutes
   - b. 4 hours
   - c. 8 hours
   - d. 12 hours

6. Used engine oil should be disposed of by all except the following method.
   - a. Disposed of in regular trash
   - b. Shipped offsite for recycling
   - c. Burned onsite in a waste oil-approved heater
   - d. Burned offsite in a waste oil-approved heater

7. All of the following are the proper ways to dispose of a drained oil filter **except** _____.
   - a. sent for recycling
   - b. picked up by a service contract company
   - c. disposed of in regular trash
   - d. considered to be hazardous waste and disposed of accordingly

8. Which act or organization regulates air-conditioning refrigerant?
   - a. Clean Air Act (CAA)
   - b. SDS
   - c. WHMIS
   - d. Code of Federal Regulations (CFR)

9. Gasoline should be stored in approved containers that include what color(s)?
   - a. A red container with yellow lettering
   - b. A red container
   - c. A yellow container
   - d. A yellow container with red lettering

10. What automotive devices may contain mercury?
    - a. Rear seat video displays
    - b. Navigation displays
    - c. HID headlights
    - d. All of the above

chapter 3
ELECTRICAL FUNDAMENTALS

LEARNING OBJECTIVES

After studying this chapter, the reader will be able to:

1. Discuss the fundamentals of electricity and explain how electrons move through a conductor.

2. Discuss the different sources of electricity.

3. Explain conductors and resistance.

4. Explain the units of electrical measurement, and discuss the relationship among volts, amperes, and ohms.

This chapter will help you prepare for the ASE Electrical/Electronic Systems (A6) certification test content area "A" (General Electrical/Electronic System Diagnosis).

KEY TERMS

Ammeter 57
Ampere 57
Bound electrons 55
Conductors 55
Conventional theory 56
Coulomb 57
Electrical potential 57
Electricity 53
Electrochemistry 59
Electromotive force (EMF) 58
Electron theory 56
Free electrons 55
Insulators 55
Ion 54
Neutral charge 53
Ohmmeter 58

Ohms 58
Peltier effect 59
Photoelectricity 59
Piezoelectricity 59
Positive temperature coefficient (PTC) 60
Potentiometer 61
Resistance 58
Rheostat 61
Semiconductor 56
Static electricity 59
Thermocouple 59
Thermoelectricity 59
Valence ring 54
Voltmeter 58
Watt 58

INTRODUCTION

The electrical system is one of the most important systems in a vehicle today. Every year more and more components and systems use electricity. Those technicians who really know and understand automotive electrical and electronic systems will be in great demand.

Electricity may be difficult for some people to learn for the following reasons:

- It cannot be seen.
- Only the results of electricity can be seen.
- It has to be detected and measured.
- The test results have to be interpreted.

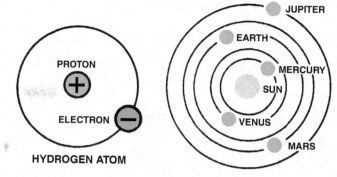

FIGURE 3–1 In an atom (left), electrons orbit protons in the nucleus just as planets orbit the sun in our solar system (right).

ELECTRICITY

BACKGROUND Our universe is composed of matter, which is *anything* that has mass and occupies space. All matter is made from slightly over 100 individual components called *elements*. The smallest particle that an element can be broken into and still retain the properties of that element is known as an atom. ● **SEE FIGURE 3–1.**

DEFINITION **Electricity** is the movement of electrons from one atom to another. The dense center of each atom is called the nucleus. The nucleus contains:

- *Protons*, which have a positive charge
- *Neutrons*, which are electrically neutral (have no charge)

Electrons, which have a negative charge, surround the nucleus in orbits. Each atom contains an equal number of electrons and protons. The physical aspect of all protons, electrons, and neutrons are the same for all atoms. It is the *number* of electrons and protons in the atom that determines the material and how electricity is conducted. Because the number of negative-charged electrons is balanced with the same number of positive-charged protons, an atom has a **neutral charge** (no charge).

NOTE: As an example of the relative sizes of the parts of an atom, consider that if an atom were magnified so that the nucleus were the size of the period at the end of this sentence, the whole atom would be bigger than a house.

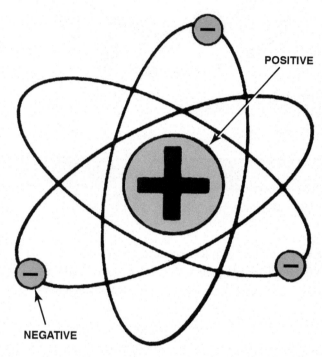

FIGURE 3–2 The nucleus of an atom has a positive (+) charge and the surrounding electrons have a negative (–) charge.

POSITIVE AND NEGATIVE CHARGES The parts of the atom have different charges. The orbiting electrons are negatively charged, while the protons are positively charged. Positive charges are indicated by the "plus" sign (+) and negative charges by the "minus" sign (–), as shown in ● **FIGURE 3–2.**

These same + and – signs are used to identify parts of an electrical circuit. Neutrons have no charge at all. They are neutral. In a normal, or balanced, atom, the number of negative particles equals the number of positive particles. That is, there are as many electrons as there are protons. ● **SEE FIGURE 3–3.**

MAGNETS AND ELECTRICAL CHARGES An ordinary magnet has two ends, or poles. One end is called the south pole and the other is called the north pole. If two magnets are brought

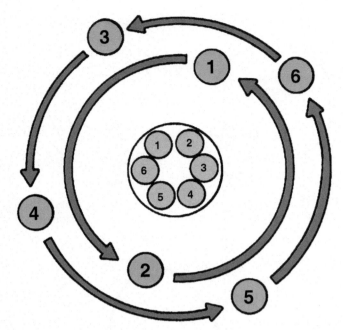

FIGURE 3–3 This figure shows a balanced atom. The number of electrons is the same as the number of protons in the nucleus.

FIGURE 3–4 Unlike charges attract and like charges repel.

close to each other with like poles together (south to south or north to north), the magnets will push each other apart, because like poles repel each other. If the opposite poles of the magnets are brought close to each other, south to north, the magnets will snap together, because unlike poles attract each other.

The positive and negative charges within an atom are like the north and south poles of a magnet. Charges that are alike will repel each other, similar to the poles of a magnet. ● **SEE FIGURE 3–4.**

That is why the negative electrons continue to orbit around the positive protons. They are attracted and held by the opposite charge of the protons. The electrons keep moving in orbit because they repel each other.

IONS When an atom loses any electrons, it becomes unbalanced. It will have more protons than electrons, and therefore will have a positive charge. If it gains more electrons than protons, the atom will be negatively charged. When an atom is not balanced, it becomes a charged particle called an **ion**. Ions try to regain their balance of equal protons and electrons by exchanging electrons with neighboring atoms. The flow of electrons during the "equalization" process is defined as the flow of electricity. ● **SEE FIGURE 3–5.**

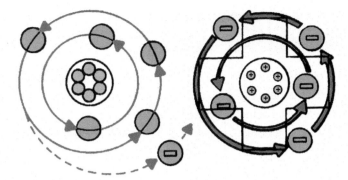

FIGURE 3–5 An unbalanced, positively charged atom (ion) will attract electrons from neighboring atoms.

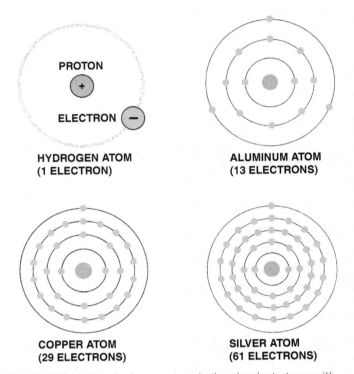

FIGURE 3–6 The hydrogen atom is the simplest atom, with only one proton, one neutron, and one electron. More complex elements contain higher numbers of protons, neutrons, and electrons.

ELECTRON SHELLS Electrons orbit around the nucleus in definite paths. These paths form shells, like concentric rings, around the nucleus. Only a specific number of electrons can orbit within each shell. If there are too many electrons for the first and closest shell to the nucleus, the others will orbit in additional shells until all electrons have an orbit within a shell. There can be as many as seven shells around a single nucleus. ● **SEE FIGURE 3–6.**

FREE AND BOUND ELECTRONS The outermost electron shell or ring, called the **valence ring**, is the most important part of understanding electricity. The number of electrons in this outer ring determines the valence of the atom and indicates its capacity to combine with other atoms.

If the valence ring of an atom has three or fewer electrons in it, the ring has room for more. The electrons there are held very loosely, and it is easy for a drifting electron to join the valence ring and push another electron away. These loosely held electrons are called **free electrons.** When the valence ring has five or more electrons in it, it is fairly full. The electrons are held tightly, and it is hard for a drifting electron to push its way into the valence ring. These tightly held electrons are called **bound electrons.** ● **SEE FIGURES 3–7 AND 3–8.**

The movement of these drifting electrons is called current. Current can be small, with only a few electrons moving, or it can be large, with a tremendous number of electrons moving. Electric current is the controlled, directed movement of electrons from atom to atom within a conductor.

CONDUCTORS
Conductors are materials with fewer than four electrons in their atom's outer orbit. ● **SEE FIGURE 3–9.**

Copper is an excellent conductor because it has only one electron in its outer orbit. This orbit is far enough away from the nucleus of the copper atom that the pull or force holding the outermost electron in orbit is relatively weak.
● **SEE FIGURE 3–10.**

Copper is the conductor most used in vehicles because the price of copper is reasonable compared to the relative cost of other conductors with similar properties. Examples of other commonly used conductors include:

- Silver
- Gold
- Aluminum
- Steel
- Cast iron

 FREQUENTLY ASKED QUESTION

Is Water a Conductor?

Pure water is an insulator; however, if anything is in the water, such as salt or dirt, then the water becomes conductive. Because it is difficult to keep it from becoming contaminated, water is usually thought of as being capable of conducting electricity, especially high-voltage household 110- or 220-volt outlets.

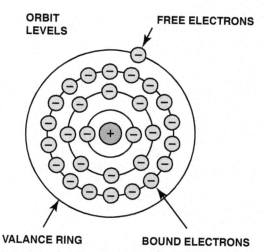

FIGURE 3–7 As the number of electrons increases, they occupy increasing energy levels that are farther from the center of the atom.

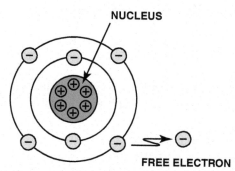

FIGURE 3–8 Electrons in the outer orbit, or shell, can often be drawn away from the atom and become free electrons.

INSULATORS
Some materials hold their electrons very tightly; therefore, electrons do not move through them very well. These materials are called insulators. **Insulators** are materials with more than four electrons in their atom's outer orbit. Because they have more than four electrons in their outer orbit, it becomes easier for these materials to acquire (gain) electrons than to release electrons.
● **SEE FIGURE 3–11.**

Examples of insulators include plastics, nylon, porcelain, fibreglass, wood, glass, rubber, ceramics (spark plugs), and varnish for covering (insulating) copper wires in alternators and starters.

SEMICONDUCTORS
Materials with exactly four electrons in their outer orbit are neither conductors nor insulators, but

CONDUCTORS

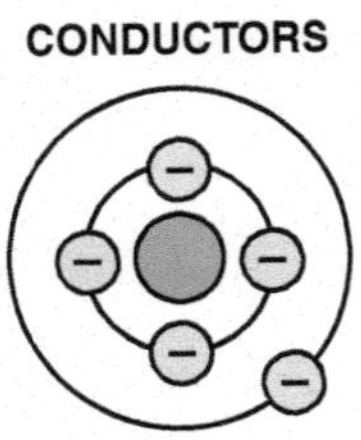

FIGURE 3–9 A conductor is any element that has one to three electrons in its outer orbit.

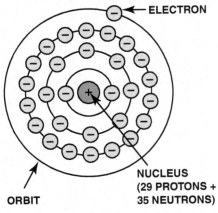
COPPER

ELECTRON

NUCLEUS
(29 PROTONS +
35 NEUTRONS)

ORBIT

FIGURE 3–10 Copper is an excellent conductor of electricity because it has just one electron in its outer orbit, making it easy to be knocked out of its orbit and flow to other nearby atoms. This causes electron flow, which is the definition of electricity.

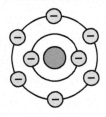
INSULATORS

FIGURE 3–11 Insulators are elements with five to eight electrons in the outer orbit.

are called **semiconductors**. Semiconductors can be either an insulator or a conductor in different design applications.
● **SEE FIGURE 3–12**.

Examples of semiconductors include:

■ Silicon

■ Germanium

■ Carbon

Semiconductors are used mostly in transistors, computers, and other electronic devices.

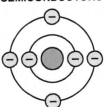
SEMICONDUCTORS

FIGURE 3–12 Semiconductor elements contain exactly four electrons in the outer orbit.

COPPER WIRE

POSITIVE
(+)
CHARGE

NEGATIVE
(−)
CHARGE

FIGURE 3–13 Current electricity is the movement of electrons through a conductor.

HOW ELECTRONS MOVE THROUGH A CONDUCTOR

CURRENT FLOW The following events occur if a source of power, such as a battery, is connected to the ends of a conductor—a positive charge (lack of electrons) is placed on one end of the conductor and a negative charge (excess of electrons) is placed on the opposite end of the conductor. For current to flow, there *must* be an imbalance of excess electrons at one end of the circuit and a deficiency of electrons at the opposite end of the circuit.

■ The negative charge will repel the free electrons from the atoms of the conductor, whereas the positive charge on the opposite end of the conductor will attract electrons.

■ As a result of this attraction of opposite charges and repulsion of like charges, electrons will flow through the conductor. ● **SEE FIGURE 3–13**.

CONVENTIONAL THEORY VERSUS ELECTRON THEORY

■ **Conventional theory.** It was once thought that electricity had only one charge and moved from positive to negative. This theory of the flow of electricity through a conductor is called the **conventional theory** of current flow. ● **SEE FIGURE 3–14**.

■ **Electron theory.** The discovery of the electron and its negative charge led to the **electron theory,** which states that there is electron flow from negative to positive. Most automotive applications use the conventional theory. We will use the conventional theory (positive to negative) unless stated otherwise.

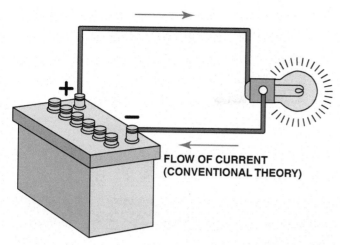

FIGURE 3–14 Conventional theory states that current flows through a circuit from positive (+) to negative (–). Automotive electricity uses the conventional theory in all electrical diagrams and schematics.

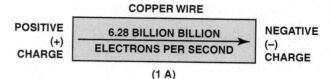

FIGURE 3–15 One ampere is the movement of 1 coulomb (6.28 billion billion electrons) past a point in 1 second.

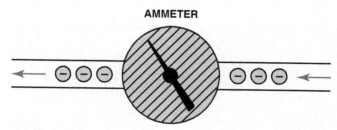

FIGURE 3–16 An ammeter is installed in the path of the electrons similar to a water meter used to measure the flow of water in gallons per minute. The ammeter displays current flow in amperes.

UNITS OF ELECTRICITY

Electricity is measured using meters or other test equipment. The three fundamentals of electricity-related units include the ampere, volt, and ohm.

AMPERES The **ampere** is the unit used throughout the world to measure current flow. When 6.28 billion billion electrons (the name for this large number of electrons is a **coulomb**) move past a certain point in 1 second, this represents 1 ampere of current. ● **SEE FIGURE 3–15**.

The ampere is the electrical unit for the amount of electron flow, just as "gallons per minute" is the unit that can be used to measure the quantity of water flow. It is named for the French electrician André Marie Ampére (1775–1836). The conventional abbreviations and measurement for amperes are as follows:

1. The ampere is the unit of measurement for the amount of current flow.

2. *A* and *amps* are acceptable abbreviations for *amperes*.

3. The capital letter *I*, for *intensity*, is used in mathematical calculations to represent amperes.

4. Amperes do the actual work in the circuit. It is the actual movement of the electrons through a lightbulb or motor that actually makes the electrical device work. Without amperage through a device it will not work at all.

5. Amperes are measured by an **ammeter** (not ampmeter). ● **SEE FIGURE 3–16**.

VOLTS The **volt** is the unit of measurement for electrical pressure. It is named for an Italian physicist, Alessandro Volta

(1745–1827). The comparable unit using water pressure as an example would be pounds per square inch (psi). It is possible to have very high pressures (volts) and low water flow (amperes). It is also possible to have high water flow (amperes) and low pressures (volts). Voltage is also called **electrical potential**, because if there is voltage present in a conductor, there is a potential (possibility) for current flow. This electrical pressure is a result of the following:

■ Excess electrons remain at one end of the wire or circuit.

■ There is a lack of electrons at the other end of the wire or circuit.

■ The natural effect is to equalize this imbalance, creating a pressure to allow the movement of electrons through a conductor.

■ It is possible to have pressure (volts) without any flow (amperes). For example, a fully charged 12-volt battery placed on a workbench has 12 volts of pressure potential, but because there is no conductor (circuit) connected between the positive and negative terminals of the battery, there is no flow (amperes). Current will only flow when there is pressure and a circuit for the electrons to flow in order to "equalize" to a balanced state.

Voltage does *not* flow through conductors, but voltage does cause current (in amperes) to flow through conductors. ● **SEE FIGURE 3–17**.

The conventional abbreviations and measurement for voltage are as follows:

1. The volt is the unit of measurement for the amount of electrical pressure.

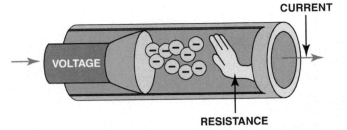

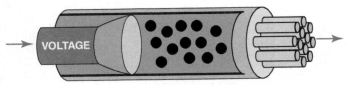

VOLTAGE IS PRESSURE

FIGURE 3–17 Voltage is the electrical pressure that causes the electrons to flow through a conductor.

FIGURE 3–19 Resistance to the flow of electrons through a conductor is measured in ohms.

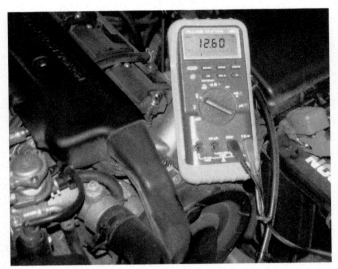

FIGURE 3–18 This digital multimeter set to read DC volts is being used to test the voltage of a vehicle battery. Most multimeters can also measure resistance (ohms) and current flow (amperes).

2. **Electromotive force**, abbreviated **EMF**, is another way of indicating voltage.

3. *V* is the generally accepted abbreviation for *volts*.

4. The symbol used in calculations is *E*, for *electromotive force*.

5. Volts are measured by a **voltmeter.** ● SEE FIGURE 3–18.

OHMS **Resistance** to the flow of current through a conductor is measured in units called **ohms,** named after the German physicist George Simon Ohm (1787–1854). The resistance to the flow of free electrons through a conductor results from the countless collisions the electrons cause within the atoms of the conductor. ● SEE FIGURE 3–19.

The conventional abbreviations and measurement for resistance are as follows:

1. The ohm is the unit of measurement for electrical resistance.

2. The symbol for ohms is Ω (Greek capital letter omega), the last letter of the Greek alphabet.

3. The symbol used in calculations is *R*, for *resistance*.

FIGURE 3–20 A display at the Henry Ford Museum in Dearborn, Michigan, which includes a hand-cranked generator and a series of lightbulbs. This figure shows a young man attempting to light as many bulbs as possible. The crank gets harder to turn as more bulbs light because it requires more power to produce the necessary watts of electricity.

4. Ohms are measured by an **ohmmeter**.

5. Resistance to electron flow depends on the material used as a conductor.

WATTS A **watt** is the electrical unit for *power,* the capacity to do work. It is named after a Scottish inventor, James Watt (1736–1819). The symbol for power is *P*. Electrical power is calculated as amperes times volts:

$$P \text{ (power)} = I \text{ (amperes)} \times E \text{ (volts)}$$

The formula can also be used to calculate the amperage if the wattage and the voltage are known. For example, a 100-watt lightbulb powered by 120-volts AC in the shop requires how many amperes?

$$A \text{ (amperes)} = P \text{ (watts)} \div E \text{ (volts)}$$

$$A = 0.83 \text{ amperes}$$

● SEE FIGURE 3–20.

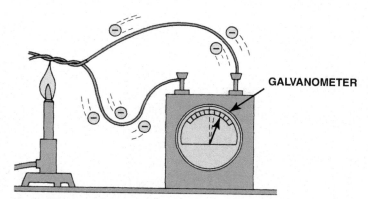

FIGURE 3–21 Electron flow is produced by heating the connection of two different metals. A galvanometer is an analog (needle-type) meter designed to detect weak voltage signals.

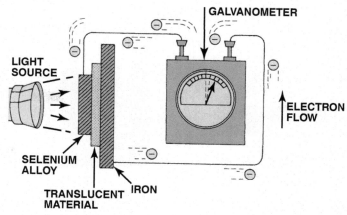

FIGURE 3–22 Electron flow is produced by light striking a light-sensitive material.

SOURCES OF ELECTRICITY

FRICTION When certain different materials are rubbed together, the friction causes electrons to be transferred from one to the other. Both materials become electrically charged. These charges are not in motion, but stay on the surface where they were deposited. Because the charges are stationary, or static, this type of voltage is called **static electricity.** Walking across a carpeted floor creates a buildup of a static charge in your body, which is an insulator, and then the charge is discharged when you touch a metal conductor. Vehicle tires rolling on pavement often create static electricity that interferes with radio reception.

HEAT When pieces of two different metals are joined together at both ends and one junction is heated, current passes through the metals. The current is very small, only millionths of an ampere, but this is enough to use in a temperature-measuring device called a **thermocouple.** ● **SEE FIGURE 3–21.**

Some engine temperature sensors operate in this manner. This form of voltage is called **thermoelectricity**.

Thermoelectricity was discovered and has been known for over a century. In 1823, a German physicist, Thomas Johann Seebeck, discovered that a voltage was developed in a loop containing two dissimilar metals, provided the two junctions were maintained at different temperatures. A decade later, a French scientist, Jean Charles Athanase Peltier, found that electrons moving through a solid can carry heat from one side of the material to the other side. This effect is called the **Peltier effect**. A Peltier effect device is often used in portable coolers to keep food items cool if the current flows in one direction, and keep items warm if the current flows in reverse.

LIGHT In 1839, Edmond Becquerel noticed that by shining a beam of sunlight over two different liquids, he could develop an electric current. When certain metals are exposed to light, some of the light energy is transferred to the free electrons of the metal. This excess energy breaks the electrons loose from the surface of the metal. They can then be collected and made to flow in a conductor. ● **SEE FIGURE 3–22.**

This **photoelectricity** is widely used in light-measuring devices, such as photographic exposure meters and automatic headlamp dimmers.

PRESSURE The first experimental demonstration of a connection between the generation of a voltage due to pressure applied to a crystal was published in 1880 by Pierre and Jacques Curie. Their experiment consisted of voltage being produced when prepared crystals, such as quartz, topaz, and Rochelle salt, had a force applied. ● **SEE FIGURE 3–23**.

This current is used in crystal microphones, underwater hydrophones, and certain stethoscopes. The voltage created is called **piezoelectricity**. A gas grill igniter uses the principle of piezoelectricity to produce a spark, and engine knock sensors (KS) use piezoelectricity to create a voltage signal for use as an input for an engine computer input signal.

CHEMICAL Two different materials (usually metals) placed in a conducting and reactive chemical solution create a difference in potential, or voltage, between them. This principle is called **electrochemistry** and is the basis of the automotive battery.

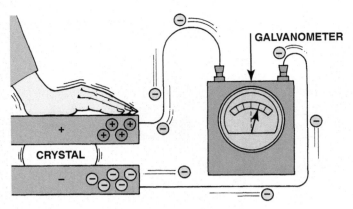

FIGURE 3–23 Electron flow is produced by pressure on certain crystals.

1	Silver
2	Copper
3	Gold
4	Aluminum
5	Tungsten
6	Zinc
7	Brass (copper and zinc)
8	Platinum
9	Iron
10	Nickel
11	Tin
12	Steel
13	Lead

CHART 3–1

Conductor ratings (starting with the best).

MAGNETISM Electricity can be produced if a conductor is moved through a magnetic field or a moving magnetic field is moved near a conductor. This is the principle on which many automotive devices work, including the following:

- Starter motor
- Alternator
- Ignition coils
- Solenoids and relays

? **FREQUENTLY ASKED QUESTION**

Why Is Gold Used If Copper Has Lower Resistance?

Copper is used for most automotive electrical components and wiring because it has low resistance and is reasonably priced. Gold is used in airbag connections and sensors because it does not corrode. Gold can be buried for hundreds of years and, when dug up, it is just as shiny as ever.

CONDUCTORS AND RESISTANCE

All conductors have some resistance to current flow. The following are principles of conductors and their resistance:

- **If the conductor length is doubled, its resistance doubles.** This is the reason why battery cables are designed to be as short as possible.

- **If the conductor diameter is increased, its resistance is reduced.** This is the reason starter motor cables are larger in diameter than other wiring in the vehicle.

- **As the temperature increases, the resistance of the conductor also increases.** This is the reason for installing heat shields on some starter motors. The heat shield helps to protect the conductors (copper wiring inside the starter) from excessive engine heat and so reduces the resistance of starter circuits. Because the resistance in a conductor increases with increase in temperature, the conductor is called a **positive temperature coefficient (PTC)** resistor.

- **Materials used in the conductor have an impact on its resistance.** Silver has the lowest resistance among all materials used as conductors, but is expensive. Copper is the next lowest in resistance and is reasonably priced.
- **SEE CHART 3–1** for a comparison of materials.

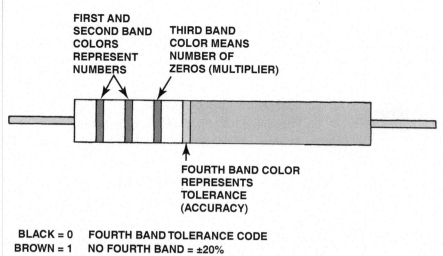

FIRST AND SECOND BAND COLORS REPRESENT NUMBERS

THIRD BAND COLOR MEANS NUMBER OF ZEROS (MULTIPLIER)

FOURTH BAND COLOR REPRESENTS TOLERANCE (ACCURACY)

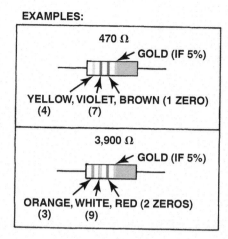

EXAMPLES:

470 Ω
GOLD (IF 5%)
YELLOW, VIOLET, BROWN (1 ZERO)
(4)   (7)

3,900 Ω
GOLD (IF 5%)
ORANGE, WHITE, RED (2 ZEROS)
(3)   (9)

BLACK = 0	**FOURTH BAND TOLERANCE CODE**
BROWN = 1	NO FOURTH BAND = ±20%
RED = 2	SILVER = ±10%
ORANGE = 3	* GOLD = ±5%
YELLOW = 4	RED = ±2%
GREEN = 5	BROWN = ±1%
BLUE = 6	* GOLD IS THE MOST
VIOLET = 7	COMMONLY AVAILABLE
GRAY = 8	RESISTOR TOLERANCE.
WHITE = 9	

FIGURE 3–24 This figure shows a resistor color-code interpretation.

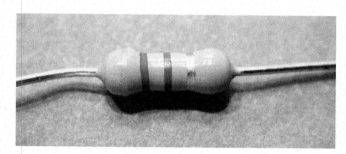

FIGURE 3–25 A typical carbon resistor.

RESISTORS

FIXED RESISTORS Resistance is the opposition to current flow. Resistors represent an electrical load, or resistance to current flow. Most electrical and electronic devices use resistors of specific values to limit and control the flow of current. Resistors can be made from carbon or other materials that restrict the flow of electricity and are available in various sizes and resistance values. Most resistors have a series of painted color bands around them. These color bands are coded to indicate the degree of resistance. ● **SEE FIGURES 3–24 AND 3–25**.

VARIABLE RESISTORS Two basic types of mechanically operated variable resistors are used in automotive applications.

■ A **potentiometer** is a three-terminal variable resistor where a wiper contact provides a variable voltage output. ● **SEE FIGURE 3–26**. Potentiometers are most commonly used as throttle position (TP) sensors on computer-equipped

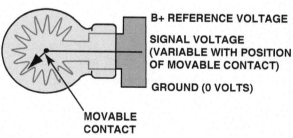

B+ REFERENCE VOLTAGE
SIGNAL VOLTAGE (VARIABLE WITH POSITION OF MOVABLE CONTACT)
GROUND (0 VOLTS)
MOVABLE CONTACT

FIGURE 3–26 A three-wire variable resistor is called a potentiometer.

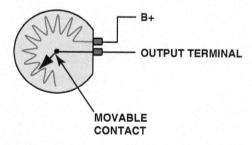

B+
OUTPUT TERMINAL
MOVABLE CONTACT

FIGURE 3–27 A two-wire variable resistor is called a rheostat.

engines. A potentiometer is also used to control audio volume, bass, treble, balance, and fade.

■ Another type of mechanically operated variable resistor is the **rheostat.** A rheostat is a *two*-terminal unit in which all of the current flows through the movable arm. ● **SEE FIGURE 3–27**. A rheostat is commonly used for a dash light dimmer control.

1. Electricity is the movement of electrons from one atom to another.

2. In order for current to flow in a circuit or wire, there must be an excess of electrons at one end and a deficiency of electrons at the other end.

3. Automotive electricity uses the conventional theory that electricity flows from positive to negative.

4. The ampere is the measure of the amount of current flow.

5. Voltage is the unit of electrical pressure.

6. The ohm is the unit of electrical resistance.

7. Sources of electricity include friction, heat, light, pressure, and chemical.

REVIEW QUESTIONS

1. What is electricity?

2. What are ampere, volt, and ohm?

3. Give three examples of conductors and three examples of insulators.

4. What are the five sources of electricity?

5. Why is copper used for wire in vehicles?

CHAPTER QUIZ

1. An electrical conductor is an element with _____ electrons in its outer orbit.
   a. less than 2
   b. less than 4
   c. exactly 4
   d. more than 4

2. Like charges _____.
   a. attract
   b. repel
   c. neutralize each other
   d. add

3. Carbon and silicon are examples of _____.
   a. semiconductors
   b. insulators
   c. conductors
   d. photoelectric materials

4. Which unit of electricity does the work in a circuit?
   a. Volt
   b. Ampere
   c. Ohm
   d. Coulomb

5. As temperature increases, _____.
   a. the resistance of a conductor decreases
   b. the resistance of a conductor increases
   c. the resistance of a conductor remains the same
   d. the voltage of the conductor decreases

6. The _____ is a unit of electrical pressure.
   a. coulomb
   b. volt
   c. ampere
   d. ohm

7. Technician A says that a two-wire variable resistor is called a rheostat. Technician B says that a three-wire variable resistor is called a potentiometer. Which technician is correct?
   a. Technician A only
   b. Technician B only
   c. Both Technicians A and B
   d. Neither Technician A nor B

8. Creating electricity by exerting a force on a crystal is called _____.
   a. electrochemistry
   b. piezoelectricity
   c. thermoelectricity
   d. photoelectricity

9. The fact that a voltage can be created by exerting force on a crystal is used in which type of sensor?
   a. Throttle position (TP)
   b. Manifold absolute pressure (MAP)
   c. Barometric pressure (BARO)
   d. Knock sensor (KS)

10. A potentiometer, a three-wire variable resistor, is used in which type of sensor?
    a. Throttle position (TP)
    b. Manifold absolute pressure (MAP)
    c. Barometric pressure (BARO)
    d. Knock sensor (KS)

chapter 4
ELECTRICAL CIRCUITS AND OHM'S LAW

LEARNING OBJECTIVES

After studying this chapter, the reader will be able to:

1. Identify the parts of a complete circuit.
2. Describe the characteristics of different types of circuits.
3. Explain Ohm's law as it applies to automotive circuits.
4. Explain Watt's law as it applies to automotive circuits.

This chapter will help you prepare for the ASE Electrical/Electronic Systems (A6) certification test content area "A" (General Electrical/Electronic System Diagnosis).

KEY TERMS

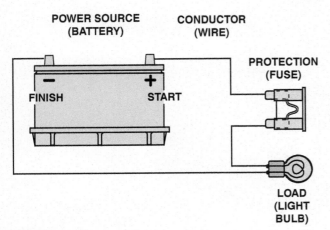

FIGURE 4–1 All complete circuits must have a power source, a power path, protection (fuse), an electrical load (lightbulb in this case), and a return path back to the power source.

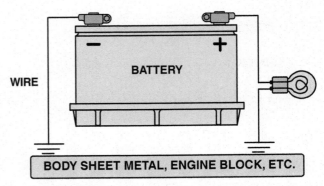

FIGURE 4–2 The return path back to the battery can be any electrical conductor, such as a copper wire or the metal frame or body of the vehicle.

CIRCUITS

DEFINITION A **circuit** is a complete path that electrons travel from a power source (such as a battery) through a **load** (such as a lightbulb) and back to the power source. It is called a *circuit* because the current must start and finish at the same place (power source).

For *any* electrical circuit to work at all, it must be continuous from the battery (power), through all the wires and components, and back to the battery (ground). A circuit that is continuous throughout is said to have **continuity.**

PARTS OF A COMPLETE CIRCUIT Every **complete circuit** contains the following parts. ● **SEE FIGURE 4–1.**

1. A **power source,** such as a vehicle's battery.

2. Protection from harmful overloads (excessive current flow). (Fuses, circuit breakers, and fusible links are examples of electrical circuit protection devices.)

3. The power path for the current to flow through from the power source to the resistance. (This path from a power source to the load—a lightbulb in this example—is usually an insulated copper wire.)

4. The **electrical load** or resistance, which converts electrical energy into heat, light, or motion.

5. A **return path (ground)** for the electrical current from the load back to the power source so there is a *complete* circuit. (This return, or ground, path is usually the metal body, frame, ground wires, and engine block of the vehicle.) ● **SEE FIGURE 4–2.**

6. Switches and controls that turn the circuit on and off. ● **SEE FIGURE 4–3.**

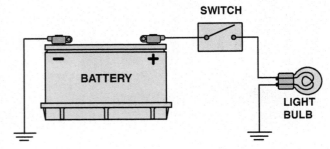

FIGURE 4–3 An electrical switch opens the circuit and no current flows. The switch could also be on the return (ground) path wire.

CIRCUIT FAULT TYPES

OPEN CIRCUITS An **open circuit** is any circuit that is *not* complete, or that lacks continuity, such as a broken wire. ● **SEE FIGURE 4–4.**

Open circuits have the following features:

1. *No current at all* will flow through an open circuit.

2. An open circuit may be created by a break in the circuit or by a switch that opens (turns off) the circuit and prevents the flow of current.

3. In any circuit containing a power load and ground, an opening anywhere in the circuit will cause the circuit not to work.

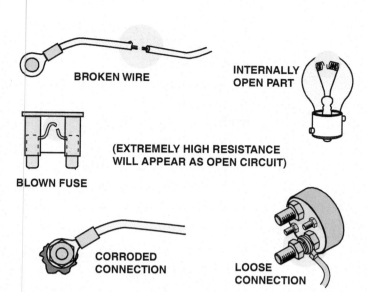

BROKEN WIRE

INTERNALLY OPEN PART

(EXTREMELY HIGH RESISTANCE WILL APPEAR AS OPEN CIRCUIT)

BLOWN FUSE

CORRODED CONNECTION

LOOSE CONNECTION

FIGURE 4–4 Examples of common causes of open circuits. Some of these causes are often difficult to find.

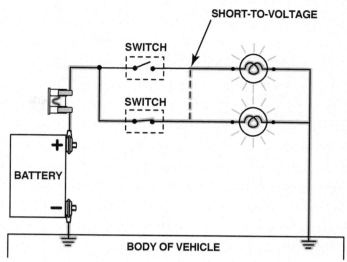

SHORT-TO-VOLTAGE

SWITCH

SWITCH

BATTERY

BODY OF VEHICLE

FIGURE 4–5 A short circuit permits electrical current to bypass some or all of the resistance in the circuit.

4. A light switch in a home and the headlight switch in a vehicle are examples of devices that open a circuit to control its operation.

5. A fuse will blow (open) when the current in the circuit exceeds the fuse rating. This stops the current flow to prevent any harm to the components or wiring as a result of the fault.

SHORT-TO-VOLTAGE
If a wire (conductor) or component is shorted to voltage, it is commonly referred to as being **shorted**. A **short-to-voltage** occurs when the power side of one circuit is electrically connected to the power side of another circuit. ● **SEE FIGURE 4–5**.

A short circuit has the following features:

1. It is a complete circuit in which the current usually bypasses *some* or *all* of the resistance in the circuit.

2. It involves the power side of the circuit.

3. It involves a copper-to-copper connection (two power-side wires touching together).

4. It is also called a *short-to-voltage*.

5. It usually affects more than one circuit. In this case, if one circuit is electrically connected to another circuit,

TECH TIP

"Open" Is a Four-Letter Word

An open in a circuit breaks the path of current flow. The open can be any break in the power side, load, or ground side of a circuit. A switch is often used to close and open a circuit to turn it on and off. Just remember,

Open = no current flow

Closed = current flow

Trying to locate an open circuit in a vehicle is often difficult and may cause the technician to use other four-letter words, such as "HELP"!

one of the circuits may operate when it is not supposed to because it is being supplied power from another circuit.

6. It *may* or *may not* blow a fuse. ● **SEE FIGURE 4–6**.

SHORT-TO-GROUND
A **short-to-ground** is a type of short circuit that occurs when the current bypasses part of the normal circuit and flows directly to ground. A short-to-ground has the following features:

1. Because the ground return circuit is metal (vehicle frame, engine, or body), it is often identified as having current flowing from copper to steel.

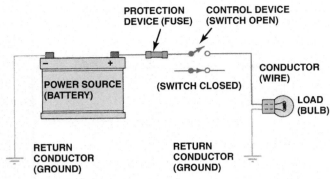

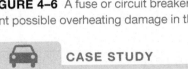

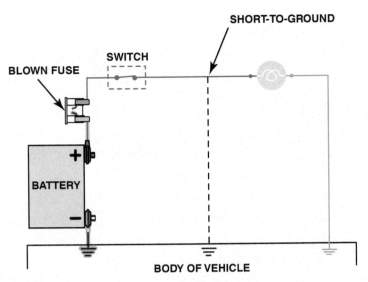

FIGURE 4–6 A fuse or circuit breaker opens the circuit to prevent possible overheating damage in the event of a short circuit.

FIGURE 4–7 A short-to-ground affects the power side of the circuit. Current flows directly to the ground return, bypassing some or all of the electrical loads in the circuit. There is no current in the circuit past the short. A short-to-ground will also cause the fuse to blow.

CASE STUDY

The Short-to-Voltage Story

A technician was working on a Chevrolet pickup truck with the following unusual electrical problems:

1. When the brake pedal was depressed, the dash light and the side marker lights would light.
2. The turn signals caused all lights to blink and the fuel gauge needle to bounce up and down.
3. When the brake lights were on, the front parking lights also came on.

NOTE: Using a single-filament bulb (such as a #1156) in the place of a dual-filament bulb (such as a #1157) could also cause many of these same problems.

Because most of the trouble occurred when the brake pedal was depressed, the technician decided to trace all the wires in the brake light circuit. The technician discovered the problem near the exhaust system. A small hole in the tailpipe (after the muffler) directed hot exhaust gases to the wiring harness containing all of the wires for circuits at the rear of the truck. The heat had melted the insulation and caused most of the wires to touch. Whenever one circuit was activated (such as when the brake pedal was applied), the current had a complete path to several other circuits. A fuse did not blow because there was enough resistance in the circuits being energized, so the current (in amperes) was too low to blow any fuses.

Summary:

- **Complaint**—Customer stated that the truck lights were doing strange things when the brake pedal was depressed.
- **Cause**—Melted wires caused by a small hole in the exhaust was found during a visual inspection.
- **Correction**—Performing a wire repair and fixing the exhaust leak corrected the customer concern.

2. It occurs at any place where a power path wire accidentally touches a return path wire or conductor. ● **SEE FIGURE 4–7**.

3. A defective component or circuit that is shorted to ground is commonly called **grounded**.

4. A short-to-ground almost always results in a blown fuse, damaged connectors, or melted wires.

HIGH RESISTANCE High resistance can be caused by any of the following:

- Corroded connections or sockets
- Loose terminals in a connector
- Loose ground connections

If there is high resistance anywhere in a circuit, it may cause the following problems:

1. Slow operation of a motor-driven unit, such as the windshield wipers or blower motor
2. Dim lights
3. "Clicking" of relays or solenoids.
4. No operation of a circuit or electrical component.

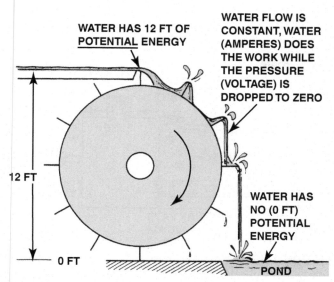

WATER HAS 12 FT OF POTENTIAL ENERGY

WATER FLOW IS CONSTANT, WATER (AMPERES) DOES THE WORK WHILE THE PRESSURE (VOLTAGE) IS DROPPED TO ZERO

WATER HAS NO (0 FT) POTENTIAL ENERGY

12 FT

0 FT

POND

FIGURE 4–8 Electrical flow through a circuit is similar to water flowing over a waterwheel. The more the water (amperes in electricity), the greater the amount of work (waterwheel). The amount of water remains constant, yet the pressure (voltage in electricity) drops as the current flows through the circuit.

 TECH TIP

Think of a Waterwheel

A beginner technician cleaned the positive terminal of the battery when the starter was cranking the engine slowly. When questioned by the shop foreman as to why only the positive post had been cleaned, the technician responded that the negative terminal was "only a ground." The foreman reminded the technician that the current, in amperes, is constant throughout a series circuit (such as the cranking motor circuit). If 200 amperes leave the positive post of the battery, then 200 amperes must return to the battery through the negative post.

The technician could not understand how electricity can do work (crank an engine), yet return the same amount of current, in amperes, as left the battery. The shop foreman explained that even though the current is constant throughout the circuit, the voltage (electrical pressure or potential) drops to zero in the circuit. To explain further, the shop foreman drew a waterwheel. ● SEE FIGURE 4–8.

As water drops from a higher level to a lower level, high potential energy (or voltage) is used to turn the waterwheel and results in low potential energy (or lower voltage). The same amount of water (or amperes) reaches the pond under the waterwheel as started in the fall above the waterwheel. As current (amperes) flows through a conductor, it performs work in the circuit (turns the waterwheel) while its voltage (potential) drops.

OHM'S LAW

DEFINITION The German physicist George Simon Ohm established that electric pressure (EMF) in volts, electrical resistance in ohms, and the amount of current in amperes flowing through any circuit are all related. **Ohm's law** states:

It requires 1 volt to push 1 ampere through 1 ohm of resistance.

This means that if the voltage is doubled, the number of amperes of current flowing through a circuit will also double if the resistance of the circuit remains the same.

FORMULAS Ohm's law can also be stated as a simple formula used to calculate one value of an electrical circuit if the other two are known. If, for example, the current (*I*) is unknown but the voltage (*E*) and resistance (*R*) are known, Ohm's law can be used to find the answer. ● **SEE FIGURE 4–9**.

$$I = \frac{E}{R}$$

where

I = Current in amperes (A)

E = Electromotive force (EMF) in volts (V)

R = Resistance in ohms (Ω), represented by the Greek letter Omega (pronounced oh-MAY-guh).

1. Ohm's law can determine the resistance if the volts and amperes are known: $R = \frac{E}{I}$

2. Ohm's law can determine the *voltage* if the resistance (ohms) and amperes are known: $E = I \times R$

3. Ohm's law can determine the amperes if the resistance and voltage are known: $I = \frac{E}{R}$

NOTE: Before applying Ohm's law, be sure that each unit of electricity is converted into base units. For example, 10 KΩ should be converted to 10,000 Ω and 10 mA should be converted into 0.010 A.

● **SEE CHART 4–1.**

OHM'S LAW APPLIED TO SIMPLE CIRCUITS If a battery with 12 volts is connected to a resistor of 4 ohms, as shown in ● **FIGURE 4–10**, how many amperes will flow through the circuit?

Using Ohm's law, we can calculate the number of amperes that will flow through the wires and the resistor. Remember, if two factors are known (volts and ohms in this

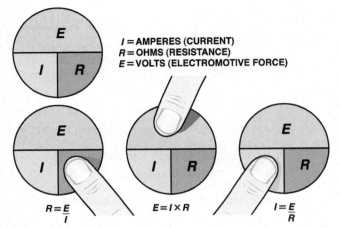

FIGURE 4–9 To calculate one unit of electricity when the other two are known, simply use your finger and cover the unit you do not know. For example, if both voltage (*E*) and resistance (*R*) are known, cover the letter *I* (amperes). Notice that the letter *E* is above the letter *R*, so divide the resistor's value into the voltage to determine the current in the circuit.

VOLTAGE	RESISTANCE	AMPERAGE
Up	Down	Up
Up	Same	Up
Up	Up	Same
Same	Down	Up
Same	Same	Same
Same	Up	Down
Down	Up	Down
Down	Same	Down

CHART 4–1

Ohm's law relationship with the three units of electricity.

example), the remaining factor (amperes) can be calculated using Ohm's law.

$$I = \frac{E}{R} = \frac{12V}{4\Omega} = A$$

The values for the voltage (12) and the resistance (4) were substituted for the variables *E* and *R*, and *I* is thus 3 amperes

$$\left(\frac{12}{4} = 3\right)$$

If we want to connect a resistor to a 12-volt battery, we now know that this simple circuit requires 3 amperes to operate. This may help us for two reasons.

1. We can now determine the wire diameter that we will need based on the number of amperes flowing through the circuit.

2. The correct fuse rating can be selected to protect the circuit.

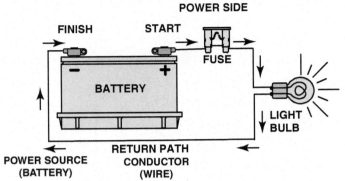

FIGURE 4–10 This closed circuit includes a power source, power-side wire, circuit protection (fuse), resistance (bulb), and return path wire. In this circuit, if the battery has 12 volts and the electrical load has 4 ohms, then the current through the circuit is 3 amperes.

WATT'S LAW

BACKGROUND James Watt (1736–1819), a Scottish inventor, first determined the power of a typical horse while measuring the amount of coal being lifted out of a mine. The power of one horse was determined to be 33,000 foot-pounds per minute. Electricity can also be expressed in a unit of power called a **watt** and the relationship is known as **Watt's law,** which states:

A **watt** is a unit of electrical power represented by a current of 1 ampere through a circuit with a potential difference of 1 volt.

FORMULAS The symbol for a watt is the capital letter *W*. The formula for watts is:

$$W = I \times E$$

Another way to express this formula is to use the letter *P* to represent the unit of power. The formula then becomes:

$$P = I \times E$$

NOTE: An easy way to remember this equation is that it spells "pie."

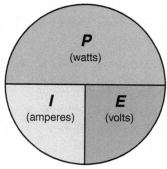

FIGURE 4–11 To calculate one unit when the other two are known, simply cover the unknown unit to see what unit needs to be divided or multiplied to arrive at the solution.

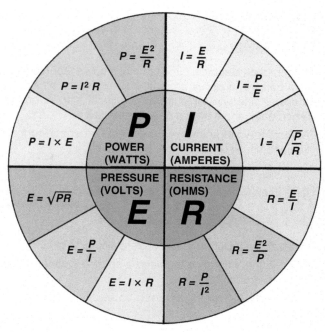

FIGURE 4–12 "Magic circle" of most formulas for problems involving Ohm's law. Each quarter of the "pie" has formulas used to solve for a particular unknown value: current (amperes), in the upper right segment; resistance (ohms), in the lower right; voltage (E), in the lower left; and power (watts), in the upper left.

Engine power is commonly rated in watts or kilowatts (1,000 watts equal 1 kilowatt), because 1 horsepower is equal to 746 watts. For example, a 200 horsepower engine can be rated as having the power equal to 149,200 watts or 149.2 kilowatts (kW).

To calculate watts, both the current in amperes and the voltage in the circuit must be known. If any two of these factors are known, then the other remaining factor can be determined by the following equations:

$P = I \times E$ **(watts equal amperes times voltage)**

$I = \dfrac{P}{E}$ **(amperes equal watts divided by voltage)**

$E = \dfrac{P}{I}$ **(voltage equals watts divided by amperes)**

A Watt's circle can be drawn and used like the Ohm's law circle diagram. ● **SEE FIGURE 4–11**.

MAGIC CIRCLE The formulas for calculating any combination of electrical units are shown in ● **FIGURE 4–12**.

It is almost impossible to remember all of these formulas, so this one circle showing all of the formulas is nice to have available if needed.

🔧 **TECH TIP**

Wattage Increases by the Square of the Voltage

The brightness of a lightbulb, such as an automotive headlight or courtesy light, depends on the number of watts available. The watt is the unit by which electrical power is measured. If the battery voltage drops, even slightly, the light becomes noticeably dimmer. The formula for calculating power (P) in watts is $P = I \times E$. This can also be expressed as Watts = Amps × Volts.

According to Ohm's law, $I = \dfrac{E}{R}$. Therefore, $\dfrac{E}{R}$ can be substituted for I in the previous formula resulting in $P = \dfrac{E}{R} \times E$ or $P = \dfrac{E^2}{R}$.

E^2 means E multiplied by itself. A small change in the voltage (E) has a big effect on the total brightness of the bulb. (Remember, household lightbulbs are sold according to their wattage.) Therefore, if the voltage to an automotive bulb is reduced, such as by a poor electrical connection, the brightness of the bulb is greatly affected. A poor electrical ground causes a voltage drop. The voltage at the bulb is reduced and the bulb's brightness is reduced.

1. All complete electrical circuits have a power source (such as a battery), a circuit protection device (such as a fuse), a power-side wire or path, an electrical load, a ground return path, and a switch or a control device.

2. A short-to-voltage involves a copper-to-copper connection and usually affects more than one circuit.

3. A short-to-ground usually involves a power path conductor coming in contact with a return (ground) path conductor and usually causes the fuse to blow.

4. An open is a break in the circuit resulting in absolutely no current flow through the circuit.

REVIEW QUESTIONS

1. What all are included in a complete electrical circuit?

2. What is the difference between a short-to-voltage and a short-to-ground?

3. What is the difference between an electrical open and a short?

4. What is Ohm's law?

5. What happens to current flow (amperes) and wattage if the resistance of a circuit is increased because of a corroded connection?

CHAPTER QUIZ

1. If an insulated (power side) wire gets rubbed through a part of the insulation and the wire conductor touches the steel body of a vehicle, the type of failure would be called a(n) _____.
   a. short-to-voltage
   b. short-to-ground
   c. open
   d. chassis ground

2. If two insulated (power side) wires were to melt together at the point where the copper conductors touched each other, the type of failure would be called a(n) _____.
   a. short-to-voltage
   b. short-to-ground
   c. open
   d. floating ground

3. If 12 volts are being applied to a resistance of 3 ohms, _____ amperes will flow.
   a. 12
   b. 3
   c. 4
   d. 36

4. How many watts are consumed by a lightbulb if 1.2 amperes are measured when 12 volts are applied?
   a. 14.4 watts
   b. 144 watts
   c. 10 watts
   d. 0.10 watt

5. How many watts are consumed by a starter motor if it draws 150 amperes at 10 volts?
   a. 15 watts
   b. 150 watts
   c. 1,500 watts
   d. 15,000 watts

6. High resistance in an electrical circuit can cause _____.
   a. dim lights
   b. slow motor operation
   c. clicking of relays or solenoids
   d. All of the above

7. If the voltage increases in a circuit, what happens to the current (amperes) if the resistance remains the same?
   a. Increases
   b. Decreases
   c. Remains the same
   d. Cannot be determined

8. If 200 amperes flow from the positive terminal of a battery and operate the starter motor, how many amperes will flow back to the negative terminal of the battery?
   a. Cannot be determined
   b. Zero
   c. One half (about 100 amperes)
   d. 200 amperes

9. What is the symbol for voltage used in calculations?
   a. R
   b. E
   c. EMF
   d. I

10. Which circuit failure is most likely to cause the fuse to blow?
   a. Open
   b. Short-to-ground
   c. Short-to-voltage
   d. High resistance

chapter 5

SERIES, PARALLEL, AND SERIES-PARALLEL CIRCUITS

LEARNING OBJECTIVES

After studying this chapter, the reader will be able to:

1. Identify a series circuit.
2. Identify a parallel circuit.
3. Identify a series-parallel circuit.
4. Calculate the total resistance in a parallel circuit.
5. State Kirchhoff's voltage law.
6. Calculate voltage drops in a series circuit.
7. Explain series and parallel circuit laws.
8. State Kirchhoff's current law.
9. Identify where faults in a series-parallel circuit can be detected or determined.

Prepare for ASE Electrical/Electronic Systems (A6) certification test content area "A" (General Electrical/ Electronic System Diagnosis).

KEY TERMS

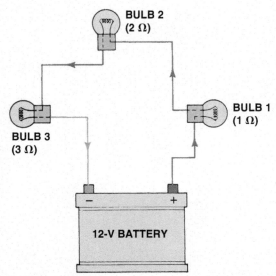

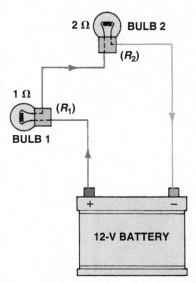

FIGURE 5–1 A series circuit with three bulbs. All current flows through all resistances (bulbs). The total resistance of the circuit is the sum of the total resistance of the bulbs. The bulbs will light dimly because of the increased resistance and the reduction of current flow (amperes) through the circuit.

FIGURE 5–2 A series circuit with two bulbs.

SERIES CIRCUITS

A **series circuit** is a complete circuit that has more than one electrical load where all of the current has only one path to flow through all of the loads. Electrical components, such as fuses and switches, are generally not considered to be included in the determination of a series circuit. The circuit must be continuous or have continuity in order for current to flow through the circuit.

NOTE: Because an electrical load needs both a power and a ground to operate, a break (open) anywhere in a series circuit will cause the current in the circuit to stop.

OHM'S LAW AND SERIES CIRCUITS

As explained earlier, a series circuit is a circuit containing more than one resistance in which all current must flow through all resistances in the circuit. Ohm's law can be used to calculate the value of one unknown (voltage, resistance, or amperes) if the other two values are known.

Because *all* current flows through all resistances, the total resistance is the sum (addition) of all resistances. ● **SEE FIGURE 5–1**. The total resistance of the circuit shown here is

Farsighted Quality of Electricity

Electricity almost seems to act as if it "knows" what resistances are ahead on the long trip through a circuit. If the trip through the circuit has many high-resistance components, very few electrons (amperes) will choose to attempt to make the trip. If a circuit has little or no resistance (e.g., a short circuit), as many electrons (amperes) as possible attempt to flow through the complete circuit. If the flow exceeds the capacity of the fuse or the circuit breaker, the circuit is opened and all current flow stops.

6 ohms ($1\ \Omega + 2\ \Omega + 3\ \Omega$). The formula for total resistance (R_T) for a series circuit is:

$$R_T = R_1 + R_2 + R_3 + \cdots$$

Using Ohm's law to find the current flow, we have

$$I = E/R + 12\,V/6\ \Omega + 2\,A$$

Therefore, with a total resistance of 6 ohms using a 12-volt battery in the series circuit shown, 2 amperes of current will flow through the entire circuit. If the amount of resistance in a circuit is reduced, more current will flow.

In ● **FIGURE 5–2**, one resistance has been eliminated and now the total resistance is 3 ohms ($1\ \Omega + 2\ \Omega$). Using Ohm's law to calculate current flow yields 4 amperes.

$$I = E/R = 12\,V/3\ \Omega = 4\,A$$

Notice that the current flow was doubled (4 amperes instead of 2 amperes) when the resistance was cut in half (from 6 to 3 ohms).

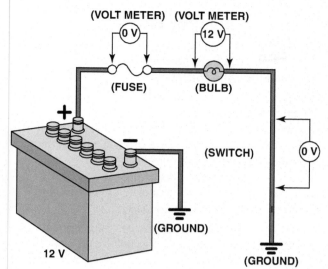

FIGURE 5–3 As current flows through a circuit, the voltage drops in proportion to the amount of resistance in the circuit. Most, if not all, of the resistance should occur across the load, such as the bulb in this circuit. All of the other components and wiring should produce little, if any, voltage drop. If a wire or connection did cause a voltage drop, less voltage would be available to light the bulb and the bulb would be dimmer than normal.

KIRCHHOFF'S VOLTAGE LAW

The voltage that is applied through a series circuit drops with each resistor in a manner similar to that in which the strength of an athlete drops each time a strenuous physical feat is performed. The greater the resistance, the greater the drop in voltage.

A German physicist, Gustav Robert Kirchhoff (1824–1887), developed laws about electrical circuits. His second law, **Kirchhoff's voltage law**, concerns voltage drops. It states: *The voltage around any closed circuit is equal to the sum (total) of the voltage drops across the resistances.*

APPLYING KIRCHHOFF'S VOLTAGE LAW
Kirchhoff states in his second law that the voltage will drop in proportion to the resistance and that the total of all voltage drops will equal the applied voltage. ● **SEE FIGURE 5–3**. Using ● **FIGURE 5–4**, the total resistance of the circuit can be determined by adding the individual resistances ($2\ \Omega + 4\ \Omega + 6\ \Omega = 12\ \Omega$). The current through the circuit is determined by using Ohm's law, $I = E/R = 12\ V/12\ \Omega = 1\ A$. Therefore, in the circuit shown, the following values are known:

Resistance = 12 Ω

Voltage = 12 V

Current = 1 A

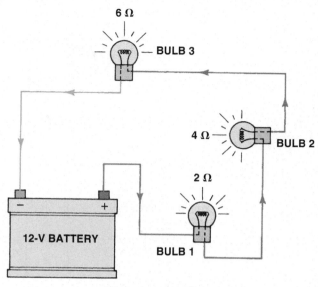

SERIES CIRCUIT

FIGURE 5–4 In a series circuit, the voltage is dropped or lowered by each resistance in the circuit. The higher the resistance, the greater the drop in voltage.

Everything is known *except* the voltage drop caused by each resistance. The **voltage drop** can be determined by using Ohm's law and calculating for voltage (*E*) using the value of each resistance individually:

$$E = I \times R$$

where

E = Voltage

I = Current in the circuit (remember, the current is constant in a series circuit; only the voltage varies)

R = Resistance of only one of the resistances

The voltage drops are as follows:

Voltage drop for bulb 1: $E = I \times R = 1A \times 2\ \Omega = 2\ V$

Voltage drop for bulb 2: $E = I \times R = 1A \times 4\ \Omega = 4\ V$

Voltage drop for bulb 3: $E = I \times R = 1A \times 6\ \Omega = 6\ V$

NOTE: Notice that the voltage drop is proportional to the resistance. In other words, the higher the resistance, the greater the voltage drop. A 6-ohm resistance dropped the voltage three times as much as the voltage drop created by the 2-ohm resistance.

According to Kirchhoff, the sum (addition) of the voltage drops should equal the applied voltage (battery voltage):

Total of voltage drops = 2 V + 4 V + 6 V = 12 V = Battery voltage

This illustrates Kirchhoff's second (voltage) law. Another example is illustrated in ● **FIGURE 5–5**.

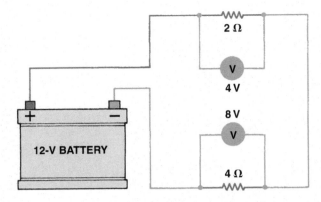

A. $I = E/R$ (TOTAL "R" = 6 Ω)
   = 12 V/6 Ω = 2 A

B. $E = IXR$ (VOLTAGE DROP)
   AT 2 Ω RESISTANCE =
   $E = 2 \times 2 = 4$ V
   AT 4 Ω RESISTANCE =
   $E = 2 \times 4 = 8$ V

C. $4 + 8 = 12$ V
   SUM OF VOLTAGE DROP
   EQUALS APPLIED VOLTAGE

FIGURE 5–5 A voltmeter reads the differences of voltage between the test leads. The voltage read across a resistance is the voltage drop that occurs when current flows through a resistance. A voltage drop is also called an "*IR*" drop because it is calculated by multiplying the current (*I*) through the resistance (electrical load) by the value of the resistance (*R*).

USE OF VOLTAGE DROPS Voltage drops, due to built-in resistance, are used in automotive electrical systems to drop the voltage in the following examples:

1. **Intentional Voltage Drop in Automotive Circuits.** An example of an intentional voltage drop is the blower motor resistor, used in some heater or air-conditioning fans. Speeds are usually controlled by a fan switch sending current through medium 2-, medium 1-, or low-resistance wire resistors. The highest resistance will drop the voltage the most, causing the motor to run at the lowest speed. The speed of the motor changes as current is switched through 1, 2, or 3 resistors in the circuit.

2. **Unintentional Voltage Drop in Automotive Circuits.** Unintentional voltage drop occurs when there is a resistance in a circuit that is not supposed to be there, such as a loose connection or dirty switch contacts.

SERIES CIRCUIT LAWS

Law 1 The total resistance in a series circuit is the sum total of the individual resistances. The resistance values of each electrical load are simply added together.

Law 2 The current is constant throughout the entire circuit. ● **SEE FIGURE 5–6**. If 2 amperes of current leave the battery, 2 amperes of current return to the battery.

? **FREQUENTLY ASKED QUESTION**

Why Check the Voltage Drop Instead of Measuring the Resistance?

Imagine a wire with all strands cut except for one. An ohmmeter can be used to check the resistance of this wire and the resistance would be low, indicating that the wire was okay. But this one small strand cannot properly carry the current (amperes) in the circuit. A voltage drop test is a better test to determine the resistance in components for following two reasons:

- An ohmmeter can only test a wire or component that has been disconnected from the circuit and is not carrying current. The resistance can, and does, change when current flows.
- A voltage drop test is a dynamic test because as the current flows through a component, the conductor increases in temperature, which in turn increases resistance. This means that a voltage drop test is testing the circuit during normal operation and is therefore the most accurate way of determining circuit conditions.

A voltage drop test is also easier to perform because the resistance does not have to be known, only that the unwanted loss of voltage in a circuit should be less than 3% or less than about 0.14 volts for any 12-volt circuit.

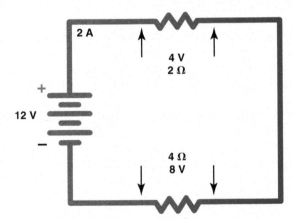

FIGURE 5–6 In this series circuit with a 2-ohm resistor and a 4-ohm resistor, current (2 amperes) is the same throughout even though the voltage drops across each resistor.

Law 3 Although the current (in amperes) is constant, the voltage drops across each resistance in the circuit. The voltage drop across each load is proportional to the value of the resistance compared to the total resistance. For example, if the resistance is one-half of the total resistance, the voltage drop across that resistance will be one-half of the applied voltage. The sum total of all individual voltage drops equals the applied source voltage.

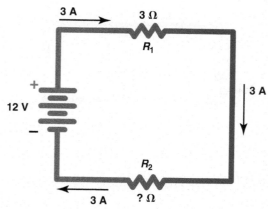

FIGURE 5–7 Example 1.

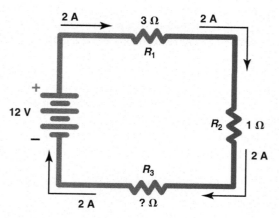

FIGURE 5–8 Example 2.

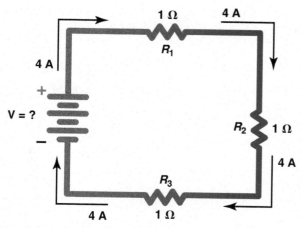

FIGURE 5–9 Example 3.

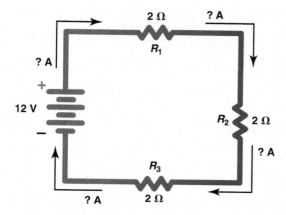

FIGURE 5–10 Example 4.

SERIES CIRCUIT EXAMPLES

Each of the four examples discussed below includes solving for the following:

- Total resistance in the circuit
- Current flow (amperes) through the circuit
- Voltage drop across each resistance

Example 1:

● **SEE FIGURE 5–7**.

The unknown in this problem is the value of R_2. The total resistance, however, can be calculated using Ohm's law.

$$R_{Total} = E/I = 12\ V/3\ A = 4\ \Omega$$

Because R_1 is 3 ohms and the total resistance is 4 ohms, the value of R_2 is 1 ohm.

Example 2:

● **SEE FIGURE 5–8**.

The unknown in this problem is the value of R_3. The total resistance, however, can be calculated using Ohm's law.

$$R_{Total} = E/I = 12\ V/2\ A = 6\ \Omega$$

The total resistance of R_1 (3 ohms) and R_2 (1 ohm) equals 4 ohms so that the value of R_3 is the difference between the total resistance (6 ohms) and the value of the known resistance (4 ohms).

$$6 - 4 = 2\ \Omega = R_3$$

Example 3:

● **SEE FIGURE 5–9**.

The unknown value in this problem is the voltage of the battery. To solve for voltage, use Ohm's law ($E = I \times R$). The "R" in this problem refers to the total resistance (R_T). The total resistance of a series circuit is determined by adding the values of the individual resistors.

$$R_T = 1\ \Omega + 1\ \Omega + 1\ \Omega$$
$$R_T = 3\ \Omega$$

Placing the value for the total resistance (3 Ω) into the equation results in a battery voltage of 12 volts.

$$E = 4\ A \times 3\ \Omega$$
$$E = 12\ V$$

Example 4:

● **SEE FIGURE 5–10**.

The unknown in this example is the current (amperes) in the circuit. To solve for current, use Ohm's law.

$$I = E/R = 12\ V/6\ \Omega = 2\ A$$

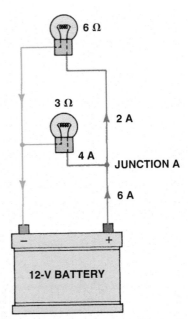

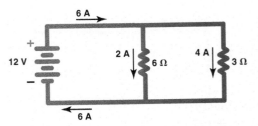

FIGURE 5–12 The current in a parallel circuit splits (divides) according to the resistance in each branch.

FIGURE 5–11 The amount of current flowing into junction point A equals the total amount of current flowing out of the junction.

Notice that the total resistance in the circuit (6 ohms) was used in this example, which is the total of the three individual resistors ($2\,\Omega + 2\,\Omega + 2\,\Omega = 6\,\Omega$). The current through the circuit is 2 amperes.

PARALLEL CIRCUITS

A **parallel circuit** is a complete circuit that has more than one path for the current. The separate paths which split and meet at junction points are called **branches, legs,** or **shunts.** The current flow through each branch or leg varies, depending on the resistance in that branch. A break or open in one leg or section of a parallel circuit does not stop the current flow through the remaining legs of the parallel circuit.

KIRCHHOFF'S CURRENT LAW

Kirchhoff's current law (his first law) states: *The current flowing into any junction of an electrical circuit is equal to the current flowing out of that junction.* This first law can be illustrated using Ohm's law, as seen in ● **FIGURE 5–11.** Kirchhoff's law states that the amount of current flowing into junction A will equal the current flowing out of junction A.

Because the 6-ohm leg requires 2 amperes and the 3-ohm resistance leg requires 4 amperes, it is necessary that the wire from the battery to junction A be capable of handling 6 amperes. Also notice that the sum of the current flowing *out* of a junction ($2 + 4 = 6$ A) is equal to the current flowing *into* the junction (6 A), proving Kirchhoff's current law.

 **TECH TIP**

The Path of Least Resistance

There is an old saying that electricity will always take the path of least resistance. This is true, especially if there is a fault, such as in the secondary (high-voltage) section of the ignition system. If there is a path to ground that is lower than the path to the spark plug, the high-voltage spark will take the path of least resistance. In a parallel circuit where there is more than one path for the current to flow, most of the current will flow through the branch with the lower resistance. This does not mean that all of the current will flow through the lowest resistance, because the other path does provide a path to ground, and the amount of current flow through the other branches is determined by the resistance and the applied voltage according to Ohm's law.

Therefore, the only place where electricity takes the path of least resistance is in a series circuit where there are no other paths for the current to flow.

PARALLEL CIRCUIT LAWS

Law 1 The total resistance of a parallel circuit is always less than that of the smallest-resistance leg. This occurs because not all of the current flows through each leg or branch. With many branches, more current can flow from the battery just as more vehicles can travel on a road with five lanes compared to a road with only one or two lanes.

Law 2 The voltage is the same for each leg of a parallel circuit.

Law 3 The sum of the individual currents in each leg will equal the total current. The amount of current flow through a parallel circuit may vary for each leg depending on the resistance of that leg. The current flowing through each leg results in the same voltage drop (from the power side to the ground side) as for every other leg of the circuit. ● **SEE FIGURE 5–12.**

NOTE: A parallel circuit drops the voltage from source voltage to zero (ground) across the resistance in each leg of the circuit.

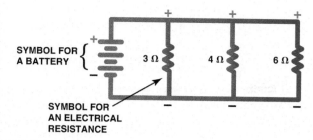

FIGURE 5–13 In a typical parallel circuit, each resistance has power and ground and each leg operates independently of the other legs of the circuit.

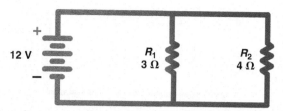

FIGURE 5–14 A schematic showing two resistors in parallel connected to a 12-volt battery.

DETERMINING TOTAL RESISTANCE IN A PARALLEL CIRCUIT

There are five methods commonly used to determine total resistance in a parallel circuit.

NOTE: Determining the total resistance of a parallel circuit is very important in automotive service. Electronic fuel-injector and diesel engine glow plug circuits are two of the most commonly tested circuits where parallel circuit knowledge is required. Also, when installing extra lighting, the technician must determine the proper gauge wire and protection device.

METHOD 1 The total *current* (in amperes) can be calculated first by treating each leg of the parallel circuit as a simple circuit. ● **SEE FIGURE 5–13.** Each leg has its own power and ground (−), and therefore, the current through each leg is independent of the current through any other leg.

Current through the 3-Ω resistance =
$$I = E/R = 12 \text{ V}/3 \ \Omega = 4 \text{ A}$$

Current through the 4-Ω resistance =
$$I = E/R = 12 \text{ V}/4 \ \Omega = 3 \text{ A}$$

Current through the 6-Ω resistance =
$$I = E/R = 12 \text{ V}/6 \ \Omega = 2 \text{ A}$$

The total current flowing from the battery is the sum total of the individual currents for each leg. Total current from the battery is, therefore, 9 amperes (4 A + 3 A + 2 A = 9 A).

If **total circuit resistance** (R_T) is needed, Ohm's law can be used to calculate it because voltage (E) and current (I) are now known.

$$R_T = E/I = 12 \text{ V}/9 \text{ A} = 1.33 \ \Omega$$

Note that the total resistance (1.33 Ω) is smaller than that of the smallest-resistance leg of the parallel circuit. This characteristic of a parallel circuit holds true because not all current flows through all resistances as in a series circuit.

Because the current has alternative paths to ground through the various legs of a parallel circuit, as additional resistances (legs) are added to a parallel circuit, the total current from the battery (power source) *increases.*

Additional current can flow when resistances are added in parallel, because each leg of a parallel circuit has its own power and ground and the current flowing through each leg is strictly dependent on the resistance of *that* leg.

METHOD 2 If only two resistors are connected in parallel, the total resistance (R_T) can be found using the formula $R_T = (R_1 \times R_2)/(R_1 + R_2)$. For example, using the circuit in ● **FIGURE 5–14** and substituting 3 ohms for R_1 and 4 amperes for R_2, $R_T = (3 \times 4)/(3 + 4) = 12/7 = 1.7 \ \Omega$. Note that the total resistance (1.7 Ω) is smaller than that of the smallest-resistance leg of the circuit.

NOTE: Which resistor is R_1 and which is R_2 is not important. The position in the formula makes no difference in the multiplication and addition of the resistor values.

This formula can be used for more than two resistances in parallel, but only two resistances can be calculated at a time. After solving for R_T for two resistors, use the value of R_T as R_1 and the additional resistance in parallel as R_2. Then solve for another R_T. Continue the process for all resistance legs of the parallel circuit. However, note that it might be easier to solve for R_T when there are more than two resistances in parallel by using Method 3 or 4.

METHOD 3 A formula that can be used to find the total resistance for any number of resistances in parallel is $1/R_T = 1/R_1 + 1/R_2 + 1/R_3 + \cdots$

To solve for R_T for the three resistance legs in ● **FIGURE 5–15**, substitute the values of the resistances for R_1, R_2, and R_3: $1/R_T = 1/3 + 1/4 + 1/6$. The fractions cannot be added together unless they all have the same denominator. The lowest common denominator in this example is 12. Therefore, 1/3 becomes 4/12, 1/4 becomes 3/12, and 1/6 becomes 2/12. $1/R_T = 4/12 + 3/12 + 2/12$ or 9/12. Cross multiplying $R_T = 12/9 = 1.33 \ \Omega$. Note that the result (1.33 Ω) is the same regardless of

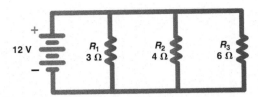

FIGURE 5-15 A parallel circuit with three resistors connected to a 12-volt battery.

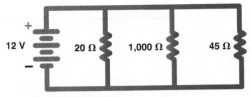

USE AN ELECTRONIC CALCULATOR TO SOLVE

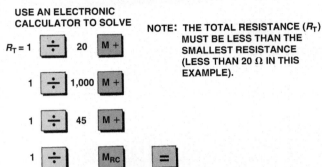

NOTE: THE TOTAL RESISTANCE (R_T) MUST BE LESS THAN THE SMALLEST RESISTANCE (LESS THAN 20 Ω IN THIS EXAMPLE).

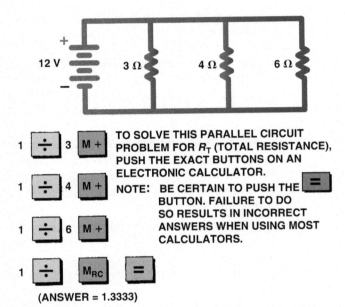

TO SOLVE THIS PARALLEL CIRCUIT PROBLEM FOR R_T (TOTAL RESISTANCE), PUSH THE EXACT BUTTONS ON AN ELECTRONIC CALCULATOR.

NOTE: BE CERTAIN TO PUSH THE [=] BUTTON. FAILURE TO DO SO RESULTS IN INCORRECT ANSWERS WHEN USING MOST CALCULATORS.

(ANSWER = 1.3333)

FIGURE 5-16 Using an electronic calculator to determine the total resistance of a parallel circuit.

FIGURE 5-17 Another example of how to use an electronic calculator to determine the total resistance of a parallel circuit. The answer is 13.45 ohms. Notice that the effective resistance of this circuit is less than the resistance of the lowest branch (20 ohms).

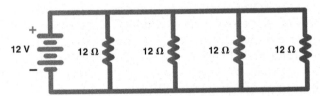

FIGURE 5-18 A parallel circuit containing four 12-ohm resistors. When a circuit has more than one resistor of equal value, the total resistance can be determined by simply dividing the value of the resistance (12 ohms in this example) by the number of equal-value resistors (4 in this example) to get 3 ohms.

the method used (see Method 1). The most difficult part of using this method (besides using fractions) is determining the lowest common denominator, especially for circuits containing a wide range of resistance values for the various legs. For an easier method using a calculator, see Method 4.

METHOD 4 This method uses an electronic calculator, commonly available at very low cost. Instead of determining the lowest common denominator as in Method 3, one can use the electronic calculator to convert the fractions to decimal equivalents. The memory buttons on most calculators can be used to keep a running total of the fractional values. Use ● **FIGURE 5-16** and calculate the total resistance (R_T) by pushing the indicated buttons on the calculator. Also ● **SEE FIGURE 5-17**.

NOTE: This method can be used to find the total resistance of *any number* of resistances in parallel.

The memory recall (MRC) and equals (=) buttons invert the answer to give the correct value for total resistance (1.33 Ω). The inverse (1/X, or X^{-1}) button can be used with the sum (SUM) button on scientific calculators without using the memory button.

METHOD 5 This method can be easily used whenever two or more resistances connected in parallel are of the same value. ● **SEE FIGURE 5-18**. To calculate the total resistance (R_T) of equal-value resistors, divide the number of equal resistors into the value of the resistance. R_T = Value of equal resistance/Number of equal resistances = 12 Ω/4 = 3 Ω.

NOTE: Since most automotive and light-truck electrical circuits involve multiple use of the same resistance, this method is the most useful. For example, if six additional 12-ohm lights were added to a vehicle, the additional lights would represent just 2 ohms of resistance (12 Ω/6 lights = 2). Therefore, 6 amperes of additional current would be drawn by the additional lights (I = E/R = 12 V/2 Ω = 6 A).

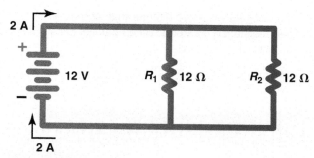

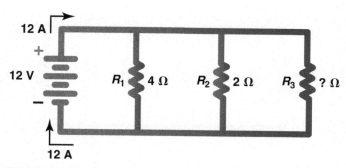

FIGURE 5–19 Example 1.

FIGURE 5–20 Example 2.

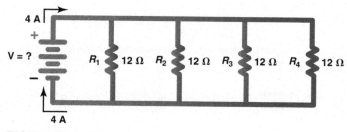

FIGURE 5–21 Example 3.

PARALLEL CIRCUIT EXAMPLES

Each of the four examples discussed below includes solving for the following:

- Total resistance
- Current flow (amperes) through each branch as well as total current flow
- Voltage drop across each resistance

Example 1:

● SEE FIGURE 5–19.

In this example, the voltage of the battery is unknown and the equation to be used is $E = I \times R$ where R represents the total resistance of the circuit. Using the equation for two resistors in parallel, the total resistance is 6 ohms.

$$R_T = \frac{R_1 \times R_2}{R_1 + R_2} = \frac{12 \times 12}{12 + 12} = \frac{144}{24} = 6\ \Omega$$

Placing the value of the total resistors into the equation results in a value for the battery voltage of 12 volts.

$$E = I \times R$$
$$E = 2\,A \times 6\,\Omega$$
$$E = 12\,V$$

Example 2:

● SEE FIGURE 5–20.

In this example, the value of R_3 is unknown. Because the voltage (12 volts) and the current (12 A) are known, it is easier to solve for the unknown resistance by treating each branch or leg as a separate circuit. Using Kirchhoff's law, the total current equals the total current flow through each branch. The current flow through R_1 is 3 A ($I = E/R = 12\ V/4\ \Omega = 3\ A$) and the current flow through R_2 is 6 A ($I = E/R = 12\ V/2\ \Omega = 6\ A$). Therefore, the total current through the two known branches equals 9 A (3 A + 6 A = 9 A). Because there are 12 A leaving and returning to the battery, the current flow through R_3 must be 3 A (12 A − 9 A = 3 A).

The resistance must therefore be 4 Ω because the current through the unknown resistance is 3 A ($I = E/R = 12\ V/4\ \Omega = 3\ A$).

Example 3:

● SEE FIGURE 5–21.

In this example, the voltage of the battery is unknown. The equation to solve for voltage according to Ohm's law is:

$$E = I \times R$$

The R in this equation refers to the total resistance. Because there are four resistors of equal value, the total can be determined by the following equation:

$$R_{Total} = \textbf{Value of Resistors/Number}$$
$$\textbf{of Equal Resistors} = 12\ \Omega/4 = 3\ \Omega$$

Inserting the value of the total resistance of the parallel circuit (3 Ω) into Ohm's law results in a battery voltage of 12 V.

$$E = 4\,A \times 3\,\Omega$$
$$E = 12\,V$$

Example 4:

● SEE FIGURE 5–22.

The unknown is the amount of current in the circuit. The Ohm's law equation for determining current is:

$$I = E/R$$

The R represents the total resistance. Because there are two equal resistances (8 Ω), these two can be replaced by one resistance of 4 Ω (R_{Total} = Value/Number = 8 Ω/2 = 4 Ω).

The total resistance of this parallel circuit containing two 8-ohm resistors and one 4-ohm resistor is 2 ohms. (Two 8-ohm resistors in parallel equals 4 ohms. Then you have two 4-ohm resistors in parallel that equals 2 ohms.) The current flow from the battery is then calculated to be 6 A.

$$I = E/R = 12\ V/2\ \Omega = 6\ A$$

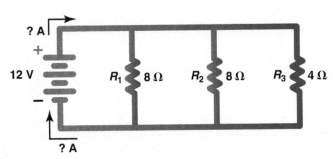

FIGURE 5-22 Example 4.

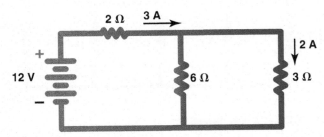

FIGURE 5-23 A series-parallel circuit.

SERIES-PARALLEL CIRCUITS

Series-parallel circuits are a combination of series and parallel segments in one complex circuit. A series-parallel circuit is also called a **compound** or a **combination circuit**. Many automotive circuits include sections that are in parallel and in series.

A series-parallel circuit includes both parallel loads or resistances, plus additional loads or resistances that are electrically connected in series. There are two basic types of series-parallel circuits.

■ A circuit where the load is in series with other loads in parallel. ● **SEE FIGURE 5-23.** An example of this type of series-parallel circuit is a dash light dimming circuit. The variable resistor is used to limit current flow to the dash light bulbs, which are wired in parallel.

■ A circuit where a parallel circuit contains resistors or loads that are in series with one or more branches.

SERIES-PARALLEL CIRCUIT FAULTS If a conventional parallel circuit, such as a taillight circuit, had an electrical fault that increased the resistance in one branch of the circuit, the amount of current flow through that branch will be reduced. The added resistance, due to corrosion or other similar cause, would create a voltage drop. As a result of this drop in voltage, a lower voltage would be applied and the bulb in the taillight would be dimmer than normal. If, however, the added resistance occurred in a part of the circuit that fed both taillights,

then both taillights would be dimmer than normal. In this case, the added resistance created a series-parallel circuit that was originally just a simple parallel circuit.

SOLVING SERIES-PARALLEL CIRCUIT PROBLEMS

The key to solving series-parallel circuit problems is to combine or simplify as much as possible. For example, if there are two loads or resistances in series within a parallel branch or leg, the circuit can be made simpler if the two are first added together before attempting to solve the parallel section. ● **SEE FIGURE 5-24.**

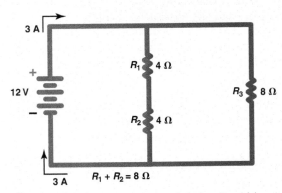

FIGURE 5-24 Solving a series-parallel circuit problem.

SERIES-PARALLEL CIRCUIT EXAMPLES

Each of the four examples discussed below includes solving for the following:

■ Total resistance

■ Current flow (amperes) through each branch, as well as total current flow

■ Voltage drop across each resistance

Example 1:

● **SEE FIGURE 5-25.**

The unknown resistor is in series with the other two resistances, which are connected in parallel. The Ohm's law equation to determine resistance is:

$$R = E/I = 12 \text{ V}/3 \text{ A} = 4 \text{ } \Omega$$

The total resistance of the circuit is therefore 4 ohms, and the value of the unknown can be determined by subtracting the value of the two resistors that are connected in parallel. The parallel branch resistance is 2 Ω.

$$R_T = \frac{4 \times 4}{4 + 4} = \frac{16}{8} = 2\ \Omega$$

The value of the unknown resistance is therefore 2 Ω.

$$\text{Total }\ R = 4\ \Omega - 2\ \Omega = 2\ \Omega$$

Example 2:

● **SEE FIGURE 5–26.**

The unknown unit in this circuit is the voltage of the battery. The Ohm's law equation is:

$$E = I \times R$$

Before solving the problem, the total resistance must be determined. Because each branch contains two 4-ohm resistors in series, the value in each branch can be added to help simplify the circuit. By adding the resistors in each branch together, the parallel circuit now consists of two 8-ohm resistors.

$$R_T = \frac{R_1 \times R_2}{R_1 + R_2} = \frac{8 \times 8}{8 + 8} = \frac{64}{16} = 4\ \Omega$$

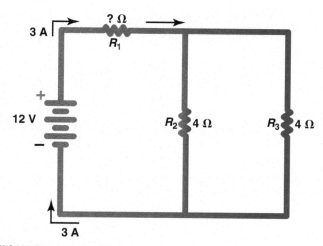

FIGURE 5–25 Example 1.

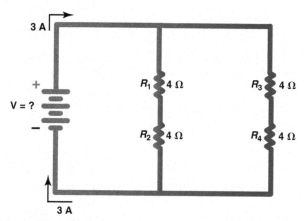

FIGURE 5–26 Example 2.

Inserting the value for the total resistance into the Ohm's law equation results in a value of 12 volts for the battery voltage.

$$E = I \times R$$
$$E = 3\,A \times 4\ \Omega$$
$$E = 12\,V$$

Example 3:

● **SEE FIGURE 5–27.**

In this example, the total current through the circuit is unknown. The Ohm's law equation to solve for it is:

$$I = E/R$$

The total resistance of the parallel circuit must be determined before the equation can be used to solve for current (amperes). To solve for total resistance, the circuit can first be simplified by adding R_3 and R_4 together because these two resistors are in series in the same branch of the parallel circuit. To simplify even more, the resulting parallel section of the circuit, now containing two 8-ohm resistors in parallel, can be replaced with one 4-ohm resistor.

$$R_T = \frac{R_1 \times R_2}{R_1 + R_2} = \frac{8 \times 8}{8 + 8} = \frac{64}{16} = 4\ \Omega$$

With the parallel branches now reduced to just one 4-ohm resistor, this can be added to the 2-ohm (R_1) resistor because it is in series, creating a total circuit resistance of 6 ohms. Now the current flow can be determined from Ohm's law:

$$I = E/R = 12\,V/6\ \Omega = 2\,A$$

Example 4:

● **SEE FIGURE 5–28.**

In this example, the value of resistor R_1 is unknown. Using Ohm's law, the total resistance of the circuit is 3 ohms.

$$R = E/I = 12\,V/4\,A = 3\ \Omega$$

However, knowing the total resistance is not enough to determine the value of R_1. To simplify the circuit, R_2 and R_5 can combine to create a parallel branch resistance value of 8 ohms because they are in series. To simplify even further, the two 8-ohm branches can be reduced to one branch of 4 ohms.

$$R_T = \frac{R_1 \times R_2}{R_1 + R_2} = \frac{8 \times 8}{8 + 8} = \frac{64}{16} = 4\ \Omega$$

Now the circuit has been simplified to one resistor in series (R_1) with two branches with 4 ohms in each branch. These two branches can be reduced to the equal of one 2-ohm resistor.

$$R_T = \frac{R_1 \times R_2}{R_1 + R_2} = \frac{4 \times 4}{4 + 4} = \frac{16}{8} = 2\ \Omega$$

Now the circuit includes just one 2-ohm resistor plus the unknown R_1. Because the total resistance is 3 ohms, the value of R_1 must be 1 ohm.

$$3\ \Omega - 2\ \Omega = 1\ \Omega$$

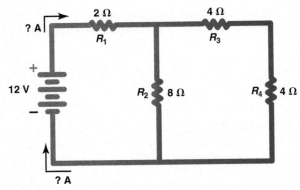

FIGURE 5–27 Example 3.

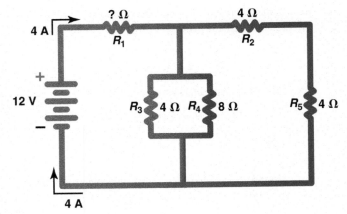

FIGURE 5–28 Example 4.

1. Series circuits:
   a. In a simple series circuit, the current remains constant throughout, but the voltage drops as current flows through the resistances of the circuit.
   b. The voltage drop across each resistance or load is directly proportional to the value of the resistance compared to the total resistance in the circuit.
   c. The sum (total) of the voltage drops equals the applied voltage (Kirchhoff's voltage law).
   d. An open or a break anywhere in a series circuit stops all current from flowing.

2. Parallel circuits:
   a. A parallel circuit, such as is used for all automotive lighting, has the same voltage available to each resistance (bulb).
   b. The total resistance of a parallel circuit is always lower than the smallest resistance.
   c. The separate paths that split and meet at junction points are called branches, legs, or shunts.
   d. Kirchhoff's current law states: "The current flowing into a junction of an electrical circuit is equal to current flowing out of that junction."

3. Series-parallel circuits:
   a. A series-parallel circuit is also called a compound circuit or a combination circuit.
   b. A series-parallel circuit is a combination of a series and a parallel circuit, which does not include fuses or switches.
   c. A fault in a series portion of the circuit would affect the operation if the series part was in the power or the ground side of the parallel portion of the circuit.
   d. A fault in one leg of a series-parallel circuit will affect just the component(s) in that one leg.

REVIEW QUESTIONS

1. What is Kirchhoff's voltage law?
2. What would current (amperes) do if the voltage were doubled in a circuit?
3. Why is the total resistance of a parallel circuit less than the smallest resistance?
4. What would be the effect of an open circuit in one leg of a parallel portion of a series-parallel circuit?
5. What would be the effect of an open circuit in a series portion of a series-parallel circuit?

1. The amperage in a series circuit is _____.
   a. the same anywhere in the circuit
   b. varies in the circuit due to the different resistances
   c. high at the beginning of the circuit and decreases as the current flows through the resistance
   d. always less returning to the battery than leaving the battery

2. The sum of the voltage drops in a series circuit equals the _____.
   a. amperage
   b. resistance
   c. source voltage
   d. wattage

3. If the resistance and the voltage are known, what is the formula for finding the current (amperes)?
   a. $E = I \times R$
   b. $I = E \times R$
   c. $R = E \times I$
   d. $I = E/R$

4. A series circuit has three resistors of 4 ohms each. The voltage drop across each resistor is 4 volts. Technician A says that the source voltage is 12 volts. Technician B says that the total resistance is 18 ohms. Which technician is correct?
   a. Technician A only
   b. Technician B only
   c. Both Technicians A and B
   d. Neither Technician A nor B

5. If a 12-volt battery is connected to a series circuit with three resistors of 2, 4, and 6 ohms, how much current will flow through the circuit?
   a. 1 ampere
   b. 2 amperes
   c. 3 amperes
   d. 4 amperes

6. A series circuit has two 10-ohm bulbs. A third bulb is added in series. Technician A says that the three bulbs will be dimmer than when only two bulbs were in the circuit. Technician B says that the current in the circuit will increase. Which technician is correct?
   a. Technician A only
   b. Technician B only
   c. Both Technicians A and B
   d. Neither Technician A nor B

7. Technician A says that the sum of the voltage drops in a series circuit should equal the source voltage. Technician B says that the current (amperes) varies depending on the value of the resistance in a series circuit. Which technician is correct?
   a. Technician A only
   b. Technician B only
   c. Both Technicians A and B
   d. Neither Technician A nor B

8. Two bulbs are connected in parallel to a 12-volt battery. One bulb has a resistance of 6 ohms and the other bulb has a resistance of 2 ohms. Technician A says that only the 2-ohm bulb will light because all of the current will flow through the path with the least resistance and no current will flow through the 6-ohm bulb. Technician B says that the 6-ohm bulb will be dimmer than the 2-ohm bulb. Which technician is correct?
   a. Technician A only
   b. Technician B only
   c. Both Technicians A and B
   d. Neither Technician A nor B

9. Calculate the total resistance and current in a parallel circuit with three resistors of 4, 8, and 16 ohms, using any one of the five methods (calculator suggested). What is the total resistance and current?
   a. 27 ohms (0.4 ampere)
   b. 14 ohms (0.8 ampere)
   c. 4 ohms (3.0 amperes)
   d. 2.3 ohms (5.3 amperes)

10. A vehicle has four parking lights all connected in parallel and one of the bulbs burns out. Technician A says that this could cause the parking light circuit fuse to blow (open). Technician B says that it would decrease the current in the circuit. Which technician is correct?
    a. Technician A only
    b. Technician B only
    c. Both Technicians A and B
    d. Neither Technician A nor B

chapter 6

CIRCUIT TESTERS AND DIGITAL METERS

After studying this chapter, the reader will be able to:

1. Discuss diode check, pulse width, and frequency.

2. Describe the prefixes used with electrical units and how to read digital meters.

3. Discuss how to safely set up and use a fused jumper wire, a test light, and a logic probe.

4. Explain how to safely and properly use a digital meter to read voltage, resistance, and current and compare to factory specifications.

This chapter will help you prepare for the ASE Electrical/Electronic Systems (A6) certification test content area "A" (General Electrical/Electronic System Diagnosis).

KEY TERMS

AC/DC clamp-on DMM 92

Continuity light 86

DMM 87

DVOM 87

High-impedance test meter 87

IEC 99

Inductive ammeter 92

Kilo (k) 94

LED test light 86

Logic probe 87

Mega (M) 94

Meter accuracy 98

Meter resolution 97

Milli (m) 94

OL 89

RMS 97

Test light 85

FUSED JUMPER WIRE

DEFINITION A fused jumper wire is used to check a circuit by bypassing the switch or to provide a power or ground to a component. A fused jumper wire, also called a test lead, can be purchased or made by the service technician.
● **SEE FIGURE 6–1.**

It should include the following features:

- **Fuse.** A typical fused jumper wire has a blade-type fuse that can be easily replaced. A 10-ampere fuse (red color) is often the value used.

- **Alligator clip ends.** Alligator clips at the ends allow the fused jumper wire to be clipped to a ground or power source while the other end is attached to the power side or ground side of the unit being tested.

- **Good-quality insulated wire.** Most purchased jumper wire is about 14 gauge stranded copper wire with a flexible rubberized insulation to allow it to move easily even in cold weather.

USES OF A FUSED JUMPER WIRE A fused jumper wire can be used to help diagnose a component or circuit by performing the following procedures:

- **Supply power or ground.** If a component, such as a horn, does not work, a fused jumper wire can be used to supply a temporary power and/or ground. Start by unplugging the electrical connector from the device and connect a fused jumper lead to the power terminal. Another fused jumper wire may be needed to provide the ground. If the unit works, the problem is in the power-side or ground-side circuit.

CAUTION: Never use a fused jumper wire to bypass any resistance or load in the circuit. The increased current flow could damage the wiring and could blow the fuse on the jumper lead.

FIGURE 6–1 A technician-made fused jumper lead, which is equipped with a red 10-ampere fuse. This fused jumper wire uses terminals for testing circuits at a connector instead of alligator clips.

TEST LIGHTS

NONPOWERED TEST LIGHT A 12-volt test light is one of the simplest testers that can be used to detect electricity. A **test light** is simply a lightbulb with a probe and a ground wire attached. ● **SEE FIGURE 6–2.**

It is used to detect battery voltage potential at various test points. Battery voltage cannot be seen or felt and can be detected only with test equipment.

The ground clip is connected to a clean ground on either the negative terminal of the battery or a clean metal part of the body and the probe touched to terminals or components. If the test light comes on, this indicates that voltage is available. ● **SEE FIGURE 6–3.**

A purchased test light could be labeled a "12-volt test light." Do not purchase a test light designed for household current (110 or 220 volts), as it will not light with 12 to 14 volts.

USES OF A 12-VOLT TEST LIGHT A 12-volt test light can be used to check the following:

- **Electrical power.** If the test light comes on, there is power available. It will not, however, indicate the voltage level or if there is enough current available to operate an electrical load. This only indicates that there is enough voltage and current to light the test light (about 0.25 A).

- **Grounds.** A test light can be used to check for grounds by attaching the clip of the test light to the positive terminal of

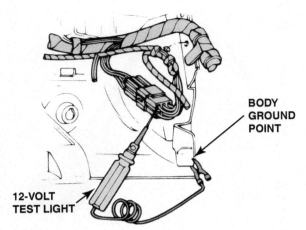

FIGURE 6–2 A 12-volt test light is attached to a good ground while probing for power.

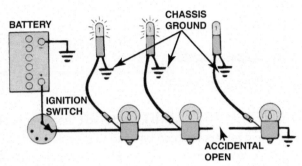

FIGURE 6–3 A test light can be used to locate an open in a circuit. Note that the test light is grounded at a different location than the circuit itself.

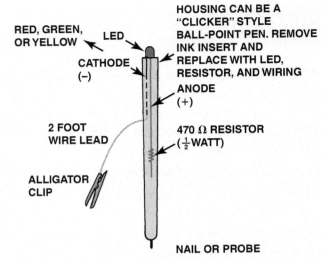

FIGURE 6–4 An LED test light can be easily made using low cost components and an old ink pen. With the 470 ohm resistor in series with the LED, this tester only draws 0.025 ampere (25 milliamperes) from the circuit being tested. This low current draw helps assure the technician that the circuit or component being tested will not be damaged by excessive current flow.

the battery or to any 12-volt electrical terminal. The tip of the test light can then be used to touch the ground wire. If there is a ground connection, the test light will come on.

CAUTION: The use of a self-powered (continuity) test light is not recommended on any electronic circuit, because a continuity light contains a battery and applies voltage; therefore, it may harm delicate electronic components.

HIGH-IMPEDANCE TEST LIGHT
A high-impedance test light has a high internal resistance and therefore draws very low current in order to light. High-impedance test lights are safe to use on computer circuits because they will not affect the circuit current in the same way as conventional 12-volt test lights when connected to a circuit. There are two types of high-impedance test lights.

- Some test lights use an electronic circuit to limit the current flow to avoid causing damage to electronic devices.
- An **LED test light** uses a light-emitting diode (LED) instead of a standard automotive bulb for a visual indication of voltage. An LED test light requires only about 25 milliamperes (0.025 ampere) to light; therefore, it can be used on electronic circuits, as well as, on standard circuits.

● **SEE FIGURE 6–4** for construction details for a home-made LED test light.

PURPOSE AND FUNCTION A **logic probe** is an electronic device that lights up a red (usually) LED if the probe is touched to battery voltage. If the probe is touched to ground, a green (usually) LED lights up. ● **SEE FIGURE 6–5**.

A logic probe can "sense" the difference between high- and low-voltage levels, which explains the name *logic*.

- A typical logic probe can also light another light (often amber color) when a change in voltage occurs.
- Some logic probes will flash the red light when a pulsing voltage signal is detected.
- Some will flash the green light when a pulsing ground signal is detected.

This feature is helpful when checking for a variable voltage output from a computer or ignition sensor.

USING A LOGIC PROBE A logic probe must first be connected to a power and ground source, such as the vehicle battery. This connection powers the probe and gives it a reference low (ground).

Most logic probes also make a distinctive sound for each high- and low-voltage level. This makes troubleshooting easier when probing connectors or component terminals. A sound (usually a beep) is heard when the probe tip is touched to a changing voltage source. The changing voltage also usually lights the pulse light on the logic probe. Therefore, the probe can be used to check components such as:

- Pickup coils
- Hall-effect sensors
- Magnetic sensors

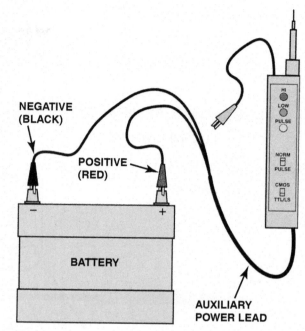

FIGURE 6–5 A logic probe connected to the vehicle battery. When the tip probe is connected to a circuit, it can check for power, ground, or a pulse.

DIGITAL MULTIMETERS

TERMINOLOGY **Digital multimeter (DMM)** and **digital volt-ohm-meter (DVOM)** are terms commonly used for electronic **high-impedance test meters**. *High impedance* means that the electronic internal resistance of the meter is high enough to prevent excessive current draw from any circuit being tested. Most meters today have a minimum of 10 million ohms (10 megohms) of resistance. This high internal resistance between the meter leads is present only when measuring volts. The high resistance in the meter itself reduces the amount of current flowing through the meter when it is being used to measure voltage, leading to more accurate test results because the meter does not change the load on the circuit. High-impedance meters are required for measuring computer circuits.

CAUTION: Analog (needle-type) meters are almost always lower than 10 megohms and should not be used to measure any computer or electronic circuit. Connecting an analog meter to a computer circuit could damage the computer or other electronic modules.

A high-impedance meter can be used to measure any automotive circuit within the ranges of the meter. ● **SEE FIGURE 6–6**.

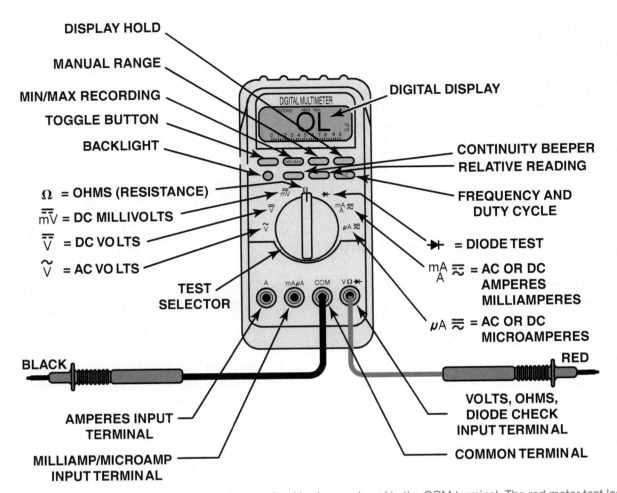

DISPLAY HOLD

MANUAL RANGE

MIN/MAX RECORDING

TOGGLE BUTTON

BACKLIGHT

Ω = OHMS (RESISTANCE)

$\overline{mV}$ = DC MILLIVOLTS

$\overline{V}$ = DC VOLTS

$\sim V$ = AC VOLTS

TEST SELECTOR

DIGITAL DISPLAY

CONTINUITY BEEPER

RELATIVE READING

FREQUENCY AND DUTY CYCLE

$\rightarrowtail$ = DIODE TEST

$\dfrac{mA}{A} \approx$ = AC OR DC AMPERES MILLIAMPERES

$\mu A \approx$ = AC OR DC MICROAMPERES

BLACK

RED

VOLTS, OHMS, DIODE CHECK INPUT TERMINAL

AMPERES INPUT TERMINAL

MILLIAMP/MICROAMP INPUT TERMINAL

COMMON TERMINAL

FIGURE 6–6 Typical digital multimeter. The black meter lead is always placed in the COM terminal. The red meter test lead should be in the volt-ohm terminal except when measuring current in amperes.

SYMBOL	MEANING
AC	Alternating current or voltage
DC	Direct current or voltage
V	Volts
mV	Millivolts (1/1,000 volts)
A	Ampere (amps), current
mA	Milliampere (1/1,000 amps)
%	Percent (for duty cycle readings only)
Ω	Ohms, resistance
kΩ	Kilohm (1,000 ohms), resistance
MΩ	Megohm (1,000,000 ohms), resistance
Hz	Hertz (cycles per second), frequency
kHz	Kilohertz (1,000 cycles/sec.), frequency
ms	Milliseconds (1/1,000 sec.) for pulse width measurements

CHART 6–1

Common symbols and abbreviations used on digital meters.

The common abbreviations for the units that many meters can measure are often confusing. ● **SEE CHART 6–1** for the most commonly used symbols and their meanings.

MEASURING VOLTAGE A voltmeter measures the *pressure* or potential of electricity in units of volts. A voltmeter is connected to a circuit in parallel. Voltage can be measured by selecting either AC or DC volts.

- **DC volts (DCV).** This setting is the most common for automotive use. Use this setting to measure battery voltage and voltage to all lighting and accessory circuits.

- **AC volts (ACV).** This setting is used to check for unwanted AC voltage from alternators and some sensors.

- **Range.** The range is automatically set for most meters but can be manually ranged if needed.

● **SEE FIGURES 6–7 AND 6–8.**

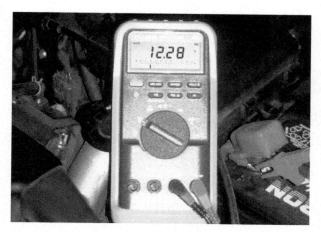

FIGURE 6-7 Typical digital multimeter (DMM) set to read DC volts.

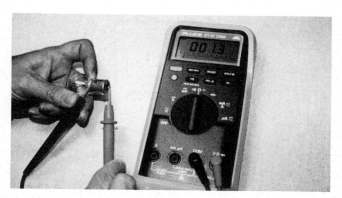

FIGURE 6-9 Using a digital multimeter set to read ohms (Ω) to test this lightbulb. The meter reads the resistance of the filament.

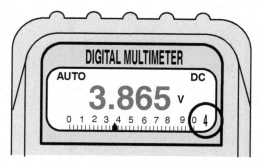

BECAUSE THE SIGNAL READING IS BELOW 4 VOLTS, THE METER AUTORANGES TO THE 4-VOLT SCALE. IN THE 4-VOLT SCALE, THIS METER PROVIDES THREE DECIMAL PLACES.

(a)

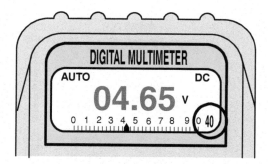

WHEN THE VOLTAGE EXCEEDS 4 VOLTS, THE METER AUTORANGES INTO THE 40-VOLT SCALE. THE DECIMAL POINT MOVES ONE PLACE TO THE RIGHT LEAVING ONLY TWO DECIMAL PLACES.

(b)

FIGURE 6-8 A typical autoranging digital multimeter automatically selects the proper scale to read the voltage being tested. The scale selected is usually displayed on the meter face. (a) Note that the display indicates "4," meaning that this range can read up to 4 volts. (b) The range is now set to the 40-volt scale, meaning that the meter can read up to 40 volts on the scale. Any reading above this level will cause the meter to reset to a higher scale. If not set on autoranging, the meter display would indicate OL if a reading exceeds the limit of the scale selected.

MEASURING RESISTANCE An ohmmeter measures the resistance in ohms of a component or circuit section when no current is flowing through the circuit. An ohmmeter contains a battery (or other power source) and is connected in series with the component or wire being measured. When the leads are connected to a component, current flows through the test leads and the difference in voltage (voltage drop) between the leads is measured as resistance. Note the following facts about using an ohmmeter:

- Zero ohms on the scale means that there is no resistance between the test leads, thus indicating continuity or a continuous path for the current to flow in a closed circuit.

- Infinity means no connection, as in an open circuit.

- Ohmmeters have no required polarity even though red and black test leads are used for resistance measurement.

CAUTION: The circuit must be electrically open with no current flowing when using an ohmmeter. If current is flowing when an ohmmeter is connected, the reading will be incorrect and the meter can be destroyed.

Different meters have different ways of indicating infinite resistance, or a reading higher than the scale allows. Examples of an over limit display include:

- **OL**, meaning **over limit** or overload

- Flashing or solid number 1

- Flashing or solid number 3 on the left side of the display

Check the meter instructions for the exact display used to indicate an open circuit or over range reading. ● **SEE FIGURES 6-9 AND 6-10.**

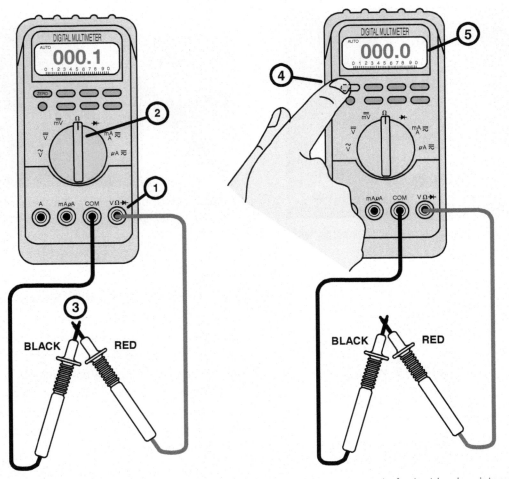

FIGURE 6–10 Many digital multimeters can have the display indicate zero to compensate for test lead resistance. (1) Connect leads in the V Ω and COM meter terminals. (2) Select the Ω scale. (3) Touch the two meter leads together. (4) Push the "zero" or "relative" button on the meter. (5) The meter display will now indicate zero ohms of resistance.

To summarize, open and zero readings are as follows:

0.00 Ω = Zero resistance (component or circuit has continuity)

OL = An open circuit or reading is higher than the scale selected (no current flows)

MEASURING AMPERES An ammeter measures the flow of *current* through a complete circuit in units of amperes. The ammeter has to be installed in the circuit (in series) so that it can measure all the current flow in that circuit, just as a water flow meter would measure the amount of water flow (cubic feet per minute, for example). ● **SEE FIGURE 6–11.**

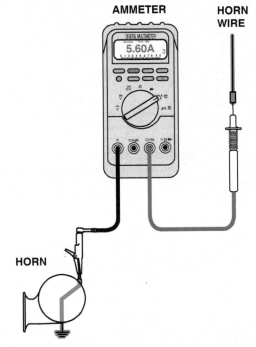

FIGURE 6–11 Measuring the current flow required by a horn requires that the ammeter be connected to the circuit in series and the horn button be depressed by an assistant.

FREQUENTLY ASKED QUESTION

How Much Voltage Does an Ohmmeter Apply?

Most digital meters that are set to measure ohms (resistance) apply 0.3 to 1 volt to the component being measured. The voltage comes from the meter itself to measure the resistance. Two things are important to remember about an ohmmeter.

1. The component or circuit must be disconnected from any electrical circuit while the resistance is being measured.

2. Because the meter itself applies a voltage (even though it is relatively low), a meter set to measure ohms can damage electronic circuits. Computer or electronic chips can be easily damaged if subjected to only a few milliamperes of current, similar to the amount an ohmmeter applies when a resistance measurement is being performed.

CAUTION: An ammeter must be installed in series with the circuit to measure the current flow in the circuit. If a meter set to read amperes is connected in parallel, such as across a battery, the meter or the leads may be destroyed, or the fuse will blow, by the current available across the battery. Some digital multimeters (DMMs) beep if the unit selection does not match the test lead connection on the meter. However, in a noisy shop, this beep sound may be inaudible.

Digital meters require that the meter leads be moved to the ammeter terminals. Most digital meters have an ampere scale that can accommodate a maximum of 10 amperes. See the Tech Tip "Fuse Your Meter Leads!"

TECH TIP

Fuse Your Meter Leads!

Most digital meters include an ammeter capability. When reading amperes, the leads of the meter must be changed from volts or ohms (V or Ω) to amperes (A), milliamperes (mA), or microamperes (µA).

A common problem may then occur the next time voltage is measured. Although the technician may switch the selector to read volts, often the leads are not switched back to the volt or ohm position. Because the ammeter lead position results in zero ohms of resistance to current flow through the meter, the meter or the fuse inside the meter will be destroyed if the meter is connected to a battery. Many meter fuses are expensive and difficult to find.

To avoid this problem, simply solder an inline 10-ampere blade-fuse holder into one meter lead.
 SEE FIGURE 6–12.

Do not think that this technique is for beginners only. Experienced technicians often get in a hurry and forget to switch the lead. A blade fuse is faster, easier, and less expensive to replace than a meter fuse or the meter itself. Also, if the soldering is done properly, the addition of an inline fuse holder and fuse does not increase the resistance of the meter leads. All meter leads have some resistance. If the meter is measuring very low resistance, touch the two leads together and read the resistance (usually no more than 0.2 ohm). Simply subtract the resistance of the leads from the resistance of the component being measured.

FREQUENTLY ASKED QUESTION

What Does "CE" Mean on Many Meters?

The "CE" means that the meter meets the newest European Standards and the CE mark stands for *Conformité Européenne,* which is French for "European Conformity."

FIGURE 6–12 Note the blade-type fuse holder soldered in series with one of the meter leads. A 10-ampere fuse helps protect the internal meter fuse (if equipped) and the meter itself from damage that may result from excessive current flow if accidentally used incorrectly.

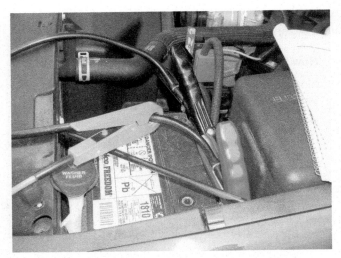

FIGURE 6–13 An inductive ammeter clamp is used with all starting and charging testers to measure the current flow through the battery cables.

INDUCTIVE AMMETERS

OPERATION **Inductive ammeters** do not make physical contact with the circuit. They measure the strength of the magnetic field surrounding the wire carrying the current, and use a Hall-effect sensor to measure current. The Hall-effect sensor detects the strength of the magnetic field that surrounds the wire carrying an electrical current. ● SEE FIGURE 6–13.

This means that the meter probe surrounds the wire(s) carrying the current and measures the strength of the magnetic field that surrounds any conductor carrying a current.

AC/DC CLAMP-ON DIGITAL MULTIMETERS An **AC/ DC clamp-on digital multimeter (DMM)** is a useful meter for automotive diagnostic work. ● SEE FIGURE 6–14.

The major advantage of the clamp-on-type meter is that there is no need to break the circuit to measure current (amperes). Simply clamp the jaws of the meter around the power lead(s) or ground lead(s) of the component being measured and read the display. Most clamp-on meters can also

FIGURE 6–14 A typical mini clamp-on-type digital multimeter. This meter is capable of measuring alternating current (AC) and direct current (DC) without requiring that the circuit be disconnected to install the meter in series. The jaws are simply placed over the wire and current flow through the circuit is displayed.

measure alternating current, which is helpful in the diagnosis of an alternator problem. Volts, ohms, frequency, and temperature can also be measured with the typical clamp-on DMM, but use conventional meter leads. The inductive clamp is only used to measure amperes.

FIGURE 6–15 Typical digital multimeter showing OL (over limit) on the readout with the ohms (Ω) unit selected. This usually means that the unit being measured is open (infinite resistance) and has no continuity.

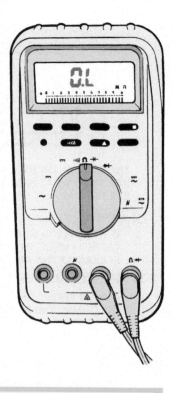

DIODE CHECK, DUTY CYCLE AND FREQUENCY

DIODE CHECK Diode check is a meter function that can be used to check diodes including light-emitting diodes (LEDs). The meter is able to test diodes in the following way:

- The meter applies roughly a 3-volt DC signal to the test leads.
- The voltage is high enough to cause a diode to work and the meter will display:

  1. 0.4 to 0.7 volt when testing silicon diodes, such as those found in alternators
  2. 1.5 to 2.3 volts when testing LEDs, such as those found in some lighting applications

DUTY CYCLE Duty Cycle is the amount of time by percentage that a signal is on compared to being off.

- 100% indicates that a device is being commanded on all of the time.
- 50% indicates that a device is being commanded on half of the time.
- 25% indicates that a device is being commanded on just 25% of the time.

Duty Cycle is used to measure the on time for fuel injectors and other computer-controlled solenoid and devices.

FREQUENCY Frequency is a measure of how many times per second a signal changes. Frequency is measured in a unit called hertz, formerly termed "cycles per second."

Frequency measurements are used when checking the following:

- Mass airflow (MAF) sensors for proper operation
- Ignition primary pulse signals when diagnosing a no-start condition
- Checking a wheel speed sensor

 **TECH TIP**

Over Limit Display Does Not Mean the Meter Is Reading "Nothing"

The meaning of the over limit display on a digital meter often confuses beginning technicians. When asked what the meter is reading when an over limit (OL) is displayed on the meter face, the response is often, "Nothing." Many meters indicate *over limit* or *over load*, which simply means that the reading is over the maximum that can be displayed for the selected range. For example, the meter will display OL if 12 volts are being measured, but the meter has been set to read a maximum of 4 volts.

Autoranging meters adjust the range to match what is being measured. Here OL means a value higher than the meter can read (unlikely on the voltage scale for automobile usage), or infinity when measuring resistance (ohms). Therefore, OL means infinity when measuring resistance or an open circuit is being indicated. The meter will read 00.0 if the resistance is zero, so "nothing" in this case indicates continuity (zero resistance), whereas OL indicates infinite resistance. Therefore, when talking with another technician about a meter reading, make sure you know exactly what the reading on the face of the meter means. Also be sure that you are connecting the meter leads correctly. ● **SEE FIGURE 6–15**.

ELECTRICAL UNIT PREFIXES

DEFINITIONS Electrical units are measured in numbers such as 12 volts, 150 amperes, and 470 ohms. Large units over 1,000 may be expressed in kilo units. **Kilo (k)** means 1,000.
● **SEE FIGURE 6–16**.

47,00 ohms = 4.7 kilohms (kΩ)

If the value is over 1 million (1,000,000), the prefix **mega (M)** is often used. For example,

1,100,000 volts = 1.1 megavolts (MV)

4,700,000 ohms = 4.7 mega ohms (MΩ)

Sometimes a circuit conducts so little current that a smaller unit of measure is required. Small units of measure expressed in 1/1,000 are prefixed by **milli (m)**. To summarize,

mega (M) = 1,000,000 (decimal point six places to the right = 1,000,000)

kilo (k) = 1,000 (decimal point three places to the right = 1,000)

milli (m) = 1/1,000 (decimal point three places to the left = 0.001)

NOTE: Lowercase *m* equals a small unit (milli), whereas a capital *M* represents a large unit (mega).

● **SEE CHART 6–2**.

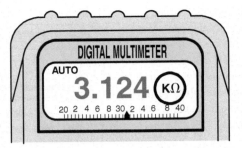

THE SYMBOL ON THE RIGHT SIDE OF THE DISPLAY INDICATES WHAT RANGE THE METER HAS BEEN SET TO READ.

Ω = OHMS

IF THE ONLY SYMBOL ON THE DISPLAY IS THE OHMS SYMBOL, THE READING ON THE DISPLAY IS EXACTLY THE RESISTANCE IN OHMS.

KΩ = KILOHMS = OHMS TIMES 1,000

A "K" IN FRONT OF THE OHMS SYMBOL MEANS "KILOHMS"; THE READING ON THE DISPLAY IS IN KILOHMS. YOU HAVE TO MULTIPLY THE READING ON THE DISPLAY BY 1,000 TO GET THE RESISTANCE IN OHMS.

MΩ = MEGOHMS = OHMS TIMES 1,000,000

AN "M" IN FRONT OF THE OHMS SYMBOL MEANS "MEGOHMS"; THE READING ON THE DISPLAY IS IN MEGOHMS. YOU HAVE TO MULTIPLY THE READING ON THE DISPLAY BY 1,000,000 TO GET THE RESISTANCE IN OHMS.

FIGURE 6–16 Always look at the meter display when a measurement is being made, especially if using an autoranging meter.

TO/ FROM	MEGA	KILO	BASE	MILLI
Mega	0 places	3 places to the right	6 places to the right	9 places to the right
Kilo	3 places to the left	0 places	3 places to the right	6 places to the right
Base	6 places to the left	3 places to the left	0 places	3 places to the right
Milli	9 places to the left	6 places to the left	3 places to the left	0 places

CHART 6–2

A conversion chart showing the decimal point location for the various prefixes.

PREFIXES The prefixes can be confusing because most digital meters can express values in more than one unit, especially if the meter is autoranging. For example, an ammeter reading may show 36.7 mA on autoranging. When the scale is changed to amperes ("A" in the window of the display), the number displayed will be 0.037 A. Note that the resolution of the value is reduced.

NOTE: Always check the face of the meter display for the unit being measured. To best understand what is being displayed on the face of a digital meter, select a manual scale and move the selector until *whole units appear*, such as "A" for amperes instead of "mA" for milliamperes.

Think of Money

Digital meter displays can often be confusing. The display for a battery measured as 12 1/2 volts would be 12.50 V, just as $12.50 is 12 dollars and 50 cents. A 1/2-volt reading on a digital meter will be displayed as 0.50 V, just as $0.50 is half of a dollar.

It is more confusing when low values are displayed. For example, if a voltage reading is 0.063 volt, an autoranging meter will display 63 millivolts (63 mV), or 63/1,000 of a volt, or $63 of $1,000. (It takes 1,000 mV to equal 1 volt.) Think of millivolts as one-tenth of a cent, with 1 volt being $1.00. Therefore, 630 millivolts are equal to $0.63 of $1.00 (630 tenths of a cent, or 63 cents).

To avoid confusion, try to manually range the meter to read base units (whole volts). If the meter is ranged to base unit volts, 63 millivolts would be displayed as 0.063 or maybe just 0.06, depending on the display capabilities of the meter.

HOW TO READ DIGITAL METERS

STEPS TO FOLLOW Getting to know and use a digital meter takes time and practice. The first step is to read, understand, and follow all safety and operational instructions that come with the meter. Use of the meter usually involves the following steps:

STEP 1 **Select the proper unit of electricity for what is being measured.** This unit could be volts, ohms (resistance), or amperes (amount of current flow). If the meter is not autoranging, select the proper scale for the anticipated reading. For example, if a 12-volt battery is being measured, select a meter reading range that is higher than the voltage but not too high. A 20- or 30-volt range will accurately show the voltage of a 12-volt battery. If a 1,000 volt scale is selected, a 12-volt reading may not be accurate.

STEP 2 **Place the meter leads into the proper input terminals.**

- The black lead is inserted into the common (COM) terminal. This meter lead usually stays in this location for all meter functions.
- The red lead is inserted into the volt, ohm, or diode check terminal usually labeled "VΩ" when voltage, resistance, or diodes are being measured.
- When current flow in amperes is being measured, most digital meters require that the red test lead be inserted in the ammeter terminal, usually labeled "A" or "mA."

CAUTION: If the meter leads are inserted into ammeter terminals, even though the selector is set to volts, the meter may be damaged or an internal fuse may blow if the test leads touch both terminals of a battery.

STEP 3 Measure the component being tested. Carefully note the decimal point and the unit on the face of the meter.

- **Meter lead connections.** If the meter leads are connected to a battery backwards (red to the battery negative, for example), the display will still show the correct reading, but a negative sign (−) will be displayed in front of the number. The correct polarity is not important when measuring resistance (ohms) except where indicated, such as measuring a diode.
- **Autorange.** Many meters automatically default to the autorange position and the meter will display the value in the most readable scale. The meter can be manually ranged to select other levels or to lock in a scale for a value that is constantly changing.

   If a 12-volt battery is measured with an autoranging meter, the correct reading of 12.0 is given. "AUTO" and "V" should show on the face of the meter. For example, if a meter is manually set to the

Scale Selected	0.01 V (10 mV)	0.150 V (150 mV)	1.5 V	10.0 V	12.0 V	120 V
	Voltmeter will display:					
200 mV	10.0	150.0	OL	OL	OL	OL
2 V	0.100	0.150	1.500	OL	OL	OL
20 V	0.1	1.50	1.50	10.00	12.00	OL
200 V	00.0	01.5	01.5	10.0	12.0	120.0
2 kV	00.00	00.00	000.1	00.10	00.12	0.120
Autorange	10.0 mV	15.0 mV	1.50	10.0	12.0	120.0

RESISTANCE BEING MEASURED

Scale Selected	10 OHMS	100 OHMS	470 OHMS	1 KILOHM	220 KILOHMS	1 MEGOHM
	Ohmmeter will display:					
400 ohms	10.0	100.0	OL	OL	OL	OL
4 kilohms	010	100	0.470 k	1000	OL	OL
40 kilohms	00.0	0.10 k	0.47 k	1.00 k	OL	OL
400 kilohms	000.0	00.1 k	00.5 k	0.10 k	220.0 k	OL
4 megohms	00.00	0.01 M	0.05 M	00.1 M	0.22 M	1.0 M
Autorange	10.0	100.0	470.0	1.00 k	220 k	1.00 M

CURRENT BEING MEASURED

Scale Selected	50 mA	150 mA	1.0 A	7.5 A	15.0 A	25.0 A
	Ammeter will display:					
40 mA	OL	OL	OL	OL	OL	OL
400 mA	50.0	150	OL	OL	OL	OL
4 A	0.05	0.00	1.00	OL	OL	OL
40 A	0.00	0.000	01.0	7.5	15.0	25.0
Autorange	50.0 mA	150.0 mA	1.00	7.5	15.0	25.0

CHART 6–3

Sample meter readings using manually set and autoranging selection on the digital meter control.

2 kilohm scale, the highest that the meter will read is 2,000 ohms. If the reading is over 2,000 ohms, the meter will display OL. ● **SEE CHART 6–3.**

STEP 4 Interpret the reading. This is especially difficult on autoranging meters, where the meter itself selects the proper scale. The following are two examples of different readings:

Example 1: A voltage drop is being measured. The specifications indicate a maximum voltage drop of 0.2 volt. The meter reads "AUTO" and "43.6 mV." This reading means that the voltage drop is 0.0436 volt, or 43.6 mV, which is far lower than the 0.2 volt (200 mV). Because the number showing on the meter face is much larger than the specifications, many beginner technicians are led to believe that the voltage drop is excessive.

NOTE: Pay attention to the units displayed on the meter face and convert to whole units.

Example 2: A spark plug wire is being measured. The reading should be less than 10,000 ohms for each foot in length if the wire is okay. The wire being tested is 3 ft long (maximum allowable resistance is 30,000 ohms). The meter reads "AUTO" and "14.85 kΩ." This reading is equivalent to 14,850 ohms.

NOTE: When converting from kilohms to ohms, make the decimal point a comma.

Because this reading is well below the specified maximum allowable, the spark plug wire is okay.

RMS VERSUS AVERAGE Alternating current voltage waveforms can be true sinusoidal or nonsinusoidal. A true

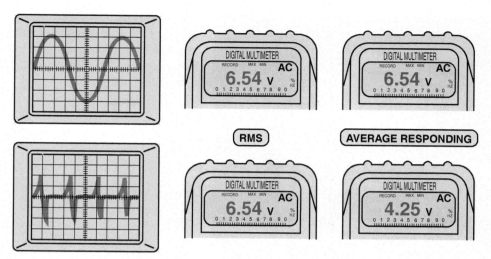

FIGURE 6–17 When reading AC voltage signals, a true RMS meter (such as a Fluke 87) provides a different reading than an average responding meter (such as a Fluke 88). The only place this difference is important is when a reading is to be compared with a specification.

Purchase a Digital Meter That Will Work for Automotive Use

Try to purchase a digital meter that is capable of reading the following:

- DC volts
- AC volts
- DC amperes (up to 10 A or more is helpful)
- Ohms (Ω) up to 40 MΩ (40 million ohms)
- Diode check

Additional features for advanced automotive diagnosis include:

- Frequency (hertz, abbreviated Hz)
- Temperature probe (°F and/or °C)
- Pulse width (millisecond, abbreviated ms)
- Duty cycle (%)

sine wave pattern measurement will be the same for both **root-mean-square (RMS)** and average reading meters. RMS and averaging are two methods used to measure the true effective rating of a signal that is constantly changing. ● SEE **FIGURE 6–17**.

Only true RMS meters are accurate when measuring nonsinusoidal AC waveforms, which are seldom used in automotive applications.

RESOLUTION, DIGITS, AND COUNTS   Meter resolution

refers to how small or fine a measurement the meter can make. By knowing the resolution of a DMM, you can determine whether the meter could measure down to only 1 volt or down to 1 millivolt (1/1,000 of a volt).

You would not buy a ruler marked in 1 inch segments (or centimeters) if you had to measure down to 1/4 inch (or 1 mm). A thermometer that only measured in whole degrees is not of much use when your normal temperature is 98.6°F. You need a thermometer with 0.1° *resolution*.

The terms *digits* and *counts* are used to describe a meter's resolution. DMMs are grouped by the number of counts or digits they display.

- A 3 1/2-digit meter can display three full digits ranging from 0 to 9, and one "half" digit that displays only a 1 or is left blank. A 3 1/2-digit meter will display up to 1,999 counts of resolution.

FIGURE 6–18 This meter display shows 052.2 AC volts. Notice that the zero beside the 5 indicates that the meter can read over 100 volts AC with a resolution of 0.1 volt.

- A 4 1/2-digit meter can display up to 19,000 counts of resolution. It is more precise to describe a meter by counts of resolution than by 3 1/2 or 4 1/2 digits. Some 3 1/2-digit meters have enhanced resolution of up to 3,200 or 4,000 counts.

Meters with more counts offer better resolution for certain measurements. For example, a 1,999 count meter will not be able to measure down to a tenth of a volt when measuring 200 volts or more. ● **SEE FIGURE 6–18.**

However, a 3,200 count meter will display a tenth of a volt up to 320 volts. Digits displayed to the far right of the display may at times flicker or constantly change. This is called *digit rattle* and represents a changing voltage being measured on the ground (COM terminal of the meter lead). High-quality meters are designed to reject this unwanted voltage.

ACCURACY **Meter accuracy** is the largest allowable error that will occur under specific operating conditions. In other words, it is an indication of how close the DMM's displayed measurement is to the actual value of the signal being measured.

Accuracy for a DMM is usually expressed as a percent of reading. An accuracy of ±1% of reading means that for a displayed reading of 100.0 V, the actual value of the voltage could be anywhere between 99.0 V and 101.0 V. Thus, the lower the percent of accuracy is, the better.

- Unacceptable = 1.00%
- Okay = 0.50% (1/2%)
- Good = 0.25% (1/4%)
- Excellent = 0.10% (1/10%)

For example, if a battery had 12.6 volts, a meter could read between the following, based on its accuracy.

± 0.1%	high =	12.61
	low =	12.59
± 0.25%	high =	12.63
	low =	12.57
± 0.50%	high =	12.66
	low =	12.54
± 1.00%	high =	12.73
	low =	12.47

Before you purchase a meter, check the accuracy. Accuracy is usually indicated on the specifications sheet for the meter.

SAFETY TIP

Meter Usage on Hybrid Electric Vehicles

Many hybrid electric vehicles use system voltage as high as 650 volts DC. Be sure to follow all vehicle manufacturer's testing procedures; and if a voltage measurement is needed, be sure to use a meter and test leads that are designed to insulate against high voltages. The **International Electrotechnical Commission (IEC)** has several categories of voltage standards for meter and meter leads. These categories are ratings for overvoltage protection and are rated CAT I, CAT II, CAT III, and CAT IV. The higher the category, the greater the protection against voltage spikes caused by high-energy circuits. Under each category there are various energy and voltage ratings.

CAT I Typically a CAT I meter is used for low-energy voltage measurements such as at wall outlets in the home. Meters with a CAT I rating are usually rated at 300 to 800 volts.

CAT II This higher rated meter would be typically used for checking higher energy level voltages at the fuse panel in the home. Meters with a CAT II rating are usually rated at 300 to 600 volts.

CAT III This minimum rated meter should be used for hybrid vehicles. The CAT III category is designed for high-energy levels and voltage measurements at the service pole at the transformer. Meters with this rating are usually rated at 600 to 1,000 volts.

CAT IV CAT IV meters are for clamp-on meters only. If a clamp-on meter also has meter leads for voltage measurements, that part of the meter will be rated as CAT III.

NOTE: Always use the highest CAT rating meter, especially when working with hybrid vehicles. A CAT III, 600-volt meter is safer than a CAT II, 1,000 volt meter because of the energy level of the CAT ratings.

Therefore, for best personal protection, use only meters and meter leads that are CAT III or CAT IV rated when measuring voltage on a hybrid vehicle. ● **SEE FIGURES 6–19 AND 6–20.**

FIGURE 6–19 Be sure to use only a meter that is CAT III rated when taking electrical voltage measurements on a hybrid vehicle.

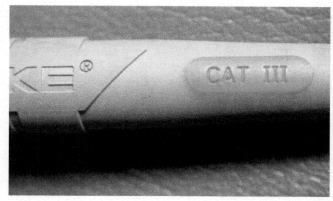

FIGURE 6–20 Always use meter leads that are CAT III rated on a meter that is also CAT III rated, to maintain the protection needed when working on hybrid vehicles.

DIGITAL METER USAGE

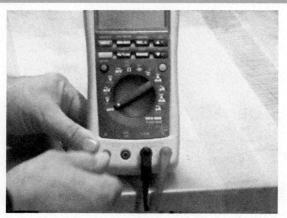

1 For most electrical measurements, the black meter lead is inserted in the terminal labeled "COM" and the red meter lead is inserted into the terminal labeled "V".

2 To use a digital meter, turn the power switch and select the unit of electricity to be measured. In this case, the rotary switch is turned to select DC volts V.

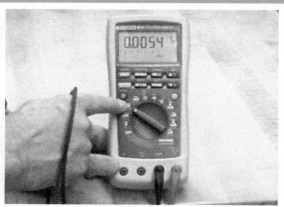

3 For most automotive electrical use, such as measuring battery voltage, select DC volts.

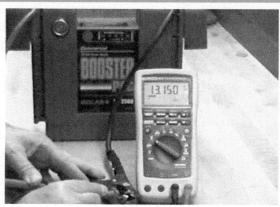

4 Connect the red meter lead to the positive (+) terminal of a battery and the black meter lead to the negative (−) terminal. The meter reads the voltage difference between the leads.

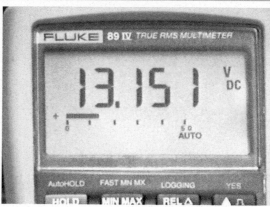

5 This jump start battery unit measures 13.151 volts with the meter set on autoranging on the DC voltage scale.

6 Another meter (Fluke 87 III) displays four digits when measuring the voltage of the battery jump start unit.

CONTINUED ▶

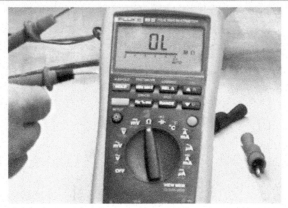

7 To measure resistance, turn the rotary dial to the ohm (Ω) symbol. With the meter leads separated, the meter display reads OL (over limit).

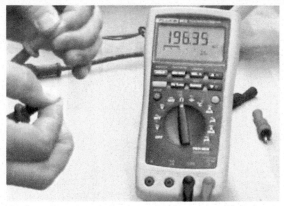

8 The meter can read your own body resistance if you grasp the meter lead terminals with your fingers. The reading on the display indicates 196.35 kΩ.

9 When measuring anything, be sure to read the symbol on the meter face. In this case, the meter reading is 291.10 kΩ.

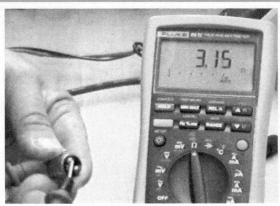

10 A meter set on ohms can be used to check the resistance of a light bulb filament. In this case, the meter reads 3.15 ohms. If the bulb were bad (filament open), the meter would display OL.

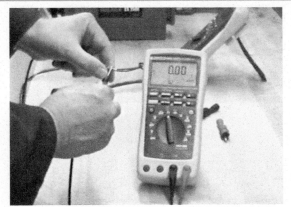

11 A digital meter set to read ohms should measure 0.00 as shown when the meter leads are touched together.

12 The large letter V means volts and the wavy symbol over the V means that the meter measures alternating current (AC) voltage if this position is selected.

13 The next symbol is a V with a dotted and a straight line overhead. This symbol stands for direct current (DC) volts. This position is most used for automotive service.

14 The symbol mV indicates millivolts or 1/1,000 of a volt (0.001). The solid and dashed line above the mV means DC mV.

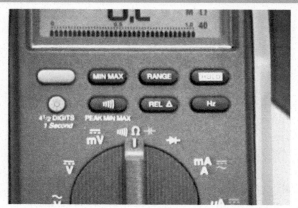

15 The rotary switch is turned to Ω (ohms) unit of resistance measure. The symbol to the left of the Ω symbol is the beeper or continuity indicator.

16 Notice that AUTO is in the upper left and the MΩ is in the lower right. MΩ means megaohms or that the meter is set to read in millions of ohms.

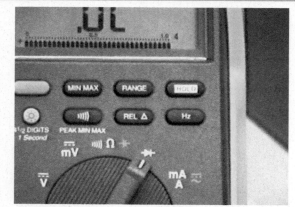

17 The symbol shown is that of a diode. In this position, the meter applies a voltage to a diode and the meter reads the voltage drop across the junction of a diode.

18 One of the most useful features of this meter is the MIN/MAX feature. By pushing the MIN/MAX button, the meter will be able to display the highest (MAX) and the lowest (MIN) reading.

CONTINUED ▶

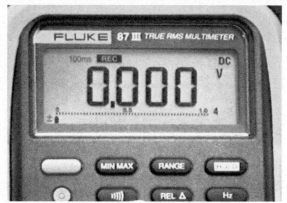

19 Pushing the MIN/MAX button puts the meter into record mode. Note the 100 ms and "rec" on the display. In this position, the meter is capturing any voltage change that lasts 100 ms (0.1 sec.) or longer.

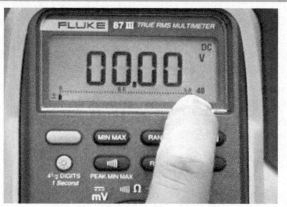

20 To increase the range of the meter, touch the range button. Now the meter is set to read voltage up to 40 volts DC.

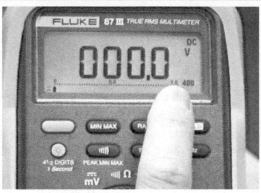

21 Pushing the range button one more time changes the meter scale to the 400 voltage range. Notice that the decimal point has moved to the right.

22 Pushing the range button again changes the meter to the 4,000 volt range. This range is not suitable to use in automotive applications.

23 By pushing and holding the range button, the meter will reset to autorange. Autorange is the preferred setting for most automotive measurements except when using MIN/MAX record mode.

1. Circuit testers include test lights and fused jumper leads.

2. Digital multimeter (DMM) and digital volt-ohm-meter (DVOM) are terms commonly used for electronic high-impedance test meters.

3. Use of a high-impedance digital meter is required on any computer-related circuit or component.

4. Ammeters measure current and must be connected in series in the circuit.

5. Voltmeters measure voltage and are connected in parallel.

6. Ohmmeters measure resistance of a component and must be connected in parallel, with the circuit or component disconnected from power.

7. Logic probes can indicate the presence of power, ground, or pulsed signals.

REVIEW QUESTIONS

1. Why should high-impedance meters be used when measuring voltage on computer-controlled circuits?

2. How is an ammeter connected to an electrical circuit?

3. Why must an ohmmeter be connected to a disconnected circuit or component?

4. What is duty cycle of a signal?

5. What are the prefixes used in most digital meter displays?

CHAPTER QUIZ

1. Inductive ammeters work because of what principle?
   a. Magic
   b. Electrostatic electricity
   c. A magnetic field surrounds any wire carrying a current
   d. Voltage drop as it flows through a conductor

2. A meter used to measure amperes is called a(n) _____.
   a. amp meter
   b. ampmeter
   c. ammeter
   d. coulomb meter

3. A voltmeter should be connected to the circuit being tested _____.
   a. in series
   b. in parallel
   c. only when no power is flowing
   d. Both a and c

4. An ohmmeter should be connected to the circuit or component being tested _____.
   a. with current flowing in the circuit or through the component
   b. when connected to the battery of the vehicle to power the meter
   c. only when no power is flowing (electrically open circuit)
   d. Both b and c

5. A high-impedance meter _____.
   a. measures a high amount of current flow
   b. measures a high amount of resistance
   c. can measure a high voltage
   d. has a high internal resistance

6. A meter is set to read DC volts on the 4-volt scale. The meter leads are connected at a 12-volt battery. The display will read _____.
   a. 0.00
   b. OL
   c. 12 V
   d. 0.012 V

7. What could happen if the meter leads were connected to the positive and negative terminals of the battery while the meter and leads were set to read amperes?
   a. Could blow an internal fuse or damage the meter
   b. Would read volts instead of amperes
   c. Would display OL
   d. Would display 0.00

8. Which is the highest reading?
   a. 38.7 mV
   b. 0.01 V
   c. 0.1 V
   d. 0.387 V

9. If a digital meter face shows 0.93 when set to read $k\Omega$, the reading means _____.
   a. 93 ohms
   b. 930 ohms
   c. 9,300 ohms
   d. 93,000 ohms

10. A reading of 432 shows on the face of the meter set to the millivolt scale. The reading means _____.
    a. 0.432 volt
    b. 4.32 volts
    c. 43.2 volts
    d. 4,320 volts

chapter 7

OSCILLOSCOPES AND GRAPHING MULTIMETERS

LEARNING OBJECTIVES

After studying this chapter, the reader will be able to:

1. Compare the different types of oscilloscopes and explain how to set up and adjust oscilloscopes.

2. Explain time base and volts per division settings.

3. Explain how to use a scope and discuss graphing multimeters and graphing scan tools.

This chapter will help you prepare for the ASE Electrical/Electronic Systems (A6) certification test content area "A" (General Electrical/Electronic System Diagnosis).

KEY TERMS

AC coupling 108
BNC connector 111
Cathode ray tube (CRT) 106
Channel 109
DC coupling 108
Digital storage oscilloscope (DSO) 106
Division 106
Duty cycle 108
External trigger 111

Frequency 108
GMM 111
Graticule 106
Hertz 108
Oscilloscope (scope) 106
Pulse train 108
Pulse width 108
PWM 108
Time base 106
Trigger level 111
Trigger slope 111

TYPES OF OSCILLOSCOPES

TERMINOLOGY An **oscilloscope** (usually called a **scope**) is a visual voltmeter with a timer that shows when a voltage changes. Following are two types of oscilloscopes.

- An *analog scope* uses a **cathode ray tube (CRT)** similar to a television screen to display voltage patterns. The scope screen displays the electrical signal constantly.

- A *digital scope* commonly uses a liquid crystal display (LCD), but a CRT may also be used on some digital scopes. A digital scope takes samples of the signals that can be stopped or stored and is therefore called a **digital storage oscilloscope, or DSO.**

  - A digital scope does not capture each change in voltage, but instead captures voltage levels over time and stores them as dots. Each dot is a voltage level. Then the scope displays the waveforms using the thousands of dots (each representing a voltage level) and electrically connects the dots to create a waveform.

  - A DSO can be connected to a sensor output signal wire and can record the voltage signals over a long period of time. Then, it can be replayed and a technician can see if any faults were detected. This feature makes a DSO the perfect tool to help diagnose intermittent problems.

  - A digital storage scope, however, can sometimes miss faults called *glitches* that may occur between samples captured by the scope. This is why a DSO with a high "sampling rate" is preferred. Sampling rate means that a scope is capable of capturing voltage changes that occur over a very short period of time. Some digital storage scopes have a capture rate of 25 million (25,000,000) samples per second. The scope can capture a glitch (fault) that lasts just 40 nano (0.00000040) seconds.

  - A scope has been called "a voltmeter with a clock."

    - The voltmeter part means that a scope can capture and display changing voltage levels.

    - The clock part means that the scope can display these changes in voltage levels within a specific time period; and with a DSO, it can be replayed so that any faults can be seen and studied.

OSCILLOSCOPE DISPLAY GRID A typical scope face usually has eight or ten grids vertically (up and down) and ten grids horizontally (left to right). The transparent scale (grid), used for reference measurements, is called a **graticule**. This arrangement is commonly 8 × 10 or 10 × 10 divisions. ● **SEE FIGURE 7–1**.

NOTE: These numbers originally referred to the metric dimensions of the graticule in centimeters. Therefore, an 8 × 10 display would be 8 cm (80 mm or 3.14 inch) high and 10 cm (100 mm or 3.90 inch) wide.

- Voltage is displayed on a scope starting with zero volts at the bottom and higher voltage being displayed vertically.

- The scope illustrates time left to right. The pattern starts on the left and sweeps across the screen from left to right.

SCOPE SETUP AND ADJUSTMENTS

SETTING THE TIME BASE Most scopes use 10 graticules from left to right on the display. Setting the **time base** means setting how much time will be displayed in each block called a **division**. For example, if the scope is set to read 2 seconds per division (referred to as *s/div*), then the total time displayed would be 20 seconds (2 × 10 divisions = 20 sec.). The time base should be set to an amount of time that allows two to four events to be displayed. Milliseconds (0.001 sec.) are commonly used in scopes when adjusting the time base. Sample time is milliseconds per division (indicated as *ms/div*) and total time. ● **SEE CHART 7–1**.

MILLISECONDS PER DIVISION (ms/DIV)	TOTAL TIME DISPLAYED
1 ms	10 ms (0.010 sec.)
10 ms	100 ms (0.100 sec.)
50 ms	500 ms (0.500 sec.)
100 ms	1 sec. (1.000 sec.)
500 ms	5 sec. (5.0 sec.)
1,000 ms	10 sec. (10.0 sec.)

CHART 7–1

The time base is milliseconds (ms) and total time of an event that can be displayed.

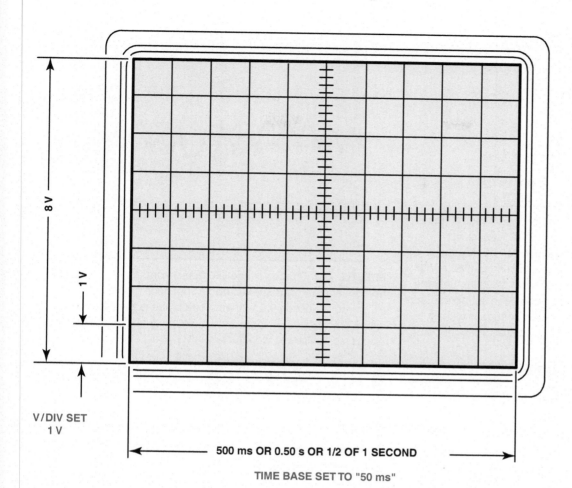

8 V

1 V

V/DIV SET
1 V

500 ms OR 0.50 s OR 1/2 OF 1 SECOND

TIME BASE SET TO "50 ms"

FIGURE 7–1 A scope display allows technicians to take measurements of voltage patterns. In this example, each vertical division is 1 volt and each horizontal division is set to represent 50 milliseconds.

NOTE: Increasing the time base reduces the number of samples per second.

The horizontal scale is divided into 10 divisions (sometimes called *grats*). If each division represents 1 second of time, then the total time period displayed on the screen will be 10 seconds. The time per division is selected so that several events of the waveform are displayed. Time per division settings can vary greatly in automotive use, including:

- MAP/MAF sensors: 2 ms/div (20 ms total)

- Network (CAN) communications network: 2 ms/div (20 ms total)

- Throttle position (TP) sensor: 100 ms per division (1 sec. total)

- Fuel injector: 2 ms/div (20 ms total)

- Oxygen sensor: 1 sec. per division (10 sec. total)

- Primary ignition: 10 ms/div (100 ms total)

- Secondary ignition: 10 ms/div (100 ms total)

- Voltage measurements: 5 ms/div (50 ms total)

The total time displayed on the screen allows comparisons to see if the waveform is consistent or is changing. Multiple waveforms shown on the display at the same time also allow for measurements to be seen more easily. ● **SEE FIGURE 7–2** for an example of a throttle position sensor waveform created by measuring the voltage output as the throttle was depressed and then released.

VOLTS PER DIVISION The volts per division, abbreviated *V/div*, should be set so that the entire anticipated waveform can be viewed. Examples include:

Throttle position (TP) sensor: 1 V/div (8 V total)

Battery, starting and charging: 2 V/div (16 V total)

Oxygen sensor: 200 mV/div (1.6 V total)

Notice from the examples that the total voltage to be displayed exceeds the voltage range of the component being tested. This ensures that all the waveform will be displayed. It also allows for some unexpected voltage readings. For example, an oxygen sensor should read between 0 V and 1 V (1,000 mV). By setting the V/div to 200 mV, up to 1.6 V (1,600 mV) will be displayed.

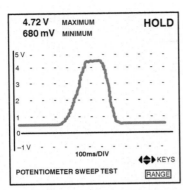

FIGURE 7–2 The digital storage oscilloscope (DSO) displays the entire waveform of a throttle position (TP) sensor from idle to wide-open throttle and then returns to idle. The display also indicates the maximum (4.72 V) and minimum (680 mV or 0.68 V) readings. The display does not show anything until the throttle is opened, because the scope has been set up to start displaying a waveform only after a certain voltage level has been reached. This voltage is called the trigger or trigger point.

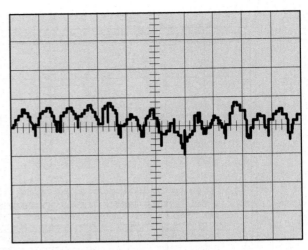

FIGURE 7–3 Ripple voltage is created from the AC voltage from an alternator. Some AC ripple voltage is normal, but if the AC portion exceeds 0.5 V, then a bad diode is the most likely cause. Excessive AC ripple can cause many electrical and electronic devices to work incorrectly.

DC AND AC COUPLING

DC COUPLING **DC coupling** is the most used position on a scope because it allows the scope to display both alternating current (AC) voltage signals and direct current (DC) voltage signals present in the circuit. The AC part of the signal will ride on top of the DC component. For example, if the engine is running and the charging voltage is 14.4 volts DC, this will be displayed as a horizontal line on the screen. Any AC ripple voltage leaking past the alternator diodes will be displayed as an AC signal on top of the horizontal DC voltage line. Therefore, both components of the signal can be observed at the same time.

AC COUPLING When the **AC coupling** position is selected, a capacitor is placed into the meter lead circuit, which effectively blocks all DC voltage signals, but allows the AC portion of the signal to pass and be displayed. AC coupling can be used to show output signal waveforms from sensors such as:

- Distributor pickup coils
- Magnetic wheel speed sensors
- Magnetic crankshaft position sensors
- Magnetic camshaft position sensors
- The AC ripple from an alternator. ● **SEE FIGURE 7–3**.
- Magnetic vehicle speed sensors

NOTE: Check the instructions from the scope manufacturer for the recommended settings to use. Sometimes it is necessary to switch from DC coupling to AC coupling or from AC coupling to DC coupling to properly see some waveforms.

PULSE TRAINS

DEFINITION Scopes can show all voltage signals. Among the most commonly found in automotive applications is a DC voltage that varies up and down and does not go below zero like an AC voltage. A DC voltage that turns on and off in a series of pulses is called a **pulse train**. Pulse trains differ from an AC signal in that they do not go below zero. An alternating voltage goes above and below zero voltage. Pulse train signals can vary in several ways. ● **SEE FIGURE 7–4**.

FREQUENCY **Frequency** is the number of cycles per second measured in **hertz**. The engine revolutions per minute (RPM) is an example of a signal that can occur at various frequencies. At low engine speed, the ignition pulses occur fewer times per second (lower frequency) than when the engine is operated at higher engine speeds (RPM).

DUTY CYCLE **Duty cycle** refers to the percentage of on-time of the signal during one complete cycle. As on-time increases, the amount of time the signal is off decreases and is usually measured in percentage. Duty cycle is also called **pulse-width modulation (PWM)** and can be measured in degrees. ● **SEE FIGURE 7–5**.

PULSE WIDTH The **pulse width** is a measure of the actual on-time measured in milliseconds. Fuel injectors are usually controlled by varying the pulse width. ● **SEE FIGURE 7–6**.

1. FREQUENCY—FREQUENCY IS THE NUMBER OF CYCLES THAT TAKE PLACE PER SECOND. THE MORE CYCLES THAT TAKE PLACE IN ONE SECOND, THE HIGHER THE FREQUENCY READING. FREQUENCIES ARE MEASURED IN HERTZ, WHICH IS THE NUMBER OF CYCLES PER SECOND. AN 8-HERTZ SIGNAL CYCLES EIGHT TIMES PER SECOND.

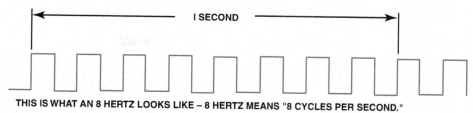

THIS IS WHAT AN 8 HERTZ LOOKS LIKE – 8 HERTZ MEANS "8 CYCLES PER SECOND."

2. DUTY CYCLE—DUTY CYCLE IS A MEASUREMENT COMPARING THE SIGNAL ON-TIME TO THE LENGTH OF ONE COMPLETE CYCLE. AS ON-TIME INCREASES, OFF-TIME DECREASES. DUTY CYCLE IS MEASURED IN PERCENTAGE OF ON-TIME. A 60% DUTY CYCLE IS A SIGNAL THAT IS ON 60% OF THE TIME AND OFF 40% OF THE TIME. ANOTHER WAY TO MEASURE DUTY CYCLE IS DWELL, WHICH IS MEASURED IN DEGREES INSTEAD OF PERCENT.

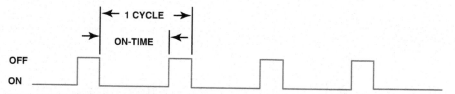

DUTY CYCLE IS THE RELATIONSHIP BETWEEN ONE COMPLETE CYCLE AND THE SIGNAL IS ON-TIME. A SIGNAL CAN VARY IN DUTY CYCLE WITHOUT AFFECTING THE FREQUENCY.

3. PULSE WIDTH—PULSE WIDTH IS THE ACTUAL ON-TIME OF A SIGNAL, MEASURED IN MILLISECONDS. WITH PULSE WIDTH MEASUREMENTS, OFF-TIME DOESN'T REALLY MATTER—THE ONLY REAL CONCERN IS HOW LONG THE SIGNAL IS ON. THIS IS A USEFUL TEST FOR MEASURING CONVENTIONAL INJECTOR ON-TIME, TO SEE THAT THE SIGNAL VARIES WITH LOAD CHANGE.

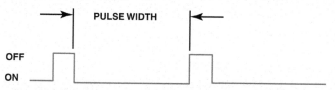

PULSE WIDTH IS THE ACTUAL TIME A SIGNAL IS ON, MEASURED IN MILLISECONDS. THE ONLY THING BEING MEASURED IS HOW LONG THE SIGNAL IS ON.

FIGURE 7–4 A pulse train is any electrical signal that turns on and off, or goes high and low in a series of pulses. Ignition module and fuel-injector pulses are examples of a pulse train signal.

NUMBER OF CHANNELS

DEFINITION Scopes are available that allow the viewing of more than one sensor or event at the same time on the display. The number of events, which require leads for each, is called a **channel**. A channel is an input to a scope. Commonly available scopes include:

- **Single channel.** A single-channel scope is capable of displaying only one sensor signal waveform at a time.

- **Two channel.** A two-channel scope can display the waveform from two separate sensors or components at the same time. This feature is very helpful when testing the camshaft and crankshaft position sensors on an engine to see if they are properly timed. ● **SEE FIGURE 7–7**.

- **Four channel.** A four-channel scope allows the technician to view up to four different sensors or actuators on one display.

NOTE: Often the capture speed of the signals is slowed when using more than one channel.

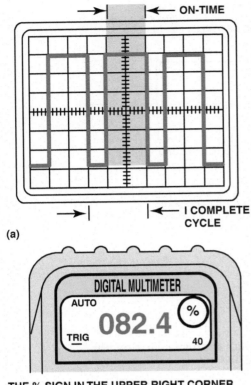

(a)

(b)

THE % SIGN IN THE UPPER RIGHT CORNER
OF THE DISPLAY INDICATES THAT THE METER
IS READING A DUTY CYCLE SIGNAL.

FIGURE 7–5 (a) A scope representation of a complete cycle showing both on-time and off-time. (b) A meter display indicating the on-time duty cycle in percentage (%). Note the trigger and negative (–) symbol. This indicates that the meter started recording the percentage of on-time when the voltage dropped (start of on-time).

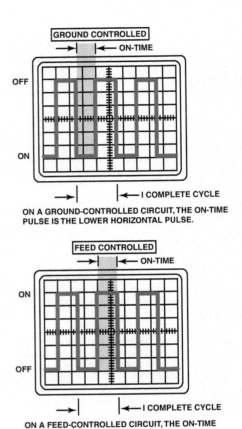

ON A GROUND-CONTROLLED CIRCUIT, THE ON-TIME
PULSE IS THE LOWER HORIZONTAL PULSE.

ON A FEED-CONTROLLED CIRCUIT, THE ON-TIME
PULSE IS THE UPPER HORIZONTAL PULSE.

FIGURE 7–6 Most automotive computer systems control the device by opening and closing the ground to the component.

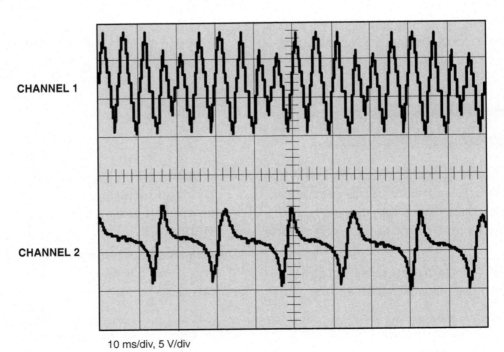

10 ms/div, 5 V/div

FIGURE 7–7 A two-channel scope being used to compare two signals on the same vehicle.

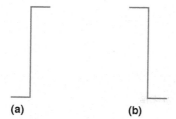

FIGURE 7–8 (a) A symbol for a positive trigger—a trigger occurs at a rising (positive) edge of the signal (waveform). (b) A symbol for a negative trigger—a trigger occurs at a falling (negative) edge of the signal (waveform).

TRIGGERS

EXTERNAL TRIGGER An **external trigger** is when the waveform starts as a signal is received from another external source rather than from the signal pickup lead. A common example of an external trigger comes from the probe clamp around the cylinder #1 spark plug wire to trigger the start of an ignition pattern.

TRIGGER LEVEL **Trigger level** is the voltage that must be detected by the scope before the pattern will be displayed. A scope will start displaying a voltage signal only when it is triggered or is told to start. The trigger level must be set to start the display. If the pattern starts at 1 volt, the trace will begin displaying on the left side of the screen *after* the trace has reached 1 volt.

TRIGGER SLOPE The **trigger slope** is the voltage direction that a waveform must have in order to start the display. Most often, the trigger to start a waveform display is taken from the signal itself. Besides trigger voltage level, most scopes can be adjusted to trigger only when the voltage rises past the trigger-level voltage. This is called a *positive slope*. When the voltage falling past the higher level activates the trigger, this is called a *negative slope*.

The scope display indicates both a positive and a negative slope symbol. For example, if a waveform, such as a magnetic sensor used for crankshaft position or wheel speed starts moving upward, a positive slope should be selected. If a negative slope is selected, the waveform will not start showing until the voltage reaches the trigger level in a downward direction. A negative slope should be used when a fuel-injector circuit is being analyzed. In this circuit, the computer provides the ground and the voltage level drops when the computer commands the injector on. Sometimes the technician needs to change from negative to positive or positive to negative trigger if a waveform is not being shown correctly. ● **SEE FIGURE 7–8**.

USING A SCOPE

USING SCOPE LEADS Most scopes, both analog and digital, normally use the same test leads. These leads usually attach to the scope through a **BNC connector**, which is a miniature standard coaxial cable connector. BNC is an international standard that is used in the electronics industry. If using a BNC connector, be sure to connect one lead to a good clean, metal engine ground. The probe of the scope lead attaches to the circuit or component being tested. Many scopes use one ground lead and each channel has its own signal pickup lead.

MEASURING BATTERY VOLTAGE WITH A SCOPE

One of the easiest things to measure and observe on a scope is battery voltage. A lower voltage can be observed on the scope display as the engine is started, and a higher voltage should be displayed after the engine starts. ● **SEE FIGURE 7–9**.

An analog scope displays rapidly and cannot be set to show or freeze a display. Therefore, even though an analog scope shows all voltage signals, it is easy to miss a momentary glitch on an analog scope.

CAUTION: Check the instructions for the scope being used before attempting to scope household AC circuits. Some scopes, such as the Snap-On MODIS, are not designed to measure high-voltage AC circuits.

GRAPHING MULTIMETER

A **graphing multimeter**, abbreviated **GMM**, is a cross between a digital meter and a digital storage oscilloscope. A graphing multimeter displays the voltage levels at two places:

- On a display screen
- In a digital readout

It is usually not capable of capturing very short duration faults or glitches that would likely be captured with a digital storage oscilloscope. ● **SEE FIGURE 7–10**.

GRAPHING SCAN TOOLS

Many scan tools are capable of displaying the voltage levels captured by the scan tool through the data link connector (DLC) on a screen. This feature is helpful where changes in voltage levels are difficult to detect by looking at numbers that are constantly changing. Read and follow the instructions for the scan tool being used.

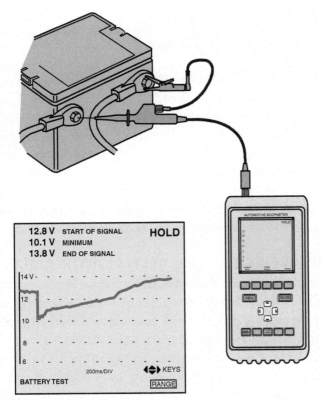

12.8 V	START OF SIGNAL	HOLD
10.1 V	MINIMUM	
13.8 V	END OF SIGNAL	

BATTERY TEST
200ms/DIV
◄▲▼► KEYS
RANGE

FIGURE 7–9 Constant battery voltage is represented by a flat horizontal line. In this example, the engine was started and the battery voltage dropped to about 10 V as shown on the left side of the scope display. When the engine started, the alternator started to charge the battery and the voltage is shown as climbing.

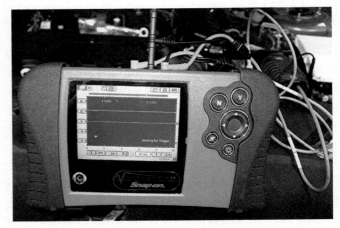

FIGURE 7–10 A typical graphing multimeter that can be used as a digital meter, plus it can show the voltage levels on the display screen.

SUMMARY

1. Analog oscilloscopes use a cathode ray tube to display voltage patterns.

2. The waveforms shown on an analog oscilloscope cannot be stored for later viewing.

3. A digital storage oscilloscope (DSO) creates an image or waveform on the display by connecting thousands of dots captured by the scope leads.

4. An oscilloscope display grid is called a graticule. Each of the 8 × 10 or 10 × 10 dividing boxes is called a division.

5. Setting the time base means establishing the amount of time each division represents.

6. Setting the volts per division allows the technician to view either the entire waveform or just part of it.

7. DC coupling and AC coupling are two selections that can be made to observe different types of waveforms.

8. A graphing multimeter is not capable of capturing short duration faults, but can display usable waveforms.

9. Oscilloscopes display voltage over time. A DSO can capture and store a waveform for viewing later.

REVIEW QUESTIONS

1. What are the differences between an analog and a digital oscilloscope?

2. What is the difference between DC coupling and AC coupling?

3. Why are DC signals that change called pulse trains?

4. What is the difference between an oscilloscope and a graphing multimeter?

5. What is the symbol used to show a positive or negative trigger?

1. Technician A says an analog scope can store the waveform for viewing later. Technician B says that the trigger level has to be set on most scopes to be able to view a changing waveform. Which technician is correct?
   a. Technician A only
   b. Technician B only
   c. Both Technicians A and B
   d. Neither Technician A nor B

2. An oscilloscope display is called a _____.
   a. grid
   b. graticule
   c. division
   d. box

3. A signal showing the voltage of a battery displayed on a digital storage oscilloscope (DSO) is being discussed. Technician A says that the display will show one horizontal line above the zero line. Technician B says that the display will show a line sloping upward from zero to the battery voltage level. Which technician is correct?
   a. Technician A only
   b. Technician B only
   c. Both Technicians A and B
   d. Neither Technician A nor B

4. Setting the time base to 50 ms per division will allow the technician to view a waveform how long in duration?
   a. 50 ms
   b. 200 ms
   c. 400 ms
   d. 500 ms

5. A throttle position sensor waveform is going to be observed. At what setting should the volts per division be set to see the entire waveform from 0 to 5 volts?
   a. 0.5 V/div
   b. 1.0 V/div
   c. 2.0 V/div
   d. 5.0 V/div

6. Two technicians are discussing the DC coupling setting on a DSO. Technician A says that the position allows both the DC and AC signals of the waveform to be displayed. Technician B says that this setting allows just the DC part of the waveform to be displayed. Which technician is correct?
   a. Technician A only
   b. Technician B only
   c. Both Technicians A and B
   d. Neither Technician A nor B

7. Voltage signals (waveforms) that do not go below zero are called _____.
   a. AC signals
   b. pulse trains
   c. pulse width
   d. DC coupled signals

8. Cycles per second are expressed in _____.
   a. hertz
   b. duty cycle
   c. pulse width
   d. slope

9. Oscilloscopes use what type of lead connector?
   a. Banana plugs
   b. Double banana plugs
   c. Single conductor plugs
   d. BNC

10. A digital meter that can show waveforms is called a _____.
    a. DVOM
    b. DMM
    c. GMM
    d. DSO

chapter 8

AUTOMOTIVE WIRING AND WIRE REPAIR

LEARNING OBJECTIVES

After studying this chapter, the reader will be able to:

1. Explain the purpose of ground wires, battery cables, and jumper cables.
2. Explain automotive wiring and the wire gauge systems.
3. Describe how fusible links and fuses protect circuits and wiring.
4. Discuss circuit breakers and PTC electronic circuit protection devices.
5. List the steps for performing a proper wire repair.
6. Perform solder repair of electrical wiring.
7. Explain the types of electrical conduit.

This chapter will help you prepare for the ASE Electrical/Electronic Systems (A6) certification test content area "A" (General Electrical/Electronic System Diagnosis).

KEY TERMS

Adhesive-lined heat shrink tubing 126
American wire gauge (AWG) 115
Auto link 120
Battery cables 117
Braided ground straps 116
Circuit breakers 120
Cold solder joint 125
CPA 123
Crimp-and-seal connectors 126
Fuse link 120

Fuses 118
Fusible link 122
Heat shrink tubing 126
Jumper cables 117
Lock tang 123
Metric wire gauge 115
Pacific fuse element 120
Primary wire 116
PTC circuit protection 121
Rosin-core solder 125
Terminal 123
Twisted pair 117

AUTOMOTIVE WIRING

DEFINITION AND TERMINOLOGY Most automotive wire is made from strands of copper covered by plastic insulation. Copper is an excellent conductor of electricity that is reasonably priced and very flexible. However, solid copper wire can break when moved repeatedly; therefore, most copper wiring is constructed of multiple small strands that allow for repeated bending and moving without breaking. Solid copper wire is generally used for components, such as starter armature and alternator stator windings that do not bend or move during normal operation. Copper is the best electrical conductor besides silver, which is a great deal more expensive. The conductivity of various metals is rated in ● **CHART 8–1**.

AMERICAN WIRE GAUGE Wiring is sized and purchased according to gauge size as assigned by the **American wire gauge (AWG)** system. AWG numbers can be confusing because as the gauge number *increases,* the size of the conductor wire *decreases.* Therefore, a 14-gauge wire is smaller than a 10-gauge wire. The *greater* the amount of current (in amperes) that is flowing through a wire, the *larger the diameter (smaller gauge number)* that will be required. ● **SEE CHART 8–2,** which compares the AWG number to the actual wire diameter in inches. The diameter refers to the diameter of the metal conductor and does not include the insulation.

Following are general applications for the most commonly used wire gauge sizes. Always check the installation instructions or the manufacturer's specifications for wire gauge size before replacing any automotive wiring.

- 20 to 22 gauge: radio speaker wires
- 18 gauge: small bulbs and short leads
- 16 gauge: taillights, gas gauge, turn signals, windshield wipers
- 14 gauge: horn, radio power lead, headlights, cigarette lighter, brake lights
- 12 gauge: headlight switch to fuse box, rear window defogger, power windows and locks
- 10 gauge: alternator to battery
- 4, 2, or 0 (1/0) gauge: battery cables

METRIC WIRE GAUGE Most manufacturers indicate on the wiring diagrams the **metric wire gauge** sizes measured in square millimeters (mm^2) of cross-sectional area. The following

1. Silver
2. Copper
3. Gold
4. Aluminum
5. Tungsten
6. Zinc
7. Brass (copper and zinc)
8. Platinum
9. Iron
10. Nickel
11. Tin
12. Steel
13. Lead

CHART 8–1

The list of relative conductivity of metals, showing silver to be the best.

WIRE GAUGE DIAMETER TABLE	
AMERICAN WIRE GAUGE (AWG)	**WIRE DIAMETER IN INCHES**
20	0.03196118
18	0.040303
16	0.0508214
14	0.064084
12	0.08080810
10	0.10189
8	0.128496
6	0.16202
5	0.18194
4	0.20431
3	0.22942
2	0.25763
1	0.2893
0	0.32486
00	0.3648

CHART 8–2

American wire gauge (AWG) number and the actual conductor diameter in inches.

Why Is There a Ground Strap on My Exhaust System?

The ground strap is only there to dissipate static electricity. Static electricity is created when the flow of the exhaust gases travels through the system. Using a ground strap connected to the exhaust system helps prevent the static charge from building up that could cause a spark to jump to the body or frame of the vehicle.

The exhaust is insulated electrically from the rest of the vehicle by rubber hangers and gaskets at the exhaust manifold, thereby causing the entire exhaust system to be electrically isolated from chassis ground.

If a vehicle is equipped with a ground strap, be sure that it is connected at both ends to help ensure long exhaust system life. If static electricity is allowed to discharge from the exhaust system to the body or frame of the vehicle, the resulting arcing points can cause rust or corrosion, thereby shortening the life of the exhaust system.

If a new exhaust system is installed, be sure to reattach the ground strap. Most vehicles also use a ground strap connected to the fuel filler tube for the same reason.

METRIC SIZE (MM²)	AWG SIZE
0.5	20
0.8	18
1.0	16
2.0	14
3.0	12
5.0	10
8.0	8
13.0	6
19.0	4
32.0	2
52.0	0

CHART 8–3

Metric wire size in square millimeters (mm²) conversion chart to American wire gauge (AWG).

chart gives conversions or comparisons between metric gauge and AWG sizes. Notice that the metric wire size increases with size (area), whereas the AWG size gets smaller with larger size wire. ● **SEE CHART 8–3.**

12 V	RECOMMENDED WIRE GAUGE (AWG) (FOR LENGTH IN FEET)*						
AMPS	3'	5'	7'	10'	15'	20'	25'
5	18	18	18	18	18	18	18
7	18	18	18	18	18	18	16
10	18	18	18	18	16	16	16
12	18	18	18	18	16	16	14
15	18	18	18	18	14	14	12
18	18	18	16	16	14	14	12
20	18	18	16	16	14	12	10
22	18	18	16	16	12	12	10
24	18	18	16	16	12	12	10
30	18	16	16	14	10	10	10
40	18	16	14	12	10	10	8
50	16	14	12	12	10	10	8
100	12	12	10	10	6	6	4
150	10	10	8	8	4	4	2
200	10	8	8	6	4	4	2

* When mechanical strength is a factor, use the next larger wire gauge.

CHART 8–4

Recommended AWG wire size increases as the length increases because all wires have internal resistance. The longer the wire is, the greater is the resistance. The larger the diameter is, the lower is the resistance.

The AWG number should be decreased (wire size increased) with increased lengths of wire. ● **SEE CHART 8–4.**

For example, a trailer may require 14-gauge wire to light all the trailer lights, but if the wire required is over 25-feet long, 12-gauge wire should be used. Most automotive wire, except for spark plug wire, is often called **primary wire** (named for the voltage range used in the primary ignition circuit) because it is designed to operate at or near battery voltage.

GROUND WIRES

PURPOSE AND FUNCTION All vehicles use ground wires between the engine and body and/or between the body and the negative terminal of the battery. The two types of ground wires are the following:

- Insulated copper wire
- Braided ground straps

Braided ground straps are uninsulated. It is not necessary to insulate a ground strap because it does not matter if it touches metal, as it already attaches to ground. Braided ground straps are more flexible than stranded wire. Because the engine will move slightly on its mounts, the braided ground strap must be able to flex without breaking. ● **SEE FIGURE 8–1.**

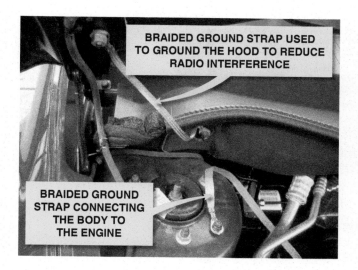

FIGURE 8–1 All lights and accessories are grounded to the body of the vehicle. Body ground wires, such as this one, are needed to conduct all of the current from these components back to the negative terminal of the battery. The body ground wire connects the body to the engine. Most battery negative cables attach to the engine.

SKIN EFFECT The braided strap also dampens out some radio-frequency interference that otherwise might be transmitted through standard stranded wiring due to the skin effect.

The *skin effect* is the term used to describe how high-frequency AC electricity flows through a conductor. Direct current flows through a conductor, but alternating current tends to travel through the outside (skin) of the conductor. Because of the skin effect, most audio (speaker) cable is constructed of many small-diameter copper wires instead of fewer larger strands, because the smaller wire has a greater surface area and, therefore, results in less resistance to the flow of AC voltage.

NOTE: Body ground wires are necessary to provide a circuit path for the lights and accessories that ground to the body and flow to the negative battery terminal.

 FREQUENTLY ASKED QUESTION

What Is a Twisted Pair?

A **twisted pair** is used to transmit low-voltage signals, using two wires that are twisted together. Electromagnetic interference can create a voltage in a wire and twisting the two signal wires cancels out the induced voltage. A twisted pair means that the two wires have at least nine turns per foot (turns per meter). A rule of thumb is a twisted pair should have one twist per inch of length.

FIGURE 8–2 Battery cables are designed to carry heavy starter current and are usually 4-gauge or larger wire. Note that this battery has a thermal blanket covering to help protect the battery from high underhood temperatures. The wiring is also covered with a plastic conduit called split-loom tubing.

BATTERY CABLES

Battery cables are the largest wires used in the automotive electrical system. The cables are usually 4-gauge, 2-gauge, or 1-gauge wires (19 mm² or larger). ● **SEE FIGURE 8–2**.

Wires larger than 1 gauge are called 0 gauge (pronounced "ought"). Larger cables are labeled 2/0 or 00 (2 ought) and 3/0 or 000 (3 ought). Electrical systems that are 6 volts require battery cables two sizes larger than those used for 12-volt electrical systems, because the lower voltage used in antique vehicles resulted in twice the amount of current (amperes) to supply the same electrical power.

JUMPER CABLES

Jumper cables are 4-to 2/0-gauge electrical cables with large clamps attached and are used to connect the discharged battery of one vehicle to the good battery of another vehicle. Good-quality jumper cables are necessary to prevent excessive voltage drops caused by cable resistance. Aluminum wire jumper cables should not be used, because even though aluminum is a good electrical conductor (although not as good as copper), it is less flexible and can crack and break when bent or moved repeatedly. The size should be 6 gauge or larger.

1/0-AWG welding cable can be used to construct an excellent set of jumper cables using welding clamps on both

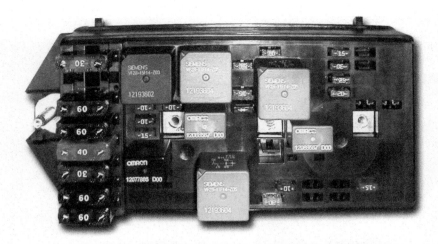

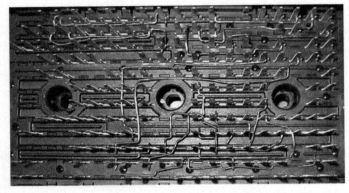

FIGURE 8–3 A typical Underhood Electrical Center (UHEC). Most are referred to as an "intelligent power distribution box" or a "smart junction box" because underneath (lower figure) are wires that join the circuits from the maxi fuses to other fuses and to or from relays. Because of these interconnected circuits, if there is a fault due to a collision or water intrusion, most experts suggest replacing the entire assembly rather than trying to repair the assembly. Always check service information for the exact procedures to follow when working with an underhood fuse panel.

FUSES AND CIRCUIT PROTECTION DEVICES

ends. Welding cable is usually constructed of many very fine strands of wire, which allow for easier bending of the cable as the strands of fine wire slide against each other inside the cable.

NOTE: Always check the wire gauge of any battery cables or jumper cables and do not rely on the outside diameter of the wire. Many lower-cost jumper cables use smaller gauge wire, but may use thick insulation to make the cable look as if it is the correct size wire.

CONSTRUCTION **Fuses** should be used in every circuit to protect the wiring from overheating and damage caused by excessive current flow as a result of a short circuit or other malfunction. The symbol for a fuse is a wavy line between two points: ⌇.

A fuse is constructed of a fine tin conductor inside a glass, plastic, or ceramic housing. The tin is designed to melt and open the circuit if excessive current flows through the fuse. Each fuse is rated according to its maximum current-carrying capacity.

Many fuses are used to protect more than one circuit of the automobile. ● **SEE FIGURE 8–3.**

A typical example is the fuse for the cigarette lighter that also protects many other circuits, such as those for the courtesy lights, clock, and other circuits. A fault in one of these circuits can cause this fuse to melt, which will prevent the operation of all other circuits that are protected by the fuse.

NOTE: The SAE term for a cigarette lighter is cigar lighter because the diameter of the heating element is large enough for a cigar. Most vehicle manufacturers now call the former lighter plug a 12-volt power plug.

FUSE RATINGS Fuses are used to protect the wiring and components in the circuit from damage if an excessive amount of current flows. The fuse rating is normally about 20% higher than the normal current in the circuit. ● **SEE CHART 8–5** for a typical fuse

NORMAL CURRENT IN THE CIRCUIT (AMPERES)	FUSE RATING (AMPERES)
7.5	10
16	20
24	30

CHART 8–5

The fuse rating should be 20% higher than the maximum current in the circuit to provide the best protection for the wiring and the component being protected.

AMPERAGE RATING	COLOR
1	Dark green
2	Gray
2.5	Purple
3	Violet
4	Pink
5	Tan
6	Gold
7.5	Brown
9	Orange
10	Red
14	Black
15	Blue
20	Yellow
25	White
30	Green

CHART 8–6

The amperage rating and the color of the blade fuse are standardized.

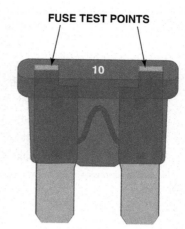

FUSE TEST POINTS

FIGURE 8–4 Blade-type fuses can be tested through openings in the plastic at the top of the fuse.

rating based on the normal current in the circuit. In other words, the normal current flow should be about 80% of the fuse rating. Current flow higher than the fuse rating will cause the fuse to blow.

BLADE FUSES Colored blade-type fuses are also referred to as ATO fuses and have been used since 1977. The color of the plastic of blade fuses indicates the maximum current flow, measured in amperes.

● **SEE CHART 8–6** for the color and the amperage rating of blade fuses.

Each fuse has an opening in the top of its plastic portion to allow access to its metal contacts for testing purposes. ● **SEE FIGURE 8–4.**

MINI FUSES To save space, many vehicles use mini (small) blade fuses. Not only do they save space, but they also allow the vehicle design engineer to fuse individual circuits instead of grouping many different components on one fuse. This improves customer satisfaction because if one component fails, it only affects that circuit without stopping electrical power to several other circuits as well. This makes troubleshooting a lot easier too, because each circuit is separate. ● **SEE CHART 8–7** for the amperage rating and corresponding fuse color for mini fuses.

AMPERAGE RATING	COLOR
5	Tan
7.5	Brown
10	Red
15	Blue
20	Yellow
25	Natural
30	Green

CHART 8–7

Mini fuse amperage rating and colors.

AMPERAGE RATING	COLOR
20	Yellow
30	Green
40	Amber
50	Red
60	Blue
70	Brown
80	Natural

CHART 8–8

Maxi fuse amperage rating and colors.

FIGURE 8–5 Three sizes of blade-type fuses: mini on the left, standard or ATO type in the center, and maxi on the right.

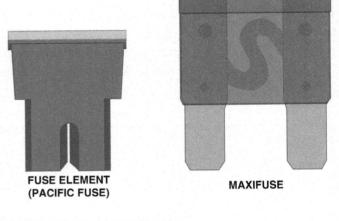

FUSE ELEMENT
(PACIFIC FUSE)   MAXIFUSE

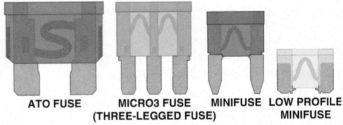

ATO FUSE   MICRO3 FUSE   MINIFUSE LOW PROFILE
               (THREE-LEGGED FUSE)   MINIFUSE

FIGURE 8–6 A comparison of the various types of protective devices used in most vehicles.

MAXI FUSES

Maxi fuses are a large version of blade fuses and are used to replace fusible links in many vehicles. Maxi fuses are rated up to 80 amperes or more. ● **SEE CHART 8–8** for the amperage rating and corresponding color for maxi fuses.

● **SEE FIGURE 8–5** for a comparison of the various sizes of blade-type fuses.

PACIFIC FUSE ELEMENT

First used in the late 1980s, **Pacific fuse elements** (also called a **fuse link** or **auto link**) are used to protect wiring from a direct short-to-ground. The housing contains a short link of wire sized for the rated current load. The transparent top allows inspection of the link inside. ● **SEE FIGURE 8–6**.

TESTING FUSES

It is important to test the condition of a fuse if the circuit being protected by the fuse does not operate. Most blown fuses can be detected quickly because the center conductor is melted. Fuses can also fail and open the circuit because of a poor connection in the fuse itself or in the fuse holder. Therefore, just because a fuse "looks okay" does not mean that it *is* okay. All fuses should be tested with a test light. The test light should be connected to first one side of the fuse and then the other. A test light should light on both sides. If the test light only lights on one side, the fuse is blown or open. If the test light does not light on either side of the fuse, that circuit is not being supplied power. ● **SEE FIGURE 8–7**. An ohmmeter can be used to test fuses.

CIRCUIT BREAKERS

Circuit breakers are used to prevent harmful overload (excessive current flow) in a circuit by opening the circuit and stopping the current flow to prevent overheating and possible fire caused by hot wires or electrical components. **Circuit breakers** are mechanical units made of two different

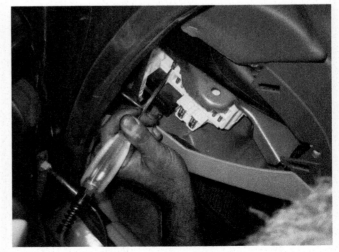

FIGURE 8–7 To test a fuse, use a test light to check for power at the power side of the fuse. The ignition switch and lights may have to be on before some fuses receive power. If the fuse is good, the test light should light on both sides (power side and load side) of the fuse.

metals (bimetallic) that deform when heated and open a set of contact points that work in the same manner as an "off" switch. ● **SEE FIGURE 8–8**.

Cycling-type circuit breakers, therefore, are reset when the current stops flowing, which causes the bimetallic strip to cool and the circuit to close again. A circuit breaker is used in circuits that could affect the safety of passengers if a conventional nonresetting fuse were used. The headlight circuit is an excellent example of the use of a circuit breaker rather than a fuse. A short or grounded circuit anywhere in the headlight circuit could cause excessive current flow and, therefore, the opening of the circuit. Obviously, a sudden loss of headlights at night could have disastrous results. A circuit breaker opens and closes the circuit rapidly, thereby protecting the circuit from overheating and also providing sufficient current flow to maintain at least partial headlight operation.

Circuit breakers are also used in other circuits where conventional fuses could not provide for the surges of high current commonly found in those circuits. ● **SEE FIGURE 8–9** for the electrical symbols used to represent a circuit breaker.

Examples are the circuits for the following accessories.

1. Power seats
2. Power door locks
3. Power windows

PTC CIRCUIT PROTECTORS   Positive temperature coefficient (PTC) circuit protectors are solid state (without moving parts). Like all other circuit protection devices, PTCs are installed in series in the circuit being protected. If excessive current flows, the temperature and resistance of the PTC increase.

This increased resistance reduces current flow (amperes) in the circuit and may cause the electrical component in the circuit not to function correctly. For example, when a PTC circuit protector is used in a power window circuit, the increased resistance causes the operation of the power window to be much slower than normal.

Unlike circuit breakers or fuses, PTC circuit protection devices do *not* open the circuit, but rather provide a very high resistance between the protector and the component. ● **SEE FIGURE 8–10**.

In other words, voltage will be available to the component. This fact has led to a lot of misunderstanding about how these circuit protection devices actually work. It is even more confusing when the circuit is opened and the PTC circuit protector cools down. When the circuit is turned back on, the component

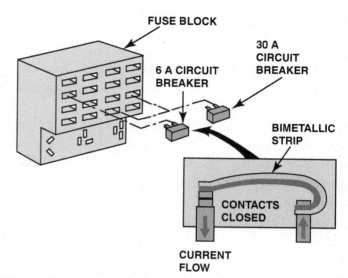

FIGURE 8–8 Typical blade circuit breaker fits into the same space as a blade fuse. If excessive current flows through the bimetallic strip, the strip bends and opens the contacts and stops current flow. When the circuit breaker cools, the contacts close again, completing the electrical circuit.

FIGURE 8–9 Electrical symbols used to represent circuit breakers.

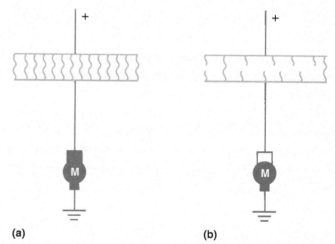

FIGURE 8–10 (a) The normal operation of a PTC circuit protector such as in a power window motor circuit showing the many conducting paths. With normal current flow, the temperature of the PTC circuit protector remains normal. (b) When current exceeds the amperage rating of the PTC circuit protector, the polymer material that makes up the electronic circuit protector increases in resistance. As shown, a high-resistance electrical path still exists even though the motor will stop operating as a result of the very low current flow through the very high resistance. The circuit protector will not reset or cool down until voltage is removed from the circuit.

may operate normally for a short time; however, the PTC circuit protector will again get hot because of too much current flow. Its resistance again increases to limit current flow.

The electronic control unit (computer) used in most vehicles today incorporates thermal overload protection devices. ● **SEE FIGURE 8–11**.

Therefore, when a component fails to operate, do not blame the computer. The current control device is controlling current flow to protect the computer. Components that do not operate correctly should be checked for proper resistance and current draw.

FUSIBLE LINKS

A **fusible link** is a type of fuse that consists of a short length (6 to 9 inch long) of standard copper-strand wire covered with a special nonflammable insulation. This wire is usually four wire numbers smaller than the wire of the circuits it protects. For example, a 12-gauge circuit is protected by a 16-gauge fusible link. The special thick insulation over the wire may make it look larger than other wires of the same gauge number. ● **SEE FIGURE 8–12**.

If excessive current flow (caused by a short-to-ground or a defective component) occurs, the fusible link will melt in half and open the circuit to prevent a fire hazard. Some fusible links are identified with "fusible link" tags at the junction between the fusible link and the standard chassis wiring, which represent only the junction. Fusible links are the backup system for circuit protection. All current except the current used by the starter motor flows through fusible links and then through individual circuit fuses. It is possible that a fusible link will melt and not blow a fuse. Fusible links are installed as close to the battery as possible so that they can protect the wiring and circuits coming directly from the battery.

MEGA FUSES

Many newer vehicles are equipped with mega fuses instead of fusible links to protect high-amperage circuits. Circuits often controlled by mega fuses include:

- Charging circuit
- HID headlights
- Heated front or rear glass
- Multiple circuits usually protected by mega fuses
- Mega fuse rating for vehicles, including 80, 100, 125, 150, 175, 200, 225, and 250 amperes

  ● **SEE FIGURE 8–13**.

FIGURE 8–11 PTC circuit protectors are used extensively in the power distribution center of this Chrysler vehicle.

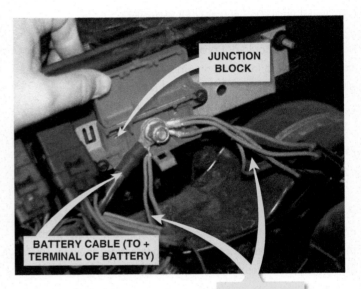

JUNCTION BLOCK

BATTERY CABLE (TO + TERMINAL OF BATTERY)

FUSIBLE LINKS

FIGURE 8–12 Fusible links are usually located close to the battery and are usually attached to a junction block. Notice they are only 6 to 9 inches long and feed more than one fuse from each fusible link.

FIGURE 8–13 A 125-ampere-rated mega fuse used to protect the circuit from the alternator.

CHECKING FUSIBLE LINKS AND MEGA FUSES Fusible links and mega fuses are usually located near where electrical power is sent to other fuses or circuits, such as the following:

- Starter solenoid battery terminals
- Power distribution centers
- Output terminals of alternators
- Positive terminals of the battery

Fusible links can melt and not show any external evidence of damage. To check a fusible link, gently pull on each end to see if it stretches. If the insulation stretches, the wire inside has melted and the fusible link must be replaced after determining what caused the link to fail.

Another way to check a fusible link is to use a test light or a voltmeter and check for available voltage at both ends of the fusible link. If voltage is available at only one end, the link is electrically open and should be replaced.

REPLACING A FUSIBLE LINK
If a fusible link is found to be melted, perform the following steps.

STEP 1 Determine why the fusible link failed and repair the fault.

STEP 2 Check service information for the exact length, gauge, and type of fusible link required.

STEP 3 Replace the fusible link with the specified fusible link wire and according to the instructions found in the service information.

CAUTION: Always use the exact length of fusible link wire required because if it is too short, it will not have enough resistance to generate the heat needed to melt the wire and protect the circuits or components. If the wire is too long, it could melt during normal operation of the circuits it is protecting. Fusible link wires are usually longer than 6 inches and shorter than 9 inches.

TERMINALS AND CONNECTORS

A **terminal** is a metal fastener attached to the end of a wire, which makes the electrical connection. The term *connector* usually refers to the plastic portion that snaps or connects together, thereby making the mechanical connection. Wire terminal ends usually snap into and are held by a connector. Male and female connectors can then be snapped together, thereby completing an electrical connection. Connectors exposed to the environment are also equipped with a weather-tight seal. ● **SEE FIGURE 8–14.**

Terminals are retained in connectors by the use of a **lock tang.** Removing a terminal from a connector includes the following steps.

STEP 1 Release the **connector position assurance (CPA)**, if equipped, that keeps the latch of the connector from releasing accidentally.

STEP 2 Separate the male and female connector by opening the lock. ● **SEE FIGURE 8–15.**

STEP 3 Release the secondary lock, if equipped. ● **SEE FIGURE 8–16.**

STEP 4 Using a pick, look for the slot in the plastic connector where the lock tang is located, depress the lock tang, and gently remove the terminal from the connector. ● **SEE FIGURE 8–17.**

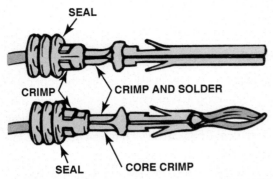

FIGURE 8–14 Some terminals have seals attached to help seal the electrical connections.

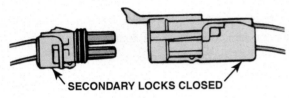

FIGURE 8–15 Separate a connector by opening the lock and pulling the two apart.

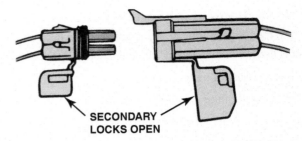

FIGURE 8–16 The secondary locks help retain the terminals in the connector.

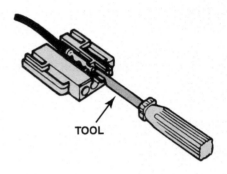

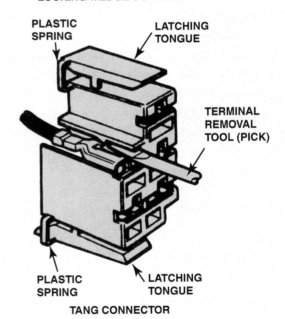

FIGURE 8–17 Use a small removal tool, sometimes called a pick, to release terminals from the connector.

TECH TIP

Look for the "Green Crud"

Corroded connections are a major cause of intermittent electrical problems and open circuits. The usual sequence of conditions is as follows:

1. **Heat causes expansion.** This heat can be from external sources, such as connectors being too close to the exhaust system. Another possible source of heat is a poor connection at the terminal, causing a voltage drop and heat due to the electrical resistance.

2. **Condensation occurs when a connector cools.** The moisture from condensation causes rust and corrosion.

3. **Water gets into the connector.** The solution is, if corroded connectors are noticed, the terminal should be cleaned and the condition of the electrical connection to the wire terminal end(s) confirmed. Many vehicle manufacturers recommend using a dielectric silicone or lithium-based grease inside connectors to prevent moisture from getting into and attacking the connector.

FIGURE 8–18 Always use rosin-core solder for electrical or electronic soldering. Also, use small-diameter solder for small soldering irons. Use large-diameter solder only for large-diameter (large-gauge) wire and higher-wattage soldering irons (guns).

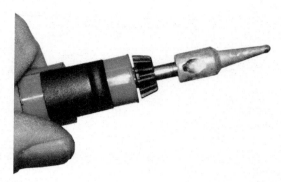

FIGURE 8–19 A butane-powered soldering tool. The cap has a built-in striker to light a converter in the tip of the tool. This handy soldering tool produces the equivalent of 60 watts of heat. It operates for about 1/2 hour on one charge from a commonly available butane refill dispenser.

WIRE REPAIR

SOLDER Many manufacturers recommend that all wiring repairs be soldered. Solder is an alloy of tin and lead used to make a good electrical contact between two wires or connections in an electrical circuit. However, a flux must be used to help clean the area and to help make the solder flow. Therefore, solder is made with a resin (rosin) contained in the center, called **rosin-core solder.**

CAUTION: Never use acid-core solder to repair electrical wiring as the acid will cause corrosion.

● **SEE FIGURE 8–18.**

An acid-core solder is also available, but should only be used for soldering sheet metal. Solder is available with various percentages of tin and lead in the alloy. Ratios are used to identify these various types of solder, with the first number denoting the percentage of tin in the alloy and the second number giving the percentage of lead. The most commonly used solder is 50/50, which means that 50% of the solder is tin and the other 50% is lead. The percentages of each alloy primarily determine the melting point of the solder.

- 60/40 solder (60% tin/40% lead) melts at 361°F (183°C).
- 50/50 solder (50% tin/50% lead) melts at 421°F (216°C).
- 40/60 solder (40% tin/60% lead) melts at 460°F (238°C).

NOTE: The melting points stated here can vary depending on the purity of the metals used.

Because of the lower melting point, 60/40 solder is the most highly recommended solder to use, followed by 50/50.

SOLDERING GUNS When soldering wires, be sure to heat the wires (not the solder) using:

- An electric soldering gun or soldering pencil (60 to 150 watt rating)
- Butane-powered tool that uses a flame to heat the tip (about 60 watt rating) ● **SEE FIGURE 8–19**.

SOLDERING PROCEDURE Soldering a wiring splice includes the following steps.

STEP 1 While touching the soldering gun to the splice, apply solder to the junction of the gun and the wire.

STEP 2 The solder will start to flow. Do not move the soldering gun.

STEP 3 Just keep feeding more solder into the splice as it flows into and around the strands of the wire.

STEP 4 After the solder has flowed throughout the splice, remove the soldering gun and the solder from the splice and allow the solder to cool slowly.

The solder should have a shiny appearance. Dull-looking solder may be caused by not reaching a high enough temperature, which results in a **cold solder joint.** Reheating the splice and allowing it to cool often restores the shiny appearance.

CRIMPING TERMINALS Terminals can be crimped to create a good electrical connection if the proper type of crimping

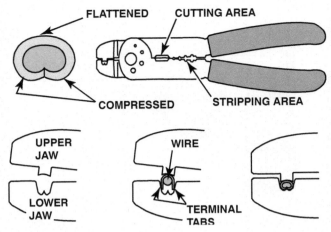

FIGURE 8–20 Notice that to create a good crimp the open part of the terminal is placed in the jaws of the crimping tool toward the anvil or the W-shape part.

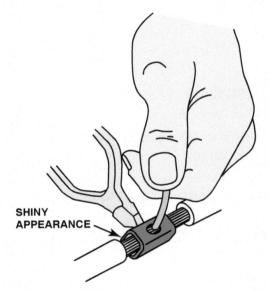

FIGURE 8–21 All hand-crimped splices or terminals should be soldered to be assured of a good electrical connection.

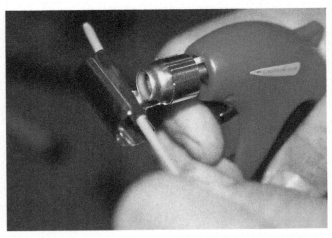

FIGURE 8–22 A butane torch especially designed for use on heat shrink applies heat without an open flame, which could cause damage.

FIGURE 8–23 A typical crimp-and-seal connector. This type of connector is first lightly crimped to retain the ends of the wires and then it is heated. The tubing shrinks around the wire splice, and thermoplastic glue melts on the inside to provide an effective weather-resistant seal.

tool is used. Most vehicle manufacturers recommend that a W-shaped crimp be used to force the strands of the wire into a tight space. ● SEE FIGURE 8–20.

Most vehicle manufacturers also specify that all hand-crimped terminals or splices be soldered. ● SEE FIGURE 8–21.

HEAT SHRINK TUBING   Heat shrink tubing is usually made from polyvinyl chloride (PVC) or polyolefin and shrinks to about half of its original diameter when heated; this is usually called a 2:1 shrink ratio. Heat shrink by itself does not provide protection against corrosion, because the ends of the tubing are not sealed against moisture. DaimlerChrysler Corporation recommends that all wire repairs that may be exposed to the

elements be repaired and sealed using **adhesive-lined heat shrink tubing**. The tubing is usually made from flame-retardant flexible polyolefin with an internal layer of special thermoplastic adhesive. When heated, this tubing shrinks to one-third of its original diameter (3:1 shrink ratio) and the adhesive melts and seals the ends of the tubing. ● SEE FIGURE 8–22.

CRIMP-AND-SEAL CONNECTORS   General Motors Corporation recommends the use of crimp-and-seal connectors as the method for wire repair. **Crimp-and-seal connectors** contain a sealant and shrink tubing in one piece and are **not** simply butt connectors. ● SEE FIGURE 8–23.

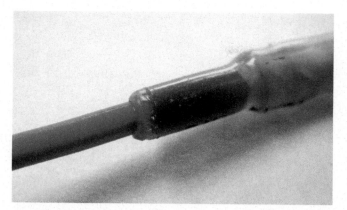

FIGURE 8–24 Heating the crimp-and-seal connector melts the glue and forms an effective seal against moisture.

The usual procedure specified for making a wire repair using a crimp-and-seal connector is as follows:

STEP 1 Strip the insulation from the ends of the wire (about 5/16 inch or 8 mm).

STEP 2 Select the proper size of crimp-and-seal connector for the gauge of wire being repaired. Insert the wires into the splice sleeve and crimp.

NOTE: Use only the specified crimping tool to help prevent the pliers from creating a hole in the cover.

STEP 3 Apply heat to the connector until the sleeve shrinks down around the wire and a small amount of sealant is observed around the ends of the sleeve, as shown in ● **FIGURE 8–24**.

ALUMINUM WIRE REPAIR Some vehicle manufacturers used plastic-coated solid aluminum wire for some body wiring. Because aluminum wire is brittle and can break as a result of vibration, it is used only where there is no possible movement of the wire, such as along the floor or sill area. This section of wire is stationary, and the wire changes back to copper at a junction terminal after the trunk or rear section of the vehicle, where movement of the wiring may be possible.

If any aluminum wire must be repaired or replaced, the following procedure should be used to be assured of a proper repair. The aluminum wire is usually found protected in a plastic conduit. This conduit is then normally slit, after which the wires can easily be removed for repair.

STEP 1 Carefully strip only about 1/4 inch (6 mm) of insulation from the aluminum wire, being careful not to nick or damage the aluminum wire case.

STEP 2 Use a crimp connector to join two wires together. Do *not* solder an aluminum wire repair. Solder will not

What Method of Wire Repair Should I Use?

Good question. Vehicle manufacturers recommend all wire repairs performed under the hood, or where the repair could be exposed to the elements, be weatherproof. The most commonly recommended methods include:

- **Crimp-and-seal connector.** These connectors are special and are not like low-cost insulated-type crimp connectors. This type of connector is recommended by General Motors and others and is sealed using heat after the mechanical crimp has secured the wire ends together.

- **Solder and adhesive-lined heat shrink tubing.** This method is recommended by Chrysler and it uses the special heat shrink that has glue inside that melts when heated to form a sealed connection. Regular heat shrink tubing can be used inside a vehicle, but should not be used where it can be exposed to the elements.

- **Solder and electrical tape.** This is acceptable to use inside the vehicle where the splice will not be exposed to the outside elements. It is best to use a crimp and seal even on the inside of the vehicle for best results.

What Is in Lead-Free Solder?

Lead is an environmental and a health concern and all vehicle manufacturers are switching to lead-free solder. Lead-free solder does not contain lead, but usually a very high percentage of tin. Several formulations of lead-free solder include:

- 95% tin; 5% antimony (melting temperature 450°F (245°C))

- 97% tin; 3% copper (melting temperature 441°F (227°C))

- 96% tin; 4% silver (melting temperature 443°F (228°C))

readily adhere to aluminum because the heat causes an oxide coating on the surface of the aluminum.

STEP 3 The spliced, crimped connection must be coated with petroleum jelly to prevent corrosion.

STEP 4 The coated connection should be covered with shrinkable plastic tubing or wrapped with electrical tape to seal out moisture.

FIGURE 8–25 Conduit that has a paint stripe is constructed of plastic that can withstand high underhood temperatures.

(a)

(b)

FIGURE 8–26 (a) Blue conduit is used to cover circuits that carry up to 42 volts. (b) Yellow conduit can also be used to cover 42-volt wiring.

ELECTRICAL CONDUIT

Electrical conduit covers and protects wiring. The color used on electrical convoluted conduit tells the technician a lot if some information is known, such as the following:

- **Black conduit with a green or blue stripe.** This conduit is designed for high temperatures and is used under the hood and near hot engine parts. Do not replace high-temperature conduit with low-temperature conduit that does not have a stripe when performing wire repairs. ● **SEE FIGURE 8–25**.

- **Blue or yellow conduit.** This color conduit is used to cover wires that have voltages ranging from 12 to 42 volts. Circuits that use this high voltage usually are for the electric power steering. While 42 volts does not represent a shock hazard, an arc will be maintained if a line circuit is disconnected. Use caution around these circuits. ● **SEE FIGURE 8–26**.

- **Orange conduit.** This color conduit is used to cover wiring that carries high-voltage current higher than 60 volts. These circuits are found in hybrid electric vehicles (HEVs). An electric shock from these wires can be fatal, so extreme caution has to be taken when working on or near the components that have orange conduit. Follow the vehicle manufacturer's instruction for de-powering the high-voltage circuits before work begins on any of the high-voltage components. ● **SEE FIGURE 8–27**.

FIGURE 8–27 Always follow the vehicle manufacturer's instructions which include the use of linesman's (high-voltage) gloves if working on circuits that are covered in orange conduit.

1. The higher the AWG size number, the smaller the wire diameter.
2. Metric wire is sized in square millimeters (mm^2) and the higher the number, the larger the wire.
3. All circuits should be protected by a fuse, fusible link, or circuit breaker. The current in the circuit should be about 80% of the fuse rating.
4. A terminal is the metal end of a wire, whereas a connector is the plastic housing for the terminal.
5. All wire repair should use either soldering or a crimp-and-seal connector.

REVIEW QUESTIONS

1. What is the difference between the American wire gauge (AWG) system and the metric system?
2. What is the difference between a wire and a cable?
3. What is the difference between a terminal and a connector?
4. How do fuses, PTC circuit protectors, circuit breakers, and fusible links protect a circuit?
5. How should a wire repair be done if the repair is under the hood where it is exposed to the outside?

CHAPTER QUIZ

1. The higher the AWG number, _____.
   a. the smaller the wire diameter
   b. the larger the wire diameter
   c. the thicker the insulation
   d. the more strands in the conductor core

2. Metric wire size is measured in units of _____.
   a. meters
   b. cubic centimeters
   c. square millimeters
   d. cubic millimeters

3. Which statement is true about fuse ratings?
   a. The fuse rating should be less than the maximum current for the circuit.
   b. The fuse rating should be higher than the normal current for the circuit.
   c. The fuse rating is about 20% higher than the normal current in the circuit.
   d. Both b and c

4. Which statements are true about wire, terminals, and connectors?
   a. Wire is called a lead, and the metal end is a connector.
   b. A connector is usually a plastic piece where terminals lock in.
   c. A lead and a terminal are the same thing.
   d. Both a and c

5. The type of solder that should be used for electrical work is _____.
   a. rosin core
   b. acid core
   c. 60/40 with no flux
   d. 50/50 with acid paste flux

6. A technician is performing a wire repair on a circuit under the hood of the vehicle. Technician A says to use solder and adhesive-lined heat shrink tubing or a crimp-and-seal connector. Technician B says to solder and use electrical tape. Which technician is correct?
   a. Technician A only
   b. Technician B only
   c. Both Technicians A and B
   d. Neither Technician A nor B

7. Two technicians are discussing fuse testing. Technician A says that a test light should light on both test points of the fuse if it is okay. Technician B says the fuse is defective if a test light only lights on one side of the fuse. Which technician is correct?
   a. Technician A only
   b. Technician B only
   c. Both Technicians A and B
   d. Neither Technician A nor B

8. If a wire repair, such as that made under the hood or under the vehicle, is exposed to the elements, which type of repair should be used?
   a. Wire nuts and electrical tape
   b. Solder and adhesive-lined heat shrink or crimp-and-seal connectors
   c. Butt connectors
   d. Rosin-core solder and electrical tape

9. Many ground straps are uninsulated and braided because _____.
   a. they are more flexible to allow movement of the engine without breaking the wire.
   b. they are less expensive than conventional wire.
   c. they help dampen radio-frequency interference (RFI).
   d. Both a and c

10. What causes a fuse to blow?
    a. A decrease in circuit resistance
    b. An increase in the current flow through the circuit
    c. A sudden decrease in current flow through the circuit
    d. Both a and b

chapter 9

WIRING SCHEMATICS AND CIRCUIT TESTING

LEARNING OBJECTIVES

After studying this chapter, the reader will be able to:

1. Interpret wiring schematics and explain the procedure to identify relay terminals.

2. Locate shorts, grounds, opens, and resistance problems in electrical circuits, and determine necessary action.

3. Explain the different methods to locate a short circuit, and the procedure to troubleshoot an electrical problem.

This chapter will help you prepare for the ASE Electrical/Electronic Systems (A6) certification test content area "A" (General Electrical/Electronic System Diagnosis).

KEY TERMS

Coil 138
DPDT 136
DPST 136
Gauss gauge 145
Momentary switch 137
N.C. 136
N.O. 136
Poles 136
Relay 138

Short circuit 144
SPDT 136
SPST 136
Terminal 133
Throws 136
Tone generator tester 145
Wiring schematic 131

FIGURE 9–1 The center wire is a solid color wire, meaning that the wire has no other identifying tracer or stripe color. The two end wires could be labeled "BLU/WHT," indicating a blue wire with a white tracer or stripe.

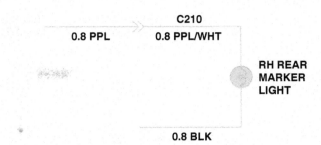

FIGURE 9–2 Typical section of a wiring diagram. Notice that the wire color changes at connection C210. The "0.8" represents the metric wire size in square millimeters.

WIRING SCHEMATICS AND SYMBOLS

TERMINOLOGY The service manuals of automotive manufacturers include wiring schematics of every electrical circuit in a vehicle. A **wiring schematic**, sometimes called a *diagram*, shows electrical components and wiring using symbols and lines to represent components and wires. A typical wiring schematic may include all of the circuits combined on several large foldout sheets, or they may be broken down to show individual circuits. All circuit schematics or diagrams include the following:

- Power-side wiring of the circuit
- All splices
- Connectors
- Wire size
- Wire color
- Trace color (if any)
- Circuit number
- Electrical components
- Ground return paths
- Fuses and switches

CIRCUIT INFORMATION Many wiring schematics include numbers and letters near components and wires that may confuse readers of the schematic. Most letters used near or on a wire identify the color or colors of the wire.

- The first color or color abbreviation is the color of the wire insulation.
- The second color (if mentioned) is the color of the stripe or tracer on the base color. ● **SEE FIGURE 9–1**.

Wires with different color tracers are indicated by a slash (/) between them. For example, GRN/WHT means a green wire with a white stripe or tracer. ● **SEE CHART 9–1**.

ABBREVIATION	COLOR
BRN	Brown
BLK	Black
GRN	Green
WHT	White
PPL	Purple
PNK	Pink
TAN	Tan
BLU	Blue
YEL	Yellow
ORN	Orange
DK BLU	Dark blue
LT BLU	Light blue
DK GRN	Dark green
LT GRN	Light green
RED	Red
GRY	Gray
VIO	Violet

CHART 9–1

Typical abbreviations used on schematics to show wire color. Some vehicle manufacturers use two letters to represent a wire color. Check service information for the color abbreviations used.

WIRE SIZE Wire size is shown on all schematics. ● **FIGURE 9–2** illustrates a rear side-marker bulb circuit diagram where "0.8" indicates the metric wire gauge size in square millimeters (mm^2) and "PPL" indicates a solid purple wire.

The wire diagram also shows that the color of the wire changes at number C210. This stands for "connector #210" and is used for reference purposes. The symbol for the connection can vary depending on the manufacturer. The color change from purple (PPL) to purple with a white tracer (PPL/WHT) is not important except for knowing where the wire changes color in the circuit. The wire gauge has remained the same on both sides of the connection (0.8 mm^2 or 18 gauge). The ground circuit is the "0.8 BLK" wire. ● **FIGURE 9–3** shows many of the electrical and electronic symbols that are used in wiring and circuit diagrams.

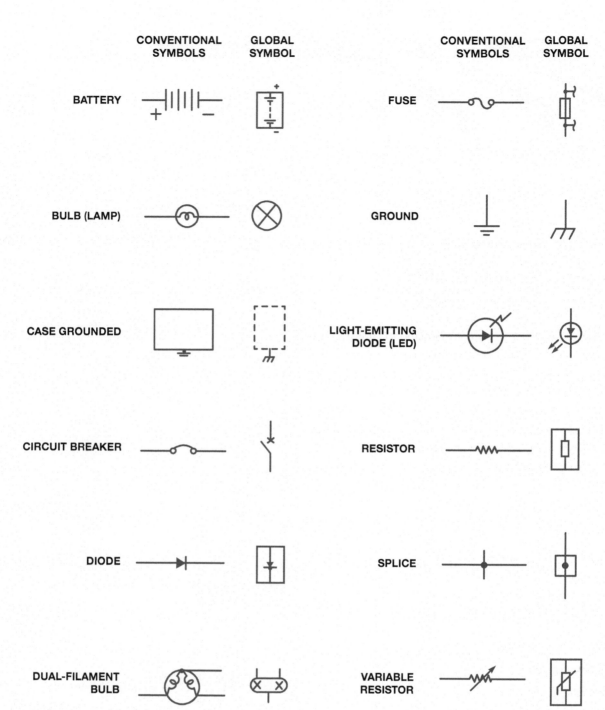

	CONVENTIONAL SYMBOLS	GLOBAL SYMBOL		CONVENTIONAL SYMBOLS	GLOBAL SYMBOL
BATTERY			FUSE		
BULB (LAMP)			GROUND		
CASE GROUNDED			LIGHT-EMITTING DIODE (LED)		
CIRCUIT BREAKER			RESISTOR		
DIODE			SPLICE		
DUAL-FILAMENT BULB			VARIABLE RESISTOR		

FIGURE 9–3 Typical electrical and electronic symbols used in automotive wiring and circuit diagrams. Both the conventional and the global symbols are shown side-by-side to make reading schematics easier. The global symbols are used by many vehicle manufacturers.

FIGURE 9–4 In this typical connector, note that the positive terminal is usually a female connector.

🔧 **TECH TIP**

Read the Arrows

Wiring diagrams indicate connections by symbols that look like arrows. ● **SEE FIGURE 9–4**.

    Do *not* read these "arrows" as pointers showing the direction of current flow. Also observe that the power side (positive side) of the circuit is usually the female end of the connector. If a connector becomes disconnected, it will be difficult for the circuit to become shorted to ground or to another circuit because the wire is recessed inside the connector.

SCHEMATIC SYMBOLS

In a schematic drawing, photos or line drawings of actual components are replaced with a symbol that represents the actual component. The following discussion centers on these symbols and their meanings.

BATTERY The plates of a battery are represented by long and short lines. ● **SEE FIGURE 9–5**.

    The longer line represents the positive plate of a battery and the shorter line represents the negative plate. Therefore, each pair of short and long lines represents one cell of a battery. Because each cell of a typical automotive lead–acid battery has 2.1 volts, a battery symbol showing a 12-volt battery should have six pairs of lines. However, most battery symbols simply use two or three pairs of long and short lines and list the voltage of the battery next to the symbol. As a result, the battery symbols are shorter and yet clear, because the voltage is stated. The positive terminal of the battery is often indicated with a plus sign (+), representing the positive post of the battery, and is placed next to the long line of the end cell. The negative terminal of the battery is represented by a negative sign (−) and is placed next to the shorter cell line. The negative battery terminal is connected to ground. ● **SEE FIGURE 9–6**.

WIRING Electrical wiring is shown as straight lines and with a few numbers and/or letters to indicate the following:

- **Wire size.** This can be either AWG, such as 18 gauge, or in square millimeters, such as 0.8 mm^2.

FIGURE 9–5 The symbol for a battery. The positive plate of a battery is represented by the longer line and the negative plate by the shorter line. The voltage of the battery is usually stated next to the symbol.

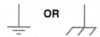

FIGURE 9–6 The ground symbol on the left represents an earth ground. The ground symbol on the right represents a chassis ground.

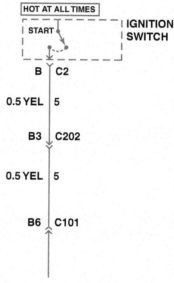

FIGURE 9–7 Starting at the top, the wire from the ignition switch is attached to terminal B of connector C2, the wire is 0.5 mm^2 (20-gauge AWG), and is yellow. The circuit number is 5. The wire enters connector C202 at terminal B3.

- **Circuit numbers.** Each wire in part of a circuit is labeled with the circuit number to help the service technician trace the wiring and to provide an explanation of how the circuit should work.

- **Wire color.** Most schematics also indicate an abbreviation for the color of the wire and place it next to the wire. Many wires have two colors: a solid color and a stripe color. In this case, the solid color is listed, followed by a dark slash (/) and the color of the stripe. For example, Red/Wht would indicate a red wire with a white tracer. ● **SEE FIGURE 9–7**.

- **Terminals.** The metal part attached at the end of a wire is called a **terminal.** A symbol for a terminal is shown in ● **FIGURE 9–8**.

- **Splices.** When two wires are electrically connected, the junction is shown with a black dot. The identification

FIGURE 9–8 The electrical terminals are usually labeled with a letter or number.

SPLICE

FIGURE 9–9 Two wires that cross at the dot indicate that the two are electrically connected.

WIRES NOT ELECTRONICALLY CONNECTED

FIGURE 9–10 Wires that cross, but do not electrically contact each other, are shown with one wire bridging over the other.

of the splice is an "S" followed by three numbers, such as S103. ● **SEE FIGURE 9–9.** When two wires cross in a schematic that are not electrically connected, one of the wires is shown as going over the other wire and does not connect. ● **SEE FIGURE 9–10.**

■ **Connectors.** An electrical connector is a plastic part that contains one or more terminals. Although the terminals provide the electrical connection in a circuit, it is the plastic connector that keeps the terminals together mechanically.

■ **Location.** Connections are usually labeled "C" followed by three numbers. The three numbers indicate the general location of the connector. Normally, the connector number represents the general area of the vehicle, such as the following:

100–199	Under the hood
200–299	Under the dash
300–399	Passenger compartment
400–499	Rear package or trunk area
500–599	Left-front door
600–699	Right-front door
700–799	Left-rear door
800–899	Right-rear door

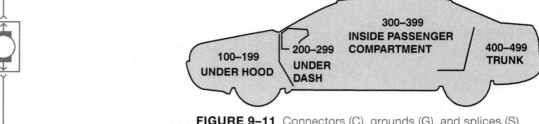

FIGURE 9–11 Connectors (C), grounds (G), and splices (S) are followed by a number, generally indicating the location in the vehicle. For example, G209 is a ground connection located under the dash.

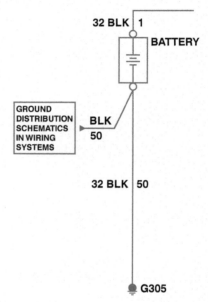

FIGURE 9–12 The ground for the battery is labeled G305 indicating the ground connector is located in the passenger compartment of the vehicle. The ground wire is black (BLK), the circuit number is 50, and the wire is 32 mm^2 (2-gauge AWG).

Even-numbered connectors are on the right (passenger side) of the vehicle and odd-numbered connectors are on the left (driver's side) of the vehicle. For example, C102 is a connector located under the hood (between 100 and 199) on the right side of the vehicle (even number 102). ● **SEE FIGURE 9–11.**

■ **Grounds and splices.** These are also labeled using the same general format as connectors. Therefore, a ground located in the passenger compartment could be labeled G305 (G means "ground" and "305" means that it is located in the passenger compartment). ● **SEE FIGURE 9–12.**

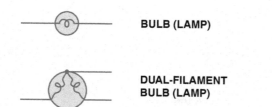

BULB (LAMP)

DUAL-FILAMENT
BULB (LAMP)

FIGURE 9–13 The symbol for lightbulbs shows the filament inside a circle, which represents the glass ampoule of the bulb.

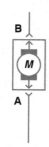

B

A

FIGURE 9–14 An electric motor symbol shows a circle with the letter *M* in the center and two black sections that represent the brushes of the motor. This symbol is used even though the motor is a brushless design.

ELECTRICAL COMPONENTS
Most electrical components have their own unique symbol that shows the basic function or parts.

- **Bulbs.** Lightbulbs often use a filament, which heats and then gives off light when electrical current flows. The symbol used for a lightbulb is a circle with a filament inside. A dual-filament bulb, such as is used for taillights and brake light/turn signals, is shown with two filaments. ● **SEE FIGURE 9–13.**

ELECTRIC MOTORS
An electric motor symbol shows a circle with the letter *M* in the center and two electrical connections, one at the top and the other at the bottom. ● **SEE FIGURE 9–14** for an example of a cooling fan motor.

RESISTORS
Although resistors are usually part of another component, the symbol appears on many schematics and wiring diagrams. A resistor symbol is a jagged line representing resistance to current flow. If the resistor is variable, such as a thermistor, an arrow is shown running through the symbol of a fixed resistor. A potentiometer is a three-wire variable resistor, shown with an arrow pointing toward the resistance part of a fixed resistor. ● **SEE FIGURE 9–15.**

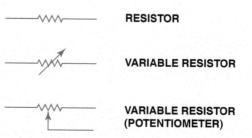

RESISTOR

VARIABLE RESISTOR

VARIABLE RESISTOR
(POTENTIOMETER)

FIGURE 9–15 Resistor symbols vary depending on the type of resistor.

FIGURE 9–16 A rheostat uses only two wires—one is connected to a voltage source and the other is attached to the movable arm.

OR

FIGURE 9–17 Symbols used to represent capacitors. If one of the lines is curved, the capacitor being used has a polarity, while the one without a curved line can be installed in the circuit without concern about polarity.

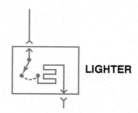

LIGHTER

FIGURE 9–18 The grid-like symbol represents an electrically heated element.

A two-wire rheostat is usually shown as part of another unit, such as a fuel-level sensing unit. ● **SEE FIGURE 9–16.**

CAPACITORS
Capacitors are usually part of an electronic component, but not a replaceable component unless the vehicle is an older model. Many older vehicles used capacitors to reduce radio interference and were installed inside alternators or were attached to wiring connectors. ● **SEE FIGURE 9–17.**

ELECTRIC HEATED UNIT
Electric grid-type rear window defoggers and cigarette lighters are shown with a square box-type symbol. ● **SEE FIGURE 9–18.**

BOXED COMPONENTS
If a component is shown in a box using a solid line, the box is the entire component. If a box uses dashed lines, it represents part of a component. A commonly

FIGURE 9–19 A dashed outline represents a portion (part) of a component.

FIGURE 9–20 A solid box represents an entire component.

FIGURE 9–21 This symbol represents a component that is case grounded.

used dashed-line box is a fuse panel. Often, just one or two fuses are shown in a dashed-line box. This means that a fuse panel has more fuses than shown. ● **SEE FIGURES 9–19 AND 9–20.**

SEPARATE REPLACEABLE PART
Often components are shown on a schematic that cannot be replaced, but are part of a complete assembly. When looking at a schematic of General Motors vehicles, the following is shown:

- If a part name is underlined, it is a replaceable part.
- If a part is not underlined, it is not available as a replaceable part, but is included with other components shown and sold as an assembly.
- If the case itself is grounded, the ground symbol is attached to the component as shown in ● **FIGURE 9–21**.

SWITCHES
Electrical switches are drawn on a wiring diagram in their normal position. This can be one of two possible positions.

- **Normally open.** The switch is not connected to its internal contacts and no current will flow. This type of switch is labeled **N.O.**
- **Normally closed.** The switch is electrically connected to its internal contacts and current will flow through the switch. This type of switch is labeled **N.C.**

Other switches can use more than two contacts.

The **poles** refer to the number of circuits completed by the switch and the **throws** refer to the number of output circuits.

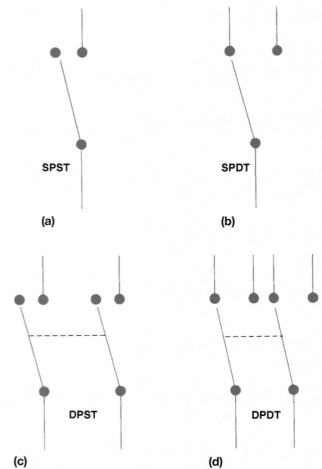

FIGURE 9–22 (a) A symbol for a single-pole, single-throw (SPST) switch. This type of switch is normally open (N.O.) because nothing is connected to the terminal that the switch is contacting in its normal position. (b) A single-pole, double-throw (SPDT) switch has three terminals. (c) A double-pole, single-throw (DPST) switch has two positions (off and on) and can control two separate circuits. (d) A double-pole, double-throw (DPDT) switch has six terminals—three for each pole. Note: Both (c) and (d) also show a dotted line between the two arms indicating that they are mechanically connected, called a "ganged switch."

A **single-pole, single-throw (SPST)** switch has only two positions, on or off. A **single-pole, double-throw (SPDT)** switch has three terminals, one wire in and two wires out. A headlight dimmer switch is an example of a typical SPDT switch. In one position, the current flows to the low-filament headlight; in the other, the current flows to the high-filament headlight.

NOTE: A SPDT switch is not an on or off type of switch, but instead directs power from the source to either the high-beam lamps or the low-beam lamps.

There are also **double-pole, single-throw (DPST)** switches and **double-pole, double-throw (DPDT)** switches. ● **SEE FIGURE 9–22.**

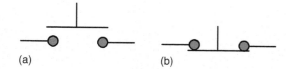

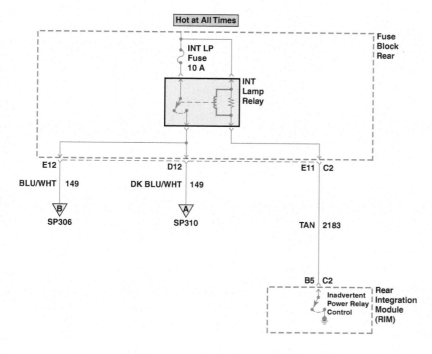

(a)   (b)

FIGURE 9–23 (a) A symbol for a normally open (N.O.) momentary switch. (b) A symbol for a normally closed (N.C.) momentary switch.

FIGURE 9–24 Color the parts of the circuit that have 12 volts, then take it to the vehicle to see if power is available at each location marked.

NOTE: All switches are shown on schematics in their normal position. The headlight switch will be shown normally off, as are most other switches and controls.

MOMENTARY SWITCH

A **momentary switch** is a switch primarily used to send a voltage signal to a module or controller to request that a device be turned on or off. The switch makes momentary contact and returns to the open position. A horn switch is a commonly used momentary switch. The symbol that represents a momentary switch uses two dots for the contact with a switch above them. A momentary switch can be either normally open or normally closed. ● **SEE FIGURE 9–23.**

A momentary switch, for example, can be used to lock or unlock a door or to turn the air conditioning on or off. If the device is currently operating, the signal from the momentary switch will turn it off, and if it is off, the switch will signal the module to turn it on. The major advantage of momentary switches is that they can be lightweight and small, because the switch does not carry any heavy electrical current, just a small voltage signal. Most momentary switches use a membrane constructed of foil and plastic.

 **TECH TIP**

Color-Coding Is Key to Understanding

Whenever diagnosing an electrical problem, it is common practice to print out the schematic of the circuit and take it to the vehicle. A meter is then used to check for voltage at various parts of the circuit to help determine if there is a fault. The diagnosis can be made easier if the parts of the circuit are first color-coded, using markers or color pencils.

The colors represent voltage conditions in various parts of a circuit. Once the circuit has been color-coded, it can be tested using the factory wire colors as a guide. ● **SEE FIGURE 9–24.**

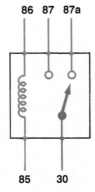

86—POWER SIDE OF THE COIL
85—GROUND SIDE OF THE COIL

(MOSTLY RELAY COILS HAVE BETWEEN 60–100 Ω OF RESISTANCE)

30—COMMON POWER FOR RELAY CONTACTS
87—NORMALLY OPEN OUTPUT (N.O.)
87a—NORMALLY CLOSED OUTPUT (N.C.)

FIGURE 9–25 A relay uses a movable arm to complete a circuit whenever there is a power at terminal 86 and a ground at terminal 85. A typical relay only requires about 1/10 ampere through the relay coil. The movable arm then closes the contacts (#30 to #87) and can relay 30 amperes or more.

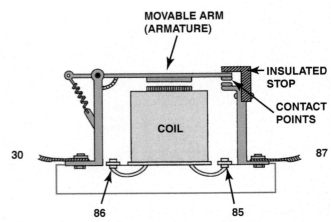

FIGURE 9–26 A cross-sectional view of a typical four-terminal relay. Current flowing through the coil (terminals 86 and 85) causes the movable arm (called the armature) to be drawn toward the coil magnet. The contact points complete the electrical circuit connected to terminals 30 and 87.

RELAY TERMINAL IDENTIFICATION

DEFINITION A **relay** is a magnetic switch that uses a movable armature to control a high-amperage circuit by using a low-amperage electrical switch.

ISO RELAY TERMINAL IDENTIFICATION Most automotive relays adhere to common terminal identification. The primary source for this common identification comes from the standards established by the International Standards Organization (ISO). Knowing this terminal information will help in the correct diagnosis and troubleshooting of any circuit containing a relay. ● **SEE FIGURES 9–25 AND 9–26.**

Relays are found in many circuits because they are capable of being controlled by computers, yet are able to handle enough current to power motors and accessories. Relays include the following components and terminals.

RELAY OPERATION

1. **Coil** (terminals 85 and 86)
   - A coil provides the magnetic pull to a movable armature (arm).
   - The resistance of most relay coils ranges from 50 to 150 ohms, but is usually between 60 and 100 ohms.

   - The ISO identification of the coil terminals are 86 and 85. The terminal number 86 represents the power to the relay coil and the terminal labeled 85 represents the ground side of the relay coil.
   - The relay coil can be controlled by supplying either power or ground to the relay coil winding.
   - The coil winding represents the *control circuit*, which uses low current to control the higher current through the other terminals of the relay. ● **SEE FIGURE 9–27.**

2. Other terminals used to control the load current
   - The higher amperage current flow through a relay flows through terminals 30 and 87, and often 87a.
   - Terminal 30 is usually where power is applied to a relay. Check service information for the exact operation of the relay being tested.
   - When the relay is at rest, without power and ground to the coil, the armature inside the relay electrically connects terminals 30 and 87a if the relay has five terminals. When there is power at terminal 85 and a ground at terminal 86 of the relay, a magnetic

Divide the Circuit in Half

When diagnosing any circuit that has a relay, start testing at the relay and divide the circuit in half.

- **High current portion:** Remove the relay and check that there are 12 volts at the terminal 30 socket. If there is, the power side is okay. Use an ohmmeter and check between terminal 87 socket and ground. If the load circuit has continuity, there should be some resistance. If OL, the circuit is electrically open.

- **Control circuit (low current):** With the relay removed from the socket, check that there are 12 volts to terminal 86 with the ignition on and the control switch on. If not, check service information to see if power should be applied to terminal 86, then continue troubleshooting the switch power and related circuit.

- **Check the relay itself:** Use an ohmmeter and measure for continuity and resistance.
  - Between terminals 85 and 86 (coil), there should be 60 to 100 ohms. If not, replace the relay.
  - Between terminals 30 and 87 (high-amperage switch controls), there should be continuity (low ohms) when there is power applied to terminal 85 and a ground applied to terminal 86 that operates the relay. If OL is displayed on the meter set to read ohms, the circuit is open, which requires that the relay be replaced.
  - Between terminals 30 and 87a (if equipped), with the relay turned off, there should be low resistance (less than 5 ohms).

FIGURE 9–27 A typical relay showing the schematic of the wiring in the relay.

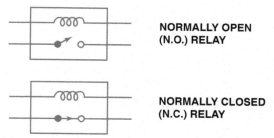

NORMALLY OPEN (N.O.) RELAY

NORMALLY CLOSED (N.C.) RELAY

FIGURE 9–28 All schematics are shown in their normal, nonenergized position.

field is created in the coil winding, which draws the armature of the relay toward the coil. The armature, when energized electrically, connects terminals 30 and 87.

The maximum current through the relay is determined by the resistance of the circuit, and relays are designed to safely handle the designed current flow. ● **SEE FIGURES 9–28 AND 9–29.**

RELAY VOLTAGE SPIKE CONTROL Relays contain a coil and when power is removed, the magnetic field surrounding the coil collapses, creating a voltage to be induced in the coil winding. This induced voltage can be as high as 100 volts or more and can cause problems with other electronic devices in the vehicle. For example, the short high-voltage surge can be heard as a "pop" in the radio. To reduce the induced voltage, some relays contain a diode connected across the coil. ● **SEE FIGURE 9–30.**

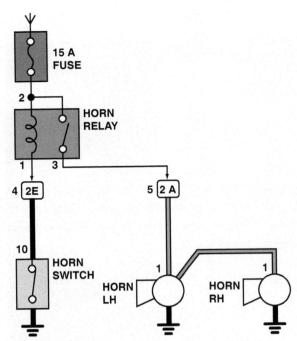

FIGURE 9–29 A typical horn circuit. Note that the relay contacts supply the heavy current to operate the horn when the horn switch simply completes a low-current circuit to ground, causing the relay contacts to close.

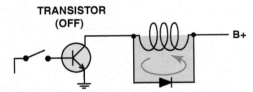

FIGURE 9–30 When the relay or solenoid coil current is turned off, the stored energy in the coil flows through the clamping diode and effectively reduces voltage spike.

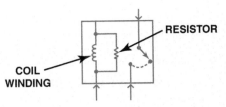

FIGURE 9–31 A resistor used in parallel with the coil windings is a common spike reduction method used in many relays.

What Is the Difference between a Relay and a Solenoid?

Often, these terms are used differently among vehicle manufacturers, which can lead to some confusion.

Relay: A relay is an electromagnetic switch that uses a movable arm. Because a relay uses a movable arm, it is generally limited to current flow not exceeding 30 amperes.

Solenoid: A solenoid is an electromagnetic switch that uses a movable core. Because of this type of design, a solenoid is capable of handling 200 amperes or more. It is used in the starter motor circuit and other high-amperage applications, such as in the glow plug circuit of diesel engines.

When the current flows through the coil, the diode is not part of the circuit because it is installed to block current. However, when the voltage is removed from the coil, the resulting voltage induced in the coil windings has a reversed polarity to the applied voltage. Therefore, the voltage in the coil is applied to the coil in a forward direction through the diode, which conducts the current back into the winding. As a result, the induced voltage spike is eliminated.

Most relays use a resistor connected in parallel with the coil winding. The use of a resistor, typically about 400 to 600 ohms, reduces the voltage spike by providing a path for the voltage created in the coil to flow back through the coil windings when the coil circuit is opened. ● **SEE FIGURE 9–31.**

LOCATING AN OPEN CIRCUIT

TERMINOLOGY An open circuit is a break in the electrical circuit that prevents current from flowing and operating an electrical device. Examples of open circuits include the following:

- Blown (open) lightbulbs
- Cut or broken wires
- Disconnected or partially disconnected electrical connectors
- Electrically open switches
- Loose or broken ground connections or wires
- Blown fuse

PROCEDURE TO LOCATE AN OPEN CIRCUIT The typical procedure for locating an open circuit involves the following steps.

STEP 1 **Perform a thorough visual inspection.** Check the following:

- Look for evidence of a previous repair. Often, an electrical connector or ground connection can be accidentally left disconnected.
- Look for evidence of recent body damage or body repairs. Movement due to a collision can cause metal to move, which can cut wires or damage connectors or components.

STEP 2 **Print out the schematic.** Trace the circuit and check for voltage at certain places. This will help pinpoint the location of the open circuit.

STEP 3 **Check everything that does and does not work.** Often, an open circuit will affect more than one component. Check the part of the circuit that is common to the other components that do not work.

STEP 4 **Check for voltage.** Voltage is present up to the location of the open circuit fault. For example, if there is battery voltage at the positive terminal and the negative (ground) terminal of a two-wire lightbulb socket with the bulb plugged in, the ground circuit is open.

COMMON POWER OR GROUND

When diagnosing an electrical problem that affects more than one component or system, check the electrical schematic for a common power source or a common ground.

● **SEE FIGURE 9–32** for an example of lights being powered by one fuse (power source).

- Underhood light
- Inside lighted mirrors
- Dome light
- Left-side courtesy light
- Right-side courtesy light

Therefore, if a customer complains about one or more of the items listed, check the fuse and the common part of the circuit that feeds all of the affected lights. Check for a common ground if several components that seem unrelated are not functioning correctly.

 CASE STUDY

The Electric Mirror Fault Story

A customer noticed that the electric mirrors stopped working. The service technician checked all electrical components in the vehicle and discovered that the interior lights were also not working.

The interior lights were not mentioned by the customer as being a problem most likely because the driver only used the vehicle in daylight hours.

The service technician found the interior light and power accessory fuse blown. Replacing the fuse restored the proper operation of the electric outside mirror and the interior lights. However, what caused the fuse to blow? A visual inspection of the dome light, next to the electric sunroof, showed an area where a wire was bare. Evidence showed the bare wire had touched the metal roof, which could cause the fuse to blow. The technician covered the bare wire with a section of vacuum hose and then taped the hose with electrical tape to complete the repair.

Summary:

- **Complaint**—The electric power mirrors stopped working.
- **Cause**—A blown fuse due to a fault in the wiring at the dome light.
- **Correction**—Repaired the wiring at the dome light which restored the proper operation of the electric mirrors that shared the same fuse as the dome light.

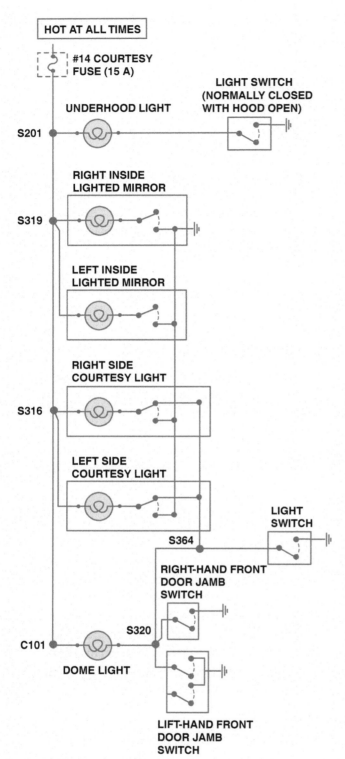

#14 COURTESY FUSE (15 A)

UNDERHOOD LIGHT

S201

LIGHT SWITCH (NORMALLY CLOSED WITH HOOD OPEN)

RIGHT INSIDE LIGHTED MIRROR

S319

LEFT INSIDE LIGHTED MIRROR

RIGHT SIDE COURTESY LIGHT

S316

LEFT SIDE COURTESY LIGHT

LIGHT SWITCH

S364

RIGHT-HAND FRONT DOOR JAMB SWITCH

S320

C101

DOME LIGHT

LIFT-HAND FRONT DOOR JAMB SWITCH

FIGURE 9–32 A typical wiring diagram showing multiple switches and bulbs powered by one fuse.

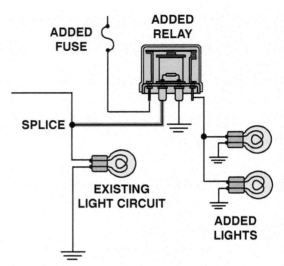

ADDED FUSE

ADDED RELAY

SPLICE

EXISTING LIGHT CIRCUIT

ADDED LIGHTS

FIGURE 9–33 To add additional lighting, simply tap into an existing light wire and connect a relay. Whenever the existing light is turned on, the coil of the relay is energized. The arm of the relay then connects power from another circuit (fuse) to the auxiliary lights without overloading the existing light circuit.

🔧 **TECH TIP**

Do It Right—Install a Relay

Often the owners of vehicles, especially owners of pickup trucks and sport utility vehicles (SUVs), want to add additional electrical accessories or lighting. It is tempting in these cases to simply splice into an existing circuit. However, when another circuit or component is added, the current that flows through the newly added component is also added to the current for the original component. This additional current can easily overload the fuse and wiring. Do not simply install a larger amperage fuse; the wire gauge size was not engineered for the additional current and could overheat.

The solution is to install a relay, which uses a small coil to create a magnetic field that causes a movable arm to switch on a higher current circuit. The typical relay coil has 50 to 150 ohms (usually 60 to 100 ohms) of resistance and requires just 0.24 to 0.08 ampere when connected to a 12-volt source. This small additional current will not be enough to overload the existing circuit. ● **SEE FIGURE 9–33** for an example of how additional lighting can be added.

FIGURE 9–34 Always check the simple things first. Check the fuse for the circuit you are testing. Maybe a fault in another circuit controlled by the same fuse could have caused the fuse to blow. Use a test light to check that both sides of the fuse have voltage.

CIRCUIT TROUBLESHOOTING PROCEDURE

Follow these steps when troubleshooting wiring problems.

STEP 1 Verify the malfunction. If, for example, the backup lights do not operate, make certain that the ignition is on (key on, engine off), with the gear selector in reverse, and check for operation of the backup lights.

STEP 2 Check everything else that does or does not operate correctly. For example, if the taillights are also not working, the problem could be a loose or broken ground connection in the trunk area that is shared by both the backup lights and the taillights.

STEP 3 Check the fuse for the backup lights. ● **SEE FIGURE 9–34**.

STEP 4 Check for voltage at the backup light socket. This can be done using a test light or a voltmeter.

Where to Start?

The common question is, where does a technician start the troubleshooting when using a wiring diagram (schematic)?

HINT 1 If the circuit contains a relay, start your diagnosis at the relay. The entire circuit can be tested at the terminals of the relay.

HINT 2 The easiest first step is to locate the unit on the schematic that is not working at all or not working correctly.

    a. Trace where the unit gets its ground connection.

    b. Trace where the unit gets its power connection.

Often a ground is used by more than one component. Therefore, ensure that everything else is working correctly. If not, then the fault may lie at the common ground (or power) connection.

HINT 3 Divide the circuit in half by locating a connector or a part of the circuit that can be accessed easily. Then check for power and ground at this midpoint. This step could save you much time.

HINT 4 Use a fused jumper wire to substitute a ground or a power source to replace a suspected switch or section of wire.

If voltage is available at the socket, the problem is either a defective bulb or a poor ground at the socket or a ground wire connection to the body or frame. If no voltage is available at the socket, consult a wiring diagram for the type of vehicle being tested. The wiring diagram should show all of the wiring and components included in the circuit. For example, the backup light current must flow through the fuse and ignition switch to the gear selector switch before traveling to the rear backup light socket. As stated in the second step, the fuse used for the backup lights may also be used for other vehicle circuits.

The wiring diagram can be used to determine all other components that share the same fuse. If the fuse is blown (open circuit), the cause can be a short in any of the circuits sharing the same fuse. Because the backup light circuit current must be switched on and off by the gear selector switch, an open in the switch can also prevent the backup lights from functioning.

LOCATING A SHORT CIRCUIT

TERMINOLOGY A short circuit usually blows a fuse, and a replacement fuse often also blows in the attempt to locate the source of the short circuit. A **short circuit** is an electrical connection to another wire or to ground before the current flows through some or all of the resistance in the circuit. A short-to-ground will always blow a fuse and usually involves a wire on the power side of the circuit coming in contact with metal. Therefore, a thorough visual inspection should be performed around areas involving heat or movement, especially if there is evidence of a previous collision or previous repair that may not have been properly completed.

A short-to-voltage may or may not cause the fuse to blow and usually affects another circuit. Look for areas of heat or movement where two power wires could come in contact with each other. Several methods can be used to locate the short.

FUSE REPLACEMENT METHOD Disconnect one component at a time and then replace the fuse. If the new fuse blows, continue the process until you determine the location of the short. This method uses many fuses and is *not* a preferred method for finding a short circuit.

CIRCUIT BREAKER METHOD Another method is to connect an automotive circuit breaker to the contacts of the fuse holder with alligator clips. Circuit breakers are available that plug directly into the fuse panel, replacing a blade-type fuse. The circuit breaker will alternately open and close the circuit, protecting the wiring from possible overheating damage while still providing current flow through the circuit.

NOTE: A heavy-duty (HD) flasher can also be used in place of a circuit breaker to open and close the circuit. Wires and terminals must be made to connect the flasher unit where the fuse normally plugs in.

All components included in the defective circuit should be disconnected, one at a time, until the circuit breaker stops clicking. The unit that was disconnected and stopped the circuit breaker clicking is the unit causing the short circuit. If the circuit breaker continues to click with all circuit components unplugged, the problem is in the wiring *from* the fuse panel *to* any one of the units in the circuit. Visual inspection of all the wiring or further disconnecting will be necessary to locate the problem.

TEST LIGHT METHOD To use the test light method, simply remove the blown fuse and connect a test light to the terminals of the fuse holder (polarity does not matter). If there is a short circuit, current will flow from the power side of the fuse holder through the test light and on to ground through the short circuit, and the test light will then light. Unplug the connectors or components protected by the fuse until the test light goes out. The circuit that was disconnected, which caused the test light to go out, is the circuit that is shorted.

BUZZER METHOD The buzzer method is similar to the test light method, but uses a buzzer to replace a fuse and act as an electrical load. The buzzer will sound if the circuit is shorted and will stop when the part of the circuit that is grounded is unplugged.

OHMMETER METHOD The fifth method uses an ohmmeter connected to the fuse holder and ground. This is the recommended method of finding a short circuit, as an ohmmeter will indicate low ohms when connected to a short circuit. However, an ohmmeter should never be connected to an operating circuit. The correct procedure for locating a short using an ohmmeter is as follows:

1. Connect one lead of an ohmmeter (set to a low scale) to a good clean metal ground and the other lead to the circuit (load) side of the fuse holder.

   CAUTION: Connecting the lead to the power side of the fuse holder will cause current to flow through and damage the ohmmeter.

2. The ohmmeter will read zero or almost zero ohms if the circuit or a component in the circuit is shorted.

3. Disconnect one component in the circuit at a time and watch the ohmmeter. If the ohmmeter reading shoots to a high value or infinity, the component just unplugged was the source of the short circuit.

4. If all of the components have been disconnected and the ohmmeter still reads low ohms, then disconnect electrical connectors until the ohmmeter reads high ohms. The location of the short-to-ground is then between the ohmmeter and the disconnected connector.

(a)

(b)

FIGURE 9–35 (a) After removing the blown fuse, a pulsing circuit breaker is connected to the terminals of the fuse. (b) The circuit breaker causes current to flow, then stop, then flow again, through the circuit up to the point of the short-to-ground. By observing the Gauss gauge, the location of the short is indicated near where the needle stops moving due to the magnetic field created by the flow of current through the wire.

NOTE: Some meters, such as the Fluke 87, can be set to beep (alert) when the circuit closes or when the circuit opens—a very useful feature.

GAUSS GAUGE METHOD If a short circuit blows a fuse, a special pulsing circuit breaker (similar to a flasher unit) can be installed in the circuit in place of the fuse. Current will flow through the circuit until the circuit breaker opens the circuit. As soon as the circuit breaker opens the circuit, it closes again. This on-and-off current flow creates a pulsing magnetic field around the wire carrying the current. A **Gauss gauge** is a handheld meter that responds to weak magnetic fields. It is used to observe this pulsing magnetic field, which is indicated on the gauge as needle movement. This pulsing magnetic field will register on the Gauss gauge even through the metal body of the vehicle. A needle-type compass can also be used to observe the pulsing magnetic field. ● **SEE FIGURES 9–35 AND 9–36**.

ELECTRONIC TONE GENERATOR TESTER An electronic tone generator tester can be used to locate a short-to-ground or an open circuit. Similar to test equipment used to test telephone and cable television lines, a **tone generator tester** generates a tone that can be heard through a receiver (probe). ● **SEE FIGURE 9–37**.

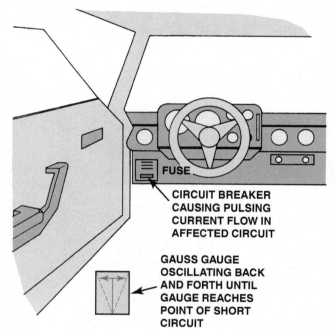

FIGURE 9–36 A Gauss gauge can be used to determine the location of a short circuit even behind a metal panel.

The tone will be generated as long as there is a continuous electrical path along the circuit. The signal will stop if there is a short-to-ground or an open in the circuit. ● **SEE FIGURE 9–38**.

The windings in the solenoids and relays will increase the strength of the signal in these locations.

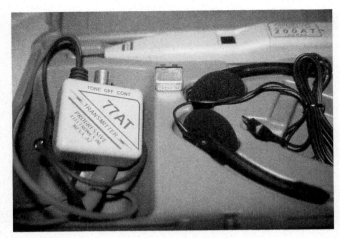

FIGURE 9–37 A tone generator–type tester used to locate open circuits and circuits that are shorted-to-ground. Included with this tester is a transmitter (tone generator), receiver probe, and headphones for use in noisy shops.

 **TECH TIP**

Heat or Movement

Electrical shorts are commonly caused either by movement, which causes the insulation around the wiring to be worn away, or by heat melting the insulation. When checking for a short circuit, first check the wiring that is susceptible to heat, movement, and damage.

1. **Heat.** Wiring near heat sources, such as the exhaust system, cigarette lighter, or alternator
2. **Wire movement.** Wiring that moves, such as in areas near the doors, trunk, or hood
3. **Damage.** Wiring subject to mechanical injury, such as in the trunk, where heavy objects can move around and smash or damage wiring; can also occur as a result of an accident or a previous repair

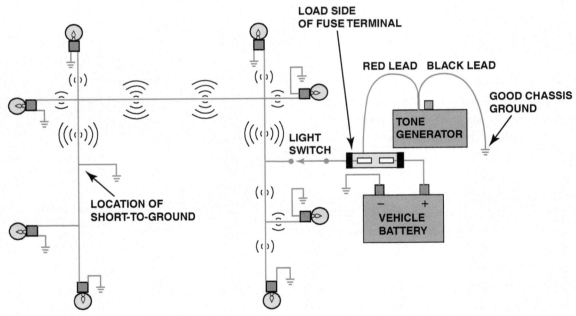

FIGURE 9–38 To check for a short-to-ground using a tone generator, connect the black transmitter lead to a good chassis ground and the red lead to the load side of the fuse terminal. Turn the transmitter on and check for tone signal with the receiver. Using a wiring diagram, follow the strongest signal to the location of the short-to-ground. There will be no signal beyond the fault, either a short-to-ground as shown or an open circuit.

Wiggle Test

Intermittent electrical problems are common yet difficult to locate. To help locate these hard-to-find problems, try operating the circuit and start wiggling the wires and connections that control the circuit. If in doubt where the wiring goes, try moving all the wiring starting at the battery. Pay particular attention to wiring running near the battery or the windshield washer container. Corrosion can cause wiring to fail, and battery acid fumes and alcohol-based windshield washer fluid can start or contribute to the problem. If you notice any change in the operation of the device being tested while wiggling the wiring, look closer in the area you were wiggling until you locate and correct the actual problem.

ELECTRICAL TROUBLE-SHOOTING GUIDE

When troubleshooting any electrical component, remember the following hints to identify the problem faster and more easily.

1. For a device to work, it must have two things: power and ground.

2. If there is no power to a device, an open power side (blown fuse, etc.) is indicated.

3. If there is power on both sides of a device, an open ground is indicated.

4. If a fuse blows immediately, a grounded power-side wire is indicated.

5. Most electrical faults result from heat or movement.

6. Most noncomputer–controlled devices operate by opening and closing the power side of the circuit (power-side switch).

7. Most computer-controlled devices operate by opening and closing the ground side of the circuit (ground-side switch).

STEP-BY-STEP TROUBLESHOOTING PROCEDURE

Knowing what should be done and when it should be done is a major concern for many technicians trying to repair an electrical problem. The following field-tested procedure provides a step-by-step guide for troubleshooting an electrical fault.

STEP 1 Determine the customer concern (complaint) and get as much information as possible from the customer or service advisor.
  a. When did the problem start?
  b. Under what conditions does the problem occur?
  c. Have there been any recent previous repairs to the vehicle which could have created the problem?

STEP 2 Verify the customer's concern by actually observing the fault.

STEP 3 Perform a thorough visual inspection and be sure to check everything that does and does not work.

STEP 4 Check for technical service bulletins (TSBs).

STEP 5 Locate the wiring schematic for the circuit being diagnosed.

STEP 6 Check the factory service information and follow the troubleshooting procedure.
  a. Determine how the circuit works.
  b. Determine which part of the circuit is good, based on what works and what does not work.
  c. Isolate the problem area.

NOTE: Split the circuit in half to help isolate the problem and start at the relay (if the circuit has a relay).

STEP 7 Determine the root cause and repair the vehicle.

STEP 8 Verify the repair and complete the work order by listing the three Cs (complaint, cause, and correction).

Shocking Experience

A customer complained that after driving for a while, he got a static shock whenever he grabbed the door handle when exiting the vehicle. The customer thought that there must be an electrical fault and that the shock was coming from the vehicle itself. In a way, the shock was caused by the vehicle, but it was not a fault. The service technician sprayed the cloth seats with an anti-static spray and the problem did not reoccur. Obviously, a static charge was being created by the movement of the driver's clothing on the seats and discharged when the driver touched the metal door handle. ● **SEE FIGURE 9–39.**

Summary:

- **Complaint**—Vehicle owner complained that he got shocked when the door handle was touched.
- **Cause**—Static electricity was found to be the cause and not a fault with the vehicle.
- **Correction**—The seats and carpet were sprayed with an anti-static spray and this corrected the concern.

FIGURE 9–39 Anti-static spray can be used by customers to prevent being shocked when they touch a metal object like the door handle.

SUMMARY

1. Most wiring diagrams include the wire color, circuit number, and wire gauge.
2. The number used to identify connectors, grounds, and splices usually indicates where they are located in the vehicle.
3. All switches and relays on a schematic are shown in their normal position either normally closed (N.C.) or normally open (N.O.).
4. A typical relay uses a small current through a coil (terminals 85 and 86) to operate the higher current part (terminals 30 and 87).
5. A short-to-voltage affects the power side of the circuit and usually involves more than one circuit.
6. A short-to-ground usually causes the fuse to blow and usually affects only one circuit.
7. Most electrical faults are a result of heat or movement.

REVIEW QUESTIONS

1. List the numbers used on schematics to indicate grounds, splices, and connectors and where they are used in the vehicle.
2. List and identify the terminals of a typical ISO type relay.
3. List three methods that can be used to help locate a short circuit.
4. How can a tone generator be used to locate a short circuit?
5. Why do most experts suggest that the technician start at the relay when diagnosing any circuit that contains a relay?

1. On a wiring diagram, S110 with a "0.8 BRN/BLK" means
   _____.
   a. circuit #.8, spliced under the hood
   b. a connector with 0.8 mm² wire
   c. a splice of a brown with black stripe, wire size being 0.8 mm² (18-gauge AWG)
   d. Both a and b

2. Where is connector C250?
   a. Under the hood
   b. Under the dash
   c. In the passenger compartment
   d. In the trunk

3. All switches illustrated in schematics are _____.
   a. shown in their normal position
   b. always shown in their on position
   c. always shown in their off position
   d. shown in their on position except for lighting switches

4. When testing a relay using an ohmmeter, which two terminals should be touched to measure the coil resistance?
   a. 87 and 30   c. 87a and 87
   b. 86 and 85   d. 86 and 87

5. Technician A says that a good relay should measure between 60 and 100 ohms across the coil terminals. Technician B says that OL should be displayed on an ohmmeter when touching terminals 30 and 87. Which technician is correct?
   a. Technician A only
   b. Technician B only
   c. Both Technicians A and B
   d. Neither Technician A nor B

6. Which relay terminal is the normally closed (N.C.) terminal?
   a. 30   c. 87
   b. 85   d. 87a

7. Technician A says that there is often more than one circuit being protected by each fuse. Technician B says that more than one circuit often shares a single ground connector. Which technician is correct?
   a. Technician A only
   b. Technician B only
   c. Both Technicians A and B
   d. Neither Technician A nor B

8. Two technicians are discussing finding a short-to-ground using a test light. Technician A says that the test light, connected in place of the fuse, will light when the circuit that has the short is disconnected. Technician B says that the test light should be connected to the positive (+) and negative (−) terminals of the battery during this test. Which technician is correct?
   a. Technician A only
   b. Technician B only
   c. Both Technicians A and B
   d. Neither Technician A nor B

9. A short circuit can be located using a _____.
   a. test light
   b. gauss gauge
   c. tone generator
   d. Any of the above

10. For an electrical device to operate, it must have _____.
    a. Power and a ground
    b. A switch and a fuse
    c. A ground and fusible link
    d. A relay to transfer the current to the device

chapter 10
CAPACITANCE AND CAPACITORS

FIGURE 10–1 A Leyden jar can be used to store an electrical charge.

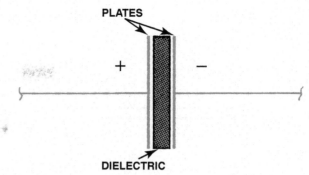

FIGURE 10–2 This simple capacitor is made of two plates separated by an insulating material called a dielectric.

MATERIAL	DIELECTRIC CONSTANT
Vacuum	1
Air	1.00059
Polystyrene	2.5
Paper	3.5
Mica	5.4
Flint glass	9.9
Methyl alcohol	35
Glycerin	56.2
Pure water	81

CHART 10–1

The higher the dielectric constant is, the better are the insulating properties between the plates of the capacitor.

CAPACITANCE

DEFINITION **Capacitance** is the ability of an object or surface to store an electrical charge. Around 1745, Ewald Christian von Kliest and Pieter van Musschenbroek independently discovered capacitance in an electric circuit. While engaged in separate studies of electrostatics, they discovered that an electric charge could be stored for a period of time. They used a device, now called a **Leyden jar**, for their experimentation, which consisted of a glass jar filled with water, with a nail piercing the stopper and dipping into the water. ● **SEE FIGURE 10–1**.

The two scientists connected the nail to an electrostatic charge. After disconnecting the nail from the source of the charge, they felt a shock by touching the nail, demonstrating that the device had stored the charge.

In 1747, John Bevis lined both the inside and outside of the jar with foil. This created a capacitor with two conductors (the inside and outside metal foil layers) equally separated by the insulating glass. The Leyden jar was also used by Benjamin Franklin to store the charge from lightning as well as in other experiments. The natural phenomenon of lightning includes capacitance, because huge electrical fields develop between cloud layers or between clouds and the earth prior to a lightning strike.

NOTE: Capacitors are also called condensers. This term developed because electric charges collect, or condense, on the plates of a capacitor much like water vapor collects and condenses on a cold bottle or glass.

CAPACITOR CONSTRUCTION AND OPERATION

CONSTRUCTION A capacitor (also called a condenser) consists of two conductive plates with an insulating material between them. The insulating material is commonly called a **dielectric.** This substance is a poor conductor of electricity and can include air, mica, ceramic, glass, paper, plastic, or any similar nonconductive material. The dielectric constant is the relative strength of a material against the flow of electrical current. The higher the number is, the better are the insulating properties. ● **SEE CHART 10–1**.

OPERATION When a capacitor is placed in a closed circuit, the voltage source (battery) forces electrons around the circuit. Because electrons cannot flow through the dielectric of the capacitor, excess electrons collect on what becomes the negatively charged plate. At the same time, the other plate loses electrons and, therefore, becomes positively charged. ● **SEE FIGURE 10–2**.

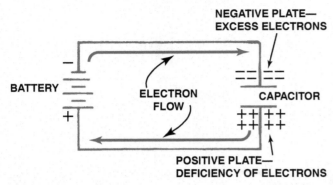

FIGURE 10–3 As the capacitor is charging, the battery forces electrons through the circuit.

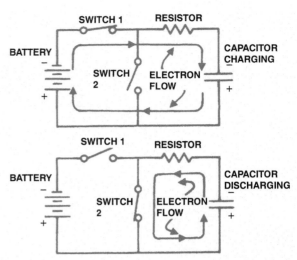

FIGURE 10–5 The capacitor is charged through one circuit (top) and discharged through another (bottom).

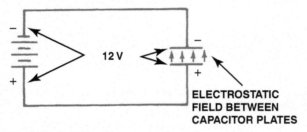

FIGURE 10–4 When the capacitor is charged, there is equal voltage across the capacitor and the battery. An electrostatic field exists between the capacitor plates. No current flows in the circuit.

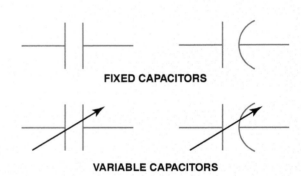

FIGURE 10–6 Capacitor symbols as shown in electrical diagrams. The negative plate is often shown curved.

Current continues until the voltage charge across the capacitor plates becomes the same as the source voltage. At that time, the negative plate of the capacitor and the negative terminal of the battery are at the same negative potential. ● SEE FIGURE 10–3.

The positive plate of the capacitor and the positive terminal of the battery are also at equal positive potentials. There is then a voltage charge across the battery terminals and an equal voltage charge across the capacitor plates. The circuit is in balance, and there is no current. An electrostatic field now exists between the capacitor plates because of their opposite charges. It is this field that stores energy. In other words, a charged capacitor is similar to a charged battery. ● SEE FIGURE 10–4.

If the circuit is opened, the capacitor will hold its charge until it is connected into an external circuit through which it can discharge. When the charged capacitor is connected to an external circuit, it discharges. After discharging, both plates of the capacitor are neutral because all the energy from a circuit stored in a capacitor is returned when it is discharged. ● SEE FIGURE 10–5.

Theoretically, a capacitor holds its charge indefinitely. Actually, the charge slowly leaks off the capacitor through the dielectric. The better the dielectric, the longer the capacitor holds its charge. To avoid an electrical shock, any capacitor should be treated as if it were charged until it is proven to be discharged. To safely discharge a capacitor, use a test light with the clip attached to a good ground, and touch the pigtail or terminal with the point of the test light. ● SEE FIGURE 10–6 for the symbol for capacitors as used in electrical schematics.

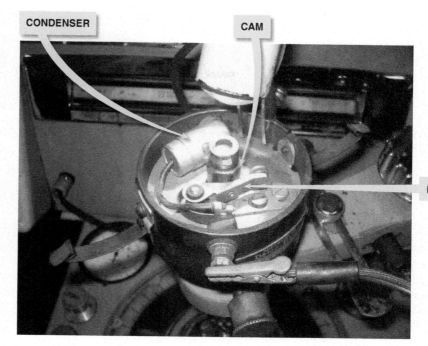

CONDENSER

CAM

POINTS

FIGURE 10–7 A point-type distributor shown with the condenser from an old vehicle being tested on a distributor machine.

? **FREQUENTLY ASKED QUESTION**

What Are "Points and Condenser"?

Points and condenser are used in point-type ignition systems.

Points. A set of points uses one stationary contact and a movable contact that is opened by a cam lobe inside the ignition distributor. When the points are closed, current flows through the primary windings of the ignition coil and creates a strong magnetic field. As the engine rotates, the distributor can open the contact points, which opens the circuit to the coil. The stored magnetic field in the coil collapses and generates a high-voltage arc from the secondary winding of the coil. It is this spark that is sent to the spark plugs that ignite the air-fuel mixture inside the engine.

Condenser. The condenser (capacitor) is attached to the points and the case of the condenser is grounded. When the points start to open, the charge built up in the primary winding of the coil would likely start to arc across the opening points. To prevent the points from arcing and to increase how rapidly the current is turned off, the condenser stores the current temporarily.

Points and condenser were used in vehicles and small gasoline engines until the mid-1970s. ● **SEE FIGURE 10–7.**

FACTORS OF CAPACITANCE

Capacitance is governed by three factors.

- The surface area of the plates
- The distance between the plates
- The dielectric material

The larger the surface area of the plates is, the greater the capacitance, because more electrons collect on a larger plate area than on a small one. The closer the plates are to each other, the greater the capacitance, because a stronger electrostatic field exists between charged bodies that are close together. The insulating qualities of the dielectric material also affect capacitance. The capacitance of a capacitor is higher if the dielectric is a very good insulator.

MEASUREMENT OF CAPACITANCE Capacitance is measured in **farads,** which is named after Michael Faraday (1791–1867), an English physicist. The symbol for farads is the letter *F*. If a charge of 1 coulomb is placed on the plates of a capacitor and the potential difference between them is 1 volt, the capacitance is defined to be 1 farad, or 1 F. One coulomb is equal to the charge of 6.25×10^{18} electrons. One farad is an extremely large quantity of capacitance. Microfarads (0.000001 farad), or μF, are more commonly used.

The capacitance of a capacitor is proportional to the quantity of charge that can be stored in it for each volt difference in potential.

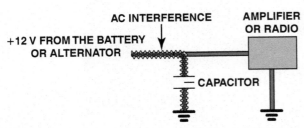

FIGURE 10–8 A capacitor blocks direct current (DC) but passes alternating current (AC). A capacitor makes a very good noise suppressor because most of the interference is AC and the capacitor will conduct this AC to ground before it can reach the radio or amplifier.

FIGURE 10–9 A 1 farad capacitor used to boost the power to large speakers.

USES FOR CAPACITORS

SPIKE SUPPRESSION A capacitor can be used in parallel to a coil to reduce the resulting voltage spike that occurs when the circuit is opened. The energy stored to the magnet field of the coil is rapidly released at this time. The capacitor acts to absorb the high voltage produced and stop it from interfering with other electronic devices, such as automotive radio and video equipment.

NOISE FILTERING Interference in a sound system or radio is usually due to alternating current (AC) voltage created somewhere in the vehicle, such as in the alternator. A capacitor does the following:

- Blocks the flow of direct current (DC)
- Allows alternating current (AC) to pass

By connecting a capacitor (condenser) to the power lead of the radio or sound system amplifier, the AC voltage passes through the capacitor to the ground where the other end of the capacitor is connected. Therefore, the capacitor provides a path for the AC without affecting the DC power circuit. ● **SEE FIGURE 10–8**.

Because a capacitor stores a voltage charge, it opposes or slows any voltage change in a circuit. Therefore, capacitors are often used as voltage "shock absorbers." You sometimes find a capacitor attached to one terminal of an ignition coil. In this application, the capacitor absorbs and dampens changes in ignition voltage that interferes with radio reception.

SUPPLEMENTAL POWER SOURCE A capacitor can be used to supply electrical power for short bursts in an audio

system to help drive the speakers. Woofers and subwoofers require a lot of electrical current that often cannot be delivered by the amplifier itself. ● **SEE FIGURE 10–9**.

TIMER CIRCUITS Capacitors are used in electronic circuits as part of a timer, to control window defoggers, interior lighting, pulse wipers, and automatic headlights. The capacitors store energy and are allowed to discharge through a resistance load. The greater the capacity of the capacitor and the higher the resistance load, the longer the time it takes for the capacitor to discharge.

COMPUTER MEMORY In most cases, the main memory of a computer is a high-speed random-access memory (RAM). One type of main memory called dynamic random-access memory (DRAM) is the most commonly used type of RAM. A single memory chip is made up of several million memory cells. In a DRAM chip, each memory cell consists of a capacitor. When a capacitor is electrically charged, it is said to store the binary digit 1, and when discharged, it represents 0.

CONDENSER MICROPHONES A microphone converts sound waves into an electric signal. All microphones have a diaphragm that vibrates as sound waves strike. The vibrating diaphragm in turn causes an electrical component to create an output flow of current at a frequency proportional to the sound waves. A condenser microphone uses a capacitor for this purpose.

In a condenser microphone, the diaphragm is the negatively charged plate of a charged capacitor. When a sound wave compresses the diaphragm, the diaphragm is moved closer to the positive plate. Decreasing the distance between the plates increases the electrostatic attraction between them, which results in a flow of current to the negative plate. As the diaphragm moves out in response to sound waves, it also moves further from the positive plate. Increasing the distance between the plates decreases the electrostatic attraction between them. This results in a flow of current back to the positive plate. These alternating flows of current provide weak electronic signals that travel to an amplifier and then to a loudspeaker.

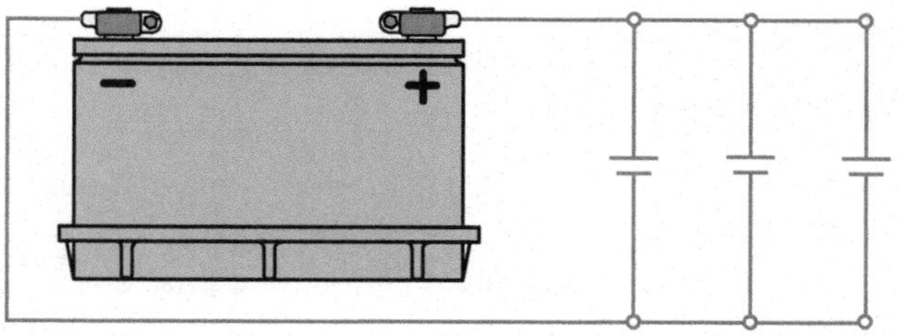

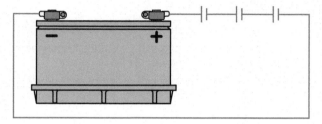

FIGURE 10–10 Capacitors in parallel effectively increase the capacitance.

CAPACITORS IN CIRCUITS

CAPACITORS IN PARALLEL CIRCUITS Capacitance can be increased in a circuit by connecting capacitors in parallel. For example, if a greater boost is needed for a sound system, then additional capacitors should be connected in parallel because their value adds together. ● **SEE FIGURE 10–10**.

Capacitance of a capacitor can be increased by increasing the size of its plates. Connecting two or more capacitors in parallel in effect increases plate size. Increasing plate area makes it possible to store more charge and, therefore, creates greater capacitance. To determine total capacitance of several parallel capacitors, simply add up their individual values. The following is the formula for calculating total capacitance in a circuit containing capacitors in parallel.

$$C_T = C_1 + C_2 + C_3 \ldots$$

For example, 220 µF + 220 µF = 400 µF when connected in parallel.

CAPACITORS IN SERIES CIRCUITS Capacitance in a circuit can be decreased by placing capacitors in series, as shown in ● **FIGURE 10–11**.

We know that capacitance of a capacitor can be decreased by placing the plates further apart. Connecting two or more capacitors in series in effect increases the distance between the plates and thickness of the dielectric, thereby decreasing the amount of capacitance.

Following is the formula for calculating total capacitance in a circuit containing two capacitors in series.

$$C_T = \frac{C_1 \times C_2}{C_1 + C_2}$$

FIGURE 10–11 Capacitors in series decrease the capacitance.

For example, $\dfrac{220 \ \mu F \times 220 \ \mu F}{220 \ \mu F + 220 \ \mu F} = \dfrac{48,400}{440} = 110 \ \mu F$

NOTE: Capacitors are often used to reduce radio interference or to improve the performance of a high-power sound system. Additional capacitance can, therefore, be added by attaching another capacitor in parallel.

SUPPRESSION CAPACITORS Capacitors are installed across many circuits and switching points to absorb voltage fluctuations. Among other applications, they are used across the following:

- The primary circuit of some electronic ignition modules
- The output terminal of most alternators
- The armature circuit of some electric motors

Radio choke coils reduce current fluctuations resulting from self-induction. They are often combined with capacitors to act as electromagnetic interference (EMI) filter circuits for windshield wiper and electric fuel pump motors. Filters also may be incorporated in wiring connectors.

SUMMARY

1. Capacitors (condensers) are used in numerous automotive applications.
2. Capacitors can block direct current and pass alternating current.
3. Capacitors are used to control radio-frequency interference and are installed in various electronic circuits to control unwanted noise.
4. Capacitors connected in series reduce the capacitance, whereas if connected in parallel increase the capacitance.

REVIEW QUESTIONS

1. How does a capacitor store an electrical charge?
2. How should two capacitors be electrically connected if greater capacitance is needed?
3. Where can a capacitor be used as a power source?
4. How can a capacitor be used as a noise filter?
5. In what units is capacitance measured?

CHAPTER QUIZ

1. A capacitor _____.
   a. stores electrons
   b. passes AC
   c. blocks DC
   d. All of the above

2. Capacitors are often used as "suppression capacitors". What does a capacitor suppress?
   a. Excessive current
   b. Voltage fluctuations
   c. Resistance
   d. Noise

3. Capacitors are commonly used as a _____.
   a. voltage supply
   b. timer
   c. noise filter
   d. All of the above

4. A charged capacitor acts like a _____.
   a. switch
   b. battery
   c. resistor
   d. coil

5. The unit of measurement for capacitor rating is the _____.
   a. ohm
   b. volt
   c. farad
   d. ampere

6. Two technicians are discussing the operation of a capacitor. Technician A says that a capacitor can create electricity. Technician B says that a capacitor can store electricity. Which technician is correct?
   a. Technician A only
   b. Technician B only
   c. Both Technicians A and B
   d. Neither Technician A nor B

7. Capacitors block the flow of _____ current but allow _____ current to pass.
   a. strong; weak
   b. AC; DC
   c. DC; AC
   d. weak; strong

8. To increase the capacity, what could be done?
   a. Connect another capacitor in series.
   b. Connect another capacitor in parallel.
   c. Add a resistor between two capacitors.
   d. Both a and b

9. A capacitor can be used in what components?
   a. Microphone
   b. Radio
   c. Speaker
   d. All of the above

10. A capacitor used for spike protection will normally be placed in _____ to the load or circuit.
    a. series
    b. parallel
    c. either series or parallel
    d. parallel with a resistor in series

chapter 11
MAGNETISM AND ELECTROMAGNETISM

FIGURE 11-1 A freely suspended natural magnet (lodestone) will point toward the magnetic north pole.

FIGURE 11-2 If a magnet breaks or is cracked, it becomes two weaker magnets.

FUNDAMENTALS OF MAGNETISM

DEFINITION **Magnetism** is a form of energy that is caused by the motion of electrons in some materials. It is recognized by the attraction it exerts on other materials. Like electricity, magnetism cannot be seen. It can be explained in theory, however, because it is possible to see the results of magnetism and recognize the actions that it causes. Magnetite is the most naturally occurring magnet. Naturally magnetized pieces of magnetite, called *lodestone,* will attract and hold small pieces of iron. ● **SEE FIGURE 11-1**.

Many other materials can be artificially magnetized to some degree, depending on their atomic structure. Soft iron is very easy to magnetize, whereas some materials, such as aluminum, glass, wood, and plastic, cannot be magnetized at all.

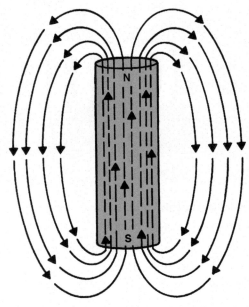

FIGURE 11-3 Magnetic lines of force leave the north pole and return to the south pole of a bar magnet.

TECH TIP

A Cracked Magnet Becomes Two Magnets

Magnets are commonly used in vehicle crankshaft, camshaft, and wheel speed sensors. If a magnet is struck and cracks or breaks, the result is two smaller-strength magnets. Because the strength of the magnetic field is reduced, the sensor output voltage is also reduced. A typical problem occurs when a magnetic crankshaft sensor becomes cracked, resulting in a no-start condition. Sometimes the cracked sensor works well enough to start an engine that is cranking at normal speeds, but will not work when the engine is cold. ● **SEE FIGURE 11-2**.

LINES OF FORCE The lines that create a field of force around a magnet are believed to be caused by the way groups of atoms are aligned in the magnetic material. In a bar magnet, the lines are concentrated at both ends of the bar and form closed, parallel loops in three dimensions around the magnet. Force does not flow along these lines the way electrical current flows, but the lines *do* have direction. They come out of the north end, or **pole**, of the magnet and enter at the other end. ● **SEE FIGURE 11-3**.

The opposite ends of a magnet are called its north and south poles. In reality, they should be called the "north seeking" and "south seeking" poles, because they seek the earth's North Pole and South Pole, respectively.

The more lines of force that are present, the stronger the magnet becomes. The magnetic lines of force, also called **magnetic flux** or **flux lines,** form a magnetic field. The terms *magnetic field, lines of force, flux,* and *flux lines* are used interchangeably.

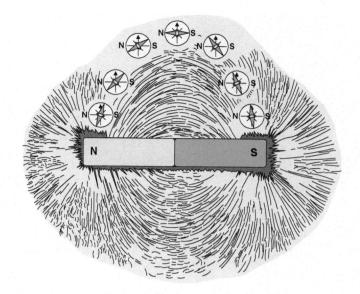

FIGURE 11–4 Iron filings and a compass can be used to observe the magnetic lines of force.

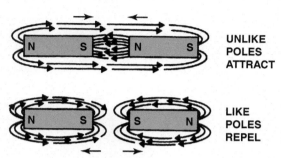

UNLIKE POLES ATTRACT

LIKE POLES REPEL

FIGURE 11–5 Magnetic poles behave like electrically charged particles—unlike poles attract and like poles repel.

Flux density refers to the number of flux lines per unit area. A magnetic field can be measured using a Gauss gauge, named for German scientist, Johann Carl Friedrick Gauss (1777–1855).

Magnetic lines of force can be seen by spreading fine iron filings or dust on a piece of paper laid on top of a magnet. A magnetic field can also be observed by using a compass. A compass is simply a thin magnet or magnetized iron needle balanced on a pivot. The needle will rotate to point toward the opposite pole of a magnet. The needle can be very sensitive to small magnetic fields. Because it is a small magnet, a compass usually has one north end (marked N) and one south end (marked S). ● **SEE FIGURE 11–4**.

MAGNETIC INDUCTION

If a piece of iron or steel is placed in a magnetic field, it will also become magnetized. This process of creating a magnet by using a magnetic field is called **magnetic induction.**

If the metal is then removed from the magnetic field, and it retains some magnetism, this is called **residual magnetism.**

ATTRACTING OR REPELLING

The poles of a magnet are called north (N) and south (S) because when a magnet is suspended freely, the poles tend to point toward the earth's North Pole and South Pole. Magnetic flux lines exit from the north pole and bend around to enter the south pole. An equal number of lines exit and enter, so magnetic force is equal at both

Magnetize a Steel Needle

A piece of steel can be magnetized by rubbing a magnet in one direction along the steel. This causes the atoms to line up in the steel, so it acts like a magnet. The steel often will not remain magnetized, whereas the true magnet is permanently magnetized.

When soft iron or steel is used, such as a paper clip, it will lose its magnetism quickly. The atoms in a magnetized needle can be disturbed by heating it or by dropping the needle on a hard object, which would cause the needle to lose its magnetism. Soft iron is used inside ignition coils because it will not keep its magnetism.

poles of a magnet. Flux lines are concentrated at the poles, and therefore, magnetic force (flux density) is stronger at the ends.

Magnetic poles behave like positively and negatively charged particles. When unlike poles are placed close together, the lines exit from one magnet and enter the other. The two magnets are pulled together by flux lines. If like poles are placed close together, the curving flux lines meet head-on, forcing the magnets apart. Therefore, like poles of a magnet repel and unlike poles attract. ● **SEE FIGURE 11–5**.

FIGURE 11–6 A crankshaft position sensor and reluctor (notched wheel).

CRANKSHAFT POSITION (CKP) SENSOR

RELUCTOR

PERMEABILITY Magnetic flux lines cannot be insulated. There is no known material through which magnetic force does not pass, if the force is strong enough. However, some materials allow the force to pass through more easily than others. This degree of passage is called **permeability.** Iron allows magnetic flux lines to pass through much more easily than air, so iron is highly permeable.

An example of this characteristic is the use of a reluctor wheel in magnetic-type camshaft position (CMP) and crankshaft position (CKP) sensors. The teeth on a reluctor cause the magnetic field to increase as each tooth gets closer to the sensor and decrease as the tooth moves away, thus creating an AC voltage signal. ● **SEE FIGURE 11–6.**

RELUCTANCE Although there is no absolute insulation for magnetism, certain materials resist the passage of magnetic force. This can be compared to resistance without an electrical circuit. Air does not allow easy passage, so air has a high **reluctance.** Magnetic flux lines tend to concentrate in permeable materials and avoid materials with high reluctance. As with electricity, magnetic force follows the path of least resistance.

ELECTROMAGNETISM

DEFINITION Scientists did not discover that current-carrying conductors also are surrounded by a magnetic field until 1820. These fields may be made many times stronger than those surrounding conventional magnets. Also, the magnetic field strength around a conductor may be controlled by changing the current.

- As current increases, more flux lines are created and the magnetic field expands.
- As current decreases, the magnetic field contracts. The magnetic field collapses when the current is shut off.
- The interaction and relationship between magnetism and electricity is known as electromagnetism.

CREATING AN ELECTROMAGNET An easy way to create an electromagnet is to wrap a nail with 20 turns of insulated wire and connect the ends to the terminals of a 1.5-volt dry cell battery. When energized, the nail will become a magnet and will be able to pick up tacks or other small steel objects.

STRAIGHT CONDUCTOR The magnetic field surrounding a straight, current-carrying conductor consists of several concentric cylinders of flux that are the length of the wire. The

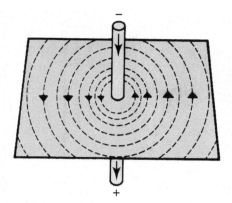

FIGURE 11-7 A magnetic field surrounds a straight, current-carrying conductor.

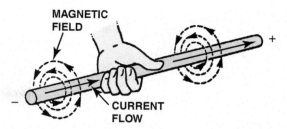

FIGURE 11-8 The left-hand rule for magnetic field direction is used with the electron flow theory.

FIGURE 11-9 The right-hand rule for magnetic field direction is used with the conventional theory of electron flow.

amount of current flow (amperes) determines how many flux lines (cylinders) there will be and how far out they extend from the surface of the wire. ● SEE FIGURE 11-7.

LEFT-HAND AND RIGHT-HAND RULES Magnetic flux cylinders have direction, just as the flux lines surrounding a bar magnet have direction. The **left-hand rule** is a simple way to determine this direction. When you grasp a conductor with your left hand so that your thumb points in the direction of electron flow (− to +) through the conductor, your fingers curl around the wire in the direction of the magnetic flux lines. ● SEE FIGURE 11-8.

Most automotive circuits use the conventional theory of current (+ to −) and, therefore, the right-hand rule is used to determine the direction of the magnetic flux lines. ● SEE FIGURE 11-9.

FIELD INTERACTION The cylinders of flux surrounding current-carrying conductors interact with other magnetic fields. In the following illustrations, the cross symbol (+) indicates current moving inward, or away from you. It represents the tail of an arrow. The dot symbol (•) represents an arrowhead and indicates current moving outward. If two conductors carry current in opposite directions, their magnetic fields also carry current in opposite directions (according to the left-hand rule). If they are placed side by side, then the opposing flux lines between the conductors create a strong magnetic field. Current-carrying conductors tend to move out of a strong field into a weak field, so the conductors move away from each other. ● SEE FIGURE 11-10.

If the two conductors carry current in the same direction, their fields are in the same direction. The flux lines between the two conductors cancel each other out, leaving a very weak field between them. The conductors are drawn into this weak field, and they tend to move toward each other.

FIGURE 11-10 Conductors with opposing magnetic fields will move apart into weaker fields.

TECH TIP

Electricity and Magnetism

Electricity and magnetism are closely related because any electrical current flowing through a conductor creates a magnetic field. Any conductor moving through a magnetic field creates an electrical current. This relationship can be summarized as follows:

- Electricity creates magnetism.
- Magnetism creates electricity.

From a service technician's point of view, this relationship is important because wires carrying current should always be routed as the factory intended to avoid causing interference with another circuit or electronic component. This is especially important when installing or servicing spark plug wires, which carry high voltages and can cause high electromagnetic interference.

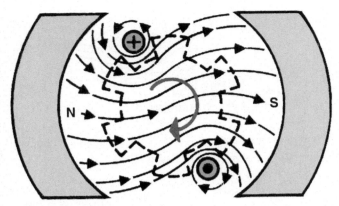

FIGURE 11–11 Electric motors use the interaction of magnetic fields to produce mechanical energy.

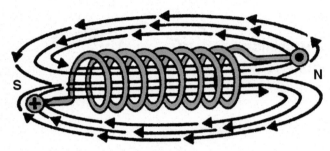

FIGURE 11–12 The magnetic lines of flux surrounding a coil look similar to those surrounding a bar magnet.

MOTOR PRINCIPLE Electric motors, such as vehicle starter motors, use this magnetic field interaction to convert electrical energy into mechanical energy. If two conductors carrying current in opposite directions are placed between strong north and south poles, the magnetic field of the conductor interacts with the magnetic fields of the poles. The counterclockwise field of the top conductor adds to the fields of the poles and creates a strong field beneath the conductor. The conductor then tries to move up to get out of this strong field. The clockwise field of the lower conductor adds to the field of the poles and creates a strong field above the conductor. The conductor then tries to move down to get out of this strong field. These forces cause the center of the motor, where the conductors are mounted, to turn clockwise. ● **SEE FIGURE 11–11**.

COIL CONDUCTOR If several loops of wire are made into a coil, the magnetic flux density is strengthened. Flux lines around a coil are the same as the flux lines around a bar magnet. ● **SEE FIGURE 11–12**.

They exit from the north pole and enter at the south pole. Use the left-hand rule to determine the north pole of a coil, as shown in ● **FIGURE 11–13**.

Grasp the coil with your left hand so that your fingers point in the direction of electron flow; your thumb will point toward the north pole of the coil.

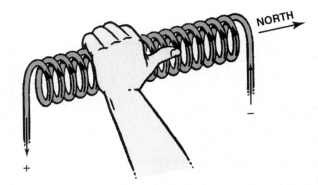

FIGURE 11–13 The left-hand rule for coils is shown.

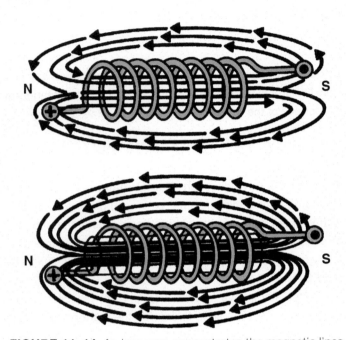

FIGURE 11–14 An iron core concentrates the magnetic lines of force surrounding a coil.

ELECTROMAGNETIC STRENGTH The magnetic field surrounding a current-carrying conductor can be strengthened (increased) in three ways:

■ Place a soft iron core in the center of the coil.

■ Increase the number of turns of wire in the coil.

■ Increase the current flow through the coil windings.

Because soft iron is highly permeable, magnetic flux lines pass through it easily. If a piece of soft iron is placed inside a coiled conductor, the flux lines concentrate in the iron core, rather than pass through the air, which is less permeable. The concentration of force greatly increases the strength of the magnetic field inside the coil. Increasing the number of turns in a coil and/or increasing the current flow through the coil results in greater field strength and is proportional to the number of turns. The magnetic field strength is often expressed in the units called **ampere-turns.** Coils with an iron core are called electromagnets. ● **SEE FIGURE 11–14**.

USES OF ELECTROMAGNETISM

RELAYS As mentioned in the previous chapter, a **relay** is a control device that allows a small amount of current to control a large amount of current in another circuit. A simple relay contains an electromagnetic coil in series with a battery and a switch. Near the electromagnet is a movable flat arm, called an *armature*, of some material that is attracted by a magnetic field. ● **SEE FIGURE 11–15**.

The armature pivots at one end and is held a small distance away from the electromagnet by a spring (or by the spring steel of the movable arm itself). A contact point, made of a good conductor, is attached to the free end of the armature. Another contact point is fixed a small distance away. The two contact points are wired in series with an electrical load and the battery.

When the switch is closed, the following occurs:

1. Current travels from the battery through a coil, creating an electromagnet.

2. The magnetic field created by the current attracts the armature, pulling it down until the contact points close.

3. Closing the contacts allows current in the heavy current circuit from the battery to the load.

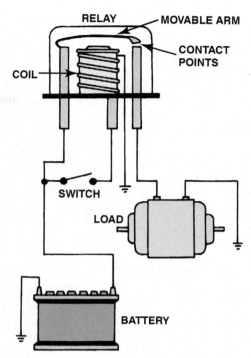

FIGURE 11–15 An electromagnetic switch that has a movable arm is referred to as a relay.

When the switch is open, the following occurs:

1. The electromagnet loses its magnetism when the current is shut off.

2. Spring pressure lifts the arm back up.

3. The heavy current circuit is broken by the opening of the contact points.

Relays may also be designed with normally closed contacts that open when current passes through the electromagnetic coil.

SOLENOID A solenoid is an example of an electromagnetic switch. A solenoid uses a movable core rather than a movable arm and is generally used in high-amperage applications. A solenoid can be a separate unit or attached to a starter, such as a starter solenoid. ● **SEE FIGURE 11–16**.

? FREQUENTLY ASKED QUESTION

Solenoid or Relay?

Often, either term is used to describe the same part in service information. ● **SEE CHART 11–1** for a summary of the differences.

	CONSTRUCTION	AMPERAGE RATING (AMPERE)	USES	CALLED IN SERVICE INFORMATION
Relay	Uses a movable arm Coil: 60–100 ohms requiring 0.12–0.20 ampere to energize	1–30	Lower current switching, lower cost, more commonly used	Electromagnetic switch or relay
Solenoid	Uses a movable core Coil(s): 0.2–0.6 ohm requiring 20–60 amperes to energize	30–400	Higher cost, used in starter motor circuits and other high-amperage applications	Solenoid, relay, or electromagnetic switch

CHART 11–1

Comparison between a relay and a solenoid.

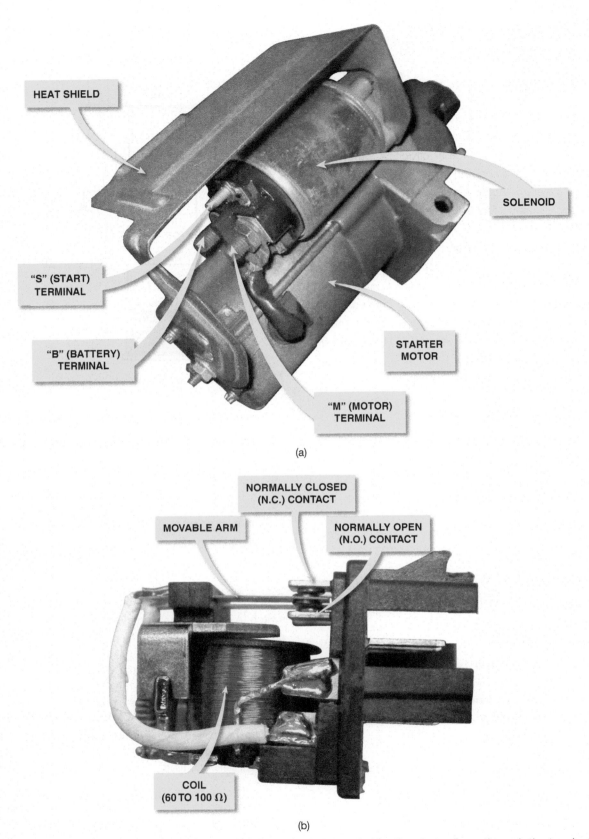

FIGURE 11–16 (a) A starter with attached solenoid. All of the current needed by the starter flows through the two large terminals of the solenoid and through the solenoid contacts inside. (b) A relay is designed to carry lower current compared to a solenoid and uses a movable arm.

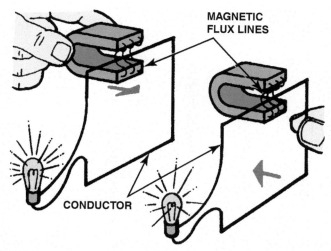

FIGURE 11–17 Voltage can be induced by the relative motion between a conductor and magnetic lines of force.

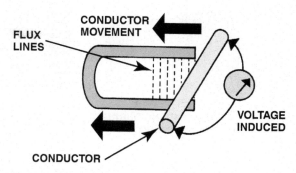

FIGURE 11–18 Maximum voltage is induced when conductors cut across the magnetic lines of force (flux lines) at a 90-degree angle.

ELECTROMAGNETIC INDUCTION

PRINCIPLES INVOLVED Electricity can be produced by using the relative movement of an electrical conductor and a magnetic field. The following three items are necessary to produce electricity (voltage) from magnetism:

1. Electrical conductor (usually a coil of wire)
2. Magnetic field
3. Movement of either the conductor or the magnetic field
   Therefore,

- Electricity creates magnetism.
- Magnetism can create electricity.

Magnetic flux lines create an electromotive force, or voltage, in a conductor if either the flux lines or the conductor is moving. This movement is called *relative motion*. This process is called induction, and the resulting electromotive force is called *induced voltage*. This creation of a voltage (electricity) in a conductor by a moving magnetic field is called electromagnetic induction. ● SEE FIGURE 11–17.

VOLTAGE INTENSITY Voltage is induced when a conductor cuts across magnetic flux lines. The amount of the voltage depends on the rate at which the flux lines are broken. The more flux lines that are broken per unit of time, the greater the induced voltage. If a single conductor breaks 1 million flux lines per second, 1 volt is induced.

There are four ways to increase induced voltage:

- Increase the strength of the magnetic field, so there are more flux lines.
- Increase the number of conductors that are breaking the flux lines.
- Increase the speed of the relative motion between the conductor and the flux lines so that more lines are broken per time unit.
- Increase the angle between the flux lines and the conductor to a maximum of 90 degrees. There is no voltage induced if the conductors move parallel to, and do not break, any flux lines.

Maximum voltage is induced if the conductors break flux lines at 90 degrees. Induced voltage varies proportionately at angles between 0 and 90 degrees. ● SEE FIGURE 11–18.

Voltage can be induced electromagnetically and can be measured. Induced voltage creates current. The direction of induced voltage (and the direction in which current moves) is called *polarity* and depends upon the direction of the flux lines, as well as the direction of relative motion.

LENZ'S LAW An induced current moves so that its magnetic field opposes the motion that induced the current. This principle is called **Lenz's law.** The relative motion of a conductor and a magnetic field is opposed by the magnetic field of the current it has induced.

SELF-INDUCTION When current begins to flow in a coil, the flux lines expand as the magnetic field forms and strengthens. As current increases, the flux lines continue to expand, cutting across the wires of the coil and actually inducing another voltage within the same coil. Following Lenz's law, this self-induced voltage tends to *oppose* the current that produces it. If

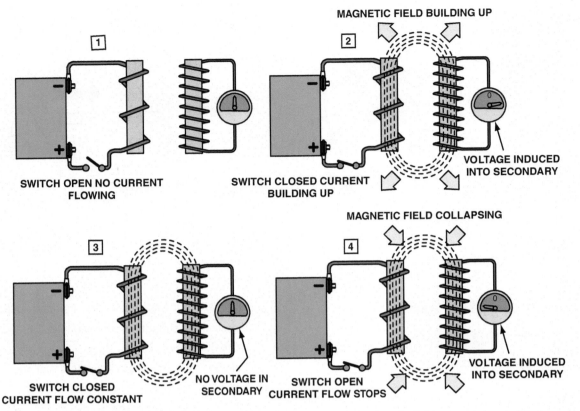

FIGURE 11–19 Mutual induction occurs when the expansion or collapse of a magnetic field around one coil induces a voltage in a second coil.

the current continues to increase, the second voltage opposes the increase. When the current stabilizes, the countervoltage is no longer induced because there are no more expanding flux lines (no relative motion). When current to the coil is shut off, the collapsing magnetic flux lines self-induce a voltage in the coil that tries to maintain the original current. The self-induced voltage *opposes* and *slows* the *decrease* in the original current. The self-induced voltage that opposes changes in current flow in an inductor is called **counter electromotive force (CEMF).**

MUTUAL INDUCTION When two coils are close together, energy may be transferred from one to the other by magnetic coupling called mutual induction. **Mutual induction** means that the expansion or collapse of the magnetic field around one coil induces a voltage in the second coil.

IGNITION COILS

IGNITION COIL WINDINGS Ignition coils use two windings and are wound on the same iron core:

- One coil winding is connected to a battery through a switch and is called the *primary winding*.

- The other coil winding is connected to an external circuit and is called the *secondary winding*.

When the switch is open, there is no current in the primary winding. There is no magnetic field and, therefore, no voltage in the secondary winding. When the switch is closed, current is introduced and a magnetic field builds up around both windings. The primary winding thus changes electrical energy from the battery into magnetic energy of the expanding field. As the field expands, it cuts across the secondary winding and induces a voltage in it. A meter connected to the secondary circuit shows current. ● **SEE FIGURE 11–19.**

When the magnetic field has expanded to its full strength, it remains steady as long as the same amount of current exists. The flux lines have stopped their cutting action. There is no relative motion and no voltage in the secondary winding, as shown on the meter.

When the switch is opened, primary current stops and the field collapses. As it does, flux lines cut across the secondary winding, but in the opposite direction. This induces a secondary voltage with current in the opposite direction, as shown on the meter.

Mutual induction is used in ignition coils. In an ignition coil, low-voltage primary current induces a very high

FIGURE 11–20 Some ignition coils are electrically connected, called "married" (top figure), whereas others use separated primary and secondary windings, called "divorced" (lower figure).

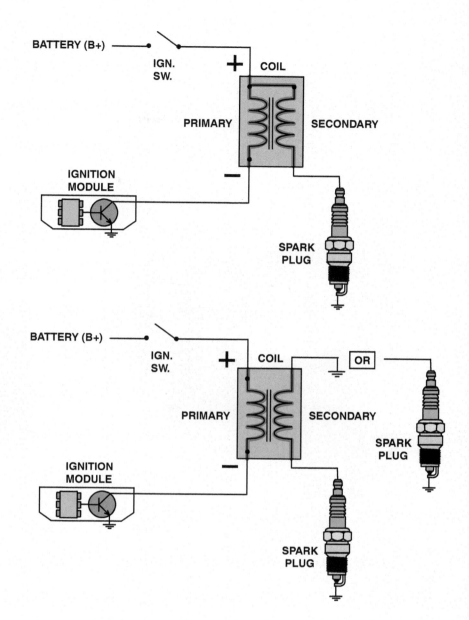

secondary voltage because of the different number of turns in the primary and secondary windings. Because the voltage is increased, an ignition coil is also called a *step-up transformer*.

■ **Electrically connected windings.** Many ignition coils contain two separate but electrically connected windings of copper wire. This type of coil is called a "married" type and is used in older distributor-type ignition systems and in many coil-on-plug (COP) designs.

■ **Electrically insulated windings.** Other coils are true transformers in which the primary and secondary windings are not electrically connected. This type of coil is often called a "divorced" type and is used in all waste-spark-type ignition systems.

● **SEE FIGURE 11–20**.

IGNITION COIL CONSTRUCTION The center of an ignition coil contains a core of laminated soft iron (thin strips of soft iron). This core increases the magnetic strength of the coil. Surrounding the laminated core are approximately 20,000 turns of fine wire (approximately 42 gauge). These windings are called the secondary coil windings. Surrounding the secondary windings are approximately 150 turns of heavy wire (approximately 21 gauge). These windings are called the primary coil windings. The secondary winding has about 100 times the number of turns of the primary winding, referred to as the **turns ratio** (approximately 100:1). In many coils, these windings are surrounded with a thin metal shield and insulating paper and placed into a metal container. The metal container and shield help retain the magnetic field produced in the coil windings. The primary and secondary windings produce heat because of the electrical resistance in

FIGURE 11–21 A GM waste-spark ignition coil showing the section of laminations that is shaped like the letter *E*. These mild steel laminations improve the efficiency of the coil.

FIGURE 11–22 The coil-on-plug (COP) design typically uses a bobbin-type coil.

the turns of wire. Many coils contain oil to help cool the ignition coil. Other coil designs include the following:

- **Air-cooled, epoxy-sealed *E* coil.** The *E* coil is so named because the laminated, soft iron core is E shaped, with the coil wire turns wrapped around the center "finger" of the *E* and the primary winding wrapped inside the secondary winding. ● **SEE FIGURE 11–21.**

- **Spool design.** Used mostly for coil-on-plug design, the coil windings are wrapped around a nylon or plastic spool or bobbin. ● **SEE FIGURE 11–22.**

IGNITION COIL OPERATION The negative terminal is attached to an **ignition control module (ICM, or igniter),** which opens and closes the primary ignition circuit by opening or closing the ground return path of the circuit. When the ignition

switch is on, voltage should be available at *both* the positive terminal and the negative terminal of the coil if the primary windings of the coil have continuity.

A spark is created by the following sequence of events:

- A magnetic field is created in the primary winding of the coil when there are 12 volts applied to the primary coil winding and the ignition control module grounds the other end on the coil.

- When the ignition control module (or powertrain control module) opens the ground circuit, the stored magnetic field collapses and creates a high-voltage pulse (up to 40,000 volts or more) in the secondary winding.

- The high-voltage pulse then flows to the spark plug and creates a spark at the ground electrode inside the engine that ignites the air–fuel mixture inside the cylinder.

ELECTROMAGNETIC INTERFERENCE

DEFINITION Until the advent of onboard computers, **electromagnetic interference (EMI)** was not a source of real concern to automotive engineers. The problem was mainly one of *radio-frequency interference* (RFI), caused primarily by the use of secondary ignition cables. Using spark plug wires that contained a high-resistance, nonmetallic core made of carbon, linen, or fiberglass strands impregnated with graphite mostly solved RFI from the secondary ignition system. RFI is a part of electromagnetic interference, which deals with interference that affects radio reception. All electronic devices used in vehicles are affected by EMI/RFI.

HOW EMI IS CREATED Whenever there is current in a conductor, an electromagnetic field is created. When current stops and starts, as in a spark plug cable or a switch that opens and closes, the field strength changes. Each time this happens, it creates an electromagnetic signal wave. If it happens rapidly enough, the resulting high-frequency signal waves, or EMI, interfere with radio and television transmission or with other electronic systems, such as those under the hood. This is an undesirable side effect of the phenomenon of electromagnetism.

Static electric charges caused by friction of the tires with the road, or the friction of engine drive belts contacting their pulleys, also produce EMI. Drive axles, driveshafts, and clutch or brake lining surfaces are other sources of static electric charges.

There are four ways of transmitting EMI, all of which can be found in a vehicle:

- Conductive coupling is actual physical contact through circuit conductors.

- Capacitive coupling is the transfer of energy from one circuit to another through an electrostatic field between two conductors.

- Inductive coupling is the transfer of energy from one circuit to another as the magnetic fields between two conductors form and collapse.

- Electromagnetic radiation is the transfer of energy by the use of radio waves from one circuit or component to another.

EMI SUPPRESSION DEVICES There are four general ways in which EMI is reduced:

- **Resistance suppression.** Adding resistance to a circuit to suppress RFI works only for high-voltage systems. This has been done by the use of resistance spark plug cables, resistor spark plugs, and the silicone grease used on the distributor cap and rotor of some electronic ignitions.

- **Suppression capacitors and coils.** Capacitors are installed across many circuits and switching points to absorb voltage fluctuations. Among other applications, they are used across the following:

  - The primary circuit of some electronic ignition modules

  - The output terminal of most alternators

  - The armature circuit of some electric motors

  Coils reduce current fluctuations resulting from self-induction. They are often combined with capacitors to act as EMI filter circuits for windshield wiper and electric fuel pump motors. Filters also may be incorporated in wiring connectors.

- **Shielding.** The circuits of onboard computers are protected to some degree from external electromagnetic waves by their metal housings.

- **Ground wires or straps.** Ground wires or braided straps between the engine and chassis of an automobile help suppress EMI conduction and radiation by providing a low-resistance circuit ground path. Such suppression ground straps are often installed between rubber-mounted components and body parts. On some models, ground straps are installed between body parts, such as between the hood and a fender panel, where no electrical circuit exists. The strap has no other job than to suppress EMI. Without it, the sheet-metal body and hood could function as a large capacitor. The space between the fender and hood could form an electrostatic field and couple with the computer circuits in the wiring harness routed near the fender panel. ● **SEE FIGURE 11–23**.

FIGURE 11–23 To help prevent underhood electromagnetic devices from interfering with the antenna input, it is important that all ground wires, including the one from this power antenna, be properly grounded.

 **TECH TIP**

Cell Phone Interference

A cellular phone emits a weak signal if it is turned on, even though it is not being used. This signal is picked up and tracked by cell phone towers. When the cell phone is called, it emits a stronger signal to notify the tower that it is on and capable of receiving a phone call. It is this "handshake" signal that can cause interference in the vehicle. Often this signal causes some static in the radio speakers even though the radio is off, but it can also cause a false antilock brake (ABS) trouble code to set. These signals from the cell phone create a voltage that is induced in the wires of the vehicle. Because the cell phone usually leaves with the customer, the service technician is often unable to verify the customer concern.

Remember, the interference occurs right *before* the cell phone rings. To fix the problem, check that all of the body-to-engine ground wires are clean and tight and add additional ground wires if needed.

SUMMARY

1. Most automotive electrical components use magnetism, the strength of which depends on both the amount of current (amperes) and the number of turns of wire of each electromagnet.
2. The strength of electromagnets is increased by using a soft iron core.
3. Voltage can be induced from one circuit to another.
4. Electricity creates magnetism and magnetism creates electricity.
5. Radio-frequency interference (RFI) is a part of electromagnetic interference (EMI).

REVIEW QUESTIONS

1. What is the relationship between electricity and magnetism?
2. What is the difference between mutual induction and self-induction?
3. What is the result if a magnet cracks?
4. How can EMI be reduced or controlled?
5. What units is a magnetic field strength measured?

CHAPTER QUIZ

1. Technician A says that magnetic lines of force can be seen by placing iron filings on a piece of paper and then holding them over a magnet. Technician B says that the effects of magnetic lines of force can be seen using a compass. Which technician is correct?
   a. Technician A only
   b. Technician B only
   c. Both Technicians A and B
   d. Neither Technician A nor B

2. Unlike magnetic poles _____, and like magnetic poles _____.
   a. repel; attract
   b. attract; repel
   c. repel; repel
   d. attract; attract

3. The conventional theory for current flow is being used to determine the direction of magnetic lines of force. Technician A says that the left-hand rule should be used. Technician B says that the right-hand rule should be used. Which technician is correct?
   a. Technician A only
   b. Technician B only
   c. Both Technicians A and B
   d. Neither Technician A nor B

4. Technician A says that a relay is an electromagnetic switch. Technician B says that a solenoid uses a movable core. Which technician is correct?
   a. Technician A only
   b. Technician B only
   c. Both Technicians A and B
   d. Neither Technician A nor B

5. Two technicians are discussing electromagnetic induction. Technician A says that the induced voltage can be increased if the speed is increased between the conductor and the magnetic lines of force. Technician B says that the induced voltage can be increased by increasing the strength of the magnetic field. Which technician is correct?
   a. Technician A only
   b. Technician B only
   c. Both Technicians A and B
   d. Neither Technician A nor B

6. An ignition coil operates using the principle(s) of _____.
   a. electromagnetic induction
   b. self-induction
   c. mutual induction
   d. All of the above

7. Electromagnetic interference can be reduced by using a _____.
   a. resistance
   b. capacitor
   c. coil
   d. Any of the above

8. An ignition coil is an example of a _____.
   a. solenoid
   b. step-down transformer
   c. step-up transformer
   d. relay

9. Magnetic field strength is measured in _____.
   a. ampere-turns
   b. flux
   c. density
   d. coil strength

10. Two technicians are discussing ignition coils. Technician A says that some ignition coils have the primary and secondary windings electrically connected. Technician B says that some coils have totally separate primary and secondary windings that are not electrically connected. Which technician is correct?
    a. Technician A only
    b. Technician B only
    c. Both Technicians A and B
    d. Neither Technician A nor B

chapter 12

ELECTRONIC FUNDAMENTALS

LEARNING OBJECTIVES

After studying this chapter, the reader will be able to:

1. Identify semiconductor components.

2. Explain necessary precautions when working with semiconductor circuits.

3. Describe how diodes and transistors work, and how to test them.

4. Identify the causes of failure of electronic components.

This chapter will help you prepare for the ASE Electrical/Electronic Systems (A6) certification test content area "A" (General Electrical/Electronic System Diagnosis).

Electronic components are the heart of computers. Knowing how electronic components work helps take the mystery out of automotive electronics.

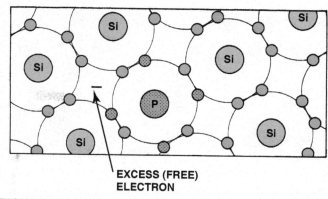

FIGURE 12–1 N-type material. Silicon (Si) doped with a material (such as phosphorus) with five electrons in the outer orbit results in an extra free electron.

SEMICONDUCTORS

DEFINITION Semiconductors are neither conductors nor insulators. The flow of electrical current is caused by the movement of electrons in materials known as conductors, having *fewer* than four electrons in their atom's outer orbit. Insulators contain *more* than four electrons in their outer orbit and cannot conduct electricity because their atomic structure is stable (no free electrons).

Semiconductors are materials that contain exactly four electrons in the outer orbit of their atom structure and are, therefore, neither good conductors nor good insulators.

EXAMPLES OF SEMICONDUCTORS Two examples of semiconductor materials are **germanium** and **silicon**, which have exactly four electrons in their valance ring and no free electrons to provide current flow. However, both of these semiconductor materials can be made to conduct current if another material is added to provide the necessary conditions for electron movement.

CONSTRUCTION When another material is added to a semiconductor material in very small amounts, it is called **doping**. The doping elements are called **impurities**; therefore, after their addition, the germanium and silicon are no longer considered *pure* elements. The material added to pure silicon or germanium to make it electrically conductive represents only one atom of impurity for every *100 million* atoms of the pure semiconductor material. The resulting atoms are still electrically *neutral,* because the number of electrons still equals the number of protons of the combined materials. These combined materials are classified into two groups depending on the number of electrons in the bonding between the two materials.

- N-type materials
- P-type materials

N-TYPE MATERIAL **N-type material** is silicon or germanium that is doped with an element such as *phosphorus*, *arsenic*, or *antimony*, each having five electrons in its outer orbit. These five electrons are combined with the four electrons of the silicon or germanium to total nine electrons. There is room for only eight electrons in the bonding between the semiconductor material and the doping material. This leaves extra electrons, and even though the material is still electrically neutral, these extra electrons tend to repel other electrons outside the material. ● **SEE FIGURE 12–1**.

P-TYPE MATERIAL **P-type material** is produced by doping silicon or germanium with the element *boron* or the element *indium*. These impurities have only three electrons in their outer shell and, when combined with the semiconductor material, result in a material with seven electrons, one electron *less* than is required for atom bonding. This lack of one electron makes the material able to attract electrons, even though the material still has a neutral charge. This material tends to attract electrons to fill the holes for the missing eighth electron in the bonding of the materials. ● **SEE FIGURE 12–2**.

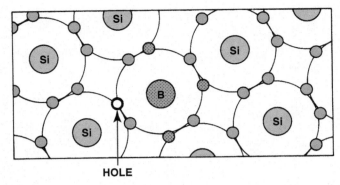

FIGURE 12–2 P-type material. Silicon (Si) doped with a material, such as boron (B), with three electrons in the outer orbit results in a hole capable of attracting an electron.

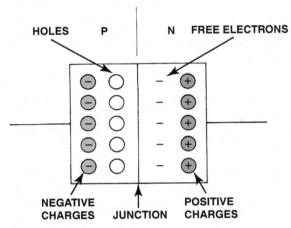

FIGURE 12–3 Unlike charges attract and the current carriers (electrons and holes) move toward the junction.

? **FREQUENTLY ASKED QUESTION**

What Is the Hole Theory?

Current flow is expressed as the movement of electrons from one atom to another. In semiconductor and electronic terms, the movement of electrons fills the holes of the P-type material. Therefore, as the holes are filled with electrons, the unfilled holes move opposite to the flow of the electrons. This concept of hole movement is called the **hole theory** of current flow. The holes move in the direction opposite to that of electron flow. For example, think of an egg carton, where if an egg is moved in one direction, the holes created move in the opposite direction. ● **SEE FIGURE 12–3.**

SUMMARY OF SEMICONDUCTORS

The following is a summary of semiconductor fundamentals:

1. The two types of semiconductor materials are P type and N type. N-type material contains extra electrons; P-type material contains holes due to missing electrons. The number of excess electrons in an N-type material must remain constant, and the number of holes in the P-type material must also remain constant. Because electrons are interchangeable, movement of electrons in or out of the material is possible to maintain a balanced material.

2. In P-type semiconductors, electrical conduction occurs mainly as a result of holes (absence of electrons). In N-type semiconductors, electrical conduction occurs mainly as a result of electrons (excess of electrons).

3. Hole movement results from the jumping of electrons into new positions.

4. Under the effect of a voltage applied to the semiconductor, electrons travel toward the positive terminal and holes move toward the negative terminal. The direction of hole current agrees with the conventional direction of current flow.

DIODES

CONSTRUCTION A **diode** is an electrical one-way check valve made by combining a P-type material and an N-type material. The word *diode* means "having two electrodes." Electrodes are electrical connections: The positive electrode is called the **anode**; the negative electrode is called the **cathode**. The point where the two types of materials join is called the **junction**. ● **SEE FIGURE 12–4.**

OPERATION The N-type material has one extra electron, which can flow into the P-type material. The P type requires electrons to fill its holes. If a battery's positive terminal (+) were connected to the diode's P-type material and negative (−) to the N-type material, then the electrons that left the N-type material and flowed into the P-type material to fill the holes would be

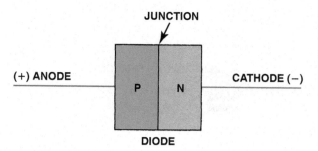

FIGURE 12–4 A diode is a component with P-type and N-type materials together. The negative electrode is called the cathode and the positive electrode is called the anode.

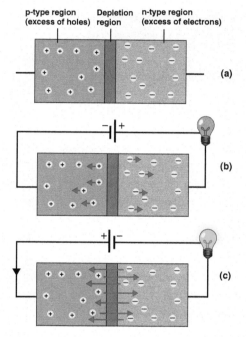

FIGURE 12–5 (a) A diode consist of P-type and N-type materials separated by a depletion region. (b) When connected to a voltage source in the reverse bias situation, the charge carriers are forced apart and no current flows across the depletion region. (c) When the diode is connected in the forward bias direction, the charge carriers are allowed to cross the depletion region and current can flow from the anode (+) to the cathode (-).

quickly replaced by the electron flow from the battery. Current flows through a forward-bias diode for the following reasons:

■ Electrons move toward the holes (P-type material).

■ Holes move toward the electrons (N-type material).

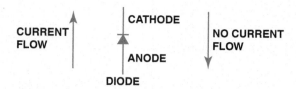

FIGURE 12–6 Diode symbol and electrode names. The stripe on one end of a diode represents the cathode end of the diode.

? FREQUENTLY ASKED QUESTION

What Is the Difference between Electricity and Electronics?

Electronics usually means that solid-state devices are used in the electrical circuits. Electricity as used in automotive applications usually means electrical current flow through resistance and loads without the use of diodes, transistors, or other electronic devices.

As a result, current would flow through the diode with low resistance. This condition is called **forward bias**.

If the battery connections were reversed and the positive side of the battery was connected to the N-type material, the electrons would be pulled toward the battery and away from the junction of the N-type and P-type materials. (Remember, unlike charges attract, whereas like charges repel.) Because electrical conduction requires the flow of electrons across the junction of the N-type and P-type materials and because the battery connections are actually reversed, the diode offers very high resistance to current flow. This condition is called **reverse bias**. ● **SEE FIGURE 12–5**.

Therefore, diodes allow current flow only when current of the correct polarity is connected to the circuit.

■ Diodes are used in alternators to control current flow in one direction, which changes the AC voltage generated into DC voltage.

■ Diodes are also used in computer controls, relays, air-conditioning circuits, and many other circuits to prevent possible damage due to reverse current flows that may be generated within the circuit. ● **SEE FIGURE 12–6**.

TECH TIP

"Burn In" to Be Sure

A common term heard in the electronic and computer industry is **burn in**, which means to operate an electronic device, such as a computer, for a period from several hours to several days.

Most electronic devices fail in infancy, or during the first few hours of operation. This early failure occurs if there is a manufacturing defect, especially at the P-N junction of any semiconductor device. The junction will usually fail after only a few operating cycles.

What does this information mean to the average person? When purchasing a personal or business computer, have the computer burned in before delivery. This step helps ensure that all of the circuits have survived infancy and that the chances of chip failure are greatly reduced. Purchasing sound or television equipment that has been on display may be a good value, because during its operation as a display model, the burn-in process has been completed. The automotive service technician should be aware that if a replacement electronic device fails shortly after installation, the problem may be a case of early electronic failure.

NOTE: Whenever there is a failure of a replacement part, the technician should always check for excessive voltage or heat to and around the problem component.

ZENER DIODES

CONSTRUCTION A **zener diode** is a specially constructed diode designed to operate with a reverse-bias current. Zener diodes were named in 1934 for their inventor, Clarence Melvin Zener, an American professor of physics.

OPERATION A zener diode acts as any diode in that it blocks reverse-bias current, but only up to a certain voltage. Above this certain voltage (called the *breakdown voltage* or the *zener region*), a zener diode will conduct current in the opposite direction without damage to the diode. A zener diode is heavily doped, and the reverse-bias voltage does not harm the material. The voltage drop across a zener diode remains practically the same before and after the breakdown voltage, and this factor makes a zener diode perfect for voltage regulation. Zener diodes can be constructed

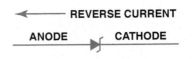

ZENER DIODE SYMBOL

FIGURE 12–7 A zener diode blocks current flow until a certain voltage is reached, then it permits current to flow.

for various breakdown voltages and can be used in a variety of automotive and electronic applications, especially for electronic voltage regulators used in the charging system. ● **SEE FIGURE 12–7.**

HIGH-VOLTAGE SPIKE PROTECTION

CLAMPING DIODES Diodes can be used as a high-voltage clamping device when the power (+) is connected to the cathode (−) of the diode. If a coil is pulsed on and off, a high-voltage spike is produced whenever the coil is turned off. To control and direct this possibly damaging high-voltage spike, a diode can be installed across the leads to the coil to redirect the high-voltage spike back through the coil windings to prevent possible damage to the rest of the vehicle's electrical or electronic circuits. A diode connected across the terminals of a coil to control voltage spikes is called a **clamping diode**. Clamping diodes can also be called **despiking** or **suppression diodes**. ● **SEE FIGURE 12–8.**

CLAMPING DIODE APPLICATION Diodes were first used on A/C compressor clutch coils at the same time electronic devices were first used. The diode was used to help prevent the high-voltage spike generated inside the A/C clutch coil from damaging delicate electronic circuits anywhere in the vehicle's electrical system. ● **SEE FIGURE 12–9.**

Because most automotive circuits eventually are electrically connected to each other in parallel, a high-voltage surge anywhere in the vehicle could damage electronic components in other circuits.

The circuits most likely to be affected by the high-voltage surge, if the diode fails, are the circuits controlling the operation of the A/C compressor clutch and any component that uses a coil, such as those of the blower motor and climate control units.

Many relays are equipped with a diode to prevent a voltage spike when the contact points open and the magnetic field in the coil winding collapses. ● **SEE FIGURE 12–10.**

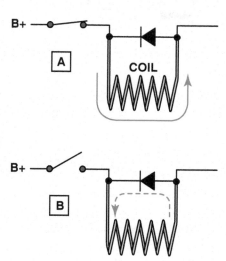

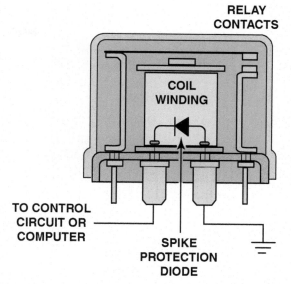

FIGURE 12–8 (a) Notice that when the coil is being energized, the diode is reverse biased and the current is blocked from passing through the diode. The current flows through the coil in the normal direction. (b) When the switch is opened, the magnetic field surrounding the coil collapses, producing a high-voltage surge in the reverse polarity of the applied voltage. This voltage surge forward biases the diode, and the surge is dissipated harmlessly back through the windings of the coil.

FIGURE 12–10 Spike protection diodes are commonly used in computer-controlled circuits to prevent damaging high-voltage surges that occur any time current flowing through a coil is stopped.

FIGURE 12–9 A diode connected to both terminals of the air-conditioning compressor clutch used to reduce the high-voltage spike that results when a coil (compressor clutch coil) is de-energized.

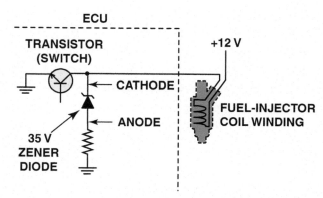

FIGURE 12–11 A zener diode is commonly used inside automotive computers to protect delicate electronic circuits from high-voltage spikes. A 35-volt zener diode will conduct any voltage spike higher than 35 volts resulting from the discharge of the fuel-injector coil safely to ground through a current-limiting resistor in series with the zener diode.

DESPIKING ZENER DIODES
Zener diodes can also be used to control high-voltage spikes and keep them from damaging delicate electronic circuits. Zener diodes are most commonly used in electronic fuel-injection circuits that control

the firing of the injectors. If clamping diodes were used in parallel with the injection coil, the resulting clamping action would tend to delay the closing of the fuel-injector nozzle. A zener diode is commonly used to clamp only the higher voltage portion of the resulting voltage spike without affecting the operation of the injector. ● **SEE FIGURE 12–11.**

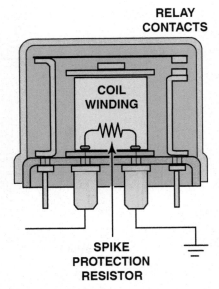

RELAY
CONTACTS

COIL
WINDING

SPIKE
PROTECTION
RESISTOR

FIGURE 12–12 A despiking resistor is used in many automotive applications to help prevent harmful high-voltage surges from being created when the magnetic field surrounding a coil collapses when the coil circuit is opened.

DESPIKING RESISTORS
All coils must use some protection against high-voltage spikes that occur when the voltage is removed from any coil. Instead of a diode installed in parallel with the coil windings, a resistor can be used, called a **spike protection resistor**. ● **SEE FIGURE 12–12.**

Resistors are preferred instead of diodes for voltage spike protection for two reasons:

Reason 1	Coils will usually fail when shorted rather than open, as this shorted condition results in greater current flow in the circuit. A diode installed in the reverse-bias direction cannot control this extra current, whereas a resistor in parallel can help reduce potentially damaging current flow if the coil becomes shorted.
Reason 2	The protective diode can also fail, and diodes usually fail by shorting before they blow open. If a diode becomes shorted, excessive current can flow through the coil circuit, perhaps causing damage. A resistor usually fails open and, therefore, even in failure could not in itself cause a problem.

Resistors on coils are often used in relays and in climate-control circuit solenoids to control vacuum to the various air management system doors, as well as other electronically controlled appliances.

SPECIFICATIONS Most diodes are rated according to the following:

- Maximum current flow in the forward-bias direction. Diodes are sized and rated according to the amount of current they are designed to handle in the forward-bias direction. This rating is normally from 1 to 5 amperes for most automotive applications.

- This rating of resistance to reverse-bias voltage is called the **peak inverse voltage (PIV)** rating, or the **peak reverse voltage (PRV)** rating. It is important that the service technician specifies and uses only a replacement diode that has the same or a higher rating than specified by the vehicle manufacturer for both amperage and PIV rating. Typical 1 ampere diodes use an industry numbering code that indicates the PIV rating. For example,

  1N 4001-50 V PIV

  1N 4002-100 V PIV

  1N 4003-200 V PIV (most commonly used)

  1N 4004-400 V PIV

  1N 4005-600 V PIV

- "1N" means that the diode has one P-N junction. A higher rating diode can be used with no problems (except for slightly higher cost, even though the highest rated diode generally costs less than $1). Never substitute a *lower* rated diode than is specified.

DIODE VOLTAGE DROP The voltage drop across a diode is about the same voltage as that required to forward bias the diode. If the diode is made from germanium, the forward voltage is 0.3 to 0.5 volt. If the diode is made from silicon, the forward voltage is 0.5 to 0.7 volt.

NOTE: When diodes are tested using a digital multimeter, the meter will display the voltage drop across the P-N junction (about 0.5 to 0.7 volt) when the meter is set to the *diode-check* position.

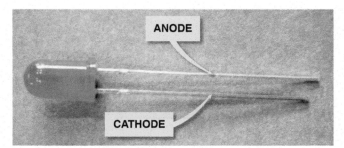

FIGURE 12–13 A typical light-emitting diode (LED). This particular LED is designed with a built-in resistor so that 12-volts DC may be applied directly to the leads without an external resistor. Normally a 300 to 500 ohm, 0.5-watt resistor is required to be attached in series with the LED, to control current flow to about 0.020 ampere (20 milliamperes) or damage to the P-N junction may occur.

LIGHT-EMITTING DIODES

OPERATION All diodes radiate some energy during normal operation. Most diodes radiate heat because of the junction barrier voltage drop (typically 0.6 volt for silicon diodes). A **Light-emitting diode (LED)** radiate light when current flows through the diode in the forward-bias direction. ● **SEE FIGURE 12–13**.

The forward-bias voltage required for an LED ranges between 1.5 and 2.2 volts.

An LED will only light if the voltage at the anode (positive electrode) is at least 1.5 to 2.2 volts higher than the voltage at the cathode (negative electrode).

NEED FOR CURRENT LIMITING If an LED were connected across a 12-volt automotive battery, the LED would light brightly, but only for a second or two. Excessive current (amperes) that flows across the P-N junction of any electronic device can destroy the junction. A resistor *must* be connected in series with every diode (including LEDs) to control current flow across the P-N junction. This protection should include the following:

1. The value of the resistor should be from 300 to 500 ohms for each P-N junction. Commonly available resistors in this range include 470, 390, and 330 ohm resistors.

2. The resistors can be connected to either the anode or the cathode end. (Polarity of the resistor does not matter.) Current flows through the LED in series with the resistor, and the resistor will control the current flow through the LED regardless of its position in the circuit.

3. Resistors protecting diodes can be actual resistors or other current-limiting loads, such as lamps or coils. With the current-limiting devices to control the current, the average LED will require about 20 to 30 milliamperes (mA), or 0.020 to 0.030 ampere.

? FREQUENTLY ASKED QUESTION

How Does an LED Emit Light?

An LED contains a chip that houses P-type and N-type materials. The junction between these regions acts as a barrier to the flow of electrons between the two materials. When a voltage of 1.5 to 2.2 volts is applied to the correct polarity, current will flow across the junction. As the electrons enter the P-type material, it combines with the holes in the material and releases energy in the form of light (called **photons**). The intensity and color the light produces depends on materials used in the manufacture of the semiconductor.

LEDs are very efficient compared to conventional incandescent bulbs, which depend on heat to create light. LEDs generate very little heat, with most of the energy consumed converted directly into light. LEDs are reliable and are being used for taillights, brake lights, daytime running lights, and headlights in some vehicles.

PHOTODIODES

PURPOSE AND FUNCTION All semiconductor P-N junctions emit energy, mostly in the form of heat or light such as with an LED. In fact, if an LED is exposed to bright light, a voltage potential is established between the anode and the cathode. **Photodiodes** are specially constructed to respond to various wavelengths of light with a "window" built into the housing. ● **SEE FIGURE 12–14**.

Photodiodes are frequently used in steering wheel controls for transmitting tuning, volume, and other information from the steering wheel to the data link and the unit being controlled. If several photodiodes are placed on the steering column end and LEDs or phototransistors are placed on the steering wheel side, then data can be transmitted between the two moving points without the interference that could be caused by physical contact types of units.

CONSTRUCTION A photodiode is sensitive to light. When light energy strikes the diode, electrons are released and the diode will conduct in the forward-bias direction. (The light energy is used to overcome the barrier voltage.)

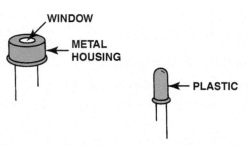

FIGURE 12–14 Typical photodiodes. They are usually built into a plastic housing so that the photodiode itself may not be visible.

FIGURE 12–15 Symbol for a photodiode. The arrows represent light striking the P-N junction of the photodiode.

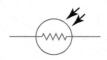

FIGURE 12–16 Either symbol may be used to represent a photoresistor.

The resistance across the photodiode decreases as the intensity of the light increases. This characteristic makes the photodiode a useful electronic device for controlling some automotive lighting systems, such as automatic headlights. The symbol for a photodiode is shown in ● **FIGURE 12–15.**

PHOTORESISTORS

A **photoresistor** is a semiconductor material (usually cadmium sulfide) that changes resistance with the presence or absence of light.

Dark = High resistance

Light = Low resistance

Because resistance is reduced when the photoresistor is exposed to light, the photoresistor can be used to control headlight dimmer relays and automotive headlights. ● **SEE FIGURE 12–16.**

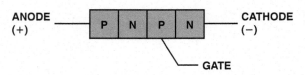

FIGURE 12–17 Symbol and terminal identification of an SCR.

SILICON-CONTROLLED RECTIFIERS

CONSTRUCTION A **silicon-controlled rectifier (SCR)** is commonly used in the electronic circuits of various automotive applications. An SCR is a semiconductor device that looks like two diodes connected end to end. ● **SEE FIGURE 12–17.**

If the anode is connected to a higher voltage source than the cathode in a circuit, no current will flow as would occur with a diode. If, however, a positive voltage source is connected to the gate of the SCR, then current can flow from anode to cathode with a typical voltage drop of 1.2 volts (double the voltage drop of a typical diode, at 0.6 volt).

Voltage applied to the gate is used to turn the SCR on. However, if the voltage source at the gate is shut off, the current will still continue to flow through the SCR until the source current is stopped.

USES OF AN SCR SCRs can be used to construct a circuit for a **center high-mounted stoplight (CHMSL)**. If this third stoplight were wired into either the left- or the right-side brake light circuit, the CHMSL would also flash whenever the turn signals were used for the side that was connected to the CHMSL. When two SCRs are used, both brake lights must be activated to supply current to the CHMSL. The current to the CHMSL is shut off when both SCRs lose their power source (when the brake pedal is released, which stops the current flow to the brake lights). ● **SEE FIGURE 12–18.**

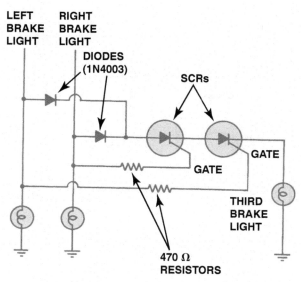

FIGURE 12–18 Wiring diagram for a center high-mounted stoplight (CHMSL) using SCRs.

	COPPER WIRE	NTC THERMISTOR
Cold	Lower resistance	Higher resistance
Hot	Higher resistance	Lower resistance

CHART 12–1

The resistance changes opposite to that of a copper wire with changes in temperature.

THERMISTORS

CONSTRUCTION A **thermistor** is a semiconductor material, such as silicon that has been doped to provide a given resistance. When the thermistor is heated, the electrons within the crystal gain energy and electrons are released. This means that a thermistor actually produces a small voltage when heated. If voltage is applied to a thermistor, its resistance decreases because the thermistor itself is acting as a current carrier rather than as a resistor at higher temperatures.

USES OF THERMISTORS A thermistor is commonly used as a temperature-sensing device for coolant temperature and intake manifold air temperature. Because thermistors operate in a manner opposite to that of a typical conductor, they are called **negative temperature coefficient (NTC)** thermistors; their resistance decreases as the temperature increases. ● **SEE CHART 12–1.**

Thermistor symbols are shown in ● **FIGURE 12–19.**

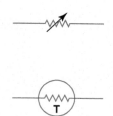

FIGURE 12–19 Symbols used to represent a thermistor.

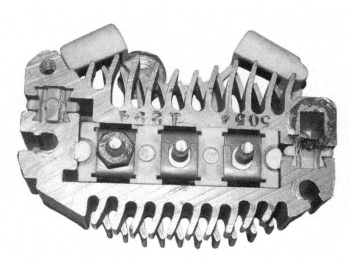

FIGURE 12–20 This rectifier bridge contains six diodes; the three on each side are mounted in an aluminum-finned unit to help keep the diode cool during alternator operation.

RECTIFIER BRIDGES

DEFINITION The word *rectify* means "to set straight"; therefore, a rectifier is an electronic device (such as a diode) used to convert a changing voltage into a straight or constant voltage. A **rectifier bridge** is a group of diodes that is used to change alternating current (AC) into direct current (DC). A rectifier bridge is used in alternators to rectify the AC voltage produced in the stator (stationary windings) of the alternator into DC voltage. These rectifier bridges contain six diodes: one pair of diodes (one positive and one negative) for each of the three stator windings. ● **SEE FIGURE 12–20.**

TRANSISTORS

PURPOSE AND FUNCTION

A **transistor** is a semiconductor device that can perform the following electrical functions:

1. Act as an electrical switch in a circuit
2. Act as an amplifier of current in a circuit
3. Regulate the current in a circuit

The word *transistor,* derived from the words *transfer* and *resistor,* is used to describe the transfer of current across a resistor. A transistor is made of three alternating sections or layers of P-type and N-type materials. This type of transistor is usually called a **bipolar transistor**.

CONSTRUCTION

A transistor that has P-type material on each end with N-type material in the center is called a **PNP transistor**. Another type, with the exact opposite arrangement, is called an **NPN transistor**.

The material at one end of a transistor is called the **emitter** and the material at the other end is called the **collector**. The **base** is in the center and the voltage applied to the base is used to control current through a transistor.

TRANSISTOR SYMBOLS

All transistor symbols contain an arrow indicating the emitter part of the transistor. The arrow points in the direction of current flow (conventional theory).

When an arrowhead appears in any semiconductor symbol, it stands for a P-N junction and it points from the P-type material toward the N-type material. The arrow on a transistor is always attached to the *emitter* side of the transistor. ● **SEE FIGURE 12–21**.

HOW A TRANSISTOR WORKS

A transistor is similar to two back-to-back diodes that can conduct current in only one direction. As in a diode, N-type material can conduct electricity by means of its supply of free electrons, and P-type material conducts by means of its supply of positive holes.

A transistor will allow current flow if the electrical conditions allow it to switch on, in a manner similar to the working of an electromagnetic relay. The electrical conditions are determined, or switched, by means of the base, or *B*. The base will carry current only when the proper voltage and polarity are applied. The main circuit current flow travels through the other two parts of the transistor: the emitter *E* and the collector *C*. ● **SEE FIGURE 12–22**.

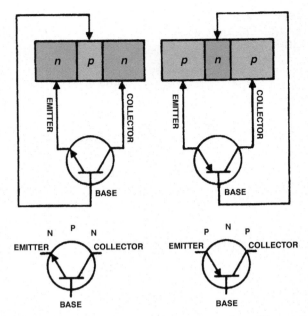

FIGURE 12–21 Basic transistor operation. A small current flowing through the base and emitter of the transistor turns on the transistor and permits a higher amperage current to flow from the collector and the emitter.

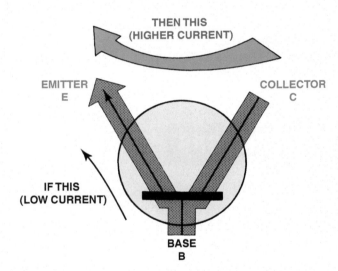

FIGURE 12–22 Basic transistor operation. A small current flowing through the base and emitter of the transistor turns on the transistor and permits a higher amperage current to flow from the collector and the emitter.

If the base current is turned off or on, the current flow from collector to emitter is turned off or on. The current controlling the base is called the control current. The control current must be high enough to switch the transistor on or off. (This control voltage, called the **threshold voltage**, must be above approximately

	RELAY	TRANSISTOR
Low-current circuit	Coil (terminals 85 and 86)	Base and emitter
High-current circuit	Contacts terminals 30 and 87	Collector and emitter

CHART 12–2

Comparison between the control (low-current) and high-current circuits of a transistor compared to a mechanical relay.

FREQUENTLY ASKED QUESTION

Is a Transistor Similar to a Relay?

Yes, in many cases a transistor is similar to a relay.

Both use a low current to control a higher current circuit. ● **SEE CHART 12–2**.

A relay can only be on or off. A transistor can provide a variable output if the base is supplied a variable current input.

0.3 volt for germanium and 0.6 volt for silicon transistors.) This control current can also "throttle" or regulate the main circuit, in a manner similar to the operation of a water faucet.

HOW A TRANSISTOR AMPLIFIES A transistor can amplify a signal if the signal is strong enough to trigger the base of a transistor on and off. The resulting on–off current flow through the transistor can be connected to a higher powered electrical circuit. This results in a higher-powered circuit being controlled by a lower-powered circuit. This low-powered circuit's cycling is exactly duplicated in the higher-powered circuit, and therefore, any transistor can be used to amplify a signal. However, because some transistors are better than others for amplification, specialized types of transistors are used for each specialized circuit function.

FREQUENTLY ASKED QUESTION

What Does the Arrow Mean on a Transistor Symbol?

The arrow on a transistor symbol is always on the emitter and points toward the N-type material. The arrow on a diode also points toward the N-type material. To know which type of transistor is being shown, note which direction the arrow points.

• PNP: pointing in
• NPN: not pointing in

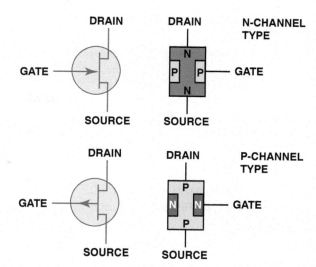

FIGURE 12–23 The three terminals of a field-effect transistor (FET) are called the source, gate, and drain.

FIELD-EFFECT TRANSISTORS

Field-effect transistors (FETs) have been used in most automotive applications since the mid-1980s. They use less electrical current and rely mostly on the strength of a small voltage signal to control the output. The parts of a typical FET include the *source, gate,* and *drain.* ● **SEE FIGURE 12–23**.

Many field-effect transistors are constructed of metal oxide semiconductor (MOS) materials, called **MOSFETs**. MOSFETs are highly sensitive to static electricity and can be easily damaged if exposed to excessive current or high-voltage surges (spikes). Most automotive electronic circuits use MOSFETs, which explains why it is vital for the service technician to use caution to avoid doing anything that could result in a high-voltage spike and perhaps destroy an expensive computer module. Some vehicle manufacturers recommend that technicians wear an antistatic wristband when working with modules that contain MOSFETs. Always follow the vehicle manufacturer's instructions found in service information to avoid damaging electronic modules or circuits.

PHOTOTRANSISTORS

Similar in operation to a photodiode, a **phototransistor** uses light energy to turn on the base of a transistor. A phototransistor is an NPN transistor that has a large exposed base area to permit light to act as the control for the transistor. Therefore, a

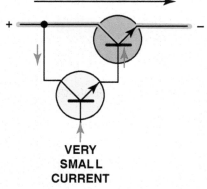

VERY LARGE CURRENT

VERY
SMALL
CURRENT

FIGURE 12–24 A Darlington pair consists of two transistors wired together, allowing for a very small current to control a larger current flow circuit.

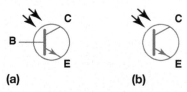

(a)   (b)

FIGURE 12–25 Symbols for a phototransistor. (a) This symbol uses the line for the base; (b) this symbol does not.

 FREQUENTLY ASKED QUESTION

What Is a Darlington Pair?

A **Darlington pair** consists of two transistors wired together. This arrangement permits a very small current flow to control a large current flow. The Darlington pair is named for Sidney Darlington, an American physicist for Bell Laboratories from 1929 to 1971. Darlington amplifier circuits are commonly used in electronic ignition systems, computer engine control circuits, and many other electronic applications. ● **SEE FIGURE 12–24.**

phototransistor may or may not have a base lead. If not, then it has only a collector and emitter lead. When the phototransistor is connected to a powered circuit, the light intensity is amplified by the gain of the transistor. Phototransistors, along with photo diodes, are frequently used in steering wheel controls. ● **SEE FIGURE 12–25.**

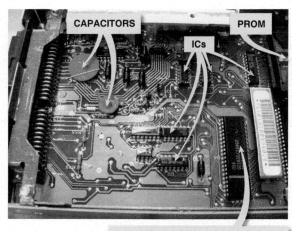

FIGURE 12–26 A typical automotive computer with the case removed to show all of the various electronic devices and integrated circuits (ICs). The CPU is an example of a DIP chip and the large red and orange devices are ceramic capacitors.

INTEGRATED CIRCUITS

PURPOSE AND FUNCTION Solid-state components are used in many electronic semiconductors and/or circuits. They are called "solid state" because they have no moving parts, just higher or lower voltage levels within the circuit. Discrete (individual) diodes, transistors, and other semiconductor devices were often used to construct early electronic ignition and electronic voltage regulators. Newer style electronic devices use the same components, but they are now combined (integrated) into one group of circuits, and are thus called an **integrated circuit (IC)**.

CONSTRUCTION Integrated circuits are usually encased in a plastic housing called a CHIP with two rows of inline pins. This arrangement is called the **dual inline pins (DIP)** chips. ● **SEE FIGURE 12–26.**

Therefore, most computer circuits are housed as an integrated circuit in a DIP chip.

HEAT SINK **Heat sink** is a term used to describe any area around an electronic component that, because of its shape or design, can conduct damaging heat away from electronic parts. Examples of heat sinks include the following:

What Causes a Transistor or Diode to Blow?

Every automotive diode and transistor is designed to operate within certain voltage and amperage ranges for individual applications. For example, transistors used for switching are designed and constructed differently from transistors used for amplifying signals.

Because each electronic component is designed to operate satisfactorily for its particular application, any severe change in operating current (amperes), voltage, or heat can destroy the *junction*. This failure can cause either an open circuit (no current flows) or a short (current flows through the component all the time when the component should be blocking the current flow).

1. Ribbed electronic ignition control units
2. Cooling slits and cooling fan attached to an alternator
3. Special heat-conducting grease under the electronic ignition module in General Motors HEI distributor ignition systems and other electronic systems

Heat sinks are necessary to prevent damage to diodes, transistors, and other electronic components due to heat buildup. Excessive heat can damage the junction between the N-type and P-type materials used in diodes and transistors.

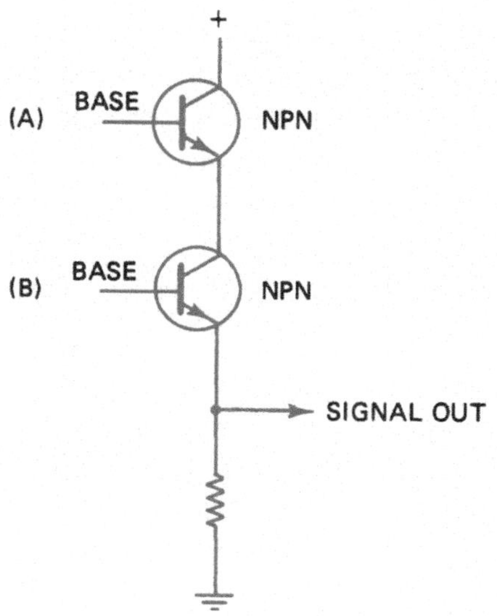

FIGURE 12–27 Typical AND gate circuit using two transistors. The emitter is always the line with the arrow. Notice that both transistors must be turned on before there is voltage present at the point labeled "signal out."

TRANSISTOR GATES

PURPOSE AND FUNCTION Knowledge of the basic operation of electronic gates is important in understanding how computers work. A gate is an electronic circuit whose output depends on the location and voltage of two inputs.

CONSTRUCTION Whether a transistor is on or off depends on the voltage at the base of the transistor. For the transistor to turn on, a voltage difference between the base of the transmitter and the emitter should be at least a 0.6 volt. Most electronic and computer circuits use 5 volts as a power source. If two transistors are wired together, several different outputs can be received depending on how the two transistors are wired. ● **SEE FIGURE 12–27**.

OPERATION If the voltage at A is higher than that of the emitter, the top transistor is turned on; however, the bottom transistor is off unless the voltage at B is also higher. If both transistors are turned on, the output signal voltage will be high. If only one of the two transistors is on, the output will be zero (off or no voltage). Because it requires both A and B to be on to result in a voltage output, this circuit is called an *AND gate*. In other words, both transistors have to be on before the gate opens and allows a voltage output. Other types of gates can be constructed using various connections to the two transistors. For example,

> **AND gate.** Requires both transistors to be on to obtain an output.
>
> **OR gate.** Requires either transistor to be on to obtain an output.
>
> **NAND (NOT-AND) gate.** Output is on unless both transistors are on.
>
> **NOR (NOT-OR) gate.** Output is on only when both transistors are off.

What Are Logic Highs and Lows?

All computer circuits and most electronic circuits (such as gates) use various combinations of high and low voltages. High voltages are typically those above 5 volts, and low is generally considered zero (ground). However, high voltages do not *have* to begin at 5 volts. *High, or the number 1, to a computer is the presence of voltage above a certain level.* For example, a circuit could be constructed where any voltage higher than 3.8 volts would be considered high. *Low, or the number 0, to a computer is the absence of voltage or a voltage lower than a certain value.* For example, a voltage of 0.62 volt may be considered low. Various associated names and terms can be summarized.

- Logic low = Low voltage = Number 0 = Reference low
- Logic high = Higher voltage = Number 1 = Reference high

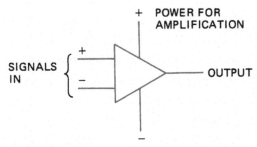

FIGURE 12–28 Symbol for an operational amplifier (op-amp).

OPERATIONAL AMPLIFIERS

Operational amplifiers (op-amps) are used in circuits to control and amplify digital signals. Op-amps are frequently used for motor control for airflow door operation as part of the climate control system. Op-amps can provide the proper voltage polarity and current (amperes) to control the direction of permanent magnetic (PM) motors. The symbol for an op-amp is shown in ● **FIGURE 12–28**.

ELECTRONIC COMPONENT FAILURE CAUSES

Gates represent logic circuits that can be constructed so that the output depends on the voltage (on or off; high or low) of the inputs to the bases of transistors. Their inputs can come from sensors or other circuits that monitor sensors, and their outputs can be used to operate an output device if amplified and controlled by other circuits. For example, the blower motor will be commanded on when the following events occur, to cause the control module to turn it on:

1. The ignition must be on (input).
2. The air conditioning is commanded on.
3. The engine coolant temperature is within a predetermined limit.

If all of these conditions are met, then the control module will command the blower motor on. If any of the input signals are incorrect, the control module will not be able to perform the correct command.

Electronic components, such as electronic ignition modules, electronic voltage regulators, onboard computers, and any other electronic circuit are generally quite reliable; however, failure can occur. Frequent causes of premature failure include the following:

- **Poor connections.** It has been estimated that most engine computers returned as defective have simply had poor connections at the wiring harness terminal ends. These faults are often intermittent and hard to find.

  NOTE: When cleaning electronic contacts, use a pencil eraser. This cleans the contacts without harming the thin, protective coating used on most electronic terminals.

- **Heat.** The operation and resistance of electronic components and circuits are affected by heat. Electronic components should be kept as cool as possible and never hotter than 260°F (127°C).

- **Voltage spikes.** A high-voltage spike can literally burn a hole through semiconductor material. The source of these high-voltage spikes is often the discharge of a coil without proper (or with defective) despiking protection. A poor electrical connection at the battery or other major electrical connection can cause high-voltage spikes to occur, because the *entire wiring harness creates its own magnetic field*, similar to that formed around a coil. If the connection is loose and momentary loss of contact occurs, a high-voltage surge can occur through the entire electrical system. To help prevent this type of damage, ensure that all electrical connections, including grounds, are properly clean and tight.

CAUTION: One of the major causes of electronic failure occurs during jump starting a vehicle. Always check that the ignition switch is off on both vehicles when making the connection. Always double-check that the correct battery polarity (+ to + and − to −) is being performed.

■ **Excessive current.** All electronic circuits are designed to operate within a designated range of current (amperes). If a solenoid or relay is controlled by a computer circuit, the resistance of that solenoid or relay becomes part of that control circuit. If a coil winding inside the solenoid or relay becomes shorted, the resulting lower resistance will increase the current through the circuit. Even though individual components are used with current-limiting resistors in series, the coil winding resistance is also used as a current-control component in the circuit. If a computer fails, always measure the resistance across all computer-controlled relays and solenoids. The resistance should be within specifications (generally *over* 20 ohms) for each component that is computer controlled.

NOTE: Some computer-controlled solenoids are pulsed on and off rapidly. This type of solenoid is used in many electronically shifted transmissions. Their resistance is about half of the resistance of a simple on–off solenoid, usually between 10 and 15 ohms. Because the computer controls the on-time of the solenoid, the solenoid and its circuit control are called pulse-width modulated (PWM).

RED LED STARTS TO FLASH WHENEVER IGNITION IS TURNED OFF

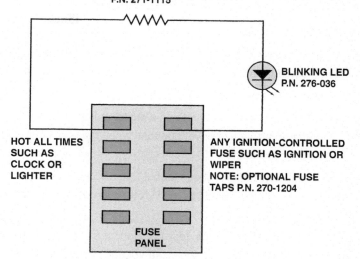

470 Ω 0.5 WATT RESISTOR
P.N. 271-1115

BLINKING LED
P.N. 276-036

HOT ALL TIMES SUCH AS CLOCK OR LIGHTER

ANY IGNITION-CONTROLLED FUSE SUCH AS IGNITION OR WIPER
NOTE: OPTIONAL FUSE TAPS P.N. 270-1204

FUSE PANEL

*ALL PART NUMBERS ARE FROM RADIO SHACK

FIGURE 12–29 Schematic for a blinking LED theft deterrent.

 **TECH TIP**

Blinking LED Theft Deterrent

A blinking (flashing) LED consumes only about 5 milliamperes (5/1,000 of 1 ampere, or 0.005 A). Most alarm systems use a blinking red LED to indicate that the system is armed. A fake alarm indicator is easy to make and install.

A 470 ohm, 0.5 watt resistor limits current flow to prevent battery drain. The positive terminal (anode) of the diode is connected to a fuse that is hot at all times, such as the cigarette lighter. The negative terminal (cathode) of the LED is connected to any ignition-controlled fuse. ● **SEE FIGURE 12–29.**

When the ignition is turned off, the power flows through the LED to ground and the LED flashes. To prevent distraction during driving, the LED goes out when the ignition is on. Therefore, this fake theft deterrent is "auto setting" and no other action is required to activate it when you leave your vehicle except to turn off the ignition and remove the key as usual.

HOW TO TEST DIODES AND TRANSISTORS

TESTERS Diodes and transistors can be tested with an ohmmeter. The diode or transistor being tested must be disconnected from the circuit for the results to be meaningful.

- Use the *diode-check* position on a digital multimeter.
- In the diode-check position on a digital multimeter, the meter applies a higher voltage than when the ohms test function is selected.
- This slightly higher voltage (about 2 to 3 volts) is enough to forward bias a diode or the P-N junction of transistors.

DIODES Using the diode test position, the meter applies a voltage. The display will show the voltage drop across the diode P-N junction. A good diode should give an over limit (OL) reading with the test leads attached to each lead of the diode in one way, and a voltage reading of 0.400 to 0.600 volt when the leads are reversed. This reading is the voltage drop or the barrier voltage across the P-N junction of the diode.

1. A low-voltage reading with the meter leads attached both ways across a diode means that the diode is *shorted* and must be replaced.

2. An OL reading with the meter leads attached both ways across a diode means that the diode is *open* and must be replaced.

   ● **SEE FIGURE 12–30**.

TRANSISTORS Using a digital meter set to the diode-check position, a good transistor should show a voltage drop of 0.400 to 0.600 volt between the following:

- The emitter (*E*) and the base (*B*) and between the base (*B*) and the collector (*C*) with a meter connected one way, and OL when the meter test leads are reversed.
- An OL reading (no continuity) in both directions when a transistor is tested between the emitter (*E*) and the collector (*C*). (A transistor tester can also be used if available.)

   ● **SEE FIGURE 12–31**.

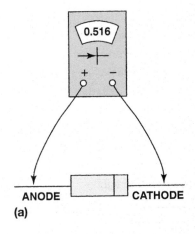
(a)

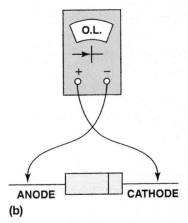
(b)

FIGURE 12–30 To check a diode, select "diode check" on a digital multimeter. The display will indicate the voltage drop (difference) between the meter leads. The meter itself applies a low-voltage signal (usually about 3 volts) and displays the difference on the display. (a) When the diode is forward biased, the meter should display a voltage between 0.500 and 0.700 volt (500 to 700 millivolts). (b) When the meter leads are reversed, the meter should read OL (over limit) because the diode is reverse biased and blocking current flow.

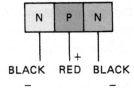

FIGURE 12–31 If the red (positive) lead of the ohmmeter (or a multimeter set to diode check) is touched to the center and the black (negative lead) touched to either end of the electrode, the meter should forward bias the P-N junction and indicate on the meter as low resistance. If the meter reads high resistance, reverse the meter leads, putting the black on the center lead and the red on either end lead. If the meter indicates low resistance, the transistor is a good PNP type. Check all P-N junctions in the same way.

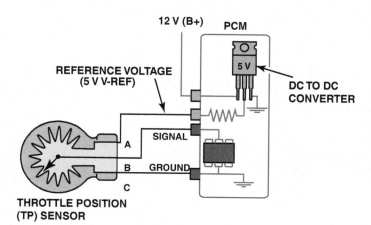

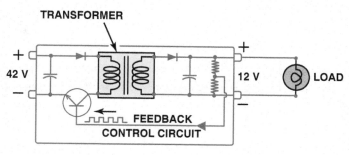

FIGURE 12–32 A DC to DC converter is built into most powertrain control modules (PCMs) and is used to supply the 5-volt reference called V-ref to many sensors used to control the internal combustion engine.

FIGURE 12–33 This DC–DC converter is designed to convert 42 volts to 14 volts, to provide 12-volts power to accessories on a hybrid electric vehicle operating with a 42-volt electrical system.

CONVERTERS AND INVERTERS

CONVERTERS DC to DC converters (usually written as DC–DC converter) are electronic devices used to transform DC voltage from one level to another higher or lower level. They are used to distribute various levels of DC voltage throughout a vehicle from a single power bus (or voltage source).

EXAMPLES OF USE One example of a DC–DC converter circuit is the circuit the PCM uses to convert 14 to 5 volts. The 5 volts is called the reference voltage, abbreviated V-ref, and is used to power many sensors in a computer-controlled engine management system. The schematic of a typical 5-volt V-ref interfacing with the TP sensor circuit is shown in ● **FIGURE 12–32**.

The PCM operates on 14 volts, using the principle of DC conversion to provide a constant 5 volts of sensor reference voltage to the TP sensor and others. The TP sensor demands little current, so the V-ref circuit is a low-power DC voltage converter in the range of 1 watt. The PCM uses a DC–DC converter, which is a small semiconductor device called a voltage regulator, and is designed to convert battery voltage to a constant 5 volts regardless of changes in the charging voltage.

Hybrid electric vehicles use DC–DC converters to provide higher or lower DC voltage levels and current requirements.

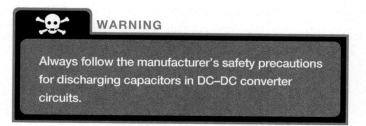

☠ WARNING

Always follow the manufacturer's safety precautions for discharging capacitors in DC–DC converter circuits.

A high-power DC–DC converter schematic is shown in ● **FIGURE 12–33** and represents how a nonelectronic DC–DC converter works.

The central component of a converter is a transformer that physically isolates the input (42 volts) from the output (14 volts). The power transistor pulses the high-voltage coil of the transformer, and the resulting changing magnetic field induces a voltage in the coil windings of the lower-voltage side of the transformer. The diodes and capacitors help control and limit the voltage and frequency of the circuit.

DC–DC CONVERTER CIRCUIT TESTING Usually a DC control voltage is used, which is supplied by a digital logic circuit to shift the voltage level to control the converter. A voltage test can indicate if the correct voltages are present when the converter is on and off.

Voltage measurements are usually specified to diagnose a DC–DC converter system. A digital multimeter (DMM) that is CAT III rated should be used.

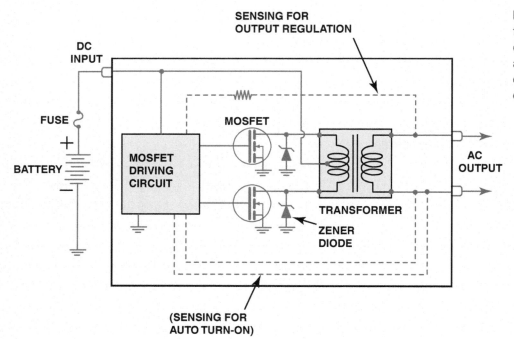

SENSING FOR
OUTPUT REGULATION

DC
INPUT

FUSE

BATTERY

MOSFET
DRIVING
CIRCUIT

MOSFET

TRANSFORMER

ZENER
DIODE

AC
OUTPUT

(SENSING FOR
AUTO TURN-ON)

FIGURE 12–34 A typical circuit for an inverter designed to change direct current from a battery to alternating current for use by the electric motors used in a hybrid electric vehicle.

HIGH VOLTAGE CIRCUIT PRECAUTIONS

Whenever working on or near potential high-voltage circuits, adhere to the following:

1. Always follow the manufacturer's safety precautions when working with high-voltage circuits. These circuits are usually indicated by orange wiring.

2. Never tap into wires in a DC–DC converter circuit to access power for another circuit.

3. Never tap into wires in a DC–DC converter circuit to access a ground for another circuit.

4. Never block airflow to a DC–DC converter heat sink.

5. Never use a heat sink for a ground connection for a meter, scope, or accessory connection.

6. Never connect or disconnect a DC–DC converter while the converter is powered up.

7. Never connect a DC–DC converter to a larger voltage source than specified.

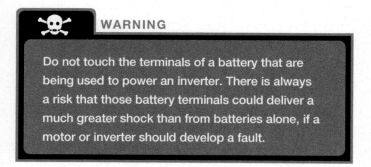

☠ WARNING

Do not touch the terminals of a battery that are being used to power an inverter. There is always a risk that those battery terminals could deliver a much greater shock than from batteries alone, if a motor or inverter should develop a fault.

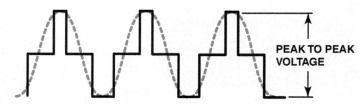

PEAK TO PEAK
VOLTAGE

FIGURE 12–35 The switching (pulsing) MOSFETs create a waveform called a modified sine wave (solid lines) compared to a true sine wave (dotted lines).

INVERTERS

An **inverter** is an electronic circuit that changes direct current (DC) into alternating current (AC). In most DC-AC inverters, the switching transistors, which are usually MOSFETs, are turned on alternately for short pulses. As a result, the transformer produces a modified sine wave output, rather than a true sine wave. ● SEE FIGURE 12–34.

The waveform produced by an inverter is not the perfect sine wave of household AC, but is rather more like a pulsing DC that reacts similar to sine wave AC in transformers and in induction motors. ● SEE FIGURE 12–35.

Inverters power AC motors. An inverter converts DC power to AC power at the required frequency and amplitude. The inverter consists of three half-bridge units, and the output voltage is mostly created by a pulse-width modulation (PWM) technique. The three-phase voltage waves are shifted 120 degrees to each other to power each of the three phases.

ELECTROSTATIC DISCHARGE

DEFINITION **Electrostatic discharge (ESD)** is created when static charges build up on the human body when movement occurs. The friction of the clothing and the movement of shoes against carpet or vinyl floors cause a high voltage to build. Then when we touch a conductive material, such as a doorknob, the static charge is rapidly discharged. These charges, although just slightly painful to us, can cause severe damage to delicate electronic components. The following are typical static voltages:

- If you can feel it, it is at least 3,000 volts.
- If you can hear it, it is at least 5,000 volts.
- If you can see it, it is at least 10,000 volts.

Although these voltages seem high, the current, in amperes, is extremely low. However, sensitive electronic components, such as vehicle computers, radios, and instrument panel clusters can be ruined if exposed to as little as 30 volts. This is a problem because components can be harmed at voltages lower than we can feel.

AVOIDING ESD To help prevent damage to components, follow these easy steps:

1. Keep the replacement electronic component in the protective wrapping until just before installation.
2. Before handling any electronic component, ground yourself by touching a metal surface to drain away any static charge.
3. Do not touch the terminals of electronic components.
4. If working in an area where you could come in contact with terminals, wear a static electrically grounding wrist strap available at most electronic parts stores, such as Radio Shack.

If these precautions are observed, ESD damage can be eliminated or reduced. Remember, just because the component works even after being touched does not mean that damage has not occurred. Often, a section of the electronic component may be damaged, yet will not fail until several days or weeks later.

SUMMARY

1. Semiconductors are constructed by doping semiconductor materials such as silicon.
2. N-type and P-type materials can be combined to form diodes, transistors, SCRs, and computer chips.
3. Diodes can be used to direct and control current flow in circuits and to provide despiking protection.
4. Transistors are electronic relays that can also amplify signals.
5. All semiconductors can be damaged if subjected to excessive voltage, current, or heat.
6. Never touch the terminals of a computer or electronic device; static electricity can damage electronic components.

REVIEW QUESTIONS

1. What is the difference between P-type material and N-type material?
2. How can a diode be used to suppress high-voltage surges in automotive components or circuits containing a coil?
3. How does a transistor work?
4. To what precautions should all service technicians adhere, to avoid damage to electronic and computer circuits?
5. What is the difference between forward bias and reverse bias when discussing a diode?

CHAPTER QUIZ

1. A semiconductor is a material _____.
   a. with fewer than four electrons in the outer orbit of its atoms
   b. with more than four electrons in the outer orbit of its atoms
   c. with exactly four electrons in the outer orbit of its atoms
   d. determined by other factors besides the number of electrons

2. The arrow in a symbol for a semiconductor device _____.
   a. points toward the negative
   b. points away from the negative
   c. is attached to the emitter on a transistor
   d. Both a and c

3. A diode installed across a coil with the cathode toward the battery positive is called a(n) _____.
   a. clamping diode
   b. forward-bias diode
   c. SCR
   d. transistor

4. A transistor is controlled by the polarity and current at the _____.
   a. collector
   b. emitter
   c. base
   d. Both a and b

5. A transistor can _____.
   a. switch on and off
   b. amplify
   c. throttle
   d. All of the above

6. Clamping diodes _____.
   a. are connected into a circuit with the positive (+) voltage source to the cathode and the negative (−) voltage to the anode
   b. are also called despiking diodes
   c. can suppress transient voltages
   d. All of the above

7. A zener diode is normally used for voltage regulation. A zener diode, however, can also be used for high-voltage spike protection if connected _____.
   a. positive to anode, negative to cathode
   b. positive to cathode, ground to anode
   c. negative to anode, cathode to a resistor then to a lower voltage terminal
   d. Both a and c

8. The forward-bias voltage required for an LED is _____.
   a. 0.3 to 0.5 volt
   b. 0.5 to 0.7 volt
   c. 1.5 to 2.2 volts
   d. 4.5 to 5.1 volts

9. An LED can be used in a _____.
   a. headlight
   b. taillight
   c. brake light
   d. All of the above

10. Another name for a ground is _____.
    a. logic low
    b. zero
    c. reference low
    d. Any of the above

chapter 13

COMPUTER FUNDAMENTALS

LEARNING OBJECTIVES

After studying this chapter, the reader will be able to:

1. List the various parts of onboard computers.
2. Explain the purpose and function of onboard computers.
3. Explain the parts and characteristics of digital computers.
4. List input sensors to an automotive computer and output devices (actuators) controlled by the computer.

KEY TERMS

Actuator 195
Analog-to-digital (AD) converter 194
Baud rate 197
Binary system 197
Clock generator 196
Controller 194
CPU 195
Digital computer 196
Duty cycle 200
E²PROM 195
ECA 194
ECM 194
ECU 194
EEPROM 195
Engine mapping 196
Input 194
Input conditioning 194
KAM 195
Nonvolatile RAM 195
Output drivers 199
Powertrain control module (PCM) 194
PROM 195
PWM 199
RAM 195
ROM 195
SAE 194

COMPUTER FUNDAMENTALS

PURPOSE AND FUNCTION Modern automotive control systems consist of a network of electronic sensors, actuators, and computer modules designed to regulate the powertrain and vehicle support systems. The onboard automotive computer has many names. It may be called an **electronic control unit (ECU)**, **electronic control module (ECM)**, **electronic control assembly (ECA)**, or a **controller**, depending on the manufacturer and the computer application. The **Society of Automotive Engineers (SAE)** bulletin J1930 standardizes the name as a **powertrain control module (PCM)**. The PCM coordinates engine and transmission operation, processes data, maintains communications, and makes the control decisions needed to keep the vehicle operating. Not only is it capable of operating the engine and transmission, but it is also able to perform the following:

- Undergo self-tests (40% of the computing power is devoted to diagnosis)
- Set and store diagnostic trouble codes (DTCs)
- Communicate with the technician using a scan tool

VOLTAGE SIGNALS Automotive computers use voltage to send and receive information. Voltage is electrical pressure and does not flow through circuits, but it can be used as a signal. A computer converts input information or data into voltage signal combinations that represent number combinations. A computer processes the input voltage signals it receives by computing what they represent, and then delivering the data in computed or processed form.

COMPUTER FUNCTIONS

BASIC FUNCTIONS The operation of every computer can be divided into four basic functions. ● **SEE FIGURE 13–1.**

- **Input.** Receives voltage signals from sensors
- **Processing.** Performs mathematical calculations
- **Storage.** Includes short-term and long-term memory
- **Output.** Controls an output device by either turning it on or off

INPUT FUNCTIONS First, the computer receives a voltage signal (input) from an input device. **Input** is a signal from a device that can be as simple as a button or a switch on an instrument panel, or a sensor on an automotive engine. See ● **SEE FIGURE 13–2** for a typical type of automotive sensor.

Vehicles use various mechanical, electrical, and magnetic sensors to measure factors, such as vehicle speed, throttle position, engine RPM, air pressure, oxygen content of exhaust gas, airflow, engine coolant temperature, and status of electrical circuits (on-off). Each sensor transmits its information in the form of voltage signals. The computer receives these voltage signals, but before it can use them, the signals must undergo a process called **input conditioning**. This process includes amplifying voltage signals that are too small for the computer circuitry to handle. Input conditioners generally are located inside the computer, but a few sensors have their own input conditioning circuitry.

A digital computer changes the analog input signals (voltage) to digital bits (*binary digits*) of information through an **analog-to-digital (AD) converter** circuit. The binary digital number is used by the computer in its calculations or logic networks. ● **SEE FIGURE 13–3.**

PROCESSING The term *processing* is used to describe how input voltage signals received by a computer are handled through a series of electronic logic circuits maintained in its programmed instructions. These logic circuits change the input voltage signals, or data, into output voltage signals or commands.

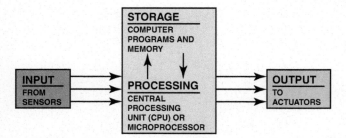

FIGURE 13–1 All computer systems perform four basic functions: input, processing, storage, and output.

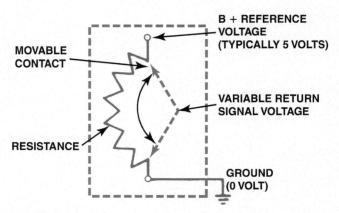

FIGURE 13–2 A potentiometer uses a movable contact to vary resistance and send an analog voltage right to the PCM.

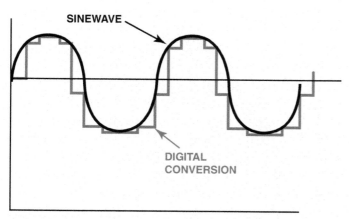

FIGURE 13–3 An AD converter changes analog (variable) voltage signals into digital signals that the PCM can process.

STORAGE Storage is the place where the program instructions for a computer are stored in electronic memory. Some programs may require that certain input data be stored for later reference or future processing. In others, output commands may be delayed or stored before they are transmitted to devices elsewhere in the system.

Computers have two types of memory.

1. Permanent memory is called **read-only memory (ROM)** because the computer can only read the contents; it cannot change the data stored in it. This data is retained even when power to the computer is shut off. Part of the ROM is built into the computer, and the rest is located in an integrated circuit (IC) chip called a **programmable read-only memory (PROM)** or calibration assembly. Many chips are erasable, meaning that the program can be changed. These chips are called erasable programmable read-only memory, or EPROM. Since the early 1990s, most programmable memory has been electronically erasable, meaning that the program in the chip can be reprogrammed by using a scan tool and the proper software. This computer reprogramming is usually called *reflashing*. These chips are electrically erasable programmable read-only memory, abbreviated **EEPROM** or **E²PROM**.

    All vehicles equipped with onboard diagnosis second generation, called OBD-II, are equipped with EEPROMs.

2. Temporary memory is called **random-access memory (RAM)**, because the computer can write or store new data into it as directed by the computer program, as well as read the data already in it. Automotive computers use two types of RAM memory.

    - Volatile RAM memory is lost whenever the ignition is turned off. However, a type of volatile RAM called **keep-alive memory (KAM)** can be wired directly to battery power. This prevents its data from being erased when the ignition is turned off. One example of RAM and KAM is the loss of station settings in a programmable radio when the battery is disconnected. Because all the settings are stored in RAM, they have to be reset when the battery is reconnected. System trouble codes are commonly stored in RAM and can be erased by disconnecting the battery.

    - **Nonvolatile RAM** memory can retain its information even when the battery is disconnected. One use for this type of RAM is the storage of odometer information in an electronic speedometer. The memory chip retains the mileage accumulated by the vehicle. When speedometer replacement is necessary, the odometer chip is removed and installed in the new speedometer unit. KAM is used primarily in conjunction with adaptive strategies.

OUTPUT FUNCTIONS After the computer has processed the input signals, it sends voltage signals or commands to other devices in the system, such as system actuators. An **actuator** is an electrical or mechanical output device that converts electrical energy into a mechanical action, such as:

- Adjusting engine idle speed
- Operating fuel injectors
- Ignition timing control
- Altering suspension height

COMPUTER COMMUNICATION A typical vehicle can have many computers, also called modules or controllers. Computers also can communicate with, and control, each other through their output and input functions. This means that the output signal from one computer system can be the input signal for another computer system through a data network.

DIGITAL COMPUTERS

PARTS OF A COMPUTER The software consists of the programs and logic functions stored in the computer's circuitry. The hardware is the mechanical and electronic parts of a computer.

- **Central processing unit.** The microprocessor is the **central processing unit (CPU)** of a computer. Because it performs the essential mathematical operations and logic decisions that make up its processing function, the CPU can be considered the brain of a computer. Some computers use more than one microprocessor, called a coprocessor. The digital computer can process thousands of digital signals per second because its circuits are able to switch voltage signals on and off in billionths of a second. It is called a **digital computer** because it processes zeros and ones (digits) and needs to have any variable input signals, called analog inputs, converted to digital form before it can function. ● **SEE FIGURE 13–4.**

- **Computer memory.** Other integrated circuit (IC) devices store the computer operating program, system sensor input data, and system actuator output data—information that is necessary for CPU operation.

- **Computer programs.** By operating a vehicle on a dynamometer and manually adjusting the variable factors such as speed, load, and spark timing, it is possible to determine the optimum output settings for the best driveability, economy, and emission control. This is called engine mapping. ● **SEE FIGURE 13–5.**

Engine mapping creates a three-dimensional performance graph that applies to a given vehicle and powertrain combination. Each combination is mapped in this manner to produce a PROM or EEPROM calibration. This allows an automaker to use one basic computer for all models.

Many older-vehicle computers used a single PROM that plugged into the computer.

NOTE: If the computer needs to be replaced, the PROM or calibration module must be removed from the defective unit and installed in the replacement computer. Since the mid-1990s, PCMs do not have removable calibration PROMs, and must be programmed or *flashed* using a scan tool before being put into service.

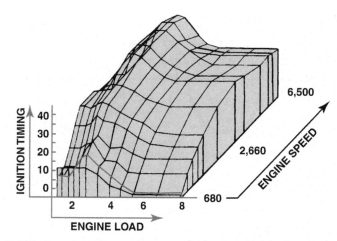

FIGURE 13–5 Typical engine map developed from testing and used by the vehicle computer to provide the optimum ignition timing for all engine speeds and load combinations.

CLOCK RATES AND TIMING The microprocessor receives sensor input voltage signals, processes them by using information from other memory units, and then sends voltage signals to the appropriate actuators. The microprocessor communicates by transmitting long strings of 0s and 1s in a language called binary code; but the microprocessor must have some way of knowing when one signal ends and another begins. That is the job of a crystal oscillator called a **clock generator.** ● **SEE FIGURE 13–6.**

The computer's crystal oscillator generates a steady stream of one-bit-long voltage pulses. Both the microprocessor and the memories monitor the clock pulses while they are communicating. Because they know how long each voltage pulse should be, they can distinguish between a 01 and a 0011. To complete the process, the input and output circuits also watch the clock pulses.

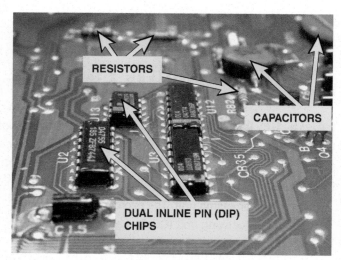

FIGURE 13–4 Many electronic components are used to construct a typical vehicle computer including chips, resistors, and capacitors.

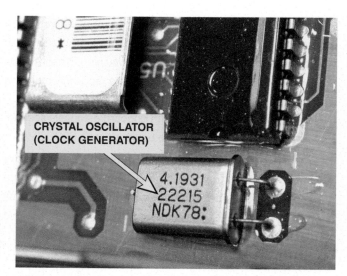

FIGURE 13–6 The clock generator produces a series of pulses that are used by the microprocessor and other components to stay in step with each other at a steady rate.

COMPUTER SPEEDS Not all computers operate at the same speed; some are faster than others. The speed at which a computer operates is specified by the cycle time, or clock speed, required to perform certain measurements. Cycle time or clock speed is measured in megahertz (4.7 MHz, 8 MHz, 15 MHz, 18 MHz, and 32 MHz, which is the clock speed of most vehicle computers today).

BAUD RATE The computer transmits bits of a serial datastream at precise intervals. The computer's speed is called the **baud rate**, or bits per second. The term *baud* was named after J. M. Emile Baudot (1845–1903), a French telegraph operator who developed a five-bit-per-character code of telegraph. Just as mph helps in estimating the length of time required to travel a certain distance, the baud rate is useful in estimating how long a given computer will need to transmit a specified amount of data to another computer.

Automotive computers have evolved from a baud rate of 160 used in the early 1980s to a baud rate as high as 500,000 for some networks. The speed of data transmission is an important factor both in system operation and in system troubleshooting.

CONTROL MODULE LOCATIONS The computer hardware is all mounted on one or more circuit boards and installed in a metal case to help shield it from electromagnetic interference (EMI). The wiring harnesses that link the computer to sensors and actuators connect to multipin connectors or edge connectors on the circuit boards.

Onboard computers range from single-function units that control a single operation to multifunction units that manage all of the separate (but linked) electronic systems in the vehicle.

They vary in size from a small module to a notebook-size box. Most other computers are installed in the passenger compartment either under the instrument panel or in a side kick panel where they can be shielded from physical damage caused by temperature extremes, dirt, and vibration, or interference by the high currents and voltages of various underhood systems.
● **SEE FIGURE 13–7.**

? FREQUENTLY ASKED QUESTION

What Is a Binary System?

In a digital computer the signals are simple high-low, yes-no, on-off signals. The digital signal voltage is limited to two voltage levels: high voltage and low voltage. Since there is no stepped range of voltage or current in between, a digital binary signal is a "square wave." The signal is called "digital" because the on and off signals are processed by the computer as the digits or numbers 0 and 1. The number system containing only these two digits is called the **binary system**. Any number or letter from any number system or language alphabet can be translated into a combination of binary 0s and 1s for the digital computer. A digital computer changes the analog input signals (voltage) to digital bits (*binary digits*) of information through an analog-to-digital (AD) converter circuit. The binary digital number is used by the computer in its calculations or logic networks. Output signals usually are digital signals that turn system actuators on and off.

FIGURE 13–7 A powertrain control module (PCM) under the hood where it can be exposed to air for cooling.

COMPUTER INPUT SENSORS

The vehicle computer uses signals (voltage levels) from the following sensors:

- **Engine speed (revolutions per minute, or RPM) sensor.** This signal comes from the primary ignition signal in the ignition control module (ICM) or directly from the crankshaft position (CKP) sensor.

- **Switches or buttons for accessory operation.** Many accessories use control buttons that signal the body computer to turn on or off an accessory, such as the windshield wiper or heated seats.

- **Manifold absolute pressure (MAP) sensor.** This sensor detects engine load by using a signal from a sensor that measures the vacuum in the intake manifold.

- **Mass airflow (MAF) sensor.** This sensor measures the mass (weight and density) of the air flowing through the sensor and entering the engine.

- **Engine coolant temperature (ECT) sensor.** This sensor measures the temperature of the engine coolant. This is a sensor used for engine controls and for automatic air-conditioning control operation.

- **Oxygen sensor (O2S).** This sensor measures the oxygen in the exhaust stream. There are as many as four oxygen sensors in some vehicles.

- **Throttle position (TP) sensor.** This sensor measures the throttle opening and is used by the computer for engine control and the shift points of the automotive transmission/transaxle.

- **Vehicle speed (VS) sensor.** This sensor measures the vehicle speed using a sensor located at the output of the transmission/transaxle or by monitoring sensors at the wheel speed sensors. This sensor is used by the speedometer, cruise control, and airbag systems.

COMPUTER OUTPUTS

OUTPUT CONTROLS After the computer has processed the input signals, it sends voltage signals or commands to other devices in the system, as follows:

- **Operate actuators.** An actuator is an electrical or mechanical device that converts electrical energy into heat, light, or motion to control engine idle speed, suspension height, ignition timing, and other output devices.

- **Network communication.** Computers also can communicate with another computer system through a network.

A vehicle computer can do only two things.

1. Turn a device on.

2. Turn a device off.

Typical output devices include the following:

- **Fuel injectors.** The computer can vary the amount of time in milliseconds the injectors are held open, thereby controlling the amount of fuel supplied to the engine.

- **Blower motor control.** Many blower motors are controlled by the body computer by pulsing the current on and off to maintain the desired speed.

- **Transmission shifting.** The computer provides a ground to the shift solenoids and torque converter clutch (TCC) solenoid. The operation of the automatic transmission/transaxle is optimized based on vehicle sensor information.

- **Idle speed control.** The computer can control the idle air control (IAC) or electronic throttle control (ETC) to maintain engine idle speed and to provide an increased idle speed as needed.

- **Evaporative emission control solenoids.** The computer can control the flow of gasoline fumes from the charcoal canister to the engine and seal off the system to perform a fuel system leak detection test as part of the OBD-II system requirements.

Most outputs work electrically in one of three ways:

1. Digital

2. Pulse-width modulated

3. Switched

Digital control is mostly used for computer communications and involves voltage signals that are transmitted and received in packets.

Pulse-width control allows a device, such as a blower motor, to be operated at variable speed by changing the amount of time electrical power is supplied to the device.

A switched output is an output that is either on or off. In many circuits, the PCM uses a relay to switch a device on or off, because the relay is a low-current device that can switch to a higher current device. Most computer circuits cannot handle high amounts of current. By using a relay circuit, the PCM provides the output control to the relay, which in turn provides the output control to the device.

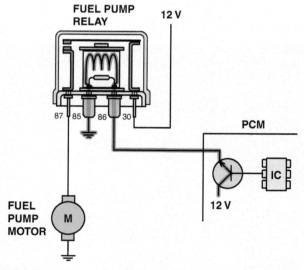

FIGURE 13–8 A typical output driver. In this case, the PCM applies voltage to the fuel pump relay coil to energize the fuel pump.

The relay coil, which the PCM controls, typically draws less than 0.5 ampere. The device that the relay controls may draw 30 amperes or more. The PCM switches are actually transistors, and are often called **output drivers**. ● SEE FIGURE 13–8.

OUTPUT DRIVERS There are two basic types of output drivers.

1. **Low-side drivers.** The low-side drivers (LSDs) are transistors inside the computer that complete the ground path of the relay coil. Ignition (key-on) voltage and battery voltage are supplied to the relay. The ground side of the relay coil is connected to the transistor inside the computer. In the example of a fuel pump relay, when the transistor turns "on," it will complete the ground for the relay coil, and the relay will then complete the power circuit between the battery power and the fuel pump. A relatively low current flows through the relay coil and transistor that is inside the computer. This causes the relay to switch and provides the fuel pump with battery voltage. The majority of switched outputs have typically been low-side drivers. ● SEE FIGURE 13–9.

    Low-side drivers can often perform a diagnostic circuit check by monitoring the voltage from the relay to check that the control circuit for the relay is complete. A low-side driver, however, cannot detect a short-to-ground.

2. **High-side drivers.** The high-side drivers (HSDs) control the power side of the circuit. In these applications when the transistor is switched on, voltage is applied to the device. A ground has been provided to the device so when the high-side driver switches, the device will be energized. In some applications, high-side drivers are used instead of low-side drivers to provide better circuit protection. General Motors vehicles use a high-side driver to control the fuel pump relay instead of a low-side driver. In the event of an accident, should the circuit to the fuel pump relay become grounded, a high-side driver will cause a short circuit, which will cause the fuel pump relay to de-energize. High-side drivers inside modules can detect electrical faults such as a lack of continuity when the circuit is not energized. ● SEE FIGURE 13–10.

PULSE-WIDTH MODULATION Pulse-width modulation (PWM) is a method of controlling an output using a digital signal. Instead of just turning devices on or off, the computer can control the amount of on-time. For example, a solenoid could be a PWM device. If, for example, a vacuum solenoid is controlled by a switched driver, switching either on or off would mean that either full vacuum would flow through the solenoid

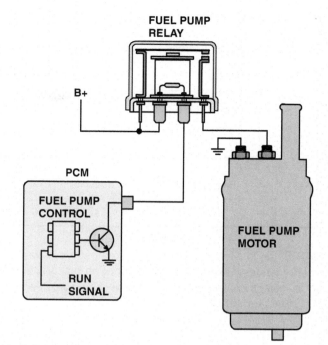

FIGURE 13–9 A typical low-side driver (LSD) which uses a control module to control the ground side of the relay coil.

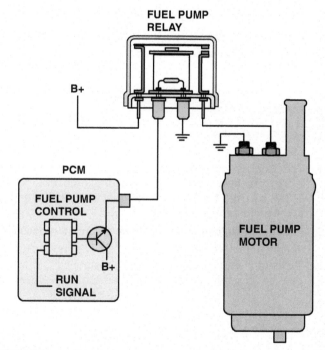

FIGURE 13–10 A typical module-controlled high-side driver (HSD) where the module itself supplies the electrical power to the device. The logic circuit inside the module can detect circuit faults including continuity of the circuit and if there is a short-to-ground in the circuit being controlled.

or no vacuum would flow through the solenoid. However, to control the amount of vacuum that flows through the solenoid, pulse-width modulation could be used. A PWM signal is a digital signal, usually 0 and 12 volts, which is cycling at a

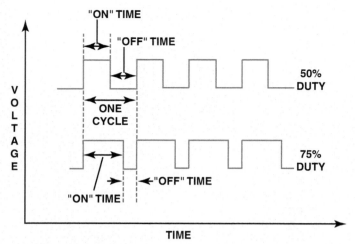

FIGURE 13–11 Both the top and bottom pattern have the same frequency. However, the amount of on-time varies. Duty cycle is the percentage of the time during a cycle that the signal is turned on.

fixed frequency. Varying the length of time that the signal is on provides a signal that can vary the on- and off-time of an output. The ratio of on-time relative to the period of the cycle is referred to as **duty cycle**. ● **SEE FIGURE 13–11.**

Depending on the frequency of the signal, which is usually fixed, this signal will turn the device on and off a fixed number of times per second. When, for example, the voltage is high (12 volts) 90% of the time and low (0 volt) the other 10% of the time, the signal has a 90% duty cycle. In other words, if this signal were applied to the vacuum solenoid, the solenoid would be on 90% of the time. This would allow more vacuum to flow through the solenoid. The computer has the ability to vary this on- and off-time or pulse-width modulation at any rate between 0% and 100%. A good example of pulse-width modulation is the cooling fan speed control. The speed of the cooling fan is controlled by varying the amount of on-time that the battery voltage is applied to the cooling fan motor.

- 100% duty cycle: fan runs at full speed
- 75% duty cycle: fan runs at 3/4 speed
- 50% duty cycle: fan runs at 1/2 speed
- 25% duty cycle: fan runs at 1/4 speed

The use of PWM, therefore, results in precise control of an output device to achieve the amount of cooling needed and conserve electrical energy compared to simply timing the cooling fan on high when needed. PWM may be used to control vacuum through a solenoid, the amount of purge of the evaporative purge solenoid, the speed of a fuel pump motor, control of a linear motor, or even the intensity of a light bulb.

SUMMARY

1. The Society of Automotive Engineers (SAE) standard J1930 specifies that the term powertrain control module (PCM) be used for the computer that controls the engine and transmission in a vehicle.

2. The four basic computer functions are input, processing, storage, and output.

3. Types of memory include read-only memory (ROM) which can be programmable (PROM), erasable (EPROM), or electrically erasable (EEPROM); random-access memory (RAM); and keep-alive memory (KAM).

4. Computer input sensors include engine speed (RPM), MAP, MAF, ECT, O2S, TP, and VS.

5. A computer can only turn a device on or turn a device off, but it can do either operation rapidly.

REVIEW QUESTIONS

1. What part of the vehicle computer is considered to be the brain?

2. What is the difference between volatile and nonvolatile RAM?

3. What are four input sensors?

4. What are four output devices?

5. How does using pulse-width modulation control devices?

1. What unit of electricity is used as a signal for a computer?
   a. Volt
   c. Ampere
   b. Ohm
   d. Watt

2. The four basic computer functions include _____ .
   a. writing, processing, printing, and remembering
   b. input, processing, storage, and output
   c. data gathering, processing, output, and evaluation
   d. sensing, calculating, actuating, and processing

3. All OBD-II vehicles use what type of read-only memory?
   a. ROM
   c. EPROM
   b. PROM
   d. EEPROM

4. The "brain" of the computer is the _____ .
   a. PROM
   b. RAM
   c. CPU
   d. AD converter

5. Computer speed is measured in _____ .
   a. baud rate
   c. voltage
   b. clock speed (Hz)
   d. bytes

6. Which item is a computer input sensor?
   a. RPM
   b. Throttle position
   c. Engine coolant temperature
   d. All of the above

7. Which item is a computer output device?
   a. Fuel injector
   b. Transmission shift solenoid
   c. Evaporative emission control solenoid
   d. All of the above

8. The SAE term for the vehicle computer is _____ .
   a. PCM
   c. ECA
   b. ECM
   d. Controller

9. What two things can a vehicle computer actually perform (output)?
   a. Store and process information
   b. Turn something on or turn something off
   c. Calculate and vary temperature
   d. Control fuel and timing only

10. Analog signals from sensors are changed to digital signals for processing by the computer through which type of circuit?
    a. Digital
    b. Analog
    c. Analog-to-digital converter
    d. PROM.

chapter 14
CAN AND NETWORK COMMUNICATIONS

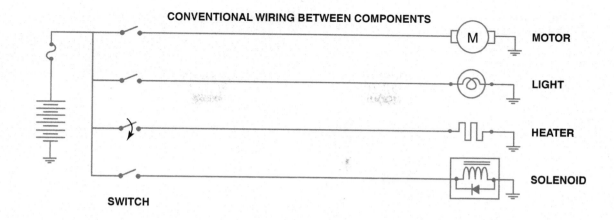

CONVENTIONAL WIRING BETWEEN COMPONENTS

MOTOR

LIGHT

HEATER

SOLENOID

SWITCH

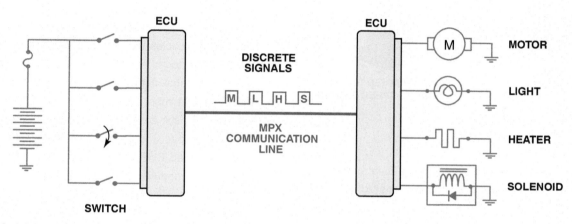

ECU

ECU

DISCRETE
SIGNALS

MPX
COMMUNICATION
LINE

SWITCH

MOTOR

LIGHT

HEATER

SOLENOID

FIGURE 14–1 Module communications makes controlling multiple electrical devices and accessories easier by utilizing simple low-current switches to signal another module, which does the actual switching of the current to the device.

MODULE COMMUNICATIONS AND NETWORKS

NEED FOR NETWORK Since the 1990s, vehicles have used modules to control the operation of most electrical components. A typical vehicle will have 10 or more modules and they communicate with each other over data lines or hard wiring, depending on the application:

ADVANTAGES Most modules are connected together in a network because of the following advantages:

- A decreased number of wires are needed, thereby saving weight and cost, as well as helping with installation at the factory and decreased complexity, making servicing easier.

- Common sensor data can be shared with those modules that may need the information, such as vehicle speed, outside air temperature, and engine coolant temperature.

- **SEE FIGURE 14–1.**

NETWORK FUNDAMENTALS

MODULES AND NODES Each module, also called a **node**, must communicate to other modules. For example, if the driver depresses the window-down switch, the power window switch sends a window-down message to the body control module. The body control module then sends the request to the driver's side window module. This module is responsible for actually performing the task by supplying power and ground to the window lift motor in the current polarity to cause the window to go down. The module also contains a circuit that monitors the current flow through the motor and will stop and/or reverse the window motor if an obstruction causes the window motor to draw more than the normal amount of current.

TYPES OF COMMUNICATION The types of communications include the following:

- **Differential.** In the differential form of BUS communication, a difference in voltage is applied to two wires, which

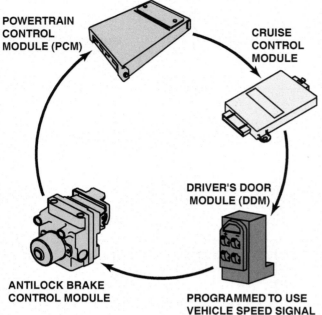

PROGRAMMED TO USE
VEHICLE SPEED SIGNAL

POWERTRAIN
CONTROL
MODULE (PCM)

CRUISE
CONTROL
MODULE

DRIVER'S DOOR
MODULE (DDM)

ANTILOCK BRAKE
CONTROL MODULE

PROGRAMMED TO USE
VEHICLE SPEED SIGNAL

FIGURE 14–2 A network allows all modules to communicate with other modules.

are twisted to help reduce electromagnetic interference (EMI). These transfer wires are called a **twisted pair**.

- **Parallel.** In the parallel type of BUS communication, the send and receive signals are on different wires.

- **Serial data.** The **serial data** is data transmitted by a series of rapidly changing voltage signals pulsed from low to high or from high to low.

- **Multiplexing.** The process of **multiplexing** involves the sending of multiple signals of information at the same time over a signal wire and then separating the signals at the receiving end.

This system of intercommunication of computers or processors is referred to as a **network**. ● SEE FIGURE 14–2.

By connecting the computers together on a communications network, they can easily share information back and forth. This multiplexing has the following advantages:

- Elimination of redundant sensors and dedicated wiring for these multiple sensors

- Reduction of the number of wires, connectors, and circuits

- Addition of more features and option content to new vehicles

- Weight reduction due to fewer components, wires, and connectors, thereby increasing fuel economy

- Changeable features with software upgrades versus component replacement

MODULE COMMUNICATIONS CONFIGURATION

The three most common types of networks used on vehicles include the following:

1. **Ring link networks.** In a ring-type network, all modules are connected to each other by a serial data line (in a line) until all are connected in a ring. ● SEE FIGURE 14–3.

2. **Star link networks.** In a star link network, a serial data line attaches to each module and then each is connected to a central point. This central point is called a **splice pack**, abbreviated SP such as in "SP 306." The splice pack uses a bar to splice all of the serial lines together. Some GM vehicles use two or more splice packs to tie the modules together. When more than one splice pack is used, a serial data line connects one splice pack to the others. In most applications, the BUS bar used in each splice pack can be removed. When the BUS bar is removed, a special tool (J 42236) can be installed in place of the removed BUS bar. Using this tool, the serial data line for each module can be isolated and tested for a possible problem. Using the special tool at the splice pack makes diagnosing this type of network easier than many others. ● SEE FIGURE 14–4.

3. **Ring/star hybrid.** In a ring/star network, the modules are connected using both types of network configurations. Check service information (SI) for details on how this network is connected on the vehicle being diagnosed and always follow the recommended diagnostic steps.

? FREQUENTLY ASKED QUESTION

What Is a BUS?

A **BUS** is a term used to describe a communications network. Therefore, there are *connections to the BUS* and *BUS communications*, both of which refer to digital messages being transmitted among electronic modules or computers.

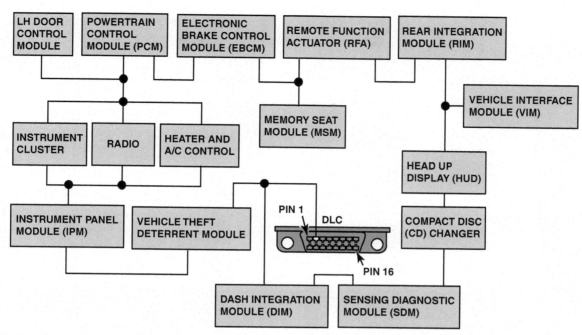

FIGURE 14–3 A ring link network reduces the number of wires it takes to interconnect all of the modules.

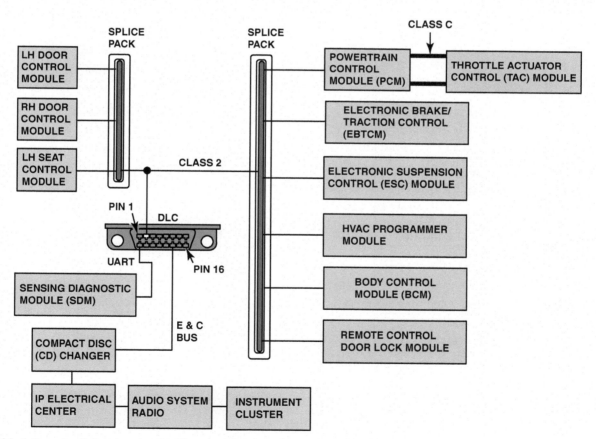

FIGURE 14–4 In a star link network, all of the modules are connected using splice packs.

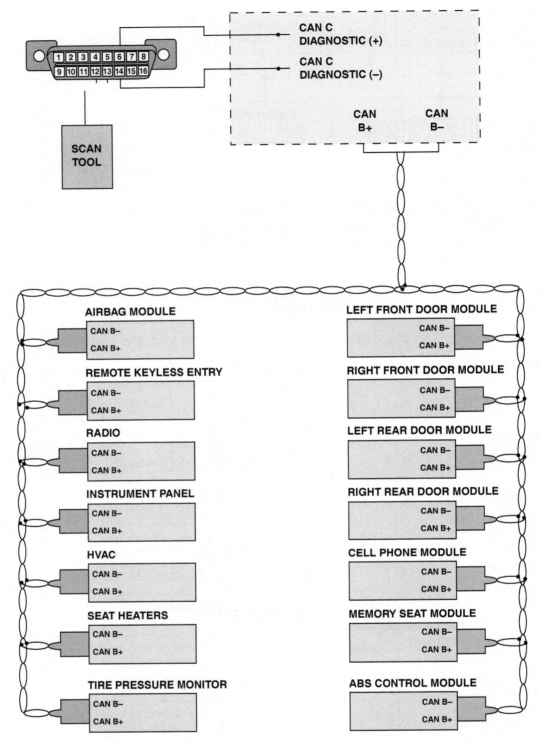

FIGURE 14–5 A typical BUS system showing module CAN communications and twisted pairs of wire.

> ## FREQUENTLY ASKED QUESTION
>
> **What Is a Protocol?**
>
> A protocol is a set of rules or a standard used between computers or electronic control modules. Protocols include the type of electrical connectors, voltage levels, and frequency of the transmitted messages. Protocols, therefore, include both the hardware and software needed to communicate between modules.

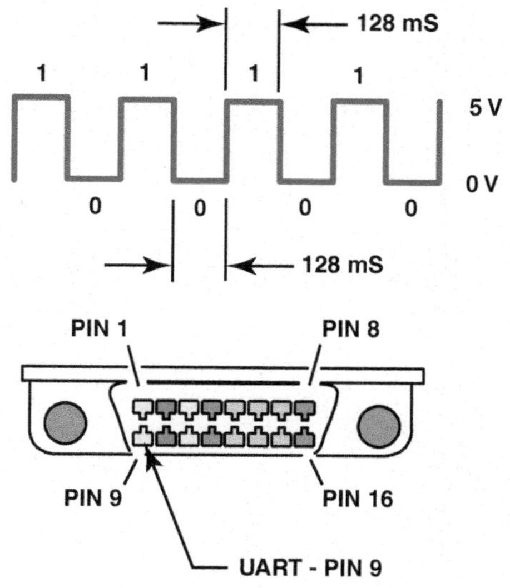

FIGURE 14–6 UART serial data master control module is connected to the data link connector (DLC) at pin 9.

NETWORK COMMUNICATIONS CLASSIFICATIONS

The Society of Automotive Engineers (SAE) standards include the following three categories of in-vehicle network communications:

CLASS A Low-speed networks, meaning less than 10,000 bits per second (bps, or 10 Kbs), are generally used for trip computers, entertainment, and other convenience features.

CLASS B Medium-speed networks, meaning 10,000 to 125,000 bps (10 to 125 Kbs), are generally used for information transfer among modules, such as instrument clusters, temperature sensor data, and other general uses.

CLASS C High-speed networks, meaning 125,000 to 1,000,000 bps, are generally used for real-time powertrain and vehicle dynamic control. High-speed BUS communication systems now use a **controller area network (CAN)**. ● **SEE FIGURE 14–5**.

GENERAL MOTORS COMMUNICATIONS PROTOCOLS

UART General Motors and others use UART communications for some electronic modules or systems. **UART** is a serial data communications protocol that stands for **universal asynchronous receive and transmit**. UART uses a master control module connected to one or more remote modules. The master control module is used to control message traffic on the data line by poling all of the other UART modules. The remote modules send a response message back to the master module.

UART uses a fixed pulse-width switching between 0 and 5 volts. The UART data BUS operates at a baud rate of 8,192 bps. ● **SEE FIGURE 14–6**.

ENTERTAINMENT AND COMFORT COMMUNICATION

The GM **entertainment and comfort (E & C)** serial data is similar to UART, but uses a 0- to 12-volts toggle. Like UART, the E & C serial data uses a master control module connected to other remote modules, which could include the following:

- Compact disc (CD) player
- Instrument panel (IP) electrical center
- Audio system (radio)

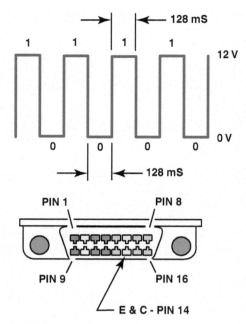

FIGURE 14–7 The E & C serial data is connected to the data link connector at pin 14.

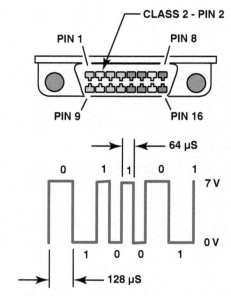

FIGURE 14–8 Class 2 serial data communication is accessible at the data link connector at pin 2.

- Heating, ventilation, and air-conditioning (HVAC) programmer and control head
- Steering wheel controls
  - **SEE FIGURE 14–7**.

CLASS 2 COMMUNICATIONS Class 2 is a serial communications system that operates by toggling between 0 and 7 volts at a transfer rate of 10.4 Kbs. Class 2 is used for most high-speed communications between the powertrain control module and other control modules, plus to the scan tool. Class 2 is the primary high-speed serial communications system used by GMCAN (CAN). ● **SEE FIGURE 14–8**.

KEYWORD COMMUNICATION Keyword 81, 82, and 2000 serial data are also used for some module-to-module communication on GM vehicles. Keyword data BUS signals are toggled from 0 to 12 volts when communicating. The voltage or the datastream is 0 volt when not communicating. Keyword serial communication is used by the seat heater module and others, but is not connected to the data link connector (DLC). ● **SEE FIGURE 14–9**.

GMLAN General Motors, like all vehicle manufacturers, must use high-speed serial data to communicate with scan tools on all vehicles effective with the 2008 model year. As mentioned, the standard is called controller area network

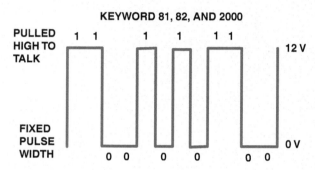

FIGURE 14–9 Keyword 82 operates at a rate of 8,192 bps, similar to UART, and keyword 2000 operates at a baud rate of 10,400 bps (the same as a Class 2 communicator).

(CAN), which General Motors calls **GMLAN**, which stands for **GM local area network.**

General Motors uses two versions of GMLAN.

- **Low-speed GMLAN.** The low-speed version is used for driver-controlled functions, such as power windows and door locks. The baud rate for low-speed GMLAN is 33,300 bps. The GMLAN low-speed serial data is not connected directly to the data link connector and uses one wire. The voltage toggles between 0 and 5 volts after an initial 12-volts spike, which indicates to the modules to turn on or wake-up and listen for data on the line. Low-speed GMLAN is also known as **single-wire CAN,** or **SWCAN,** and is located at pin 1 of the DLC.
- **High-speed GMLAN.** The baud rate is almost real time at 500 Kbs. This serial data method uses a two-twisted-wire circuit that is connected to the data link connector on pins 6 and 14. ● **SEE FIGURE 14–10**.

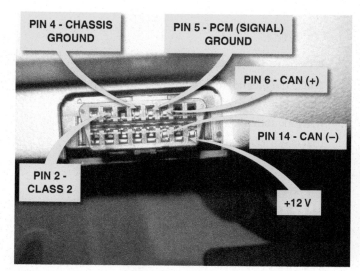

FIGURE 14–10 GMLAN uses pins at terminals 6 and 14. Pin 1 is used for low-speed GMLAN on 2006 and newer GM vehicles.

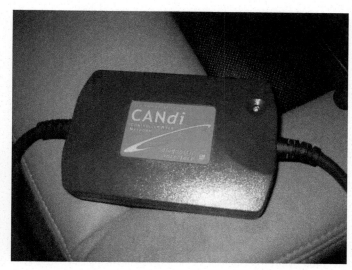

FIGURE 14–12 A CANDi module will flash the green LED rapidly if communication is detected.

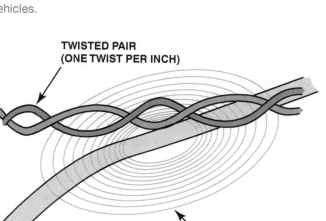

FIGURE 14–11 A twisted pair is used by several different network communications protocols to reduce interference that can be induced in the wiring from nearby electromagnetic sources.

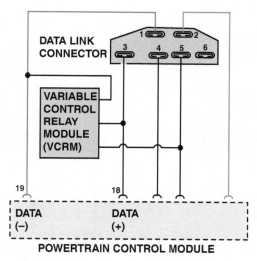

FIGURE 14–13 A Ford OBD-I diagnostic link connector showing that SCP communication uses terminals in cavities 1 (upper left) and 3 (lower left).

FREQUENTLY ASKED QUESTION

Why Is a Twisted Pair Used?

A twisted pair is where two wires are twisted to prevent electromagnetic radiation from affecting the signals passing through the wires. By twisting the two wires about once every inch (9 to 16 times per foot), the interference is canceled by the adjacent wire. ● **SEE FIGURE 14–11.**

A CANDi (CAN diagnostic interface) module is required to be used with the Tech 2 to be able to connect a GM vehicle equipped with GMLAN. ● **SEE FIGURE 14–12.**

FORD NETWORK COMMUNICATIONS PROTOCOLS

STANDARD CORPORATE PROTOCOL Only a few Fords had scan tool data accessible through the OBD-I data link connector. To identify an OBD-I (1988–1995) on a Ford vehicle that is equipped with **standard corporate protocol (SCP)** and be able to communicate through a scan tool, look for terminals in cavities 1 and 3 of the DLC. ● **SEE FIGURE 14–13.**

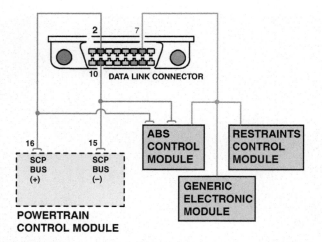

FIGURE 16–14 A scan tool can be used to check communications with the SCP BUS through terminals 2 and 10 and to the other modules connected to terminal 7 of the data link connector.

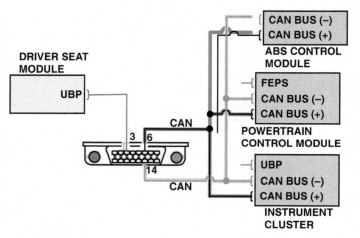

FIGURE 14–15 Many Fords use UBP module communications along with CAN.

SCP uses the J-1850 protocol and is active with the key on. The SCP signal is from 4 volts negative to 4.3 volts positive, and a scan tool does not have to be connected for the signal to be detected on the terminals. OBD-II (EECV) Ford vehicles use terminals 2 (positive) and 10 (negative) of the 16 pin data link connector for network communication, using the SCP module communications.

UART-BASED PROTOCOL Newer Fords use the CAN for scan tool diagnosis, but still retain SCP and **UART-based protocol (UBP)** for some modules. ● **SEE FIGURES 14–14 AND 14–15.**

What Are U Codes?

The U diagnostic trouble codes were at first "undefined" but are now network-related codes. Use the network codes to help pinpoint the circuit or module that is not working correctly.

CHRYSLER COMMUNICATIONS PROTOCOLS

CCD Since the late 1980s, the Chrysler Collision Detection (CCD) multiplex network is used for scan tool and module communications. It is a differential-type communication and uses a twisted pair of wires. The modules connected to the network apply a bias voltage on each wire. CCD signals are divided into plus and minus (CCD+ and CCD–) and the voltage difference does not exceed 0.02 volt. The baud rate is 7,812.5 bps.

NOTE: The "collision" in the Chrysler Collision detection BUS communications refers to the program that avoids conflicts of information exchange within the BUS, and does not refer to airbags or other accident-related circuits of the vehicle.

The circuit is active without a scan tool command. ● **SEE FIGURE 14–16.**

The modules on the CCD BUS apply a bias voltage on each wire by using termination resistors. ● **SEE FIGURE 14–17.**

The difference in voltage between CCD+ and CCD– is less than 20 millivolts. For example, using a digital meter with the black meter lead attached to ground and the red meter lead attached at the data link connector, a normal reading could include the following:

■ Terminal 3 = 2.45 volts

■ Terminal 11 = 2.47 volts

This is an acceptable reading because the readings are 20 millivolts (0.020 volt) of each other. If both had been exactly 2.5 volts, then this could indicate that the two data lines are shorted together. The module providing the bias voltage is usually the body control module on passenger cars and the front control module on jeeps and trucks.

PROGRAMMABLE CONTROLLER INTERFACE The Chrysler **programmable controller interface (PCI)** is a one-wire communication protocol that connects at the OBD-II DLC

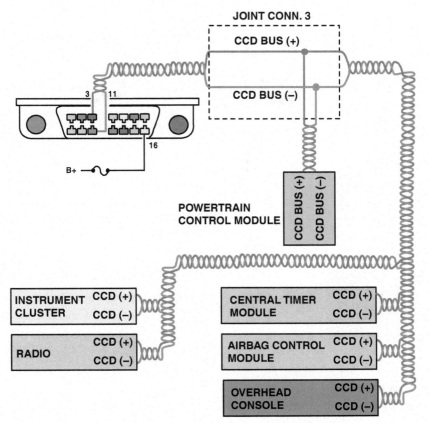

FIGURE 14–16 CCD signals are labeled plus (+) and minus (–) and use a twisted pair of wires. Notice that terminals 3 and 11 of the data link connector are used to access the CCD BUS from a scan tool. Pin 16 is used to supply 12 volts to the scan tool.

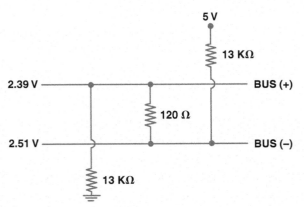

FIGURE 14–17 The differential voltage for the CCD BUS is created by using resistors in a module.

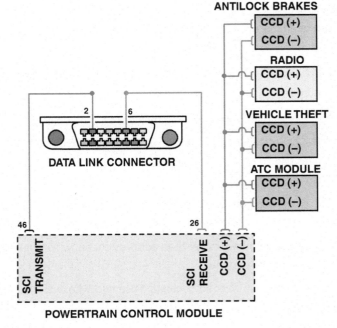

FIGURE 14–18 Many Chrysler vehicles use both SCI and CCD for module communication.

at terminal 2. The PCI BUS is connected to all modules on the BUS in a star configuration and operates at a baud rate of 10,200 bps. The voltage signal toggles between 7.5 and 0 volt. If this voltage is checked at terminal 2 of the OBD-II DLC, a voltage of about 1 volt indicates the average voltage and means that the BUS is functioning and is not shorted-to-ground. PCI and CCD are often used in the same vehicle. ● **SEE FIGURE 14–18**.

SERIAL COMMUNICATIONS INTERFACE Chrysler used **serial communications interface (SCI)** for most scan tool and flash reprogramming functions until it was replaced

with CAN. SCI is connected at the OBD-II data link connector (DLC) at terminals 6 (SCI receive) and 2 (SCI transmit). A scan tool must be connected to test the circuit.

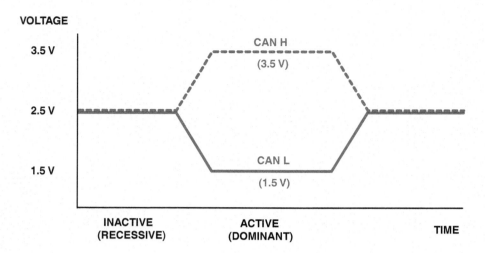

FIGURE 14–19 CAN uses a differential type of module communication where the voltage on one wire is the equal but opposite voltage on the other wire. When no communication is occurring, both wires have 2.5 volts applied. When communication is occurring, CAN H goes up 1 to 3.5 volts and CAN L goes down 1 to 1.5 volts.

CONTROLLER AREA NETWORK

BACKGROUND Robert Bosch Corporation developed the CAN protocol, which was called CAN 1.2, in 1993. The CAN protocol was approved by the Environmental Protection Agency (EPA) for 2003 and newer vehicle diagnostics, and became a legal requirement for all vehicles by 2008. The CAN diagnostic systems use pins 6 and 14 in the standard 16 pin OBD-II (J-1962) connector. Before CAN, the scan tool protocol had been manufacturer specific.

CAN FEATURES The CAN protocol offers the following features:

- Faster than other BUS communication protocols
- Cost effective because it is an easier system than others to use
- Less affected by electromagnetic interference (Data is transferred on two wires that are twisted together, called twisted pair, to help reduce EMI interference.)
- Message based rather than address based, which makes it easier to expand
- No wake-up needed because it is a two-wire system
- Supports up to 15 modules plus a scan tool
- Uses a 120-ohm resistor at the ends of each pair to reduce electrical noise
- Applies 2.5 volts on both wires:
  H (high) goes to 3.5 volts when active
  L (low) goes to 1.5 volts when active
  ● **SEE FIGURE 14–19**.

CAN CLASS A, B, AND C There are three classes of CAN and they operate at different speeds. The CAN A, B, and C networks can all be linked using a gateway within the same vehicle. The gateway is usually one of the many modules in the vehicle.

- **CAN A.** This class operates on only one wire at slow speeds and is therefore less expensive to build. CAN A operates a data transfer rate of 33.33 Kbs in normal mode and up to 83.33 Kbs during reprogramming mode. CAN A uses the vehicle ground as the signal return circuit.

- **CAN B.** This class operates on a two-wire network and does not use the vehicle ground as the signal return circuit. CAN B uses a data transfer rate of 95.2 Kbs. Instead, CAN B (and CAN C) uses two network wires for differential signaling. This means that the two data signal voltages are opposite to each other and used for error detection by constantly being compared. In this case, when the signal voltage at one of the CAN data wires goes high (CAN H), the other one goes low (CAN L), hence the name *differential signaling*. Differential signaling is also used for redundancy, in case one of the signal wires shorts out.

- **CAN C.** This class is the highest speed CAN protocol with speeds up to 500 Kbs. Beginning with 2008 models, all vehicles sold in the United States must use CAN BUS for scan tool communications. Most vehicle manufacturers started using CAN in older models, and it is easy to determine if a vehicle is equipped with CAN. The CAN BUS communicates to the scan tool through terminals 6 and 14 of the DLC indicating that the vehicle is equipped with CAN. ● **SEE FIGURE 14–20**.

The total voltage remains constant at all times and the electromagnetic field effects of the two data BUS lines cancel each other out. The data BUS line is protected against received radiation and is virtually neutral in sending radiation.

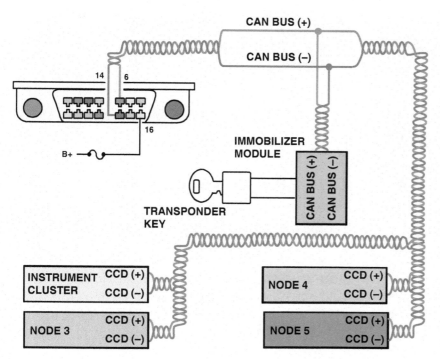

FIGURE 14–20 A typical (generic) system showing how the CAN BUS is connected to various electrical accessories and systems in the vehicle.

FIGURE 14–21 A DLC from a pre-CAN Acura. It shows terminals in cavities 4, 5 (grounds), 7, 10, 14, and 16 (B+).

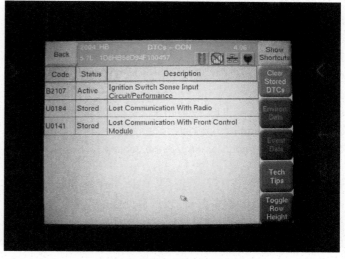

FIGURE 14–22 A Honda scan display showing a B and two U codes, all indicating a BUS-related problem(s).

HONDA/TOYOTA COMMUNICATIONS

The primary BUS communication on pre-CAN-equipped vehicles is ISO 9141-2 using terminals 7 and 15 at the OBD-II DLC. ● SEE FIGURE 14–21.

A factory scan tool or an aftermarket scan tool equipped with enhanced original equipment (OE) software is needed to access many of the BUS messages. ● SEE FIGURE 14–22.

EUROPEAN BUS COMMUNICATIONS

UNIQUE DIAGNOSTIC CONNECTOR Many different types of module communications protocols are used on European vehicles, such as Mercedes and BMW.

Most of these communication BUS messages cannot be accessed through the data link connector. To check the operation of the individual modules, a scan tool equipped with

FIGURE 14-23 A typical 38-cavity diagnostic connector as found on many BMW and Mercedes vehicles under the hood. The use of a breakout box (BOB) connected to this connector can help gain access to module BUS information.

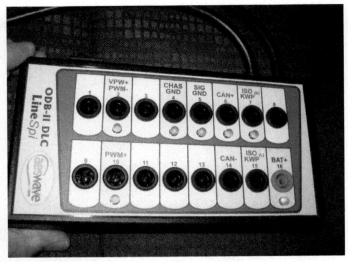

FIGURE 14-24 A breakout box (BOB) used to access the BUS terminals while using a scan tool to activate the modules. This breakout box is equipped with LEDs that light when circuits are active.

factory-type software will be needed to communicate with the module through the gateway module. ● **SEE FIGURE 14-23** for an alternative access method to the modules.

MEDIA-ORIENTED SYSTEM TRANSPORT BUS
The media-oriented system transport (MOST) BUS uses fiber optics for module-to-module communications in a ring or star configuration. This BUS system is currently being used for entertainment equipment data communications for videos, CDs, and other media systems in the vehicle.

MOTOROLA INTERCONNECT BUS
Motorola interconnect (MI) is a single-wire serial communications protocol, using one master control module and many slave modules. Typical application of the MI BUS protocol is with power and memory mirrors, seats, windows, and headlight levelers.

DISTRIBUTED SYSTEM INTERFACE BUS
Distributed system interface (DSI) BUS protocol was developed by Motorola and uses a two-wire serial BUS. This BUS protocol is currently being used for safety-related sensors and components.

BOSCH-SIEMANS-TEMIC BUS
The Bosch-Siemans-Temic (BST) BUS is another system that is used for safety-related components and sensors in a vehicle, such as airbags. The BST BUS is a two-wire system and operates up to 250,000 bps.

FREQUENTLY ASKED QUESTION

How Do You Know What System Is Used?

Use service information to determine which network communication protocol is used. However, due to the various systems on some vehicles, it may be easier to look at the data link connection to determine the system. All OBD-II vehicles have terminals in the following cavities.

Terminal 4: chassis ground

Terminal 5: computer (signal) ground

Terminal 16: 12-volts positive

The terminals in cavities 6 and 14 mean that this vehicle is equipped with CAN as the only module communication protocol available at the DLC. To perform a test of the BUS, use a **breakout box (BOB)** to gain access to the terminals while connecting to the vehicle, using a scan tool. ● **SEE FIGURE 14-24** or a typical OBD-II connector breakout box.

BYTEFLIGHT BUS
The byteflight BUS is used in safety critical systems, such as airbags, and uses the time division multiple access (TDMA) protocol, which operates at 10 million bps using a plastic optical fiber (POF).

FLEXRAY BUS
FlexRay BUS is a version of byteflight and is a high-speed serial communication system for in-vehicle networks. FlexRay is commonly used for steer-by-wire and brake-by-wire systems.

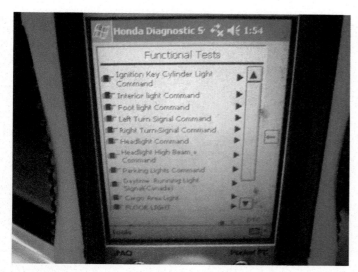

FIGURE 14–25 This Honda scan tool allows the technician to turn on individual lights and operate individual power windows and other accessories that are connected to the BUS system.

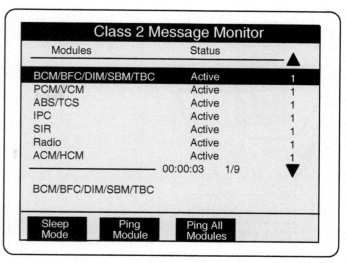

FIGURE 14–26 Modules used in a General Motors vehicle can be "pinged" using a Tech 2 scan tool.

DOMESTIC DIGITAL BUS The domestic digital BUS, commonly designated D2B, is an optical BUS system connecting audio, video, computer, and telephone components in a single-ring structure with a speed of up to 5,600,000 bps.

LOCAL INTERCONNECT NETWORK BUS Local interconnect network (LIN) is a BUS protocol used between intelligent sensors and actuators and has a BUS speed of 19,200 bps.

NETWORK COMMUNICATIONS DIAGNOSIS

STEPS TO FINDING A FAULT When a network communications fault is suspected, perform the following steps:

STEP 1 **Check everything that does and does not work.** Often accessories that do not seem to be connected can help identify which module or BUS circuit is at fault.

STEP 2 **Perform module status test.** Use a factory level scan tool or an aftermarket scan tool equipped with enhanced software that allows OE-like functions. Check if the components or systems can be operated through the scan tool. ● **SEE FIGURE 14–25**.

TECH TIP

No Communication? Try Bypass Mode.

If a Tech 2 scan tool shows "no communication," try using the bypass mode to see what should be on the data display. To enter bypass mode, perform the following steps:

STEP 1 Select tool option (F3).

STEP 2 Set communications to bypass (F5).

STEP 3 Select enable.

STEP 4 Input make/model and year of vehicle.

STEP 5 Note all parameters that should be included, as shown. The values will not be shown.

■ **Ping modules.** Start the Class 2 diagnosis by using a scan tool and select *diagnostic circuit check*. If no diagnostic trouble codes (DTCs) are shown, there could be a communication problem. Select *message monitor,* which will display the status of all of the modules on the Class 2 BUS circuit. The modules that are awake will be shown as active and the scan tool can be used to ping individual modules or command all modules. The ping command should change the status from "active" to "inactive." ● **SEE FIGURE 14–26**.

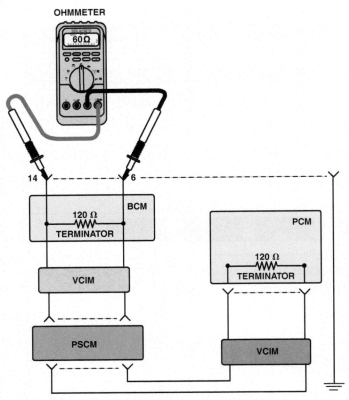

FIGURE 14–27 Checking the terminating resistors using an ohmmeter at the DLC.

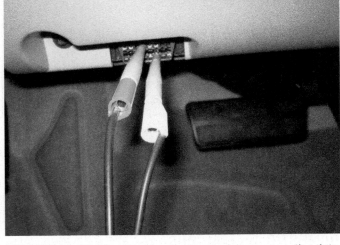

FIGURE 14–28 Use front-probe terminals to access the data link connector. Always follow the specified back-probe and front-probe procedures as found in service information.

NOTE: If an excessive parasitic draw is being diagnosed, use a scan tool to ping the modules is one way to determine if one of the modules is not going to sleep and cause excessive battery drain.

■ **Check state of health.** All modules on the Class 2 BUS circuit have at least one other module responsible for reporting **state of health (SOH)**. If a module fails to send a state of health message within five seconds, the companion module will set a diagnostic trouble code for the module that did not respond. The defective module is not capable of sending this message.

STEP 3 **Check the resistance of the terminating resistors.** Most high-speed BUS systems use resistors at each end, called **terminating resistors**. These resistors are used to help reduce interference into other systems in the vehicle. Usually two 120-ohm resistors are installed at each end and are therefore connected electrically in parallel. Two 120-ohm resistors connected in parallel would measure 60 ohms if tested using an ohmmeter. ● **SEE FIGURE 14–27.**

STEP 4 **Check data BUS for voltages.** Use a digital multimeter set to DC volts to monitor communications and check the BUS for proper operation. Some BUS conditions and possible causes include the following:

■ **Signal is zero volt all of the time.** Check for short-to-ground by unplugging modules one at a time to check if one module is causing the problem.

■ **Signal is high or 12 volts all of the time.** The BUS circuit could be shorted to 12 volts. Check with the customer to see if any service or body repair work was done recently. Try unplugging each module one at a time to pin down which module is causing the communications problem.

■ **A variable voltage usually indicates that messages are being sent and received.** CAN and Class 2 can be identified by looking at the data link connector for a terminal in cavity number 2. Class 2 is active all of the time the ignition is "on," and therefore voltage variation between 0 and 7 volts can be measured using a DMM set to read DC volts. ● **SEE FIGURE 14–28.**

HIGH

LOW

(a)

FIGURE 14–29 (a) Data is sent in packets, so it is normal to see activity and then a flat line between messages. (b) A CAN BUS should show voltages that are opposite when there is normal communications. CAN H circuit should go from 2.5 volts at rest to 3.5 volts when active. The CAN L circuit goes from 2.5 volts at rest to 1.5 volts when active.

CAN BUS LOOKS GOOD

CAN LOW

CAN HIGH

(b)

STEP 5 **Use a digital storage oscilloscope to monitor the waveforms of the BUS circuit.** Using a scope on the data line terminals can show if communication is being transmitted. Typical faults and their causes include the following:

- **Normal operation.** Normal operation shows variable voltage signals on the data lines. It is impossible to know what information is being transmitted, but if there is activity with short sections of inactivity, this indicates normal data line transmission activity. ● **SEE FIGURE 14–29**.
- **High voltage.** If there is a constant high-voltage signal without any change, this indicates that the data line is shorted-to-voltage.
- **Zero or low voltage.** If the data line voltage is zero or almost zero and not showing any higher voltage signals, then the data line is short-to-ground.

STEP 6 **Follow factory service information instructions to isolate the cause of the fault.** This step often involves disconnecting one module at a time to see if it is the cause of a short-to-ground or an open in the BUS circuit.

CASE STUDY

The Radio Caused No-Start Story

A 2005 Chevrolet Cobalt did not start. A technician checked with a subscription-based helpline service and discovered that a fault with the Class 2 data circuit could prevent the engine from starting. The advisor suggested that a module should be disconnected one at a time to see if one of them was taking the data line to ground. The first one the technician disconnected was the radio. The engine started and ran. Apparently the Class 2 serial data line was shorted-to-ground inside the radio, which took the entire BUS down. When BUS communication is lost, the PCM is not able to energize the fuel pump, ignition, or fuel injectors so the engine would not start. The radio was replaced to solve the no-start condition.

Summary:
- **Complaint**—The engine did not start.
- **Cause**—A hot line service helped the technician narrow the cause to a fault in the radio that took the Class 2 data line to ground.
- **Correction**—The radio was replaced that restored proper operation of the Class 2 data bus.

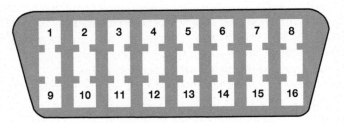

Pin 2 - J1850 Bus+
Pin 4 - Chassis Ground
Pin 5 - Signal Ground
Pin 6 - CAN High (J-2284)
Pin 7 - ISO 9141-2 K Line

Pin 10 - J1850 Bus
Pin 14 - CAN Low (J-2284)
Pin 15 - ISO 9141-2 L Line
Pin 16 - Battery Power

FIGURE 14–30 A 16 pin OBD-II DLC with terminals identified. Scan tools use the power pin (16) and ground pin (4) for power so that a separate power plug is not necessary on OBD-II vehicles.

FREQUENTLY ASKED QUESTION

Which Module Is the Gateway Module?

The gateway module is responsible for communicating with other modules and acts as the main communications module for scan tool data. Most General Motors vehicles use the body control module (BCM) or the instrument panel control (IPC) module as the gateway. To verify which module is the gateway, check the schematic and look for one that has voltage applied during all of the following conditions:

- Key on, engine off
- Engine cranking
- Engine running

OBD-II DATA LINK CONNECTOR

All OBD-II vehicles use a 16 pin connector that includes the following::

   Pin 4 = chassis ground

   Pin 5 = signal ground

   Pin 16 = battery power (4 A max)

   ● **SEE FIGURE 14–30**.

GENERAL MOTORS VEHICLES

- SAE J-1850 (VPW, Class 2, 10.4 Kbs) standard, which uses pins 2, 4, 5, and 16, but not 10
- GM Domestic OBD-II

   Pins 1 and 9: CCM (comprehensive component monitor) slow baud rate, 8,192 UART (prior to 2006)

   Pin 1 (2006+): low-speed GMLAN

   Pins 2 and 10: OEM enhanced, fast rate, 40,500 baud rate

   Pins 7 and 15: generic OBD-II, ISO 9141, 10,400 baud rate

   Pins 6 and 14: GMLAN

ASIAN, CHRYSLER, AND EUROPEAN VEHICLES

- ISO 9141-2 standard, which uses pins 4, 5, 7, 15, and 16
- Chrysler Domestic Group OBD-II

   Pins 2 and 10: CCM

   Pins 3 and 14: OEM enhanced, 60,500 baud rate

   Pins 7 and 15: generic OBD-II, ISO 9141, 10,400 baud rate

FORD VEHICLES

- SAE J-1850 (PWM, 41.6 Kbs) standard, which uses pins 2, 4, 5, 10, and 16
- Ford Domestic OBD-II

   Pins 2 and 10: CCM

   Pins 6 and 14: OEM enhanced, Class C, 40,500 baud rate

   Pins 7 and 15: generic OBD-II, ISO 9141, 10,400 baud rate

 TECH TIP

Check Computer Data Line Circuit Schematic

Many General Motors vehicles use more than one type of BUS communications protocol. Check service information (SI) and look at the schematic for computer data line circuits, which should show all of the data BUSes and their connectors to the diagnostic link connector (DLC). ● **SEE FIGURE 14–31**.

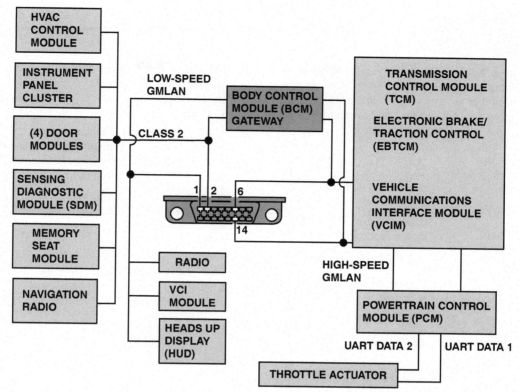

FIGURE 14–31 This schematic of a Chevrolet Equinox shows that the vehicle uses a GMLAN BUS (DLC pins 6 and 14), plus a Class 2 (pin 2) and UART. Pin 1 connects to the low-speed GMLAN network.

SUMMARY

1. The use of a network for module communications reduces the number of wires and connections needed.

2. Module communication configurations include ring link, star link, and ring/star hybrid systems.

3. The SAE communication classifications for vehicle communications systems include Class A (low speed), Class B (medium speed), and Class C (high speed).

4. Various module communications used on General Motors vehicles include UART, E & C, Class 2, keyword communications, and GMLAN (CAN).

5. Types of module communications used on Ford vehicles include SCP, UBP, and CAN.

6. Chrysler brand vehicles use SCI, CCD, PCI, and CAN communications protocols.

7. Many European vehicles use an underhood electrical connector that can be used to access electrical components and modules using a breakout box (BOB) or special tester.

8. Diagnosis of network communications includes checking the terminating resistor value and checking for changing voltage signals at the DLC.

REVIEW QUESTIONS

1. Why is a communication network used?

2. Why are the two wires twisted if used for network communications?

3. Why is a gateway module used?

4. What are U codes?

5. What is the purpose of the terminating resistors?

1. Technician A says that module communications networks are used to reduce the number of wires in a vehicle. Technician B says that a communications network is used to share data from sensors, which can be used by many different modules. Which technician is correct?
   a. Technician A only
   b. Technician B only
   c. Both Technicians A and B
   d. Neither Technician A nor B

2. A module is also known as a _____.
   a. BUS
   b. node
   c. terminator
   d. resistor pack

3. A high-speed CAN BUS communicates with a scan tool through which terminal(s)?
   a. 6 and 14
   b. 2
   c. 7 and 15
   d. 4 and 16

4. UART uses a _____ signal that toggles 0 volt.
   a. 5 volts
   b. 7 volts
   c. 8 volts
   d. 12 volts

5. GM Class 2 communication toggles between _____.
   a. 5 and 7 volts
   b. 0 and 12 volts
   c. 7 and 12 volts
   d. 0 and 7 volts

6. Which terminal of the data link connector does General Motors use for Class 2 communication?
   a. 1
   b. 2
   c. 3
   d. 4

7. GMLAN is the General Motors term for which type of module communication?
   a. UART
   b. Class 2
   c. High-speed CAN
   d. Keyword 2000

8. How do CAN H and CAN L operate?
   a. CAN H is at 2.5 volts when not transmitting.
   b. CAN L is at 2.5 volts when not transmitting.
   c. CAN H goes to 3.5 volts when transmitting.
   d. All of the above

9. Which terminal of the OBD-II data link connector is the signal ground for all vehicles?
   a. 1
   b. 3
   c. 4
   d. 5

10. Terminal 16 of the OBD-II data link connector is used for what?
    a. Chassis ground
    b. 12-V positive
    c. Module (signal ground)
    d. Manufacturer's discretion

chapter 15
BATTERIES

221

LEARNING OBJECTIVES

After studying this chapter, the reader will be able to:

1. Describe how a battery works.
2. Describe the construction of a battery.
3. Discuss valve regulated batteries and the causes of battery failure.
4. Discuss how charge indicators work.
5. List battery ratings and battery sizes.

This chapter will help you prepare for the ASE Electrical/Electronic Systems (A6) certification test content area "B" (Battery Diagnosis and Repair).

KEY TERMS

AGM 227
Ampere hour 229
Battery Council International (BCI) 229
CA 228
CCA 228
Cells 223
Deep cycling 229
Electrolyte 224
Enhanced Flooded Batteries (EFB) 227
Flooded lead acid (FLA) 226
Gassing 222
Gel battery 227
Grid 222
Low-water-loss battery 222

Maintenance-free battery 222
MCA 228
Partitions 224
Porous lead 222
Recombinant battery 227
Reserve capacity 228
Sediment chamber 222
SLA 227
SLI 222
Specific gravity 225
Sponge lead 222
SVR 227
VRLA 227

INTRODUCTION

PURPOSE AND FUNCTION   Every electrical component in a vehicle is supplied current from the battery. The battery is one of the most important parts of a vehicle because it is the heart or foundation of the electrical system. The primary purpose of an automotive battery is to provide a source of electrical power for starting and for electrical demands that exceed alternator output.

WHY BATTERIES ARE IMPORTANT   The battery also acts as a voltage stabilizer for the entire electrical system. The battery is a voltage stabilizer because it acts as a reservoir from where large amounts of current (amperes) can be used quickly during starting, and replaced back gradually by the alternator during charging.

- The battery *must* be in good (serviceable) condition before the charging and cranking systems can be tested. For example, if a battery is discharged, the cranking circuit (starter motor) could test as being defective because the battery voltage might drop below specifications.
- The charging circuit could also test as being defective because of a weak or discharged battery. It is important to test the vehicle battery before further testing of the cranking or charging system.

BATTERY CONSTRUCTION

CASE   Most automotive battery cases (container or covers) are constructed of polypropylene, a thin (approximately 0.08 inch or 0.02 millimeter thick), strong, and lightweight plastic. In contrast, containers for industrial batteries and some truck batteries are constructed of a hard, thick rubber material.

Inside the case are six cells (for a 12-volt battery). Each cell has positive and negative plates. Built into the bottom of many batteries are ribs that support the lead-alloy plates and provide a space for sediment to settle, called the **sediment chamber**. This space prevents spent active material from causing a short circuit between the plates at the bottom of the battery. ● **SEE FIGURE 15–1.**

A **maintenance-free battery** uses little water during normal service because of the alloy material used to construct the battery plate grids. Maintenance-free batteries are also called **low-water-loss batteries**.

GRIDS   Each positive and negative plate in a battery is constructed on a framework, or **grid**, made primarily of lead. Lead is a soft material and must be strengthened for use in an automotive battery grid. Adding antimony or calcium to the pure lead adds strength to the lead grids. ● **SEE FIGURE 15–2.**

Battery grids hold the active material and provide the electrical pathways for the current created in the plate.

Maintenance-free batteries use calcium instead of antimony, because 0.2% calcium has the same strength as 6% antimony. A typical lead–calcium grid uses only 0.09% to 0.12% calcium. Using low amounts of calcium instead of higher amounts of antimony reduces **gassing**. Gassing is the release of hydrogen and oxygen from the battery that occurs during charging and results in water usage.

Low-maintenance batteries use a low percentage of antimony (about 2% to 3%), or use antimony only in the positive grids and calcium in the negative grids. *The percentages that make up the alloy of the plate grids constitute the major difference between standard and maintenance-free batteries.* The chemical reactions that occur inside each battery are identical regardless of the type of material used to construct the grid plates.

POSITIVE PLATES   The positive plates have *lead dioxide (peroxide)* placed onto the grid framework. This process is called *pasting*. This active material can react with the sulfuric acid of the battery and is dark brown in color.

NEGATIVE PLATES   The negative plates are pasted to the grid with a pure **porous lead**, called **sponge lead**, and are gray in color.

SEPARATORS   The positive and the negative plates must be installed alternately next to each other without touching. Nonconducting *separators* are used, which allow room for the reaction of the acid with both plate materials, yet insulate the plates to prevent shorts. These separators are porous (with many small holes) and have ribs facing the positive plate. Separators can be made from resin-coated paper, porous rubber, fiberglass, or expanded plastic. Many batteries use

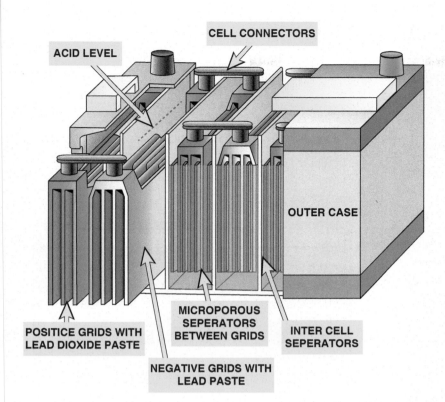

FIGURE 15–1 Batteries are constructed of plates grouped into cells and installed in a plastic case.

Labels (Figure 15–1):
- ACID LEVEL
- CELL CONNECTORS
- OUTER CASE
- POSITICE GRIDS WITH LEAD DIOXIDE PASTE
- MICROPOROUS SEPERATORS BETWEEN GRIDS
- INTER CELL SEPERATORS
- NEGATIVE GRIDS WITH LEAD PASTE

FIGURE 15–2 A grid from a battery used in both positive and negative plates.

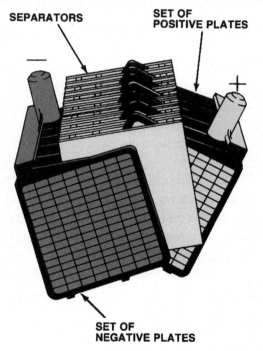

Labels (Figure 15–3):
- SEPARATORS
- SET OF POSITIVE PLATES
- SET OF NEGATIVE PLATES

FIGURE 15–3 Two groups of plates are combined to form a battery element.

envelope-type separators that encase the entire plate. This helps prevent any material that may shed from the plates from causing a short circuit between plates at the bottom of the battery.

CELLS **Cells** are constructed of positive and negative plates with insulating separators between each plate. Most batteries use one more negative plate than positive plate in each cell. However, many newer batteries use the same number of positive and negative plates. A cell is also called an element. Each cell is actually a 2.1-volt battery, regardless of the number of positive or negative plates used. The greater the number of plates used in each cell, the greater the amount of *current* that can be produced. Typical batteries contain four positive plates

and five negative plates per cell. A 12-volt battery contains six cells connected in series, which produce 12.6 volts ($6 \times 2.1 =$ 12.6) and contain 54 plates (9 plates per cell $\times$ 6 cells). If the same 12-volt battery had five positive plates and six negative plates, for a total of 11 plates per cell (5 + 6), or 66 plates (11 plates $\times$ 6 cells), it would have the same voltage, but the amount of current that the battery could produce would be increased. ● **SEE FIGURE 15–3.**

FIGURE 15–4 A cutaway battery showing the connection of the cells to each other through the partition.

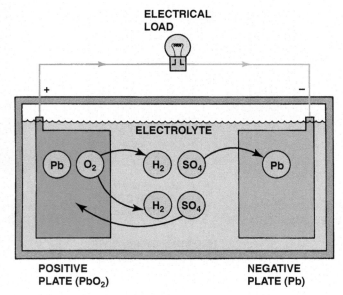

FIGURE 15–5 Chemical reaction for a lead–acid battery that is fully charged being discharged by the attached electrical load.

The amperage capacity of a battery is determined by the amount of active plate material in the battery and the area of the plate material exposed to the electrolyte in the battery.

PARTITIONS Each cell is separated from the other cells by **partitions**, which are made of the same material as that used for the outside case of the battery. Electrical connections between cells are provided by lead connectors that loop over the top of the partition and connect the plates of the cells together. Many batteries connect the cells directly through the partition connectors, which provide the shortest path for the current and the lowest resistance. ● **SEE FIGURE 15–4**.

ELECTROLYTE **Electrolyte** is the term used to describe the acid solution in a battery. The electrolyte used in automotive batteries is a solution (liquid combination) of 36% sulfuric acid and 64% water. This electrolyte is used for both lead–antimony and lead–calcium (maintenance-free) batteries. The chemical symbol for this sulfuric acid solution is H_2SO_4.

H_2 = Symbol for hydrogen (the subscript 2 means that there are two atoms of hydrogen)

S = Symbol for sulfur

O_4 = Symbol for oxygen (the subscript 4 indicates that there are four atoms of oxygen)

Electrolyte is sold premixed in a proper proportion and is factory installed or added to the battery when the battery is sold. Additional electrolyte must *never* be added to any battery after the original electrolyte fill. It is normal for some water (H_2O) to escape during charging as a result of the chemical reactions. The escape of gases from a battery during charging or discharging is called gassing. Only pure distilled water should be added to a battery. If distilled water is not available, clean drinking water can be used.

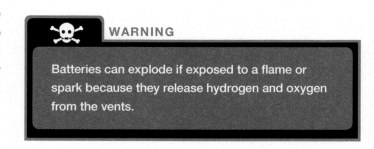

WARNING

Batteries can explode if exposed to a flame or spark because they release hydrogen and oxygen from the vents.

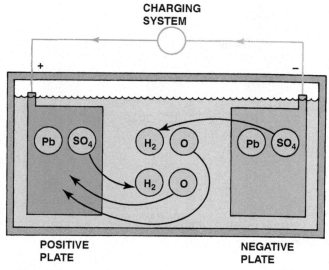

FIGURE 15–6 Chemical reaction for a lead–acid battery that is fully discharged being charged by the attached generator.

? FREQUENTLY ASKED QUESTION

Is There an Easy Way to Remember How a Battery Works?

Yes. Think of the sulfuric acid solution in the electrolyte being deposited, then removed from the plates.

- **During discharge.** The acid (SO_4) is leaving the electrolyte and getting onto both plates.
- **During charging.** The acid (SO_4) is being forced from both plates and enters the electrolyte.

HOW A BATTERY WORKS

PRINCIPLE INVOLVED The principle on which a battery works is based on a scientific principle discovered years ago, which states that:

- When two dissimilar metals are placed in an acid, electrons flow between the metals if a circuit is connected between them.
- This can be demonstrated by pushing a steel nail and a piece of solid copper wire into a lemon. Connect a voltmeter to the ends of the copper wire and the nail, and voltage will be displayed.

A fully charged lead–acid battery has a positive plate of lead dioxide (peroxide) and a negative plate of lead surrounded by a sulfuric acid solution (electrolyte). The difference in potential (voltage) between lead peroxide and lead in acid is approximately 2.1 volts.

DURING DISCHARGING The positive plate lead dioxide (PbO_2) combines with the SO_4, forming $PbSO_4$ from the electrolyte and releases its O_2 into the electrolyte, forming H_2O. The negative plate also combines with the SO_4 from the electrolyte and becomes lead sulfate ($PbSO_4$). ● **SEE FIGURE 15–5.**

FULLY DISCHARGED STATE When the battery is fully discharged, both the positive and the negative plates are $PbSO_4$ (lead sulfate) and the electrolyte has become water (H_2O). As the battery is being discharged, the plates and the electrolyte approach the completely discharged state. There is also the danger of freezing when a battery is discharged, because the electrolyte is mostly water.

CAUTION: Never charge or jump start a frozen battery because the hydrogen gas can get trapped in the ice and ignite if a spark is caused during the charging process. The result can be an explosion.

DURING CHARGING During charging, the sulfate from the acid leaves both the positive and the negative plates and returns to the electrolyte, where it becomes a normal-strength sulfuric acid solution. The positive plate returns to lead dioxide (PbO_2), the negative plate is again pure lead (Pb), and the electrolyte becomes H_2SO_4. ● **SEE FIGURE 15–6.**

SPECIFIC GRAVITY

DEFINITION The amount of sulfate in the electrolyte is determined by the electrolyte's **specific gravity**, which is the ratio of the weight of a given volume of a liquid to the weight of an equal volume of water. In other words, the more dense the liquid is, the higher its specific gravity. Pure water is the basis for this measurement and is given a specific gravity of 1.000 at 80°F (27°C). Pure sulfuric acid has a specific gravity of 1.835; the *correct* concentration of water and sulfuric acid

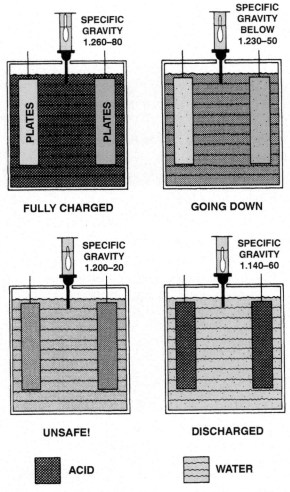

FIGURE 15-7 As the battery becomes discharged, the specific gravity of the battery acid decreases. Because the electrolyte is close to water when discharged, a dead battery can freeze in cold weather.

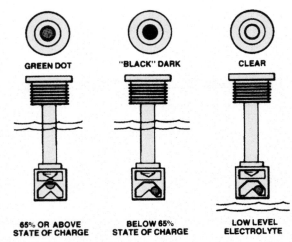

FIGURE 15-8 Typical battery charge indicator. If the specific gravity is low (battery discharged), the ball drops away from the reflective prism. When the battery is charged enough, the ball floats and reflects the color of the ball (usually green) back up through the sight glass and the sight glass is dark.

SPECIFIC GRAVITY	STATE OF CHARGE	BATTERY VOLTAGE (V)
1.265	Fully charged	12.6 or higher
1.225	75% charged	12.4
1.190	50% charged	12.2
1.155	25% charged	12.0
Lower than 1.120	Discharged	11.9 or lower

CHART 15-1

A comparison showing the relationship among specific gravity, battery voltage, and state of charge.

(called electrolyte—64% water, 36% acid) is 1.260 to 1.280 at 80°F. The higher the battery's specific gravity, the more fully it is charged. ● SEE FIGURE 15-7.

CHARGE INDICATORS Some batteries are equipped with a built-in state-of-charge indicator, commonly called *green eyes.* This indicator is simply a small, ball-type hydrometer that is installed in one cell. This hydrometer uses a plastic ball that floats if the electrolyte density is sufficient (which it is when the battery is about 65% charged). When the ball floats, it appears in the hydrometer's sight glass, changing its color. ● SEE FIGURE 15-8.

Because the hydrometer is testing only one cell (out of six on a 12-volt battery), and because the hydrometer ball can easily stick in one position, do not trust that this is accurate information about a state of charge (SOC) of the battery.

Values of specific gravity, state of charge, and battery voltage at 80°F (27°C) are given in ● CHART 15-1.

BATTERY CONSTRUCTION TYPES

FLOODED BATTERIES Conventional batteries use a liquid electrolyte and are called **flooded lead acid (FLA)** batteries., In this design, vents are used to allow the gases (hydrogen and oxygen) to escape. It is this loss of the hydrogen and oxygen that results in a battery using water during normal use.

ENHANCED FLOODED BATTERIES.

Enhanced Flooded Battery (EFB) is a flooded battery (NOT an absorbed glass mat battery) that is optimized to work with stop/start vehicle systems. Using wet cells, the design allows for improved charge acceptance and greater durability when being operated in a vehicle that uses a stop/start system. This operation requires a robust battery and starter motor to function correctly over an estimated life of over 500,000 stops and starts.

ABSORBED GLASS MAT.

The acid used in an **absorbed glass mat (AGM)** battery is totally absorbed into the separator, making the battery leak proof and spill proof. The battery is assembled by compressing the cell about 20%, then inserting it into the container. The compressed cell helps reduce damage caused by vibration and helps keep the acid tightly against the plates. The sealed maintenance-free design uses a pressure release valve in each cell. Unlike conventional batteries that use a liquid electrolyte, called flooded cell batteries, most of the hydrogen and oxygen given off during charging remains inside the battery. The separator or mat is only 90% to 95% saturated with electrolyte, thereby allowing a portion of the mat to be filled with gas. The gas spaces provide channels to allow the hydrogen and oxygen gases to recombine rapidly and safely. Because the acid is totally absorbed into the glass mat separator, an AGM battery can be mounted in any direction. AGM batteries also have a longer service life, often lasting 7 to 10 years. Absorbed glass mat batteries are used as standard equipment in some vehicles such as the Chevrolet Corvette and in most Toyota/Lexus hybrid electric vehicles. ● **SEE FIGURES 15-9 and 15-10.**

GELLED ELECTROLYTE BATTERY.

In a gelled electrolyte battery, silica is added to the electrolyte, which turns the electrolyte into a substance similar to gelatin. This type of battery is also called a **gel battery**. Gel batteries are usually used in electric scooters and bicycles and not used for automotive applications.

VALVE-REGULATED LEAD-ACID BATTERIES.

Both AGM and gel batteries are called **Valve-regulated lead-acid (VRLA)**, also called **Sealed valve-regulated (SVR)** or **Sealed lead-acid (SLA)**, batteries. These batteries use a low-pressure venting system that releases excess gas and automatically reseals if a buildup of gas is created due to overcharging.

Both types of valve-regulated lead-acid batteries are also called **recombinant battery** design. A recombinant-type battery means that the oxygen gas generated at the positive plate travels through the dense electrolyte to the negative plate. When the oxygen reaches the negative plate, it reacts with the lead, which consumes the oxygen gas and prevents the formation of hydrogen gas. It is because of this oxygen recombination that VRLA batteries do not use water.

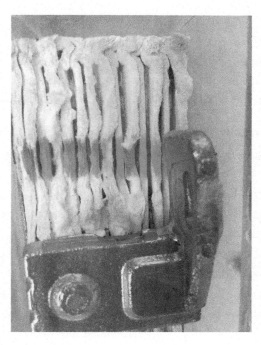

FIGURE 15-9 A close up of a AGM cell showing the mat totally encasing the plates.

FIGURE 15-10 A AGM battery under the floor next to the spare tire on a Lexus NX300h hybrid electric vehicle.

CAUSES AND TYPES OF BATTERY FAILURE

NORMAL LIFE Most automotive batteries have a useful service life of three to seven years; however, proper care can help increase the life of a battery, but abuse can shorten it. The major cause of premature battery failure is overcharging.

BATTERY SULFATION During charging of a battery, the lead sulfate is converted back to lead. When a battery is left in a discharged condition, the lead sulfate re-crystallizes into hard lead sulfate. This process is called "sulfation" or a "*sulfated battery*."

CHARGING VOLTAGE The automotive charging circuit, consisting of an alternator and connecting wires, must operate correctly to prevent damage to the battery.

- Charging voltages higher than 15.5 volts can damage a battery by warping the plates as a result of the heat of overcharging.
- AGM batteries can be damaged if charged at a voltage higher than 14.5 volts.

Overcharging also causes the active plate material to disintegrate and fall out of the supporting grid framework. Vibration or bumping can also cause internal damage similar to that caused by overcharging. It is important, therefore, to ensure that all automotive batteries are securely clamped with the battery hold-down bracket in the vehicle. The shorting of cell plates can occur without notice. If one of the six cells of a 12-volt battery is shorted, the resulting voltage of the battery is only 10 volts (12 − 2 = 10). With only 10 volts available, the starter *usually* will not be able to start the engine.

BATTERY HOLD-DOWNS All batteries must be attached securely to the vehicle to prevent battery damage. Normal vehicle vibrations can cause the active materials inside the battery to shed. Battery hold-down clamps or brackets help reduce vibration, which can greatly reduce the capacity and life of any battery. ● **SEE FIGURE 15–11.**

BATTERY VENT TUBES If a battery is installed inside a vehicle, vent tubes are used to route battery fumes to the outside so they don't get into the passenger compartment. ● **SEE FIGURE 15–12.**

BATTERY RATINGS

Batteries are rated according to the amount of current they can produce under specific conditions.

COLD-CRANKING AMPERES Every automotive battery must be able to supply electrical power to crank the engine in cold weather and still provide battery voltage high enough to operate the ignition system for starting. The cold-cranking ampere rating of a battery is the number of amperes that can be supplied by a battery at 0°F (−18°C) for 30 seconds while the battery still maintains a voltage of 1.2 volts per cell or higher. This means that the battery voltage would be 7.2 volts for a 12-volt battery and 3.6 volts for a 6-volt battery. The cold-cranking performance rating is called **cold-cranking amperes (CCA)**. Try to purchase a battery with the highest CCA for the money. See the vehicle manufacturer's specifications for recommended battery capacity.

CRANKING AMPERES The designation **CA** refers to the number of amperes that can be supplied by a battery at 32°F (0°C). This rating results in a higher number than the more stringent CCA rating. ● **SEE FIGURE 15–13.**

MARINE CRANKING AMPERES Marine cranking amperes **(MCA)** is similar to cranking amperes and is tested at 32°F (0°C).

RESERVE CAPACITY The **reserve capacity** rating for batteries is *the number of minutes* for which the battery can produce 25 amperes and still have a battery voltage of 1.75 volts per cell (10.5 volts for a 12-volt battery). This rating is actually a measurement of the time a vehicle can be driven in the event of a charging system failure.

BATTERY HOLD-DOWN BRACKET

FIGURE 15–11 A typical battery hold-down bracket. All batteries should use a bracket to prevent battery damage due to vibration and shock.

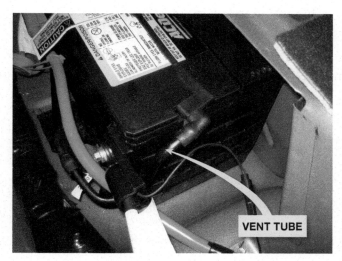

FIGURE 15–12 A battery installed under the rear seat of a Cadillac showing the vent tubes.

FIGURE 15–13 This battery has a cranking amperes (CA) rating of 1,000. This means that this battery is capable of cranking an engine for 30 seconds at a temperature of 32°F (0°C) at a minimum of 1.2 volts per cell (7.2 volts for a 12-volt battery).

AMPERE HOUR **Ampere hour** is an older battery rating system that measures how many amperes of current the battery can produce over a period of time. For example, a battery that has a 50 amp-hour (A-H) rating can deliver 50 amperes for 1 hour or 1 ampere for 50 hours or any combination that equals 50 amp-hours.

 FREQUENTLY ASKED QUESTION

What Determines Battery Capacity?

The capacity of any battery is determined by the amount of active plate material in the battery. A battery with a large number of thin plates can produce high current for a short period. If a few thick plates are used, the battery can produce low current for a long period. A trolling motor battery used for fishing must supply a low current for a long period of time. An automotive battery is required to produce a high current for a short period for cranking. Therefore, every battery is designed for a specific application.

 FREQUENTLY ASKED QUESTION

What Is Deep Cycling?

Deep cycling is almost fully discharging a battery and then completely recharging it. Golf cart batteries are an example of lead–acid batteries that must be designed to be deep cycled. A golf cart must be able to cover two 18-hole rounds of golf and then be fully recharged overnight. Charging is hard on batteries because the internal heat generated can cause plate warpage, so these specially designed batteries use thicker plate grids that resist warpage. Normal automotive batteries are not designed for repeated deep cycling.

BATTERY SIZES

BCI GROUP SIZES Battery sizes are standardized by the **Battery Council International (BCI)**. When selecting a replacement battery, check the specified group number in service information, battery application charts at parts stores, or the owner's manual.

TYPICAL GROUP SIZE APPLICATIONS

- **24/24F (top terminals).** Fits many Honda, Acura, Infiniti, Lexus, Nissan, and Toyota vehicles.
- **34/78 (dual terminals, both side and top posts).** Fits many General Motors pickups and SUVs, as well as midsize and larger GM sedans and large Chrysler/Dodge vehicles.

- **35 (top terminals).** Fits many Japanese brand vehicles.
- **65 (top terminals).** Fits most large Ford/Mercury passenger cars, trucks, and SUVs.
- **75 (side terminals).** Fits some General Motors small and midsize cars and some Chrysler/Dodge vehicles.

- **78 (side terminals).** Fits many General Motors pickups and SUVs, as well as midsize and larger GM sedans.

Exact dimensions can be found on the Internet by searching for BCI battery sizes.

SUMMARY

1. Maintenance-free batteries use lead–calcium grids instead of lead–antimony grids to reduce gassing.
2. When a battery is being discharged, the acid (SO4) is leaving the electrolyte and being deposited on the plates.
3. All batteries give off hydrogen and oxygen when being charged.
4. Batteries are rated according to CCA and reserve capacity. When the battery is being charged, the acid (SO4) is forced off the plates and goes back into the electrolyte.

REVIEW QUESTIONS

1. Why can discharged batteries freeze?
2. What are the battery-rating methods?
3. Why can a battery explode if it is exposed to an open flame or spark?
4. What is meant by a sulfated battery?
5. What does the BCI group number mean?

CHAPTER QUIZ

1. When a battery becomes completely discharged, both positive and negative plates become _____ and the electrolyte becomes _____.
   a. H_2SO_4/Pb
   b. $PbSO_4$/H_2O
   c. PbO_2/H_2SO_4
   d. $PbSO_4$/H_2SO_4

2. A fully charged 12-volt battery should indicate _____.
   a. 12.6 volts or higher
   b. A specific gravity of 1.265 or higher
   c. 12 volts
   d. Both a and b

3. Deep cycling means _____.
   a. Overcharging the battery
   b. Overfilling or underfilling the battery with water
   c. The battery is fully discharged and then recharged
   d. The battery is overfilled with acid (H_2SO_4)

4. What makes a battery "low maintenance" or "maintenance free"?
   a. The material that is used to construct the grids
   b. The plates are constructed of different metals.
   c. The electrolyte is hydrochloric acid solution.
   d. The battery plates are smaller, making more room for additional electrolytes.

5. The positive battery plate is _____.
   a. Lead dioxide
   b. Brown in color
   c. Sometimes called lead peroxide
   d. All of the above

6. Which battery rating is tested at 0°F (−18°C)?
   a. Cold-cranking amperes (CCA)
   b. Cranking amperes (CA)
   c. Reserve capacity
   d. Battery voltage test

7. Which battery rating is expressed in minutes?
   a. Cold-cranking amperes (CCA)
   b. Cranking amperes (CA)
   c. Reserve capacity
   d. Battery voltage test

8. What battery rating is tested at 32°F (0°C)?
   a. Cold-cranking amperes (CCA)
   b. Cranking amperes (CA)
   c. Reserve capacity
   d. Battery voltage test

9. What gases are released from a battery when it is being charged?
   a. Oxygen
   b. Hydrogen
   c. Nitrogen and oxygen
   d. Hydrogen and oxygen

10. A charge indicator (eye) operates by showing green or red when the battery is charged and dark if the battery is discharged. This charge indicator detects _____.
    a. Battery voltage
    b. Specific gravity
    c. Electrolyte water pH
    d. Internal resistance of the cells

chapter 16
BATTERY TESTING AND SERVICE

LEARNING OBJECTIVES

After studying this chapter, the reader will be able to:

1. List the precautions necessary when working with batteries.
2. Describe how to inspect and clean terminals and hold-downs.
3. Discuss how to test batteries for open circuit voltage and specific gravity.
4. Describe how to perform a battery load test and a conductance test.
5. Explain how to safely charge or jump start a battery.
6. Discuss how to perform a battery drain test.

This chapter will help you prepare for the ASE Electrical/Electronic Systems (A6) certification test content area "B" (Battery Diagnosis and Service).

KEY TERMS

Battery electrical drain test 241
Dynamic voltage 233
Hydrometer 235
IOD 241
Load test 235
Open circuit voltage 233
Parasitic load test 241
Three-minute charge test 235

BATTERY SERVICE SAFETY CONSIDERATIONS

HAZARDS Batteries contain acid and release explosive gases (hydrogen and oxygen) during normal charging and discharging cycles.

SAFETY PROCEDURES To help prevent physical injury or damage to the vehicle, always adhere to the following safety procedures:

1. When working on any electrical component on a vehicle, disconnect the negative battery cable from the battery. When the negative cable is disconnected, all electrical circuits in the vehicle will be open, which will prevent accidental electrical contact between an electrical component and ground. Any electrical spark has the potential to cause explosion and personal injury.

2. Wear eye protection (goggles preferred) when working around any battery.

3. Wear protective clothing to avoid skin contact with battery acid.

4. Always adhere to all safety precautions as stated in the service procedures for the equipment used for battery service and testing.

5. Never smoke or use an open flame around any battery.

6. Never attempt to jump start or charge a frozen battery.

SYMPTOMS OF A WEAK OR DEFECTIVE BATTERY

The following warning signs indicate that a battery is near the end of its useful life:

- **Uses water in one or more cells.** This indicates that the plates are sulfated and that during the charging process, the water in the electrolyte is being turned into separate hydrogen and oxygen gases. ● **SEE FIGURE 16–1.**

- **Excessive corrosion on battery cables or connections.** Corrosion is more likely to occur if the battery is sulfated, creating hot spots on the plates. When the battery is

FIGURE 16–1 A visual inspection on this battery shows the electrolyte level is below the plates in all cells. Not many batteries can be checked for the electrolyte level and if low, the battery is likely at the end of its normal service life.

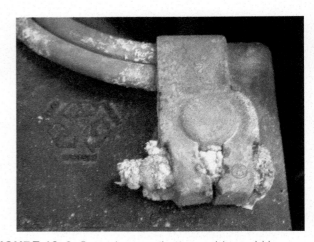

FIGURE 16–2 Corrosion on a battery cable could be an indication that the battery itself is either being overcharged or is sulfated, creating a lot of gassing of the electrolyte.

being charged, the acid fumes are forced out of the vent holes and onto the battery cables, connections, and even on the battery tray underneath the battery. ● **SEE FIGURE 16–2.**

- **Slower than normal engine cranking.** When the capacity of the battery is reduced due to damage or age, it is less likely to be able to supply the necessary current for starting the engine, especially during cold weather.

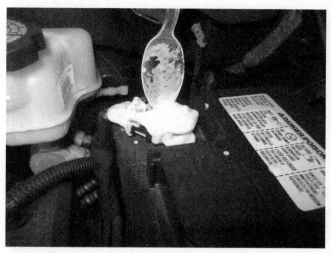

FIGURE 16–3 Using a baking soda and water paste to remove the corrosion on a battery terminal.

BATTERY MAINTENANCE

NEED FOR MAINTENANCE Most new-style batteries are of a maintenance-free design that uses lead–calcium instead of lead–antimony plate grid construction. Because lead–calcium batteries do not release as much gas as the older-style, lead–antimony batteries, there is less consumption of water during normal service. Also, with less gassing, less corrosion is observed on the battery terminals, wiring, and support trays. If the electrolyte level can be checked, and if it is low, add only distilled water. Distilled water is recommended by all battery manufacturers, but if distilled water is not available, clean ordinary drinking water, low in mineral content, can be used.

Battery maintenance includes making certain that the battery case is clean and checking that the battery cables and hold-down fasteners are clean and tight.

BATTERY TERMINAL CLEANING Many battery-related faults are caused by poor electrical connections at the battery. Battery cable connections should be checked and cleaned to prevent voltage drop at the connections. One common reason for an engine to not start is loose or corroded battery cable connections. Perform an inspection and check for the following conditions:

- Loose or corroded connections at the battery terminals (should not be able to be moved by hand)
- Loose or corroded connections at the ground connector on the engine block
- Wiring that has been modified to add auxiliary power for a sound system or other electrical accessory

If the connections are loose or corroded, use 1 tablespoon of baking soda in 1 quart (liter) of water and brush this mixture onto the battery and housing to neutralize the acid. Mechanically clean the connections and wash the area with water. ● **SEE FIGURE 16–3**.

BATTERY HOLD-DOWN The battery should also be secured with a hold-down bracket to prevent vibration from damaging the plates inside the battery. The hold-down bracket should be snug enough to prevent battery movement, yet not so tight as to cause the case to crack. Factory-original hold-down brackets are often available through local automobile dealers, and universal hold-down units are available through local automotive parts stores.

(a)

(b)

FIGURE 16–4 (a) A voltage reading of 12.28 volts indicates that the battery is not fully charged and should be charged before testing. (b) A battery that measures 12.6 volts or higher after the surface charge has been removed is 100% charged.

BATTERY VOLTAGE TEST

STATE OF CHARGE Testing the battery voltage with a voltmeter is a simple method for determining the state of charge of any battery. ● **SEE FIGURE 16–4.** The voltage of a battery does not necessarily indicate whether the battery can perform satisfactorily, but it does indicate to the technician more about the battery's condition than a simple visual inspection. A battery that "looks good" may not be good. This test is commonly called an *open circuit battery voltage test* because it is conducted with an open circuit, no current flowing, and no load applied to the battery.

1. If the battery has just been charged or the vehicle has recently been driven, it is necessary to remove the surface charge from the battery before testing. A surface charge is a charge of higher-than-normal voltage that is just on the surface of the battery plates. The surface charge is quickly removed when the battery is loaded and therefore does not accurately represent the true state of charge of the battery.

2. To remove the surface charge, turn the headlights on high beam (brights) for one minute, then turn the headlights off and wait two minutes.

BATTERY VOLTAGE (V)	STATE OF CHARGE
12.6 or higher	100% charged
12.4	75% charged
12.2	50% charged
12.0	25% charged
11.9 or lower	Discharged

CHART 16–1

The estimated state of charge of a 12-volt battery after the surface charge has been removed.

3. With the engine and all electrical accessories off, and the doors shut (to turn off the interior lights), connect a voltmeter to the battery posts. Connect the red positive lead to the positive post and the black negative lead to the negative post.

   NOTE: If the meter reads negative (−), the battery has been reverse charged (has reversed polarity) and should be replaced, or the meter has been connected incorrectly.

4. Read the voltmeter and compare the results with the state of charge (SOC). The voltages shown are for a battery at or near room temperature (70°F to 80°F, or 21°C to 27°C). ● **SEE CHART 16–1.**

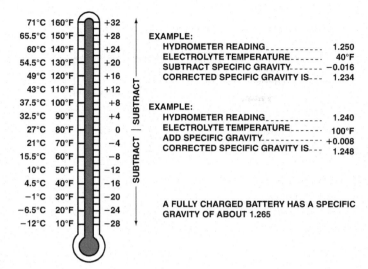

71°C	160°F	+32
65.5°C	150°F	+28
60°C	140°F	+24
54.5°C	130°F	+20
49°C	120°F	+16
43°C	110°F	+12
37.5°C	100°F	+8
32.5°C	90°F	+4
27°C	80°F	0
21°C	70°F	−4
15.5°C	60°F	−8
10°C	50°F	−12
4.5°C	40°F	−16
−1°C	30°F	−20
−6.5°C	20°F	−24
−12°C	10°F	−28

EXAMPLE:
HYDROMETER READING _____ 1.250
ELECTROLYTE TEMPERATURE _____ 40°F
SUBTRACT SPECIFIC GRAVITY _____ −0.016
CORRECTED SPECIFIC GRAVITY IS ___ 1.234

EXAMPLE:
HYDROMETER READING _____ 1.240
ELECTROLYTE TEMPERATURE _____ 100°F
ADD SPECIFIC GRAVITY _____ +0.008
CORRECTED SPECIFIC GRAVITY IS ___ 1.248

A FULLY CHARGED BATTERY HAS A SPECIFIC GRAVITY OF ABOUT 1.265

FIGURE 16–5 When testing a battery using a hydrometer, the reading must be corrected if the temperature is above or below 80°F (27°C).

SPECIFIC GRAVITY	BATTERY VOLTAGE (V)	STATE OF CHARGE
1.265	12.6 or higher	100% charged
1.225	12.4	75% charged
1.190	12.2	50% charged
1.155	12.0	25% charged
Lower than 1.120	11.9 or lower	Discharged

CHART 16–2

Measuring the specific gravity can detect a defective battery. A battery should be at least 75% charged before being load tested.

HYDROMETER TESTING

If the battery has removable filler caps, the specific gravity of the electrolyte can also be checked. A **hydrometer** is a tester that measures the specific gravity. ● **SEE FIGURE 16–5**.

This test can also be performed on batteries that are equipped with caps that can be removed to get access to the electrolytic. The specific gravity test indicates the state of battery charge and can indicate a defective battery if the specific gravity of one or more cells varies by more than 0.050 from the value of the highest-reading cell. ● **SEE CHART 16–2**.

? **FREQUENTLY ASKED QUESTION**

What Is the Three-Minute Charge Test?

A **three-minute charge test** is used to check if a battery is sulfated and is performed as follows:

- Connect a battery charger and a voltmeter to the battery terminals.
- Charge the battery at a rate of 40 amperes for three minutes.
- At the end of three minutes, read the voltmeter.

Results: If the voltage is above 15.5 volts, replace the battery. If the voltage is below 15.5 volts, the battery is not sulfated and should be charged and retested.

This is *not* a valid test for many maintenance-free batteries. Due to the high internal resistance, a discharged battery may not start to accept a charge for several hours. Always use another alternative battery test before discarding a battery based on the results of the three-minute charge test.

BATTERY LOAD TESTING

TERMINOLOGY One test to determine the condition of any battery is the **load test.** Most automotive starting and charging testers use a carbon pile to create an electrical load on the battery. The amount of the load is determined by the original CCA rating of the battery, which should be at least 75% charged before performing a load test. The capacity is measured in cold-cranking amperes, which is the number of amperes that a battery can supply at 0°F (−18°C) for 30 seconds.

TEST PROCEDURE To perform a battery load test, take the following steps:

STEP 1 **Determine the CCA rating of the battery.** The proper electrical load used to test a battery is half of the CCA rating or three times the ampere-hour rating, with a minimum 150 ampere load. ● **SEE FIGURE 16–6**.

STEP 2 **Connect the load tester to the battery.** Follow the instructions for the tester being used.

STEP 3 **Apply the load for a full 15 seconds.** Observe the voltmeter during the load testing and check the voltage at the end of the 15 seconds period while the battery is still under load. A good battery should indicate above 9.6 volts.

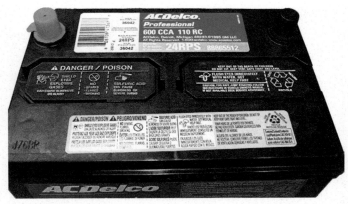

FIGURE 16–6 This battery has a CCA rating of 600 amperes and a reserve capacity (RC) of 110 minutes.

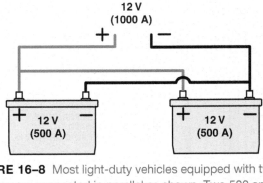

FIGURE 16–8 Most light-duty vehicles equipped with two batteries are connected in parallel as shown. Two 500 amperes, 12-volt batteries are capable of supplying 1,000 amperes at 12 volts, which is needed to start many diesel engines.

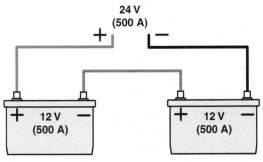

FIGURE 16–9 Many heavy-duty trucks and buses use two 12-volt batteries connected in series to provide 24 volts.

FIGURE 16–7 A Snap-on battery tester that is capable of performing a battery load test as well as starter and alternator amperage tests.

STEP 4 **Repeat the test.** Many battery manufacturers recommend performing the load test twice, using the first load period to remove the surface charge on the battery and the second test to provide a truer indication of the condition of the battery. Wait 30 seconds between tests to allow time for the battery to recover. ● SEE FIGURE 16–7.

Results: If the battery fails the load test, recharge the battery and retest. If the load test is failed again, replacement of the battery is required.

? **FREQUENTLY ASKED QUESTION**

How Should You Test a Vehicle Equipped with Two Batteries?

Many vehicles equipped with a diesel engine use two batteries. These batteries are usually electrically connected in parallel to provide additional current (amperes) at the same voltage. ● SEE FIGURE 16–8.

Some heavy-duty trucks and buses connect two batteries in series to provide about the same current as one battery, but with twice the voltage, as shown in ● FIGURE 16–9.

To successfully test the batteries, they should be disconnected and tested separately. If just one battery is found to be defective, most experts recommend that both be replaced to help prevent future problems. Because the two batteries are electrically connected, a fault in one battery can cause the good battery to discharge into the defective battery, thereby affecting both even if just one battery is defective.

FIGURE 16–10 A conductance tester is very easy to use and has proved to accurately determine battery condition if the connections are properly made. Follow the instructions on the display exactly for best results.

WARNING

Never Charge or Jump Start a Frozen Battery

A discharged battery can freeze because the electrolyte becomes mostly water. Never attempt to charge or jump start a vehicle that has a frozen battery. When the battery freezes, it often bulges at the sides because water expands about 9% when it freezes, forming ice crystals that occupy more space than water. The crystals can trap bubbles of hydrogen and oxygen that are created during the chemical processes in a battery. When attempting to charge or jump start the frozen battery, these pockets of gases can explode. Because the electrolyte expands, the freezing action usually destroys the plates and can loosen the active material from the grids. It is rare for a frozen battery to be restored to useful service.

ELECTRONIC CONDUCTANCE TESTING

TERMINOLOGY General Motors Corporation, Chrysler Corporation, and Ford specify that an electronic conductance tester be used to test batteries in vehicles still under factory warranty. Conductance is a measure of how well a battery can create current. This tester sends a small signal through the battery and then measures a part of the AC response. As a battery ages, the plates can become sulfated and shed active materials from the grids, thus reducing the battery capacity. Conductance testers can be used to test flooded or absorbed glass mat-type (AGM) batteries. The unit can determine the following information about a battery:

- CCA
- State of charge
- Voltage of the battery
- Defects such as shorts and opens

However, a conductance tester is not designed to accurately determine the state of charge or CCA rating of a new battery. Unlike a battery load test, a conductance tester can be used on a battery that is discharged. This type of tester should only be used to test batteries that have been in service. ● **SEE FIGURE 16–10**.

TEST PROCEDURE

STEP 1 Connect the unit to the positive and negative terminals of the battery. If testing a side post battery, always use the lead adapters and *never* use steel bolts as these can cause an incorrect reading.

NOTE: Test results can be incorrectly reported on the display if proper, clean connections to the battery are not made. Also be sure that all accessories and the ignition switch are in the off position.

STEP 2 Enter the CCA rating (if known) and push the arrow keys.

STEP 3 The tester determines and displays one of the following:
- **Good battery.** The battery can return to service.
- **Charge and retest.** Fully recharge the battery and return it to service.
- **Replace the battery.** The battery is not serviceable and should be replaced.
- **Bad cell–replace.** The battery is not serviceable and should be replaced.

Some conductance testers can check the charging and cranking circuits, too. ● **SEE FIGURE 16–11**.

OPEN CIRCUIT VOLTAGE	BATTERY SPECIFIC GRAVITY*	STATE OF CHARGE	CHARGING TIME TO FULL CHARGE AT 80°F**					
			at 60 amps	at 50 amps	at 40 amps	at 30 amps	at 20 amps	at 10 amps
12.6	1.265	100%	FULL CHARGE					
12.4	1.225	75%	15 min.	20 min.	27 min.	35 min.	48 min.	90 min.
12.2	1.190	50%	35 min.	45 min.	55 min.	75 min.	95 min.	160 min.
12.0	1.155	25%	50 min.	65 min.	85 min.	115 min.	145 min.	260 min.
11.8	1.120	0%	65 min.	85 min.	110 min.	150 min.	195 min.	370 min.

CHART 16–3

Battery charging guideline showing the charging times that vary according to state of charge, temperature, and charging rate. It may take eight hours or more to charge a fully discharged battery:
*Correct for temperature.
**If colder, it'll take longer.

FIGURE 16–11 A Midtronics tester that can not only test the battery but can also detect faults with the starter and alternator.

FIGURE 16–12 A typical industrial battery charger. Be sure that the ignition switch is in the off position before connecting any battery charger. Connect the cables of the charger to the battery before plugging the charger into the outlet. This helps prevent a voltage spike and spark that could occur if the charger happened to be accidentally left on. Always follow the battery charger manufacturer's instructions.

BATTERY CHARGING

CHARGING PROCEDURE If the state of charge of a battery is low, it must be recharged. It is best to slow charge any battery to prevent possible overheating damage to the battery. Perform the following steps:

STEP 1 **Determine the charge rate.** The charge rate is based on the current state of charge and charging rate. ● **SEE CHART 16–3** for the recommended charging rate.

STEP 2 **Connect a battery charger to the battery.** Be sure the charger is not plugged in when connecting a charger to a battery. Always follow the battery charger's instructions for proper use.

STEP 3 **Set the charging rate.** The initial charge rate should be about 35 amperes for 30 minutes to help start the charging process. Fast charging a battery increases the temperature of the battery and can cause warping

of the plates inside the battery. Fast charging also increases the amount of gassing (release of hydrogen and oxygen), which can create a health and fire hazard. The battery temperature should not exceed 125°F (hot to the touch).

- Fast charge: 15 amperes maximum
- Slow charge: 5 amperes maximum
- ● **SEE FIGURE 16–12**.

CHARGING AGM BATTERIES Charging an AGM battery requires a different charger than is used to recharge a flooded-type battery. The differences include:

■ The AGM can be charged with high current, up to 75% of the ampere-hour rating due to lower internal resistance.

- The charging voltage has to be kept at or below 14.4 volts to prevent damage.

Because most conventional battery chargers use a charging voltage of 16 volts or higher, a charger specifically designed to charge AGM batteries must be used.

Absorbed glass mat batteries are often used as auxiliary batteries in hybrid electric vehicles when the battery is located inside the vehicle.

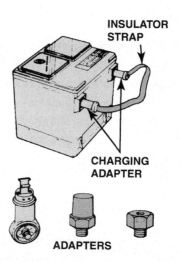

FIGURE 16–13 Adapters should be used on side terminal batteries whenever charging.

TECH TIP

Charge Batteries at 1% of Their CCA Rating

Many batteries are damaged due to overcharging. To help prevent damages, such as warped plates and excessive release of sulfur smell gases, charge batteries at a rate equal to 1% of the battery's CCA rating. For example, a battery with a 700 CCA rating should be charged at 7 amperes ($700 \times 0.01 = 7$ amperes). No harm will occur to the battery at this charge rate even though it may take longer to achieve a full charge. This means that a battery may require eight or more hours to become fully charged depending on the battery capacity and state of charge (SOC).

For example, if a 10 amperes charge rate is applied to a discharged battery that has a 90-minute reserve capacity, the time needed to charge the battery will be nine hours.

90 minutes ÷ 10 amperes = 9 hours

TECH TIP

Always Use Adapters on Side Post Batteries

Side post batteries require that an adapter be used when charging the battery, if it is removed from the vehicle. Do not use steel bolts. If a bolt is threaded into the terminal, only the parts of the threads that contact the battery terminal will be conducting all of the charging current. An adapter or a bolt with a nut attached is needed to achieve full contact with the battery terminals. ● **SEE FIGURE 16–13**.

BATTERY CHARGE TIME

The time needed to charge a completely discharged battery can be estimated by using the reserve capacity rating of the battery in minutes divided by the charging rate.

Hours needed to charge the battery =
Reserve capacity ÷ Charge current

FREQUENTLY ASKED QUESTION

Should Batteries Be Kept Off of Concrete Floors?

All batteries should be stored in a cool, dry place when not in use. Many technicians have been warned not to store or place a battery on concrete. According to battery experts, it is the temperature difference between the top and the bottom of the battery that causes a difference in the voltage potential between the top (warmer section) and the bottom (colder section). It is this difference in temperature that causes self-discharge to occur.

In fact, submarines cycle seawater around their batteries to keep all sections of the battery at the same temperature to help prevent self-discharge.

Therefore, always store or place batteries up off the floor and in a location where the entire battery can be kept at the same temperature, avoiding extreme heat and freezing temperatures. Concrete cannot drain the battery directly because the case of the battery is a very good electrical insulator.

To jump start another vehicle with a dead battery, connect good-quality copper jumper cables or a jump box to the good battery and the dead battery, as shown in ● FIGURE 16–14.

When using jumper cables or a battery jump box, the last connection made should always be on the engine block or an engine bracket on the dead vehicle as far from the battery as possible.

It is normal for a spark to occur when the jumper cables finally complete the jumping circuit, and this spark could cause an explosion of the gases around the battery. Many newer vehicles have special ground and/or positive power connections built away from the battery just for the purpose of jump starting. Check the owner's manual or service information for the exact location.

FIGURE 16–15 The sticker on this battery indicates that it was shipped from the factory January, 2015.

FIGURE 16–14 A typical battery jump box used to jump start vehicles. These hand-portable units have almost made jumper cables obsolete.

 TECH TIP

Look at the Battery Date Code

All major battery manufacturers' stamp codes on the battery case give the date of manufacture and other information about the battery. Most battery manufacturers use a number to indicate the year of manufacture and a letter to indicate the month of manufacture, except the letter I, because it can be confused with the number 1. For example,

A = January   G = July
B = February   H = August
C = March   J = September
D = April   K = October
E = May   L = November
F = June   M = December

The shipping date from the manufacturing plant is usually indicated by a *sticker* on the body of the battery. Almost every battery manufacturer uses just one letter and one number to indicate the month and year. ● SEE FIGURE 16–15.

BATTERY ELECTRICAL DRAIN TEST

TERMINOLOGY The **battery electrical drain test** determines if any component or circuit in a vehicle is causing a drain on the battery when everything is off. This test is also called the **ignition off draw (IOD)** or **parasitic load test.**

Many electronic components draw a continuous, slight amount of current from the battery when the ignition is off.

This test should be performed when one of the following conditions exists:

1. When a battery is being charged or replaced (a battery drain could be the cause for charging or replacing the battery)

2. When the battery is suspected of being drained

PROCEDURE FOR BATTERY ELECTRICAL DRAIN TEST

■ **Inductive DC ammeter.** The fastest and easiest method to measure battery electrical drain is to connect an inductive DC ammeter that is capable of measuring low current (10 milliamperes). ● **SEE FIGURE 16–16** for an example of a clamp-on digital multimeter being used to measure battery drain.

■ **DMM set to read milliamperes.** Following is the procedure for performing the battery electrical drain test using a DMM set to read DC amperes:

STEP 1 Make certain that all lights, accessories, and ignition are off.

STEP 2 Check all vehicle doors to be certain that the interior courtesy (dome) lights are off.

STEP 3 Disconnect the *negative* (–) battery cable and install a parasitic load tool, as shown in ● **FIGURE 16–17.**

STEP 4 Start the engine and drive the vehicle about 10 minutes, being sure to turn on all the lights and accessories including the radio.

STEP 5 Turn the engine and all accessories off including the underhood light.

STEP 6 Connect an ammeter across the parasitic load tool switch and wait 20 minutes for all computers and circuits to shut down.

STEP 7 Open the switch on the load tool and read the battery electrical drain on the meter display.

FIGURE 16–16 This mini clamp-on digital multimeter is being used to measure the amount of battery electrical drain that is present. In this case, a reading of 20 milliamperes (displayed on the meter as 00.02 ampere) is within the normal range of 20 to 30 milliamperes. Be sure to clamp around all of the positive battery cables or all of the negative battery cables, whichever is easiest to get the clamp around.

FIGURE 16–17 After connecting the shut-off tool, start the engine and operate all accessories. Stop the engine and turn off everything. Connect the ammeter across the shut-off switch in parallel. Wait 20 minutes. This time allows all electronic circuits to "time out" or shut down. Open the switch—all current now will flow through the ammeter. A reading greater than specified (usually greater than 50 milliamperes, or 0.05 ampere) indicates a problem that should be corrected.

SPECIFICATIONS Results:

■ Normal = 20 to 30 milliamperes (0.02 to 0.03 ampere)

■ Maximum allowable = 50 milliamperes (0.05 ampere)

BATTERY DRAIN AND RESERVE CAPACITY It is normal for a battery to self-discharge even if there is not an electrical load, such as computer memory to drain the battery.

CASE STUDY

The Chevrolet Battery Story

A 2011 Chevrolet Impala was being diagnosed for a dead battery. Testing for a battery drain (parasitic draw) showed 2.25 amperes, which was clearly over the acceptable value of 0.050 or less. At the suggestion of the shop foreman, the technician used a Tech 2 scan tool to check if all of the computers and modules went to sleep after the ignition was turned off. The scan tool display indicated that the instrument panel (IP) showed that it remained awake after all of the others had gone into sleep mode. The IP cluster was unplugged and the vehicle was tested for an electrical drain again. This time, it was only 32 milliamperes (0.032 ampere), well within the normal range. Replacing the IP cluster solved the excessive battery drain.

Summary:
- **Complaint**–The battery was dead.
- **Cause**–Excessive battery drain (parasitic draw) was found. Using a scan tool to test the modules, it was discovered that the instrument panel cluster (IPC) remained awake and never powered down when the ignition was turned off.
- **Correction**–The IPC was replaced, which corrected the excessive battery drain problem.

According to General Motors, this self-discharge is about 13 milliamperes (0.013 ampere).

Some vehicle manufacturers specify a maximum allowable parasitic draw or battery drain be based on the reserve capacity of the battery. The calculation used is the reserve capacity of the battery divided by 4; this equals the maximum allowable battery drain. For example, a battery rated at 120 minutes reserve capacity should have a maximum battery drain of 30 milliamperes.

120 minutes reserve capacity ÷ 4 = 30 mA

FINDING THE SOURCE OF THE DRAIN If there is a drain,
check and temporarily disconnect the following components:

1. Underhood light
2. Glove compartment light
3. Trunk light

If after disconnecting these three components the battery drain draws more than 50 milliamperes (0.05 ampere), disconnect one fuse at a time from the fuse box until the excessive drain drops to normal.

NOTE: Do not reinsert fuses after they have been removed as this action can cause modules to "wake-up," leading to an inconclusive test.

If the excessive battery drain stops after one fuse is disconnected, the source of the drain is located in that particular circuit, as labeled on the fuse box. Continue to disconnect the *power-side* wire connectors from each component included in that particular circuit until the test light goes off. The source of the battery drain can then be traced to an individual component or part of one circuit.

WHAT TO DO IF A BATTERY DRAIN STILL EXISTS

If all the fuses have been disconnected and the drain still exists, the source of the drain has to be between the battery and the fuse box. The most common sources of drain under the hood include the following:

1. **The alternator.** Disconnect the alternator wires and retest. If the ammeter now reads a normal drain, the problem is a defective diode(s) in the alternator.

2. **PCM or Control module.** Staying on and not going to sleep. The procedure usually involves disconnecting one module at a time then checking to see if the battery drain has been reduced or eliminated. Check service information for the exact procedures to follow to determine if the modules are staying awake.

MAINTAINING ELECTRONIC MEMORY FUNCTIONS

BATTERY DISCONNECT ISSUES Whenever a battery is disconnected or replaced, many electrical/electronic modules may lose their memory including:

Radio presets and clock functions plus antitheft (if equipped) ● **SEE FIGURE 16–18**.

FIGURE 16–18 The battery was replaced in this Ford and the radio displayed "enter code" when the replacement battery was installed. Thankfully, the owner had the code required to unlock the radio.

- Security system
- PCM engine idle learn
- Auto power windows/sunroof

To prevent having to reinitialize these modules, a "memory saver" can be used keep power applied to the electrical system when the battery is disconnected.

MAINTAINING MEMORY METHODS
There are two ways to connect power to prevent the loss of memory function.

Connect a battery (9-volt dry cell or 12-volt auxiliary battery) to the power (cigarette lighter) plug. ● SEE FIGURE 16–19.

Connect a 12 volt auxiliary battery to terminals 4 and 16 of the data link connector (DLC). Use a commercially available memory saver for this procedure to help prevent possible damage that could occur if 12-volt power is accidently applied to data lines at the DLC.

Make the connections to the vehicle using either method before disconnecting the vehicle battery. The applied voltage which is connected the electrical system through the power plug or DLC will keep all memory functions so they do not need to be reset. ● SEE FIGURE 16–20.

REINITIALIZATION/REGISTRATION
If a memory saver was not used and the battery was disconnected, then the memory functions will need to be reinitialization which can include the following:

- **Auto power windows**—To reset proper operation, use the window control for each window and hold the down button for a few seconds after the window reaches the bottom. Repeat for the up button if the vehicle is equipped with auto up function

- **Radio antitheft**—To unlock an antitheft radio that has lost power, a code number is needed to get the radio to function again. Check service information for the exact procedure to follow if the owner does not have the radio code number which is usually with the owner's manual.

- **Intelligent battery systems**— Some vehicles, usually European brands, use an intelligent battery system that monitors the battery operation including state-of charge, voltage and temperature. As the battery ages, the system can compensate by changing the charging voltage. When a new battery is installed, the vehicle must have the new

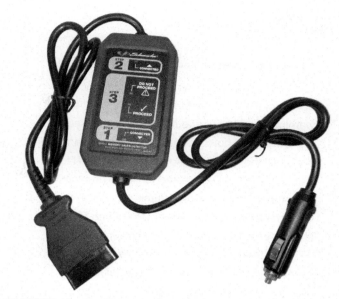

FIGURE 16–19 A special tool that includes a lighter plug what can be plugged into a jump-start battery unit and the other end connected to the data link connector (DLC) of the vehicle to maintain the memory functions.

FIGURE 16–20 A memory saver tool that uses a 12 volt battery to connect to the power and ground terminals of the DLC.

battery registered so that the system will be reset and will not overcharge the new battery. The replacement battery must be the same type (flooded or AGM) as the original to avoid potential issues.

A scan tool is needed to register the new battery to the vehicle. Always follow the vehicle manufacturer's recommended procedures when replacing a battery.

It Could Happen to You!

The owner of a Toyota replaced the battery. After doing so, the owner noted that the "airbag" amber warning lamp was lit and the radio was locked out. The owner had purchased the vehicle used and did not know the four-digit security code needed to unlock the radio. Determined to fix the problem, the owner tried three four-digit numbers, hoping that one of them would work. However, after three tries, the radio became permanently disabled.

Frustrated, the owner went to a dealer. It cost over $300 to fix the problem. A special tool was required to easily reset the airbag lamp. The radio had to be removed and sent out of state to an authorized radio service center and then reinstalled into the vehicle.

Therefore, before disconnecting the battery, check to be certain that the owner has the security code for a security-type radio. A "memory saver" may be needed to keep the radio powered up when the battery is being disconnected. ● SEE FIGURE 16–21.

Dead Batteries Can Freeze

If a battery becomes discharged, the electrolyte can freeze. This can occur because when a battery is discharged, the "acid" ($PbSO_4$) leaves the electrolyte and is deposited on both the negative and positive plates leaving just water. Never attempt to charge or place into service a battery that is frozen. Often the case is spilt requiring the battery to be replaced. If a battery is found to be frozen, place the battery into a warm room with good ventilation and allowed to thaw.

If the case is not cracked, then it may be able to be restored to useful service if charged at a low rate for several hours. Test and recharge as needed.

? FREQUENTLY ASKED QUESTION

Where Is the Battery?

Many vehicle manufacturers today place the battery under the backseat, under the front fender, or in the trunk. ● SEE FIGURE 16–22.

Often, the battery is not visible even if it is located under the hood. When testing or jump starting a vehicle, look for a battery access point.

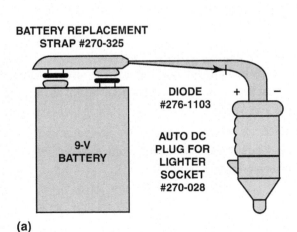

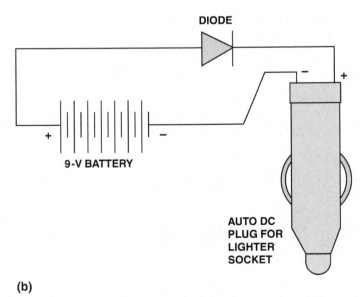

FIGURE 16–21 (a) Memory saver. The part numbers represent components from RadioShack. (b) A schematic drawing of the same memory saver. Some experts recommend using a 12-volt lantern battery instead of a small 9-volt battery to help ensure that there will be enough voltage in the event that a door is opened while the vehicle battery is disconnected. Interior lights could quickly drain a small 9-volt battery.

FIGURE 16–22 Many newer vehicles have batteries that are sometimes difficult to find. Some are located under plastic panels under the hood, under the front fender, or even under the rear seat as shown here.

The following list will assist technicians in troubleshooting batteries:

Problem	Possible Causes and/or Solutions
1. Headlights are dimmer than normal	1. Discharged battery or poor connections on the battery, engine, or body
2. Solenoid clicks	2. Discharged battery or poor connections on the battery or an engine fault, such as coolant on top of the pistons, causing a hydrostatic lock
3. Engine is slow in cranking	3. Discharged battery, high-resistance battery cables, or defective starter or solenoid
4. Battery will not accept a charge	4. Possible loose battery cable connections. (If the battery is a maintenance-free type, attempt to fast charge the battery for several hours. If the battery still will not accept a charge, replace the battery.)
5. Battery is using water	5. Check charging system for too high a voltage. (If the voltage is normal, the battery is showing signs of gradual failure. Load test and replace the battery, if necessary.)

SUMMARY

1. All batteries should be securely attached to the vehicle with hold-down brackets to prevent vibration damage.
2. Batteries can be tested with a voltmeter to determine the state of charge. A battery load test loads the battery to half of its CCA rating. A good battery should be able to maintain higher than 9.6 volts for the entire 15 seconds test period.
3. Batteries can be tested with a conductance tester even if discharged.
4. A battery drain test should be performed if the battery runs down.
5. Be sure that the battery charger is unplugged from power outlet when making connections to a battery.

REVIEW QUESTIONS

1. What are the results of a voltmeter test of a battery and its state of charge?
2. What are the steps for performing a battery load test?
3. How is a battery drain test performed?
4. Why should a battery not be fast charged?
5. Why do some vehicles need to have a new battery registered?

1. Technician A says that distilled or clean drinking water should be added to a battery when the electrolyte level is low. Technician B says that fresh electrolyte (solution of acid and water) should be added. Which technician is correct?
   a. Technician A only
   b. Technician B only
   c. Both Technicians A and B
   d. Neither Technician A nor B

2. Battery maintenance includes _____.
   a. battery terminals should be clean and tight
   b. add distilled water if low on electrolyte
   c. battery should be secured with a hold-down bracket
   d. All of the above

3. A battery date code sticker indicates D8. What does this mean?
   a. The date it was shipped from the factory was December 2018
   b. The date it was shipped from the factory was April 2018
   c. The battery expires in December, 2018
   d. It was built the second day of the week (Tuesday).

4. Many vehicle manufacturers recommend that a special electrical connector be installed between the battery and the battery cable when testing for _____.
   a. battery drain (parasitic drain)
   b. specific gravity
   c. battery voltage
   d. battery charge rate

5. When load testing a battery, which battery rating is often used to determine how much load to apply to the battery?
   a. CA
   b. RC
   c. MCA
   d. CCA

6. When measuring the specific gravity of the electrolyte, the maximum allowable difference between the highest and lowest hydrometer reading is _____.
   a. 0.010
   b. 0.020
   c. 0.050
   d. 0.50

7. A battery high-rate discharge (load capacity) test is being performed on a 12-volt battery. Technician A says that a good battery should have a voltage reading of higher than 9.6 volts while under load at the end of the 15 seconds test. Technician B says that the battery should be discharged (loaded) to twice its CCA rating. Which technician is correct?
   a. Technician A only
   b. Technician B only
   c. Both Technicians A and B
   d. Neither Technician A nor B

8. When charging a lead–acid (flooded-type) battery, _____.
   a. the initial charging rate should be about 35 amperes for 30 minutes
   b. the battery may not accept a charge for several hours, yet may still be a good (serviceable) battery
   c. the battery temperature should not exceed 125°F (hot to the touch)
   d. All of the above

9. Normal battery drain (parasitic drain) in a vehicle with many computer and electronic circuits is _____.
   a. 20 to 30 milliamperes
   b. 2 to 3 amperes
   c. 150 to 300 milliamperes
   d. None of the above

10. When jump starting, _____.
    a. the last connection should be the positive post of the dead battery
    b. the last connection should be the engine block of the dead vehicle
    c. the alternator must be disconnected on both vehicles
    d. Both a and c

chapter 17
CRANKING SYSTEM

FIGURE 17–1 A typical solenoid-operated starter.

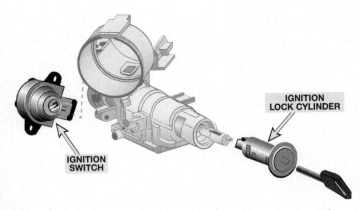

FIGURE 17–2 The lock cylinder is often a separate part from the electrical ignition switch and operates it directly or uses a link between two components.

CRANKING CIRCUIT

PARTS INVOLVED For any engine to start, it must first be rotated using an external power source. It is the purpose and function of the cranking circuit to create the necessary power and transfer it from the battery to the starter motor, which rotates the engine.

The cranking circuit includes those mechanical and electrical components that are required to crank the engine for starting. The cranking force in the early 1900s was the driver's arm, because the driver had to physically crank the engine until it started. Modern cranking circuits include the following:

1. **Starter motor.** The starter is normally a 0.5 to 2.6 horsepower (0.4 to 2 kilowatts) electric motor that can develop nearly 8 horsepower (6 kilowatts) for a very short time when first cranking a cold engine. ● **SEE FIGURE 17–1**.

2. **Battery.** The battery must be of the correct capacity and be at least 75% charged to provide the necessary current and voltage for correct starter operation.

3. **Starter solenoid or relay.** The high current required by the starter must be able to be turned on and off. A large switch would be required if the current were controlled by the driver directly. Instead, a small current switch (ignition switch) operates a solenoid or relay that controls the high current to the starter.

4. **Starter drive.** The starter drive uses a small pinion gear that contacts the engine flywheel gear teeth and transmits starter motor power to rotate the engine.

5. **Ignition switch.** The ignition switch and safety control switches control the starter motor operation. ● **SEE FIGURE 17–2**.

CONTROL CIRCUIT PARTS AND OPERATION The engine is cranked by an electric motor that is controlled by an ignition switch. The ignition switch will not operate the starter unless the automatic transmission is in neutral or park, or the clutch pedal is depressed on manual transmission/transaxle vehicles. This is to prevent any accident that might result from the vehicle moving forward or rearward when the engine is started. The types of controls that are used to be sure that the vehicle will not move when being cranked include the following:

- Many automobile manufacturers use an electric switch called a **neutral safety switch**, which opens the circuit between the ignition switch and the starter to prevent starter motor operation, unless the gear selector is in neutral or park. The safety switch can be attached either to the steering column inside the vehicle near the floor or on the side of the transmission.

- Many manufacturers use a mechanical blocking device in the steering column to prevent the driver from engaging the start position unless the gear selector is in neutral or park.

- Many manual transmission vehicles also use a safety switch to permit cranking only if the clutch is depressed. This switch is commonly called the *clutch safety switch*. ● **SEE FIGURE 17–3**.

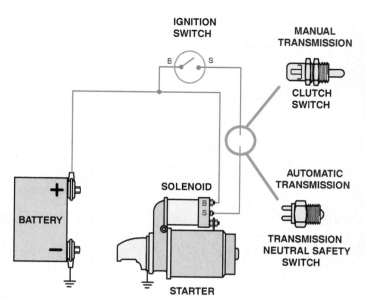

FIGURE 17–3 To prevent the engine from cranking, an electrical switch is usually installed to open the circuit between the ignition switch and the starter solenoid. The control circuit includes the small wiring and components needed to control the solenoid. The starter solenoid controls the electrical current flow through the large battery cables of the power circuit that operates the starter motor.

COMPUTER-CONTROLLED STARTING

OPERATION Many key-operated ignition systems and most push-button-to-start systems use the computer to crank the engine. The ignition switch start position on the push-to-start button is used as an input signal to the powertrain control module (PCM). Before the PCM cranks the engine, the following conditions must be met:

- The brake pedal is depressed.
- The gear selector is in park or neutral.
- The correct key fob (code) is present in the vehicle.

A typical computer-controlled system includes the following sequence:

- The ignition key can be turned to the start position, released, and the PCM cranks the engine until it senses that the engine has started.
- The PCM can detect that the engine has started by looking at the engine speed signal.
- Normal cranking speed can vary between 100 and 250 RPM. If the engine speed exceeds 400 RPM, the PCM determines that the engine has started and opens the circuit to the "S" (start) terminal of the starter solenoid that stops the starter motor.

FIGURE 17–4 Instead of using an ignition key to start the engine, some vehicles are using a start button, which is also used to stop the engine, as shown on this Jaguar.

FIGURE 17–5 The top button on this key fob is the remote start button.

Computer-controlled starting is almost always part of the system if a push-button start is used. ● **SEE FIGURE 17–4**.

REMOTE STARTING Remote starting, sometimes called **remote vehicle start (RVS)**, is a system that allows the driver to start the engine of the vehicle from inside the house or a building at a distance of about 200 ft (65 m). The doors remain locked to reduce the possibility of theft. This feature allows the heating or air-conditioning system to start before the driver arrives. ● **SEE FIGURE 17–5**.

NOTE: Most remote start systems will turn off the engine after 10 minutes of run time unless reset by using the remote.

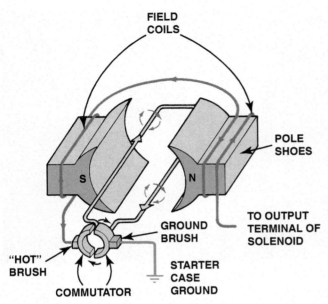

FIGURE 17–6 This series-wound electric motor shows the basic operation with only two brushes: one hot brush and one ground brush. The current flows through both field coils, then through the hot brush and the loop winding of the armature, before reaching ground through the ground brush.

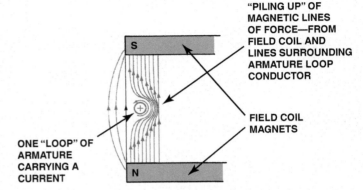

FIGURE 17–7 The interaction of the magnetic fields of the armature loops and field coils creates a stronger magnetic field on the right side of the conductor, causing the armature loop to move toward the left.

STARTER MOTOR OPERATION

PRINCIPLES A starter motor uses electromagnetic principles to convert electrical energy from the battery (up to 300 amperes) to mechanical power (up to 8 horsepower [6 kilowatts]) to crank the engine. Current for the starter motor or power circuit is controlled by a solenoid or relay, which is itself controlled by the driver-operated ignition switch.

The current travels through the brushes and into the armature windings, where other magnetic fields are created around each copper wire loop in the armature. The two strong magnetic fields created inside the starter housing create the force that rotates the armature.

Inside the starter housing is a strong magnetic field created by the field coil magnets. The armature, a conductor, is installed inside this strong magnetic field, with little clearance between the armature and the field coils.

The two magnetic fields act together, and their lines of force "bunch up" or are strong on one side of the armature loop wire and become weak on the other side of the conductor. This causes the conductor (armature) to move from the area of strong magnetic field strength toward the area of weak magnetic field strength. ● SEE FIGURES 17–6 AND 17–7.

The difference in magnetic field strength causes the armature to rotate. This rotation force (torque) is increased as the current flowing through the starter motor increases. The torque of a starter is determined by the strength of the magnetic fields inside the starter. Magnetic field strength is measured in ampere-turns. If the current or the number of turns of wire is increased, the magnetic field strength is increased.

The magnetic field of the starter motor is provided by two or more pole shoes and field windings. The pole shoes are made of iron and are attached to the frame with large screws. ● SEE FIGURE 17–8.

● FIGURE 17–9 shows the paths of magnetic flux lines within a four-pole motor.

The field windings are usually made of a heavy copper ribbon to increase their current-carrying capacity and electromagnetic field strength. ● SEE FIGURE 17–10.

Automotive starter motors usually have four pole shoes and two to four field windings to provide a strong magnetic field within the motor. Pole shoes that do not have field windings are magnetized by flux lines from the wound poles.

SERIES MOTORS A series motor develops its maximum torque at the initial start (0 RPM) and develops less torque as the speed increases.

■ A series motor is commonly used for an automotive starter motor because of its high starting power characteristics.

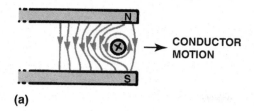

(a)

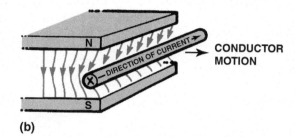

(b)

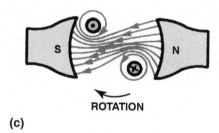

(c)

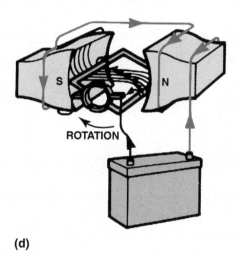

(d)

FIGURE 17–8 The armature loops rotate due to the difference in the strength of the magnetic field. The loops move from a strong magnetic field strength toward a weaker magnetic field strength.

- A series starter motor develops less torque at high RPM, because a current is produced in the starter itself that acts against the current from the battery. Because this current works against battery voltage, it is called **counter-electromotive force**, or **CEMF**. This CEMF is produced by electromagnetic induction in the armature conductors, which are cutting across the magnetic lines of force formed by the field coils. This induced voltage operates

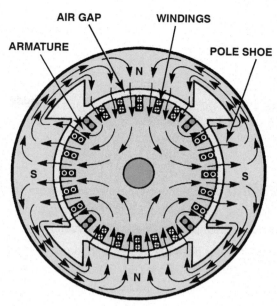

FIGURE 17–9 Magnetic lines of force in a four-pole motor.

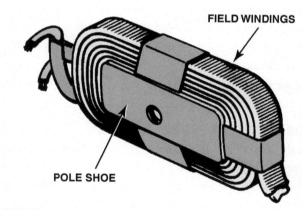

FIGURE 17–10 A pole shoe and field winding.

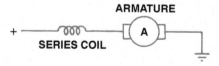

FIGURE 17–11 This wiring diagram illustrates the construction of a series-wound electric motor. Notice that all current flows through the field coils, then through the armature (in series) before reaching ground.

against the applied voltage supplied by the battery, which reduces the strength of the magnetic field in the starter.

- Because the power (torque) of the starter depends on the strength of the magnetic fields, the torque of the starter decreases as the starter speed increases. A series-wound starter also draws less current at higher speeds and will keep increasing in speed under light loads. This could lead to the destruction of the starter motor unless controlled or prevented. ● **SEE FIGURE 17–11.**

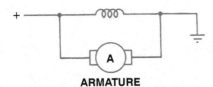

FIGURE 17–12 This wiring diagram illustrates the construction of a shunt-type electric motor and shows the field coils in parallel (or shunt) across the armature.

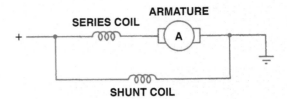

FIGURE 17–13 A compound motor is a combination of series and shunt types, using part of the field coils connected electrically in series with the armature and part in parallel (shunt).

SHUNT MOTORS Shunt-type electric motors have the field coils in parallel (or shunt) across the armature.

A shunt-type motor has the following features:

■ A shunt motor does not decrease in torque at higher motor RPM, because the CEMF produced in the armature does not decrease the field coil strength.

■ A shunt motor, however, does not produce as high a starting torque as that produced by a series-wound motor and is not used for starters. Some small electric motors, such as those used for windshield wiper, use a shunt motor but most use permanent magnets rather than electromagnets.
● **SEE FIGURE 17–12**.

PERMANENT MAGNET MOTORS A permanent magnet (PM) starter uses permanent magnets that maintain constant field strength, the same as a shunt-type motor, so they have similar operating characteristics. To compensate for the lack of torque, all PM starters use gear reduction to multiply starter motor torque. The permanent magnets used are an alloy of neodymium, iron, and boron and are almost 10 times more powerful than previously used permanent magnets.

COMPOUND MOTORS A compound-wound, or compound, motor has the operating characteristics of a series motor *and* a shunt-type motor, because some of the field coils are connected to the armature in series and some (usually only one) are connected directly to the battery in parallel (shunt) with the armature.

Compound-wound starter motors are commonly used in Ford, Chrysler, and some GM starters. The shunt-wound field coil is called a shunt coil and is used to limit the maximum speed of the starter. Because the shunt coil is energized as soon as the battery current is sent to the starter, it is used to engage the starter drive on older Ford positive engagement-type starters. ● **SEE FIGURE 17–13**.

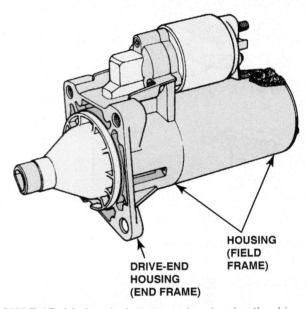

FIGURE 17–14 A typical starter motor showing the drive-end housing.

HOW THE STARTER MOTOR WORKS

PARTS INVOLVED A starter consists of the main structural support called the **field housing**, one end of which is called a **commutator-end (or brush-end) housing** and the other end a **drive-end housing**. The drive-end housing contains the drive pinion gear, which meshes with the engine flywheel gear teeth to start the engine. The commutator-end plate supports the end containing the starter brushes. **Through bolts** hold the three components together. ● **SEE FIGURE 17–14**.

■ **Field coils.** The steel housing of the starter motor contains permanent magnets or four electromagnets that are connected directly to the positive post of the battery to provide a strong magnetic field inside the starter. The four electromagnets use heavy copper or aluminum wire wrapped around a soft-iron core, which is contoured to fit against the rounded internal surface of the starter frame. The soft-iron cores are called **pole shoes**. Two of the four pole

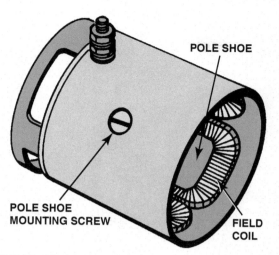

FIGURE 17–15 Pole shoes and field windings installed in the housing.

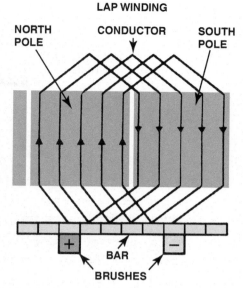

FIGURE 17–17 An armature showing how its copper wire loops are connected to the commutator.

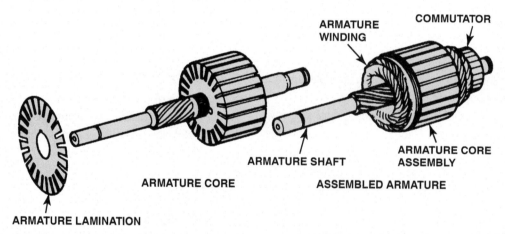

FIGURE 17–16 A typical starter motor armature. The armature core is made from thin sheet metal sections assembled on the armature shaft, which is used to increase the magnetic field strength.

shoes are wrapped with copper wire in one direction to create a north pole magnet, and the other two pole shoes are wrapped in the opposite direction to create a south pole magnet. These magnets, when energized, create strong magnetic fields inside the starter housing and, therefore, are called **field coils**. The soft-iron cores (pole shoes) are often called **field poles**. ● SEE FIGURE 17–15.

■ **Armature.** Inside the field coils is an **armature** that is supported with either bushings or ball bearings at both ends, which permit it to rotate. The armature is constructed of thin, circular disks of steel laminated together and wound lengthwise with heavy-gauge insulated copper wire. The laminated iron core supports the copper loops of wire and helps concentrate the magnetic field produced by the coils. ● SEE FIGURE 17–16.

Insulation between the laminations helps to increase the magnetic efficiency in the core. For reduced resistance, the armature conductors are made of a thick copper wire. The two ends of each conductor are attached to two adjacent commutator bars.

The commutator is made of copper bars insulated from each other by mica or some other insulating material. ● SEE FIGURE 17–17.

The armature core, windings, and commutator are assembled on a long armature shaft. This shaft also carries the pinion gear that meshes with the engine flywheel ring gear.

STARTER BRUSHES To supply the proper current to the armature, a four-pole motor must have four brushes riding on the commutator. Most automotive starters have two

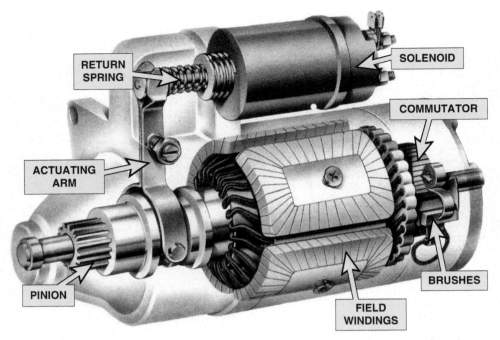

FIGURE 17-18 A cutaway of a typical starter motor showing the commutator, brushes, and brush spring.

grounded and two insulated brushes, which are held against the commutator by spring force.

The ends of the copper armature windings are soldered to **commutator segments**. The electrical current that passes through the field coils is then passed to the commutator of the armature by brushes that can move over the segments of the rotating armature. These **brushes** are made of a combination of copper and carbon.

- The copper used here is a good conductor material.

- The carbon added to the starter brushes helps provide the graphite-type lubrication needed to reduce wear of the brushes and the commutator segments.

The starter uses four brushes—two brushes to transfer the current from the field coils to the armature and two brushes to provide the ground return path for the current that flows through the armature.

The two sets of brushes include the following:

1. Two **insulated brushes**, which are in holders and are insulated from the housing.

2. Two **ground brushes**, which use bare, stranded copper wire connections to the brushes. The ground brush holders are not insulated and attach directly to the field housing or brush-end housing.

● **SEE FIGURE 17-18.**

PERMANENT MAGNET FIELDS Permanent magnets are used in place of the electromagnetic field coils and pole shoes in many starters today. This eliminates the motor field circuit, which in turn eliminates the potential for field coil faults and other electrical problems. The motor has only an armature circuit.

 **TECH TIP**

Don't Hit That Starter!

In the past, it was common to see service technicians hitting a starter in their effort to diagnose a no-crank condition. Often the shock of the blow to the starter aligned or moved the brushes, armature, and bushings. Many times, the starter functioned after being hit, even if only for a short time.

However, most starters today use permanent magnet fields, and the magnets can be easily broken if hit. A magnet that is broken becomes two weaker magnets. Some early permanent magnet starters used magnets that were glued or bonded to the field housing. If struck with a heavy tool, the magnets could be broken with parts of the magnet falling onto the armature and into the bearing pockets, making the starter impossible to repair or rebuild.

● **SEE FIGURE 17-19.**

FIGURE 17–19 This starter permanent magnet field housing was ruined when someone used a hammer on the field housing in an attempt to "fix" a starter that would not work. A total replacement is the only solution in this case.

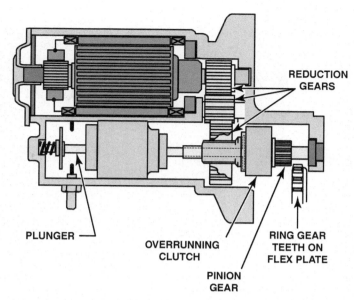

FIGURE 17–20 A typical gear-reduction starter.

GEAR-REDUCTION STARTERS

PURPOSE AND FUNCTION Gear-reduction starters are used by many automotive manufacturers. The purpose of the gear reduction (typically 2:1 to 4:1) is to increase starter motor speed and provide the torque multiplication necessary to crank an engine.

As a series-wound motor increases in rotational speed, the starter produces less power, and less current is drawn from the battery because the armature generates greater CEMF as the starter speed increases. However, a starter motor's maximum torque occurs at 0 RPM and torque decreases with increasing RPM. A smaller starter using a gear-reduction design can produce the necessary cranking power with reduced starter amperage requirements. Lower current requirements mean that smaller battery cables can be used. Many permanent magnet starters use a planetary gear set (a type of gear reduction) to provide the necessary torque for starting. ● **SEE FIGURE 17–20.**

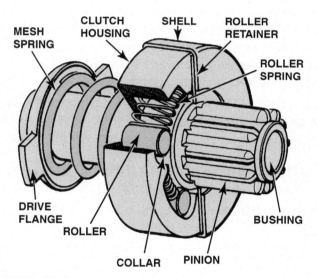

FIGURE 17–21 A cutaway of a typical starter drive showing all of the internal parts.

STARTER DRIVES

PURPOSE AND FUNCTION A **starter drive** includes small pinion gears that mesh with and rotate the larger gear on the engine flywheel or flex plate for starting. The pinion gear must engage with the engine gear slightly *before* the starter motor rotates to prevent serious damage to either the starter gear or the engine, but must be disengaged after the engine starts. The ends of the starter pinion gear are tapered to help the teeth mesh more easily without damaging the flywheel ring gear teeth. ● **SEE FIGURE 17–21.**

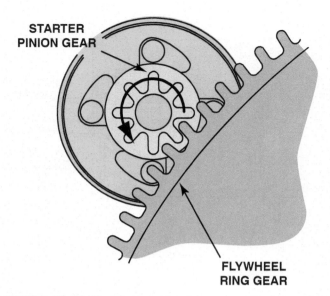

STARTER PINION GEAR

FLYWHEEL RING GEAR

FIGURE 17–22 The ring gear to pinion gear ratio is usually 15:1 to 20:1.

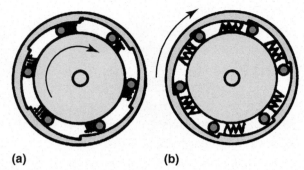

(a)   **(b)**

FIGURE 17–23 Operation of the overrunning clutch. (a) Starter motor is driving the starter pinion and cranking the engine. The rollers are wedged against spring force into their slots. (b) The engine has started and is rotating faster than the starter armature. Spring force pushes the rollers so they can rotate freely.

STARTER DRIVE GEAR RATIO The ratio of the number of teeth on the engine ring gear to the number on the starter pinion is between 15:1 and 20:1. A typical small starter pinion gear has 9 teeth that turn an engine ring gear with 166 teeth. This provides an 18:1 gear reduction; thus, the starter motor is rotating approximately 18 times faster than the engine. Normal cranking speed for the engine is 200 RPM (varies from 70 to 250 RPM). This means that the starter motor speed is 18 times faster, or 3,600 starter RPM ($200 \times 18 = 3,600$). If the engine starts and is accelerated to 2,000 RPM (normal cold engine speed), the starter will be destroyed by the high speed (36,000 RPM) if the starter was not disengaged from the engine. ● **SEE FIGURE 17–22**.

STARTER DRIVE OPERATION All starter drive mechanisms use a type of one-way clutch that allows the starter to rotate the engine, but then turns freely if the engine speed is greater than the starter motor speed. This clutch, called an **overrunning clutch**, protects the starter motor from damage if the ignition switch is held in the start position after the engine starts. The overrunning clutch, which is built in as a part of the starter drive unit, uses steel balls or rollers installed in tapered notches. ● **SEE FIGURE 17–23**.

This taper forces the balls or rollers tightly into the notch when rotating in the direction necessary to start the engine. When the engine rotates faster than the starter pinion, the balls or rollers are forced out of the narrow tapered notch, allowing the pinion gear to turn freely (overrun).

The spring between the drive tang or pulley and the overrunning clutch and pinion is called a **mesh spring**. It helps to cushion and control the engagement of the starter drive pinion with the engine flywheel gear. This spring is also called a **compression spring**, because the starter solenoid or starter yoke compresses the spring and the spring tension causes the starter pinion to engage the engine flywheel.

FAILURE MODE A starter drive is generally a dependable unit and does not require replacement unless defective or worn. The major wear occurs in the overrunning clutch section of the starter drive unit. The steel balls or rollers wear and often do not wedge tightly into the tapered notches as is necessary for engine cranking. A worn starter drive can cause the starter motor to operate and then stop cranking the engine further creating a "whining" noise. The whine indicates that the starter motor is operating and that the starter drive is not rotating the engine flywheel. The entire starter drive is replaced as a unit. The overrunning clutch section of the starter drive cannot be serviced or repaired separately because the drive is a sealed unit. Starter drives are most likely to fail intermittently at first and then more frequently, until replacement becomes necessary to start the engine. Intermittent starter drive failure (starter whine) is often most noticeable during cold weather.

FREQUENTLY ASKED QUESTION

What Is a Bendix?

Older-model starters often used a Bendix drive mechanism, which used inertia to engage the starter pinion with the engine flywheel gear. Inertia is the tendency of a stationary object to remain stationary, because of its weight, unless forced to move. On these older-model starters, the small starter pinion gear was attached to a shaft with threads, and the weight of this gear caused it to be spun along the threaded shaft and mesh with the flywheel whenever the starter motor spun. If the engine speed was greater than the starter speed, the pinion gear was forced back along the threaded shaft and out of mesh with the flywheel gear. The Bendix drive mechanism has generally not been used since the early 1960s, but some technicians use this term when describing a starter drive.

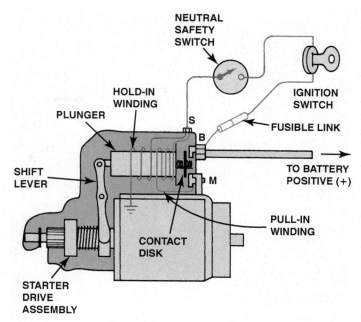

FIGURE 17–24 Wiring diagram of a typical starter solenoid. Notice that both the pull-in winding and the hold-in winding are energized when the ignition switch is first turned to the "start" position. As soon as the solenoid contact disk makes electrical contact with both the B and M terminals, the battery current is conducted to the starter motor and electrically neutralizes the pull-in winding.

STARTER SOLENOIDS

SOLENOID OPERATION A **starter solenoid** is an electromagnetic switch containing two separate, but connected, electromagnetic windings. This switch is used to engage the starter drive and control the current from the battery to the starter motor.

SOLENOID WINDINGS The two internal windings contain approximately the same number of turns but are made from different-gauge wire. Both windings together produce a strong magnetic field that pulls a metal plunger into the solenoid. The plunger is attached to the starter drive through a shift fork lever. When the ignition switch is turned to the start position, the motion of the plunger into the solenoid causes the starter drive to move into mesh with the flywheel ring gear.

1. The heavier-gauge winding (called the **pull-in winding**) is needed to draw the plunger into the solenoid and is grounded through the starter motor.

2. The lighter-gauge winding (called the **hold-in winding**), which is grounded through the starter frame, produces enough magnetic force to keep the plunger in position. The main purpose of using two separate windings

is to permit as much current as possible to operate the starter, and yet provide the strong magnetic field required to move the starter drive into engagement. ● **SEE FIGURE 17–24.**

OPERATION

1. The solenoid operates as soon as the ignition or computer-controlled relay energizes the "S" (start) terminals. At that instant, the plunger is drawn into the solenoid enough to engage the starter drive.

2. The plunger makes contact with a metal disk that connects the battery terminal post of the solenoid to the motor terminal. This permits full battery current to flow through the solenoid to operate the starter motor.

3. The contact disk also electrically disconnects the pull-in winding. The solenoid *has* to work to supply current to the starter. Therefore, if the starter motor operates at all, the solenoid is working, even though it may have high external resistance that could cause slow starter motor operation.

FIGURE 17–25 A palm-size starter armature.

? **FREQUENTLY ASKED QUESTION**

How Are Starters Made So Small?

Starters and most components in a vehicle are being made as small and as light in weight as possible to help increase vehicle performance and fuel economy. A starter can be constructed smaller due to the use of gear reduction and permanent magnets to achieve the same cranking torque as a straight drive starter, but using much smaller components.
● **SEE FIGURE 17–25** for an example of an automotive starter armature that is palm size.

STOP/START SYSTEMS

PURPOSE AND FUNCTION **Stop/start** systems are designed to increase fuel economy and reduce exhaust emissions. Fuel economy and the reduction of CO_2 emissions are estimated to be 5% to 10%, depending on the vehicle and how it is being operated. With stop/start mechanism, the engine is stopped to reduce the fuel consumption when the vehicle is stopped at traffic signals or in stop and go traffic conditions. Various vehicle manufacturers refer to stop/start

FIGURE 17–26 A Buick Auto Stop system lets the driver know when the engine is stopped.

systems using different terms including. Auto Stop ● **SEE FIGURE 17–26**

- Stop/Start
- Idle-Stop (Honda)
- Smart Stop (Toyota)
- Intelligent Stop and Go (Kia)
- Auto Start/Stop (BMW)
- Engine Stop-Start (ESS) -Chrysler

CONDITIONS FOR STOP/START TO OCCUR Before the PCM will engage the stop/start function, the following parameters must be achieved:

- Engine speed is within idling range.
- Accelerator pedal is not depressed.
- Vehicle speed is low or zero depending on the type of starter used.
- Battery state of charge (SOC) is above threshold.
- Hood is closed.

START/STOP SYSTEM COMPONENTS It is estimated that a stop/start system will start the engine about 500,000 times in the life of the vehicle compared to about 5,000 times for a conventional starting system. A typical stop/start system includes the following components:

1. An absorbed glass-mat (AGM) or enhanced lead-acid (ELA) battery

2. Battery sensor—Used by the PCM to determine the current entering and leaving the battery in order to estimate the battery SOC.

3. At lower engine speeds.

4. Hood switch—Used by the PCM to disengage stop/start if the hood is open.

5. HVAC control unit—Used to start the engine if cooling or heat is required in the passenger compartment.

STARTER MOTOR DESIGNS Because the engine needs to be restarted many times a day, if driving in heavy congested traffic, the starter used must be durable and capable of starting the engine over 500,000 times during the life of the system. There are three designs of starters used in stop/start system including the following:

1. **Advanced Engagement (AE) Starter.** An advanced engagement starter works like a typical starter. When energized, the pinion shifts forward by the starter solenoid and engages with the engine's ring gear/flywheel, and immediately spins. This starter design requires that the engine speed needs to be zero before re-engagement and engine restart can occur. To survive the increased usage requires long-life electrical brushes, plus an enhanced pinion spring mechanism that reduces ring gear/flywheel wear.

2. **Tandem Solenoid (TS) Starter.** Using a starter that has two solenoids allows the starter to engage the flywheel of the engine when it is still moving, such as when the vehicle is coasting to a stop. A tandem solenoid starter design is also able to start the engine within 0.5 and 1.5 seconds compared to about 3 seconds for a conventional starter. A conventional starter uses the solenoid to engage the starter pinion, and when it is being held by the hold-in winding, the solenoid then energizes the starter motor cranking the engine. The use of a dual solenoid allows the two functions of the starter solenoid to work independently. One solenoid is used to engage the starter drive into the engine ring gear and the other solenoid is used to engage the operation of the starter motor. ● SEE FIGURE 17–27.

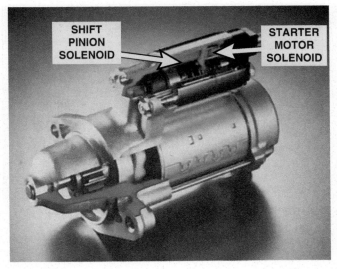

FIGURE 17–27 Using two solenoids allows independent control of the pinion gear and motor energization. This allows the engine to be re-engaged (and re-started) by the starter motor when the engine RPM is falling from idle (about 600 RPM) to zero RPM. A tandem solenoid starter is almost identical in size and shape so it can be used on almost any engine.

3. **Permanently Engaged (PE) Starter.** A permanently engaged starter delivers the quickest and quietest restart times of all starter motor-based systems. In this system, the starter and flywheel gears are permanently connected, so there are no concerns with gear engagement and disengagement. The PE starter eliminates the starter pinion gear shifting mechanism with its slight delay in activating by mounting the starter to the engine permanently engaged with the flywheel. When a restart is needed, the motor is simply energized, which immediately re-cranks the engine. There is no waiting or delay since the starter gear is already mated to the flywheel. The flywheel does require a special clutching mechanism to disconnect it from engine RPM after engine start.

FIGURE 17–28 The stop/start system on this Ford F-150 pickup truck can be turned off using a switch on the dash.

FREQUENTLY ASKED QUESTION

Can a Stop/Start System Be Turned Off?

Sometimes. Some vehicles equipped with a stop/start system can be turned off using a button on the dash or center stack. ● **SEE FIGURE 17–28.**

SUMMARY

1. All starter motors use the principle of magnetic interaction between the field coils attached to the housing and the magnetic field of the armature.

2. The control circuit includes the ignition switch, neutral safety (clutch) switch, and solenoid.

3. The power circuit includes the battery, battery cables, solenoid, and starter motor.

4. The parts of a typical starter include the main field housing, commutator-end (or brush-end) housing, drive-end housing, brushes, armature, and starter drive.

REVIEW QUESTIONS

1. What is the difference between the control circuit and the power (motor) circuit sections of a typical cranking circuit?

2. What are the parts of a typical starter?

3. What are the terms used to describe a stop-start system?

4. What moves the starter drive into mesh with the engine ring gear?

5. Why are there two windings in the starter solenoid?

CHAPTER QUIZ

1. Starter motors operate on the principle that _____.
   a. the field coils rotate in the opposite direction from the armature
   b. opposite magnetic poles repel
   c. like magnetic poles repel
   d. the armature rotates from a strong magnetic field toward a weaker magnetic field

2. Series-wound electric motors _____.
   a. produce electrical power
   b. produce maximum power at 0 RPM
   c. produce maximum power at high RPM
   d. use a shunt coil

3. What conditions are needed before the stop-start system functions?
   a. Engine speed is within idling range.
   b. Accelerator pedal is not depressed.
   c. Hood is closed
   d. All of the above

4. The neutral safety switch is located _____.
   a. between the starter solenoid and the starter motor
   b. inside the ignition switch itself
   c. between the ignition switch and the starter solenoid
   d. in the battery cable between the battery and the starter solenoid

5. The brushes are used to transfer electrical power between _____.
   a. field coils and the armature
   b. the commutator segments
   c. the solenoid and the field coils
   d. the armature and the solenoid

6. The faster a starter motor rotates, _____.
   a. the more current it draws from the battery
   b. the less CEMF is generated
   c. the less current it draws from the battery
   d. the greater the amount of torque produced

7. Normal cranking speed of the engine is about _____.
   a. 2,000 RPM
   b. 1,500 RPM
   c. 1,000 RPM
   d. 200 RPM

8. A starter motor rotates about _____ times faster than the engine.
   a. 18
   b. 10
   c. 5
   d. 2

9. Permanent magnets are commonly used for what part of the starter?
   a. Armature
   b. Solenoid
   c. Field coils
   d. Commutator

10. Which unit contains a hold-in winding and a pull-in winding?
    a. Field coil
    b. Starter solenoid
    c. Armature
    d. Ignition switch

chapter 18
CRANKING SYSTEM DIAGNOSIS AND SERVICE

LEARNING OBJECTIVES

After studying this chapter, the reader will be able to:

1. Discuss how to perform a voltage drop test on the cranking circuit.

2. Perform control circuit testing and starter amperage test, and determine necessary action.

3. Explain starter motor service and bench testing.

This chapter will help you prepare for the ASE Electrical/Electronic Systems (A6) certification test content area "C" (Starting Systems Diagnosis and Repair).

KEY TERMS

Bench testing 269

Growler 268

Shims 270

Voltage drop 264

STARTING SYSTEM TROUBLESHOOTING PROCEDURE

OVERVIEW The proper operation of the starting system depends on a good battery, good cables and connections, and a good starter motor. Because a starting problem can be caused by a defective component anywhere in the starting circuit, it is important to check for the proper operation of each part of the circuit to diagnose and repair the problem quickly.

STEPS INVOLVED Following are the steps involved in the diagnosis of a fault in the cranking circuit.

STEP 1 **Verify the customer concern.** Sometimes the customer is not aware of how the cranking system is supposed to work, especially if it is computer controlled.

STEP 2 **Visually inspect the battery and battery connections.** The starter is the highest amperage draw device used in a vehicle and any faults, such as corrosion on battery terminals, can cause cranking system problems.

STEP 3 **Test battery condition.** Perform a battery load or conductance test on the battery to be sure that the battery is capable of supplying the necessary current for the starter.

STEP 4 **Check the control circuit.** An open or high resistance anywhere in the control circuit can cause the starter motor to not engage. Items to check include the following:
- "S" terminal of the starter solenoid
- Neutral safety or clutch switch

THEFT DETERRENT INDICATOR LAMP

FIGURE 18–1 A theft deterrent indicator lamp of the dash. A flashing lamp usually indicates a fault in the system, and the engine may not start.

- Starter enable relay (if equipped)
- Antitheft system fault (If the engine does not crank or start and the theft indicator light is on or flashing, there is likely a fault in the theft deterrent system. Check service information for the exact procedures to follow before attempting to service the cranking circuit. ● **SEE FIGURE 18–1.**)

STEP 5 **Check voltage drop of the starter circuit.** Any high resistance in either the power side or ground side of the starter circuit will cause the starter to rotate slowly or not at all.

 TECH TIP

Voltage Drop Is Resistance

Many technicians have asked, "Why measure voltage drop when the resistance can be easily measured using an ohmmeter?" Think of a battery cable with all the strands of the cable broken, except for one strand. If an ohmmeter were used to measure the resistance of the cable, the reading would be very low, probably less than 1 ohm. However, the cable is not capable of conducting the amount of current necessary to crank the engine. In less severe cases, several strands can be broken, thereby affecting the operation of the starter motor. Although the resistance of the battery cable will not indicate an increase, the restriction to current flow will cause heat and a drop in voltage available at the starter. Because resistance is not effective until current flows, measuring the voltage drop (differences in voltage between two points) is the most accurate method of determining the true resistance in a circuit.

How much is too much? According to Bosch Corporation, all electrical circuits should have a maximum of 3% loss of the circuit voltage to resistance. Therefore, in a 12-volt circuit, the maximum loss of voltage in cables and connections should be 0.36 volt ($12 \times 0.03 = 0.36$ volt). The remaining 97% of the circuit voltage (11.64 volts) is available to operate the electrical device (load). Just remember:
- Low-voltage drop = Low resistance
- High-voltage drop = High resistance

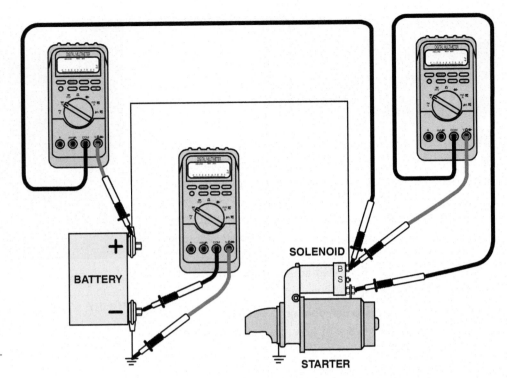

FIGURE 18–2 Voltmeter hookups for voltage drop testing of a solenoid-type cranking circuit.

VOLTAGE DROP TESTING

PURPOSE **Voltage drop** is the drop in voltage that occurs when current is flowing through a resistance. That is, a voltage drop is the difference between voltage at the source and voltage at the electrical device to which it is flowing. The higher the voltage drop is, the greater is the resistance in the circuit. Even though voltage drop testing can be performed on any electrical circuit, the most common areas of testing include the cranking circuit and the charging circuit wiring and connections. Voltage drop testing should be performed on both the power side and ground side of the circuit.

A high-voltage drop (high resistance) in the cranking circuit wiring can cause slow engine cranking with less than normal starter amperage drain as a result of the excessive circuit resistance. If the voltage drop is high enough, such as that caused by dirty battery terminals, the starter may not operate. A typical symptom of high resistance in the cranking circuit is a "clicking" of the starter solenoid.

TEST PROCEDURE Voltage drop testing of the wire involves connecting a voltmeter set to read DC volts to the suspected high-resistance cable ends and cranking the engine.
● **SEE FIGURES 18–2 THROUGH 18–4.**

NOTE: Before a difference in voltage (voltage drop) can be measured between the ends of a battery cable, current must be flowing through the cable. Resistance is not effective unless current is flowing. If the engine is not being cranked, current is not flowing through the battery cables and the voltage drop cannot be measured.

STEP 1 Disable the ignition or fuel injection as follows:
- Disconnect the primary (low-voltage) electrical connection(s) from the ignition module or ignition coils.
- Remove the fuel-injection fuse or relay, or the electrical connection leading to all of the fuel injectors.

CAUTION: Never disconnect the high-voltage ignition wires unless they are connected to ground. The high voltage that could occur when cranking can cause the ignition coil to fail (arc internally).

STEP 2 Connect one lead of the voltmeter to the starter motor battery terminal and the other end to the positive battery terminal.

STEP 3 Crank the engine and observe the reading while cranking. (Disregard the first higher reading.) The reading should be less than 0.20 volt (200 millivolts).

STEP 4 If accessible, test the voltage drop across the "B" and "M" terminals of the starter solenoid with the engine cranking. The voltage drop should be less than 0.20 volt (200 millivolts).

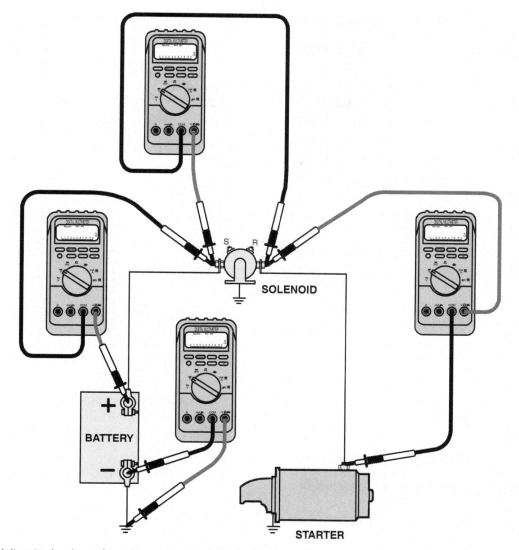

FIGURE 18–3 Voltmeter hookups for voltage drop testing of a Ford cranking circuit.

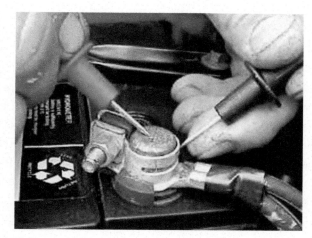

FIGURE 18–4 To test the voltage drop of the battery cable connection, place one voltmeter lead on the battery terminal and the other voltmeter lead on the cable end and crank the engine. The voltmeter will read the difference in voltage between the two leads, which should not exceed 0.20 volt (200 millivolts).

STEP 5 Repeat the voltage drop on the ground side of the cranking circuit by connecting one voltmeter lead to the negative battery terminal and the other at the starter housing. Crank the engine and observe the voltmeter display. The voltage drop should be less than 0.2 volt (200 millivolts).

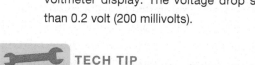

TECH TIP

A Warm Cable Equals High Resistance

If a cable or connection is warm to the touch, there is electrical resistance in the cable or connection. The resistance changes electrical energy into heat energy. Therefore, if a voltmeter is not available, touch the battery cables and connections while cranking the engine. If any cable or connection is hot to the touch, it should be cleaned or replaced.

CONTROL CIRCUIT TESTING

PARTS INVOLVED The control circuit for the starting circuit includes the battery, ignition switch, neutral or clutch safety switch, theft deterrent system, and starter solenoid. When the ignition switch is rotated to the start position, current flows through the ignition switch and neutral safety switch to activate the solenoid. High current then flows directly from the battery through the solenoid and to the starter motor. Therefore, an open or break anywhere in the control circuit will prevent the operation of the starter motor.

If a starter is inoperative, first check for voltage at the "S" (start) terminal of the starter solenoid. Check for faults with the following:

- Neutral safety or clutch switch
- Blown crank fuse
- Open at the ignition switch in the crank position
- Starter relay or module, if equipped

Some models with antitheft controls use a relay to open this control circuit to prevent starter operation.

STARTER AMPERAGE TEST

REASON FOR A STARTER AMPERAGE TEST A starter should be tested to see if the reason for slow or no cranking is due to a fault with the starter motor or another problem. A voltage drop test is used to find out if the battery cables and connections are okay. A starter amperage draw test determines if the starter motor is the cause of a no or slow cranking concern.

TEST PREPARATION Before performing a starter amperage test, be certain that the battery is sufficiently charged (75% or more) and capable of supplying adequate starting current. Connect a starter amperage tester following the tester's instructions. ● **SEE FIGURE 18–5.**

A starter amperage test should be performed when the starter fails to operate normally (is slow in cranking) or as part of a routine electrical system inspection.

SPECIFICATIONS Some service manuals specify normal starter amperage for starter motors being tested on the vehicle; however, most service manuals only give the specifications for bench testing a starter without a load applied. These

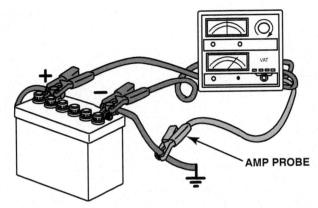

FIGURE 18–5 A starter amperage tester uses an amp probe around the positive or negative battery cables.

TECH TIP

Watch the Dome Light

When diagnosing any starter-related problem, open the door of the vehicle and observe the brightness of the dome or interior light(s).

The brightness of any electrical lamp is proportional to the voltage of the battery.

Normal operation of the starter results in a slight dimming of the dome light.

If the light remains bright, the problem is usually an open in the control circuit.

If the light goes out or almost goes out, there could be a problem with the following:

- A shorted or grounded armature of field coils inside the starter
- Loose or corroded battery connections or cables
- Weak or discharged battery

specifications are helpful in making certain that a repaired starter meets exact specifications, but they do not apply to starter testing on the vehicle. If exact specifications are not available, the following can be used as general *maximum* amperage draw specifications for testing a starter on the vehicle ignoring the initial surge of current when the engine is first cranked.

- **4-cylinder engines** = 150 to 185 amperes (normally less than 100 amperes) at room temperature
- **6-cylinder engines** = 160 to 200 amperes (normally less than 125 amperes) at room temperature
- **8-cylinder engines** = 185 to 250 amperes (normally less than 150 amperes) at room temperature

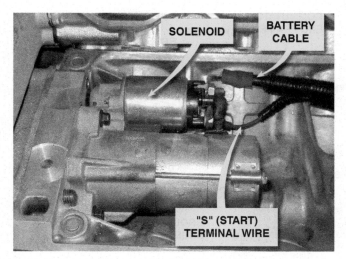

FIGURE 18–6 The starter is located under the intake manifold on this Cadillac Northstar engine.

Excessive current draw may indicate one or more of the following:

1. Binding of starter armature as a result of worn bushings
2. Oil too thick (viscosity too high) for weather conditions
3. Shorted or grounded starter windings or cables
4. Tight or seized engine
5. Shorted starter motor (usually caused by fault with the field coils or armature)

   - High mechanical resistance = High starter amperage draw
   - High electrical resistance = Low starter amperage draw

Lower amperage draw and slow or no cranking may indicate one or more of the following:

- Dirty or corroded battery connections
- High internal resistance in the battery cable(s)
- High internal starter motor resistance
- Poor ground connection between the starter motor and the engine block

 CASE STUDY

The Case of the No-Crank Camaro

The owner of a Camaro SS equipped with a 6.2 liter V-8 and a six-speed manual transmission had the car towed to a shop for a no crank, no start condition. The technician used a scan tool and was able to retrieve a stored diagnostic trouble code (DTC) P0807. This code indicated a fault with the clutch pedal position

(CPP) sensor. The clutch pedal position sensor was removed and it was found to be internally shorted. A new sensor was installed and the technician performed a relearn procedure as specified in service information. The car was then able to crank and start and the verified that no codes were present.

Summary:

- **Complaint**—The customer stated that the engine would not crank or start
- **Cause**—A shorted clutch pedal position (CPP) sensor
- **Correction**—The clutch pedal position sensor was replaced and a relearn procedure was performed.

STARTER REMOVAL

PROCEDURE After testing has confirmed that a starter motor may need to be replaced, most vehicle manufacturers recommend the following general steps and procedures:

STEP 1 Disconnect the negative battery cable.

STEP 2 Hoist the vehicle safely.

> **NOTE: This step may not be necessary. Check service information for the specified procedure for the vehicle being serviced. Some starters are located under the intake manifold. ● SEE FIGURE 18–6.**

STEP 3 Remove the starter retaining bolts and lower the starter to gain access to the wire(s) connection(s) on the starter.

STEP 4 Disconnect and label the wire(s) from the starter and remove the starter.

STEP 5 Inspect the flywheel (flexplate) for ring gear damage. Also check that the mounting holes are clean and the mounting flange is clean and smooth. Service as needed.

STARTER MOTOR SERVICE

PURPOSE Most starter motors are replaced as an assembly or not easily disassembled or serviced. However, some starters, especially on classic muscle or collector vehicles, can be serviced.

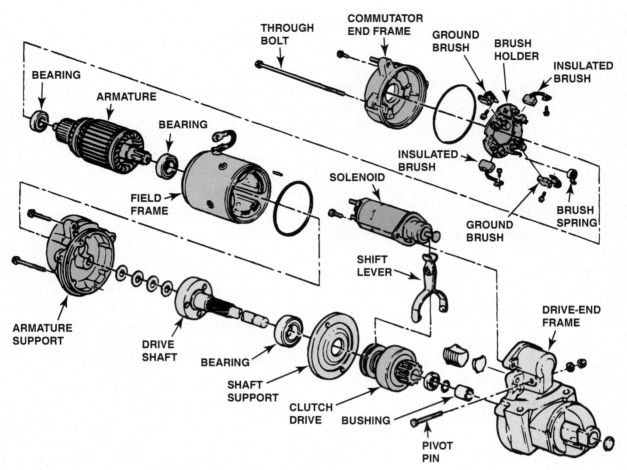

FIGURE 18–7 An exploded view of a typical solenoid-operated starter.

DISASSEMBLY PROCEDURE Disassembly of a starter motor usually includes the following steps:

STEP 1 Remove the starter solenoid assembly.

STEP 2 Mark the location of the through bolts on the field housing to help align them during reassembly.

STEP 3 Remove the drive-end housing and then the armature assembly.

● **SEE FIGURE 18–7.**

INSPECTION AND TESTING The various parts should be inspected and tested to see if the components can be used to restore the starter to serviceable condition.

- **Solenoid.** Check the resistance of the solenoid winding. The solenoid can be tested using an ohmmeter to check for the proper resistance in the hold-in and pull-in windings. ● **SEE FIGURE 18–8.**

Most technicians replace the solenoid whenever the starter is replaced and is usually included with a replacement starter.

- **Starter armature.** After the starter drive has been removed from the armature, it can be checked for runout using a dial indicator and V-blocks, as shown in ● **FIGURE 18–9.**

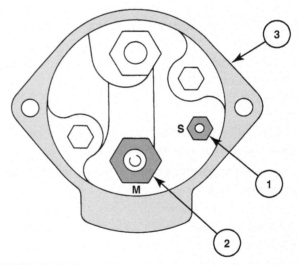

FIGURE 18–8 GM solenoid ohmmeter check. The reading between 1 and 3 (S terminal and ground) should be 0.4 to 0.6 ohm (hold-in winding). The reading between 1 and 2 (S terminal and M terminal) should be 0.2 to 0.4 ohm (pull-in winding).

- **Growler.** Because the loops of copper wire are interconnected in the armature of a starter, an armature can be accurately tested only by use of a **growler**. A

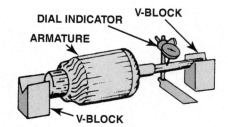

FIGURE 18–9 Measuring an armature shaft for runout using a dial indicator and V-blocks.

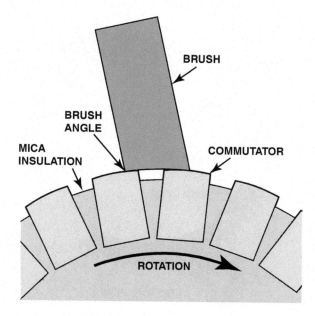

FIGURE 18–10 Replacement starter brushes should be installed so the beveled edge matches the rotation of the commutator.

growler is a 110-volt AC test unit that generates an alternating (60 hertz) magnetic field around an armature. A starter armature is placed into the V-shaped top portion of a laminated soft-iron core surrounded by a coil of copper wire. Plug the growler into a 110-volt outlet and then follow the instructions for testing the armature.

- **Starter motor field coils.** With the armature removed from the starter motor, the field coils should be tested for opens and grounds using a powered test light or an ohmmeter. To test for a grounded field coil, touch one lead of the tester to a field brush (insulated or hot) and the other end to the starter field housing. The ohmmeter should indicate infinity (no continuity), and the test light should *not* light. If there is continuity, replace the field coil housing assembly. The ground brushes should show continuity to the starter housing.

NOTE: **Many starters use removable field coils. These coils must be rewound using the proper equipment and insulating materials. Usually, the cost involved in replacing defective field coils exceeds the cost of a replacement starter.**

- **Starter brush inspection.** Starter brushes should be replaced if the brush length is less than half of its original length (less than 0.5 inch [13 millimeters]). On some models of starter motors, the field brushes are serviced with the field coil assembly and the ground brushes with the brush holder. Many starters use brushes that are held in with screws and are easily replaced, whereas other starters may require soldering to remove and replace the brushes. ● **SEE FIGURE 18–10.**

BENCH TESTING

Every starter should be tested before installation in a vehicle. **Bench testing** is the usual method and involves clamping the starter in a vise to prevent rotation during operation and connecting heavy-gauge jumper wires (minimum 4 gauge) to both a good battery and the starter. The starter motor should rotate as fast as specifications indicate and not draw more than the free-spinning amperage permitted. A typical amperage specification for a starter being tested on a bench (not installed in a vehicle) usually ranges from 60 to 100 amperes.

STARTER INSTALLATION

After verifying that the starter assembly is functioning correctly, verify that the negative battery cable has been disconnected. Safely hoist the vehicle, if necessary. Following are the usual steps to install a starter. Be sure to check service information for the exact procedures to follow for the vehicle being serviced.

STEP 1 Check service information for the exact wiring connections to the starter and/or the solenoid.

STEP 2 Verify that all electrical connections on the starter-motor and/or the solenoid are correct for the vehicle and that they are in good condition.

NOTE: Be sure that the locking nuts for the studs are tight. Often, the retaining nut that holds the wire to the stud will be properly tightened, but if the stud itself is loose, cranking problems can occur.

STEP 3 Attach the power and control wires.

STEP 4 Install the starter, and torque all the fasteners to factory specifications and tighten evenly.

STEP 5 Perform a starter amperage draw test and check for proper engine cranking.

CAUTION: Be sure to install all factory heat shields to help ensure problem-free starter operation under all weather and driving conditions.

STARTER DRIVE-TO-FLYWHEEL CLEARANCE

NEED FOR SHIMS For the proper operation of the starter and absence of abnormal starter noise, there must be a slight clearance between the starter pinion and the engine flywheel ring gear. Many starters use **shims**, which are thin metal strips between the flywheel and the engine block mounting pad to provide the proper clearance. ● **SEE FIGURE 18-11.**

Some manufacturers use shims under the starter drive-end housings during production. Other manufacturers *grind* the mounting pads at the factory for proper starter pinion gear

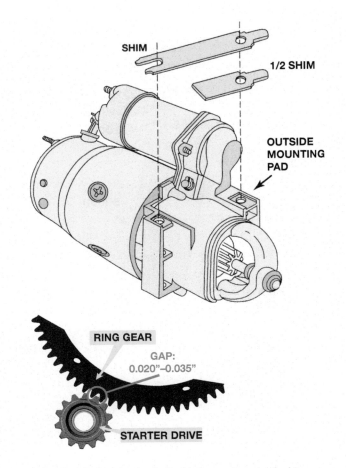

FIGURE 18-11 A shim (or half shim) may be needed to provide the proper clearance between the flywheel teeth of the engine and the pinion teeth of the starter.

clearance. If a GM starter is replaced, the starter pinion should be checked and corrected as necessary to prevent starter damage and excessive noise.

SYMPTOMS OF CLEARANCE PROBLEMS

- If the clearance is too great, the starter will produce a high-pitched whine *during* cranking.

- If the clearance is too small, the starter may bind, crank slowly, or produce a high-pitched whine *after* the engine starts, just as the ignition is released.

PROCEDURE FOR PROPER CLEARANCE To be sure that the starter is shimmed correctly, use the following procedure.

STEP 1 Place the starter in position and finger-tighten the mounting bolts.

Reuse Drive-End Housing to Be Sure

Most GM starter motors use a pad mount and attach to the engine with bolts through the drive-end (nose) housing. Many times when a starter is replaced on a GM vehicle, the starter makes noise because of improper starter pinion-to-engine flywheel ring gear clearance. Instead of spending a lot of time shimming the new starter, simply remove the drive-end housing from the original starter and install it on the replacement starter. Service the bushing in the drive-end housing if needed. Because the original starter did not produce excessive gear engagement noise, the replacement starter will also be okay. Reuse any shims that were used with the original starter. This is preferable to removing and reinstalling the replacement starter several times until the proper clearance is determined.

STEP 2 Use a 1/8-inch diameter drill bit (or gauge tool) and insert between the armature shaft and a tooth of the engine flywheel.

STEP 3 If the gauge tool cannot be inserted, use a full-length shim across both mounting holes to move the starter away from the flywheel.

STEP 4 Remove a shim (or shims) if the gauge tool is loose between the shaft and the tooth of the engine flywheel.

STEP 5 If no shims have been used and the fit of the gauge tool is too loose, add a half shim to the outside pad only. This moves the starter closer to the teeth of the engine flywheel.

STARTING SYSTEM SYMPTOM GUIDE

The following list will assist technicians in troubleshooting starting systems.

Problem	Possible Causes
1. Starter motor whines	1. Possible defective starter drive; worn starter drive engagement yoke; defective flywheel; improper starter drive to flywheel clearance
2. Starter rotates slowly	2. Possible high resistance in the battery cables or connections; possible defective or discharged battery; possible worn starter bushings, causing the starter armature to drag on the field coils; possible worn starter brushes or weak brush springs; possible defective (open or shorted) field coil
3. Starter fails to rotate	3. Possible defective ignition switch or neutral safety switch, or open in the starter motor control circuit; theft deterrent system fault; possible defective starter solenoid
4. Starter produces grinding noise	4. Possible defective starter drive unit; possible defective flywheel; possible incorrect distance between the starter pinion and the flywheel; possible cracked or broken starter drive-end housing; worn or damaged flywheel or ring gear teeth
5. Starter clicks when engaged	5. Low battery voltage; loose or corroded battery connections

1 This dirty and greasy starter can be restored to useful service.

2 The connecting wire between the solenoid and the starter is removed.

3 An old starter field housing is being used to support the drive-end housing of the starter as it is being disassembled. This rebuilder is using an electric impact wrench to remove the solenoid fasteners.

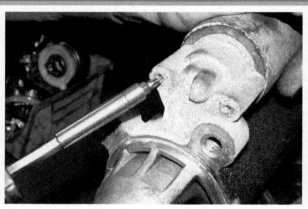

4 A Torx driver is used to remove the solenoid attaching screws.

5 After the retaining screws have been removed, the solenoid can be separated from the starter motor. This rebuilder always replaces the solenoid.

6 The through bolts are being removed.

7 The brush end plate is removed.

8 The armature assembly is removed from the field frame.

9 Notice that the length of a direct-drive starter armature (top) is the same length as the overall length of a gear-reduction armature except smaller in diameter.

10 A light tap with a hammer dislodges the armature thrust ball (in the palm of the hand) from the center of the gear-reduction assembly.

11 This figure shows the planetary ring gear and pinion gears.

12 A close-up of one of the planetary gears, which shows the small needle bearings on the inside.

CONTINUED ▶

13 The clip is removed from the shaft so the planetary gear assembly can be separated and inspected.

14 The shaft assembly is being separated from the stationary gear assembly.

15 The commutator on the armature is discolored and the brushes may not have been making good contact with the segments.

16 All of the starter components are placed in a tumbler with water-based cleaner. The armature is installed in a lathe and the commutator is resurfaced using emery cloth.

17 The finished commutator looks like new.

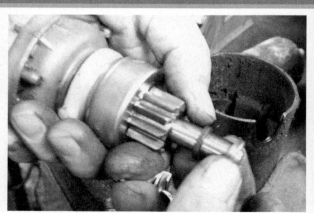

18 Starter reassembly begins by installing a new starter drive on the shaft assembly. The stop ring and stop ring retainer are then installed.

19 The gear-reduction assembly is positioned along with the shift fork (drive lever) into the cleaned drive-end housing.

20 After gear retainer has been installed over the gear-reduction assembly, the armature is installed.

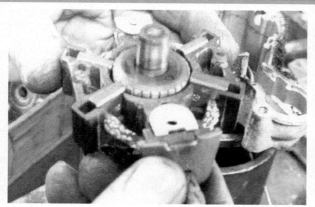

21 New brushes are being installed into the brush holder assembly.

22 The brush end plate and the through bolts are installed, being sure that the ground connection for the brushes is clean and tight.

23 This starter was restored to useful service by replacing the solenoid, the brushes, and the starter drive assembly plus a thorough cleaning and attention to detail in the reassembly.

SUMMARY

1. Proper operation and testing of the starter motor depends on the battery being at least 75% charged and the battery cables being of the correct size (gauge) and having no more than a 0.2 volt drop.

2. Voltage drop testing includes cranking the engine, measuring the drop in voltage from the battery to the starter, and measuring the drop in voltage from the negative terminal of the battery to the engine block.

3. The cranking circuit should be tested for proper amperage draw.

4. An open in the control circuit can prevent starter motor operation.

REVIEW QUESTIONS

1. What are the steps involved in troubleshooting the cranking circuit?

2. What are the steps taken to perform a voltage drop test of the cranking circuit?

3. What are the steps necessary to replace a starter?

4. What are typical starter amperage draw for four, six and eight cylinder engines?

5. What could be the cause of excessive starter current draw?

CHAPTER QUIZ

1. A growler is used to test what starter component?
   a. Field coils
   b. Armatures
   c. Commutator
   d. Solenoid

2. Two technicians are discussing what could be the cause of slow cranking and excessive current draw. Technician A says that an engine mechanical fault could be the cause. Technician B says that the starter motor could be binding or defective. Which technician is correct?
   a. Technician A only
   b. Technician B only
   c. Both Technicians A and B
   d. Neither Technician A nor B

3. A V-6 is being checked for starter amperage draw. The initial surge current was about 210 amperes and about 160 amperes during cranking. Technician A says the starter is defective and should be replaced because the current flow exceeds 200 amperes. Technician B says this is normal current draw for a starter motor on a V-6 engine. Which technician is correct?
   a. Technician A only
   b. Technician B only
   c. Both Technicians A and B
   d. Neither Technician A nor B

4. What component or circuit can keep the engine from cranking?
   a. Antitheft system
   b. Solenoid
   c. Ignition switch
   d. All of the above

5. Technician A says that a discharged battery (lower than normal battery voltage) can cause solenoid clicking. Technician B says that a discharged battery or dirty (corroded) battery cables can cause solenoid clicking. Which technician is correct?
   a. Technician A only
   b. Technician B only
   c. Both Technicians A and B
   d. Neither Technician A nor B

6. Slow cranking by the starter can be caused by all except _____.
   a. a low or discharged battery
   b. corroded or dirty battery cables
   c. engine mechanical problems
   d. an open neutral safety switch

7. Bench testing of a starter should be done _____.
   a. after reassembling an old starter
   b. before installing a new starter
   c. after removing the old starter
   d. Both a and b

8. If the clearance between the starter pinion and the engine flywheel is too great, _____.
   a. the starter will produce a high-pitched whine during cranking
   b. the starter will produce a high-pitched whine after the engine starts
   c. the starter drive will not rotate at all
   d. the solenoid will not engage the starter drive unit

9. A technician connects one lead of a digital voltmeter to the positive (+) terminal of the battery and the other meter lead to the battery terminal (B) of the starter solenoid and then cranks the engine. During cranking, the voltmeter displays a reading of 878 millivolts. Technician A says that this reading indicates that the positive battery cable has too high resistance. Technician B says that this reading indicates that the starter is defective. Which technician is correct?
   a. Technician A only
   b. Technician B only
   c. Both Technicians A and B
   d. Neither Technician A nor B

10. A vehicle equipped with a V-8 engine does not crank fast enough to start. Technician A says the battery could be discharged or defective. Technician B says that the negative cable could be loose at the battery. Which technician is correct?
    a. Technician A only
    b. Technician B only
    c. Both Technicians A and B
    d. Neither Technician A nor B

chapter 19
CHARGING SYSTEM

LEARNING OBJECTIVES

After studying this chapter, the reader will be able to:

1. Describe an alternator's overrunning pulleys.
2. Describe the components and operation of an alternator.
3. Discuss how an alternator works.
4. Explain how the voltage produced by an alternator is regulated.
5. Discuss computer-controlled alternators.

This chapter will help you prepare for the ASE Electrical/Electronic Systems (A6) certification test content area "C" (Starting System Diagnosis and Repair).

KEY TERMS

Alternator 278
Claw poles 280
Delta winding 283
Diodes 281
Drive-end (DE)
   housing 278
Duty cycle 289
EPM 288

OAD 279
OAP 278
Rotor 280
Slip-ring-end (SRE)
   housing 278
Stator 281
Thermistor 287

FIGURE 19–1 A typical alternator on a Chevrolet V-8 engine and is driven by the accessory drive belt at the front of the engine.

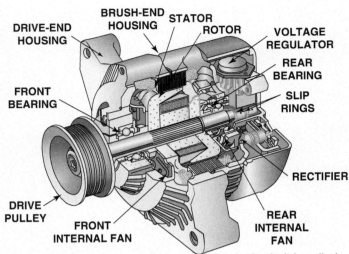

FIGURE 19–2 The end frame toward the drive belt is called the drive-end housing and the rear section is called the slip-ring-end housing.

PRINCIPLE OF ALTERNATOR OPERATION

TERMINOLOGY It is the purpose and function of the charging system to keep the battery fully charged. The Society of Automotive Engineers (SAE) term for the unit that generates electricity is *generator.* The term **alternator** is most commonly used in the trade and will be used here as well.

PRINCIPLES All electrical alternators use the principle of electromagnetic induction to generate electrical power from mechanical power. Electromagnetic induction involves the generation of electric current in a conductor when the conductor is moved through a magnetic field. The amount of current generated can be increased by the following factors.

1. Increasing the *speed* of the conductors through the magnetic field

2. Increasing the *number* of conductors passing through the magnetic field

3. Increasing the *strength* of the magnetic field

CHANGING AC TO DC An alternator generates an alternating current (AC) because the current changes polarity during the alternator's rotation. However, a battery cannot "store" alternating current; therefore, this alternating current is changed to direct current (DC) by diodes inside the alternator. Diodes are one-way electrical check valves that permit current to flow in only one direction.

ALTERNATOR CONSTRUCTION

HOUSING An alternator is constructed using a two-piece cast aluminum housing. Aluminum is used because of its lightweight, nonmagnetic properties and heat transfer properties needed to help keep the alternator cool. A front ball bearing is pressed into the front housing, called the **drive-end (DE) housing**, to provide the support and friction reduction necessary for the belt-driven rotor assembly. The rear housing, or the **slip-ring-end (SRE) housing**, usually contains either a roller bearing or ball bearing support for the rotor and mounting for the brushes, diodes, and internal voltage regulator (if so equipped). ● **SEE FIGURES 19–1 AND 19–2.**

ALTERNATOR OVERRUNNING PULLEYS

PURPOSE AND FUNCTION Many alternators are equipped with an **overrunning alternator pulley (OAP)**, also called an *overrunning clutch pulley* or an *alternator clutch pulley.* The purpose of this pulley is to help eliminate noise and vibration in the accessory drive belt system, especially when the engine is at idle speed. At idle, engine impulses are transmitted to the alternator through the accessory drive belt. The mass of the rotor of the alternator tends to want to keep spinning, but the engine crankshaft speeds up and slows down

FIGURE 19–3 An OAP on a Chevrolet Corvette alternator.

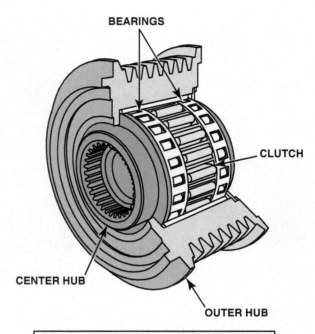

OVERRUNNING ALTERNATOR PULLEY (OAP)

FIGURE 19–4 An exploded view of an overrunning alternator pulley showing all of the internal parts.

TECH TIP

Alternator Horsepower and Engine Operation

Many technicians are asked how much power certain accessories require. A 100 ampere alternator requires about 2 horsepower from the engine. One horsepower is equal to 746 watts. Watts are calculated by multiplying amperes times volts.

Power in watts = 100 A × 14.5 V = 1,450 W

1 hp = 746 W

Therefore, 1,450 watts is about 2 horsepower.

Allowing about 20% for mechanical and electrical losses adds another 0.4 horsepower. Therefore, when someone asks how much power it takes to produce 100 amperes from an alternator, the answer is 2.4 horsepower.

Many alternators delay the electrical load to prevent the engine from stumbling when a heavy electrical load is applied. The voltage regulator or vehicle computer is capable of gradually increasing the output of the alternator over a period of several minutes. Even though 2 horsepower does not sound like much, a sudden demand for 2 horsepower from an idling engine can cause the engine to run rough or stall. The difference in part numbers of various alternators is often an indication of the time interval over which the load is applied. Therefore, using the wrong replacement alternator could cause the engine to stall!

slightly due to the power impulses. Using a one-way clutch in the alternator pulley allows the belt to apply power to the alternator in only one direction, thereby reducing fluctuations in the belt. ● **SEE FIGURES 19–3 AND 19–4.**

A conventional drive pulley attaches to the alternator (rotor) shaft with a nut and lock washer. In the overrunning clutch pulley, the inner race of the clutch acts as the nut as it screws on to the shaft. Special tools are required to remove and install this type of pulley.

Another type of alternator pulley uses a dampener spring inside, plus a one-way clutch. These units have the following names. ● **SEE FIGURE 19-5.**

- Isolating Decoupler Pulley (IDP)
- Active Alternator Pulley (AAP)
- Alternator Decoupler Pulley (ADP)
- Alternator Overrunning Decoupler Pulley
- **Overrunning Alternator Dampener (OAD)** (most common term)

OAP or OAD pulleys are primarily used on vehicles equipped with diesel engines or on luxury vehicles where noise and vibration need to be kept at a minimum. Both are designed to do the following:

- Reduce accessory drive belt noise
- Improve the life of the accessory drive belt
- Improve fuel economy by allowing the engine to be operated at a low idle speed

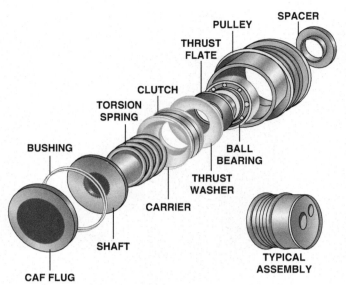

FIGURE 19–5 An overrunning alternator damper (OAD) is not a simple one-way clutch or a solid pulley, but instead is engineered to dampen noises and vibrations in the front accessory drive belt system.

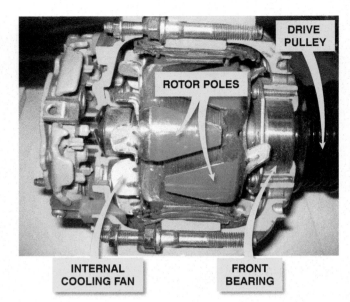

FIGURE 19–6 A cutaway of an alternator, showing the rotor and cooling fan that is used to force air through the unit to remove the heat created when it is charging the battery and supplying electrical power for the vehicle.

 FREQUENTLY ASKED QUESTION

Can I Install an OAP or an OAD to My Alternator?

Usually, no. An alternator needs to be equipped with the proper shaft to allow the installation of an OAP or OAD. This also means that a conventional pulley often cannot be used to replace a defective overrunning alternator pulley or dampener. Check service information for the exact procedure to follow.

ALTERNATOR COMPONENTS AND OPERATION

ROTOR CONSTRUCTION The **rotor** is the rotating part of the alternator and is driven by the accessory drive belt. The rotor creates the magnetic field of the alternator and produces a current by electromagnetic induction in the stationary stator windings. The rotor is constructed of many turns of copper wire coated with a varnish insulation wound over an iron core. The iron core is attached to the rotor shaft.

At both ends of the rotor windings are heavy-gauge metal plates bent over the windings with triangular fingers called **claw poles**. These pole fingers do not touch, but alternate or interlace, as shown in ● **FIGURE 19–6.**

HOW ROTORS CREATE MAGNETIC FIELDS The two ends of the rotor winding are connected to the rotor's slip rings. Current for the rotor flows from the battery into one brush that rides on one of the slip rings, then flows through the rotor winding, and exits the rotor through the other slip ring and brush. One alternator brush is considered to be the "positive" brush and one is considered to be the "negative" or "ground" brush. The voltage regulator is connected to either the positive or the negative brush and controls the field current through the rotor that controls the output of the alternator.

If current flows through the rotor windings, the metal pole pieces at each end of the rotor become electromagnets. Whether a north or a south pole magnet is created depends on the *direction* in which the wire coil is wound. Because the pole pieces are attached to each end of the rotor, one pole piece will be a north pole magnet. The other pole piece is on the opposite end of the rotor, and therefore, is viewed as being wound in the opposite direction, creating a south pole. Therefore, the rotor fingers are alternating north and south magnetic poles. The magnetic fields are created between the alternating pole piece fingers. These individual magnetic fields produce a current by electromagnetic induction in the stationary stator windings. ● **SEE FIGURE 19–7.**

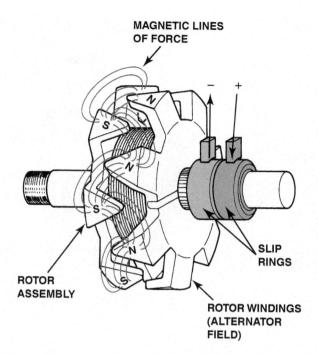

FIGURE 19–7 Rotor assembly of a typical alternator. Current through the slip rings causes the "fingers" of the rotor to become alternating north and south magnetic poles. As the rotor revolves, these magnetic lines of force induce a current in the stator windings.

ROTOR CURRENT The current necessary for the field (rotor) windings is conducted through slip rings with carbon brushes. The maximum rated alternator output in amperes depends on the number and gauge of the rotor windings. Substituting rotors from one alternator to another can greatly affect maximum output. Many commercially rebuilt alternators are tested and then display a sticker to indicate their tested output. The original rating stamped on the housing is then ground off.

The current for the field is controlled by the voltage regulator and is conducted to the slip rings through carbon brushes. The brushes conduct only the field current, which is usually between 2 and 5 amperes.

STATOR CONSTRUCTION The **stator** consists of the stationary coil windings inside the alternator. The stator is supported between the two halves of the alternator housing, with three copper wire windings that are wound on a laminated metal core.

As the rotor revolves, its moving magnetic field induces a current in the stator windings. ● **SEE FIGURE 19–8.**

DIODES **Diodes** are constructed of a semiconductor material (usually silicon) and operate as a one-way electrical check valve that permits the current to flow in only one direction. Alternators often use six diodes (one positive and one negative set for each of the three stator windings) to convert alternating current to direct current.

Diodes used in alternators are included in a single part called a rectifier, or *rectifier bridge*. A rectifier includes not only the diodes (usually six), but also the cooling fins and connections for the stator windings and the voltage regulator. ● **SEE FIGURE 19–9.**

DIODE TRIO Some alternators are equipped with a diode trio that supplies current to the brushes from the stator windings. A diode trio uses three diodes in one housing, with one diode for each of the three stator windings and then one output terminal.

HOW AN ALTERNATOR WORKS

FIELD CURRENT IS PRODUCED A rotor inside an alternator is turned by a belt and drive pulley which are turned by the engine. Field current flowing through the slip rings to the rotor creates an alternating north and south pole on the rotor, with a magnetic field between each finger of the rotor. The magnetic field of the rotor generates a current in the stator windings by electromagnetic induction. ● **SEE FIGURE 19–10.**

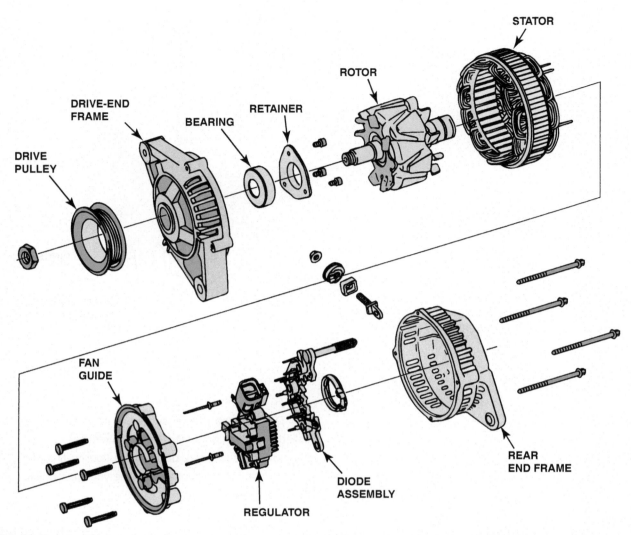

FIGURE 19–8 An exploded view of a typical alternator showing all of its internal parts including the stator windings.

FIGURE 19–9 A rectifier usually includes six diodes in one assembly and is used to rectify AC voltage from the stator windings into DC voltage suitable for use by the battery and electrical devices in the vehicle.

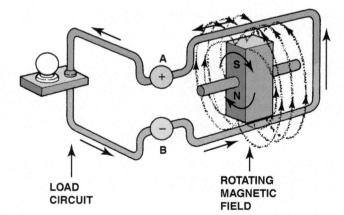

FIGURE 19–10 Magnetic lines of force cutting across a conductor induce a voltage and current in the conductor.

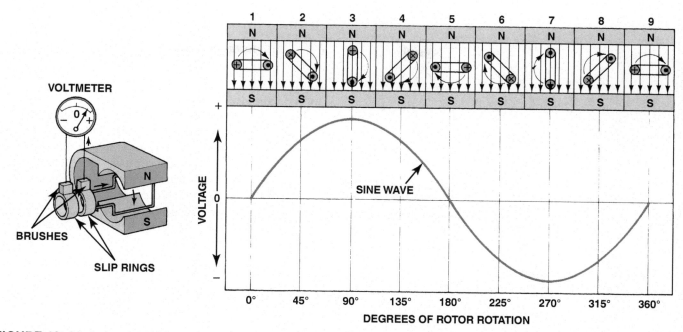

FIGURE 19–11 A sine wave (shaped like the letter *S* on its side) voltage curve is created by one revolution of a winding as it rotates in a magnetic field.

CURRENT IS INDUCED IN THE STATOR The induced current in the stator windings is an alternating current because of the alternating magnetic field of the rotor. The induced current starts to increase as the magnetic field starts to induce current in each winding of the stator. The current then peaks when the magnetic field is the strongest and starts to decrease as the magnetic field moves away from the stator winding. Therefore, the current generated is described as being of a sine wave or alternating current pattern. ● **SEE FIGURE 19–11**.

As the rotor continues to rotate, this sine wave current is induced in each of the three windings of the stator.

Because each of the three windings generates a sine wave current, as shown in ● **FIGURE 19–12**, the resulting currents combine to form a three-phase voltage output.

The current induced in the stator windings connects to diodes (one-way electrical check valves) that permit the alternator output current to flow in only one direction. All alternators contain six diodes, one pair (a positive and a negative diode) for each of the three stator windings. Some alternators contain eight diodes with another pair connected to the center connection of a wye-type stator.

WYE-CONNECTED STATORS The Y (pronounced "wye" and generally so written) type or star pattern is the most commonly used alternator stator winding connection. ● **SEE FIGURE 19–13**.

The output current with a wye-type stator connection is constant over a broad alternator speed range.

Current is induced in each winding by electromagnetic induction from the rotating magnetic fields of the rotor. In a wye-type stator connection, the currents must combine because two windings are always connected in series. ● **SEE FIGURE 19–14**.

The current produced in each winding is added to the other windings' current and then flows through the diodes to the alternator output terminal. The diodes convert the AC voltage created in the stator to DC voltage. One-half of the current produced is available at the neutral junction (usually labeled "STA" for stator).

DELTA-CONNECTED STATORS The **delta winding** is connected in a triangular shape. Delta is a Greek letter shaped like a triangle. ● **SEE FIGURE 19–15**.

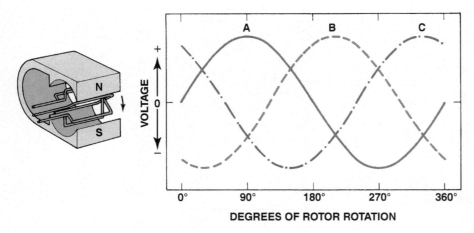

FIGURE 19–12 When three windings (A, B, and C) are present in a stator, the resulting current generation is represented by the three sine waves. The voltages are 120 degrees out of phase. The connection of the individual phases produces a three-phase alternating voltage.

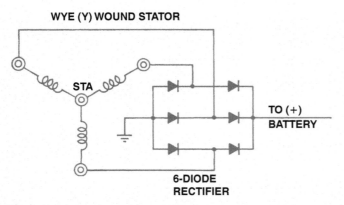

FIGURE 19–13 Wye-connected stator winding.

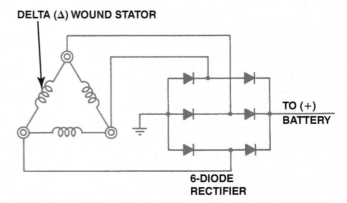

FIGURE 19–15 Delta-connected stator winding.

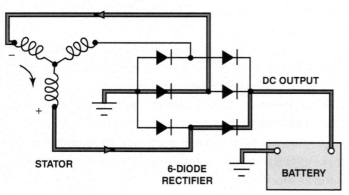

FIGURE 19–14 As the magnetic field, created in the rotor, cuts across the windings of the stator, a current is induced. Notice that the current path includes passing through one positive (+) diode on the way to the battery and one negative (−) diode as a complete circuit is completed through the rectifier and stator. It is the flow of current through the diodes that converts the AC voltage produced in the stator windings to DC voltage available at the output terminal of the alternator.

Current induced in each winding flows to the diodes in a parallel circuit. More current can flow through two parallel circuits than can flow through a series circuit (as in a wye-type stator connection).

Delta-connected stators are used on alternators where high output at high-alternator revolutions per minute (RPM) is required. The delta-connected alternator can produce 73% more current than the same alternator with wye-type stator connections. For example, if an alternator with a wye-connected stator can produce 55 amperes, the *same* alternator with delta-connected stator windings can produce 73% more current, or 95 amperes (55 × 1.73 = 95). The delta-connected alternator, however, produces lower current at low speed and must be operated at high speed to produce its maximum output.

FIGURE 19–16 A stator assembly with six, rather than the normal three, windings.

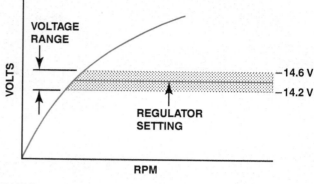

FIGURE 19–17 Typical voltage regulator range.

ALTERNATOR OUTPUT FACTORS

The output voltage and current of an alternator depend on the following factors:

1. **Speed of rotation.** Alternator output is increased with alternator rotational speed up to the alternator's maximum possible ampere output. Alternators normally rotate at a speed two to three times faster than engine speed, depending on the relative pulley sizes used for the belt drive. For example, if an engine is operating at 5,000 RPM, the alternator will be rotating at about 15,000 RPM.

2. **Number of conductors.** A high-output alternator contains more turns of wire in the stator windings. Stator winding connections (whether wye or delta) also affect the maximum alternator output. ● **SEE FIGURE 19–16** for an example of a stator that has six rather than three windings, which greatly increase the amperage output of the alternator.

3. **Strength of the magnetic field.** If the magnetic field is strong, a high output is possible because the current generated by electromagnetic induction is dependent on the number of magnetic lines of force that are cut.

   a. The strength of the magnetic field can be increased by increasing the number of turns of conductor wire wound on the rotor. A higher output alternator rotor has more turns of wire than an alternator rotor with a low rated output.

   b. The strength of the magnetic field also depends on the current through the field coil (rotor). Because magnetic field strength is measured in ampere-turns, the greater the amperage or the number of turns, or both, the greater the alternator output.

ALTERNATOR VOLTAGE REGULATION

PRINCIPLES An automotive alternator must be able to produce electrical pressure (voltage) higher than battery voltage to charge the battery. Excessively high voltage can damage the battery, electrical components, and the lights of a vehicle. Basic principles include the following:

- If no (zero) amperes of current existed throughout the field coil of the alternator (rotor), alternator output would be zero because without field current, a magnetic field does not exist.

- The field current required by most automotive alternators is less than 3 amperes. It is the *control* of the *field* current that controls the output of the alternator.

- Current for the rotor flows from the battery positive post, through the rotor positive brush, into the rotor field winding, and exits the rotor winding through the rotor ground brush. Most voltage regulators control field current by controlling the amount of field current through the ground brush.

- The voltage regulator simply opens the field circuit if the voltage reaches a predetermined level, then closes the field circuit again as necessary to maintain the correct charging voltage. ● **SEE FIGURE 19–17**.

- The electronic circuit of the voltage regulator cycles between 10 and 7,000 times per *second* as needed to accurately control the field current through the rotor, and therefore control the alternator output.

FIGURE 19–18 A typical electronic voltage regulator with the cover removed showing the circuits inside.

REGULATOR OPERATION

- The control of the field current is accomplished by opening and closing the *ground* side of the field circuit through the rotor on most alternators.

- The zener diode is a major electronic component that makes voltage regulation possible. A zener diode blocks current flow until a specific voltage is reached, then it permits current to flow. Alternator voltage from the stator and diodes is first sent through a thermistor, which changes resistance with temperature, and then to a zener diode. When the upper-limit voltage is reached, the zener diode conducts current to a transistor, which then opens the field (rotor) circuit. The electronics are usually housed in a separate part inside the alternator. ● **SEE FIGURES 19–18 AND 19–19.**

BATTERY CONDITION AND CHARGING VOLTAGE

If the automotive battery is discharged, its voltage will be lower than the voltage of a fully charged battery. The alternator will supply charging current, but it may not reach the maximum charging voltage. For example, if a vehicle is jump started and run at a fast idle (2,000 RPM), the charging voltage may be only 12 volts. In this case, the following may occur:

- As the battery becomes charged and the battery voltage increases, the charging voltage will also increase, until the voltage regulator limit is reached.

- Then the voltage regulator will start to control the charging voltage. A good, but discharged, battery should be able to convert into chemical energy all the current the alternator can produce. As long as alternator voltage is higher than battery voltage, current will flow from the alternator (high voltage) to the battery (lower voltage).

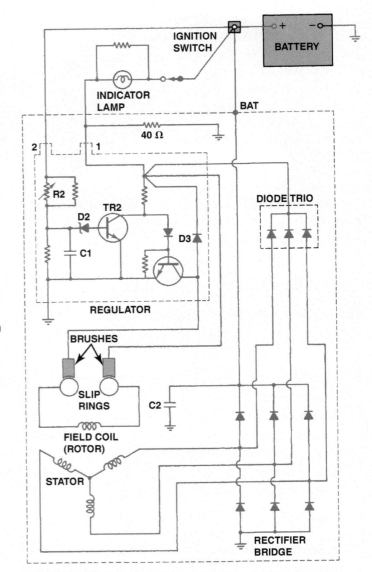

FIGURE 19–19 Typical General Motors SI-style alternator with an integral voltage regulator. Voltage present at terminal 2 is used to reverse bias the zener diode (D2) that controls TR2. The positive brush is fed by the ignition current (terminal 1) plus current from the diode trio.

- Therefore, if a voltmeter is connected to a discharged battery with the engine running, it may indicate charging voltage that is lower than normally acceptable.

In other words, the condition and voltage of the battery *do* determine the charging rate of the alternator. It is often stated that the battery is the true "voltage regulator" and that the voltage regulator simply acts as the upper-limit voltage control.

This is the reason why all charging system testing *must* be performed with a reliable and known to be good battery, at least 75% charged, to be assured of accurate test results. If a discharged battery is used during charging system testing, tests could mistakenly indicate a defective alternator and/or voltage regulator.

TEMPERATURE COMPENSATION All voltage regulators (mechanical or electronic) provide a method for increasing the charging voltage slightly at low temperatures and for lowering the charging voltage at high temperatures. A battery requires a higher charging voltage at low temperatures because of the resistance to chemical reaction changes. However, the battery would be overcharged if the charging voltage were not reduced during warm weather. Electronic voltage regulators use a temperature-sensitive resistor in the regulator circuit. This resistor, called a **thermistor**, provides lower resistance as the temperature increases. A thermistor is used in the electronic circuits of the voltage regulator to control charging voltage over a wide range of underhood temperatures.

NOTE: Voltmeter test results may vary according to temperature. Charging voltage tested at 32°F (0°C) will be higher than for the same vehicle tested at 80°F (27°C) because of the temperature-compensation factors built into voltage regulators.

ALTERNATOR COOLING

Alternators create heat during normal operation and this heat must be removed to protect the components inside, especially the diodes and voltage regulator. The types of cooling include the following:

- External fan
- Internal fan(s)
- Both an external fan and an internal fan
- Coolant cooled ● **SEE FIGURE 19–20.**

COOLANT CONNECTIONS

FIGURE 19–20 A coolant-cooled alternator showing the hose connections where coolant from the engine flows through the rear frame of the alternator.

COMPUTER-CONTROLLED ALTERNATORS

TYPES OF SYSTEMS Computers can interface with the charging system in three ways:

1. The computer can *activate* the charging system by turning on and off the field current to the rotor. In other words, the computer, usually the powertrain control module (PCM), controls the field current to the rotor.

2. The computer can *monitor* the operation of the alternator and increase engine speed if needed during conditions when a heavy load is demanded by the alternator.

3. The computer can *control* the alternator by controlling alternator output to match the needs of the electrical system. This system detects the electrical needs of the vehicle and commands the alternator to charge only when needed to improve fuel economy.

COMPUTER-CONTROLLED CHARGING SYSTEMS
Computer control of the charging system has the following advantages:

1. The computer controls the field of the alternator, which can pulse it on or off as needed for maximum efficiency, thereby saving fuel.

Note: Some vehicle manufacturers, such as Honda/Acura, use an *electronic load control (ELC)*, which turns on the alternator when decelerating, where the additional load on the engine is simply used to help slow the vehicle. This allows the battery to be charged without placing a load on the engine, helping to increase fuel economy.

2. Engine idle can also be improved by turning on the alternator slowly, rather than all at once, if an electrical load is switched on, such as the air-conditioning system.

3. Most computers can also reduce the load on the electrical system if the demand exceeds the capacity of the charging system by reducing fan speed, shutting off rear window defoggers, or increasing engine speed to cause the alternator to increase the amperage output.

   Note: A commanded higher-than-normal idle speed may be the result of the computer compensating for an abnormal electrical load. This higher idle speed could indicate a defective battery or other electrical system faults.

4. The computer can monitor the charging system and set diagnostic trouble codes (DTCs) if a fault is detected. Many systems allow the service technician to control the charging of the alternator using a scan tool.

5. Because the charging system is computer controlled, it can be checked using a scan tool. Some vehicle systems allow the scan tool to activate the alternator field and then monitor the output to help detect fault locations. Always follow the vehicle manufacturer's diagnostic procedure.

GM ELECTRICAL POWER MANAGEMENT SYSTEM A typical system used on some General Motors vehicles is called **electrical power management (EPM)**. It uses a Hall-effect sensor attached to the negative or positive battery cable to measure the current leaving and entering the battery.
● **SEE FIGURE 19–21**.

The engine control module (ECM) controls the alternator by changing the on-time of the current through the rotor.
● **SEE FIGURE 19–22**.

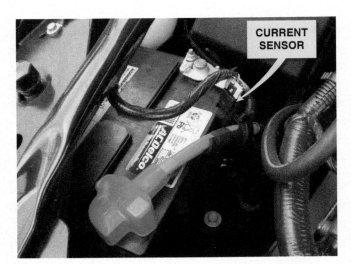

FIGURE 19–21 A Hall-effect current sensor attached to the positive battery cable is used as part of the EPM system.

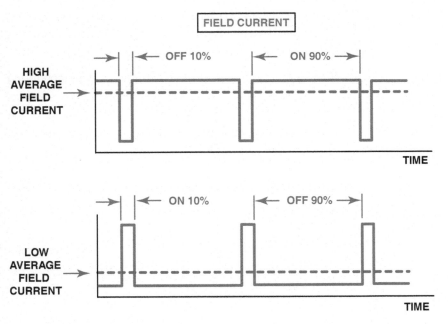

FIGURE 19–22 The amount of time current is flowing through the field (rotor) determines the alternator output.

COMMAND DUTY CYCLE	ALTERNATOR OUTPUT VOLTAGE
10%	11.0 V
20%	11.6 V
30%	12.1 V
40%	12.7 V
50%	13.3 V
60%	13.8 V
70%	14.4 V
80%	14.9 V
90%	15.5 V

CHART 19–1

The output voltage is controlled by varying the duty cycle as controlled by the PCM.

The on-time, called **duty cycle**, varies from 5% to 95%.
● **SEE CHART 19–1.**

This system has six modes of operation:

1. **Charge mode.** The charge mode is activated when any of the following occurs.
   ■ Electric cooling fans are on high speed.
   ■ Rear window defogger is on.
   ■ Battery state of charge (SOC) is less than 80%.
   ■ Outside (ambient) temperature is less than 32°F (0°C).

2. **Fuel economy mode.** This mode reduces the load on the engine from the alternator for maximum fuel economy. This mode is activated when the following conditions are met:
   ■ Ambient temperature is above 32°F (0°C).
   ■ The SOC of the battery is 80% or higher.
   ■ The cooling fans and rear defogger are off.
   The target voltage is 13 volts and will return to the charge mode, if needed.

3. **Voltage reduction mode.** This mode is commanded to reduce the stress on the battery during low-load conditions. This mode is activated when the following conditions are met:
   ■ Ambient temperature is above 32°F (0°C).
   ■ Battery discharge rate is less than 7 amperes.
   ■ Rear defogger is off.
   ■ Cooling fans are on low or off.
   ■ Target voltage is limited to 12.7 volts.

4. **Start-up mode.** This mode is selected after engine start and commands a charging voltage of 14.5 volts for 30 seconds. After 30 seconds, the mode is changed depending on conditions.

5. **Battery sulfation mode.** This mode is commanded if the output voltage is less than 13.2 volts for 45 minutes, which can indicate that sulfated plates could be the cause. The target voltage is 13.9 to 15.5 volts for three minutes. After three minutes, the system returns to another mode based on conditions.

6. **Headlight mode.** This mode is selected when the headlights are on and the target voltage is 14.5 volts.

 **TECH TIP**

The Voltage Display Can Be a Customer Concern

A customer may complain that the voltmeter reading on the dash fluctuates up and down. This may be normal as the computer-controlled charging system commands various modes of operation based on the operating conditions. Follow the vehicle manufacturer's recommended procedures to verify proper operation.

SUMMARY

1. Alternator output is increased if the speed of the alternator is increased.
2. The parts of a typical alternator include the drive-end (DE) housing, slip-ring-end (SRE) housing, rotor assembly, stator, rectifier bridge, brushes, and voltage regulator.
3. The magnetic field is created in the rotor.
4. The alternator output current is created in the stator windings.
5. The voltage regulator controls the current flow through the rotor winding.

1. How can a small electronic voltage regulator control the output of a typical 100 ampere alternator?
2. What are the component parts of a typical alternator?
3. How is the computer used to control an alternator?
4. How is AC voltage inside the alternator changed to DC voltage at the output terminal?
5. What is the purpose of an OAP or OAD?

CHAPTER QUIZ

1. Technician A says that the diodes regulate the alternator output voltage. Technician B says that the field current can be computer controlled. Which technician is correct?
   a. Technician A only
   b. Technician B only
   c. Both Technicians A and B
   d. Neither Technician A nor B

2. A magnetic field is created in the _____ in an alternator (AC alternator).
   a. stator
   b. diodes
   c. rotor
   d. drive-end frame

3. The voltage regulator controls current through the _____.
   a. alternator brushes
   b. rotor
   c. alternator field
   d. All of the above

4. Technician A says that two diodes are required for each stator winding lead. Technician B says that diodes change alternating current into direct current. Which technician is correct?
   a. Technician A only
   b. Technician B only
   c. Both Technicians A and B
   d. Neither Technician A nor B

5. The alternator output current is produced in the _____.
   a. stator
   b. rotor
   c. brushes
   d. diodes (rectifier bridge)

6. Alternator brushes are constructed from _____.
   a. copper
   b. aluminum
   c. carbon
   d. silver-copper alloy

7. How much current flows through the alternator brushes?
   a. All of the alternator output flows through the brushes
   b. 25 to 35 amperes, depending on the vehicle
   c. 10 to 15 amperes
   d. Less than 3 amperes

8. Technician A says that an alternator overrunning pulley is used to reduce vibration and noise. Technician B says that an overrunning alternator pulley or dampener uses a one-way clutch. Which technician is correct?
   a. Technician A only
   b. Technician B only
   c. Both Technicians A and B
   d. Neither Technician A nor B

9. Which part of the alternator is driven by the accessory drive belt?
   a. Diodes (rectifier bridge)
   b. Stator
   c. Rotor
   d. Brushes

10. Technician A says that a wye-wound stator produces more maximum output than the same alternator equipped with a delta-wound stator. Technician B says that an alternator equipped with a delta-wound stator produces more maximum output than a wye-wound stator. Which technician is correct?
    a. Technician A only
    b. Technician B only
    c. Both Technicians A and B
    d. Neither Technician A nor B

chapter 20
CHARGING SYSTEM DIAGNOSIS AND SERVICE

LEARNING OBJECTIVES

After studying this chapter, the reader will be able to:

1. Discuss the various methods to test the charging system.

2. Discuss the alternator output test.

3. Explain how to disassemble an alternator and test its component parts.

This chapter will help you prepare for the ASE Electrical/Electronic Systems (A6) certification test content area "D" (Charging System Diagnosis and Repair).

KEY TERMS

AC ripple voltage 295   Cores 304

Charging voltage
   test 292

FIGURE 20–1 The digital multimeter should be set to read DC volts, with the red lead connected to the positive (+) battery terminal and the black meter lead connected to the negative (–) battery terminal.

FIGURE 20–2 A scan tool can be used to diagnose charging system problems.

CHARGING SYSTEM TESTING AND SERVICE

BATTERY STATE OF CHARGE The charging system can be tested as part of a routine vehicle inspection or to determine the reason for a no-charge or reduced charging circuit performance. The battery *must* be at least 75% charged before testing the alternator and the charging system. A weak or defective battery will cause inaccurate test results. If in doubt, replace the battery with a known good shop battery for testing.

CHARGING VOLTAGE TEST The **charging voltage test** is the easiest way to check the charging system voltage at the battery. Use a digital multimeter to check the voltage, as follows:

STEP 1 Select DC volts.

STEP 2 Connect the red meter lead to the positive (+) terminal of the battery and the black meter lead to the negative (–) terminal of the battery.

> NOTE: The polarity of the meter leads is not too important when using a digital multimeter. If the meter leads are connected backward on the battery, the resulting readout will simply have a negative (–) sign in front of the voltage reading.

STEP 3 Start the engine and increase the engine speed to about 2,000 RPM (fast idle) and record the charging voltage. ● SEE FIGURE 20–1.

Specifications for charging voltage = 13.5 to 15 volts

- If the voltage is too high, check that the alternator is properly grounded.

- If the voltage is lower than specifications, then there is a fault with the wiring or the alternator.

- If the wiring fuses, and the connections are okay, then additional testing is required to help pinpoint the root cause. Replacement of the alternator and/or battery is often required if the charging voltage is not within factory specifications.

- If the alternator is computer controlled, a defective current sensor or PCM could be the reason for a no-charge condition.

SCAN TESTING THE CHARGING CIRCUIT Most vehicles that use a computer-controlled charging system can be diagnosed using a scan tool. Not only can the charging voltage be monitored, but also in many vehicles, the field circuit can be controlled and the output voltage monitored to check that the system is operating correctly. ● **SEE FIGURE 20–2.**

NOTE: Some charging systems, such as those on many Honda/Acura vehicles, use an electronic load detection circuit that energizes the field circuit only when an electrical load is detected. For example, if the engine is running and there are no accessories on, the voltage reading at the battery may be 12.6 volts, which could indicate that the charging system is not operating. In this situation, turning on the headlights or an accessory should cause the computer to activate the field circuit, and the alternator should produce normal charging voltage.

FREQUENTLY ASKED QUESTION

What Is a Full-Fielding Test?

Full fielding is a procedure used on older non-computerized vehicles for bypassing the voltage regulator that could be used to determine if the alternator is capable of producing its designed output. This test is no longer performed for the following reasons:

- The voltage regulator is built into the alternator, therefore, requiring that the entire assembly be replaced even if just the regulator is defective.
- When the regulator is bypassed, the alternator can produce a high voltage (over 100 volts in some cases) that could damage all of the electronic circuits in the vehicle.

Always follow the vehicle manufacturer's recommended testing procedures.

TECH TIP

Use a Test Light to Check for a Defective Fusible Link

Most alternators use a fusible link or mega fuse between the output terminal and the positive (+) terminal of the battery. If this fusible link or fuse is defective (blown), then the charging system will not operate at all. Many alternators have been replaced repeatedly because of a blown fusible link that was not discovered until later. A quick and easy test to check if the fusible link is okay is to touch a test light to the output terminal. With the other end of the test light attached to a good ground, the fusible link or mega fuse is okay if the light comes on. This test confirms that the circuit between the alternator and the battery has continuity. ● **SEE FIGURE 20–3.**

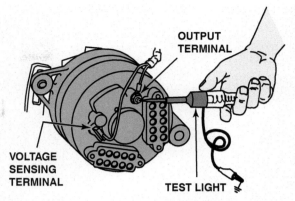

FIGURE 20–3 Before replacing an alternator, the wise technician checks that battery voltage is present at the output and battery voltage sense terminals. if no voltage is detected, then there is a fault in the wiring.

DRIVE BELT INSPECTION AND ADJUSTMENT

BELT VISUAL INSPECTION It is generally recommended that all belts be inspected regularly and replaced as needed. Replace any serpentine belt that has more than three cracks in any one rib that appears in a 3-inch span. Check service information for the specified procedure and recommended replacement interval. ● **SEE FIGURE 20–4.**

BELT TENSION MEASUREMENT If the vehicle does not use a belt tensioner, then a belt tension gauge is needed to achieve the specified belt tension. Install the belt and operate the engine with all of the accessories turned on to "run-in" the belt for at least five minutes. Adjust the tension of the accessory drive belt to factory specifications or use the following table for an example of the proper tension based on the size of the belt.

There are four ways that vehicle manufacturers specify that the belt tension is within factory specifications:

1. **Belt tension gauge.** A belt tension gauge is needed to determine if it is at the specified belt tension. Install the belt and operate the engine with all of the accessories turned on to "run-in" the belt for at least five minutes. Adjust the tension of the accessory drive belt to factory specifications, or see ● **CHART 20–1** for an example of the proper tension based on the size of the belt.

2. **Marks on a tensioner.** Many tensioners have marks that indicate the normal operating tension range for the accessory drive belt. Check service information for the preferred location of the tensioner mark. ● **SEE FIGURE 20–5.**

(a)

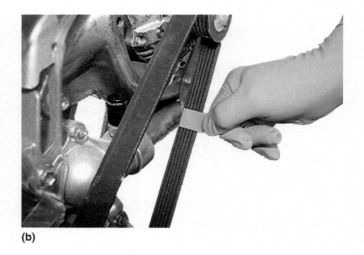

(b)

FIGURE 20–4 (a) This accessory drive belt is worn and requires replacement. Newer belts are made from ethylene propylene diene monomer (EPDM). This rubber does not crack like older belts and may not show wear even though the ribs do wear and can cause slippage. (b) A belt wear gauge being used to check a belt. It should fit tightly but if it is able to be moved side to side, then the belt is worn and should be replaced.

FIGURE 20–5 Check service information for the exact marks where the tensioner should be located for proper belt tension.

SERPENTINE BELTS	
NUMBER OF RIBS USED	TENSION RANGE (LB)
3	45–60
4	60–80
5	75–100
6	90–125
7	105–145
V-BELTS	
V-BELT TOP WIDTH (in.)	TENSION RANGE (LB)
1/4	45–65
5/16	60–85
25/64	85–115
31/64	105–145

CHART 20–1

Typical belt tension for various widths of belts. Tension is the force needed to depress the belt as displayed on a belt tension gauge.

3. **Torque wrench reading.** Some vehicle manufacturers specify that a beam-type torque wrench be used to determine the torque needed to rotate the tensioner. If the torque reading is below specifications, the tensioner must be replaced.

4. **Deflection.** Depress the belt between the two pulleys that are the farthest apart; the flex or deflection should be 1/2 inch (13 mm).

OVERRUNNING CLUTCH If low or no alternator output is found, remove the alternator drive belt and check the overrunning alternator pulley (OAP) or overrunning alternator dampener (OAD) for proper operation. Both types of overrunning clutches use a one-way clutch. Therefore, the pulley should freewheel in one direction and rotate the alternator rotor when rotated in the opposite direction.● **SEE FIGURE 20–6.**

A special tool such as Lisle No. 57650 or Gates No. 91024. ● **SEE FIGURE 20–7.**

FIGURE 20–6 This overrunning alternator dampener (OAD) is longer than an overrunning alternator pulley (OAP) because it contains a dampener spring as well as a one-way clutch. Be sure to check that it locks in one direction.

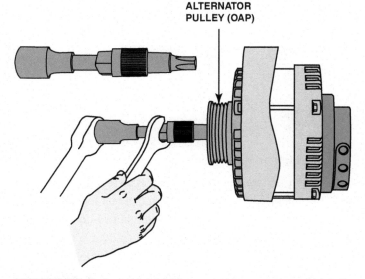

OVERUNNING ALTERNATOR PULLEY (OAP)

FIGURE 20–7 A special tool is needed to remove and install overrunning alternator pulleys or dampeners.

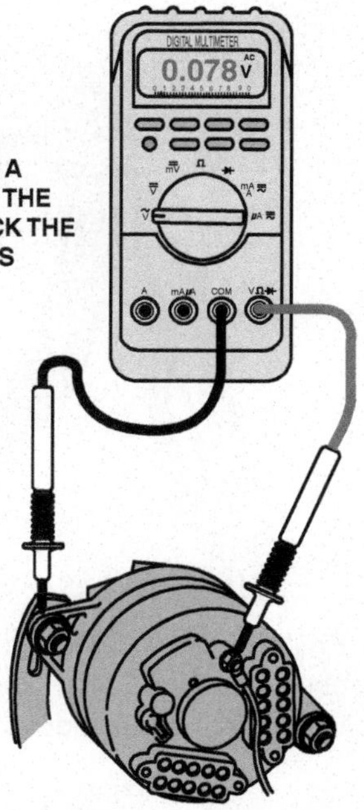

MEASURING THE AC RIPPLE FROM THE ALTERNATOR TELLS A LOT ABOUT ITS CONDITION. IF THE AC RIPPLE IS ABOVE 500 MILLIVOLTS, OR 0.5 VOLT, LOOK FOR A PROBLEM IN THE DIODES OR STATOR. IF THE RIPPLE IS BELOW 500 MILLIVOLTS, CHECK THE ALTERNATOR OUTPUT TO DETERMINE ITS CONDITION.

FIGURE 20–8 Testing AC ripple at the output terminal of the alternator is more accurate than testing at the battery due to the resistance of the wiring between the alternator and the battery. The reading shown on the meter, set to AC volts, is only 78 millivolts (0.078 volt), far below what the reading would be if a diode were defective.

AC RIPPLE VOLTAGE CHECK

PRINCIPLES A good alternator should produce very little AC voltage or current output. It is the purpose of the diodes in the alternator to rectify or convert most AC voltage into DC voltage. While it is normal to measure some AC voltage from an alternator, excessive AC voltage, called AC ripple, is undesirable and indicates a fault with the rectifier diodes or stator windings inside the alternator.

TESTING AC RIPPLE VOLTAGE The procedure to check for **AC ripple voltage** includes the following steps.

STEP 1 Set the digital meter to read AC volts.

STEP 2 Start the engine and operate it at 2,000 RPM (fast idle).

STEP 3 Connect the voltmeter leads to the positive and negative battery terminals.

STEP 4 Turn on the headlights to provide an electrical load on the alternator.

NOTE: A more accurate reading can be obtained by touching the meter lead to the output or "battery" terminal of the alternator. ● SEE FIGURE 20–8.

The results should be interpreted as follows: If the rectifier diodes are good, the voltmeter should read *less* than 400 millivolts (0.4 volt) AC. If the reading is over 500 millivolts (0.5 volt) AC, the rectifier diodes are defective.

NOTE: Many conductance testers, such as Midtronic and Snap-On, automatically test for AC ripple.

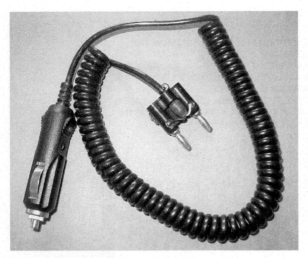

FIGURE 20–9 Charging system voltage can be easily checked at the lighter plug by connecting a lighter plug to the voltmeter through a double banana plug.

FIGURE 20–10 A mini clamp-on meter can be used to measure alternator output as shown here (105.2 amperes). Then the meter can be used to check AC current ripple by selecting AC amps on the rotary dial. AC ripple current should be less than 10% of the DC current output.

TESTING AC RIPPLE CURRENT

All alternators should create direct current (DC) if the diodes and stator windings are functioning correctly. A mini clamp-on meter capable of measuring AC amperes can be used to check the alternator. A good alternator should produce less than 10% of its rated amperage output in AC ripple amperes. For example, an alternator rated at 100 amperes should not produce more than 10 amperes AC ripple (100 × 10% = 10). It is normal for a good alternator to produce 3 or 4 amperes of AC ripple current to the battery. Only if the AC ripple current exceeds 10% of the rating of the alternator should the alternator be repaired or replaced.

TEST PROCEDURE To measure the AC current to the battery, perform the following steps:

STEP 1 Start the engine and turn on the lights to create an electrical load on the alternator.

STEP 2 Using a mini clamp-on digital multimeter, place the clamp around either all of the positive (+) battery cables or all of the negative (–) battery cables.

An AC/DC current clamp adapter can also be used with a conventional digital multimeter set on the DC millivolts scale.

STEP 3 To check for AC current ripple, switch the meter to read AC amperes and record the reading. Read the meter display.

STEP 4 The results should be within 10% of the specified alternator rating. A reading of greater than 10 amperes AC indicates defective alternator diodes.
● **SEE FIGURE 20–10.**

  TECH TIP

The Lighter Plug Trick

Battery voltage measurements can be read through the lighter socket. Simply construct a test tool using a lighter plug at one end of a length of two-conductor wire and the other end connected to a double banana plug. The double banana plug will fit most meters in the common (COM) terminal and the volt terminal of the meter. This is handy to use while road testing the vehicle under real-life conditions. Both DC voltage and AC ripple voltage can be measured. ● **SEE FIGURE 20–9.**

CHARGING SYSTEM VOLTAGE DROP TESTING

ALTERNATOR WIRING For the proper operation of any charging system, there must be good electrical connections between the battery positive terminal and the alternator output terminal. The alternator must also be properly grounded to the engine block.

Many manufacturers of vehicles run the lead from the output terminal of the alternator to other connectors or junction

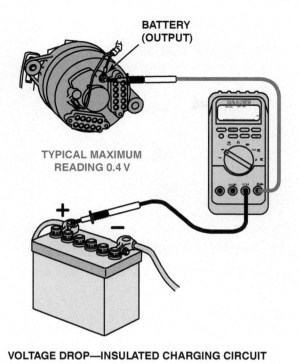

BATTERY
(OUTPUT)

TYPICAL MAXIMUM
READING 0.4 V

VOLTAGE DROP—INSULATED CHARGING CIRCUIT

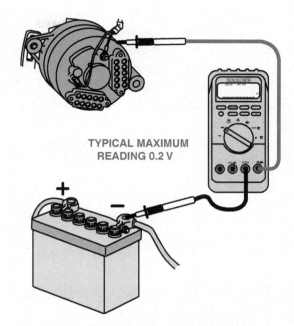

ENGINE AT 2000 RPM.
CHARGING SYSTEM
LOADED TO 20 A

TYPICAL MAXIMUM
READING 0.2 V

VOLTAGE DROP—CHARGING GROUND CIRCUIT

FIGURE 20–11 Voltmeter hookup to test the voltage drop of the charging circuit.

blocks that are electrically connected to the positive terminal of the battery. If there is high resistance (a high voltage drop) in these connections or in the wiring itself, the battery will not be properly charged.

VOLTAGE DROP TEST PROCEDURE When there is a suspected charging system problem (with or without a charge indicator light on), simply follow these steps to measure the voltage drop of the insulated (power-side) charging circuit:

STEP 1 Start the engine and run it at a fast idle (about 2,000 engine RPM).

STEP 2 Turn on the headlights to ensure an electrical load on the charging system.

STEP 3 Using any voltmeter set to read DC volts, connect the positive test lead (red) to the output terminal of the alternator. Attach the negative test lead (black) to the positive post of the battery.

The results should be interpreted as follows:

1. If there is less than a 0.4 volt (400 millivolts) reading, all wiring and connections are satisfactory.

2. If the voltmeter reads higher than 0.4 volt, there is excessive resistance (voltage drop) between the alternator output terminal and the positive terminal of the battery.

3. If the voltmeter reads battery voltage (or close to battery voltage), there is an open circuit between the battery and the alternator output terminal.

To determine whether the alternator is correctly grounded, maintain the engine speed at 2,000 RPM with the headlights on. Connect the positive voltmeter lead to the case of the alternator and the negative voltmeter lead to the negative terminal of the battery. The voltmeter should read less than 0.2 volt (200 millivolts) if the alternator is properly grounded. If the reading is over 0.2 volt, connect one end of an auxiliary ground wire to the case of the alternator and the other end to a good engine ground. ● **SEE FIGURE 20–11.**

TECH TIP

Use a Fused Jumper Wire as a Diagnostic Tool

When diagnosing an alternator charging problem, try using a fused jumper wire to connect the positive and negative terminals of the alternator directly to the positive and negative terminals of the battery. If a definite improvement is noticed, the problem is in the wiring of the vehicle. High resistance, due to corroded connections or loose grounds, can cause low alternator output, repeated regulator failures, slow cranking, and discharged batteries. A voltage drop test of the charging system can also be used to locate excessive resistance (high voltage drop) in the charging circuit, but using a fused jumper wire is often faster and easier.

FIGURE 20–12 A typical tester used to test batteries as well as the cranking and charging system. Always follow the operating instructions.

ALTERNATOR OUTPUT TEST

PRELIMINARY CHECKS An alternator output test measures the current (amperes) of the alternator. A charging circuit may be able to produce correct charging circuit voltage, but not be able to produce adequate amperage output. If in doubt about charging system output, first check the condition of the alternator drive belt. With the engine off, attempt to rotate the fan of the alternator by hand. Replace or tighten the drive belt if the alternator fan can be rotated this way.

CARBON PILE TEST PROCEDURE A carbon pile tester uses plates of carbon to create an electrical load. A carbon pile tester is used to load test a battery and/or an alternator. ● **SEE FIGURE 20–12.**

The testing procedure for alternator output is as follows:

STEP 1 Connect the starting and charging test leads according to the manufacturer's instructions, which usually include installing the amp clamp around the output wire near the alternator.

STEP 2 Turn off all electrical accessories to be sure that the tester is measuring the true output of the alternator.

STEP 3 Start the engine and operate it at 2,000 RPM (fast idle). Turn the load increase control slowly to obtain the highest reading on the ammeter scale. Do not allow the voltage to drop below 12.6 volts. Note the ampere reading.

STEP 4 Add 5 to 7 amperes to the reading because this amount of current is used by the ignition system to operate the engine.

STEP 5 Compare the output reading to factory specifications. The rated output may be stamped on the alternator or can be found in service information.

CAUTION: *NEVER* disconnect a battery cable with the engine running. All vehicle manufacturers warn not to do this, because this was an old test, before alternators, to see if a generator could supply current to operate the ignition system without a battery. When a battery cable is removed, the alternator (or PCM) will lose the battery voltage sense signal. Without a battery voltage sense circuit, the alternator will do one of two things, depending on the make and model of vehicle:

- The alternator output can exceed 100 volts. This high voltage may damage not only the alternator but also electrical components in the vehicle, including the PCM and all electronic devices.
- The alternator stops charging as a fail-safe measure to protect the alternator and all of the electronics in the vehicle from being damaged due to excessively high voltage.

MINIMUM REQUIRED ALTERNATOR OUTPUT

PURPOSE All charging systems must be able to supply the electrical demands of the electrical system. If lights and accessories are used constantly and the alternator cannot supply the necessary ampere output, the battery will be drained. To determine the minimum electrical load requirements, connect an inductive ammeter probe around either battery cable or the alternator output cable. ● **SEE FIGURE 20–13**.

NOTE: If using an inductive pickup ammeter, be certain that the pickup is over all the wires leaving the battery terminal.

Failure to include the small body ground wire from the negative battery terminal to the body or the small positive wire (if testing from the positive side) will greatly decrease the current flow readings.

PROCEDURE After connecting an ammeter correctly in the battery circuit, continue as follows:

1. Start the engine and operate to about 2,000 RPM (fast idle).
2. Turn the heat selector to air-conditioning (if the vehicle is so equipped).
3. Turn the blower motor to high speed.
4. Turn the headlights on bright.
5. Turn on the rear defogger.
6. Turn on the windshield wipers.
7. Turn on any other accessories that may be used continuously (do not operate the horn, power door locks, or other units that are not used for more than a few seconds).
8. Observe the ammeter. The current indicated is the electrical load that the alternator is able to exceed to keep the battery fully charged.

TEST RESULTS The minimum acceptable alternator output is 5 amperes greater than the accessory load. A negative (discharge) reading indicates that the alternator is not capable of supplying the current (amperes) that may be needed.

FIGURE 20–13 The best place to install a charging system tester amp probe is around the alternator output terminal wire, as shown in the figure.

 **TECH TIP**

Bigger Is Not Always Better

Many technicians are asked to install a higher output alternator to allow the use of emergency equipment or other high-amperage equipment, such as a high-wattage sound system.

Although many higher output units can be physically installed, it is important not to forget to upgrade the wiring and the fusible link(s) in the alternator circuit. Failure to upgrade the wiring could lead to overheating. The usual failure locations are at junctions or electrical connectors.

ALTERNATOR REMOVAL

After diagnosis of the charging system has determined that there is a fault with the alternator, it must be removed safely from the vehicle. Always check service information for the exact procedure to follow on the vehicle being serviced. A typical removal procedure includes the following steps:

STEP 1 Before disconnecting the negative battery cable, use a test light or a voltmeter and check for battery voltage at the output terminal of the alternator. A complete circuit must exist between the alternator and the battery. If there is no voltage at the alternator output terminal, check for a blown fusible link or other electrical circuit fault.

STEP 2 Disconnect the negative (−) terminal from the battery. (Use a memory saver to maintain radio, memory seats, and other functions.)

FIGURE 20–14 Replacing an alternator is not always as easy as it is from a Buick with a 3800 V-6, where the alternator is easy to access. Many alternators are difficult to access and require the removal of other components.

 **TECH TIP**

The Sniff Test

When checking for the root cause of an alternator failure, one test that a technician could do is to sniff (smell) the alternator. If the alternator smells like a dead rat (rancid smell), the stator windings have been overheated by trying to charge a discharged or defective battery. If the battery voltage is continuously low, the voltage regulator will continue supplying full-field current to the alternator. The voltage regulator is designed to cycle on and off to maintain a narrow charging system voltage range.

If the battery voltage is continually below the cutoff point of the voltage regulator, the alternator is continually producing current in the stator windings. This constant charging can often overheat the stator and burn the insulating varnish covering the stator windings. If the alternator fails the sniff test, the technician should replace the stator and other alternator components that are found to be defective *and* replace or recharge and test the battery.

STEP 3 Remove the accessory drive belt that drives the alternator.

STEP 4 Remove electrical wiring, fasteners, spacers, and brackets, as necessary, and remove the alternator from the vehicle. ● **SEE FIGURE 20–14.**

ALTERNATOR DISASSEMBLY

DISASSEMBLY PROCEDURE

STEP 1 Mark the case with a scratch or with chalk to ensure proper reassembly of the alternator case.

STEP 2 After the through bolts have been removed, carefully separate the two halves. The stator windings must stay with the rear case. When this happens, the brushes and springs will fall out.

STEP 3 Remove the rectifier assembly and voltage regulator.

ROTOR TESTING The slip rings on the rotor should be smooth and round (within 0.002 inch of being perfectly round).

- If grooved, the slip rings can be machined to provide a suitable surface for the brushes. Do not machine beyond the minimum slip-ring dimension as specified by the manufacturer.

- If the slip rings are discolored or dirty, they can be cleaned with 400-grit or fine emery (polishing) cloth. The rotor must be turned while being cleaned to prevent flat spots on the slip rings.

- Measure the resistance between the slip rings using an ohmmeter. Typical resistance values and results include the following:

  1. The resistance measured between either slip ring and the steel rotor shaft should be infinity (OL). If there is continuity, then the rotor is shorted-to-ground.

 FREQUENTLY ASKED QUESTION

What Is a "Clock Position"?

Most alternators of a particular manufacturer can be used on a variety of vehicles, which may require wiring connections placed in various locations. For example, a Chevrolet and a Buick alternator may be identical except for the position of the rear section containing the electrical connections. The four through bolts that hold the two halves together are equally spaced; therefore, the rear alternator housing *can* be installed in any one of four positions to match the wiring needs of various models. Always check the clock position of the original and be sure that it matches the replacement unit. ● **SEE FIGURE 20–15.**

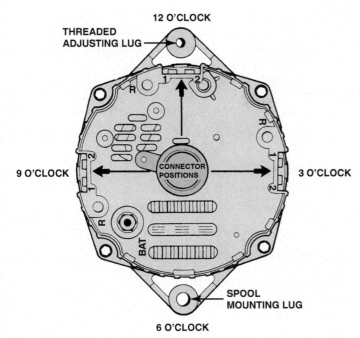

FIGURE 20–15 Explanation of clock positions. Because the four through bolts are equally spaced, it is possible for an alternator to be installed in one of four different clock positions. The connector position is determined by viewing the alternator from the diode end with the threaded adjusting lug in the up or 12 o'clock position. Select the 3 o'clock, 6 o'clock, 9 o'clock, or 12 o'clock position to match the unit being replaced.

2. Rotor resistance range is normally between 2.4 and 6 ohms.

3. If the resistance is below specification, the rotor is shorted.

4. If the resistance is above specification, the rotor connections are corroded or open.

If the rotor is found to be bad, it must be replaced or repaired at a specialized shop. ● SEE FIGURE 20–16.

NOTE: The cost of a replacement rotor may exceed the cost of an entire rebuilt alternator. Be certain, however, that the rebuilt alternator is rated at the same output as the original or higher.

STATOR TESTING The stator must be disconnected from the diodes (rectifiers) before testing. Because all three windings of the stator are electrically connected (either wye or delta), an ohmmeter can be used to check a stator.

- There should be low resistance at all three stator leads (continuity).

- There should *not* be continuity (in other words, there should be a meter reading of infinity ohms) when the stator is tested between any stator lead and the metal stator core.

- If there is continuity, the stator is shorted-to-ground and must be repaired or replaced. ● SEE FIGURE 20–17.

TESTING AN ALTERNATOR ROTOR USING AN OHMMETER

CHECKING FOR GROUNDS (SHOULD READ INFINITY IF ROTOR IS NOT GROUNDED)

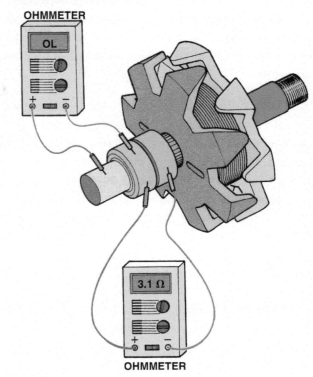

FIGURE 20–16 Testing an alternator rotor using an ohmmeter.

TESTING STATOR (CHECK FOR OPENS)

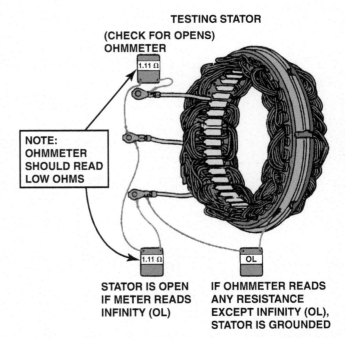

FIGURE 20–17 If the ohmmeter reads infinity between any two of the three stator windings, the stator is open and, therefore, defective. The ohmmeter should read infinity between any stator lead and the steel laminations. If the reading is less than infinity, the stator is grounded. Stator windings cannot be tested if shorted because the normal resistance is very low.

NOTE: Because the resistance is very low for a normal stator, it is generally not possible to test for a shorted (copper-to-copper) stator. A shorted stator will, however, greatly reduce alternator output. An ohmmeter cannot detect an open stator if the stator is delta wound. The ohmmeter will still indicate low resistance because all three windings are electrically connected.

TESTING THE DIODE TRIO Many alternators are equipped with a diode trio. A diode is an electrical one-way check valve that permits current to flow in only one direction. Because *trio* means "three," a diode trio is three diodes connected together. ● **SEE FIGURE 20–18**.

The diode trio is connected to all three stator windings. The current generated in the stator flows through the diode trio to the internal voltage regulator. The diode trio is designed to supply current for the field (rotor) and turns off the charge indicator light when the alternator voltage equals or exceeds the battery voltage. If one of the three diodes in the diode trio is defective (usually open), the alternator may produce close-to-normal output; however, the charge indicator light will be "on" dimly.

A diode trio should be tested with a digital multimeter. The meter should be set to the diode-check position. The multimeter should indicate 0.5 to 0.7 volt (500 to 700 millivolts) one way and OL (overlimit) after reversing the test leads and touching all three connectors of the diode trio.

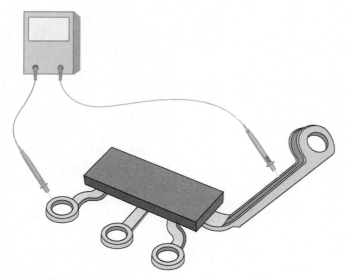

FIGURE 20–18 A diode trio can be tested using an analog (needle-type) ohmmeter or a digital meter set to "diode check".

FIGURE 20–19 A typical rectifier bridge that contains all six diodes in one replaceable assembly.

TESTING THE RECTIFIER

TERMINOLOGY The rectifier assembly usually is equipped with six diodes including three positive diodes and three negative diodes (one positive and one negative for each winding of the stator).

METER SETUP The rectifier(s) (diodes) should be tested using a multimeter that is set to "diode check" position on the digital multimeter (DMM).

Because a diode (rectifier) should allow current to flow in only one direction, each diode should be tested to determine if the diode allows current flow in one direction and blocks current flow in the opposite direction. To test some alternator diodes, it may be necessary to unsolder the stator connections. ● **SEE FIGURE 20–19**.

Accurate testing is not possible unless the diodes are separated electrically from other alternator components.

TESTING PROCEDURE Connect the leads to the leads of the diode (pigtail and housing of the rectifier bridge). Read the meter. Reverse the test leads. A good diode should have high resistance (OL) one way (reverse bias) and low voltage drop of 0.5 to 0.7 volt (500 to 700 millivolts) the other way (forward bias).

RESULTS Open or shorted diodes must be replaced. Most alternators group or combine all positive and all negative diodes in one replaceable rectifier component.

BRUSH RETAINER
PIN HOLE

FIGURE 20–20 A brush holder assembly with new brushes installed. The holes in the brushes are used to hold the brushes up in the holder when it is installed in the alternator. After the rotor has been installed, the retaining pin is removed, which allows the brushes to contact the slip rings of the rotor.

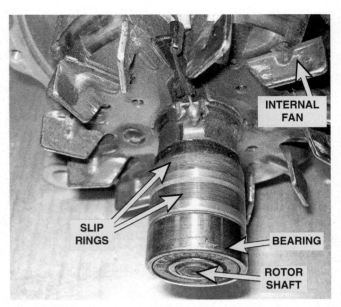

INTERNAL FAN

SLIP RINGS

BEARING

ROTOR SHAFT

FIGURE 20-21 An example of a rotor assembly that, if tested to be within specification, is suitable to be reinstalled after the slip rings have been cleaned.

REASSEMBLING THE ALTERNATOR

BRUSH HOLDER REPLACEMENT Alternator carbon brushes often last for many years and require no scheduled maintenance. The life of the alternator brushes is extended because they conduct only the field (rotor) current, which is normally only 2 to 5 amperes. The alternator brushes should be inspected when the alternator is disassembled and should be replaced when worn to less than 1/2-inch long. Brushes are commonly purchased assembled together in a brush holder. After the brushes are installed (usually retained by two or three screws) and the rotor is installed in the alternator housing, a brush retainer pin can be pulled out through an access hole in the rear of the alternator, allowing the brushes to be pressed against the slip rings by the brush springs. ● **SEE FIGURE 20–20.**

BEARING SERVICE AND REPLACEMENT The bearings of an alternator must be able to support the rotor and reduce friction. An alternator must be able to rotate at up to 15,000 RPM and withstand the forces created by the drive belt. The front bearing is usually a ball bearing type and the rear can be either a smaller roller or ball bearing.

The old or defective bearing can sometimes be pushed out of the front housing and the replacement pushed in by applying pressure with a socket or pipe against the outer edge of the bearing (outer race). Replacement bearings are usually prelubricated and seated. Many alternator front bearings must be removed from the rotor using a special puller.

What is Considered to be Normal Rotor Slip Ring Wear?

Many alternators can be restored to useful service by replacing the only wear item that they have, which are the brushes. The brushes ride on the surface of the slip rings of the rotor and these need to be round with a surface that is free from grooves, which would reduce the contact surface area where the brushes ride. Slight wear or discoloration is usually normal and can be cleaned using fine sandpaper. The slip rings also need to be perfectly round. ● **SEE FIGURE 20–21.**

ALTERNATOR ASSEMBLY After testing or servicing, the alternator rectifier(s), regulator, stator, and brush holder must be reassembled using the following steps:

STEP 1   If the brushes are internally mounted, insert a wire through the holes in the brush holder to hold the brushes against the springs.

STEP 2   Install the rotor and front-end frame in proper alignment with the mark made on the outside of the alternator housing. Install the through bolts. Before removing the wire pin holding the brushes, spin the alternator pulley. If the alternator is noisy or not rotating freely, the alternator can easily be disassembled again to check for the cause. After making certain the alternator is free to rotate, remove the brush holder pin and spin the alternator again by hand. The noise level may be slightly higher with the brushes released onto the slip rings.

STEP 3 Alternators should be tested on a bench tester, if available, before they are reinstalled on a vehicle. When installing the alternator on the vehicle, be certain that all mounting bolts and nuts are tight. The battery terminal should be covered with a plastic or rubber protective cap to help prevent accidental shorting to ground, which could seriously damage the alternator.

 FREQUENTLY ASKED QUESTION

What is done to an alternator when it is remanufactured?

Remanufactured or rebuilt alternators are totally disassembled and rebuilt. Even though there are many smaller rebuilders who may not replace all worn parts, the major national remanufacturers *totally* remanufacture the alternator. Old alternators (called **cores**) are totally disassembled and cleaned. Both bearings are replaced and all components are tested. Rotors are rewound to original specifications if required. The rotor windings are not counted but are rewound on the rotor "spool," using the correct-gauge copper wire, to the *weight* specified by the original manufacturer. New slip rings are replaced as required, soldered to the rotor spool windings, and machined. The rotors are also balanced and measured to ensure that the outside diameter of the rotor meets specifications. An undersized rotor will produce less alternator output because the field must be close to the stator windings for maximum output. Bridge rectifiers are replaced, if required. Every alternator is then assembled and tested for proper output, boxed, and shipped to a warehouse. Individual parts stores (called jobbers) purchase parts from various regional or local warehouses.

ALTERNATOR INSTALLATION

Before installing a replacement alternator, check service information for the exact procedure to follow for the vehicle being serviced. A typical installation procedure includes the following steps:

STEP 1 Verify that the replacement alternator is the correct unit for the vehicle.

 CASE STUDY

The Two-Minute Alternator Repair

A Chevrolet pickup truck was brought to a shop for routine service. The customer stated that the battery required a jump start after a weekend of sitting. The technician tested the battery and the charging system voltage using a small handheld digital multimeter. The battery voltage was 12.4 volts (about 75% charged), but the charging voltage was also 12.4 volts at 2,000 RPM. Because normal charging voltage should be 13.5 to 15 volts, it was obvious that the charging system was not operating correctly.

The technician checked the dash and found that the "charge" light was not on. Before removing the alternator for service, the technician checked the wiring connection on the alternator. When the connector was removed, it was discovered to be rusty. After the contacts were cleaned, the charging system was restored to normal operation. The technician had learned that the simple things should always be checked first before tearing into a big or expensive repair.

Summary:

- **Complaint**—Customer stated that the truck battery had to be jump-started after sitting for a weekend.

- **Cause**—Tests confirmed that the alternator was not charging and a rusty connection at the alternator was found during a visual inspection.

- **Correction**—Cleaning the electrical terminals at the alternator restored proper operation of the charging system.

STEP 2 Install the alternator wiring on the alternator and install the alternator.

STEP 3 Check the condition of the drive belt and replace, if necessary. Install the drive belt over the drive pulley.

STEP 4 Properly tension the drive belt.

STEP 5 Tighten all fasteners to factory specifications.

STEP 6 Double-check that all fasteners are correctly tightened and remove all tools from the engine compartment area.

STEP 7 Reconnect the negative battery cable.

STEP 8 Start the engine and verify proper charging circuit operation.

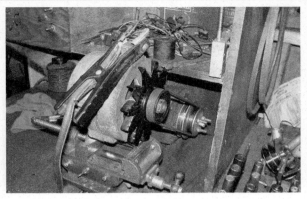

1 Before the alternator is disassembled, it is spin tested and connected to a scope to check for possible defective components.

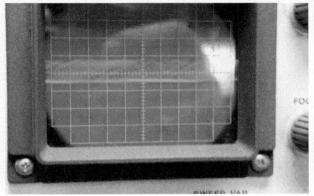

2 The scope pattern shows that the voltage output is far from being a normal pattern. This pattern indicates serious faults in the rectifier diodes.

3 The first step is to remove the drive pulley. This rebuilder is using an electric impact wrench to accomplish the task.

4 Carefully inspect the drive galley for damage of embedded rubber from the drive belt. The slightest fault can cause a vibration, noise, or possible damage to the alternator.

5 Remove the external fan (if equipped) and then the spacers as shown.

6 Next pop off the plastic cover (shield) covering the stator/rectifier connection.

CONTINUED ▶

7 After the cover has been removed, the stator connections to the rectifier can be seen.

8 Using a diagonal cutter, cut the weld to separate the stator from the rectifier.

9 Before separating the halves of the case, this technician uses a punch to mark both halves.

10 After the case has been marked, the through bolts are removed.

11 The drive-end (DE) housing and the stator are being separated from the rear (slip-ring-end) housing.

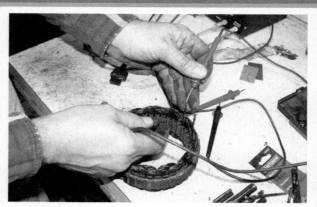

12 The stator is checked by visual inspection for discoloration or other physical damage, and then checked with an ohmmeter to see if the windings are shorted-to-ground.

13 The front bearing is removed from the drive-end housing using a press.

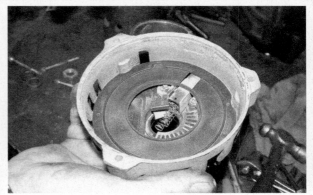

14 A view of the slip-ring-end (SRE) housing showing the black plastic shield, which helps direct air flow across the rectifier.

15 A punch is used to dislodge the plastic shield retaining clips.

16 After the shield has been removed, the rectifier, regulator, and brush holder assembly can be removed by removing the retaining screws.

17 The heat transfer grease is visible when the rectifier assembly is lifted out of the rear housing.

18 The parts are placed into a tumbler where ceramic stones and a water-based solvent are used to clean the parts.

CONTINUED ▶

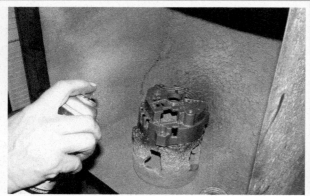

19 This rebuilder is painting the housing using a high-quality industrial grade spray paint to make the rebuilt alternator look like new.

20 The slip rings on the rotor are being machined on a lathe.

21 The rotor is being tested using an ohmmeter. The specifications for the resistance between the slip rings on the CS-130 are 2.2 to 3.5 ohms.

22 The rotor is also tested between the slip ring and the rotor shaft. This reading should be infinity.

23 A new rectifier. This replacement unit is significantly different than the original but is designed to replace the original unit and meets the original factory specifications.

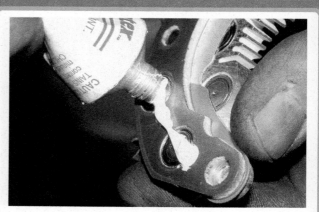

24 Silicone heat transfer compound is applied to the heat sink of the new rectifier.

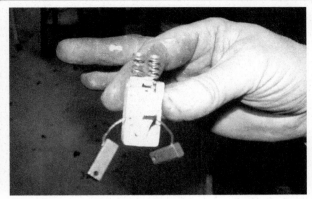

25 Replacement brushes and springs are assembled into the brush holder.

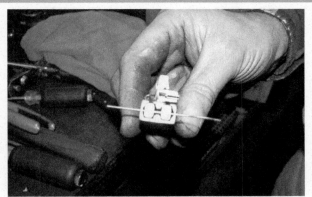

26 The brushes are pushed into the brush holder and retained by a straight wire, which extends through the rear housing of the alternator. This wire is then pulled out when the unit is assembled.

27 Here is what the CS alternator looks like after installing the new brush holder assembly, rectifier bridge, and voltage regulator.

28 The junction between the rectifier bridge and the voltage regulator is soldered.

29 The plastic deflector shield is snapped back into location using a blunt chisel and a hammer. This shield directs the airflow from the fan over the rectifier bridge and voltage regulator.

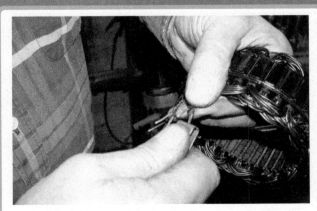

30 Before the stator windings can be soldered to the rectifier bridge, the varnish insulation is removed from the ends of the leads.

CONTINUED ▶

31 After the stator has been inserted into the rear housing, the stator leads are soldered to the copper lugs of the rectifier bridge.

32 New bearings are installed. A spacer is placed between the bearing and the slip rings to help prevent the possibility that the bearing could move on the shaft and short against the slip ring.

33 The slip-ring-end housing is aligned with the marks made during disassembly and is pressed into the drive-end housing.

34 The retaining bolts, which are threaded into the drive-end housing from the back of the alternator, are installed.

35 The external fan and drive pulley are installed and the retaining nut is tightened on the rotor shaft.

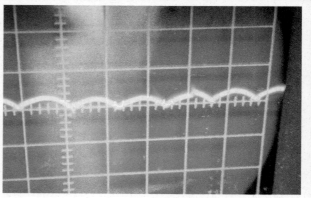

36 The scope pattern shows that the diodes and stator are functioning correctly and voltage check indicates that the voltage regulator is also functioning correctly.

1. Charging system testing requires that the battery be at least 75% charged to be assured of accurate test results. Normal charging voltage (at 2000 engine RPM) is 13.5 to 15 volts.

2. To check for excessive resistance in the wiring between the alternator and the battery, a voltage drop test should be performed.

3. Alternators do not produce their maximum rated output unless required by circuit demands. Therefore, to test for maximum alternator output, the battery must be loaded to force the alternator to produce its maximum output.

4. Each alternator should be marked across its case before disassembly to ensure proper clock position during reassembly. After disassembly, all alternator internal components should be tested using an ohmmeter. The following components should be tested:
   a. Stator
   b. Rotor
   c. Diodes
   d. Diode trio (if the alternator is so equipped)
   e. Bearings
   f. Brushes (should be more than 1/2 inch long)

REVIEW QUESTIONS

1. How does a technician test the voltage drop of the charging circuit?

2. How does a technician measure the amperage output of an alternator?

3. What tests can be performed to determine whether a diode or stator is defective before removing the alternator from the vehicle?

4. Why could a defective overrunning alternator pulley (OAP) or dampener (OAD) cause a lack of proper charging?

5. What is the procedure for replacing an alternator?

CHAPTER QUIZ

1. To check the charging voltage, connect a digital multimeter (DMM) to the positive (+) and the negative (−) terminals of the battery and select _____.
   a. DC volts
   b. AC volts
   c. DC amps
   d. AC amps

2. To check for ripple voltage from the alternator, connect a digital multimeter (DMM) and select _____.
   a. DC volts
   b. AC volts
   c. DC amps
   d. AC amps

3. The maximum allowable alternating current (AC) in amperes that is being sent to the battery from the alternator is _____.
   a. 0.4 ampere
   b. 1 to 3 amperes
   c. 3 to 4 amperes
   d. 10% of the rated output of the alternator

4. Why should the lights be turned on when checking for ripple voltage or alternating current from the alternator?
   a. To warm the battery
   b. To check that the battery is fully charged
   c. To create an electrical load for the alternator
   d. To test the battery before conducting other tests

5. An acceptable charging circuit voltage on a 12 volt system is _____.
   a. 13.5 to 15 volts
   b. 12.6 to 15.6 volts
   c. 12 to 14 volts
   d. 14.9 to 16.1 volts

6. Technician A says that the alternator case should be marked if it is to be disassembled. Technician B says that a DMM should be set to "diode check" when checking the rectifier assembly. Which technician is correct?
   a. Technician A only
   b. Technician B only
   c. Both Technicians A and B
   d. Neither Technician A nor B

7. Technician A says that a voltage drop test of the charging circuit should only be performed when current is flowing through the circuit. Technician B says to connect the leads of a voltmeter to the positive and negative terminals of the battery to measure the voltage drop of the charging system. Which technician is correct?
   a. Technician A only
   b. Technician B only
   c. Both Technicians A and B
   d. Neither Technician A nor B

8. When testing an alternator rotor, if an ohmmeter shows zero ohms with one meter lead attached to the slip rings and the other meter lead touching the rotor shaft, the rotor is _____.
   a. okay (normal)
   b. defective (shorted-to-ground)
   c. defective (shorted-to-voltage)
   d. okay (rotor windings are open)

9. An alternator diode is being tested using a digital multimeter set to the diode-check position. A good diode will read _____ if the leads are connected one way across the diode and _____ if the leads are reversed.
   a. 300/300
   b. 0.475/0.475
   c. OL/OL
   d. 0.551/OL

10. An overrunning alternator pulley or overrunning alternator dampener should be checked for proper operation is _____.
    a. There is excessive AC ripple voltage
    b. low or no alternator output is found
    c. the drive belt if loose or slipping
    d. Any of the above

LIGHTING AND SIGNALING CIRCUITS

After studying this chapter, the reader will be able to:

1. Explain adaptive front lighting and other lighting systems in an automobile.
2. Describe how an exterior lighting system works.
3. Read and interpret a bulb chart.
4. Discuss the operation of brake lights and turn signals.
5. Inspect, replace, and aim headlights and bulbs.
6. Discuss troubleshooting procedures for lighting and signaling circuits.

This chapter will help you prepare for the ASE Electrical/Electronic Systems (A6) certification test content area "E" (Lighting Systems Diagnosis and Repair).

Adaptive Front Lighting Systems (AFS) 324
Automatic headlight 325
Courtesy lights 329
Color shift 324
Composite head-light 321
Daytime running lights (DRLs) 320
Hazard warning 320
High-intensity discharge (HID) 323
Kelvin (K) 323
Light-emitting diode (LED) 316
Trade number 315
Troxler effect 329

CIRCUITS INVOLVED

CIRCUITS INVOLVED A vehicle has many different lighting and signaling systems, each with its own specific components and operating characteristics. The major light-related circuits and systems covered in this chapter include the following:

- Exterior lighting
- Headlights
- Bulb trade numbers
- Brake lights
- Turn signals and flasher units
- Courtesy lights
- Light-dimming rearview mirrors

NONCOMPUTER CONTROLLED LIGHTING Older vehicles used the headlight switch to operate all of the lights including the following:

1. Headlights
2. Taillights
3. Side-marker lights
4. Front parking lights
5. Dash lights
6. Interior (dome) light(s)

The headlight switch assembly on older vehicles carried a heavy current and was mechanical. Most contained a built-in circuit breaker for the headlights that would cause them to flicker on and off if a short circuit occurred in the headlight circuit. ● **SEE FIGURE 21–1.**

BODY CONTROL MODULE CONTROLLED LIGHTING

The **Body Control Module (BCM)** is often referred to as a *central organizational module*. Using a BCM results in the following benefits:

1. It simplifies the manufacturing and troubleshooting aspects of electronic modules.
2. It coordinates the operating functions of many related items, as well as security features.

All recent vehicles use a controller, usually the BCM to control the lights. The switches to turn on the lights are simply a request from the switch to the BCM to turn on the lights. The communication between the switches and the BCM is over serial data lines. Many vehicles use front and rear lighting modules so the BCM sends a message over the data lines to the front or rear lighting module to turn on the commanded lights. The controller can control either the power side or the ground side of the circuit and performs the following:

- Monitors the current flow through the circuit and will turn on a bulb failure warning light if it detects an open bulb or a fault in the circuit.

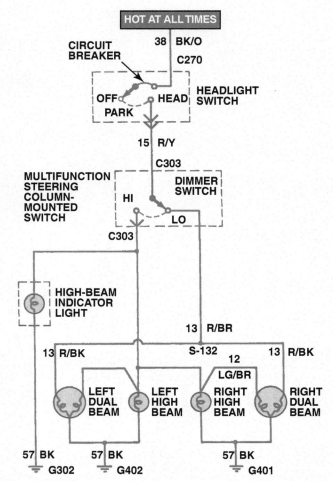

FIGURE 21–1 A Typical headlight circuit diagram on an older vehicle that does not use a controller, such as the body control module (BCM) to control the operation of the lights. Note that the headlight switch is represented by a dotted outline indicating that other circuits (such as dash lights) also operate from the switch.

- After the ignition has been turned off, the modules will turn off the lights after a time delay to prevent the battery from being drained.
- In the event of a communication failure, most module controlled exterior lighting systems will default to on position for safety.

Many electronic components are controlled by the BCM, including the following lighting circuits:

- Brake lights
- Courtesy lamps
- Dome lamps
- Exterior and interior lamps
- Fog lamps
- Hazard warning lamps
- Low- and high-beam head lamps
- Parking lamps
- Turn signal lamps
    ● **SEE FIGURE 21–2.**

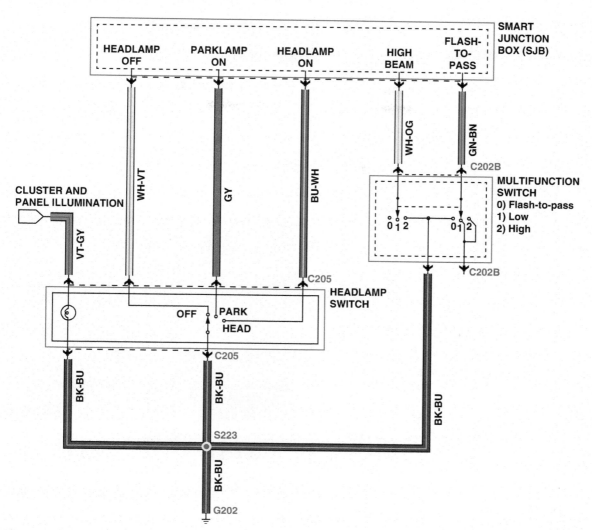

FIGURE 21–2 A schematic showing the inputs from the multi-function switch and the headlight switch to the smart junction box (SJB). The SJB then uses the body control module (BCM) to operate the lights.

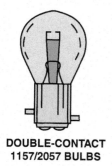

DOUBLE-CONTACT 1157/2057 BULBS

SINGLE-CONTACT 1156 BULBS

WEDGE 194 BULB

FIGURE 21–3 Dual-filament (double-contact) bulbs contain both a low-intensity filament for taillights or parking lights, and a high-intensity filament for brake lights and turn signals. Bulbs come in a variety of shapes and sizes. The numbers shown are the trade numbers.

BULB NUMBERS

TRADE NUMBER The number used on automotive bulbs is called the bulb **trade number**, as recorded with the American National Standards Institute (ANSI). The number is the same regardless of the manufacturer. ● **SEE FIGURE 21–3**.

The amount of light produced by a bulb is determined by the resistance of the filament wire, which also affects the amount of current (in amperes) required by the bulb. The correct trade number of a bulb should always be used for replacement to prevent circuit or component damage. Check service information or the owner's manual for the exact replacement bulb to use. ● **SEE CHART 21–1**.

BULB NUMBER SUFFIXES Many bulbs have suffixes that indicate some feature of the bulb, while keeping the same size and light output specifications. Typical bulb suffixes include the following:

- A: amber (painted glass)
- B: blue
- G: green

BULB NUMBER	FILAMENTS	AMPERAGE	WATTAGE
1156	1	2.1	26.9
1157	2	0.6/2/1	8.3/26.9
2057	2	0.5/2.1	6.9/26.9
3057	2	0.5/2.1	6.7/26.9
4157	2	0.6/2/1	8.3/26.9
7440	1	1.8	21.0
7443	2	0.4/1.8	5.0/21.0
67	1	0.6	8.0
161	1	0.2	2.7
168	1	0.4	4.9
192	1	0.3	4.3
194	1	0.3	3.8
585	1	0.04	1.1
921	1	1.4	18
9003	2	4.6/5.0	55.0/60.0
9006	1	4.3	55.0

CHART 21–1

Some automotive bulb trade numbers with their amperage and wattage rating. Check service information for the exact bulb to use.

- HD: heavy duty
- IF: inside frosted
- LL: long life
- NA: natural amber (amber glass)
- Q: Quartz halogen
- R: red
  - ● **SEE FIGURE 21–4**.

LED LIGHTING

PARTS AND OPERATION A **light-emitting diode (LED)** is a two-lead semiconductor light source. An LED is a P-N junction diode that emits light when a suitable voltage is applied to the leads. The electrons are able to recombine with electron holes within the device, releasing energy in the form of photons.
● **SEE FIGURE 21–5**.

FIGURE 21–4 Bulbs that have the same trade number have the same operating voltage and wattage. NA means that the bulb uses a natural amber glass ampoule with clear turn signal lenses.

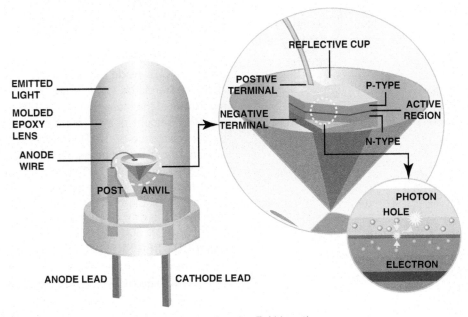

FIGURE 21–5 An LED emits light when a photon is released at the P-N junction.

FIGURE 21–6 A replacement LED taillight bulb is constructed of many small, individual light-emitting diodes.

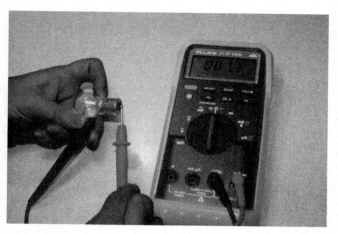

FIGURE 21–7 This single-filament bulb is being tested with a digital multimeter set to read resistance in ohms. The reading of 1.1 ohms is the resistance of the bulb when cold. As soon as current flows through the filament, the resistance increases about 10 times. It is the initial surge of current flowing through the filament, when the bulb is cool, that causes many bulbs to fail in cold weather as a result of the reduced resistance. As the temperature increases, the resistance increases.

LED FEATURES   Light-emitting diode (LED) lights are frequently used in newer vehicles for the following reasons.

1. **Faster illumination.** Using LEDs in brake lights will light up 200 ms faster than an incandescent bulb, which requires some time to heat the filament before it is hot enough to create light. This faster illumination, when used in brake lights, can mean the difference in stopping distances at 60 MPH (100 km/h) by about 18 feet (6 m) due to the reduced reaction time for the driver of the vehicle behind.

2. **Longer service life.** LEDs are solid-state devices that do not use a filament to create light. As a result, they are less susceptible to vibration and will often last the life of the vehicle.

3. **Lower current draw.** LEDs draw less current compared to incandescent bulbs and the result is less electrical drain from the charging system to operate all of the lights in the vehicle. This helps improve fuel economy and lowers exhaust emissions by reducing the electrical load created by the alternator on the engine.

NOTE: Aftermarket replacement LED bulbs that are used to replace conventional bulbs may require the use of a different type of flasher unit due to the reduced current draw of the LED bulbs. ● SEE FIGURE 21–6.

TESTING BULBS   Bulbs can be tested using two basic tests.

1. Perform a visual inspection of any bulb. Many faults, such as a shorted filament, a corroded connector, or moisture, can cause weird problems that are often thought to be wiring issues.

2. Bulbs can be tested using an ohmmeter and checking the resistance of the filament(s). Most bulbs will read low resistance, between 0.5 and 20 ohms (incandescent bulbs), at room temperature, depending on the bulb. Test results include the following:

   Normal resistance. The bulb is good. Check both filaments if it is a two-filament bulb. ● **SEE FIGURE 21–7.**

   ■ Zero ohms. It is unlikely, but possible for the bulb filament to be shorted.

   ■ OL (electrically open). The reading indicates that the bulb filament is broken.

NOTE: If testing LED lights, check service information for the specified testing procedure.

BRAKE LIGHTS

TERMINOLOGY   Brake lights, also called *stop lights*, use the high-intensity filament of a double-filament bulb or LEDs. The brake lights are lit when the driver depresses the brake pedal. On older vehicles, the brake switch receives current from a fuse that is hot all the time. The brake light switch is a normally open (N.O.) switch, but is closed when the driver depresses the brake pedal. Newer brake switches have more than one set of contacts. In many cases, one set is normally open and the other set is normally closed.

   ■ **One-filament stop/Turn bulbs.** In some vehicles, the stop and turn signals are both provided by one filament.

   ■ **Two-filament stop/Turn bulbs.** In systems using separate filaments for the stop and turn lamps, the brake and turn signal switches are not connected.

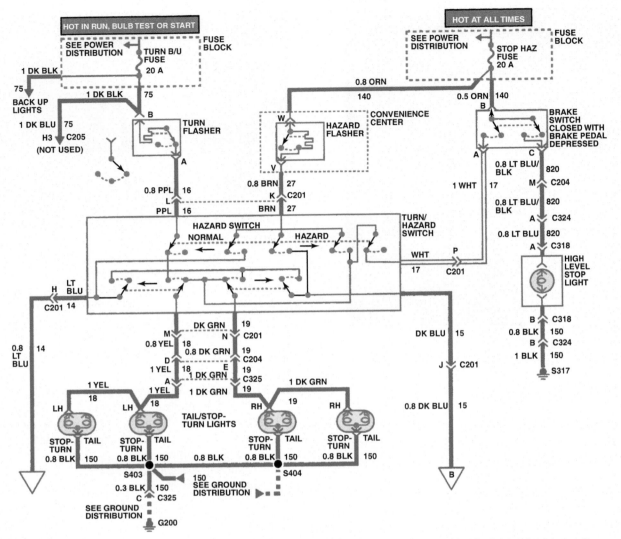

FIGURE 21–8 A typical older-type brake light circuit showing the brake switch and all of the related circuit components.

All vehicles sold in the United States have a third brake light commonly referred to as the *center high-mounted stop light (CHMSL)*. ● **SEE FIGURE 21–8.**

BCM-CONTROLLED BRAKE LIGHTS
When the brake pedal is depressed, the signal is sent to the brake light controller, usually the BCM, which then signals the rear light module to actuate the brake lights. The input from the brake pedal switch or sensor is used by other systems in the vehicle as an input signal for the following systems:

1. **Shift interlock.** On vehicles equipped with an automatic transmission, the gear selector cannot be moved out of the park position unless the brake pedal is depressed.

2. **Push-button start.** Vehicles equipped with a push-button start will not start unless the brake pedal is depressed.

3. **Cruise control.** If the brake pedal is depressed, the cruise control function is disabled.

4. **Antilock braking system (ABS).** When the brake pedal is depressed, the ABS system is ready to intervene, if needed, to control wheel slippage.

On some vehicles, the key must be in the on position for all the brake lights to illuminate. This is particularly important to know when performing diagnostics. Check service information for the specified procedure to follow on the vehicle being tested. ● **SEE FIGURE 21–9.**

TURN SIGNALS

MECHANICAL SYSTEM OPERATION
In older systems, the turn signal circuit is supplied power from the ignition switch and operated by a lever and a switch. When the turn signal switch is moved in either direction, the corresponding turn signal lamps receive current through the flasher unit. The flasher

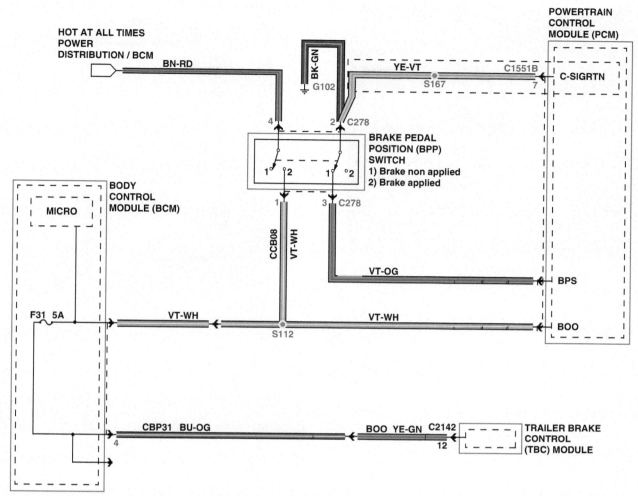

FIGURE 21-9 A schematic of the BCM-controlled brake light circuit that includes the brake pedal position (BPP) switch, which creates signals to the powertrain control module (PCM) with inputs labeled BPS (brake pedal position) and BOO (brake on-off).

unit causes the current to start and stop as the turn signal lamp flashes on and off with the interrupted current.

A turn signal flasher unit is a metal or plastic can, containing a switch that opens and closes the turn signal circuit. It is often installed in a metal clip attached to the dash panel to allow the "clicking" noise of the flasher to be heard by the driver. Most flashers have a lamp current-sensing circuit, which will cause the flash rate to double when a bulb is burned out. ● **SEE FIGURE 21-10.**

BCM-CONTROLLED TURN SIGNALS

Starting in the early 2000s, many vehicles use the turn signal as an input to the body control module (BCM). ● **SEE FIGURE 21-11.**

The BCM sends a signal through the data lines to the lighting module(s) to flash the lights. With these systems, the BCM also sends a signal to the radio, which sends a clicking sound to the driver's side speaker even if the radio is off.

BULB OUTAGE WARNING

The lighting module, usually the body control module (BCM), monitors the current flow though all of the lights. These circuits measure the current and, if there is a change that is not expected, it can turn on a warning light to warn the driver. If this current is below some threshold value, the bulb is assumed to be burned out. The bulb failure

FIGURE 21-10 Three styles of flasher units.

system works using a resistance value for each circuit. When diagnosing a bulb outage concern, perform the following steps:

STEP 1 Visually check the exterior lights for proper operation. Check all of the following:

- Backup light(s)
- Brake lights, including the center high-mounted stop light

FIGURE 21–11 A steering column with the steering wheel removed, showing the turn signal canceling cam used to return the lever to the neutral position after a turn. The switches are an input to the body control module for left and right turn signal operation.

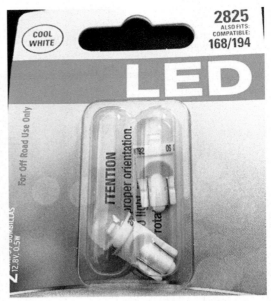

FIGURE 21–12 Replacement side marker LED lamps that could be used to replace standard bulbs. However, the current draw is lower and using these bulbs could cause the lamp outage warning lamp to be turned on.

- Driving lights, if equipped
- Fog lights, if equipped
- High-beam headlights
- License plate light(s)
- Low-beam headlights
- Park lights
- Puddle lights
- Side marker lights, front and rear, and left and right sides
- Taillights
- Turn signals front and rear

STEP 2 If one or more are not lighting, check or replace the bulb. Verify that the affected bulb is not an LED where a non-LED bulb is specified. ● **SEE FIGURE 21–12**.

STEP 3 If the warning lamp is still on, check the sockets for corrosion, proper voltage, and ground at the socket.

HAZARD WARNING LIGHTS The **hazard warning**, also called *four-way flashers*, is a device installed in a vehicle lighting system with the primary function of causing both the left and right turn signal lamps to flash when the hazard warning switch is activated. Secondary functions may include visible dash indicators for the hazard system and an audible signal to indicate when the flasher is operating. In older systems, a separate hazard warning flasher is used. Current vehicles use the body control module (BCM) to operate all four turn signal lights when the hazard (four-way) flasher switch is turned on by the driver.

DAYTIME RUNNING LIGHTS

PURPOSE AND FUNCTION Daytime **running lights (DRLs)** are lights at the front of the vehicle that are on all the time the engine is running, unless they are turned off, or when the headlights are on. DRLs involve operation of the following:

- Front parking lights
- Separate DRL lamps
- Headlights (usually at reduced current and voltage) when the vehicle is running

Studies have shown that DRLs have reduced accidents where used. Daytime running lights primarily use a control module that turns on either the low- or high-beam headlights wired in series or separate daytime running lights. The lights on some vehicles come on when the engine starts. Other vehicles will turn on the lamps when the engine is running, but delay their operation until a signal from the vehicle speed sensor indicates that the vehicle is moving. To avoid having the lights on during servicing, some systems will turn off the headlights when the parking brake is applied, and the ignition switch is cycled off and then back on. Others will only light the headlights when the vehicle is in a drive gear. ● **SEE FIGURE 21–13**.

The DRLs will operate when the following conditions are met:

- The ignition is in the RUN or CRANK position
- The shift lever is out of the PARK position for vehicles equipped with automatic transmissions or the parking brake is released for vehicles with manual transmissions
- The low and high beam headlamps are OFF

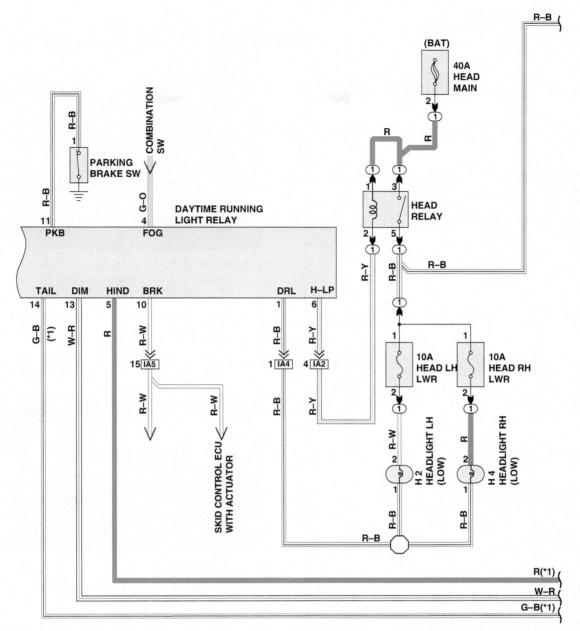

FIGURE 21-13 A schematic showing a DRL circuit that uses the headlights. Also notice that each headlight has its own fuse to protect the circuit. Check service information for how the DRLs operate on the vehicle being serviced.

HEADLIGHTS

HEADLIGHT SWITCHES Older vehicles use the headlight switch to operate the exterior and interior lights. On these systems, the headlight switch is connected directly to the battery through a fusible link, and has continuous power or is "hot" all the time. ● **SEE FIGURE 21-14.**

COMPOSITE HEADLIGHTS Sealed beam headlights were used for many years and, then in the 1990s, were replaced with composite headlights. **Composite headlights** are constructed using a replaceable bulb and a fixed lens cover that is part of the vehicle. Composite headlights

are the result of changes in the aerodynamic styling of vehicles where sealed beam lamps could no longer be used. ● **SEE FIGURE 21-15.**

The replaceable bulbs are usually bright halogen bulbs. Halogen bulbs get very hot during operation, between 500°F and 1,300°F (260°C and 700°C). It is important to never touch the glass of any halogen bulb with bare fingers because the natural oils of the skin on the glass bulb can cause the bulb to break when it heats during normal operation. ● **SEE FIGURE 21-16.**

BULB FAULTS Halogen bulbs can fail for various reasons. Some causes for halogen bulb failure and their indications include the following:

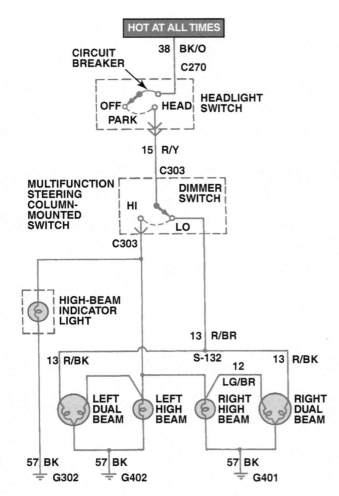

FIGURE 21–14 A Typical headlight circuit diagram on an older vehicle that does not use a controller, such as the BCM to control the operation of the lights. Note that the headlight switch is represented by a dotted outline, indicating that other circuits (such as dash lights) also operate from the switch.

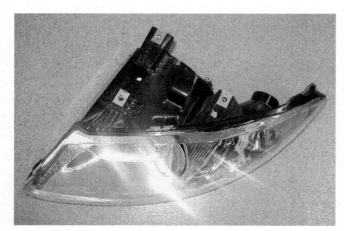

FIGURE 21–15 A typical composite headlamp assembly. The lens, housing, and bulb sockets are usually included as a complete assembly.

- **Gray color.** Low voltage to the bulb (check for corroded socket or connector)
- **White (cloudy) color.** Indication of an air leak

FIGURE 21–16 Handle a halogen bulb by the base to prevent the skin's oil from getting on the glass.

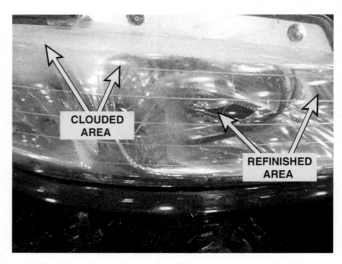

FIGURE 21–17 The right side of this headlight assembly has been restored, but still needs to be polished. The left is side is cloudy and not yet restored.

- **Broken filament.** Usually caused by excessive vibration
- **Blistered glass.** Indication that someone has touched the glass

CLOUDY HEADLIGHT RESTORATION The bulb covering of composite headlights is made from acrylic plastic. This material tends to fade, turn yellow, and discolor over a period of time due primarily to constant exposure to the sun's ultraviolet (UV) rays. The problem tends to be most serious in warmer, sunny climates. This clouding of the surface is more than a cosmetic issue because it can reduce the available light, reducing night vision. There are many brands and types of headlight restoration products available. Most products involve sanding the surface of the lens, using fine sandpaper and applying a UV protectant to help prevent further damage to the plastic lens. Always follow the instructions for the product or procedure used to restore the headlights. ● **SEE FIGURE 21–17.**

HIGH-INTENSITY DISCHARGE HEADLIGHTS

PARTS AND OPERATION High-intensity discharge **(HID)** headlights produce light that is crisper, clearer, and brighter than light produced by a halogen headlight. High-intensity discharge lamps do not use a filament like conventional electrical bulbs, but contain two electrodes about 0.2 inch (5 mm) apart. A high-voltage pulse is sent to the bulb, which arcs across the tips of electrodes producing light. It creates light from an electrical discharge between two electrodes in a gas-filled arc tube. An HID produces twice the light with less electrical current (amperage) than conventional halogen bulbs. The HID lighting system consists of the discharge arc source, igniter, ballast, and headlight assembly.
● **SEE FIGURE 21–18**.

The two electrodes are contained in a tiny quartz capsule filled with xenon gas, mercury, and metal halide salts. HID headlights are also called *xenon* headlights. The lights and support electronics are expensive, but they should last the life of the vehicle unless physically damaged.

HID headlights produce a white light giving the lamp a blue-white color. The color of light is expressed in temperature using the Kelvin scale. **Kelvin (K)** temperature is the Celsius

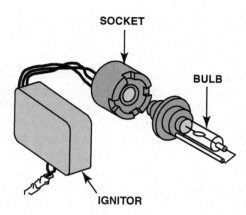

FIGURE 21–18 The igniter contains the ballast and transformer needed to provide high-voltage pulses to the arc tube bulb.

temperature plus 273 degrees. Typical color temperatures include the following:

- Daylight: 5,400°K
- HID: 4,100°K
- Halogen: 3,200°K
- Incandescent (tungsten): 2,800°K

● **SEE FIGURE 21–19**.

? **FREQUENTLY ASKED QUESTION**

What Is the Difference between the Temperature of the Light and the Brightness of the Light?

The temperature of the light indicates the color of the light. The brightness of the light is measured in lumens. A standard 100-watt incandescent light bulb emits about 1,700 lumens. A typical halogen headlight bulb produces about 2,000 lumens, and a typical HID bulb produces about 2,800 lumens.

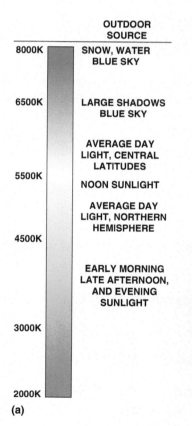

OUTDOOR SOURCE

8000K	SNOW, WATER BLUE SKY
6500K	LARGE SHADOWS BLUE SKY
5500K	AVERAGE DAY LIGHT, CENTRAL LATITUDES
	NOON SUNLIGHT
	AVERAGE DAY LIGHT, NORTHERN HEMISPHERE
4500K	
	EARLY MORNING LATE AFTERNOON, AND EVENING SUNLIGHT
3000K	
2000K	

(a)

(b)

FIGURE 21–19 (a) The color of light is measured in degrees Kelvin (K). The higher the temperature of the light is, the bluer the appearance. (Line drawing to be drafted) (b) HID (xenon) headlights emit a whiter light than halogen headlights and usually look blue compared to halogen bulbs.

STAGES OF HID HEADLIGHT OPERATION The HID ballast is powered voltage from the headlight switch or the body control module. The HID headlights operate in three stages or states.

1. **Start-up or stroke state.** When the headlight switch is turned to the on position, the ballast may draw up to 20 amperes at 12 volts. The ballast sends multiple high-voltage pulses to the arc tube to start the arc inside the bulb. The voltage provided by the ballast during the start-up state ranges from - 600 to + 600 volts, which is increased by a transformer to about 25,000 volts. The increased voltage is used to create an arc between the electrodes in the bulb.

2. **Run-up state.** After the arc is established, the ballast provides a higher than steady state voltage to the arc tube to keep the bulb illuminated. On a cold bulb, this state could last as long as 40 seconds. On a hot bulb, the run-up state may last only 15 seconds. The current requirements during the run-up state are about 360 volts from the ballast and a power level of about 75 watts.

3. **Steady state.** The steady state phase begins when the power requirement of the bulb drops to 35 watts. The ballast provides a minimum of 55 volts to the bulb during steady state operation.

BI-XENON HEADLIGHTS Some vehicles are equipped with bi-xenon headlights, which use a shutter to block some of the light during low-beam operation, and then mechanically move to expose more of the light from the bulb for high-beam operation. Because xenon lights are relatively slow to start working, vehicles equipped with bi-xenon headlights use two halogen lights for the "flash-to-pass" feature.

HID HEADLIGHT FAILURE SYMPTOMS The following symptoms indicate bulb failure:

- A light flickers
- Lights go out (caused when the ballast assembly detects repeated bulb restrikes)
- Color changes to a dim pink glow

Bulb failures are often intermittent and difficult to repeat. However, bulb failure is likely if the symptoms get worse over time. Always follow the vehicle manufacturer's recommended testing and service procedures.

DIAGNOSIS AND SERVICE High-intensity discharge headlights will change slightly in color with age. This color shift is usually not noticeable unless one headlight arc tube assembly has been replaced due to a collision repair, and then the difference in color may be noticeable. The difference in color will gradually change as the arc tube ages and should not be too noticeable by most customers. If the arc tube assembly is near the end of its life, it may not light immediately if it is turned off and then back on immediately. This test is called a "hot restrike" and if it fails, a replacement arc tube assembly may be needed, or there is another fault, such as a poor electrical connection that should be checked.

FIGURE 21–20 LED headlights usually require multiple units to provide the needed light as seen on this Lexus LS600h.

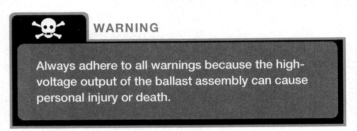

WARNING

Always adhere to all warnings because the high-voltage output of the ballast assembly can cause personal injury or death.

LED HEADLIGHTS

Many newer vehicles use LED headlights either as standard equipment or optional equipment. ● **SEE FIGURE 21–20**.

The advantages of LED headlights compared to other types include the following:

- Long service life
- Reduced electrical power required

The disadvantages of LED headlights include the following:

- Higher cost
- Many small LEDs are required to create the necessary light output

ADAPTIVE FRONT LIGHTING SYSTEM

PURPOSE AND FUNCTION An **adaptive (or advanced) front lighting system or AFS** is a system that mechanically moves the headlights to follow the direction of the front wheels. The purpose is to provide improved lighting during cornering. The AFS headlights are usually capable of rotating 15 degrees to the

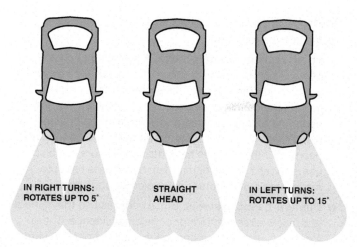

FIGURE 21–21 Adaptive front lighting systems rotate the low-beam headlight in the direction of travel.

FIGURE 21–23 Typical dash-mounted switch that allows the driver to turn off the front lighting system.

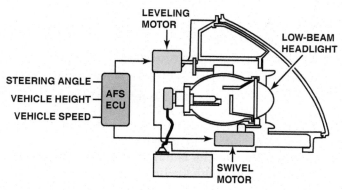

FIGURE 21–22 A typical adaptive front lighting system uses two motors: one for the up and down movement and the other for rotating the low-beam headlight to the left and right.

left and 5 degrees to the right (some systems rotate 14 degrees and 9 degrees, respectively). Vehicles that use AFS include Lexus, Mercedes, and certain domestic models, usually as an extra cost option. ● SEE FIGURE 21–21.

NOTE: These angles are reversed on vehicles sold in countries that drive on the left side of the road, such as Great Britain, Japan, Australia, and New Zealand.

PARTS AND OPERATION
The vehicle has to be moving above a predetermined speed, usually above 20 mph (30 km/h), and the lights stop moving when the speed drops below about 3 mph (5 km/h). AFS is often used in addition to self-leveling motors so that the headlights remain properly aimed regardless of how the vehicle is loaded. Without self-leveling, headlights would shine higher than normal if the rear of the vehicle is heavily loaded. ● SEE FIGURE 21–22.

When a vehicle is equipped with an adaptive front lighting system, the lights are moved by the headlight controller outward and then inward, as well as up and down as a test of the system. This action is quite noticeable to the driver and is normal operation of the system.

DIAGNOSIS AND SERVICE
The first step when diagnosing an AFS fault is to perform the following visual inspection:

■ Start by checking that the AFS is switched on. Most AFS headlights are equipped with a switch that allows the driver to turn the system on and off. ● SEE FIGURE 21–23.

■ Check that the system performs a self-test during start-up.

■ Verify that both low-beam and high-beam lights function correctly. The system may be disabled if a fault with one of the headlights is detected.

■ Use a scan tool to test for any AFS-related diagnostic trouble codes. Some systems allow the AFS to be checked and operated using a scan tool.

Always follow the recommended testing and service procedures as specified by the vehicle manufacturer in service information.

AUTOMATIC HEADLIGHTS

PURPOSE AND FUNCTION
Automatic headlights will automatically turn on the headlights when the light sensor detects low ambient light level. These sensors are usually located on the dash of the vehicle. If the light level is low, the headlights turn on automatically when the engine starts. The ambient light sensor is used to monitor outside lighting conditions. The ambient light sensor provides a voltage signal that will vary between 0.2 and 4.9 volts, depending on outside lighting conditions. The body control module (BCM) provides a 5-volt reference signal to the ambient light sensor. The BCM monitors the ambient light sensor signal circuit to determine if outside lighting conditions are correct for either daytime running lights, or automatic lamp control (ALC) when the headlamp switch is in the AUTO position.

FIGURE 21–24 A dash symbol used to inform the driver that the automatic headlights are on. (New Halderman line drawing)

CONTROLS Most vehicles allow the driver to select the headlights in the "AUTO" position or turn them on and off manually. If the headlights are on, a dash symbol is often displayed on the dash to inform the driver. ● **SEE FIGURE 21–24**.

HEADLIGHT HIGH/LOW BEAM SWITCH

DIMMER SWITCH Headlights use a high-intensity bulb or lamp and a low-intensity bulb or lamp. The switch used to switch between the two circuits is often called the *dimmer switch* or the high/low switch. An indicator light illuminates on the dash when the high beams are selected. The dimmer switch is usually hand operated by a lever on the steering column. Some steering column switches are actually attached to the outside of the steering column and are spring loaded. To replace these types of dimmer switches, the steering column needs to be lowered slightly to gain access to the switch itself.

AUTO DIMMING HEADLIGHTS

PURPOSE AND FUNCTION An **automatic headlight dimmer** (also called *automatic beam control* or *automatic high beams*) is a system that causes the headlights to switch from high-intensity beams to low-intensity beams when the system detects the headlights from an approaching vehicle.

TYPES OF SYSTEMS Types of automatic headlight dimming include the following:

- **Photo resistor-based system.** A system that uses a photo resistor usually mounted at the top of the windshield inside the vehicle. This system automatically adjusts the headlight beams from "high beam" to "low beam" when approaching oncoming vehicles during nighttime driving. The system also switches back to high beam after the vehicles have passed. Drivers can also use standard headlight dimmers to override the automatic headlight dimmer on vehicles so equipped.

- **Camera-based systems.** Some vehicles use the camera and lasers already fitted for collision avoidance. These systems can detect an oncoming vehicle from 400 yards (m) away, and detect the tail lights of a car in front from more than 120 yards (m).

CONDITIONS NEEDED TO FUNCTION For the automatic operation to turn on the high beams, the following conditions are usually required:

- Vehicle speed above 20 MPH
- Dark conditions with few streetlights
- There are no approaching vehicles with the headlights on
- There are no taillights from the vehicle in front

NOTE: High beams may not automatically turn off when an approaching vehicle is hidden from view due to a hill or a curve. This inability is not a fault with the system, but instead is due to the limiting factors of the system.

HEADLIGHT SYSTEM DIAGNOSIS

VISUAL INSPECTION All of the lights, including the operation of the headlights, should be a part of any vehicle inspection process. During a visual inspection, check the headlights for the following:

- Are they functioning as designed? (Check service information or a similar vehicle to make sure that the system is actually not working as designed).
- Check the brightness to see if they are dim.
- Check if the headlights are too bright.

DIAGNOSTIC PROCEDURE If the headlights are not working at all, perform the following steps:

STEP 1 Use a factory or factory-level scan tool to turn the headlights on using the bi-directional command from the scan tool. If the headlights work, the headlights and the headlight circuit is working normally. The problem is likely the control input to the controller that actually operates the headlights.

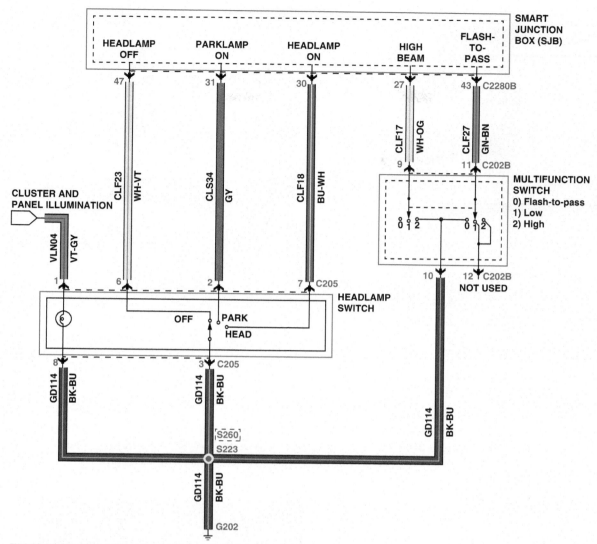

FIGURE 21–25 A Ford headlight circuit showing the control of the power side of the circuit comes from the smart junction box (SCB).

STEP 2 Check the schematic for the headlight circuit and check for voltage at various parts to help pinpoint the location of the open circuit. Always follow the vehicle manufacturer's specified procedures. ● **SEE FIGURE 21–25**.

■ If the headlights are brighter than normal, the battery voltage may be higher than normal. Check the charging system voltage to make sure that it is less than 15.5 volts on most vehicles. Check service information for the exact specifications.

■ If the headlight(s) is/are dimmer than normal, check the electrical circuits to the headlights for excessive circuit resistance, such any of the following:

1. Loose electrical connector
2. Corroded socket
3. Poor electrical ground connection

TECH TIP

The Weirder the Problem, the More Likely It Is a Poor Ground Connection

Bad grounds are often the cause for feedback or lamps operating at full or partial brilliance. At first, the problem looks weird, because often the switch for the lights that are on dimly is not even turned on. When an electrical device is operating, and it lacks a proper ground connection, the current will try to find ground and will often cause other circuits to work. Check all grounds before replacing parts.

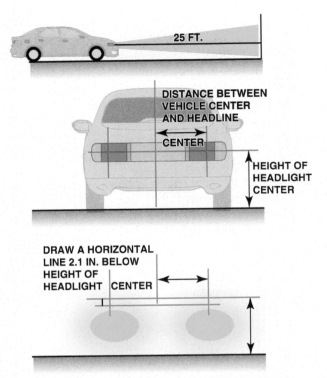

DISTANCE BETWEEN VEHICLE CENTER AND HEADLINE CENTER

HEIGHT OF HEADLIGHT CENTER

DRAW A HORIZONTAL LINE 2.1 IN. BELOW HEIGHT OF HEADLIGHT CENTER

THE LOW BEAMS SHOULD INTERSECT THE LOWER LINE AND VERTICAL LINES WHERE THE ANGLE OF THE BEAM BEGINS TO SLOPE UPWARD.

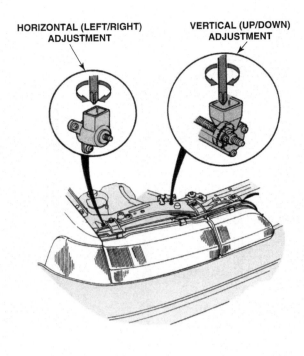

HORIZONTAL (LEFT/RIGHT) ADJUSTMENT

VERTICAL (UP/DOWN) ADJUSTMENT

FIGURE 21–26 (a) A typical headlight aiming diagram as found in service information. (b) Adjustments to move the headlight aiming point left or right or up and down are usually made using a screwdriver to move the headlight housing.

HEADLIGHT AIMING

According to U.S. federal law, all headlights, regardless of shape, must be able to be aimed using headlight aiming equipment. The headlights are equipped with adjusting screws that can be used to aim the headlights. Some are also equipped with a bubble level to help make sure that the lights are level. Older vehicles equipped with sealed beam headlights used a headlight aiming system that attached to the headlight itself. Check service information for the exact procedure and specifications to follow when aiming headlights. ● **SEE FIGURE 21–26.**

FOG AND DRIVING LIGHTS

FOG LIGHTS The light from regular headlights can reflect off the fog, snow, or dust particles in the air, causing glare. When driving in fog, the use of fog lights reduces the glare. Fog lights have a unique beam that is flat and wide, and is positioned low on the vehicle, usually near the front bumper. Fog lights are also useful where there is dust and snow on the road, either drifting in through the air or being churned up from the surface of the road. Fog lights are usually white, though they can also be yellow or blue. Fog lights in the rear are always red. ● **SEE FIGURE 21–27.**

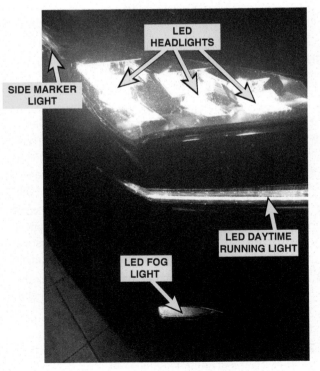

LED HEADLIGHTS

SIDE MARKER LIGHT

LED DAYTIME RUNNING LIGHT

LED FOG LIGHT

FIGURE 21–27 Fog lights are often included on many vehicles, such as these on a Lexus NX SUV.

What Are Rear Fog Lights?

Some vehicles, usually European vehicles, are equipped with rear (red) fog lights. These are used so that drivers behind can see the vehicle in front. These could be on whenever the fog lights are turned on, or they could be on a separate switch. These rear fog lights are sometimes confused with brake lights being on because they are often as bright as brake lights. Check the owner's manual or service information if a fault is reported about the rear fog lights.

NOTE: Fog lights should only be used when visibility is poor and then turned off.

DRIVING LIGHTS Driving lights have a narrow, straight beam, and are used while off-roading or traversing dark, deserted country roads. Driving lights are designed to send powerful beams far ahead, illuminating the next stretch of road. Driving lights are usually installed by the vehicle owner and are usually not available from the factory unless a special off-road equipment package is ordered. If installed, they should be wired to work only when the high beams are in use. Check local and state regulations in regards to the mounting and use of driving lights.

AUTOMATIC DIMMING MIRRORS

PARTS AND OPERATION Automatic dimming mirrors use electrochromic technology to dim the mirror in proportion to the amount of headlight glare from other vehicles at the rear. The electrochromic technology developed by Gentex Corporation uses a gel that changes with light between two pieces of glass. One piece of glass acts as a reflector and the other has a transparent (clear) electrically conductive coating. The inside rearview mirror also has a forward-facing light sensor that is used to detect darkness. It will signal the rearward-facing sensor to begin to check for excessive glare from headlights behind the vehicle. The rearward-facing sensor sends a voltage to the electrochromic gel in the mirror that is in proportion to the amount of glare detected. The mirror dims in proportion to the glare, and becomes like a standard rearview mirror when the glare is no longer detected. If automatic dimming mirrors are used on the exterior, the sensors in the interior mirror and electronics are used to control both the interior and exterior mirrors. ● **SEE FIGURE 21–28**.

DIAGNOSIS AND SERVICE If a customer concern states that the mirrors do not dim when exposed to bright headlights from the vehicle behind, the cause could be sensors or the mirror itself. Be sure that the mirror is getting electrical power. Most automotive dimming mirrors have a green light to indicate the presence of electrical power. If no voltage is found at the mirror, follow standard troubleshooting procedures to find the cause. If the mirror is getting voltage, start the diagnosis by placing a strip of tape over the forward-facing light sensor. Turn the ignition key on, engine off (KOEO), and observe the operation of the mirror when a flashlight or trouble light is directed onto the mirror. If the mirror reacts and dims, the forward-facing sensor is defective. Most often, the entire mirror assembly has to be replaced if any sensor or mirror faults are found.

One typical fault with automatic dimming mirrors is that a crack can occur in the mirror assembly, allowing the gel to escape from between the two layers of glass. This gel can drip onto the dash or center console and harm these surfaces. The mirror should be replaced at the first sign of any gel leakage.

What Is the Troxler Effect?

The **Troxler effect**, also called *Troxler fading*, is a visual effect where an image remains on the retina of the eye for a short time after the image has been removed. The effect was discovered in 1804 by Igney Paul Vital Troxler (1780–1866), a Swiss physician. Because of the Troxler effect, headlight glare can remain on the retina of the eye and create a blind spot. At night, this fading away of the bright light from the vehicle in the rear reflected by the rearview mirror can cause a hazard.

COURTESY LIGHTS

Courtesy lights are a generic term primarily used for interior lights, including overhead (dome) and under-the-dash (courtesy) lights. These interior lights are controlled by switches located in the door handle of the vehicle or by a switch on the dash. Many newer vehicles operate the interior lights through the body control module (BCM) or through an electronic module. Because the exact wiring and operation of these units differ, check the service information for the exact model of the vehicle being serviced.

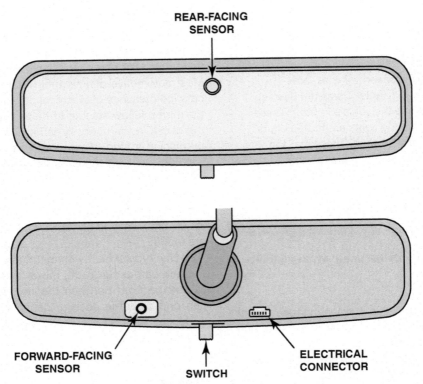

FIGURE 21–28 An automatic dimming mirror compares the amount of light toward the front of the vehicle to the rear of the vehicle and allows a voltage to cause the gel to darken the mirror.

ILLUMINATED ENTRY

Some vehicles are equipped with illuminated entry, meaning the interior lights are turned on for a given amount of time when the outside door handle or remote keyless entry (RKE) fob is operated while the doors are locked.

Most vehicles equipped with illuminated entry also light the exterior door lights called "puddle lights" that shine downward so people entering a vehicle in the dark can see the ground near the vehicle. The input from the door handle or key fob remote is used to "wake up" the power supply for the body control module (BCM) and usually turns on the interior lights.

LIGHTING SYSTEM DIAGNOSIS

Diagnosing any faults in the lighting and signaling systems usually includes the following steps.

STEP 1 Verify the customer concern.

STEP 2 Perform a visual inspection, checking for collision damage or other possible causes that would affect the operation of the lighting circuit.

STEP 3 Connect a factory or enhanced scan tool with bidirectional control of the control modules to check for proper operation of the affected lighting circuit.

STEP 4 Follow the diagnostic procedure as found in service information to determine the root cause of the problem.

1 The driver noticed that the taillight fault indicator (icon) on the dash was on any time the lights were on.

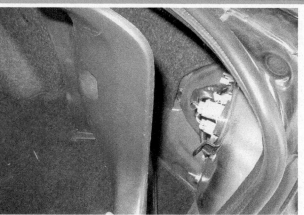

2 A visual inspection at the rear of the vehicle indicated that the right rear taillight bulb did not light. Removing a few screws from the plastic cover revealed the taillight assembly.

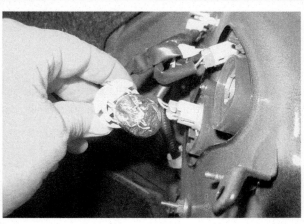

3 The bulb socket is removed from the taillight assembly by gently twisting the base of the bulb counterclockwise.

4 The bulb is removed from the socket by gently grasping the bulb and pulling the bulb straight out of the socket. Many bulbs required that you rotate the bulb 90° (1/4 turn) to release the retaining bulbs.

5 The new 7443 replacement bulb is being checked with an ohmmeter to be sure that it is okay before it is installed in the vehicle.

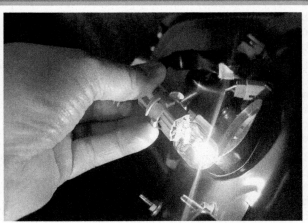

6 The replacement bulb in inserted into the taillight socket and the lights are turned on to verify proper operation before putting the components back together

1. Lighting systems used in older vehicle are not controlled by a computer, usually the body-control module (BCM) as are most of the lighting system on newer vehicles.

2. The number used on automotive bulbs is called the bulb trade number, as recorded with the American National Standards Institute (ANSI). The number is the same regardless of the manufacturer.

3. LEDs are used in many newer vehicles because they light faster, have a longer service life and draw lower amount of current.

4. Turn signals can be operated through a flasher unit or the BCM depending on the make, model and year of the vehicle.

5. Daytime running lights (DRLs) are lights at the front of the vehicle that are on all the time the engine is running, unless they are turned off, or when the headlights are on.

6. High-intensity discharge (HID) headlights produce light that is crisper, clearer, and brighter than light produced by a halogen headlight.

7. An adaptive (or advanced) front lighting system or AFS is a system that mechanically moves the headlights to follow the direction of the front wheels.

8. Automatic headlights will automatically turn on the headlights when the light sensor detects low ambient light level.

9. Automatic dimming mirrors use electrochromic technology to dim the mirror in proportion to the amount of headlight glare from other vehicles at the rear.

REVIEW QUESTIONS

1. Why should the exact same trade number of bulb be used as a replacement?

2. Why is it important to avoid touching a halogen bulb with your fingers?

3. What are the advantages of LED lights?

4. Why are lights controlled by the BCM in many vehicles?

5. What are the conditions needed for an auto dimming headlight system to work?

CHAPTER QUIZ

1. Technician A says that the bulb trade number is the same for all bulbs of the same size.
   Technician B says that a dual-filament bulb has different wattage ratings for each filament. Which technician is correct?
   a. Technician A only
   b. Technician B only
   c. Both Technicians A and B
   d. Neither Technician A nor B

2. Light emitting diodes (LEDs) are used for lighting because they _____.
   a. light quicker (faster illumination)
   b. have longer service life
   c. have lower current draw
   d. Any of the above

3. The correct trade number of bulb always is used for replacement because it _____.
   a. prevents circuit or component damage.
   b. keeps the circuit resistance the same
   c. keeps the circuit current (amperes) the same
   d. All of the above

4. Daytime running lights (DRLs) turn on the _____ when in operation.
   a. headlights in series or separate lights
   b. side marker lights
   c. driving lights
   d. fog lights

5. According to Chart 21–1, which of the following bulbs has two filaments?
   a. 194
   b. 168
   c. 194NA
   d. 1157

6. Which of the lighting systems could result in an electrical shock hazard if proper precautions are not followed?
   a. LED lights
   b. HID lights
   c. Rear fog lights
   d. Driving lights

7. What type of light bulb should not be touched using bare hands?
   a. 1157 or 2057 bulbs
   b. Halogen bulbs
   c. LED bulbs
   d. HID bulbs

8. The "color" of light produced by a light bulb is measured in what unit?
   a. Kelvin degrees
   b. Amperes
   c. Watts
   d. Volts

9. An ambient light sensor is used to control _____.
   a. automatic dimming headlights
   b. automatic headlights
   c. fog lights
   d. daytime running lights (DRLs)

10. A vehicle has a defective brake switch. Which of these systems may not operate properly?
    a. Cruise control
    b. ABS brakes
    c. Shift interlock
    d. Any of the above

DRIVER INFORMATION AND NAVIGATION SYSTEMS

LEARNING OBJECTIVES

After studying this chapter, the reader should be able to:

Help prepare for the ASE Electrical/Electronic Systems (A6) certification test content area "F" (Gauges, Warning Devices, and Driver Information System Diagnosis and Repair).

1. Discuss the diagnosis of oil pressure lamp, temperature lamp, brake warning lamp, and other analog dash instruments.
2. Discuss the operation of head-up display, night vision, and digital electronic displays.
3. Identify the meaning of dash warning symbols.
4. Explain the operation and diagnosis of Telematics systems, backup camera, backup sensor, and lane departure warning system.
5. Describe how a navigation system works.

KEY TERMS

Analog display 337
Backup camera 344
Blind spot monitor 346
Bulb test 335
Digital display 337
EEPROM 342
Electromagnetic parking sensors (EPS) 346
Global positioning system (GPS) 346
Head-up display (HUD) 338
Instrument panel (IP) 335
Instrument panel cluster (IPC) 337
Lane departure warning system (LDWS) 346
Liquid crystal display (LCD) 340

Light-emitting diode (LED) 339
Night vision 338
Nonvolatile random access memory (NVRAM) 342
OnStar 349
Parking assist systems 345
Steering wheel controls 336
Stepper motor 337
Telematics 348
Ultrasonic object sensors 345
Virtual display 340
Voice activation 336
Vacuum tube fluorescent (VTF) 339
WOW display 340

DASH WARNING SYMBOLS

PURPOSE AND FUNCTION

All vehicles are equipped with warning lights on the **instrument panel (IP)** and they are often confusing to drivers. Symbols are used instead of words because they are universal in a global vehicle market. The dash warning lights are often called *telltale* lights as they are used to notify the driver of a situation or fault.

NOTE: Not all vehicles use all of the symbols. Check the owner's manual or service information for the symbols used on the vehicle being checked.

BULB TEST

A **bulb test** is performed when the ignition is first turned on. All of the warning lights come on as part of a self-test, and to help the driver or technician spot any warning light that may be burned out or not operating. Technicians or drivers who are familiar with what lights should light may be able to determine if one or more warning lights are not on when the ignition is first turned on. Most factory scan tools can be used to command all of the warning lights on to help determine if one is not working.

GREEN OR WHITE SYMBOLS

Green or white symbols are used to notify the driver that certain functions are working, such as the headlights are on, or the turn signals have been activated. None of the green or white symbols need any further action by the driver. The blue symbol is used to indicate the high-beam headlights are on. ● **SEE FIGURE 22–1.**

AMBER SYMBOLS

Amber-colored symbols mean that a fault or an issue has occurred that may require attention soon. These can include a warning of low air pressure in a tire, or that the powertrain control module (PCM) has detected a fault in the engine that could affect the exhaust emissions.

While these issues should be addressed, there is no urgency and it is not necessary to stop the vehicle. ● **See FIGURE 22–2.**

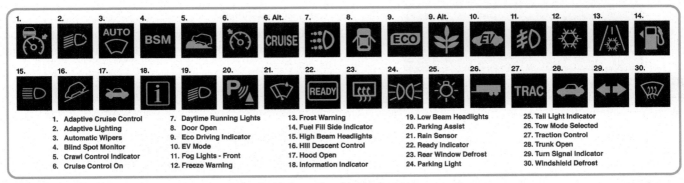

1. Adaptive Cruise Control
2. Adaptive Lighting
3. Automatic Wipers
4. Blind Spot Monitor
5. Crawl Control Indicator
6. Cruise Control On
7. Daytime Running Lights
8. Door Open
9. Eco Driving Indicator
10. EV Mode
11. Fog Lights - Front
12. Freeze Warning
13. Frost Warning
14. Fuel Fill Side Indicator
15. High Beam Headlights
16. Hill Descent Control
17. Hood Open
18. Information Indicator
19. Low Beam Headlights
20. Parking Assist
21. Rain Sensor
22. Ready Indicator
23. Rear Window Defrost
24. Parking Light
25. Tail Light Indicator
26. Tow Mode Selected
27. Traction Control
28. Trunk Open
29. Turn Signal Indicator
30. Windshield Defrost

FIGURE 22–1 Green and blue symbols are used to inform the driver what is in operation.

1. Adaptive Cruise Control
2. Alert Notice
3. All Wheel Lock
4. All Wheel Steer
5. Anti-Lock Brake System Warning
6. Auto Braking Indicator
7. Auxiliary Brake Active
8. Blind Spot Indicator
9. Brake Fluid Low
10. Brake Warning Light Fault
11. Brake Pad Wear Warning
12. Brake Pad Warning - Front
13. Brake Pad Warning - Rear
14. Collision Warning Off
15. Convertible Top Warning
16. Crosswind Assist
17. Diesel Engine Preheat
18. Diesel Particulate Filter Warning
19. Dirty Air Filter
20. Electric Shift Malfunction
21. Exterior Light Fault
22. Four-Wheel-Drive Fault
23. Gas Cap Loose
24. Glow Plug
25. Headlight Range Control
26. Key Fob Battery Low
27. Key Not In Vehicle
28. Lane Departure Warning
29. Low Coolant Level Detected
30. Low Fuel
31. Malfunction Indicator Lamp (MIL)
32. Needs To Be Towed
33. Parking Brake
34. Passenger Airbag Deactivated
35. Press Brake Pedal
36. Press Clutch Pedal
37. Rear Differential Lock
38. Reduced Power
39. Service Required
40. Speed Reduced
41. Stability Control Activated
42. TPMS Warning Lamp
43. Tail Light Out
44. Theft Deterrent
45. Time for Maintenance Indicator
46. Traction Control Fault
47. Trailer Towing Mode
48. Transmission Warning
49. Washer Fluid Low
50. Water in Diesel Fuel
51. Water in Fuel Filter

FIGURE 22–2 Amber warning symbols inform the driver of a potential concern.

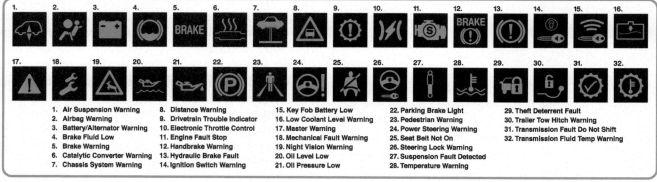

1. Air Suspension Warning	8. Distance Warning	15. Key Fob Battery Low	22. Parking Brake Light	29. Theft Deterrent Fault
2. Airbag Warning	9. Drivetrain Trouble Indicator	16. Low Coolant Level Warning	23. Pedestrian Warning	30. Trailer Tow Hitch Warning
3. Battery/Alternator Warning	10. Electronic Throttle Control	17. Master Warning	24. Power Steering Warning	31. Transmission Fault Do Not Shift
4. Brake Fluid Low	11. Engine Fault Stop	18. Mechanical Fault Warning	25. Seat Belt Not On	32. Transmission Fluid Temp Warning
5. Brake Warning	12. Handbrake Warning	19. Night Vision Warning	26. Steering Lock Warning	
6. Catalytic Converter Warning	13. Hydraulic Brake Fault	20. Oil Level Low	27. Suspension Fault Detected	
7. Chassis System Warning	14. Ignition Switch Warning	21. Oil Pressure Low	28. Temperature Warning	

FIGURE 22–3 Red dash symbols are used to warn the driver of a fault requiring immediate action.

FIGURE 22–4 Steering wheel controls allow the driver to select a function while keeping their hands on the wheel and their eyes on the road.

RED WARNING SYMBOLS Red symbols mean that a serious fault has been detected and that immediate attention is required. An example of a serious fault that requires the driver's attention is the red brake warning light, or the oil pressure warning light. Both of these indicate that a fault has been detected and the vehicle should not be driven further until the cause has been found and corrected. ● **See FIGURE 22–3**

STEERING WHEEL CONTROLS

PURPOSE **Steering wheel controls** are steering wheels that include buttons to allow the driver to control certain audio, vehicle information, and HVAC functions. The purpose of having steering wheel controls is to allow the driver to keep their hands on the wheel and their eyes on the road at all times. Steering wheels that have controls are often called *multi-function steering wheels.* ● **See FIGURE 22–4.**

FUNCTIONS Some of the functions on the steering wheel include the following:

- Radio controls, such as volume up and down and mode selection
- Cruise control
- Telephone answering and calling
- Voice Commands

Check service information for the specified tests and procedures to follow if the steering wheel controls do not operate as designed.

VOICE ACTIVATION

PURPOSE Most recent vehicles include *voice commands,* commonly called **voice activation** that can be used to perform various functions or settings in the vehicle. Most system includes a list of phrases to use to achieve the best results.

FUNCTIONS The typical functions that can be performed using voice commands include the following:

- Phone calls with outgoing or incoming usually tied by Bluetooth to a cell phone in the vehicle.
- Text messages can be read and a response sent using Bluetooth
- Climate control settings, including desired temperature in many vehicles
- Select source of audio, such as radio, USB, or satellite
- Navigation system, including destination and points of interest

Check service information for the specified tests and procedures to follow if the voice commands or the controls do not operate as designed.

MAINTENANCE INDICATORS

PURPOSE AND FUNCTION The purpose of the maintenance reminders is to inform the driver that routine maintenance is needed. The message can include what type of maintenance is needed, such as a minor or a major service, but most messages simply state that service is required soon or service is required now. ● **See FIGURE 22–5.**

RESET MAINTENANCE INDICATORS To reset the maintenance reminder light or message, check the owner's manual, service information. Or visit www.jameshalderman.com and click on "classroom content," and then select "service information" for the procedure to follow for all vehicles.

ANALOG AND DIGITAL DISPLAYS

TERMINOLOGY Vehicle information is displayed on the **instrument panel cluster (IPC)**.

- An **analog display** uses a needle to show the values, such as engine RPM
- A **digital display** uses numbers to indicate values, such as vehicle speed

Analog electromagnetic dash instruments use small electromagnetic coils that are connected to a sending unit for such things as fuel level, water temperature, and oil pressure. The sensors are the same regardless of the type of display used. The resistance of the sensor varies with what is being measured.

STEPPER MOTOR ANALOG GAUGES Most analog dash displays use a stepper motor to move the needle. A **stepper motor** is a type of electric motor that is designed to rotate in small steps

based on the signal from a computer. This type of gauge is very accurate. A digital output is used to control stepper motors. Stepper motors are direct current motors that move in fixed steps or increments from de-energized (no voltage) to fully energized (full voltage). A stepper motor often has as many as 120 steps of motion.

A typical stepper motor uses a permanent magnet and two electromagnets. Each of the two electromagnetic windings is controlled by the computer. The computer pulses the windings and changes the polarity of the windings to cause the armature of the stepper motor to rotate a degree at a time. Each degree pulse is recorded by the computer as a "count" or "step," which explains the name given to this type of motor. ● **See FIGURE 22–6.**

NOTE: Many electronic gauge clusters are checked when the ignition is first turned on, the dash display needles are commanded to 1/4, 1/2, 3/4, and full positions before returning to their normal readings. This self-test allows the service technician to check the operation of each individual gauge, even though replacing the entire instrument panel cluster is usually necessary to repair an inoperative gauge.

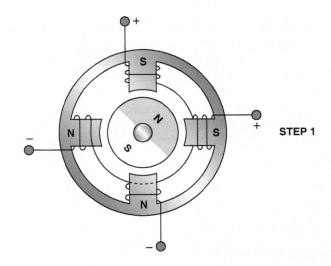

FIGURE 22–5 Maintenance reminders are often messages displayed on the instrument panel informing the driver of needed service, such as the need to change the engine oil.

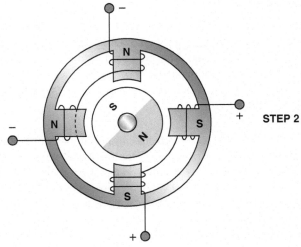

FIGURE 22–6 Most stepper motors use four wires which are pulsed by the computer to rotate the armature in steps.

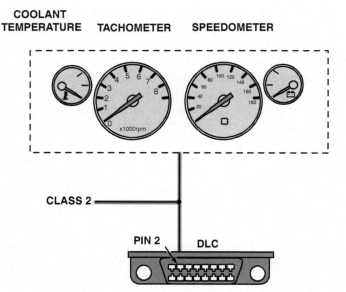

FIGURE 22–7 A typical instrument display uses data from the sensors over serial data lines to the individual gauges.

NETWORK COMMUNICATION Many instrument panels are operated by electronic control units that communicate with the powertrain control module (PCM) for engine data, such as revolutions per minute (RPM) and engine coolant temperature (ECT). The PCM use the voltage changes from variable-resistance sensors, such as that of the fuel gauge, to determine fuel level. The data is transmitted to the instrument cluster, as well as to the PCM through serial data lines. Because all sensor inputs are interconnected, the technician should always follow the factory recommended diagnostic procedures. ● **See FIGURE 22–7**.

HEAD-UP DISPLAY

PURPOSE The **head-up display (HUD)**, also called a *heads-up display*, is a supplemental display that projects the vehicle speed and sometimes other data, such as turn signal information onto the windshield. The projected image looks as if it is some distance ahead, making it easy for the driver to see without having to refocus on a closer dash display. ● **SEE FIGURES 22–8 AND 22–9**.

OPERATION On many vehicles, the brightness of the HUD can be controlled to make it easier for the driver to see the information. The HUD unit is installed in the instrument panel (IP) and uses a mirror to project vehicle information onto the inside surface of the windshield. ● **SEE FIGURE 22–10**.

Follow the vehicle manufacturer's recommended diagnostic and testing procedures if any faults are found with the HUD.

FIGURE 22–8 A typical HUD showing zero miles per hour, which is actually projected on the windshield from the head-up display in the dash.

FIGURE 22–9 The dash-mounted control for the HUD on this Cadillac allows the driver to move the image up and down on the windshield for best viewing.

NIGHT VISION

PURPOSE AND FUNCTION **Night vision** systems use a camera that is capable of observing objects in the dark to assist the driver while driving at night. The primary night viewing illumination devices are the headlights. The night vision option uses a HUD to improve the vision of the driver beyond the scope of the headlights. Using a HUD display allows the driver to keep eyes on the road and hands on the wheel for maximum safety. Besides the HUD, the night vision camera uses a special thermal

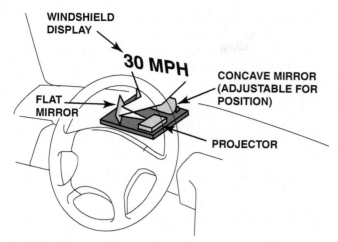

FIGURE 22–10 A typical HUD unit.

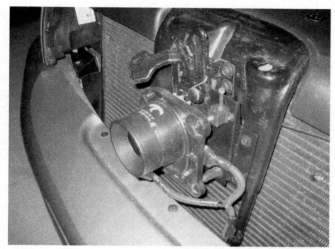

FIGURE 22–11 A night vision camera behind the grille of a Cadillac.

imaging or infrared technology. The camera is mounted behind the grille in the front of the vehicle. ● **SEE FIGURE 22–11**.

OPERATION The camera creates pictures based on the heat energy emitted by objects rather than from light reflected on an object, as in a normal optical camera. The image looks like a black and white photo negative when hot objects (higher thermal energy) appear light or white, and cool objects appear dark or black. Other parts of the night vision system include:

- On/off and dimming switch. This allows the driver to adjust the brightness of the display and to turn it on or off as needed.

- Up/down switch. The night vision HUD system has an electric tilt-adjust motor that allows the driver to adjust the image up or down on the windshield within a certain image.

CAUTION: Becoming accustomed to night vision can be difficult and may take several nights to get used to looking at the HUD.

DIAGNOSIS AND SERVICE The first step when diagnosing a fault with the night vision system is to verify the concern. Check the owner's manual or service information for proper operation. For example, the Cadillac night vision system requires the following actions to function.

1. The ignition has to be in the on (run) position.
2. The Twilight Sentinel photo cell must indicate that it is dark.
3. The headlights must be on.
4. The switch for the night vision system must be on and the brightness adjusted so the image is properly displayed.

Even though the night vision system camera is protected from road debris by a grille, small stones or other debris can get past the grille and damage the lens of the camera. The operation of the night vision can also be affected by an accumulation of heavy ice or snow. If the camera is damaged, it must be replaced as an assembly because no separate parts are available. Always follow the vehicle manufacturer's recommended testing and servicing procedures.

ELECTRONIC DISPLAYS

LIGHT-EMITTING DIODE (LED) All diodes emit some form of energy during operation. The **light-emitting diode (LED)** is a semiconductor that is constructed to release energy in the form of light. Many colors of LEDs can be constructed, but the most popular are red, green, and yellow. Red is difficult to see in direct sunlight, therefore if an LED is used, most vehicle manufacturers use yellow. Light-emitting diodes can be arranged in a group of seven, which then can be used to display both numbers and letters. ● **SEE FIGURE 22–12**.

An LED display requires more electrical power than other types of electronic displays. A typical LED display requires 30 milliamperes for each *segment;* therefore, each number or letter displayed could require 210 milliamperes (0.210 ampere).

VACUUM TUBE FLUORESCENT DISPLAYS The **vacuum tube fluorescent (VTF)** display is a popular automotive and household appliance display because it is very bright and can easily be viewed in strong sunlight.

- The VTF display generates its bright light in a manner similar to that of a TV screen, where a chemical-coated light-emitting element called phosphor is hit with high-speed electrons.

- VTF displays are very bright and must be dimmed by use of dense filters or by controlling the voltage applied to the display. A typical VTF dash is dimmed to 75% brightness whenever the parking lights or headlights are turned on. Some displays use a photocell to monitor and adjust the intensity of the display during daylight viewing. Most VTF displays are green for best viewing under most lighting conditions.

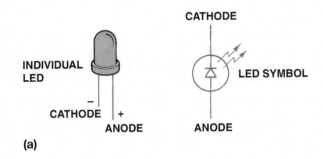

(a)

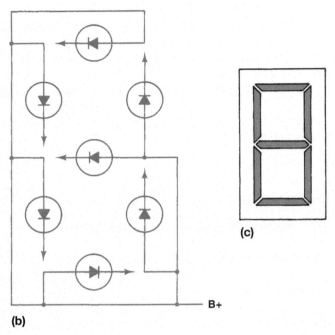

(b)

(c)

FIGURE 22–12 (a) Symbol and line drawing of a typical light-emitting diode (LED). (b) Grouped in seven segments, this array is called a seven-segment LED display with a common anode (positive connection). The dash computer toggles the cathode (negative) side of each individual segment to display numbers and letters. (c) When all segments are turned on, the number 8 is displayed.

LIQUID CRYSTAL DISPLAYS A **Liquid crystal display (LCD)** can be arranged into a variety of forms, letters, numbers, and bar graph displays.

- LCD construction consists of a special fluid sandwiched between two sheets of polarized glass. The special fluid between the glass plates will permit light to pass if a small voltage is applied to the fluid through a conductive film laminated to the glass plates.

- The light from a very bright halogen bulb behind the LCD shines through those segments of the LCD that have been polarized to let the light through, which then show numbers or letters. Color filters can be placed in front of the display to change the color of certain segments of the display, such as the maximum engine speed on a digital tachometer.

- LCD displays can be used to present data in the form of numbers, text messages, or graphical gauges. The

high-resolution screen can be programmed to show several functions, such as navigation, radio and media, as well as Google Earth 3-D graphics, and traffic data. This is in addition to the usual functions of showing speed, engine revolutions, outside temperature and the fuel level.

CAUTION: When cleaning an LCD, be careful not to push on the glass plate covering the special fluid. If excessive pressure is exerted on the glass, the display may be permanently distorted. If the glass breaks, the fluid will escape and could damage other components in the vehicle, as a result of its strong alkaline nature. Use only a soft, damp cloth to clean these displays.

- The major disadvantage of an LCD digital dash is that the numbers or letters are slow to react or change at low temperatures. ● **SEE FIGURE 22–13**.

WOW DISPLAY When a vehicle equipped with a digital dash is started, all segments of the electronic display are turned on at full brilliance for 1 or 2 seconds. This is commonly called the **WOW display** and is used to show off the brilliance of the display. If numbers are part of the display, the number 8 is shown, because this number uses all segments of a number display. Technicians can also use the WOW display to determine if all segments of the electronic display are functioning correctly.

VIRTUAL DISPLAY

PURPOSE AND FUNCTION A **virtual display** is a dash that allows the driver to select what data is being displayed. Many vehicles are equipped with an LCD dash display that can be changed to display various functions based on the driver's preference. This allows the dash display to be totally customized to what the driver wishes to see displayed. For example, a typical display can show any four of the following:

FIGURE 22–13 A typical LCD navigation system display.

FIGURE 22–14 A virtual dash being used to show a navigation screen that takes up all of the center dash area. This driver selectable dash display can show almost any combination of dash instruments to meet the desires of the driver.

- Coolant temperature
- Voltmeter
- Oil pressure
- Vehicle speed (speedometer)
- Engine speed (tachometer)
- Automatic transmission fluid temperature
- Tire pressures for all four tires

OPERATION The dash display is all that is really different because all of the data comes to the IPC on the data bus. The only difference is that the display can be changed to meet the needs of the driver. For example, if a driver is towing a trailer, displaying the automatic transmission fluid temperature would be very helpful so that overheating of the transmission can be avoided. ● **SEE FIGURE 22–14**.

TOUCH SCREENS

PURPOSE A **touch screen** is a dash display, usually LCD, which allows the driver or passenger to use a finger to perform functions that are displayed on the screen.

OPERATION A capacitive touch screen panel consists of an insulator, such as glass, coated with a transparent conductor, such as indium tin oxide (ITO). Because the human body is also an electrical conductor, touching the surface of the screen results in a distortion of the screen's electrostatic field. The location is then sent to the controller for processing. Placing a finger near the electric fields, adds conductive surface area to the capacitive system. This is measurable as a change in capacitance. The capacitance can be changed and measured at every individual point on the grid (intersection). ● **SEE FIGURE 22–15**.

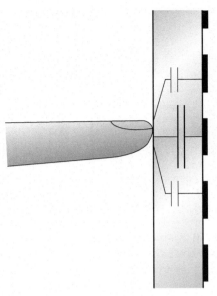

FIGURE 22–15 Schematic of a capacitive touch screen.

TECH TIP

Touch Screen Tip

Most vehicle navigation systems use a touch screen for use by the driver (or passenger) to input information or other on-screen prompts. Most touch screens use a change in capacitance at the surface of the screen to determine when and where some action is being performed. Do not push harder on the display if the unit does not respond, or the display unit may be damaged. If no response is detected when lightly touching the screen, rotate the finger to cause the capacitance area to increase so it can be easily detected.

TOUCH SCREEN FEEDBACK Many touch screens include feedback to the user by either using a beep or a small vibration when the screen is touched. This is called *haptic* response system and helps improve the user experience by giving immediate feedback.

SPEEDOMETERS/ODOMETERS

OPERATION Dash displays use an electric vehicle speed sensor on the output of the transmission or from the input from the wheel speed sensors (WSS). Some vehicles use the ABS WSS to get vehicle speed rather than a dedicated vehicle speed sensor. Many speed sensors contain a permanent magnet and generate a voltage in proportion to the vehicle speed. These speed sensors are commonly called permanent magnet (PM) generators. ● **SEE FIGURE 22–16**.

FIGURE 22–16 A vehicle speed sensor located in the extension housing of the transmission. Some vehicles use the wheel speed sensors for vehicle speed information.

 TECH TIP

Keep the Same Overall Tire Diameter

Whenever larger (or smaller) wheels or tires are installed, the speedometer and odometer calibration are thrown off. This can be summarized as follows:

- **Larger diameter tires.** The speed showing on the speedometer is slower than the actual speed.
- The odometer reading will show fewer miles than actual.
- **Smaller diameter tires.** The speed showing on the speedometer is faster than the actual speed. The odometer reading will show more miles than actual.

To avoid speedometer and odometer issues, select a wheel/tire combination that has the same outside diameter (OD) of the original wheel/tire combination. Many newer vehicles can use the scan tool to change the tire size (from a select group of sizes) to minimize the effects of tires size change on odometer and speedometer readings.

To determine the exact effects of a replacement size wheel or tire, perform an Internet search for a tire size comparison chart.

The output of a PM generator speed sensor is an AC voltage that varies in frequency and amplitude with increasing vehicle speed. The PM generator speed signal is sent to the instrument cluster electronic circuits. These specialized electronic circuits include a buffer amplifier circuit that converts the variable sine wave voltage from the speed sensor to an on/off signal that can be used by other electronic circuits to indicate a vehicle's speed. The vehicle speed is then displayed by either an electronic needle-type speedometer or by numbers on a digital display.

ODOMETERS An odometer is a dash display that indicates the total miles traveled by the vehicle. Electronic dash displays can use either an electrically driven mechanical

(a)

(b)

FIGURE 22–17 (a) Some odometers are mechanical and are operated by a stepper motor. (b) Many vehicles are equipped with an electronic odometer.

odometer or a digital display odometer to indicate miles traveled. On mechanical type odometers, a small electric motor, called a stepper motor, is used to turn the number wheels of a mechanical-style odometer. A pulsed voltage is fed to this stepper motor, which moves in relation to the miles traveled. ● SEE FIGURE 22–17.

Digital odometers use LED, LCD, or VTF displays to indicate miles traveled in the instrument cluster. Because total miles must be retained when the ignition is turned off or the battery is disconnected, a special electronic chip must be used that will retain the miles traveled. These special chips are called **nonvolatile random access memory (NVRAM)**. *Nonvolatile* means that the information stored in the electronic chip is not lost when electrical power is removed. Some vehicles use a chip called electronically erasable programmable read-only memory **(EEPROM)**. Most digital odometers can read up to 999,999.9 miles or kilometers (km), and then the display indicates error. If the chip is damaged or exposed to static electricity, it may fail to operate and "error" may appear.

SPEEDOMETER/ODOMETER SERVICE

If the speedometer and odometer fail to operate, check the following:

- Use a scan tool and monitor the vehicle speed as displayed on the scan tool. If the speed is zero, then check the output from the vehicle, speed sensor. With the vehicle safely raised off the ground and supported so the drive wheels rotate, check the vehicle speed using a scan tool.

- If a scan tool is not available, disconnect the wires from the speed sensor near the output shaft of the transmission. Connect a multimeter set on AC volts to the terminals of the speed sensor, and rotate the drive wheels with the transmission in neutral. A good speed sensor should indicate approximately 2 volts AC if the drive wheels are rotated by hand.

- If the speed sensor is working, check the wiring from the speed sensor to the dash cluster. If the wiring is good, the instrument panel (IP) should be sent to a specialized repair facility.

- If the speedometer operates correctly, but the mechanical odometer does not work, the odometer stepper motor, the number wheel assembly, or the circuit controlling the stepper motor is defective. If the digital odometer does not operate, but the speedometer operates correctly, the dash cluster must be removed and sent to a specialized repair facility.

 CASE STUDY

The Speedometer Works as if It Is a Tachometer

The owner of a Ford F-150 pickup truck complained that all of a sudden the speedometer needle went up and down with engine speed, rather than vehicle speed. In fact, the speedometer needle went up and down with engine speed, even though the gear selector was in "park" and the vehicle was not moving. After hours of troubleshooting, the service technician went back and started checking the basics and discovered that the alternator had a bad diode. The technician measured over 1 volt AC and over 10 amperes AC ripple current using a clamp-on AC/DC ammeter. Replacing the alternator restored the proper operation of the speedometer.

Summary:

- **Complaint**—Customer stated that the speedometer would move in relation to engine speed and not vehicle speed.
- **Cause**—Tests confirmed that the alternator was producing excessive AC voltage due to a bad diode.
- **Correction**—Replacing the alternator restored proper operation of the speedometer.

DASH GAUGES

FUEL LEVEL Fuel level gauges use a fuel tank sending unit that consists of a float attached to a variable resistor. When the fuel level changes, the resistance of the fuel level sending unit also changes. As the resistance of the tank unit changes, the dash-mounted gauge also changes to show the level of the fuel in the tank.

OIL PRESSURE The oil pressure lamp operates through use of an oil pressure sending unit, which is a switch screwed into the engine block, and grounds the electrical circuit. It lights the dash warning lamp in the event of low oil pressure, that is, 3 to 7 PSI (20 to 50 kilopascals [kPa]). Normal oil pressure is generally between 10 and 60 PSI (70 and 400 kPa). Some vehicles are equipped with variable voltage oil pressure sensors rather than a simple pressure switch. ● SEE FIGURE 22–18.

To test the operation of the oil pressure warning circuit, unplug the wire from the oil pressure sending unit, usually located near the oil filter, with the ignition switch on. With the wire disconnected from the sending unit, the warning lamp should be off. If the wire is touched to a ground, the warning lamp should be on. If there is *any* doubt of the operation of the oil pressure warning lamp, always check the actual engine oil pressure, using a mechanical gauge that can be screwed into the opening that is left after unscrewing the oil pressure sending unit. For removing the sending unit, special sockets are available at most auto parts stores, or a 1 inch or 1 1/16 inches 6-point socket may be used for most sending units.

COOLANT TEMPERATURE The "hot" lamp, or engine coolant overheat warning lamp, warns the driver whenever

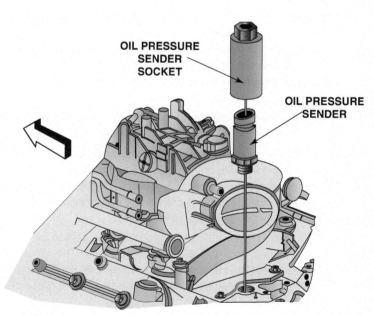

FIGURE 22–18 A sending unit socket being used to remove an oil pressure sender unit.

FIGURE 22–19 A temperature gauge showing normal operating temperature between 180°F and 215°F, depending on the specific vehicle and engine.

the engine coolant temperature is between 248°F and 258°F (120°C and 126°C). Most vehicles use the engine coolant temperature (ECT) sensor for engine temperature gauge operation. To test this sensor, use a scan tool to verify proper engine temperature and follow the vehicle manufacturer's recommended testing procedures. ● **SEE FIGURE 22–19**.

DASH INSTRUMENT DIAGNOSIS If one or more electronic dash gauges do not work correctly, first perform a bulb check. If on a digital dash, check the WOW display that lights all segments to full brilliance whenever the ignition switch is first switched on. If all segments of the display do not operate, the entire electronic cluster must be replaced in most cases. If all segments operate during the WOW display, but do not function correctly afterward, the problem is most often a defective sensor or defective wiring to the sensor. All dash instruments, except the voltmeter, use a variable resistance unit as a sensor for the system being monitored. The electronic dash instruments can be tested using the following procedure:

1. Use a factory or factory level scan tool check for any "B" (body) or "C" (chassis) diagnostic trouble codes (DTCs) that may be set and stored. If a DTC is stored, follow the service information instructions to find the root cause.

2. Use the bidirectional control features on the scan tool to actuate the dash display to see if they function. If not, the replacement of the entire IPC may be required.

3. If just one gauge works when commanded, but does not work in the vehicle, unplug the wire(s) from the sensor for the function being tested. For example, if the oil pressure gauge is not functioning correctly, unplug the wire connector at the oil pressure sending unit.

4. With the sensor wire unplugged, turn the ignition switch on and wait until the WOW display stops. The display for the affected unit should show either fully lighted segments, or no lighted segments, depending on the make of the vehicle and the type of sensor.

Always follow the specified testing and diagnostic procedures found in service information for the vehicle being tested.

BACKUP CAMERA

PARTS AND OPERATION A **backup camera** is used to display the area at the rear of the vehicle in a screen display on the dash, or in the inside rear view mirror when the gear selector is placed in reverse. Backup cameras are also called:

- *Reversing cameras*
- *Rearview cameras*

Backup cameras are different from normal cameras because the image displayed on the dash is flipped so it is a mirror image of the scene at the rear of the vehicle. This reversing of the image is needed because the driver and the camera are facing in opposite directions. Backup cameras were first used in large vehicles with limited rearward visibility, such as motor homes. Many vehicles equipped with navigation systems today include a backup camera for added safety while reversing. ● **SEE FIGURE 22–20**.

The backup camera contains a wide-angle or fisheye lens to give the largest viewing area. Most backup cameras are pointed downward so that objects on the ground, as well as walls, are displayed. ● **SEE FIGURE 22–21**.

REAR CAMERA IMAGE ISSUES The quality of the image projected on the display may be not be clear if any of the following conditions occur:

FIGURE 22–20 A typical view displayed on the navigation screen from the backup camera.

FIGURE 22–21 A typical fisheye-type backup camera usually located near the center on the rear of the vehicle near the license plate.

- Dark conditions
- Damage to the rear camera or the rear of the vehicle, affecting the aiming of the camera
- Dirt, mud, ice, or snow blocking the camera view
- Excessive high or low temperature that could affect the camera or lens
- Glare caused by the sun or a nearby bright light source, such as headlights of another vehicle.

DIAGNOSIS AND SERVICE Faults in the backup camera system can be related to the camera itself, the display, or the connecting wiring. The main input to the display unit comes from the transmission range switch, which signals the backup camera when the transmission is shifted into reverse.

To check the transmission range switch, perform the following:

1. Check if the backup (reverse) lights function when the gear selector is placed in reverse with the key on, engine off (KOEO).
2. Check that the transmission/transaxle is fully engaged in reverse when the selector is placed in reverse.

Most of the other diagnosis involves visual inspection:

1. Check the backup camera for damage.
2. Check the screen display for proper operation.
3. Check that the wiring from the rear camera to the body is not cut or damaged.

Always follow the vehicle manufacturer's recommended diagnosis and repair procedures.

PARKING ASSIST SYSTEMS

COMPONENTS The **parking assist system** is used to help drivers avoid contact with another object while moving slowly. When backing up at speed of less than 5 mph (8 km/h), the system constantly monitors for objects located around the vehicle. The parking assist system can usually detect objects that are greater than 3 inches (8 cm) wide and 10 inches (25 cm) tall, but the system cannot detect objects below the bumper or underneath the vehicle. As the vehicle gets closer to an object, there will be an audible beep out of the speakers, and the time between the beeps becomes shorter. The parking assist system usually includes the following components.

- **Ultrasonic object sensors** built into the fender and front and rear bumper assembly. The ultrasonic proximity detectors are used to measure the distances to nearby objects. The sensors send out acoustic pulses and a control unit measures the return interval of each reflected signal, calculating object distances. ● **SEE FIGURE 22–22**.
- The system warns the driver with warning tones with the frequency indicating object distance. The faster the tone sounds the closer to the object. A continuous tone indicates a minimal predefined distance. Systems may also include visual aids, such as LED or LCD readouts to indicate object distance. A vehicle may include a vehicle pictogram on the infotainment screen. ● **SEE FIGURE 22–23**.

FIGURE 22–22 The small round buttons in the rear bumper are ultrasonic sensors used to sense distance to an object.

FIGURE 22–23 The dash display on a Chevrolet pickup truck showing that an object is being detected at the front and left-front of the vehicle.

 **TECH TIP**

Check for Repainted Bumper

The ultrasonic sensors embedded in the bumper are sensitive to paint thickness because the paint covers the sensors. If the system does not seem to be responding to objects, and if the bumper has been repainted, measure the paint thickness using a nonferrous paint thickness gauge. The maximum allowable paint thickness is 6 mils (0.006 inch or 0.15 millimeter).

■ **Electromagnetic parking sensors (EPS)** detect when a vehicle is moving slowly and towards an object. Once detected, the sensor continues to give signal of presence of the obstacle. If the vehicle then continues to move toward the object, the alarm signal becomes more and more impressive as the obstacle approaches. Electromagnetic parking sensors do not require any holes in the bumper and cannot be seen from the outside of the vehicle.

A **blind spot monitor** is an option that may include more than monitoring the front, rear, and sides of the vehicle. It can include *cross traffic alert*, which can sound an alarm when backing out of a parking space when traffic is approaching from either side.

OPERATION The system is activated automatically when the vehicle is started. The indicator light on the dash or driver information center indicates the system is on. The parking assist system is active from the time the engine is started until the vehicle exceeds a speed of approximately 6 mph (10 km/h). It is also active when the vehicle is backing up. The parking assist system will be automatically reactivated the next time the engine is started, even if the system was turned off by the driver the last time the vehicle was driven.

DIAGNOSIS The parking assist control module is capable of detecting faults and storing diagnostic trouble codes. If a fault has been detected by the control module, the red lamp flashes and the system is disabled. Follow service information diagnostic procedures because the parking assist module cannot usually be accessed using a scan tool.

LANE DEPARTURE WARNING

PARTS AND OPERATION The **lane departure warning system (LDWS)** uses cameras to detect if the vehicle is crossing over lane marking lines on the pavement. Some systems use two cameras, one mounted on each outside rearview mirror. Some systems use infrared sensors located under the front bumper to monitor the lane markings on the road surface. The system names also vary according to vehicle manufacturer, including the following:

Honda/Acura: Lane keep assist system (LKAS)

Toyota/Lexus: Lane monitoring system (LMS)

General Motors: Lane departure warning (LDW)

Ford: Lane departure warning (LDW)

Nissan/Infiniti: Lane departure prevention (LDP) system

If the cameras detect that the vehicle is starting to cross over a lane dividing line, a warning chime will sound or a vibrating mechanism mounted in the driver's seat cushion is triggered on the side where the departure is being detected. This warning will not occur if the turn signal is on in the same direction as detected. ● **SEE FIGURE 22–24.**

DIAGNOSIS AND SERVICE Before attempting to service or repair a lane departure warning system fault, check service information for an explanation on how the system is supposed to work. If the system is not working as designed, perform a visual inspection of the sensors or cameras, checking for damage from road debris or evidence of body damage, which could affect the sensors. After a visual inspection, follow the vehicle manufacturer's recommended diagnosis procedures to locate and repair the fault in the system.

NAVIGATION AND GPS

PURPOSE AND FUNCTION The **global positioning system (GPS)** uses 24 satellites in orbit around the earth to provide signals for navigation devices. GPS is funded and controlled by the U.S. Department of Defense (DOD). While the system can be used by anyone with a GPS receiver, it was designed for and is operated by the U.S. military. ● **SEE FIGURE 22–25.**

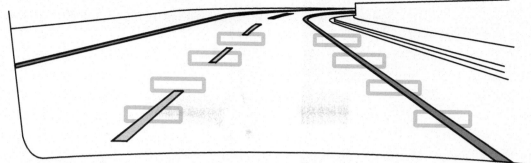

FIGURE 22–24 A lane departure warning system often uses cameras to sense the road lines and warns the driver if the vehicle is not staying within the lane, unless the turn signal is on.

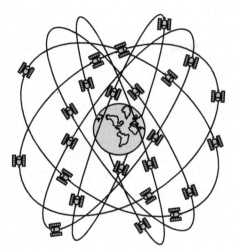

FIGURE 22–25 Global positioning systems use 24 satellites in high earth orbit whose signals are picked up by navigation systems. The navigation system computer then calculates the location based on the position of the satellite overhead.

FIGURE 22–26 A typical GPS display screen showing the location of the vehicle.

1. Screen display ● **SEE FIGURE 22–26.**
2. GPS antenna
3. Navigation control unit, usually with map information on a DVD or memory card.

The memory card includes street names and the following information:

1. Points of interest (POI), including automated teller machines (ATMs), restaurants, schools, colleges, museums, shopping mall, and airports, as well as vehicle dealer locations.
2. Business addresses and telephone numbers, including hotels and restaurants (If the telephone number is listed in the business telephone book, it can usually be displayed on the navigation screen. If the telephone number of the business is known, the location can be displayed.)

NOTE: Private residences or cellular telephone numbers are not included in the database of telephone numbers stored on the navigation system memory card.

3. Turn-by-turn directions to addresses that are selected by the following:
   ■ POI
   ■ Typed in using a keyboard shown on the display

NAVIGATION SYSTEM PARTS AND OPERATION

Navigation systems use the GPS satellites for basic location information. The navigation controller uses other sensors, including a digitized map to display the location of the vehicle.

■ **GPS satellite signals.** Signals from at least three satellites are needed to locate the vehicle.

■ **Yaw sensor.** This sensor is often used inside the navigation unit to detect movement of the vehicle during cornering. This sensor is also called a "g" sensor because it measures force; 1 g is the force of gravity.

■ **Vehicle speed sensor.** A yaw sensor is a device, usually a chip that measures the movement of a vehicle around its vertical axis. This sensor input is used by the navigation controller to determine the speed and distance the vehicle travels. This information is compiled and compared to the digital map and GPS satellite inputs to locate the vehicle.

■ **Audio output/input.** Voice-activated factory units use a built-in microphone at the center top of the windshield and the audio speakers speech output.

Navigation systems include the following components:

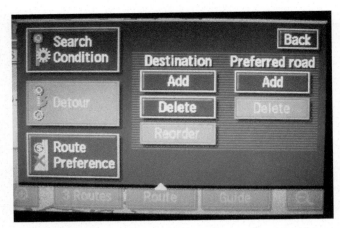

FIGURE 22–27 A typical navigation display showing various options. Some systems do not allow access to these if the vehicle is in gear and/or moving.

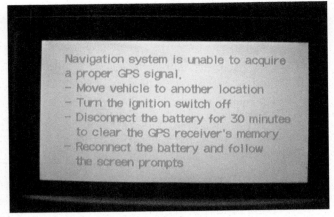

FIGURE 22–28 A screen display of a navigation system that is unable to acquire usable signals from GPS satellites.

The navigation unit then often allows the user to select the fastest way to the destination, as well as the shortest way, or assists in how to avoid toll roads. ● **SEE FIGURE 22–27**.

DIAGNOSIS AND SERVICE For the correct functioning of the navigation system, three inputs are needed:

- Location
- Direction
- Speed

The navigation system uses the GPS satellite and map data to determine a location. Direction and speed are determined by the navigation computer from inputs from the satellite, plus the yaw sensor and vehicle speed sensor. The following symptoms may occur and be a customer complaint. Knowing how the system malfunctions helps to determine the most likely cause.

- If the vehicle symbol jumps down the road, a fault with the vehicle speed (VS) sensor input is usually indicated.
- If the symbol rotates on the screen, but the vehicle is not being driven in circles, a fault with the yaw sensor or yaw sensor input to the navigation controller is likely.
- If the symbol goes off course and shows the vehicle on a road that it is not on, a fault with the GPS antenna is the most common reason.
- Most factory-installed navigation systems use a GPS antenna inside the rear back glass or under the rear package shelf. If a metalized window tint is applied to the rear glass, the signal strength from the GPS satellites can be reduced. If the customer concern includes inaccurate or nonfunctioning navigation, check for window tint.

Sometimes the navigation system itself will display a warning that views from the satellite are not being received. Always follow the displayed instructions. ● **SEE FIGURE 22–28**.

 FREQUENTLY ASKED QUESTION

What Is Navigation-Enhanced Climate Control?

Some vehicles use data from the navigation system to help control the automatic climate control system. Data about the location of the vehicle includes the following:

- Time and date. This information allows the automatic climate control system to determine where the sun is located.
- Direction of travel. The navigation system can also help the climate control system determine the direction of travel.

As a result of the input from the navigation system, the automatic climate control system can control cabin temperature in addition to various other sensors in the vehicle. For example, if the vehicle was traveling south in the late afternoon in July, the climate control system could assume that the passenger side of the vehicle would be warmed more by the sun than the driver's side and could increase the airflow to the passenger side to help compensate for the additional solar heating.

TELEMATICS

WHAT IS TELEMATICS? **Telematics** is an interconnected system that combines telecommunications (cellular systems) and global position system (GPS) navigation satellite system technology. Telematics is a method of monitoring a vehicle by combining a GPS system with on-board diagnostic systems. It is possible to record and map exactly where a vehicle is located and how fast it's traveling.

A typical telematics system includes the following:

- Telecommunications, such as cell phone communication
- Vehicle technologies, such as self-diagnostics
- Electrical sensors, instrumentation, wireless communications
- Multimedia and Internet

Telematics, such as **OnStar**, can be a manufacturer-installed system or an aftermarket-installed system. The systems offer a variety of features, including the following:

1. **Vehicle tracking.** Used by the GPS, an onboard telematics system can track the vehicle location.

2. **User based Insurance (UBI).** Insurance companies want to control their cost so many offer a discount if the vehicle owner allows a tracking device to be installed on their vehicle. This unit usually plugs into the data link connector (DLC) under the dash for its power and ground, as well as, some of the data that is available on the data stream, such as throttle position and vehicle speed.

    NOTE: This type of add-on tracking device is sometimes responsible for some false diagnostic trouble codes. The devices should be removed when diagnosing any suspected vehicle network faults.

3. **Security Services.** Services, such as vehicle-collision notification and emergency services, are the core telematics features found on all systems. When an airbag deploys or other sensors are trigged, the vehicle-collision notification sends an alert to a telematics command center. An operator then contacts the vehicle's occupants through the telematics system's built-in cellular modem to assess the situation. Once the occupants confirm there's been an accident—or if the operator doesn't get a response—the command center dispatches emergency-response personnel. A telematics system also pinpoints the vehicle's location using GPS.

4. **Convenience Services.** Telematics systems offer various convenience features to help vehicle owners out of a non-emergency jam, or just make their lives easier. The system can remotely unlock a car's door after you've accidentally left the keys inside, for example. A telematics system can also flash a car's lights and sound the horn in a crowded parking lot to help you find it.

TELEMATICS SYSTEMS
There are many brand names for what is considered to be a telematics system including the following:

- Acura Link
- Audi Connect
- Blue Link (Hyundai)
- BMW Assist
- Care Track (Volvo)
- Car-Net (VW)
- CUE (Cadillac)

- Honda Link
- InControl (Jaguar)
- IntelliLink (Buick and GMC)
- Lexus Enform
- Mbrace (Mercedes)
- OnStar (Chevrolet and others)
- Porsche Car Connect
- Starlink (Subaru)
- Sync (Ford)
- T Connect (Toyota)
- UVO (Kia)

PARTS AND OPERATION One example of a telematics system is OnStar. OnStar was first introduced in 1996 as an option on some Cadillac models. This is a system that includes the following functions:

1. Cellular telephone
2. Global positioning antenna and computer

The cellular telephone is used to communicate with the driver from advisors at service centers. The advisor at the service center is able to see the location of the vehicle as transmitted from the GPS antenna and computer system in the vehicle on a display.

OnStar does not display the location of the vehicle to the driver unless the vehicle is also equipped with a navigation system. Unlike most navigation systems, the OnStar system requires a monthly fee. The driver interface unit is a group of three buttons mounted on the inside rearview mirror and a hands-free cellular telephone. ● **SEE FIGURE 22–29.**

The OnStar system includes the following features, which can vary, depending on the level of service desired and cost per month.

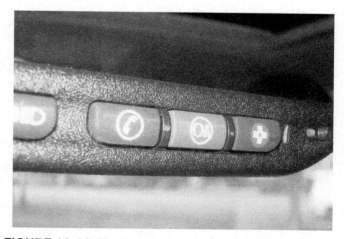

FIGURE 22–29 The three-button OnStar control is located on the inside rearview mirror. The left button (telephone handset icon) is pushed if a hands-free cellular call is to be made. The center button is depressed to contact an OnStar advisor and the right emergency button is used to request that help be sent to the vehicle's location.

- **Automatic notification of airbag deployment.** If the airbag is deployed, the advisor is notified immediately and attempts to call the vehicle. If there is no reply, or if the occupants report an emergency, the advisor will contact emergency services and give them the location of the vehicle.

- **Emergency services.** If the red button is pushed, OnStar immediately locates the vehicle and contacts the nearest emergency service agency.

- **Stolen vehicle location assistance.** If a vehicle is reported stolen, a call center advisor can track the vehicle.

- **Remote door unlock.** An OnStar advisor can send a cellular telephone message to the vehicle to unlock the vehicle if needed.

- **Roadside assistance.** When called, an OnStar advisor can locate a towing company or locate a provider who can bring gasoline or change a flat tire.

- **Accident assistance.** An OnStar advisor is able to help with the best way to handle an accident. The advisor can supply a step-by-step checklist of the things that should be done, plus call the insurance company, if desired.

- **Remote horn and lights.** The OnStar system is tied into the lights and horn circuits so an advisor can activate them if requested to help the owner locate the vehicle in a parking lot or garage.

- **Vehicle diagnosis.** Because the OnStar system is tied to the PCM, an OnStar advisor can help with diagnosis if there is a fault detected. The system works as follows:

- The malfunction indicator light (MIL) (check engine) comes on to warn the driver that a fault has been detected. The driver can depress the OnStar button to talk to an advisor and ask for a diagnosis.

- The OnStar advisor will send a signal to the vehicle requesting the status from the powertrain control module, as well as the controller for the antilock brakes and the airbag module.

- The vehicle then sends any diagnostic trouble codes (DTCs) to the advisor. The advisor can then inform the driver about the importance of the problem and give advice as to how to resolve the problem.

DIAGNOSIS AND SERVICE The OnStar system can fail to meet the needs of the customer if any of the following conditions occur:

1. Lack of cellular telephone service in the area

2. Poor GPS signals, which can prevent an OnStar advisor from determining the position of the vehicle

3. Transport of the vehicle by truck or ferry so that it is out of contact with the GPS satellite in order for an advisor to properly track the vehicle

If all of the above are normal and the problem still exists, follow service information diagnostic and repair procedures. If a new vehicle communication interface module (VCIM) is installed in the vehicle, the electronic serial number (ESN) must be tied to the vehicle. Check service information instructions for the exact procedures to follow.

SUMMARY

1. Green or white symbols are used to notify the driver that certain functions are working. Amber-colored symbols mean that a fault or an issue has occurred that may require attention soon. Red symbols mean that a serious fault has been detected and that immediate attention is required.

2. Most recent vehicles include voice commands, commonly called voice activation that can be used to perform various functions or settings in the vehicle.

3. The purpose of the maintenance reminders is to inform the driver that routine maintenance is needed.

4. The head-up display (HUD), also called a heads-up display, is a supplemental display that projects the vehicle speed and sometimes other data, such as turn signal information onto the windshield.

5. Night vision systems use a camera that is capable of observing objects in the dark to assist the driver while driving at night.

6. Touch screen is a dash display, usually LCD, which allows the driver or passenger to use a finger to perform functions that are displayed on the screen.

7. Dash displays use an electric vehicle speed sensor on the output of the transmission or from the input from the wheel speed sensors (WSS).

8. Fuel level gauges use a fuel tank sending unit that consists of a float attached to a variable resistor.

9. The parking assist system is used to help drivers avoid contact with another object while moving slowly.

10. The lane departure warning system (LDWS) uses cameras to detect if the vehicle is crossing over lane marking lines on the pavement.

11. The global positioning system (GPS) uses 24 satellites in orbit around the earth to provide signals for navigation devices.

12. Telematics is an interconnected system that combines telecommunications (cellular systems) and global position system (GPS) navigation satellite system technology.

1. How does a stepper motor analog dash gauge work?
2. What do the colors of the dash symbols mean?
3. Night vision is used to detect what type of objects?
4. Parking assist systems use what type of sensor?
5. How does a navigation system determine the location of the vehicle?

CHAPTER QUIZ

1. Which color symbol requires immediate attention by the driver?
   a. Red
   b. Amber
   c. Green
   d. White

2. Technician A says that LCDs may be slow to work at low temperatures. Technician B says that an LCD dash display can be damaged if pressure is exerted on the front of the display during cleaning. Which technician is correct?
   a. Technician A only
   b. Technician B only
   c. Both Technicians A and B
   d. Neither Technician A nor B

3. Technician A says that metal-type tinting can affect the navigation system. Technician B says most navigation systems require a monthly payment for use of the GPS satellite. Which technician is correct?
   a. Technician A only
   b. Technician B only
   c. Both Technicians A and B
   d. Neither Technician A nor B

4. Technician A says that the data displayed on the dash can come from the powertrain control module (PCM). Technician B says that the entire dash assembly may have to be replaced even if just one unit fails. Which technician is correct?
   a. Technician A only
   b. Technician B only
   c. Both Technicians A and B
   d. Neither Technician A nor B

5. The WOW display is used to _____.
   a. impress the driver
   b. used as a bulb check to the driver
   c. used as a bulb check for the service technician
   d. Any of the above

6. What do most touch screens use to detect the presence of a human finger?
   a. Infrared sensors
   b. A change in the capacitance
   c. Temperature
   d. Radio frequency interference (RFI)

7. Where are the total miles traveled stored in a vehicle equipped with an electronic odometer?
   a. LCD
   b. NVRAM
   c. LED
   d. VTF

8. A backup camera can show a poor quality image on the interior display if what occurs?
   a. Ice or snow on the camera
   b. Bright lights aimed at the camera
   c. Extreme temperatures
   d. Any of the above

9. The vehicle symbol jumps down the road on a vehicle equipped with an on-board navigation. What is the most likely cause?
   a. A defective yaw sensor
   b. A defective vehicle speed (VS) sensor or a fault in the circuits
   c. A fault with the GPS antenna
   d. Metalized window tint

10. A parking assist system works to warn the driver if the vehicle is getting closed to an object. What type of object cannot be detected by most systems?
    a. Objects larger than 3 inches (8 cm) wide
    b. Objects larger than 10 inches (25 cm) high
    c. Objects under the vehicle
    d. Any of the above

chapter 23

SAFETY, COMFORT, AND CONVENIENCE CIRCUITS

LEARNING OBJECTIVES

After studying this chapter, the reader should be able to:

1. Describe how the horn operates and diagnose faulty horn operation.
2. Explain the testing and diagnosis of windshield wipers and windshield washers.
3. Describe the operation of cruise control, including radar cruise control systems.
4. Discuss electrically heated rear window defogger systems.
5. Explain the operation and testing procedures for power windows and locks.
6. Discuss the operation of power sunroofs, moon roofs, and sun shades.
7. Describe the operation of power seats and heated/cooled seats, plus heated steering wheels and mirrors.
8. Explain the operation of adjustable pedals.
9. Describe the operation and diagnosis of remote keyless entry and remote start systems.

This chapter will help you prepare for the ASE Electrical/Electronic Systems (A6) certification test content area "G" (Repair Body Electrical Systems Diagnosis and Repair).

KEY TERMS

Automatic reversal systems (ARS) 368
Cruise control 360
Electric adjustable pedals (EAP) 374
Heated rear window defogger 365
Heated seats 373
Heated steering wheel 374
Horns 353
Lumbar support 372

Moon roof 370
Power windows 366
Pulse wipers 355
Radar cruise control system 362
Rain-sense wipers 358
Remote start 378
Sun roof 370
Sun shades 370
Variable-delay wipers 355
Windshield wipers 354

HORNS

PURPOSE AND FUNCTION **Horns** are electric devices that emit a loud sound to alert other drivers or persons in the area. Horns are manufactured in several different tones, ranging from 1,800 to 3,550 Hz, and must be heard from a minimum distance of 200 feet (60 meters). Vehicle manufacturers select from various horn tones for a particular vehicle sound. ● **SEE FIGURE 23–1.**

When two horns are used, each has a different tone, yet the sound combines when both are operated. Most horns since 2000 have used the body control module (BCM) to control the actual operation.

HORN CIRCUITS Automotive horns usually operate on full battery voltage wired from the battery, through a fuse, switch, and then to the horns. Most vehicles use a horn relay and the horn button on the steering wheel or column completes a circuit to ground that closes the control side of the relay. The heavy current flow required to operate the horn travels through the load side of the relay to the horn. ● **SEE FIGURE 23–2.**

COMPUTER-CONTROLLED HORNS On most recent model vehicles, the horn button is an input to the BCM or electronic control unit (ECU). The BCM controls the operation of the horn relay. The horn relay may also be controlled by the BCM, which "beeps" the horn when the vehicle is locked or unlocked, using the key fob remote and can be sounded by the alarm system. Check service information for the exact details about the horn circuit for the vehicle being checked. ● **SEE FIGURE 23–3.**

HORN OPERATION A vehicle horn is an actuator that converts an electrical signal to sound. The horn circuit has an armature (a coil of wire) and contacts that are attached to a diaphragm. When energized, the armature causes the diaphragm to move up, which then opens a set of contact points that de-energize the armature circuit. As the diaphragm moves down, the contact points close re-energizing the armature circuit, and the diaphragm moves up

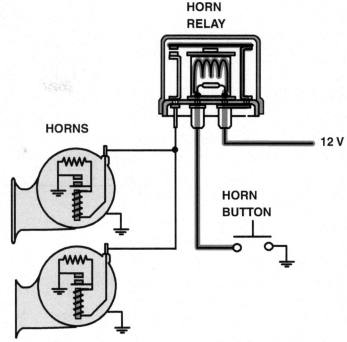

FIGURE 23–2 A simplified horn circuit where the horn button completes the ground circuit of the relay coil.

again. This rapid opening and closing of the contact points causes the diaphragm to vibrate at an audible frequency. The sound created by the diaphragm is magnified as it travels through a trumpet attached to the diaphragm chamber. Most horn systems typically use one or two horns, but some have up to four. Those with multiple horns use both high- and low-pitch units to achieve a harmonious tone. Only a high-pitched unit is used in single-horn applications. The horn assembly is marked with an "H" or "L" for pitch identification.

HORN DIAGNOSIS

SCAN TOOL TESTING A scan tool can be used to test a horn that is computer controlled by using the bi-directional feature of a factory or factory-level aftermarket scan tool. Because most horn buttons are an input to the BCM or similar module, a scan tool can often be used to command the horn to sound. Check service information for the vehicle being tested for the exact tests and testing procedures to follow.

HORN CIRCUIT TESTING Once the cause of an inoperative horn has been reduced to the horn wiring circuit, the wiring needs to be checked. Typically, a digital multimeter (DMM) is used to perform voltage drop and continuity checks to isolate the failure. A momentary contact switch, horn button, is used to sound the horn. The horn switch is mounted to the steering wheel in or near the center of the steering column.

FIGURE 23–1 Two horns are used on this vehicle. Many vehicles use only one horn, often hidden underneath the vehicle.

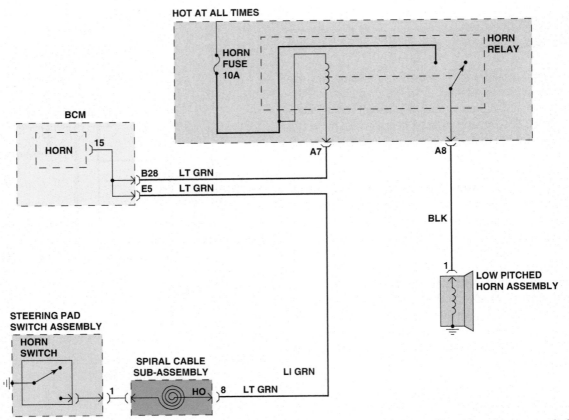

FIGURE 23–3 A typical schematic of a horn circuit. Note that the horn relay can be activated by either the horn switch in the steering wheel or by the BCM.

CAUTION: If the steering wheel needs to be removed for diagnosis or repair of the horn circuit, follow service information procedures for disarming the airbag circuit prior to removing the steering wheel, and for the specified test equipment to use.

On most recent-model vehicles, the horn relay is located in a centralized power distribution center along with other relays, circuit breakers, and fuses. Check the relay to determine if the coil is being energized and if current passes through the power circuit when the horn switch is depressed. Check service information for the exact diagnosis and horn replacement procedures to follow.

HORN REPLACEMENT Horns are generally mounted on the radiator core support by bolts and nuts or sheet metal screws. To replace a horn, remove the fasteners and lift the old horn from its mounting bracket. Clean the attachment area on the mounting bracket and chassis before installing the new horn. Some models use a corrosion-resistant mounting bolt to ensure a ground connection.

WINDSHIELD WIPERS

PURPOSE AND FUNCTION **Windshield wipers** are used to keep the viewing area of the windshield clear of rain. Windshield wiper systems and circuits vary greatly between manufacturers,

as well as between models. Some vehicles combine the windshield wiper and windshield washer functions into a single system. Many minivans and sport utility vehicles (SUVs) also have a rear window wiper and washer system that works independently of the windshield system. Generally, all windshield and rear window wiper and washer systems operate in a similar fashion. Wiper control switches are installed on the steering column usually as part of a multifunction switch that controls several other functions.

COMPUTER-CONTROLLED WIPERS Most wipers, since the 1990s, have used the BCM to control the actual operation of the wiper. The wiper controls are an input to the control module and may also turn on the headlights whenever the wipers are on, which is the law in some states. ● **SEE FIGURE 23–4.**

WIPER AND WASHER COMPONENTS A typical combination wiper and washer system consists of the following:

- Wiper motor(s)
- Gearbox
- Wiper arms and linkage
- Wiper blades
- Washer pump
- Hoses and jets (nozzles)
- Fluid reservoir

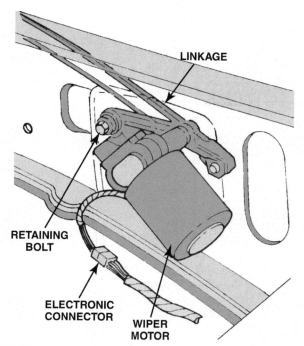

FIGURE 23–4 The motor and linkage bolt to the body and connect to the switch with a wiring harness.

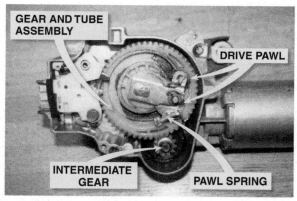

FIGURE 23–5 A typical wiper motor with the housing cover removed. The motor itself has a worm gear on the shaft that turns the small intermediate gear, which then rotates the gear and tube assembly, which rotates the crank arm (not shown) that connects to the wiper linkage.

- Combination switch
- Wiring and electrical connectors
  - ● SEE FIGURE 23–5.

WINDSHIELD WIPER MOTORS
The windshield wipers ordinarily use a special two-speed electric motor. Some are compound-wound motors, a motor type which provides for two different speeds.

- Series-wound field
- Shunt field

One speed is achieved in the series-wound field and the other speed in the shunt-wound field. Other wiper motors are of the permanent magnet-type. ● SEE FIGURE 23–6.

WIPER MOTOR OPERATION
Wiper motors using a permanent magnet motor have a low-speed positive brush, a high-speed positive brush and a ground (negative) brush. The brushes connect the battery to the internal windings of the motor, and the two brushes provide for two different motor speeds. The ground brush is directly opposite the low-speed brush. The high-speed brush is off to the side of the low speed brush. When current flows through the high-speed brush, there are fewer turns on the armature between the hot and ground brushes, and therefore, the resistance is less. With less resistance, more current flows and the armature revolves faster.

PARK POSITION
Windshield wiper motor park operation is controlled by the wiper motor module using an input from the park switch within the wiper motor assembly. When the windshield wiper/washer switch is turned to the OFF position while the wiper blades are somewhere on the windshield, the wiper motor module will continue to operate the wiper motor until the wipers reach the park position. Check service information for the exact operation for the vehicle being serviced.

VARIABLE WIPERS
The **variable-delay wipers** (also called **pulse wipers**) is a term used to describe the operation of the wipers that operate on an interval that can be delayed when the rain is light. Older vehicles use an electronic circuit with a variable resistor that controls the time of the charge and discharge of a capacitor. The charging and discharging of the capacitor controls the circuit for the operation of the wiper motor. On newer vehicles the wipers are controlled by the BCM with input from the driver using a knob or dial to adjust the wiper interval.

WINDSHIELD WIPER DIAGNOSIS
If the windshield wipers are not working, use a factory or factory-level scan tool and check for operation using the bi-directional controls.

- If the wipers function when commanded by the scan tool, check service information for the exact procedures

 FREQUENTLY ASKED QUESTION

How Do Wipers Park?
Some vehicles have wiper arms that park lower than the normal operating position so they are hidden below the hood when not in operation. This is called a *depressed park position*. When the wiper motor is turned off, the park switch allows the motor to continue to turn until the wiper arms reach the bottom edge of the windshield. Then the park switch reverses the current flow through the wiper motor, which makes a partial revolution in the opposite direction.

The wiper linkage pulls the wiper arms down below the level of the hood and the park switch is opened, stopping the wiper motor.

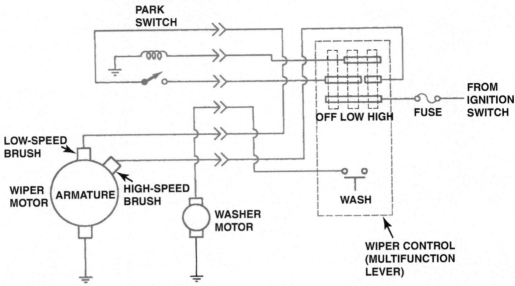

RUN—CLOSED BY RELAY
PARK—OPENED BY MECHANICAL LEVER

FIGURE 23–6 A wiring diagram of a two-speed windshield wiper circuit using a three-brush, two-speed motor. The dashed line for the multifunction lever indicates that the circuit shown is only part of the total function of the steering column lever.

to follow when checking the switch input and BCM connections.

- If the wipers do not function when being commanded by the scan tool, perform circuit testing, which usually includes determining if the fault is electrical or mechanical. ● **SEE FIGURE 23–7**.

To determine if there is an electrical or mechanical problem, access the motor assembly and disconnect the wiper arm linkage from the motor and gearbox. If the motor operates, but the wipers do not, check for the following:

- Stripped gears in the gearbox or stripped linkage connection
- Loose or separated motor-to-gearbox connection
- Loose linkage to the motor connection

If the motor does not shut off, check for the following:

- Defective park switch inside the motor
- Defective wiper switch
- Poor ground connection at the wiper switch

WIPER MOTOR REPLACEMENT Wiper motors are replaced if defective. The motor usually mounts on the bulkhead (firewall). Bulkhead-mounted units are accessible from under the hood, while the cowl panel needs to be removed to service a motor mounted in the cowl. ● **SEE FIGURE 23–8**.

REAR WIPERS Rear window wiper motors are generally located inside the rear hatch panel on vehicles with a hatchback or lift gate. After removing the trim panel covering the motor, replacement is essentially the same as replacing the front wiper motor.

WINDSHIELD WASHERS

OPERATION Windshield washers are used to squirt washer fluid onto the surface of the windshield where it can help dissolve debris and clean the viewing area of the windshield when the wipers are used. Most vehicle windshield washers use a positive-displacement or centrifugal-type washer pump located in the washer reservoir. A momentary contact switch, which is often part of a steering column–mounted combination switch assembly, energizes the washer pump. Washer pump switches are installed either on the steering column or on the instrument panel. The nozzles can be located on the bulkhead, in the hood or mounted as part of the wiper arms, depending on the vehicle.

REAR WASHERS Vehicles equipped with a rear wiper will also be equipped with a rear washer. The rear washer may share a fluid reservoir with the front wipers or it may have its own reservoir. The rear washer switch is located on either the steering column or on the instrument panel.

HEADLIGHT WASHERS Many vehicles are equipped with headlight washers that spray washer fluid into the surface of the headlights when actuated. Some systems even include small wiper blades. Headlight washers are usually operated from the main headlight control switch, if equipped. Most headlight washers use the same windshield washer reservoir as is used for the front windshield washers.

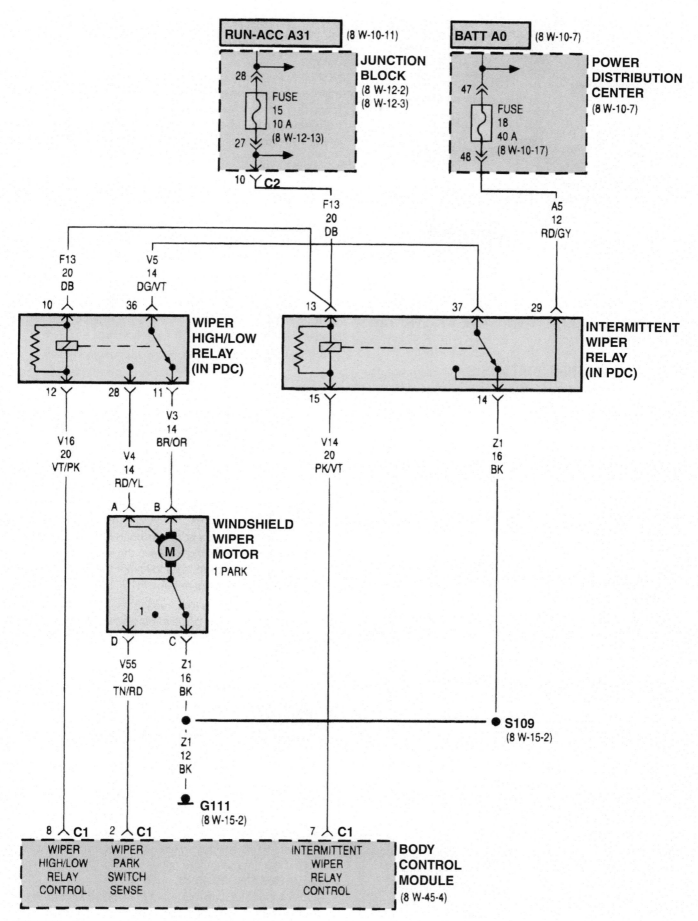

FIGURE 23–7 A circuit diagram is necessary to troubleshoot a windshield wiper problem.

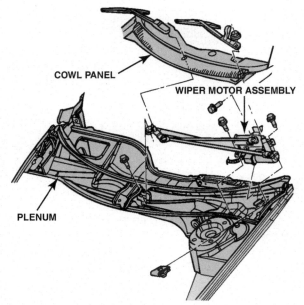

FIGURE 23–8 The wiper motor and linkage mount under the cowl panel on many vehicles.

WINDSHIELD WASHER DIAGNOSIS To diagnose the washer system, follow service information procedures that usually include the following steps:

TECH TIP

Scan Tool Bidirectional Control

Most vehicles built since 2000 can have the lighting and accessory circuits checked using a scan tool. A technician can use the following:
Factory scan tool, such as the following:

- Tech 2 or Multiple Diagnostic Interface (MDI) (General Motors vehicle)
- DRB III, Star Scan, Star Mobile, WiTech or MicroPOD II (Chrysler-Jeep vehicles)
- New Generation Star or IDS (Ford)
- Honda Diagnostic System (HDS)
- TIS Tech Stream (Toyota/Lexus)

An enhanced aftermarket scan tool has body bidirectional control capability, including the following:

- Snap-on Modis, Solus, or Verus
- OTC Genisys
- AutoEnginuity

Using a bidirectional scan tool allows the technician to command the operation of electrical accessories, such as horns, windows, lights, door locks, and wipers. ● SEE FIGURE 23–9.

If the circuit operates correctly when commanded by the scan tool and does not function using the switch(s), follow service information instructions for the exact tests and testing procedures to follow for the vehicle being tested.

STEP 1 To quick check any washer system, make sure the reservoir has fluid and is not frozen. Then, disconnect the pump hose and operate the washer switch.

NOTE: Always use good-quality windshield washer fluid from a closed container to prevent contaminated fluid from damaging the washer pump. Radiator antifreeze (ethylene glycol) should *never* be used in any windshield wiper system.

● SEE FIGURE 23–10.

STEP 2 If fluid squirts from the pump, the delivery system is at fault, not the motor, switch, or the electrical circuits (switch input, BCM etc.).

STEP 3 If no fluid squirts from the pump, the problem is most likely a circuit failure, defective pump, or faulty switch.

STEP 4 A clogged reservoir screen also may be preventing fluid from entering the pump.

WINDSHIELD WASHER SERVICE When a fluid delivery problem is indicated, check for the following:

- Blocked, pinched, broken, or disconnected hoses
- Clogged nozzles
- Blocked washer pump outlet

If the pump motor does not operate, check for battery voltage available at the pump while operating the washer switch.

- If voltage is available and the pump does not run, check for continuity on the pump ground circuit.
- If there is no voltage drop on the ground circuit, replace the pump motor. If battery voltage is not available at the motor, check for power through the washer switch.
- If voltage is available at and through the switch, there is a problem in the wiring between the switch and pump. Perform voltage drop tests to locate the fault. Repair the wiring as needed and retest.

Washer motors are not repairable and are replaced if defective. Centrifugal or positive-displacement pumps are located on or inside the washer reservoir tank or cover. ● SEE FIGURE 23–11.

RAIN-SENSE WIPERS

PARTS AND OPERATION **Rain-sense wiper** systems use a sensor located on the inside and at the top of the windshield to detect rain droplets. This sensor is often called the *rain-sense module (RSM)*. It determines and adjusts the time delay of the wiper based on how much moisture it detects on the windshield. The wiper switch can be left on the sense position all of the time, and if no rain is sensed, the wipers will not swipe. ● SEE FIGURE 23–12.

The control knob is rotated to the desired wiper sensibility level. The microprocessor in the RSM sends a command to the

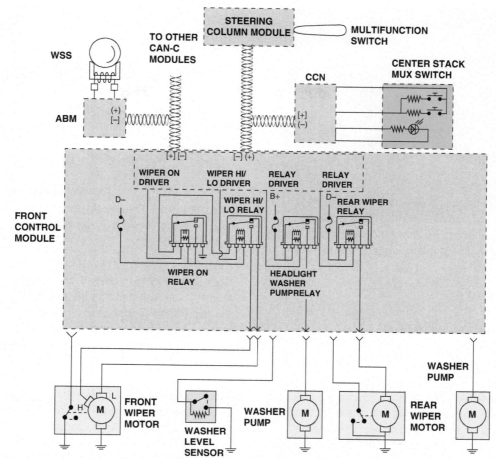

FIGURE 23–9 A typical schematic showing how a scan tool connected to the CAN bus could be used to operate the components connected to the bus.

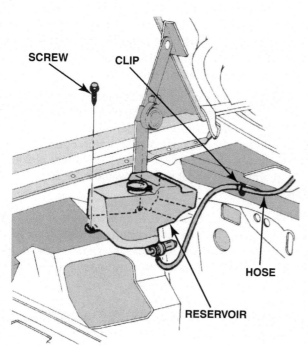

FIGURE 23–10 A typical windshield washer reservoir and pump assembly.

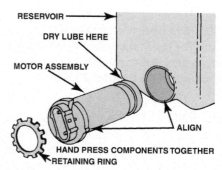

FIGURE 23–11 Washer pumps usually install into the reservoir and are held in place with a retaining ring.

body control module. The rain-sense module is a triangular- or rectangle -shaped black plastic housing. Fine openings on the windshield side of the housing are fitted with eight convex clear plastic lenses. The unit contains four infrared (IR) diodes, two photocells, and a microprocessor.

The IR diodes generate IR beams that are aimed by four of the convex optical lenses near the base of the module through the windshield glass. Four additional convex lenses near the top of the RSM are focused on the IR light beam on the outside of the windshield glass and allow the two photocells to sense changes

FIGURE 23–12 A typical rain-sensing module located on the inside of the windshield near the inside rearview mirror.

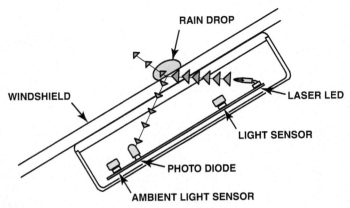

FIGURE 23–13 The electronics in the rain-sense wiper module can detect the presence of rain drops under various lighting conditions.

TECH TIP

Rain Sense and Cruise Control

The rain-sense wiper module communicates with the BCM over the data links and if the rain is heavy, a signal is sent to deactivate the cruise control. A message is then displayed on the instrument panel warning that the cruise control is not available. This is normal operation and is used to help prevent the vehicle from hydroplaning during heavy rain. Normal cruise control operation will resume when the rain intensity is reduced. This is normal operation and not a fault with the cruise control system.

in the intensity of the IR light beam. When sufficient moisture accumulates, the RSM detects a change in the monitored IR light beam intensity. The RSM processes the rain-intensity signal and sends it over the data BUS to the BCM, which then commands a swipe of the wiper. ● **SEE FIGURE 23–13.**

DIAGNOSIS AND SERVICE
If there is a complaint about the rain-sense wipers not functioning correctly, check the owner's manual to be sure that they are properly set. Also, verify that the windshield wipers are functioning correctly on all speeds before diagnosing the rain sensor circuits. Most rain-sensing wiper systems can be tested by misting water on the windshield in the area of the sensor. Always follow the vehicle manufacturer's recommended diagnosis and testing procedures.

CRUISE CONTROL

PURPOSE AND FUNCTION
Cruise control, also called vehicle *speed control*, is used to maintain a preset vehicle speed even up gentle grades. Some vehicles are programmed to downshift the transmission to maintain the vehicle speed

when descending grades if the speed increases more than 5 mph (7 km/h) faster than the preset speed. Using cruise control avoids the tendency to drive at varying speeds, helps to reduce driver fatigue, and allows for driver position changes when driving for a long period of time. Cruise control should be avoided if driving on curving roads or when it is raining.

CRUISE CONTROL OPERATION
A typical cruise control system can be set only if the vehicle speed is 25 mph (40 km/h) or more. Older systems use a throttle actuator to control the throttle opening, control switches for driver control of cruise control functions, and electrical brake and clutch (if equipped) pedal release switches. The typical actuator uses is a stepper motor to move the throttle linkage based on commands from the cruise control module, which is often inside the cruise control assembly. ● **SEE FIGURE 23–14.**

NOTE: Older Toyota-built vehicles do not retain the set speed in memory if the vehicle speed drops below 25 mph (40 km/h). The driver is required to set the desired speed again. This is normal operation and not a fault with the cruise control system.

Most computer-controlled cruise control systems use the vehicle's speed sensor input to the powertrain control module (PCM) for speed reference. Older cruise control systems also use an actuator to control the throttle opening, as well as control switches for driver control, electrical brake, and clutch (if equipped) pedal release switches. ● **SEE FIGURE 23–15.**

CAUTION: Always follow the manufacturer's recommended safety switch adjustment procedures. If the brake safety switch(s) is misadjusted, it could keep pressure applied to the master brake cylinder, resulting in severe damage to the braking system.

ELECTRONIC THROTTLE CRUISE CONTROL
Many vehicles are equipped with an electronic throttle control (ETC) system. Vehicles equipped with such a system do not use throttle actuators for the cruise control; instead, they use the electronic throttle to control vehicle speed. ● **SEE FIGURE 23–16.**

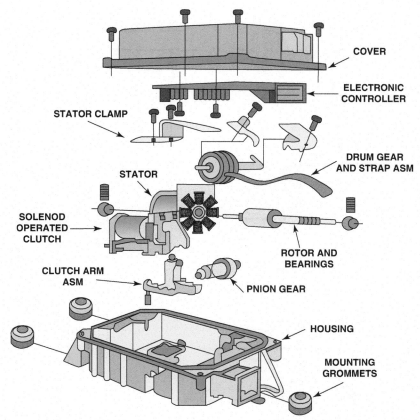

COVER

ELECTRONIC CONTROLLER

STATOR CLAMP

DRUM GEAR AND STRAP ASM

STATOR

SOLENOD OPERATED CLUTCH

ROTOR AND BEARINGS

CLUTCH ARM ASM

PNION GEAR

HOUSING

MOUNTING GROMMETS

FIGURE 23–14 An exploded view of a cruise control assembly used on a vehicle that does not have an electronic throttle. The stepper motor is connected to the throttle of the engine and is used to increase or decrease engine speed to maintain the set speed.

TECH TIP

Bump Problems

Cruise control problem diagnosis can involve a complex series of checks and tests. The troubleshooting procedures vary among manufacturers (and year), so a technician should always check service information for the exact vehicle being serviced. However, every cruise control system uses a brake safety switch and, if the vehicle has manual transmission, a clutch safety switch. The purpose of these safety switches is to ensure that the cruise control system is disabled if the brakes or the clutch are applied. Some systems use a redundant brake pedal safety switch. If the cruise control "cuts out" or disengages itself while traveling over bumpy roads, the most common cause is a misadjusted brake (and/or clutch) safety switch(s). Often, a simple readjustment of these safety switches will cure the intermittent cruise control disengagement problems.

The cruise control on a vehicle equipped with an electronic throttle control system consists of a switch to set the desired speed. The PCM receives the vehicle speed information from the vehicle speed (VS) sensor. The PCM then commands the ETC throttle to open or close the throttle valve as needed to maintain desired vehicle speed.

DIAGNOSIS AND SERVICE Any fault in the accelerator pedal position (APP) sensor, brake switch, or ETC system will disable the cruise control function. Always follow the specified troubleshooting procedures, which will usually include the use of a scan tool to properly diagnose the ETC system.

TECH TIP

Check the Brake Lights

On many vehicles, the cruise control will not work if the brake lights are not working. This includes the third brake light, commonly called the center high-mounted stop light (CHMSL). Always check for the proper operation of the brake lights first if the cruise control does not work.

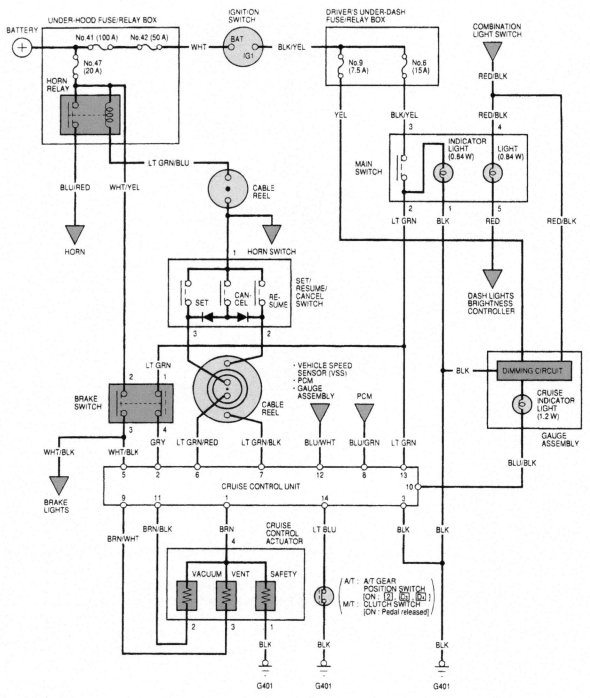

FIGURE 23–15 Circuit diagram of a typical electronic cruise control system.

RADAR CRUISE CONTROL

PURPOSE AND FUNCTION The purpose of a **radar cruise control system**, often called *adaptive cruise control (ACC)*, is to give the driver more control over the vehicle by keeping an assured clear distance, usually 2 to 3 seconds, behind the vehicle in front. If the vehicle in front slows, the radar cruise control detects the slowing vehicle and automatically reduces the speed of the vehicle to keep a safe distance. Then, if the vehicle speeds up, the

radar cruise control also allows the vehicle to increase to the preset speed. This makes driving in congested areas easier and less tiring.

TERMINOLOGY Depending on the manufacturer, radar cruise control is also referred to as the following:

- Adaptive cruise control (Audi, Chrysler, Ford, General Motors, and Hyundai)
- Dynamic cruise control (BMW, Toyota/Lexus)
- Active cruise control (Mini Cooper, BMW)
- Autonomous cruise control (Mercedes)

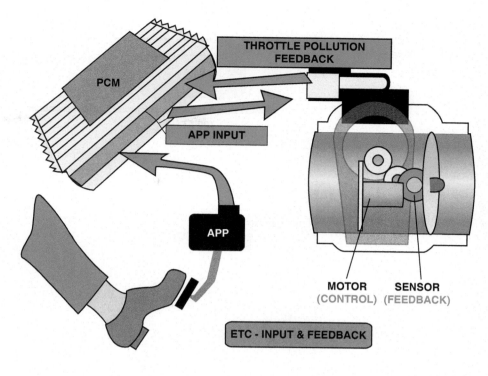

FIGURE 23–16 The electronic throttle control (ETC) system uses a sensor that measures the position and the speed of the driver's foot on the accelerator pedal. A throttle position sensor measures the throttle angle. An electric motor operates the movement of the throttle plate using commands from the PCM.

THROTTLE POLLUTION FEEDBACK

PCM

APP INPUT

APP

MOTOR
(CONTROL)

SENSOR
(FEEDBACK)

ETC - INPUT & FEEDBACK

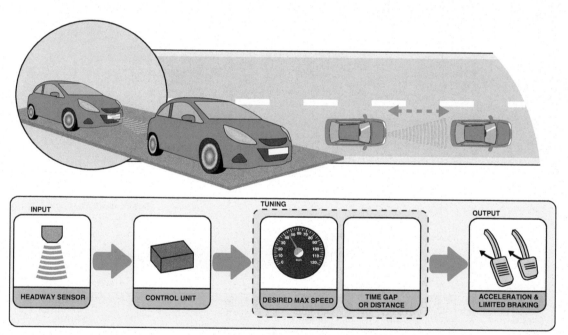

INPUT

TUNING

OUTPUT

HEADWAY SENSOR

CONTROL UNIT

DESIRED MAX SPEED

TIME GAP OR DISTANCE

ACCELERATION & LIMITED BRAKING

FIGURE 23–17 Adaptive cruise control can use radar to determine the distance of another vehicle in front. The control unit then checks the driver selected speed and the sets the distance between the vehicles to determine what action is needed. The PCM then can operate the throttle or the brakes through the antilock brake/electronic stability control system to slow the vehicle if needed to maintain the set distance.

Radar cruise control uses forward-looking radar to sense the distance to the vehicle in front and maintains an assured clear distance. This type of cruise control system works within the following conditions.

1. Speeds from 20 to 100 mph (30 to 161 km/h)

2. Designed to detect objects as far away as 500 ft. (150 m)

The cruise control system is able to sense both distance and relative speed. ● **SEE FIGURE 23–17.**

PARTS AND OPERATION Radar cruise control systems use long-range radar (LRR) to detect faraway objects in front of the moving vehicle. Some systems use a short-range radar (SRR) and/or infrared (IR), or optical cameras to detect

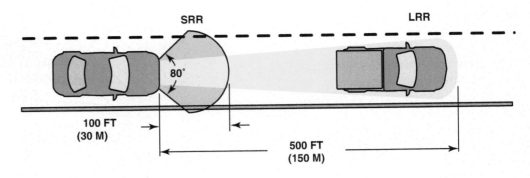

FIGURE 23–18 Most radar cruise control systems use radar, both long and short range. Some systems use optical or infrared cameras to detect objects.

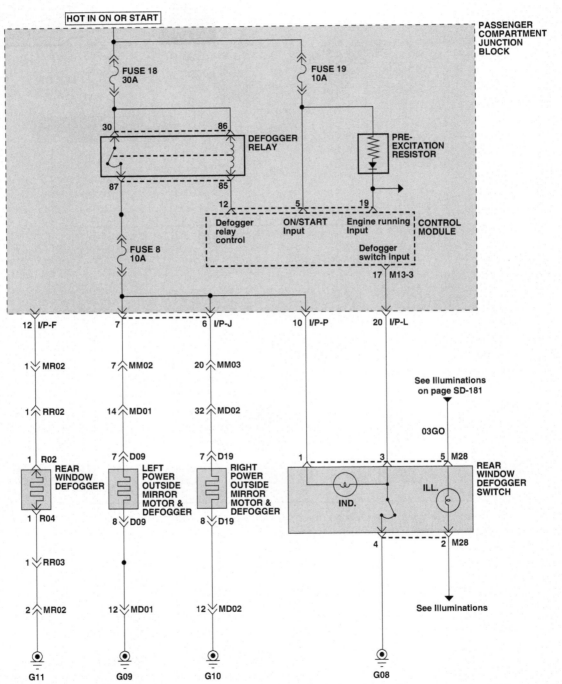

FIGURE 23–19 A schematic showing that the side view mirrors are heated along with the rear window defogger whenever the rear window switch (lower right) is turned to the on position.

Will Radar Cruise Control Set Off My Radar Detector?

It is doubtful. The radar used for radar cruise control systems operates on frequencies that are not detectable by police radar detector units. Cruise control radar works on the following frequencies:

- 76 to 77 GHz (long range)
- 24 GHz (short range)

The frequencies used for the various types of police radar include the following:

- X-band: 8 to 12 GHz
- K-band: 24 GHz
- Ka-band: 33 to 36 GHz

The only time there may be interference is when the radar cruise control, as part of a pre-collision system, starts to use SRR in the 24 GHz frequency. This would trigger the radar detector, but would be an unlikely event and just before a possible collision with a vehicle coming toward you.

FIGURE 23–20 A typical image captured using an infrared camera of a rear defogger that is working as designed.

 TECH TIP

The Infrared Camera Test

It is difficult to test for the proper operation of all grids of a rear window defogger unless the rear window happens to be covered with fog. A common trick that works is to turn on the rear defogger and look at the outside of the rear window glass using an infrared camera. The image will show if all sections of the rear grids are working. ● **SEE FIGURE 23–20**.

distances for when the distance between the moving vehicle and another vehicle in front is reduced. ● **SEE FIGURE 23–18**.

DIAGNOSIS AND SERVICE If the radar cruise control is not working properly, begin by making sure the sensor, which is usually behind the grille on most vehicles, is not covered. The system will not operate if the system is covered by heavy mud, ice, or snow. Additionally, some aftermarket vehicle front covers will obstruct the sensor view. If the sensor is replaced, some systems require a re-alignment using special tools. Always refer to the manufacturer's service information for specific instructions.

HEATED REAR WINDOW DEFOGGERS

PARTS AND OPERATION An electrically **heated rear window defogger** system uses an electrical grid baked on the glass that warms the glass to about 85°F (29°C) and clears it of fog or frost. The rear window is also called a *backlight*. The rear window defogger system is controlled by a driver-operated switch and a timer relay. ● **SEE FIGURE 23–19**.

The timer relay is necessary because the window grid can draw up to 30 amperes, and continued operation would put a strain on the battery and the charging system. Generally, the timer relay permits current to flow through the rear window grid for only 10 minutes. If the window is still not clear of fog after 10 minutes, the driver can turn the defogger on again, but after the first 10 minutes, any additional defogger operation is limited to 5 minutes.

The electrical current through the grids depends, in part, on the temperature of the conductor grids. As the temperature decreases, the resistance of the grids decreases and the current flow increases, helping to warm the rear glass. As the temperature of the glass increases, the resistance of the conductor grids increases and the current flow decreases. Therefore, the defogger system tends to self-regulate the electrical current requirements to match the need for defogging.

NOTE: Some vehicles use the wire grid of the rear window defogger as the radio antenna. Therefore, if the grid is damaged, radio reception can also be affected.

HEATED REAR WINDOW DEFOGGER DIAGNOSIS Troubleshooting a nonfunctioning rear window defogger unit involves using a test light or a voltmeter to check for voltage to the grid. If no voltage is present at the rear window, check for voltage at the switch and relay timer assembly. A poor ground connection on the opposite side of the grid from the power side can also cause the rear defogger not to operate. Because most defogger circuits use an indicator light switch and a relay timer, it is possible to have the indicator light on, even if the wires are disconnected at the rear window grid. A voltmeter can be used to test the operation of the rear window defogger grid. ● **SEE FIGURE 23–21**.

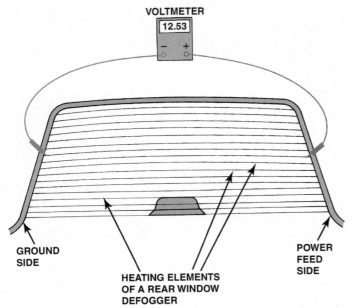

FIGURE 23–21 A rear window defogger electrical grid can be tested using a voltmeter to check for a decreasing voltage as the meter lead is moved from the power side toward the ground side. As the voltmeter positive lead is moved along the grid (on the inside of the vehicle), the voltmeter reading should steadily decrease as the meter approaches the ground side of the grid.

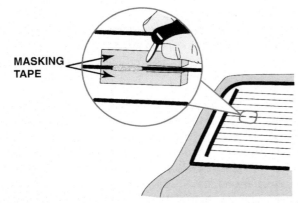

FIGURE 23–22 The typical repair material contains conductive silver-filled polymer, which dries in 10 minutes and is usable in 30 minutes.

With the negative meter lead attached to a good body ground, carefully touch the positive meter lead to the grid conductors. There should be a decreasing voltage reading as the meter lead is moved from the power ("hot") side of the grid toward the ground side of the grid.

REPAIR OR REPLACEMENT Electric grid-type rear window defoggers can be damaged easily by careless cleaning or scraping of the inside of the rear window glass. If there is a broken grid wire, it can be repaired using an electrically conductive substance available in a repair kit. Most vehicle manufacturers recommend that grid wire less than 2 inches (5 cm) long be repaired. If a bad section is longer than 2 inches, the entire rear window will need to be replaced. ● **SEE FIGURE 23–22**.

HEATED MIRRORS

PURPOSE AND FUNCTION The purpose and function of heated outside mirrors is to heat the surface of the mirror, which evaporates moisture on the surface. Heated mirrors may be an option for the left outside mirror or both the left and right side outside mirrors, depending on the vehicle. The heat helps keep ice and fog off the mirrors to allow for better driver visibility.

PARTS AND OPERATION Heated outside mirrors are often tied into the same electrical circuit as the rear window defogger. Therefore, when the rear defogger is turned on, the heating grid on the backside of the mirror is also turned on. On some vehicles, the heated mirrors are activated when the heating, ventilation, and cooling (HVAC) system is placed in the defrost mode. Some vehicles use a switch for each mirror.

DIAGNOSIS The first step in any diagnosis procedure is to verify the customer concern. Check the owner's manual or service information for the proper method to use to turn on the heated mirrors.

NOTE: Heated mirrors are *not* designed to melt snow or a thick layer of ice.

If a fault has been detected, check service information instructions for the exact procedure to follow. If the mirror itself is found to be defective, it is usually replaced as an assembly instead of being repaired.

POWER WINDOWS

SWITCHES AND CONTROLS **Power windows** use electric motors to raise and lower door glass. They can be operated by both a master control switch located beside the driver and additional independent switches located at each electric window. Some power window systems use a lockout/child safety switch located on the driver's controls to prevent operation of the power windows from the independent switches. Power windows are designed to operate only with the ignition switch in the on (run) position, although some manufacturers use a time delay for accessory power after the ignition switch is turned off. This feature permits the driver and passengers an opportunity to close all windows or operate other accessories for about 10 minutes or until a vehicle door is opened after the ignition has been turned off. This feature is often called *retained accessory power (RAP)*.

POWER WINDOW MOTORS Most power window systems use permanent magnet (PM) electric motors. It is possible to run a PM motor in the reverse direction by reversing the polarity of the two wires going to the motor. Most power window motors do not require that the motor be grounded to the body (door) of the vehicle. The ground for all the power windows is most often centralized near the driver's master control

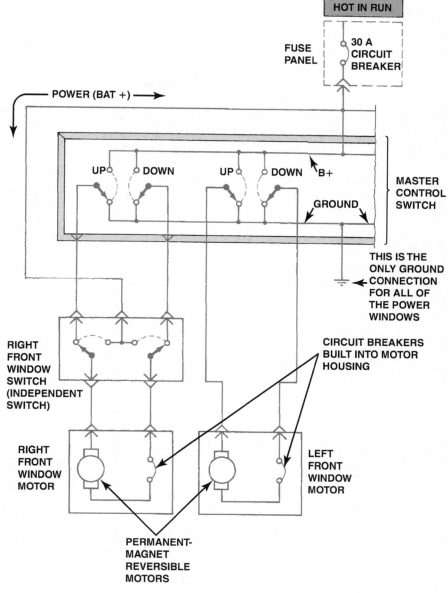

FIGURE 23–23 A typical power window circuit using PM motors. Control of the direction of window operation is achieved by directing the polarity of the current through the nongrounded motors. The only ground for the entire system is located at the master control (driver's side) switch assembly.

switch. The up-and-down motion of the individual window motors is controlled by double-pole, double-throw (DPDT) switches. These DPDT switches have five contacts and permit battery voltage to be applied to the power window motor, as well as reverse the polarity and direction of the motor.

Each motor is protected by a positive temperature coefficient (PTC) electronic circuit breaker. These circuit breakers are built into the motor assembly and are not a separate replaceable part. ● **SEE FIGURE 23–23**.

The power window motors rotate a mechanism called a *window regulator*. The window regulator is attached to the door glass and controls opening and closing of the glass. Door glass adjustments, such as glass tilt and upper and lower stops are usually the same for both power and manual windows. ● **SEE FIGURE 23–24**.

AUTO DOWN/UP FEATURES Many power windows are equipped with an auto down feature that allows windows to be lowered all of the way if the control switch is moved to a detent

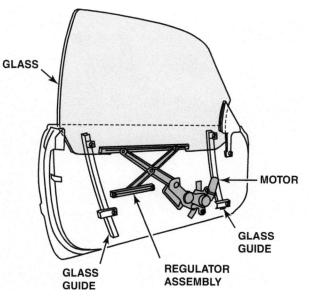

FIGURE 23–24 An electric motor and a regulator assembly raise and lower the glass on a power window.

Programming Auto Down/Up Power Windows

Many vehicles are equipped with automatic operation that can cause the window to go all the way down (or up) if the switch is depressed beyond a certain point or held for a fraction of a second. Sometimes this feature is lost if the battery in the vehicle has been disconnected. Although this programming procedure can vary depending on the make and model, many times the window(s) can be reprogrammed without using a scan tool by depressing and holding the down button for 10 seconds. If the vehicle is equipped with an auto up feature, repeat the procedure by holding the button up for 10 seconds. Always check exact service information for the vehicle being serviced.

or held down for longer than 0.3 second. The window will then move down all the way to the bottom, and then the motor stops.

Public Law 110-189, also known as the Cameron Gulbransen Kids Transportation Safety Act, mandated the use of power window **automatic reversal systems (ARS)**. The automatic reversal system is designed to prevent windows from causing injury when they are closing, if the vehicle is equipped with power windows. The Department of Transportation (DOT) established a limit of 136 ft-lb (100 NM) of force be exerted by the window before the window retracts. There are two methods used for controlling ARS and auto up and auto down windows including:

1. An encoder wheel and position sensor is used to monitor the speed and position of the window as it travels up and down.

2. The current (amperes) required is measured by the power window control module.

The window direction will reverse if the current draw exceeds a pre-determined value. If an object is in the path of the window, the current draw and or slowing of the window will cause the control module to reverse. The system is designed to expect increased current flow and slower window movement in cold weather conditions. However, sudden vehicle movement, such as hitting a bump in the road as the window is moving upward or a fault in the window track, can cause the window to reverse.

A factory or factory-level scan tool is used to diagnose this system, which can monitor switch operation and can be used to control the operation of the windows using bidirectional controls. ● **SEE FIGURE 23–25**.

TROUBLESHOOTING POWER WINDOWS Before troubleshooting a power window problem, check for proper operation of all power windows. Also check that the child-proof switch is not in the disable position, which prevents the windows from being operated from any position except the driver's master control. Check service information for the exact procedure to follow. In a newer system, a scan tool can be used to perform the following:

- Check for B (body) or U (network) diagnostic trouble codes (DTCs)
- Operate the power windows using the bidirectional control feature
- Relearn or program the operation of the power windows after a battery disconnect

Always follow the diagnosis and repair procedures as specified in service information.

ELECTRIC POWER DOOR LOCKS

PARTS AND OPERATION Electric power door locks use a PM reversible motor to lock or unlock all vehicle door locks from a control switch or switches. The electric motor uses a built-in

FIGURE 23–25 A master power window control panel with the buttons and the cover removed.

circuit breaker and operates the lock-activating rod. PM reversible motors do not require grounding because, as with power windows, the motor control is determined by the polarity of the current through the two motor wires. ● **SEE FIGURE 23–26**.

Some two-door vehicles do not use a power door lock relay because the current flow for only two PM motors can be handled through the door lock switches. However, most four-door vehicles and vans with power locks on rear and side doors, use a relay to control the current flow necessary to operate four or more power door lock motors. The door lock relay is controlled by the door lock switch and is commonly the location of the one and only *ground* connection for the entire door lock circuit.

TROUBLESHOOTING POWER LOCKS
If all power door locks are inoperative, use a factory or factory-level aftermarket scan tool and try operating the locks using the bidirectional control. If the door locks do not operate using a scan tool, refer to service information for the exact procedure to follow.

If only the power door lock is inoperative, check for the power and ground, as well as possible physical binding of the lock mechanism. Repair or replace as needed.

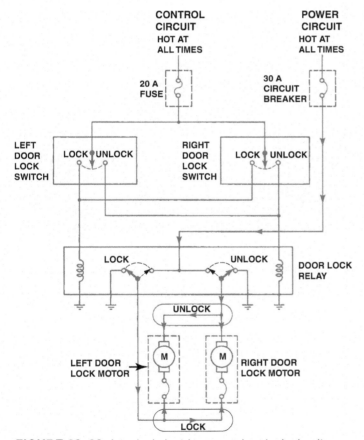

FIGURE 23–26 A typical electric power door lock circuit diagram. Note that the control circuit is protected by a fuse, whereas the power circuit is protected by a circuit breaker. As with the operation of power windows, power door locks typically use reversible PM nongrounded electric motors. These motors are geared mechanically to the lock–unlock mechanism.

TRUNK/LIFT GATE LOCKS

CIRCUIT DESCRIPTION The electric power trunk/lift gate lock uses a PM reversible motor to lock or unlock the trunk/lift gate lock from a control switch or through the use of the remote. The electric motor uses a built-in circuit breaker and operates the lock-activating rod. PM reversible motors do not require grounding because, as with power windows and door locks, the motor control is determined by the polarity of the current through the two motor wires.

 TECH TIP

Check the Glove Box Switch Position
A common customer complaint is that the trunk or lift gate can be opened manually, but it cannot be opened using the remote. Most vehicles are equipped with a lock-out switch in the glove compartment (instrument panel compartment) that can be switched off, and the glove box door locked to limit access when the vehicle is parked and the valet has the key to the ignition. If the switch is in the locked position, the trunk cannot be opened using the remote. Check that first before following the recommended diagnostic procedures found in service information. ● **SEE FIGURE 23–27**.

POWER SUN ROOF/ MOON ROOF

DEFINITIONS While they are similar in nature and often used interchangeably, there is a difference between a sun roof and a moon roof.

FIGURE 23–27 The switch to disable the outside opening of the trunk/lift gate is often in the glove box.

- **Sun roof** – A sun roof is basically any kind of panel on the roof of a car that permits light, air, or both to come into a vehicle, but only if the panel is opened. A sunroof includes two types of panels:
  1. One panel may be made of either metal or the same material as the ceiling of the car, and can be retracted to expose the glass panel above.
  2. The other panel is made of glass that can be either tilted open or completely retracted to essentially serve as an open window in the roof.

- **Moon roof** – A moon roof is made of a tinted glass panel that can be either tilted open or completely retracted to operate as an open window in the roof. The majority of new cars have moon roofs.

OPERATION Most moon or sun roof systems use PM electric motors to open and close the moveable glass panel. The open and close, or tilt up or down, motion of the moon roof motors is controlled by DPDT switches. These DPDT switches have five contacts and permit battery voltage to be applied to the power moon roof motor, as well as reverse the polarity and direction of the motor. Each motor is protected by an electronic circuit breaker. These circuit breakers are built into the motor assembly and are not a separate replaceable part.

DIAGNOSIS AND SERVICE Always check service information for the exact procedure to use because the moon roofs have many different service items that are likely to need service or repair including:

- **Water leaks.** Engineers refer to water seals around moon roofs as "controlling the flow of water" and not necessarily trying to provide a waterproof seal. Because the roof of a vehicle flexes when the being driven, no seal is able to prevent water from leaking around the area around the moon roof. Instead, the water is directed to a tray under the outer seal and then tubes are installed at the four corners of the moon roof to drain the water from the tray to the ground. If water is entering the passenger compartment, make sure the drain tubes are not clogged. The tubes are routed though the two front "A" pillars and the two rear "C" pillars. ● **SEE FIGURE 23–28.**

- **Electrical/Mechanical Issues.** Electrical or mechanical issues can prevent the moon roof from opening or closing. Most vehicle manufacturers include a crank or a way to close the roof if the roof fails to close due to an electrical fault.

Always follow the vehicle manufacturer's recommended service and repair instructions and procedures.

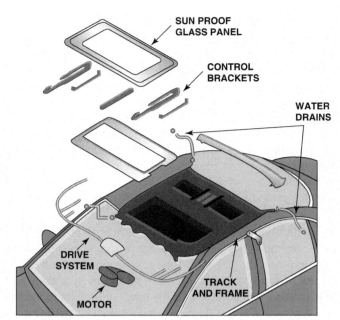

FIGURE 23–28 An exploded view of a typical moveable roof showing the location of the motor and the drain tubes, which direct the water to the ground.

FIGURE 23–29 The control for the operation of the powered inside sun shade on this Chevrolet Impala is located in the overhead control panel. Sun shades are vehicle specific, so check service information for the exact procedures to follow when servicing or repairing a sun shade.

are operated manually and either can be pulled down from the top of the inside of the door or up from the inner part of the door panel. Sun shades used to block the sun in the rear backlight or moon roof are often electrically powered and use a reversible PM motor to drive the roll holding the fabric. ● **SEE FIGURE 23–29.**

SUN SHADES

DESCRIPTION **Sun shades** are fabric or screen-like material installed on the inside of the vehicle that can be raised, lowered, or moved to block the rays of the sun from entering the interior of the vehicle. Most of the sun shades used on the side windows

POWER SEATS

PARTS AND OPERATION A typical power-operated seat includes a reversible electric motor and a transmission assembly that may have three solenoids or motors,

FIGURE 23–30 A power seat uses electric motors under the seat, which drive cables that extend to operate screw jacks (up and down) or gears to move the seat forward and back.

and six drive cables that turn the six seat adjusters. A six-way power seat offers seat movement forward and backward, plus seat cushion movement up and down at the front and the rear. The drive cables rotate inside a cable housing and connect the power output of the seat transmission

to a gear or screw jack assembly that moves the seat. ● **SEE FIGURE 23–30**.

A *screw jack assembly* is often called a *gear nut*. It is used to move the front or back of the seat cushion up and down. A rubber coupling, usually located between the electric motor and the transmission, prevents electric motor damage in the event of a jammed seat. This coupling is designed to prevent motor damage. Most power seats use a permanent magnet motor that can be reversed by reversing the polarity of the current sent to the motor by the seat switch. ● **SEE FIGURE 23–31**.

POWER SEAT MOTOR(S) Power seats use a PM motor to power the movement of the seat. Most PM motors have a built-in circuit breaker or PTC circuit protector to protect the motor from overheating. Some older Ford power seat motors use three separate armatures inside one large permanent magnet field housing. Some power seats use a series-wound electric motor with two separate field coils, one field coil for each direction of rotation. This type of power seat motor typically uses a relay to control the direction of current from the seat switch to the corresponding field coil of the seat motor. This type of power seat can be identified by the "click" heard when the seat switch is changed from up to down or front to back, or vice versa. The click is the sound of the relay switching the field coil current. Some power seats use as many as eight separate PM motors that operate all functions of the seat, including headrest height, seat length, and side bolsters, in addition to the usual six-way power seat functions.

FIGURE 23–31 A typical power seat circuit diagram. Notice that each motor has a built-in electronic (solid-state) PTC circuit protector. The seat control switch can change the direction in which the motor(s) runs by reversing the direction in which the current flows through the motor.

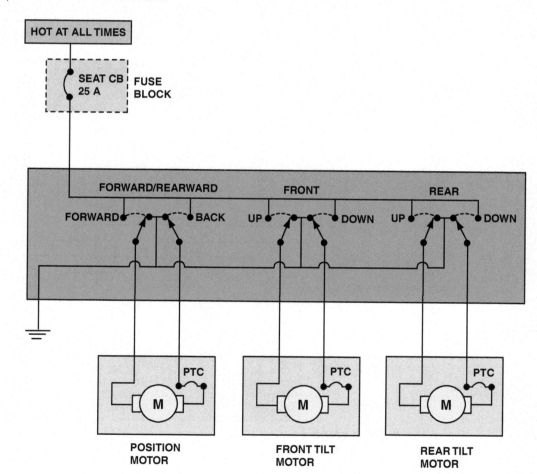

Easy Exit Seat Programming

Some vehicles are equipped with memory seats that allow the seat to move rearward when the ignition is turned off to allow easy exit from the vehicle. Vehicles equipped with this feature include an exit/entry button that is used to program the desired exit/entry position of the seat for each of two drivers. If the vehicle is not equipped with this feature and only one driver primarily uses the vehicle, the second memory position can be programmed for easy exit and entry. Set position 1 to the desired seat position and position 2 to the entry/exit position. When exiting the vehicle, press memory 2 to allow easy exit and easy entry the next time. Press memory 1 to return the seat memory to the desired driving position.

NOTE: Some power seats use a small air pump to inflate a bag (or bags) in the lower part of the back of the seat, called the **lumbar**, because it supports the lumbar section of the lower back. The lumbar section of the seat can also be changed, using a lever or knob that the driver can move to change the seat section for the lower back.

MEMORY SEAT Memory seats use a potentiometer to sense the position of the seat. The seat position can be programmed into the BCM or memory seat module, and stored by position number 1, 2, or 3. The driver pushes the desired button and the seat moves to the stored position. On some vehicles, the memory seat position is also programmed into the remote keyless entry (RKE) key fob. ● **SEE FIGURE 23–32.**

Check service information for the exact procedure to follow when diagnosing power seats.

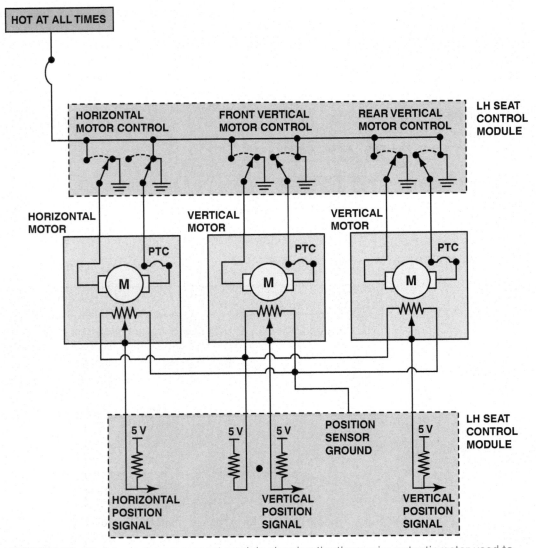

FIGURE 23–32 A typical memory seat module showing the three-wire potentiometer used to determine seat position.

What Every Driver Should Know About Power Seats

Power seats use an electric motor or motors to move the position of the seat. These electric motors turn small cables, gears, and/or shafts that operate mechanisms that move the seat. Never place rags, newspapers, or any other object under a power seat. Even ice scrapers can get caught between moving parts of the seat and can often cause serious damage or jamming of the power seat. In many cases, after the object is removed that caused the seat jam, the memory function will need to be relearned for proper operation to resume.

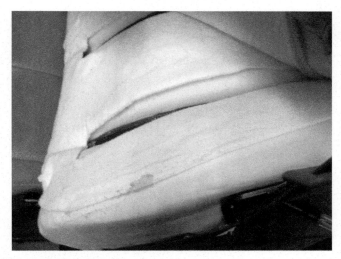

FIGURE 23–33 The heating element of a heated seat is a replaceable part, but service requires that the upholstery be removed. The yellow part is the seat foam material and the entire white cover is the replaceable heating element. This is then covered by the seat material.

ELECTRICALLY HEATED SEATS

PARTS AND OPERATION **Heated seats** use electric heating elements in the seat bottom, as well as in the seat back in many vehicles. The heating element is designed to warm the seat and/or back of the seat to about 100°F (37°C) or close to normal body temperature (98.6°F). Many heated seats also include a high-position or a variable temperature setting, so the temperature of the seats can therefore be as high as 110°F (44°C).

A temperature sensor in the seat cushion is used to regulate the temperature. The sensor is a variable resistor, which changes with temperature and is used as an input signal to a heated seat control module. The heated seat module uses the seat temperature input, as well as the input from the high–low (or variable) temperature control, to turn the current on or off to the heating element in the seat. Some vehicles are equipped with heated seats in both the front and the rear seats.

DIAGNOSIS AND SERVICE When diagnosing a heated seat concern, start by verifying that the switch is in the on position and that the temperature of the seat is below normal body temperature. Using service information, check for power and ground at the control module and to the heating element in the seat. Most vehicle manufacturers recommend replacing the entire heating element if it is defective. ● **SEE FIGURE 23–33**.

HEATED AND COOLED SEATS

PARTS AND OPERATION Most electrically heated and cooled seats use a thermoelectric device (TED) located under the seat cushion and seat back. The TED consists of positive and negative connections between two ceramic plates. Each ceramic

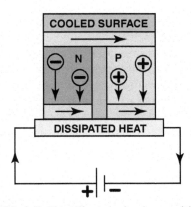

FIGURE 23–34 A Peltier effect device is capable of heating or cooling, depending on the polarity of the applied current.

plate has copper fins to allow the transfer of heat to or from air passing over the device and directed into the seat cushion. The thermoelectric device uses the Peltier effect, named after the inventor Jean C. A. Peltier (1785–1845), a French clockmaker. When electrical current flows through the module, one side is heated and the other side is cooled. Reversing the polarity of the current changes the side to be heated. ● **SEE FIGURE 23–34**.

Most vehicles equipped with heated and cooled seats use two modules per seat, one for the seat cushion and one for the seat back. When the heated and cooled seats are turned on, air is forced through a filter and then through the thermoelectric modules. The air is then directed through passages in the foam of the seat cushion and seat back. Each thermoelectric device has a temperature sensor called a thermistor. The control module uses sensors to determine the temperature of the fins in the thermoelectric device so the controller can maintain the set temperature. ● **SEE FIGURE 23–35**.

Always follow the vehicle manufacturer's recommended diagnosis and service procedures for the repair of heated and cooled seat systems.

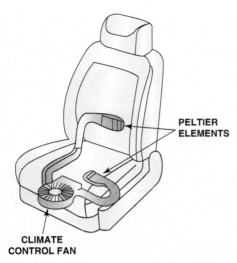

FIGURE 23-35 A fan is used to move the heated or cooled air to heat or cool the bottom or the back of the seat.

FIGURE 23-36 The heated steering wheel is controlled by a switch on the steering wheel in this vehicle.

 TECH TIP

Check the Seat Filter

Heated and cooled seats often use a filter to trap dirt and debris to help keep the air passages clean. If a customer complains of a slow heating or cooling of the seat, check the air filter and replace or clean as necessary. Check service information for the exact location of the seat filter and for instructions on how to remove and/or replace it.

Always follow the vehicle manufacturer's recommended diagnosis and testing procedures for heated steering wheel diagnosis and repair.

ADJUSTABLE PEDALS

PURPOSE AND FUNCTION Adjustable pedals, also called *pedal height* or **electric adjustable pedals (EAP)**, place the brake pedal and the accelerator pedal on movable brackets that are motor operated. The height of the accelerator pedal and the brake pedal are adjusted together and cannot be adjusted individually. A typical adjustable pedal system includes the following components:

- Adjustable pedal position switch. Allows the driver to position the pedals
- Adjustable pedal assembly. Includes the motor, threaded adjustment rods, and a pedal position sensor. ● **SEE FIGURE 23-37**.

The position of the pedals, as well as the position of the seat system, is usually included as part of the memory seat function and can be set for two or more drivers.

DIAGNOSIS AND SERVICE The first step when there is a customer concern about the functioning of the adjustable pedals is to verify that the unit is not working as designed. Check the owner's

HEATED STEERING WHEEL

PARTS INVOLVED A **heated steering wheel** usually consists of the following components:

- Steering wheel with a built-in heater in the rim
- Heated steering wheel control switch
- Heated steering wheel control module

OPERATION When the steering wheel heater control switch is turned on, a signal is sent to the control module and electrical current flows through the heating element in the rim of the steering wheel. ● **SEE FIGURE 23-36**.

The system remains on until the ignition switch is turned off or the driver turns off the control switch. The temperature of the steering wheel is usually calibrated to stay at about 90°F (32°C), and it requires three to four minutes to reach that temperature, depending on the outside temperature. Most heated steering wheels only heat a part and often not all of the steering wheel. Before trying to repair a condition where just some sections of the steering wheel are being warmed, check service information for what parts are normally heated.

 TECH TIP

Check the Remote

The memory function may be programmed to a particular key fob remote, which would command the adjustable pedals to move to the position set in memory. Always check the settings of all remotes before attempting to repair a problem that may not be a problem.

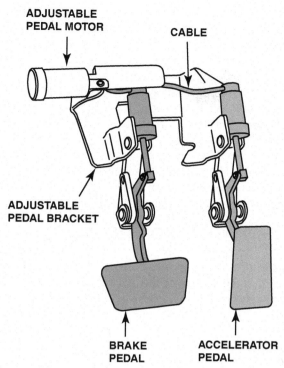

FIGURE 23–37 A typical adjustable pedal assembly. Both the accelerator and the brake pedal can be moved forward and rearward by using the adjustable pedal position switch.

FIGURE 23–38 Electrically folded mirror in the folded position.

FIGURE 23–39 The electric mirror control is located on the driver's side door panel on this Cadillac Escalade.

 CASE STUDY

The Case of the Haunted Mirrors

The owner complained that while driving, either one or the other, outside mirror would fold in without any button being depressed. Unable to verify the customer concern, the service technician looked at the owner's manual to find out exactly how the mirrors were supposed to work. In the manual, a caution statement said that if the mirror is electrically folded inward and then manually pushed out, the mirror will not lock into position. The power folding mirrors must be electrically cycled outward, using the mirror switches to lock them in position. After cycling both mirrors inward and outward electrically, the problem was solved. ● **SEE FIGURES 23–38 AND 23–39.**

Summary:

- **Complaint**—Customer stated that the outside power folding mirror would fold by itself at times.
- **Cause**—The mirrors have to moved electrically, not manually, to work correctly.
- **Correction**—Cycling the mirrors electrically restored proper operation.

manual or service information for the proper operation. Follow the vehicle manufacturer's recommended troubleshooting procedure. Many diagnostic procedures include the use of a factory scan tool with bidirectional control capabilities to test this system.

FOLDING OUTSIDE MIRRORS

Mirrors that can be electrically folded inward are a popular feature, especially on larger sport utility vehicles. A control inside is used to fold both mirrors inward when needed, such as when entering a garage or a tight parking spot. For diagnosis and servicing of outside folding mirrors, check service information for details.

KEYLESS ENTRY

SYSTEM DESCRIPTION Even though some Ford vehicles use a keypad located on the outside of the door, most keyless entry systems use a wireless transmitter built into the key fob or remote. A key fob is a decorative item on a key chain. ● **SEE FIGURE 23-40.**

FIGURE 23–40 A key fob remote.

The transmitter broadcasts a signal that is received by the electronic control module, which is generally mounted in the trunk or under the instrument panel. ● SEE FIGURE 23–41.

The electronic control unit sends a voltage signal to the door lock actuator(s) located in the doors. Generally, if the transmitter unlock button is depressed once, only the driver's door is unlocked. If the unlock button is depressed twice, then all doors unlock.

ROLLING CODE RESET PROCEDURE Many keyless remote systems use a rolling code type of transmitter and receiver. In a conventional system, the transmitter emits a certain fixed frequency, which is received by the vehicle control module. This single frequency can be intercepted and rebroadcast to open the vehicle. A rolling code type of transmitter emits a different frequency every time the transmitter button is depressed and then rolls over to another frequency so that it cannot be intercepted. Both the transmitter and the receiver must be kept in synchronized order so that the remote will function correctly. If the transmitter is depressed when it is out of range from the vehicle, the proper frequency may not be recognized by the receiver, which did not roll over to the new frequency when the transmitter was depressed. If the transmitter does not work, try to resynchronize the transmitter to the receiver by depressing and holding both the lock and the unlock button for 10 seconds when within range of the receiver.

PASSIVE KEYLESS ENTRY SYSTEM A passive system uses the key fob as a transmitter, which communicates with the vehicle as it comes close. The key is identified using one of several antennas around the body of the vehicle and a radio pulse generator in the key housing. Depending on the system, the vehicle is automatically unlocked when a button or sensor on the door handle or trunk release is depressed. ● SEE FIGURE 23–42.

A passive system can also be used to unlock and open a rear lift gate on an SUV if a foot is moved under the edge of the vehicle allowing it to open the slider or the rear hatch. Vehicles with a passive (smart) key system can also have a mechanical backup, usually in the form of a key blade built into the key fob.

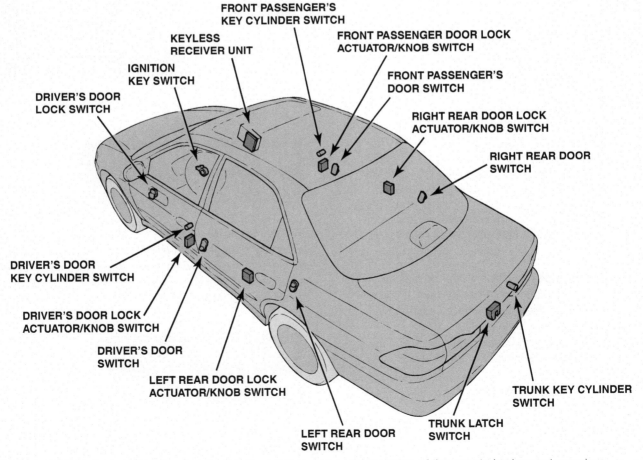

FIGURE 23–41 A typical vehicle showing the location of the various components of the remote keyless entry system.

FIGURE 23-42 (a) If the passive key is within about 15 feet (5 m) of the vehicle when the door handle is touched, the door will unlock allowing access to the interior (b) The engine will start if the smart key is detected being inside the vehicle.

(a)   ▉ = PASSIVE KEY   (b)

Vehicles with a smart key system can be started without inserting a key in the ignition, provided the driver has the key fob inside the vehicle. On most vehicles, this is done most often by pressing a start button. When leaving a vehicle equipped with a smart key system, the vehicle is locked, depending on the make, model, and year of manufacture of vehicle, by:

- Pressing a button on one of the door handles
- Touching a capacitive area on a door handle
- Walking away from the vehicle and the door will lock when the key fob is further away than 15 feet (5 m).

KEYLESS ENTRY DIAGNOSIS A small battery powers the transmitter, and a weak battery is a common cause of remote power locks failing to operate. If the keyless entry system fails to operate after the transmitter battery has been replaced, check the following items.

- Mechanical binding in the door lock
- Low vehicle battery voltage
- Blown fuse
- Open circuit to the control module
- Defective control module
- Defective transmitter

PROGRAMMING A NEW REMOTE If a new or additional remote transmitter is to be used, it must be programmed to the vehicle. Generally, all remotes previously programmed to the vehicle must be present during the programming or they will no longer work. The programming procedure varies and may require the use of a scan tool. Check service information for the exact procedure to follow.

GARAGE DOOR OPENER

OPERATION HomeLink or Car2U is a device installed in many new vehicles that duplicates the radio-frequency code of the original garage door opener. The frequency range is 288 to 418 MHz. The typical vehicle garage door opening system has three buttons that can be used to operate one or more of the following devices.

- Garage doors equipped with a radio transmitter electric opener
- Gates

- Entry door locks
- Lighting or small appliances

The devices include both fixed-frequency devices, usually older units, and rolling (encrypted) code devices. ● **SEE FIGURE 23-43**.

PROGRAMMING A VEHICLE GARAGE DOOR OPENER When a vehicle is purchased, it must be programmed using the transmitter for the garage door opener or other device.

NOTE: The garage door opening controller can only be programmed by using a transmitter. If an automatic garage door system does not have a remote transmitter, the system cannot be programmed.

Normally, the customer is responsible for programming the garage door opener. However, some customers may find that help is needed from the service department. The steps that are usually involved in programming a garage door opener in the vehicle to the garage door opener are as follows:

STEP 1 Unplug the garage door opener during programming to prevent it from being cycled on and off, which could damage the motor.

STEP 2 Check that the frequency of the handheld transmitter is between 288 and 418 MHz.

STEP 3 Install new batteries in the transmitter to be assured of a strong signal being transmitted to the garage door opener module in the vehicle.

FIGURE 23-43 Typical HomeLink garage door opener buttons. Notice that three different units can be controlled from the vehicle using the HomeLink system.

FIGURE 23–44 A remote start system allows the engine to be started from a distance usually from inside the house before leaving for the day. Most systems only allow the engine for run for 10 minutes.

STEP 4 Turn the ignition on, engine off (KOEO).

STEP 5 While holding the transmitter 4 to 6 inches away from the opener button, press and hold the button while pressing and releasing the handheld transmitter every 2 seconds. Continue pressing and releasing the transmitter until the indicator light near the opener button changes from a slow blink to a rapid flash.

STEP 6 Verify that the vehicle garage door system (HomeLink or Car2U) button has been programmed. Press and hold the garage door button. If the indicator light blinks rapidly for 2 seconds and then comes on steady, the system has been successfully programmed using a rolling code design. If the indicator light is on steady, then it has been successfully programmed to a fixed frequency device.

DIAGNOSIS AND SERVICE If a fault occurs with the garage door opening system, first verify that the garage door opener is functioning correctly. Also, check if the garage door opener remote control is capable of operating the door. Repair the garage door opener system as needed. If the problem still exists, attempt reprogramming the HomeLink/Car2U vehicle system, being sure that the remote has a newly purchased battery.

REMOTE START

PURPOSE AND FUNCTION A **remote start** is the ability to start the engine of the vehicle from a distance by using a remote control. This a popular option, especially in cold climates, which allows the driver to start the engine when inside the house or office to start the warm-up process before even entering the vehicle. It is also popular in the warm weather areas where the interior can be cooled by the air conditioning before entering the vehicle. Most factory-installed remote start systems use the same key fob that it used to unlock the doors. ● **SEE FIGURE 23–44**.

PARTS AND OPERATION The remote start system uses a signal from the transmitter (usually the key fob on factory systems) to start the engine. The engine will run for about 10 minutes depending on the system and then shut off. The vehicle needs to be setup ahead of time with the HVAC system set

☠ WARNING:

Never use the remote start to start the engine if the vehicle is located inside a garage or an area without proper ventilation, or if a car cover is covering the body of the vehicle.

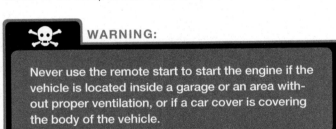 **TECH TIP**

Try to Purchase an Aftermarket System That Has a Long Range

Most factory remote start systems have a range of 400 to 600 feet (120–180 m) and may work as far away as 1,500 feet (450 m) in open areas. The distance is affected by buildings and walls which can greatly reduce the effective range. If purchasing an aftermarket remote start device, look for a high transmitter power rating because this is the value that determines the range of the remote. Many units are advertised as having a 500-foot range or 3,000-foot range but these numbers are for areas without any obstructions. While few vehicle owners need to start their vehicles from more than 1,000 feet away, most want to start a vehicle from inside a building. A longer range (more transmitter power) will be needed if it will be used from a mall, sporting events, parking garages, hospitals, or restaurants. If in doubt, pay a little more to get a more powerful unit.

to heat or A/C and the transmission gear selector in park, or in neutral on vehicles equipped with a manual transmission. Always check service information for the conditions that allow remote starting, which often includes the following:

- The keyless remote is not inside the vehicle.
- The gearshift lever is in the "P" (Park) position.
- The security warning system is not activated.
- The brake pedal is not depressed.

- The engine hood is closed.
- All the doors are closed and locked.
- The trunk or tailgate is closed.
- The ignition key is removed from the ignition switch.
- The vehicle battery is not low.

Check service information for the exact procedures to follow when diagnosing a fault with the remote engine start system.

SUMMARY

1. Horns are manufactured in several different tones, ranging from 1,800 to 3,550 Hz, and must be heard from a minimum distance of 200 feet (60 meters).

2. Most wipers, since the 1990s, have used the BCM to control the actual operation of the wiper. The wiper controls are an input to the control module and may also turn on the headlights whenever the wipers are on, which is the law in some states.

3. Most vehicle windshield washers use a positive-displacement or centrifugal-type washer pump located in the washer reservoir.

4. The electronics in the rain-sense wiper module can detect the presence of rain drops under various lighting conditions.

5. Cruise control, also called vehicle speed control, is used to maintain a preset vehicle speed even up gentle grades.

6. Most radar cruise control systems use radar, both long and short range. Some systems use optical or infrared cameras to detect objects.

7. A rear window defogger electrical grid can be tested using a voltmeter to check for a decreasing voltage as the meter lead is moved from the power side toward the ground side.

8. A typical power window circuit using PM motors. Control of the direction of window operation is achieved by directing the polarity of the current through the non-grounded motors.

9. A power seat uses electric motors under the seat, which drive cables that extend to operate screw jacks (up and down) or gears to move the seat forward and back.

10. The heating element of a heated seat is a replaceable part, but service requires that the upholstery be removed.

11. Most electrically heated and cooled seats use a thermo-electric device (TED) located under the seat cushion and seat back.

12. Many keyless remote systems use a rolling code type of transmitter and receiver.

13. A remote start system allows the engine to be started from a distance usually form inside the house before leaving for the day.

REVIEW QUESTIONS

1. What are the advantages of using the BCM to operate the horns?

2. How do rain-sense wipers work?

3. What is the purpose of a radar cruise control system?

4. How can an infrared camera be used to test a rear window defogger?

5. What is meant by a "rolling code"?

CHAPTER QUIZ

1. The owner of a vehicle equipped with cruise control complains that the cruise control often stops working when driving over rough or bumpy pavement. What is the most likely fault?
   a. A defective BCM
   b. A worn throttle plate in the throttle body assembly
   c. A misadjusted brake or clutch safety switch
   d. Normal operation designed to discourage the use of cruise control when driving over bumpy roads

2. Technician A says that the cruise control on a vehicle that uses an electronic throttle control (ETC) system uses a servo to move the throttle. Technician B says that the cruise control on a vehicle with ETC uses the APP sensor to set the speed. Which technician is correct?
   a. Technician A only
   b. Technician B only
   c. Both Technicians A and B
   d. Neither Technician A nor B

3. All power windows fail to operate from the independent switches, but all power windows operate from the master switch. Technician A says the window lockout switch may be on. Technician B says the power window relay could be defective. Which technician is correct?
   a. Technician A only
   b. Technician B only
   c. Both Technicians A and B
   d. Neither Technician A nor B

4. Technician A says that a defective ground connection at the master control switch (driver's side) could cause the failure of all power windows. Technician B says that if *one* control wire is disconnected, all windows will fail to operate. Which technician is correct?
   a. Technician A only
   b. Technician B only
   c. Both Technicians A and B
   d. Neither Technician A nor B

5. A typical radar cruise control system uses _____.
   a. long-range radar (LRR)
   b. short-range radar (SRR)
   c. ETC system to control vehicle speed
   d. All of the above

6. When checking the operation of a rear window defogger with a voltmeter, _____.
   a. the voltmeter should be set to read AC volts
   b. the voltmeter should read close to battery voltage anywhere along the grid
   c. voltage should be available anytime at the power side of the grid because the control circuit just completes the ground side of the heater grid circuit
   d. the voltmeter should indicate decreasing voltage when the grid is tested across the width of the glass.

7. PM motors used in power windows, mirrors, and seats can be reversed by _____.
   a. sending current to a reversed field coil
   b. reversing the polarity of the current to the motor
   c. using a reverse relay circuit
   d. using a relay and a two-way clutch

8. If only one power door lock is inoperative, a possible cause is a _____.
   a. poor ground connection at the power door lock relay
   b. defective door lock motor (or solenoid)
   c. defective (open) circuit breaker for the power circuit
   d. defective (open) fuse for the control circuit

9. A keyless remote control stops working. Technician A says the battery in the remote could be dead. Technician B says that the key fob may have to be resynchronized. Which technician is correct?
   a. Technician A only
   b. Technician B only
   c. Both Technicians A and B
   d. Neither Technician A nor B

10. Remote start systems include what restriction that could prevent the engine from being started?
    a. The remote is inside the vehicle
    b. The distance away from the vehicle exceeds the range of the transmitter.
    c. The doors are not locked
    d. Any of the above

chapter 24
AIR MANAGEMENT SYSTEM

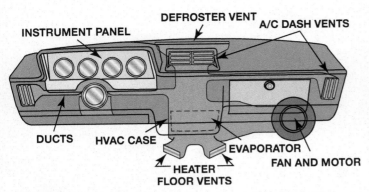

FIGURE 24–1 The HVAC airflow is directed toward the windshield, dash or floor vents, or combinations depending on the system settings.

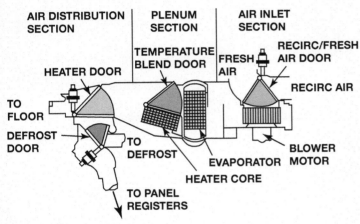

FIGURE 24–2 The three major portions of the A/C and heat system are air inlet, plenum, and air distribution. The shaded portions show the paths of the four control doors.

INTRODUCTION

TERMINOLOGY A system that contains the heating, ventilation, and cooling (HVAC) plenum, ducts, and **air doors** is called the **air management system**, or *air distribution system*, and controls the airflow to the passenger compartment. ● **SEE FIGURE 24–1.**

Air flows into the case that contains the evaporator and heater core from two possible inlets:

1. **Outside air**, often called *fresh air*
2. **Inside air**, usually called **recirculation**.

Proper temperature control to enhance passenger comfort during heating should maintain an air temperature in the footwell about 7°F to 14°F (4°C to 8°C) above the temperature around the upper body. This is done by directing the heated airflow to the floor. During A/C operation, the upper body should be cooler, so the airflow is directed to the instrument panel registers. Airflow is usually controlled by three or more doors, which are called *flap doors* or valves by some manufacturers. The three doors include the following:

■ **Air inlet** door is used to select outside or inside air inlet
■ **Temperature-blend door** is used to adjust air temperature
■ **Mode door** is used to select air discharge location ● **SEE FIGURE 24–2.**

The use of these components allows the system to provide airflow under the following conditions:

1. Fresh outside air or recirculated air
2. Air conditioning
3. Defrost
4. Heat

HEAT For heat position, the following can be done:

■ Temperature set to the desired setting
■ Air intake—select outside air for faster heating
■ Air conditioning set to off
■ Set airflow to floor
■ Fan speed to desired speed

AIR CONDITIONING For air conditioning position, the following can be done:

■ Temperature set to the desired setting
■ Air intake—set to outside air or recirculation under high humidity conditions.
■ Airflow—select dash vents (also called panel vents)
■ Air conditioning set to on
■ Fan speed set to desired speed

VENTILATION For ventilation position, the following can be done:

■ Temperature set to desired temperature
■ Air intake—select outside air
■ Airflow—set to dash (panel) vents
■ Air conditioning set to off
■ Fan speed set to desired speed

DEFOGGING OR DEFROSTING THE INSIDE OF THE WINDSHIELD For defogging or defrosting position, the following can be done:

■ Temperature set to high temperature
■ Air intake set to outside air
■ Airflow set to windshield (defrost)
■ Fan speed set to desired speed. ● **SEE FIGURE 24–3.**

HVAC CONTROL HEAD The HVAC control head or panel is mounted in the instrument panel cluster or console. The control head includes the following controls:

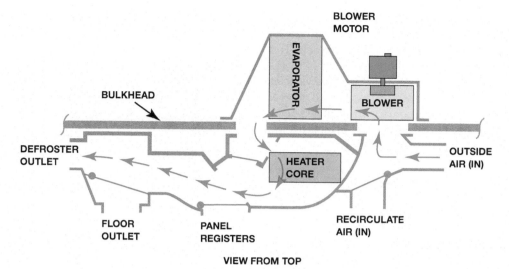

VIEW FROM TOP

FIGURE 24–3 In the defog or defrost mode position, the air is directed through the evaporator to remove the moisture from the air before being sent through the heater core to warm the air.

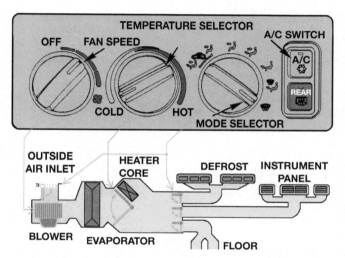

FIGURE 24–4 Most HVAC control heads include a control for turning units on and setting the mode of operation, a control for adjusting the temperature, and a control for the fan speed.

- System on and off
- Outside or recirculated air
- Mode position (floor, vent, or defrost)
- Temperature desired
- Blower speed

The control head is connected to various parts through electrical connections, vacuum connections, mechanical cables, or a combination of these. ● **SEE FIGURE 24–4.**

AIRFLOW CONTROL

OPERATION The amount or volume of HVAC air is controlled by blower speed. A multispeed blower is used to force air through the ductwork when the vehicle is moving at

? **FREQUENTLY ASKED QUESTION**

What Does the Snowflake Button on the Dash Do?

Some people, such as those who drive vehicles that are equipped with automatic climate control systems, sometimes find it hard to figure out how to engage the A/C compressor on a rental car or a vehicle that they have not driven before. Often the driver will turn the fan to high and the mode selector to the dash vent position, but no cool air is being delivered. For the compressor to function, the button that looks like a snowflake has to be pushed. The snowflake button is actually the air conditioning on/off button. ● **SEE FIGURE 24–5.**

FIGURE 24–5 The A/C compressor is turned on or off by depressing the "snow flake" button on the dash.

low speeds or to increase the airflow at any speed. At highway speeds, most systems have a natural airflow from ram air pressure created by the forward movement of the vehicle. This is the pressure generated at the base of the windshield by the speed of the vehicle. This airflow is improved in some vehicles by outlet registers placed in low-pressure areas toward the rear of the vehicle. Higher speeds move more air. The inlet and outlet directions of the airflow and the discharge air temperature are controlled by swinging, sliding, or rotating doors.

TYPES OF DOORS
Most systems use a flap door that swings about 45° to 90°. Swinging doors are very simple and require little maintenance. ● **SEE FIGURE 24–6.**

Another design uses a *rotary door*. This pan-shaped door has openings at the side and edge, and the door rotates about 100° to one of four different positions. Each position directs airflow to the desired outlet(s).

The space under the instrument panel is very crowded, and some vehicles use a smaller HVAC case using a *sliding mode door* also called a *rolling door*. Some of these door designs roll up, similar to a window shade, and unroll to block a passage. ● **SEE FIGURE 24–7.**

AIR TEMPERATURE CONTROL

TEMPERATURE CONTROL USING AIRFLOW Most HVAC systems are considered *reheat* systems in that the incoming air is chilled as it passes through the evaporator. The air is then heated as part or all of the flow passes through the heater core so it reaches the desired in-vehicle temperature. ● **SEE FIGURE 24–8.**

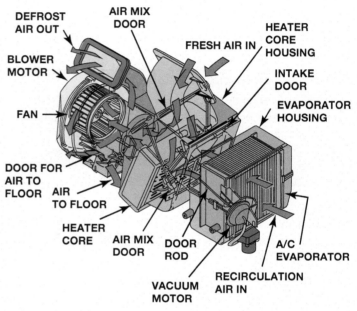

FIGURE 24–8 The blower motor forces air to flow through the A/C evaporator to remove moisture from the air before it is sent through the heater core where the air is heated before being directed to the defrost and floor vents.

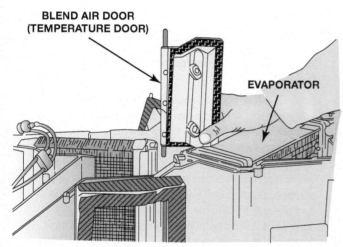

FIGURE 24–6 Many air control doors swing on their upper and lower pivots, in red.

FIGURE 24–7 (a) A typical rolling-door type HVAC door that is shown almost fully closed. (b) The same door is shown about half open.

FIGURE 24–9 An extremely dirty cabin filter removed a Subrau Legency. The owner had complained about a lack of airflow from the air conditioning vents. A new cabin filter corrected the concern.

TEMPERATURE CONTROL USING A VARIABLE COMPRESSOR There is an increasing trend to use an electronically controlled variable displacement compressor with an air temperature sensor after the evaporator. Compressor displacement is adjusted to cool the evaporator just enough to cool the air to the desired temperature. Cooling the incoming air no more than necessary will reduce compressor load on the engine and should improve fuel economy.

AIR FILTRATION

TERMINOLOGY Most HVAC systems include a **cabin filter** to remove small dust or pollen particles from the incoming airstream. This filter is also called a/an

- HVAC air filter
- Interior ventilation filter
- Micron filter
- Particulate filter
- Pollen filter

These filters require periodic replacement. If they are not serviced properly, they will cause an airflow reduction when plugged. ● SEE FIGURE 24–9.

CASES AND DUCTS

CONSTRUCTION The evaporator and heater housing is molded from reinforced plastic and contains the following components:

- Evaporator
- Heater core
- Blower motor
- Most of the air control doors

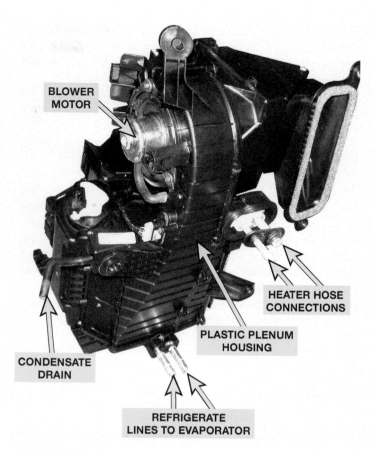

FIGURE 24–10 A typical HVAC housing that often has to be removed from the vehicle as an assembly to get access to the heater core and evaporator.

The housing, called a **plenum**, is connected to the air inlets and outlets using formed plastic. These parts are required to contain and direct airflow, reduce noise, keep outside water and debris from entering, and isolate engine fumes and noises. ● SEE FIGURE 24–10.

Air can enter the duct system from either the plenum chamber in front of the vehicle's windshield (outside air) or from the *recirc* (short for *recirculation*) or return register (inside air). The return register is often positioned below the right end of the instrument panel. (The right and left sides of the vehicle are always described as seen by the driver.) The outside air plenum often includes a screen to keep leaves and other large debris from entering with the air. ● SEE FIGURE 24–11.

PLENUM AND CONTROL DOORS

AIR INLET CONTROL DOOR The **air inlet control** door is also called

- Fresh air door
- Recirculation door
- Outside air door

FIGURE 24–11 The air inlet to the HVAC system is usually at the base of the windshield and covered with a plastic screen (grille) to help keep debris such as leaves from entering the system.

 **TECH TIP**

Keep the Air Screen Clean

The outside air inlet screen must be kept in good condition to prevent debris and small animals from entering the HVAC case. Leaves and pine needles can enter, decay, and mold. Mice have been known to enter and build nests and/or die. Any of these conditions can create a bad smell and are very difficult to clean.

This door is normally positioned so it allows airflow from one source while it shuts off the other. It can be positioned to allow

- Fresh air to enter while shutting off the recirculation opening
- Air to return or recirculate from inside the vehicle while shutting off fresh air
- A mix of fresh air and return air.

In many newer vehicles, the door is set to the fresh air position in all function lever positions except off, max heat, and max A/C. Max A/C and max heat settings position the door to recirculate in-vehicle air.

NOTE: In some vehicles, the recirculation door blocks most of the outside air and allows 80% of the air to be recirculated from the passenger compartment. About 20% of the air entering the passenger compartment is outside air to help keep the air in the passenger compartment fresh and keep the CO_2 levels low.

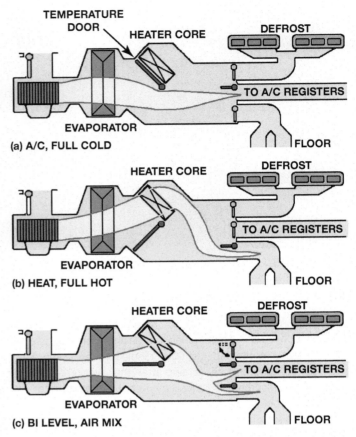

(a) A/C, FULL COLD

(b) HEAT, FULL HOT

(c) BI LEVEL, AIR MIX

FIGURE 24–12 (a) The temperature and mode doors swing to direct all of the cool air past the heater core, (b) through the core to become hot, (c) or to blend hot and cool air.

TEMPERATURE-BLEND DOOR Most systems position the evaporator so all air must pass through it. This allows removal of moisture by the evaporator's cold temperature. Many systems operate the A/C when defrost is selected to dry the air. The heater core is placed downstream so that air can be routed either through or around it using one or two doors to control this airflow. The door used to control interior temperature is called the temperature-blend door. Some other names for this door include the following:

- Air-mix door
- Temperature door
- Blend door
- Diverter door
- Bypass door ● **SEE FIGURE 24–12.**

The temperature-blend door is connected to the temperature knob or lever at the control head using a mechanical cable or an electric actuator. When the temperature lever is set to the coldest setting, the temperature-blend door routes all air so it bypasses the heater core. This causes the air entering the passenger compartment to be the coldest, coming straight from the evaporator. When the temperature lever is set to the hottest setting, the temperature-blend door routes all air through the heater core, and heated air goes to the passenger

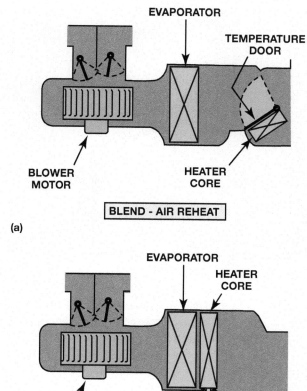

BLEND - AIR REHEAT

(a)

STACKED CORE REHEAT

(b)

FIGURE 24–13 (a) In a blend-air system, all of the air is cooled. Then some of it is reheated and blended with the cool air to get the right temperature. (b) In a reheat system, all of the air is cooled and then reheated to the correct temperature.

compartment. Setting the control lever to somewhere between cold and hot will mix or *temper* cold and hot air, allowing the driver to adjust the temperature to whatever is desired.

In the past in some vehicles, the evaporator was placed or stacked right next to the heater core. These systems controlled the air temperature by regulating the amount of reheat at the heater core. ● **SEE FIGURE 24–13.**

AIR DISTRIBUTION AND OUTLETS Air from the plenum can flow into one or two of three outlet paths:

1. The A/C registers (vents) in the face of the instrument panel
2. The defroster registers at the base of the windshield
3. The heater outlets at the floor under the instrument panel.

Most vehicles include two ducts under the front seats or in the center console to transfer air to the rear seat area. Most vehicles also direct airflow to the side windows to defog the side windows. ● **SEE FIGURE 24–14.**

Airflow to these ducts is controlled by one or more mode doors controlled by the function lever or buttons. Mode doors are also called *function, floor-defrost,* and *panel-defrost* doors. Mode/function control sets the doors as follows:

- A/C: in-dash registers with outside air inlet
- Max A/C: in-dash registers with recirculation
- Heat: floor level with outside air inlet
- Max Heat: floor level with recirculation
- Bi-level: both in-dash and floor discharge
- Defrost: windshield registers

In many systems, a small amount of air is directed to the defroster ducts when in the heat mode, and while in defrost mode, a small amount of air goes to the floor level.

DUAL-ZONE AIR DISTRIBUTION **Dual-zone** air distribution allows the driver and passenger to select different temperature settings. The temperature choices can be as much as 30°F (16°C) different. Dual-zone systems split the duct and airflow past the heater core and use two air mix valves or doors with each air mix valve/temperature door controlled by a separate actuator.

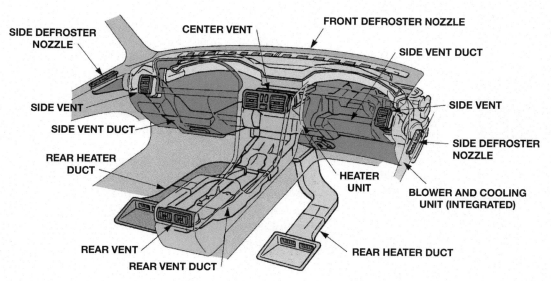

FIGURE 24–14 Ducts are placed in the center console or on the floor under the front seats to provide heated and cooled air to the rear seat passengers.

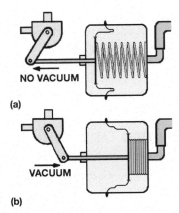

FIGURE 24–15 (a) With no vacuum signal, the spring extends the actuator shaft to place the door in a certain position. (b) A vacuum signal pulls the shaft inward and moves the door to the other position.

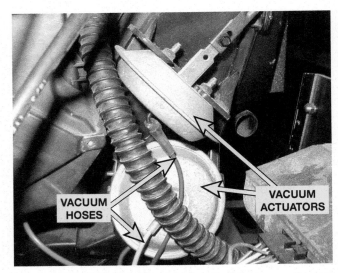

FIGURE 24–16 Many older vehicles used vacuum actuators to move the HVAC doors. When vacuum actuators operate, they alter the air–fuel mixture in the engine. Because vacuum controls affect engine operation and therefore emissions, recent vehicles use electric control systems.

NONELECTRICAL HVAC CONTROLS

CABLE-OPERATED SYSTEMS Mechanical systems are the least expensive. Most early control heads used purely mechanical operation for the doors, and one or more cables connected the function lever to the air inlet and mode doors. The temperature lever was also connected to the temperature-blend door by another cable. These mechanical levers were rather simple and usually trouble free, but they had some disadvantages. They tended to bind and could require a good deal of effort to operate.

VACUUM-OPERATED SYSTEMS Many vehicles use **vacuum actuators,** sometimes called *vacuum motors,* to operate the air inlet and mode doors. ● **SEE FIGURE 24–15.**

The doors are controlled by a vacuum valve that is operated by the control head. Vacuum controls operate more easily than cables, and vacuum hoses are much easier to route through congested areas than cables. ● **SEE FIGURE 24–16.**

ELECTRONIC HVAC CONTROLS

OVERVIEW Most recent vehicles use electrical function switches at the HVAC control head. These are often called *electromechanical controls.* These switches operate a group of solenoid valves that control the vacuum flow to the vacuum motors or use an electric actuator (motor) to operate the air distribution and temperature-blend doors. ● **SEE FIGURE 24–17.**

🔧 **TECH TIP**

Defrost All the Time? Check the Vacuum

A common problem with older vehicles that use vacuum actuators involves airflow from the defroster ducts even though the selector lever is in other positions. The defrost setting is the default position in the event of a failure with the vacuum supply. The defrost position is used because it is the *safest* position. For safety, the windshield must remain free from frost. Heat is also supplied to the passenger compartments not only through defrost ducts but also through the heater vents at floor level. If the airflow is mostly directed to the windshield, check under the hood for a broken, disconnected, or missing vacuum hose. Check the vacuum reserve container for cracks or rust (if metal) that could prevent the container from holding vacuum. Check all vacuum hose connections at the intake manifold and trace each carefully, inspecting for cracks, splits, or softened areas that may indicate a problem.

NOTE: This problem of incorrect airflow inside the vehicle often occurs after another service procedure has been performed, such as air filter or cabin filter replacement. The movement of the technician's body and arms can cause a hose to be pulled loose or a vacuum fitting to break without the service technician being aware that anything wrong has occurred.

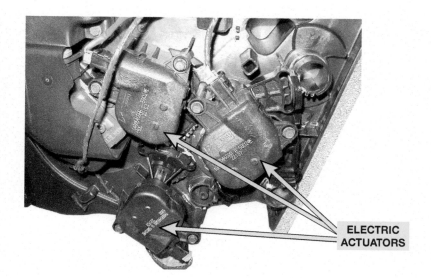

FIGURE 24–17 Three compact, electric actuators/servomotors operate the doors in this part of the HVAC case.

ELECTRIC ACTUATORS

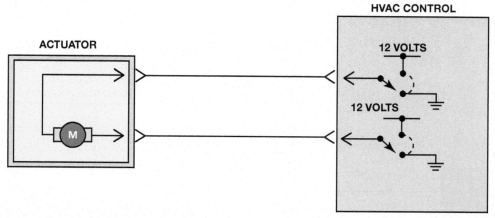

FIGURE 24–18 A two-wire HVAC electronic actuator where the direction of rotation is controlled by the HVAC control head or module, which changes the direction of rotation by changing the polarity of the power and ground connection at the motor.

TWO-WIRE ACTUATORS A typical two-wire actuator rotates when electric impulses are sent to the brushes by the HVAC control head. The direction of rotation, and therefore the movement of the HVAC door position, is changed by changing the wire that is pulsed with power and the other brush is then connected to ground. ● **SEE FIGURE 24–18.**

THREE-WIRE ACTUATORS A typical three-wire actuator uses a power, ground, and an input signal wire from the HVAC control module. There is a module (logic chip) inside the motor assembly that receives a 0 to 5-volt signal from the HVAC control module. When the actuator gets a 0-volt signal from the control module, it rotates in one direction and when it receives a 5-volt signal, it rotates in the opposite direction. If the motor receives a 2.5-volt signal, the motor stops rotating. ● **SEE FIGURE 24–19.**

FIVE-WIRE ACTUATORS A five-wire actuator uses two wires to power the motor (power and ground) and three wires for a potentiometer that is used to signal the HVAC control module of the motor's location. The potentiometer

may be a separate gear-driven part attached to the motor or a part of the printed circuit board where a slider moves across resistive paint to create the potentiometer signal voltage. ● **SEE FIGURE 24–20.**

Most HVAC control modules convert the potentiometer signal voltage to a binary number ranging from 0 to 255, which is often seen on a scan tool display. The HVAC control module monitors the feedback signal to determine the actual location of the door and to determine if the door is stuck. If the motor position falls outside of the expected range, there can be two things that can occur, depending on the vehicle.

1. The controller, usually the HVAC control module, will drive the motor until it reaches its desired location. This action can result a ticking sound being heard as the motor attempts to reach the desired position.

2. The controller will move the motor to a default position and then stop working, making the HVAC controls inoperative.

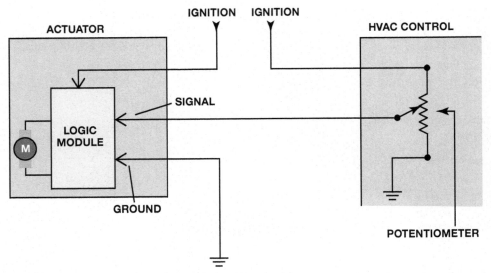

FIGURE 24–19 Three-wire actuators include a logic chip inside the motor assembly. The HVAC control module then sends a 0-volt to 5-volt signal to the motor assembly to control the direction of rotation.

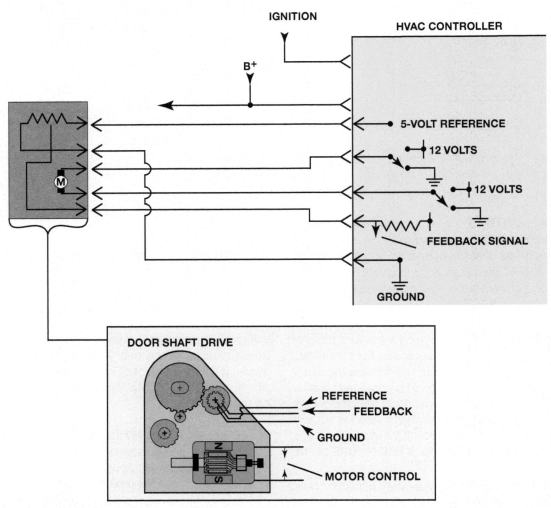

FIGURE 24–20 A typical five-wire HVAC actuator showing the two wires used to power the motor and the three wires used for the motor position potentiometer.

ACTUATOR CALIBRATION PROCEDURES

An HVAC actuator may need to be calibrated after the actuator has been replaced. Check service information for the specified procedure to follow to perform a calibration if needed.

A typical calibration procedure to use when installing a new actuator using a scan tool includes the following steps:

STEP 1 Clear all diagnostic trouble codes (DTCs).

STEP 2 Turn the ignition switch to the off position.

STEP 3 Install the replacement actuator and reconnect all mechanical and electrical connections.

STEP 4 Start the engine and select motor recalibration program on the scan tool under the functions menu.

STEP 5 Verify that no diagnostic trouble codes have been set.

CAUTION: Do not operate an actuator prior to installation to "test it" because many actuators operate until they are stopped mechanically by the door being fully open or fully closed. If operated using a battery and jumper wires without being installed, the actuator can be moved beyond its normal range of motion and will not operate correctly, if at all, when placed into the HVAC housing.

FIGURE 24–21 A squirrel cage blower motor. A replacement blower motor usually does not come equipped with the squirrel cage blower, so it has to be switched from the old motor.

BLOWER MOTOR

PURPOSE AND FUNCTION The same blower motor moves air inside the vehicle for the following:

1. Air conditioning
2. Heat
3. Defrosting
4. Defogging
5. Venting of the passenger compartment

The motor turns a squirrel cage-type fan. A squirrel cage-type fan is able to move air without creating a lot of noise. The fan switch controls the path that the current follows to the blower motor. ● **SEE FIGURE 24–21**

PARTS AND OPERATION The motor is usually a permanent magnet, one-speed motor that operates at its maximum speed with full battery voltage. The switch gets current from the fuse panel with the ignition switch on, and then directs full battery voltage to the blower motor for high speed and to the blower motor through resistors for lower speeds.

VARIABLE SPEED CONTROL The fan switch controls the path of current through a resistor pack to obtain different fan speeds of the blower motor. The electrical path can be the following:

- Full battery voltage for high-speed operation
- Through one or more resistors to reduce the voltage and the current to the blower motor which then rotates at a slower speed. The resistors are

located near the blower motor and mounted in the duct where the airflow from the blower can cool the resistors. The current flow through the resistor is controlled by the switch and often uses a relay to carry the heavy current (10 to 12 amperes) needed to power the fan. Normal operation includes the following:

- Low speed. Current flows through three resistors in series to drop the voltage to about 4 volts and 4 amperes.
- Medium-low speed. Current is directed through two resistors in series to lower the voltage to about 6 volts and 6 amperes.
- Medium-high speed. Current is directed through one resistor resulting in a voltage of about 9 volts and a current of 9 amperes.
- High speed. Full battery voltage, usually through a relay, is applied to the blower motor resulting in a current of about 12 amperes. ● **SEE FIGURES 24-22 AND 24-23.**

Some blower motors are electronically controlled by the body control module and include electronic circuits to achieve a variable speed. ● **SEE FIGURE 24-24.**

BLOWER MOTOR DIAGNOSIS If the blower motor does not operate at any speed, the problem could be any of the following:

1. Defective ground wire or ground wire connection
2. Defective blower motor (not repairable; must be replaced)
3. Open circuit in the power-side circuit, including fuse, wiring, or fan switch If the blower works on lower speeds but not on high speed, the problem is usually an in-line fuse or high-speed relay that controls the heavy current flow for high-speed operation. The high-speed fuse or relay usually

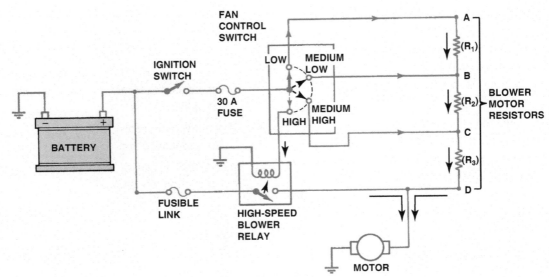

FIGURE 24–22 A blower motor circuit with four speeds controlled using resistors. The three lowest fan speeds (low, medium-low, and medium-high) use the blower motor resistors to drop the voltage to the motor and reduce current to the motor. On high, the resistors are bypassed. The "high" position on the fan switch energizes a relay, which supplies the current for the blower on high through a fusible link or maxi fuse.

FIGURE 24–23 A blower motor resistor pack used to control blower motor speed. Some blower motor resistors are flat and look like a credit card and are called "credit card resistors."

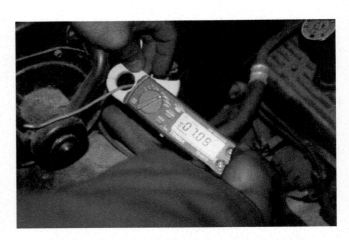

FIGURE 24–25 Using a mini AC/DC clamp-on multimeter to measure the current drawn by a blower motor.

FIGURE 24–24 A brushless DC motor that uses the body computer to control the speed.

fails as a result of internal blower motor bushing wear, which causes excessive resistance to motor rotation. At slow blower speeds, the resistance is not as noticeable and the blower operates normally. The blower motor is a sealed unit, and if defective, must be replaced as a unit. The squirrel cage fan usually needs to be removed from the old motor and attached to the replacement motor. If the blower motor operates normally at high speed but not at any of the lower speeds, the problem could be melted wire resistors or a defective switch. The blower motor can be tested using a clamp-on DC ammeter. ● SEE FIGURE 24–25.

Most blower motors do not draw more than 15 amperes on high speed. A worn or defective motor usually draws more current than normal and could damage the blower motor resistors or blow a fuse if not replaced.

1. Air flows into the case that contains the evaporator and heater core from two possible inlets:
   - Outside air, often called fresh air
   - Inside air, usually called recirculation air.

2. The HVAC case contains a blower, A/C evaporator, the heater core, and doors to control the air temperature and flow.

3. The control head allows the driver to change blower speed, adjust the temperature, turn A/C on or off, and direct the airflow.

4. Control heads transfer motion to the HVAC case through cables, vacuum control, or electronics and electric motors.

5. Most HVAC systems include a filter to remove particles and odors from the air.

REVIEW QUESTIONS

1. What do the three main HVAC doors do?

2. In the heating mode, why is heat directed toward the floor?

3. Where is the air directed when the control panel is set to defog/defrost position?

4. How does a "reheat" system work and why?

5. Where does the air enter the vehicle when outside air is selected?

CHAPTER QUIZ

1. "Outside air" is also called _____ air.
   - a. recirculation
   - b. fresh
   - c. plenum
   - d. mode

2. The _____ door is used to select air discharge location such as floor, vent, or defrost.
   - a. mode
   - b. recirculation
   - c. fresh air
   - d. Any of the above

3. What does the snowflake button on the dash do?
   - a. Selects defrost
   - b. Selects defog
   - c. Turns on the A/C compressor
   - d. Selects fresh outside air

4. The ram air that enters the vehicle from the outside enters the HVAC system from _____.
   - a. beside the headlight
   - b. behind the grille
   - c. the side vents
   - d. the base of the windshield

5. Most systems use a flap door that swings about _____ degrees.
   - a. 10 to 25
   - b. 25 to 40
   - c. 45 to 90
   - d. 90 to 120

6. The air inlet control door is also called _____.
   - a. fresh air door
   - b. recirculation door
   - c. outside air door
   - d. Any of the above

7. The door used to control interior temperature is called the _____ door.
   - a. temperature-blend
   - b. recirculation
   - c. outside (fresh) air
   - d. mode

8. A five-wire actuator uses two wires to power the motor (power and ground) and three wires for _____.
   - a. direction control
   - b. a feedback potentiometer
   - c. static electricity protection
   - d. redundant control

9. How is the speed of the blower motor controlled?
   - a. A 3 or 4 speed motor is used
   - b. A series of resistors are used to drop the voltage and the current to the blower motor.
   - c. A variable resistor in the blower speed control switch is used to change the speed
   - d. Any of the above depending on the make and model of vehicle.

10. A typical blower motor draws _____ on high speed?
    - a. 5 to 7 amperes
    - b. 12 amperes
    - c. 20 to 25 amperes
    - d. 30 to 40 amperes

chapter 25

IMMOBILIZER SYSTEMS

LEARNING OBJECTIVES

After studying this chapter, the reader will be able to:

1. Describe the purpose and function of a security system.
2. Explain how an immobilizer system works.
3. List the engine-related faults that can be caused by the immobilizer system when it malfunctions.
4. Identify the major components that could be involved with an immobilizer system.
5. Explain how to diagnose a fault with an immobilizer system.

Prepare for ASE Engine Performance (A8) certification test content area "A" (General Diagnosis).

KEY TERMS

Key fob 396
Radio frequency
    identification
    (RFID) 396
Remote keyless entry
    (RKE) 396

Sentry Key Immobilizer
    System (SKIS) 398
Transceiver 396
Transponder 396

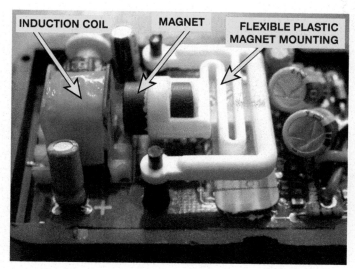

FIGURE 25–1 A shock sensor used in alarm and antitheft systems. If the vehicle is moved, the magnet will move relative to the coil, inducing a small voltage that will trigger the alarm.

FIGURE 25–2 The security system symbol used on a Ford. The symbol varies by make, model, and year; so check service information to determine what symbol is used on the vehicle being diagnosed.

VEHICLE SECURITY SYSTEMS

PURPOSE AND FUNCTION The purpose and function of a security system on a vehicle is to prevent the unauthorized use (theft) of the vehicle. This function is accomplished by installing the following locks:

1. A lock on the doors to help prevent unauthorized entry to the interior of the vehicle.

2. A lock for the ignition so a key is needed to crank and start the engine and unlock the steering wheel, starting in 1970.

While these locks have worked, vehicles can still be easily stolen if access to the interior and the ignition switch is accessible. It is the purpose and function of an immobilizer system to prevent the vehicle from being started if the correct ignition key is not used, even if an intruder gains access to the interior of the vehicle and tries to use a key that fits the lock cylinder.

POSSIBLE IMMOBILIZER CAUSED FAULTS Faults with the immobilizer system can be the cause of one of the following conditions depending on the exact make and model of a vehicle:

- No crank condition (the starter motor does not operate)
- The engine cranks but does not start (fuel disabled in most vehicles)
- The engine starts, but then almost immediately stalls.

Therefore, if a customer concern involves any of these situations, a fault in the immobilizer system is a possible cause rather than a fault with the ignition or fuel system.

IMMOBILIZER SYSTEMS

NORMAL OPERATION A vehicle equipped with an immobilizer system operates normally as follows:

- When a valid key is used, and is rotated to the start position, the engine cranks and starts and the immobilizer symbol on the dash will flash on and off for about two seconds, and then go off. ● **SEE FIGURE 25–2**.
- If there is a fault with an invalid key, the dash symbol will flash continuously and the engine will not start or if it does crank and start, the engine will not continue to run.

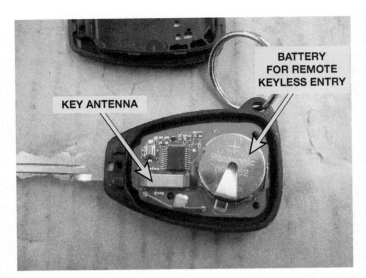

FIGURE 25–3 A typical key with the cover removed showing the battery used to power the door lock and the antenna used for the immobilizer system.

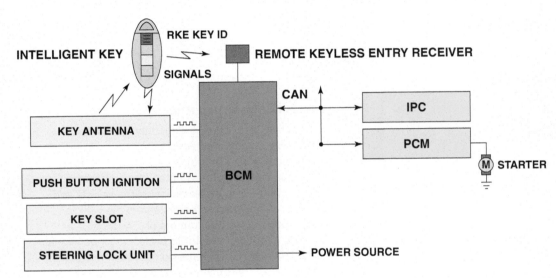

FIGURE 25–4 The remote keyless entry is used to unlock the doors, as well as create the signals to the powertrain control module (PCM) used to control the starter motor and/ or the fuel system and the warning lamp on the instrument panel cluster (IPC).

IMMOBILIZER SYSTEM PARTS

Most security systems today use a **Radio Frequency Identification (RFID)** security system, which has two main components:

1. A **key fob** is the object that is a decoration on a key ring and usually contains a transmitter used to unlock a vehicle. While the **remote keyless entry (RKE)** part of the key fob has a battery to power the transmitter, the RFID chip part of the key fob does not require a battery to function. The **transponder** is mounted in the key or the body of the key fob. A transponder has an antenna, which consists of a coil of wire, as well as a circuit board containing the processing electronics and data memory. ● **SEE FIGURE 25–3.**

2. The transponder key has the transponder electronics integrated in its plastic body. It consists of the following components:

   ■ A microchip contains the unique internal identification (ID) number. To prevent an unauthorized scanning of the ID number, the code changes with each transfer and uses several million different coding possibilities. ● **SEE FIGURE 25–4.**

■ The coil antenna in the key consists of a copper coil wound up in a ring case and an integrated circuit to create a high-frequency alternating voltage for the inductive coupling. Through inductive (electromagnetic) coupling, the data from the key is transferred to the immobilizer module.

■ Another coil is installed around the lock cylinder and connected to the control module of the immobilizer system. This coil transfers and receives all data signals to and from the immobilizer control module, using the coil antenna/transceiver. It does not need to be reprogrammed to the immobilizer system in case of replacement.

■ A **transceiver** is inside the vehicle and receives the signal transmitted by the transponder in the key. A "transceiver" functions as both a reviewer and a transmitter. The transceiver is usually mounted on the steering column assembly. The antenna for the transceiver is a coil of wire mounted within the plastic ring that mounts around the lock cylinder. ● **SEE FIGURE 25–5 AND 25–6.**

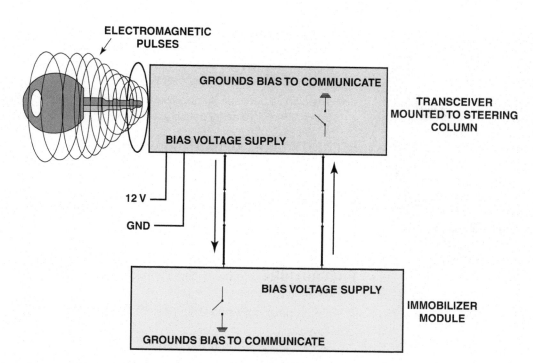

FIGURE 25–5 A typical immobilizer circuit showing the communication between the key and the transceiver. The transceiver then communicates with the immobilizer module over data lines.

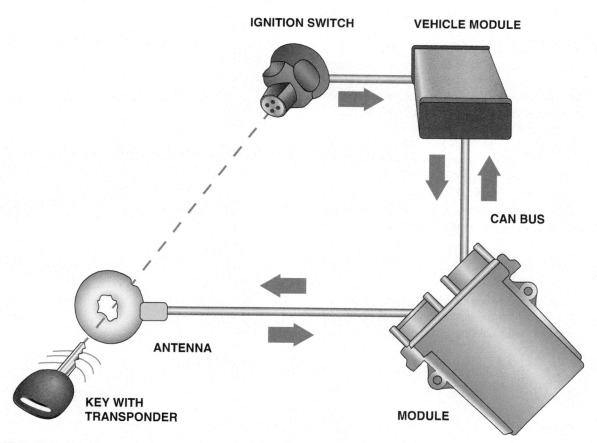

FIGURE 25–6 The communication between the components and modules of the security system use a combination of hard wired and data bus messages.

What Is a Passive Keyless Entry System?

A passive system uses the key fob as a transmitter, which communicates with the vehicle as it comes close. The key is identified using one of several antennas around the body of the vehicle and a radio pulse generator in the key housing. Depending on the system, the vehicle is automatically unlocked when a button or sensor on the door handle or trunk release is depressed.

Vehicles with a passive (smart) key system can also have a mechanical backup, usually in the form of a key blade built into the key fob. Vehicles with a smart key system can be started without inserting a key in the ignition, provided the driver has the key fob inside the vehicle. On most vehicles, this is done most often by pressing a start button. When leaving a vehicle equipped with a smart key system, the vehicle is locked, depending on the make, model, and year of manufacture of vehicle, by:

- pressing a button on one of the door handles,
- touching a capacitive area on a door handle, or
- simply walking away from the vehicle and will lock the doors when the key fob is further away than 15 feet (5m).

IMMOBILIZER SYSTEM OPERATION When the ignition key in inserted, the transceiver sends out an electromagnetic energy pulse. This energy pulse is received by the coil inside the key transponder, which creates a voltage. The information or data in the magnetic pulses is in the form of a frequency modulated signal.

A typical immobilizer system consists of transponder key, coil antenna, key reminder switch, separate immobilizer module, PCM, and security light. Most immobilizer systems work as follows:

- The key identification (ID) numbers are stored in a non-volatile memory of the immobilizer module. At each start, the module compares the ID number of the transponder key used with those stored in the memory.
- If the verification has been successful, the immobilizer module sends a request signal to the PCM to compare the key ID number with the numbers registered in the PCM.
- Each immobilizer module has its unique code word that is stored in the PCM. After the verification of the ID number, the immobilizer module requests the code word from the PCM.

- The immobilizer module controls the starter circuit and the security light and signals the PCM to activate fuel injection and ignition when the ID number and code word verification have been successful.
- The signals between immobilizer module and PCM are transmitted via a serial data line.

SECURITY LIGHT OPERATION Normal operation of the security light includes a self-test and flashes a few times then goes out. However, if a fault is detected, the security light will continue to flash and the engine may not start. If a fault occurs with the immobilizer system when the engine is running, then the security light will come on, but the engine will not be shut off as this condition is not a theft attempt.

PRECAUTIONS To avoid damage to the key, do not allow the following to happen to the key:

- Be dropped onto a hard surface
- Get wet
- Be exposed to any kind of magnetic field
- Be exposed to high temperatures on places, such as the top of the dash under direct sunlight.

A system malfunction may occur if any of the following items are touching the key or are near the key head:

- A metal object
- Spare keys or keys for other vehicles equipped with an immobilizer system
- An electronic device, such as cards with magnetic strips

TECH TIP

Do Not Have Other Keys Near

Whenever diagnosing an immobilizer system, keep other key fobs away from the area. If another key fob is close, it could be transmitting a signal that is not recognized by the vehicle and the security system could prevent proper vehicle operation. Even having other metal objects near the key can affect the strength of the electromagnetic pulses and could interfere with the immobilizer system and prevent it from working as designed. ● **SEE FIGURE 25–7.**

(a)

(b)

(c)

FIGURE 25–7 (a) Avoid using a key where the key ring is over the top of the key, which can interfere with the operation of the immobilizer system. (b) Do not angle another key upward from the key being used to help prevent interference with the magnetic field used to energize the key. (c) Do not have the keys from another vehicle near the key being used.

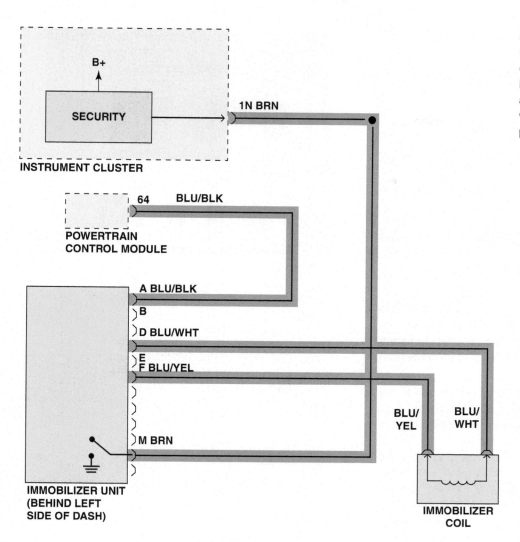

FIGURE 25–8 Check service information for the exact wiring diagram (schematic) for the vehicle being tested. Highlighting the wires and noting their color will help when following the specified testing procedures.

TYPICAL IMMOBILIZER CIRCUITS The diagnostic process involved with positively identifying the defective security system component can be quick and accurate. At the transceiver check for power, ground, and proper communication on data transmission lines. ● **SEE FIGURE 25–8.**

CAUTION: Do not leave the key in the ignition as this will often keep the immobilizer system alive and will drain the vehicle battery. If leaving the vehicle, take the key out of the ignition and best to place it 15 feet (5m) away to help avoid possible issues.

CHRYSLER IMMOBILZER SYSTEM

Beginning in 1998, Chrysler started a security system known as the **Sentry Key Immobilizer System (SKIS)**. When an attempt to start a vehicle arises, the onboard computer sends out a radio-frequency (RF) signal that is read by the electronic transponder chip embedded in the key. The transponder then returns a unique signal back to the SKIM, giving it the okay for the vehicle to start and continue to run. This all happens in under a second, and is completely transparent to the vehicle driver. For additional security, two preprogrammed keys are needed in order to register additional keys into the system. In the event of the loss of all keys, special programming equipment is needed to register new keys into the system.

CHRYSLER SELF-PROGRAMMING ADDITIONAL SENTRY KEYS (REQUIRES TWO ORIGINAL KEYS)

Quick steps:

STEP 1 Purchase a blank key and have it cut to fit the lock cylinder.

STEP 2 Insert the original key #1 into the ignition and turn to ON.

STEP 3 Wait 5 seconds and turn the key to OFF.

STEP 4 Immediately insert the original key #2 into the ignition and turn to ON.

STEP 5 Wait 10 seconds for the SKIS indicator in the dash to start to flash.

STEP 6 Turn the ignition off, insert the new blank key, and turn the ignition back on.

STEP 7 Once the SKIS light stops flashing and turns off, the new key is programmed.

FORD PATS SYSTEM

Ford uses a responder key for their antitheft system, which is called the **Passive Antitheft System** (**PATS**).

FORD PROGRAMMING FOR ADDITIONAL (PATS) KEYS

This procedure will work only if two or more programmed ignition keys are available. The steps include the following:

STEP 1 Insert the first programmed ignition key into the ignition lock cylinder. Turn the ignition switch from the LOCK to RUN position (ignition switch must stay in the run position for 1 second). Turn the ignition switch to the LOCK position and remove the ignition key from the ignition lock cylinder.

STEP 2 Within 5 seconds of turning the ignition switch to the LOCK position, insert the second programmed ignition key into the ignition lock cylinder. Turn the ignition switch from the LOCK to RUN position (ignition switch must stay in the RUN position for 1 second). Turn the ignition switch to the LOCK position and remove the second ignition key from the ignition lock cylinder.

STEP 3 Within 5 seconds of turning the ignition switch to the LOCK position, insert a new un-programmed ignition key into the ignition lock cylinder. Turn the ignition switch from the LOCK to RUN position (the ignition switch must stay in the RUN position for 1 second). Turn the ignition switch to the LOCK position and remove the ignition key from the ignition lock cylinder. The new ignition key should now be programmed. To program additional key(s), repeat the key programming procedure from Step 1.

GENERAL MOTORS ANTITHEFT SYSTEM

The type of antitheft system used on General Motors vehicles has included many different systems starting with an antitheft system that used a resistor pellet in the ignition key. If the key fit the lock cylinder and the resistance was the correct value, the engine would crank and start. This system was called the **Vehicle Antitheft System** or (**VATS**). A special tester was required to test this system. ● **SEE FIGURE 25–9**.

Newer systems include the **Passkey I** and **Passkey II**, which also use a resistor pellet in the ignition key. **Passlock I**, **Passlock II**, and **Passlock III** systems use a Hall-effect sensor and magnets in the lock cylinder with a conventional key. ● **SEE FIGURE 25–10**.

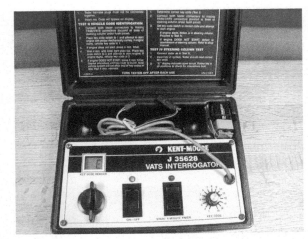

FIGURE 25–9 A special tool is needed to diagnose a General Motors VATS security system and special keys that contain a resistor pellet.

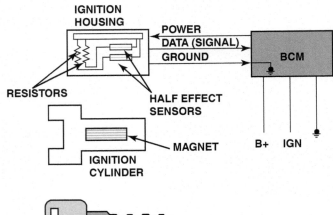

FIGURE 25–10 The Passlock series of General Motors security systems uses a conventional key. The magnet is located in the ignition lock cylinder and triggers the Hall-effect sensors.

Passkey III systems use a transponder embedded into the head of the key, which is stamped "SK3." Most of the systems disable the starter and the fuel injectors, but Passlock I disables fuel after the engine starts and the security light will then flash. Due to the various systems, service information must be used and followed to diagnose and repair a fault in these systems.

TESTING IMMOBILIZER SYSTEMS

DIAGNOSTIC STEPS Most vehicle manufacturers recommend a series of steps that a technician should follow when diagnosing a fault with the immobilizer system.

STEP 1 **Verify the Customer Concern.** A fault with the immobilizer system will often cause the engine to not start

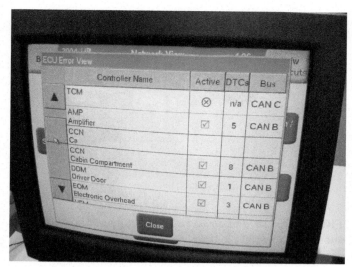

FIGURE 25–11 Scan tools, such as this factory tool being used on a BMW, are capable of many diagnostic functions that can help the technician zero in on the root cause of a problem.

DTC	DESCRIPTION OF FAULT
P0513	Incorrect Immobilizer Key
P1570	Fault in antenna detected
P1517	Reference code not compatible with ECM
P1572	Communications failure with ECM
B2957	Security System Data Circuit Low
B2960	Security System Data Wrong But Valid

CHART 25–1

Sample DTCs for an immobilizer system. These codes vary by make, model, and year of manufacture, so check service information for the exact vehicle being diagnosed.

TECH TIP

Look for DTCs in "Body" and "Chassis"

Whenever diagnosing a customer concern with the immobilizer system, check for diagnostic trouble codes (DTCs) under chassis and body systems. A global or generic scan tool that can read only "P" codes is not suitable for diagnosing many faults with the immobilizer system. Engine or emission control-type codes are "P" codes, whereas module communications are "U" codes. These are most often found when looking for DTCs under chassis or body systems. Chassis-related codes are labeled "C" and body system-related codes are labeled "B" codes and these can cause an immobilizer issue if they affect a sensor that is used by the system. ● SEE FIGURE 25–11.

■ **Normal.** The security dash lamp comes on for 2 to 5 seconds for a bulb check when the ignition is turned on, then goes out.

■ **Tamper mode.** The security lamp flashes about once per second if the system detects a bad key, lock cylinder, or security-related wiring problem. The engine will not start or if it does start, will not continue to run.

■ **Fail enable mode.** If a fault with the security system occurs when the vehicle is running, the security light will remain on but the immobilizer system will be disabled because it is apparently, not a theft attempt. Therefore, the engine will start and run as normal except that the security warning light on the dash will be on all the time.

Check for the presence of aftermarket accessories such as an add-on remote starter system. These systems require the use of a spare key that is held near the lock cylinder, thereby allowing the engine to start using a remote control. A fault with the aftermarket system could have an effect on the proper operation of the immobilizer system.

STEP 3 **Check for DTCs.** Use a factory or enhanced factory level aftermarket scan tool and retrieve DTCs. Check service information for the exact codes for the vehicle being checked. ● SEE CHART 25–1 for some sample DTCs and their meaning.

STEP 4 **Check for Technical Service Bulletins.** Technical service bulletins (TSBs) are issued by vehicle and aftermarket manufacturers to inform technicians of a situation or technical problem and give the corrective steps and a list of parts needed to solve the problem. Any DTCs should be retrieved before looking at the technical service bulletins because many bulletins include what DTCs may or may not be present. ● SEE FIGURE 25–12.

While some of these TSBs concern minor problems covering few vehicles, many contain very helpful solutions to hard-to-find problems that cover many vehicles. TSBs can also be purchased through aftermarket companies that are licensed and available on a website. Visit the National Automotive Service Task

or start and then stall. Faults can also be intermittent because many systems will "time out" after 20 minutes if an error occurs and then works normally after the wait period. A "no-start" condition can also occur that is not associated with the immobilizer system and should be handled using normal diagnostic procedures as specified by the vehicle manufacturer for a no-start condition.

STEP 2 **Visual Inspection.** Most vehicle manufacturers specify that the first step after the customer concern has been verified is that a visual inspection be performed. A visual inspection includes checking the security light status. A typical security light status includes the following:

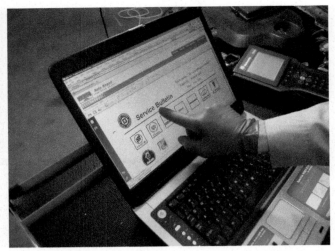

FIGURE 25–12 After checking for stored diagnostic trouble codes (DTCs), the wise technician checks service information for any technical service bulletins (TSBs) that may relate to the vehicle being serviced.

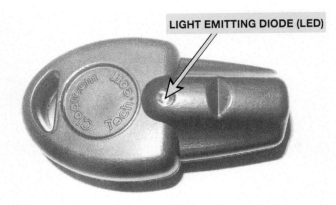

LIGHT EMITTING DIODE (LED)

FIGURE 25–13 Immobilizer coil detectors can be found on line by searching for immobilizer transponder coil detector.

Force (NASTF) website (www.NASTF.org) for a list of the Web addresses for all vehicle manufacturers' sites where the full text of TSBs can be purchased directly. Factory TSBs can often save the technician many hours of troubleshooting.

STEP 5 **Perform Pinpoint Tests.** Following the specified diagnostic steps found in service information, check for the system for proper voltage at each of the components.

STEP 6 **Determine the Root Cause.** By following the specified diagnostic routine, the root cause can often be determined. If a module is replaced, it will usually have to be programmed to accept the ignition key and this can be a huge problem if a used module is chosen instead of a new one. Always check service information for the exact procedure to follow.

STEP 7 **Verify the Repair.** After the repairs or service procedures have been performed, verify that the system is working as designed. If needed, operate the

vehicle under the same conditions that it was when the customer concern was corrected to verify the repair. Document the work order and return the vehicle to the customer in clean condition.

SUMMARY

1. Faults with the immobilizer system can cause one of the following conditions:
   - No crank condition (the starter motor does not operate)
   - The engine cranks but does not start
   - The engine starts but then almost immediately stalls.

2. Most security systems today use a Radio Frequency Identification (RFID) security system.

3. The transponder key has the transponder electronic integrated in its plastic handle where it is encapsulated in a glass or plastic body.

4. The transceiver is usually mounted to the steering column assembly. The antenna for the transceiver is a coil of wire mounted within the plastic ring that mounts around the lock cylinder.

5. A typical immobilizer system consists of transponder key, coil antenna, key reminder switch, separate immobilizer module, PCM, and security light.

6. Normal operation of the security light includes a self-test and flashes a few times then goes out. However, if a fault is detected, the security light will continue to flash and the engine may not start.

7. To diagnosis an immobilizer system, use a factory or enhanced factory level aftermarket scan tool and retrieve DTCs, then follow the specified diagnostic procedures.

REVIEW QUESTIONS

1. What faults will an immobilizer system cause?
2. How is the security information transferred from the key to the vehicle?
3. A typical immobilizer system consists of what parts?
4. To avoid damage to the key, what precautions are needed to be performed?
5. What is a passive keyless entry system?

CHAPTER QUIZ

1. What is the purpose and function of an immobilizer system?
   a. To prevent entry inside the vehicle
   b. Only allows the use of the ignition key that is properly matched to the lock cylinder
   c. Prevents the vehicle from starting or running if the correct key is not used
   d. Requires that the driver enter a password to start the vehicle

2. What does the battery in the key fob power?
   a. The shock sensor
   b. The remote keyless entry (RKE)
   c. The immobilizer circuit
   d. Both the remote keyless entry and the immobilizer circuit

3. What can occur if the immobilizer system is not working as designed?
   a. No crank condition (the starter motor does not operate)
   b. The engine cranks but does not start
   c. The engine starts but then almost immediately stalls
   d. Any of the above

4. An immobilizer fault may occur if the _____.
   a. the key is dropped onto a hard surface
   b. the key gets wet
   c. the key is exposed to any kind of magnetic field
   d. Any of the above

5. How is data transmitted between the key and the steering column (lock cylinder)?
   a. By inductive coupling
   b. By electrical contacts inside the lock cylinder
   c. Transmitted from the key to the vehicle using the battery inside the key
   d. Transferred from the key to the BCM using a small transmitter in the key

6. A typical Ford immobilizer system is called _____.
   a. VATS
   b. PATS
   c. Passlock
   d. SKIS

7. A typical Chrysler immobilizer system is called _____.
   a. VATS
   b. PATS
   c. Passlock
   d. SKIS

8. The security dash lamp comes on for 2 to 5 seconds and then goes out. This indicates what condition?
   a. A fault has been detected in the key transponder
   b. A fault has been detected in the wiring near the ignition lock cylinder
   c. Normal security light operation
   d. The system has entered tamper mode

9. Immobilizer DTCs are often found under what area?
   a. Engine-related "P" codes
   b. Body-related "B" codes
   c. Chassis-related "C" codes
   d. Any of the above

10. Tamper mode is when what occurs?
    a. The security lamp flashes about once per second if the system detects a bad key, lock cylinder, or security-related wiring problem. The engine will not start or if it does start, will not continue to run.
    b. The security dash lamp comes on for 2 to 5 seconds for a bulb check when the ignition is turned on, then goes out.
    c. The engine will start and run as normal except that the security warning light on the dash will be on all the time.
    d. Any of the above, depending on the make, model and year of vehicle.

chapter 26

AIRBAG AND PRETENSIONER CIRCUITS

LEARNING OBJECTIVES

After studying this chapter, the reader will be able to:

1. Diagnose and repair faulty safety belts and retractors.
2. Explain the operation of front airbags.
3. Describe the procedures to diagnose and repair common faults in airbag systems.
4. Disarm and enable the airbag system for vehicle service.
5. Explain how the passenger presence system works.

This chapter will help you prepare for the ASE Electrical/Electronic Systems (A6) certification test content area "F" (Body Electrical Systems Diagnosis and Repair).

KEY TERMS

Airbag 406
Arming sensor 407
Clockspring 410
Deceleration sensors 409
Dual-stage airbags 410
EDR 417
Integral sensors 409
Occupant detection system (ODS) 415
Passenger presence system (PPS) 415
Pretensioners 406
SAR 406
SIR 406
Squib 407
SRS 406

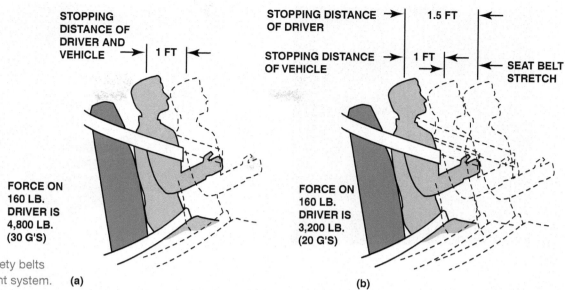

FIGURE 26–1 (a) Safety belts are the primary restraint system. (b) During a collision, the stretching of the safety belt slows the impact to help reduce bodily injury.

CRASH SCENARIO WITH A VEHICLE STOPPING IN ONE FOOT DISTANCE FROM A SPEED OF 30 MPH.

SAFETY BELTS AND RETRACTORS

SAFETY BELTS Safety belts are used to keep the driver and passengers secured to the vehicle in the event of a collision. Most safety belts include three-point support and are constructed of nylon webbing about 2 inches (5 cm) wide. The three support points include two points on either side of the seat for the belt over the lap and one crossing over the upper torso, which is attached to the "B" pillar or seat back. Every crash consists of three types of collisions:

Collision 1: The vehicle strikes another vehicle or object.

Collision 2: The driver and/or passengers hit objects inside the vehicle if unbelted.

Collision 3: The internal organs of the body hit other organs or bones, which causes internal injuries.

If a safety belt is being worn, the belt stretches, absorbing a lot of the impact, thereby preventing collision with other objects in the vehicle and reducing internal injuries. ● **SEE FIGURE 26–1**.

BELT RETRACTORS Safety belts are also equipped with one of the following types of retractors:

■ Emergency locking retractors, which lock the position of the safety belt in the event of a collision or rollover

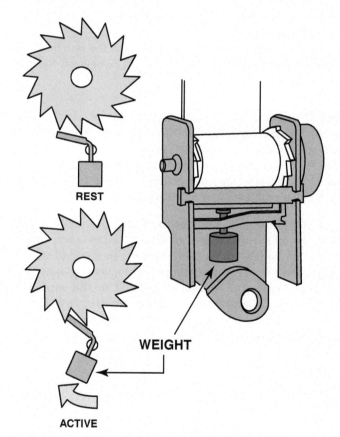

FIGURE 26–2 Most safety belts have an inertia-type mechanism that locks the belt in the event of rapid movement.

■ Emergency and web speed-sensitive retractors, which allow freedom of movement for the driver and passenger but lock if the vehicle is accelerating too fast or if the vehicle is decelerating too fast

● **SEE FIGURE 26–2** for an example of an inertia-type seat belt locking mechanism.

FIGURE 26–3 A typical safety belt warning light.

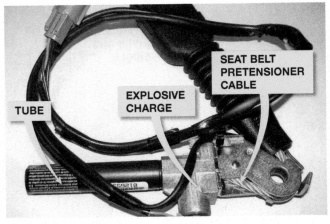

FIGURE 26–4 A small explosive charge in the pretensioner forces the end of the seat belt down the tube, which removes any slack in the seat belt.

SAFETY BELT LIGHTS AND CHIMES All late-model vehicles are equipped with a safety belt warning light on the dash and a chime that sounds if the belt is not fastened. ● **SEE FIGURE 26–3.**

Some vehicles will intermittently flash the reminder light and sound a chime until the driver and sometimes the front passenger fasten their safety belts.

PRETENSIONERS A **pretensioner** is an explosive (pyrotechnic) device that is part of the seat belt retractor assembly and tightens the seat belt as the airbag is being deployed. The purpose of the pretensioning device is to force the occupant back into position against the seat back and to remove any slack in the seat belt. ● **SEE FIGURE 26–4.**

CAUTION: The seat belt pretensioner assemblies must be replaced in the event of an airbag deployment. Always follow the vehicle manufacturer's recommended service procedure. Pretensioners are explosive devices that could be ignited if voltage is applied to the terminals. Do not use a jumper wire or powered test light around the seat belt latch wiring. Always follow the vehicle manufacturer's recommended test procedures.

FRONT AIRBAGS

PURPOSE AND FUNCTION **Airbag** passive restraints are designed to cushion the driver (or passenger, if the passenger side is so equipped) during a frontal collision. The system consists of one or more nylon bags folded up in compartments located in the steering wheel, dashboard, interior panels, or side pillars of the vehicle. During a crash of sufficient force, pressurized gas instantly fills the airbag and then deploys out of the storage compartment to protect the occupant from serious injury. These airbag systems may be known by many different names, including the following:

1. **Supplemental restraint system (SRS)**
2. **Supplemental inflatable restraints (SIR)**
3. **Supplemental air restraints (SAR)**

Most airbags are designed to supplement the safety belts in the event of a collision, and front airbags are meant to be deployed only in the event of a frontal impact within 30 degrees of center. Front (driver and passenger side) airbag systems are *not* designed to inflate during side or rear impact. The force required to deploy a typical airbag is approximately equal to the force of a vehicle hitting a wall at over 10 mph (16 km/h).

The force required to trigger the sensors within the system prevents accidental deployment if curbs are hit or the brakes are rapidly applied. The system requires a substantial force to deploy the airbag to help prevent accidental inflation.

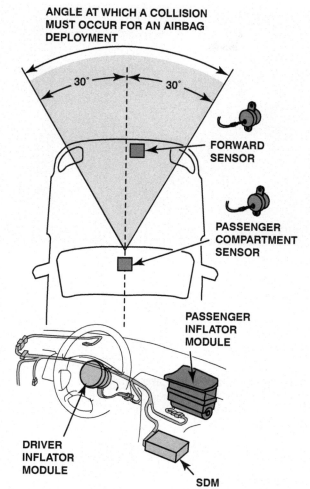

FIGURE 26–5 A typical airbag system showing many of the components. The SDM is the "sensing and diagnostic module" and includes the arming sensor as well as the electronics that keep checking the circuits for continuity and the capacitors that are discharged to deploy the airbags.

PARTS INVOLVED ● SEE FIGURE 26–5 for an overall
view of the parts included in a typical airbag system.

The parts include the following:

1. Sensors
2. Airbag (inflator) module
3. Clockspring wire coil in the steering column
4. Control module
5. Wiring and connectors

OPERATION   To cause inflation, the following events must
occur:

- To cause a deployment of the airbag, two sensors must be triggered at the same time. The **arming sensor** is used to provide electrical power, and a *forward* or *discriminating sensor* is used to provide the ground connection.
- The arming sensor provides the electrical power to the airbag heating unit, called a **squib**, inside the inflator module.

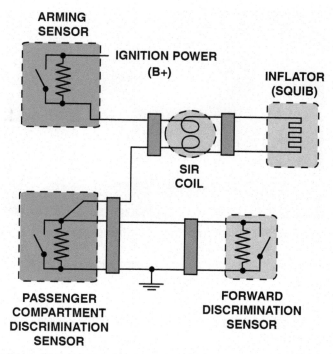

FIGURE 26–6 A simplified airbag deployment circuit. Note that both the arming sensor and at least one of the discriminating sensors must be activated at the same time. The arming sensor provides the power, and either one of the discriminating sensors can provide the ground for the circuit.

- The squib uses electrical power and converts it into heat for ignition of the propellant used to inflate the airbag.
- Before the airbag can inflate, however, the squib circuit also must have a ground provided by the forward or the discriminating sensor. In other words, two sensors (arming and forward sensors) *must* be triggered *at the same time* before the airbag will be deployed. ● SEE FIGURE 26–6.

TYPES OF AIRBAG INFLATORS   There are two different
types of inflators used in airbags:

1. **Solid fuel.** This type uses sodium azide pellets, and when ignited, generates a large quantity of nitrogen gas that quickly inflates the airbag. This was the first type used and is still commonly used in driver and passenger side airbag inflator modules. ● SEE FIGURE 26–7. The squib is the electrical heating element used to ignite the gas-generating material, usually sodium azide. It requires about 2 amperes of current to heat the heating element and ignite the inflator.

2. **Compressed gas.** Commonly used in passenger side airbags and roof-mounted systems, the compressed gas-system uses a canister filled with argon gas, plus a small percentage of helium at 3,000 PSI (435 kPa). A small igniter ruptures a burst disc to release the gas when energized. The compressed gas inflators are long cylinders that can be installed inside the instrument panel, seat back, door

FIGURE 26-7 The inflator module is being removed from the airbag housing. The squib, inside the inflator module, is the heating element that ignites the pyrotechnic gas generator that rapidly produces nitrogen gas to fill the airbag.

FIGURE 26-8 This figure shows a deployed side curtain airbag on a training vehicle.

panel, or along any side rail or pillar of the vehicle. ● **SEE FIGURE 26-8**.

Once the inflator is ignited, the nylon bag quickly inflates (in about 30 ms or 0.030 sec.) with nitrogen gas generated by the inflator. During an actual frontal collision accident, the driver is being thrown forward by the driver's own momentum toward the steering wheel. The strong nylon bag inflates at the same time. Personal injury is reduced by the spreading of the stopping force over the entire upper-body region. The normal collapsible steering column remains in operation and collapses in a collision when equipped with an airbag system. The bag is equipped with two large side vents that allow the bag to deflate immediately after inflation, once the bag has cushioned the occupant in a collision.

TIMELINE FOR AIRBAG DEPLOYMENT Following are the times necessary for an airbag deployment in milliseconds (each ms is equal to 0.001 sec. or 1/1,000 of a sec.).

1. Collision occurs: 0.0 millisecond
2. Sensors detect collision: 16 milliseconds (0.016 sec.)
3. Airbag is deployed and seam cover rips: 40 milliseconds (0.040 sec.)
4. Airbag is fully inflated: 100 milliseconds (0.100 sec.)
5. Airbag deflated: 250 milliseconds (0.250 sec.)

In other words, an airbag deployment occurs and is over in about a quarter of a sec.

SENSOR OPERATION All three sensors are basically switches that complete an electrical circuit when activated. The sensors are similar in construction and operation, and the *location* of the sensor determines its name. All airbag sensors are rigidly mounted to the vehicle and *must* be mounted with the arrow pointing toward the front of the vehicle to ensure that the sensor can detect rapid forward deceleration.

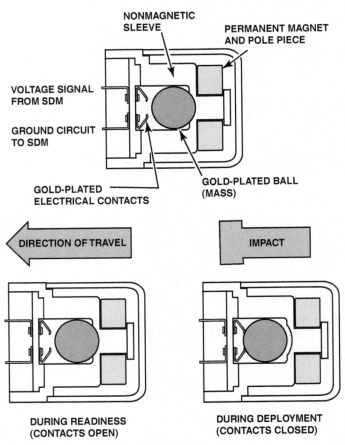

FIGURE 26-9 An airbag magnetic sensor.

There are three basic styles (designs) of airbag sensors.

1. **Magnetically retained gold-plated ball sensor.** This sensor uses a permanent magnet to hold a gold-plated steel ball away from two gold-plated electrical contacts. ● **SEE FIGURE 26-9**.

CRASH SENSOR

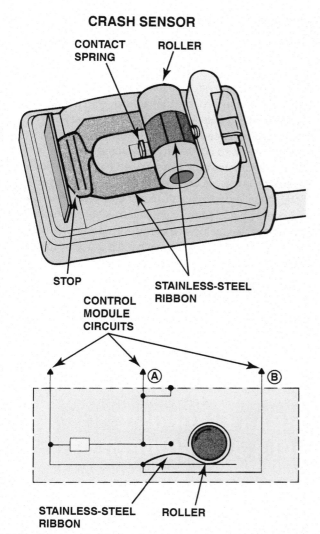

FIGURE 26–10 Some vehicles use a ribbon-type crash sensor.

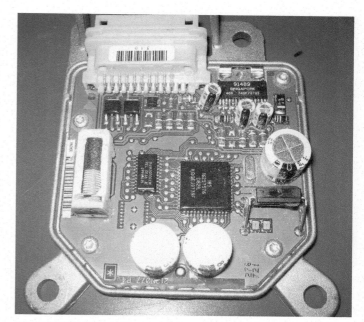

FIGURE 26–11 A sensing and diagnostic module that includes an accelerometer.

If the vehicle (and the sensor) stops rapidly enough, the steel ball is released from the magnet because the inertia force of the crash was sufficient to overcome the magnetic pull on the ball and then makes contact with the two gold-plated electrodes. The steel ball only remains in contact with the electrodes for a relatively short time because the steel ball is drawn back into contact with the magnet.

2. **Rolled up stainless-steel ribbon-type sensor.** This sensor is housed in an airtight package with nitrogen gas inside to prevent harmful corrosion of the sensor parts. If the vehicle (and the sensor) stops rapidly, the stainless-steel roll "unrolls" and contacts the two gold-plated contacts. Once the force is stopped, the stainless-steel roll will roll back into its original shape. ● **SEE FIGURE 26–10**.

3. **Integral sensor.** Some vehicles use electronic **deceleration sensors** built into the inflator module, called **integral sensors**. For example, General Motors uses the term *sensing and diagnostic module* (SDM) to describe their integrated sensor/module assembly. These units contain an accelerometer-type sensor that measures the rate of deceleration and, through computer logic, determines if the airbags should be deployed. ● **SEE FIGURE 26–11**.

TWO-STAGE AIRBAGS   Two-stage airbags, often called advanced airbags or smart airbags, use an accelerometer-type of sensor to detect force of the impact. This type of sensor measures the actual amount of deceleration rate of the vehicle and is used to determine whether one or both elements of a two-stage airbag should be deployed.

- **Low-stage deployment.** This lower force deployment is used if the accelerometer detects a low-speed crash.

- **High-stage deployment.** This stage is used if the accelerometer detects a higher speed crash or a more rapid deceleration rate.

- **Both low- and high-stage deployment.** Under severe high-speed crashes, both stages can be deployed.
  ● **SEE FIGURE 26–12**.

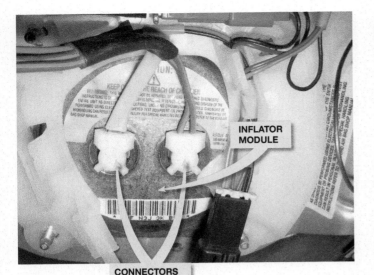

CONNECTORS TO EACH STAGE

INFLATOR MODULE

FIGURE 26–12 A driver's side airbag showing two inflator connectors. One is for the lower force inflator and the other is for the higher force inflator. Either can be ignited or both at the same time if the deceleration sensor detects a severe impact.

WIRING Wiring and connectors are very important for proper identification and long life. Airbag-related circuits have the following features:

- All electrical wiring connectors and conduit for airbags are colored yellow.
- To ensure proper electrical connection to the inflator module in the steering wheel, a coil assembly is used in the steering column. This coil is a ribbon of copper wires that operates much like a window shade when the steering wheel is rotated. As the steering wheel is rotated, this coil, usually called a **clockspring**, prevents the lack of continuity between the sensors and the inflator assembly that might result from a horn-ring type of sliding conductor.
- Inside the yellow plastic airbag connectors are gold-plated terminals that are used to prevent corrosion.

  ● **SEE FIGURE 26–13.**

Most airbag systems also contain a diagnostic unit that often includes an auxiliary power supply, which is used to provide the current to inflate the airbag if the battery is disconnected from the vehicle during a collision. This auxiliary power supply normally uses capacitors that are discharged through the squib of the inflation module. When the ignition is turned off, these capacitors are discharged. Therefore, after a few minutes, an airbag system will not deploy if the vehicle is hit while parked.

Dual-Stage Airbag Caution

Many vehicles are equipped with **dual-stage airbags** (two-stage airbags) that actually contain two separate inflators, one for less severe crashes and one for higher speed collisions. These systems are sometimes called smart airbag systems because the accelerometer-type sensor used can detect how severe the impact is and deploy one or both stages. If one stage is deployed, the other stage is still active and could be accidentally deployed. A service technician cannot tell by looking at the airbag whether both stages have deployed. Always handle a deployed airbag as if it has not been deployed and take all precautions necessary to keep any voltage source from getting close to the inflator module terminals.

AIRBAG DIAGNOSIS TOOLS AND EQUIPMENT

SELF-TEST PROCEDURE The electrical portion of airbag systems is constantly checked by the circuits within the airbag-energizing power unit or through the airbag controller. The electrical airbag components are monitored by applying a small-signal voltage from the airbag controller through the various sensors and components. Each component and sensor uses a resistor in parallel with the load or open sensor switch for use by the diagnostic signals. If continuity exists, the testing circuits will measure a small voltage drop. If an open or short circuit occurs, a dash warning light is lighted and a possible diagnostic trouble code (DTC) is stored. Follow exact manufacturer's recommended procedures for accessing and erasing airbag diagnostic trouble codes.

Diagnosis and service of airbag systems usually require some or all of the following items:

- Digital multimeter (DMM)
- Airbag simulator, often called a load tool
- Scan tool
- Shorting bar or shorting connector(s)
- Airbag system tester
- Vehicle-specific test harness

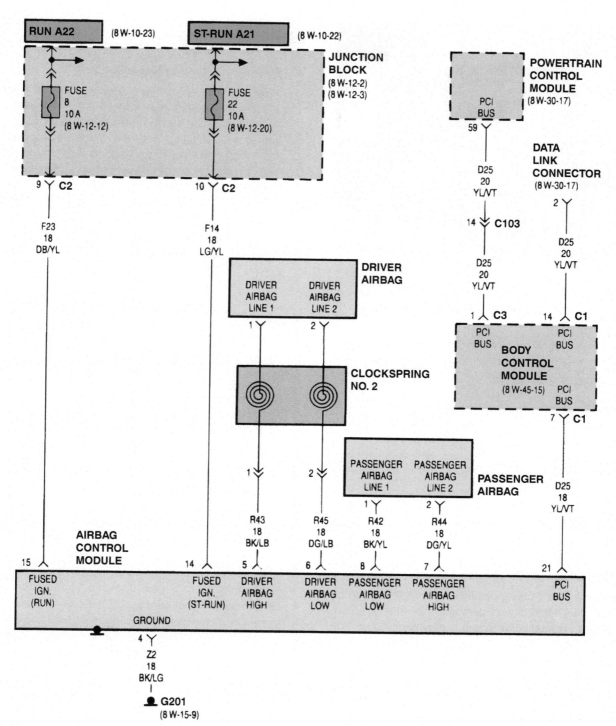

FIGURE 26–13 The airbag control module is linked to the powertrain control module (PCM) and the body control module (BCM) on this Chrysler system. Notice the airbag wire connecting the module to the airbag through the clockspring. Both power, labeled "driver airbag high," and ground, labeled "driver airbag low," are conducted through the clockspring.

FIGURE 26-14 An airbag diagnostic tester. Included in the plastic box are electrical connectors and a load tool that substitutes for the inflator module during troubleshooting.

- Special wire repair tools or connectors, such as crimp-and-seal weatherproof connectors
  - **SEE FIGURE 26-14.**

CAUTION: Most vehicle manufacturers specify that the negative battery terminal be removed when testing or working around airbags. Be aware that a memory saver device used to keep the computer and radio memory alive can supply enough electrical power to deploy an airbag.

PRECAUTIONS Take the following precautions when working with or around airbags:

1. Always follow all precautions and warning stickers on vehicles equipped with airbags.
2. Maintain a safe working distance from all airbags to help prevent the possibility of personal injury in the unlikely event of an unintentional airbag deployment.
   - Side impact airbag: 5 inches (13 cm) distance
   - Driver front airbag: 10 inches (25 cm) distance
   - Passenger front airbag: 20 inches (50 cm) distance
3. In the event of a collision in which the bag(s) is deployed, the inflator module *and* all sensors usually must be replaced to ensure proper future operation of the system.
4. Avoid using a self-powered test light around the yellow airbag wiring. Even though it is highly unlikely, a self-powered test light could provide the necessary current to accidentally set off the inflator module and cause an airbag deployment.
5. Use care when handling the inflator module section when it is being removed from the steering wheel. Always hold the inflator away from your body.

TECH TIP

Pocket the Ignition Key to Be Safe

When replacing any steering gear such as a rack-and-pinion steering unit, be sure that no one accidentally turns the steering wheel. If the steering wheel is turned without being connected to the steering gear, the airbag wire coil (clockspring) can become off center. This can cause the wiring to break when the steering wheel is rotated after the steering gear has been replaced. To help prevent this from occurring, simply remove the ignition key from the ignition and keep it in your pocket while servicing the steering gear.

 FREQUENTLY ASKED QUESTION

What Are Smart Airbags?

Smart airbags use the information from sensors to determine the level of deployment. Sensors used include the following:

- **Vehicle speed (VS) sensors.** This type of sensor has a major effect on the intensity of a collision. The higher the speed is, the greater is the amount of impact force.
- **Seat belt fastened switch.** If the seat belt is fastened, as determined by the seat belt buckle switch, the airbag system will deploy accordingly. If the driver or passenger is not wearing a seat belt, the airbag system will deploy with greater force compared to when the seat belt is being worn.
- **Passenger seat sensor.** The sensor in the seat on the passenger's side determines the force of deployment. If there is not a passenger detected, the passenger side airbag will not deploy on the vehicle equipped with a passenger seat sensor system.

6. If handling a deployed inflator module, always wear gloves and safety glasses to avoid the possibility of skin irritation from the sodium hydroxide dust, which is used as a lubricant on the bag(s), that remains after deployment.
7. Never jar or strike a sensor. The contacts inside the sensor may be damaged, preventing the proper operation of the airbag system in the event of a collision.
8. When mounting a sensor in a vehicle, make certain that the arrow on the sensor is pointing toward the front of the vehicle. Also be certain that the sensor is securely mounted.

AIRBAG SYSTEM SERVICE

DIS-ARMING The airbags should be dis-armed (temporarily disconnected) whenever performing service work on any of the following locations:

- Steering wheel
- Dash or instrument panel
- Glove box (instrument panel storage compartment)

Check service information for the exact procedure, which usually includes the following steps:

STEP 1 Disconnect the negative battery cable.

STEP 2 Remove the airbag fuse (has a yellow cover).

STEP 3 Disconnect the yellow electrical connector located at the base of the steering column to disable the driver's side airbag.

STEP 4 Disconnect the yellow electrical connector for the passenger side airbag.

This procedure is called "disabling airbags" in most service information. Always follow the vehicle manufacturer's specified procedures.

DIAGNOSTIC AND SERVICE PROCEDURE Airbag system components and their location in the vehicle vary according to system design, but the basic principles of testing are the same as for other electrical circuits. Use service information to determine how the circuit is designed and the correct sequence of tests to be followed.

- Some airbag systems require the use of special testers. The built-in safety circuits of such testers prevent accidental deployment of the airbag.
- If such a tester is not available, follow the recommended alternative test procedures specified by the manufacturer.
- Access the self-diagnostic system and check for diagnostic trouble code records.
- The scan tool is needed to access the data stream on most systems.

SELF-DIAGNOSIS All airbag systems can detect system electrical faults, and if found, will disable the system and notify the driver through an airbag warning lamp in the instrument cluster. Depending on circuit design, a system fault may cause the warning lamp to fail to illuminate, remain lit continuously, or flash. Some systems use a tone generator that produces an audible warning when a system fault occurs or if the warning lamp is inoperative.

 ? FREQUENTLY ASKED QUESTION

Why Change Knee Bolsters If Switching to Larger Wheels?

Larger wheels and tires can be installed on vehicles, but the powertrain control module (PCM) needs to be reprogrammed so the speedometer and other systems that are affected by a change in wheel/tire size can work effectively. When 20 inch wheels are installed on General Motors (GM) trucks or sport utility vehicles (SUVs), GM specifies that replacement knee bolsters be installed. Knee bolsters are the padded area located on the lower part of the dash where a driver or passenger's knees would hit in the event of a front collision. The reason for the need to replace the knee bolsters is to maintain the crash testing results. The larger 20 inches wheels would tend to be forced further into the passenger compartment in the event of a front-end collision. Therefore, to maintain the frontal crash rating standard, the larger knee bolsters are required.

WARNING: Failure to perform the specified changes when changing wheels and tires could result in the vehicle not being able to provide occupant protection as designed by the crash test star rating that the vehicle originally achieved.

The warning lamp should illuminate with the ignition key on and engine off as a bulb check. If not, the diagnostic module is likely disabling the system. If the airbag warning light remains on, the airbags may or may not be disabled, depending on the specific vehicle and the fault detected. Some warning lamp circuits have a timer that extinguishes the lamp after a few seconds. The airbag system generally does not require service unless there is a failed component. However, a steering wheel–mounted airbag module is routinely removed and replaced in order to service switches and other column-mounted devices.

KNEE AIRBAGS Some vehicles are equipped with knee airbags usually on the driver's side. Use caution if working under the dash and always follow the vehicle manufacturer's specified service procedures.

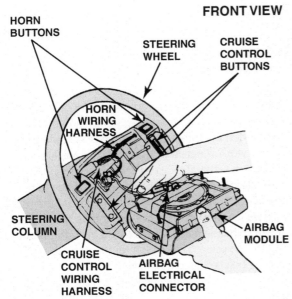

FRONT VIEW

HORN BUTTONS

STEERING WHEEL

CRUISE CONTROL BUTTONS

HORN WIRING HARNESS

STEERING COLUMN

CRUISE CONTROL WIRING HARNESS

AIRBAG ELECTRICAL CONNECTOR

AIRBAG MODULE

FIGURE 26–15 After disconnecting the battery and the yellow connector at the base of the steering column, the airbag inflator module can be removed from the steering wheel and the yellow airbag electrical connector at the inflator module can be disconnected.

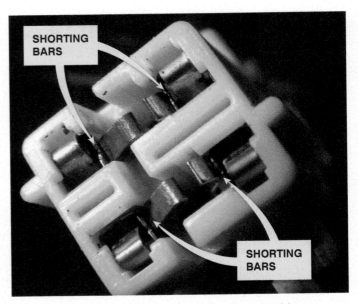

SHORTING BARS

SHORTING BARS

FIGURE 26–16 Shorting bars are used in most airbag connectors. These spring-loaded clips short across both terminals of an airbag connector when it is disconnected to help prevent accidental deployment of the airbag. If electrical power was applied to the terminals, the shorting bars would simply provide a low-resistance path to the other terminal and not allow current to flow past the connector. The mating part of the connector has a tapered piece that spreads apart the shorting bars when the connector is reconnected.

DRIVER SIDE AIRBAG MODULE REPLACEMENT

For the specific model being serviced, carefully follow the procedures provided by the vehicle manufacturer to disable and remove the airbag module. Failure to do so may result in serious injury and extensive damage to the vehicle. Replacing a discharged airbag is costly. The following procedure reviews the basic steps for removing an airbag module. Do not substitute these general instructions for the specific procedure recommended by the manufacturer.

1. Turn the steering wheel until the front wheels are positioned straight ahead. Some components on the steering column are removed only when the front wheels are straight.

2. Switch the ignition off and disconnect the negative battery cable, which cuts power to the airbag module.

3. Once the battery is disconnected, wait as long as recommended by the manufacturer before continuing. When in doubt, wait at least 10 minutes to make sure the capacitor is completely discharged.

4. Loosen and remove the nuts or screws that hold the airbag module in place. On some vehicles, these fasteners are located on the back of the steering wheel. On other vehicles, they are located on each side of the steering wheel.

The fasteners may be concealed with plastic finishing covers that must be pried off with a small screwdriver to access them.

5. Carefully lift the airbag module from the steering wheel and disconnect the electrical connector. Connector location varies: Some are below the steering wheel behind a plastic trim cover; others are at the top of the column under the module. ● **SEE FIGURES 26–15 AND 26–16.**

6. Store the module pad side up in a safe place where it will not be disturbed or damaged while the vehicle is being serviced. Do not attempt to disassemble the airbag module. If the airbag is defective, replace the entire assembly.

When installing the airbag module, make sure the clockspring is correctly positioned to ensure module-to-steering-column continuity. ● **SEE FIGURE 26–17.**

Always route the wiring exactly as it was before removal. Also, make sure the module seats completely into the steering wheel. Secure the assembly using new fasteners, if specified.

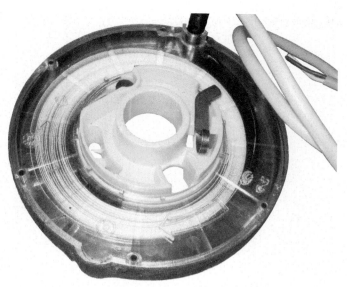

FIGURE 26–17 An airbag clockspring showing the flat conductor wire. It must be properly positioned to ensure proper operation.

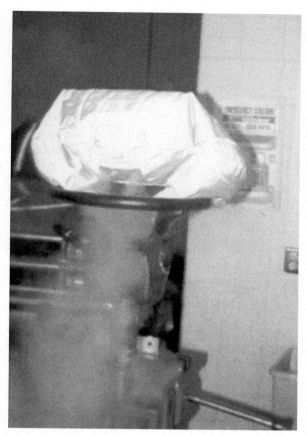

FIGURE 26–18 An airbag being deployed as part of a demonstration in an automotive laboratory. Notice that the airbag quickly deflates due to the large vent openings in the backside of the bag.

SAFETY WHEN MANUALLY DEPLOYING AIRBAGS

Airbag modules cannot be disposed of unless they are deployed. Do the following to prevent injury when manually deploying an airbag:

- When possible, deploy the airbag outside of the vehicle. Follow the vehicle manufacturer's recommendations.
- Follow the vehicle manufacturer's procedures and equipment recommendations.
- Wear the proper hearing and eye protection.
- Deploy the airbag with the trim cover facing up.
- Stay at least 20 feet (6 m) from the airbag. (Use long jumper wires attached to the wiring and routed outside the vehicle to a battery.)
- Allow the airbag module to cool.
  ● **SEE FIGURE 26–18.**

FIGURE 26–19 A dash warning lamp will light if the passenger side airbag is off because no passenger was detected by the seat sensor.

OCCUPANT DETECTION SYSTEMS

PURPOSE AND FUNCTION The U.S. Federal Motor Vehicle Safety Standard 208 (FMVSS) specifies that the passenger side airbag be disabled or deployed with reduced force under the following conditions. This system is referred to as an **occupant detection system (ODS)** or the **passenger presence system (PPS)**.

- When there is no weight on the seat and no seat belt is fastened, the passenger side airbag will not deploy

and the passenger airbag light should be off. ● **SEE FIGURE 26–19.**

- The passenger side airbag will be disabled and the disabled airbag light will be "on" only if at least 10 to 37 lb (4.5 to 17 kg) is on the passenger seat, which would generally represent a seated child.

FIGURE 26–20 The passenger side airbag "on" lamp will light if a passenger is detected on the passenger seat.

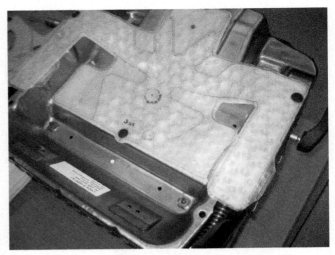

FIGURE 26–21 A gel-filled (bladder-type) occupant detection sensor showing the pressure sensor and wiring.

- If 38 to 99 lb (17 to 45 kg) is detected on the passenger seat, which represents a child or small adult, the airbag will deploy at a decreased force.
- If 99 lb (45 kg) or more is detected on the passenger seat, the airbag will deploy at full force, depending on the severity of the crash, speed of the vehicle, and other factors which may result in the airbag deploying at a reduced force.

  ● SEE FIGURE 26–20.

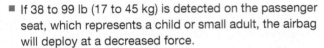

FIGURE 26–22 A resistor-type occupant detection sensor. The weight of the passenger strains these resistors, which are attached to the seat, thereby signaling to the module the weight of the occupant.

TYPE OF SEAT SENSOR The passenger presence system uses one of three types of sensors:

- **Gel-filled bladder sensor.** This type of occupant sensor uses a silicone-filled bag that has a pressure sensor attached. The weight of the passenger is measured by the pressure sensor, which sends a voltage signal to the module controlling the airbag deployment. A safety belt tension sensor is also used with a gel-filled bladder system to monitor the tension on the belt. The module then uses the information from both the bladder and the seat belt sensor to determine if a tightened belt may be used to restrain a child seat.

  ● SEE FIGURE 26–21.

- **Capacitive strip sensors.** This type of occupant sensor uses several flexible conductive metal strips under the seat cushion. These sensor strips transmit and receive a low-level electric field, which changes due to the weight of the front passenger seat occupant. The module determines the weight of the occupant based on the sensor values.

- **Force-sensing resistor sensors.** This type of occupant sensor uses resistors, which change their resistance based on the stress that is applied. These resistors are

part of the seat structure, and the module can determine the weight of the occupant based on the change in the resistance of the sensors. ● SEE FIGURE 26–22.

CAUTION: Because the resistors are part of the seat structure, it is very important that all seat fasteners be torqued to factory specifications to ensure proper operation of the occupant detection system. A *seat track position* (STP) *sensor* is used by the airbag controller to determine the position of the seat. If the seat is too close to the airbag, the controller may disable the airbag.

DIAGNOSING OCCUPANT DETECTION SYSTEMS

A fault in the system may cause the passenger side airbag light to turn on when there is no weight on the seat. A scan tool is often used to check or calibrate the seat, which must be empty, by commanding the module to rezero the seat sensor. Some systems, such as those on Chrysler vehicles, use a unit that has various weights along with a scan tool to calibrate and diagnose the occupant detection system. ● SEE FIGURE 26–23.

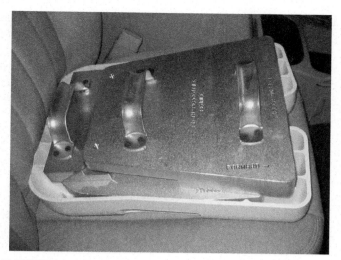

FIGURE 26–23 A test weight is used to calibrate the occupant detection system on a Chrysler vehicle.

FIGURE 26–24 A typical seat (side) airbag that deploys from the side of the seat.

SEAT AND SIDE CURTAIN AIRBAGS

SEAT AIRBAGS Side and/or *curtain airbags* use a variety of sensors to determine if they need to be deployed. Side airbags are mounted in one of two general locations:

■ In the side bolster of the seat (● **SEE FIGURE 26–24.**)

■ In the door panel

Most side airbag sensors use an electronic accelerometer to detect when to deploy the airbags, which are usually mounted to the bottom of the left and right "B" pillars (where the front doors latch) behind a trim panel on the inside of the vehicle.

CAUTION: Avoid using a lockout tool (e.g., a "slim jim") in vehicles equipped with side airbags to help prevent damage to the components and wiring in the system.

SIDE CURTAIN AIRBAGS Side curtain airbags are usually deployed by a module based on input from many different sensors, including a lateral acceleration sensor and wheel speed sensors. For example, in one system used by Ford, the ABS controller commands that the brakes on one side of the vehicle be applied, using down pressure while monitoring the wheel speed sensors. If the wheels slow down with little brake pressure, the controller assumes that the vehicle could roll over, thereby deploying the side curtain airbags.

TECH TIP

Aggressive Driving and OnStar

If a vehicle equipped with the OnStar system is being driven aggressively and the electronic stability control system has to intercede to keep the vehicle under control, OnStar may call the vehicle to see if there has been an accident. The need for a call from OnStar usually will be determined if the accelerometer registers slightly over 1 g-force, which could be achieved while driving on a race track.

EVENT DATA RECORDERS

PARTS AND OPERATION As part of the airbag controller on many vehicles, the **event data recorder (EDR)** is used to record parameters just before and slightly after an airbag deployment. The following parameters are recorded:

■ Vehicle speed

■ Brake on/off

■ Seat belt fastened

■ G-forces as measured by the accelerometer

Unlike an airplane event data recorder, a vehicle unit is not a separate unit and does not record voice conversations and does not include all crash parameters. This means that additional crash data, such as skid marks and physical evidence at the crash site, will be needed to fully reconstruct the incident.

The EDR is embedded into the airbag controller and receives data from many sources and at varying sample rates. The data is constantly being stored in a memory buffer and not recorded into the EPROM unless an airbag deployment has been commanded. The combined data is known as an *event file.* The airbag is commanded on, based on input mainly from the accelerometer sensor. This sensor, usually built into the airbag controller, is located inside the vehicle. The accelerometer calculates the rate of change of the speed of the vehicle. This determines the acceleration rate and is used to predict if that rate is high enough to deploy the frontal airbags. The airbags will be deployed if the threshold g-value is exceeded. The passenger side airbag will also be deployed unless it is suppressed by either of the following:

- No passenger is detected.

- The passenger side airbag switch is off.

DATA EXTRACTION Data extraction from the event data recorder in the airbag controller can only be achieved using a piece of equipment known as the Crash Data Retrieval System, manufactured by Vetronics Corporation. This is the only authorized method for retrieving event files and only certain organizations are allowed access to the data. These groups or organizations include the following:

- Original equipment manufacturer's representatives

- National Highway Traffic Safety Administration

- Law enforcement agencies

- Accident reconstruction companies

Crash data retrieval must only be done by a trained crash data retrieval (CDR) technician or analyst. A technician undergoes specialized training and must pass an examination. An analyst must attend additional training beyond that of a technician to achieve CDR analyst certification.

SUMMARY

1. Airbags use a sensor(s) to determine if the rate of deceleration is enough to cause bodily harm.

2. All airbag electrical connectors and conduit are yellow and all electrical terminals are gold plated to protect against corrosion.

3. Always follow the manufacturer's procedure for disabling the airbag system prior to any work performed on the system.

4. Frontal airbags operate only within 30 degrees from center and do not deploy in the event of a rollover, side, or rear collision.

5. Two sensors must be triggered at the same time for an airbag deployment to occur. Many newer systems use an accelerometer-type crash sensor that actually measures the amount of deceleration.

6. Pretensioners are explosive (pyrotechnic) devices that remove the slack from the seat belt and help position the occupant.

7. Occupant detection systems use sensors in the seat to determine whether the airbag will be deployed and with full or reduced force.

REVIEW QUESTIONS

1. What are the safety precautions to follow when working around an airbag?

2. What sensor(s) must be triggered for an airbag deployment?

3. How should deployed inflation modules be handled?

4. What is the purpose of pretensioners?

5. What is the purpose and function of the event data recorder (EDR)?

1. A vehicle is being repaired after an airbag deployment. Technician A says that the inflator module should be handled as if it is still live. Technician B says rubber gloves should be worn to prevent skin irritation. Which technician is correct?
   a. Technician A only
   b. Technician B only
   c. Both Technicians A and B
   d. Neither Technician A nor B

2. A seat belt pretensioner is _____.
   a. a device that contains an explosive charge
   b. used to remove slack from the seat belt in the event of a collision
   c. used to force the occupant back into position against the seat back in the event of a collision
   d. All of the above

3. What conducts power and ground to the driver's side airbag?
   a. Twisted-pair wires
   b. Clockspring
   c. Carbon contact and brass surface plate on the steering column
   d. Magnetic reed switch

4. Two technicians are discussing dual-stage airbags. Technician A says that a deployed airbag is safe to handle regardless of which stage caused the deployment of the airbag. Technician B says that both stages ignite, but at different speeds depending on the speed of the vehicle. Which technician is correct?
   a. Technician A only
   b. Technician B only
   c. Both Technicians A and B
   d. Neither Technician A nor B

5. Where are shorting bars used?
   a. In pretensioners
   b. At the connectors for airbags
   c. In the crash sensors
   d. In the airbag controller

6. Technician A says that a deployed airbag can be repacked, reused, and reinstalled in the vehicle. Technician B says that a deployed airbag should be discarded and replaced with an entire new assembly. Which technician is correct?
   a. Technician A only
   b. Technician B only
   c. Both Technicians A and B
   d. Neither Technician A nor B

7. What color are the airbag electrical connectors and conduit?
   a. Blue
   b. Red
   c. Yellow
   d. Orange

8. Driver and/or passenger front airbags will only deploy if a collision occurs how many degrees from straight ahead?
   a. 10 degrees
   b. 30 degrees
   c. 60 degrees
   d. 90 degrees

9. How many sensors must be triggered at the same time to cause an airbag deployment?
   a. One
   b. Two
   c. Three
   d. Four

10. The electrical terminals used for airbag systems are unique because they are _____.
    a. solid copper
    b. tin-plated heavy-gauge steel
    c. silver plated
    d. gold plated

chapter 27

AUDIO SYSTEM OPERATION AND DIAGNOSIS

AUDIO FUNDAMENTALS

INTRODUCTION The audio system of today's vehicles is a complex combination of antenna system, receiver, amplifier, and speakers, all designed to provide living room–type music reproduction while the vehicle is traveling in city traffic or at highway speed.

Audio systems produce audible sounds and include the following:

- Radio (AM, FM, and satellite)
- Antenna systems that are used to capture electronic energy broadcast to radios
- Speaker systems
- Aftermarket enhancement devices that increase the sound energy output of an audio system
- Diagnosis of audio-related problems

Many audio-related problems can be addressed and repaired by a service technician.

TYPES OF ENERGY There are two types of energy that affect audio systems.

- **Electromagnetic energy or radio waves.** Antennas capture the radio waves, which are then sent to the radio or receiver to be amplified.
- **Acoustical energy, usually called sound.** Radios and receivers amplify the radio wave signals and drive speakers, which reproduce the original sound as transmitted by radio waves.
  ● **SEE FIGURE 27–1.**

TERMINOLOGY Radio waves travel at approximately the speed of light (186,272,000 miles per second) and are electromagnetic. Radio waves are measured in two ways, wavelength and frequency. A radio wave has a series of high points and low points. A wavelength is the time and distance between two consecutive points, either high or low. Wavelength is measured in meters. **Frequency**, also known as **radio frequency (RF)**, is the number of times a particular waveform repeats itself in a given amount of time and is measured in **hertz (Hz)**. A signal with a frequency of 1 Hz is one radio wavelength per second. Radio frequencies are measured in kilohertz (kHz), thousands of wavelengths per second, and megahertz (MHz), millions of wavelengths per second. ● **SEE FIGURE 27–2.**

- The higher the frequency, the shorter the wavelength.
- The lower the frequency, the longer the wavelength.

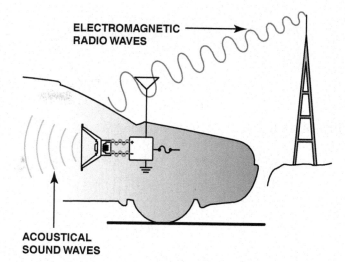

FIGURE 27–1 Audio systems use both electromagnetic radio waves and sound waves to reproduce sound inside the vehicle.

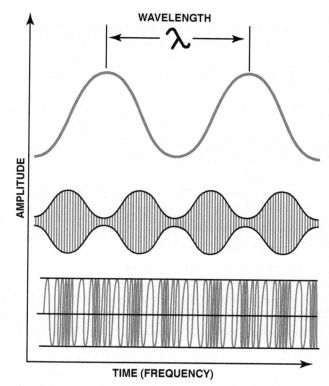

FIGURE 27–2 The relationship among wavelength, frequency, and amplitude.

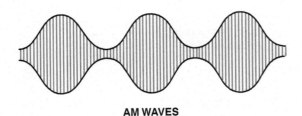

AM WAVES

FIGURE 27–3 The amplitude changes in AM broadcasting.

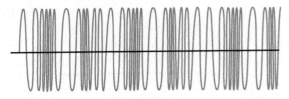

FM WAVES

FIGURE 27–4 The frequency changes in FM broadcasting and the amplitude remains constant.

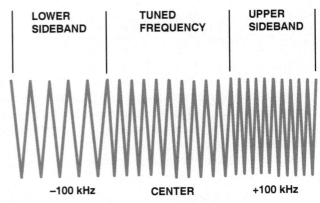

FIGURE 27–5 Using upper and lower sidebands allows stereo to be broadcast. The receiver separates the signals to provide left and right channels.

A longer wavelength can travel a further distance than a shorter wavelength. Therefore, lower frequencies provide better reception at further distances.

- AM radio frequencies range from 530 to 1,710 kHz.
- FM radio frequencies range from 87.9 to 107.9 MHz.

MODULATION Modulation is the term used to describe when information is added to a constant frequency. The base radio frequency used for RF is called the *carrier wave.* A carrier is a radio wave that is changed to carry information. The two types of modulation are:

- **Amplitude modulation (AM)**
- **Frequency modulation (FM)**

AM waves are radio waves that have amplitude that can be varied, transmitted, and detected by a receiver. Amplitude is the height of the wave as graphed on an oscilloscope. ● **SEE FIGURE 27–3.**

FM waves are also radio waves that have a frequency that can be varied, transmitted, and detected by a receiver. This type of modulation changes the number of cycles per second, or frequency, to carry the information. ● **SEE FIGURE 27–4.**

RADIO WAVE TRANSMISSION More than one signal can be carried by a radio wave. This process is called *sideband operation.* Sideband frequencies are measured in kilohertz.

The amount of the signal above the assigned frequency is referred to as the upper sideband. The amount of the signal below the assigned frequency is called the lower sideband. This capability allows radio signals to carry stereo broadcasts. Stereo broadcasts use the upper sideband to carry one channel of the stereo signal and the lower sideband to carry the other channel. When the signal is decoded by the radio, these two signals become the right and left channels. ● **SEE FIGURE 27–5.**

NOISE Because radio waves are a form of electromagnetic energy, other forms of energy can impact them. For example, a bolt of lightning generates broad radio-frequency bandwidths known as radio-frequency interference (RFI). RFI is one type of electromagnetic interference (EMI) and is the frequency that interferes with radio transmission.

AM CHARACTERISTICS AM radio reception can be achieved over long distances from the transmitter because the waves can bounce off the ionosphere, usually at night. Even during the day, the AM signals can be picked up some distance from the transmitter. AM radio reception depends on a good antenna. If there is a fault in the antenna circuit, AM reception is affected the most.

FM CHARACTERISTICS Because FM waves have a high RF and a short wavelength, they travel only a short distance. The waves cannot follow the shape of the earth but instead travel in a straight line from the transmitter to the receiver. FM waves will travel through the ionosphere and into space and do not reflect back to earth like AM waves.

What Does a "Capture" Problem Mean?

A capture problem affects only FM reception and means that the receiver is playing more than one station if two stations are broadcasting at the same frequency. Most radios capture the stronger signal and block the weaker signal. However, if the stronger signal is weakened due to being blocked by buildings or mountains, the weaker signal will then be used. When this occurs, it will sound as if the radio is changing stations by itself. This is not a fault with the radio, but simply a rare occurrence with FM radio.

MULTIPATH Multipath is caused by reflected, refracted, or line of sight signals reaching an antenna at different times. Multipath results from the radio receiving two signals to process on the same frequency. This causes an echo effect in the speakers. *Flutter,* or *picket fencing a*s it is sometimes called, is caused by the blocking of part of the FM signal. This blocking causes a weakening of the signal resulting in only part of the signal getting to the antenna, causing an on-again off-again radio sound. Flutter also occurs when the transmitter and the receiving antenna are far apart.

RADIOS AND RECEIVERS

The antenna receives the radio wave where it is converted into very weak fluctuating electrical current. This current travels along the antenna lead-in to the radio that amplifies the signal and sends the new signal to the speakers where it is converted into acoustical energy.

Most late-model radios and receivers use five input/output circuits:

1. **Power.** Usually a constant 12-volt feed to keep the internal clock alive.
2. **Ground.** This is the lowest voltage in the circuit and connects indirectly to the negative terminal of the battery.
3. **Serial data.** Used to turn the unit on and off and provide other functions, such as steering wheel control operation.
4. **Antenna input.** From one or more antennas.
5. **Speaker outputs.** These wires connect the receiver to the speakers or as an input to an amplifier.

ANTENNAS

TYPES OF ANTENNAS The typical radio electromagnetic energy from the broadcast antenna induces a signal in the antenna that is very small, only about 25 microvolts AC (0.000025 VAC), in strength. The radio contains amplifier circuits that increase the received signal strength into usable information.

For example, the five types of antennas used on vehicles include the following:

- **Slot antenna.** The slot antenna is concealed in the roof of some plastic body vehicles, such as older General Motors plastic body vans. This antenna is surrounded by metal on a Mylar sheet.
- **Rear window defogger grid.** This type of system uses the heating wires to receive the signals and special circuitry to separate the RF from the DC heater circuit.
- **Powered mast.** These antennas are controlled by the radio. When the radio is turned on, the antenna is raised; when the radio is shut off, the antenna is retracted. The antenna system consists of an antenna mast and a drive motor controlled by the radio "on" signal through a relay.
- **Fixed mast antenna.** This antenna offers the best overall performance currently available. The mast is simply a vertical rod. Mast antennas are typically located on the fender or rear quarter panel of the vehicle.
- **Integrated antenna.** This type of antenna is sandwiched in the windshield and an appliqué on the rear window glass. The antenna in the rear window is the primary antenna and receives both AM and FM signals. The secondary antenna is located in the front windshield typically on the passenger side of the vehicle. This antenna receives only FM signals.

● **SEE FIGURE 27–6.**

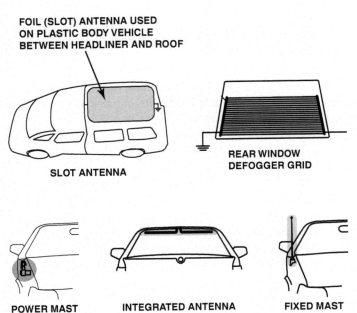

FOIL (SLOT) ANTENNA USED
ON PLASTIC BODY VEHICLE
BETWEEN HEADLINER AND ROOF

SLOT ANTENNA

REAR WINDOW
DEFOGGER GRID

POWER MAST   INTEGRATED ANTENNA   FIXED MAST

FIGURE 27–6 The five types of antennas used on General Motors vehicles include the slot antenna, fixed mast antenna, rear window defogger grid antenna, a powered mast antenna, and an integrated antenna.

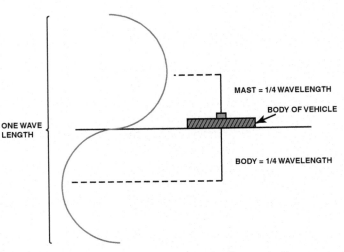

ONE WAVE LENGTH

MAST = 1/4 WAVELENGTH

BODY OF VEHICLE

BODY = 1/4 WAVELENGTH

FIGURE 27–7 The ground plane is actually one-half of the antenna.

? **FREQUENTLY ASKED QUESTION**

What Is a Ground Plane?

Antennas designed to pick up the electromagnetic energy that is broadcast through the air to the transmitting antenna are usually one-half wavelength high, and the other half of the wavelength is the **ground plane**. This one-half wavelength in the ground plane is literally underground.

For ideal reception, the receiving antenna should also be the same as the wavelength of the signal. Because this length is not practical, a design compromise uses the length of the antenna as one-fourth of the wavelength; in addition, the body of the vehicle itself is one-fourth of the wavelength. The body of the vehicle, therefore, becomes the ground plane. ● **SEE FIGURE 27–7**.

Any faulty condition in the ground plane circuit will cause the ground plane to lose effectiveness, such as:

• Loose or corroded battery cable terminals
• Acid buildup on battery cables
• Engine grounds with high resistance
• Loss of antenna or audio system grounds
• Defective alternator, causing an AC ripple exceeding 50 millivolts (0.050 volt)

ANTENNA DIAGNOSIS

ANTENNA HEIGHT The antenna collects all radio-frequency signals. An AM radio operates best with as long an antenna as possible, but FM reception is best when the antenna height is exactly 31 inches (79 cm). Most fixed-length antennas are, therefore, exactly this height. Even the horizontal section of a windshield antenna is 31 inches (79 cm) long.

A defective antenna

■ Will greatly affect AM radio reception
■ May affect FM radio reception

ANTENNA TESTING If the antenna or lead-in cable is broken (open), FM reception will be heard but may be weak, and there will be *no* AM reception. An ohmmeter should read infinity between the center antenna lead and the antenna case. For proper reception and lack of noise, the case of the antenna must be properly grounded to the vehicle body. ● **SEE FIGURE 27–8**.

POWER ANTENNA TESTING AND SERVICE Most power antennas use a circuit breaker and a relay to power a reversible, permanent magnet (PM) electric motor that moves a nylon cord attached to the antenna mast. Some vehicles have a dash-mounted control that can regulate antenna mast height and/or operation, whereas many operate automatically when the radio is turned on and off. The power antenna assembly is usually mounted between the outer and inner front fender or in the rear quarter panel. The unit contains the motor, a spool for the cord, and upper- and lower-limit switches. The power antenna mast is tested in the same way as a fixed-mast

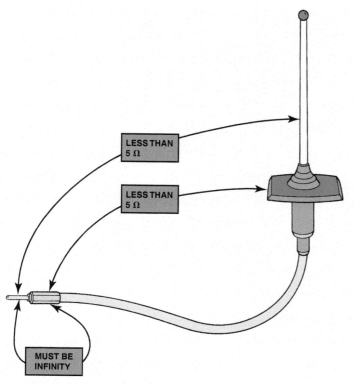

FIGURE 27–8 If all ohmmeter readings are satisfactory, the antenna is good.

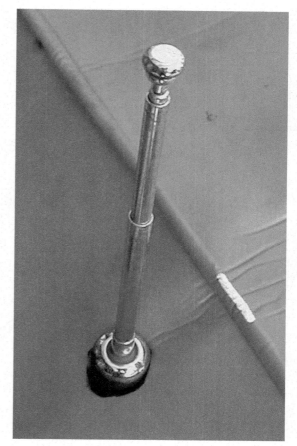

FIGURE 27–9 Cutting a small hole in a fender cover helps to protect the vehicle when replacing or servicing an antenna.

TECH TIP

The Hole in the Fender Cover Trick

A common repair is to replace the mast of a power antenna. To help prevent the possibility of causing damage to the body or paint of the vehicle, cut a hole in a fender cover and place it over the antenna.
● **SEE FIGURE 27–9**.

If a wrench or tool slips during the removal or installation process, the body of the vehicle will be protected.

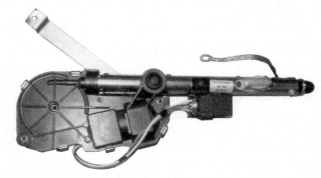

FIGURE 27–10 A typical power antenna assembly. Note the braided ground wire used to ensure that the antenna has a good ground plane.

antenna. (An infinity reading should be noted on an ohmmeter when the antenna is tested between the center antenna terminal and the housing or ground.) Except in the case of cleaning or mast replacement, most power antennas are either replaced as a unit or repaired by specialty shops. ● **SEE FIGURE 27–10**.

Making certain that the drain holes in the motor housing are not plugged with undercoating, leaves, or dirt can prevent many power antenna problems. All power antennas should be kept clean by wiping the mast with a soft cloth and lightly oiling with light oil such as WD-40 or a similar grade oil.

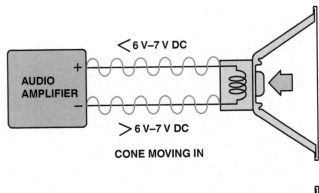

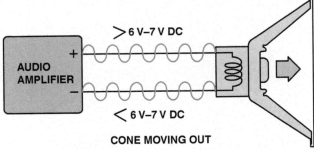

FIGURE 27–11 Between 6 and 7 volts is applied to each speaker terminal, and the audio amplifier then increases the voltage on one terminal and at the same time decreases the voltage on the other terminal causing the speaker cone to move. The moving cone then moves the air, causing sound.

FIGURE 27–12 A typical automotive speaker with two terminals. The polarity of the speakers can be identified by looking at the wiring diagram in the service manual or by using a 1.5-volt battery to check. When the battery positive is applied to the positive terminal of the speaker, the cone will move outward. When the battery leads are reversed, the speaker cone will move inward.

SPEAKERS

PURPOSE AND FUNCTION The purpose of any **speaker** is to reproduce the original sound as accurately as possible. Speakers are also called *loudspeakers*. The human ear is capable of hearing sounds from a very low frequency of 20 Hz (cycles per second) to as high as 20,000 Hz. No one speaker is capable of reproducing sound over such a wide frequency range. ● **SEE FIGURE 27–11.**

Good-quality speakers are the key to a proper sounding radio or sound system. Replacement speakers should be securely mounted and wired according to the correct *polarity*. ● **SEE FIGURE 27–12.**

IMPEDANCE MATCHING All speakers used on the same radio or amplifier should have the same internal coil resistance, called **impedance**. If unequal-impedance speakers are used,

sound quality may be reduced and serious damage to the radio may result. ● **SEE FIGURE 27–13.**

All speakers should have the same impedance. For example, if two 4-ohm speakers are being used for the rear and they are connected in parallel, the total impedance is 2 ohms.

$$R_T = \frac{4\ \Omega\ \text{(Impedance of each speaker)}}{2\ \text{(number of speakers in parallel)}} = 2\ \text{ohms}$$

The front speakers should also represent a 2-ohm load from the radio or amplifier. See the following example:

Two front speakers: each 2 ohms

Two rear speakers: each 8 ohms

Solution: Connect the front speakers in series (connect the positive [+] of one speaker to the negative [−] of the other) for a total impedance of 4 ohms (2 Ω + 2 Ω = 4 Ω).

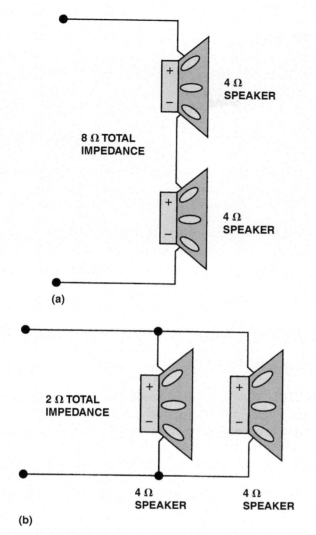

8 Ω TOTAL IMPEDANCE

4 Ω SPEAKER

4 Ω SPEAKER

(a)

2 Ω TOTAL IMPEDANCE

4 Ω SPEAKER

4 Ω SPEAKER

(b)

FIGURE 27–13 (a) Two 4-ohm speakers connected in series result in total impedance of 8 ohms. (b) Two 4-ohm speakers connected in parallel result in total impedance of 2 ohms.

Connect the two rear speakers in parallel (connect the positive [+] of each speaker together and the negative [−] of each speaker together) for a total impedance of 4 ohms (8 Ω ÷ 2 = 4 Ω).

SPEAKER WIRING The wire used for speakers should be as large a wire (as low an AWG gauge number) as is practical in order to be assured that full power is reaching the speakers. Typical "speaker wire" is about 22 gauge (0.35 mm^2), yet tests conducted by audio engineers have concluded that increasing the wire gauge—up to 4 gauge (19 mm^2) or larger—greatly increases sound quality. All wiring connections should be soldered after making certain that all speaker connections have the correct polarity.

TECH TIP

Skin Effect

When a high-frequency signal (AC voltage) is transmitted through a wire, the majority of it travels on the outside surface of the wire. This characteristic is called skin effect. The higher the frequency is, the closer to the outer surface the signal moves. To increase audio system output, most experts recommend the use of wire that has many strands of very fine wire to increase the surface area or the skin area of the conductor. Therefore, most aftermarket speaker wires are stranded with many small-diameter copper strands.

CAUTION: Be careful when installing additional audio equipment on a General Motors vehicle system that uses a two-wire speaker connection called a floating ground system. Other systems run only one power (hot) lead to each speaker and ground the other speaker lead to the body of the vehicle.

This arrangement helps prevent interference and static that could occur if these components were connected to a chassis (vehicle) ground. If the components are chassis grounded, there may be a difference in the voltage potential (voltage); this condition is called a *ground loop*.

CAUTION: Regardless of radio speaker connections used, *never* operate any radio without the speakers connected, or the speaker driver section of the radio may be damaged as a result of the open speaker circuit.

SPEAKER TYPES

INTRODUCTION   No one speaker is capable of reproducing sound over such a wide frequency range. Therefore, speakers are available in three basic types:

1. Tweeters are for high-frequency ranges.
2. Midrange are for mid-frequency ranges.
3. Woofers and subwoofers are for low-frequency ranges.

TWEETER   A **tweeter** is a speaker designed to reproduce high-frequency sounds, usually between 4,000 and 20,000 Hz (4 and 20 kHz). Tweeters are very directional. This means that the human ear is most likely to be able to detect the location of the speaker while listening to music. This also means that a tweeter should be mounted in the vehicle where the sound can be directed in line of sight to the listener. Tweeters are usually mounted on the inside door near the top, windshield "A" pillar or similar locations.

MIDRANGE   A midrange speaker is designed and manufactured to be able to best reproduce sounds in the middle of the human hearing range, from 400 to 5,000 Hz. Most people are sensitive to the sound produced by these midrange speakers. These speakers are also directional in that the listener can usually locate the source of the sound.

SUBWOOFER   A **subwoofer**, sometimes called a *woofer,* produces the lowest frequency of sounds, usually 125 Hz and lower. A *midbass* speaker may also be used to reproduce those frequencies between 100 and 500 Hz. Low-frequency sounds from these speakers are *not* directional. This means that the listener usually cannot detect the source of the sound from these speakers. The low-frequency sounds seem to be everywhere in the vehicle, so the location of the speakers is not as critical as with the higher frequency speakers.

The subwoofer can be placed almost anywhere in the vehicle. Most subwoofers are mounted in the rear of the vehicle where there is more room for the larger subwoofer speakers.

SPEAKER FREQUENCY RESPONSE   Frequency response is how a speaker responds to a range of frequencies. A typical frequency response for a midrange speaker may be 500 to 4,000 Hz.

WARNING

Hearing loss is possible if exposed to loud sounds. According to noise experts (audiologists), hearing protection should be used whenever the following occurs.

1. You must raise your voice to be heard by others next to you.
2. You cannot hear someone else speaking who is less than 3 feet (1 m) away.
3. You are operating power equipment, such as a lawnmower.

SOUND LEVELS

DECIBEL SCALE   A **decibel (dB)** is a measure of sound power, and it is the faintest sound a human can hear in the midband frequencies. The dB scale is not linear (straight line) but logarithmic, meaning that a small change in the dB reading results in a large change in volume of noise. An increase of 10 dB in sound pressure is equal to doubling the perceived volume. Therefore, a small difference in dB rating means a big difference in the sound volume of the speaker.

EXAMPLES   Some examples of decibel sound levels include the following:

■Quiet, faint	30 dB: whisper, quiet library
	40 dB: quiet room
■Moderate	50 dB: moderate range sound
	60 dB: normal conversation
■Loud	70 dB: city traffic
	80 dB: busy noisy traffic, vacuum cleaner
■Extremely loud	90 dB: lawnmower, shop tools
	100 dB: chain saw, air drill
■Hearing loss possible	110 dB: loud rock music

What Is a Bass Blocker?

A bass blocker is a capacitor and coil assembly that effectively blocks low frequencies. A bass blocker is normally used to block low frequencies being sent to the smaller front speakers. Using a bass blocker allows the smaller front speakers to more efficiently reproduce the midrange and high-range frequency sounds.

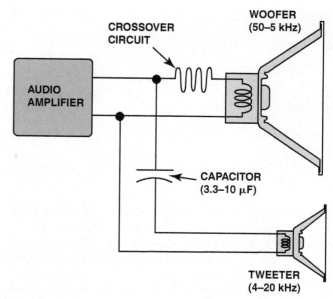

FIGURE 27–14 Crossovers are used in audio systems to send high-frequency sounds to the small (tweeter) speakers and low-frequency sounds to larger (woofer) speakers.

CROSSOVERS

DEFINITION A **crossover** is designed to separate the frequency of a sound and send a certain frequency range, such as low-bass sounds, to a woofer designed to reproduce these low-frequency sounds. There are two types of crossovers: passive and active.

PASSIVE CROSSOVER A passive crossover does not use an external power source. Rather it uses a coil and a capacitor to block certain frequencies that a particular type of speaker cannot handle and allow just those frequencies that it can handle to be applied to the speaker. For example, a 6.6-millihenry coil and a 200-microfarad capacitor can effectively pass 100-Hz frequency sound to a large 10-inches subwoofer. This type of passive crossover is called a **low-pass filter**, because it passes (transfers) only the low-frequency sounds to the speaker and blocks all other frequencies. A **high-pass filter** is used to transfer higher frequency (over 100 Hz) to smaller speakers.

ACTIVE CROSSOVER **Active crossovers** use an external power source and produce superior performance. An active crossover is also called an *electronic crossover* or *crossover network*. These units include many powered filters and are considerably more expensive than passive crossovers. Two amplifiers are necessary to fully benefit from an active crossover. One amplifier is for the higher frequencies and midrange and the other amplifier is for the subwoofers. If you are on a budget and plan to use just one amplifier, then use passive crossover. If you can afford to use two or more amplifiers, then consider using the electronic (active) crossover. ● **SEE FIGURE 27–14** for an example of crossovers used in factory-installed systems.

AFTERMARKET SOUND SYSTEM UPGRADE

POWER AND GROUND UPGRADES If adding an amplifier and additional audio components, be sure to include the needed power and ground connections. These upgrades can include the following:

- A separate battery for the audio system
- An inline fuse near the battery to protect the wiring and the components
- Wiring that is properly sized to the amperage draw of the system and the length of wire (The higher the output wattage, the greater the amperage required and the larger the wire gauge needed. The longer the distance between the battery and the components, the larger the wire gauge needed for best performance.)
- Ground wires at least the same gauge as the power-side wiring (Some experts recommend using extra ground wires for best performance.)

Read, understand, and follow all instructions that come with audio system components.

POWERLINE CAPACITOR A **powerline capacitor**, also called a **stiffening capacitor**, refers to a large capacitor (often abbreviated CAP) of 0.25 farad or larger connected to an amplifier power wire. The purpose and function of this capacitor is to provide the electrical reserve energy needed by the amplifier to provide deep bass notes. ● **SEE FIGURE 27–15**.

FIGURE 27–15 Two capacitors connected in parallel provide the necessary current flow to power large subwoofer speakers.

Battery power is often slow to respond; and when the amplifier attempts to draw a large amount of current, the capacitor will try to stabilize the voltage level at the amplifier by discharging stored current as needed.

A rule of thumb is to connect a capacitor with a capacity of 1 farad for each 1,000 watts of amplifier power. ● **SEE CHART 27–1**.

CAPACITOR INSTALLATION A powerline capacitor connects to the power leads between the inline fuse and the amplifier. ● **SEE FIGURE 27–16**.

If the capacitor were connected to the circuit as shown without "precharging," the capacitor would draw so much current that it would blow the inline fuse. To safely connect a large capacitor, it must be *precharged.* To precharge the capacitor, follow these steps.

STEP 1 Connect the negative (2) terminal of the capacitor to a good chassis ground.

STEP 2 Insert an automotive 12-volts lightbulb, such as a headlight or parking light, between the positive (1) terminal of the capacitor and the positive terminal of the battery. The light will come on as the capacitor is being charged and then go out when the capacitor is fully charged.

STEP 3 Disconnect the light from the capacitor, then connect the power lead to the capacitor. The capacitor is now fully charged and ready to provide the extra power necessary to supplement battery power to the amplifier.

POWERLINE CAPACITOR USAGE GUIDE	
WATTS (AMPLIFIER)	**RECOMMENDED CAPACITOR IN FARADS (MICROFARADS)**
100 W	0.10 farad (100,000 μF)
200 W	0.20 farad (200,000 μF)
250 W	0.25 farad (250,000 μF)
500 W	0.50 farad (500,000 μF)
750 W	0.75 farad (750,000 μF)
1,000 W	1.00 farad (1,000,000 μF)

CHART 27–1

The rating of the capacitor needed to upgrade an audio system is directly related to the wattage of the system.

? **FREQUENTLY ASKED QUESTION**

What Do the Amplifier Specifications Mean?

RMS power	**RMS** means root-mean-square and is the rating that indicates how much power the amplifier is capable of producing continuously.
RMS power at 2 ohms	This specification in watts indicates how much power the amplifier delivers into a 2-ohm speaker load. This 2-ohm load is achieved by wiring two 4-ohm speakers in parallel or by using 2-ohm speakers.
Peak power	Peak power is the maximum wattage an amplifier can deliver in a short burst during a musical peak.
THD	**Total harmonic distortion (THD)** represents the amount of change of the signal as it is being amplified. The lower the number, the better the amplifier (e.g., a 0.01% rating is better than a 0.07% rating).
Signal-to-noise ratio	This specification is measured in decibels (dB) and compares the strength of the signal with the level of the background noise (hiss). A higher volume indicates less background noise (e.g., a 105-dB rating is better than a 100-dB rating).

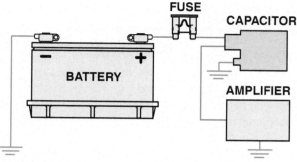

FIGURE 27–16 A powerline capacitor should be connected through the power wire to the amplifier as shown. When the amplifier requires more electrical power (watts) than the battery can supply, the capacitor will discharge into the amplifier and supply the necessary current for the fraction of a second it is needed by the amplifier. At other times when the capacitor is not needed, it draws current from the battery to keep it charged.

VOICE RECOGNITION

PARTS AND OPERATION **Voice recognition** is an expanding technology. It allows the driver of a vehicle to perform tasks, such as locate an address in a navigation system by using voice commands rather than buttons. In the past, users had to say the exact words to make it work, such as the following examples listed from an owner's manual for a vehicle equipped with a voice-actuated navigation system.

"Go home"

"Repeat guidance"

"Nearest ATM"

The problem with these simple voice commands was that the exact wording had to be spoken. The voice recognition software would compare the voice command to a specific list of words or phrases stored in the system in order for a match to occur. Newer systems recognize speech patterns and take action based on learned patterns. Voice recognition can be used for the following functions:

1. Navigation system operation (● **SEE FIGURE 27–17.**)
2. Sound system operation
3. Climate control system operation
4. Telephone dialing and other related functions (● **SEE FIGURE 27–18.**)

A microphone is usually placed in the driver's side sun visor or in the overhead console in the center top portion of the windshield area.

FIGURE 27–17 Voice commands can be used to control many functions, including navigation systems, climate control, telephone, and radio.

FIGURE 27–18 The voice command icon on the steering wheel of a Cadillac.

DIAGNOSIS AND SERVICE Voice recognition is usually incorporated into many functions of the vehicle. If a problem occurs with the system, perform the following steps:

1. Verify the customer complaint (concern). Check the owner's manual or service information for the proper voice commands and verify that the system is not functioning correctly.
2. Check for any aftermarket accessories that may interfere or were converted to components used by the voice recognition system, such as remote start units, MP3 players, or any other electrical component.
3. Check for stored diagnostic trouble codes (DTCs) using a scan tool.
4. Follow the recommended troubleshooting procedures as stated in service information.

FIGURE 27–19 Bluetooth earpiece that contains a microphone and speaker unit that is paired to a cellular phone. The telephone has to be within 33 feet (10 m) of the earpiece.

BLUETOOTH

OPERATION **Bluetooth** is a (radio frequency) standard for short-range communications. The range of a typical Bluetooth device is 33 feet (10 m) and it operates in the ISM (industrial, scientific, and medical) band between 2.4000 and 2.4835 MHz.

Bluetooth is a wireless standard that works on two levels.

- It provides physical communication using low power, requiring only about 1 milliwatt (1/1,000 of a watt) of electrical power, making it suitable for use with small handheld or portable devices, such as an ear-mounted speaker/microphone.

- It provides a standard protocol for how bits of data are sent and received.

The Bluetooth standard is an advantage because it is wireless, low cost, and automatic. The automotive use of Bluetooth technology is in the operation of a cellular telephone being tied into the vehicle. The vehicle allows the use of hands-free telephone usage. A vehicle that is Bluetooth telephone equipped has the following components.

- A Bluetooth receiver can be built into the navigation or existing sound system.

- A microphone allows the driver to use voice commands as well as telephone conversations from the vehicle to the cell via Bluetooth wireless connections.

Many cell phones are equipped with Bluetooth, which may allow the caller to use an ear-mounted microphone and speaker. ● **SEE FIGURE 27–19**.

If the vehicle and the cell phone are equipped with Bluetooth, the speaker and microphone can be used as a hands-free telephone when the phone is in the vehicle. The cell phone can be activated in the vehicle by using voice commands.

? FREQUENTLY ASKED QUESTION

Where Did Bluetooth Get Its Name?

The early adopters of the standard used the term "Bluetooth," and they named it for Harold Bluetooth, the king of Denmark in the late 900s. The king was able to unite Denmark and part of Norway into a single kingdom.

 FREQUENTLY ASKED QUESTION

Can Two Bluetooth Telephones Be Used in a Vehicle?

Usually. In order to use two telephones, the second phone needs to be given a name. When both telephones enter the vehicle, check which one is recognized. Say "phone status" and the system will tell you to which telephone the system is responding. If it is not the one you want, simply say, "next phone" and it will move to the other one.

SATELLITE RADIO

PARTS AND OPERATION Satellite radio, also called **Satellite Digital Audio Radio Services** or **SDARS**, is a fee-based system that uses satellites to broadcast high-quality radio. SDARS broadcasts on the S-band of 2.1320 to 2.345 GHz.

SIRIUS/XM RADIO Sirius/XM radio is standard equipment, but is optional in most vehicles. XM radio uses two satellites launched in 2001 called Rock (XM-2) and Roll (XM-1) in a geosynchronous orbit above North America. Two replacement satellites, Rhythm (XM-3) and Blues (XM-4), were launched in 2006. Sirius and XM radio combined in 2008 and now share some programming. The two types of satellite radios use different protocols and, therefore, require separate radios unless a combination unit is purchased.

RECEPTION Reception from satellites can be affected by tall buildings and mountains. To help ensure consistent reception, both SDARS providers do the following:

- Include in the radio itself a buffer circuit that can store several seconds of broadcasts to provide service when traveling out of a service area

- Provide land-based repeater stations in most cities (● **SEE FIGURE 27–20**.)

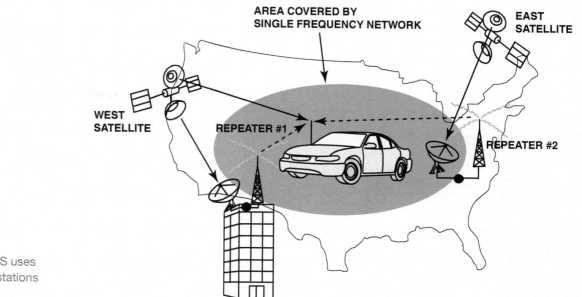

FIGURE 27–20 SDARS uses satellites and repeater stations to broadcast radio.

FIGURE 27–21 An aftermarket XM radio antenna mounted on the rear deck lid. The deck lid acts as the ground plane for the antenna.

FIGURE 27–22 A shark-fin-type factory antenna used for both XM and OnStar.

ANTENNA To be able to receive satellite radio, the antenna needs to be able to receive signals from both the satellite and the repeater stations located in many large cities. There are various types and shapes of antennas, including those shown in ● **FIGURES 27–21 AND 27–22.**

DIAGNOSIS AND SERVICE The first step in any diagnosis is to verify the customer complaint (concern). If no satellite service is being received, first check with the customer to verify that the monthly service fee has been paid and the account is up to date. If poor reception is the cause, carefully check the antenna for damage or faults with the lead-in wire. The antennas must be installed on a metal surface to provide the proper ground plane.

For all other satellite radio fault problems, check service information for the exact tests and procedures. Always follow the factory recommended procedures. Check the following websites for additional information:

- **www.xmradio.com**
- **www.sirius.com**
- **www.siriusxm.com**

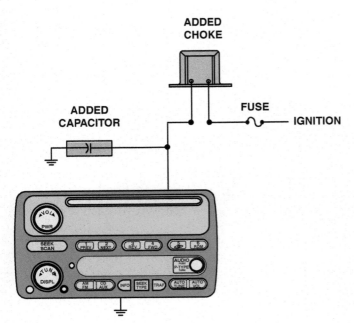

FIGURE 27-23 A radio choke and/or a capacitor can be installed in the power feed lead to any radio, amplifier, or equalizer.

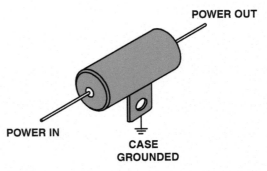

FIGURE 27-24 Many automobile manufacturers install a coaxial capacitor, like this one, in the power feed wire to the blower motor to eliminate interference caused by the blower motor.

RADIO INTERFERENCE

DEFINITION Radio interference is caused by variations in voltage in the powerline or may be picked up by the antenna. A "whine" that increases in frequency with increasing engine speed is usually referred to as an **alternator whine**, and is eliminated by installing a radio choke or a filter capacitor in the power feed wire to the radio. ● **SEE FIGURE 27-23**.

CAPACITOR USAGE Ignition noise is usually a raspy sound that varies with the speed of the engine. This noise is usually eliminated by the installation of a capacitor on the positive side of the ignition coil. The capacitor should be connected to the power feed wire to either the radio or the amplifier, or both. The capacitor *has* to be grounded. A capacitor allows AC interference to pass through to ground while blocking the flow of DC current. Use a 470-μF 50-volt electrolytic capacitor, which is readily available from most radio supply stores. A special coaxial capacitor can also be used in the powerline. ● **SEE FIGURE 27-24**.

RADIO CHOKE A **radio choke**, which is a coil of wire, can also be used to reduce or eliminate radio interference. Again, the radio choke is installed in the power feed wire to the radio equipment. Radio interference being picked up by the antenna can best be eliminated by stopping the source of the interference and making certain that all units containing a coil, such as electric motors, have a capacitor or diode attached to the power-side wire.

BRAIDED GROUND WIRE Using a braided ground wire is usually specified when electrical noise is a concern. The radio-frequency signals travel on the surface of a conductor rather than through the core of the wire. A braided ground strap is used because the overlapped wires short out any radio-frequency signals traveling on the surface.

AUDIO NOISE SUMMARY

- Radio noise can be broadcast or caused by noise (voltage variations) in the power circuit to the radio.

- Most radio interference complaints come when someone installs an amplifier, power booster, equalizer, or other radio accessory.

- *A major cause of this interference is the variation in voltage through the ground circuit wires. To prevent or reduce this interference, make sure all ground connections are clean and tight.*

- Placing a capacitor in the ground circuit also may be beneficial.

CAUTION: Amplifiers sold to boost the range or power of an antenna often increase the level of interference and radio noise to a level that disturbs the driver.

FIGURE 27–25 A "sniffer" can be made from an old antenna lead-in cable by removing about 3 inches of the outer shielding from the end. Plug the lead-in cable into the antenna input of the radio and tune the radio to a weak station. Move the end of the antenna wire around the vehicle dash area. The sniffer is used to locate components that may not be properly shielded or grounded and can cause radio interference through the case (housing) of the radio itself.

TECH TIP

The Separate Battery Trick
Whenever diagnosing sound system interference, try running separate 14 gauge wire(s) from the sound system power lead and ground to a separate battery outside of the vehicle. If the noise is still heard, the interference is *not* due to an alternator diode or other source in the wiring of the vehicle.

AUDIO NOISE CONTROL SYMPTOM CHART

NOISE SOURCE	WHAT IT SOUNDS LIKE	WHAT TO TRY
Alternator	A whine whose pitch changes with engine speed	Install a capacitor to a ground at the alternator output
Ignition	Ticking that changes with engine speed	Use a sniffer to further localize the source of the problem
Turn signals	Popping in time with the turn signals	Install a capacitor across the turn signal flasher
Brake lights	Popping whenever the brake pedal is depressed	Install a capacitor across the brake light switch contacts
Blower motor	Ticking in time with the blower motor	Install a capacitor to ground at the motor hot lead
Dash lamp dimmer	A buzzy whine whose pitch changes with the dimmer setting	Install a capacitor to ground at the dimmer hot lead
Horn switch	Popping when the horn is sounded	Install a capacitor between the hot lead and horn lead at the horn relay
Horn	Buzzing synchronized with the horn	Install a capacitor to ground at each horn hot lead
Amplifier power supply	A buzz, not affected by engine speed	Ground the amplifier chassis using a braided ground strap

CHART 27–2

Radio noise can have various causes, and knowing where or when the noise occurs helps pin down the location.

Capacitor and/or radio chokes are the most commonly used components. Two or more capacitors can be connected in parallel to increase the capacity of the original capacitor. A "sniffer" can be used to locate the source of the radio noise. A sniffer is a length of antenna wire with a few inches of insulation removed from the antenna end. The sniffer is attached to the antenna input terminal of the radio, and the radio is turned on and set to a weak station. The other end of the sniffer is then moved around areas of the dash to locate where the source of the interference originates. The radio noise will greatly increase if the end of the sniffer comes close to where electromagnetic leakage is occurring. ● **SEE FIGURE 27–25.**

● **SEE CHART 27–2.**

CASE STUDY

Lightning Damage

A radio failed to work in a vehicle that was outside during a thunderstorm. The technician checked the fuses and verified that power was reaching the radio. Then the technician noticed the antenna. It had been struck by lightning. Obviously, the high voltage from the lightning strike traveled to the radio receiver and damaged the circuits. Both the radio and the antenna were replaced to correct the problem. ● **SEE FIGURE 27–26**.

Summary:

- **Complaint**—Customer stated that the radio did not work.
- **Cause**—Visual inspection showed an antenna that had been stuck by lightning.
- **Correction**—Replacing the radio and the antenna restored proper operation.

FIGURE 27–26 The tip of this antenna was struck by lightning.

 CASE STUDY

The General Motors Security Radio Problem

A customer replaced the battery in a General Motors vehicle and now the radio display shows "LOC." This means that the radio is locked and there is a customer code stored in the radio.

Other displays and their meaning include the following:

"InOP"	This display indicates that too many incorrect codes have been entered and the radio must be kept powered for one hour and the ignition turned on before any more attempts can be made.
"SEC"	This display means there is a customer's code stored and the radio is unlocked, secured, and operable.
"---"	This means there is no customer code stored and the radio is unlocked.
"REP"	This means the customer's code has been entered once and the radio now is asking that the code be repeated to verify it was entered correctly the first time.

To unlock the radio, the technician used the following steps (the code number being used is 4321).

STEP 1 Press the "HR" (hour) button: "000" is displayed.

STEP 2 Set the first two digits using the hour button: "4300" is displayed.

STEP 3 Set the last two digits of the code using the "MIN" (minutes) button: "4321" is displayed.

STEP 4 Press the AM-FM button to enter the code. The radio is unlocked and the clock displays "1:00."

Thankfully, the owner had the security code. If the owner had lost the code, the technician would have to secure a scrambled factory backup code from the radio and then call a toll-free number to obtain another code for the customer. The code will only be given to authorized dealers or repair facilities.

Summary:

- **Complaint**—Customer stated that the radio was locked out after a battery replacement.
- **Cause**—Normal operation for radios equipped with security features.
- **Correction**—After installing the security code, the radio operation was restored.

1. Radios receive AM (amplitude modulation) and FM (frequency modulation) signals that are broadcast through the air.

2. The radio antenna is used to induce a very small voltage signal as an input into the radio from the electromagnetic energy via the broadcast station.

3. AM requires an antenna, whereas FM may be heard from a radio without an antenna.

4. Speakers reproduce the original sound, and the impedance of all speakers should be equally matched.

5. Crossovers are used to block certain frequencies to allow each type of speaker to perform its job better. A low-pass filter is used to block high-frequency sounds being sent to large woofer speakers, and a high-pass filter blocks low-frequency sounds being sent to tweeters.

6. Radio interference can be caused by many different things, such as a defective alternator, a fault in the ignition system, a fault in a relay or solenoid, or a poor electrical ground connection.

REVIEW QUESTIONS

1. Why do AM signals travel farther than FM signals?
2. What are the purpose and function of the ground plane?
3. How do you match the impedance of speakers?
4. What two items may need to be added to the wiring of a vehicle to control or reduce radio noise?
5. What is the first step when diagnosing a satellite radio customer complaint?

CHAPTER QUIZ

1. Technician A says that a radio can receive AM signals, but not FM signals, if the antenna is defective. Technician B says that a good antenna should give a reading of about 500 ohms when tested with an ohmmeter between the center antenna wire and ground. Which technician is correct?
   a. Technician A only
   b. Technician B only
   c. Both Technicians A and B
   d. Neither Technician A nor B

2. An antenna lead-in wire should have how many ohms of resistance between the center terminal and the grounded outer covering?
   a. Less than 5 ohms
   b. 5 to 50 ohms
   c. 300 to 500 ohms
   d. Infinity (OL)

3. Technician A says that a braided ground wire is best to use for audio equipment to help reduce interference. Technician B says to use insulated 14 gauge or larger ground wire to reduce interference. Which technician is correct?
   a. Technician A only
   b. Technician B only
   c. Both Technicians A and B
   d. Neither Technician A nor B

4. What maintenance should be performed to a power antenna to help keep it working correctly?
   a. Remove it from the vehicle and lubricate the gears and cable.
   b. Clean the mast with a soft cloth and lubricate with a light oil.
   c. Disassemble the mast and pack the mast with silicone grease (or equal).
   d. Loosen and then retighten the retaining nut.

5. If two 4-ohm speakers are connected in parallel, meaning positive (+) to positive (+) and negative (−) to negative (−), the total impedance will be _____.
   a. 8 ohms
   b. 4 ohms
   c. 2 ohms
   d. 1 ohm

6. If two 4-ohm speakers are connected in series, meaning the positive (+) of one speaker connected to the negative (−) of the other speaker, the total impedance will be _____.
   a. 8 ohms
   b. 5 ohms
   c. 4 ohms
   d. 1 ohm

7. An aftermarket satellite radio has poor reception. Technician A says that a lack of a proper ground plane on the antenna could be the cause. Technician B says that mountains or tall buildings can interfere with reception. Which technician is correct?
   a. Technician A only
   b. Technician B only
   c. Both Technicians A and B
   d. Neither Technician A nor B

8. 100,000 µF means _____.
   a. 0.10 farad
   b. 0.01 farad
   c. 0.001 farad
   d. 0.0001 farad

9. A radio choke is actually a _____.
   a. resistor
   b. capacitor
   c. coil (inductor)
   d. transistor

10. What device passes AC interference to ground and blocks DC voltage, and is used to control radio interference?
    a. Resistor
    b. Capacitor
    c. Coil (inductor)
    d. Transistor

chapter 28

GASOLINE, ALTERNATIVE FUELS, AND DIESEL FUELS

INTRODUCTION

Using the proper fuel is important for the proper operation of any engine. Although gasoline is the most commonly used fuel today, there are several alternative fuels that can be used in some vehicles. Diesel fuel contains much lower amounts of sulfur than before 2007 and this allows the introduction of many new clean burning diesel engines.

GASOLINE

Gasoline is a term used to describe a complex mixture of various hydrocarbons refined from crude petroleum oil for use as a fuel in engines. Gasoline and air burns in the cylinder of the engine and produces heat and pressure, which is transferred to rotary motion inside the engine and eventually powers the drive wheels of a vehicle. When the combustion process in the engine is perfect, all of the fuel and air are consumed and only carbon dioxide and water are produced.

REFINING

DISTILLATION In the late 1800s, crude was separated into different products by boiling in a process called **distillation**. Distillation works because crude oil is composed of hydrocarbons with a broad range of boiling points.

In a distillation column, the vapor of the lowest boiling hydrocarbons, propane and butane, rises to the top. The straight-run gasoline (also called naphtha), kerosene, and diesel fuel cuts are drawn off at successively lower positions in the column.

CRACKING **Cracking** is the process during which hydrocarbons with higher boiling points can be broken down (cracked) into lower boiling hydrocarbons by treating them to very high temperatures. This process, called *thermal cracking,* was used to increase gasoline production starting in 1913.

Today, instead of high heat, cracking is performed using a catalyst and is called **catalytic cracking**. A catalyst is a material that speeds up or otherwise facilitates a chemical reaction without undergoing a permanent chemical change itself. Catalytic cracking produces gasoline of higher quality than thermal cracking.

Hydrocracking is similar to catalytic cracking in that it uses a catalyst, but the catalyst is in a hydrogen atmosphere. Hydrocracking can break down hydrocarbons that are resistant to catalytic cracking alone and it is used to produce diesel fuel rather than gasoline.

Other types of refining processes include the following:

- Reforming
- Alkylation
- Isomerization
- Hydrotreating
- Desulfurization
  ● **SEE FIGURE 28–1.**

SHIPPING The gasoline is transported to regional storage facilities by tank railway car or by pipeline. In the pipeline method, all gasoline from many refiners is often sent through the same pipeline and can become mixed. All gasoline is said to be **fungible**, meaning that it is capable of being interchanged because each grade is created to specification so there is no reason to keep the different gasoline brands separated except for grade. Regular grade, midgrade, and premium grades are separated by using a device, called a *pig*, in the pipeline and sent to regional storage facilities. ● **SEE FIGURE 28–2.**

It is at these regional or local storage facilities where the additives and dye (if any) are added and then shipped by truck to individual gas stations.

VOLATILITY

DEFINITION **Volatility** describes how easily the gasoline evaporates (forms a vapor). The definition of volatility assumes that the vapors will remain in the fuel tank or fuel line and will cause a certain pressure based on the temperature of the fuel.

REID VAPOR PRESSURE **Reid vapor pressure (RVP)** is the pressure of the vapor above the fuel when the fuel is at 100°F (38°C). Increased vapor pressure permits the engine to start in cold weather. Gasoline without air will not burn. Gasoline must be vaporized (mixed with air) to burn in an engine. ● **SEE FIGURE 28–3.**

SEASONAL BLENDING Cold temperatures reduce the normal vaporization of gasoline; therefore, winter-blended gasoline is specially formulated to vaporize at lower temperatures for proper starting and driveability at low ambient temperatures.

- **Winter blend.** The **American Society for Testing and Materials (ASTM)** standards for winter-blend gasoline allow volatility of up to 15 pounds per square inch (PSI) RVP.
- **Summer blend.** At warm ambient temperatures, gasoline vaporizes easily. However, the fuel system (fuel pump, fuel-injector nozzles, etc.) is designed to operate with liquid gasoline. The volatility of summer-grade gasoline should be about 7 PSI RVP. According to ASTM standards, the maximum RVP should be 10.5 PSI for summer-blend gasoline.

VOLATILITY-RELATED PROBLEMS If using winter-grade fuel during warm weather, the following may occur.

- Heat causes some fuel to evaporate, thereby causing bubbles.
- When the fuel is full of bubbles (sometimes called *vapor lock*), the engine is not being supplied with enough fuel and the engine runs lean. A lean engine will lead to the following:

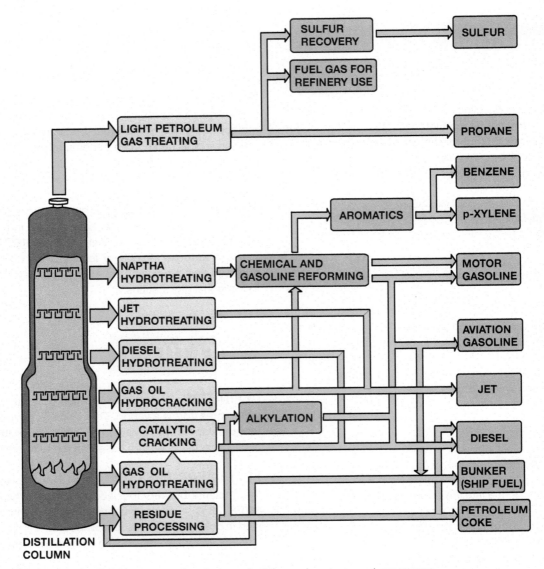

FIGURE 28-1 The crude oil refining process showing most of the major steps and processes.

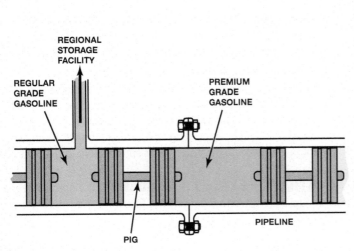

FIGURE 28-2 A pig is a plug-like device that is placed in a pipeline to separate two types or grades of fuel.

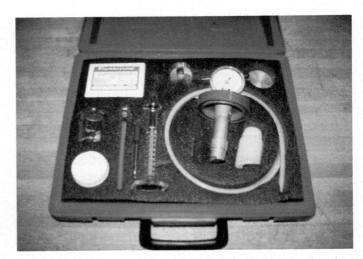

FIGURE 28-3 A gasoline testing kit, including an insulated container where water at 100°F is used to heat a container holding a small sample of gasoline. The reading on the pressure gauge is the Reid vapor pressure (RVP).

Why Do I Get Lower Gas Mileage in the Winter?

Several factors cause the engine to use more fuel in the winter than in the summer.

- Gasoline that is blended for use in cold climates is designed for ease of starting and contains fewer heavy molecules, which contribute to fuel economy. The heat content of winter gasoline is lower than summer-blend gasoline.
- In cold temperatures, all lubricants are stiff, causing more resistance. These lubricants include the engine oil, as well as the transmission and differential gear lubricants.
- Heat from the engine is radiated into the outside air more rapidly when the temperature is cold, resulting in longer run time until the engine has reached normal operating temperature.
- Road conditions, such as ice and snow, can cause tire slippage or additional drag on the vehicle.

1. Rough idle
2. Stalling
3. Hesitation on acceleration
4. Surging

If using summer-grade fuel in cold temperatures, the engine will be hard to start (long cranking before starting) due to the lack of volatility to allow the engine to start easily.

AIR-FUEL RATIOS

DEFINITION The **air-fuel ratio** is the proportion by weight of air and gasoline that the injection system mixes as needed for engine combustion. Air-fuel ratios in which a gasoline engine can operate without stalling range from 8:1 to 18.5:1.
● **SEE FIGURE 28–4**.

These ratios are usually stated by weight, as follows:

- 8 parts of air by weight combined with 1 part of gasoline by weight (8:1), which is the richest mixture that an engine can tolerate and still fire reliably
- 18.5 parts of air mixed with 1 part of gasoline (18.5:1), which is the leanest practical ratio

Richer or leaner air-fuel ratios cause the engine to misfire badly or not run at all.

STOICHIOMETRIC AIR-FUEL RATIO The ideal mixture or ratio at which all of the fuel combines with all of the oxygen in the air and burns completely is called the **stoichiometric** ratio, a chemically perfect combination. In theory, this ratio for gasoline is an air-fuel mixture of 14.7:1. The stoichiometric ratio is a compromise between maximum power and maximum economy. ● **SEE FIGURE 28–5**.

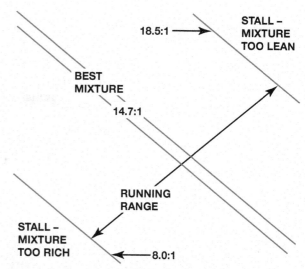

FIGURE 28–4 An engine will not run if the air-fuel mixture is either too rich or too lean.

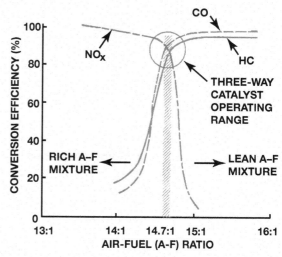

FIGURE 28–5 With a three-way catalytic converter, emission control is most efficient with an air-fuel ratio between 14.65:1 and 14.75:1.

NORMAL AND ABNORMAL COMBUSTION

TERMINOLOGY The **octane rating** of gasoline is the measure of its antiknock properties. **Spark knock** (also called **detonation** or **ping**) is a metallic noise an engine makes, usually during acceleration, resulting from abnormal or uncontrolled combustion inside the cylinder. Normal combustion occurs smoothly and progresses across the combustion chamber from the point of ignition.
● **SEE FIGURE 28–6**.

Normal flame-front combustion travels between 45 and 90 mph (72 and 145 km/h). The speed of the flame front depends on air-fuel ratio, combustion chamber design (determining amount of turbulence), and temperature.

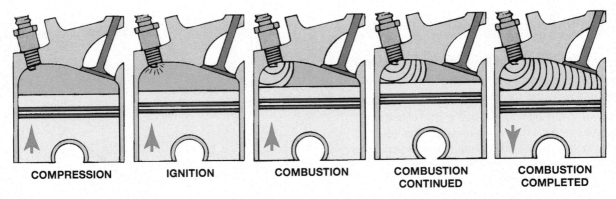

COMPRESSION   IGNITION   COMBUSTION   COMBUSTION CONTINUED   COMBUSTION COMPLETED

FIGURE 28–6 Normal combustion is a smooth, controlled burning of the air-fuel mixture.

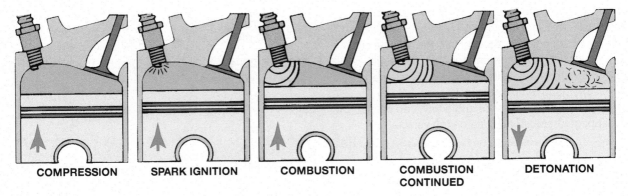

COMPRESSION   SPARK IGNITION   COMBUSTION   COMBUSTION CONTINUED   DETONATION

FIGURE 28–7 Detonation is a secondary ignition of the air-fuel mixture. It is also called spark knock or pinging.

ABNORMAL COMBUSTION During periods of abnormal combustion, called spark knock or detonation, the combustion speed increases by up to 10 times to near the speed of sound. The increased combustion speed also causes increased temperatures and pressures, which can damage pistons, gaskets, and cylinder heads. ● **SEE FIGURE 28–7.**

CONTROLLING SPARK KNOCK Spark knock was commonly heard in older engines, especially when under load and in warm weather temperatures. Most engines built since the 1990s are equipped with a knock sensor that is used to signal the powertrain control module (PCM) to retard the ignition timing if knock is detected. Using the proper octane fuel helps to ensure that spark knock does not occur.

OCTANE RATING

RATING METHODS The two basic methods used to rate gasoline for antiknock properties (octane rating) include the *Research method* and the *Motor method.*

Each uses a model of the special *cooperative fuel research* (CFR) single-cylinder engine to test the octane of a fuel sample, and the two methods use different engine settings. The research method typically results in readings that are 6 to 10 points higher than those of the motor method. For example, a fuel with a research octane number (RON) of 93 might have a motor octane number (MON) of 85.

GASOLINE GRADES The octane rating posted on pumps in the United States is the average of the two methods and is referred to as R + M ÷ 2, meaning that, for the fuel used in the previous example, the rating posted on the pumps would be the following:

$$\frac{RON + MON}{2} = \frac{93 + 85}{2} = 89$$

This pump octane rating is often called the **antiknock index (AKI).**
● **SEE FIGURE 28–8.**

FIGURE 28–8 A pump showing regular with a pump octane of 87, plus rated at 89, and premium rated at 93. These ratings can vary with brand, as well as in different parts of the country.

Except in high-altitude areas, the grades and octane ratings are shown in ● SEE CHART 28–1.

GRADES	OCTANE RATING
Regular	87
Midgrade (also called Plus)	89
Premium	91 or higher

CHART 28–1

The octane rating displayed on the fuel pumps can vary depending on climate.

OCTANE EFFECTS OF ALTITUDE As the altitude increases, atmospheric pressure drops. The air is less dense because a pound of air takes more volume. The octane rating of fuel does not need to be as high because the engine cannot take in as much air. This process will reduce the combustion (compression) pressures inside the engine. In mountainous areas, gasoline (R + M) ÷ 2 octane ratings are two or more numbers lower than normal (according to the SAE, about one octane number lower per 1,000 ft (300 m) in altitude). ● SEE FIGURE 28–9.

A second reason for the lowered octane requirement of engines running at higher altitudes is the normal enrichment of the air-fuel ratio and lower engine vacuum with the decreased air density. Some problems, therefore, may occur when driving out of high-altitude areas into lower areas where the octane rating must be higher. Most electronic fuel injection systems can compensate for changes in altitude and modify air-fuel ratio and ignition timing for best operation.

Because the combustion burn rate slows at high altitude, the ignition (spark) timing can be advanced to improve power. The amount of timing advance can be about 1 degree per 1,000 ft over 5,000 ft. Therefore, if driving at 8,000 ft of altitude, the ignition timing can be advanced 3 degrees.

VOLATILITY EFFECTS OF ALTITUDE High altitude also allows fuel to evaporate more easily. The volatility of fuel should be reduced at higher altitudes to prevent vapor from forming in sections of the fuel system, which can cause driveability and stalling problems. The extra heat generated in climbing to higher altitudes plus the lower atmospheric pressure at higher altitudes combine to cause possible driveability problems as the vehicle goes to higher altitudes.

FREQUENTLY ASKED QUESTION

What Grade of Gasoline Does the EPA Use When Testing Engines?

Due to the various grades and additives used in commercial fuel, the government (EPA) uses a liquid called indolene, which has a research method octane number of 96.5 and a motor method octane rating of 88, resulting in a (R + M) ÷ 2 rating of 92.25.

TECH TIP

Horsepower and Fuel Flow

To produce 1 hp, the engine must be supplied with 0.50 lb of fuel per hour (lb/hr). Fuel injectors are rated in pounds per hour. For example, a V-8 engine equipped with 25 lb/hr fuel injectors could produce 50 hp per cylinder (per injector) or 400 hp. Even if the cylinder head or block is modified to produce more horsepower, the limiting factor may be the injector flow rate.

The following are flow rates and resulting horsepower for a V-8 engine.

- 30 lb/hr: 60 hp per cylinder, or 480 hp
- 35 lb/hr: 70 hp per cylinder, or 560 hp
- 40 lb/hr: 80 hp per cylinder, or 640 hp

Of course, injector flow rate is only one of many variables that affect power output. Installing larger injectors without other major engine modifications could decrease engine output and drastically increase exhaust emissions.

FIGURE 28–9 The posted octane rating in most high-altitude areas shows regular at 85 instead of the usual 87.

GASOLINE ADDITIVES

DYE Dye is usually added to gasoline at the distributor to help identify the grade and/or brand of fuel. Fuels are required to be colored using a fuel soluble dye in many countries. In the United States and Canada, diesel fuel used for off-road use and not taxed is required to be dyed red for identification. Gasoline sold for off-road use in Canada is dyed purple.

OXYGENATED FUEL ADDITIVES **Oxygenated fuels** contain oxygen in the molecule of the fuel itself. Examples of oxygenated fuels include the following:

- **Methyl tertiary butyl ether (MTBE).** This fuel is manufactured by means of the chemical reaction of methanol and isobutylene. Unlike methanol, MTBE does not increase the volatility of the fuel, and is not as sensitive to water as are other alcohols. The maximum allowable volume level, according to the EPA, is 15% but is currently being phased out due to health concerns, as well as MTBE contamination of drinking water if spilled from storage tanks.

- **Tertiary-amyl methyl ether (TAME).** This fuel contains an oxygen atom bonded to two carbon atoms, and is added to gasoline to provide oxygen to the fuel. It is slightly soluble in water, very soluble in ethers and alcohol, and soluble in most organic solvents including hydrocarbons.

- **Ethyl tertiary butyl ether (ETBE).** This fuel is derived from ethanol. The maximum allowable volume level is 17.2%. The use of ETBE is the cause of much of the odor from the exhaust of vehicles if using reformulated gasoline, as mandated for use in some parts of the country.

- **Ethanol.** Also called *ethyl alcohol,* **ethanol** is drinkable alcohol and is usually made from grain. Adding 10% ethanol (ethyl alcohol or grain alcohol) increases the $(R + M) \div 2$ octane rating by three points.

The alcohol added to the base gasoline, however, also raises the volatility of the fuel about 0.5 PSI. Most automobile manufacturers permit up to 10% ethanol if driveability problems are not experienced.

The oxygen content of a 10% blend of ethanol in gasoline, called **E10**, is 3.5% oxygen by weight. ● **SEE FIGURE 28–10**.

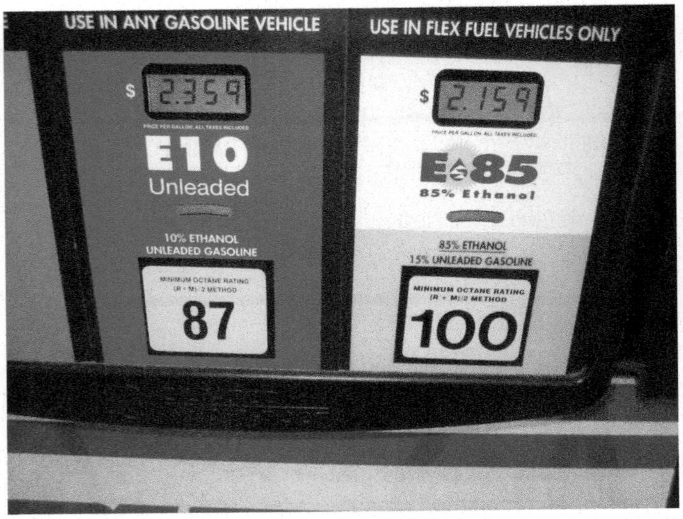

GASOLINE BLENDING

Gasoline additives, such as ethanol and dyes, are usually added to the fuel at the distributor. Adding ethanol to gasoline is a way to add oxygen to the fuel itself. There are three basic methods used to blend ethanol with gasoline to create E10 (10% ethanol, 90% gasoline).

FIGURE 28–10 This fuel pump indicates that the gasoline is blended with 10% ethanol (ethyl alcohol) and can be used in any gasoline vehicle. E85 contains 85% ethanol and can only be used in vehicles specifically designed to use it.

? **FREQUENTLY ASKED QUESTION**

What Is Meant by "Phase Separation"?

All alcohols absorb water, and the alcohol-water mixture can separate from the gasoline and sink to the bottom of the fuel tank. This process is called phase separation. To help avoid engine performance problems, try to keep at least a quarter tank of fuel at all times, especially during seasons when there is a wide temperature span between daytime highs and nighttime lows. These conditions can cause moisture to accumulate in the fuel tank as a result of condensation of the moisture in the air. Keeping the fuel tank full reduces the amount of air and moisture in the tank. ● **SEE FIGURE 28–11**.

FIGURE 28–11 A container with gasoline containing water and alcohol. Notice the separation line where the alcohol-water mixture separated from the gasoline and sank to the bottom.

1. **In-line blending.** Gasoline and ethanol are mixed in a storage tank or in the tank of a transport truck while it is being filled. Because the quantities of each can be accurately measured, this method is most likely to produce a well-mixed blend of ethanol and gasoline. ● **SEE FIGURE 28–12.**

2. **Sequential blending.** This method is usually performed at the wholesale terminal and involves adding a measured amount of ethanol to a tank truck followed by a measured amount of gasoline. ● **SEE FIGURE 28–13.**

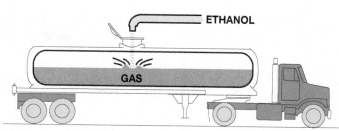

FIGURE 28–14 Splash blending occurs when the ethanol is added to a tanker with gasoline and is mixed as the truck travels to the retail outlet.

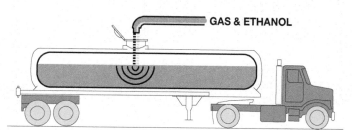

FIGURE 28–12 In-line blending is the most accurate method for blending ethanol with gasoline because computers are used to calculate the correct ratio.

3. **Splash blending.** This method can be done at the retail outlet or distributor and involves separate purchases of ethanol and gasoline. In a typical case, a distributor can purchase gasoline, and then drive to another supplier and purchase ethanol. The ethanol is added (splashed) into the tank of gasoline. This method is the least accurate method of blending and can result in ethanol concentration for E10 that should be 10% to range from 5% to over 20% in some cases. ● **SEE FIGURE 28–14.**

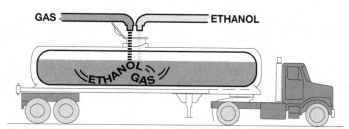

FIGURE 28–13 Sequential blending uses a computer to calculate the correct ratio, as well as the prescribed order that the products are loaded.

TESTING GASOLINE FOR ALCOHOL CONTENT

Take the following steps when testing gasoline for alcohol content:

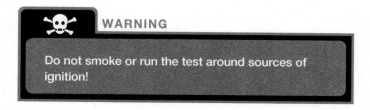

WARNING

Do not smoke or run the test around sources of ignition!

1. Pour suspect gasoline into a graduated cylinder.
2. Carefully fill the graduated cylinder to the 90 mL mark.
3. Add 10 mL of water to the graduated cylinder by counting the number of drops from an eyedropper.
4. Put the stopper in the cylinder and shake vigorously for one minute. Relieve built-up pressure by occasionally removing the stopper. Alcohol dissolves in water and will drop to the bottom of the cylinder.
5. Place the cylinder on a flat surface and let it stand for two minutes.
6. Take a reading near the bottom of the cylinder at the boundary between the two liquids.

? FREQUENTLY ASKED QUESTION

Is Water Heavier than Gasoline?

Yes. Water weighs about 8 lb per gallon, whereas gasoline weighs about 6 lb per gallon. The density as measured by specific gravity includes the following:

Water = 1.000 (the baseline for specific gravity)

Gasoline = 0.730 to 0.760

This means that any water that gets into the fuel tank will sink to the bottom.

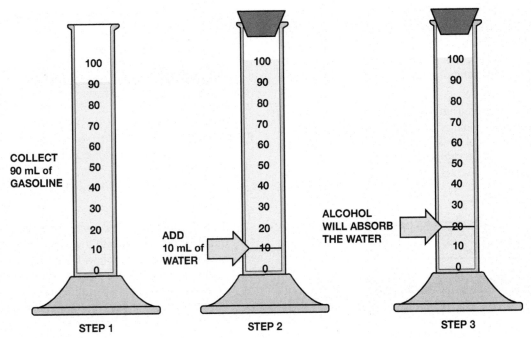

COLLECT 90 mL of GASOLINE	ADD 10 mL of WATER	ALCOHOL WILL ABSORB THE WATER
STEP 1	STEP 2	STEP 3

FIGURE 28–15 Checking gasoline for alcohol involves using a graduated cylinder and adding water to check if the alcohol absorbs the water.

7. For percentage of alcohol in gasoline, subtract 10 to get the percentage.

For example,

The reading is 20 mL: 20 − 10 = 10% alcohol

If the increase in volume is 0.2% or less, it may be assumed that the test gasoline contains no alcohol. ● **SEE FIGURE 28–15.**

Alcohol content can also be checked using an electronic tester. See the photo sequence at the end of the chapter.

GENERAL GASOLINE RECOMMENDATIONS

The fuel used by an engine is a major expense in the operation cost of the vehicle. The proper operation of the engine depends on clean fuel of the proper octane rating and vapor pressure for the atmospheric conditions.

To help ensure proper engine operation and keep fuel costs to a minimum, follow these guidelines:

1. Purchase fuel from a busy station to help ensure that it is fresh and less likely to be contaminated with water or moisture.

2. Keep the fuel tank above one-quarter full, especially during seasons in which the temperature rises and falls by more than 20°F between daytime highs and nighttime lows. This helps to reduce condensed moisture in the fuel tank and could prevent gas line freeze-up in cold weather.

NOTE: Gas line freeze-up occurs when the water in the gasoline freezes and forms an ice blockage in the fuel line.

3. Do not purchase fuel with a higher octane rating than is necessary. Try using premium high-octane fuel to check for operating differences. Most newer engines are equipped with a detonation (knock) sensor that signals the vehicle computer to retard the ignition timing when spark knock occurs. Therefore, an operating difference may not be noticeable to the driver when using a low-octane fuel, except for a decrease in power and fuel economy. In other words, the engine with a knock sensor will tend to operate knock free on regular fuel, even if premium, higher octane fuel is specified. Using premium fuel may result in more

 FREQUENTLY ASKED QUESTION

What Is "Top-Tier" Gasoline?

Top-tier gasoline has specific standards for quality, including enough detergent to keep all intake valves clean. Four automobile manufacturers (BMW, General Motors, Honda, and Toyota) developed the standards. Top-tier gasoline exceeds the quality standards developed by the **World Wide Fuel Charter (WWFC)** in 2002 by vehicle and engine manufacturers. The gasoline companies that agreed to make fuel that matches or exceeds the standards as a top-tier fuel include ChevronTexaco, Shell, and ConocoPhillips. ● **SEE FIGURE 28–16.**

FIGURE 28-16 Not all top-tier gas stations mention that they are top-tier like this station. For more information and the list of top-tier gasoline stations, visit www.toptiergas.com.

power and greater fuel economy. The increase in fuel economy, however, would have to be substantial to justify the increased cost of high-octane premium fuel. Some drivers find a good compromise by using midgrade (plus) fuel to benefit from the engine power and fuel economy gains without the cost of using premium fuel all the time.

4. Try to avoid using gasoline with alcohol in warm weather, even though many alcohol blends do not affect engine driveability. If warm-engine stumble, stalling, or rough idle occurs, change brands of gasoline.

5. Do not purchase fuel from a retail outlet when a tanker truck is filling the underground tanks. During the refilling procedure, dirt, rust, and water may be stirred up in the underground tanks. This undesirable material may be pumped into your vehicle's fuel tank.

6. Do not overfill the gas tank. After the nozzle clicks off, add just enough fuel to round up to the next dime. Adding additional gasoline will cause the excess to be drawn into the charcoal canister. This can lead to engine flooding and excessive exhaust emissions.

7. Be careful when filling gasoline containers. Always fill a gas can on the ground to help prevent the possibility of static electricity buildup during the refueling process. ● **SEE FIGURE 28-17**.

FIGURE 28-17 Many service stations have signs posted warning customers to place plastic fuel containers on the ground while filling. If placed in a trunk or pickup truck bed equipped with a plastic liner, static electricity could build up during fueling and discharge from the container to the metal nozzle, creating a spark and possible explosion. Some service stations have warning signs not to use cell phones while fueling to help avoid the possibility of an accidental spark creating a fire hazard.

 TECH TIP

The Sniff Test

Problems can occur with stale gasoline from which the lighter parts of the gasoline have evaporated. Stale gasoline usually results in a no-start situation. If stale gasoline is suspected, sniff it. If it smells rancid, replace it with fresh gasoline.

NOTE: If storing a vehicle, boat, or lawnmower over the winter, put some gasoline stabilizer into the gasoline to reduce the evaporation and separation that can occur during storage. Gasoline stabilizer is frequently available at most automotive parts stores.

Why Should I Keep the Fuel Gauge Above One-Quarter Tank?

The fuel pickup inside the fuel tank can help keep water from being drawn into the fuel system unless water is all that is left at the bottom of the tank. Over time, moisture in the air inside the fuel tank can condense, causing liquid water to drop to the bottom of the fuel tank. (Recall that water is heavier than gasoline–about 8 pound per gallon for water and about 6 pound per gallon for gasoline.) If alcohol-blended gasoline is used, the alcohol can absorb the water and the alcohol-water combination can be burned inside the engine. However, when water combines with alcohol, a separation layer occurs between the gasoline at the top of the tank and the alcohol-water combination at the bottom. When the fuel level is low, the fuel pump will draw from this concentrated level of alcohol and water. Because alcohol and water do not burn as well as pure gasoline, severe driveability problems can occur such as stalling, rough idle, hard starting, and missing.

 TECH TIP

Do Not Overfill the Fuel Tank

Gasoline fuel tanks have an expansion volume area at the top. The volume of this expansion area is equal to 10% to 15% of the volume of the tank. This area is normally not filled with gasoline, but rather is designed to provide a place for the gasoline to expand into, if the vehicle is parked in the hot sun and the gasoline expands. This prevents raw gasoline from escaping from the fuel system. A small restriction is usually present to control the amount of air and vapors that can escape the tank and flow to the charcoal canister.

This volume area could be filled with gasoline if the fuel is slowly pumped into the tank. Since it can hold an extra 10% (2 gallons in a 20 gallon tank), some people deliberately try to fill the tank completely. When this expansion volume is filled, liquid fuel (rather than vapors) can be drawn into the charcoal canister. When the purge valve opens, liquid fuel can be drawn into the engine, causing an excessively rich air-fuel mixture. Not only can this liquid fuel harm vapor recovery parts, but overfilling the gas tank could also cause the vehicle to fail an exhaust emission test, particularly during an enhanced test when the tank could be purged while on the rollers.

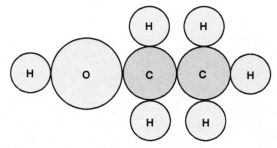

FIGURE 28–18 The ethanol molecule showing two carbon atoms, six hydrogen atoms, and one oxygen atom.

FIGURE 28–19 E85 has 85% ethanol mixed with 15% gasoline.

E85

WHAT IS E85? Vehicle manufacturers have available vehicles that are capable of operating on gasoline plus ethanol or a combination of gasoline and ethanol called **E85**, composed of 85% ethanol and 15% gasoline. Ethanol is also called **ethyl alcohol** or **grain alcohol**, because it is usually made from grain and is the type of alcohol found in alcoholic drinks such as beer, wine, and distilled spirits like whiskey. Ethanol is composed of two carbon atoms and six hydrogen atoms with one added oxygen atom. ● SEE FIGURE 28–18.

Pure ethanol has an octane rating of about 113. E85, which contains 35% oxygen by weight, has an octane rating of 100 to 105. This compares to a regular unleaded gasoline which has a rating of 87. ● SEE FIGURE 28–19.

NOTE: The octane rating of E85 depends on the exact percentage of ethanol used, which can vary from 81% to 85%. It also depends on the octane rating of the gasoline used to make E85.

HEAT ENERGY OF E85 E85 has less heat energy than gasoline.

Purchase a Flex Fuel Vehicle

If purchasing a new or used vehicle, try to find a flex fuel vehicle. Even though you may not want to use E85, a flex fuel vehicle has a more robust fuel system than a conventional fuel system designed for gasoline or E10. The enhanced fuel system components and materials usually include:

- Stainless steel fuel rail
- Graphite commutator bars instead of copper in the fuel pump motor (ethanol can oxidize into acetic acid, which can corrode copper)
- Diamondlike carbon (DLC) corrosion-resistant fuel injectors
- Alcohol resistant O-rings and hoses

The cost of a flex fuel vehicle compared with the same vehicle designed to operate on gasoline is a no-cost or a low-cost option.

Gasoline: 114,000 BTUs per gallon

E85: 87,000 BTUs per gallon

This means that the fuel economy is reduced by 20% to 30% if E85 is used instead of gasoline.

Example: A Chevrolet Tahoe 5.3-liter V-8 with an automatic transmission has an EPA rating using gasoline of 15 mpg in the city and 20 mpg on the highway. If this same vehicle is fueled with E85, the EPA fuel economy rating drops to 11 mpg in the city and 15 mpg on the highway.

ALTERNATIVE FUEL VEHICLES

The 15% gasoline in the E85 blend helps the engine start, especially in cold weather. Vehicles equipped with this capability are commonly referred to as the following:

- **Alternative fuel vehicles (AFVs)**
- **Flex fuels**
- **Flexible fuel vehicles (FFVs)**

Using E85 in a flex fuel vehicle can result in a power increase of about 5%. For example, an engine rated at 200 hp using gasoline or E10 could produce 210 hp if using E85.

NOTE: E85 may test as containing less than 85% ethanol if tested because it is often blended according to outside temperature. A lower percentage of ethanol with a slightly higher percentage of gasoline helps engines start in cold climates.

These vehicles are equipped with an electronic sensor in the fuel supply line that detects the presence and percentage of ethanol. The PCM then adjusts the fuel injector on-time and ignition timing to match the needs of the fuel being used.

E85 contains less heat energy, and therefore will use more fuel, but the benefits include a lower cost of the fuel and less environmental impact associated with using an oxygenated fuel.

General Motors, Ford, Chrysler, and Mazda are a few of the manufacturers offering E85 compatible vehicles. E85 vehicles use fuel system parts designed to withstand the additional alcohol content, modified driveability programs that adjust fuel delivery and timing to compensate for the various percentages of ethanol fuel, and a **fuel compensation sensor** that measures both the percentage of ethanol blend and the temperature of the fuel. This sensor is also called a **variable fuel sensor**. ● **SEE FIGURES 28–20 AND 28–21.**

E85 FUEL SYSTEM REQUIREMENTS Most E85 vehicles are very similar to non-E85 vehicles. Fuel system components may be redesigned to withstand the effects of higher

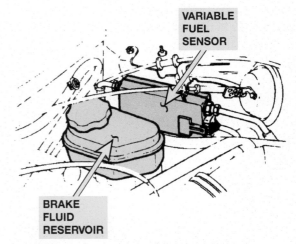

FIGURE 28–20 The location of the variable fuel sensor can vary, depending on the make and model of vehicle, but it is always in the fuel line between the fuel tank and the fuel injectors.

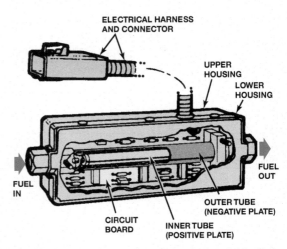

FIGURE 28–21 A cutaway view of a typical variable fuel sensor.

concentrations of ethanol. In addition, since the stoichiometric point for ethanol is 9:1 instead of 14.7:1 as for gasoline, the air-fuel mixture has to be adjusted for the percentage of ethanol present in the fuel tank.

The benefits of E85 vehicles include the following:

- Reduced pollution
- Less CO_2 production
- Less dependence on imported oil

FLEX FUEL VEHICLE IDENTIFICATION
Flexible fuel vehicles (FFVs) can be identified by the following:

- Emblems on the side, front, and/or rear of the vehicle
- Yellow fuel cap showing E85/gasoline (● **SEE FIGURE 28–22.**)
- Vehicle emission control information (VECI) label under the hood (● **SEE FIGURE 28–23.**)
- Vehicle identification number (VIN)

FIGURE 28–22 A flex fuel vehicle often has a yellow gas cap, which is labeled E85/gasoline.

FIGURE 28–23 This flexible fuel vehicle (FFV) vehicle emission control information (VECI) sticker located under the hood indicates that it can operate on either gasoline or ethanol.

 FREQUENTLY ASKED QUESTION

How Does a Sensorless Flex Fuel System Work?

Many General Motors flex fuel vehicles do not use a fuel compensation sensor and instead use the oxygen sensor to detect the presence of the lean mixture and the extra oxygen in the fuel.

The powertrain control module (PCM) then adjusts the injector pulse width and the ignition timing to optimize engine operation to the use of E85. This type of vehicle is called a **virtual flexible fuel vehicle (V-FFV)**. It can operate on pure gasoline or blends up to 85% ethanol.

 FREQUENTLY ASKED QUESTION

How Long Can Oxygenated Fuel Be Stored Before All of the Oxygen Escapes?

The oxygen in oxygenated fuels, such as E10 and E85, is not in a gaseous state like the CO_2 in soft drinks. The oxygen is part of the molecule of ethanol or other oxygenates and does not bubble out of the fuel. Oxygenated fuels, like any fuel, have a shelf life of about 90 days.

NOTE: For additional information on E85 and for the location of E85 stations in your area, go to www.e85fuel.com.

METHANOL

METHANOL TERMINOLOGY Methanol, also known as *methyl alcohol, wood alcohol,* or *methyl hydrate,* is a chemical compound formula that includes one carbon atom, four hydrogen atoms, and one oxygen atom. ● **SEE FIGURE 28–24.**

Methanol is a light, volatile, colorless, tasteless, flammable, poisonous liquid with a very faint odor. Methanol can be used in the following ways:

- As an antifreeze, a solvent, or a fuel
- To denature ethanol (to make undrinkable)

Methanol burns in air, forming CO_2 (carbon dioxide) and H_2O (water). A methanol flame is almost colorless. Methanol is often called wood alcohol because it was once produced chiefly as a by-product of the destructive distillation of wood. ● **SEE FIGURE 28–25.**

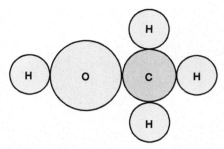

FIGURE 28–24 The molecular structure of methanol showing the one carbon atom, four hydrogen atoms, and one oxygen atom.

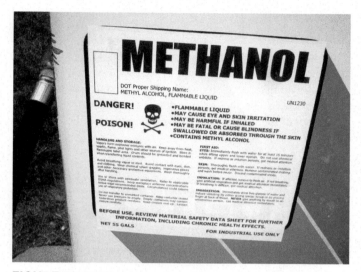

FIGURE 28–25 Sign on methanol pump shows that methyl alcohol is a poison and can cause skin irritation and other personal injury. Methanol is used in industry, as well as being a fuel.

PRODUCTION OF METHANOL The biggest source of methanol in the United States is coal. Using a simple reaction between coal and steam, a gas mixture called **syn-gas** (synthesis gas) is formed. The components of this mixture are carbon monoxide and hydrogen, which, through an additional chemical reaction, are converted to methanol.

Natural gas can also be used to create methanol and is reformed or converted to synthesis gas, which is later made into methanol.

Biomass can be converted to synthesis gas by a process called partial oxidation, and later converted to methanol. Biomass is organic material and includes the following:

- Urban wood wastes
- Primary mill residues
- Forest residues
- Agricultural residues
- Dedicated energy crops (e.g., sugarcane and sugar beets) that can be made into fuel

Electricity can be used to convert water into hydrogen, which is then reacted with carbon dioxide to produce methanol.

Methanol is toxic and can cause blindness and death. It can enter the body by ingestion, inhalation, or absorption through the skin. Dangerous doses will build up if a person is regularly exposed to fumes or handles liquid without skin protection. If methanol has been ingested, a doctor should be contacted immediately. The usual fatal dose is 4 fl oz (100 to 125 mL).

M85 Some flexible fuel vehicles are designed to operate on 85% methanol and 15% gasoline, called **M85**. Methanol is very corrosive and requires that the fuel system components be constructed of stainless steel and other alcohol-resistant rubber and plastic components. The heat content of M85 is about 60% of that of gasoline.

PROPANE

Propane is the most widely used of all the alternative fuels mainly because of its use in fleets, which utilize a central refueling station. Propane is normally a gas, but is easily compressed into a liquid and stored in inexpensive containers. When sold as a fuel, it is also known as **liquified petroleum gas (LPG)** or **LP gas**, because the propane is often mixed with about 10% of other gases, including the following:

- Butane
- Propylene
- Butylenes
- Mercaptan, to give the colorless and odorless propane a smell

Propane is nontoxic, but if inhaled can cause asphyxiation through lack of oxygen. Propane is heavier than air and lays near the floor if released into the atmosphere. Propane is commonly used in forklifts and other equipment located inside warehouses and factories, because the exhaust from the engine using propane is not harmful. Propane is a by-product of petroleum refining of natural gas. In order to liquefy the fuel, it is stored in strong tanks at about 300 PSI (2,000 kPa). The heating value of propane is less than that of gasoline; therefore, more is required, which reduces the fuel economy. ● SEE FIGURE 28–26.

COMPRESSED NATURAL GAS

CNG VEHICLE DESIGN Another alternative fuel that is often used in fleet vehicles is **compressed natural gas (CNG)**. Vehicles using this fuel are often referred to as **natural gas vehicles (NGVs)**. Look for the blue CNG label on vehicles designed to operate on compressed natural gas. ● SEE FIGURE 28–27.

FIGURE 28–26 Propane fuel storage tank in the trunk of a Ford taxi.

FIGURE 28–28 A CNG storage tank from a Honda Civic GX shown with the fixture used to support it while it is being removed or installed in the vehicle. Honda specifies that three technicians be used to remove or install the tank through the rear door of the vehicle due to the size and weight of the tank.

FIGURE 28–27 The blue sticker on the rear of this vehicle indicates that it is designed to use compressed natural gas. This Ford truck also has a sticker that allows it to be driven in the high occupancy vehicle (HOV) lane, even if there is just the driver, because it is a CNG vehicle.

Because natural gas must be compressed to 3,000 PSI (20,000 kPa) or more, the weight and cost of the storage container are major factors when it comes to preparing a vehicle to run on CNG. The tanks needed for CNG are typically constructed of 0.5 inch (3 mm) thick aluminum reinforced with fiberglass. ● **SEE FIGURE 28–28.**

The octane rating of CNG is about 130 and the cost per gallon is roughly half of the cost of gasoline. However, the heat value of CNG is also less, and therefore more is required to produce the same power; and the miles per gallon is less.

CNG COMPOSITION Compressed natural gas is a blend of the following:

- Methane
- Propane
- Ethane
- N-butane
- Carbon dioxide
- Nitrogen

Once it is processed, compressed natural gas is at least 93% methane. Natural gas is nontoxic, odorless, and colorless in its natural state. It is odorized during processing, using ethyl mercaptan ("skunk"), to allow for easy leak detection. Natural gas is lighter than air and will rise when released into the air. Since CNG is already a vapor, it does not need heat to vaporize before it will burn, which improves cold start-up and results in lower emissions during cold operation. However, because

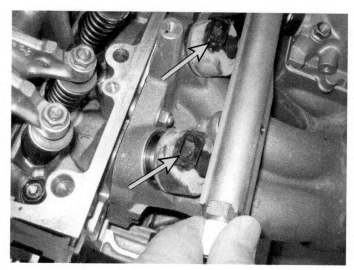

FIGURE 28–29 The fuel injectors used on this Honda Civic GX CNG engine are designed to flow gaseous fuel instead of liquid fuel and cannot be interchanged with any other type of injector.

it is already in a gaseous state, it displaces some of the air charge in the intake manifold, leading to a 10% reduction in engine power as compared to an engine operating on gasoline. Natural gas also burns slower than gasoline; therefore, the ignition timing must be advanced more when the vehicle operates on natural gas. The stoichiometric ratio, the point at which all the air and fuel is used or burned, is 16.5:1 compared to 14.7:1 for gasoline. This means that more air is required to burn 1 pound of natural gas than is required to burn 1 pound of gasoline. ● **SEE FIGURE 28–29**.

The CNG engine is designed to include:

- Increased compression ratio
- Strong pistons and connecting rods
- Heat-resistant valves
- Fuel injectors designed for gaseous fuel instead of liquid fuel

CNG FUEL SYSTEMS When completely filled, the CNG tank has 3,600 PSI of pressure in the tank. When the ignition is turned on, the alternate fuel electronic control unit activates the high-pressure lock-off, which allows high-pressure gas to pass to the high-pressure regulator.

- The high-pressure regulator reduces the high-pressure CNG to approximately 150 to 170 PSI and sends it to the low-pressure lock-off. The low-pressure lock-off is also controlled by the alternate fuel electronic control unit and is activated at the same time as the high-pressure lock-off.
- From the low-pressure lock-off, the CNG is directed to the low-pressure regulator. This is a two-stage regulator that first reduces the pressure to approximately 4 to 6 PSI in the first stage and then to about 0.5 PSI in the second stage.

- From here, the low-pressure gas is delivered to the gas mass sensor/mixture control valve. This valve controls the air-fuel mixture. The CNG gas distributor adapter then delivers the gas to the intake stream.

CNG vehicles are designed for fleet use that usually have their own refueling capabilities. One of the drawbacks to using CNG is the time that it takes to refuel a vehicle. The ideal method of refueling is the slow-fill method. The slow filling method compresses the natural gas as the tank is being fueled. This method ensures that the tank will receive a full charge of CNG; however, this method can take three to five hours to accomplish. If more than one vehicle needs filling, the facility will need multiple CNG compressors to refuel the vehicles.

There are three commonly used CNG refilling station pressures:

P24: 2,400 PSI

P30: 3,000 PSI

P36: 3,600 PSI

Try to find and use a station with the highest refilling pressure. Filling at lower pressures will result in less compressed natural gas being installed in the storage tank, thereby reducing the driving range. ● **SEE FIGURE 28–30**.

The fast-fill method uses CNG that is already compressed. However, as the CNG tank is filled rapidly, the internal temperature of the tank will rise, which causes a rise in tank pressure.

FIGURE 28–30 This CNG pump is capable of supplying compressed natural gas at either 3,000 PSI or 3,600 PSI. The price per gallon is higher for the higher pressure.

Once the temperature drops in the CNG tank, the pressure in the tank also drops, resulting in an incomplete charge in the CNG tank. This refueling method may take only about five minutes, but it will result in an incomplete charge to the CNG tank, reducing the driving range. ● **SEE CHART 28–2** for a comparison of the most frequently used alternative fuels.

ALTERNATE FUEL COMPARISON CHART

CHARACTERISTIC	PROPANE	CNG	METHANOL	ETHANOL	REGULAR UNLEADED GAS
Octane	104	130	100	100	87–93
BTU per gallon	91,000	NA	70,000	83,000	114,000–125,000
Gallon equivalent	1.15	122 ft³–1 gallon of gasoline	1.8	1.5	1
Onboard fuel storage	Liquid	Gas	Liquid	Liquid	Liquid
Miles/gallon as compared to gas	85%	Varies with pressure	55%	70%	100%
Relative tank size required to yield driving range equivalent to gas	Tank is 1.25 times larger	Tank is 3.5 times larger	Tank is 1.8 times larger	Tank is 1.5 times larger	
Pressure	200 PSI	3,000–3,600 PSI	NA	NA	NA
Cold weather capability	Good	Good	Poor	Poor	Good
Vehicle power	5%–10% power loss	10%–20% power loss	4% power increase	5% power increase	Standard
Toxicity	Nontoxic	Nontoxic	Highly toxic	Toxic	Toxic
Corrosiveness	Noncorrosive	Noncorrosive	Corrosive	Corrosive	Minimally corrosive
Source	Natural gas/ petroleum refining	Natural gas/ crude oil	Natural gas/coal	Sugar and starch crops/biomass	Crude oil

CHART 28–2

The characteristics of alternative fuels compared to regular unleaded gasoline show that all have advantages and disadvantages.

LIQUEFIED NATURAL GAS

Natural gas can be turned into a liquid if cooled to below −260°F (−127°C). The natural gas condenses into a liquid at normal atmospheric pressure and the volume is reduced by about 600 times. This means that the natural gas can be more efficiently transported over long distances where no pipelines are present when liquefied.

Because the temperature of liquefied natural gas (LNG) must be kept low, it is best used for fleets where a central LPG station can be used to refuel the vehicles.

P-SERIES FUELS

P-series alternative fuel is patented by Princeton University and is a nonpetroleum or natural gas based fuel suitable for use in flexible fuel vehicles or any vehicle designed to operate on E85 (85% ethanol, 15% gasoline). P-series fuel is recognized by the U.S. Department of Energy as being an alternative fuel, but is not yet available to the public. P-series fuels are blends of the following:

- Ethanol (ethyl alcohol)
- Methyltetrahydrofuran (MTHF)
- Natural gas liquids, such as pentanes
- Butane

The ethanol and MTHF are produced from renewable feedstocks, such as corn, waste paper, biomass, agricultural waste, and wood waste (scraps and sawdust). The components used in P-series fuel can be varied to produce regular grade, premium grade, or fuel suitable for cold climates. ● SEE CHART 28–3 for the percentages of the ingredients based on fuel grade.

COMPOSITION OF P-SERIES FUELS (BY VOLUME)

COMPONENT	REGULAR GRADE (%)	PREMIUM GRADE (%)	COLD WEATHER (%)
Pentanes plus	32.5	27.5	16
MTHF	32.5	17.5	26
Ethanol	35	55	47
Butane	0	0	11

CHART 28–3

P-series fuel varies in composition, depending on the octane rating and temperature.

SYNTHETIC FUELS

INTRODUCTION Synthetic fuels can be made from a variety of products, using several different processes. Synthetic fuel must, however, make these alternatives practical only when conventional petroleum products are either very expensive or not available.

FISCHER-TROPSCH Synthetic fuels were first developed using the **Fischer-Tropsch** method, and have been in use since the 1920s to convert coal, natural gas, and other fossil fuel products into a fuel that is high in quality and clean burning. The process for producing Fischer-Tropsch fuels was patented by two German scientists, Franz Fischer and Hans Tropsch, during World War I. The Fischer-Tropsch method uses carbon monoxide and hydrogen (the same synthesis gas used to produce hydrogen fuel) to convert coal and other hydrocarbons to liquid fuels in a process similar to hydrogenation, another method for hydrocarbon conversion. The process using natural gas, also called **gas-to-liquid (GTL)** technology, uses a catalyst, usually iron or cobalt, and incorporates steam reforming to give

FREQUENTLY ASKED QUESTION

What Is a Tri-Fuel Vehicle?

In Brazil, most vehicles are designed to operate on ethanol or gasoline, or any combination of the two. In this South American country, ethanol is made from sugarcane, is commonly available, and is lower in price than gasoline. Compressed natural gas (CNG) is also being made available so many vehicle manufacturers in Brazil, such as General Motors and Ford, are equipping vehicles to be capable of using gasoline, ethanol, or CNG. These vehicles are called tri-fuel vehicles.

off the by-products of carbon dioxide, hydrogen, and carbon monoxide. ● **SEE FIGURE 28–31**.

Whereas traditional fuels emit environmentally harmful particulates and chemicals, namely sulfur compounds, Fischer-Tropsch fuels combust with no soot or odors and emit only low levels of toxins. Fischer-Tropsch fuels can also be blended with traditional transportation fuels with little equipment modification, as they use the same engine and equipment technology as traditional fuels.

The fuels contain a very low sulfur and aromatic content and they produce virtually no particulate emissions. Researchers also expect reductions in hydrocarbon and carbon monoxide emissions. Fischer-Tropsch fuels do not differ in fuel performance from gasoline and diesel. At present, Fischer-Tropsch fuels are very expensive to produce on a large scale, although research is under way to lower processing costs. Diesel fuel created using the **Fischer-Tropsch diesel (FTD)** process is often called *GTL diesel*. GTL diesel can also be combined with petroleum diesel to produce a GTL blend. This fuel product is currently being sold in Europe and plans are in place to introduce it in North America.

COAL TO LIQUID Coal is very abundant in the United States and can be converted to a liquid fuel through a process called **coal to liquid (CTL)**. The huge cost of processing is the main obstacle to this type of fuel. The need to invest $1.4 billion per plant before it can make product is the reason no one has built a CTL plant yet in the United States. Investors need to be convinced that the cost of oil is going to remain high in order to get them to commit this kind of money.

A large plant might be able to produce 120,000 barrels of liquid fuel a day and would consume about 50,000 tons of coal per day. However, such a plant would create about 6,000 tons of CO_2 per day, which could contribute to global warming. With this factor and with the costs involved, CTL technology is not likely to expand.

Despite the limitations, two procedures can be used to convert CTL fuel.

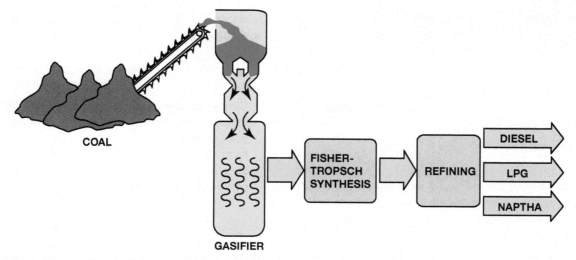

FIGURE 28–31 A Fischer-Tropsch processing plant is able to produce a variety of fuels from coal.

1. **Direct method**. In the direct method, coal is broken down to create liquid products. First the coal is reacted with hydrogen (H_2) at high temperatures and pressure with a catalyst. This process creates a synthetic crude, called **syncrude**, which is then refined to produce gasoline or diesel fuel.

2. **Indirect method.** In the indirect method, coal is first turned into a gas and the molecules are reassembled to create the desired product. This process involves turning coal into syngas, which is then converted into liquid, using the Fischer-Tropsch diesel (FTD) process.

Russia has been using CTL by injecting air into the underground coal seams. Ignition is provided and the resulting gases are trapped and converted to liquid gasoline and diesel fuel through the Fischer-Tropsch process. This underground method is called **underground coal gasification (UCG)**.

METHANOL TO GASOLINE Exxon Mobil has developed a process for converting methanol (methyl alcohol) into gasoline in a process called **methanol to gasoline (MTG)**. The MTG process was discovered by accident when a gasoline additive made from methanol was being created. The process instead created olefins, paraffins (alkenes), and aromatic compounds, which in combination are known as gasoline. The process uses a catalyst and is currently being produced in New Zealand.

FUTURE OF SYNTHETIC FUELS Producing gasoline and diesel fuels by other methods besides refining from crude oil has usually been more expensive. With the increasing cost of crude oil, alternative methods are now becoming economically feasible. Whether the diesel fuel or gasoline is created from coal, natural gas, or methanol, or created by refining crude oil, the transportation and service pumps are already in place. Compared to using compressed natural gas or other similar alternative fuels, synthetic fuels represent the lowest cost.

SAFETY PROCEDURES WHEN WORKING WITH ALTERNATIVE FUELS

All fuels are flammable and many are explosive under certain conditions. Whenever working around compressed gases of any kind (CNG, LNG, propane, or LPG), always wear personal protective equipment (PPE), including at least the following items:

1. Safety glasses and/or face shield
2. Protective gloves
3. Long-sleeve shirt and pants, to help protect bare skin from the freezing effects of gases under pressure in the event that the pressure is lost

If a spill should occur, take the following actions.

1. If any fuel gets on the skin, the area should be washed immediately.

2. If fuel spills on clothing, change into clean clothing as soon as possible.

3. If fuel spills on a painted surface, flush the surface with water and air dry. If simply wiped off with a dry cloth, the paint surface could be permanently damaged.

4. As with any fuel-burning vehicle, always vent the exhaust to the outside. If methanol fuel is used, the exhaust contains *formaldehyde,* which has a sharp odor and can cause severe burning of the eyes, nose, and throat.

 WARNING

Do not smoke or have an open flame in the area when working around or refueling any vehicle.

DIESEL FUEL

FEATURES OF DIESEL FUEL Diesel fuel must meet an entirely different set of standards than gasoline. Diesel fuel contains 12% more heat energy than the same amount of gasoline. The fuel in a diesel engine is not ignited with a spark, but is ignited by the heat generated by high compression. The pressure of compression (400 to 700 PSI, or 2,800 to 4,800 kPa) generates temperatures of 1,200°F to 1,600°F (700°C to 900°C), which speeds the preflame reaction to start the ignition of fuel injected into the cylinder.

DIESEL FUEL REQUIREMENTS All diesel fuel must have the following characteristics:

- **Cleanliness.** It is imperative that the fuel used in a diesel engine be clean and free from water. Unlike the case with gasoline engines, the fuel is the lubricant and coolant for the diesel injector pump and injectors. Good-quality diesel fuel contains additives, such as oxidation inhibitors, detergents, dispersants, rust preventatives, and metal deactivators.

- **Low-temperature fluidity.** Diesel fuel must be able to flow freely at all expected ambient temperatures. One specification for diesel fuel is its "pour point," which is the temperature below which the fuel will stop flowing.

- **Cloud point.** Another concern with diesel fuel at lower temperatures concerns **cloud point**, the low-temperature point when the waxes present in most diesel fuels tend to form crystals that can clog the fuel filter. Most diesel fuel suppliers distribute fuel with the proper pour point and cloud point for the climate conditions of the area.

CETANE NUMBER The cetane number for diesel fuel is the opposite of the octane number for gasoline. The **cetane number** is a measure of the ease with which the fuel can be ignited. The cetane rating of the fuel determines, to a great extent, its ability to start the engine at low temperatures and to provide smooth warmup and even combustion. The cetane rating of diesel fuel should be between 45 and 50. The higher the cetane rating, the more easily the fuel is ignited.

SULFUR CONTENT

The sulfur content of diesel fuel is very important to the life of the engine. Sulfur in the fuel creates sulfuric acid during the combustion process, which can damage engine components and cause piston ring wear. Federal regulations are getting extremely tight on sulfur content to less than 15 parts per million (ppm). High-sulfur fuel contributes to acid rain.

DIESEL FUEL COLOR

Diesel fuel intended for use on the streets and highways is either clear or green. Diesel fuel to be used on farms and off-road use is dyed red. ● SEE FIGURE 28-32.

(a)

(b)

FIGURE 28-32 (a) Regular diesel fuel on the left has a clear or greenish tint, whereas fuel for off-road use is tinted red for identification. (b) This fuel pump in a farming area clearly states the red diesel fuel is for off-road use only because it is not taxed.

GRADES OF DIESEL FUEL

ASTM also classifies diesel fuel by volatility (boiling range) into the following grades:

Grade 1 This grade of diesel fuel has the lowest boiling point and the lowest cloud and pour points, as well as a lower BTU content (less heat per pound of fuel). As a result, grade 1 is suitable for use during low-temperature (winter) operation. Grade 1 produces less heat per pound of fuel compared to grade 2, and may be specified for use in diesel engines involved in frequent changes in load and speed, such as those found in city buses and delivery trucks.

Grade 2 This grade has a higher boiling point, cloud point, and pour point as compared with grade 1. It is usually specified where constant speed and high loads are encountered, such as in long-haul trucking and automotive diesel applications.

DIESEL FUEL SPECIFIC GRAVITY TESTING

The density of diesel fuel should be tested whenever there is a driveability concern. The density or specific gravity of diesel fuel is measured in units of **API gravity**, which is an arbitrary scale expressing the gravity or density of liquid petroleum products devised jointly by the American Petroleum Institute and the National Bureau of Standards. The measuring scale is calibrated in terms of degrees API. Oil with the least specific gravity has the highest API gravity. The formula for determining API gravity is as follows:

$$\text{Degrees API gravity} = (141.5 \div \text{Specific gravity at } 60°\text{F}) - 131.5$$

The normal API gravity for grade 1 diesel fuel is 39 to 44 (typically 40). The normal API gravity for grade 2 diesel fuel is 30 to 39 (typically 35). A hydrometer calibrated in API gravity units should be used to test diesel fuel. ● SEE FIGURE 28-33.

FIGURE 28-33 Testing the API viscosity of a diesel fuel sample using a hydrometer.

ULTRA-LOW-SULFUR DIESEL FUEL Diesel fuel is used in diesel engines and is usually readily available throughout the United States, Canada, and Europe, where many more cars are equipped with diesel engines. Diesel engines manufactured to 2007 or newer standards must use **ultra-low-sulfur diesel (ULSD)** fuel containing less than 15 ppm of sulfur compared to the older, low-sulfur specification of 500 ppm. The purpose of the lower sulfur amount in diesel fuel is to reduce emissions of sulfur oxides (SOx) and particulate matter (PM) from heavy-duty highway engines and vehicles that use diesel fuel. The emission controls used on 2007 and newer diesel engines require the use of ULSD for reliable operation.

DIESEL FUEL ADDITIVES These types of additives include:

Winter Conditioners—Winter conditioners are designed to reduce the **Cold Filter Plugging Point (CFPP).** CFPP is lowest temperature at that a specified volume of diesel type of fuel can pass through a standardized filtration device in a specified time when cooled under certain conditions.

Multi-functional Conditioners—Many multifunctional additives increase the cetane rating of the fuel and helps keep injectors clean. By raising the cetane rating of the diesel fuel, engine power and fuel economy is improved. This type of additive is designed to be used year-round.

Microbicide—Microbes can grow in diesel fuel at the junction between the water and the diesel. Water is heavier than the diesel fuel and is near the bottom of the tank. Water in the fuel can be caused by condensation of moist air in the fuel tank and during transport and storage. A microbicide is designed to kill microorganisms including bacteria and fungi.

BIODIESEL

DEFINITION OF BIODIESEL **Biodiesel** is a domestically produced, renewable fuel that can be manufactured from vegetable oils, animal fats, or recycled restaurant greases. Biodiesel is safe, biodegradable, and reduces serious air pollutants such as PM, carbon monoxide, and hydrocarbons. Biodiesel is defined as mono-alkyl esters of long-chain fatty acids derived from vegetable oils or animal fats which conform to ASTM D6751 specifications for use in diesel engines. Biodiesel refers to the pure fuel before blending with diesel fuel. ● **SEE FIGURE 28–34.**

Biodiesel blends are denoted as BXX, with the "XX" representing the percentage of biodiesel contained in the blend (i.e., **B20** is 20% biodiesel, 80% petroleum diesel). Blends of 5% biodiesel with 95% petroleum diesel, called **B5,** can generally be used in unmodified diesel engines. Some diesel-powered vehicles can use B20 (20% biodiesel). Dodge, for example, allows the use of B5 in all diesel vehicles and B20 only if the optional additional fuel filter is installed. Biodiesel can also be used in its pure form (B100), but it may require certain engine modifications to avoid maintenance and performance problems and may not be suitable for wintertime use. Users should

FIGURE 28–34 A biodiesel pump decal indicating that the diesel fuel is ultra-low-sulfur diesel (ULSD) and must be used in 2007 and newer diesel vehicles.

consult their engine warranty statement for more information on fuel blends of greater than 20% biodiesel.

In general, B20 costs 30 to 40 cents more per gallon than conventional diesel. Although biodiesel costs more than regular diesel fuel, often called **petrodiesel,** fleet managers can make the switch to alternative fuels without purchasing new vehicles, acquiring new spare parts inventories, rebuilding refueling stations, or hiring new service technicians.

FEATURES OF BIODIESEL Biodiesel has the following characteristics:

1. Purchasing biodiesel in bulk quantities decreases the cost of fuel.

2. Biodiesel maintains similar horsepower, torque, and fuel economy.

3. Biodiesel has a higher cetane number than conventional diesel, which increases the engine's performance.

4. Biodiesel has a high flash point and low volatility so it does not ignite as easily as petrodiesel, which increases the margin of safety in fuel handling. In fact, it degrades four times faster than petrodiesel and is not particularly soluble in water.

5. It is nontoxic, which makes it safe to handle, transport, and store. Maintenance requirements for B20 vehicles and petrodiesel vehicles are the same.

6. Biodiesel acts as a lubricant, which can add to the life of the fuel system components.

NOTE: For additional information on biodiesel and the locations where it can be purchased, visit www. biodiesel.org.

I Thought Biodiesel Was Vegetable Oil?

Biodiesel is vegetable oil with the glycerin component removed by means of reacting the vegetable oil with a catalyst. The resulting hydrocarbon esters are 16 to 18 carbon atoms in length, almost identical to the petroleum diesel fuel atoms. This allows the use of biodiesel fuel in a diesel engine with no modifications needed. Biodiesel-powered vehicles do not need a second fuel tank, whereas vehicles powered with vegetable oil do.

There are three main types of fuel used in diesel engines:

- Petroleum diesel, a fossil hydrocarbon with a carbon chain length of about 16 carbon atoms
- Biodiesel, a hydrocarbon with a carbon chain length of 16 to 18 carbon atoms
- Vegetable oil, a triglyceride with a glycerin component joining three hydrocarbon chains of 16 to 18 carbon atoms each, called **straight vegetable oil (SVO)**

Other terms used when describing vegetable oil include the following:

- **Pure plant oil (PPO),** a term most often used in Europe to describe SVO
- **Waste vegetable oil (WVO),** which could include animal or fish oils from cooking
- **Used cooking oil (UCO),** a term used when the oil may or may not be pure vegetable oil

Vegetable oil is not liquid enough at common ambient temperatures for use in a diesel engine fuel delivery system designed for the lower viscosity petroleum diesel fuel. Vegetable oil needs to be heated to obtain a similar viscosity to biodiesel and petroleum diesel. This means a heat source needs to be provided before the fuel can be used in a diesel engine. This is achieved by starting on petroleum diesel or biodiesel fuel until the engine heat can be used to sufficiently warm a tank containing the vegetable oil. It also requires purging the fuel system of vegetable oil with petroleum diesel or biodiesel fuel prior to stopping the engine to avoid the vegetable oil thickening and solidifying in the fuel system away from the heated tank. The use of vegetable oil in its natural state does, however, eliminate the need to remove the glycerin component.

Many vehicle and diesel engine fuel system suppliers permit the use of biodiesel fuel that is certified as meeting testing standards. None permit the use of vegetable oil in its natural state.

FUEL	NOZZLE DIAMETER	PUMP HANDLE COLOR (VARIES—NO ESTABLISHED STANDARD)
Gasoline	13/16 inch (21 mm)	Black, red, white, green, or blue
E10	13/16 inch (21 mm)	Black, red, white, green, or blue
E85	13/16 inch (21 mm)	Yellow or black
Diesel fuel	15/16 inch (24 mm)	Yellow, green, or black
Biodiesel	15/16 inch (24 mm)	Green
Truckstop diesel	1 1/4 or 1 1/2 inch (32 or 38 mm)	Varies

CHART 28–4

Fuel pump nozzle size is standardized except for use by over-the-road truckstops where high fuel volumes and speedy refills require larger nozzle sizes compared to passenger vehicle filling station nozzles.

E-DIESEL FUEL

DEFINITION E-diesel, also called **diesohol** outside of the United States, is standard No. 2 diesel fuel that contains up to 15% ethanol. While E-diesel can have up to 15% ethanol by volume, typical blend levels are from 8% to 10%.

CETANE RATING OF E-DIESEL The higher the cetane number, the shorter the delay between injection and ignition. Normal diesel fuel has a cetane number of about 50. Adding 15% ethanol lowers the cetane number. To increase the cetane number back to that of conventional diesel fuel, a cetane-enhancing additive is added to E-diesel. The additive used to increase the cetane rating of E-diesel is ethylhexyl nitrate or ditertbutyl peroxide.

E-diesel has better cold-flow properties than conventional diesel. The heat content of E-diesel is about 6% less than conventional diesel, but the PM emissions are reduced by as much as 40%, carbon monoxide by 20%, and oxides of nitrogen (NO_x) by 5%.

Currently, E-diesel is considered to be experimental and can be used legally in off-road applications or in mass-transit buses with EPA approval. For additional information, visit www.e-diesel.org.

What Are the Pump Nozzle Sizes?

Unleaded gasoline nozzles are smaller than those used for diesel fuel to help prevent fueling errors. However, it is still possible to fuel a diesel vehicle with gasoline.

● **SEE CHART 28–4** for the sizes and colors used for fuel pump nozzles.

TESTING FOR ALCOHOL CONTENT IN GASOLINE

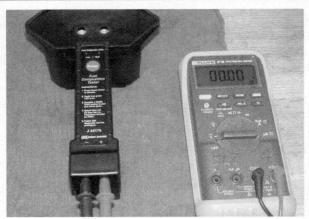

1 A fuel composition tester (SPX Kent-Moore J-44175) is the recommended tool to use to test the alcohol content of gasoline.

2 This battery-powered tester uses light-emitting diodes (LEDs), meter lead terminals, and two small openings for the fuel sample.

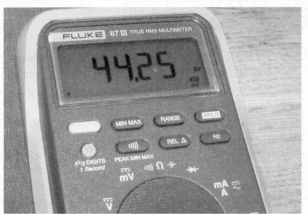

3 The first step is to verify the proper operation of the tester by measuring the air frequency by selecting AC hertz on the meter. The air frequency should be between 35 Hz and 48 Hz.

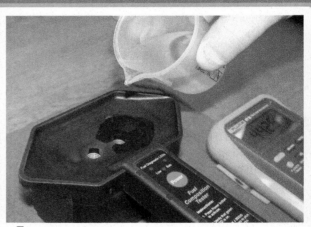

4 After verifying that the tester is capable of correctly reading the air frequency, gasoline is poured into the testing cell of the tool.

5 Record the AC frequency as shown on the meter and subtract 50 from the reading (e.g., 60.50 – 50.00 = 10.5). This number (10.5) is the percentage of alcohol in the gasoline sample.

6 Adding additional amounts of ethyl alcohol (ethanol) increases the frequency reading.

1. Gasoline is a complex blend of hydrocarbons. Gasoline is blended for seasonal usage to achieve the correct volatility for easy starting and maximum fuel economy under all driving conditions.

2. Winter-blend fuel used in a vehicle during warm weather can cause a rough idle and stalling because of its higher Reid vapor pressure (RVP).

3. Abnormal combustion (also called detonation or spark knock) increases both the temperature and the pressure inside the combustion chamber.

4. Most regular grade gasoline today, using the (R + M) ÷ 2 rating method, is 87 octane; midgrade (plus) is 89 and premium grade is 91 or higher.

5. Oxygenated fuels contain oxygen to lower CO exhaust emissions.

6. Flexible fuel vehicles (FFVs) are designed to operate on gasoline or gasoline-ethanol blends up to 85% ethanol (E85).

7. E85 has fewer BTUs of energy per gallon compared with gasoline and will therefore provide lower fuel economy.

8. Methanol is also called methyl alcohol or wood alcohol and, while it can be made from wood, it is mostly made from natural gas.

9. Propane is the most widely used alternative fuel. Propane is also called liquefied petroleum gas (LPG).

10. Compressed natural gas (CNG) is available for refilling in several pressures, including 2,400 PSI, 3,000 PSI, and 3,600 PSI.

11. Safety procedures when working around alternative fuel include wearing the necessary personal protective equipment (PPE), including safety glasses and protective gloves.

12. Diesel fuel requirements include cleanliness, low-temperature fluidity, and proper cetane rating.

13. Emission control devices used on 2007 and newer engines require the use of ultra-low-sulfur diesel (ULSD) that has less than 15 parts per million (ppm) of sulfur.

14. Biodiesel is the blend of vegetable-based liquid with regular diesel fuel. Most diesel engine manufacturers allow the use of a 5% blend, called B5, without any changes to the fuel system or engine.

REVIEW QUESTIONS

1. What does the (R + M) ÷ 2 gasoline pump octane rating indicate?

2. What is stoichiometric?

3. How is a flexible fuel vehicle identified?

4. Why is it desirable to fill a compressed natural gas (CNG) vehicle with the highest pressure available?

5. Biodiesel blends are identified by what designation?

CHAPTER QUIZ

1. Winter-blend gasoline _____.
   a. vaporizes more easily than summer-blend gasoline
   b. has a higher RVP
   c. can cause engine driveability problems if used during warm weather
   d. All of the above

2. Technician A says that spark knock, ping, and detonation are different names for abnormal combustion. Technician B says that any abnormal combustion raises the temperature and pressure inside the combustion chamber and can cause severe engine damage. Which technician is correct?
   a. Technician A only
   b. Technician B only
   c. Both Technicians A and B
   d. Neither Technician A nor B

3. Technician A says that the research octane number is higher than the motor octane number. Technician B says that the octane rating posted on fuel pumps is an average of the two ratings. Which technician is correct?
   a. Technician A only
   b. Technician B only
   c. Both Technicians A and B
   d. Neither Technician A nor B

4. Technician A says that in going to high altitudes, engines produce lower power. Technician B says that most engine control systems can compensate the air-fuel mixture for changes in altitude. Which technician is correct?
   a. Technician A only
   b. Technician B only
   c. Both Technicians A and B
   d. Neither Technician A nor B

5. Which method of blending ethanol with gasoline is the most accurate?
   a. In-line
   b. Sequential
   c. Splash
   d. All of the above

6. What can be used to measure the alcohol content in gasoline?
   a. Graduated cylinder
   b. Electronic tester
   c. Scan tool
   d. Both a and b

7. E85 means that the fuel is made from _____.
   a. 85% gasoline and 15% ethanol
   b. 85% ethanol and 15% gasoline
   c. ethanol that has 15% water
   d. pure ethyl alcohol

8. A flex fuel vehicle can be identified by _____.
   a. emblems on the side, front, and/or rear of the vehicle
   b. VECI
   c. VIN
   d. All of the above

9. When refueling a CNG vehicle, why is it recommended that the tank be filled to a high pressure?
   a. The range of the vehicle is increased.
   b. The cost of the fuel is lower.
   c. Less of the fuel is lost to evaporation.
   d. Both a and c.

10. What color is diesel fuel dyed if it is for off-road use only?
    a. Red
    b. Green
    c. Blue
    d. Yellow

IGNITION SYSTEM COMPONENTS AND OPERATION

LEARNING OBJECTIVES

After studying this chapter, the reader will be able to:

1. Explain how the ignition system and ignition coils work.
2. Discuss crankshaft position sensor and pickup coil operation.
3. Discuss knock sensors and ignition control circuits.
4. Describe the operation of distributor ignition.
5. Describe the operation of waste-spark and coil-on-plug ignition systems.

This chapter will help you prepare for Engine Repair (A8) ASE certification test content area "B" (Ignition System Diagnosis and Repair).

KEY TERMS

Bypass ignition 474

Coil-on-plug (COP) ignition (also coil-by-plug, coil-near-plug, coil-over-plug) 475

Companion cylinder 472

Compression-sensing ignition 475

Crankshaft Position (CKP) sensor 467

Camshaft position (CMP) sensor 467

Detonation 478

Distributorless ignition system (DIS) 471

Distributor ignition (DI) 465

Dwell 474

Electromagnetic interference (EMI) 475

Electronic control unit (ECU) 471

Electronic ignition (EI) 465

Electronic ignition system (EIS) 471

Electronic spark timing (EST) 474

Hall-effect switch 467

Igniter 465

Ignition coil 465

Ignition control module (ICM) 465

Ignition timing 477

Inductive reactance 466

Initial timing 477

Ion-sensing ignition 476

Iridium spark plugs 479

Knock sensor (KS) 478

Magnetic sensor 467

Mutual induction 466

Paired cylinder 472

Ping 478

Platinum spark plugs 479

Polarity 465

Primary ignition circuit 466

Saturation 466

Schmitt trigger 467

Secondary ignition circuit 466

Self-induction 466

Spark knock 478

Spark output (SPOUT) 474

Switching 467

Transistor 467

Turns ratio 465

Up-integrated ignition 474

Waste-spark ignition 471

IGNITION SYSTEM

PURPOSE AND FUNCTION   The ignition system includes components and wiring necessary to create and distribute a high voltage (up to 40,000 volts or more) and send to the spark plug. A high-voltage arc occurs across the gap of a spark plug inside the combustion chamber. The spark raises the temperature of the air–fuel mixture and starts the combustion process inside the cylinder.

BACKGROUND   All ignition systems apply battery voltage (close to 12 volts) to the positive side of the ignition coil(s) and pulse the negative side to ground on and off.

EARLY IGNITION SYSTEMS.   Before the mid-1970s, ignition systems used a mechanically opened set of contact points to make and break the electrical connection to ground. A cam lobe, located and driven by the distributor, opened the points. There was one lobe for each cylinder. The points used a rubbing block that was lubricated by applying a thin layer of grease on the cam lobe at each service interval. Each time the points opened, a spark was created in the ignition coil. The high-voltage spark then traveled to each spark plug through the distributor cap and rotor and the spark plug wires. The distributor was used twice in the creation of the spark.

1. The distributor was connected to the camshaft that rotated the distributor cam causing the points to open and close.

2. The distributor used a rotor to direct the high-voltage spark from the coil entering the center of the distributor cap to inserts connected to spark plug wires to each cylinder. ● **SEE FIGURE 29–1.**

ELECTRONIC IGNITION.   Since the mid-1970s, ignition systems have used sensors, such as a pickup coil and reluctor (trigger wheel), to trigger or signal an electronic module that switches the primary ground circuit of the ignition coil.

DISTRIBUTOR IGNITION (DI)   is the term specified by the Society of Automotive Engineers (SAE) for an ignition system that uses a distributor.

ELECTRONIC IGNITION (EI)   is the term specified by the SAE for an ignition system that does not use a distributor. Types of EI systems include:

1. **Waste-spark system.** This type of system uses one ignition coil to fire the spark plugs for two cylinders at the same time. ● **SEE FIGURE 29–2.**

2. **Coil-on-plug system.** This type of system uses a single ignition coil for each cylinder with the coil placed above or near the spark plug.

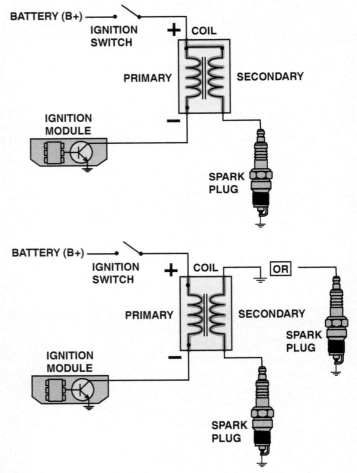

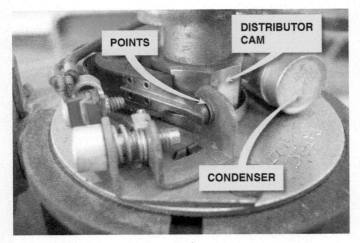

FIGURE 29–1 A point-type ignition system showing the distributor cam which opens the points.

FIGURE 29–2 Some ignition coils are electrically connected, called married (top figure), whereas others use separate primary and secondary windings, called divorced (lower figure). The polarity (positive or negative) of a coil is determined by the direction in which the coil is wound.

IGNITION SYSTEM OPERATION

The ignition system includes components and wiring necessary to create and distribute a high voltage (up to 40,000 volts or more). All ignition systems apply voltage close to battery voltage (12 volts) to the positive side of the ignition coil and pulse the negative side to ground. When the coil negative lead is grounded, the primary (low-voltage) circuit of the coil is complete and a magnetic field is created around the coil windings. When the circuit is opened, the magnetic field collapses and induces a high-voltage spark in the secondary winding of the ignition coil. Early ignition systems used a mechanically opened set of contact points to make and break the electrical connection to ground. Electronic ignition uses a sensor, such as a pickup coil and reluctor (trigger wheel), or trigger to signal an electronic module that makes and breaks the primary connection of the ignition coil.

NOTE: Distributor ignition (DI) is the term specified by the Society of Automotive Engineers (SAE) for an ignition system that uses a distributor. Electronic ignition (EI) is the term specified by the SAE for an ignition system that does not use a distributor.

IGNITION COILS

PURPOSE AND FUNCTION The heart of any ignition system is the **ignition coil**. The coil creates a high-voltage spark by electromagnetic induction. Many ignition coils contain two separate, but electrically connected, windings of copper wire. Other coils are true transformers in which the primary and secondary windings are not electrically connected.

COIL CONSTRUCTION The center of an ignition coil contains a core of laminated soft iron (thin strips of soft iron). This core increases the magnetic strength of the coil. Surrounding the laminated core are approximately 20,000 turns of fine wire (approximately 42 gauge). These windings are called the secondary coil windings. Surrounding the secondary windings are approximately 150 turns of heavy wire (approximately 21 gauge). These windings are called the primary coil windings. The secondary winding has about 100 times the number of turns of the primary winding, referred to as the **turns ratio** (approximately 100:1). The E coil is so named because the laminated, soft-iron core is E-shaped, with the coil wire turns wrapped around the center "finger" of the E and the primary winding wrapped inside the secondary winding. ● **SEE FIGURES 29–3 AND 29–4.**

The primary windings of the coil extend through the case of the coil and are labeled as "positive" and "negative." The positive terminal of the coil attaches to the ignition switch,

FIGURE 29–3 The steel lamination used in an E coil helps increase the magnetic field strength, which helps the coil produce higher energy output for a more complete combustion in the cylinders.

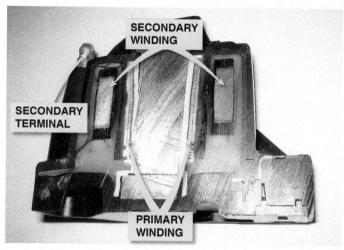

FIGURE 29–4 The primary windings are inside the secondary windings on this General Motors coil.

which supplies current from the positive battery terminal. The negative terminal is attached to an **ignition control module (ICM** or **igniter)**, which opens and closes the primary ignition circuit by opening or closing the ground return path of the circuit. When the ignition switch is on, voltage should be available at *both* the positive terminal and the negative terminal of the coil if the primary windings of the coil have continuity. The labeling of positive (+) and negative (−) of the coil indicates that the positive terminal is *more* positive (closer to the positive terminal of the battery) than the negative terminal of the coil. This condition is called the coil **polarity**. The polarity of the coil must be correct to ensure that electrons will flow from the hot center electrode of the spark plug on DI systems. *The polarity of an ignition coil is determined by the direction of rotation of the coil windings.* The correct polarity is then indicated on the primary terminals of the coil. If the coil primary leads are reversed, the voltage required to fire the spark plugs is increased by 40%. The coil output voltage is directly proportional to the ratio of primary to secondary turns of wire used in the coil.

SELF-INDUCTION When current starts to flow into a coil, an opposing current is created in the windings of the coil. This opposing current generation is caused by **self-induction** and is called **inductive reactance**. Inductive reactance is similar to resistance because it opposes any changes (increase or decrease) in current flow in a coil. Therefore, when an ignition coil is first energized, there is a slight delay of approximately 0.01 second before the ignition coil reaches its maximum magnetic field strength. The point at which a coil's maximum magnetic field strength is reached is called **saturation**.

MUTUAL INDUCTION In an ignition coil there are two windings, a primary and a secondary winding. When a *change* occurs in the magnetic field of one coil winding, a change also occurs in the other coil winding. Therefore, if the current is stopped from flowing (circuit is opened), the collapsing magnetic field cuts across the turns of the secondary winding and creates a high voltage in the secondary winding. This generation of an electric current in both coil windings is called **mutual induction**. The collapsing magnetic field also creates a voltage of up to 250 volts in the primary winding.

HOW IGNITION COILS CREATE 40,000 VOLTS All ignition systems use electromagnetic induction to produce a high-voltage spark from the ignition coil. Electromagnetic induction means that a current can be created in a conductor (coil winding) by a moving magnetic field. The magnetic field in an ignition coil is produced by current flowing through the primary windings of the coil. The current for the primary winding is supplied through the ignition switch to the positive terminal of the ignition coil. The negative terminal is connected to the ground return through an electronic ignition module (igniter).

If the primary circuit is completed, current (approximately 2 to 6 A) can flow through the primary coil windings. This flow creates a strong magnetic field inside the coil. When the primary coil winding ground return path connection is opened, the magnetic field collapses and induces a voltage of 250 to 400 volts in the primary winding of the coil, and a high-voltage (20,000 to 40,000 volts) low-amperage (20 to 80 mA) current in the secondary coil windings. This high-voltage pulse flows through the coil wire (if the vehicle is so equipped), distributor cap, rotor, and spark plug wires to the spark plugs. For each spark that occurs, the coil must be charged with a magnetic field and then discharged. The ignition components that regulate the current in the coil primary

winding by turning it on and off are known collectively as the **primary ignition circuit**. The components necessary to create and distribute the high voltage produced in the secondary windings of the coil are called the **secondary ignition circuit**. ● **SEE FIGURE 29–4**. These circuits include the following components:

PRIMARY IGNITION CIRCUIT

1. Battery
2. Ignition switch
3. Primary windings of coil
4. Pickup coil (crank sensor)
5. Ignition module (igniter)
6. PCM

SECONDARY IGNITION CIRCUIT

1. Secondary windings of coil
2. Distributor cap and rotor (if the vehicle is so equipped)
3. Spark plug wires
4. Spark plugs

● **SEE FIGURE 29–5.**

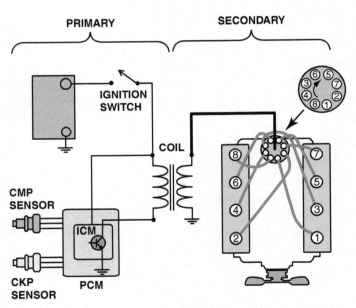

FIGURE 29–5 The primary ignition system is used to trigger, and therefore create the secondary (high-voltage) spark from the ignition coil.

How Does the Computer Control the Ignition?

The Powertrain Control Module (PCM) plays a key role in the final functioning of the ignition circuits. The PCM receives signals from all of the engine sensors and based on this information, uses an algorithm (computer program) to determine the best time to fire the spark plugs. For example, the sensors and how they could affect when the spark occurs include:

Engine Coolant Temperature (ECT)—The colder the engine, the more spark advance may be needed to achieve the highest possible engine output torque with lowest exhaust emissions.

Throttle Position (TP) sensor—The PCM uses the TP sensor information to not only determine where the accelerator position is located but also at what rate it is changing. If the accelerator pedal is rapidly being depressed, spark timing may be delayed (retarded slightly) to help prevent spark knock.

Manifold Absolute Pressure (MAP) sensor—The MAP sensor is used to detect engine load. During a heavy load, less spark advance is needed to help prevent spark knock, whereas more spark advance is needed under light load conditions for the engine to achieve maximum fuel economy and the lowest possible exhaust emissions.

IGNITION SWITCHING AND TRIGGERING

For any ignition system to function, the primary current must be turned on to charge the coil and off to allow the coil to discharge, creating a high-voltage spark. This turning on and off of the primary circuit is called **switching**. The unit that does the switching is an electronic switch, such as a power transistor. This power transistor can be located in any of the following locations:

- In the ignition control module (ICM) as part of the coil-on-plug assembly
- In the ignition control module (ICM)
- In the Powertrain control module (PCM)

The device that signals the switching of the coil on and off, or just on in most instances, is called the trigger.

A trigger is typically a pickup coil in some distributor-type ignitions and a crankshaft position sensor (CKP) on electronic (waste-spark and coil-on-plug) and many distributor-type ignitions. There are two types of devices used for triggering, including the magnetic sensor or Hall-effect switch.

PRIMARY CIRCUIT OPERATION

To get a spark out of an ignition coil, the primary coil circuit must be turned on and off. This primary circuit current is controlled by a **transistor** (electronic switch) inside the ignition module or (igniter)

The following are used as **crankshaft position (CKP) sensors** or **camshaft position (CMP) sensors**.

- **Hall-effect switch**—A **Hall-effect switch** also uses a stationary sensor and rotating trigger wheel (shutter). The Hall-effect switch requires a small input voltage to generate an output or signal voltage. Hall effect is the ability to generate a voltage signal in semiconductor material (gallium arsenate crystal) by passing current through it in one direction, and applying a magnetic field to it at a right angle to its surface. If the input current is held steady and the magnetic field fluctuates, an output voltage is produced that changes in proportion to field strength. Most Hall-effect switches have a Hall element or device, a permanent magnet, and a rotating ring of metal blades (shutters) similar to a trigger wheel (another method uses a stationary sensor with a rotating magnet). When the shutter blade enters the gap between the magnet and the Hall element, it creates a magnetic shunt that changes the field strength through the Hall element. This analog signal is sent to a **Schmitt trigger** inside the sensor itself, which converts the analog signal into a digital signal. A digital (on or off) voltage signal is created at a varying frequency to the ignition module or onboard computer. ● **SEE FIGURES 29–6 AND 29–7.**

- **Magnetic crankshaft position sensor**—A **magnetic sensor** uses the changing strength of the magnetic field surrounding a coil of wire to signal the module and computer. This signal is used by the electronics in the module and computer as to piston position and engine speed (RPM). ● **SEE FIGURES 29–8 AND 29–9.**

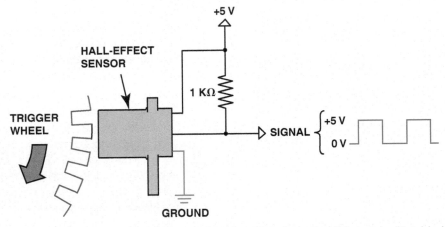

FIGURE 29–6 A Hall-effect sensor produces a digital on-off voltage signal whether it is used with a blade or a notched wheel.

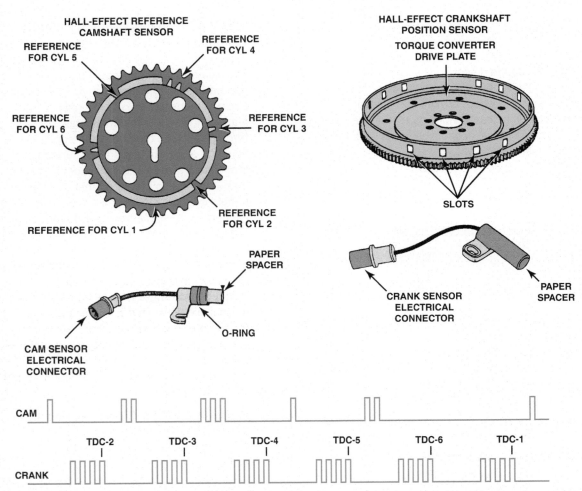

FIGURE 29–7 Some Hall-effect sensors look like magnetic sensors. This Hall-effect camshaft reference sensor and crankshaft position sensor have an electronic circuit built in that creates a 0 to 5 volt signal as shown at the bottom. These Hall-effect sensors have three wires: a power supply (8 volts) from the computer (controller); a signal (0 to 5 volts); and a signal ground.

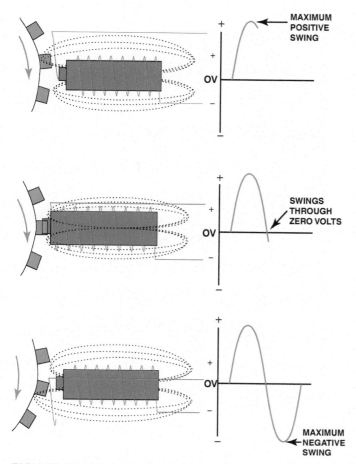

FIGURE 29–8 A magnetic sensor uses a permanent magnet surrounded by a coil of wire. The notches of the crankshaft (or camshaft) create a variable magnetic field strength around the coil. When a metallic section is close to the sensor, the magnetic field is stronger because metal is a better conductor of magnetic lines of force than air.

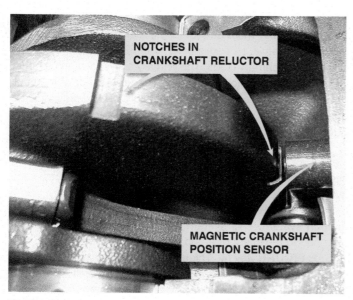

NOTCHES IN CRANKSHAFT RELUCTOR

MAGNETIC CRANKSHAFT POSITION SENSOR

FIGURE 29–9 A typical magnetic crankshaft position sensor.

DISTRIBUTOR IGNITION SYSTEMS

PURPOSE AND FUNCTION An ignition distributor was used for three purposes in older engines:

- To distribute the high-voltage spark from the ignition coil to the spark plugs located at each cylinder.
- Provide a method for switching the primary ignition circuit first using mechanical points and later by the use of a sensor.
- The distributor was driven by a gear from the end of the camshaft inside the engine which rotated at the same speed as the camshaft which is half crankshaft speed. The distributor also drove the oil pump in many engines.

DISTRIBUTOR CAP AND ROTOR The high-voltage pulse from the ignition coil enters the distributor cap and is sent to the individual spark plug wires by the rotating rotor. The rotor is attached to the distributor shaft and rotates as the engine runs. The main body of a distributor cap is typically made from molded plastic. A typical cap has one metal, usually aluminum or brass, insert per cylinder and one central contact for the coil. The center contact is a stationary or a spring-loaded carbon brush that contacts the rotor. Carbon is used because not only is it a conductor of electricity, it is also a lubricant so that there is minimum wear between the center insert of the distributor

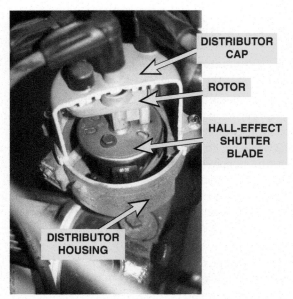

FIGURE 29-10 (a) A cutaway of a Ford distributor showing the Hall-effect shutter blade that is used to trigger the ignition control module and the rotor. (b) A rotor from a GM HEI system.

cap and the rotor. The other inserts are spaced evenly around the top of the cap. There is about a 0.020 inch (0.5mm) between the tip of the rotor and the inserts in the distributor cap. This is the first gap that the high voltage has to jump. The second gap is at the spark plug. Rotors are attached to distributor shafts using press-on spring clip fittings or screws. Most distributor rotors are made out of injection-molded plastics with a spring steel metal tab that provides electrical contact between the central (coil) distributor insert and each outer (spark plug) inserts. ● **SEE FIGURE 29-10.**

FIRING ORDER
Firing order means the order that the spark is distributed to the correct spark plug at the right time. The firing order of an engine is determined by crankshaft and camshaft design. The firing order is determined by the location of the spark plug wires in the distributor cap of an engine equipped with a distributor. The firing order is often cast into the intake manifold for easy reference. ● **SEE FIGURES 29-11.**

FIGURE 29-11 The firing order is cast or stamped on the intake manifold on most engines that have a distributor ignition.

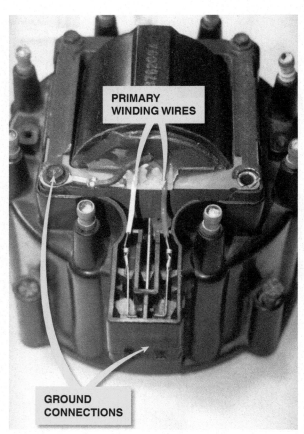

FIGURE 29-12 A typical General Motors HEI coil installed in the distributor cap. When the coil or distributor cap is replaced, check that the ground clip is transferred from the old distributor cap to the new. Without proper grounding, coil damage is likely. There are two designs of HEI coils. One uses red and white wire as shown, and the other design, which has reversed polarity, uses red and yellow wire for the coil primary.

GENERAL MOTORS HEI ELECTRONIC IGNITION
General Motor's HEI distributors use 8-mm-diameter spark plug wires that use female connections to the distributor cap towers. HEI coils must be replaced (if defective) with the exact replacement style. HEI coils differ and can be identified by the colors of the primary leads. The primary coil leads can be either white and red or yellow and red. The correct color of lead coil must be used for replacement. The colors of the leads indicate the direction in which the coil is wound, and therefore its polarity. ● **SEE FIGURES 29-12 AND 29-13.**

FORD ELECTRONIC IGNITION Ford electronic ignition systems all function similarly, even though over the years the system has been called by various names.

The EEC IV system uses the thick-film-integration (TFI) ignition system. This system uses a smaller control module attached to the distributor and uses an air-cooled epoxy E coil. ● **SEE FIGURE 29-14.** Thick-film integration means that all electronics are manufactured on small layers built up to form a thick film. Construction includes using pastes of different electrical resistances that are deposited on a thin, flat ceramic

FIGURE 29-13 This distributor ignition system uses a remotely mounted ignition coil.

material by a process similar to silk-screen printing. These resistors are connected by tracks of palladium silver paste. Then the chips that form the capacitors, diodes, and integrated circuits are soldered directly to the palladium silver tracks. The thick-film manufacturing process is highly automated.

CHRYSLER DISTRIBUTOR IGNITION Chrysler was the first domestic manufacturer to produce electronic ignition as standard equipment. The Chrysler system consists of a pulse generator unit in the distributor (pickup coil and reluctor). Chrysler's name for their electronic ignition is **electronic ignition system (EIS)**, and the control unit (module) is called the **electronic control unit (ECU)**.

The pickup coil in the distributor (pulse generator) generates the signal to open and close the primary coil circuit.
● **SEE FIGURE 29-15.**

WASTE-SPARK IGNITION SYSTEMS

Waste-spark ignition is another name for **distributorless ignition system (DIS)** or electronic ignition (EI). Waste-spark ignition was introduced in the mid-1980s and uses the on-board computer to fire the ignition coils. These systems were

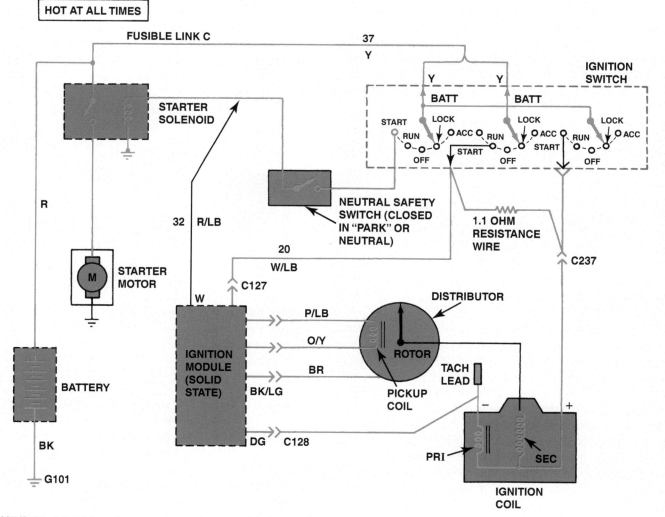

FIGURE 29-14 Wiring diagram of a typical Ford electronic ignition.

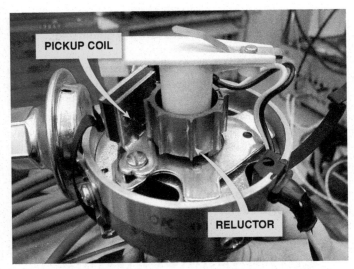

FIGURE 29-15 A Chrysler electronic ignition distributor. This unit is equipped with a vacuum advance mechanism that advances the ignition timing under light engine load conditions.

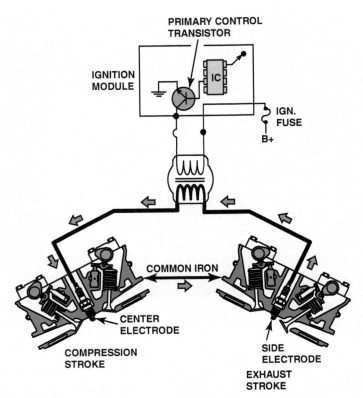

FIGURE 29-16 A waste-spark system fires one cylinder while its piston is on the compression stroke and into paired or companion cylinders while it is on the exhaust stroke. In a typical engine, it requires only about 2 to 3 kV to fire the cylinder on the exhaust strokes. The remaining coil energy is available to fire the spark plug under compression (typically about 8 to 12 kV).

first used on some Saabs and General Motors engines. A four-cylinder engine uses two ignition coils and a six-cylinder engine uses three ignition coils. Each coil is a true transformer in which the primary winding and secondary winding are not electrically connected. Each end of the secondary winding is connected to a cylinder exactly opposite the other in the firing order, which is called a **companion (paired) cylinder**.
● **SEE FIGURE 29-16**. This means that *both* spark plugs fire at the same time (within nanoseconds of each other). When one cylinder (e.g., 6) is on the compression stroke, the other cylinder (3) is on the exhaust stroke. This spark that occurs on the exhaust stroke is called the waste spark, because it does no useful work and is only used as a ground path for the secondary winding of the ignition coil. The voltage required to jump the spark plug gap on cylinder 3 (the exhaust stroke) is only 2 to 3 kV and provides the *ground circuit* for the secondary coil circuit. The remaining coil energy is used by the cylinder on the compression stroke. One spark plug of each pair always fires straight polarity and the other cylinder always fires reverse polarity. Spark plug life is not greatly affected by the reverse polarity. If there is only one defective spark plug wire or spark plug, two cylinders may be affected.

The coil polarity is determined by the direction the coil is wound (left-hand rule for conventional current flow) and cannot be changed. ● **SEE FIGURE 29-17**. Each spark plug for a particular cylinder always will be fired either with straight or reversed polarity, depending on its location in the engine and how the coils are wired. However, the compression and waste-spark condition flip-flops. When one cylinder is on compression, such as cylinder number 1, the paired cylinder (number 4) is on the exhaust stroke. During the next rotation of the crankshaft, cylinder number 4 is on the compression stroke and cylinder number 1 is on the exhaust stroke.

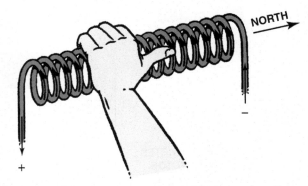

FIGURE 29-17 The left-hand rule states that if a coil is grasped with the left hand, the fingers will point in the direction of current flow and the thumb will point toward the north pole.

| Cylinder 1 | Always fires straight polarity, one time, requiring 10 to 12 kV and one time, requiring 3 to 4 kV. |
| Cylinder 4 | Always fires reverse polarity, one time, requiring 10 to 12 kV and one time, requiring 3 to 4 kV. |

NOTE: With a distributor-type ignition system, the coil has two air gaps to fire: one between the rotor tip and the distributor insert (not under compression forces)

and the other in the gap at the firing tip of the spark plug (under compression forces). A DIS also fires two gaps: one under compression (compression stroke plug) and one not under compression (exhaust stroke plug).

COMPRESSION-SENSING IGNITION

Some waste-spark ignition systems, use the voltage required to fire the cylinders to determine cylinder position. It requires a higher voltage to fire a spark plug under compression than it does when the spark plug is being fired on the exhaust stroke. The electronics in the coil and the PCM can detect which of the two companion (paired) cylinders that are fired at the same time requires the higher voltage, and therefore indicates the cylinder that is on the compression stroke. For example, a typical four-cylinder engine equipped with a waste-spark ignition system will fire both cylinders 1 and 4. If cylinder 4 requires a higher voltage to fire, as determined by the electronics connected to the coil, the PCM assumes that cylinder 4 is on the compression stroke. Engines equipped with compression-sensing ignition systems do not require the use of a camshaft position sensor to determine specific cylinder numbers. ● SEE FIGURE 29–18.

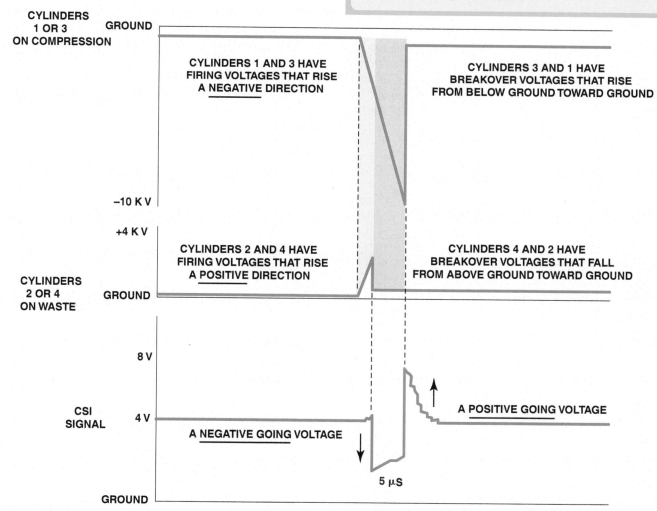

FIGURE 29–18 The slight (5 microsecond) difference in the firing of the companion cylinders is enough time to allow the PCM to determine which cylinder is firing on the compression stroke. The compression sensing ignition (CSI) signal is processed by the PCM, which then determines which cylinder is on the compression stroke.

IGNITION CONTROL CIRCUITS

Ignition control (IC) is the OBD-II terminology for the output signal from the PCM to the ignition system that controls engine timing. Previously, each manufacturer used a different term to describe this signal. For instance, Ford referred to this signal as **spark output (SPOUT)** and General Motors referred to this signal as **electronic spark timing (EST)**. This signal is now referred to as the ignition control (IC) signal. The ignition control signal is usually a digital output that is sent to the ignition system as a timing signal. If the ignition system is equipped with an ignition module, this signal is used by the ignition module to vary the timing as engine speed and load changes. If the PCM directly controls the coils, such as most coil-on-plug ignition systems, this IC signal directly controls the coil primary and there is a separate IC signal for each ignition coil. The IC signal controls the time that the coil fires; it either advances or retards the timing. On many systems, this signal controls the duration of the primary current flow in the coil, which is referred to as the **dwell**.

BYPASS IGNITION CONTROL A bypass-type ignition control means that the engine starts using the ignition module for timing control and switches to the PCM for timing control after the engine starts. A **bypass ignition** is commonly used on General Motors engines equipped with distributor ignition (DI), as well as those equipped with waste-spark ignition. ● **SEE FIGURE 29–19.** The bypass circuit includes four wires:

- **Tach reference (purple/white).** This wire comes from the ignition control (IC) module and is used by the PCM as engine speed information.
- **Ground (black/white).** This ground wire is used to ensure that both the PCM and the ignition control module share the same ground.
- **Bypass (tan/black).** This wire is used to conduct a 5-volt DC signal from the PCM to the ignition control module to switch the timing control from the module to the PCM.
- **EST (ignition control) (white wire).** This is the ignition timing control signal from the PCM to the ignition control module.

NOTE: It is this bypass wire that is disconnected before the ignition timing can be set on many General Motors engines equipped with a distributor ignition.

DIAGNOSING A BYPASS IGNITION SYSTEM One advantage of a bypass-type ignition is that the engine will run without the computer because the module can do the coil switching and can, through electronic circuits inside the module, provide for some spark advance as the engine speed increases. This is a safety feature that helps protect the catalytic converter if the ignition control from the PCM is lost. Therefore, if there is a problem, use a digital meter and check for the presence of 5 volts on the tan bypass wire. If there is not 5 volts present with the engine running, then the PCM or the wiring is at fault.

UP-INTEGRATED IGNITION CONTROL Most coil-on-plug and many waste-spark-type ignition systems use the PCM for ignition timing control. This type of ignition control is called **up-integrated** because all timing functions are interpreted in

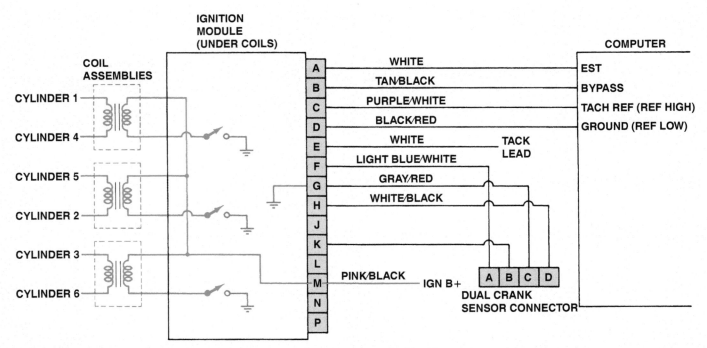

FIGURE 29–19 Typical wiring diagram of a V-6 distributorless (direct fire) ignition system.

the PCM, rather than being split between the ignition control module and the PCM. The ignition module, if even used, contains the power transistor for coil switching. The signal as to when the coil fires, is determined and controlled from the PCM.

Unlike a bypass ignition control circuit, it is not possible to separate the PCM from the ignition coil control to help isolate a fault.

COMPRESSION-SENSING IGNITION

Some waste-spark ignition systems, use the voltage required to fire the cylinders to determine cylinder position. It requires a higher voltage to fire a spark plug under compression than it does when the spark plug is being fired on the exhaust stroke. The electronics in the coil and the PCM can detect which of the two cylinders that are fired at the same time requires the higher voltage, which indicates the cylinder on the compression stroke. For example, a typical four-cylinder engine equipped with a waste-spark ignition system will fire both cylinders 1 and 4. If cylinder number 4 requires a higher voltage to fire, as determined by the electronics

connected to the coil, then the PCM assumes that cylinder number 4 is on the compression stroke. Engines equipped with **compression-sensing ignition** systems, do not require the use of a camshaft position sensor to determine cylinder number.

COIL-ON-PLUG IGNITION

Coil-on-plug (COP) ignition uses one ignition coil for each spark plug. This system is also called coil-by-plug, coil-near-plug, or coil-over-plug ignition. ● **SEE FIGURES 29–20 AND 29–21.** The coil-on-plug system eliminates the spark plug wires, which are often sources of **electromagnetic interference (EMI)** that can cause problems to some computer signals. The vehicle computer controls the timing of the spark. Ignition timing also can be changed (retarded or advanced) on a cylinder-by-cylinder basis for maximum performance and to respond to knock sensor signals. ● **SEE FIGURE 29–22.**

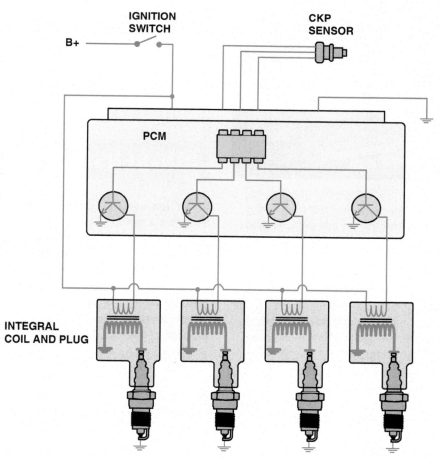

FIGURE 29–20 A typical two-wire coil-on-plug ignition system showing the triggering and the switching being performed by the PCM from input from the crankshaft position sensor.

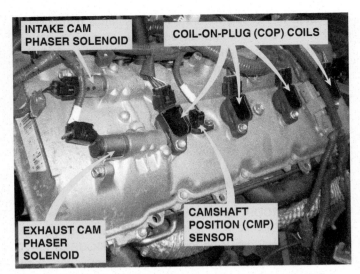

FIGURE 29–21 An overhead camshaft engine equipped with variable valve timing on both the intake and exhaust camshafts and coil-on-plug ignition.

FIGURE 29–22 Chrysler Hemi V-8 that has two spark plugs per cylinder. The coil on top of one spark fires that plug plus, through a spark plug wire, fires a plug in the companion cylinder.

There are two basic types of coil-on-plug ignition:

■ **Two-wire** —This design uses the vehicle computer to control the firing of the ignition coil. The two wires include ignition voltage feed and the pulse ground wire, which is controlled by the computer. All ignition timing and dwell control are handled by the computer.

■ **Three-wire** —This design includes an ignition module at each coil. The three wires are:

  ■ Ignition voltage

  ■ Ground

  ■ Pulse from the computer to the built-in module

General Motors vehicles use a variety of coil-on-plug-type ignition systems. Many V-8 engines use a coil-near-plug system with individual coils and modules for each individual cylinder that are placed on the valve covers. Short secondary ignition spark plug wires are used to connect the output terminal of the ignition coil to the spark plug.

Most newer Chrysler engines use coil-over-plug-type ignition systems. Each coil is controlled by the PCM, which can vary the ignition timing separately for each cylinder based on signals the PCM receives from the knock sensor(s). For example, if the knock sensor detects that a spark knock has occurred after firing cylinder 3, then the PCM will continue to monitor cylinder 3 and retard timing on just this one cylinder if necessary to prevent engine-damaging detonation.

ION-SENSING IGNITION

In an **ion-sensing ignition** system, the spark plug itself becomes a sensor. The ignition control (IC) module applies a voltage of about 100 to 400 volts DC across the spark plug gap after the ignition event to sense the plasma inside the cylinder.
● **SEE FIGURE 29–23.** The coil discharge voltage (10 to 15 kV) is electrically isolated from the ion-sensing circuit. The combustion flame is ionized and will conduct some electricity, which can be accurately measured at the spark plug gap. The purpose of this circuit includes:

■ Misfire detection (required by OBD-II regulations)

■ Knock detection (eliminates the need for a knock sensor)

■ Ignition timing control (to achieve the best spark timing for maximum power with lowest exhaust emissions)

■ Exhaust gas recirculation (EGR) control

■ Air–fuel ratio control on an individual cylinder basis

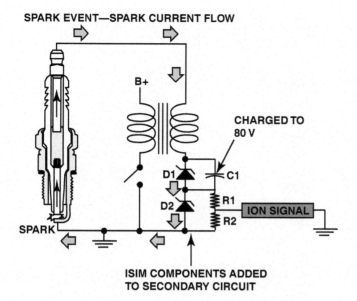

SPARK EVENT—SPARK CURRENT FLOW

CHARGED TO 80 V

B+

D1 C1

D2 R1

R2 ION SIGNAL

SPARK

ISIM COMPONENTS ADDED TO SECONDARY CIRCUIT

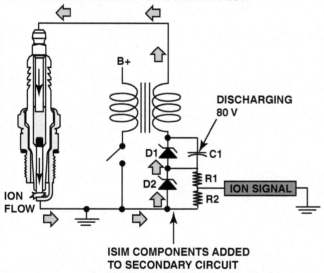

MEASUREMENT PERIOD—ION CURRENT FLOW

B+

DISCHARGING 80 V

D1 C1

D2 R1

R2 ION SIGNAL

ION FLOW

ISIM COMPONENTS ADDED TO SECONDARY CIRCUIT

FIGURE 29–23 A DC voltage is applied across the spark plug gap after the plug fires and the circuit can determine if the correct air–fuel ratio was present in the cylinder and if knock occurred.

Ion-sensing ignition systems still function the same as conventional coil-on-plug designs, but the engine does not need to be equipped with a camshaft position sensor for misfire detection, or a knock sensor because both of these faults are achieved using the electronics inside the ignition control circuits. Ion-sensing ignition is used in the Saab four- and six-cylinder engines and on many Harley-Davidson motorcycles.

THE NEED FOR SPARK ADVANCE **Ignition timing** refers to when the spark plug fires in relation to piston position. The time when the spark occurs depends on engine speed, and therefore, must be advanced (spark plugs fire some) as the engine rotates faster. The ignition in the cylinder takes a certain amount of time, usually 30 milliseconds (30/1000 of a second). This burning time is relatively constant throughout the entire engine speed range. For maximum efficiency from the expanding gases inside the combustion chamber, the burning of the air–fuel mixture should end by about 10° after top dead center (ATDC). If the burning of the mixture is still occurring after that point, the expanding gases do not exert much force on the piston because it is moving away from the gases (the gases are "chasing" the piston).

Therefore, to achieve the goal of having the air–fuel mixture be completely burned by the time the piston reaches 10° after top dead center, the spark must be advanced (occur sooner) as the engine speed increases. This timing advance is determined and controlled by the PCM on most vehicles. ● SEE FIGURE 29–24.

INITIAL TIMING If the engine is equipped with a distributor, it may be possible to adjust the base or the **initial timing**. The initial timing is usually set to fire the spark plug between zero degrees (top dead center or TDC) or slightly before TDC (BTDC). Ignition timing does change as the timing chain or gear wears and readjustment is often necessary on high-mileage engines. ● SEE FIGURE 29–25. Waste-spark and coil-on-plug ignitions cannot be adjusted.

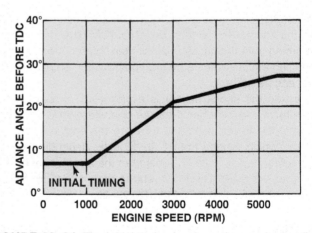

FIGURE 29–24 The initial timing is where the spark plug fires at idle speed. The computer then advances the timing based on engine speed and other factors.

FIGURE 29–25 Ignition timing marks are found on the harmonic balancers that are equipped with distributor ignition.

KNOCK SENSORS

Knock sensors are used to detect abnormal combustion, often called **ping**, **spark knock**, or **detonation**. Whenever abnormal combustion occurs, a rapid pressure increase occurs in the cylinder, creating a vibration in the engine block. It is this vibration that is detected by the knock sensor. The signal from the knock sensor is used by the PCM to retard the ignition timing until the knock is eliminated, thereby reducing the damaging effects of the abnormal combustion on pistons and other engine parts.

Inside the knock sensor is a piezoelectric element that generates a voltage when pressure or a vibration is applied to the unit. The knock sensor is tuned to the engine knock frequency, which ranges from 5 to 10 kHz, depending on the engine design. The voltage signal from the **knock sensor (KS)** is sent to the PCM. The PCM retards the ignition timing until the knocking stops. ● **SEE FIGURE 29–26.**

DIAGNOSING THE KNOCK SENSOR If a knock sensor diagnostic trouble code (DTC) is present, follow the specified testing procedure in the service information. A scan tool can be used to check the operation of the knock sensor, using the following procedure:

STEP 1 Start the engine and connect a scan tool to monitor ignition timing and/or knock sensor activity.

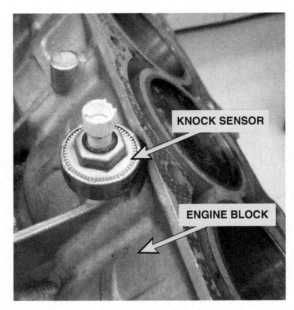

FIGURE 29–26 A knock sensor which is used by the powertrain control module (PCM) to detect engine detonation.

STEP 2 Create a simulated engine knocking sound by tapping on the engine block or cylinder head with a soft-faced mallet.

STEP 3 Observe the scan tool display. The vibration from the tapping should have been interpreted by the knock sensor as a knock, resulting in a knock sensor signal and a reduction in the spark advance.

A knock sensor also can be tested using a digital storage oscilloscope. ● **SEE FIGURE 29–27.**

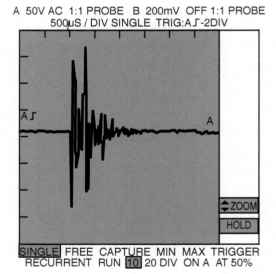

FIGURE 29–27 A typical waveform from a knock sensor during a spark knock event. This signal is sent to the computer which in turn retards the ignition timing. This timing retard is accomplished by an output command from the computer to either a spark advance control unit or directly to the ignition module.

NOTE: Some engine computers are programmed to ignore knock sensor signals when the engine is at idle speed to avoid having the noise from a loose accessory drive belt, or other accessory, interpreted as engine knock. Always follow the vehicle manufacturer's recommended testing procedure.

REPLACING A KNOCK SENSOR If replacing a knock sensor, be sure to purchase the exact replacement needed, because they often look the same, but the frequency range can vary according to engine design, as well as where it is located on the engine. Always tighten the knock sensor using a torque wrench and tighten to the specified torque to avoid causing damage to the piezoelectric element inside the sensor.

SPARK PLUGS

Spark plugs are manufactured from ceramic insulators inside a steel shell. The threads of the shell are rolled and a seat is formed to create a gastight seal with the cylinder head. ● **SEE FIGURE 29–28.** The physical difference in spark plugs includes:

- **Reach.** This is the length of the threaded part of the plug.
- **Heat range.** The heat range of the spark plug refers to how rapidly the heat created at the tip is transferred to the cylinder head. A plug with a long ceramic insulator path will run hotter at the tip than a spark plug that has a

shorter path because the heat must travel farther. ● **SEE FIGURE 29–29.**

- **Type of seat.** Some spark plugs use a gasket and others rely on a tapered seat to seal.

RESISTOR SPARK PLUGS Most spark plugs include a resistor in the center electrode, which helps to reduce electromagnetic noise or radiation from the ignition system. The closer the resistor is to the actual spark or arc, the more effective it becomes. The value of the resistor is usually between 2,500 and 7,500 ohms.

PLATINUM SPARK PLUGS **Platinum spark plugs** have a small amount of the precious metal platinum welded onto the end of the center electrode, as well as on the ground or side electrode. Platinum is a grayish-white metal that does not react with oxygen and therefore, will not erode away as can occur with conventional nickel alloy spark plug electrodes. Platinum is also used as a catalyst in catalytic converters where it is able to start a chemical reaction without itself being consumed.

IRIDIUM SPARK PLUGS Iridium is a white precious metal and is the most corrosion-resistant metal known. Most **iridium spark plugs** use a small amount of iridium welded onto the tip of a small center electrode 0.0015 to 0.002 inches (0.4 to 0.6 mm) in diameter. The small diameter reduces the voltage required to jump the gap between the center and the side electrode, thereby reducing possible misfires. The ground or side electrode is usually tipped with platinum to help reduce electrode gap wear.

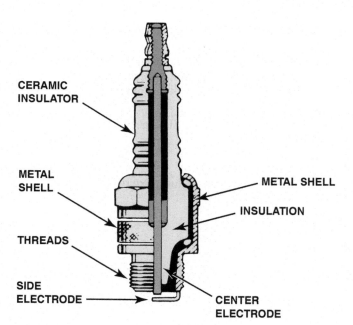

FIGURE 29–28 Parts of a typical spark plug.

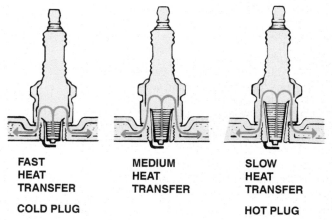

FIGURE 29–29 The heat range of a spark plug is determined by the distance the heat has to flow from the tip to the cylinder head.

1. All inductive ignition systems supply battery voltage to the positive side of the ignition coil and pulse the negative side of the coil on and off to ground to create a high-voltage spark.

2. If an ignition system uses a distributor, it is a distributor ignition (DI) system.

3. If an ignition system does not use a distributor, it is called an electronic ignition (EI) system.

4. A waste-spark ignition system fires two spark plugs at the same time.

5. A coil-on-plug ignition system uses an ignition coil for each spark plug.

1. How can 12 volts from a battery be changed to 40,000 volts for ignition?

2. How does a magnetic sensor work?

3. How does a Hall-effect sensor work?

4. How does a waste-spark ignition system work?

5. What does the heat range of a spark plug refer to?

1. The primary (low-voltage) ignition system must be working correctly before any spark occurs from a coil. Which component is *not* in the primary ignition circuit?
   a. Spark plug wiring
   b. Ignition module (igniter)
   c. Pickup coil (pulse generator)
   d. Ignition switch

2. The ignition module has direct control over the firing of the coil(s) of an EI system. Which component(s) triggers (controls) the module?
   a. Pickup coil
   b. Computer
   c. Crankshaft sensor
   d. Either a or c

3. A reluctor is a _____.
   a. type of sensor used in the secondary circuit.
   b. notched ring or pointed wheel
   c. type of optical sensor
   d. type of Hall effect sensor

4. HEI and EIS are examples of _____.
   a. waste-spark systems
   b. coil-on-plug ignition systems
   c. distributor ignition systems
   d. pickup coil types

5. Coil polarity is determined by the _____.
   a. direction of rotation of the coil windings
   b. turns ratio
   c. direction of laminations
   d. saturation direction

6. Because of _____, an ignition coil cannot be fully charged (reach magnetic saturation) until after a delay of about 10 milliseconds
   a. voltage drop across the ignition switch and related wiring
   b. resistance in the coil windings
   c. inductive reactance
   d. saturation

7. A COP ignition system can be called _____.
   a. coil-by-plug
   b. coil-near-plug
   c. coil-over-plug
   d. any of the above

8. A compression-sensing ignition is what type?
   a. Distributor
   b. Waste spark
   c. Coil-on-plug
   d. Any of the above

9. A waste-spark-type ignition system _____.
   a. fires two spark plugs at the same time
   b. fires one spark plug with reverse polarity
   c. fires one spark plug with straight polarity
   d. All of the above

10. An ion-sensing ignition system allows the ignition system itself to be able to _____.
    a. detect misfire
    b. detect spark knock
    c. detect rich or lean air–fuel mixture
    d. All of the above

chapter 30
IGNITION SYSTEM DIAGNOSIS AND SERVICE

FIGURE 30–1 An adjustable spark tester that can be adjusted and should be set to at least 25,000 volts. The tester is connected to a disconnected spark plug wire or coil and the the pigtail clipped to a good chassis ground. Cranking the engine should cause a spark to be seen from the spark tester.

FIGURE 30–2 A close-up showing the recessed center electrode on a spark tester. It is recessed 3/8 inch into the shell and the spark must then jump another 3/8 inch to the shell for a total gap of 3/4 inch.

CHECKING FOR SPARK

In the event of a no-start condition, the first step should be to check for secondary voltage out of the ignition coil or to the spark plugs. If the engine is equipped with a separate ignition coil, remove the coil wire from the center of the distributor cap, install a **spark tester,** and crank the engine. See the Tech Tip "Always Use a Spark Tester." A good coil and ignition system should produce a blue spark at the spark tester. ● **SEE FIGURES 30–1 AND 30–2.**

If the ignition system being tested does not have a separate ignition coil, disconnect any spark plug wire from a spark plug and, while cranking the engine, test for spark available at the spark plug wire, again using a spark tester.

NOTE: An intermittent spark should be considered a no-spark condition.

Typical causes of a no-spark (intermittent spark) condition include the following:

1. Weak ignition coil
2. Low or no voltage to the primary (positive) side of the coil
3. High resistance or open coil wire, or spark plug wire
4. Negative side of the coil not being pulsed by the ignition module, also called an ignition control module (ICM)
5. Defective pickup coil
6. Defective module

TECH TIP

Always Use a Spark Tester

A spark tester looks like a spark plug except it has a recessed center electrode and no side electrode. The tester commonly has an alligator clip attached to the shell so that it can be clamped on a good ground connection on the engine. A good ignition system should be able to cause a spark to jump this wide gap at atmospheric pressure. Without a spark tester, a technician might assume that the ignition system is okay, because it can spark across a normal, grounded spark plug. The voltage required to fire a standard spark plug when it is out of the engine and not under pressure is about 3,000 volts or less. An electronic ignition spark tester requires a minimum of 25,000 volts to jump the 3/4 inch gap. Therefore, never assume that the ignition system is okay because it fires a spark plug—always use a spark tester. *Remember that an intermittent spark across a spark tester should be interpreted as a no-spark condition.*

ELECTRONIC IGNITION TROUBLESHOOTING PROCEDURE

When troubleshooting any electronic ignition system for no spark, follow these steps to help pinpoint the exact cause of the problem:

STEP 1 Turn the ignition on (engine off) and, using either a voltmeter or a test light, test for battery voltage available at the positive terminal of the ignition coil. If the voltage is not available, check for an open circuit at the ignition switch or wiring. Also check the condition of the ignition fuse (if used).

NOTE: Many Chrysler group products use an automatic shutdown (ASD) relay to power the ignition coil. The ASD relay will not supply voltage to the coil unless the engine is cranking and the computer senses a crankshaft sensor signal. This little known fact has fooled many technicians.

STEP 2 Connect the voltmeter or test light to the negative side of the coil and crank the engine. The voltmeter should fluctuate or the test light should blink, indicating that the primary coil current is being turned on and off. If there is no pulsing of the negative side of the coil, the problem is a defective pickup, electronic control module, or wiring.

IGNITION COIL TESTING USING AN OHMMETER

If an ignition coil is suspected of being defective, a simple ohmmeter check can be performed to test the resistance of the primary and secondary winding inside the coil. For accurate resistance measurements, the wiring to the coil should be removed before testing. To test the primary coil winding resistance, take the following steps (● **SEE FIGURE 30–3**):

STEP 1 Set the meter to read low ohms.

STEP 2 Measure the resistance between the positive terminal and the negative terminal of the ignition coil. Most coils will give a reading between 1 and 3 ohms; however, some coils should indicate less than 1 ohm. Check the manufacturer's specifications for the exact resistance values.

To test the secondary coil winding resistance, follow these steps:

STEP 1 Set the meter to read kilohms (kΩ).

STEP 2 Measure the resistance between primary terminal and the secondary coil tower. The normal resistance of most coils ranges between 6,000 and 30,000 ohms. Check the manufacturer's specifications for the exact resistance values.

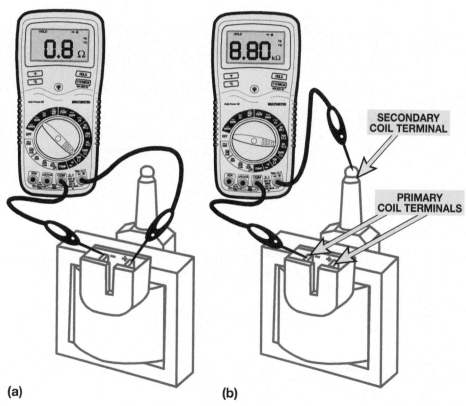

(a)   **(b)**

FIGURE 30–3 (a) Set the digital meter to read Ohms and measure between the two primary terminals of the coil. Most coils are less than 1 Ohm. (b) To measure the secondary winding, connect 1 meter lead to one of the primary terminals and the other to the secondary terminal.

TESTING MAGNETIC SENSORS

First of all, magnetic sensors must be tested to see if they will stick to iron or steel, indicating that the magnetic strength of the sensors is okay. If the permanent magnet inside the sensor has cracked, the result is two weak magnets.

If the sensor is removed from the engine, hold a metal (steel) object against the end of the sensor. It should exert a strong magnetic pull on the steel object. If not, replace the sensor. Second, the sensor can be tested using a digital meter set to read AC volts. ● **SEE FIGURE 30–4**.

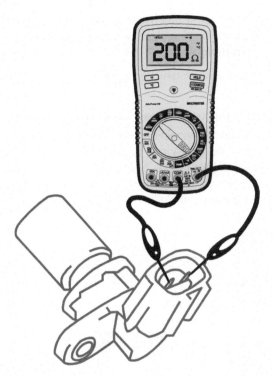

FIGURE 30–4 Measuring the resistance of an magnetic crankshaft position (CKP) sensor using an ohmmeter.

The Weird Running Chevrolet Truck

An older Chevrolet pickup truck equipped with a V-8 engine was towed into a shop because it would not start. A quick check of the ignition system showed that the pickup coil had a broken wire between it and the ignition control module. The distributor was removed from the engine and the distributor shaft was removed, cleaned, and a replacement pickup coil was installed. The engine started, but ran rough and hesitated when the accelerator pedal was depressed. After an hour of troubleshooting, a careful inspection of the new pickup coil showed that the time core had six instead of eight points, meaning that the new pickup coil was meant for a V-6 instead of a V-8 engine. Replacing the pickup coil again solved the problem.

Summary:

- **Complaint**—Customer stated that the truck would not start.
- **Cause**—A visual inspection was used to determine a that a pickup coil wire was broken and was replaced but with the wrong part that was in the correct box.
- **Correction**—Replacing the pickup coil with the right part fixed the truck.

TESTING HALL-EFFECT SENSORS

As with any other sensor, the output of the Hall-effect sensor should be tested first. Using a digital voltmeter, check for the presence of changing voltage (pulsed on and off or digital DC) when the engine is being cranked. The best test is to use an oscilloscope and observe the waveform. ● **SEE FIGURE 30–5**.

FIGURE 30–5 A Hall Effect sensor produces a square waveform, whereas a magnetic sensor produces an analog waveform when viewed on the scope.

Crankshaft Position Sensor (CPK) and Camshaft Position Sensor (CMP)

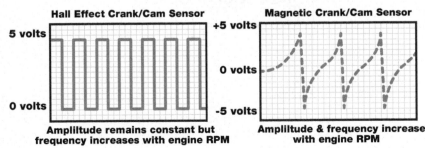

Hall Effect Crank/Cam Sensor
5 volts
0 volts
Ampliltude remains constant but frequency increases with engine RPM

Magnetic Crank/Cam Sensor
+5 volts
0 volts
-5 volts
Amplitude & frequency increase with engine RPM

Bad Wire? Replace the Coil!

When performing engine testing (such as a compression test), always ground the coil wire. Never allow the coil to discharge without a path to ground for the spark. High-energy electronic ignition systems can produce 40,000 volts or more of electrical pressure. If the spark cannot arc to ground, the coil energy can (and usually does) arc inside the coil itself, creating a low-resistance path to the primary windings or the steel laminations of the coil. ● **SEE FIGURE 30–6**. This low-resistance path is called a track and could cause an engine misfire under load even though all of the remaining component parts of the ignition system are functioning correctly. Often these tracks do not show up on any coil test, including most scopes. Because the track is a lower-resistance path to ground than normal, it requires that the ignition system be put under a load for it to be detected, and even then, the problem (engine misfire) may be intermittent.

Therefore, when disabling an ignition system, perform one of the following procedures to prevent possible ignition coil damage:

1. Remove the power source wire from the ignition system to prevent any ignition operation.
2. On distributor-equipped engines, remove the secondary coil wire from the center of the distributor cap and connect a jumper wire between the disconnected coil wire and a good engine ground. This ensures that the secondary coil energy will be safely grounded and prevents high-voltage coil damage.

IGNITION SYSTEM DIAGNOSIS USING VISUAL INSPECTION

One of the first steps in the diagnosis process is to perform a thorough visual inspection of the ignition system, including the following:

- Check all spark plug wires for proper routing. All plug wires should be in the factory wiring separator and be clear of any metallic object that could cause damage to the insulation and cause a short-to-ground fault.
- Check that all spark plug wires are securely attached to the spark plugs and to the distributor cap or ignition coil(s).
- Check that all spark plug wires are clean and free from excessive dirt or oil. Check that all protective covers normally covering the coil and/or distributor cap are in place and not damaged.
- Remove the distributor cap and carefully check the cap and distributor rotor for faults.
- Remove the spark plugs and check for excessive wear or other visible faults. Replace if needed.

NOTE: According to research conducted by General Motors, about one-fifth (20%) of all faults are detected during a *thorough visual inspection*!

TECH TIP

The Magnetic Pickup Tool Test

All ignition coils are pulsed on and off by the ignition control module or PCM. When the coil charges and discharges, the magnetic field around the coil changes. This pulsing of the coil can be observed by holding the magnetic end of a pickup tool near an operating ignition coil. The magnet at the end of the pickup tool will move as the magnetic field around the coil changes. ● **SEE FIGURE 30–7**.

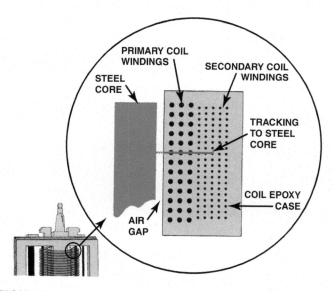

FIGURE 30–6 A track inside an ignition coil is not a short, but rather it is a low-resistance path or hole that has been burned through from the secondary wiring to the steel core.

FIGURE 30–7 If the coil is working, the end of the magnetic pickup tool will move with the changes in the magnetic field around the coil.

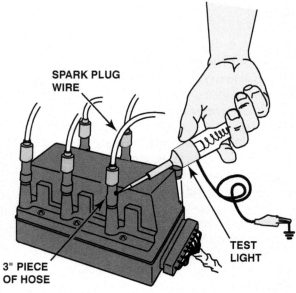

SPARK PLUG WIRE

3" PIECE OF HOSE

TEST LIGHT

FIGURE 30–8 Using a vacuum hose and a grounded testlight to ground one cylinder at a time on a DIS. This works on all types of ignition systems and provides a method for grounding out one cylinder at a time without fear of damaging any component. Use a standard 12-volt test light that uses a bulb because if an LED test light is used, the high-voltage with harm the electronic circuit inside the test light.

TESTING FOR POOR PERFORMANCE

Many diagnostic equipment manufacturers offer methods for testing distributorless ignition systems on an oscilloscope. If using this type of equipment, follow the manufacturer's recommended procedures and interpretation of the specific test results.

A simple method of testing distributorless (waste-spark systems) ignition with the engine off involves removing the spark plug wires (or connectors) from the spark plugs (or coils or distributor cap) and installing short lengths (2 inches) of rubber vacuum hose in series.

NOTE: For best results, use rubber hose that is electrically conductive. Measure the vacuum hose with an ohmmeter. Suitable vacuum hose should give a reading of less than 10,000 ohms (10 kΩ) for a length of about 2 inches. ● **SEE FIGURES 30–7 AND 30–8.**

STEP 1 Start the engine and ground out each cylinder one at a time by touching the tip of a grounded test light to the rubber vacuum hose. Even though the computer will increase idle speed and fuel delivery to compensate for the grounded spark plug wire, a technician should watch for a change in the operation of the engine. If no change is observed or heard, the cylinder being grounded is obviously weak or defective. Check the spark plug wire or connector with an ohmmeter to be certain of continuity.

STEP 2 Check all cylinders by grounding them out one at a time. If one weak cylinder is found (very little RPM drop), check the other cylinder using the same ignition coil (except on engines that use an individual coil for each cylinder). If both cylinders are affected, the problem could be an open spark plug wire, defective spark plug, or defective ignition coil.

STEP 3 To help eliminate other possible problems and determine exactly what is wrong, switch the suspected ignition coil to another position (if possible).
- If the problem now affects the other cylinders, the ignition coil is defective and must be replaced.
- If the problem does not "change positions" with changing the position of the ignition coil, the control module affecting the suspected coil or either cylinder's spark plug or spark plug wire could be defective.

TESTING FOR A NO-START CONDITION

A no-start condition (with normal engine cranking speed) can be the result of either no spark or no fuel delivery.

Computerized engine control systems use the ignition primary pulses as a signal to inject fuel—a port or throttle-body injection (TBI) style of fuel—injection system. If there is no pulse, there is no squirt of fuel. To determine exactly what is wrong, follow these steps:

STEP 1 Test the output signal from the crankshaft sensor. Most computerized engines with distributorless ignitions use a crankshaft position sensor. These sensors are either the Hall-effect type or the magnetic type. The sensors must be able to produce either a sine or a digital signal. A meter set on AC volts should read a voltage across the sensor leads when the engine is being cranked. If there is no AC voltage output, replace the sensor.

STEP 2 If the sensor tests okay in step 1, check for a changing AC voltage signal at the ignition module.

NOTE: Step 2 checks the wiring between the crankshaft position sensor and the ignition control module.

STEP 3 If the ignition control module is receiving a changing signal from the crankshaft position sensor, it must be capable of switching the power to the ignition coils on and off. Remove a coil or coil package, and with the ignition switched to on (run), check for voltage at the positive terminal of the coil(s).

NOTE: Several manufacturers program the current to the coils to be turned off within several seconds of the ignition being switched to on if no pulse is received by the computer. This circuit design helps prevent ignition coil damage in the event of a failure in the control circuit or driver error, by keeping the ignition switch on (run) without operating the starter (start position). Some Chrysler engines do not supply power to the positive (+) side of the coil until a crank pulse is received by the computer, which then energizes the coil(s) and injectors through the automatic shutdown (ASD) relay.

STEP 4 If the module is not pulsing the negative side of the coil or not supplying battery voltage to the positive side of the coil, replace the ignition control module.

NOTE: Before replacing the ignition control module, be certain that it is properly grounded (where applicable) and that the module is receiving ignition power from the ignition circuit.

CAUTION: Most distributorless (waste-spark) ignition systems can produce 40,000 volts or more, with energy levels high enough to cause personal injury. Do not open the circuit of an electronic ignition secondary wire, because damage to the system (or to you) can occur.

DISTRIBUTOR INDEXING

A few engines that use a distributor also use it to house a camshaft position (CMP) sensor. One purpose of this sensor is to properly initiate the fuel-injection sequence. Some of these engines use a positive distributor position notch or clamp that allows the distributor to be placed in only one position, while others use a method of indexing to verify the distributor position. If a distributor is not indexed correctly, the following symptoms may occur:

- Surging (especially at idle speed)
- Light bucking
- Intermittent engine misfiring

This will most likely occur when the vehicle is at operating temperature, and under a light load at approximately 2,000 RPM.

A misindexed distributor may cause these conditions.

NOTE: This is *not* the same as setting the ignition timing. Indexing the distributor does not affect the ignition timing.

Always use the factory procedure as stated in service information.

Some of the methods may require a scan tool, while others require the use of a voltmeter to verify position. Jeep, late model Chrysler V-6 and V-8 engines, and some GM trucks require indexing. ● **SEE FIGURE 30–9.**

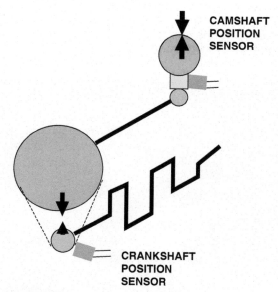

CAMSHAFT POSITION SENSOR

CRANKSHAFT POSITION SENSOR

FIGURE 30–9 The relationship between the crankshaft position (CKP) sensor and the camshaft position (CMP) sensor is affected by wear in the timing gear and/or chain.

SECONDARY IGNITION INSPECTION

DISTRIBUTOR CAP AND ROTOR Inspect a **distributor cap** for a worn or cracked center carbon insert, excessive side insert wear or corrosion, cracks, or carbon tracks, and check the towers for burning or corrosion by removing spark plug wires from the distributor cap one at a time. Remember, a defective distributor cap affects starting and engine performance, especially in high-moisture conditions. If a carbon track is detected, it is most likely the result of a high-resistance or open spark plug wire. Replacement of a distributor cap because of a carbon track without checking and replacing the defective spark plug wire(s) often will result in the new distributor cap failing in a short time. It is recommended that the distributor cap and rotor be inspected every year and replaced if defective. The rotor should be replaced every time the spark plugs are replaced, because all ignition current flows through the rotor. Generally, distributor caps should only need replacement after every three or four years of normal service.

COP AND WASTE SPARK INSPECTION If a misfire is being diagnosed, perform a thorough visual inspection of the coil-on-plug (COP) assembly and look for evidence of carbon track or heat-related faults to the plug boot.
● **SEE FIGURE 30–10**.

Check ignition coils of waste spark and coil-on-plug (COP) systems for signs of carbon tracks (black lines) or corrosion.

When checking a waste spark-type ignition system, check that the coils are clean and that the spark plug wires are attached to the specified coil and coil terminal. ● **SEE FIGURES 30–11 AND 30–12**.

FIGURE 30–11 When checking a waste spark-type ignition system, check that the secondary wires are attached to the correct coil terminal and that the wiring is correctly routed to help avoid cross-fire.

FIGURE 30–12 Corroded terminals on a waste-spark coil can cause misfire diagnostic trouble codes to be set.

SPARK PLUG WIRE INSPECTION Spark plug wires should be visually inspected for cuts or defective insulation and checked for resistance with an ohmmeter. Good spark plug wires should measure less than 10,000 ohms per foot of length. ● **SEE FIGURES 30–13 AND 30–14**. Faulty spark plug wire insulation can cause hard starting or no starting in damp weather conditions.

FIGURE 30–10 When checking a coil-on-plug (COP) assembly, check that the primary and secondary wiring looks normal and that the coil is not discolored from arcing or corrosion.

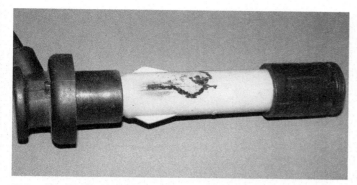

FIGURE 30–13 This spark plug boot on an overhead camshaft engine has been arcing to the valve cover causing a misfire to occur.

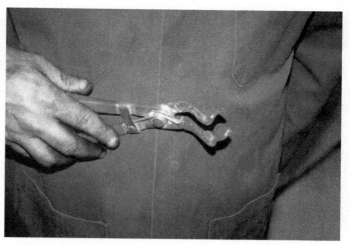

FIGURE 30–15 Spark plug wire boot pliers are a handy addition to any tool box.

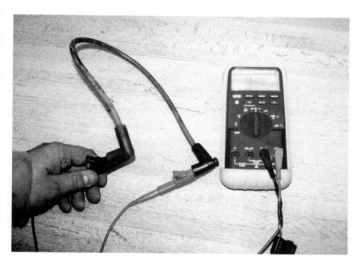

FIGURE 30–14 Measuring the resistance of a spark plug wire with a multimeter set to the ohms position. The reading of 16.03 kO (16.030 ohms) is okay because the wire is about 2 feet long. Maximum allowable resistance for a spark plug wire this long would be 20 kO (20,000 ohms). High resistance spark plug wires can cause an engine misfire especially during acceleration.

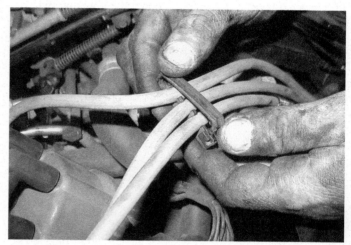

FIGURE 30–16 Always take the time to install spark plug wires back into the original holding brackets (wiring combs).

 **TECH TIP**

Route the Wires Right!

High voltage is present through spark plug wires when the engine is running. Surrounding the spark plugs in a magnetic field that can affect other circuits or components of the vehicle. For example, if a spark plug wire is routed too closely to the signal wire from a mass airflow (MAF) sensor, the induced signal from the ignition wire could create a false MAF signal to the computer. The computer, not able to detect that the signal was false, would act on the MAF signal and command the appropriate amount of fuel based on the false MAF signal.

To prevent any problems associated with high-voltage spark plug wires, be sure to route them as manufactured, using all the factory holding brackets and wiring combs. ● **SEE FIGURE 30–16**. If the factory method is unknown, most factory service information shows the correct routing.

 **TECH TIP**

Spark Plug Wire Pliers Are a Good Investment

Spark plug wires are often difficult to remove. Using a good-quality spark plug wire plier, such as shown in ● **FIGURE 30–15**, saves time and reduces the chance of harming the wire during removal.

SPARK PLUG SERVICE

THE NEED FOR SERVICE

Spark plugs should be inspected when an engine performance problem occurs and should be replaced at specified intervals to ensure proper ignition system performance. Most spark plugs have a service life of over 20,000 miles (32,000 kilometers). Platinum-tipped original equipment spark plugs have a typical service life of 60,000 to 100,000 miles (100,000 to 160,000 kilometers). Used spark plugs should *not* be cleaned and reused unless absolutely necessary. The labor required to **remove and replace (R & R)** spark plugs is the same whether the spark plugs are replaced or cleaned. Although cleaning spark plugs often restores proper engine operation, the service life of cleaned spark plugs is definitely shorter than that of new spark plugs. *Platinum-tipped spark plugs should not be regapped!* Using a gapping tool can break the platinum after it has been used in an engine.

Be certain that the engine is cool before removing spark plugs, especially on engines with aluminum cylinder heads. To help prevent dirt from getting into the cylinder of an engine while removing a spark plug, use compressed air or a brush to remove dirt from around the spark plug before removal. ● **SEE FIGURES 30–17 THROUGH 30–19.**

FIGURE 30–17 When removing spark plugs, it is wise to arrange them so that they can be compared and any problem can be identified with a particular cylinder.

FIGURE 30–18 A spark plug thread chaser is a low-cost tool that hopefully will not be used often, but is necessary to use to clean the threads before new spark plugs are installed.

FIGURE 30–19 Since 1991, General Motors engines have been equipped with slightly (1/8 inch or 3 mm) longer spark plugs. This requires that a longer spark plug socket should be used to prevent the possibility of cracking a spark plug during installation. The longer socket is shown next to a normal 5/8 inch spark plug socket.

SPARK PLUG INSPECTION

Spark plugs are the windows to the inside of the combustion chamber. A thorough visual inspection of the spark plugs often can lead to the root cause of an engine performance problem. Two indications on spark plugs and their possible root causes in engine performance include the following:

1. **Carbon fouling.** If the spark plug(s) has *dry black carbon* (soot), the usual causes include:
   - Excessive idling
   - Slow-speed driving under light loads that keeps the spark plug temperatures too low to burn off the deposits
   - Overrich air–fuel mixture
   - Weak ignition system output

2. **Oil fouling.** If the spark plug has *wet, oily* deposits with little electrode wear, oil may be getting into the combustion chamber from the following:
   - Worn or broken piston rings
   - Defective or missing valve stem seals

NOTE: If the deposits are heavier on the side of the plug facing the intake valve, the cause is usually due to excessive valve stem clearance or defective intake valve stem seals.

When removing spark plugs, place them in order so that they can be inspected to check for engine problems that might affect one or more cylinders. All spark plugs should be in the same condition, and the color of the center insulator should be light tan or gray. If all the spark plugs are black or dark, the engine should be checked for conditions that could cause an overly rich air–fuel mixture or possible oil burning. If only one or a few spark plugs are black, check those cylinders for proper firing (possible defective spark plug wire) or an engine condition affecting only those particular cylinders. ● **SEE FIGURES 30–20 THROUGH 30–23.**

If all spark plugs are white, check for possible overadvanced ignition timing or a vacuum leak causing a lean air–fuel mixture. If only one or a few spark plugs are white, check for a vacuum leak affecting the fuel mixture only to those particular cylinders.

NOTE: The engine computer "senses" rich or lean air–fuel ratios by means of input from the oxygen sensor. If one cylinder is lean, the computer may make all other cylinders richer to compensate.

Inspect all spark plugs for wear by first checking the condition of the center electrode. As a spark plug wears, the center electrode becomes rounded. If the center electrode is rounded, higher ignition system voltage is required to fire the spark plug. When installing spark plugs, always use the correct tightening torque to ensure proper heat transfer from the spark plug shell to the cylinder head. ● **SEE CHART 30–1.**

FIGURE 30–22 A spark plug from an engine that had a blown head gasket. The white deposits could be from the additives in the coolant.

FIGURE 30–20 A normally worn spark plug that has a tapered platinum-tipped center electrode.

FIGURE 30–21 A worn spark plug showing fuel and/or oil deposits.

FIGURE 30–23 A platinum tipped spark plug that is fuel soaked indicating a fault with the fuel system or the ignition system causing the spark plug to not fire.

SPARK PLUG	TORQUE WITH TORQUE WRENCH (LB-FT)		TORQUE WITHOUT TORQUE WRENCH (TURNS)	
	CAST-IRON HEAD	ALUMINUM HEAD	CAST-IRON HEAD	ALUMINUM HEAD
Gasket				
14 mm	26–30	18–22	1/4	1/4
18 mm	32–38	28–34	1/4	1/4
Tapered seat				
14 mm	7–15	7–15	1/16 (snug)	1/16 (snug)
18 mm	15–20	15–20	1/16 (snug)	1/16 (snug)

CHART 30–1

Typical spark plug tightening torque based on type of spark plug and the cylinder head material.

TECH TIP

Two-Finger Trick

To help prevent overtightening a spark plug when a torque wrench is not available, simply use two fingers on the ratchet handle. Even the strongest service technician cannot overtighten a spark plug by using two fingers.

TECH TIP

Use Original Equipment Manufacturer's Spark Plugs

A technician at an independent service center replaced the spark plugs in a Buick with new Champion brand spark plugs of the correct size, reach, and heat range. When the customer returned to pay the bill, he inquired as to the brand name of the replacement parts used for the tune-up. When told that Champion spark plugs were used, he stopped signing his name on the check he was writing. He said that he owned 1,000 shares of General Motors stock and he owned two General Motors vehicles and he expected to have General Motors parts used in his General Motors vehicles. The service manager had the technician replace the spark plugs with AC brand spark plugs because this brand was used in the engine when the vehicle was new. Even though most spark plug manufacturers produce spark plugs that are correct for use, many customers prefer that original equipment manufacturer (OEM) spark plugs be used in their engines.

NOTE: General Motors does not recommend the use of antiseize compound on the threads of spark plugs being installed in an aluminum cylinder head, because the spark plug will be overtightened. This excessive tightening torque places the threaded portion of the spark plug too far into the combustion chamber where carbon can accumulate and result in the spark plugs being difficult to remove. If antiseize compound is used on spark plug threads, reduce the tightening torque by 40%. Always follow the vehicle manufacturer's recommendations.

QUICK AND EASY SECONDARY IGNITION TESTS

Engine running problems often are caused by defective or out-of-adjustment ignition components. Many ignition problems involve the high-voltage secondary ignition circuit. Following are some quick and easy secondary ignition tests:

TEST 1 If there is a crack in a distributor cap, coil, or spark plug, or if there is a defective spark plug wire, a spark may be visible at night. Because the highest voltage is required during partial throttle acceleration, the technician's assistant should accelerate the engine slightly with the gear selector in drive or second gear (if manual transmission) and the brake firmly applied. If any spark is visible or a "snapping" sound is heard, the location should be closely inspected and the defective parts replaced. A blue glow or "corona" around the shell of the spark plug is normal and not an indication of a defective spark plug.

TEST 2 For intermittent problems, use a spray bottle to apply a water mist to the spark plugs, distributor cap, and spark plug wires. ● **SEE FIGURE 30–24**. With the engine

FIGURE 30–24 A water spray bottle is an excellent diagnostic tool to help find an intermittent engine misfire caused by a break in a secondary ignition circuit component.

FIGURE 30–25 Typical timing marks. The numbers of the degrees are on the stationary plate and the notch is on the harmonic balancer.

running, the water may cause an arc through any weak insulating materials and cause the engine to misfire or stall.

NOTE: Adding a little salt or liquid soap to the water makes the water more conductive and also makes it easier to find those hard-to-diagnose intermittent ignition faults.

TEST 3 To determine if the rough engine operation is due to secondary ignition problems, connect a 12-volt test light to the negative side (sometimes labeled "tach") of the coil. Connect the other lead of the test light to the positive lead of the coil. With the engine running, the test light should be dim and steady in brightness. If there is high resistance in the secondary circuit (such as that caused by a defective spark plug wire), the test light will pulse brightly at times. If the test light varies noticeably, this indicates that the secondary voltage cannot find ground easily and is feeding back through the primary windings of the coil. This feedback causes the test light to become brighter.

IGNITION TIMING

PURPOSE Ignition timing refers to when the spark plug fires in relation to piston position. The time when the spark occurs depends on engine speed and, therefore, must be advanced (spark plugs fire sooner) as the engine rotates faster. The ignition in the cylinder takes a certain amount of time, usually 30 milliseconds (30/1,000 of a second) and remains constant regardless of engine speed. Therefore, to maintain the most efficient combustion, the ignition sequence has to occur sooner as the engine speed increases. For maximum efficiency from the expanding gases inside the combustion chamber, the burning of the air-fuel mixture should end by about 10 degrees after top

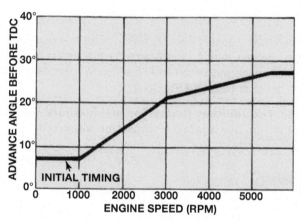

FIGURE 30–26 The initial (base) timing is where the spark plug fires at idle speed. The PCM then advances the timing based primarily on engine speed.

dead center (ATDC). If the burning of the mixture is still occurring after that point, the expanding gases do not exert much force on the piston because the gases are "chasing" the piston as it moves downward. Therefore, to achieve the goal of having the air-fuel mixture be completely burned by the time the piston reaches 10 degrees after top dead center, the spark must be advanced (occur sooner) as the engine speed increases. This timing advance is determined and controlled by the PCM on most vehicles.
● **SEE FIGURES 30–25 AND 30–26.**

If the engine is equipped with a distributor, it may be possible to adjust the base or the initial timing. The initial timing is usually set to fire the spark plug between zero degrees (TDC) or slightly before TDC (BTDC). Ignition timing changes as mechanical wear occurs to the following:

■ Timing chain

■ Distributor gear

■ Camshaft drive gear

"Turn the Key" Test

If the ignition timing is correct, a warm engine should start immediately when the ignition key is turned to the start position. If the engine cranks a long time before starting, the ignition timing may be retarded. If the engine cranks slowly, the ignition timing may be too far advanced. However, if the engine starts immediately, the ignition timing, although it may not be exactly set according to specification, is usually adjusted fairly close to specifications. When a starting problem is experienced, check the ignition timing first, before checking the fuel system or the cranking system for a possible problem. This procedure can be used to help diagnose a possible ignition timing problem quickly without tools or equipment.

CHECKING IGNITION TIMING To be assured of the proper ignition timing, follow exactly the timing procedure indicated on the underhood vehicle emission control information (VECI) decal. ● **SEE FIGURE 30–27.**

NOTE: The ignition timing for waste-spark and coil-on-plug ignition systems cannot be adjusted.

Two Marks Are the Key to Success

When a distributor is removed from an engine, always mark the direction the rotor is pointing to ensure that the distributor is reinstalled in the correct position. Because of the helical cut on the distributor drive gear, the rotor rotates as the distributor is being removed from the engine. To help reinstall a distributor without any problems, simply make another mark where the rotor is pointing just as the distributor is lifted out of the engine. Then to reinstall, simply line up the rotor to the second mark and lower the distributor into the engine. The rotor should then line up with the original mark as a double check.

SCOPE-TESTING THE IGNITION SYSTEM

Any automotive scope with the correct probes or adapters will show an ignition system pattern. All ignition systems must charge and discharge an ignition coil. With the

(a)

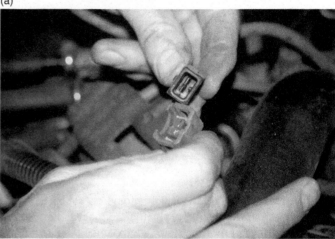

(b)

FIGURE 30–27 (a) Typical SPOUT connector as used on many Ford engines equipped with distributor ignition (DI). (b) The connector must be opened (disconnected) to check and/or adjust the ignition timing. On DIS/EDIS systems, the connector is called SPOUT/SAW (spark output/spark angle word).

engine off, most scopes will display a horizontal line. With the engine running, this horizontal (zero) line is changed to a pattern that will have sections both above and below the zero line. Sections of this pattern that are above the zero line indicate that the ignition coil is discharging. Sections of the scope pattern below the zero line indicate charging of the ignition coil. The height of the scope pattern indicates voltage. The length (from left to right) of the scope pattern indicates time. ● **SEE FIGURES 30–28 AND 30–29** for typical scope hookups.

FIRING LINE The leftmost vertical (upward) line is called the **firing line.** The height of the firing line should be between 5,000 and 15,000 volts (5 and 15 kV) with not more than a 3 kV difference between the highest and the lowest cylinder's firing line. ● **SEE FIGURES 30–30 AND 30–31.**

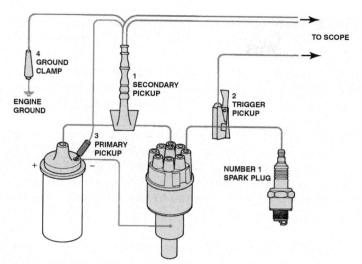

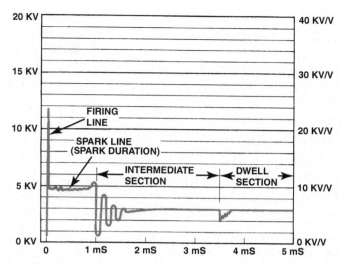

FIGURE 30–28 Typical engine analyzer hookup that includes a scope display. (1) Coil wire on top of the distributor cap if integral type of coil; (2) number 1 spark plug connection; (3) negative side of the ignition coil; (4) ground (negative) connection of the battery.

FIGURE 30–30 Typical secondary ignition oscilloscope pattern.

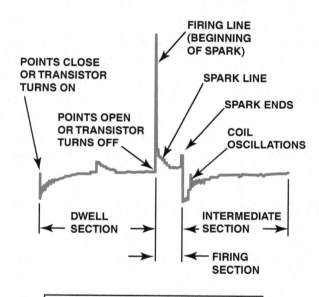

SECONDARY CONVENTIONAL (SINGLE)

SECONDARY CONVENTIONAL (PARADE)

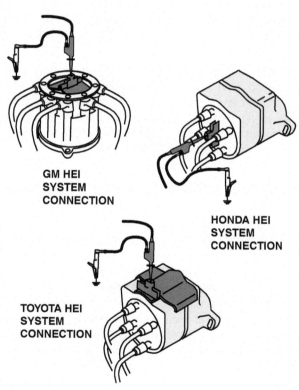

GM HEI SYSTEM CONNECTION

HONDA HEI SYSTEM CONNECTION

TOYOTA HEI SYSTEM CONNECTION

FIGURE 30–29 Clip-on adapters are used with an ignition system that uses an integral ignition coil.

FIRING LINES SHOULD BE EQUAL. A SHORT LINE INDICATES LOW RESISTANCE IN THE WIRE. A HIGH LINE INDICATES HIGH RESISTANCE IN THE WIRE.

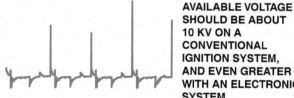

AVAILABLE VOLTAGE SHOULD BE ABOUT 10 KV ON A CONVENTIONAL IGNITION SYSTEM, AND EVEN GREATER WITH AN ELECTRONIC SYSTEM

SPARK LINES CAN BE VIEWED SIDE-BY-SIDE FOR EASE OF COMPARISON

CYLINDERS ARE DISPLAYED IN FIRING ORDER

FIGURE 30–31 A single cylinder is shown at the top and a four-cylinder engine at the bottom.

The height of the firing line indicates the *voltage* required to fire the spark plug. It requires a high voltage to make the air inside the cylinder electrically conductive (to ionize the air). A higher than normal height (or height higher than that of other cylinders) can be caused by one or more of the following:

1. Spark plug gapped too wide
2. Lean fuel mixture
3. Defective spark plug wire

If the firing lines are higher than normal for *all* cylinders, possible causes include one or more of the following:

1. Worn distributor cap and/or rotor (if the vehicle is so equipped)
2. Excessive wearing of all spark plugs
3. Defective coil wire (the high voltage could still jump across the open section of the wire to fire the spark plugs)

SPARK LINE

The **spark line** is a short horizontal line immediately after the firing line. The height of the spark line represents the voltage required to maintain the spark across the spark plug after the spark has started. The height of the spark line should be one-fourth of the height of the firing line (between 1.5 and 2.5 kV). The length (from left to right) of the line represents the length of time for which the spark lasts (duration or burn time). The spark duration should be between 0.8 and 2.2 milliseconds (usually between 1.0 and 2.0 ms). The spark stops at the end (right side) of the spark line, as shown in ● **FIGURE 30–32**.

INTERMEDIATE OSCILLATIONS

After the spark has stopped, some energy remains in the coil. This remaining energy dissipates in the coil windings and the entire secondary circuit. The **intermediate oscillations** are also called the "ringing" of the coil as it is pulsed.

The secondary pattern amplifies any voltage variation occurring in the primary circuit because of the turns ratio between the primary and secondary windings of the ignition coil. A correctly operating ignition system should display five or more "bumps" (oscillations) (three or more for a GM HEI system).

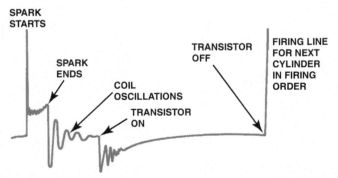

SPARK STARTS

SPARK ENDS

COIL OSCILLATIONS

TRANSISTOR ON

TRANSISTOR OFF

FIRING LINE FOR NEXT CYLINDER IN FIRING ORDER

FIGURE 30–32 Drawing shows what is occurring electrically at each part of the scope pattern.

TRANSISTOR-ON POINT

After the intermediate oscillations, the coil is empty (not charged), as indicated by the scope pattern being on the zero line for a short period. When the transistor turns on an electronic system, the coil is being charged. Note that the charging of the coil occurs slowly (coil-charging oscillations) because of the inductive reactance of the coil.

DWELL SECTION

Dwell is the amount of time that the current is charging the coil from the transistor-on point to the transistor-off point. At the end of the **dwell section** is the beginning of the next firing line. This point is called "transistor off" and indicates that the primary current of the coil is stopped, resulting in a high-voltage spark out of the coil.

PATTERN SELECTION

Ignition oscilloscopes use three positions to view certain sections of the basic pattern more closely. These three positions are as follows:

1. **Superimposed.** This **superimposed** position is used to look at differences in patterns between cylinders in all areas except the firing line. There are no firing lines illustrated in superimposed positions. ● **SEE FIGURE 30–33**.

2. **Raster (stacked).** Cylinder 1 is at the bottom on most scopes. Use the **raster** (stacked) position to look at the spark line length and transistor-on point. The raster pattern shows all areas of the scope pattern except the firing lines. ● **SEE FIGURE 30–34**.

3. **Display (parade).** Display (parade) is the only position in which firing lines are visible. The firing line section for cylinder 1 is on the far right side of the screen, with the remaining portions of the pattern on the left side. This selection is used to compare the height of firing lines among all cylinders. ● **SEE FIGURE 30–35**.

READING THE SCOPE ON DISPLAY (PARADE)

Start the engine and operate at approximately 1,000 RPM to ensure a smooth and accurate scope pattern. Firing lines are visible only on the display (parade) position. The firing lines should all be 5 to 15 kV in height and be within 3 kV of each other. If one or more cylinders have high firing lines, this could indicate a defective (open) spark plug wire, a spark plug gapped too far, or a lean fuel mixture affecting only those cylinders.

A lean mixture (not enough fuel) requires a higher voltage to ignite because there are fewer droplets of fuel in the cylinder for the spark to use as "stepping stones" for the voltage to jump across. Therefore, a lean mixture is less conductive than a rich mixture.

READING THE SPARK LINES

Spark lines can easily be seen on either superimposed or raster (stacked) position. On the raster position, each individual spark line can be viewed.

The spark lines should be level and one-fourth as high as the firing lines (1.5 to 2.5 kV, but usually less than 2 kV). The spark line voltage is called the **burn kV.** The *length* of the spark line is the critical factor for determining proper operation of the engine because it represents the spark duration or burn time.

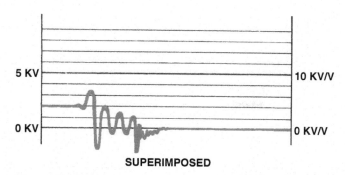

FIGURE 30–33 Typical secondary ignition pattern. Note the lack of firing lines on superimposed pattern.

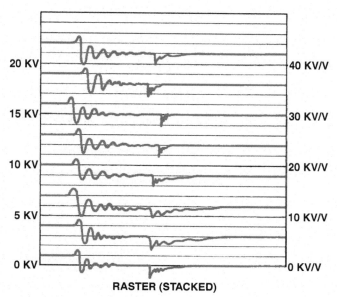

FIGURE 30–34 Raster is the best scope position to view the spark lines of all the cylinders to check for differences. Most scopes display the cylinder 1 at the bottom. The other cylinders are positioned by firing order above cylinder 1.

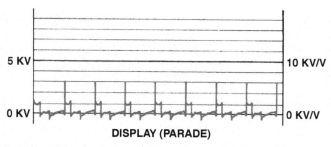

FIGURE 30–35 Display is the only position to view the firing lines of all cylinders. Cylinder 1 is displayed on the left (except for its firing line, which is shown on the right). The cylinders are displayed from left to right by firing order.

There is only a limited amount of energy in an ignition coil. If most of the energy is used to ionize the air gaps of the rotor and the spark plug, there may not be enough energy remaining to create a spark duration long enough to completely burn the air–fuel mixture. Many scopes are equipped with a **millisecond (ms) sweep.** This means that the scope will sweep only that portion of the pattern that can be shown during a 5- or 25-ms setting. Following are guidelines for spark line length:

- 0.8 ms—too short
- 1.5 ms—average
- 2.2 ms—too long

If the spark line is too short, possible causes include the following:

1. Spark plug(s) gap is too wide
2. Rotor tip to distributor cap insert distance gap is too wide (worn cap or rotor)
3. High-resistance spark plug wire
4. Air–fuel mixture too lean (vacuum leak, broken valve spring, etc.)

If the spark line is too long, possible causes include the following:

1. Fouled spark plug(s)
2. Spark plug(s) gap is too narrow
3. Shorted spark plug or spark plug wire

Many scopes do not have a millisecond scale. Some scopes are labeled in degrees and/or percentage (%) of dwell. The following chart can be used to determine acceptable spark line length. ● **SEE CHART 30–2.**

SPARK LINE SLOPE Downward-sloping spark lines indicate that the voltage required to maintain the spark duration is decreasing during the firing of the spark plug. This downward slope usually indicates that the spark energy is finding ground through spark plug deposits (the plug is fouled) or other ignition problems. ● **SEE FIGURE 30–36.**

Normal Spark Line Length (at 700 to 1,200 RPM)

NUMBER OF CYLINDERS	MILLISECONDS	PERCENTAGE (%) OF DWELL SCALE	DEGREES (°)
4	1.0–2.0	3–6	3–5
6	1.0–2.0	4–9	2–5
8	1.0–2.0	6–13	3–6

CHART 30–2

Spark line length depends on the number of cylinders and the engine speed.

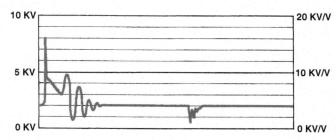

FIGURE 30–36 A downward-sloping spark line usually indicates high secondary ignition system resistance or an excessively rich air–fuel mixture.

A Technician's Toughie

The owner of a Honda Civic complained that the engine did not run smoothly and the "Check Engine" light was on. The service technician retrieved a P0300 (random misfire detected) as well as a P0303 (cylinder number three misfire detected). A scope was connected to each of the coils one at a time and the secondary pattern looked perfect on all four cylinders. All four coils and spark plugs were removed, yet they all looked normal. The spark plug for cylinder #3 was moved to cylinder #1 and the coils were re-installed and the vehicle driven on a test drive. A P0301 was retrieved which indicated that the problem was due to the spark plug itself. Replacing the spark plug with a new one solved the misfire problem. The plug was apparently cracked, yet not seen. The scope showed a normal secondary pattern because the voltage needed to jump to ground through the crack in the plug was about the same as would be required to jump the gap inside the combustion chamber.

Summary:

- **Complaint**—Customer stated that the engine ran poorly.
- **Cause**—Tests confirmed that one spark plug was found to be cracked.
- **Correction**—Replacing the spark plug solved the engine misfire problem.

An upward-sloping spark line usually indicates a mechanical engine problem. A defective piston ring or valve would tend to seal better in the increasing pressures of combustion. As the spark plug fires, the effective increase in pressures increases the voltage required to maintain the spark, and the height of the spark line rises during the duration of the spark. ● **SEE FIGURE 30–37**.

An upward-sloping spark line can also indicate a lean air-fuel mixture. Typical causes include:

1. Clogged injector(s)
2. Vacuum leak
3. Sticking intake valve

● **SEE FIGURE 30–38** for an example showing the relationship between the firing line and the spark line.

READING THE INTERMEDIATE SECTION
The intermediate section should have three or more oscillations (bumps) for a correctly operating ignition system. Because approximately 250 volts are in the primary ignition circuit

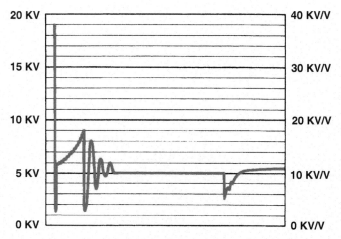

FIGURE 30–37 An upward-sloping spark line usually indicates a mechanical engine problem or a lean air–fuel mixture.

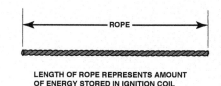

LENGTH OF ROPE REPRESENTS AMOUNT OF ENERGY STORED IN IGNITION COIL

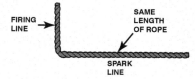

SAME LENGTH OF ROPE

FIRING LINE

SPARK LINE

SAME LENGTH OF ROPE (ENERGY). IF HIGH VOLTAGE IS REQUIRED TO IONIZE SPARK PLUG CAP, LESS ENERGY IS AVAILABLE FOR SPARK DURATION. (A LEAN CYLINDER IS AN EXAMPLE OF WHERE HIGHER VOLTAGE IS REQUIRED TO FIRE WITH A SHORTER-THAN-NORMAL DURATION.)

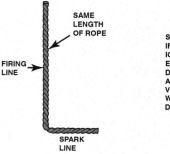

FIRING LINE

SAME LENGTH OF ROPE

SPARK LINE

IF LOW VOLTAGE IS REQUIRED TO FIRE THE SPARK PLUG (LOW FIRING LINE), MORE OF THE COIL'S ENERGY IS AVAILABLE TO PROVIDE A LONG-DURATION SPARK LINE. (A FOULED SPARK PLUG IS AN EXAMPLE OF LOW VOLTAGE TO FIRE, WITH A LONGER-THEN-NORMAL DURATION.)

FIGURE 30–38 The relationship between the height of the firing line and length of the spark line can be illustrated using a rope. Because energy cannot be destroyed, the stored energy in an ignition coil must dissipate totally, regardless of engine operating conditions.

when the spark stops flowing across the spark plugs, this voltage is reduced by about 75 volts per oscillation. Additional resistances in the primary circuit would decrease the number of oscillations. If there are fewer than three oscillations, possible problems include the following:

1. Shorted ignition coil
2. Loose or high-resistance primary connections on the ignition coil or primary ignition wiring

ELECTRONIC IGNITION AND THE DWELL SECTION

Electronic ignitions also use a dwell period to charge the coil. Dwell is not adjustable with electronic ignition, but it does change with increasing RPM with many electronic ignition systems. This change in dwell with RPM should be considered normal.

Many EI systems also produce a "hump" in the dwell section, which reflects a current-limiting circuit in the control module. These current-limiting humps may have slightly different shapes depending on the exact module used. For example, the humps produced by various GM HEI modules differ slightly.

DWELL VARIATION (ELECTRONIC IGNITION) A worn distributor gear, worn camshaft gear, or other distributor problem may cause engine performance problems, because the signal created in the distributor will be affected by the inaccurate distributor operation. However, many electronic ignitions vary the dwell electronically in the module to maintain acceptable current flow levels through the ignition coil and module without the use of a ballast resistor.

NOTE: Distributorless ignition systems also vary dwell time electronically within the engine computer or ignition module.

COIL POLARITY With the scope connected and the engine running, observe the scope pattern in the superimposed mode. If the pattern is upside down, the primary wires on the coil may be reversed, causing the coil polarity to be reversed.

NOTE: Check the scope hookup and controls before deciding that the coil polarity is reversed.

ACCELERATION CHECK With the scope selector set on the display (parade) position, rapidly accelerate the engine (gear selector in park or neutral with the parking brake on). The results should be interpreted as follows:

1. All firing lines should rise evenly (not to exceed 75% of maximum coil output) for properly operating spark plugs.

2. If the firing lines on one or more cylinders fail to rise, this indicates fouled spark plugs.

ROTOR GAP VOLTAGE The **rotor gap** voltage test measures the voltage required to jump the gap (0.030 to 0.050 inch or 0.8 to 1.3 mm) between the rotor and the inserts (segments) of the distributor cap. Select the display (parade) scope pattern and remove a spark plug wire using a jumper wire to provide a good ground connection.

Start the engine and observe the height of the firing line for the cylinder being tested. Because the spark plug wire is connected directly to ground, the firing line height on the scope will indicate the voltage required to jump the air gap between the rotor and the distributor cap insert. The normal rotor gap voltage is 3 to 7 kV, and the voltage should not exceed 8 kV. If the rotor gap voltage indicated is near or above 8 kV, inspect and replace the distributor cap and/or rotor as required.

SCOPE-TESTING A WASTE-SPARK IGNITION SYSTEM

A handheld digital storage oscilloscope can be used to check the pattern of each individual cylinder. Some larger scopes can be connected to all spark plug wires, and therefore are able to display both power and waste-spark waveforms. ● **SEE FIGURE 30–39.** Because the waste spark does not require as high a voltage level as the cylinder on the power stroke, the waste form will be normally lower.

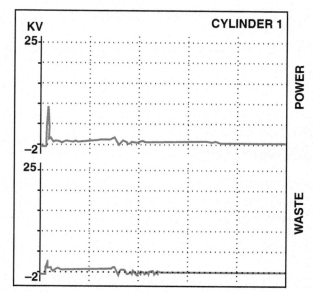

FIGURE 30–39 A dual-trace scope pattern showing both the power and the waste spark from the same coil (cylinders 1 and 6). Note that the firing line is higher on the cylinder that is under compression (power); otherwise, both patterns are almost identical.

SCOPE-TESTING A COIL-ON-PLUG IGNITION SYSTEM

On a coil-on-plug type of ignition system, each individual coil can be shown on a scope and using the proper cables and adapters, the waveform for all of the cylinders can be viewed at the same time. Always follow the scope equipment manufacturer's instructions. Many Ford coil-on-plug systems use a triple-strike secondary spark event. The spark plugs are fired three times when the engine is at idle speed to improve idle quality and to reduce exhaust emissions. Above certain engine speeds, the ignition system switches to a single-fire event.
● **SEE FIGURE 30–40**.

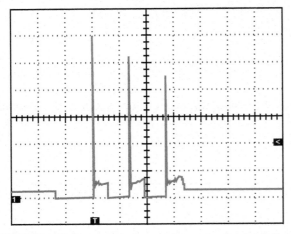

FIGURE 30–40 A secondary waveform of a Ford 4.6 liter V-8, showing three sparks occurring at idle speed.

IGNITION SYSTEM SYMPTOM GUIDE

Problem	Possible Causes and/or Solutions
No spark out of the coil	• Possible open in the ignition switch circuit • Possible defective ignition module (if electronic ignition coil) • Possible defective pickup coil or Hall-effect switch (if electronic ignition) • Possible shorted condenser
Weak spark out of the coil	• Possible high-resistance coil wire or spark plug wire • Possible poor ground between the distributor or module and the engine block
Engine misfire	• Possible defective (open) spark plug wire • Possible worn or fouled spark plugs • Possible defective pickup coil • Possible defective module • Possible poor electrical connections at the pickup coil and/or module

SUMMARY

1. A thorough visual inspection should be performed on all ignition components when diagnosing an engine performance problem.
2. Platinum spark plugs should not be regapped after use in an engine.
3. A secondary ignition scope pattern includes a firing line, spark line, intermediate oscillations, and transistor-on and transistor-off points.
4. The slope of the spark line can indicate incorrect air–fuel ratio or other engine problems.

REVIEW QUESTIONS

1. Why should a spark tester be used to check for spark rather than a standard spark plug?
2. How do you test a pickup coil for resistance and AC voltage output?
3. What harm can occur if the engine is cranked or run with an open (defective) spark plug wire?
4. What are the sections of a secondary ignition scope pattern?
5. What can the slope of the spark line indicate about the engine?

1. A spark tester should be used to check for spark because _____.
   a. a spark tester requires at least 25,000 volts to fire
   b. it is connected to the CKP sensor to check its output
   c. it can detect a cracked spark plug
   d. it can detect the gap of the spark plugs

2. Technician A says that a defective spark plug wire or boot can cause an engine misfire. Technician B says that a tracked ignition coil can cause an engine misfire. Which technician is correct?
   a. Technician A only
   b. Technician B only
   c. Both Technicians A and B
   d. Neither Technician A nor B

3. Poor engine performance could be the result of a _____.
   a. defective coil
   b. distributor ignition with the CMP and CKP not correctly indexed
   c. a high-voltage spark leak
   d. any of the above

4. Typical primary coil resistance specifications usually range from _____ ohms.
   a. 100 to 450
   b. 500 to 1,500
   c. less than 1 to 3
   d. 6,000 to 30,000

5. Typical secondary coil resistance specifications usually range from _____ ohms.
   a. 100 to 450
   b. 500 to 1,500
   c. 1 to 3
   d. 6,000 to 30,000

6. What should be inspected as part of a visual inspection of the ignition system?
   a. Spark plug wires for proper routing
   b. Spark plug gap
   c. Coil polarity
   d. All of the above

7. What part of the scope pattern shows the duration of the spark?
   a. Firing line
   b. Spark line
   c. Intermediate section
   d. Dwell section

8. Which can be used to test for a fault with a cylinder on a waste-spark system?
   a. Using a timing light to check for spark
   b. Using short sections of rubber hose attached to the coil terminals
   c. An LED test light
   d. Any of the above

9. Two technicians are discussing a no-start (no-spark) condition. Technician A says that an open pickup coil could be the cause. Technician B says that a defective ignition control module (ICM) could be the cause. Which technician is correct?
   a. Technician A only
   b. Technician B only
   c. Both Technicians A and B
   d. Neither Technician A nor B

10. As engine speed increases, the timing of the spark in the cylinder must be _____.
    a. advanced
    b. maintained the same
    c. set at 10 degrees BTDC
    d. retarded slightly

chapter 31
TEMPERATURE SENSORS

LEARNING OBJECTIVES

After studying this chapter, the reader will be able to:

1. Describe the purpose and function of engine coolant temperature sensors.
2. Describe how to inspect and test temperature sensors.
3. Diagnose emissions and driveability problems resulting from malfunctions in the intake air temperature control systems.
4. Discuss how automatic fluid temperature sensor values can affect transmission operation.

This chapter will help you prepare for Engine Repair (A8) ASE certification test content area "E" (Computerized Engine Controls Diagnosis and Repair).

KEY TERMS

Cylinder head temperature (CHT) 512

Engine coolant temperature (ECT) 503

Engine fuel temperature (EFT) 512

Negative temperature coefficient (NTC) 503

Throttle-body temperature (TBT) 510

Transmission fluid temperature (TFT) 511

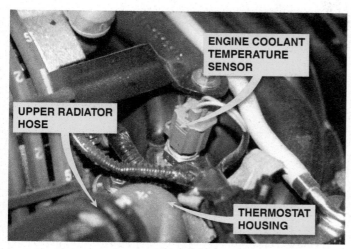

FIGURE 31–1 A typical engine coolant temperature (ECT) sensor. ECT sensors are located near the thermostat housing on most engines.

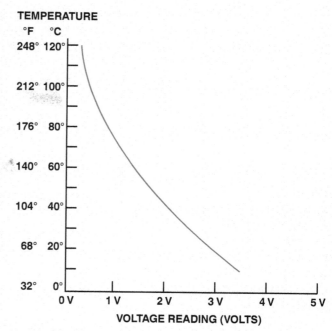

FIGURE 31–2 A typical ECT sensor temperature versus voltage curve.

ENGINE COOLANT TEMPERATURE SENSORS

PURPOSE AND FUNCTION Computer-equipped vehicles use an **engine coolant temperature (ECT)** sensor. When the engine is cold, the fuel mixture must be richer to prevent stalling and engine stumble. When the engine is warm, the fuel mixture can be leaner to provide maximum fuel economy with the lowest possible exhaust emissions. Because the computer controls spark timing and fuel mixture, it will need to know the engine temperature. An engine coolant temperature sensor screwed into the engine coolant passage will provide the computer with this information. ● **SEE FIGURE 31–1.** This will be the most important (high-authority) sensor while the engine is cold. The ignition timing can also be tailored to engine (coolant) temperature. A hot engine cannot have the spark timing as far advanced as can a cold engine. The ECT sensor is also used as an important input for the following:

■ Idle air control (IAC) position

■ Oxygen sensor closed-loop status

■ Canister purge on/off times

■ Idle speed

ECT SENSOR CONSTRUCTION Engine coolant temperature sensors are constructed of a semiconductor material that decreases in resistance as the temperature of the sensor increases. Coolant sensors have very high resistance when the coolant is cold and low resistance when the coolant is hot. This is referred to as having a **negative temperature coefficient (NTC)**,

which is opposite to the situation with most other electrical components. ● **SEE FIGURE 31–2.** Therefore, if the coolant sensor has a poor connection (high resistance) at the wiring connector, the computer will supply a richer-than-normal fuel mixture based on the resistance of the coolant sensor. Poor fuel economy and a possible-rich code can be caused by a defective sensor or high resistance in the sensor wiring. If the sensor was shorted or defective and had too low a resistance, a leaner-than-normal fuel mixture would be supplied to the engine. A too-lean fuel mixture can cause driveability problems and a possible-lean computer code.

STEPPED ECT CIRCUITS Some vehicle manufacturers use a step-up resistor to effectively broaden the range of the ECT sensor. Chrysler and General Motors vehicles use the same sensor as a non-stepped ECT circuit, but instead apply the sensor voltage through two different resistors.

■ When the temperature is low, usually below 120°F (50°C), the ECT sensor voltage is applied through a high-value resistor inside the PCM.

■ When the temperature is high, usually above 120°F (50°C), the ECT sensor voltage is applied through a much lower resistance value inside the PCM. ● **SEE FIGURE 31–3.**

The purpose of this extra circuit is to give the PCM a more accurate reading of the engine coolant temperature compared to the same sensor with only one circuit. ● **SEEFIGURE 31–4.**

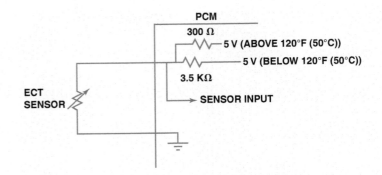

FIGURE 31–3 A typical two-step ECT circuit showing that when the coolant temperature is low, the PCM applies a 5 volt reference voltage to the ECT sensor through a higher resistance compared to when the temperature is higher.

FIGURE 31–4 The transition between steps usually occurs at a temperature that would not interfere with cold engine starts or the cooling fan operation. In this example, the transition occurs when the sensor voltage is about 1 volt and rises to about 3.6 volts.

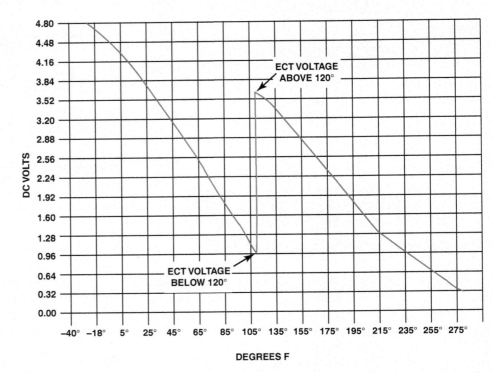

TESTING THE ENGINE COOLANT TEMPERATURE SENSOR

TESTING THE ENGINE COOLANT TEMPERATURE BY VISUAL INSPECTION The correct functioning of the engine coolant temperature sensor depends on the following items that should be checked or inspected:

- **Properly filled cooling system.** Check that the radiator reservoir bottle is full and that the radiator itself is filled to the top.

   CAUTION: Be sure that the radiator is cool before removing the radiator cap to avoid being scalded by hot coolant.

   The ECT sensor must be submerged in coolant to be able to indicate the proper coolant temperature.

- **Proper pressure maintained by the radiator cap.** If the radiator cap is defective and cannot allow the cooling system to become pressurized, air pockets could develop. These air pockets could cause the engine to operate at a hotter-than-normal temperature and prevent proper temperature measurement, especially if the air pockets occur around the sensor.

- **Proper antifreeze-water mixture.** Most vehicle manufacturers recommend a 50/50 mixture of antifreeze and water as the best compromise between freezing protection and heat transfer ability.

- **Proper operation of the cooling fan.** If the cooling fan does not operate correctly, the engine may overheat.

TESTING THE ECT USING A MULTIMETER Both the resistance (in ohms) and the voltage drop across the sensor can be measured and compared with specifications. ● **SEE FIGURE 31–5.** See the following charts showing

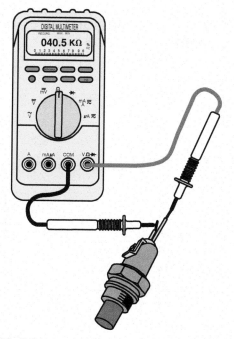

FIGURE 31–5 Measuring the resistance of the ECT sensor. The resistance measurement can then be compared with specifications. (Courtesy of Fluke Corporation)

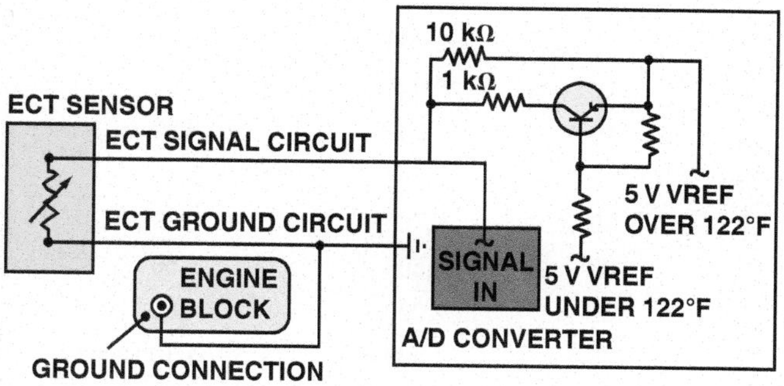

FIGURE 31–6 When the voltage drop reaches approximately 1.20 volts, the PCM turns on a transistor. The transistor connects a 1 kΩ resistor in parallel with the 10 kΩ resistor. Total circuit resistance now drops to around 909 ohms. This function allows the PCM to have full binary control at cold temperatures up to approximately 122°F, and a second full binary control at temperatures greater than 122°F.

examples of typical engine coolant temperature sensor specifications. Some vehicles use the PCM to attach another resistor in the ECT circuit to provide a more accurate measure of the engine temperature. ● **SEE FIGURE 31–6**.

If resistance values match the approximate coolant temperature and there is still a coolant sensor trouble code, the problem is generally in the wiring between the sensor and the computer. Always consult the manufacturers' recommended procedures for checking this wiring. If the resistance values do not match, the sensor may need to be replaced.

GENERAL MOTORS ECT SENSOR WITHOUT PULL-UP RESISTOR			
°F	°C	OHMS	VOLTAGE DROP ACROSS SENSOR
−40	−40	100,000 +	4.95
18	−8	14,628	4.68
32	0	9,420	4.52
50	10	5,670	4.25
68	20	3,520	3.89
86	30	2,238	3.46
104	40	1,459	2.97
122	50	973	2.47
140	60	667	2.00
158	70	467	1.59
176	80	332	1.25
194	90	241	0.97
212	100	177	0.75

GENERAL MOTORS ECT SENSOR WITH PULL-UP RESISTOR

°F	°C	OHMS	VOLTAGE DROP ACROSS SENSOR
−40	−40	100,000	5
−22	−30	53,000	4.78
−4	−20	29,000	4.34
14	−10	16,000	3.89
32	0	9,400	3.45
50	10	5,700	3.01
68	20	3,500	2.56
86	30	2,200	1.80
104	40	1,500	1.10
122	50	970	3.25
140	60	670	2.88
158	70	470	2.56
176	80	330	2.24
194	90	240	1.70
212	100	177	1.42
230	110	132	1.15
248	120	100	0.87

FORD ECT SENSOR

°F	°C	RESISTANCE (Ω)	VOLTAGE (V)
50	10	58,750	3.52
68	20	37,300	3.06
86	30	24,270	2.26
104	40	16,150	2.16
122	50	10,970	1.72
140	60	7,600	1.35
158	70	5,370	1.04
176	80	3,840	0.80
194	90	2,800	0.61
212	100	2,070	0.47
230	110	1,550	0.36
248	120	1,180	0.28

CHRYSLER ECT SENSOR WITHOUT PULL-UP RESISTOR

°F	°C	VOLTAGE (V)
130	54	3.77
140	60	3.60
150	66	3.40
160	71	3.20
170	77	3.02
180	82	2.80
190	88	2.60
200	93	2.40
210	99	2.20
220	104	2.00
230	110	1.80
240	116	1.62
250	121	1.45

CHRYSLER ECT SENSOR WITH PULL-UP RESISTOR

°F	°C	VOLTS
−20	−29	4.70
−10	−23	4.57
0	−18	4.45
10	−12	4.30
20	−7	4.10
30	−1	3.90
40	4	3.60
50	10	3.30
60	16	3.00
70	21	2.75
80	27	2.44
90	32	2.15
100	38	1.83
		PULL-UP RESISTOR SWITCHED BY PCM
110	43	4.20
120	49	4.10
130	54	4.00
140	60	3.60
150	66	3.40
160	71	3.20
170	77	3.02
180	82	2.80
190	88	2.60
200	93	2.40
210	99	2.20
220	104	2.00
230	110	1.80
240	116	1.62
250	121	1.45

NISSAN ECT SENSOR

°F	°C	RESISTANCE (Ω)
14	−10	7,000–11,400
68	20	2,100–2,900
122	50	680–1,000
176	80	260–390
212	100	180–200

MERCEDES ECT

°F	°C	VOLTAGE (DCV)
60	20	3.5
86	30	3.1
104	40	2.7
122	50	2.3
140	60	1.9
158	70	1.5
176	80	1.2
194	90	1.0
212	100	0.8

EUROPEAN BOSCH ECT SENSOR

°F	°C	RESISTANCE (Ω)
32	0	6,500
50	10	4,000
68	20	3,000
86	30	2,000
104	40	1,500
122	50	900
140	60	650
158	70	500
176	80	375
194	90	295
212	100	230

HONDA ECT SENSOR (RESISTANCE CHART)

°F	°C	RESISTANCE (Ω)
0	−18	15,000
32	0	5,000
68	20	3,000
104	40	1,000
140	60	500
176	80	400
212	100	250

HONDA ECT SENSOR (VOLTAGE CHART)

°F	°C	VOLTAGE (V)
0	−18	4.70
10	−12	4.50
20	−7	4.29
30	−1	4.10
40	4	3.86
50	10	3.61
60	16	3.35
70	21	3.08
80	27	2.81
90	32	2.50
100	38	2.26
110	43	2.00
120	49	1.74
130	54	1.52
140	60	1.33
150	66	1.15
160	71	1.00
170	77	0.88
180	82	0.74
190	88	0.64
200	93	0.55
210	99	0.47

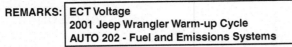

REMARKS: ECT Voltage
2001 Jeep Wrangler Warm-up Cycle
AUTO 202 - Fuel and Emissions Systems

METER ID: FLUKE 189 V2.02 0085510089

SHOW DATA: ALL GRAPH VIEW: ALL

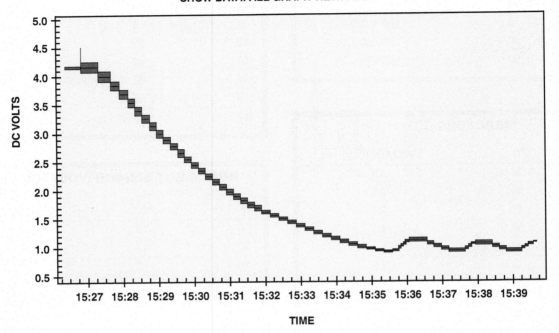

FIGURE 31–7 An ECT sensor being tested using a digital meter set to DC volts. A chart showing the voltage decrease of the ECT sensor as the temperature increases from a cold start. The bumps at the bottom of the waveform represent temperature decreases when the thermostat opens and is controlling coolant temperature.

Normal operating temperature varies with vehicle make and model. Some vehicles are equipped with a thermostat with an opening temperature of 180°F (82°C), whereas other vehicles use a thermostat that is 195°F (90°C) or higher. Before replacing the ECT sensor, be sure that the engine is operating at the temperature specified by the manufacturer. Most manufacturers recommend checking the ECT sensor after the cooling fan has cycled twice, indicating a fully warmed engine. To test for voltage at the ECT sensor, select DC volts on a digital meter and carefully back probe the sensor wire and read the voltage. ● **SEE FIGURE 31–7.**

NOTE: Many manufacturers install another resistor in parallel inside the computer to change the voltage drop across the ECT sensor. This is done to expand the scale of the ECT sensor and to make the sensor more sensitive. Therefore, if measuring *voltage* at the ECT sensor, check with the service manual for the proper voltage at each temperature.

TESTING THE ECT SENSOR USING A SCAN TOOL Follow the scan tool manufacturer's instructions and connect a scan tool to the data link connector (DLC) of the vehicle. Comparing the temperature of the engine coolant as displayed on a scan tool with the actual temperature of the engine is an excellent method to test an engine coolant temperature sensor.

1. Record the scan tool temperature of the coolant (ECT).

2. Measure the actual temperature of the coolant using an infrared pyrometer or contact-type temperature probe.

NOTE: Often the coolant temperature gauge in the dash of the vehicle can be used to compare with the scan tool temperature. Although not necessarily accurate, it may help to diagnose a faulty sensor, especially if the temperature shown on the scan tool varies greatly from the temperature indicated on the dash gauge.

The maximum difference between the two readings should be 10°F (5°C). If the actual temperature varies by more than 10°F from the temperature indicated on the scan tool, check the ECT sensor wiring and connector for damage or corrosion. If the connector and wiring are okay, check the sensor with a DVOM for resistance and compare with the actual engine temperature chart. If that checks out okay, check the computer.

NOTE: Some manufacturers use two coolant sensors, one for the dash gauge and one for the computer.

FIGURE 31–8 The IAT sensor on this General Motors 3800 V-6 engine is in the air passage duct between the air cleaner housing and the throttle body.

INTAKE AIR TEMPERATURE SENSOR

PURPOSE AND FUNCTION   The intake air temperature (IAT) sensor is a negative temperature coefficient (NTC) thermistor that decreases in resistance as the temperature of the sensor increases. The IAT sensor can be located in one of the following locations:

- In the air cleaner housing
- In the air duct between the air filter and the throttle body, as shown in ● **FIGURE 31–8**
- Built into the mass air flow (MAF) or airflow sensor. Most MAF sensors use three wires. If a MAF sensor has five wires, it also includes an IAT sensor built in as part of the assembly. If more than five wires, the MAF sensor may be equipped with a humidity sensor also.
- Screwed into the intake manifold where it senses the temperature of the air entering the cylinders

NOTE: An IAT installed in the intake manifold is the most likely to suffer damage due to an engine backfire, which can often destroy the sensor.

The purpose and function of the intake air temperature sensor is to provide the engine computer (PCM) the temperature of the air entering the engine. The IAT sensor information is used for fuel control (adding or subtracting fuel) and spark timing, depending on the temperature of incoming air.

The IAT sensor is used as an input sensor by the PCM to control many functions including:

- If the air temperature is low, the PCM will modify the amount of fuel delivery and add fuel.
- If the air temperature is high, the PCM will subtract the calculated amount of fuel.
- Spark timing is also changed, depending on the temperature of the air entering the engine. The timing is advanced if the temperature is cold and retarded from the base-programmed timing if the temperature is hot.
- Cold air is more dense, contains more oxygen, and therefore requires a richer mixture to achieve the proper air-fuel mixture. Air at 32°F (0°C) is 14% denser than air at 100°F (38°C).
- Hot air is less dense, contains less oxygen, and therefore requires less fuel to achieve the proper air-fuel mixture.

The IAT sensor is a low-authority sensor and is used by the computer to modify the amount of fuel and ignition timing as determined by the engine coolant temperature sensor.

The IAT sensor is used by the PCM as a backup in the event that the ECT sensor is determined to be inoperative.

Poor Fuel Economy? Black Exhaust Smoke? Look at the IAT

If the intake air temperature sensor is defective, it may be signaling the computer that the intake air temperature is extremely cold when in fact it is warm. In such a case, the computer will supply a mixture that is much richer than normal.

If a sensor is physically damaged or electrically open, the computer will often set a diagnostic trouble code (DTC). This DTC is based on the fact that the sensor temperature did not change for a certain amount of time, usually about nine minutes. If, however, the wiring or the sensor itself has excessive resistance, a DTC will not be set and the result will be lower-than-normal fuel economy, and in serious cases, black exhaust smoke from the tailpipe during acceleration.

TESTING THE INTAKE AIR TEMPERATURE SENSOR

If the intake air temperature sensor circuit is damaged or faulty, a diagnostic trouble code is set and the malfunction indicator lamp (MIL) may or may not turn on depending on the condition and the type and model of the vehicle. To diagnose the IAT sensor follow these steps:

STEP 1 After the vehicle has been allowed to cool for several hours, use a scan tool, observe the IAT, and compare it to the engine coolant temperature. The two temperatures should be within 5°F of each other.

STEP 2 Perform a thorough visual inspection of the sensor and the wiring. If the IAT is screwed into the intake manifold, remove the sensor and check for damage.

STEP 3 Check the voltage and compare to the following chart.

NOTE: Some engines use a throttle-body temperature (TBT) sensor to sense the temperature of the air entering the engine, instead of an intake air temperature sensor.

Engine temperature is most accurately determined by looking at the engine coolant temperature sensor. In certain conditions, the IAT has an effect on performance and driveability. One such condition is a warm engine being stopped in very cold weather. In this case, when the engine is restarted, the ECT may be near normal operating temperature such as 200°F (93°C) yet the air temperature could be −20°F (−30°C). In this case, the engine requires a richer mixture due to the cold air than the ECT would seem to indicate.

INTAKE AIR TEMPERATURE SENSOR TEMPERATURE VS. RESISTANCE AND VOLTAGE DROP (APPROXIMATE)			
°F	°C	OHMS	VOLTAGE DROP ACROSS THE SENSOR
−40	−40	100,000	4.95
+18	−8	15,000	4.68
32	0	9,400	4.52
50	10	5,700	4.25
68	20	3,500	3.89
86	30	2,200	3.46
104	40	1,500	2.97
122	50	1,000	2.47
140	60	700	2.00
158	70	500	1.59
176	80	300	1.25
194	90	250	0.97
212	100	200	0.75

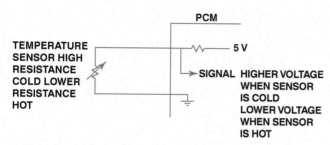

FIGURE 31–9 A typical temperature sensor circuit.

PCM

TEMPERATURE
SENSOR HIGH
RESISTANCE
COLD LOWER
RESISTANCE
HOT

5 V

SIGNAL HIGHER VOLTAGE
WHEN SENSOR
IS COLD
LOWER VOLTAGE
WHEN SENSOR
IS HOT

 FREQUENTLY ASKED QUESTION

What Exactly Is an NTC Sensor?

A negative temperature coefficient (NTC) thermistor is a semiconductor whose resistance decreases as the temperature increases. In other words, the sensor becomes more electrically conductive as the temperature increases. Therefore, when a voltage is applied, typically 5 volts, the signal voltage is high when the sensor is cold because the sensor has a high resistance and little current flows through to ground. ● **SEE FIGURE 31–9**.

However, when the temperature increases, the sensor becomes more electrically conductive and takes more of the 5 volts to ground, resulting in a lower signal voltage as the sensor warms.

TRANSMISSION FLUID TEMPERATURE SENSOR

The **transmission fluid temperature (TFT)**, also called *transmission oil temperature (TOT)*, sensor is an important sensor for the proper operation of the automatic transmission. A TFT sensor is a NTC thermistor that decreases in resistance as the temperature of the sensor increases.

GENERAL MOTORS Transaxle Sensor—Temperature to Resistance (approximate)		
°F	**°C**	**RESISTANCE (Ω)**
32	0	7,987–10,859
50	10	4,934–6,407
68	20	3,106–3,923
86	30	1,991–2,483
104	40	1,307–1,611
122	50	878–1,067
140	60	605–728
158	70	425–507
176	80	304–359
194	90	221–259
212	100	163–190

CHRYSLER Sensor Resistance (Ohms)—Transmission Temperature Sensor		
°F	**°C**	**RESISTANCE (Ω)**
−40	−40	291,490–381,710
−4	−20	85,850–108,390
14	−10	49,250–61,430
32	0	29,330–35,990
50	10	17,990–21,810
68	20	11,370–13,610
77	25	9,120–10,880
86	30	7,370–8,750
104	40	4,900–5,750
122	50	3,330–3,880
140	60	2,310–2,670
158	70	1,630–1,870
176	80	1,170–1,340
194	90	860–970
212	100	640–720
230	110	480–540
248	120	370–410

FORD		
Transmission Fluid Temperature		
°F	°C	RESISTANCE (Ω)
−40 to −4	−40 to −20	967–284 K
−3 to 31	−19 to −1	284–100 K
32 to 68	0 to 20	100–37 K
69 to 104	21 to 40	37–16 K
105 to 158	41 to 70	16–5 K
159 to 194	71 to 90	5–2.7 K
195 to 230	91 to 110	2.7–1.5 K
231 to 266	111 to 130	1.5–0.8 K
267 to 302	131 to 150	0.8–0.54 K

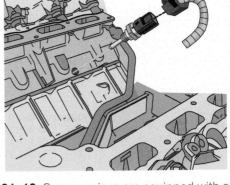

FIGURE 31–10 Some engines are equipped with a cylinder head temperature (CHT) sensor, which is used by the PCM along with the ECT to determine the temperature of the engine.

The transmission fluid temperature signal is used by the Powertrain Control Module (PCM) to perform certain strategies based on the temperature of the automatic transmission fluid. For example:

- If the temperature of the automatic transmission fluid is low (typically below 32°F [0°C]), the shift points may be delayed and overdrive disabled. The torque converter clutch also may not be applied to assist in the heating of the fluid.
- If the temperature of the automatic transmission fluid is high (typically above 260°F [130°C]), the overdrive is disabled and the torque converter clutch is applied to help reduce the temperature of the fluid.

NOTE: Check service information for the exact shift strategy based on high and low transmission fluid temperatures for the vehicle being serviced.

CYLINDER HEAD TEMPERATURE SENSOR

Some vehicles are equipped with **cylinder head temperature (CHT)** sensors.
VW Golf

$$14°F (−10°C) = 11,600 \ \Omega$$

$$68°F (20°C) = 2,900 \ \Omega$$

$$176°F (80°C) = 390 \ \Omega$$

ENGINE FUEL TEMPERATURE (EFT) SENSOR

Some vehicles, such as many Ford vehicles that are equipped with an electronic returnless type of fuel injection, use an **engine fuel temperature (EFT)** sensor to give the PCM information regarding the temperature and, therefore, the density of the fuel. Check service information for the exact location, if equipped, and how to test and service the sensor.

EXHAUST GAS RECIRCULATION (EGR) TEMPERATURE SENSOR

Some engines, such as Toyota, are equipped with exhaust gas recirculation (EGR) temperature sensors. EGR is a well-established method for reduction of NO_X emissions in internal combustion engines. The exhaust gas contains unburned hydrocarbons, which are recirculated in the combustion process. Recirculation is controlled by valves, which operate as a function of exhaust gas speed, load, and temperature. The gas reaches a temperature of about 850°F (450°C) for which a special heavy-duty glass-encapsulated NTC sensor is available.

The PCM monitors the temperature in the exhaust passage between the EGR valve and the intake manifold. If the temperature increases when the EGR is commanded on, the PCM can determine that the valve or related components are functioning.

ENGINE OIL TEMPERATURE SENSOR

Engine oil temperature sensors are used on many General Motors vehicles and are used as an input to the oil life monitoring system. The computer program inside the PCM calculates engine oil life based on run time, engine RPM, and oil temperature.

TEMPERATURE SENSOR DIAGNOSTIC TROUBLE CODES

The OBD-II diagnostic trouble codes that relate to temperature sensors include both high- and low-voltage codes, as well as intermittent codes. ● **SEE CHART 31-1**.

DIAGNOSTIC TROUBLE CODE	DESCRIPTION	POSSIBLE CAUSES
P0112	IAT sensor low voltage	▪ IAT sensor internally shorted-to-ground ▪ IAT sensor wiring shorted-to-ground ▪ IAT sensor damaged by backfire (usually associated with IAT sensors that are mounted in the intake manifold) ▪ Possible defective PCM
P0113	IAT sensor high voltage	▪ IAT sensor internally (electrically) open ▪ IAT sensor signal, circuit, or ground circuit open ▪ Possible defective PCM
P0117	ECT sensor low voltage	▪ ECT sensor internally shorted-to-ground ▪ The ECT sensor circuit wiring shorted-to-ground ▪ Possible defective PCM
P0118	ECT sensor high voltage	▪ ECT sensor internally (electrically) open ▪ ECT sensor signal, circuit, or ground circuit open ▪ Engine operating in an overheated condition ▪ Possible defective PCM

CHART 31-1

Selected temperature sensor-related diagnostic trouble codes.

SUMMARY

1. The ECT sensor is a high-authority sensor at engine start-up and is used for closed-loop control, as well as idle speed.

2. All temperature sensors decrease in resistance as the temperature increases. This is called negative temperature coefficient (NTC).

3. The ECT and IAT sensors can be tested visually, as well as by using a digital multimeter or a scan tool.

4. Some vehicle manufacturers use a stepped ECT circuit inside the PCM to broaden the accuracy of the sensor.

5. Other temperature sensors include transmission fluid temperature (TFT), engine fuel temperature (EFT), exhaust gas recirculation (EGR) temperature, and engine oil temperature.

REVIEW QUESTIONS

1. How does a typical NTC temperature sensor work?
2. What is the difference between a stepped and a non-stepped ECT circuit?
3. What temperature should be displayed on a scan tool if the ECT sensor is unplugged with the key on, engine off?
4. What are the three ways that temperature sensors can be tested?
5. If the transmission fluid temperature (TFT) sensor were to fail open (as if it were unplugged), what would the PCM do to the transmission shifting points?

CHAPTER QUIZ

1. The sensor that most determines fuel delivery when a fuel-injected engine is first started is the _____.
   a. O2S
   b. ECT sensor
   c. engine MAP sensor
   d. IAT sensor

2. What happens to the voltage measured at the ECT sensor when the thermostat opens?
   a. Increases slightly
   b. Increases about 1 volt
   c. Decreases slightly
   d. Decreases about 1 volt

3. Two technicians are discussing a stepped ECT circuit. Technician A says that the sensor used for a stepped circuit is different than one used in a non-stepped circuit. Technician B says that a stepped ECT circuit uses different internal resistance inside the PCM. Which technician is correct?
   a. Technician A only
   b. Technician B only
   c. Both Technicians A and B
   d. Neither Technician A nor B

4. When testing an ECT sensor on a vehicle, a digital multimeter can be used and the signal wires back probed. What setting should the technician use to test the sensor?
   a. AC volts
   b. DC volts
   c. Ohms
   d. Hz (hertz)

5. When testing the ECT sensor with the connector disconnected, the technician should select what position on the DMM?
   a. AC volts
   b. DC volts
   c. Ohms
   d. Hz (hertz)

6. When checking the ECT sensor with a scan tool, about what temperature should be displayed if the connector is removed from the sensor with the key on, engine off?
   a. 284°F (140°C)
   b. 230°F (110°C)
   c. 120°F (50°C)
   d. −40°F (−40°C)

7. Two technicians are discussing the IAT sensor. Technician A says that the IAT sensor is more important to the operation of the engine (higher authority) than the ECT sensor. Technician B says that the PCM will add fuel if the IAT indicates that the incoming air temperature is cold. Which technician is correct?
   a. Technician A only
   b. Technician B only
   c. Both Technicians A and B
   d. Neither Technician A nor B

8. A typical IAT or ECT sensor reads about 3,000 ohms when tested using a DMM. This resistance represents a temperature of about _____.
   a. −40°F (−40°C)
   b. 70°F (20°C)
   c. 120°F (50°C)
   d. 284°F (140°C)

9. If the transmission fluid temperature (TFT) sensor indicates cold automatic transmission fluid temperature, what would the PCM do to the shifts?
   a. Normal shifts and normal operation of the torque converter clutch
   b. Disable torque converter clutch; normal shift points
   c. Delayed shift points and torque converter clutch disabled
   d. Normal shifts but overdrive will be disabled

10. A P0118 DTC is being discussed. Technician A says that the ECT sensor could be shorted internally. Technician B says that the signal wire could be open. Which technician is correct?
    a. Technician A only
    b. Technician B only
    c. Both Technicians A and B
    d. Neither Technician A nor B

chapter 32

THROTTLE POSITION (TP) SENSORS

LEARNING OBJECTIVES

After studying this chapter, the reader will be able to:

1. Discuss how throttle position sensors work.
2. Describe how to test the TP sensor using a scan tool.
3. Describe how the operation of the TP sensor affects vehicle operation.
4. Discuss the PCM uses for the TP sensor.

This chapter will help you prepare for Engine Repair (A8) ASE certification test content area "E" (Computerized Engine Controls Diagnosis and Repair).

KEY TERMS

Potentiometer 516
Skewed 518

Throttle position (TP) sensor 516

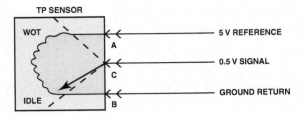

FIGURE 32–1 A typical TP sensor mounted on the throttle plate of this port-injected engine.

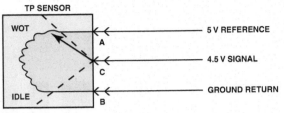

FIGURE 32–2 The signal voltage from a throttle position increases as the throttle is opened because the wiper arm is closer to the 5-volt reference. At idle, the resistance of the sensor winding effectively reduces the signal voltage output to the computer.

THROTTLE POSITION SENSOR CONSTRUCTION

PURPOSE AND FUNCTION Before the introduction of electronic throttle control (ECT) systems (throttle-by-wire), engines used a single **throttle position (TP) sensor** to signal to the powertrain control module (PCM) the position of the throttle.

POTENTIOMETERS A potentiometer is a variable-resistance sensor with three terminals. One end of the resistor receives reference voltage, while the other end is grounded. The third terminal is attached to a movable contact that slides across the resistor to vary its resistance. Depending on whether the contact is near the supply end or the ground end of the resistor, return voltage is high or low. ● **SEE FIGURE 32–2**.

Throttle position (TP) sensors are among the most common potentiometer-type sensors. The computer uses their input to determine the amount of throttle opening and the rate of change.

A typical sensor has three wires:

- A 5-volt reference feed wire from the computer
- Signal return (a ground wire back to the computer)
- A voltage signal wire back to the computer; as the throttle is opened, the voltage to the computer changes

Normal throttle position voltage on most vehicles is about 0.5 volt at idle (closed throttle) and 4.5 volts at wide-open throttle (WOT).

NOTE: The TP sensor voltage at idle is usually about 10% of the TP sensor voltage when the throttle is wide open, but can vary from as low as 0.3 to 1.2 volts, depending on the make and model of vehicle.

TP SENSOR COMPUTER INPUT FUNCTIONS

- The computer senses any change in throttle position and changes the fuel mixture and ignition timing. The actual change in fuel mixture and ignition timing is also partly determined by the other sensors, such as the manifold pressure (engine vacuum), engine RPM, the coolant temperature, and oxygen sensor(s). Some throttle position sensors are adjustable and should be set according to the exact engine manufacturer's specifications.

- The throttle position sensor signals the PCM to pulse additional fuel from the injectors when the throttle is depressed. Because the air can quickly flow into the engine when the throttle is opened, additional fuel must be supplied to prevent the air–fuel mixture from going lean, causing the engine to hesitate when the throttle is depressed. If the TP sensor is unplugged or defective, the engine may still operate satisfactorily, but hesitate upon acceleration.

- The PCM supplies the TP sensor with a regulated voltage that ranges from 4.8 to 5.1 volts. This reference voltage is usually referred to as a 5-volt reference or "Vref." The TP output signal is an input to the PCM, and the TP sensor ground also flows through the PCM.

See the Ford throttle position sensor chart for an example of how sensor voltage changes with throttle angle.

Ford Throttle Position (TP) Sensor Chart

THROTTLE ANGLE (DEGREES)	VOLTAGE (V)
0	0.50
10	0.97
20	1.44
30	1.90
40	2.37
50	2.84
60	3.31
70	3.78
80	4.24

NOTE: Generally, any reading higher than 80% represents wide-open throttle to the computer.

PCM USES FOR THE TP SENSOR

The TP sensor is used by the Powertrain Control Module (PCM) for the following reasons.

- **Clear Flood Mode** If the throttle is depressed to the floor during engine cranking, the PCM will either greatly reduce or entirely eliminate any fuel-injector pulses to aid in clearing a flooded engine. If the throttle is depressed to the floor and the engine is not flooded with excessive fuel, the engine may not start.

- **Torque Converter Clutch Engagement and Release** The torque converter clutch will be released if the PCM detects rapid acceleration to help the transmission deliver maximum torque to the drive wheels. The torque converter clutch is applied when the vehicle is lightly accelerating and during cruise conditions to improve fuel economy.

- **Rationality Testing for MAP and MAF Sensors** As part of the rationality tests for the MAP and/or MAF sensor, the TP sensor signal is compared to the reading from other sensors to determine if they match. For example, if the throttle position sensor is showing wide-open throttle, the MAP and/or MAF reading should also indicate that this engine is under a heavy load. If not,

a diagnostic trouble code could be set for the TP, as well as the MAP and/or MAF sensors.

- **Automatic Transmission Shift Points** The shift points are delayed if the throttle is opened wide to allow the engine speed to increase, thereby producing more power and aiding in the acceleration of the vehicle. If the throttle is barely open, the shift point occurs at the minimum speed designed for the vehicle.

- **Target Idle Speed (Idle Control Strategy)** When the TP sensor voltage is at idle, the PCM controls idle speed using the idle air control (IAC) and/or spark timing variation to maintain the commanded idle speed. If the TP sensor indicates that the throttle has moved off idle, fuel delivery and spark timing are programmed for acceleration. Therefore, if the throttle linkage is stuck or binding, the idle speed may not be correct.

- **Air-Conditioning Compressor Operation** The TP sensor is also used as an input sensor for air-conditioning compressor operation. If the PCM detects that the throttle is at or close to wide open, the air-conditioning compressor is disengaged.

- **Backs Up Other Sensors** The TP sensor is used as a backup to the MAP sensor and/or MAF in the event the PCM detects that one or both are not functioning correctly. The PCM then calculates fuel needs and spark timing based on the engine speed (RPM) and throttle position.

TESTING THE THROTTLE POSITION SENSOR

A TP sensor can be tested using one or more of the following tools:

- A digital voltmeter with three test leads connected in series between the sensor and the wiring harness connector or back probing using T-pins or other recommended tool that will not cause harm to the connector or wiring.

- A scan tool or a specific tool recommended by the vehicle manufacturer.

- An oscilloscope.

Use jumper wires, T-pins to back-probe the wires, or a breakout box to gain electrical access to the wiring to the TP sensor. ● **SEE FIGURE 32–3.**

FIGURE 32–3 A meter lead connected to a T-pin that was gently pushed along the signal wire of the TP sensor until the point of the pin touched the metal terminal inside the plastic connector.

NOTE: The procedure that follows is the usual method used by many manufacturers. Always refer to service information for the exact recommended procedure and specifications for the vehicle being tested.

The procedure for testing the sensor using a digital multimeter is as follows:

1. Turn the ignition switch on (engine off).

2. Set the digital meter to read to DC volts and measure the voltage between the signal wire and ground (reference low) wire. The voltage should be about 0.5 volt.

   NOTE: Consult the service information for exact wire colors or locations.

3. With the engine still not running (but with the ignition still on), slowly increase the throttle opening. The voltage signal from the TP sensor should also increase. Look for any "dead spots" or open circuit readings as the throttle is increased to the wide-open position. ● **SEE FIGURE 32–4** for an example of how a good TP sensor would look when tested with a digital storage oscilloscope (DSO).

   NOTE: Use the accelerator pedal to depress the throttle because this applies the same forces on the TP sensor as the driver does during normal driving. Moving the throttle by hand under the hood may not accurately test the TP sensor.

4. With the voltmeter still connected, slowly return the throttle down to the idle position. The voltage from the TP sensor should also decrease evenly on the return to idle.

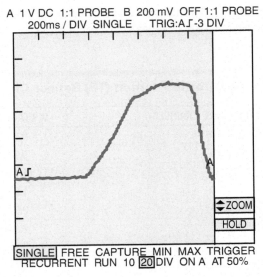

FIGURE 32–4 A typical waveform of a TP sensor signal as recorded on a DSO when the accelerator pedal was depressed with the ignition switch on (engine off). Clean transitions and the lack of any glitches in this waveform indicate a good sensor.

The TP sensor voltage at idle should be within the acceptable range as specified by the manufacturer. Some TP sensors can be adjusted by loosening their retaining screws and moving the sensor in relation to the throttle opening. This movement changes the output voltage of the sensor.

All TP sensors should also provide a smooth transition voltage reading from idle to WOT and back to idle. Replace the TP sensor if erratic voltage readings are obtained or if the correct setting at idle cannot be obtained.

 TECH TIP

Check Power and Ground Before Condemning a Bad Sensor

Most engine sensors use a 5-volt reference and a ground. If the 5 volts to the sensor is too high (shorted to voltage) or too low (high resistance), the sensor output will be **skewed** or out of range. Before replacing the sensor that did not read correctly, measure both the 5-volt reference and ground. To measure the ground, simply turn the ignition on (engine off) and touch one test lead of a DMM set to read DC volts to the sensor ground and the other to the negative terminal of the battery. Any reading higher than 0.2 volt (200 mV) represents a poor ground. ● **SEE FIGURES 32–5 AND 32–6.**

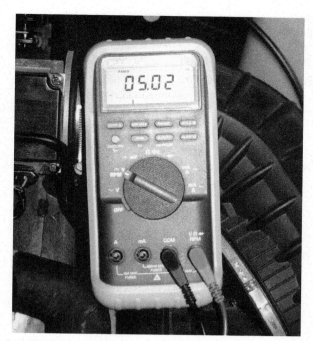

FIGURE 32–5 Checking the 5-volt reference from the computer being applied to the TP sensor with the ignition switch on (engine off).

FIGURE 32–6 Checking the voltage drop between the TP sensor ground and a good engine ground with the ignition on (engine off). A reading of greater than 0.2 volt (200 mV) represents a bad computer ground.

TESTING A TP SENSOR USING THE MIN/MAX FUNCTION

Many digital multimeters are capable of recording voltage readings over time and then displaying the minimum, maximum, and average readings. To perform a MIN/MAX test of the TP sensor, manually set the meter to read higher than 4 volts.

STEP 1 Connect the red meter lead to the signal wire and the black meter lead to a good ground on the ground return wire at the TP sensor.

STEP 2 With the ignition on, engine off, slowly depress and release the accelerator pedal from inside the vehicle.

STEP 3 Check the minimum and maximum voltage reading on the meter display. Any 0- or 5-volt reading would indicate a fault or short in the TP sensor.

TESTING THE TP SENSOR USING A SCAN TOOL

A scan tool can be used to check for proper operation of the throttle position sensor using the following steps:

STEP 1 With the key on, engine off, the TP sensor voltage display should be about 0.5 volt, but can vary from as low as 0.3 volt to as high as 1.2 volts.

STEP 2 Check the scan tool display for the percentage of throttle opening. The reading should be zero and gradually increase in percentage as the throttle is depressed.

STEP 3 The idle air control (IAC) counts should increase as the throttle is opened and decrease as the throttle is closed. Start the engine and observe the IAC counts as the throttle is depressed.

STEP 4 Start the engine and observe the TP sensor reading. Use a wedge or thin object to increase the throttle opening slightly. The throttle percentage reading should increase. Shut off and restart the engine. If the percentage of throttle opening returns to 0%, the PCM determines that the increased throttle opening is now the new minimum and resets the idle position of the TP sensor. Remove the wedge and cycle the ignition key. The throttle position sensor should again read zero percentage.

NOTE: Some engine computers are not capable of resetting the throttle position sensor.

TP SENSOR DIAGNOSTIC TROUBLE CODES

The diagnostic trouble codes (DTCs) associated with the throttle position sensor include the following:

DIAGNOSTIC TROUBLE CODE	DESCRIPTION	POSSIBLE CAUSES
P0122	TP sensor low voltage	▪ TP sensor internally shorted-to-ground ▪ TP sensor wiring shorted-to-ground ▪ TP sensor or wiring open
P0123	TP sensor high voltage	▪ TP sensor internally shorted to 5-volt reference ▪ TP sensor ground open ▪ TP sensor wiring shorted-to-voltage
P0121	TP sensor signal does not agree with MAP	▪ Defective TP sensor ▪ Incorrect vehicle-speed (VS) sensor signal ▪ MAP sensor out-of-calibration or defective

SUMMARY

1. A throttle position (TP) sensor is a three-wire variable resistor called a potentiometer.

2. The three wires on the TP sensor include a 5-volt reference voltage from the PCM, plus the signal wire to the PCM, and a ground, which also goes to the PCM.

3. The TP sensor is used by the PCM for clear flood mode, torque converter engagement and release, and automotive transmission shift points, as well as for rationality testing for the MAP and MAF sensors.

4. The TP sensor signal voltage should be about 0.5 volt at idle and increase to about 4.5 volts at wide-open throttle (WOT).

5. A TP sensor can be tested using a digital multimeter, a digital storage oscilloscope (DSO), or a scan tool.

REVIEW QUESTIONS

1. What is the purpose of each of the three wires on a typical TP sensor?

2. What all does the PCM do with the TP sensor signal voltage?

3. What is the procedure to follow when checking the 5-volt reference and TP sensor ground?

4. How can a TP sensor be diagnosed using a scan tool?

5. What diagnostic trouble codes (DTCs) are usually associated with a fault with the throttle position (TP) sensor?

1. Which sensor is used to measure the position of the throttle?
   a. O2S
   b. ECT sensor
   c. Engine MAP sensor
   d. TP sensor

2. Typical TP sensor voltage at idle is about _____.
   a. 2.50 to 2.80 volts
   b. 0.5 volt or 10% of WOT TP sensor voltage
   c. 1.5 to 2.8 volts
   d. 13.5 to 15.0 volts

3. A TP sensor is what type of sensor?
   a. Rheostat
   b. Voltage generating
   c. Potentiometer
   d. Piezoelectric

4. Most TP sensors have how many wires?
   a. 1
   b. 2
   c. 3
   d. 4

5. Which sensor does the TP sensor back up if the PCM determines that a failure has occurred?
   a. Oxygen sensor
   b. MAF sensor
   c. MAP sensor
   d. Either b or c

6. Which wire on a TP sensor should be back-probed to check the voltage signal to the PCM?
   a. 5 volt reference (Vref)
   b. Signal
   c. Ground
   d. Meter should be connected between the 5-volt reference and the ground

7. After a TP sensor has been tested using the MIN/MAX function on a DMM, a reading of zero volts is displayed. What does this reading indicate?
   a. The TP sensor is open at one point during the test.
   b. The TP sensor is shorted.
   c. The TP sensor signal is shorted to 5-volt reference.
   d. Both b and c are possible.

8. After a TP sensor has been tested using the MIN/MAX function on a DMM, a reading of 5 volts is displayed. What does this reading indicate?
   a. The TP sensor is open at one point during the test.
   b. The TP sensor is shorted.
   c. The TP sensor signal is shorted to 5-volt reference.
   d. Both b and c are possible.

9. A technician attaches one lead of a digital voltmeter to the ground terminal of the TP sensor and the other meter lead to the negative terminal of the battery. The ignition is switched to on, engine off and the meter displays 37.3 mV. Technician A says that this is the signal voltage and is a little low. Technician B says that the TP sensor ground circuit has excessive resistance. Which technician is correct?
   a. Technician A only
   b. Technician B only
   c. Both Technicians A and B
   d. Neither Technician A nor B

10. A P0122 DTC is retrieved using a scan tool. This DTC means _____.
    a. the TP sensor voltage is low
    b. the TP sensor could be shorted-to-ground
    c. the TP sensor signal circuit could be shorted-to-ground
    d. All of the above.

chapter 33

MAP/BARO SENSORS

AIR PRESSURE—HIGH AND LOW

Think of an internal combustion engine as a big air pump. As the pistons move up and down in the cylinders, they pump in air and fuel for combustion and pump out exhaust gases. They do this by creating a difference in air pressure. The air outside an engine has weight and exerts pressure, as does the air inside an engine.

As a piston moves down on an intake stroke with the intake valve open, it creates a larger area inside the cylinder for the air to fill. This lowers the air pressure within the engine. Because the pressure inside the engine is lower than the pressure outside, air flows into the engine to fill the low-pressure area and equalize the pressure.

The low pressure within the engine is called **vacuum** and is measured in inches of Mercury, abbreviated in. Hg. Vacuum causes the higher-pressure air on the outside to flow into the low-pressure area inside the cylinder. The difference in pressure between the two areas is called a **pressure differential**. ● SEE FIGURE 33–1.

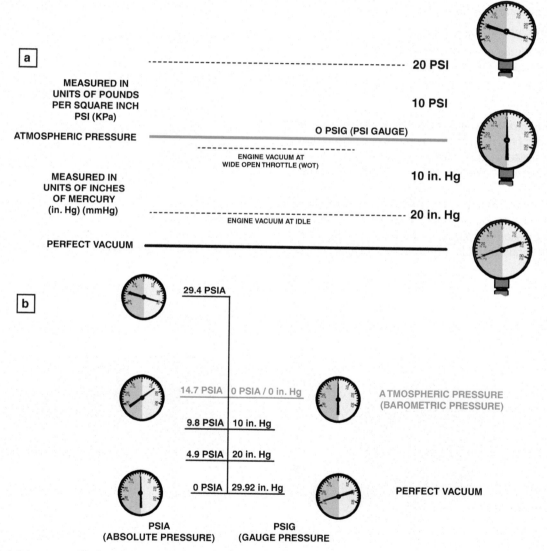

FIGURE 33–1 (a) As an engine is accelerated under a load, the engine vacuum drops. This drop in vacuum is actually an increase in absolute pressure in the intake manifold. A MAP sensor senses all pressures greater than that of a perfect vacuum. (b) The relationship between absolute pressure, vacuum, and gauge pressure.

PRINCIPLES OF PRESSURE SENSORS

Intake manifold pressure changes with changing throttle positions. At wide-open throttle, manifold pressure is almost the same as atmospheric pressure. On deceleration or at idle, manifold pressure is below atmospheric pressure, thus creating a vacuum. In cases where turbo- or supercharging is used, under part- or full-load condition, intake manifold pressure rises above atmospheric pressure. Also, oxygen content and barometric pressure change with differences in altitude, and the computer must be able to compensate by making changes in the flow of fuel entering the engine. To provide the computer with changing airflow information, a fuel-injection system may use the following:

- Manifold absolute pressure (MAP) sensor
- Manifold absolute pressure sensor plus barometric absolute pressure (BARO) sensor
- Barometric and manifold absolute pressure sensors combined (BMAP)

The **manifold absolute pressure (MAP) sensor** may be a ceramic capacitor diaphragm, an aneroid bellows, or a piezoresistive crystal. It has a sealed vacuum reference input on one side; the other side is connected (vented) to the intake manifold. This sensor housing also contains signal conditioning circuitry. ● **SEE FIGURE 33–2**. Pressure changes in the manifold cause the sensor to deflect, varying its analog or digital return signal to the computer. As the air pressure increases, the MAP sensor generates a higher voltage or frequency return signal to the computer.

CONSTRUCTION OF MANIFOLD ABSOLUTE PRESSURE SENSORS

The manifold absolute pressure sensor is used by the engine computer to sense engine load. The typical MAP sensor consists of a ceramic or silicon wafer sealed on one side with a perfect vacuum and exposed to intake manifold vacuum on the other side. As the engine vacuum changes, the pressure difference on the wafer changes the output voltage or frequency of the MAP sensor.

A manifold absolute pressure sensor is used on many engines for the PCM to determine the load on the engine. The relationship among barometer pressure, engine vacuum, and MAP sensor voltage includes the following:

- Absolute pressure is equal to barometric pressure minus intake manifold vacuum.
- A decrease in manifold vacuum means an increase in manifold pressure.
- The MAP sensor compares manifold vacuum to a perfect vacuum.
- Barometric pressure minus MAP sensor reading equals intake manifold vacuum. Normal engine vacuum is 17–21 inch Hg.
- Supercharged and turbocharged engines require a MAP sensor that is calibrated for pressures above atmospheric, as well as for vacuum. ● **SEE FIGURE 33–3**.

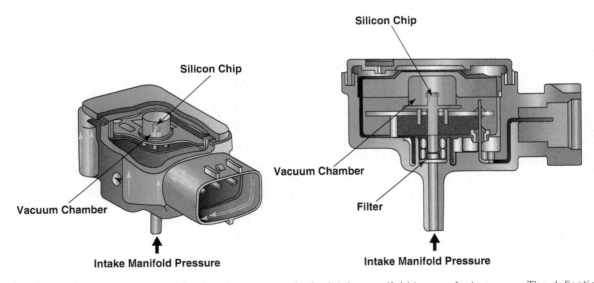

FIGURE 33–2 A MAP sensor compares the absolute pressure in the intake manifold to a perfect vacuum. The deflection of the silicon chip is converted to a an absolute pressure reading by the electronics in the sensor itself.

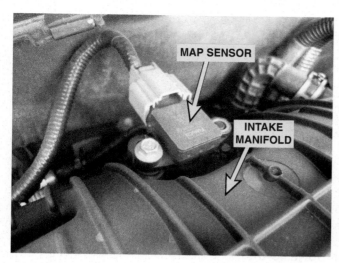

FIGURE 33–3 A typical MAP sensor installed in the intake manifold.

A typical General Motors MAP sensor voltage varies from 0.88 to 1.62 at engine idle.

- 17 inch Hg is equal to about 1.62 volts
- 21 inch Hg is equal to about 0.88 volts

Therefore, a good reading should be about 1.0 volt from the MAP sensor on a sound engine at idle speed. See the following chart that shows engine load, engine vacuum, and MAP. ● **SEE CHART 33–1.**

CERAMIC DISC MAP SENSOR The ceramic disc MAP sensor is used by Chrysler and it converts manifold pressure into a capacitance discharge. The discharge controls the amount of voltage delivered by the sensor to the PCM. The output is the same as the previously used strain gauge/Wheatstone bridge design and is interchangeable. ● **SEE FIGURE 33–4.** Also ● **SEE CHART 33–2.**

ENGINE LOAD	MANIFOLD VACUUM	MANIFOLD ABSOLUTE PRESSURE	MAP SENSOR VOLT SIGNAL
Heavy (WOT)	Low (almost 0 inch Hg)	High (almost atmospheric)	High (4.6–4.8 V)
Light (idle)	High (17–21 inch Hg)	Low (lower than atmospheric)	Low (0.8–1.6 V)

CHART 33–1

Engine load and how it is related to engine vacuum, and MAP sensor reading.

SILICON-DIAPHRAGM STRAIN GAUGE MAP SENSOR This is the most commonly used design for a MAP sensor and the output is a DC analog (variable) voltage. One side of a silicon wafer is exposed to engine vacuum and the other side is exposed to a perfect vacuum.

There are four resistors attached to the silicon wafer, which changes in resistance when strain is applied to the wafer. This change in resistance due to strain is called **piezoresistivity**. The resistors are electrically connected to a Wheatstone bridge circuit and then to a differential amplifier, which creates a voltage in proportion to the vacuum applied.

FIGURE 33–4 Shown is the electronic circuit inside a ceramic disc MAP sensor used on many Chrysler engines. The black areas are carbon resistors that are applied to the ceramic, and lasers are used to cut lines into these resistors during testing to achieve the proper operating calibration.

Chrysler MAP Sensor Chart

VACUUM (IN. HG)	MAP SENSOR SIGNAL VOLTAGE (V)
0.5	4.8
1.0	4.6
3.0	4.1
5.0	3.8
7.0	3.5
10.0	2.9
15.0	2.1
20.0	1.2
25.0	0.5

CHART 33-2

Chyrsler MAP sensor values compared to engine vacuum.

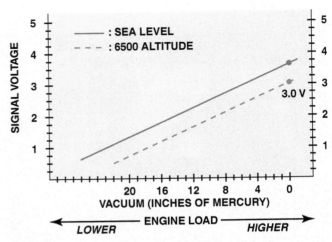

FIGURE 33-5 Altitude affects the MAP sensor voltage.

 TECH TIP

If It's Green, It's a Signal Wire
Ford-built vehicles usually use a green wire as the signal wire back to the computer from the sensors. It may not be a solid green, but if there is green somewhere on the wire, then it is the signal wire. The other wires are the power and ground wires to the sensor.

PCM USES OF THE MAP SENSOR

The PCM uses the MAP sensor to determine the following:

- **The load on the engine.** The MAP sensor is used on a **speed density**-type fuel-injection system to determine the load on the engine, and therefore the amount of fuel needed. On engines equipped with a mass air flow (MAF) sensor, the MAP is used as a backup to the MAF, for diagnosis of other sensors, and systems such as the EGR system.
- **Altitude, fuel, and spark control calculations.** At key on, the MAP sensor determines the altitude (acts as a BARO sensor) and adjusts the fuel delivery and spark timing accordingly.
  - If the altitude is high, generally over 5,000 feet (1,500 meters), the PCM will reduce fuel delivery and advance the ignition timing.

- The altitude is also reset when the engine is accelerated to wide-open throttle and the MAP sensor is used to reset the altitude reading. ● **SEE FIGURE 33-5**.
- **EGR system operation.** As part of the OBD-II standards, the exhaust gas recirculation (EGR) system must be checked for proper operation. One method used by many vehicle manufacturers is to command the EGR valve on and then watch the MAP sensor signal. The opening of the EGR pintle should decrease engine vacuum. If the MAP sensor does not react with the specified drop in manifold vacuum (increase in manifold pressure), an EGR flow rate problem diagnostic trouble code is set.
- **Detect deceleration (vacuum increases).** The engine vacuum rises when the accelerator is released, which changes the MAP sensor voltage. When deceleration is detected by the PCM, fuel is either stopped or greatly reduced to improve exhaust emissions.
- **Monitor engine condition.** As an engine wears, the intake manifold vacuum usually decreases. The PCM is programmed to detect the gradual change in vacuum and is able to keep the air-fuel mixture in the correct range. If the PCM were not capable of making adjustments for engine wear, the lower vacuum could be interpreted as increased load on the engine, resulting in too much fuel being injected, thereby reducing fuel economy and increasing exhaust emissions.
- **Load detection for returnless-type fuel injection.** On fuel delivery systems that do not use a return line back to the fuel tank, the engine load calculation for the fuel needed is determined by the signals from the MAP sensor.

Use the MAP Sensor as a Vacuum Gauge

A MAP sensor measures the pressure inside the intake manifold compared with absolute zero (perfect vacuum). For example, an idling engine that has 20 inches of mercury (inch Hg) of vacuum has a lower pressure inside the intake manifold than when the engine is under a load and the vacuum is at 10 inch Hg. A decrease in engine vacuum results in an increase in manifold pressure. A normal engine should produce between 17 and 21 inch Hg at idle. Comparing the vacuum reading with the voltage reading output of the MAP sensor indicates that the reading should be between 1.62 and 0.88 volt. Therefore, a digital multimeter (DMM), scan tool, or scope can be used to measure the MAP sensor voltage and be used instead of a vacuum gauge.

NOTE: This chart was developed by testing a MAP sensor at a location about 600 feet above sea level. For best results, a chart based on your altitude should be made by applying a known vacuum, and reading the voltage of a known-good MAP sensor. Vacuum usually drops about 1 inch per 1,000 feet of altitude.

Vacuum (in. Hg)	GM (DC volts)
0	4.80
1	4.52
2	4.46
3	4.26
4	4.06
5	3.88
6	3.66
7	3.50
8	3.30
9	3.10
10	2.94
11	2.76
12	2.54
13	2.36
14	2.20
15	2.00
16	1.80
17	1.62
18	1.42
19	1.20
20	1.10
21	0.88
22	0.66

Altitude and MAP Sensor Voltage	
ALTITUDE	MAP SENSOR VOLTAGE (KEY ON, ENGINE OFF)
Sea level	4.6–4.8 V
2,500 (760 m)	4.0 V
5,000 (1,520 m)	3.7 V
7,500 (2,300 m)	3.35 V
10,000 (3,050 m)	3.05 V
12,500 (3,800 m)	2.80 V
15,000 (4,600 m)	2.45 V

CHART 33–3

Comparison between MAP sensor voltage and altitude.

■ **Altitude and MAP sensor values.** On an engine equipped with a speed density–type fuel injection, the MAP sensor is the most important sensor needed to determine injection pulse width. Changes in altitude change the air density as well as weather conditions. Barometric pressure and altitude are inversely related:

■ As altitude increases—barometric pressure decreases
■ As altitude decreases—barometric pressure increases

As the ignition switch is turned from off to the start position, the PCM reads the MAP sensor value to determine atmospheric and air pressure conditions. This barometric pressure reading is updated every time the engine is started and whenever wide-open throttle is detected. The barometric pressure reading at that time is updated. ● **SEE CHART 33–3.**

BAROMETRIC PRESSURE SENSOR

A **barometric pressure (BARO) sensor** is similar in design, but senses more subtle changes in barometric absolute pressure (atmospheric air pressure). It is vented directly to the atmosphere. The **barometric manifold absolute pressure (BMAP) sensor** is actually a combination of a BARO and MAP sensor in the same housing. The BMAP sensor has individual circuits to measure barometric and manifold pressure. This input not only allows the computer to adjust for changes in atmospheric pressure due to weather, but also is the primary sensor used to determine altitude.

The Case of the No-Start Lexus

The owner of a Lexus IS250 had the car towed to a shop as a no-start. The technician discovered that the "check engine" light would not come on even with key on, engine off (KOEO). A scan tool would not communicate either. Checking the resources on www.iatn.net, the technician read of a similar case where the fuel pressure sensor was shorted, which disabled all serial data communications. The technician disconnected the fuel pressure sensor located on the backside of the engine and the communications were restored and the engine started. The fuel pressure sensor was replaced and returned to the happy owner.

Summary:

- **Complaint**—The vehicle owner stated that the engine would not start.
- **Cause**—A shorted fuel pressure sensor was found as per a previous similar case.
- **Correction**—The fuel pressure sensor was replaced and this corrected the serial data fault that caused the no-start condition.

NOTE: A MAP sensor and a BARO sensor are usually the same sensor, but the MAP sensor is connected to the manifold and a BARO sensor is open to the atmosphere. The MAP sensor is capable of reading barometric pressure just as the ignition switch is turned to the on position before the engine starts. Therefore, altitude and weather changes are available to the computer. During mountainous driving, it may be an advantage to stop and restart the engine so that the engine computer can take another barometric pressure reading and recalibrate fuel delivery based on the new altitude. See the Ford/BARO altitude chart for an example of how altitude affects intake manifold pressure. The computer on some vehicles will monitor the throttle position sensor and use the MAP sensor reading at wide-open throttle (WOT) to update the BARO sensor if it has changed during driving. ● SEE CHART 33–4.

NOTE: Some older Chrysler brand vehicles were equipped with a combination BARO and IAT sensor. The sensor was mounted on the bulkhead (firewall) and sensed the underhood air temperature.

Ford MAP/BARO Altitude Chart	
ALTITUDE (FEET)	VOLTS (V)
0	1.59
1,000	1.56
2,000	1.53
3,000	1.50
4,000	1.47
5,000	1.44
6,000	1.41
7,000	1.39

CHART 33–4

Comparison between Ford MAP/BARO sensor voltage and altitude.

TESTING THE MAP SENSOR

Most pressure sensors operate on 5 volts from the computer and return a signal (voltage or frequency) based on the pressure (vacuum) applied to the sensor. If a MAP sensor is being tested, make certain that the vacuum hose and hose fittings are sound and making a good, tight connection to a manifold vacuum source on the engine.

Three different types of test instruments can be used to test a pressure sensor:

1. A digital voltmeter with three test leads connected in series between the sensor and the wiring harness connector or back-probe the terminals.

2. A scope connected to the sensor output, power, and ground.

3. A scan tool or a specific tool recommended by the vehicle manufacturer.

NOTE: Always check service information for the exact testing procedures and specifications for the vehicle being tested.

TESTING THE MAP SENSOR USING A DMM OR SCOPE
Use jumper wires, T-pins to back-probe the connector, or a breakout box to gain electrical access to the wiring to the pressure sensor. Most pressure sensors use three wires:

1. A 5-volt wire from the computer

2. A variable-signal wire back to the computer

3. A ground or reference low wire

MAP Sensor Circuit

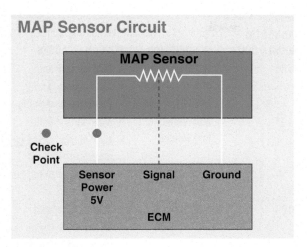

FIGURE 33–6 When checking a MAP sensor, first verify that the sensor is receiving a 5-volt reference voltage and then check for the output (signal) voltage.

The procedure for testing the sensor is as follows:

1. Turn the ignition on (engine off)
2. Measure the voltage (or frequency) of the sensor output
3. Using a hand-operated vacuum pump (or other variable vacuum source), apply vacuum to the sensor

A good pressure sensor should change voltage in relation to the applied vacuum. If the signal does not change or the values are out of range according to the manufacturers' specifications, the sensor must be replaced. ● **SEE FIGURE 33–6.**

TESTING THE MAP SENSOR USING A SCAN TOOL

A scan tool can be used to test a MAP sensor by monitoring the injector pulse width (in milliseconds) when vacuum is being applied to the MAP sensor using a hand-operated vacuum pump. ● **SEE FIGURE 33–7.**

STEP 1 Apply about 20 inch Hg of vacuum to the MAP sensor and start the engine.

STEP 2 Observe the injector pulse width. On a warm engine, the injector pulse width will normally be 1.5 to 3.5 milliseconds.

STEP 3 Slowly reduce the vacuum to the MAP sensor and observe the pulse width. A lower vacuum to the MAP sensor indicates a heavier load on the engine and the injector pulse width should increase.

NOTE: If 23 inch Hg or more vacuum is applied to the MAP sensor with the engine running, this high vacuum will often stall the engine. The engine stalls because the high vacuum is interpreted by the PCM to indicate that the engine is being decelerated, which shuts off the fuel. During engine deceleration, the PCM shuts off the fuel injectors to reduce exhaust emissions and increase fuel economy.

FIGURE 33–7 A typical hand-operated vacuum pump.

MAP/BARO DIAGNOSTIC TROUBLE CODES

The diagnostic trouble codes (DTCs) associated with the MAP and BARO sensors include:

DIAGNOSTIC TROUBLE CODE	DESCRIPTION	POSSIBLE CAUSES
P0106	BARO sensor out-of-range at key on	• MAP sensor fault • MAP sensor O-ring damaged or missing
P0107	MAP sensor low voltage	• MAP sensor fault • MAP sensor signal circuit shorted-to-ground • MAP sensor 5-volt supply circuit open
P0108	Map sensor high voltage	• MAP sensor fault • MAP sensor O-ring damaged or missing • MAP sensor signal circuit shorted-to-voltage

SUMMARY

1. Pressure below atmospheric pressure is called vacuum and is measured in inches of mercury.

2. A manifold absolute pressure sensor uses a perfect vacuum (zero absolute pressure) in the sensor to determine the pressure.

3. Three types of MAP sensors include:
   - Silicon-diaphragm strain gauge
   - Capacitor-capsule design
   - Ceramic disc design

4. A heavy engine load results in low intake manifold vacuum and a high MAP sensor signal voltage.

5. A light engine load results in high intake manifold vacuum and a low MAP sensor signal voltage.

6. A MAP sensor is used to detect changes in altitude, as well as check other sensors and engine systems.

7. A MAP sensor can be tested by visual inspection, testing the output using a digital meter or scan tool.

REVIEW QUESTIONS

1. What is the relationship among atmospheric pressure, and engine vacuum?

2. What are two types (construction) of MAP sensors?

3. What is the MAP sensor signal voltage at idle?

4. What are three uses of a MAP sensor by the PCM?

5. What diagnostic trouble codes are associated with faults with the MAP sensor?

1. As the load on an engine increases, the manifold vacuum decreases and the manifold absolute pressure _____.
   a. increases
   b. decreases
   c. changes with barometric pressure only (altitude or weather)
   d. remains constant (absolute)

2. A typical MAP sensor compares the vacuum in the intake manifold to _____.
   a. atmospheric pressure
   b. a perfect vacuum
   c. barometric pressure
   d. the value of the IAT sensor

3. Which statement is *false?*
   a. Absolute pressure is equal to barometric pressure plus intake manifold vacuum.
   b. A decrease in manifold vacuum means an increase in manifold pressure.
   c. The MAP sensor compares manifold vacuum to a perfect vacuum.
   d. Barometric pressure minus the MAP sensor reading equals intake manifold vacuum.

4. Which design of MAP sensor is used on turbocharged or supercharged engines?
   a. Manifold absolute pressure (MAP) sensor
   b. Manifold absolute pressure sensor plus barometric absolute pressure (BARO) sensor
   c. Barometric and manifold absolute pressure sensors combined (BMAP)
   d. A MAP sensor calibrated for pressures above atmospheric

5. Vacuum is measured in what unit of measure?
   a. Pounds per square inch (PSI)
   b. Inches of Mercury (inch Hg)
   c. PSIA
   d. PSIG

6. Which is *not* a purpose or function of the MAP sensor?
   a. Measures the load on the engine
   b. Measures engine speed
   c. Calculates fuel delivery based on altitude
   d. Helps diagnose the EGR system

7. When measuring the output signal of a MAP sensor on a General Motors vehicle, the digital multimeter should be set to read _____.
   a. DC V
   b. AC V
   c. Hz
   d. DC A

8. Two technicians are discussing testing MAP sensors. Technician A says that the MAP sensor voltage on a General Motors vehicle at idle should be about 1.0 volt. Technician B says that the MAP sensor voltage can be used to determine the intake manifold vacuum. Which technician is correct?
   a. Technician A only
   b. Technician B only
   c. Both Technicians A and B
   d. Neither Technician A nor B

9. Technician A says that MAP sensors use a 5 volt reference voltage from the PCM. Technician B says that the MAP sensor voltage will be higher at idle at high altitudes compared to when the engine is operating at near sea level. Which technician is correct?
   a. Technician A only
   b. Technician B only
   c. Both Technicians A and B
   d. Neither Technician A nor B

10. A P0107 DTC is being discussed. Technician A says that a defective MAP sensor could be the cause. Technician B says that a MAP sensor signal wire shorted-to-ground could be the cause. Which technician is correct?
    a. Technician A only
    b. Technician B only
    c. Both Technicians A and B
    d. Neither Technician A nor B

chapter 34
MASS AIR FLOW SENSORS

LEARNING OBJECTIVES

After studying this chapter, the reader will be able to:

1. Discuss how MAF sensors work.
2. List the methods that can be used to test MAF sensors.
3. Describe the symptoms of a failed MAF sensor.

This chapter will help you prepare for Engine Repair (A8) ASE certification test content area "E" (Computerized Engine Controls Diagnosis and Repair).

KEY TERMS

False air 536
Mass airflow (MAF) sensor 533

Speed density 533
Tap test 536

SPEED DENSITY SYSTEMS

Engines that do not use an airflow meter or sensor rely on calculating the amount of air entering the engine by using the MAP sensor and engine speed as the major factors. The method of calculating the amount of fuel needed by the engine is called **speed density**.

MASS AIRFLOW SENSOR TYPES

PURPOSE AND FUNCTION The purpose and function of mass air flow sensors is to measure the amount of air entering the engine.

There are several types of mass airflow sensors.

HOT FILM SENSOR The hot film sensor uses a temperature-sensing resistor (thermistor) to measure the temperature of the incoming air. Through the electronics within the sensor, a conductive film is kept at a temperature 70°C above the temperature of the incoming air. ● **SEE FIGURE 34–1.**

Because the amount and density of the air both tend to contribute to the cooling effect as the air passes through the sensor, this type of sensor can actually produce an output based on the *mass* of the airflow. *Mass equals volume times density.* For example, cold air is denser than warm air so a small amount of cold air may have the same mass as a larger amount of warm air. Therefore, a mass airflow sensor is designed to measure the mass, not the volume, of the air entering the engine.

The output of this type of sensor is usually a frequency based on the amount of air entering the sensor. The more air that enters the sensor, the more the hot film is cooled. The electronics inside the sensor, therefore, increase the current flow through the hot film to maintain the 70°C temperature differential between the air temperature and the temperature of the hot film. This change in current flow is converted to a frequency output that the computer can use as a measurement of airflow. Most of these types of sensors are referred to as **mass airflow (MAF) sensors** because, unlike the air vane sensor, the MAF sensor takes into account relative humidity, altitude, and temperature of the air. The denser the air, the greater the cooling effect on the hot film sensor and the greater the amount of fuel required for proper combustion.

HOT WIRE SENSOR The hot wire sensor is similar to the hot film type, but uses a hot wire to sense the mass airflow instead of the hot film. Like the hot film sensor, the hot wire sensor uses a temperature-sensing resistor (thermistor) to measure the temperature of the air entering the sensor. ● **SEE FIGURE 34–2.** The electronic circuitry within the sensor keeps the temperature of the wire at 70°C above the temperature of the incoming air.

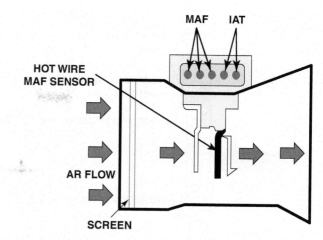

FIGURE 34–1 This five-wire mass air flow sensor consists of a metal foil sensing unit, an intake air temperature (IAT) sensor, and the electronic module.

FIGURE 34–2 The sensing wire in a typical hot wire mass air flow sensor.

Both designs operate in essentially the same way. A resistor wire or screen installed in the path of intake airflow is heated to a constant temperature by electric current provided by the computer. Air flowing past the screen or wire cools it. The degree of cooling varies with air velocity, temperature, density, and humidity. These factors combine to indicate the mass of air entering the engine. As the screen or wire cools, more current is required to maintain the specified temperature. As the screen or wire heats up, less current is required. The operating principle can be summarized as follows:

- More intake air volume = cooler sensor, more current.
- Less intake air volume = warmer sensor, less current.

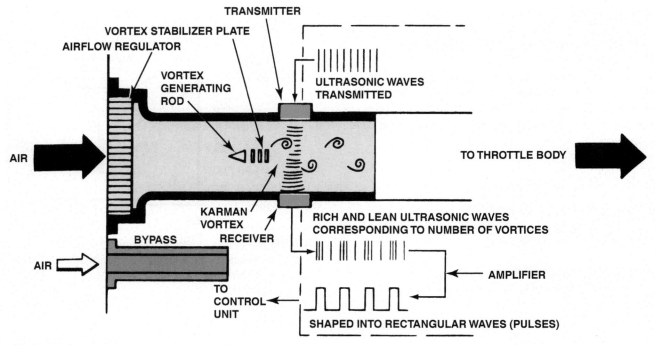

FIGURE 34–3 A Karman Vortex air flow sensor uses a triangle-shaped rod to create vortexes as the air flows through the sensor. The electronics in the sensor itself converts these vortexes to a digital square wave signal.

The computer constantly monitors the change in current and translates it into a voltage signal that is used to determine injector pulse width.

BURN-OFF CIRCUIT. Some MAF sensors use a burn-off circuit to keep the sensing wire clean of dust and dirt. A high current is passed through the sensing wire for a short time, but long enough to cause the wire to glow due to the heat. The burn-off circuit is turned on when the ignition switch is switched off after the engine has been operating long enough to achieve normal operating temperature.

KARMAN VORTEX SENSORS

In 1912, a Hungarian scientist named Theodore Van Karman observed that vortexes were created when air passed over a pointed surface. This type of sensor sends a sound wave through the turbulence created by incoming air passing through the sensor. Air mass is calculated based on the time required for the sound waves to cross the turbulent air passage.

There are two basic designs of Karman Vortex air flow sensors. The two types include the following:

- **Ultrasonic.** This type of sensor uses ultrasonic waves to detect the vortexes that are produced, and produce a digital (on-and-off) signal where frequency is proportional to the amount of air passing through the sensor. ● **SEE FIGURE 34–3.**
- **Pressure-type.** Chrysler uses a pressure-type Karman Vortex sensor that uses a pressure sensor to detect the vortexes. As the airflow through the sensor increases, so do the number of pressure variations. The electronics in the sensor convert these pressure variations to a square wave (digital DC voltage) signal, whose frequency is in proportion to the airflow through the sensor.

PCM USES FOR AIRFLOW SENSORS

The PCM uses the information from the airflow sensor for the following purposes:

- Airflow sensors are used mostly to determine the amount of fuel needed and base pulse-width numbers. The greater the mass of the incoming air, the longer the injectors are pulsed on.
- Airflow sensors back up the TP sensor in the event of a loss of signal or an inaccurate throttle position sensor signal. If the MAF sensor fails, then the PCM will calculate the fuel delivery needs of the engine based on throttle position and engine speed (RPM).

The Dirty MAF Sensor Story

The owner of a Buick Park Avenue equipped with a 3,800 V-6 engine complained that the engine would hesitate during acceleration, showed lack of power, and seemed to surge or miss at times. A visual inspection found everything to be like new, including a new air filter. There were no stored diagnostic trouble codes (DTCs). A look at the scan data showed airflow to be within the recommended 3 to 7 grams per second. A check of the frequency output showed the problem.

Idle frequency = 2.177 kHz (2,177 Hz)

Normal frequency at idle speed should be 2.37 to 2.52 kHz. Cleaning the hot wire of the MAF sensor restored proper operation. The sensor wire was covered with what looked like fine fibers, possibly from the replacement air filter.

Summary:

- **Complaint**—Customer stated that the engine hesitated when accelerating.
- **Cause**—Tests confirmed that the MAF sensor was was operating correctly but the frequency output at idle was not within the normal range.
- **Correction**—Cleaning the MAF sensor restored proper operation of the sensor and the engine now accelerates normally.

What Is Meant by a "High-Authority Sensor"?

A high-authority sensor is a sensor that has a major influence over the amount of fuel being delivered to the engine. For example, at engine start-up, the engine coolant temperature (ECT) sensor is a high-authority sensor and the oxygen sensor (O2S) is a low-authority sensor. However, as the engine reaches operating temperature, the oxygen sensor becomes a high-authority sensor and can greatly affect the amount of fuel being supplied to the engine. See the following chart:

High-Authority Sensors	Low-Authority Sensors
ECT (especially when the engine starts and is warming up)	IAT (intake air temperature) sensors modify and back up the ECT
O2S (after the engine reaches closed-loop operation)	TFT (transmission fluid temperature)
MAP	PRNDL (shift position sensor)
MAF	KS (knock sensor)
TP (high authority during acceleration and deceleration)	EFT (engine fuel temperature)

TESTING MASS AIRFLOW SENSORS

VISUAL INSPECTION Start the testing of a MAF sensor by performing a thorough visual inspection. Look at all the hoses that direct and send air, especially between the MAF sensor and the throttle body. Also check the electrical connector for the following:

- Corrosion
- Terminals that are bent or pushed out of the plastic connector
- Frayed wiring

MAF SENSOR OUTPUT TEST A digital multimeter, set to read DC volts, can be used to check the MAF sensor. See the chart that shows the voltage output compared with the grams per second of airflow through the sensor. Normal airflow is 3 to 7 grams per second. ● **SEE CHART 34-1.**

Analog MAF Sensor Grams per Second/ Voltage Chart	
GRAMS PER SECOND	**SENSOR VOLTAGE**
0	0.2
2	0.7
4	1.0 (typical idle value)
8	1.5
15	2.0
30	2.5
50	3.0
80	3.5
110	4.0
150	4.5
175	4.8

CHART 34-1

Chart showing the amount of air entering the engine in grams per second compared to the sensor output voltage.

FIGURE 34–4 Carefully check the hose between the MAF sensor and the throttle plate for cracks or splits that could create extra (false) air into the engine that is not measured by the MAF sensor.

CHECK THE SNORKEL TUBE HERE FOR CRACKS

 FREQUENTLY ASKED QUESTION

What Is False Air?

Airflow sensors and mass airflow (MAF) sensors are designed to measure *all* the air entering the engine. If an air inlet hose was loose or had a hole, extra air could enter the engine without being measured. This extra air is often called **false air**. ● SEE FIGURE 34–4.

NOTE: If the engine runs well in reverse, yet runs terrible in any forward gear, carefully look at the inlet hose for air leaks that would open when the engine torque moves the engine slightly on its mounts.

TAP TEST With the engine running at idle speed, *gently* tap the MAF sensor with the fingers of an open hand. If the engine stumbles or stalls, the MAF sensor is defective. This test is commonly called the **tap test**.

DIGITAL METER TEST OF A MAF SENSOR A digital multimeter can be used to measure the frequency (Hz) output of the sensor and compare the reading with specifications.

The frequency output and engine speed in RPM can also be plotted on a graph to check to see if the frequency and RPM are proportional, resulting in a straight line on the graph.

MAF SENSOR CONTAMINATION

Dirt, oil, silicon, or even spider webs can coat the sensing wire. Because it tends to insulate the sensing wire at low airflow rates, a contaminated sensor often overestimates the amount of air entering the engine at idle, and therefore causes the fuel system to go rich. At higher engine speeds near wide-open throttle (WOT), the contamination can cause the sensor to underestimate the amount of air entering the engine. As a result, the fuel system will go lean, causing spark knock and lack of power concerns. To check for contamination, check the fuel trim numbers.

If the fuel trim is negative (removing fuel) at idle, yet is positive (adding fuel) at higher engine speeds, a contaminated MAF sensor is a likely cause. Other tests for a contaminated MAF sensor are the following:

- At WOT, the grams per second, as read on a scan tool, should exceed 100.
- At WOT, the voltage, as read on a digital voltmeter, should exceed 4 volts for an analog sensor.
- At WOT, the frequency, as read on a meter or scan tool, should exceed 7 kHz for a digital sensor.

If the readings do not exceed these values, then the MAF sensor is contaminated.

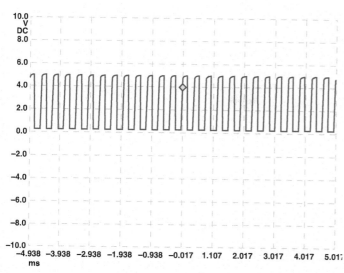

FIGURE 34–5 A scope display showing a normal Chevrolet Equinox MAF sensor at idle speed. the frequency is 2,600 Hertz (2.6 kHz).

MAF SENSOR SCOPE TESTING

A digital storage oscilloscope (DSO) can be used to monitor the operation of a MAF sensor. Connect the test leads to the signal wire and the sensor ground and following the scope instructions look for a consistent pattern that changes in frequency as the engine speed is increased. ● **SEE FIGURE 34–5**.

 TECH TIP

The Unplug It Test

If a sensor is defective yet produces a signal to the computer, the computer will often accept the reading and make the required changes in fuel delivery and spark advance. If, however, the sensor is not reading correctly, the computer will process this wrong information and perform an action assuming that information being supplied is accurate. "If in doubt, take it out."

If the engine operates better with a sensor unplugged, then suspect that the sensor is defective. A sensor that is not supplying the correct information is said to be *skewed*. The computer will not set a diagnostic trouble code for this condition because the computer can often not detect that the sensor is supplying wrong information.

MAF-RELATED DIAGNOSTIC TROUBLE CODES

The diagnostic trouble codes (DTCs) associated with the mass airflow and air vane sensors are as follows:

DIAGNOSTIC TROUBLE CODE	DESCRIPTION	POSSIBLE CAUSES
P0100	Mass or volume airflow circuit problems	■ Open or short in mass airflow circuit ■ Defective MAF sensor
P0101	Mass airflow circuit range problems	■ Defective MAF sensor (check for false air)
P0102	Mass airflow circuit low output	■ Defective MAF sensor ■ MAF sensor circuit open or shorted-to-ground ■ Open 12-volt supply voltage circuit
P0103	Mass airflow circuit high output	■ Defective MAF sensor ■ MAF sensor circuit shorted-to-voltage

1. A mass airflow sensor actually measures the density and amount of air flowing into the engine, which results in accurate engine control.

2. An air vane sensor measures the volume of the air, and the intake air temperature sensor is used by the PCM to calculate the mass of the air entering the engine.

3. A hot wire MAF sensor uses the electronics in the sensor itself to heat a wire 70°C above the temperature of the air entering the engine.

REVIEW QUESTIONS

1. How does a hot film MAF sensor work?

2. What change in the signal will occur if engine speed is increased?

3. How is a MAF sensor tested?

4. What is the purpose of a MAF sensor?

5. What are the types of mass air flow sensors?

CHAPTER QUIZ

1. A fuel-injection system that does not use a sensor to measure the amount (or mass) of air entering the engine is usually called a(n) _____ type of system.
   a. air vane-controlled
   b. speed density
   c. mass airflow
   d. hot wire

2. Which type of sensor uses a burn-off circuit?
   a. Hot wire MAF sensor
   b. Hot film MAF sensor
   c. Karman Vortex sensor
   d. Both a and b

3. The MAF sensor is used mostly to determine the amount of _____ to deliver to the engine.
   a. vacuum correction
   b. idle air
   c. spark advance
   d. fuel

4. Two technicians are discussing Karman Vortex sensors. Technician A says that they contain a burn-off circuit to keep them clean. Technician B says that they contain a movable vane. Which technician is correct?
   a. Technician A only
   b. Technician B only
   c. Both Technicians A and B
   d. Neither Technician A nor B

5. The typical MAF reading on a scan tool with the engine at idle speed and normal operating temperature is _____.
   a. 1 to 3 grams per second
   b. 3 to 7 grams per second
   c. 8 to 12 grams per second
   d. 14 to 24 grams per second

6. Two technicians are diagnosing a poorly running engine. There are no diagnostic trouble codes. When the MAF sensor is unplugged, the engine runs better. Technician A says that this means that the MAF is supplying incorrect airflow information to the PCM. Technician B says that this indicates that the PCM is defective. Which technician is correct?
   a. Technician A only
   b. Technician B only
   c. Both Technicians A and B
   d. Neither Technician A nor B

7. A MAF sensor on a General Motors 3,800 V-6 is being tested for contamination. Technician A says that the sensor should show over 100 grams per second on a scan tool display when the accelerator is depressed to WOT on a running engine. Technician B says that the output frequency should exceed 7,000 Hz when the accelerator pedal is depressed to WOT on a running engine. Which technician is correct?
   a. Technician A only
   b. Technician B only
   c. Both Technicians A and B
   d. Neither Technician A nor B

8. If the MAF sensor fails, the PCM uses _____ to calculate fuel delivery needs.
   a. MAP and throttle position
   b. RPM and throttle position
   c. throttle position and transmission RPM
   d. RPM alone

9. Air that enters the engine without passing through the airflow sensor is called _____.
   a. bypass air
   b. dirty air
   c. false air
   d. measured air

10. A P0102 DTC is being discussed. Technician A says that a sensor circuit shorted-to-ground can be the cause. Technician B says that an open sensor voltage supply circuit could be the cause. Which technician is correct?
    a. Technician A only
    b. Technician B only
    c. Both Technicians A and B
    d. Neither Technician A nor B

chapter 35
OXYGEN SENSORS

OXYGEN SENSORS

PURPOSE AND FUNCTION Automotive computer systems use a sensor in the exhaust system to measure the oxygen content of the exhaust. These sensors are called **oxygen sensors (O2S)**. The oxygen sensor is installed in the exhaust manifold or located downstream from the manifold in the exhaust pipe. ● **SEE FIGURE 35–1.**

The oxygen sensor is directly in the path of the exhaust gas stream where it monitors oxygen levels in both the exhaust stream and the ambient air. A **zirconia** oxygen sensor is made of **zirconium dioxide (ZrO2)**, an electrically conductive material capable of generating a small voltage in the presence of oxygen.

NARROW BAND A conventional zirconia oxygen sensor (O2S) is only able to detect if the exhaust is richer or leaner than 14.7:1. A conventional oxygen sensor is therefore referred to as the following:

- *Two-step sensor*, which is either rich or lean
- *Narrow-band sensor*, which informs the PCM whether the exhaust is rich or lean only

The voltage value where a zirconia oxygen sensor switches from rich to lean or from lean to rich is 0.45 V (450 mV).

- Above 0.45 V = rich
- Below 0.45 V = lean
- ● **SEE FIGURE 35–2.**

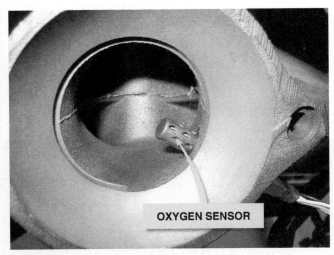

FIGURE 35–1 Many oxygen sensors are located in the exhaust manifold near its outlet so that the sensor can detect the air-fuel mixture in the exhaust stream for all cylinders that feed into the manifold.

CONSTRUCTION A typical zirconia oxygen sensor has the sensing element in the shape of a thimble; therefore, it is often referred to as one of the following:

- **Thimble design**
- **Cup design**
- **Finger design**
- ● **SEE FIGURE 35–3.**

A typical zirconia oxygen sensor has a heater inside the thimble and does not touch the inside of the sensor. The sensor is similar to a battery that has two electrodes and an electrolyte. The electrolyte is solid and is the zirconia (zirconium dioxide). There are also two porous platinum electrodes, which have the following functions:

- **Exhaust side electrode** is exposed to the exhaust stream.
- **Ambient side electrode** is exposed to outside (ambient) air and is the **signal electrode**, also called the **reference electrode**. ● **SEE FIGURE 35–4.**

The electrolyte (zirconia) is able to conduct electrons as follows:

- If the exhaust is rich, O_2 from the reference (inner) electrode wants to flow to the exhaust side electrode, which results in the generation of a voltage.
- If the exhaust is lean, O_2 flow is not needed. As a result, there is little if any electron movement and, therefore, no voltage is produced.

OPERATION Exhaust from the engine passes through the end of the sensor where the gases contact the outer side of the thimble. Atmospheric air enters through the other end of the sensor or through the wire of the sensor and contacts the inner side of the thimble. The inner and outer surfaces of the thimble are plated with platinum. The inner surface becomes a negative electrode and the outer surface is a positive electrode. The atmosphere contains a relatively constant 21% of oxygen. Exhaust gases created by burning a rich air-fuel mixture contain little oxygen. Exhaust gases from burning a lean air-fuel mixture contain more oxygen.

Negatively charged oxygen ions are drawn to the thimble where they collect on both the inner and outer surfaces.

Because the oxygen present in the atmosphere exceeds that in the exhaust gases, the air side of the thimble draws more negative oxygen ions than the exhaust side. The difference between the two sides creates an electrical potential, or voltage. When the concentration of oxygen on the exhaust side of the thimble is low, a high voltage (0.60 to 1.0 V) is generated between the electrodes. As the oxygen concentration on the exhaust side increases, the voltage generated drops low (0.0 to 0.3 V).

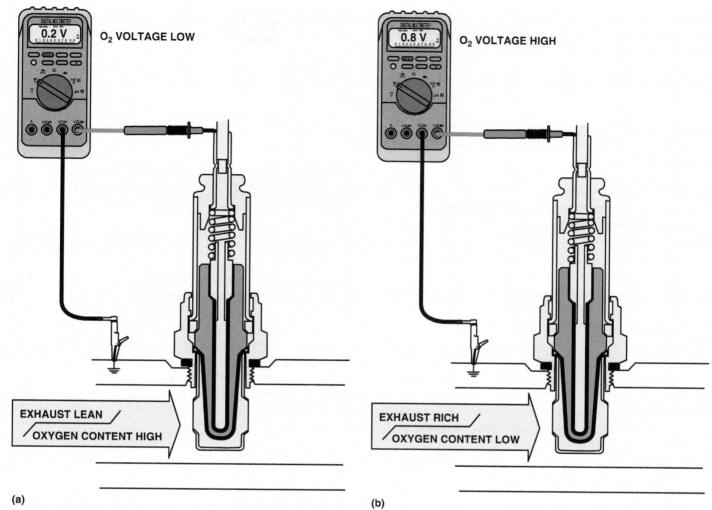

O₂ VOLTAGE LOW

O₂ VOLTAGE HIGH

EXHAUST LEAN / OXYGEN CONTENT HIGH

EXHAUST RICH / OXYGEN CONTENT LOW

(a)

(b)

FIGURE 35–2 (a) When the exhaust is lean, the output of a zirconia oxygen sensor is below 450 mV. (b) When the exhaust is rich, the output of a zirconia oxygen sensor is above 450 mV.

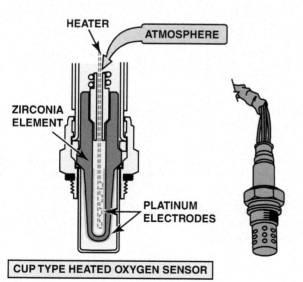

HEATER

ATMOSPHERE

ZIRCONIA ELEMENT

PLATINUM ELECTRODES

CUP TYPE HEATED OXYGEN SENSOR

FIGURE 35–3 Most conventional zirconia oxygen sensors and some wide-band oxygen sensors use the cup (finger) type of design.

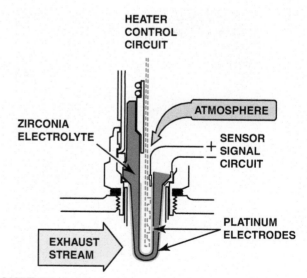

HEATER CONTROL CIRCUIT

ATMOSPHERE

ZIRCONIA ELECTROLYTE

SENSOR SIGNAL CIRCUIT

EXHAUST STREAM

PLATINUM ELECTRODES

FIGURE 35–4 A typical heated zirconia oxygen sensor, showing the sensor signal circuit that uses the outer (exhaust) electrode as the negative and the ambient air side electrode as the positive.

An O2S does not send a voltage signal until its tip reaches a temperature of about 572°F (300°C). Also, oxygen sensors provide their fastest response to mixture changes at about 1,472°F (800°C). When the engine starts and the O2S is cold, the PCM operates the engine in the open-loop mode, drawing on prerecorded data in the PROM for fuel control on a cold engine, or when O2S output is not within certain limits.

If the exhaust contains very little oxygen, the PCM assumes that the intake charge is rich (too much fuel) and reduces fuel delivery. However, when the oxygen level is high, the PCM assumes that the intake charge is lean (not enough fuel) and increases fuel delivery. ● SEE FIGURE 35–5.

There are several different designs of oxygen sensors, including the following:

- **One-wire oxygen sensor.** The single wire of the one-wire oxygen sensor is the O2S signal wire. The ground for the O2S is through the shell and threads of the sensor and through the exhaust manifold.

- **Two-wire oxygen sensor.** The two-wire sensor has a signal wire and a ground wire for the O2S.

- **Three-wire oxygen sensor.** The three-wire sensor design uses an electric resistance heater to help get the O2S up to temperature more quickly and to help keep the sensor at operating temperature even at idle speeds. The three wires include the O2S signal, the power, and ground for the heater.

- **Four-wire oxygen sensor.** The four-wire sensor is a **heated O2S (HO2S)** that uses an O2S signal wire and signal ground. The other two wires are the power and ground for the heater.

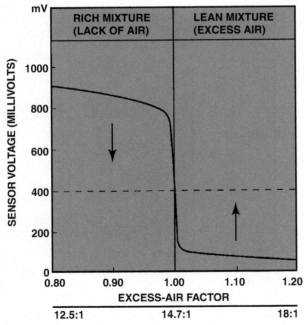

FIGURE 35–5 The oxygen sensor provides a quick response at the stoichiometric air-fuel ratio of 14.7:1.

HEATER CIRCUITS The heater circuit on conventional oxygen sensors requires 0.8 to 2.0 amperes and keeps the sensor at about 600°F (315°C).

A wide-band oxygen sensor operates at a higher temperature than a conventional HO2S, from 1,200°F to 1,400°F (650°C to 760°C). The amount of electrical current needed for a wide-band oxygen sensor is about 8 to 10 amperes.

TITANIA OXYGEN SENSOR

The **titania** (titanium dioxide) oxygen sensor does not produce a voltage, but rather changes resistance due to the presence of oxygen in the exhaust. All titania oxygen sensors use a four-terminal variable resistance unit with a heating element. A titania sensor samples exhaust air only and uses a reference voltage from the PCM. Titania oxide oxygen sensors use a 14-mm thread and are not interchangeable with zirconia oxygen sensors, which use an 18 mm thread. One volt is applied to the sensor; the changing resistance of the titania oxygen sensor changes the voltage of the sensor circuit. As with a zirconia oxygen sensor, the voltage signal is above 450 mV when the exhaust is rich and low (below 450 mV) when the exhaust is lean.

? FREQUENTLY ASKED QUESTION

What Happens to the Bias Voltage?

Some vehicle manufacturers, such as General Motors Corporation have the PCM apply 450 mV (0.45 V) to the O2S signal wire. This voltage is called the **bias voltage** and represents the threshold voltage for the transition from rich to lean.

This bias voltage is displayed on a scan tool when the ignition switch is turned on with the engine off. When the engine is started, the O2S becomes warm enough to produce a usable voltage, and bias voltage "disappears" as the O2S responds to a rich and lean mixture. What happens to the bias voltage that the PCM applies to the O2S? The voltage from the O2S simply overcomes the very weak voltage signal from the PCM. This bias voltage is so weak that even a 20 megohm impedance DMM will affect the strength enough to cause the voltage to drop to 426 mV. Other meters with only 10 megohms of impedance will cause the bias voltage to read less than 400 mV.

Therefore, even though the O2S voltage is relatively low powered, it is more than strong enough to override the very weak bias voltage the PCM sends to the O2S.

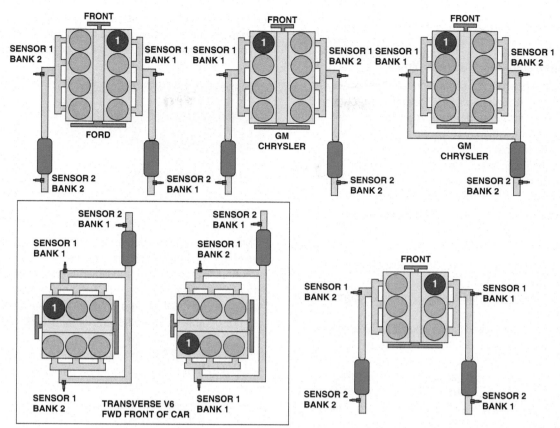

FIGURE 35–6 Number and label designations for oxygen sensors. Bank 1 is the bank where cylinder 1 is located.

The Chevrolet Pickup Truck Story

The owner of a Chevrolet pickup truck complained that the engine ran terribly. It would hesitate and surge, yet there were no diagnostic trouble codes (DTCs). After hours of troubleshooting, the technician discovered while talking to the owner that the problem started after the transmission had been repaired. However, the transmission shop said that the problem was an engine problem and not related to the transmission.

A thorough visual inspection revealed that the front and rear oxygen sensor connectors had been switched. The PCM was trying to compensate for an air-fuel mixture condition that did not exist. Reversing the O2S connectors restored proper operation of the truck.

Summary:

- **Complaint**–Vehicle owner complained that the pickup truck ran terribly.
- **Cause**–During a previous repair, the upstream and downstream oxygen sensor connectors were reversed.
- **Correction**–The connectors were moved to their correct locations, which restored proper engine operation.

Where Is HO2S1?

Oxygen sensors are numbered according to their location in the engine. On a V-type engine, heated oxygen sensor number 1 (HO2S1) is located in the exhaust system upstream of the catalytic converter on the side of the engine where cylinder 1 is located.
● **SEE FIGURE 35–6.**

PCM USES OF THE OXYGEN SENSOR

FUEL CONTROL The amount of fuel delivered to an engine is determined by the powertrain control module (PCM) based on inputs from the engine coolant temperature (ECT), throttle position (TP) sensor, and others until the oxygen sensor is capable of supplying a usable signal. When the PCM alone is determining the amount of fuel needed, it is called **open-loop** operation. As soon as the oxygen sensor (O2S) is capable of supplying rich and lean signals, PCM adjustments can be made to fine-tune the correct air-fuel mixture. This checking and adjusting of the PCM is called **closed-loop** operation.

The Oxygen Sensor Is Lying to You

A technician was trying to solve a driveability problem with an older V-6 passenger car. The car idled roughly, hesitated, and accelerated poorly. A thorough visual inspection did not indicate problems and there were no diagnostic trouble codes stored.

The technician checked the oxygen sensor activity using a DMM. The voltage stayed above 600 mV most of the time. If the technician removed a large vacuum hose, the oxygen sensor voltage would temporarily drop to below 450 mV and return to a reading of over 600 mV. Remember:

- High O2S readings = rich exhaust (low O_2 content in the exhaust)
- Low O2S readings = lean exhaust (high O_2 content in the exhaust)

As part of a thorough visual inspection, the technician removed and inspected the spark plugs. All the spark plugs were white, indicating a lean mixture, not the rich mixture that the oxygen sensor was indicating. The high O2S reading signaled the PCM to reduce the amount of fuel, resulting in an excessively lean operation.

After replacing the oxygen sensor, the engine ran great. But what killed the oxygen sensor? The technician finally learned from the owner that the head gasket had been replaced over a year ago. The silicate and phosphate additives in the antifreeze coolant had coated the oxygen sensor. Because the oxygen sensor was coated, the oxygen content of the exhaust could not be detected, resulting in a false rich signal from the oxygen sensor.

Summary:

- **Complaint**–Vehicle owner complained that the car equipped with a V-6 engine ran terribly.
- **Cause**–The oxygen sensor was contaminated by the additives in the coolant caused by a previously repaired head gasket failure.
- **Correction**–Replacing the oxygen sensors restored proper engine operation.

The upstream oxygen sensors are among the high-authority sensors used for fuel control while operating in closed loop. Before the oxygen sensors are hot enough to give accurate exhaust oxygen information to the PCM, fuel control is determined by other sensors and the anticipated injector pulse width determined by those sensors. After the control system achieves closed-loop status, the oxygen sensor provides feedback to actual exhaust gas oxygen content.

FUEL TRIM The **fuel trim** numbers are determined from the signals by the oxygen sensor(s). If the engine has been operating too lean, short-term and long-term fuel time programming inside the PCM can cause an increase in the commanded injector pulse width to bring the air-fuel mixture back into the proper range. Fuel trim can be negative (subtracting fuel) or positive (adding fuel).

OXYGEN SENSOR DIAGNOSIS

PCM SYSTEM TESTS The oxygen sensors are used for diagnosis of other systems and components. For example, the exhaust gas recirculation (EGR) system is tested by the PCM, by commanding the EGR valve to open during the test. Some PCMs determine whether enough exhaust gas flows into the engine by looking at the oxygen sensor response (fuel trim numbers). The upstream and downstream oxygen sensors are also used to determine the efficiency of the catalytic converter. Therefore, if a fault occurs with an oxygen sensor, the PCM may not be able to test other systems. ● **SEE FIGURE 35–7**.

VISUAL INSPECTION Whenever an oxygen sensor is replaced, the old sensor should be carefully inspected to help determine the cause of the failure. This is an important step because if the cause of the failure is not discovered, it could lead to another sensor failure.

Inspection may reveal the following:

1. Black sooty deposits usually indicate a rich air-fuel mixture.
2. White chalky deposits are characteristic of silica contamination. Usual causes for this type of sensor failure include silica deposits in the fuel or a technician having used the wrong type of silicone sealant during the servicing of the engine.

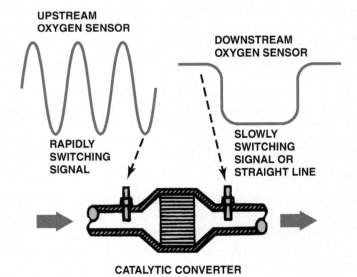

FIGURE 35–7 The OBD-II catalytic converter monitor compares the signals of the upstream and downstream oxygen sensor to determine converter efficiency.

The Missing Ford

A Ford was being analyzed for poor engine operation. The engine ran perfectly during the following conditions:

1. Engine cold or operating in open loop
2. Engine at idle
3. Engine operating at or near wide-open throttle

After hours of troubleshooting, the technician determined the cause to be a poor ground connection for the oxygen sensor. The engine ran okay during times when the PCM ignored the oxygen sensor. Unfortunately, the service technician did not have a definite plan during the diagnostic process and as a result checked and replaced many unnecessary parts. An oxygen sensor test early in the diagnostic procedure would have indicated that the oxygen (O2S) signal was not correct. The poor ground caused the oxygen sensor voltage level to be too high, indicating to the PCM that the mixture was too rich. The PCM then subtracted fuel, which caused the engine to miss and run roughly as the result of the now too lean air-fuel mixture.

Summary:

- **Complaint**–Vehicle owner complained of poor engine operation except at idle and at wide-open throttle conditions.
- **Cause**–A poor ground connection for the oxygen sensor cause the O2S to read incorrectly.
- **Correction**–The ground connection was cleaned and this restored proper engine operation under all operating conditions.

3. White sandy or gritty deposits are characteristic of antifreeze (ethylene glycol) contamination. A defective cylinder head or intake manifold gasket could be the cause, or a cracked cylinder head or engine block. Antifreeze may also cause the oxygen sensor to become green as a result of the dye used in antifreeze.

4. Dark brown deposits indicate excessive oil consumption. Possible causes include a defective positive crankcase ventilation (PCV) system or a mechanical engine problem, such as defective valve stem seals or piston rings.

DIGITAL VOLTMETER TESTING
The oxygen sensor can be checked for proper operation using a digital high-impedance voltmeter.

1. With the engine off, connect the red lead of the meter to the oxygen sensor signal wire and the black meter lead to a good engine ground. ● **SEE FIGURE 35–8**.

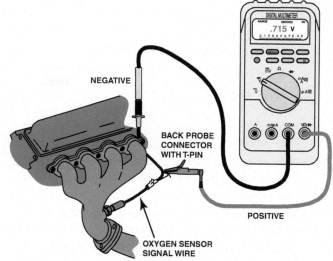

FIGURE 35–8 Testing an oxygen sensor using a DMM set on DC volts. With the engine operating in closed loop, the oxygen voltage should read over 800 mV and lower than 200 mV and be constantly fluctuating.

2. Start the engine and allow it to reach closed-loop operation.

3. In closed-loop operation, the oxygen sensor voltage should be constantly changing as the fuel mixture is being controlled.

The results should be interpreted as follows:

- If the oxygen sensor fails to respond, and its voltage remains at about 450 mV, the sensor may be defective and require replacement. Before replacing the oxygen sensor, check the manufacturer's recommended procedures.

- If the oxygen sensor reads high all the time (above 550 mV), the fuel system could be supplying too rich a fuel mixture or the oxygen sensor may be contaminated. An oxygen sensor reading that is high could be due to other things besides a rich air-fuel mixture. When the O2S reads high as a result of other factors besides a rich mixture, it is often called a **false rich** indication.

TECH TIP

Do Not Solder Oxygen Sensor Wires

Oxygen sensors must have outside oxygen to compare with the oxygen content in the exhaust. Most oxygen sensors breathe through the signal wire and, if soldered, would block the flow of outside air to the sensor. If a replacement oxygen sensor is used, always use the factory replacement, using the original connectors or a crimp-and-seal connector that will seal out any moisture and still allow air to flow through the connector.

False rich indications (high O2S readings) can be attributed to the following:

- Contaminated O2S due to additives in the engine coolant or due to silicon poisoning
- A stuck open EGR valve (especially at idle)
- A spark plug wire too close to the oxygen sensor signal wire, which can induce a higher than normal voltage in the signal wire, thereby indicating to the PCM a false rich condition
- A loose oxygen sensor ground connection, which can cause a higher than normal voltage and a false rich signal
- A break or contamination of the wiring and its connectors, which could prevent reference oxygen from reaching the oxygen sensor, resulting in a false rich indication. (All oxygen sensors require an oxygen supply inside the sensor itself for reference to be able to sense exhaust gas oxygen.)

If the oxygen sensor voltage remains low (below 350 mV), the oxygen sensor itself could be bad or the fuel system could be supplying too lean a fuel mixture. Check for a vacuum leak or partially clogged fuel injector(s). Before replacing the oxygen sensor, check the manufacturer's recommended procedures. If an oxygen sensor reads low as a result of a factor besides a lean mixture, it is often called a **false lean** indication.

False lean indications (low O2S readings) can be attributed to the following:

1. **Ignition misfires.** An ignition misfire due to a defective spark plug wire, fouled spark plug, and so forth, causes no burned air and fuel to be exhausted past the O2S. The O2S "sees" the oxygen (not the unburned gasoline) and the O2S voltage is low.

2. **Exhaust leak in front of the O2S.** An exhaust leak between the engine and the oxygen sensor causes outside oxygen to be drawn into the exhaust and past the O2S. This oxygen is "read" by the O2S and produces a lower than normal voltage. The PCM interprets the lower than normal voltage signal from the O2S as meaning that the air-fuel mixture is lean. The PCM will cause the fuel system to deliver a richer air-fuel mixture.

3. **Spark plug misfire.** The PCM does not know that the extra oxygen going past the oxygen sensor is not due to a lean air-fuel mixture. The PCM commands a richer mixture, which could cause the spark plugs to foul, increasing the rate of misfiring.

MIN/MAX TESTING A digital meter set on DC volts can be used to record the minimum and maximum voltage with the engine running. A good oxygen sensor should be able to produce a value of less than 300 mV and a maximum voltage above 800 mV. ● **SEE FIGURE 35–9.**

Replace any oxygen sensor that fails to go above 700 mV or lower than 300 mV. ● **SEE CHART 35–1.**

Why Does the Oxygen Sensor Voltage Read 5 Volts on Many Chrysler Vehicles?

Many Chrysler vehicles apply a 5-volt reference to the signal wire of the oxygen sensor. The purpose of this voltage is to allow the PCM to detect if the oxygen sensor signal circuit is open or grounded.

- If the voltage on the signal wire is 4.5 volts or more, the PCM assumes that the sensor is open.
- If the voltage on the signal wire is zero, the PCM assumes that the sensor is shorted-to-ground.

If either condition exists, the PCM can set a diagnostic trouble code (DTC).

TECH TIP

The Key On, Engine Off Oxygen Sensor Test

This test works on General Motors vehicles and may work on others if the PCM applies a bias voltage to the oxygen sensors. Zirconia oxygen sensors become more electrically conductive as they get hot. To perform this test, be sure that the vehicle has not run for several hours.

STEP 1 Connect a scan tool and get the display ready to show oxygen sensor data.

STEP 2 Key the engine on *without* starting the engine. The heater in the oxygen sensor will start heating the sensor.

STEP 3 Observe the voltage of the oxygen sensor. The applied bias voltage of 450 mV should slowly decrease for all oxygen sensors as they become more electrically conductive as the bias voltage is flowing to ground.

STEP 4 A good oxygen sensor should indicate a voltage of less than 100 mV after three minutes. Any sensor that displays a higher than usual voltage or seems to stay higher longer than the others could be defective or skewed high.

SCAN TOOL TESTING A good oxygen sensor should sense the oxygen content and change voltage outputs rapidly. How fast an oxygen sensor switches from high (above 450 mV) to low (below 350 mV) is measured as frequency, or the number of times the voltage switches per second.

NOTE: On a fuel-injected engine at 2000 engine RPM, 1 to 5 Hz (one to five switches per second) is normal.

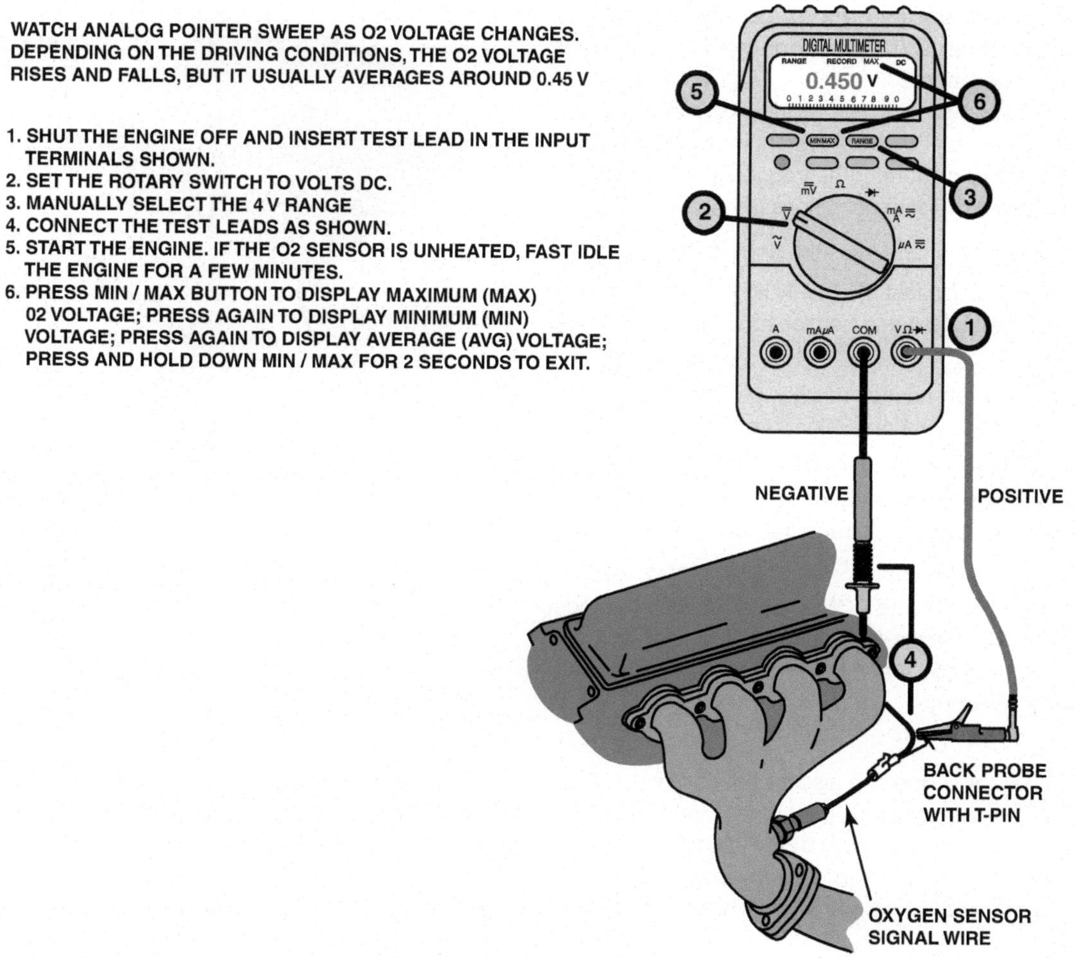
WATCH ANALOG POINTER SWEEP AS O2 VOLTAGE CHANGES. DEPENDING ON THE DRIVING CONDITIONS, THE O2 VOLTAGE RISES AND FALLS, BUT IT USUALLY AVERAGES AROUND 0.45 V
1. SHUT THE ENGINE OFF AND INSERT TEST LEAD IN THE INPUT TERMINALS SHOWN.
2. SET THE ROTARY SWITCH TO VOLTS DC.
3. MANUALLY SELECT THE 4 V RANGE
4. CONNECT THE TEST LEADS AS SHOWN.
5. START THE ENGINE. IF THE O2 SENSOR IS UNHEATED, FAST IDLE THE ENGINE FOR A FEW MINUTES.
6. PRESS MIN / MAX BUTTON TO DISPLAY MAXIMUM (MAX) 02 VOLTAGE; PRESS AGAIN TO DISPLAY MINIMUM (MIN) VOLTAGE; PRESS AGAIN TO DISPLAY AVERAGE (AVG) VOLTAGE; PRESS AND HOLD DOWN MIN / MAX FOR 2 SECONDS TO EXIT.
DIGITAL MULTIMETER
0.450 V
NEGATIVE
POSITIVE
BACK PROBE CONNECTOR WITH T-PIN
OXYGEN SENSOR SIGNAL WIRE

FIGURE 35–9 Using a digital multimeter to test an oxygen sensor using the MIN/MAX record function of the meter.

MIN/MAX OXYGEN SENSOR TEST CHART

MINIMUM VOLTAGE	MAXIMUM VOLTAGE	AVERAGE VOLTAGE	TEST RESULTS
Below 200 mV	Above 800 mV	400–500 mV	Oxygen sensor is okay.
Above 200 mV	Any reading	400–500 mV	Oxygen sensor is defective.
Any reading	Below 800 mV	400–500 mV	Oxygen sensor is defective.
Below 200 mV	Above 800 mV	Below 400 mV	System is operating lean.*
Below 200 mV	Below 800 mV	Below 400 mV	System is operating lean. (Add propane to the intake air to see if the oxygen sensor reacts. If not, the sensor is defective.)
Below 200 mV	Above 800 mV	Above 500 mV	System is operating rich.
Above 200 mV	Above 800 mV	Above 500 mV	System is operating rich. (Remove a vacuum hose to see if the oxygen sensor reacts. If not, the sensor is defective.)

CHART 35–1

The test results of using a digital meter set to read minimum and maximum values while testing a narrow-band oxygen sensor.
* Check for an exhaust leak upstream from the O2S or ignition misfire that can cause a false lean indication before further diagnosis.

Using a scan tool, observe the oxygen sensor voltages with the engine running at 2000 rpm. Look for numbers higher than 800 mV and lower than 200 mV.

If the frequency of switching is low, the oxygen sensor may be contaminated, or the fuel delivery system is delivering a constant rich or lean air-fuel mixture. If the frequency of switching is higher than 5 Hz, look for misfire conditions.

1. Connect the scan tool and start the engine.

2. Operate the engine at a fast idle (2,500 RPM) for two minutes to allow time for the oxygen sensor to warm to operating temperature.

3. Observe the oxygen sensor activity on the scan tool to verify closed-loop operation. Select the "snapshot" mode, hold the engine speed steady, and start recording.

4. Play back snapshot and place a mark beside each range of oxygen sensor voltage for each frame of the snapshot.

A good oxygen sensor and PCM should result in the most snapshot values at both ends (0 to 300 mV and 600 to 1,000 mV). If most of the readings are in the middle, the oxygen sensor is not working correctly.

SCOPE TESTING A scope can also be used to test an oxygen sensor. Connect the scope to the signal wire and ground for the sensor (if it is so equipped). ● **SEE FIGURE 35–10**.

With the engine operating in closed loop, the voltage signal of the sensor should be constantly changing. ● **SEE FIGURE 35–11**.

Check for rapid switching from rich to lean and lean to rich and change between once every two seconds and five times per second (0.5 to 5.0 Hz).

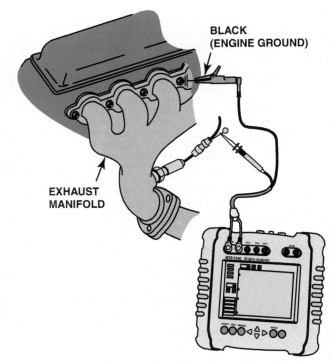

FIGURE 35–10 Connecting a handheld digital storage oscilloscope to an oxygen sensor signal wire. Check the instructions for the scope as some require the use of a filter to be installed in the test lead to reduce electromagnetic interference that can affect the oxygen sensor waveform.

NOTE: General Motors warns not to base the diagnosis of an oxygen sensor problem solely on its scope pattern. The varying voltage output of an oxygen sensor can easily be mistaken for a fault in the sensor itself, rather than a fault in the fuel delivery system.

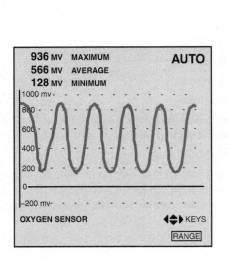

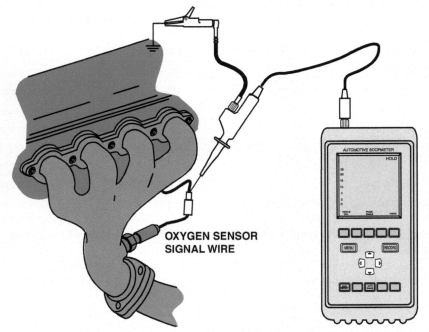

FIGURE 35–11 The waveform of a good oxygen sensor as displayed on a digital storage oscilloscope (DSO). Note that the maximum reading is above 800 mV and the minimum reading is less than 200 mV.

POST-CATALYTIC CONVERTER OXYGEN SENSOR TESTING

The oxygen sensor located behind the catalytic converter is used on OBD-II vehicles to monitor converter efficiency. A changing air-fuel mixture is required for the most efficient operation of the converter. If the converter is working correctly, the oxygen content after the converter should be fairly constant.
● **SEE FIGURE 35–12**.

The post-catalytic converter oxygen sensor also is used to modify the amount of fuel delivered to the engine to allow the converter to work efficiently. If, for example, the rear oxygen sensor voltage stayed high, the PCM will try to increase the amount of oxygen entering the converter by leaning the air-fuel mixture to the engine. This process is often called the target upstream fuel trim. Therefore, instead of the PCM commanding a target air-fuel mixture of 14.7:1, the new target may specify an air-fuel ratio of 14.9:1 or slightly leaner than normal to help provide a little extra oxygen for use by the catalytic converter. This target air-fuel ratio or fuel trim is displayed on scan tools.

TECH TIP

The Propane Oxygen Sensor Test

Adding propane to the air inlet of a running engine is an excellent way to check if the oxygen sensor is able to react to changes in air-fuel mixture. Follow these steps in performing the propane trick:

1. Connect a digital storage oscilloscope to the oxygen sensor signal wire.
2. Start and operate the engine until it reaches operating temperature and is in closed-loop fuel control.
3. While watching the scope display, add some propane to the air inlet. The scope display should read full rich (over 800 mV).
4. Shut off the propane. The waveform should drop to less than 200 mV (0.2 V).
5. Quickly add some propane while the oxygen sensor is reading low and watch for a rapid transition to rich. The transition should occur in less than 100 milliseconds (ms).

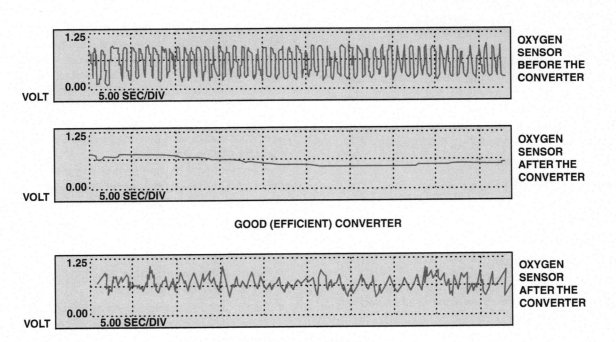

GOOD (EFFICIENT) CONVERTER

BAD (INEFFICIENT) CONVERTER

FIGURE 35–12 The post-catalytic converter oxygen sensor should display very little activity if the catalytic converter is efficient.

How Could Using Silicone Sealer on a Valve Cover Gasket Affect the Oxygen Sensor?

The wrong type of silicone **room temperature vulcanization (RTV)** sealer on a valve cover gasket gives off harmful silica fumes during the curing process. These fumes enter the crankcase area by way of the oil drainback holes in the cylinder head, as well as through pushrod openings and other passages in the engine. During engine operation, these fumes are drawn into the intake manifold through the positive crankcase ventilation (PCV) system and are burned in the engine. The harmful silica then exits through the exhaust system, where the contamination affects the oxygen sensor.

NOTE: Be careful not to spray any silicone lubricant near the engine vacuum, which might draw the fumes into the engine and cause silica damage to the oxygen sensor.

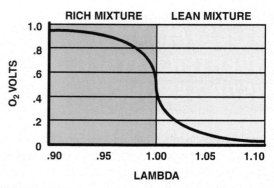

FIGURE 35–13 A conventional zirconia oxygen sensor can only reset to exhaust mixtures that are richer or leaner than 14.7:1 (lambda 1.00).

PURPOSE AND FUNCTION A wide-band oxygen sensor is capable of supplying air-fuel ratio information to the PCM over a much broader range. Compared with a conventional zirconia oxygen sensor, the wide-band oxygen sensor has the following features.

1. The ability to detect exhaust air-fuel ratio from as rich as 10:1 to as lean as 23:1 in some cases
2. Cold start activity within as little as 10 seconds

PLANAR DESIGN In 1998, Bosch introduced a wide-band oxygen sensor that is flat and thin (1.5 mm or 0.006 inch), known as a planar design and not in the shape of a thimble as previously constructed. Now several manufacturers produce a similar **planar** design wide-band oxygen sensor. Its thin design makes it easier to heat than older styles of oxygen sensors and, as a result, it can achieve closed loop in less than 10 seconds. This fast heating, called **light-off time (LOT)**, helps improve fuel economy and reduces cold-start exhaust emissions. The type of construction is not noticed by the technician, nor does it affect the testing procedures.

A conventional oxygen sensor can also be constructed using a planar design instead of the thimble-type design. A planar design has the following features:

- The elements including the zirconia electrolyte and the two electrodes and heater are stacked together in a flat-type design.
- It allows faster warm-up because the heater is in direct contact with the other elements.
- Planar oxygen sensors are the most commonly used. Some planar designs are used as a conventional narrow-band oxygen sensor.

The sandwich-type designs of the planar style of oxygen sensor have the same elements and operate the same, but are stacked in the following way from the exhaust side to the ambient air side:

Exhaust stream

Outer electrode

Zirconia (Zr_2) (electrolyte)

Inner electrode (reference or signal)

WIDE-BAND OXYGEN SENSORS

TERMINOLOGY **Wide-band oxygen sensors** have been used since 1992 on some Hondas. Today, they are used by most vehicle manufacturers to ensure that the exhaust emissions can meet the current standard. Wide-band oxygen sensors have various names, depending on the vehicle and/or oxygen sensor manufacturer, including the following:

- Wide-band oxygen sensor
- Broadband oxygen sensor
- Wide-range oxygen sensor
- Air-fuel ratio (AFR) sensor
- Wide-range air-fuel (WRAF) sensor
- Lean-air fuel (LAF) sensor
- Air-fuel (AF) sensor

Wide-band oxygen sensors are also manufactured in dual cell and single cell designs.

INTRODUCTION A conventional zirconia oxygen sensor reacts to an air-fuel mixture that is either richer or leaner than 14.7:1. This means that the sensor cannot be used to detect the exact air-fuel mixture. ●**SEE FIGURE 35–13**.

The need for more stringent exhaust emission standards, such as the national low emission vehicle (NLEV), plus the ultra low emission vehicle (ULEV) and the super ultra low emission vehicle (SULEV) require more accurate fuel control than can be provided by a traditional oxygen sensor.

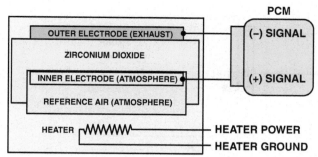

FIGURE 35–14 A planar design zirconia oxygen sensor places all of the elements together, which allows the sensor to reach operating temperature quickly.

Outside (ambient) air

Heater

● **SEE FIGURE 35–14**.

Another name for a conventional oxygen sensor is a **Nernst cell**, named for Walther Nernst, 1864–1941, a German physicist known for his work in electrochemistry.

DUAL CELL PLANAR WIDE-BAND SENSOR OPERATION

CONSTRUCTION In a conventional zirconia oxygen sensor, a bias or reference voltage can be applied to the two platinum electrodes, and then oxygen ions can be forced (pumped) from the ambient reference air side to the exhaust side of the sensor. If the polarity is reversed, the oxygen ion can be forced to travel in the opposite direction.

A **dual cell** planar-type wide-band oxygen sensor is made like a conventional planar O2S, or Nernst cell. Above the Nernst cell is another zirconia layer with two electrodes, called the **pump cell**. The two cells share a common ground, called the **reference**. There are two internal chambers:

■ The air reference chamber is exposed to ambient air.

■ The diffusion chamber is exposed to the exhaust gases.

Platinum electrodes are on both sides of the zirconia electrolyte elements, which separate the air reference chamber and the exhaust exposed diffusion chamber.

OPERATION The basic principle of operation of a typical wide-band oxygen sensor is that it uses a positive or negative voltage signal to keep a balance between two sensors. Oxygen sensors do not measure the quantity of free oxygen in the exhaust. Instead, oxygen sensors produce a voltage that is based on the ion flow between the platinum electrodes of the sensor to maintain a stoichiometric balance.

For example,

■ If there is a lean exhaust, there is oxygen in the exhaust and the ion flow from the ambient side to the exhaust side is low.

■ If there is rich exhaust, the ion flow is increased to help maintain balance between the ambient air side and the exhaust side of the sensor.

The PCM can apply a small current to the pump cell electrodes, which causes oxygen ions through the zirconia into or out of the diffusion chamber. The PCM pumps O_2 ions in and out of the diffusion chamber to bring the voltage back to 0.45 V, using the pump cell.

The operation of a wide-band oxygen sensor is best described by looking at what occurs when the exhaust is stoichiometric, rich, and lean. ● **SEE FIGURE 35–15**.

STOICHIOMETRIC

■ When the exhaust is at stoichiometric (14.7:1 air-fuel ratio), the voltage of the Nernst cell is 450 mV (0.45 V).

■ The voltage between the diffusion chamber and the air reference chamber changes from 0.45 V. This voltage will be:

■ Higher if the exhaust is rich

■ Lower if the exhaust is lean

The reference voltage remains constant, usually at 2.5 V, but can vary depending on the year, make, and model of vehicle and the type of sensor. Typical reference voltages include the following:

■ 2.2 V

■ 2.5 V

■ 2.7 V

■ 3.3 V

■ 3.6 V

RICH EXHAUST. When the exhaust is rich, the voltage between the common (reference) electrode and the Nernst cell electrode that is exposed to ambient air is higher than 0.45 V. The PCM applies a negative current in milliamperes to the pump cell electrode to bring the circuit back into balance. ● **SEE FIGURE 35–16**.

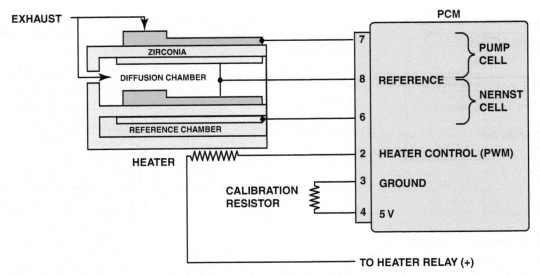

FIGURE 35–15 The reference electrodes are shared by the Nernst cell and the pump cell.

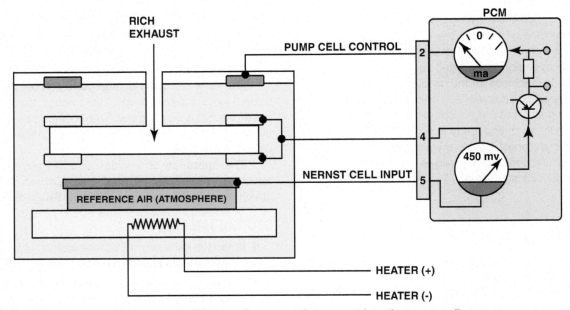

FIGURE 35–16 When the exhaust is rich, the PCM applies a negative current into the pump cell.

LEAN EXHAUST. When the exhaust is lean, the voltage between the common (reference) electrode and the Nernst cell electrode is lower than 0.45 V. The PCM applies a positive current in milliamperes to the pump cell to bring the circuit back into balance. ● **SEE FIGURE 35–17.**

DUAL CELL DIAGNOSIS

SCAN TOOL DIAGNOSIS Most service information specifies that a scan tool be used to check the wide-band oxygen sensor, because the PCM performs tests of the unit and can identify faults. However, even wide-band oxygen sensors can be fooled if there is an exhaust manifold leak or other fault, which could lead to false or inaccurate readings. If the oxygen sensor reading is false, the PCM will command an incorrect amount of fuel. The scan data shown on a generic (global) OBD-II scan tool will often be different than the reading on the factory scan tool. ● **SEE CHART 35–2** for an example of a Toyota wide-band oxygen sensor being tested using a factory scan tool and a generic OBD-II scan tool.

SCAN TOOL DATA (PID) The following information will be displayed as a scan tool when looking at data for a wide-band oxygen sensor:

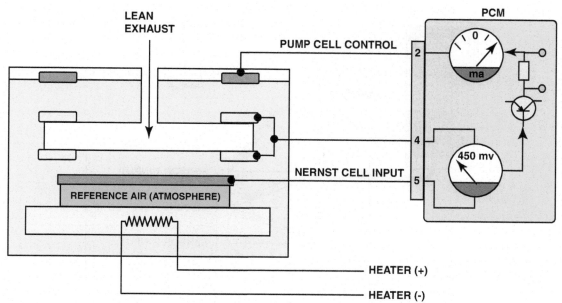

LEAN EXHAUST

PUMP CELL CONTROL

PCM

ma

450 mv

NERNST CELL INPUT

REFERENCE AIR (ATMOSPHERE)

HEATER (+)

HEATER (-)

FIGURE 35–17 When the exhaust is lean, the PCM applies a positive current into the pump cell.

FACTORY SCAN TOOL	OBD II SCAN TOOL	AIR-FUEL RATIO
2.50 V	0.50 V	12.5:1
3.00 V	0.60 V	14.0:1
3.30 V	0.66 V	14.7:1
3.50 V	0.70 V	15.5:1
4.00 V	0.80 V	18.5:1

CHART 35–2

A comparison showing what a factory scan tool and a generic OBD-II scan tool might display at various air-fuel ratios.

H02S1 = ____ mA ÷	If the current is positive, this means the PCM is pumping current in the diffusion gap due to a rich exhaust. If the current is negative, the PCM is pumping current out of the diffusion gap due to a lean exhaust.
Air-fuel ratio = ____	Usually expressed in lambda. One means that the exhaust is at stoichiometric (14.7:1 air-fuel ratio) and numbers higher than one indicate a lean exhaust and numbers lower than one indicate a rich exhaust.

DIGITAL METER TESTING When testing a wide-band oxygen sensor for proper operation, perform the following steps.

STEP 1 Check service information and determine the circuit and connector terminal identification.

STEP 2 Measure the calibration resistor. While the value of this resistor can vary widely depending on the type of sensor, the calibrating resistor should still be checked for opens and shorts.

NOTE: The calibration resistor is usually located within the connector itself.

- If open, the ohmmeter will read OL (infinity ohms).
- If shorted, the ohmmeter will read zero or close to zero.

STEP 3 Measure the heater circuit for proper resistance or current flow.

STEP 4 Measure the reference voltage relative to ground. This can vary but is generally 2.4 to 2.6 V.

STEP 5 Using jumper wires, connect an ammeter and measure the current in the pump cell control wire.

RICH EXHAUST When the exhaust is rich (lambda less than 1.00), the Nernst cell voltage will move higher than 0.45 V. The PCM will pump oxygen from the exhaust into the diffusion gap by applying a negative voltage to the pump cell.

LEAN EXHAUST When the exhaust is lean (lambda higher than 1.00), the Nernst cell voltage will move lower than 0.45 V. The PCM will pump oxygen out of the diffusion gap by applying a positive voltage to the pump cell.

Pump cell is used to pump oxygen into the diffusion gap when the exhaust is rich. The pump cell applies a negative voltage to do this.

- Positive current = lean exhaust
- Negative current = rich exhaust
- **SEE FIGURE 35–18**.

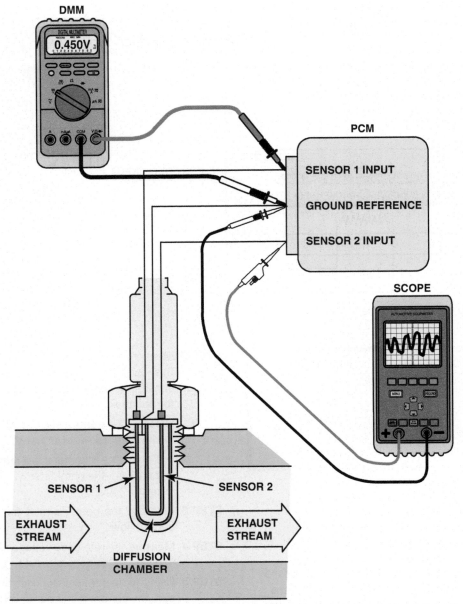

DMM

0.450V

PCM

SENSOR 1 INPUT

GROUND REFERENCE

SENSOR 2 INPUT

SCOPE

SENSOR 1   SENSOR 2

EXHAUST
STREAM

EXHAUST
STREAM

DIFFUSION
CHAMBER

FIGURE 35–18 Testing a dual cell wide-band oxygen sensor can be done using a voltmeter or a scope. The meter reading is attached to the Nernst cell and should read stoichiometric (450 mV) at all times. The scope is showing activity to the pump cell with commands from the PCM to keep the Nernst cell at 14.7:1 air-fuel ratio.

SINGLE CELL WIDE-BAND OXYGEN SENSORS

CONSTRUCTION A typical **single cell** wide-band oxygen sensor looks similar to a conventional four-wire zirconia oxygen sensor. The typical single cell wide-band oxygen sensor, usually called an **air-fuel ratio sensor**, has the following construction features.

- It can be made using the cup or planar design.
- Oxygen (O_2) is pumped into the diffusion layer similar to the operation of a dual cell wide-band oxygen sensor.
  ● **SEE FIGURE 35–19**.
- Current flow reverses positive and negative.

- There are two cell wires and two heater wires (power and ground).
- The heater usually requires 6 amperes and the ground side is pulse-width modulated.

MILLIAMMETER TESTING The PCM controls the single cell wide-band oxygen sensor by maintaining a voltage difference of 300 mV (0.3 V) between the two sensor leads. The PCM keeps the voltage difference constant under all operating conditions by increasing or decreasing current between the element of the cell.

- Zero (0 mA) represents lambda or stoichiometric air-fuel ratio of 14.7:1
- +10 mA indicates a lean condition
- −10 mA indicates a rich condition

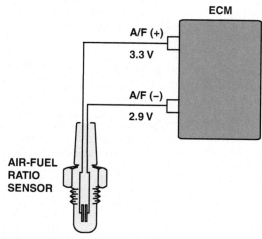

A/F (+)
3.3 V

A/F (−)
2.9 V

ECM

AIR-FUEL
RATIO
SENSOR

FIGURE 35–19 A single cell wide-band oxygen sensor has four wires with two for the heater and two for the sensor itself. The voltage applied to the sensor is 0.4 V (3.3 − 2.9 = 0.4) across the two leads of the sensor.

SCAN TOOL TESTING A scan tool will display a voltage reading but can vary depending on the type and maker of the scan tool. ● **SEE FIGURE 35–20**.

WIDE-BAND OXYGEN PATTERN FAILURES

Wide-band oxygen sensors have a long life, but they can fail. Most of the failures will cause a diagnostic trouble code (DTC) to set, usually causing the malfunction indicator (check engine) lamp to light.

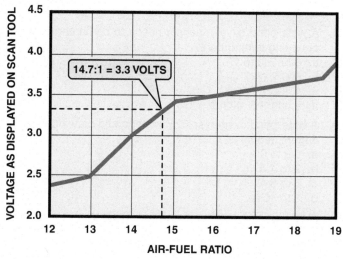

14.7:1 = 3.3 VOLTS

FIGURE 35–20 A scan tool can display various voltages, but will often show 3.3 V because the PCM is controlling the sensor through applying a low current to the sensor to achieve balance.

However, one type of failure may not set a DTC, such as when the following occurs:

1. Voltage from the heater circuit bleeds into the Nernst cell.
2. This voltage will cause the engine to operate extremely lean and may or may not set a diagnostic trouble code.
3. When testing indicates an extremely lean condition, unplug the connector to the oxygen sensor. If the engine starts to operate correctly with the sensor unplugged, this is confirmation that the wide-band oxygen sensor has failed and requires replacement.

OXYGEN SENSOR– RELATED DIAGNOSTIC TROUBLE CODES

Diagnostic trouble codes (DTCs) associated with the oxygen sensor include the following:

Diagnostic Trouble Codes	Description	Possible Causes
P0131	Upstream HO2S grounded	• Exhaust leak upstream of HO2S (bank 1) • Extremely lean air-fuel mixture • HO2S defective or contaminated • HO2S signal wire shorted-to-ground
P0132	Upstream HO2S shorted	• Upstream HO2S (bank 1) shorted • Defective HO2S • Fuel-contaminated HO2S
P0133	Upstream HO2S slow response	• Open or short in heater circuit • Defective or fuel-contaminated HO2S • EGR or fuel system fault

1. An oxygen sensor produces a voltage output signal based on the oxygen content of the exhaust stream.

2. If the exhaust has little oxygen, the voltage of the oxygen sensor will be close to 1 volt (1,000 mV) and close to zero if there is high oxygen content in the exhaust.

3. Oxygen sensors can have one, two, three, four, or more wires, depending on the style and design.

4. A wide-band oxygen sensor, also called a lean air–fuel (LAF) or linear air–fuel ratio sensor, can detect air–fuel ratios from as rich as 12:1 to as lean as 22:1.

5. The oxygen sensor signal determines fuel trim, which is used to tailor the air–fuel mixture for the catalytic converter.

6. Conditions can occur that cause the oxygen sensor to be fooled and give a false lean or false rich signal to the PCM.

7. Oxygen sensors can be tested using a digital meter, scope, or scan tool.

REVIEW QUESTIONS

1. How does an oxygen sensor detect oxygen levels in the exhaust?

2. What is the difference between open-loop and closed-loop engine operation?

3. What are three ways oxygen sensors can be tested?

4. How can the oxygen sensor be fooled and provide the wrong information to the PCM?

5. What is the purpose of a wide-band oxygen sensor?

CHAPTER QUIZ

1. The voltage output of a zirconia oxygen sensor when the exhaust stream is lean (excess oxygen) is _____.
   a. relatively high (close to 1 volt)
   b. about in the middle of the voltage range
   c. relatively low (close to 0 volt)
   d. either a or b, depending on atmospheric pressure

2. A high O2S voltage could be due to a _____.
   a. rich exhaust
   b. lean exhaust
   c. defective spark plug wire
   d. both a and c

3. A low O2S voltage could be due to a _____.
   a. rich exhaust
   b. lean exhaust
   c. defective spark plug wire
   d. Both b and c

4. An oxygen sensor is being tested with a digital multimeter (DMM), using the MIN/MAX function. The readings are: minimum = 78 mV; maximum = 932 mV; average = 442 mV. Technician A says that the engine is operating correctly. Technician B says that the oxygen sensor is skewed too rich. Which technician is correct?
   a. Technician A only
   b. Technician B only
   c. Both Technicians A and B
   d. Neither Technician A nor B

5. An oxygen sensor is being tested using a digital storage oscilloscope (DSO). A good oxygen sensor should display how many transitions (switches) per second?
   a. 1 to 5   c. 10 to 15
   b. 5 to 10   d. 15 to 20

6. A wide-band oxygen sensor was first used on a Honda in what model year?
   a. 1992   c. 2000
   b. 1996   d. 2006

7. A wide-band oxygen sensor is capable of detecting the air-fuel mixture in the exhaust from _____ (rich) to _____ (lean).
   a. 12:1; 15:1
   b. 13:1; 16.7:1
   c. 10:1; 23:1
   d. 8:1; 18:1

8. A wide-band oxygen sensor needs to be heated to what operating temperature?
   a. 600°F (315°C)
   b. 800°F (427°C)
   c. 1,400°F (760°C)
   d. 2,000°F (1,093°C)

9. A wide-band oxygen sensor heater could draw how much current (amperes)?
   a. 0.8 to 2 A
   b. 2 to 4 A
   c. 6 to 8 A
   d. 8 to 10 A

10. A P0133 DTC is being discussed. Technician A says that a defective heater circuit could be the cause. Technician B says that a contaminated sensor could be the cause. Which technician is correct?
    a. Technician A only
    b. Technician B only
    c. Both Technicians A and B
    d. Neither Technician A nor B

chapter 36

FUEL PUMPS, LINES, AND FILTERS

FUEL DELIVERY SYSTEM

Creating and maintaining a correct air–fuel mixture requires a properly functioning fuel and air delivery system. Fuel delivery (and return) systems use many, if not all, of the following components to make certain that fuel is available under the right conditions to the fuel-injection system:

- Fuel storage tank, filler neck, and gas cap
- Fuel tank pressure sensor
- Fuel pump
- Fuel filter(s)
- Fuel delivery lines and fuel rail
- Fuel-pressure regulator
- Fuel return line (if equipped with a return-type fuel delivery system)

FUEL TANKS

A vehicle fuel tank is made of corrosion-resistant steel or polyethylene plastic. Some models, such as sport utility vehicles (SUVs) and light trucks, may have an auxiliary fuel tank.

Tank design and capacity are a compromise between available space, filler location, fuel expansion room, and fuel movement. Some later-model tanks deliberately limit tank capacity by extending the filler tube neck into the tank low enough to prevent complete filling, or by providing for expansion room. ● **SEE FIGURE 36–1.** A vertical **baffle** in this same tank limits fuel sloshing as the vehicle moves.

Regardless of size and shape, all fuel tanks incorporate most if not all of the following features:

- Inlet or filler tube through which fuel enters the tank
- Filler cap with pressure holding and relief features
- An outlet to the fuel line leading to the fuel pump or fuel injector
- Fuel pump mounted within the tank
- Tank vent system
- Fuel pickup tube and fuel level sending unit

TANK LOCATION AND MOUNTING Most vehicles use a horizontally suspended fuel tank, usually mounted below the rear of the floor pan, just ahead of or behind the rear axle. Fuel tanks are located there so that frame rails and body components protect the tank in the event of a crash. To prevent squeaks, some models have insulated strips cemented on the top or sides of the tank wherever it contacts the underbody.

Fuel inlet location depends on the tank design and filler tube placement. It is located behind a filler cap and is often a hinged door in the outer side of either rear fender panel.

Generally, a pair of metal retaining straps holds a fuel tank in place. Underbody brackets or support panels hold the strap ends using bolts. The free ends are drawn underneath the tank to hold it in place and then bolted to other support brackets or to a frame member on the opposite side of the tank.

FILLER TUBES Fuel enters the tank through a large tube extending from the tank to an opening on the outside of the vehicle. ● **SEE FIGURE 36–2.**

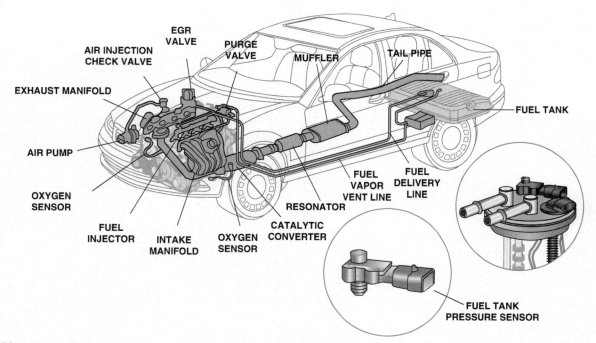

FIGURE 36–1 The fuel system includes many separate parts and components, including the fuel tank, fuel pump and lines, as well as the fuel tank pressure sensor used to measure the pressure inside the fuel tanks used by the evaporative fuel control system.

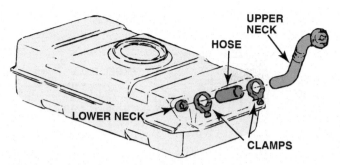

FIGURE 36–2 A three-piece filler tube assembly.

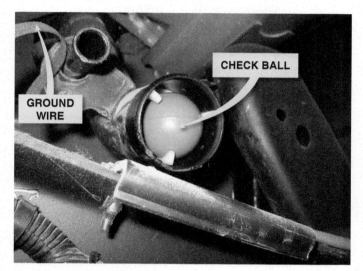

FIGURE 36–3 A view of a typical filler tube with the fuel tank removed. Notice the ground strap used to help prevent the buildup of static electricity as the fuel flows into the plastic tank. The check ball looks like a ping-pong ball.

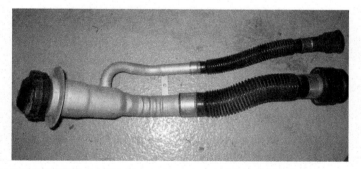

FIGURE 36–4 Vehicles equipped with onboard refueling vapor recovery usually have a reduced-size fill tube.

Effective in 1993, federal regulations require manufacturers to install a device to prevent fuel from being siphoned through the filler neck. Federal authorities recognized methanol as a poison, and methanol used in gasoline is a definite health hazard. Additionally, gasoline is a suspected carcinogen (cancer-causing agent). To prevent siphoning, manufacturers welded a filler-neck check-ball tube in fuel tanks. To drain check ball–equipped fuel tanks, a technician must disconnect the check-ball tube at the tank and attach a siphon directly to the tank. ● **SEE FIGURE 36–3**.

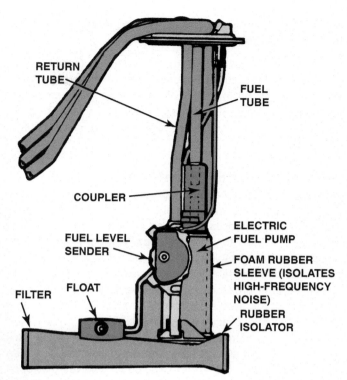

FIGURE 36–5 The fuel pickup tube is part of the fuel sender and pump assembly.

Onboard refueling vapor recovery (ORVR) systems have been developed to reduce evaporative emissions during refueling. ● **SEE FIGURE 36–4**. These systems add components to the filler neck and the tank. One ORVR system utilizes a tapered filler neck with a smaller diameter tube and a check valve. When fuel flows down the neck, it opens the normally closed check valve. The vapor passage to the charcoal canister is opened. The decreased size neck and the opened air passage allow fuel and vapor to flow rapidly into the tank and the canister, respectively. When the fuel has reached a predetermined level, the check valve closes, and the fuel tank pressure increases. This forces the nozzle to shut off, thereby preventing the tank from being overfilled.

PRESSURE-VACUUM FILLER CAP Fuel and vapors are sealed in the tank by the safety filler cap. The safety cap must release excess pressure or excess vacuum. Either condition could cause fuel tank damage, fuel spills, and vapor escape. Typically, the cap will release if the pressure is over 1.5 to 2.0 PSI (10 to 14 kPa) or if the vacuum is 0.15 to 0.30 PSI (1 to 2 kPa).

FUEL PICKUP TUBE The fuel pickup tube is usually a part of the fuel sender assembly or the electric fuel pump assembly. Since dirt and sediment eventually gather on the bottom of a fuel tank, the fuel pickup tube is fitted with a filter sock or strainer to prevent contamination from entering the fuel lines. The woven plastic strainer also acts as a water separator by preventing water from being drawn up with the fuel. The filter sock usually is designed to filter out particles that are larger than 70 to 100 microns, or 30 microns if a gerotor-type fuel pump is used. One micron is 0.000039 inch ● **SEE FIGURE 36–5**.

NOTE: The human eye cannot see anything smaller than about 40 microns.

The filter is made from woven Saran resin (copolymer of vinylidene chloride and vinyl chloride). The filter blocks any water that may be in the fuel tank, unless it is completely submerged in water. In that case, it will allow water through the filter. This filter should be replaced whenever the fuel pump is replaced.

TANK VENTING REQUIREMENTS Fuel tanks must be vented to prevent a vacuum lock as fuel is drawn from the tank. As fuel is used and its level drops in the tank, the space above the fuel increases. As the air in the tank expands to fill this greater space, its pressure drops. Without a vent, the air pressure inside the tank would drop below atmospheric pressure, developing a vacuum, which prevents the flow of fuel. Under extreme pressure variance, the tank could collapse. Venting the tank allows outside air to enter as the fuel level drops, preventing a vacuum from developing.

An EVAP system vents gasoline vapors from the fuel tank directly to a charcoal-filled vapor storage canister, and uses an unvented filler cap. Many filler caps contain valves that open to relieve pressure or vacuum above specified safety levels. Systems that use completely sealed caps have separate pressure and vacuum relief valves for venting.

Because fuel tanks are not vented directly to the atmosphere, the tank must allow for fuel expansion, contraction, and overflow that can result from changes in temperature or overfilling. One way is to use a dome in the top of the tank. Many General Motors vehicles use a design that includes a vertical slosh baffle which reserves up to 12% of the total tank capacity for fuel expansion.

ROLLOVER LEAKAGE PROTECTION

All vehicles have one or more devices to prevent fuel leaks in case of vehicle rollover or a collision in which fuel may spill.

Variations of the basic one-way check valve may be installed in any number of places between the fuel tank and the engine. The valve may be installed in the fuel return line, vapor vent line, or fuel tank filler cap.

In addition to the rollover protection devices, some vehicles use devices to ensure that the fuel pump shuts off when an accident occurs. Some pumps depend upon an oil pressure or an engine speed signal to continue operating; these pumps turn off whenever the engine dies.

Ford vehicles use an **inertia switch**. ● **SEE FIGURE 36–6**. The inertia switch is installed in the rear of the vehicle between the electric fuel pump and its power supply. With any sudden impact, such as a jolt from another vehicle in a parking lot, the inertia switch opens and shuts off power to the fuel pump. The switch must be reset manually by pushing a button to restore current to the pump.

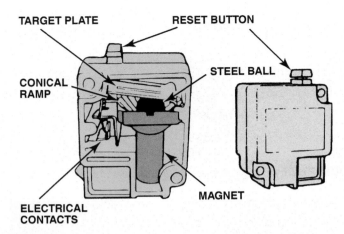

FIGURE 36–6 Ford uses an inertia switch to turn off the electric fuel pump in case of an accident.

FUEL LINES

PURPOSE AND FUNCTION Fuel and vapor lines made of steel, nylon tubing, or fuel-resistant rubber hoses connect the parts of the fuel system. Fuel lines supply fuel to the throttle body or fuel rail. They also return excess fuel and vapors to the tank. Depending on their function, fuel and vapor lines may be either rigid or flexible.

Fuel lines must remain as cool as possible. If any part of the line is located near too much heat, the gasoline passing through it vaporizes and **vapor lock** occurs. When this happens, the fuel pump supplies only vapor that passes into the injectors. Without liquid gasoline, the engine stalls and a hot restart problem develops.

The fuel delivery system supplies 10 to 15 PSI (69 to 103 kPa) or up to 35 PSI (241 kPa) to many throttle-body injection units and up to 50 PSI (345 kPa) for multiport fuel-injection systems. Fuel-injection systems retain residual or rest pressure in the lines for a half hour or longer when the engine is turned off to prevent hot engine restart problems. Higher-pressure systems such as these require special fuel lines.

RIGID LINES All fuel lines fastened to the body, frame, or engine are made of seamless steel tubing. Steel springs may be wound around the tubing at certain points to protect against impact damage.

Only steel tubing, or that recommended by the manufacturer, should be used when replacing rigid fuel lines. *Never substitute copper or aluminum tubing for steel tubing.* These materials do not withstand normal vehicle vibration and could combine with the fuel to cause a chemical reaction.

FLEXIBLE LINES Most fuel systems use synthetic rubber hose sections where flexibility is needed. Short hose sections often connect steel fuel lines to other system components. The fuel delivery hose inside diameter (ID) is generally larger (3/16 to 3/8 in. or 8 to 10 mm) than the fuel return hose ID (1/4 in. or 6 mm).

Fuel-injection systems require special-composition reinforced hoses specifically made for these higher-pressure systems. Similarly, vapor vent lines must be made of materials that

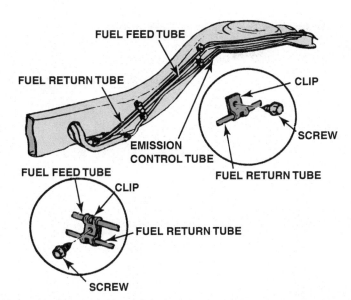

FIGURE 36–7 Fuel lines are routed along the frame or body and secured with clips.

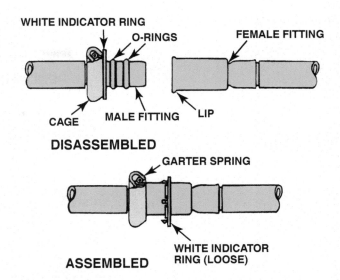

FIGURE 36–8 Some Ford metal line connections use spring-locks and O-rings.

resist fuel vapors. Replacement vent hoses are usually marked with the designation "EVAP" to indicate their intended use.

FUEL LINE MOUNTING Fuel supply lines from the tank to a throttle body or fuel rail are routed to follow the frame along the underbody of the vehicle. Vapor and return lines may be routed with the fuel supply line. All rigid lines are fastened to the frame rail or underbody with screws and clamps, or clips. ● **SEE FIGURE 36–7.**

FUEL-INJECTION LINES Hoses used for fuel-injection systems are made of materials with high resistance to oxidation and deterioration. Replacement hoses for injection systems should always be equivalent to original equipment manufacturer (OEM) hoses.

CAUTION: Do not use spring-type clamps on fuel-injected engines—they cannot withstand the fuel pressures involved.

FUEL-INJECTION FITTINGS AND NYLON LINES
Because of their operating pressures, fuel-injection systems often use special kinds of fittings to ensure leakproof connections. Some high-pressure fittings on GM vehicles with port fuel-injection systems use O-ring seals instead of the traditional flare connections. When disconnecting such a fitting, inspect the O-ring for damage and replace it if necessary. *Always* tighten O-ring fittings to the specified torque value to prevent damage.

Other manufacturers also use O-ring seals on fuel line connections. In all cases, the O-rings are made of special materials that withstand contact with gasoline and oxygenated fuel blends. Some manufacturers specify that the O-rings be replaced every time the fuel system connection is opened. When replacing one of these O-rings, a new part specifically designed for fuel system service must be used.

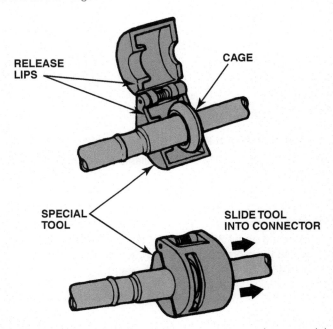

FIGURE 36–9 Ford spring-lock connectors require a special tool for disassembly.

Ford also uses spring-lock connectors to join male and female ends of steel tubing. ● **SEE FIGURE 36–8.** The coupling is held together by a garter spring inside a circular cage. The flared end of the female fitting slips behind the spring to lock the coupling together.

General Motors has used nylon fuel lines with quick-connect fittings at the fuel tank and fuel filter since the early 1990s. Like the GM threaded couplings used with steel lines, nylon line couplings use internal O-ring seals. Unlocking the metal connectors requires a special quick-connector separator tool; plastic connectors can be released without the tool. ● **SEE FIGURES 36–9 AND 36–10.**

FUEL LINE LAYOUT Fuel pressures have tended to become higher to prevent vapor lock, and a major portion of the fuel routed to the fuel-injection system returns to the tank

FIGURE 36-10 Typical quick-connect steps.

METAL COLLAR
QUICK-CONNECT FITTING

PLASTIC COLLAR
QUICK-CONNECT FITTING

REMOVAL

1. TWIST

2. BLOW

3. OR

4.

INSTALLATION

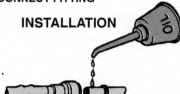

1.

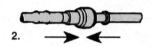

2. →←

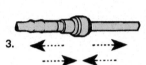

3. ←⋯⋯ ⋯⋯→
   ⋯⋯→ ⋯⋯→

Just How Much Fuel Is Recirculated?

Approximately 80% of the available fuel-pump volume is released to the fuel tank through the fuel-pressure regulator at idle speed. For example, a passenger vehicle cruising down the road at 60 mph gets 30 mpg. With a typical return-style fuel system pumping about 30 gallons per hour from the tank, it would therefore burn 2 gallons per hour, and return about 28 gallons per hour to the tank!

How Can an Electric Pump Work Inside a Gas Tank and Not Cause a Fire?

Even though fuel fills the entire pump, no burnable mixture exists inside the pump because there is no air and no danger of commutator brush arcing, igniting the fuel.

Not only must the fuel be filtered and supplied under adequate pressure, but there must also be a consistent *volume* of fuel to assure smooth engine performance even under the heaviest of loads.

by way of a fuel return line or return-type systems. This allows better control, within limits, of heat absorbed by the gasoline as it is routed through the engine compartment. Throttle-body and multiport injection systems have typically used a pressure regulator to control fuel pressure in the throttle body or fuel rail, and also allow excess fuel not used by the injectors to return to the tank. However, the warmer fuel in the tank may create problems, such as an excessive rise in fuel vapor pressures in the tank.

With late-model vehicles, there has been some concern about too much heat being sent back to the fuel tank, causing rising in-tank temperatures and increases in fuel vaporization and **volatile organic compound (VOC)** (hydrocarbon) emissions. To combat this problem, manufacturers have placed the pressure regulator back by the tank instead of under the hood on mechanical returnless systems. In this way, returned fuel is not subjected to the heat generated by the engine and the underhood environment. To prevent vapor lock in these systems, pressures have been raised in the fuel rail, and injectors tend to have smaller openings to maintain control of the fuel spray under pressure.

ELECTRIC FUEL PUMPS

The electric fuel pump is a pusher unit. When the pump is mounted in the tank, the entire fuel supply line to the engine can be pressurized. Because the fuel, when pressurized, has a higher boiling point, it is unlikely that vapor will form to interfere with fuel flow.

Most vehicles use the impeller or turbine pumps. ● **SEE FIGURE 36-11**. All electrical pumps are driven by a small electric motor, but the turbine pump turns at higher speeds and is quieter than the others.

POSITIVE DISPLACEMENT PUMP A positive displacement pump is a design that forces everything that enters the pump to leave the pump.

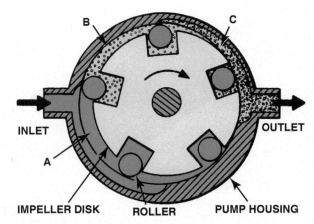

FIGURE 36–12 The pumping action of an impeller or rotary vane pump.

Labels for figure 36-12: B, C, INLET, OUTLET, A, IMPELLER DISK, ROLLER, PUMP HOUSING

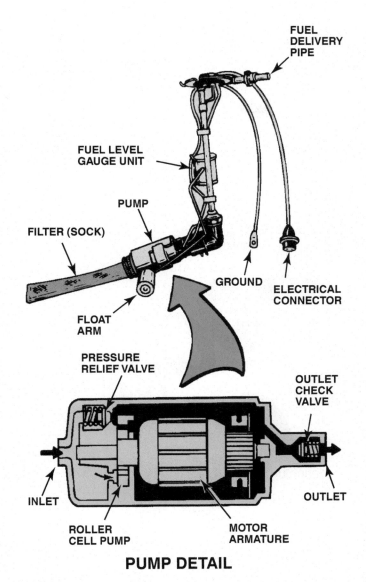

PUMP DETAIL

FIGURE 36–11 A roller cell-type electric fuel pump.

Labels for figure 36-11: FUEL DELIVERY PIPE, FUEL LEVEL GAUGE UNIT, PUMP, FILTER (SOCK), GROUND, ELECTRICAL CONNECTOR, FLOAT ARM, PRESSURE RELIEF VALVE, OUTLET CHECK VALVE, INLET, OUTLET, ROLLER CELL PUMP, MOTOR ARMATURE

In the **roller cell** or vane pump, the impeller draws fuel into the pump, and then pushes it out through the fuel line to the injection system. All designs of pumps use a variable-sized chamber to draw in fuel. When the maximum volume has been reached, the supply port closes and the discharge opens. Fuel is forced out the discharge as this volume decreases. The chambers are formed by rollers or gears in a rotor plate. Since this type of pump uses no valves to move the fuel, the fuel flows steadily through the pump housing. Since fuel flows steadily through the entire pump, including the electrical portion, the pump stays cool. Usually, only when a vehicle runs out of fuel is there a risk of pump damage.

Most electric fuel pumps are equipped with a fuel outlet check valve that closes to maintain fuel pressure when the pump shuts off. **Residual or rest pressure** prevents vapor lock and hot-start problems on these systems.

● **FIGURE 36–12** shows the pumping action of a **rotary vane pump**. The pump consists of a central impeller disk, several rollers or vanes that ride in notches in the impeller, and a pump housing that is offset from the impeller centerline. The impeller is mounted on the end of the motor armature and spins whenever

the motor is running. The rollers are free to slide in and out within the notches in the impeller to maintain sealing contact. Unpressurized fuel enters the pump, fills the spaces between the rollers, and is trapped between the impeller, the housing, and two rollers. An internal gear pump, called a **gerotor**, is another type of positive displacement pump that is often used in engine oil pumps. It uses the meshing of internal and external gear teeth to pressurize the fuel. ● **SEE FIGURE 36–13** for an example of a gerotor-type fuel pump that uses an impeller as the first stage and is used to move the fuel gerotor section where it is pressurized.

HYDROKINETIC FLOW PUMP DESIGN The word *hydro* means liquid and the term *kinetic* refers to motion, so the term **hydrokinetic pump** means that this design of pump rapidly moves the fuel to create pressure. This design of pump is a nonpositive displacement pump design.

A **turbine pump** is the most common because it tends to be less noisy. Sometimes called **turbine**, **peripheral**, and **side-channel**, these units use an impeller that accelerates the fuel particles before actually discharging them into a tract where they generate pressure via pulse exchange. Actual pump volume is controlled by using a different number of impeller blades, and in some cases a higher number of impellers, or different shapes along the side discharge channels. These units are fitted more toward lower operating pressures of less than 60 PSI. ● **SEE FIGURE 36–14** for an example of a two-stage turbine pump. The turbine impeller has a staggered blade design to minimize pump harmonic noise and to separate vapor from the liquid fuel. The end cap assembly contains a pressure relief valve and a radio-frequency interference (RFI) suppression module. The check valve is usually located in the upper fuel pipe connector assembly.

After it passes through the strainer, fuel is drawn into the lower housing inlet port by the impellers. It is pressurized and delivered to the convoluted fuel tube for transfer through a check valve into the fuel feed pipe. A typical electric fuel pump used on a fuel-injection system delivers about 40 to 50 gallons per hour or 0.6 to 0.8 gallons per minute at a pressure of 70 to 90 PSI.

MODULAR FUEL SENDER ASSEMBLY The modular fuel sender consists of a fuel level sensor, a turbine pump, and a jet pump. The reservoir housing is attached to the cover

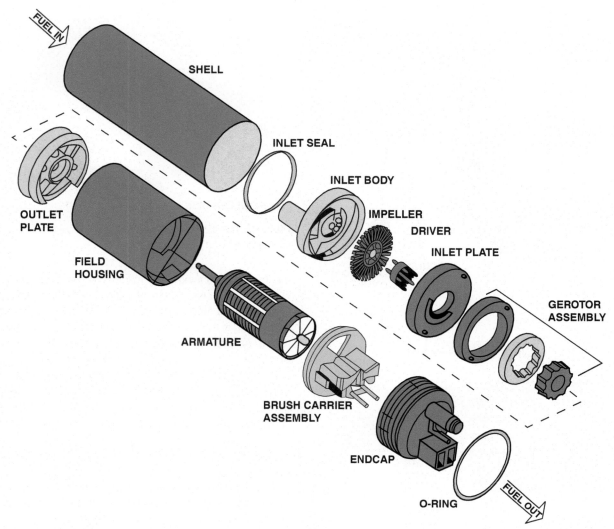

FUEL IN

SHELL

INLET SEAL

INLET BODY

OUTLET
PLATE

IMPELLER

DRIVER

INLET PLATE

FIELD
HOUSING

GEROTOR
ASSEMBLY

ARMATURE

BRUSH CARRIER
ASSEMBLY

ENDCAP

O-RING

FUEL OUT

FIGURE 36–13 An exploded view of a gerotor electric fuel pump.

containing fuel pipes and the electrical connector. Fuel is transferred from the pump to the fuel pipe through a convoluted (flexible) fuel pipe. The convoluted fuel pipe eliminates the need for rubber hoses, nylon pipes, and clamps. The reservoir dampens fuel slosh to maintain a constant fuel level available to the roller vane pump; it also reduces noise.

Some of the flow, however, is returned to the jet pump for recirculation. Excess fuel is returned to the reservoir through one of the three hollow support pipes. The hot fuel quickly mixes with the cooler fuel in the reservoir; this minimizes the possibility of vapor lock. In these modules, the reservoir is filled by the jet pump. Some of the fuel from the pump is sent through the jet pump to lift fuel from the tank into the reservoir.

ELECTRIC PUMP CONTROL CIRCUITS

Fuel-pump circuits are controlled by the fuel-pump relay. Fuel-pump relays are activated initially by turning the ignition key to on, which allows the pump to pressurize the fuel system. As a safety precaution, the relay de-energizes after a few seconds until the key is moved to the crank position. On some systems, once an ignition coil signal, or "tach" signal, is received by the engine control computer, indicating the engine is rotating, the relay remains energized even with the key released to the run position.

CHRYSLER. On older Chrysler vehicles, the PCM must receive an engine speed (RPM) signal during cranking before it can energize a circuit driver inside the power module to activate an automatic shutdown (ASD) relay to power the fuel pump, ignition coil, and injectors. As a safety precaution, if the RPM signal to the logic module is interrupted, the logic module signals the power module to deactivate the ASD, turning off the pump, coil, and injectors. In some

 FREQUENTLY ASKED QUESTION

Why Are Many Fuel-Pump Modules Spring-Loaded?

Fuel modules that contain the fuel pickup sock, fuel pump, and fuel level sensor are often spring-loaded when fitted to a plastic fuel tank. The plastic material shrinks when cold and expands when hot, so having the fuel module spring-loaded ensures that the fuel pickup sock will always be the same distance from the bottom of the tank. ● **SEE FIGURE 36–15**.

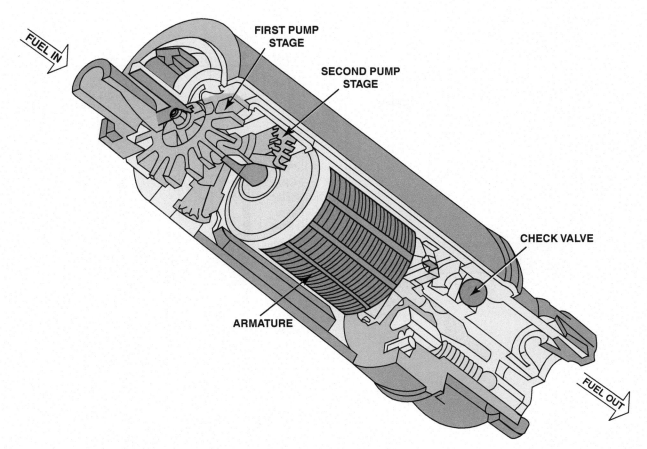

FIGURE 36–14 A cutaway view of a typical two-stage turbine electric fuel pump.

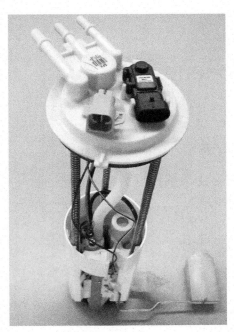

FIGURE 36–15 A typical fuel-pump module assembly, which includes the pickup strainer and fuel pump, as well as the fuel-pressure sensor and fuel level sensing unit.

vehicles, the oil pressure switch circuit may be used as a safety circuit to activate the pump in the ignition switch run position.

GENERAL MOTORS. General Motors systems energize the pump with the ignition switch to initially pressurize the fuel lines, but then deactivate the pump if an RPM signal is not received within one or two seconds. The pump is reactivated as soon as engine cranking is detected. The oil pressure sending unit serves as a backup to the fuel-pump relay on some vehicles. In case of pump relay failure, the oil pressure switch will operate the fuel pump once oil pressure reaches about 4 PSI (28 kPa).

FORD. Older fuel-injected Fords used an inertia switch between the fuel pump relay and fuel pump.

The inertia switch opens under a specified impact, such as a collision. When the switch opens, current to the pump shuts off because the fuel-pump relay will not energize. The switch must be reset manually by opening the trunk and depressing the reset button before current flow to the pump can be restored. ● **SEE FIGURE 36–16** for a schematic of a typical fuel system that uses an inertia switch in the power feed circuit to the electric fuel pump.

Since about 2008, the inertial switch has been replaced with a signal input from the airbag module. If the airbag is deployed, the circuit to the fuel pump is opened and the fuel pump stops.

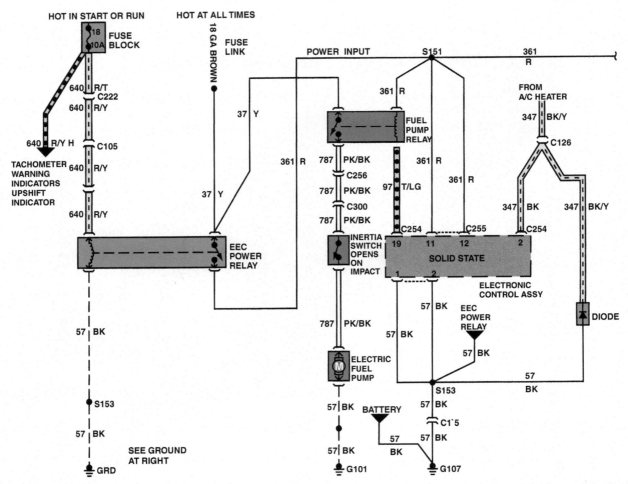

FIGURE 36–16 A schematic showing that an inertia switch is connected in series between the fuel-pump relay and the fuel pump.

PUMP PULSATION DAMPENING Some manufacturers use an **accumulator** in the system to reduce pressure pulses and noise. Others use a pulsator located at the outlet of the fuel pump to absorb pressure pulsations that are created by the pump. These pulsators are usually used on roller vane pumps and are a source of many internal fuel leaks. ● **SEE FIGURE 36–17**.

NOTE: Some experts suggest that the pulsator be removed and replaced with a standard section of fuel line to prevent the loss of fuel pressure that results when the connections on the pulsator loosen and leak fuel back into the tank.

VARIABLE SPEED PUMPS Another way to help reduce noise, current draw, and pump wear is to reduce the speed of the pump when less than maximum output is required. Pump speed and pressure can be regulated by controlling the voltage supplied to the pump with a resistor switched into the circuit, or by using a separate fuel pump driver module to supply a pulse-width modulated (PWM) voltage to the pump. With slower pump speed and pressure, less noise is produced.

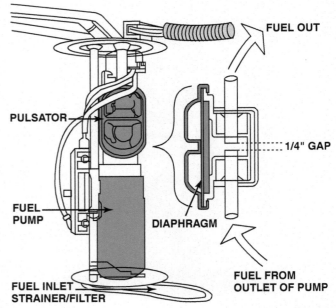

FIGURE 36–17 A typical fuel pulsator used mostly with roller vane-type pumps to help even out the pulsation in pressure that can cause noise.

FUEL FILTERS

Despite the care generally taken in refining, storing, and delivering gasoline, some impurities get into the automotive fuel system. Fuel filters remove dirt, rust, water, and other contamination from the gasoline before it can reach the fuel injectors. Most fuel filters are designed to filter particles that are 10 to 20 microns or larger in size.

The useful life of many filters is limited, but vehicles that use a returnless-type fuel-injection system usually use filters that are part of the fuel pump assembly and do not have any specified interval. This means they should last the life of the vehicle. If fuel filters are not replaced according to the manufacturer's recommendations, they can become clogged and restrict fuel flow.

In addition to using several different types of fuel filters, a single fuel system may contain two or more filters. The inline filter is located in the line between the fuel pump and the throttle body or fuel rail. ● **SEE FIGURE 36–18.** This filter protects the system from contamination, but does not protect the fuel pump. The inline filter usually is a metal or plastic container with a pleated paper element sealed inside.

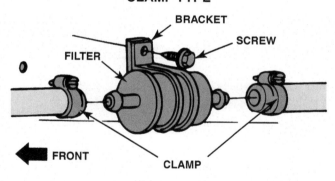

CLAMP TYPE

BRACKET

SCREW

FILTER

FRONT

CLAMP

O-RING TYPE

IDENTIFICATION LABEL

OUTLET

INLET

SSG TYPE O-RING FITTING (BOTH ENDS)

FIGURE 36–18 Inline fuel filters are usually attached to the fuel line with screw clamps or threaded connections. The fuel filter must be installed in the proper direction or a restricted fuel flow can result.

TECH TIP

Use a Headlight to Test for Power and Ground

When replacing a fuel pump, always check for proper power and ground. If the supply voltage is low due to resistance in the circuit or the ground connection is poor, the lower available voltage to the pump will result in lower pump output and could also reduce the life of the pump. While a voltage drop test can be preformed, a quick and easy test is to use a headlight connected to the circuit. If the headlight is bright, then both the power side and the ground side of the pump circuit are normal. If the headlight is dim, then more testing will be needed to find the source of the resistance in the circuit(s) ● **SEE FIGURE 36–19.**

Fuel filters may be mounted on a bracket on the fender panel, a shock tower, or another convenient place in the engine compartment. They may also be installed under the vehicle near the fuel tank. Fuel filters should be replaced according to the vehicle manufacturer's recommendations, which range from every 30,000 miles (48,000 km) to 100,000 miles (160,000 km) or longer. Fuel filters that are part of the fuel-pump module assemblies usually do not have any specified service interval.

FUEL-PUMP TESTING

Fuel-pump testing includes many different tests and procedures. Even though a fuel pump can pass one test, it does not mean that there is not a fuel-pump problem. For example, if the pump motor is rotating slower than normal, it may be able to produce the specified pressure, but not enough volume to meet the needs of the engine while operating under a heavy load.

FIGURE 36–19 A dim headlight indicates excessive resistance in fuel pump circuit.

(a)

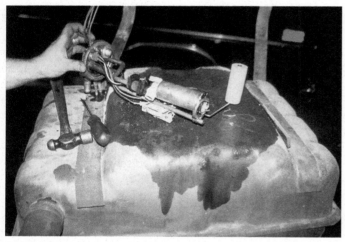

(b)

FIGURE 36–20 (a) A funnel helps in hearing if the electric fuel pump inside the gas tank is working. (b) If the pump is not running, check the wiring and current flow before going through the process of dropping the fuel tank to remove the pump.

 **TECH TIP**

The Ear Test

No, this is not a test of your hearing, but rather using your ear to check that the electric fuel pump is operating. The electric fuel pump inside the fuel tank is often difficult to hear running, especially in a noisy shop environment. A commonly used trick to better hear the pump is to use a funnel in the fuel filter neck. ● **SEE FIGURE 36–20.**

TESTING FUEL-PUMP PRESSURE Fuel pump-regulated pressure has become more important than ever with a more exact fuel control. Although an increase in fuel pressure does increase fuel volume to the engine, this is *not* the preferred method to

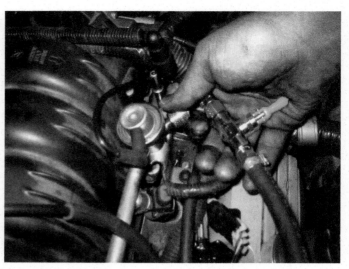

FIGURE 36–21 The Schrader valve on this General Motors 3800 V-6 is located next to the fuel-pressure regulator.

add additional fuel as some units will not open correctly at the increased fuel pressure. On the other side of the discussion, many newer engines will not start when fuel pressure is just a few PSI low. Correct fuel pressure is very important for proper engine operation. Most fuel-injection systems operate at either a low pressure of about 10 PSI or a high pressure of between 35 and 45 PSI.

Normal Operating Pressure	(PSI)	Maximum Pump Pressure (PSI)
Low-pressure TBI units	9–13	18–20
High-pressure TBI units	25–35	50–70
Port fuel-injection systems	35–45	70–90
Central port fuel injection (GM)	55–64	90–110

In both types of systems, maximum fuel-pump pressure is about double the normal operating pressure to ensure that a continuous flow of cool fuel is being supplied to the injector(s) to help prevent vapor from forming in the fuel system. Although vapor or foaming in a fuel system can greatly affect engine operation, the cooling and lubricating flow of the fuel must be maintained to ensure the durability of injector nozzles.

To measure fuel-pump pressure, locate the Schrader valve and attach a fuel-pressure gauge. ● **SEE FIGURE 36–21.**

NOTE: Some vehicles, such as those with General Motors TBI fuel-injection systems, require a specific fuel-pressure gauge that connects to the fuel system. Always follow the manufacturers' recommendations and procedures.

REST PRESSURE TEST If the fuel pressure is acceptable, then check the system for leakdown. Observe the pressure gauge

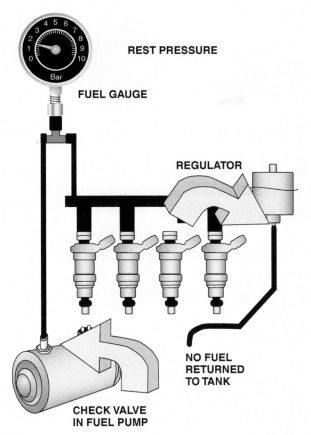

FIGURE 36–22 The fuel system should hold pressure if the system is leak free.

🔧 **TECH TIP**

The Rubber Mallet Trick

Often a no-start condition is due to an inoperative electric fuel pump. A common trick is to tap on the bottom of the fuel tank with a rubber mallet in an attempt to jar the pump motor enough to work. Instead of pushing a vehicle into the shop, simply tap on the fuel tank and attempt to start the engine. This is not a repair, but rather a confirmation that the fuel pump does indeed require replacement.

after five minutes. ● **SEE FIGURE 36–22.** The pressure should be the same as the initial reading. If not, then the pressure regulator, fuel-pump check valve, or the injectors are leaking.

DYNAMIC PRESSURE TEST
To test the pressure dynamically, start the engine. If the pressure is vacuum referenced, the pressure should change when the throttle is cycled. If it does not, check the vacuum supply circuit. Remove the vacuum line from the regulator and inspect for any presence of fuel. ● **SEE FIGURE 36–23.**

FIGURE 36–23 If the vacuum hose is removed from the fuel-pressure regulator when the engine is running, the fuel pressure should increase. If it does not increase, then the fuel pump is not capable of supplying adequate pressure or the fuel-pressure regulator is defective. If gasoline is visible in the vacuum hose, the regulator is leaking and should be replaced.

🔧 **TECH TIP**

The Fuel-Pressure Stethoscope Test

When the fuel pump is energized and the engine is not running, fuel should be heard flowing back to the fuel tank at the outlet of the fuel-pressure regulator.
● **SEE FIGURE 36–24.** If fuel is heard flowing through the return line, the fuel-pump pressure is higher than the regulator pressure. If no sound of fuel is heard, either the fuel pump or the fuel-pressure regulator is at fault.

There should never be any fuel present on the vacuum side of the regulator diaphragm. When the engine speed is increased, the pressure reading should remain within the specifications.

FIGURE 36–24 Fuel should be heard returning to the fuel tank at the fuel return line if the fuel pump and fuel-pressure regulator are functioning correctly.

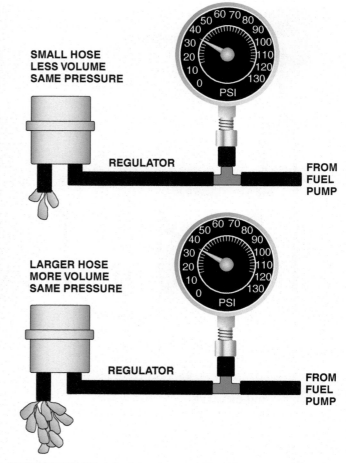

FIGURE 36–25 A fuel-pressure reading does not confirm that there is enough fuel volume for the engine to operate correctly.

Some engines do not use a vacuum-referenced regulator. The running pressure remains constant, which is typical for a mechanical returnless-type fuel system. On these systems, the pressure is higher than on return-type systems to help reduce the formation of fuel vapors in the system.

TESTING FUEL-PUMP VOLUME Fuel pressure alone is not enough for proper engine operation. ● **SEE FIGURE 36–25.** Sufficient fuel capacity (flow) should be at least 2 pints (1 L) every 30 seconds or 1 pint in 15 seconds. Fuel flow specifications are usually expressed in gallons per minute. A typical specification would be 0.5 gallons per minute or more. Volume testing is shown in ● **FIGURE 36–26.**

All fuel must be filtered to prevent dirt and impurities from damaging the fuel system components and/or engine. The first filter is inside the gas tank and is usually not replaceable separately but is attached to the fuel pump (if the pump is electric) and/or fuel gauge sending unit. The replaceable fuel filter is usually located between the fuel tank and the fuel rail or inlet to the fuel-injection system. Most vehicle manufacturers state in service information when to replace the fuel filter. Most newer vehicles, that use returnless-type fuel-injection systems, do not have replaceable filters as they are built into the fuel pump module assembly. (Check the vehicle manufacturers' recommendations for exact time and mileage intervals.)

FIGURE 36–26 A fuel system tester connected in series in the fuel system so all of the fuel used flows through the meter, which displays the rate of flow and the fuel pressure.

Quick and Easy Fuel Volume Test

Testing for pump volume involves using a specialized tester or a fuel-pressure gauge equipped with a hose to allow the fuel to be drawn from the system into a container with volume markings to allow for a volume measurement. This test can be hazardous because of expanding gasoline. An alternative test involves connecting a fuel-pressure gauge to the system with the following steps:

STEP 1 Start the engine and observe the fuel-pressure gauge. The reading should be within factory specifications (typically between 35 and 45 PSI).

STEP 2 Remove the hose from the fuel-pressure regulator. The pressure should increase if the system uses a demand-type regulator.

STEP 3 Rapidly accelerate the engine while watching the fuel-pressure gauge. If the fuel volume is okay, the fuel pressure should not drop more than 2 PSI. If the fuel pressure drops more than 2 PSI, replace the fuel filter and retest.

STEP 4 After replacing the fuel filter, accelerate the engine and observe the pressure gauge. If the pressure drops more than 2 PSI, replace the fuel pump.

NOTE: The fuel pump could still be delivering less than the specified volume of fuel, but as long as the volume needed by the engine is met, the pressure will not drop. If, however, the vehicle is pulling a heavy load, the demand for fuel volume may exceed the capacity of the pump.

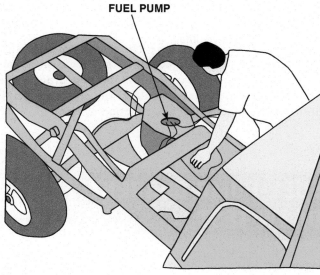
FUEL PUMP

FIGURE 36–27 Removing the bed from a pickup truck makes gaining access to the fuel pump a lot easier.

Remove the Bed to Save Time?

The electric fuel pump is easier to replace on many General Motors pickup trucks if the bed is removed. Access to the top of the fuel tank, where the access hole is located, for the removal of the fuel tank sender unit and pump is restricted by the bottom of the pickup truck bed. It would take several people (usually other technicians in the shop) to lift the truck bed from the frame after removing only a few fasteners. ● **SEE FIGURE 36–27.**

CAUTION: Be sure to clean around the fuel pump opening so that dirt or debris does not enter the tank when the fuel pump is removed.

If the fuel filter becomes partially clogged, the following are likely to occur:

1. There will be low power at higher engine speeds. The vehicle usually will not go faster than a certain speed (engine acts as if it has a built-in speed governor).
2. The engine will cut out or miss on acceleration, especially when climbing hills or during heavy-load acceleration.

A weak or defective fuel pump can also be the cause of the symptoms just listed. If an electric fuel pump for a fuel-injected engine becomes weak, additional problems include the following:

1. The engine may be hard to start.
2. There may be a rough idle and stalling.

3. There may be erratic shifting of the automatic transmission as a result of engine missing due to lack of fuel-pump pressure and/or volume.

CAUTION: Be certain to consult the vehicle manufacturers' recommended service and testing procedures before attempting to test or replace any component of a high-pressure electronic fuel-injection system.

FUEL-PUMP CURRENT DRAW TEST

Another test that can and should be performed on a fuel pump is to measure the current draw in amperes. This test is most often performed by connecting a digital multimeter set to read DC amperes and test the current draw. ● **SEE FIGURE 36–28** for the hookup for vehicles equipped with a fuel-pump relay. Compare the reading to factory specifications. ● **SEE CHART 36–1** for an example of typical fuel-pump current draw readings.

NOTE: Testing the current draw of an electric fuel pump may not indicate whether the pump is good. A pump that is not rotating may draw normal current.

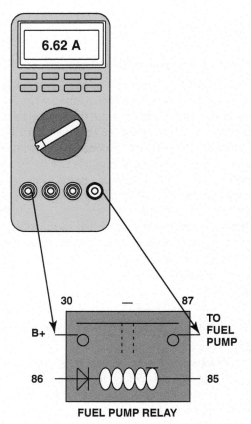

FIGURE 36–28 Hookup for testing fuel-pump current draw on any vehicle equipped with a fuel-pump relay.

Fuel-Pump Current Draw Table

AMPERAGE READING	EXPECTED VALUE	AMPERAGE TOO HIGH	AMPERAGE TOO LOW
Throttle-Body Fuel-Injection Engines	2–5 A	• Check the fuel filter. • Check for restrictions in other fuel line areas. • Replace the fuel pump.	• Check for a high-resistance connection. • Check for a high-resistance ground fault. • Replace the fuel pump.
Port Fuel-Injection Engines	4–8 A	• Check the fuel filter. • Check for restrictions in other fuel line areas. • Replace the fuel pump.	• Check for a high-resistance connection. • Check for a high-resistance ground fault. • Replace the fuel pump.
Turbo Engines	6–10 A	• Check the fuel filter. • Check for restrictions in other fuel line areas. • Replace the fuel pump.	• Check for a high-resistance connection. • Check for a high-resistance ground fault. • Replace the fuel pump.
GM CPI Truck Engines	8–12 A	• Check the fuel filter. • Check for restrictions in other fuel line areas. • Replace the fuel pump.	• Check for a high-resistance connection. • Check for a high-resistance ground fault. • Replace the fuel pump.

CHART 36–1

Fuel-pump draw and possible faults that could cause either too high or too low an amperage reading.

The Case of the Stalling Chevrolet Suburban

The owner of a Chevrolet Suburban with 187,000 miles complained that it has died several times when driving on the highway. Before it died the driver felt as if the vehicle was rumbling and had a jerky feeling. Then the truck lost power and stalls. After it was allowed to sit on the shoulder of the road for a few minutes, it started and ran normally.

The service technician checked the fuel pump for proper current draw; and while it was within specification, the technician thought that the symptoms were perfect for a fuel pump failure because it was intermittent. Using a digital storage oscilloscope (DSO) on the feed line to the pump at the fuel pump relay, it showed a pattern that indicated worn brushes. The fuel pump was replaced and the owner reported back that the intermittent stalling had not occurred since the repair.

Summary:

- **Complaint**—The owner complained that the truck would intermittently stall when driving on the highway.
- **Cause**—A worn fuel pump was the root cause of the intermittent stalling.
- **Correction**—The fuel pump was replaced that solved the stalling problem.

FUEL-PUMP REPLACEMENT

The following recommendations should be followed whenever replacing an electric fuel pump:

- The fuel-pump strainer (sock) should be replaced with the new pump.
- If the original pump had a deflector shield, it should always be used to prevent fuel return bubbles from blocking the inlet to the pump.

- Always check the interior of the fuel tank for evidence of contamination or dirt.
- Double-check that the replacement pump is correct for the application.
- Check that the wiring and electrical connectors are clean and tight.

Fuel Supply–Related Symptom Guide	
PROBLEM	**POSSIBLE CAUSES**
Pressure too high after engine start-up.	1. Defective fuel-pressure regulator 2. Restricted fuel return line 3. Excessive system voltage 4. Restricted return line 5. Wrong fuel pump
Pressure too low after engine start-up.	1. Stuck-open pressure regulator 2. Low voltage 3. Poor ground 4. Plugged fuel filter 5. Faulty inline fuel pump 6. Faulty in-tank fuel pump 7. Partially clogged filter sock 8. Faulty hose coupling 9. Leaking fuel line 10. Wrong fuel pump 11. Leaking pulsator 12. Restricted accumulator 13. Faulty pump check valves 14. Faulty pump installation
Pressure drops off with key on/ engine off. **With key off, the pressure does not hold.**	1. Leaky pulsator 2. Leaking fuel-pump coupling hose 3. Faulty fuel pump (check valves) 4. Faulty pressure regulator 5. Leaking fuel injector 6. Leaking cold-start fuel injector 7. Faulty installation 8. Lines leaking

SUMMARY

1. The fuel delivery system includes the following items:
   - Fuel tank
   - Fuel pump
   - Fuel filter(s)
   - Fuel lines

2. A fuel tank is either constructed of steel with a tin plating for corrosion resistance or polyethylene plastic.

3. Fuel tank filler tubes contain an anti-siphoning device.

4. Accident and rollover protection devices include check valves and inertia switches.

5. Most fuel lines are made of nylon plastic.
6. Electric fuel-pump types include roller cell, gerotor, and turbine.
7. Fuel filters remove particles that are 10 to 20 microns or larger in size and should be replaced regularly.

8. Fuel pumps can be tested by checking:
   - Pressure
   - Volume
   - Specified current draw

REVIEW QUESTIONS

1. What are the three most commonly used pump designs?
2. What is the proper way to disconnect and connect plastic fuel line connections?
3. Where are the fuel filters located in the fuel system?

4. What accident and rollover devices are installed in a fuel delivery system?
5. What three methods can be used to test a fuel pump?

CHAPTER QUIZ

1. The first fuel filter in the sock inside the fuel tank normally filters particles larger than _____.
   - a. 0.001 to 0.003 inch
   - b. 0.010 to 0.030 inch
   - c. 10 to 20 microns
   - d. 70 to 100 microns

2. If it is tripped, which type of safety device will keep the electric fuel pump from operating?
   - a. Rollover valve
   - b. Inertia switch
   - c. Anti-siphoning valve
   - d. Check valve

3. Fuel lines are constructed from _____.
   - a. seamless steel tubing
   - b. nylon plastic
   - c. copper and/or aluminum tubing
   - d. Both a and b

4. What prevents the fuel pump inside the fuel tank from catching the gasoline on fire?
   - a. Electricity is not used to power the pump
   - b. No air is around the motor brushes
   - c. Gasoline is hard to ignite in a closed space
   - d. All of the above

5. A good fuel pump should be able to supply how much fuel per minute?
   - a. 1/4 pint
   - b. 1/2 pint
   - c. 1 pint
   - d. 0.6 to 0.8 gallons

6. Technician A says that fuel pump modules are spring-loaded so that they can be compressed to fit into the opening. Technician B says that they are spring-loaded to allow for expansion and contraction of plastic fuel tanks. Which technician is correct?
   - a. Technician A only
   - b. Technician B only
   - c. Both Technicians A and B
   - d. Neither Technician A nor B

7. Most fuel filters are designed to remove particles larger than _____.
   - a. 10 microns
   - b. 20 microns
   - c. 70 microns
   - d. 100 microns

8. The amperage draw of an electric fuel pump is higher than specified. All of the following are possible causes *except*:
   - a. Corroded electrical connections at the pump motor
   - b. Clogged fuel filter
   - c. Restriction in the fuel line
   - d. Defective fuel pump

9. A fuel pump is being replaced for the third time. Technician A says that the gasoline could be contaminated. Technician B says that wiring to the pump could be corroded. Which technician is correct?
   - a. Technician A only
   - b. Technician B only
   - c. Both Technicians A and B
   - d. Neither Technician A nor B

10. The amperage draw of an electric fuel pump is lower than specified. What is the most likely cause?
    - a. Corroded electrical connections at the pump motor
    - b. Clogged fuel filter
    - c. Restriction in the fuel line
    - d. Stuck fuel pump impeller blades

chapter 37
FUEL-INJECTION COMPONENTS AND OPERATION

LEARNING OBJECTIVES

After studying this chapter, the reader will be able to:

1. Describe how throttle-body injection and port fuel-injection systems work.
2. Discuss the function of the fuel-pressure regulator and describe a vacuum-biased fuel-pressure regulator.
3. List the types of fuel-injection systems and explain their modes of operation.

This chapter will help you prepare for Engine Repair (A8) ASE certification test content area "C" (Fuel, Air Induction, and Exhaust Systems Diagnosis and Repair).

KEY TERMS

Demand delivery system (DDS) 583
Electronic air control (EAC) 587
Electronic returnless fuel system (ERFS) 582
Flare 587
Fuel rail 584
Gang fired 579
Idle speed control (ISC) motor 588

Mechanical returnless fuel system (MRFS) 583
Port fuel-injection 577
Pressure control valve (PCV) 583
Pressure vent valve (PVV) 582
Sequential fuel injection (SFI) 580
Throttle-body injection (TBI) 577

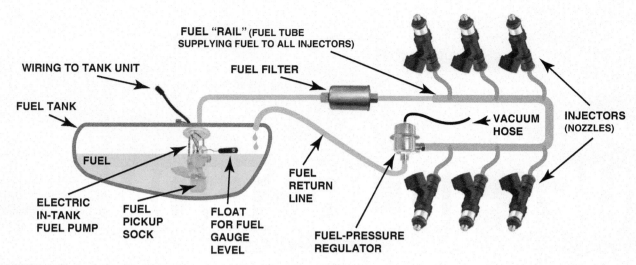

FUEL "RAIL" (FUEL TUBE
SUPPLYING FUEL TO ALL INJECTORS)

WIRING TO TANK UNIT

FUEL FILTER

FUEL TANK

INJECTORS
(NOZZLES)

VACUUM
HOSE

FUEL

FUEL
RETURN
LINE

ELECTRIC
IN-TANK
FUEL PUMP

FUEL
PICKUP
SOCK

FLOAT
FOR FUEL
GAUGE
LEVEL

FUEL-PRESSURE
REGULATOR

FIGURE 37–1 Typical port fuel-injection system, indicating the location of various components. Notice that the fuel-pressure regulator is located on the fuel return side of the system. The computer does not control fuel pressure, but does control the operation of the electric fuel pump (on most systems) and the pulsing on and off of the injectors.

ELECTRONIC FUEL-INJECTION OPERATION

Electronic fuel-injection systems use the computer to control the following operation of fuel injectors and other functions based on information sent to the computer from the various sensors. Most electronic fuel-injection systems share the following:

1. Electric fuel pump (usually located inside the fuel tank)
2. Fuel-pump relay (usually controlled by the computer)
3. Fuel-pressure regulator (mechanically operated spring-loaded rubber diaphragm maintains proper fuel pressure)
4. Fuel-injector nozzle or nozzles which are basically 12-volt solenoids

● **SEE FIGURE 37–1**. Most electronic fuel-injection systems use the computer to control the following aspects of their operation:

1. **Pulsing the fuel injectors on and off.** The longer the injectors are held open, the greater the amount of fuel injected into the intake manifold near the intake valve.
2. **Operating the fuel-pump relay circuit.** The computer usually controls the operation of the electric fuel pump located inside (or near) the fuel tank. The computer uses signals from the ignition switch and RPM signals from the ignition module or system to energize the fuel-pump relay circuit.

NOTE: This is a safety feature, because if the engine stalls and the tachometer (engine speed) signal is lost, the computer will shut off (de-energize) the fuel-pump relay and stop the fuel pump.

Computer-controlled fuel-injection systems are normally reliable systems if the proper service procedures are followed. Fuel-injection systems use the gasoline flowing through the injectors to lubricate and cool the injector electrical windings and pintle valves.

NOTE: The fuel does not actually make contact with the electrical windings because the injectors have O-rings at the top and bottom of the winding spool to keep fuel out.

 **TECH TIP**

"Two Must-Do's"

For long service life of the fuel system, always do the following:

1. Avoid operating the vehicle on a near-empty tank of fuel. The water or alcohol becomes more concentrated when the fuel level is low. Dirt that settles near the bottom of the fuel tank can be drawn through the fuel system and cause damage to the pump and injector nozzles.
2. Replace the fuel filter at regular service intervals.

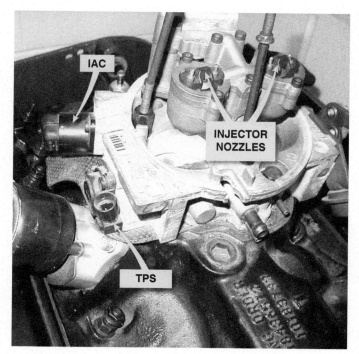

FIGURE 37–2 A dual-nozzle TBI unit on a Chevrolet 5.0 L V-8 engine. The fuel is squirted above the throttle plate where the fuel mixes with air before entering the intake manifold.

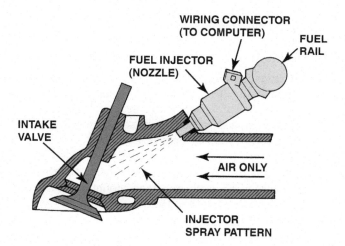

FIGURE 37–3 A typical port fuel-injection system squirts fuel into the low pressure (vacuum) of the intake manifold, about 3 inch (70 to 100 mm) from the intake valve.

There are two types of electronic fuel-injection systems:

- **Throttle-body injection (TBI) type.** A TBI system delivers fuel from a nozzle(s) into the air above the throttle plate. ● SEE FIGURE 37–2.

- **Port fuel-injection type.** A port fuel-injection design uses a nozzle for each cylinder and the fuel is squirted into the intake manifold about 2 to 3 inches (70 to 100 mm) from the intake valve. ● SEE FIGURE 37–3.

SPEED-DENSITY FUEL-INJECTION SYSTEMS

Fuel-injection computer systems require a method for measuring the amount of air the engine is breathing in, in order to match the correct fuel delivery. There are two basic methods used:

1. Speed density
2. Mass airflow

The speed-density method does not require an air quantity sensor, but rather calculates the amount of fuel required by the engine. The computer uses information from sensors such as the MAP and TP to calculate the needed amount of fuel.

- **MAP sensor.** The value of the intake (inlet) manifold pressure (vacuum) is a direct indication of engine load.

- **TP sensor.** The position of the throttle plate and its rate of change are used as part of the equation to calculate the proper amount of fuel to inject.

- **Temperature sensors.** Both engine coolant temperature (ECT) and intake air temperature (IAT) are used to calculate the density of the air and the need of the engine for fuel. A cold engine (low-coolant temperature) requires a richer air–fuel mixture than a warm engine.

On speed-density systems, the computer calculates the amount of air in each cylinder by using manifold pressure and engine RPM. The amount of air in each cylinder is the major factor in determining the amount of fuel needed. Other sensors provide information to modify the fuel requirements. The formula used to determine the injector pulse width (PW) in milliseconds (ms) is the following:

Injector pulse width = MAP/BARO × RPM/maximum RPM

The formula is modified by values from other sensors, including the following:

- Throttle position (TP)
- Engine coolant temperature (ECT)
- Intake air temperature (IAT)
- Oxygen sensor voltage (O2S)
- Adaptive memory

A fuel injector delivers atomized fuel into the airstream where it is instantly vaporized. All throttle-body (TB) fuel-injection systems and many multipoint (port) injection systems use the speed-density method of fuel calculation.

MASS AIRFLOW FUEL-INJECTION SYSTEMS

The formula used by fuel-injection systems that use a mass airflow (MAF) sensor to calculate the injection base pulse width is the following:

Injector pulse width = airflow/RPM

The formula is modified by other sensor values such as the following:

- Throttle position
- Engine coolant temperature
- Barometric pressure
- Adaptive memory

NOTE: Many four-cylinder engines do not use a MAF sensor because, due to the time interval between intake events, some reverse airflow can occur in the intake manifold. The MAF sensor would "read" this flow of air as being additional air entering the engine, giving the PCM incorrect airflow information. Therefore, most four-cylinder engines use the speed-density method of fuel control.

THROTTLE-BODY INJECTION

The computer controls injector 12 volt pulses in one of two ways:

- Synchronized
- Nonsynchronized

If the system uses a synchronized mode, the injector pulses once for each distributor reference pulse. In some vehicles, when dual injectors are used in a synchronized system, the injectors pulse alternately. In a nonsynchronized system, the injectors are pulsed once during a given period (which varies according to calibration) completely independent of distributor reference pulses.

The injector always opens the same distance, and the fuel pressure is maintained at a controlled value by the pressure regulator. The regulators used on throttle-body injection systems are not connected to a vacuum like many port fuel-injection systems. The strength of the spring inside the regulator determines at what pressure the valve is unseated, sending the fuel back to the tank and lowering the pressure. ● **SEE FIGURE 37–4.** The amount of fuel delivered by the injector depends on the amount of time (on-time) that the nozzle is open. This is the injector pulse width—the on-time in milliseconds that the nozzle is open.

The PCM commands a variety of pulse widths to supply the amount of fuel that an engine needs at any specific moment.

- A long pulse width delivers more fuel.
- A short pulse width delivers less fuel.

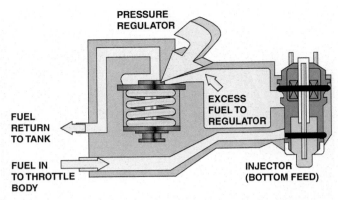

FIGURE 37–4 The tension of the spring in the fuel-pressure regulator determines the operating pressure on a throttle-body fuel-injection unit.

? FREQUENTLY ASKED QUESTION

How Do the Sensors Affect the Pulse Width?

The base pulse width of a fuel-injection system is primarily determined by the value of the MAF or MAP sensor and engine speed (RPM). However, the PCM relies on the input from many other sensors, such as the following, to modify the base pulse width as needed:

- **TP Sensor.** This sensor causes the PCM to command up to 500% (five times) the base pulse width if the accelerator pedal is depressed rapidly to the floor. It can also reduce the pulse width by about 70% if the throttle is rapidly closed.
- **ECT.** The value of this sensor determines the temperature of the engine coolant, helps determine the base pulse width, and can account for up to 60% of the determining factors.
- **BARO.** The BARO sensor compensates for altitude and adds up to about 10% under high-pressure conditions and subtracts as much as 50% from the base pulse width at high altitudes.
- **IAT.** The intake air temperature is used to modify the base pulse width based on the temperature of the air entering the engine. It is usually capable of adding as much as 20% if very cold air is entering the engine or reducing the pulse width by up to 20% if very hot air is entering the engine.
- **O2S.** This is one of the main modifiers to the base pulse width and can add or subtract up to about 20% to 25% or more, depending on the oxygen sensor activity.

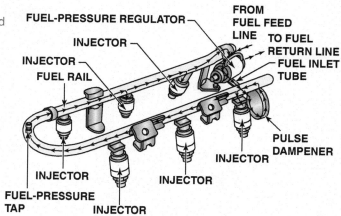

FIGURE 37–5 The injectors receive fuel and are supported by the fuel rail.

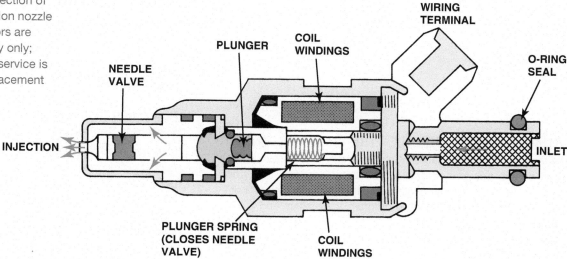

FIGURE 37–6 Cross section of a typical port fuel-injection nozzle assembly. These injectors are serviced as an assembly only; no part replacement or service is possible except for replacement of external O-ring seals.

PORT FUEL INJECTION

The advantages of port fuel-injection design also are related to characteristics of intake manifolds:

- Fuel distribution is equal to all cylinders because each cylinder has its own injector. ● **SEE FIGURE 37–5.**

- The fuel is injected almost directly into the combustion chamber, so there is no chance for it to condense on the walls of a cold intake manifold.

- Because the manifold does not have to carry fuel to properly position a TBI unit, it can be shaped and sized to tune the intake airflow to achieve specific engine performance characteristics.

An EFI injector is simply a specialized solenoid. ● **SEE FIGURE 37–6.** It has an armature winding to create a magnetic field, and a needle (pintle), a disc, or a ball valve. A spring holds the needle, disc, or ball closed against the valve seat, and when energized, the armature winding pulls open the valve when it receives a current pulse from the Powertrain Control

Module (PCM). When the solenoid is energized, it unseats the valve to inject fuel.

Electronic fuel-injection systems use a solenoid-operated injector to spray atomized fuel in timed pulses into the manifold or near the intake valve. ● **SEE FIGURE 37–7.** Injectors may be sequenced and fired in one of several ways, but their pulse width is determined and controlled by the engine computer.

Port systems have an injector for each cylinder, but they do not all fire the injectors in the same way. Domestic systems use one of three ways to trigger the injectors:

- Grouped double-fire
- Simultaneous double-fire
- Sequential

GROUPED DOUBLE-FIRE This system divides the injectors into two equalized groups. The groups fire alternately; each group fires once each crankshaft revolution, or twice per four-stroke cycle. The fuel injected remains near the intake valve and enters the engine when the valve opens. This method of pulsing injectors in groups is sometimes called **gang fired**.

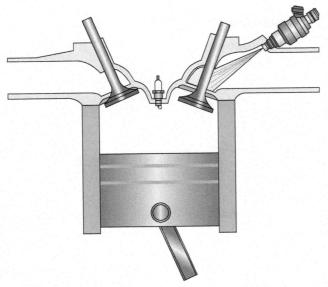

FIGURE 37-7 Port fuel injectors spray atomized fuel into the intake manifold about 3 inches (75 mm) from the intake valve.

FIGURE 37-8 A port fuel-injected engine that is equipped with long, tuned intake-manifold runners.

SIMULTANEOUS DOUBLE-FIRE This design fires all of the injectors at the same time once every engine revolution: two pulses per four-stroke cycle. Many port fuel-injection systems on four-cylinder engines use this pattern of injector firing. It is easier for engineers to program this system and it can make relatively quick adjustments in the air–fuel ratio, but it still requires the intake charge to wait in the manifold for varying lengths of time.

SEQUENTIAL Sequential firing of the injectors according to engine firing order is the most accurate and desirable method of regulating port fuel injection. However, it is also the most complex and expensive to design and manufacture. In this system, the injectors are timed and pulsed individually, much like the spark plugs are sequentially operated in firing order of the engine. This system is often called **sequential fuel injection** or **SFI**. Each cylinder receives one charge every two crankshaft revolutions, just before the intake valve opens. This means that the mixture is never static in the intake manifold and mixture adjustments can be made almost instantaneously between the firing of one injector and the next. A camshaft position sensor (CMP) signal or a special distributor reference pulse informs the PCM when the No. 1 cylinder is on its compression stroke. If the sensor fails or the reference pulse is interrupted, some injection systems shut down, while others revert to pulsing the injectors simultaneously.

The major advantage of using port injection instead of the simpler throttle-body injection is that the intake manifolds on port fuel-injected engines only contain air, not a mixture of air and fuel. This allows the engine design engineer the opportunity to design long, "tuned" intake-manifold runners that help the engine produce increased torque at low engine speeds. ● **SEE FIGURE 37-8**.

? **FREQUENTLY ASKED QUESTION**

How Can It Be Determined If the Injection System Is Sequential?

Look at the color of the wires at the injectors. If a sequentially fired injector is used, then one wire color (the pulse wire) will be a different color for each injector. The other wire is usually the same color because all injectors receive voltage from some source. If a group- or batch-fired injection system is being used, the wire colors will be the same for the injectors that are group fired. For example, a V-6 group-fired engine will have three injectors with a pink and blue wire (power and pulse) and the other three will have pink and green wires.

NOTE: Some port fuel-injection systems used on engines with four or more valves per cylinder may use two injectors per cylinder. One injector is used all the time, and the second injector is operated by the computer when high-engine speed and high-load conditions are detected by the computer. Typically, the second injector injects fuel into the high-speed intake ports of the manifold. This system permits good low-speed power and throttle responses as well as superior high-speed power.

FUEL-PRESSURE REGULATOR

PURPOSE AND FUNCTION The pressure regulator and fuel pump work together to maintain the required pressure drop at the injector tips. The fuel-pressure regulator typically consists of a spring-loaded, diaphragm-operated valve in a metal housing.

Fuel-pressure regulators on fuel-return-type fuel-injection systems are installed on the return (downstream) side of the injectors at the end of the fuel rail, or are built into or mounted upon the throttle-body housing. Downstream regulation minimizes fuel-pressure pulsations caused by pressure drop across the injectors as the nozzles open. It also ensures positive fuel pressure at the injectors at all times and holds residual pressure in the lines when the engine is off. On mechanical returnless systems, the regulator is located back at the tank with the fuel filter.

OPERATION In order for excess fuel (about 80% to 90% of the fuel delivered) to return to the tank, fuel pressure must overcome spring pressure on the spring-loaded diaphragm to uncover the return line to the tank. This happens when system pressure exceeds operating requirements. With TBI, the regulator is close to the injector tip, so the regulator senses essentially the same air pressure as the injector.

The pressure regulator used in a port fuel-injection system has an intake-manifold vacuum line connection on the regulator vacuum chamber. This allows fuel pressure to be modulated by a combination of spring pressure and manifold vacuum acting on the diaphragm. ● **SEE FIGURES 37–9 AND 37–10.**

In both TBI and port fuel-injection systems, the regulator shuts off the return line when the fuel pump is not running. This maintains pressure at the injectors for easy restarting after hot soak as well as reducing vapor lock.

Port fuel-injection systems generally operate with pressures at the injector of about 30 to 55 PSI (207 to 379 kPa).

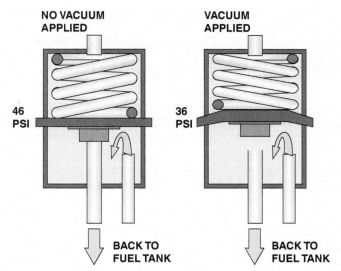

FIGURE 37–10 A typical fuel-pressure regulator that has a spring that exerts 46 pounds of force against the fuel. If 20 inches of vacuum are applied above the spring, the vacuum reduces the force exerted by the spring on the fuel, allowing the fuel to return to the tank at a lower pressure.

TECH TIP

Don't Forget the Regulator

Some fuel-pressure regulators contain a 10 micron filter. If this filter becomes clogged, a lack of fuel flow would result. ● **SEE FIGURE 37–11.**

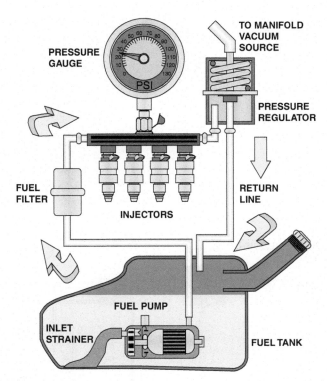

FIGURE 37–9 A typical port fuel-injected system showing a vacuum-controlled fuel-pressure regulator.

FIGURE 37–11 A lack of fuel flow could be due to a restricted fuel-pressure regulator. Notice the fine screen filter. If this filter were to become clogged, higher than normal fuel pressure would occur.

VACUUM-BIASED FUEL-PRESSURE REGULATOR

The primary reason why many port fuel-injected systems use a vacuum-controlled fuel-pressure regulator is to ensure that there is a constant pressure drop across the injectors. In a throttle-body fuel-injection system, the injector squirts into the atmospheric pressure regardless of the load on the engine. In a port fuel-injected engine, however, the pressure inside the intake manifold changes as the load on the engine increases.

ENGINE OPERATING CONDITION	INTAKE-MANIFOLD VACUUM	FUEL PRESSURE
Idle or cruise	High	Lower
Heavy load	Low	Higher

The computer can best calculate injector pulse width based on all sensors if the pressure drop across the injector is the same under all operating conditions. A vacuum-controlled fuel-pressure regulator allows the equal pressure drop by reducing the force exerted by the regulator spring at high vacuum (low-load condition), yet allowing the full force of the regulator spring to be exerted when the vacuum is low (high-engine-load condition).

ELECTRONIC RETURNLESS FUEL SYSTEM

This system is unique because it does not use a mechanical valve to regulate rail pressure. Fuel pressure at the rail is sensed by a pressure transducer, which sends a low-level signal to a controller. The controller contains logic to calculate a signal to the pump power driver. The power driver contains a high-current transistor that controls the pump speed using pulse width modulation (PWM). This system is called the **electronic returnless fuel system (ERFS).** ● SEE **FIGURE 37–12.** This transducer can be differentially referenced to manifold pressure for closed-loop feedback, correcting and maintaining the output of the pump to a desired rail setting. This system is capable of continuously varying rail pressure as a result of engine vacuum, engine fuel demand, and fuel temperature (as sensed by an external temperature transducer, if necessary). A **pressure vent valve (PVV)** is employed at the tank to relieve overpressure due to thermal expansion of fuel. In addition, a supply-side bleed, by means of an in-tank reservoir using a supply-side jet pump, is necessary for proper pump operation.

FIGURE 37–12 The fuel-pressure sensor and fuel-temperature sensor are often constructed together in one assembly to help give the PCM the needed data to control the fuel-pump speed.

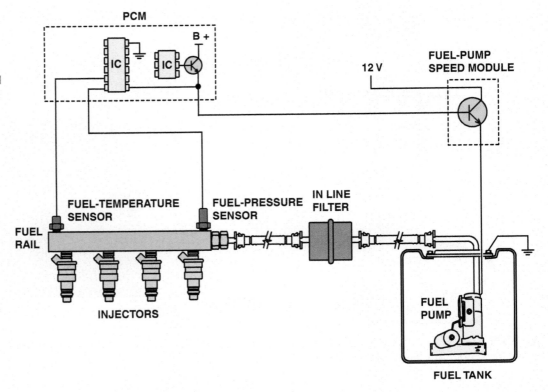

MECHANICAL RETURNLESS FUEL SYSTEM

The first production returnless systems employed the **mechanical returnless fuel system (MRFS)** approach. This system has a bypass regulator to control rail pressure that is located in close proximity to the fuel tank. Fuel is sent by the in-tank pump to a chassis-mounted inline filter with excess fuel returning to the tank through a short return line.
● **SEE FIGURE 37–13**. The inline filter may be mounted directly to the tank, thereby eliminating the shortened return line. Supply pressure is regulated on the downstream side of the inline filter to accommodate changing restrictions throughout the filter's service life. This system is limited to constant rail pressure (*CRP) system calibrations, whereas with ERFS, the pressure transducer can be referenced to atmospheric pressure for CRP systems or differentially referenced to intake-manifold pressure for constant differential injector pressure (**CIP) systems.

NOTE: *CRP is referenced to atmospheric pressure, has lower operating pressure, and is desirable for calibrations using speed/air density sensing. **CIP is referenced to manifold pressure, varies rail pressure, and is desirable in engines that use mass airflow sensing.

DEMAND DELIVERY SYSTEM (DDS)

Given the experience with both ERFS and MRFS, a need was recognized to develop new returnless technologies that could combine the speed control and constant injector pressure attributes of ERFS together with the cost savings, simplicity, and reliability of MRFS. This new technology also needed to address pulsation dampening/hammering and fuel transient response. Therefore, the **demand delivery system (DDS)** technology was developed. A different form of demand pressure regulator has been applied to the fuel rail. It mounts at the head or port entry and regulates the pressure downstream at the injectors by admitting the precise quantity of fuel into the rail as consumed by the engine. Having demand regulation at the rail improves pressure response to flow transients and provides rail pulsation dampening. A fuel pump and a low-cost, high-performance bypass regulator are used within the appropriate fuel sender. ● **SEE FIGURE 37–14**. They supply a pressure somewhat higher than the required rail set pressure to accommodate dynamic line and filter pressure losses. Electronic pump speed control is accomplished using a smart regulator as an integral flow sensor. A **pressure control valve (PCV)** may also be used and can readily reconfigure an existing design fuel sender into a returnless sender.

FIGURE 37–13 A mechanical returnless fuel system. The bypass regulator in the fuel tank controls fuel line pressure.

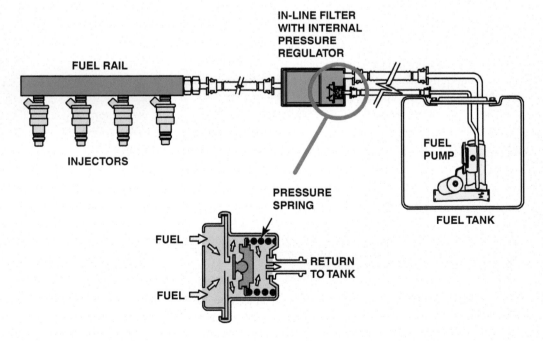

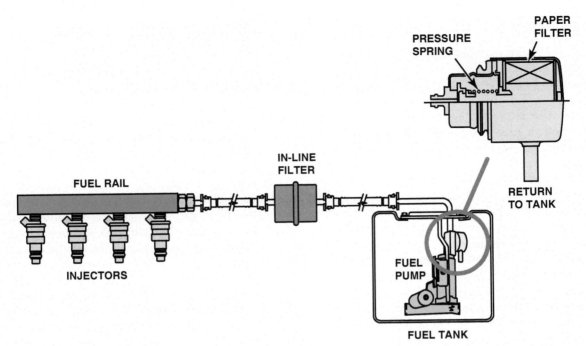

FIGURE 37–14 A demand delivery system uses a fuel-pressure regulator attached to the fuel pump assembly inside the fuel tank.

Why Are Some Fuel Rails Rectangular Shaped?

A port fuel-injection system uses a pipe or tubes to deliver fuel from the fuel line to the intended fuel injectors. This pipe or tube is called the **fuel rail**. Some vehicle manufacturers construct the fuel rail in a rectangular cross section. ● **SEE FIGURE 37–15.** The sides of the fuel rail are able to move in and out slightly, thereby acting as a fuel pulsator evening out the pressure pulses created by the opening and closing of the injectors to reduce underhood noise. A round cross-sectional fuel rail is not able to deform and, as a result, some manufacturers have had to use a separate dampener.

FIGURE 37–15 A rectangular-shaped fuel rail is used to help dampen fuel system pulsations and noise caused by the injectors opening and closing.

FUEL INJECTORS

EFI systems use 12-volt solenoid-operated injectors. ● **SEE FIGURE 37–16.** This electromagnetic device contains an armature and a spring-loaded needle valve or ball valve assembly. When the computer energizes the solenoid, voltage is applied to the solenoid coil until the current reaches a specified level. This permits a quick pull-in of the armature during turn-on. The armature is pulled off of its seat against spring force, allowing fuel to flow through the inlet filter screen to the spray nozzle, where it is sprayed in a pattern that varies with application. ● **SEE FIGURE 37–17.** The injector opens the same amount each time it is energized, so the amount of fuel injected depends on the length of time the injector remains open. By angling the director hole plates, the injector sprays fuel more directly at the intake valves, which further atomizes and vaporizes the fuel before it enters the combustion chamber. PFI injectors typically are a top-feed design in which fuel enters the top of the injector and passes through its entire length to keep it cool before being injected.

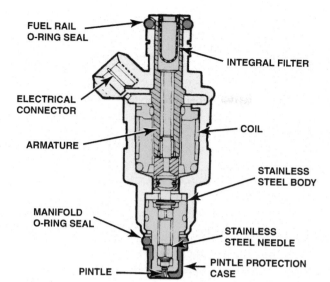

FIGURE 37–16 A multiport fuel injector. Notice that the fuel flows straight through and does not come in contact with the coil windings.

FIGURE 37–17 Each of the eight injectors shown are producing a correct spray pattern for the applications. While all throttle-body injectors spray a conical pattern, most port fuel injections do not.

Ford introduced two basic designs of deposit-resistant injectors on some engines. The design, manufactured by Bosch, uses a four-hole director/metering plate similar to that used by the Rochester Multec injectors. The design manufactured by Nippondenso uses an internal upstream orifice in the adjusting tube. It also has a redesigned pintle/seat containing a wider tip opening that tolerates deposit buildup without affecting injector performance.

FREQUENTLY ASKED QUESTION

How Can the Proper Injector Size Be Determined?

Most people want to increase the output of fuel to increase engine performance. Injector sizing can sometimes be a challenge, especially if the size of injector is not known. In most cases, manufacturers publish the rating of injectors, in pounds of fuel per hour (lb/hr). The rate is figured with the injector held open at 3 bars (43.5 PSI). An important consideration is that larger flow injectors have a higher minimum flow rating. Here is a formula to calculate injector sizing when changing the mechanical characteristics of an engine:

Flow rate = hp × BSFC/number of cylinders × maximum duty cycle (% of on-time of the injectors)

- **hp** is the projected horsepower. Be realistic!
- **BSFC** is brake-specific fuel consumption in pounds per horsepower-hour. Calculated values are used for this, 0.4 to 0.8 lb. In most cases, start on the low side for naturally aspirated engines and the high side for engines with forced induction.
- **Number of cylinders** is actually the number of injectors being used.
- **Maximum duty cycle** is considered at 0.8 (80%). Above this, the injector may overheat, lose consistency, or not work at all.

For example,

5.7 liter V-8 = 240 hp × 0.65/8 cylinders × 8 = 24.37 lb/hr injectors required

CENTRAL PORT INJECTION

A cross between port fuel injection and throttle-body injection, CPI was introduced in the early 1990s by General Motors. The CPI assembly consists of a single fuel injector, a pressure regulator, and six poppet nozzle assemblies with nozzle tubes. ● **SEE FIGURE 37–18**. The central sequential fuel injection (CSFI) system has six injectors in place of just one used on the CPI unit.

When the injector is energized, its armature lifts off of the six fuel tube seats and pressurized fuel flows through the nozzle tubes to each poppet nozzle. The increased pressure causes each poppet nozzle ball to also lift from its seat, allowing fuel to flow from the nozzle. This hybrid injection system combines the single injector of a TBI system with the equalized fuel distribution of a PFI system. It eliminates the individual fuel rail

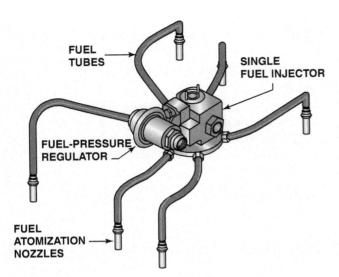

FIGURE 37–18 A central port fuel-injection system.

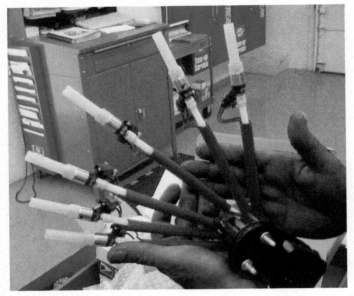

FIGURE 37–19 A factory replacement unit for a CSFI unit that has individual injectors at the ends that go into the intake manifold instead of poppet valves.

while allowing more efficient manifold tuning than is otherwise possible with a TBI system. Newer versions use six individual solenoids to fire one for each cylinder. ● **SEE FIGURE 37–19.**

FUEL-INJECTION MODES OF OPERATION

All fuel-injection systems are designed to supply the correct amount of fuel under a wide range of engine operating conditions. These modes of operation include:

Starting (cranking)	Acceleration enrichment
Clear flood	Deceleration enleanment
Idle (run)	Fuel shutoff

STARTING MODE   When the ignition is turned to the start (on) position, the engine cranks and the PCM energizes the fuel-pump relay. The PCM also pulses the injectors on, basing the pulse width on engine speed and engine coolant temperature. The colder the engine is, the greater the pulse width. Cranking mode air–fuel ratio varies from about 1.5:1 at –40°F (–40°C) to 14.7:1 at 200°F (93°C).

CLEAR FLOOD MODE   If the engine becomes flooded with too much fuel, the driver can depress the accelerator pedal to greater than 80% to enter the clear flood mode. When the PCM detects that the engine speed is low (usually below 600 RPM) and the throttle-position (TP) sensor voltage is high (WOT), the injector pulse width is greatly reduced or even shut off entirely, depending on the vehicle.

OPEN-LOOP MODE   Open-loop operation occurs during warm-up before the oxygen sensor can supply accurate information to the PCM. The PCM determines injector pulse width based on values from the MAF, MAP, TP, ECT, and IAT sensors.

CLOSED-LOOP MODE   Closed-loop operation is used to modify the base injector pulse width as determined by feedback from the oxygen sensor to achieve proper fuel control.

ACCELERATION ENRICHMENT MODE   During acceleration, the throttle-position (TP) voltage increases, indicating that a richer air–fuel mixture is required. The PCM then supplies a longer injector pulse width and may even supply extra pulses to supply the needed fuel for acceleration.

DECELERATION ENLEANMENT MODE   When the engine decelerates, a leaner air–fuel mixture is required to help reduce emissions and to prevent deceleration backfire. If the deceleration is rapid, the injector may be shut off entirely for a short time and then pulsed on enough to keep the engine running.

FUEL SHUTOFF MODE   Besides shutting off fuel entirely during periods of rapid deceleration, PCM also shuts off the injector when the ignition is turned off to prevent the engine from continuing to run.

What Is Battery Voltage Correction?

Battery voltage correction is a program built into the PCM that causes the injector pulse width to increase if there is a drop in electrical system voltage. Lower battery voltage would cause the fuel injectors to open slower than normal and the fuel pump to run slower. Both of these conditions can cause the engine to run leaner than normal if the battery voltage is low. Because a lean air–fuel mixture can cause the engine to overheat, the PCM compensates for the lower voltage by adding a percentage to the injector pulse width. This richer condition will help prevent serious engine damage. The idle speed is also increased to turn the generator (alternator) faster if low battery voltage is detected.

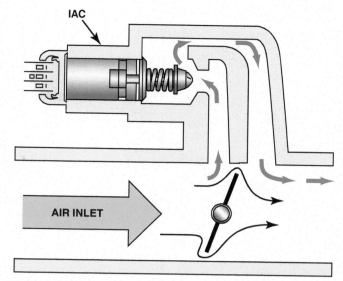

FIGURE 37–20 The small arrows indicate the air bypassing the throttle plate in the closed throttle position. This air is called minimum air. The air flowing through the IAC is the air-flow that determines the idle speed.

IDLE CONTROL

PURPOSE AND FUNCTION Before electronic throttle control (ETC) systems, the idle speed was controlled by using an air bypass control unit. ● **SEE FIGURE 37–20.** This air bypass or regulator provides needed additional airflow, and thus more fuel. The engine needs more power when cold to maintain its normal idle speed to overcome the increased friction from cold lubricating oil. It does this by opening an intake air passage to let more air into the engine just as depressing the accelerator pedal would open the throttle valve, allowing more air into the engine. The system is calibrated to maintain engine idle speed at a specified value regardless of engine temperature.

Most PFI systems use an idle air control (IAC) motor to regulate idle bypass air. The IAC is computer-controlled, and is either a solenoid-operated valve or a stepper motor that regulates the airflow around the throttle. The idle air control valve is also called an **electronic air control (EAC)** valve.

When the engine stops, most IAC units will retract outward to get ready for the next engine start. When the engine starts, the engine speed is high to provide for proper operation when the engine is cold. Then, as the engine gets warmer, the computer reduces engine idle speed gradually by reducing the number of counts or steps commanded by the IAC.

When the engine is warm and restarted, the idle speed should momentarily increase, then decrease to normal idle speed. This increase and then decrease in engine speed is often called an engine **flare**. If the engine speed does not flare, then the IAC may not be working (it may be stuck in one position).

STEPPER MOTOR OPERATION A digital output is used to control stepper motors. Stepper motors are direct-current motors that move in fixed steps or increments from de-energized (no voltage) to fully energized (full voltage). A stepper motor often has as many as 120 steps of motion.

A common use for stepper motors is as an idle air control (IAC) valve, which controls engine idle speeds and prevents stalls due to changes in engine load. When used as an IAC, the stepper motor is usually a reversible DC motor that moves in increments, or steps. The motor moves a shaft back and forth to operate a conical valve. When the conical valve is moved back, more air bypasses the throttle plates and enters the engine, increasing idle speed. As the conical valve moves inward, the idle speed decreases.

When using a stepper motor that is controlled by the PCM, it is very easy for the PCM to keep track of the position of the stepper motor. By counting the number of steps that have been sent to the stepper motor, the PCM can determine the relative position of the stepper motor. While the PCM does not actually receive a feedback signal from the stepper motor, it does know how many steps forward or backward the motor should have moved.

A typical stepper motor uses a permanent magnet and two electromagnets. Each of the two electromagnetic windings is controlled by the computer. The computer pulses the windings and changes the polarity of the windings to cause the armature of the stepper motor to rotate 90 degrees at a time. Each 90-degree pulse is recorded by the computer as a "count" or "step"; therefore, the name given to this type of motor. ● **SEE FIGURE 37–21.**

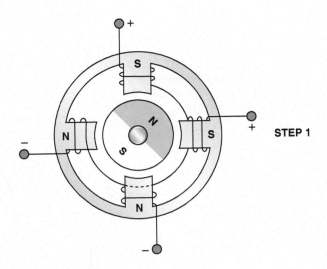

STEP 1

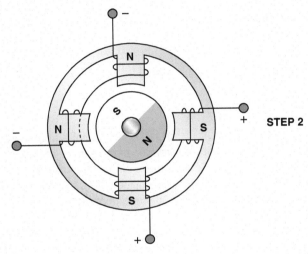

STEP 2

FIGURE 37–21 Most stepper motors use four wires, which are pulsed by the computer to rotate the armature in steps.

Idle airflow in a TBI system travels through a passage around the throttle and is controlled by a stepper motor. In some applications, an externally mounted permanent magnet motor called the **idle speed control (ISC) motor** mechanically advances the throttle linkage to advance the throttle opening.

SUMMARY

1. A fuel-injection system includes the electric fuel pump and fuel-pump relay, fuel-pressure regulator, and fuel injectors (nozzles).

2. The two types of fuel-injection systems are the throttle body design and the port fuel-injection design.

3. The two methods of fuel-injection control are the speed density system, which uses the MAP to measure the load on the engine, and the mass airflow, which uses the MAF sensor to directly measure the amount of air entering the engine.

4. The amount of fuel supplied by fuel injectors is determined by how long they are kept open. This opening time is called the pulse width and is measured in milliseconds.

5. The fuel-pressure regulator is usually located on the fuel return on return-type fuel-injection systems.

6. TBI-type fuel-injection systems do not use a vacuum-controlled fuel-pressure regulator, whereas many port fuel-injection systems use a vacuum-controlled regulator to monitor equal pressure drop across the injectors.

7. Other fuel designs include the electronic returnless, the mechanical returnless, and the demand delivery systems.

1. What are the two basic methods used for measuring the amount of air the engine is breathing in, in order to match the correct fuel delivery?

2. What is the purpose of the vacuum-controlled (biased) fuel-pressure regulator?

3. How many sensors are used to determine the base pulse width on a speed-density system?

4. How many sensors are used to determine the base pulse width on a mass airflow system?

5. What are the three types of returnless fuel-injection systems?

CHAPTER QUIZ

1. Technician A says that the fuel-pump relay is usually controlled by the PCM. Technician B says that a TBI injector squirts fuel above the throttle plate. Which technician is correct?
   a. Technician A only
   b. Technician B only
   c. Both Technicians A and B
   d. Neither Technician A nor B

2. Why are some fuel rails rectangular in shape?
   a. Increases fuel pressure
   b. Helps keep air out of the injectors
   c. Reduces noise
   d. Increases the speed of the fuel through the fuel rail

3. Which fuel-injection system uses the MAP sensor as the primary sensor to determine the base pulse width?
   a. Speed density
   b. Mass airflow
   c. Demand delivery
   d. Mechanical returnless

4. Why is a vacuum line attached to a fuel-pressure regulator on many port fuel-injected engines?
   a. To draw fuel back into the intake manifold through the vacuum hose
   b. To create an equal pressure drop across the injectors
   c. To raise the fuel pressure at idle
   d. To lower the fuel pressure under heavy engine load conditions to help improve fuel economy

5. Which sensor has the greatest influence on injector pulse width besides the MAF sensor?
   a. IAT
   b. BARO
   c. ECT
   d. TP

6. Technician A says that the port fuel-injection injectors operate using 5 volts from the computer. Technician B says that sequential fuel injectors all use a different wire color on the injectors. Which technician is correct?
   a. Technician A only
   b. Technician B only
   c. Both Technicians A and B
   d. Neither Technician A nor B

7. Which type of port fuel-injection system uses a fuel-temperature and/or fuel-pressure sensor?
   a. All port fuel-injected engines
   b. TBI units only
   c. Electronic returnless systems
   d. Demand delivery systems

8. Dampeners are used on some fuel rails to _____.
   a. increase the fuel pressure in the rail
   b. reduce (decrease) the fuel pressure in the rail
   c. reduce noise
   d. trap dirt and keep it away from the injectors

9. Where is the fuel-pressure regulator located on a vacuum-biased port fuel-injection system?
   a. In the tank
   b. At the inlet of the fuel rail
   c. At the outlet of the fuel rail
   d. Near or on the fuel filter

10. What type of device is used in a typical idle air control?
    a. DC motor
    b. Stepper motor
    c. Pulsator-type actuator
    d. Solenoid

chapter 38

GASOLINE DIRECT-INJECTION SYSTEMS

LEARNING OBJECTIVES

After studying this chapter, the reader will be able to:

1. Discuss how to troubleshoot a gasoline direct-injection system.
2. Explain how a gasoline direct-injection system works.
3. Describe the differences between port fuel-injection and gasoline direct-injection systems.
4. List the various modes of operation of a gasoline direct-injection system.

This chapter will help you prepare for Engine Repair (A8) ASE certification test content area "C" (Fuel, Air Induction, and Exhaust Systems Diagnosis and Repair).

KEY TERMS

Gasoline direct-injection (GDI) 591

Homogeneous mode 594

Spark ignition direct injection (SIDI) 591

Stratified mode 594

DIRECT FUEL INJECTION

PORT INJECTION VS. DIRECT INJECTION Unlike a port fuel-injection system, a GDI system varies the fuel pressure to achieve greater fuel delivery using a very short pulse time, which is usually less than one millisecond.

- Port Fuel Injection–Constant fuel pressure but variable injector pulse-width.
- GDI–Almost constant injector pulse-width with varying fuel pressure.

In a port fuel injection system, the fuel is squirted into the intake manifold or in the intake port upstream from the intake valve. The atomized fuel then mixes with the air entering the cylinder on the way to the combustion chamber.

In a **gasoline direct-injection (GDI)** system the fuel is squirted directly into the combustion chamber. ● **SEE FIGURE 38-1.** General Motors refers to GDI as a **spark ignition direct injection (SIDI)** system.

PARTS AND OPERATION A direct-injection system sprays high-pressure fuel, up to 2,900 PSI, into the combustion chamber as the piston approaches the top of the compression stroke. With the combination of high-pressure swirl injectors and modified combustion chamber, almost instantaneous vaporization occurs. This combined with a higher compression ratio allows a direct-injected engine to operate using a leaner-than-normal air–fuel ratio, which results in improved fuel economy with higher power output and reduced exhaust emissions. ● **SEE FIGURE 38-2.**

ADVANTAGES OF GASOLINE DIRECT INJECTION The use of direct injection compared with port fuel injection has many advantages including the following:

- Improved fuel economy due to reduced pumping losses and heat loss
- Allows a higher compression ratio for higher engine efficiency
- Allows the use of lower-octane gasoline
- The volumetric efficiency is higher
- Less need for extra fuel for acceleration
- Improved cold starting and throttle response
- Allows the use of greater percentage of EGR to reduce exhaust emissions
- Up to 25% improvement in fuel economy
- 12% to 15% reduction in exhaust emissions

DISADVANTAGES OF GASOLINE DIRECT INJECTION

- Higher cost due to high-pressure pump and injectors
- More components compared with port fuel injection
- Due to the high compression, a NO_x storage catalyst is sometimes required to meet emission standards, especially in Europe. (● **SEE FIGURE 38–3.**)
- Uses up to six operating modes depending on engine load and speed, which requires more calculations to be performed by the Powertrain Control Module (PCM).

DIRECT-INJECTION FUEL DELIVERY SYSTEM

LOW-PRESSURE SUPPLY PUMP The fuel pump in the fuel tank supplies fuel to the high-pressure fuel pump at a pressure of approximately 60 PSI. The fuel filter is located in the fuel tank and is part of the fuel pump assembly. It is not usually serviceable as a separate component; the engine control module (ECM)

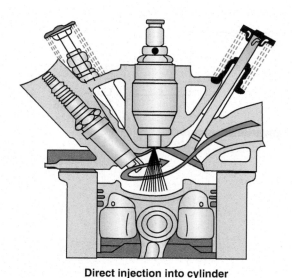

Direct injection into cylinder   Injection upstream near the valve

FIGURE 38-1 A comparison of a port fuel injection system (right) to a gasoline direct injection (GDI) system on the left.

controls the output of the high-pressure pump, which has a range between 500 PSI (3,440 kPa) and 2,900 PSI (15,200 kPa) during engine operation. ● **SEE FIGURES 38–3 AND 38–4.**

HIGH-PRESSURE PUMP

In a General Motors system, the engine control module (ECM) controls the output of the high-pressure pump, which has a range between 500 PSI (3,440 kPa) and 2,900 PSI (15,200 kPa) during engine operation. The high-pressure fuel pump connects to the pump in the fuel tank through the low-pressure fuel line. The pump consists of a single-barrel piston pump, which is driven by the engine

camshaft. The pump plunger rides on a three-lobed cam on the camshaft. The high-pressure pump is cooled and lubricated by the fuel itself. ● **SEE FIGURE 38–5.**

FUEL RAIL

The fuel rail stores the fuel from the high-pressure pump and stores high-pressure fuel for use to each injector. All injectors get the same pressure fuel from the fuel rail.

FUEL PRESSURE REGULATOR

An electric pressure-control valve is installed between the pump inlet and outlet valves. The fuel rail pressure sensor connects to the PCM with three wires:

- 5-volt reference
- ground
- signal

The sensor signal provides an analog signal to the PCM that varies in voltage as fuel rail pressure changes. Low pressure results in a low-voltage signal and high pressure results in a high-voltage signal.

The PCM uses internal drivers to control the power feed and ground for the pressure control valve. When both PCM drivers are deactivated, the inlet valve is held open by spring pressure. This causes the high-pressure fuel pump to default to low-pressure mode. The fuel from the high-pressure fuel pump flows through a line to the fuel rail and injectors. The actual operating pressure can vary from as low as 500 PSI (3,440 kPa) at idle to over 2,000 PSI (13,800 kPa) during high speed or heavy load conditions. ● **SEE FIGURE 38–6.**

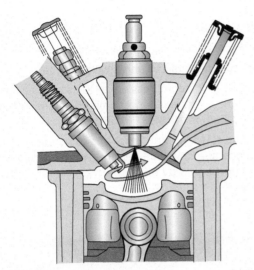

FIGURE 38–2 A gasoline direct-injection system injects fuel under high pressure directly into the combustion chamber.

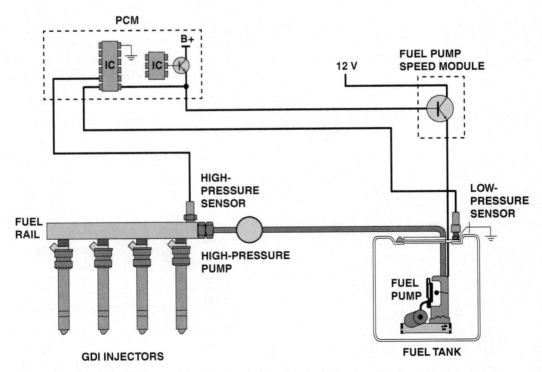

FIGURE 38–3 A GDI system uses a low-pressure pump in the gas tank similar to other types of fuel-injection systems. The PCM controls the pressure of the high-pressure pump using sensor inputs.

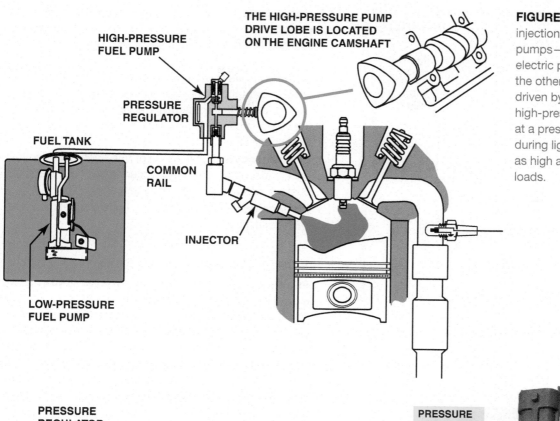

FIGURE 38–4 A typical direct-injection system uses two pumps—one low-pressure electric pump in the fuel tank and the other a high-pressure pump driven by the camshaft. The high-pressure fuel system operates at a pressure as low as 500 PSI during light load conditions and as high as 2,900 PSI under heavy loads.

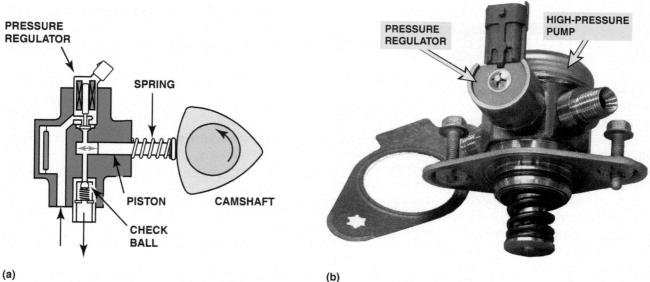

(a)

(b)

FIGURE 38–5 (a) A typical camshaft-driven high-pressure pump used to increase fuel pressure to 2,000 PSI or higher. (b) The high-pressure pump assembly removed from the engine. Many GDI engines use a roller where the high-pressure pump rides against the cam lobes to help reduce friction and wear.

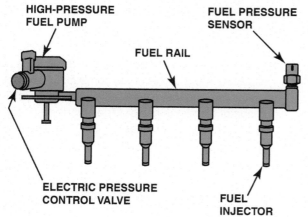

FIGURE 38–6 A GDI fuel rail and pump assembly with the electric pressure control valve.

PORT FUEL-INJECTION SYSTEM COMPARED WITH GDI SYSTEM

	PORT FUEL INJECTION	GASOLINE DIRECT INJECTION
Fuel pressure	35–60 PSI	Lift pump—50 to 60 PSI High-pressure pump—500 to 2,900 PSI
Injection pulse width at idle	1.5–3.5 ms	About 0.4 ms (400 µs)
Injector resistance	12–16 ohms	1–3 ohms
Injector voltage	6 V for low-resistance injectors, 12 V for most injectors	50–90 V
Number of injections per event	One	1–3
Engine compression ratio	8:1–11:1	11:1–13:1

CHART 38–1

A comparison chart showing the major differences between a port fuel-injection system and a GDI system.

GDI FUEL INJECTORS

Each high-pressure fuel injector assembly is an electrically magnetic injector mounted in the cylinder head. In the GDI system, the PCM controls each fuel injector with 50 to 90 volts (usually 60 to 70 volts), depending on the system, which is created by a boost capacitor in the PCM. During the high-voltage boost phase, the capacitor is discharged through an injector, allowing for initial injector opening. The injector is then held open with 12 volts. The high-pressure fuel injector has a small slit or six precision-machined holes that generate the desired spray pattern. The injector also has an extended tip to allow for cooling from a water jacket in the cylinder head.

● **SEE CHART 38–1** for an overview of the differences between a port fuel-injection system and a GDI system.

MODES OF OPERATION

The two basic modes of operation include the following:

1. **Stratified mode.** In this mode of operation, the air–fuel mixture is richer around the spark plug than it is in the rest of the cylinder.
2. **Homogeneous mode.** In this mode of operation, the air–fuel mixture is the same throughout the cylinder.

There are variations of these modes that can be used to fine-tune the air–fuel mixture inside the cylinder. For example, Bosch, a supplier to many vehicle manufacturers, uses the following six modes of operation:

- **Homogeneous mode.** In this mode, the injector is pulsed one time to create an even air–fuel mixture in the cylinder. The injection occurs during the intake stroke. This mode is used during high-speed and/or high-torque conditions.
- **Homogeneous lean mode.** Similar to the homogeneous mode except that the overall air–fuel mixture is slightly lean for better fuel economy. The injection occurs during the intake stroke. This mode is used under steady, light-load conditions.
- **Stratified mode.** In this mode of operation, the injection occurs just before the spark occurs resulting in lean combustion, reducing fuel consumption.
- **Homogeneous stratified mode.** In this mode, there are two injections of fuel:
  - The first injection is during the intake stroke.
  - The second injection is during the compression stroke.

  As a result of these double injections, the rich air–fuel mixture around the spark plug is ignited first. Then, the rich mixture ignites the leaner mixture. The advantages of this mode include lower exhaust emissions than the stratified mode and less fuel consumption than the homogeneous lean mode.
- **Homogeneous knock protection mode.** The purpose of this mode is to reduce the possibility of spark knock from occurring under heavy loads at low engine speeds. There are two injections of fuel:
  - The first injection occurs on the intake stroke.
  - The second injection occurs during the compression stroke with the overall mixture being stoichiometric.

  As a result of this mode, the PCM does not need to retard ignition timing as much to operate knock-free.
- **Stratified catalyst heating mode.** In this mode, there are two injections:
  - The first injection is on the compression stroke just before combustion.
  - The second injection is after combustion occurs to heat the exhaust. This mode is used to quickly warm the catalytic converter and to burn the sulfur from the NO_x catalyst.

PISTON TOP DESIGNS

GDI systems use a variety of shapes of piston and injector locations, depending on make and model of engine. Three of the most locations, used designs include the following:

- **Spray-guided combustion.** In this design, the injector is placed in the center of the combustion chamber and injects fuel into the dished-out portion of the piston. The shape of the piston helps guide and direct the mist of fuel in the combustion chamber. ● **SEE FIGURE 38–7**.
- **Swirl combustion.** This design uses the shape of the piston and the position of the injector at the side of the combustion chamber to create turbulence and swirl of the air–fuel mixture. ● **SEE FIGURE 38–8**.

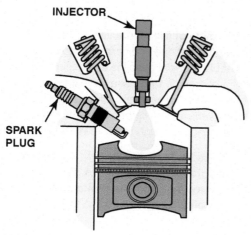

FIGURE 38–7 In this design, the fuel injector is at the top of the cylinder and sprays fuel into the cavity of the piston.

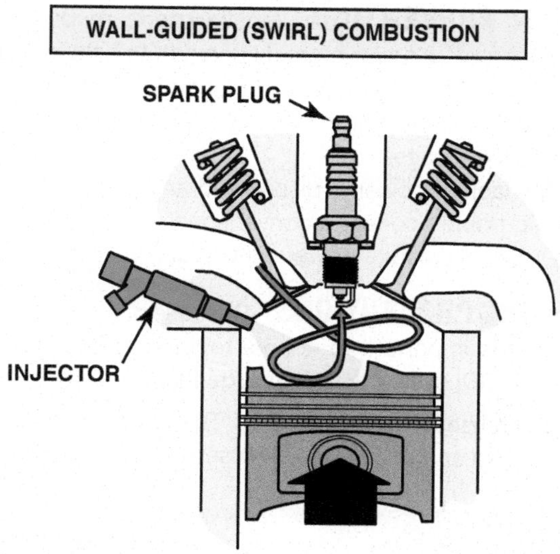

FIGURE 38–8 The side injector combines with the shape of the piston to create a swirl as the piston moves up on the compression stroke.

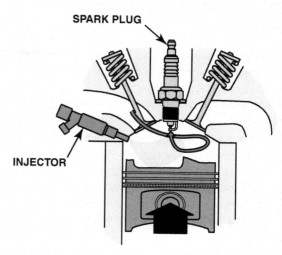

FIGURE 38–9 The piston creates a tumbling force as it moves upward.

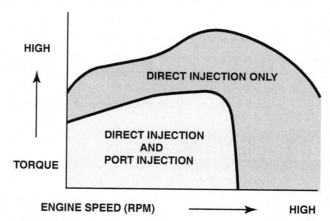

FIGURE 38–10 Notice that there are conditions when the port fuel injector, located in the intake manifold, and the gasoline direct injector, located in the cylinder, both operate to provide the proper air–fuel mixture.

- **Tumble combustion.** Depending on when the fuel is injected into the combustion chamber helps determine how the air–fuel mixture is moved or tumbled. ● **SEE FIGURE 38–9**.

PORT- AND DIRECT-INJECTION SYSTEMS

OVERVIEW Many vehicles use gasoline direct injection and in some engines they also use a conventional port fuel injection system. The system combines direct-injection injectors located in the combustion chamber with port

fuel injectors in the intake manifold near the intake valve. The two injection systems work together to supply the fuel needed by the engine. ● **SEE FIGURE 38–10** for how the two systems are used throughout the various stages of engine operation.

COLD-START WARM-UP To help reduce exhaust emissions after a cold start, the fuel system uses a stratified change mode. This results in a richer air–fuel mixture near the spark plug and allows for the spark to be retarded to increase the temperature of the exhaust. As a result of the increased exhaust temperature, the catalytic converter rapidly reaches operating temperature, which reduces exhaust emissions.

ENGINE START SYSTEM

An engine equipped with gasoline direct injection could use the system to start the engine. This is most useful during idle stop mode when the engine is stopped while the vehicle is at a traffic light to save fuel. The steps used in the Mazda start-stop system, called the *smart idle stop system (SISS)*, allow the engine to be started without a starter motor and include the following steps:

STEP 1 The engine is stopped. The normal stopping position of an engine when it stops is 70 degrees before top dead center, plus or minus 20 degrees. This is because the engine stops with one cylinder on the compression stroke and the PCM can determine the cylinder position, using the crankshaft and camshaft position sensors.

STEP 2 When a command is made to start the engine by the PCM, fuel is injected into the cylinder that is on the compression stroke and ignited by the spark plug.

STEP 3 The piston on the compression stroke is forced downward forcing the crankshaft to rotate counterclockwise or in the opposite direction to normal operation.

STEP 4 The rotation of the crankshaft forces the companion cylinder toward the top of the cylinder.

STEP 5 Fuel is injected and the spark plug is fired, forcing the piston down, causing the crankshaft to rotate in the normal (clockwise) direction. Normal combustion events continue allowing the engine to keep running.

GDI ISSUES

NOISE ISSUES GDI systems operate at high pressure and the injectors can often be heard with the engine running and the hood open. This noise can be a customer concern because the clicking sound is similar to noisy valves. If a noise issue is the customer concern, check the following:

- Check a similar vehicle to determine if the sound is louder or more noticeable than normal.
- Check that nothing under the hood is touching the fuel rail. If another line or hose is in contact with the fuel rail, the sound of the injectors clicking can be transmitted throughout the engine, making the sound more noticeable.
- Check for any technical service bulletins (TSBs) that may include new clips or sound insulators to help reduce the noise.

CARBON ISSUES Carbon is often an issue in engines equipped with GDI systems. Carbon can affect engine operation by accumulating in two places:

- **On the injector itself.** Because the injector tip is in the combustion chamber, fuel residue can accumulate on the injector, reducing its ability to provide the proper spray pattern and amount of fuel. Some injector designs are more likely to be affected by carbon than others. For example, if the injector uses small holes, these tend to become clogged more than an injector that uses a single slit opening where the fuel being sprayed out tends to blast away any carbon. ● **SEE FIGURE 38–11**.

- **The backside of the intake valve.** This is a common place for fuel residue and carbon to accumulate on engines equipped with gasoline direct injection. The accumulation of carbon on the intake valve can become so severe that the engine will start and idle, but lack power to accelerate the vehicle. The carbon deposits restrict the airflow into the cylinder enough to decrease engine power.

NOTE: Engines that use both port fuel and GDI injectors do not show intake valve deposits. It is thought that the fuel being sprayed onto the intake valve from the port fuel injector helps keep the intake valve clean.

GDI SERVICE

CARBON PREVENTION Most experts recommend the use of Techron®, a fuel system dispersant, to help keep carbon from accumulating. The use of a dispersant every six months or every 6,000 miles has proven to help prevent injector and intake valve deposits.

If the lack of power is discovered and there are no stored diagnostic trouble codes, a conventional carbon cleaning procedure will likely restore power if the intake valves are coated.

SERVICING PRECAUTIONS Because of the high pressures involved, it is important to adhere to safety precautions when working on GDI system which include the following:

- Don't reuse high-pressure lines. The ball-ends deform when tightened and will not seal if reused. ● **SEE FIGURE 38–12**.

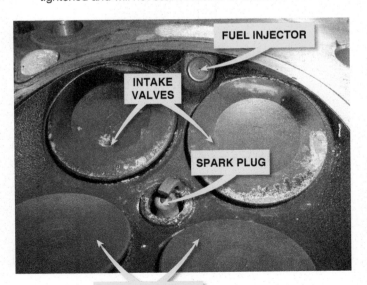

FIGURE 38–11 There may become a driveability issue because the GDI injector is exposed to combustion carbon and fuel residue.

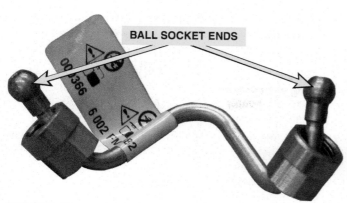

FIGURE 38-12 The high-pressure lines use a ball and socket connection. The ball end deforms when the line is tightened and must be replaced with a new part whenever it is removed.

- Always use a torque wrench when tightening fuel line fittings.
- Do not loosen any fuel fittings with the engine cranking or running.

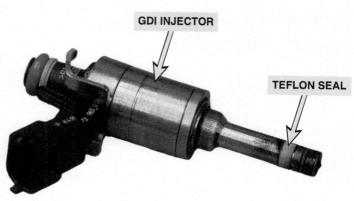

FIGURE 38-13 Whenever a GDI fuel injector is removed, a new Teflon seal must be installed to ensure a leak-free connection in the combustion chamber.

- Always replace the Teflon seal whenever replacing or re-installing an GDI injector. ● **SEE FIGURE 38-13.**

Always check service information for the exact procedures to follow when working on a GDI system.

SUMMARY

1. A gasoline direct-injection system uses a fuel injector that delivers a short squirt of fuel directly into the combustion chamber rather than in the intake manifold, near the intake valve on a port fuel-injection system.

2. The advantages of using gasoline direct injection instead of port fuel injection include:
   - Improved fuel economy
   - Reduced exhaust emissions
   - Greater engine power

3. Some of the disadvantages of gasoline direct-injection systems compared with a port fuel-injection system include:

   - Higher cost
   - The need for NOx storage catalyst in some applications
   - More components

4. The operating pressure can vary from as low as 500 PSI during some low-demand conditions to as high as 2,900 PSI.

REVIEW QUESTIONS

1. What are two advantages of gasoline direct injection compared with port fuel injection?

2. What are two disadvantages of gasoline direct injection compared with port fuel injection?

3. How is the fuel delivery system different from a port fuel-injection system?

4. What are the basic modes of operation of a GDI system?

5. What should be replaced anytime it is removed from the high-pressure GDI fuel system?

1. Where is the fuel injected in an engine equipped with gasoline direct injection?
   a. Into the intake manifold near the intake valve
   b. Directly into the combustion chamber
   c. Above the intake port
   d. In the exhaust port

2. The fuel pump inside the fuel tank on a vehicle equipped with gasoline direct injection produces about what fuel pressure?
   a. 5 to 10 PSI
   b. 10 to 20 PSI
   c. 20 to 40 PSI
   d. 50 to 60 PSI

3. The high-pressure fuel pumps used in GDI systems are powered by _____.
   a. Electricity (DC motor)
   b. Electricity (AC motor)
   c. the camshaft
   d. the crankshaft

4. The high-pressure fuel pump pressure is regulated by using _____.
   a. an electric pressure-control valve
   b. a vacuum-biased regulator
   c. a mechanical regulator at the inlet to the fuel rail
   d. a non-vacuum biased regulator

5. The fuel injectors operate under a fuel pressure of about _____.
   a. 35 to 45 PSI
   b. 90 to 150 PSI
   c. 500 to 2,900 PSI
   d. 2,000 to 5,000 PSI

6. The fuel injectors used on a GDI system are pulsed on using what voltage?
   a. 12 to 14 volt
   b. 50 to 90 volt
   c. 100 to 110 volt
   d. 200 to 220 volt

7. Which mode of operation results in a richer air–fuel mixture near the spark plug?
   a. Stoichiometric
   b. Homogeneous
   c. Stratified
   d. Knock protection

8. Some engines that use a GDI system have carbon issue _____.
   a. on the intake valves
   b. on the exhaust valves
   c. on the fuel injectors
   d. Both a and c

9. Why should any high-pressure line removed be replaced with a new part on a GDI system?
   a. The ball-ends deform when tightened and will not seal if reused
   b. The high-pressure lines are part of the high-pressure pump and must be replaced as an assembly
   c. The torque needed to remove the lines causes the lines to be damaged
   d. All of the above

10. A lack of power from an engine equipped with gasoline direct injection could be due to _____.
    a. noisy injectors
    b. carbon on the injectors
    c. carbon on the intake valves
    d. Both b and c

chapter 39
ELECTRONIC THROTTLE CONTROL SYSTEM

LEARNING OBJECTIVES

After studying this chapter, the reader will be able to:

1. Describe electronic throttle control systems and explain how the position of the accelerator pedal is detected.
2. Explain how an electronic throttle control system works.
3. List the parts of a typical electronic throttle control system.
4. Describe how to diagnose faults in an electronic throttle control system.
5. Explain how to service an electronic throttle system.

This chapter will help you prepare for ASE content area "E" (Computerized Engine Controls Diagnosis and Repair).

KEY TERMS

Accelerator pedal position (APP) sensor 600
Coast-down stall 605
Default position 601
Drive-by-wire 600
Electronic throttle control (ETC) 600
Fail safe position 602
Neutral position 602
Servomotor 601
Throttle position (TP) sensor 600

ELECTRONIC THROTTLE CONTROL (ETC) SYSTEM

ADVANTAGES OF ETC The absence of any mechanical linkage between the throttle pedal and the throttle body requires the use of an electric actuator motor. The electronic throttle system has the following advantages over the conventional cable:

- Eliminates the mechanical throttle cable, thereby reducing the number of moving parts.
- Eliminates the need for cruise control actuators and controllers.
- Helps reduce engine power for traction control (TC) and electronic stability control (ESC) systems.
- Used to delay rapid applications of torque to the transmission/transaxle to help improve driveability and to smooth shifts.
- Helps reduce pumping losses by using the electronic throttle to open at highway speeds with greater fuel economy. The ETC opens the throttle to maintain engine and vehicle speed as the Powertrain Control Module (PCM) leans the air–fuel ratio, retards ignition timing, and introduces additional exhaust gas recirculation (EGR) to reducing pumping losses.
- Used to provide smooth engine operation, especially during rapid acceleration.
- Eliminates the need for an idle air control valve.

The electronic throttle can be called **drive-by-wire**, but most vehicle manufacturers use the term **electronic throttle control (ETC)** to describe the system that opens the throttle valve electrically.

PARTS INVOLVED The typical ETC system includes the following components:

1. **Accelerator pedal position (APP)** sensor, also called *accelerator pedal sensor (APS)*
2. The electronic throttle actuator (servomotor), which is part of the electronic throttle body
3. A **throttle position (TP) sensor**
4. An electronic control unit, which is usually the PCM
   - ● **SEE FIGURE 39–1.**

NORMAL OPERATION OF THE ETC SYSTEM

Driving a vehicle equipped with an ETC system is about the same as driving a vehicle with a conventional mechanical throttle cable and throttle valve. However, the driver may notice

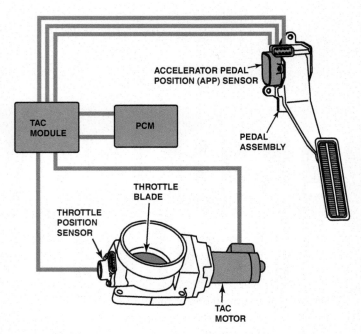

FIGURE 39–1 The throttle pedal is connected to the APP sensor. The electronic throttle body includes a throttle position sensor to provide throttle angle feedback to the vehicle computer. Some systems use a Throttle Actuator Control (TAC) module to operate the throttle blade (plate).

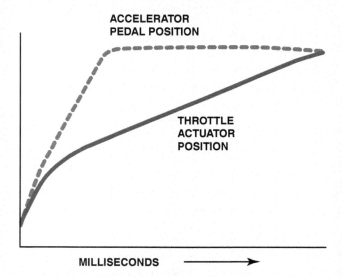

FIGURE 39–2 The opening of the throttle plate can be delayed as long as 30 milliseconds (0.030 sec) to allow time for the amount of fuel needed to catch up to the opening of the throttle plate.

some differences, which are to be considered normal. These normal conditions include the following:

- The engine may not increase above idle speed when depressing the accelerator pedal when the gear selector is in PARK.
- If the engine speed does increase when the accelerator is depressed with the transmission in PARK or NEUTRAL, the engine speed will likely be limited to less than 2,000 RPM.
- While accelerating rapidly, there is often a slight delay before the engine responds. ● **SEE FIGURE 39–2.**

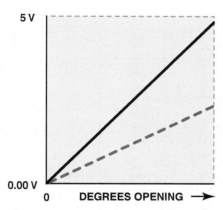

FIGURE 39–3 A typical APP sensor, showing two different output voltage signals that are used by the PCM to determine accelerator pedal position. Two (or three in some applications) are used as a double check because this is a safety-related sensor.

- While at cruise speed, the accelerator pedal may or may not cause the engine speed to increase if the accelerator pedal is moved slightly.

APP SENSOR

CABLE-OPERATED SYSTEM Honda Accords until the 2008 model year used a cable attached to the accelerator pedal to operate the APP sensor located under the hood. A similar arrangement was used in Dodge RAM trucks in 2003. In both of these applications, the throttle cable was simply moving the APP sensor and not moving the throttle plate. The throttle plate is controlled by the PCM and moved by the ETC motor.

TWO SENSORS The APP sensor uses two and sometimes three separate sensors, which act together to give accurate accelerator pedal position information to the controller, but also are used to check that the sensor is working properly. They function just like a TP sensor, and two are needed for proper system function. One APP sensor output signal increases as the pedal is depressed and the other signal decreases. The controller compares the signals with a look-up table to determine the pedal position. Using two or three signals improves redundancy should one sensor fail, and allows the PCM to quickly detect a malfunction. When three sensors are used, the third signal can either decrease or increase with pedal position, but its voltage range will still be different from the other two. ● **SEE FIGURE 39–3**.

THROTTLE BODY ASSEMBLY

The throttle body assembly contains the following components:
- Throttle plate
- Electric actuator DC motor

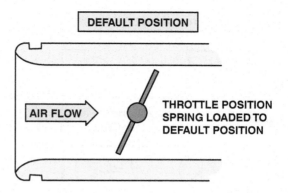

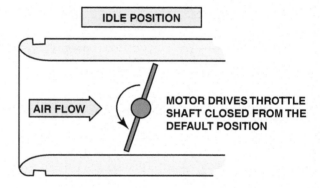

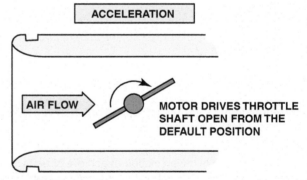

FIGURE 39–4 The default position for the throttle plate is in slightly open position. The servomotor then is used to close it for idle and open it during acceleration.

- Dual TP sensors
- Gears used to multiply the torque of the DC motor
- Springs used to hold the throttle plate in the default location

THROTTLE PLATE AND SPRING The throttle plate is held slightly open by a concentric clock spring. The spring applies a force that will close the throttle plate if power is lost to the actuator motor. The spring is also used to open the throttle plate slightly from the fully closed position.

ELECTRONIC THROTTLE BODY MOTOR The actuator is a DC electric motor and is often called a **servomotor**. The throttle plate is held in a **default position** by a spring inside the throttle body assembly. This partially open position, also called

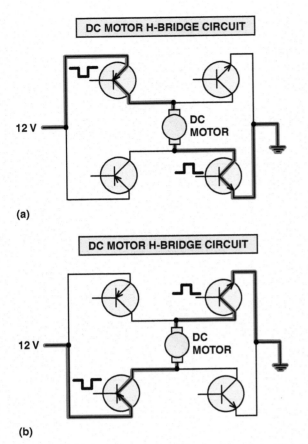

DC MOTOR H-BRIDGE CIRCUIT

12 V

DC MOTOR

(a)

DC MOTOR H-BRIDGE CIRCUIT

12 V

DC MOTOR

(b)

FIGURE 39–5 (a) An H-bridge circuit is used to control the direction of the DC electric motor of the ETC unit. (b) To reverse the direction of operation, the polarity of the current through the motor is reversed.

the **neutral position** or the **fail safe position**, is about 16% to 20% open. This default position varies, depending on the vehicle and usually results in an engine speed of 1,200 to 1,500 RPM.

- The throttle plate is driven closed to achieve speeds lower than the default position, such as idle speed.
- The throttle plate is driven open to achieve speeds higher than the default position, such as during acceleration. ● **SEE FIGURE 39–4**.

The throttle plate motor is driven by a bidirectional pulse-width modulated (PWM) signal from the PCM or ETC module using an H-bridge circuit. ● **SEE FIGURE 39–5**.

The H-bridge circuit is controlled by the PMC by the following:

- Reversing the polarity of power and ground brushes to the DC motor
- Pulse-width modulating the current through the motor

The PCM monitors the position of the throttle from the two TP sensors. The PCM then commands the throttle plate to the desired position. ● **SEE FIGURE 39–6**.

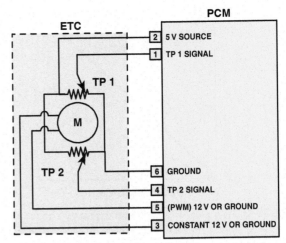

FIGURE 39–6 Schematic of a typical ETC system. Note that terminal #5 is always PWM and that terminal #3 is always constant, but both power and ground are switched to change the direction of the motor.

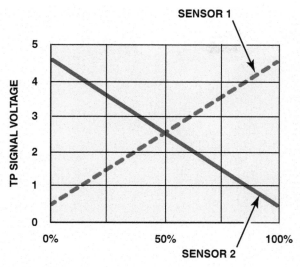

FIGURE 39–7 The two TP sensors used on the throttle body of an electronic throttle body assembly produce opposite voltage signals as the throttle is opened. The total voltage of both combined at any throttle plate position is 5 volts.

THROTTLE POSITION (TP) SENSOR

Two throttle position sensors are used in the throttle body assembly to provide throttle position signals to the PCM. Two sensors are used as a fail-safe measure and for diagnosis. There are two types of TP sensors used in ETC systems: potentiometers and Hall-effect.

THREE-WIRE POTENTIOMETER SENSORS These sensors use a 5-volt reference from the PCM and produce an analog (variable) voltage signal that is proportional to the throttle plate position. The two sensors produce opposite signals as the throttle plate opens:

- One sensor starts at low voltage (about 0.5 volt) and increases as the throttle plate is opened.
- The second sensor starts at a higher voltage (about 4.5 volt) and produces a lower voltage as the throttle plate is opened. ● **SEE FIGURE 39–7**.

HALL-EFFECT TP SENSORS Some vehicle manufacturers, such as Honda use a noncontact Hall-effect TP sensor. Because there is no physical contact, this type of sensor is less likely to fail due to wear.

DIAGNOSIS OF ETC SYSTEMS

FAULT MODE ETC systems can have faults like any other automatic system. Due to the redundant sensors in APP sensors and throttle position sensor, many faults result in a

"limp home" situation instead of a total failure. The limp home mode is also called the "fail-safe mode" and indicates the following actions performed by the PCM:

- Engine speed is limited to the default speed (about 1,200 to 1,600 RPM).
- There is slow or no response when the accelerator pedal is depressed.
- The cruise control system is disabled.
- A diagnostic trouble code (DTC) is set.
- An ETC warning lamp on the dash will light. The warning lamp may be labeled differently, depending on the vehicle manufacturer. For example,
  - **General Motors vehicle**—Reduced power lamp (● **SEE FIGURE 39–8**)
  - **Ford**—Wrench symbol (amber or green) (● **SEE FIGURE 39–9**)
  - **Chrysler**—Red lightning bolt symbol (● **SEE FIGURE 39–10**)
- The engine will run and can be driven slowly. This limp-in mode operation allows the vehicle to be driven off of the road and to a safe location.

The ETC may enter the limp-in mode if any of the following has occurred:

- Low battery voltage has been detected
- PCM failure
- One TP and the MAP sensors have failed
- Both TP sensors have failed
- The ETC actuator motor has failed
- The ETC throttle spring has failed

VACUUM LEAKS The ETC system is able to compensate for many vacuum leaks. A vacuum leak at the intake manifold,

(a)

(b)

FIGURE 39–8 (a) A "reduced power" warning light indicates a fault with the ETC system on some General Motors vehicles. (b) A symbol showing an engine with an arrow pointing down is used on some General Motors vehicles to indicate a fault with the ETC system.

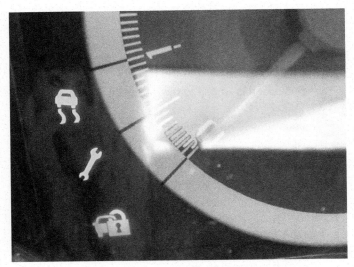

FIGURE 39–9 A wrench symbol warning lamp on a Ford vehicle. The symbol can also be green.

FIGURE 39–10 A symbol used on a Chrysler vehicle indicating a fault with the ETC.

for example, will allow air into the engine that is not measured by the mass airflow sensor. The ETC system will simply move the throttle as needed to achieve the proper idle speed to compensate for the leak.

DIAGNOSTIC PROCEDURE If a fault occurs in the ETC system, check service information for the specified procedure to follow for the vehicle being checked. Most vehicle service information includes the following steps:

STEP 1 Verify the customer concern.

STEP 2 Use a factory scan tool or an aftermarket scan tool with original equipment capability and check for DTCs.

STEP 3 If there are stored ETCs, follow service information instructions for diagnosing the system.

STEP 4 If there are no stored ETCs, check scan tool data for possible fault areas in the system.

SCAN TOOL DATA Scan data related to the ETC system can be confusing. Typical data and the meaning include the following:

■ **APP indicated angle.** The scan tool will display a percentage ranging from 0% to 100%. When the throttle is released, the indicated angle should be 0%. When the throttle is depressed to wide open, the reading should indicate 100%.

■ **TP desired angle.** The scan tool will display a percentage ranging from 0% to 100%. This represents the desired throttle angle as commanded by the driver of the vehicle.

■ **TP indicated angle.** The TP indicated angle is the angle of the measured throttle opening and it should agree with the TP desired angle.

■ **TP sensors 1 and 2.** The scan tool will display "agree" or "disagree." If the PCM or TAC module receives a voltage signal from one of the TP sensors that is not in the proper relationship to the other TP sensor, the scan tool will display *disagree*.

The High Idle Toyota

The owner of a Toyota Camry complained that the engine would idle at over 1,200 RPM compared with a normal 600 to 700 RPM. The vehicle would also not accelerate. Using a scan tool, a check for DTCs showed one code: P2101—"TAC motor circuit low."

Checking service information led to the inspection of the ETC throttle body assembly. With the ignition key out of the ignition and the inlet air duct off the throttle body, the technician used a screwdriver to see if the throttle plate worked.

Normal operation—The throttle plate should move and then spring back quickly to the default position.

Abnormal operation—If the throttle plate stays where it is moved or does not return to the default position, there is a fault with the throttle body assembly. ● SEE FIGURE 39–11.

The technician replaced the throttle body assembly with an updated version and proper engine operation was restored. The technician disassembled the old throttle body and found it was corroded inside due to moisture entering the unit through the vent hose. ● SEE FIGURE 39–12.

Summary:

- **Complaint**—Customer stated that the engine would idle at over 2,000 RPM.
- **Cause**—A stored P2101 DTC was stored indicating a fault with the throttle body assembly.
- **Correction**—The throttle body was replaced with an improved version that placed the vent tube in a different position to help avoid water getting into the assembly.

FIGURE 39–11 The throttle plate stayed where it was moved, which indicates that there is a problem with the electronic throttle body control assembly.

FIGURE 39–12 A corroded ETC assembly shown with the cover removed.

ETC THROTTLE FOLLOWER TEST

On some vehicles, such as many Chrysler vehicles, the operation of the ETC can be tested using a factory or factory-level scan tool. To perform this test, use the "throttle follower test" procedure as shown on the scan tool. An assistant is needed to check that the throttle plate is moving as the accelerator pedal is depressed. This test cannot be done normally because the PCM does not normally allow the throttle plate to be moved unless the engine is running.

SERVICING ELECTRONIC THROTTLE SYSTEMS

ETC-RELATED PERFORMANCE ISSUES The only service that an ETC system may require is a cleaning of the throttle body. Throttle body cleaning is a routine service procedure on port fuel-injected engines and is still needed when the throttle is being opened by an electric motor rather than a throttle cable tied to a mechanical accelerator pedal. The throttle body may need cleaning if one or more of the following symptoms are present:

- Lower than normal idle speed
- Rough idle
- Engine stalls when coming to a stop (called a **coast-down stall**)

If any of the above conditions exists, a throttle body cleaning will often correct these faults.

CAUTION: Some vehicle manufacturers add a non-stick coating to the throttle assembly and warn that cleaning could remove this protective coating. Always follow the vehicle manufacturer's recommended procedures.

FIGURE 39–13 Notice the small motor gear on the left drives a larger plastic gear (black), which then drives the small gear in mesh with the section of a gear attached to the throttle plate. This results in a huge torque increase from the small motor and helps explain why it could be dangerous to insert a finger into the throttle body assembly.

THROTTLE BODY CLEANING PROCEDURE Before attempting to clean a throttle body on an engine equipped with an ETC system, be sure that the ignition key is out of the vehicle and the ready light is off if working on a Toyota/Lexus hybrid electric vehicle to avoid the possibility of personal injury.

☠ **WARNING**

The electric motor that operates the throttle plate is strong enough to cut off a finger. ● SEE FIGURE 39–13.

To clean the throttle, perform the following steps:

STEP 1 With the ignition off and the key removed from the ignition, remove the air inlet hose from the throttle body.

STEP 2 Spray throttle body cleaner onto a shop cloth.

STEP 3 Open the throttle body and use the shop cloth to remove the varnish and carbon deposits from the throttle body housing and throttle plate.

   CAUTION: Do not spray cleaner into the throttle body assembly. The liquid cleaner could flow into and damage the TP sensors.

STEP 4 Reinstall the inlet hose being sure that there are no air leaks between the hose and the throttle body assembly.

STEP 5 Start the engine and allow the PCM to learn the correct idle. If the idle is not correct, check service information for the specified procedures to follow to perform a throttle relearn.

THROTTLE BODY RELEARN PROCEDURE When installing a new throttle body or PCM or sometimes after cleaning the throttle body, the throttle position has to be learned by the PCM. After the following conditions have been met, a typical throttle body relearn procedure for a General Motors vehicle includes the following:

- Accelerator pedal released
- Battery voltage higher than 8 volts
- Vehicle speed must be zero
- Engine coolant temperature (ECT) higher than 40°F (5°C) and lower than 212°F (100°C)
- Intake air temperature (IAT) higher than 40°F (5°C)
- No throttle DTCs set

If all of the above conditions are met, perform the following steps:

STEP 1 Turn the ignition on (engine off) for 30 seconds.

STEP 2 Turn the ignition off and wait 30 seconds.

Start the engine and the idle learn procedure should cause the engine to idle at the correct speed.

SUMMARY

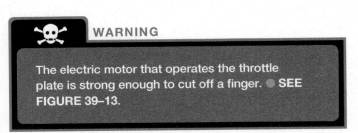

1. Using an electronic throttle control (ETC) system on an engine has many advantages over a conventional method that uses a mechanical cable between the accelerator pedal and the throttle valve.

2. The major components of an ETC system include the following:
   - Accelerator pedal position (APP) sensor
   - ETC actuator motor and spring
   - Throttle position (TP) sensor
   - Electronic control unit

3. The TP sensor is actually two sensors that share the 5-volt reference from the PCM and produce opposite signals as a redundant check.

4. Limp-in mode is commanded if there is a major fault in the system, which can allow the vehicle to be driven enough to be pulled off the road to safety.

5. The diagnostic procedure for the ETC system includes verifying the customer concern, using a scan tool to check for DTCs, and checking the value of the TP and APP sensors.

1. What parts can be deleted if an engine uses an ETC system instead of a conventional accelerator pedal and cable to operate the throttle valve?

2. How can the use of an ETC system improve fuel economy?

3. How is the operation of the throttle different on a system that uses an ETC system compared with a conventional mechanical system?

4. What component parts are included in an ETC system?

5. What is the default or limp-in position of the throttle plate?

CHAPTER QUIZ

1. The use of an ETC system allows the elimination of all *except* _____.
   a. accelerator pedal
   b. mechanical throttle cable (most systems)
   c. cruise control actuator
   d. idle air control

2. To what extent is the throttle plate spring loaded to hold the throttle slightly open?
   a. 3% to 5%
   b. 8% to 10%
   c. 16% to 20%
   d. 22% to 28%

3. What type of electric motor is the throttle plate actuator motor?
   a. Stepper motor
   b. DC motor
   c. AC motor
   d. Brushless motor

4. The actuator motor is controlled by the PCM through what type of circuit?
   a. Series
   b. Parallel
   c. H-bridge
   d. Series-parallel

5. When does the PCM perform a self-test of the ETC system?
   a. During cruise speed when the throttle is steady
   b. During deceleration
   c. During acceleration
   d. When the ignition switch is first rotated to the on position before the engine starts

6. What type is the throttle position sensor used in the throttle body assembly of an ETC system?
   a. A single potentiometer
   b. Two potentiometers that read in the opposite direction
   c. A Hall-effect sensor
   d. Either b or c

7. A green wrench symbol is displayed on the dash. What does this mean?
   a. A fault in the ETC in a Ford vehicle has been detected
   b. A fault in the ETC in a Honda vehicle has been detected
   c. A fault in the ETC in a Chrysler vehicle has been detected
   d. A fault in the ETC in a General Motors vehicle has been detected

8. A technician is checking the operation of the ETC system by depressing the accelerator pedal with the ignition in the on (run) position (engine off). What is the most likely result if the system is functioning correctly?
   a. The throttle goes to wide open when the accelerator pedal is depressed all the way
   b. No throttle movement
   c. The throttle will open partially but not all of the way
   d. The throttle will perform a self-test by closing and then opening to the default position

9. With the ignition off and the key out of the ignition, what should happen if a technician uses a screwdriver and pushes on the throttle plate in an attempt to open the valve?
   a. Nothing. The throttle should be kept from moving by the motor, which is not energized with the key off.
   b. The throttle should move and stay where it is moved and not go back unless moved back.
   c. The throttle should move, and spring back to the home position when released.
   d. The throttle should move closed, but not open further than the default position.

10. The throttle body may be cleaned (if recommended by the vehicle manufacturer) if what conditions are occurring?
    a. Coast-down stall
    b. Rough idle
    c. Lower-than-normal idle speed
    d. Any of the above

chapter 40
FUEL-INJECTION SYSTEM DIAGNOSIS AND SERVICE

PORT FUEL-INJECTION PRESSURE REGULATOR DIAGNOSIS

PURPOSE AND FUNCTION Older port fuel-injected engines use a vacuum hose connected to the fuel-pressure regulator. At idle, the pressure inside the intake manifold is low (high vacuum). Manifold vacuum is applied above the diaphragm inside the fuel-pressure regulator. This reduces the pressure exerted on the diaphragm and results in a lower, about 10 PSI (69 kPa), fuel pressure applied to the injectors.

TESTING THE REGULATOR To test a vacuum-controlled fuel-pressure regulator, follow these steps:

1. Connect a fuel-pressure gauge to monitor the fuel pressure. If the engine does not have a Schrader valve, check service information for the exact method and tools needed to perform a pressure test of the fuel-injection system.

2. Locate the fuel-pressure regulator and disconnect the vacuum hose from the regulator.

   NOTE: If gasoline drips out of the vacuum hose when removed from the fuel-pressure regulator, the regulator is defective and will require replacement.

3. With the engine running at idle speed, reconnect the vacuum hose to the fuel-pressure regulator while watching the fuel-pressure gauge. The fuel pressure should drop (about 10 PSI or 69 kPa) when the hose is reattached to the regulator.

4. Using a hand-operated vacuum pump, apply vacuum (20 inches Hg) to the regulator. The regulator should hold vacuum. If the vacuum drops, replace the fuel-pressure regulator. ● **SEE FIGURE 40–1**.

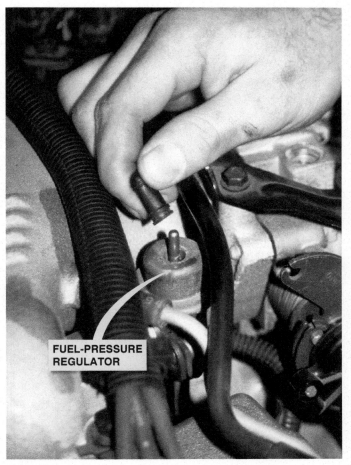

FUEL-PRESSURE REGULATOR

FIGURE 40–1 If the vacuum hose is removed from the fuel-pressure regulator when the engine is running, the fuel pressure should increase. If it does not increase, the fuel pump is not capable of supplying adequate pressure or the fuel-pressure regulator is defective. If gasoline is visible in the vacuum hose, the regulator is leaking and should be replaced.

NOTE: Some vehicles do not use a vacuum-regulated fuel-pressure regulator. Many of these vehicles use a regulator located inside the fuel tank that supplies a constant fuel pressure to the fuel injectors.

 **TECH TIP**

Pressure Transducer Fuel Pressure Test

Using a pressure transducer and a **graphing multimeter (GMM)** or digital storage oscilloscope (DSO) allows the service technician to view the fuel pressure over time. ● **SEE FIGURE 40–2(a)**. Note that the fuel pressure dropped from 15 PSI down to 6 PSI on a TBI-equipped vehicle after just one minute. A normal pressure holding capability is shown in ● **FIGURE 40–2(b)**. when the pressure dropped only about 10% after 10 minutes on a port fuel–injection system.

DIAGNOSING ELECTRONIC FUEL-INJECTION PROBLEMS

VISUAL INSPECTION All fuel-injection systems require the proper amount of clean fuel delivered to the system at the proper pressure and the correct amount of filtered air. The following items should be carefully inspected before proceeding to more detailed tests:

- Check the air filter and replace as needed.
- Check the air induction system for obstructions.
- Check the conditions of all vacuum hoses. Replace any hose that is split, soft (mushy), or brittle.

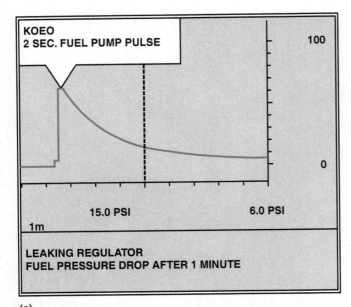

KOEO
2 SEC. FUEL PUMP PULSE

100

0

15.0 PSI   6.0 PSI

1m

LEAKING REGULATOR
FUEL PRESSURE DROP AFTER 1 MINUTE

(a)

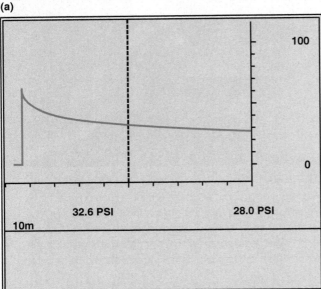

100

0

32.6 PSI   28.0 PSI

10m

(b)

FIGURE 40–2 (a) A fuel-pressure graph after key on, engine off (KOEO) on a throttle body injection (TBI) system. (b) Pressure drop after 10 minutes on a normal port fuel-injection system.

- Check the positive crankcase ventilation (PCV) valve for proper operation or replacement as needed.
  ● **SEE FIGURE 40–3.**

  NOTE: The use of an incorrect PCV valve can cause a rough idle or stalling.

- Check all fuel-injection electrical connections for corrosion or damage.
- Check for gasoline at the vacuum port of the fuel-pressure regulator if the vehicle is so equipped. Gasoline in the vacuum hose at the fuel-pressure regulator indicates that the regulator is defective and requires replacement.

FIGURE 40–3 A clogged positive crankcase ventilation (PCV) system caused the engine oil fumes to be drawn into the air cleaner assembly. This is what the technician discovered during a visual inspection.

If a vacuum leak occurs on an engine equipped with a mass airflow-type fuel-injection system, the extra air causes the following to occur:

- The engine will operate leaner than normal because the extra air has not been measured by the MAF sensor.
- The idle speed will likely be lower due to the leaner-than-normal air–fuel mixture.

 TECH TIP

Stethoscope Fuel-Injection Test

A commonly used test for injector operation is to listen to the injector using a stethoscope with the engine operating at idle speed. ● **SEE FIGURE 40–4.** All injectors should produce the same clicking sound. If any injector makes a clunking or rattling sound, it should be tested further or replaced. With the engine still running, place the end of the stethoscope probe to the return line from the fuel-pressure regulator.
● **SEE FIGURE 40–5.** Fuel should be heard flowing back to the fuel tank if the fuel-pump pressure is higher than the fuel-regulator pressure. If no sound of fuel is heard, then either the fuel pump or the fuel-pressure regulator is at fault.

 TECH TIP

Quick and Easy Leaking Injector Test

Leaking injectors may be found by disabling the ignition, unhooking all injectors, and checking exhaust for hydrocarbons (HC) using a gas analyzer while cranking the engine (maximum HC = 300 ppm).

FIGURE 40–4 All fuel injectors should make the same sound with the engine running at idle speed. A lack of sound indicates a possible electrically open injector or a break in the wiring. A defective computer could also be the cause of a lack of clicking (pulsing) of the injectors.

FUEL-PRESSURE REGULATOR

FUEL RETURN LINE TO TANK

FIGURE 40–5 Fuel should be heard returning to the fuel tank at the fuel return line if the fuel-pump and fuel-pressure regulator are functioning correctly.

TECH TIP

No Spark, No Squirt

Most electronic fuel-injection computer systems use the ignition primary (pickup coil or crank sensor) pulse as the trigger for when to inject (squirt) fuel from the injectors (nozzles). If this signal were not present, no fuel would be injected. Because this pulse is also necessary to trigger the module to create a spark from the coil, it can be said that "no spark" could also mean "no squirt." Therefore, if the cause of a no-start condition is observed to be a lack of fuel injection, do not start testing or replacing fuel-system components until the ignition system is checked for proper operation.

FUEL-INJECTION SYSTEM DIAGNOSIS

DIAGNOSTIC STEPS To determine if a port fuel-injection system—including the fuel pump, injectors, and fuel-pressure regulator—is operating correctly, take the following steps:

1. Attach a fuel-pressure gauge to the Schrader valve on the fuel rail. ● SEE FIGURE 40–6.

2. Turn the ignition key on or start the engine to build up the fuel-pump pressure (to about 35 to 45 PSI).

3. Wait 20 minutes and observe the fuel pressure retained in the fuel rail and note the PSI reading. The fuel pressure should not drop more than 20 PSI (140 kPa) in 20 minutes. If the drop is less than 20 PSI in 20 minutes, everything is okay; if the drop is *greater,* there is a possible problem with the following:

- The check valve in the fuel pump
- Injectors, lines, or fittings
- A fuel-pressure regulator

To determine which unit is defective, perform the following:

- Reenergize the electric fuel pump.

- Clamp the fuel *supply* line, and wait 10 minutes (see CAUTION). If the pressure drop does not occur, replace the fuel pump. If the pressure drop still occurs, continue with the next step.

- Repeat the pressure buildup of the electric pump and clamp the fuel return line. If the pressure drop time is now okay, replace the fuel-pressure regulator.

- If the pressure drop still occurs, one or more of the injectors is leaking. Remove the injectors with the fuel rail and hold over paper. Replace those injectors that drip one or more drops after 10 minutes with pressurized fuel.

CAUTION: Do not clamp plastic fuel lines. Connect shutoff valves to the fuel system to shut off supply and return lines. ● SEE FIGURE 40–7.

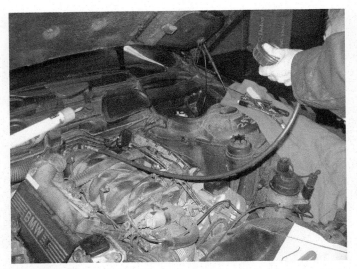

FIGURE 40–6 Checking the fuel pressure using a fuel-pressure gauge connected to the Schrader valve.

FIGURE 40–7 Shutoff valves must be used on vehicles equipped with plastic fuel lines to isolate the cause of a pressure drop in the fuel system.

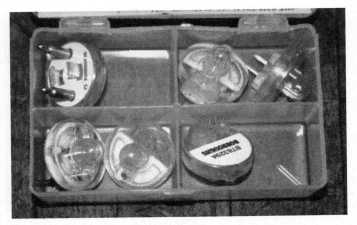

(a)

(b)

FIGURE 40–8 (a) Noid lights are usually purchased as an assortment so that one is available for any type or size of injector wiring connector. (b) The connector is unplugged from the injector and a noid light is plugged into the injector connector. The noid light should flash when the engine is being cranked if the power circuit and the pulsing to ground by the computer are functioning okay.

NOTE: The term *noid* is simply an abbreviation of the word sole*noid*. Injectors use a movable iron core and are therefore solenoids. Therefore, a noid light is a replacement for the solenoid (injector).

Possible noid light problems and causes include the following:

1. **The light is off and does not flash.** The problem is an open in either the power side or ground side (or both) of the injector circuit.

2. **The noid light flashes dimly.** A dim noid light indicates excessive resistance or low voltage available to the injector. Both the power and ground side must be checked.

3. **The noid light is on and does not flash.** If the noid light is on, both a power and a ground are present. Because the light does not flash (blink) when the engine is being

TESTING FOR AN INJECTOR PULSE

One of the first checks that should be performed when diagnosing a no-start condition is whether the fuel injectors are being pulsed by the computer. Checking for proper pulsing of the injector is also important in diagnosing a weak or dead cylinder.

A **noid light** is designed to electrically replace the injector in the circuit and to flash if the injector circuit is working correctly. ● **SEE FIGURE 40–8**. To use a noid light, disconnect the electrical connector at the fuel injector and plug the noid light into the injector harness connections. Crank or start the engine. The noid light should flash regularly.

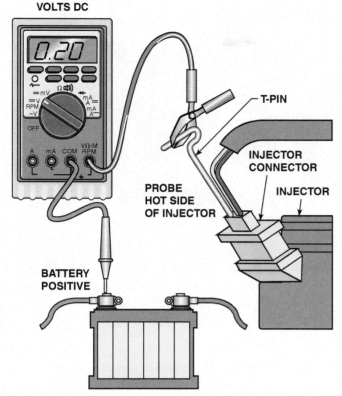

FIGURE 40–9 Use a DMM set to read DC volts to check the voltage drop of the positive circuit to the fuel injector. A reading of 0.5 volt or less is generally considered to be acceptable.

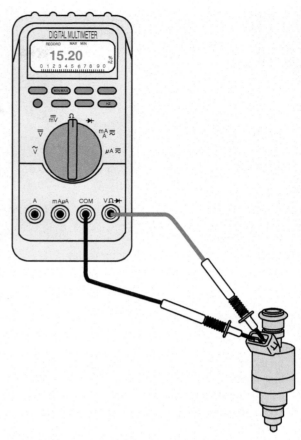

FIGURE 40–10 Connections and settings necessary to measure fuel-injector resistance.

cranked or started, a short-to-ground fault exists either in the computer itself or in the wiring between the injector and the computer.

CAUTION: A noid lamp must be used with caution. The computer may show a good noid light operation and have low supply voltage. ● SEE FIGURE 40–9.

CHECKING FUEL-INJECTOR RESISTANCE

Each port fuel injector must deliver an equal amount of fuel or the engine will idle roughly or perform poorly.

The electrical balance test involves measuring the injector coil-winding resistance. For best engine operation, all injectors should have the same electrical resistance. To measure the resistance, carefully release the locking feature of the connector and remove the connector from the injector.

NOTE: Some engines require specific procedures to gain access to the injectors. Always follow the manufacturers' recommended procedures.

With an ohmmeter, measure the resistance across the injector terminals. Be sure to lowest ohmmeter setting of the digital ohmmeter to read in tenths (0.1) of an ohm. ● **SEE FIGURES 40–10 AND 40–11.** Check service information for the resistance specification of the injectors. Measure the resistance of all of the injectors. Replace any injector that does not fall within the resistance range of the specification. The resistance of the injectors should be measured twice— once when the engine (and injectors) are cold and once after the engine has reached normal operating temperature. If any injector measures close to specification, make certain that the terminals of the injector are electrically sound, and perform other tests to confirm an injector problem before replacement.

TYPICAL RESISTANCE VALUES There are two basic types of injectors, which have an effect on their resistance, including the following:

1. **Low-resistance injectors.** The features of a low-resistance injectors include the following:

   ■ Uses a "peak and hold" type firing where a high current, usually about 4 amperes, is used to open the injector, then it is held open by using a lower current, which is usually about 1 ampere.

FIGURE 40–11 To measure fuel-injector resistance, a technician constructed a short wiring harness with a double banana plug that fits into the V and COM terminals of the meter and an injector connector at the other end. This setup makes checking resistance of fuel injectors quick and easy.

- All throttle body injection (TBI) injectors and some port fuel injectors are low-resistance injectors and are fired using a peak-and-hold circuit by the PCM.
- The resistance value of a peak-and-hold-type injector is usually 1.5 to 4.0 ohms.

 FREQUENTLY ASKED QUESTION

How Does the Fiat Chrysler Multiair System Work?

Some Chrysler and Fiat brand vehicles use a type of system that includes the following unique features:

- The engine has one overhead camshaft, but only the exhaust cam lobes actually open the exhaust, valves.
- The intake camshaft lobes are used to pressurize engine oil, which is directed to a solenoid that is pulse-width modulated.
- The oil from the solenoid is sent to a piston on top of the intake valves, which are opened by the piston.
- The timing and valve lift are determined by the PCM that pulses the control solenoid to allow oil to open the valve. ● **SEE FIGURE 40–12.**

Because the intake valves are opened using pressured engine oil, it is critical that the specified oil be used and changed at the specified interval. Some customers complain of a "clatter" from the engine, especially at idle, which is normal for this engine and is due to the operation of the control solenoids.

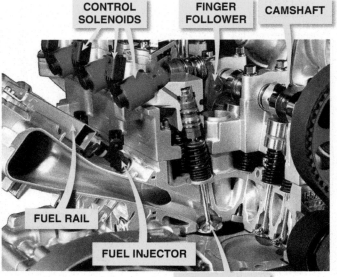

FIGURE 40–12 In a multiair engine design, the exhaust valves are opened by the exhaust camshaft lobes. Intake valves are opened by the high-pressure engine oil, the high pressure being produced by a lobe-actuated piston and controlled by a PCM-controlled solenoids.

2. **Higher-resistance injectors.** The features of a higher-resistance injectors include the following:

- Uses a constant low current, usually 1 ampere, to open the injector.
- Is called a "saturated" type of injector because the current flows until the magnetic field is strong enough to open the injector.
- Most port fuel injectors are of the saturated type.
- The resistance value of a saturated injector is usually 12 to 16 ohms.

🔧 **TECH TIP**

Equal Resistance Test

All fuel injectors should measure the specified resistance. However, the specification often indicates the temperature of the injectors be at room temperature and of course will vary according to the temperature. Rather than waiting for all of the injectors to achieve room temperature, measure the resistance and check that they are all within 0.4 ohm of each other. To determine the difference, record the resistance of each injector and subtract the lowest resistance reading from the highest resistance reading to get the difference. If more than 0.4 ohm, then further testing will be needed to verify defective injector(s). ● **SEE FIGURE 40–13.**

FIGURE 40–13 If an injector has the specified resistance, this does not mean that it is okay. This injector had the specified resistance, yet it did not deliver the correct amount of fuel because it was clogged.

FIGURE 40–14 Connect a fuel-pressure gauge to the fuel rail at the Schrader valve.

PRESSURE-DROP BALANCE TEST

The pressure balance test involves using an electrical timing device to pulse the fuel injectors on for a given amount of time, usually 500 milliseconds or 0.5 seconds, and observing the drop in pressure that accompanies the pulse. If the *fuel flow* through each injector is equal, the drop in pressure in the system will be equal. Most manufacturers recommend that the pressures be within about 1.5 PSI (10 kPa) of each other for satisfactory engine performance. This test method not only tests the electrical functioning of the injector (for definite time and current pulse), but also tests for mechanical defects that could affect fuel flow amounts.

The purpose of running this injector balance test is to determine which injector is restricted, inoperative, or delivering fuel differently than the other injectors. Replacing a complete set of injectors can be expensive. The basic tools needed are the following:

- Accurate pressure gauge with pressure relief
- Injector pulser with time control
- Necessary injector connection adapters
- Safe receptacle for catching and disposing of any fuel released

STEP 1　Attach the pressure gauge to the fuel delivery rail on the supply side. Make sure the connections are safe and leakproof.

STEP 2　Attach the injector pulser to the first injector to be tested.

STEP 3　Turn the ignition key to the on position to prime the fuel rail. Note the static fuel-pressure reading. ● **SEE FIGURE 40–14.**

STEP 4　Activate the pulser for the timed firing pulses.

STEP 5　Note and record the new static rail pressure after the injector has been pulsed.

STEP 6　Reenergize the fuel pump and repeat this procedure for all of the engine injectors.

STEP 7　Compare the two pressure readings and compute the pressure drop for each injector. Compare the pressure drops of the injectors to each other. Any variation in pressure drops will indicate an uneven fuel delivery rate between the injectors.

For example,

Injector	1	2	3	4	5	6
Initial pressure	40	40	40	40	40	40
Second pressure	30	30	35	30	20	30
Pressure drop	10	10	5	10	20	10
Possible problem	OK	OK	Restriction	OK	Leak	OK

INJECTOR VOLTAGE- DROP TESTS

Another test of injectors involves pulsing the injector and measuring the voltage drop across the windings as current is flowing. A typical voltage-drop tester is shown in ● **FIGURE 40–15.** The tester, which is recommended for use by General Motors Corporation, pulses the injector while a digital multimeter is connected to the unit, which will display the voltage drop as the current flows through the winding.

FIGURE 40–15 An injector tester being used to check the voltage drop through the injector while the tester is sending current through the injectors. This test is used to check the coil inside the injector. This same tester can be used to check for equal pressure drop of each injector by pulsing the injector on for 500 ms.

CAUTION: Do not test an injector using a pulse-type tester more than one time without starting the engine to help avoid a hydrostatic lock caused by the flow of fuel into the cylinder during the pulse test.

Record the highest voltage drop observed on the meter display during the test. Repeat the voltage-drop test for all of the injectors. The voltage drop across each injector should be within 0.1 volt of each other. If an injector has a higher-than-normal voltage drop, the injector windings have higher-than-normal resistance.

SCOPE-TESTING FUEL INJECTORS

A scope (analog or digital storage) can be connected into each injector circuit. There are three types of injector drive circuits and each type of circuit has its own characteristic pattern. ● **SEE FIGURE 40–16** for an example of how to connect a scope to read a fuel-injector waveform.

SATURATED SWITCH TYPE In a saturated switch-type injector-driven circuit, voltage (usually a full 12 volts) is applied to the injector. The ground for the injector is provided by the vehicle computer. When the ground connection is completed, current flows through the injector windings. Due to the resistance and inductive reactance of the coil itself, it requires a fraction of a second (about 3 milliseconds or 0.003 seconds) for the coil to reach **saturation** or maximum current flow. Most saturated switch-type fuel injectors have

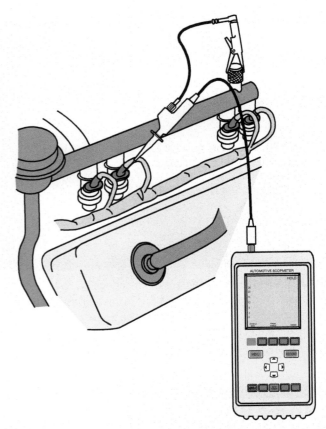

FIGURE 40–16 A DSO can be easily connected to an injector by carefully back-probing the electrical connector.

12 to 16 ohms of resistance. This resistance, as well as the computer switching circuit, control and limit the current flow through the injector. A voltage spike occurs when the computer shuts off (opens the injector ground-side circuit) the injectors. ● **SEE FIGURE 40–17.**

PEAK-AND-HOLD TYPE A **peak-and-hold** type is typically used for TBI and some port low-resistance injectors. Full battery voltage is applied to the injector and the ground side is controlled through the computer. The computer provides a high initial current flow (about 4 amperes) to flow through the injector windings to open the injector core. Then the computer reduces the current to a lower level (about 1 ampere). The hold current is enough to keep the injector open, yet conserves energy and reduces the heat buildup that would occur if the full current flow remains on as long as the injector is commanded on. Typical peak-and-hold-type injector resistance ranges from 2 to 4 ohms.

The scope pattern of a typical peak-and-hold-type injector shows the initial closing of the ground circuit, then a voltage spike as the current flow is reduced. Another voltage spike occurs when the lower level current is turned off (opened) by the computer. ● **SEE FIGURE 40–18.**

PULSE-WIDTH MODULATED TYPE A pulse-width modulated type of injector drive circuit uses lower-resistance coil injectors. Battery voltage is available at the positive terminal of the injector and the computer provides a variable-duration

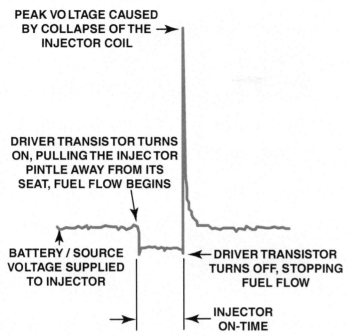

FIGURE 40–17 The injector on-time is called the pulse width.

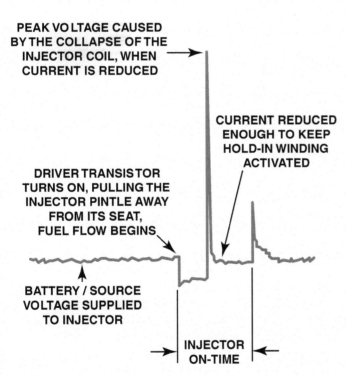

FIGURE 40–18 A typical peak-and-hold fuel-injector waveform. Most fuel injectors that measure less than 6 ohms will usually display a similar waveform.

connection to ground on the negative side of the injector. The computer can vary the time intervals that the injector is grounded for very precise fuel control.

Each time the injector circuit is turned off (ground circuit opened), a small voltage spike occurs. It is normal to see multiple voltage spikes on a scope connected to a pulse-width modulated type of fuel injector. ● SEE FIGURE 40–19.

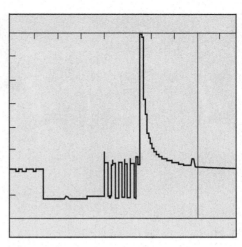

FIGURE 40–19 A waveform of a pulse-width modulated fuel injector. At the end, when the voltage is removed, there is an inductive spike created similar to the spike created but other types of injectors.

IDLE AIR SPEED CONTROL DIAGNOSIS

On older engines equipped with fuel injection (TBI or port injection), the idle speed is controlled by increasing or decreasing the amount of air bypassing the throttle plate. Again, an electronic stepper motor or pulse-width modulated solenoid is used to maintain the correct idle speed. This control is often called the **idle air control (IAC)**. ● SEE FIGURES 40–21 THROUGH 40–23.

FIGURE 40-20 A set of six reconditioned injectors. The sixth injector is barely visible at the far right.

FIGURE 40-22 A typical IAC.

FIGURE 40-23 Some IAC units are purchased with the housing as shown. Carbon buildup in these passages can cause a rough or unstable idling or stalling.

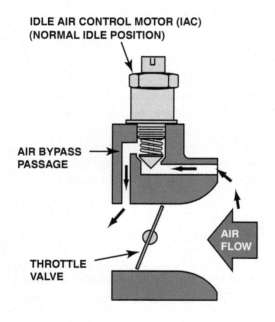

IDLE AIR CONTROL MOTOR (IAC)
(NORMAL IDLE POSITION)

AIR BYPASS
PASSAGE

AIR
FLOW

THROTTLE
VALVE

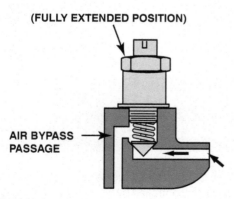

(FULLY EXTENDED POSITION)

AIR BYPASS
PASSAGE

FIGURE 40-21 An IAC controls idle speed by controlling the amount of air that passes around the throttle plate. More airflow results in a higher idle speed.

When the engine stops, most IAC units will retract outward to get ready for the next engine start. When the engine starts, the engine speed is high to provide for proper operation when the engine is cold. Then, as the engine gets warmer, the computer reduces engine idle speed gradually by reducing the number of counts or steps commanded by the IAC.

When the engine is warm and restarted, the idle speed should momentarily increase, then decrease to normal idle speed. This increase and then decrease in engine speed is often called an engine-flare. If the engine speed does not flare, then the IAC may not be working (it may be stuck in one position).

FUEL-INJECTION SERVICE

NEED FOR SERVICE All engines using fuel injection do require some type of fuel-system maintenance. Normal wear and tear with today's underhood temperatures and changes in gasoline quality contribute to the buildup of olefin wax, dirt, water, and many other additives. Unique to each engine is an air-control design that also may contribute different levels of carbon deposits, such as oil control.

FUEL-INJECTION SERVICE Fuel-injection system service should include the following operations:

FIGURE 40–24 When the cover is removed from the top of the engine, a mouse or some other animal nest is visible. The animal had already eaten through a couple of injector wires. At least the cause of the intermittent misfire was discovered.

 CASE STUDY

There Is No Substitute for a Thorough Visual Inspection

An intermittent "check engine" light and a random-misfire diagnostic trouble code (DTC) P0300 was being diagnosed. A scan tool did not provide any help because all systems seemed to be functioning normally. Finally, the technician removed the engine cover and discovered a mouse nest. ● **SEE FIGURE 40–24.**

Summary:

* **Complaint**—Customer stated that the "Check Engine" light was on.
* **Cause**—A stored P0300 DTC was stored indicating a random misfire had been detected caused by an animal that had partially eaten some fuel injector wires.
* **Correction**—The mouse nest was removed and the wiring was repaired.

1. **Check fuel-pump operating pressure and volume.** The missing link here is volume. Most working technicians assume that if the pressure is correct, the volume is also okay. Hook up a fuel-pressure tester to the fuel rail inlet to quickly test the fuel pressure with the engine running. At the same time, test the volume of the pump by sending fuel into the holding tank. (One ounce per second is the usual specification.) ● **SEE FIGURE 40–25.** A two-line system tester is the recommended procedure to use and is attached to the fuel inlet and the return on the fuel rail. The vehicle onboard system is looped and returns fuel to the tank.

2. **Test the fuel-pressure regulator for operation and leakage.** At this time, the fuel-pressure regulator would be tested for operational pressure and proper regulation, including

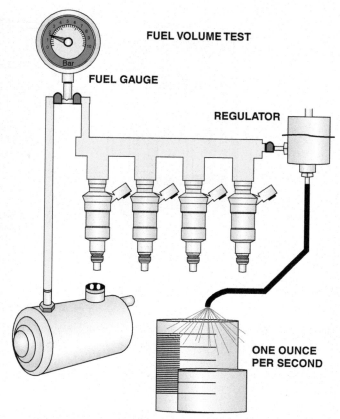

FIGURE 40–25 Checking fuel-pump volume using a hose from the outlet of the fuel-pressure regulator into a calibrated container.

leakage. (This works well as the operator has total control of rail pressure with a unit control valve.) Below are some points to consider:

■ Good pressure does not mean proper volume. For example, a clogged filter may test okay on pressure, but the restriction may not allow proper volume under load. ● **SEE FIGURE 40–26.**

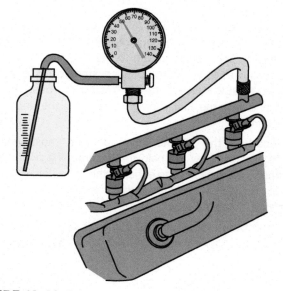

FIGURE 40–26 Testing fuel-pump volume using a fuel-pressure gauge with a bleed hose inserted into a suitable container. The engine is running during this test.

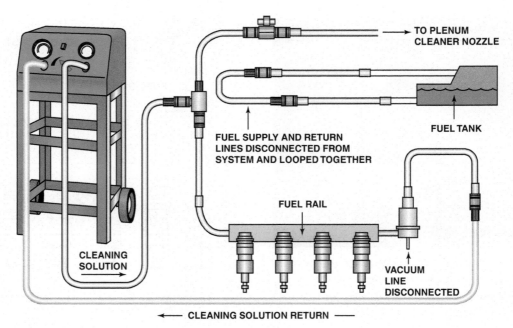

FIGURE 40–27 A typical two-line cleaning machine hookup, showing an extension hose that can be used to squirt a cleaning solution into the throttle body while the engine is running on the cleaning solution and gasoline mixture.

- It is a good idea to use the vehicle's own gasoline to service the system versus a can of shop gasoline that has been sitting around for some time.
- Pressure regulators do fail and a lot more do not properly shut off fuel, causing higher-than-normal pump wear and shorter service life.

3. **Flush the entire fuel rail and upper fuel-injector screens including the fuel-pressure regulator.** Raise the input pressure to a point above regulator setting to allow a constant flow of fuel through the inlet pressure side of the system, through the fuel rail, and out the open fuel-pressure regulator. In most cases the applied pressure is 75 to 90 PSI (517 to 620 kPa), but will be maintained by the presence of a regulator. At this point, cleaning chemical is added to the fuel at a 5:1 mixture and allowed to flow through the system for 15 to 30 minutes. ● **SEE FIGURE 40–27.** Results are best on a hot engine with the fuel supply looped and the engine not running.

4. **Decarbon the engine assembly.** On most vehicles, the injector spray will help the decarboning process. On others, you may need to enhance the operation with external addition of a mixture through the PCV hose, throttle plates, or idle air controls.

5. **Clean the throttle plate and idle air control passages.** Doing this service alone on most late-model engines will

FIGURE 40–28 To thoroughly clean a throttle body, it is sometimes best to remove it from the vehicle. The throttle plate may need to be cleaned if the engine tends to stall, hesitate or has a rough idle.

show a manifold vacuum increase of up to 2 inches Hg. ● **SEE FIGURE 40–28.** This works well as air is drawn into IAC passages on a running engine and will clean the passages without IAC removal.

6. **Relearn the onboard computer.** Some vehicles may have been running in such a poor state of operation that the onboard computer may need to be relearned. Consult service information for the suggested relearn procedures for each particular vehicle.

All of the previously listed steps may be performed using a two-line fuel-injector service unit such as Carbon Clean, Auto Care, Injector Test, DeCarbon, or Motor-Vac.

Fuel-Injection Symptom Chart

Symptom	Possible Causes
Hard cold starts	• Low fuel pressure • Leaking fuel injectors • Contaminated fuel • Low-volatility fuel • Dirty throttle plate
Garage stalls	• Low fuel pressure • Insufficient fuel volume • Restricted fuel injector • Contaminated fuel • Low-volatility fuel
Poor cold performance	• Low fuel pressure • Insufficient fuel volume • Contaminated fuel • Low-volatility fuel
Tip-in hesitation (hesitation just as the accelerator pedal is depressed)	• Low fuel pressure • Insufficient fuel volume • Intake valve deposits • Contaminated fuel • Low-volatility fuel

FIGURE 40–29 The amount each injector is able to flow is displayed in glass cylinders are each injector for a quick visual check.

 TECH TIP

Check the Injectors at the "Bends and the Ends"

Injectors that are most likely to become restricted due to clogging of the filter basket screen are the injectors at the ends of the rail, especially on returnless systems where dirt can accumulate. Also the injectors that are located at the bends of the fuel rail are also subject to possible clogging due to the dirt being deposited where the fuel makes a turn in the rail.

 TECH TIP

Use an Injector Tester

The best way to check injectors is to remove them all from the engine and test them using an injector tester. A typical injector tester uses a special nonflammable test fluid that has the same viscosity as gasoline. The tester pulses the injectors, and the amount of fuel delivered, as well as the spray pattern can be seen. Many testers are capable of varying the frequency of the pulse, as well as the duration that helps find intermittent injector faults. ● **SEE FIGURE 40–29.**

FUEL-SYSTEM SCAN TOOL DIAGNOSTICS

Diagnosing a faulty fuel system can be a difficult task. However, it can be made easier by utilizing the information available via the serial data stream. By observing the long-term fuel trim and the short-term fuel trim, a determination can be made on how the fuel system is performing. Short-term fuel trim and long-term fuel trim can help zero in on specific areas of trouble. Readings should be taken at idle and at 3,000 RPM.

 WARNING

Before opening any part of the high-pressure section of a gasoline direct injection (GDI) system, the pressure must be bled off. The high pressures of this fuel system can cause injury or death. If any of the high-pressure lines are removed, even temporarily, they MUST be replaced because the ends use a ball-fitting that deforms to create the high-pressure seal. Once this seal has been opened, a new ball end must be used to insure a proper seal. ● **SEE FIGURE 40–30.**

Always check service information for the exact procedures to follow for the vehicle being serviced.

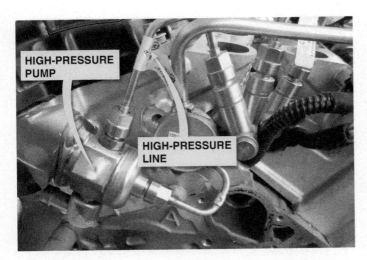

HIGH-PRESSURE PUMP

HIGH-PRESSURE LINE

FIGURE 40–30 The line that has the yellow tag is a high-pressure line and this line must be replaced with a new part if removed even for a few minutes to gain access to another part.

Condition	Long-Term Fuel Trim at Idle	Long-Term Fuel Trim at 3000 RPM
System normal	0% ± 10%	0% ± 10%
Vacuum leak	HIGH	OK
Fuel flow problem	OK	HIGH
Low fuel pressure	HIGH	HIGH
High fuel pressure	*OK or LOW	*OK or LOW

*High fuel pressure will affect trim at idle, at 3000 RPM, or both.

CHART 40–1

Fuel trim levels and possible causes if not within 10%.

1 The tools needed to diagnose a circuit containing a relay include a digital multimeter (DMM), a fused jumper wire, and an assortment of wiring terminals.

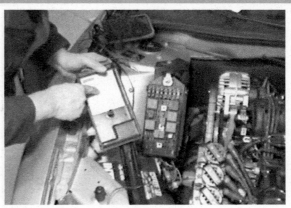

2 Start the diagnosis by locating the relay center. It is under the hood on this General Motors vehicle, so access is easy. Not all vehicles are this easy.

3 The chart under the cover for the relay center indicates the location of the relay that controls the electric fuel pump.

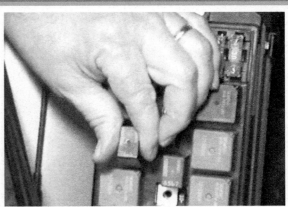

4 Locate the fuel-pump relay and remove it by using a puller if necessary. Try to avoid rocking or twisting the relay to prevent causing damage to the relay terminals or the relay itself.

5 Terminals 85 and 86 represent the coil inside the relay. Terminal 30 is the power terminal, 87a is the normally closed contact, and 87 is the normally open contact.

6 The terminals are also labeled on most relays.

CONTINUED ▶

7 To help make good electrical contact with the terminals without doing any harm, select the proper-size terminal from the terminal assortment.

8 Insert the terminals into the relay socket in 30 and 87.

9 To check for voltage at terminal 30, use a test light or a voltmeter. Start by connecting the alligator clip of the test light to the positive (+) terminal of the battery.

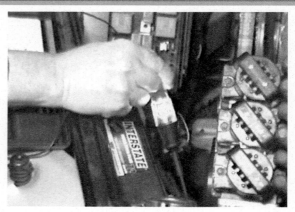

10 Touch the test light to the negative (−) terminal of the battery or a good engine ground to check the test light.

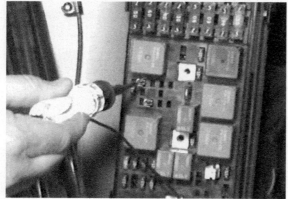

11 Use the test light to check for voltage at terminal 30 of the relay. The ignition may have to be in the on (run) position.

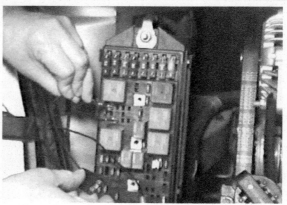

12 To check to see if the electric fuel pump can be operated from the relay contacts, use a fused jumper wire and touch the relay contacts that correspond to terminals 30 and 87 of the relay.

13 Connect the leads of the meter to contacts 30 and 87 of the relay socket. The reading of 4.7 amperes is okay because the specification is 4 to 8 amperes.

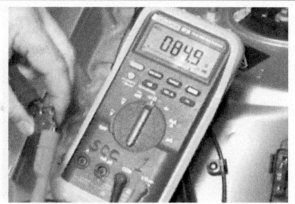

14 Set the meter to read ohms (Ω) and measure the resistance of the relay coil. The usual reading for most relays is between 60 and 100 ohms.

15 Measure between terminal 30 and 87a. Terminal 87a is the normally closed contact, and there should be little, if any, resistance between these two terminals, as shown.

16 To test the normally open contacts, connect one meter lead to terminal 30 and the other lead to terminal 87. The ohmmeter should show an open circuit by displaying OL.

17 Connect a fused jumper wire to supply 12 volts to terminal 86 and a ground to terminal 85 of the relay. If the relay clicks, then the relay coil is able to move the armature (movable arm) of the relay.

18 After testing, be sure to reinstall the relay and the relay cover.

CONTINUED ▶

FUEL INJECTOR CLEANING (CONTINUED)

1 Start the fuel injector cleaning process by bringing the vehicle's engine up to operating temperature. Shut off the engine, remove the cap from the fuel rail test port, and install the appropriate adapter.

2 The vehicle's fuel pump is disabled by removing its relay or fuse. In some cases, it may be necessary to disconnect the fuel pump at the tank if the relay or fuse powers more than just the pump.

3 Turn the outlet valve of the canister to the OFF or CLOSED position.

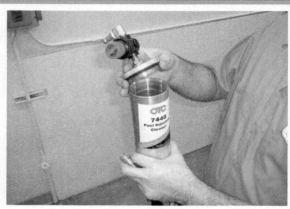

4 Remove the fuel injector cleaning canister's top and regulator assembly. Note that there is an O-ring seal located here that must be in place for the canister's top to seal properly.

5 Pour the injection system cleaning fluid into the open canister. Rubber gloves are highly recommended for this step as the fluid is toxic.

6 Replace the canister's top (making sure it is tight) and connect its hose to the fuel rail adapter. Be sure that the hose is routed away from exhaust manifolds and other hazards.

7 Hang the canister from the vehicle's hood and adjust the air pressure regulator to full OPEN position (CCW).

8 Connect shop air to the canister and adjust the air pressure regulator to the desired setting. Canister pressure can be read directly from the gauge.

9 Canister pressure should be adjusted to 5 PSI below system fuel pressure. An alternative for return-type systems is to block the fuel return line to the tank.

10 Open the outlet valve on the canister.

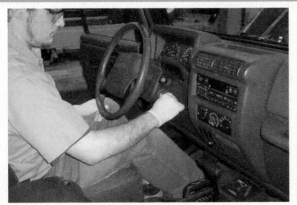

11 Start the vehicle's engine and let run at 1000–1500 RPM. The engine is now running on fuel injector cleaning fluid provided by the canister.

12 Continue the process until the canister is empty and the engine stalls. Remove the cleaning equipment, enable the vehicle's fuel pump, and run the engine to check for leaks.

1. A typical port fuel-injection system uses an individual fuel injector for each cylinder and squirts fuel directly into the intake manifold about 3 inches (80 mm) from the intake valve.

2. A typical fuel-injection system fuel pressure should not drop more than 20 PSI in 20 minutes.

3. A noid light can be used to check for the presence of an injector pulse.

4. Injectors can be tested for resistance and should be within 0.3 to 0.4 ohms of each other.

5. Different designs of injectors have a different scope waveform, depending on how the computer pulses the injector on and off.

6. An idle air control unit controls idle speed and can be tested for proper operation using a scan tool or scope.

REVIEW QUESTIONS

1. In what ways can fuel injectors be tested?

2. What steps are necessary to test a fuel-pressure regulator?

3. What is wrong if a fuel injector measures 100 ohms of resistance?

4. Why would fuel injectors at the bends and ends of the fuel rail tend to become clogged?

5. What does an injector voltage drop test indicate?

CHAPTER QUIZ

1. Most port fuel-injected engines operate on how much fuel pressure?
   a. 3 to 5 PSI (21 to 35 kPa)
   b. 9 to 13 PSI (62 to 90 kPa)
   c. 35 to 45 PSI (240 to 310 kPa)
   d. 55 to 65 PSI (380 to 450 kPa)

2. Fuel injectors can be tested using _____.
   a. an ohmmeter
   b. a stethoscope
   c. a scope
   d. Any of the above

3. Throttle-body fuel-injection systems use what type of injector driver?
   a. Peak and hold
   b. Saturated switch
   c. Pulse-width modulated
   d. Pulsed

4. Port fuel-injection systems generally use what type of injector driver?
   a. Peak and hold
   b. Saturated switch
   c. Pulse-width modulated
   d. Pulsed

5. The vacuum hose from the fuel-pressure regulator was removed from the regulator and gasoline dripped out of the hose. Technician A says that is normal and that everything is okay. Technician B says that one or more of the injectors may be defective, causing the fuel to get into the hose. Which technician is correct?
   a. Technician A only
   b. Technician B only
   c. Both Technicians A and B
   d. Neither Technician A nor B

6. The fuel pressure drops rapidly when the engine is turned off. Technician A says that one or more injectors could be leaking. Technician B says that a defective check valve in the fuel pump could be the cause. Which technician is correct?
   a. Technician A only
   b. Technician B only
   c. Both Technicians A and B
   d. Neither Technician A nor B

7. In a typical port fuel-injection system, which injectors are most subject to becoming restricted?
   a. Any of them equally
   b. The injectors at the end of the rail on a returnless system
   c. The injectors at the bends in the rail
   d. Either b or c

8. What component pulses the fuel injector on most vehicles?
   a. Electronic control unit (computer)
   b. Ignition module
   c. Crankshaft sensor
   d. Both b and c

9. Fuel-injection service is being discussed. Technician A says that the throttle plate(s) should be cleaned. Technician B says that the fuel rail should be cleaned. Which technician is correct?
   a. Technician A only
   b. Technician B only
   c. Both Technicians A and B
   d. Neither Technician A nor B

10. If the throttle plate needs to be cleaned, what symptoms will be present regarding the operation of the engine?
    a. Stalls
    b. Rough idle
    c. Hesitation on acceleration
    d. Any of the above

chapter 41

VEHICLE EMISSIONS STANDARDS, AND TESTING

After studying this chapter, the reader will be able to:

1. Discuss emissions standards.
2. Identify the reasons why excessive amounts of HC, CO, and NO_x exhaust emissions are created.
3. Diagnose driveability and emissions problems resulting from malfunctions of interrelated systems.
4. Describe how to test for various emissions products.

This chapter will help you prepare for ASE A8 certification test content area "D" (Emissions Control Systems Diagnosis and Repair) and ASE L1 certification test content area "F" (I/M Failure Diagnosis).

KEY TERMS

Carbon dioxide (CO_2) 630
Carbon monoxide (CO) 630
Federal Test Procedure (FTP) 637
Hydrocarbons (HC) 630
Lean indicator 632
Non-methane organic gases (NMOG) 636

Oxygen (O_2) 630
Oxides of Nitrogen (NO_X) 630
Ozone 634
Rich indicator 632
Smog 634
Stoichiometric ratio 630
Water (H_2O) 630

NORMAL ENGINE COMBUSTION

AIR AND GASOLINE Engines consume about 15 times more air by weight than gasoline; this ratio of air to fuel is called the **stoichiometric ratio**. This ratio, which is 14.7:1 for gasoline, is the ratio where all of the fuel is consumed in the combustion process and uses all of the available oxygen.

- Entering the engine combustion chamber is fuel (HC) plus air (**nitrogen (N$_2$)** is 78% and **oxygen (O$_2$)** is 21% of the air). ● **SEE FIGURE 41–1.**

- During combustion, the HC combines with the air to form **water (H$_2$O),** carbon dioxide (CO$_2$) plus nitrogen (N$_2$) and some other non-desirable gases.

- Engines consume about 15 times more air by with than gasoline (14.7:1 at stoichiometric ratio). Some of the other gases include the following:

- Unburned **hydrocarbons (HC)**–If perfect combustion occurs inside the engine, there should not be any left-over unburned fuel. If there is HC gas exiting the tailpipe, it indicates that all of the fuel has not been burned. ● **SEE FIGURE 41–2.**

- **Carbon monoxide (CO)**–During combustion, all of the carbon in the fuel should be converted to **carbon dioxide (CO$_2$)**, if there is enough oxygen available. If there is not enough oxygen available in the combustion chamber, incomplete combustion occurs, creating CO instead of. ● **SEE FIGURE 41–3.**

- **Oxides of Nitrogen (NO$_X$)**–Nitrogen is 78% of the air, so having some left over is normal; however, if the combustion temperatures and pressures are high enough, some of the nitrogen (N$_2$) combines with the oxygen to form NO and NO$_2$, which are harmful exhaust gases and referred to as oxides of nitrogen (NO$_X$), where the "x" represents the a number. ● **SEE FIGURE 41–4.**

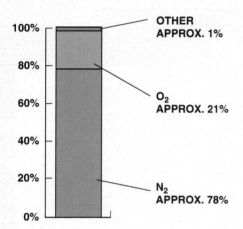

FIGURE 41–1 The air entering the engine consists of mostly nitrogen (78%) with about 21% oxygen and about 1% other gases.

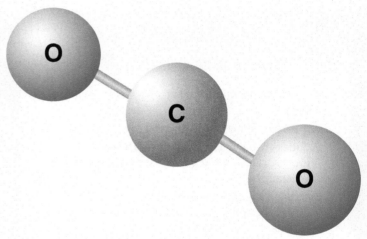

FIGURE 41–3 Carbon dioxide has two oxygen atoms attached to the one carbon atom and is a stable molecule.

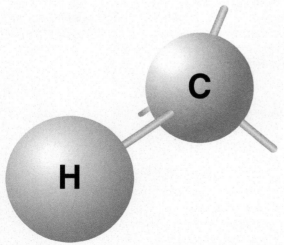

FIGURE 41–2 Hydrocarbons can include many combinations of hydrogen and carbon.

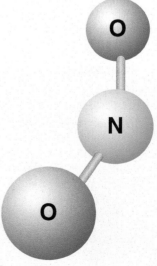

FIGURE 41–4 NO and NO$_2$ shown together are referred to as NO$_X$.

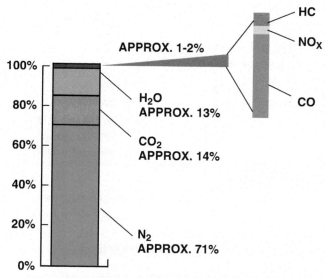

EXHAUST EMISSIONS OF GASOLINE ENGINES

FIGURE 41–5 A chart showing that about 13% of the exhaust emissions is water (H_2O) in the form of steam.

 FREQUENTLY ASKED QUESTION

Why Is Steam Seen from the Tailpipe When Cold Outside, But Not Always?

Steam is water vapor and is invisible. However, when an engine is cold, the water vapor created by combustion partially condenses into small droplets of water that are visible as "steam" from the tailpipe of vehicle when the engine is cold. After the exhaust system has been heated, the water vapor no longer condenses in the exhaust system, so it is not visible after the engine is warm. ● **SEE FIGURE 41–5.**

EXHAUST ANALYSIS AND COMBUSTION EFFICIENCY

HYDROCARBONS Hydrocarbons are unburned gasoline and are measured in parts per million (ppm). A correctly operating engine should burn (oxidize) almost all the gasoline; therefore, very little unburned gasoline should be present in the exhaust. Acceptable levels of HC are 50 ppm or less. High levels of HC could be due to excessive oil consumption caused by weak piston rings or worn valve guides. The most common cause of excessive HC emissions is a fault in the ignition system. Items that should be checked include the following:

- Spark plugs
- Secondary ignition fault such as coils, spark plug boots, or wiring

CARBON MONOXIDE Carbon monoxide (CO) is unstable and will easily combine with any oxygen to form stable CO_2. The fact that CO combines with oxygen is the reason that CO is a poisonous gas (in the lungs, it combines with oxygen to form CO_2 and deprives the brain of oxygen). CO levels of a properly operating engine should be less than 0.5%. High levels of CO can be caused by clogged or restricted crankcase ventilation devices, such as the pressure control valve (PCV) valve, hose(s), and tubes. Other items that might cause excessive CO include the following:

- Incorrect idle speed
- Too-high fuel-pump pressure
- Any other items that can cause a rich condition

CARBON DIOXIDE Carbon dioxide is the result of oxygen in the engine combining with the carbon of the gasoline. An acceptable level of CO_2 is between 12% and 15%. A high reading indicates an efficiently operating engine. If the CO_2 level is low, the mixture may be either too rich or too lean.

OXYGEN There is about 21% oxygen in the atmosphere, and most of this oxygen should be "used up" during the combustion process to oxidize all the hydrogen and carbon (hydrocarbons) in the gasoline. Levels of O_2 should be very low (about 0.5%). High levels of O_2, especially at idle, could be due to an exhaust system leak.

NOTE: Adding 10% alcohol to gasoline provides additional oxygen to the fuel and will result in lower levels of CO and higher levels of O_2 in the exhaust.

OXIDES OF NITROGEN (NO_X) An **oxide of nitrogen (NO)** is a colorless, tasteless, and odorless gas when it leaves the engine, but as soon as it reaches the atmosphere and mixes with more oxygen, nitrogen oxides (NO_2) are formed. NO_2 is reddish-brown and has an acid and pungent smell. NO and NO_2 are grouped together and referred to as NO_X, where x represents any number of oxygen atoms. NO_X, the symbol used to represent all oxides of nitrogen, is the fifth gas commonly tested using a five-gas analyzer. The exhaust gas recirculation (EGR) system is the major controlling device limiting the formation of NO_X. ● **SEE FIGURE 41–6.**

CATALYTIC CONVERTER

EFFECT ON EXHAUST GASES The catalytic converter is used to help reduce exhaust emissions by helping the oxygen in the exhaust to oxidize the HC and CO in the exhaust stream to form harmless water (H_2O) and CO_2. It also helps separate the nitrogen from the oxygen in NO_X to produce just nitrogen (N_2) and oxygen (O_2). ● **SEE FIGURE 41–7** and **CHART 41–1.**

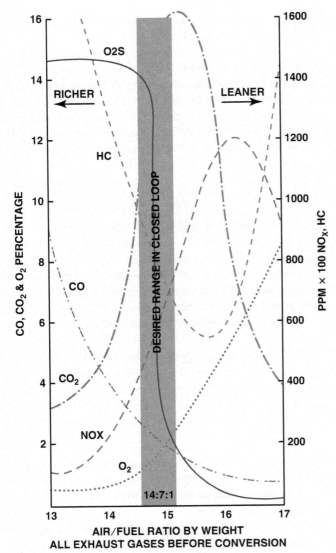

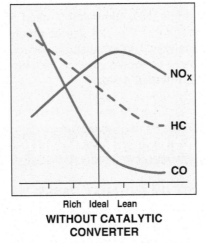

EXHAUST GAS	TYPICAL SPECIFICATIONS
Unburned hydrocarbons (HC)	30–50 ppm or less
Carbon Monoxide (CO)	0.3%–0.5% or less
Oxygen (O_2)	0%–2%
Carbon Dioxide (CO_2)	12%–15% or higher
Oxides of Nitrogen (NO_X)	Less than 100 ppm at idle and less than 1,000 ppm at wide-open throttle (WOT)

CHART 41–1

Typical specifications for gases for a vehicle equipped with a catalytic converter.

EXHAUST ANALYSIS AS A DIAGNOSTIC TOOL

RICH OR LEAN EXHAUST If the exhaust is rich, CO emissions will be higher than normal. If the exhaust is lean, O_2 emissions will be higher than normal.

- If CO is high, the exhaust is rich. This is why CO is called the **"rich indicator."**
- If O_2 is high, the exhaust is lean. This is why O_2 is called the **"lean indicator."**

Therefore, if the CO reading is the same as the O_2 reading, the engine is operating correctly. For example, if both CO and O_2 are 0.5% and the engine develops a vacuum leak, the O_2 will rise. If a fuel-pressure regulator were to malfunction, the resulting richer air–fuel mixture would increase CO emissions. Therefore, if both the rich indicator (CO) and the lean indicator (O_2) are equal, the engine is operating correctly.

If the exhaust is rich (too much fuel or not enough air), then the following can be observed:

FIGURE 41–6 Exhaust emissions are very complex. When the air–fuel mixture becomes richer, some exhaust emissions are reduced, while others increase.

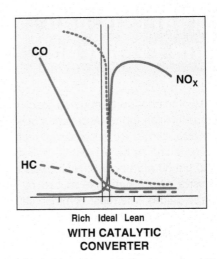

FIGURE 41–7 The image on the left shows exhaust gases exiting an engine without a catalytic converter with rich exhaust being toward the left of the vertical line and lean exhaust to the right of the line. The image on the right shows the exhaust after it has been treated by the catalytic converter.

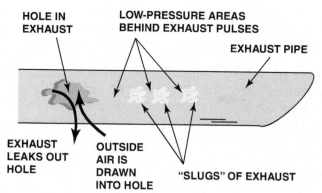

HOLE IN EXHAUST

LOW-PRESSURE AREAS BEHIND EXHAUST PULSES

EXHAUST PIPE

EXHAUST LEAKS OUT HOLE

OUTSIDE AIR IS DRAWN INTO HOLE

"SLUGS" OF EXHAUST

FIGURE 41–8 A hole in the exhaust system can cause outside air (containing oxygen) to be drawn into the exhaust system. This extra oxygen can be confusing to a service technician because the extra O_2 in the exhaust stream could be misinterpreted as a too-lean air–fuel mixture.

 TECH TIP

How to Find a Leak in the Exhaust System

A hole in the exhaust system can dilute the exhaust gases with additional oxygen (O_2). ● **SEE FIGURE 41–8.**

This additional O_2 in the exhaust can lead the service technician to believe that the air–fuel mixture is too lean. To help identify an exhaust leak, perform an exhaust analysis at idle and at 2,500 RPM (fast idle) and compare with the following:

- If the O_2 is high at idle and at 2,500 RPM, the mixture is lean at both idle and at 2,500 RPM.
- If the O_2 is low at idle and high at 2,500 RPM, this usually means the vehicle is equipped with a working AIR pump.
- If the O_2 is high at idle, but okay at 2,500 RPM, a hole in the exhaust or a small vacuum leak that is "covered up" at higher speed is indicated.

- Both CO and HC will be high
- O_2 will be low
- CO_2 will be low

If the exhaust is lean (not enough fuel or too much air), then it will result in the following:

- O_2 will be high
- CO_2 will be low

ENGINE FAULT POSSIBILITIES

HC TOO HIGH High HC exhaust emissions are usually caused by an engine misfire. What burns the fuel in an engine? The ignition system produces a spark at the spark plug to ignite

 **CASE STUDY**

O2S Shows Rich, But Pulse Width Is Low

A service technician was attempting to solve a drive-ability problem. The powertrain control module (PCM) did not indicate any diagnostic trouble codes (DTCs). A check of the oxygen sensor voltage indicated a higher-than-normal reading almost all the time. The pulse width to the port injectors was lower than normal. The lower-than- normal pulse width indicates that the PCM is attempting to reduce fuel flow into the engine by decreasing the amount of on-time for all the injectors. What could cause a rich mixture if the injectors were being commanded to deliver a lean mixture?

Finally, the technician shut off the engine and took a careful look at the entire fuel-injection system. When the vacuum hose was removed from the fuel-pressure regulator, fuel was found dripping from the vacuum hose. The problem was a defective fuel-pressure regulator that allowed an uncontrolled amount of fuel to be drawn by the intake manifold vacuum into the cylinders. While the PCM tried to reduce fuel by reducing the pulse width signal to the injectors, the extra fuel being drawn directly from the fuel rail caused the engine to operate with too rich an air–fuel mixture.

Summary:

- **Complaint**–Customer stated that the engine did not perform correctly.
- **Cause**–No stored diagnostic trouble codes (DTCs) were found but the oxygen sensor reading was higher than normal indicating that the exhaust air–fuel mixture was too rich.
- **Correction**–The fuel pressure regulator was found to be leaking causing fuel to be drawn into the intake causing the richer-then-normal air–fuel mixture. Replacing the fuel pressure regulator solved the driveability complaint.

the proper fuel–airmixture inside the combustion chamber. If a spark plug does not ignite the mixture, the resulting unburned fuel is pushed out of the cylinder on the exhaust stroke by the piston through the exhaust valves and into the exhaust system. Therefore, if any of the following ignition components or adjustments are not correct, excessive HC emission is likely:

1. Defective or worn spark plugs
2. Defective or loose spark plug boots or other faults in the primary or secondary ignition system

A lean air–fuel mixture can also cause a misfire. This condition is referred to as a *lean misfire*. A lean air–fuel mixture can be caused by low fuel pump pressure, a clogged fuel filter, or a restricted fuel injector.

CO TOO HIGH Excessive CO is an indication of too rich an air–fuel mixture. CO is the rich indicator. The higher the CO reading, the richer the air–fuel mixture. High concentrations of CO indicate that not enough oxygen was available for the amount of fuel. Common causes of high CO include the following:

- Too-high fuel pressure
- Clogged air intake or PCV valve
- Defective injectors

O_2 AND CO_2 RELATIONSHIP

Two gas exhaust analyzers (HC and CO) work well, but both HC and CO are consumed (converted) inside the catalytic converter. The amount of leftover oxygen coming out of the tailpipe is an indication of leanness. The higher the O_2 level, the leaner the exhaust. Oxygen therefore is the lean indicator. Acceptable levels of O_2 are 0% to 2%.

NOTE: A hole in the exhaust system can draw outside air (oxygen) into the exhaust system. Therefore, to be assured of an accurate reading, carefully check the exhaust system for leaks. Using a smoke machine is an easy method to locate leaks in the exhaust system.

Carbon dioxide is a measure of efficiency. The higher the level of CO_2 in the exhaust stream, the more efficiently the engine is operating. Levels of 12% to 17% are considered to be acceptable. Because CO_2 levels peak at an air–fuel mixture of 14.7:1, a lower level of CO_2 indicates either a too-rich or a too-lean condition. The CO_2 measurement by itself does not indicate which condition is present. For example, if the CO_2 is

8%, it means the combustion efficiency is low and the air–fuel mixture is not correct. Look at O_2 and CO levels; a high O_2 indicates lean and a high CO indicates rich.

SMOG AND NO_X

Oxides of nitrogen are formed by high temperature—over 2,500°F (1,370°C)—and/or pressures inside the combustion chamber. Oxides of nitrogen contribute to the formation of photochemical smog when sunlight reacts chemically with NO_X and unburned hydrocarbons. "Smog" is a term derived by combining the words *smoke* and *fog*. Ground-level ozone is a constituent of smog. Ozone is an enriched oxygen molecule with three atoms of oxygen (O_3) instead of the normal two atoms of oxygen (O_2). Ozone in the upper atmosphere is beneficial because it blocks out harmful ultraviolet rays that contribute to skin cancer.

 CASE STUDY

The Case of the Retarded Exhaust Camshaft

A Toyota equipped with a double overhead camshaft (DOHC) six-cylinder engine failed the state-mandated enhanced exhaust emissions test for NO_X. The engine ran perfectly without spark knocking (ping), which is usually a major reason for excessive NO_X emissions. The technician checked the following:

- The cylinders, which were decarbonized using top engine cleaner
- The EGR valve, which was inspected and the EGR passages cleaned

After all the items were completed, the vehicle was returned to the inspection station where the Vehicle again failed for excessive NO_X emissions (better, but still over the maximum allowable limit). After additional hours of troubleshooting, the technician decided to go back to basics and start over again. A check of the vehicle history with the owner indicated that the only previous work performed on the engine was a replacement timing belt over a year before. The technician discovered that the exhaust cam timing was retarded by two teeth, resulting in late closing of the exhaust valve. The proper exhaust valve timing resulted in a slight amount of exhaust gas being retained in the cylinder. This extra exhaust was helped reduce NO_X emissions.

After repositioning the timing belt, the vehicle passed the emissions test well within the limits.

Summary:

- **Complaint**–Customer stated that the vehicle failed an emission test due to excessive NO_X exhaust emissions.
- **Cause**–The exhaust cam was discovered to be retarded by two teeth as a result of the timing belt being incorrectly installed during a previous repair.
- **Correction**–The timing belt was properly aligned and the vehicle passed the emission test.

 **TECH TIP**

Your Nose Knows

Using the nose, a technician can often identify a major problem without having to connect the vehicle to an exhaust analyzer. For example,

- The strong smell of exhaust is due to excessive unburned hydrocarbon (HC) emissions. Look for an ignition system fault that could prevent the proper burning of the fuel.
- If your eyes start to burn or water, suspect excessive oxides of nitrogen (NO_X) emissions. The NO_X combine with the moisture in the eyes to form a mild solution of nitric acid. The acid formation causes the eyes to burn and water. Excessive NO_X exhaust emissions can be caused by a lack of proper amount of exhaust gas recirculation (EGR) or a variable valve timing issue (This is usually noticed above idle on most vehicles.)
- Dizzy feeling or headache. This is commonly caused by excessive carbon monoxide (CO) exhaust emissions. Get into fresh air as soon as possible. A probable cause of high levels of CO is an excessively rich air–fuel mixture.

CARBON MONOXIDE (CO)	CARBON DIOXIDE (CO$_2$)	HYDROCARBONS (HC)	OXYGEN (O$_2$)	POSSIBLE ISSUES
Low	High	Low	Low	Normal readings. No issues
High	Low	High	High	Rich exhaust and misfire
Low	Low	High	High	Lean exhaust and misfire
High	High	High	High	Catalytic converter not working as designed plus possible other air–fuel ratio issues
High	Low	High	High	Rich exhaust
High	Low	High	Low	Possible defective thermostat

CHART 41–2

Possible issues based on the relative readings of the four exhaust gases.

However, at ground level, this ozone (smog) is an irritant to the respiratory system. Because the formation of NO$_x$ occurs mostly under load, the most efficient method to test for NO$_x$ is to use a portable exhaust analyzer that can be carried in the vehicle while the vehicle is being driven under a variety of conditions.

A maximum reading of 1,000 ppm of NO$_x$ under loaded driving conditions will generally mean that the vehicle will pass an enhanced I/M roller test. A reading of over 100 ppm at idle should be considered excessive.

ABNORMAL GAS READINGS The exhaust gases each have their own cause for being higher than normal or lower than normal and they are interconnected. ● **SEE CHART 41–2.**

EMISSION STANDARDS

In the United States, emissions standards are managed by the Environmental Protection Agency (EPA) as well as some U.S. state governments. Some of the strictest standards in the world are formulated in California by the California Air Resources Board (CARB).

TIER 1 AND TIER 2 Federal emissions standards are set by the Clean Air Act Amendments (CAAA) of 1990 and these standards are grouped by tier. All vehicles sold in the United States must meet Tier 1 standards that went into effect in 1994 and are the least stringent. Additional Tier 2 standards which had been optional since 2001 were fully adopted by 2009. The current Tier 1 standards are different between automobiles and light trucks (SUVs, pickup trucks, and minivans), but Tier 2 standards are the same for both types.

There are several emission ratings that can be given to vehicles, and a certain percentage of a manufacturer's vehicles must meet different levels of ratings in order for the company to sell its products in affected regions. Beyond Tier 1, and in order of stringency, are the following levels:

- **TLEV** (Transitional Low-Emission Vehicle). More stringent for HC than Tier 1.
- **LEV** (also known as LEV I) (Low-Emission Vehicle). An intermediate California standard about twice as stringent as Tier 1 for HC and NO$_x$.

- **ULEV** (also known as ULEV I) (Ultra-Low-Emission Vehicle). A stronger California standard emphasizing very low HC emission.
- **ULEV II** (Ultra-Low-Emission Vehicle). A cleaner-than-average vehicle certified under the Phase II LEV standard.

Hydrocarbon and carbon monoxide emissions levels are nearly 50% lower than those of a LEV II-certified vehicle.

- **SULEV** (Super-Ultra-Low-Emission Vehicle). A California standard even tighter than ULEV, including much lower HC and NO$_x$ emissions; roughly equivalent to Tier 2 Bin 2 vehicles.
- **ZEV** (Zero-Emission Vehicle). A California standard prohibiting any tailpipe emissions. The ZEV category is largely restricted to electric vehicles and hydrogen-fueled vehicles.

In these cases, any emissions that are created are produced at another site, such as a power plant or hydrogen reforming center, unless such sites run on renewable energy.

NOTE: A battery-powered electric vehicle charged from the power grid will still be up to 10 times cleaner than even the cleanest gasoline vehicles over their respective lifetimes.

- **PZEV** (Partial Zero-Emission Vehicle). Compliant with the SULEV standard and has near-zero evaporative emissions and a 15-year/150,000-mile warranty on its emission control equipment. Tier 2 standards are even more stringent. Tier 2 variations are appended with "II," such as LEV II or SULEV II.
- **ILEV** (Inherently Low-Emission Vehicle). Used by some states that allow certain vehicles to use the HOV lanes regardless of the number of people in the vehicle. Check state and local laws and regulations for the list of vehicles included.
- **AT-PZEV** (Advanced Technology Partial Zero-Emission Vehicle). If a vehicle meets the PZEV standards and is using high-technology features, such as an electric motor or high-pressure gaseous fuel tanks for compressed natural gas, it qualifies as an AT-PZEV. Hybrid electric vehicles such as the Toyota Prius can qualify, as can internal combustion engine vehicles that run on natural gas

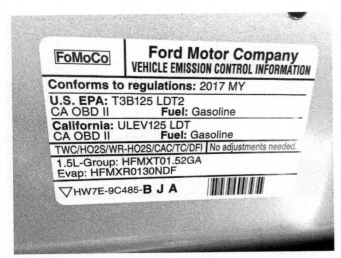

FIGURE 41–9 A vehicle emission control information (VECI) sticker for a vehicle showing that is meets Tier 3, Bin 1 (T2B3) EPA rating and California ULEV125 standard.

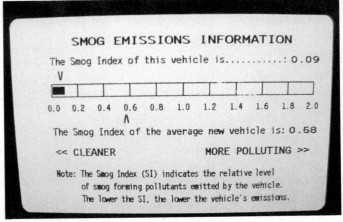

FIGURE 41–10 This label on a Toyota Camry hybrid shows the relative smog-producing emissions, but this does not include CO_2, which may increase global warming.

(CNG), such as the Honda Civic GX. These vehicles are classified as "partial" ZEV because they receive partial credit for the number of ZEV vehicles that automakers would otherwise be required to sell in California.

- **NLEV** (National Low-Emission Vehicle). All vehicles nationwide must meet this standard, which started in 2001.

FEDERAL EPA BIN NUMBER

The higher the tier number, the newer the regulation; the lower the bin number, the cleaner the vehicle. The Toyota Prius is a very clean Bin 2, while dirtier vehicles are given a higher bin number. ● **SEE FIGURE 41–9.**

SMOG EMISSION INFORMATION

New vehicles are equipped with a sticker that shows the relative level of smog-causing emissions created by the vehicle compared to others on the market. Smog-causing emissions include unburned HC and NO_X. ● **SEE FIGURE 41–10.**

CALIFORNIA STANDARDS

The pre-2004 CARB standards as a whole were known as LEV I. Within that, there were four possible ratings: Tier 1, TLEV, LEV, and ULEV. The newest CARB-rating system (since January 1, 2004) is known as LEV II. Within that rating system there are three primary ratings: LEV, ULEV, and SULEV. States other than California are given the option to use the federal EPA standards, or they can adopt California's standards.

LEV III

The latest emissions standards include maintaining the reduced emissions for 150,000 miles has several emission categories, depending on the level of emissions. The standards are more stringent than Tier 2 standards and include a number of other important changes:

- The required emission durability has been increased to 150,000 miles, up from 120,000 miles.
- Gasoline vehicles are tested—for exhaust and evaporative emissions—using gasoline containing 10% of ethanol (E10).
- Standards are for 2015–2025 vehicles sold in the United States. ● **SEE CHART 41-4.**

EMISSION CATEGORY	NMOG + NO$_X$ GRAM PER MILE (G/MI)	CO GRAM PER MILE (G/MI)	PARTICULATE MATTER (PM) GRAM PER MILE (G/MI)
LEV 160	0.160	4.2	0.01
ULEV 125	0.125	2.1	0.01
ULEV 70	0.070	1.7	0.01
ULEV 50	0.050	1.7	0.01
SULEV 30	0.030	1.0	0.01
SULEV 20	0.020	1.0	0.01

CHART 41–4

Non-methane organic gases (NMOG) and oxides of nitrogen are combined under one limit meaning that the hydrocarbons and the NO_X have to be both controlled to meet these standards. Particulate matter (PM) has in the past been associated with diesel engine emissions, but are now being tested on gasoline powered vehicles.

EUROPEAN STANDARDS

Exhaust emissions of nitrogen oxides (NO_X), total hydrocarbon (THC), non-methane hydrocarbons (NMHC), carbon monoxide (CO), and particulate matter (PM) are regulated for most vehicle types, including cars, trucks in the European Union (EU). The EU also sets limits for CO_2 emission in units of grams per kilometer with the latest standard being 95 grams per km after 2020. Carbon dioxide is created by the combustion of fuel inside an internal combustion engine. Reducing the CO_2 emissions requires the less fuel be consumed which is one way the EU is mandating fuel economy standards. The ratings include the following:

- **Euro 1** (1993)
- **Euro 2** (1996)
- **Euro 3** (2000)
- **Euro 4** (2005)
- **Euro 5** (2009)
- **Euro 6** (2014)

VEHICLE EMISSION TESTING

OBD-II TESTING In 1999, the EPA requested that states adopt OBD-II systems testing for 1996 and newer vehicles. The OBD-II system is designed to illuminate the malfunction indicator lamp (MIL) light and store trouble codes any time a malfunction exists that would cause the vehicle emissions to exceed 1 1/2 times the **Federal Test Procedure (FTP)** limits. If the OBD-II system is working correctly, the system should be able to detect a vehicle failure that would cause emissions to increase to an unacceptable level. The EPA has determined that the OBD-II system should detect emission failures of a vehicle even before that vehicle would fail an emissions test of the type that most states are employing.

The EPA has determined that, as the population of OBD-II-equipped vehicles increases and the population of older non-OBD-II-equipped vehicles decreases, tailpipe testing will no longer be necessary.

NOTE: If a state or local emission testing program still uses exhaust emission testing for older vehicles, check the information about the program and test procedures before having the vehicle tested.

The OBD-II testing program consists of a computer that can scan the vehicle OBD-II system using the DLC connector. The technician first performs a visual check of the vehicle MIL light to determine if it is working correctly. Next, the computer is connected to the vehicle's DLC connector. The computer will scan the vehicle OBD-II system and determine if there are any codes stored that are commanding the MIL light on. In addition, it will scan the status of the readiness monitors and determine if they have all run and passed. If the readiness monitors have all run and passed, it indicates that the OBD-II system has tested all the components of the emission control system. An OBD-II vehicle would fail this OBD-II test if the following conditions are present:

- The MIL light does not come on with the key on, engine off
- The MIL is commanded on

FIGURE 41–11 A partial stream sampling exhaust probe being used to measure exhaust gases in parts per million (ppm) or percent (%).

A number (varies by state) of the readiness monitors has not been run. If none of these conditions are present, the vehicle will pass the emissions test.

REMOTE SENSING The EPA requires that, in high-enhanced areas, states perform on-the-road testing of vehicle emissions. The state must sample 0.5% of the vehicle population base in high-enhanced areas. This may be accomplished by using a remote sensing device. This type of sensing may be done through equipment that projects an infrared light through the exhaust stream of a passing vehicle. The reflected beam can then be analyzed to determine the pollutant-emission levels of the vehicle. If a vehicle fails this type of test, the vehicle owner will receive notification in the mail that he or she must take the vehicle to a test facility to have the emissions tested.

RANDOM ROADSIDE TESTING Some states may implement random roadside testing that would usually involve visual checks of the emission control devices to detect tampering. Obviously, this method is not very popular as it can lead to traffic tie-ups and delays on the part of commuters. Exhaust analysis is an excellent tool to use for the diagnosis of engine performance concerns. In areas of the country that require exhaust testing to be able to get license plates, exhaust analysis must be able to carry out the following:

- Establish a baseline for failure diagnosis and service.
- Identify areas of engine performance that are and are not functioning correctly.
- Determine that the service and repair of the vehicle have been accomplished and are complete.

● **SEE FIGURE 41–11.**

SUMMARY

1. Excessive hydrocarbon (HC) exhaust emissions are created by a lack of proper combustion such as a fault in the ignition system, too lean an air–fuel mixture, or too-cold engine operation.

2. Excessive carbon monoxide (CO) exhaust emissions are usually created by a rich air–fuel mixture.

3. Excessive oxides of nitrogen (NO_x) exhaust emissions are usually created by excessive heat or pressure in the combustion chamber or a lack of the proper amount of exhaust gas recirculation (EGR).

4. Carbon dioxide (CO2) levels indicate efficiency. The higher the CO2, the more efficient the engine operation.

5. Oxygen (O2) indicates leanness. The higher the O2, the leaner the air–fuel mixture.

6. A vehicle should be driven about 20 miles, especially during cold weather, to allow the engine to be fully warm before an enhanced emissions test.

REVIEW QUESTIONS

1. What are the five exhaust gases and their maximum allowable readings for a fuel-injected vehicle equipped with a catalytic converter?

2. How is water formed during the combustion process?

3. What is the stoichiometric ratio and what does it mean?

4. How are oxides of nitrogen (NO_x) formed?

5. What information is on the vehicle emission control information (VECI) sticker?

CHAPTER QUIZ

1. Technician A says that high HC emission levels are often caused by a fault in the ignition system. Technician B says that high CO_2 emissions are usually caused by a richer than-normal air–fuel mixture. Which technician is correct?
   a. A only
   b. B only
   c. Both A and B
   d. Neither A nor B

2. HC and CO are high and CO_2 and O_2 are low. This could be caused by a_____.
   a. rich mixture
   b. iean mixture
   c. defective ignition component
   d. clogged EGR passage

3. Which gas is generally considered to be the rich indicator? (The higher the level of this gas, the richer the air–fuel mixture.)
   a. HC
   b. CO
   c. CO_2
   d. O_2

4. Which gas is generally considered to be the lean indicator? (The higher the level of this gas, the leaner the air–fuel mixture.)
   a. HC
   b. CO
   c. CO_2
   d. O_2

5. Which exhaust gas indicates efficiency? (The higher the level of this gas, the more efficient the engine operates.)
   a. HC
   b. CO
   c. CO_2
   d. O_2

6. All of the gases are measured in percentages except _____.
   a. HC
   b. CO
   c. CO_2
   d. O_2

7. After the following exhaust emissions were measured, how was the engine operating?
   HC 5,766 ppm, CO_2 58.2%, CO 54.6%, O_2 50.1%
   a. Too rich
   b. Too lean
   c. Operating at stoichiometric ratio
   d. Engine operating (coolant) temperature too high

8. Technician A says that carbon inside the engine can cause excessive NO_x to form. Technician B says that excessive NO_x could be caused by a cooling system fault causing the engine to operate too hot. Which technician is correct?
   a. A only
   b. B only
   c. Both A and B
   d. Neither A nor B

9. A clogged EGR passage could cause excessive exhaust emissions.
   a. HC
   b. CO
   c. NO_x
   d. CO_2

10. An ignition fault could cause excessive exhaust emissions.
    a. HC
    b. CO
    c. NO_x
    d. CO_2

chapter 42

EMISSION CONTROL DEVICES OPERATION AND DIAGNOSIS

After studying this chapter, the reader should be able to:

1. Explain exhaust gas recirculation systems.
2. Discuss OBD-II EGR monitoring strategies, diagnosing a defective EGR system, and EGR trouble codes.
3. Discuss crankcase ventilation, PCV system diagnosis, and PCV-related trouble codes.
4. Explain the secondary air-injection system and its diagnosis.
5. Explain the purpose and function of catalytic converters, their diagnosis, and guidelines to replace them.
6. Explain evaporative emission control system, and compare enhanced evaporative control systems and nonenhanced evaporative control systems.
7. Discuss the leak detection pump system and onboard refueling vapor recovery.
8. Discuss the diagnosis of the EVAP system and state inspection EVAP tests.
9. Describe evaporative system monitors and typical EVAP monitors.

Adsorption 659
AIR 650
Catalyst 652
Catalytic converter 652
Cerium 653
Check valves 650
Digital EGR 643
DPFE sensor 644
EGR 640
EVP 642
EVRV 645
Fuel tank pressure (FTP) 664
HO2S 654
Inert 641
Infrared thermometer (pyrometer) 656
Leak detection pump (LDP) 661
Light-off temperature 654
Linear EGR 643

LOC 654
Mini converter 654
Negative backpressure 642
NO_x 640
OSC 654
Palladium 653
PCV 646
PFE 642
Platinum 653
Positive backpressure 642
Preconverter 654
Pup converter 654
Rhodium 653
SAI 650
Smog 640
Smog pump 650
Tap test 655
Thermactor pump 650
TWC 650
Washcoat 652

INTRODUCTION

Most of the major advances in engines are a direct result of the need to improve fuel economy and reduce exhaust emissions. The engine changes needed to meet the latest emission standards include:

- More efficient combustion chambers
- Low friction engine components, such as low tension piston rings, roller camshaft followers (rockers), and roller lifters
- More precise ignition timing with coil-on-plug ignition systems, which have the ability to change ignition timing on individual cylinders as needed to achieve the highest possible efficiency
- Closer engine tolerances to reduce unburned fuel emissions and to improve power output
- Variable valve timing systems used to increase engine power and reduce exhaust emissions

It has been said that engine changes are due to the need to reduce three things.

1. Emissions
2. Emissions
3. Emissions

SMOG

DEFINITION AND TERMINOLOGY The common term used to describe air pollution is **smog**, a word that combines two words: *smoke* and *fog.* Smog is formed in the atmosphere when sunlight combines with unburned fuel (hydrocarbon, or HC) and oxides of nitrogen (NO_x) produced during the combustion process inside the cylinders of an engine. Carbon monoxide (CO) is a poisonous gas. Smog is ozone (O_3), a strong irritant to the lungs and eyes. Ozone is locatedin in two places.

1. Upper-atmospheric ozone is desirable because it blocks out harmful ultraviolet rays from the sun.
2. Ground-level ozone is considered to be unhealthy smog.

Emissions that are controlled include:

- **HC (unburned hydrocarbons).** Excessive HC emissions (unburned fuel) are controlled by the evaporative system (charcoal canister), the positive crankcase ventilation (PCV) system, the secondary air-injection (SAI) system, and the catalytic converter.
- **CO (carbon monoxide).** Excessive CO emissions are controlled by the positive crankcase ventilation (PCV) system, the secondary air-injection (SAI) system, and the catalytic converter.

FIGURE 42–1 Notice the red-brown haze which is often over many major cities. This haze is the result of oxides of nitrogen in the atmosphere.

- **NO_x (oxides of nitrogen).** Excessive NO_x emissions are controlled by the exhaust gas recirculation (EGR) system and the catalytic converter. An oxide of nitrogen (NO) is a colorless, tasteless, and odorless gas when it leaves the engine, but as soon as it reaches the atmosphere and mixes with more oxygen, nitrogen oxides (NO_2) are formed, which appear as red-brown emissions. ● **SEE FIGURE 42–1.**

EXHAUST GAS RECIRCULATION SYSTEMS

INTRODUCTION **Exhaust gas recirculation (EGR)** is an emission control system that lowers the amount of **nitrogen oxides (NO_x)** formed during combustion. In the presence of sunlight, NO_x reacts with hydrocarbons in the atmosphere to form ozone (O_3) or photochemical smog, an air pollutant.

NO_x FORMATION Nitrogen (N_2) and oxygen (O_2) molecules are separated into individual atoms of nitrogen and oxygen during the combustion process. These molecules then bond to form NO_x (NO, NO_2). When combustion flame front temperatures exceed 2,500°F (1,370°C), NO_x is formed inside the cylinders which is discharged into the atmosphere from the tailpipe.

CONTROLLING NO_x To handle the NO_x generated above 2,500°F (1,370°C), the most efficient method to meet NO_x emissions without significantly affecting engine performance, fuel economy, and other exhaust emissions is to use exhaust gas recirculation (EGR). The EGR system routes small quantities, usually between 6% and 10%, of exhaust gas into the intake manifold.

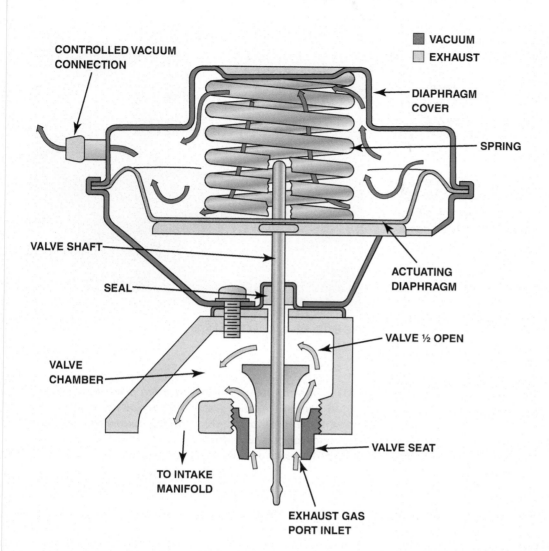

VACUUM

EXHAUST

CONTROLLED VACUUM CONNECTION

DIAPHRAGM COVER

SPRING

VALVE SHAFT

SEAL

ACTUATING DIAPHRAGM

VALVE ½ OPEN

VALVE CHAMBER

TO INTAKE MANIFOLD

VALVE SEAT

EXHAUST GAS PORT INLET

EGR VALVE

EGR CONTROL SOLENOID

FIGURE 42–3 A vacuum-operated EGR valve. The vacuum to the EGR valve is computer controlled by the EGR valve control solenoid.

Here, the exhaust gas mixes with, and takes the place of, some of the intake charge. This leaves less room for the intake charge to enter the combustion chamber. The recirculated exhaust gas is **inert** (chemically inactive) and does not enter into the combustion process. The result is a lower peak combustion temperature. When the combustion temperature is lowered, the production of oxides of nitrogen is reduced.

The EGR system has some means of interconnecting the exhaust and intake manifolds. ● **SEE FIGURES 42–2 AND 42–3.**

The EGR valve controls the flow of exhaust gases through the interconnecting passages.

- On V-type engines, the intake manifold crossover is used as a source of exhaust gas for the EGR system. A cast passage connects the exhaust crossover to the EGR valve. The exhaust gas is sent from the EGR valve to openings in the manifold.

- On inline-type engines, an external tube is generally used to carry exhaust gas to the EGR valve. This tube is often designed to be long so that the exhaust gas is cooled before it enters the EGR valve.

EGR SYSTEM OPERATION Since small amounts of exhaust are all that is needed to lower peak combustion temperatures, the orifice that the exhaust passes through is small.

EGR is usually *not* required during the following conditions because the combustion temperatures are low.

- Idle speed
- When the engine is cold
- At wide-open throttle (WOT) (Not allowing EGR allows the engine to provide extra power when demanded. While the NO_x formation is high during these times, the overall effect of not using EGR during wide-open throttle conditions is minor.)

The level of NO_x emission changes according to engine speed, temperature, and load. EGR is not used at wide-open throttle (WOT) because it would reduce engine performance and the engine does not operate under these conditions for a long period of time.

EGR BENEFITS In addition to lowering NO_x levels, the EGR system also helps control detonation. Detonation, also called spark knock or ping, occurs when high pressure and heat cause the air-fuel mixture to ignite. This uncontrolled combustion can severely damage the engine.

Using the EGR system allows for greater ignition timing advance and for the advance to occur sooner without detonation problems, which increases power and efficiency.

POSITIVE AND NEGATIVE BACKPRESSURE EGR VALVES

Some vacuum-operated EGR valves used on older engines are designed with a small valve inside that bleeds off any applied vacuum and prevents the valve from opening.

- **Positive backpressure.** These types of EGR valves require a positive backpressure in the exhaust system. At low engine speeds and light engine loads, the EGR system is not needed, and the backpressure in it is also low. Without sufficient backpressure, the EGR valve does not open even though vacuum may be present at the EGR valve.
- **Negative backpressure.** On each exhaust stroke, the engine emits an exhaust "pulse." Each pulse represents a positive pressure. Behind each pulse is a small area of low pressure. Some EGR valves react to this low-pressure area by closing a small internal valve, which allows the EGR valve to be opened by vacuum.

The following conditions must occur before a backpressure-type vacuum-controlled EGR will operate.

1. Vacuum must be applied to the EGR valve itself. The vacuum source can be ported vacuum (above the throttle plate) or manifold vacuum (below the throttle plate) and by the computer through a solenoid valve.

2. Exhaust backpressure must be present to close an internal valve inside the EGR to allow the vacuum to move the diaphragm.

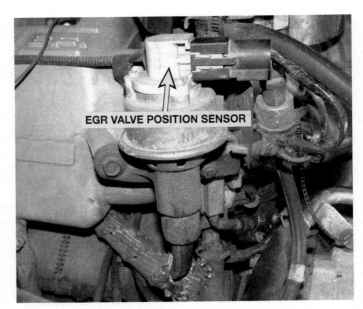

FIGURE 42–4 An EGR valve position sensor on top of an EGR valve.

NOTE: Installing a high-performance exhaust system could prevent a backpressure vacuum-operated EGR valve from opening. If this occurs, excessive combustion chamber temperature leads to severe spark knock, piston damage, or a blown head gasket.

COMPUTER-CONTROLLED EGR SYSTEMS Many computer-controlled EGR systems have one or more solenoids controlling the EGR vacuum. The computer controls a solenoid to shut off vacuum to the EGR valve at cold engine temperatures, idle speed, and wide-open throttle operation. If two solenoids are used, one acts as an off-on control of supply vacuum, while the second solenoid vents vacuum when EGR flow is not desired or needs to be reduced. The second solenoid is used to control a vacuum air bleed, allowing atmospheric pressure in to modulate EGR flow according to vehicle operating conditions.

EGR VALVE POSITION SENSORS Most computer-controlled EGR systems use a sensor to indicate EGR operation. Onboard diagnostics generation-II (OBD-II) EGR system monitors require an EGR sensor to verify that the valve opened. A linear potentiometer on the top of the EGR valve stem indicates valve position for the computer. This is called an **EGR valve position (EVP)** sensor. Some later-model Ford EGR systems, however, use a feedback signal provided by an EGR exhaust backpressure sensor that converts the exhaust backpressure to a voltage signal. This sensor is called a **pressure feedback EGR (PFE)** sensor.

On some EGR systems, the top of the valve contains a vacuum regulator and EGR pintle-position sensor in one assembly sealed inside a nonremovable plastic cover. The pintle-position sensor provides a voltage output to the PCM, which increases as the duty cycle increases, allowing the PCM to monitor valve operation. ● **SEE FIGURE 42–4.**

FIGURE 42–5 Digital EGR valve.

FIGURE 42–6 A General Motors linear EGR valve.

 FREQUENTLY ASKED QUESTION

Where Is the EGR Valve?

Most newer vehicles that are equipped with variable valve timing (VVT) use the valve overlap to keep some exhaust gases in the combustion chamber. As a result, most newer engines do not use an EGR valve.

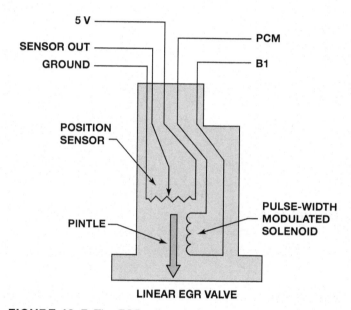

FIGURE 42–7 The EGR valve pintle is pulse-width modulated and a three-wire potentiometer provides pintle-position information back to the PCM.

DIGITAL EGR VALVES GM introduced a **digital EGR** valve design on some engines. Unlike vacuum-operated EGR valves, the digital EGR valve consists of three solenoids controlled by the powertrain control module (PCM). Each solenoid controls a different size orifice in the base—small, medium, and large. The PCM controls the ground circuit of each of the solenoids individually. It can produce any of seven different flow rates, using the solenoids to open the three valves in different combinations. The digital EGR valve offers precise control, and using a swivel pintle design helps prevent carbon deposit problems. ● SEE FIGURE 42–5.

LINEAR EGR Most General Motors and many other vehicles use a **linear EGR** that contains a pulse-width modulated solenoid to precisely regulate exhaust gas flow and a feedback potentiometer that signals the computer regarding the actual position of the valve. ● SEE FIGURES 42–6 AND 42–7.

OBD-II EGR MONITORING STRATEGIES

PURPOSE AND FUNCTION In 1996, the U.S. EPA began requiring OBD-II systems in all passenger cars and most light-duty trucks. These systems include emissions system monitors that alert the driver and the technician if an emissions system is malfunctioning. The OBD-II system performs this test by opening and closing the EGR valve. The PCM monitors an EGR function sensor for a change in signal voltage. If the EGR system

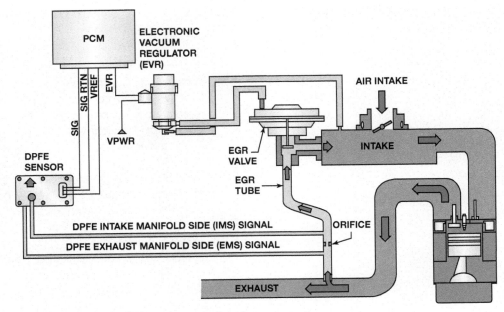

FIGURE 42–8 A DPFE sensor and related components.

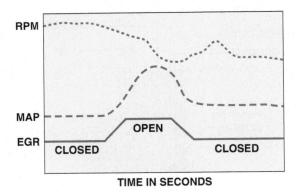

FIGURE 42–9 An OBD-II active test. The PCM opens the EGR valve and monitors the MAP sensor and/or engine speed (RPM) to verify that it meets acceptable values.

fails, a diagnostic trouble code (DTC) is set. If the system fails two consecutive times, the malfunction indicator light (MIL) is lit.

MONITORING STRATEGIES EGR monitoring strategies include the following:

- Some vehicle manufacturers, such as Chrysler, monitor the difference in the exhaust oxygen sensor voltage activity as the EGR valve opens and closes. Oxygen in the exhaust decreases when the EGR valve is open and increases when the EGR valve is closed. The PCM sets a DTC if the sensor signal does not change.

- Most Fords use an EGR monitor test sensor called a **delta pressure feedback EGR (DPFE) sensor**. This sensor measures the pressure differential between two sides of a metered orifice positioned just below the EGR valve's exhaust side. Pressure between the orifice and the EGR valve decreases when the EGR opens because it becomes exposed to the lower pressure in the intake.

The DPFE sensor recognizes this pressure drop, compares it to the relatively higher pressure on the exhaust side of the orifice, and signals the value of the pressure difference to the PCM. ● **SEE FIGURE 42–8.**

- Many vehicle manufacturers use the manifold absolute pressure (MAP) sensor as the EGR monitor on some applications. After meeting the enable criteria (operating condition requirements), the EGR monitor is run. The PCM monitors the MAP sensor while it commands the EGR valve to open. The MAP sensor signal should change in response to the sudden change in manifold pressure or the fuel trim changes created by a change in the oxygen sensor voltage. If the signal value falls outside the acceptable value in the look-up table, a DTC sets. If the EGR fails on two consecutive trips, the PCM lights the MIL. ● **SEE FIGURE 42–9.**

DIAGNOSING A DEFECTIVE EGR SYSTEM

SYMPTOMS If the EGR valve is not opening or the flow of the exhaust gas is restricted, the following symptoms are likely.

- Detonation (spark knock or ping) during acceleration or during cruise (steady-speed driving)
- Excessive oxides of nitrogen (NO_x) exhaust emissions

If the EGR valve is stuck open or partially open, the following symptoms are likely.

- Rough idle or frequent stalling
- Poor performance/low power, especially at low engine speed

FIGURE 42-10 Removing the EGR passage plugs from the intake manifold on a Honda.

 **TECH TIP**

Watch Out for Carbon Balls!

Exhaust gas recirculation (EGR) valves can get stuck partially open by a chunk of carbon. The EGR valve or solenoid will test as defective. When the valve (or solenoid) is removed, small chunks or balls of carbon often fall into the exhaust manifold passage. When the replacement valve is installed, the carbon balls can be drawn into the new valve again, causing the engine to idle roughly or stall.

To help prevent this problem, start the engine with the EGR valve or solenoid removed. Any balls or chunks of carbon will be blown out of the passage by the exhaust. Stop the engine and install the replacement EGR valve or solenoid.

EGR TESTING PROCEDURES The first step in almost any diagnosis is to perform a thorough visual inspection. To check for proper operation of a vacuum-operated EGR valve, follow these steps.

STEP 1 **Check the vacuum diaphragm of the EGR valve to see if it can hold vacuum.** Because many EGR valves require exhaust backpressure to function correctly, the engine should be running at a fast idle during this test. Always follow the specified testing procedures.

STEP 2 **Apply vacuum from a hand-operated vacuum pump and check for proper operation.** The valve itself should move when vacuum is applied, and the engine operation should be affected. The EGR valve should be able to hold the vacuum that was applied. If the vacuum drops off, the valve is likely to be defective.

 Case Study

The Blazer Story

The owner of a Chevrolet Blazer equipped with a 4.3 liter V-6 engine complained that the engine would stumble and hesitate at times. Everything seemed to be functioning correctly, except that the service technician discovered a weak vacuum going to the EGR valve at idle. This vehicle was equipped with an EGR valve-control solenoid, called an **electronic vacuum regulator valve (EVRV)** by General Motors Corporation. The computer pulses the solenoid to control the vacuum that regulates the operation of the EGR valve. The technician checked the service manual for details on how the system worked. The technician discovered that vacuum should be present at the EGR valve only when the gear selector indicates a drive gear (drive, low, reverse). Because the technician discovered the vacuum at the solenoid to be leaking, the solenoid was obviously defective and required replacement. After replacement of the solenoid (EVRV), the hesitation problem was solved.

Summary:
Complaint—Vehicle owner complained that the engine would stumble and hesitate at times.
Cause—The EGR vacuum solenoid was found to be leaking.
Correction—The EGR solenoid was replaced which restored proper engine operation.

 TECH TIP

The Snake Trick

The EGR passages on many intake manifolds become clogged with carbon, which reduces the flow of exhaust and the amount of exhaust gases in the cylinders. This reduction can cause spark knock (detonation) and increased emissions of oxides of nitrogen (NO_x) (especially important in areas with enhanced exhaust emissions testing).

To quickly and easily remove carbon from exhaust passages, cut an approximately 1 foot (30 cm) length from stranded wire, such as garage door guide wire or an old speedometer cable. Flare the end and place the end of the wire into the passage. Set your drill on reverse, turn it on, and the wire will pull its way through the passage, cleaning the carbon as it goes, just like a snake in a drain pipe. Some vehicles, such as Hondas, require that plugs be drilled out to gain access to the EGR passages, as shown in ● **FIGURE 42-10.**

STEP 3   **Monitor engine vacuum drop.** Connect a vacuum gauge to an intake manifold vacuum source and monitor the engine vacuum at idle (should be 17 to 21 inch Hg at sea level). Raise the speed of the engine to 2500 RPM and note the vacuum reading (should be 17 to 21 inch Hg or higher).

Activate the EGR valve using a scan tool or vacuum pump, if vacuum controlled, and observe the vacuum gauge. The results are as follows:

- The vacuum should drop 6 to 8 inch Hg.
- If the vacuum drops less than 6 to 8 inch Hg, the valve or the EGR passages are clogged.

Results

- If the EGR valve is able to hold vacuum, but the engine is not affected when the valve is opened, the exhaust passage(s) must be checked for restriction.

See the Tech Tip, "The Snake Trick." If the EGR valve will not hold vacuum, the valve itself is likely to be defective and requires replacement.

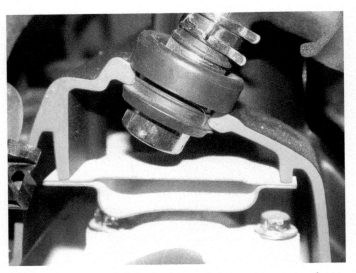

FIGURE 42–11 A PCV valve in a cutaway valve cover, showing the baffles that prevent liquid oil from being drawn into the intake manifold.

EGR-RELATED OBD-II DIAGNOSTIC TROUBLE CODES

Diagnostic Trouble Code	Description	Possible Causes
P0400	Exhaust gas recirculation flow problems	■ EGR valve ■ EGR valve hose or electrical connection ■ Defective PCM
P0401	Exhaust gas recirculation flow insufficient	■ EGR valve ■ Clogged EGR ports or passages
P0402	Exhaust gas recirculation flow excessive	■ Stuck-open EGR valve ■ Vacuum hose(s) misrouted ■ Electrical wiring shorted

CRANKCASE VENTILATION

PURPOSE AND FUNCTION The problem of crankcase ventilation has existed since the beginning of the automobile, because no piston ring, new or old, can provide a perfect seal between the piston and the cylinder wall. When an engine is running, the pressure of combustion forces the piston downward. This same pressure also forces gases and unburned fuel from the combustion chamber, past the piston rings, and into the crankcase. **Blowby** is the term used to describe when combustion gases are forced past the piston rings and into the crankcase.

These combustion by-products, particularly unburned hydrocarbons (HC) caused by blowby, must be ventilated from the crankcase. However, the crankcase cannot be vented directly to the atmosphere, because the hydrocarbon vapors add to air pollution. **Positive crankcase ventilation (PCV)** systems were developed to ventilate the crankcase and recirculate the vapors to the engine's induction system so they can be burned in the cylinders. PCV systems help reduce HC and CO emissions.

All systems use the following:

1. PCV valve, calibrated orifice, or orifice and separator
2. PCV inlet air filter plus all connecting hoses ● **SEE FIGURE 42–11.**

An oil/vapor or oil/water separator is used in some systems instead of a valve or orifice, particularly with turbocharged and fuel-injected engines. The oil/vapor separator lets oil condense and drain back into the crankcase. The oil/water separator accumulates moisture and prevents it from freezing during cold engine starts.

The air for the PCV system is drawn after the air cleaner filter, which acts as a PCV filter.

NOTE: Some older designs drew from the dirty side of the air cleaner, where a separate crankcase ventilation filter was used.

PCV VALVES The PCV valve in most systems is a one-way valve containing a spring-operated plunger that controls valve flow rate. ● **SEE FIGURE 42–12.**

Flow rate is established for each engine and a valve for a different engine should not be substituted. The flow rate is determined by the size of the plunger and the holes inside the valve. PCV valves usually are located in the valve cover or intake manifold.

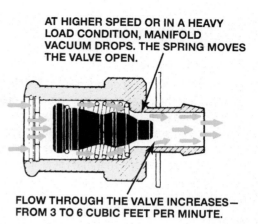

THIS END OF THE PCV VALVE IS SUBJECT TO CRANKCASE PRESSURE THAT TENDS TO CLOSE THE VALVE.

THIS END IS SUBJECT TO INTAKE MANIFOLD VACUUM THAT TENDS TO CLOSE THE VALVE.

THE SPRING FORCE OPERATES TO OPEN THE VALVE TO MANIFOLD VACUUM AND CRANKCASE PRESSURE.

FIGURE 42–12 Spring force, crankcase pressure, and intake manifold vacuum work together to regulate the flow rate through the PCV

AT HIGHER SPEED OR IN A HEAVY LOAD CONDITION, MANIFOLD VACUUM DROPS. THE SPRING MOVES THE VALVE OPEN.

FLOW THROUGH THE VALVE INCREASES— FROM 3 TO 6 CUBIC FEET PER MINUTE.

FIGURE 42–14 Air flows through the PCV valve during acceleration and when the engine is under a heavy load.

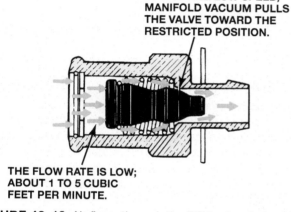

AT IDLE AND LOW SPEED, MANIFOLD VACUUM PULLS THE VALVE TOWARD THE RESTRICTED POSITION.

THE FLOW RATE IS LOW; ABOUT 1 TO 5 CUBIC FEET PER MINUTE.

FIGURE 42–13 Air flows through the PCV valve during idle, cruising, and light-load conditions.

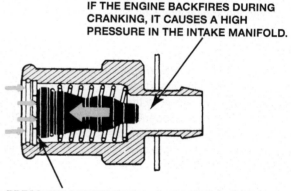

IF THE ENGINE BACKFIRES DURING CRANKING, IT CAUSES A HIGH PRESSURE IN THE INTAKE MANIFOLD.

PRESSURE CAUSES THE VALVE TO BACK-SEAT AND SEAL OFF THE INLET. THIS KEEPS THE BACKFIRE OUT OF THE CRANKCASE.

FIGURE 42–15 PCV valve operation in the event of a backfire.

The PCV valve regulates airflow through the crankcase under all driving conditions and speeds. When manifold vacuum is high (at idle, cruising, and light-load operation), the PCV valve restricts the airflow to maintain a balanced air-fuel ratio. ● **SEE FIGURE 42–13.**

It also prevents high intake manifold vacuum from pulling oil out of the crankcase and into the intake manifold. Under high speed or heavy loads, the valve opens and allows maximum airflow. ● **SEE FIGURE 42–14.**

If the engine backfires, the valve will close instantly to prevent a crankcase explosion. ● **SEE FIGURE 42–15.**

ORIFICE-CONTROLLED SYSTEMS

The closed PCV system used on some 4-cylinder engines contains a calibrated orifice instead of a PCV valve. The orifice may be located in the valve cover or intake manifold, or in a hose connected between the valve cover, air cleaner, and intake manifold.

While most orifice flow control systems work the same as a PCV valve system, they may not use fresh air scavenging of the crankcase. Crankcase vapors are drawn into the intake manifold in calibrated amounts depending on manifold

 **TECH TIP**

Check for Oil Leaks with the Engine Off

The owner of an older vehicle equipped with a V-6 engine complained to his technician that he smelled burning oil, but only *after* shutting off the engine. The technician found that the rocker cover gaskets were leaking. But why did the owner only notice the smell of hot oil when the engine was shut off? Because of the positive crankcase ventilation (PCV) system, engine vacuum tends to draw oil away from gasket surfaces. But when the engine stops, engine vacuum disappears and the oil remaining in the upper regions of the engine will tend to flow down and out through any opening. Therefore, a good technician should check an engine for oil leaks not only with the engine running but also shortly after shutdown.

The Whistling Engine

An older vehicle was being diagnosed for a whistling sound whenever the engine was running, especially at idle. It was finally discovered that the breather in the valve cover was plugged and caused high vacuum in the crankcase. The engine was sucking air from what was likely the rear main seal lip, making the "whistle" noise. After replacing the breather and PCV, the noise stopped.

Summary:

Complaint—Vehicle owner complained that the engine would make a whistling noise.

Cause—The crankcase breather was clogged.

Correction—The breather and the PCV valve were both replaced which stopped the whistling noise when the engine was running.

---

pressure and the orifice size. If vapor availability is low, as during idle, air is drawn in with the vapors. During off-idle operation, excess vapors are sent to the air cleaner.

At idle, PCV flow is controlled by a 0.05 inch (1.3 mm) orifice. As the engine moves off idle, ported vacuum pulls a spring-loaded valve off of its seat, allowing PCV flow to pass through a 0.09 inch (2.3 mm) orifice.

SEPARATOR SYSTEMS Turbocharged and many fuel-injected engines use an oil/vapor or oil/water separator and a calibrated orifice instead of a PCV valve. In the most common applications, the air intake throttle body acts as the source for crankcase ventilation vacuum and a calibrated orifice acts as the metering device.

PCV SYSTEM DIAGNOSIS

SYMPTOMS If the PCV valve or orifice is not clogged, intake air flows freely and the PCV system functions properly. Engine design includes the air and vapor flow as a calibrated part of the air-fuel mixture. In fact, some engines receive as much as 30% of the idle air through the PCV system. For this reason, a flow problem in the PCV system results in driveability problems.

A blocked or plugged PCV system can cause:

- Rough or unstable idle
- Excessive oil consumption
- Oil in the air filter housing
- Oil leaks due to excessive crankcase pressure

Before expensive engine repairs are attempted, check the condition of the PCV system.

PCV SYSTEM PERFORMANCE CHECK A properly operating positive crankcase ventilation system should be able to draw vapors from the crankcase and into the intake manifold. If the pipes, hoses, and PCV valve itself are not restricted, vacuum is applied to the crankcase. A slight vacuum is created in the crankcase (usually less than 1 inch Hg if measured at the dipstick) and is also applied to other areas of the engine. Oil drainback holes provide a path for oil to drain back into the oil pan. These holes also allow crankcase vacuum to be applied under the rocker covers and in the valley area of most V-type engines. There are several methods that can be used to test a PCV system.

RATTLE TEST The rattle test is performed by simply removing the PCV valve and shaking it in your hand.

- If the PCV valve does *not* rattle, it is definitely defective and must be replaced.
- If the PCV valve *does* rattle, it does not necessarily mean that the PCV valve is good. All PCV valves contain springs that can become weaker with age and with

The Oil Burning Chevrolet Van

An automotive instructor was driving a Chevrolet van to Fairbanks, Alaska, in January. It was pretty cold out, somewhere around −32°F (−36°C). As he pulled into Fairbanks and stopped at a traffic light, he smelled burning oil. When he stopped at the hotel he still smelled burning oil. He looked under the van and discovered a large pool of oil. After checking the oil and finding very little left, he called a local shop and was told to bring it in. The technician looked over the situation and said, "You need to put some cardboard across the grill to stop the PCV valve from freezing up." Apparently the PCV valve froze, which caused the normal blowby gases to force several quarts out the dipstick tube. After he installed the cardboard, he did not have any further problems.

CAUTION: Do not cover the radiator when driving unless under severe cold conditions and carefully watch the coolant temperature to avoid overheating the engine.

Summary:

- **Complaint**—Vehicle owner experienced oil burning when extremely cold outside.
- **Cause**—The PCV valve was frozen causing pressure to build up in the crankcase.
- **Correction**—Placing some cardboard in front of the radiator prevented the valve from freezing and allowed the crankcase ventilations system to function normally.

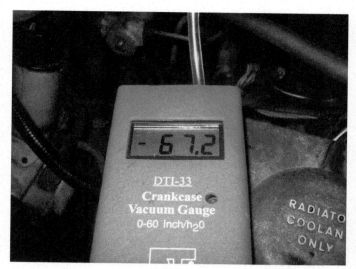

FIGURE 42–16 Using a gauge that measures vacuum in units of inches of water to test the vacuum at the dipstick tube, being sure that the PCV system is capable of drawing a vacuum on the crankcase. Note that 28 inch of water equals 1 PSI, or about 2 inch of mercury (inch Hg) of vacuum.

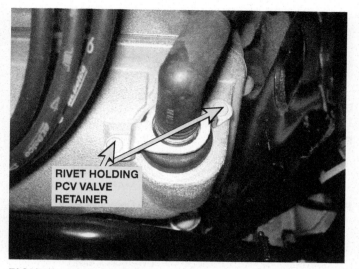

RIVET HOLDING PCV VALVE RETAINER

FIGURE 42–17 Most PCV valves used on newer vehicles are secured with fasteners, which makes it more difficult to disconnect, and therefore, less likely to increase emissions.

heating and cooling cycles. Replace any PCV valve with the *exact* replacement according to the vehicle manufacturer's recommended intervals, usually every three years or 36,000 miles (60,000 km).

THE 3 × 5 CARD TEST
Remove the oil-fill cap (where oil is added to the engine) and start the engine.

NOTE: Use care on some overhead camshaft engines. With the engine running, oil may be sprayed from the open oil-fill opening.

Hold a 3 × 5 card over the opening (a dollar bill or any other piece of paper can be used for this test).

- If the PCV system, including the valve and hoses, is functioning correctly, the card should be held down on the oil-fill opening by the slight vacuum inside the crankcase.
- If the card will not stay, carefully inspect the PCV valve, hose(s), and manifold vacuum port for carbon buildup (restriction). Clean or replace as necessary.

NOTE: On some 4-cylinder engines, the 3 × 5 card may vibrate on the oil-fill opening when the engine is running at idle speed. This is normal because of the time intervals between intake strokes on a 4-cylinder engine.

SNAP-BACK TEST
The proper operation of the PCV valve can be checked by placing a finger over the inlet hole in the valve when the engine is running and removing the finger rapidly. Repeat several times. The valve should "snap back." If the valve does not snap back, replace the valve.

CRANKCASE VACUUM TEST
Sometimes the PCV system can be checked by testing for a weak vacuum at the oil dipstick tube using an inches-of-water manometer or gauge, as follows:

STEP 1 Remove the oil-fill cap or vent PCV opening and cover the opening.

STEP 2 Remove the oil dipstick (oil level indicator).

STEP 3 Connect a water manometer or gauge to the dipstick tube.

STEP 4 Start the engine and observe the gauge at idle and at 2500 RPM.

● **SEE FIGURE 42–16.**

The gauge should show some vacuum, especially at 2500 RPM. If not, carefully inspect the PCV system for blockages or other faults.

PCV MONITOR
Starting with 2004 and newer vehicles, all vehicle PCMs monitor the PCV system for proper operation as part of the OBD-II system. The PCV monitor will fail if the PCM detects an opening between the crankcase and the PCV valve or between the PCV valve and the intake manifold. ● **SEE FIGURE 42–17.**

? FREQUENTLY ASKED QUESTION

Why Are There Wires at the PCV Valve?

Ford uses an electric heater to prevent ice from forming inside the PCV valve causing blockage. Water is a by-product of combustion and resulting moisture can freeze when the outside air temperature is low. General Motors and others clip a heater hose to the PCV hose to provide the heat needed to prevent an ice blockage.

PCV-RELATED DIAGNOSTIC TROUBLE CODE

Diagnostic Trouble Code	Description	Possible Causes
P0101	MAF or airflow circuit range problem	■ Defective PCV valve, hose/connections, or MAF circuit fault
P0505	Idle control system problem	■ Defective PCV valve or hose/connections

SECONDARY AIR-INJECTION SYSTEM

PURPOSE AND FUNCTION The **secondary air-injection (SAI)** system provides the air necessary for the oxidizing process either at the exhaust manifold or inside the catalytic converter.

NOTE: This system is commonly called AIR, meaning air-injection reaction. Therefore, an AIR pump does pump air.

PARTS AND OPERATION The SAI pump, also called an AIR pump, a **smog pump**, or a **thermactor pump**, is mounted at the front of the engine and can be driven by a belt from the crankshaft pulley. It pulls fresh air in through an external filter and pumps the air under slight pressure to each exhaust port through connecting hoses or a manifold. The typical SAI system includes the following components.

- A belt-driven pump with inlet air filter (older models) (● **SEE FIGURE 42–18.**)
- An electronic air pump (newer models)
- One or more air distribution manifolds and nozzles
- One or more exhaust check valves
- Connecting hoses for air distribution
- Air management valves and solenoids on all newer applications

With the introduction of NO_x reduction converters (also called dual-bed, **three-way converters**, or **TWC**), the output of the SAI pump is sent to the center of the converter where the extra air can help oxidize unburned hydrocarbons (HC), carbon monoxide (CO) into water vapor (H_2O), and carbon dioxide (CO_2). The computer controls the airflow from the pump by switching on and off various solenoid valves.

AIR DISTRIBUTION MANIFOLDS AND NOZZLES The secondary air-injection system sends air from the pump to a nozzle installed near each exhaust port in the cylinder head.

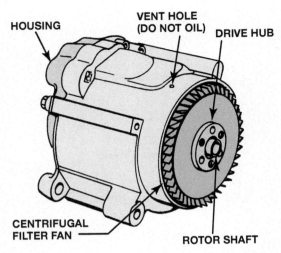

FIGURE 42–18 A typical belt-driven AIR pump. Air enters through the revolving fins behind the drive pulley. The fins act as an air filter because dirt is heavier than air and, therefore, the dirt is deflected off of the fins at the same time air is being drawn into the pump.

This provides equal air injection for the exhaust from each cylinder and makes it available at a point in the system where exhaust gases are the hottest.

Air is delivered to the exhaust system in one of two ways.

1. An external air manifold, or manifolds, distributes the air through injection tubes with stainless steel nozzles. The nozzles are threaded into the cylinder heads or exhaust manifolds close to each exhaust valve. This method is used primarily with smaller engines.

2. An internal air manifold distributes the air to the exhaust ports near each exhaust valve through passages cast in the cylinder head or the exhaust manifold. This method is used mainly with larger engines.

EXHAUST CHECK VALVES All air-injection systems use one or more one-way check valves to protect the air pump and other components from reverse exhaust flow. A **check valve** contains a spring-type metallic disc or reed that closes under exhaust backpressure. Check valves are located between the air manifold and the switching valve(s). If exhaust pressure exceeds injection pressure, or if the air pump fails, the check valve spring closes the valve to prevent reverse exhaust flow. ● **SEE FIGURE 42–19.**

NOTE: These check valves commonly fail, resulting in excessive exhaust emissions (CO especially). When the check valve fails, hot exhaust can travel up and destroy the switching valve(s) and air pump itself.

BELT-DRIVEN AIR PUMPS The belt-driven air pump uses a centrifugal filter just behind the drive pulley. As the pump rotates, underhood air is drawn into the pump and slightly compressed. The system uses either vacuum- or solenoid-controlled diverter valves to direct air to the following:

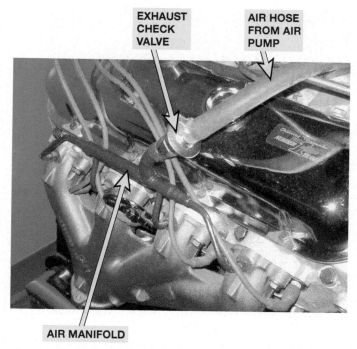

FIGURE 42–19 The external air manifold and exhaust check valve on a restored muscle car engine.

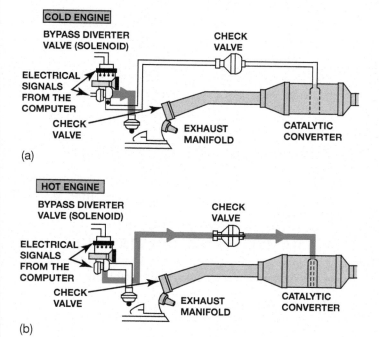

FIGURE 42–20 (a) When the engine is cold and before the oxygen sensor is hot enough to achieve closed loop, the airflow from the air pump is directed to the exhaust manifold(s) through the one-way check valves, which keep the exhaust gases from entering the switching solenoids and the pump itself. (b) When the engine achieves closed loop, the air is directed to the catalytic converter.

■ Exhaust manifold when the engine is cold to help oxidize carbon monoxide (CO) and unburned hydrocarbons (HC) into carbon dioxide (CO_2) and water vapor (H_2O)

FIGURE 42–21 A typical electric motor-driven SAI pump. This unit is on a Chevrolet Corvette and only works when the engine is cold.

■ Catalytic converter on many models to help provide the extra oxygen needed for the efficient conversion of CO and HC into CO_2 and H_2O
■ Air cleaner during deceleration or wide-open throttle (WOT) engine operation
  ● SEE FIGURE 42–20.

ELECTRIC MOTOR-DRIVEN AIR PUMPS The electric motor-driven air pump is generally used only during cold engine operation and is computer controlled. The secondary air-injection (SAI) system helps reduce hydrocarbon (HC) and carbon monoxide (CO). It also helps to warm the three-way catalytic converters quickly on engine start-up so conversion of exhaust gases may occur sooner.

■ The SAI pump solenoids are controlled by the PCM. The PCM turns on the SAI pump by providing the ground to complete the circuit, which energizes the SAI pump solenoid relay. When air to the exhaust ports is desired, the PCM energizes the relay in order to turn on the solenoid and the SAI pump. ● SEE FIGURE 42–21.
■ The PCM turns on the SAI pump during start-up any time the engine coolant temperature is above 32°F (0°C). A typical electric SAI pump operates for a maximum of four minutes, or until the system enters closed-loop operation.

SECONDARY AIR-INJECTION SYSTEM DIAGNOSIS

SYMPTOMS The air pump system should be inspected if an exhaust emissions test failure occurs. In severe cases, the exhaust will enter the air cleaner assembly, resulting in an

ENGINE OPERATION	NORMAL OPERATION OF A TYPICAL SAI SYSTEM
Cold engine (open-loop operation)	Air is diverted to the exhaust manifold(s) or cylinder head.
Warm engine (closed-loop operation)	Air is diverted to the catalytic converter.
Deceleration	Air is diverted to the air cleaner assembly.
Wide-open throttle	Air is diverted to the air cleaner assembly.

CHART 42-1

Typical SAI system operation showing the location of the airflow from the pump.

unstable running engine because the extra exhaust displaces the oxygen needed for proper combustion. With the engine running, check for normal operation. ● **SEE CHART 42-1.**

VISUAL INSPECTION Carefully inspect all secondary-air-injection (SAI) systems, including:

- Any hoses or pipes that have holes and leak air or exhaust, which require replacement
- Check valve(s), when a pump has become inoperative
- Exhaust gases that may have gotten past the check valve and damaged the pump (Look for signs of overheated areas upstream from the check valves. In severe cases, the exhaust can enter the air cleaner assembly and destroy the air filter and greatly reduce engine power.)
- Drive belt on an engine-driven pump, for wear and proper tension (If the belt is worn or damaged, check that the AIR pump rotates.)

FOUR-GAS EXHAUST ANALYSIS An SAI system can be easily tested using an exhaust gas analyzer and the following steps.

STEP 1 Start the engine and allow it to run until normal operating temperature is achieved.

STEP 2 Connect the analyzer probe to the tailpipe and observe the exhaust readings for hydrocarbons (HC) and carbon monoxide (CO).

STEP 3 Using the appropriate pinch-off pliers, shut off the airflow from the SAI system. Observe the HC and CO readings. If the SAI system is working correctly, the HC and CO should increase when the SAI system is shut off.

STEP 4 Record the O_2 reading with the SAI system still inoperative. Unclamp the pliers and watch the O_2 readings. If the system is functioning correctly, the O_2 level should increase by 1% to 4%.

SAI-RELATED DIAGNOSTIC TROUBLE CODE

Diagnostic Trouble Code	Description	Possible Causes
P0410	SAI solenoid circuit fault	■ Defective SAI solenoid ■ Loose or corroded electrical connections ■ Loose, missing, or defective rubber hose(s)

CATALYTIC CONVERTERS

PURPOSE AND FUNCTION A **catalytic converter** is an aftertreatment device used to reduce exhaust emissions outside of the engine. The catalytic converter uses a **catalyst**, which is a chemical that helps start a chemical reaction but does not enter into the chemical reaction.

- The catalyst materials on the surface of the material inside the converter help create a chemical reaction.
- The chemical reaction changes harmful exhaust emissions into nonharmful exhaust emissions.
- The converter, therefore, converts harmful exhaust gases into water vapor (H_2O) and carbon dioxide (CO_2).

This device is installed in the exhaust system between the exhaust manifold and the muffler, and usually is positioned beneath the passenger compartment. The location of the converter is important, since as much of the exhaust heat as possible must be retained for effective operation. The nearer it is to the engine, the better. ● **SEE FIGURE 42-22.**

CATALYTIC CONVERTER CONSTRUCTION Most catalytic converters are constructed of a ceramic material in a honeycomb shape with square openings for the exhaust gases.

- There are approximately 400 openings per square inch (62 openings per square centimeter) and the wall thickness is about 0.006 inch (1.5 mm).
- The substrate is coated with a porous aluminum material called the **washcoat**, which makes the surface rough.
- The catalytic materials are applied on top of the washcoat. The substrate is contained within a round or oval shell made by welding together two stamped pieces of stainless steel. ● **SEE FIGURE 42-23.**

The ceramic substrate in monolithic converters is not restrictive; however, the converter can be physically broken if exposed to shock or severe jolts. Monolithic converters can be serviced only as a unit.

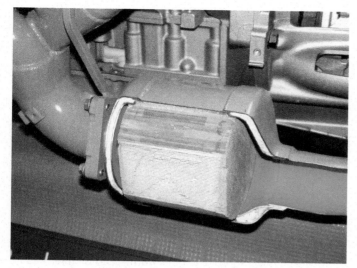

FIGURE 42–22 Most catalytic converters are located as close to the exhaust manifold as possible, as seen in this display of a Chevrolet Corvette.

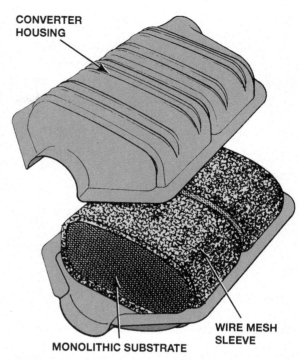

FIGURE 42–23 A typical catalytic converter with a monolithic substrate.

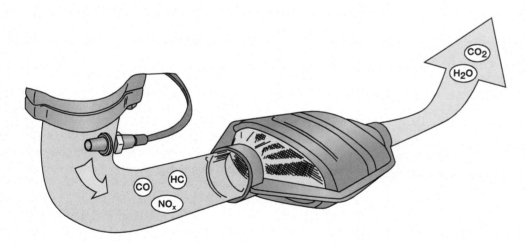

FIGURE 42–24 The three-way catalytic converter first separates the NO_x into nitrogen and oxygen and then converts the HC and CO into harmless water (H_2O) and carbon dioxide (CO_2).

An exhaust pipe is connected to the manifold or header to carry gases through a catalytic converter and then to the muffler or silencer. V-type engines can use dual converters or route the exhaust into one catalytic converter by using a Y-exhaust pipe.

CATALYTIC CONVERTER OPERATION The converter substrate contains small amounts of **rhodium, palladium**, and **platinum**. These elements act as catalysts, which, as mentioned, start a chemical reaction without becoming part of, or being consumed in, the process. In a three-way catalytic converter (TWC), all three exhaust emissions (NO_x, HC, and CO) are converted to carbon dioxide (CO_2) and water (H_2O). As the exhaust gas passes through the catalyst, oxides of nitrogen (NO_x) are chemically reduced (i.e., nitrogen and oxygen are separated) in the first section of the catalytic converter. In the second section of the catalytic converter, most of the hydrocarbons and carbon monoxide remaining in the exhaust gas are oxidized to form harmless carbon dioxide (CO_2) and water vapor (H_2O). ● **SEE FIGURE 42–24.**

Since the early 1990s, many converters also contain **cerium**, an element that can store oxygen. The purpose of the cerium is to provide oxygen to the oxidation bed of the converter when the exhaust is rich and lacks enough oxygen for proper oxidation. When the exhaust is lean, the cerium absorbs the extra oxygen. For the most efficient operation, the converter should have a 14.7:1 air-fuel ratio but can use a mixture that varies slightly.

- A rich exhaust is required for reduction—stripping the oxygen (O_2) from the nitrogen in NO_x.
- A lean exhaust is required to provide the oxygen necessary to oxidize HC and CO (combining oxygen with HC and CO to form H_2O and CO_2).

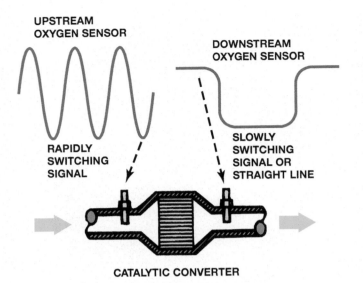

UPSTREAM
OXYGEN SENSOR

DOWNSTREAM
OXYGEN SENSOR

RAPIDLY
SWITCHING
SIGNAL

SLOWLY
SWITCHING
SIGNAL OR
STRAIGHT LINE

CATALYTIC CONVERTER

FIGURE 42–25 The OBD-II catalytic converter monitor compares the signals of the upstream and downstream HO2S to determine converter efficiency.

If the catalytic converter is not functioning correctly, check that the air-fuel mixture being supplied to the engine is correct and that the ignition system is free of defects.

CONVERTER LIGHT-OFF TEMPERATURE The catalytic converter does not work when cold, and it must be heated to its **light-off temperature** of close to 500°F (260°C) before it starts working at 50% effectiveness. When fully effective, the converter reaches a temperature range of 900°F to 1,600°F (482°C to 871°C). In spite of the intense heat, however, catalytic reactions do not generate a flame associated with a simple burning reaction. Because of the extreme heat (almost as hot as combustion chamber temperatures), a converter remains hot long after the engine is shut off. Most vehicles use a series of heat shields to protect the passenger compartment and other parts of the chassis from excessive heat. Vehicles have been known to start fires because of the hot converter causing tall grass or dry leaves beneath the just-parked vehicle to ignite, especially if the engine is idling. This is most likely to occur if the heat shields have been removed from the converter.

CONVERTER USAGE A catalytic converter must be located as close as possible to the exhaust manifold to work effectively. The farther back the converter is positioned in the exhaust system, the more the exhaust gases cool before they reach the converter. Since positioning in the exhaust system affects the oxidation process, cars that use only an oxidation converter generally locate it underneath the front of the passenger compartment.

Some vehicles have used a small, quick heating oxidation converter called a **preconverter**, a **pup converter**, or a **mini converter** that connects directly to the exhaust manifold outlet. These have a small catalyst surface area close to the engine that heats up rapidly to start the oxidation process more quickly during cold engine warm-up. For this reason, they were often called **light-off converters (LOCs)**. The larger main converter, under the passenger compartment, completes the oxidation reaction started in the LOC.

OBD-II CATALYTIC CONVERTER PERFORMANCE
With OBD-II equipped vehicles, catalytic converter performance is monitored by a **heated oxygen sensor (HO2S)**, both before and after the converter. The converters used on these vehicles have what is known as **oxygen storage capacity (OSC)**. This OSC is due mostly to the cerium coating in the catalyst rather than the precious metals used. When the three-way converter (TWC) is operating as it should, the postconverter HO2S is far less active than the preconverter sensor. The converter stores, then releases, the oxygen during normal reduction and oxidation of the exhaust gases, smoothing out the variations in O_2 being released.

Where a cycling sensor voltage output is expected before the converter, because of the converter action, the postconverter HO2S should read a steady signal without much fluctuation. ● **SEE FIGURE 42–25.**

CONVERTER-DAMAGING CONDITIONS Since converters have no moving parts, they require no periodic service. Under federal law, catalyst effectiveness is warranted for 80,000 miles or eight years.

The three main causes of premature converter failure are as follows:

- **Contamination.** Substances that can destroy the converter include exhaust that contains excess engine oil, antifreeze, sulfur (from poor fuel), and various other chemical substances.
- **Excessive temperatures.** Although a converter operates at high temperature, it can be destroyed by excessive temperatures. This most often occurs either when too much unburned fuel enters the converter, or with excessively lean mixtures. Excessive temperatures may be caused by long idling periods on some vehicles, since more heat develops at those times than when driving at normal highway speeds. Severe high temperatures can cause the converter to melt down, leading to the internal

parts breaking apart and either clogging the converter or moving downstream to plug the muffler. In either case, the restricted exhaust flow severely reduces engine power.

- **Improper air-fuel mixtures.** Rich mixtures or raw fuel in the exhaust can be caused by engine misfiring, or an excessively rich air-fuel mixture resulting from a defective coolant temp sensor or defective fuel injectors. Lean mixtures are commonly caused by intake manifold leaks. When either of these circumstances occurs, the converter can become a catalytic furnace, causing the previously described damage.

To avoid excessive catalyst temperatures and the possibility of fuel vapors reaching the converter, follow these rules.

1. Do not use fuel additives or cleaners that are not converter safe.

2. Do not crank an engine for more than 40 seconds when it is flooded or misfiring.

3. Do not turn off the ignition switch when the vehicle is in motion.

4. Do not disconnect a spark plug wire for more than 30 seconds.

5. Repair engine problems such as dieseling, misfiring, or stumbling as soon as possible.

DIAGNOSING CATALYTIC CONVERTERS

THE TAP TEST The simple **tap test** involves tapping (not pounding) on the catalytic converter using a rubber mallet. If the substrate inside the converter is broken, the converter will rattle when hit. If the converter rattles, a replacement converter is required.

TESTING BACKPRESSURE WITH A PRESSURE GAUGE Exhaust system backpressure can be measured directly by installing a pressure gauge in an exhaust opening. This can be accomplished in one of the following ways.

1. To test backpressure, remove the inside of an old, discarded oxygen sensor and thread in an adapter to convert it to a vacuum or pressure gauge.

    NOTE: An adapter can be easily made by inserting a metal tube or pipe into an old oxygen sensor housing. A short section of brake line works great. The pipe can be brazed to the oxygen sensor housing or it can be glued with epoxy. An 18 mm compression gauge adapter can also be adapted to fit into the oxygen sensor opening. ● **SEE FIGURE 42–26.**

2. To test the exhaust backpressure at the exhaust gas recirculation (EGR) valve, remove the EGR valve and fabricate a plate equipped with a fitting for a pressure gauge.

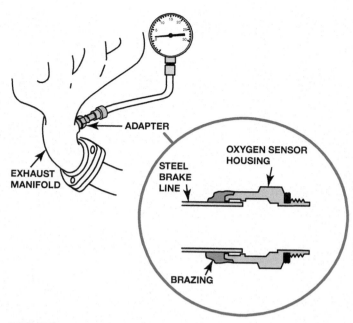

FIGURE 42–26 A back pressure tool can be made by using an oxygen sensor housing and epoxy or braze to hold the tube to the housing.

3. To test at the secondary air-injection (SAI) check valve, remove the check valve from the exhaust tubes leading to the exhaust manifold. Use a rubber cone with a tube inside to seal against the exhaust tube. Connect the tube to a pressure gauge.

At idle, the maximum backpressure should be less than 1.5 PSI (10 kPa), and it should be less than 2.5 PSI (15 kPa) at 2500 RPM. Pressure readings higher than these indicate that the exhaust system is restricted and further testing will be needed to determine the location of the restriction.

TESTING FOR BACKPRESSURE USING A VACUUM GAUGE An exhaust restriction can be tested indirectly by checking the intake manifold vacuum with the engine operating at a fast idle speed (about 2500 RPM). If the exhaust is restricted, some exhaust can pass and the effect may not be noticeable when the engine is at idle speed. However, when the engine is operating at a higher speed, the exhaust gases can build up behind the restriction and eventually will be unable to leave the combustion chamber. When some of the exhaust is left behind at the end of the exhaust stroke, the resulting pressure in the combustion chamber reduces engine vacuum. To test for an exhaust restriction using a vacuum gauge, perform the following steps.

STEP 1   Attach a vacuum gauge to an intake manifold vacuum source.

STEP 2   Start the engine. Record the engine manifold vacuum reading. The engine vacuum should read 17 to 21 inch Hg when the engine is at idle speed.

STEP 3   Increase the engine speed to 2500 RPM and hold that speed for 60 seconds while looking at the vacuum gauge.

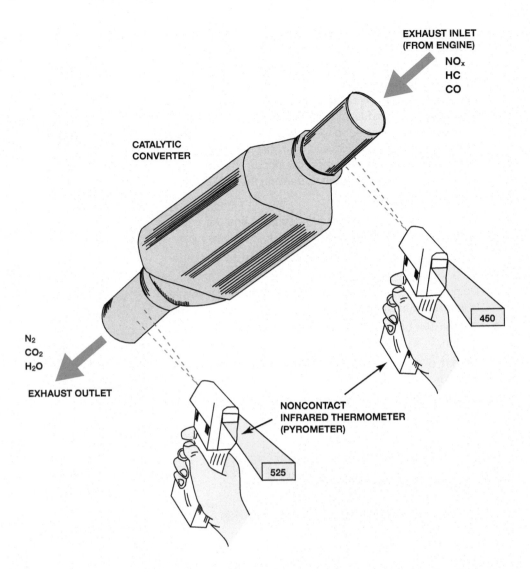

FIGURE 42–27
The temperature of the outlet should be at least 10% hotter than the temperature of the inlet. If a converter is not working, the inlet temperature will be hotter than the outlet temperature.

Results

- If the vacuum reading is equal to or higher than the vacuum reading when the engine was at idle speed, the exhaust system is *not* restricted.
- If the vacuum reading is lower than the vacuum reading when the engine was at idle speed, then the exhaust *is* restricted. Further testing will be needed to determine the location of the restriction.

TESTING A CATALYTIC CONVERTER FOR TEMPERATURE RISE
A properly working catalytic converter should be able to reduce NO_x exhaust emissions into nitrogen (N) and oxygen (O_2) and oxidize unburned hydrocarbon (HC) and carbon monoxide (CO) into harmless carbon dioxide (CO_2) and water vapor (H_2O). During these chemical processes, the catalytic converter should increase in temperature at least 10% if the converter is working properly. To test the converter, operate the engine at 2500 RPM for at least two minutes to fully warm up the converter. Measure the inlet and the outlet temperatures using an **infrared thermometer (pyrometer)**, as shown in  **FIGURE 42–27.**

TECH TIP

Aftermarket Catalytic Converters

Some replacement aftermarket (nonfactory) catalytic converters do not contain the same amount of cerium as the original part. Cerium is the element that is used in catalytic converters to store oxygen. As a result of the lack of cerium, the correlation between the oxygen storage and the conversion efficiency may be affected enough to set a false diagnostic trouble code (P0422).

NOTE: When an aftermarket converter is being installed, to be assured of proper operation, ensure that its distance from the rear of the catalyst block is the same as the distance between the rear oxygen sensor and the factory converter. Always follow the instructions that come with the replacement converter.
● **SEE FIGURE 42–28.**

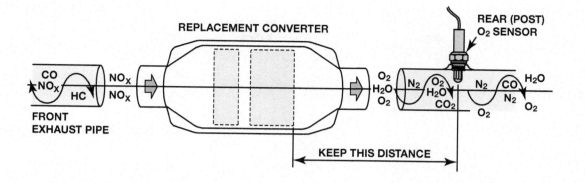

FIGURE 42–28

Whenever replacing a catalytic converter with a universal unit, first measure the distance between the rear brick and the center of the rear oxygen sensor. Be sure that the replacement unit is installed to the same dimension.

NOTE: If the engine is extremely efficient, the converter may not have any excessive unburned hydrocarbons or carbon monoxide to convert! In this case, a spark plug wire could be grounded out using a vacuum hose and a test light to create some unburned hydrocarbon in the exhaust. Do not ground out a cylinder for longer than 10 seconds or the excessive amount of unburned hydrocarbon could overheat and damage the converter.

CATALYTIC CONVERTER EFFICIENCY TESTS
The efficiency of a catalytic converter can be determined using an exhaust gas analyzer.

- **Oxygen level test.** With the engine warm and in closed loop, check the oxygen (O_2) and carbon monoxide (CO) levels. A good converter should be able to oxidize the extra hydrocarbons caused by the rapid acceleration.

  - If O_2 is zero, go to the snap-throttle test.
  - If O_2 is greater than zero, check the CO level.
  - If CO is greater than zero, the converter is *not* functioning correctly.

- **Snap-throttle test.** With the engine warm and in closed loop, snap the throttle to wide open (WOT) in park or neutral and observe the oxygen reading.

  - The O_2 reading should not exceed 1.2%; if it does, the converter is *not* working.
  - If the O_2 rises to 1.2%, the converter may have low efficiency.
  - If the O_2 remains below 1.2%, the converter is okay.

TECH TIP

Catalytic Converters Are Murdered

Catalytic converters start a chemical reaction, but do not enter into the chemical reaction. Therefore, catalytic converters do not wear out and they do not die of old age. If a catalytic converter is found to be defective (nonfunctioning or clogged), look for the *root* cause. Remember this:

"Catalytic converters do not commit suicide—they're murdered."

Items that should be checked when a defective catalytic converter is discovered include all components of the ignition and fuel systems. Excessive unburned fuel can cause the catalytic converter to overheat and fail. The oxygen sensor must be working and fluctuating from 0.5 to 5 Hz (times per second) to provide the necessary air-fuel mixture variations for maximum catalytic converter efficiency.

CATALYTIC CONVERTER REPLACEMENT GUIDELINES

Because a catalytic converter is a major exhaust gas emission control device, the Environmental Protection Agency (EPA) has strict guidelines for its replacement, including:

- If a converter is replaced on a vehicle with less than 80,000 miles or eight years, depending on the year of the vehicle, an original equipment catalytic converter *must* be used as a replacement.
- The replacement converter must be of the same design as the original. If the original had an air pump fitting, so must the replacement.
- The old converter must be kept for possible inspection by the authorities for 60 days.
- A form must be completed and signed by both the vehicle owner and a representative from the service facility. This form must state the cause of the converter failure and must remain on file for two years.

FIGURE 42–29 A capless system from a Ford Flex does not use a replaceable cap; instead, it has a spring-loaded closure.

FIGURE 42–30 A charcoal canister can be located under the hood or underneath the vehicle.

CATALYTIC CONVERTER-RELATED DIAGNOSTIC TROUBLE CODE

Diagnostic Trouble Code	Description	Possible Causes
P0420	Catalytic converter efficiency failure	1. Engine mechanical fault 2. Exhaust leaks 3. Fuel contaminants, such as engine oil, coolant, or sulfur

 FREQUENTLY ASKED QUESTION

When Filling My Fuel Tank, Why Should I Stop When the Pump Clicks Off?

Every fuel tank has an upper volume chamber that allows for expansion of the fuel when hot. The volume of the chamber is between 10% and 20% of the volume of the tank. For example, if a fuel tank had a capacity of 20 gallons, the expansion chamber volume would be from 2 to 4 gallons. A hose is attached at the top of the chamber and vented to the charcoal canister. If extra fuel is forced into this expansion volume, liquid gasoline can be drawn into the charcoal canister. This liquid fuel can saturate the canister and create an overly rich air-fuel mixture when the canister purge valve is opened during normal vehicle operation. This extra-rich air-fuel mixture can cause the vehicle to fail an exhaust emissions test, reduce fuel economy, and possibly damage the catalytic converter. To avoid problems, simply add fuel to the next dime's worth after the nozzle clicks off. This will ensure that the tank is full, yet not overfilled.

EVAPORATIVE EMISSION CONTROL SYSTEM

PURPOSE AND FUNCTION The purpose of the evaporative (EVAP) emission control system is to trap and hold gasoline vapors, also called volatile organic compounds, or VOCs. The evaporative control system includes the charcoal canister, hoses, and valves. These vapors are routed into a charcoal canister, then into the intake airflow where they are burned in the engine instead of being released into the atmosphere.

COMMON COMPONENTS The fuel tank filler caps used on vehicles with modern EVAP systems are a special design. Most EVAP fuel tank filler caps have pressure-vacuum relief built into them. When pressure or vacuum exceeds a calibrated value, the valve opens. Once the pressure or vacuum has been relieved, the valve closes. If a sealed cap is used on an EVAP system that requires a pressure-vacuum relief design, a vacuum lock may develop in the fuel system, or the fuel tank may be damaged by fuel expansion or contraction. ● **SEE FIGURE 42–29.**

EVAPORATIVE CONTROL SYSTEM OPERATION The canister is located under the hood or underneath the vehicle, and is filled with activated charcoal granules that can hold up to one-third of their own weight in fuel vapors. ● **SEE FIGURE 42–30.**

NOTE: Some vehicles with large or dual fuel tanks may have dual canisters.

Activated charcoal is an effective vapor trap because of its great surface area. Each gram of activated charcoal has a surface area of 1,100 m² (more than a quarter acre). Typical canisters hold either 300 or 625 grams of charcoal *with a surface area equivalent to 80 or 165 football fields.* By a process called **adsorption**, the fuel vapor molecules adhere to the carbon surface. This attaching force is not strong, so the system purges the vapor molecules quite simply by sending a fresh airflow through the charcoal.

- **Vapor purging.** During engine operation, stored vapors are drawn from the canister into the engine through a hose connected to the throttle body or the air cleaner. This "purging" process mixes HC vapors from the canister with the existing air-fuel charge. ● **SEE FIGURES 42–31 AND 42–32.**

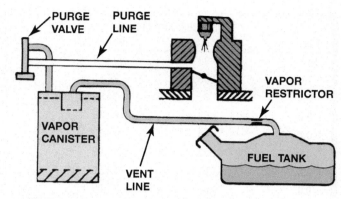

FIGURE 42–31 The evaporative emission control system includes all of the lines, hoses, and valves, plus the charcoal canister.

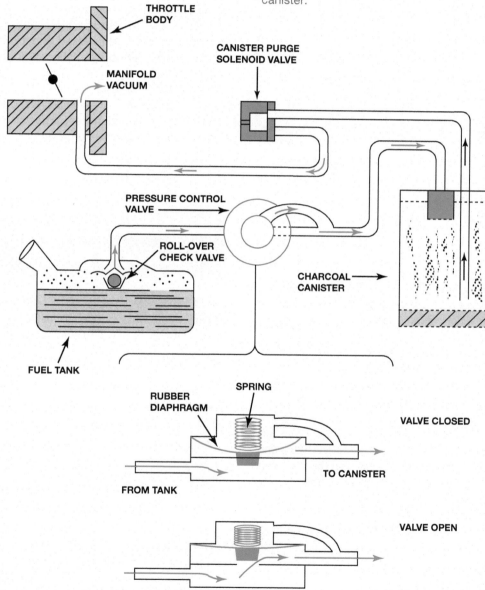

FIGURE 42–32 A typical evaporative emission control system. Note that when the computer turns on the canister purge solenoid valve, manifold vacuum draws any stored vapors from the canister into the engine. Manifold vacuum also is applied to the pressure control valve. When this valve opens, fumes from the fuel tank are drawn into the charcoal canister and eventually into the engine. When the solenoid valve is turned off (or the engine stops and there is no manifold vacuum), the pressure control valve is spring-loaded shut to keep vapors inside the fuel tank from escaping to the atmosphere.

PRESSURE CONVERSIONS		
PSI	Inches Hg	Inches H$_2$O
14.7	29.93	407.19
1.0	2.036	27.7
0.9	1.8	24.93
0.8	1.63	22.16
0.7	1.43	19.39
0.6	1.22	16.62
0.5	1.018	13.85
0.4	0.814	11.08
0.3	0.611	8.31
0.2	0.407	5.54
0.1	0.204	2.77
0.09	0.183	2.49
0.08	0.163	2.22
0.07	0.143	1.94
0.06	0.122	1.66
0.05	0.102	1.385

CHART 42–2

The conversion between Pounds per square inch (PSI) and inches of Mercury (in. Hg.) and inches of water (inches of H$_2$O).

NOTE: Pressure conversions.
1 PSI = 28 inch H$_2$O
1/4 PSI = 7 inch H$_2$O

■ **Computer-controlled purge.** The PCM controls when the canister purges on most engines. This is done by an electric vacuum solenoid, and one or more purge valves. Under normal conditions, most engine control systems permit purging only during closed-loop operation at cruising speeds. During other engine operation conditions, such as open-loop mode, idle, deceleration, or wide-open throttle, the PCM prevents canister purging.

Pressures can build inside the fuel system and are usually measured in units of inches of water (inch H$_2$O) (28 inches of water equals 1 PSI). Some scan tools display other units of measure for the EVAP system that make understanding the system difficult. ● **SEE CHART 42–2** for the conversion among PSI, inch Hg, and inch H$_2$O.

Pressure buildup in the EVAP system can be caused by:

■ Fuel evaporation rates (volatility)
■ Gas tank size (fuel surface area and volume)
■ Fuel level (liquid versus vapor)
■ Fuel slosh (driving conditions)
■ Hot temperatures (ambient, in-tank, close to the tank)
■ Returned fuel from the rail

NONENHANCED EVAPORATIVE CONTROL SYSTEMS

Prior to 1996, evaporative systems were referred to as nonenhanced evaporative (EVAP) control systems. This term refers to evaporative systems that had limited diagnostic capabilities. While they are often PCM controlled, their diagnostic capability is usually limited to their ability to detect if purge has occurred. Many systems have a diagnostic switch that could sense if purge is occurring and set a code if no purge is detected. This system does not check for leaks. On some vehicles, the PCM also has the capability of monitoring the integrity of the purge solenoid and circuit. These systems' limitations are their ability to check the integrity of the evaporative system on the vehicle. They could not detect leaks or missing or loose gas caps that could lead to excessive evaporative emissions from the vehicle. Nonenhanced evaporative systems use either a canister purge solenoid or a vapor management valve to control purge vapor.

ENHANCED EVAPORATIVE CONTROL SYSTEM

BACKGROUND Beginning in 1996, with OBD-II vehicles, manufacturers were required to install systems that are able to detect both purge flow and evaporative system leakage.

■ The systems on models produced between 1996 and 2000 must be able to detect a leak as small as 0.04 inch diameter.
■ Beginning in the model year 2000, the enhanced systems started a phase-in of 0.020 inch diameter leak detection.
■ All vehicles built after 1995 have enhanced evaporative systems that have the ability to detect purge flow and system leakage. If either of these two functions fails, the system is required to set a diagnostic trouble code (DTC) and turn on the MIL light to warn the driver of the failure.

CANISTER VENT VALVE The canister vent valve is a *normally open* valve and is only closed when commanded by the PCM during testing of the system. The vent valve is only closed during testing by the PCM as part of the mandated OBD-II standards. The vent solenoid is located under the vehicle in most cases and is exposed to the environment, making this valve subject to rust and corrosion.

 **TECH TIP**

Problems After Refueling? Check the Purge Valve

The purge valve is normally closed and open only when the PCM is commanding the system to purge. If the purge solenoid were to become stuck in the open position, gasoline fumes would be allowed to flow directly from the gas tank to the intake manifold. When refueling, this would result in a lot of fumes being forced into the intake manifold; and as a result, would cause a hard-to-start condition after refueling. This would also result in a rich exhaust (likely black) when first starting the engine after refueling. Although the purge solenoid is usually located under the hood of most vehicles and less subject to rust and corrosion, as with the vent valve, it can still fail.

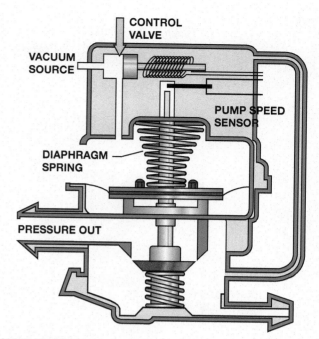

FIGURE 42–33 A leak detection pump (LDP) used on some Chrysler vehicles to pressurize (slightly) the fuel system to check for leaks.

CANISTER PURGE VALVE The purge valve, also called the **canister purge (CANP)** solenoid is *normally closed* and is pulsed open by the PCM during purging. The purge valve is connected to the intake manifold vacuum and this line is used to draw gasoline vapors from the charcoal canister into the engine when the purge valve is commanded open. Most purge valves are pulsed on and off to better control the amount of fumes being drawn into the intake manifold.

proportional to the size of the leak. The shorter the pump period, the larger the leak. The longer the pump period, the smaller the leak.

EVAP large leak (greater than 0.080 inch): less than 0.9 second
EVAP medium leak (0.040 to 0.080 inch): 0.9 to 1.2 seconds
EVAP small leak (0.020 to 0.040 inch): 1.2 to 6 seconds

LEAK DETECTION PUMP SYSTEM

PURPOSE AND FUNCTION Many vehicles use a **leak detection pump (LDP)** as part of the evaporative control system diagnosis equipment. ● **SEE FIGURE 42–33.**

OPERATION The system works to test for leaks as follows:

- The purge solenoid is normally closed.
- The vent valve in the LDP is normally open. Filtered fresh air is drawn through the LDP to the canister.
- The LDP uses a spring attached to a diaphragm to apply pressure (7.5 inch H_2O) to the fuel tank.
- The PCM monitors the LDP switch that is triggered if the pressure drops in the fuel tank.
- The time between LDP solenoid off and LDP switch close is called the pump period. This time period is inversely

ONBOARD REFUELING VAPOR RECOVERY

PURPOSE AND FUNCTION The onboard refueling vapor recovery (ORVR) system was first introduced on some 1998 vehicles. Previously designed EVAP systems allowed fuel vapor to escape to the atmosphere during refueling.

OPERATION The primary feature of most ORVR systems is the restricted tank filler tube, which is about 1 inch (25 mm) in diameter. This reduced size filler tube creates an aspiration effect, which tends to draw outside air into the filler tube. During refueling, the fuel tank is vented to the charcoal canister, which captures the gas fumes; and with air flowing into the filler tube, no vapors can escape to the atmosphere. ● **SEE FIGURE 42–34.**

FIGURE 42–34 A restricted fuel fill pipe shown on a vehicle with the interior removed.

STATE INSPECTION EVAP TESTS

In some states, a periodic inspection and test of the fuel system are mandated along with a dynamometer test. The emissions inspection includes tests on the vehicle before and during the dynamometer test. Before the running test, the fuel tank and cap, fuel lines, canister, and other fuel system components must be inspected and tested to ensure that they are not leaking gasoline vapors into the atmosphere.

- First, the fuel tank cap is tested to ensure that it is sealing properly and holds pressure within specs.
- Next, the cap is installed on the vehicle, and using a special adapter, the EVAP system is pressurized to approximately 0.5 PSI and monitored for two minutes.
- Pressure in the tank and lines should not drop below approximately 0.3 PSI.

If the cap or system leaks, hydrocarbon emissions are likely being released, and the vehicle fails the test. If the system leaks, an ultrasonic leak detector may be used to find the leak.

Finally, with the engine warmed up and running at a moderate speed, the canister purge line is tested for adequate flow using a special flow meter inserted into the system. In one example, if the flow from the canister to the intake system when the system is activated is at least 1 liter per minute, the vehicle passes the canister purge test.

FIGURE 42–35 Some vehicles will display a message if an evaporative control system leak is detected that could be the result of a loose gas cap.

DIAGNOSING THE EVAP SYSTEM

SYMPTOMS Before vehicle emissions testing began in many parts of the country, little service work was done on the evaporative emission system. Common engine-performance problems that can be caused by a fault in this system include:

- **Poor fuel economy.** A leak in a vacuum-valve diaphragm can result in engine vacuum drawing in a constant flow of gasoline vapors from the fuel tank. This usually results in a drop in fuel economy of 2 to 4 miles per gallon (mpg). Use a hand-operated vacuum pump to check that the vacuum diaphragm can hold vacuum.
- **Poor performance.** A vacuum leak in the manifold or ported vacuum section of vacuum hose in the system can cause the engine to run rough. Age, heat, and time all contribute to the deterioration of rubber hoses.

Enhanced exhaust emissions (I/M-240) testing tests the evaporative emission system. A leak in the system is tested by pressurizing the entire fuel system to a level below 1 pounds per sq. in. or 1 PSI (about 14 inch H_2O). The system is typically pressurized with nitrogen, a nonflammable gas that makes up 78% of our atmosphere. The pressure in the system is then shut off and monitored. If the pressure drops below a set standard, the vehicle fails the test. This test determines if there is a leak in the system.

NOTE: To help pass the evaporative section of an enhanced emissions test, arrive at the test site with less than one-half tank of fuel. This means the rest of the volume of the fuel tank is filled with air. It takes longer for the pressure to drop from a small leak when the volume of the air is greater compared to when the tank is full and the volume of air remaining in the tank is small.

LOCATING LEAKS IN THE SYSTEM Leaks in the evaporative emission control system will cause the malfunction check gas cap indication lamp to light on some vehicles. ● **SEE FIGURE 42–35.**

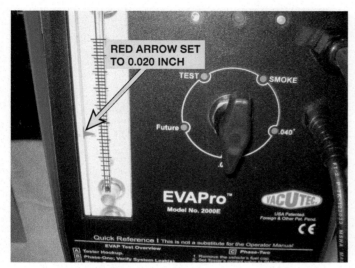

FIGURE 42–36 To test for a leak, this tester was set to the 0.020 inch hole and turned on. The ball rose in the scale on the left and the red arrow was moved to that location. When testing the system for leaks, if the ball rises higher than the arrow, the leak is larger than 0.020 inch. If the ball does not rise to the level of the arrow, the leak is smaller than 0.020 inch.

FIGURE 42–37 This unit is applying smoke to the fuel tank through an adapter and the leak was easily found to be the gas cap seal.

A leak will also cause a gas smell, which would be most noticeable if the vehicle were parked in an enclosed garage. The first step is to determine if there is a leak in the system by setting the EVAP tester to rate the system, either a 0.040 inch or a 0.020 inch hole size leak. ● **SEE FIGURE 42–36.**

After it has been determined that a leak exists and that it is larger than specified, there are two methods that can be used to check for leaks in the evaporative system.

- **Smoke machine testing.** The most efficient method of leak detection is to introduce smoke under low pressure from a machine specifically designed for this purpose. ● **SEE FIGURE 42–37.**

FIGURE 42–38 An emission tester that uses nitrogen to pressurize the fuel system.

- **Nitrogen gas pressurization.** This method uses nitrogen gas under a very low pressure (lower than 1 PSI) in the fuel system. The service technician listens for the escaping air, using amplified headphones. ● **SEE FIGURE 42–38.**

EVAPORATIVE SYSTEM MONITOR

OBD-II REQUIREMENTS OBD-II computer programs not only detect faults, but also *periodically test various systems* and alert the driver before emissions-related components are harmed by system faults.

- Serious faults cause a blinking malfunction indicator lamp (MIL) or even an engine shutdown.
- Less serious faults may simply store a code but not illuminate the MIL.

The OBD-II requirements did not affect fuel system design. However, one new component, a fuel evaporative canister purge line pressure sensor, was added for monitoring purge line pressure during tests. The OBD-II requirements state that vehicle fuel systems are to be routinely tested *while underway* by the PCM.

All OBD-II vehicles perform a canister purge system pressure test, as commanded by the PCM. While the vehicle is being driven, the vapor line between the canister and the purge valve is monitored for pressure changes.

- When the canister purge solenoid is open, the line should be under a vacuum since vapors must be drawn from the canister into the intake system. However, when the purge solenoid is closed, there should be no vacuum in the line. The pressure sensor detects if a vacuum is present, and the information is compared to the command given to the solenoid.

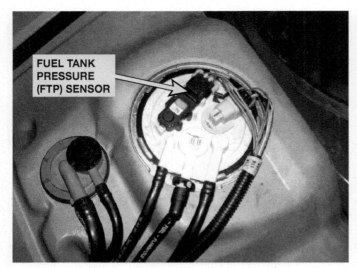

FUEL TANK PRESSURE (FTP) SENSOR

FIGURE 42–39 The fuel tank pressure sensor (black unit with three wires) looks like a MAP sensor and is usually located on top of the fuel pump module (white unit).

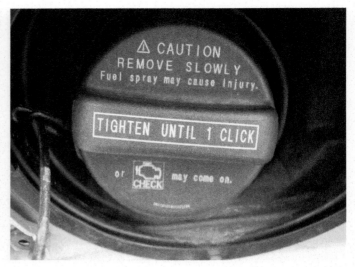

FIGURE 42–40 This Toyota cap has a warning. The check engine light will come on if not tightened until one click.

■ If, during the canister purge cycle, no vacuum exists in the canister purge line, a code is set indicating a possible fault, which could be caused by an inoperative or clogged solenoid or a blocked or leaking canister purge fuel line. Likewise, if vacuum exists when no command for purge is given, a stuck solenoid is evident, and a code is set. The EVAP system monitor tests for purge volume and leaks.

A typical EVAP monitor first closes off the system to atmospheric pressure and opens the purge valve during cruise operation. A **fuel tank pressure (FTP)** sensor then monitors the rate with which vacuum increases in the system. The monitor uses this information to determine the purge volume flow rate. To test for leaks, the EVAP monitor closes the purge valve, creating a completely closed system. The fuel tank pressure sensor monitors the leak-down rate. If the rate exceeds PCM-stored values, a leak greater than or equal to the OBD-II standard of 0.040 inch (1 mm) or 0.020 inch (0.5 mm) exists. After two consecutive failed trips testing either purge volume or the presence of a leak, the PCM lights the MIL and sets a DTC.

The fuel tank pressure sensor is similar to the MAP sensor, and instead of monitoring intake manifold absolute pressure, it is used to monitor fuel tank pressure. ● **SEE FIGURE 42–39.**

ENGINE-OFF NATURAL VACUUM
System integrity (leakage) can also be checked after the engine is shut off. The premise is that a warm evaporative system will cool down after the engine is shut off and the vehicle is stable. A slight vacuum will be created in the gas tank during this cooling period. If a specific level of vacuum is reached and maintained, the system is said to have integrity (no leakage).

TECH TIP

Always Tighten the Cap Correctly

Many diagnostic trouble codes (DTCs) are set because the gas cap has not been properly installed. To be sure that a screw-type gas cap is properly sealed, it may need to be tightened until it clicks three times. The clicking is a ratchet device and the clicking does not harm the cap. Therefore, if a P0440 or similar DTC is set, check the cap. ● **SEE FIGURE 42–40.**

TYPICAL EVAP MONITOR

The PCM will run the EVAP monitor when the following enable criteria are met.

■ Cold start
■ Barometric pressure (BARO) greater than 70 kPa (20.7 inch Hg or 10.2 PSI)
■ Intake air temperature (IAT) between 39°F and 86°F at engine start-up
■ Engine coolant temperature (ECT) between 39°F and 86°F at engine start-up
■ ECT and IAT within 39°F of each other at engine start-up
■ Fuel level within 15% to 85%
■ Throttle position (TP) sensor between 9% and 35%

FIGURE 42–41 The fuel level must be between 15% and 85% before the EVAP monitor will run on most vehicles.

 **TECH TIP**

Keep the Fuel Tank Properly Filled

Most evaporative system monitors will not run unless the fuel level is between 15% and 85%. In other words, if a driver always runs with close to an empty tank or always tries to keep the tank full, the EVAP monitor may not run. ● **SEE FIGURE 42–41.**

RUNNING THE EVAP MONITOR There are three tests that are performed during a typical EVAP monitor. A DTC is assigned to each test.

1. **Weak vacuum test (P0440—large leak).** This test identifies gross leaks. During the monitor, the vent solenoid is closed and the purge solenoid is duty cycled. The fuel tank pressure (FTP) should indicate a vacuum of approximately 6 to 10 inch H_2O.

2. **Small leak test (P0442—small leak).** After the large leak test passes, the PCM checks for a small leak by keeping the vent solenoid closed and closing the purge solenoid. The system is now sealed. The PCM measures the change in FTP voltage over time.

3. **Excess vacuum test (P0446).** This test checks for vent path restrictions. With the vent solenoid open and purge commanded, the PCM should not see excessive vacuum in the EVAP system. Typical EVAP system vacuum with the vent solenoid open is about 5 to 6 inch H_2O.

EVAP SYSTEM-RELATED DIAGNOSTIC TROUBLE CODES

Diagnostic Trouble Code	Description	Possible Causes
P0440	Evaporative system fault	■ Loose gas cap ■ Defective EVAP vent ■ Cracked charcoal canister ■ EVAP vent or purge vapor line problems
P0442	Small leak detected	■ Loose gas cap ■ Defective EVAP vent or purge solenoid ■ EVAP vent or purge line problems
P0446	EVAP canister vent blocked	■ EVAP vent or purge solenoid electrical problems ■ Restricted EVAP canister vent line

1. Recirculating 6% to 10% inert exhaust gases back into the intake system by the EGR system reduces peak temperature inside the combustion chamber and reduces NO_x exhaust emissions.

2. EGR is usually not needed at idle, at wide-open throttle, or when the engine is cold.

3. Many EGR systems use a feedback potentiometer to signal the PCM the position of the EGR valve pintle.

4. OBD-II requires that the flow rate be tested and is achieved by opening the EGR valve and observing the reaction of the MAP sensor.

5. Positive crankcase ventilation (PCV) systems use a valve or a fixed orifice to control and direct the fumes from the crankcase back into the intake system.

6. A PCV valve regulates the flow of fumes, depending on engine vacuum and seals the crankcase vent in the event of a backfire.

7. As much as 30% of the air needed by the engine at idle speed flows through the PCV system.

8. The secondary air-injection (SAI) system forces air at low pressure into the exhaust to reduce CO and HC exhaust emissions.

9. A catalytic converter is an aftertreatment device that reduces exhaust emissions outside of the engine. A catalyst is an element that starts a chemical reaction, but is not consumed in the process.

10. The catalyst material used in a catalytic converter includes rhodium, palladium, and platinum.

11. The OBD-II system monitor compares the relative activity of a rear oxygen sensor to the precatalytic oxygen sensor to determine catalytic converter efficiency.

12. The purpose of the evaporative (EVAP) emission control system is to reduce the release of volatile organic compounds (VOCs) into the atmosphere.

13. A carbon (charcoal) canister is used to trap and hold gasoline vapors until they can be purged and run into the engine to be burned.

14. OBD-II regulation requires that the evaporative emission control system be checked for leakage and proper purge flow rates.

15. External leaks can best be located by pressurizing the fuel system with low-pressure smoke.

REVIEW QUESTIONS

1. How does the use of exhaust gas recirculation reduce NO_x exhaust emission?

2. How does the DPFE sensor work?

3. What exhaust emissions does the PCV valve and SAI system control?

4. How does a catalytic converter reduce NO_x to nitrogen and oxygen?

5. How does the computer monitor catalytic converter performance?

CHAPTER QUIZ

1. Two technicians are discussing clogged EGR passages. Technician A says clogged EGR passages can cause excessive NO_x exhaust emission. Technician B says that clogged EGR passages could cause the engine to ping (spark knock or detonation). Which technician is correct?
   a. Technician A only
   b. Technician B only
   c. Both Technicians A and B
   d. Neither Technician A nor B

2. An EGR valve that is partially stuck open would *most likely* cause what condition?
   a. Rough idle/stalling
   b. Excessive NO_x exhaust emissions
   c. Ping (spark knock or detonation)
   d. Missing at highway speed

3. How much air flows through the PCV system when the engine is at idle speed?
   a. 1% to 3%
   b. 5% to 10%
   c. 10% to 20%
   d. Up to 30%

4. Technician A says that if a PCV valve rattles, it is okay and does not need to be replaced. Technician B says that if a PCV valve does not rattle, it should be replaced. Which technician is correct?
   a. Technician A only
   b. Technician B only
   c. Both Technicians A and B
   d. Neither Technician A nor B

5. The switching valves on the AIR pump have failed several times. Technician A says that a defective exhaust check valve could be the cause. Technician B says that a leaking exhaust system at the muffler could be the cause. Which technician is correct?
   a. Technician A only
   b. Technician B only
   c. Both Technicians A and B
   d. Neither Technician A nor B

6. Two technicians are discussing testing a catalytic converter. Technician A says that a vacuum gauge can be used and observed to see if the vacuum drops with the engine at 2500 RPM for 60 seconds. Technician B says that a pressure gauge can be used to check for backpressure. Which technician is correct?
   a. Technician A only
   b. Technician B only
   c. Both Technicians A and B
   d. Neither Technician A nor B

7. At about what temperature does oxygen combine with the nitrogen in the air to form NO_x?
   a. 500°F (260°C)
   b. 750°F (400°C)
   c. 1,500°F (815°C)
   d. 2,500°F (1,370°C)

8. A P0401 is being discussed. Technician A says that a stuck-closed EGR valve could be the cause. Technician B says that clogged EGR ports could be the cause. Which technician is correct?
   a. Technician A only
   b. Technician B only
   c. Both Technicians A and B
   d. Neither Technician A nor B

9. Which EVAP valve(s) is(are) normally closed?
   a. Canister purge valve
   b. Canister vent valve
   c. Both canister purge and canister vent valves
   d. Neither canister purge nor canister vent valve

10. Before an evaporative emission monitor will run, the fuel level must be where?
    a. At least 75% full
    b. Over 25%
    c. Between 15% and 85%
    d. The level of the fuel in the tank is not needed to run the monitor test

chapter 43
ON-BOARD DIAGNOSIS

LEARNING OBJECTIVES

After studying this chapter, the reader will be able to:

1. Explain the purpose and function of systems.
2. List the various continuous and noncontinuous monitors.
3. Explain the numbering designation of OBD-II diagnostic trouble codes.
4. Explain the information captured by freeze-frame and the criteria to enable an OBD monitor.
5. Describe PCM tests related to OBD systems.
6. List the operation modes of a global scan tool.

KEY TERMS

California Air Resources Board (CARB) 669

Component identification (CID) 676

Comprehensive component monitor (CCM) 670

Diagnostic executive 669

Enable criteria 672

Exponentially weighted moving average (EWMA) monitor 671

Federal Test Procedure (FTP) 669

Freeze-frame 669

Functionality 671

Malfunction indicator lamp (MIL) 669

On-board diagnosis (OBD) 669

Parameter identification (PID) 676

Rationality 671

Society of Automotive Engineers (SAE) 673

Task manager 669

Test identification (TID) 676

ON-BOARD DIAGNOSTICS GENERATION-II (OBD-II) SYSTEMS

PURPOSE AND FUNCTION OF OBD II During the 1980s, most manufacturers began equipping their vehicles with full-function control systems capable of alerting the driver of a malfunction and of allowing the technician to retrieve codes that identify circuit faults. These early diagnostic systems were meant to reduce emissions and speed up vehicle repair.

The automotive industry calls these systems **On-Board Diagnostics (OBDs)**. The **California Air Resources Board (CARB)** developed the first regulation requiring manufacturers selling vehicles in that state to install OBD. OBD Generation I (OBD I) applies to all vehicles sold in California beginning with the 1988 model year. It specifies the following requirements:

1. An instrument panel warning lamp able to alert the driver of certain control system failures, now called a **malfunction indicator lamp (MIL)**. ● **SEE FIGURE 43–1.**

2. The system's ability to record and transmit diagnostic trouble codes (DTCs) for emission-related failures.

All light-duty vehicles (less than 8,500 pounds) sold in North America since 1996, as well as medium-duty vehicles (8,500–14,000 pounds) beginning in 2005, and heavy-duty vehicles (greater than 14,000 pounds) beginning in 2010, are required to support OBD-II diagnostics, using a standardized data link connector, and a subset of the SAE J/1979 defined PIDs (or SAE J1939 as applicable for medium/heavy-duty vehicles), primarily for state-mandated emissions inspections.

OBD-II OBJECTIVES

Generally, the CARB defines an OBD-II-equipped vehicle by its ability to do the following:

1. Detect component degradation or a faulty emission-related system that prevents compliance with federal emission standards.

2. Alert the driver of needed emission-related repair or maintenance.

3. Use standardized DTCs and accept a generic scan tool.

These requirements apply to all 1996 and later-model light-duty vehicles. The Clean Air Act of 1990 directed the Environmental Protection Agency (EPA) to develop new regulations for OBD. The primary purpose of OBD II is emission-related, whereas the primary purpose of OBD I (1988) was to detect faults in sensors or sensor circuits. OBD-II regulations require that not only sensors be tested, but also all exhaust emission-control devices, and that they be verified for proper operation.

All new vehicles must pass the **Federal Test Procedure (FTP)** for exhaust emissions while being tested for 1874 seconds on dynamometer rollers that simulate the urban drive cycle around downtown Los Angeles.

FIGURE 43–1 A typical malfunction indicator lamp (MIL) often labeled "check engine" or "service engine soon" (SES).

NOTE: IM 240 is simply a shorter 240-second version of the 505-second federal test procedure.

The regulations for OBD-II vehicles state that the vehicle powertrain control module (PCM) must be capable of testing for, and determining, if the exhaust emissions are within 1.5 times the FTP limits. To achieve this goal, the PCM must do the following:

1. Test all exhaust emission system components for correct operation.

2. Actively operate the system and measure the results.

3. Continuously monitor all aspects of the engine operation to be certain that the exhaust emissions do not exceed 1.5 times the FTP.

4. Check engine operation for misfire.

5. Turn on the MIL (check engine) if the computer senses a fault in a circuit or system.

6. Record a **freeze-frame**, which is a snapshot of important engine data at the time the DTC was set.

7. Flash the MIL if an engine misfire occurs that could damage the catalytic converter.

DIAGNOSTIC EXECUTIVE AND TASK MANAGER

On OBD-II systems, the powertrain control module (PCM) incorporates a special segment of software. On Ford and GM systems, this software is called the **diagnostic executive**. On Chrysler systems, it is called the **task manager**. This software program is designed to manage the operation of all OBD-II monitors by controlling the sequence of steps necessary to execute the diagnostic tests and monitors.

MONITORS

PURPOSE AND FUNCTION A monitor is an organized method of testing a specific part of the system. Monitors are simply tests that the computer performs to evaluate components and systems. If a component or system failure is detected while a monitor is running, a DTC is stored and the MIL illuminated during the second trip. The two types of monitors are continuous and noncontinuous.

CONTINUOUS MONITORS As required conditions are met, continuous monitors begin to run. These continuous monitors run for the remainder of the vehicle drive cycle. The three continuous monitors are as follows:

- **Comprehensive component monitor (CCM).** This monitor watches the sensors and actuators in the OBD-II system. Sensor values are constantly compared with known-good values stored in the PCM's memory.

    The CCM is an internal program in the PCM designed to monitor a failure in any electronic component or circuit (including emission-related and non-emission-related circuits) that provide input or output signals to the PCM. The PCM considers that an input or output signal is inoperative when a failure exists due to an open circuit, out-of-range value, or if an on-board rationality check fails. If an emission-related fault is detected, the PCM sets a code and activates the MIL (requires two consecutive trips).

    Many PCM sensors and output devices are tested at key-on or immediately after engine start-up. However, some devices are only tested by the CCM after the engine meets certain engine conditions. The number of times the CCM must detect a fault before it activates the MIL depends upon the manufacturer, but most require two consecutive trips to activate the MIL. The components tested by the CCM include:

Four-wheel-drive low switch
Brake switch
Camshaft (CMP) and crankshaft (CKP) sensors
Clutch switch (manual transmissions/transaxles only)
Cruise servo switch
Engine coolant temperature (ECT) sensor
EVAP purge sensor or switch
Fuel composition sensor
Intake air temperature (IAT) sensor
Knock sensor (KS)
Manifold absolute pressure (MAP) sensor
Mass airflow (MAF) sensor
Throttle-position (TP) sensor
Transmission temperature sensor
Transmission turbine speed sensor
Vacuum sensor
Vehicle speed (VS) sensor
EVAP canister purge and EVAP purge vent solenoid

Idle air control (IAC)
Ignition control system
Transmission torque converter clutch solenoid
Transmission shift solenoids

- **Misfire monitor.** This monitor watches for engine misfire. The PCM uses the information received from the crankshaft position sensor (CKP) to calculate the time between the edges of the reluctor, as well as the rotational speed and acceleration. By comparing the acceleration of each firing event, the PCM can determine if a cylinder is not firing correctly.

    Misfire type A. Upon detection of a misfire type A (200 revolutions), which causes catalyst damage, the MIL blinks once per second during the actual misfire, and a DTC is stored.

    Misfire type B. Upon detection of a misfire type B (1,000 revolutions), which exceeds 1.5 times the EPA federal test procedure (FTP) standard or causes a vehicle to fail an inspection and maintenance tailpipe emissions test, the MIL illuminates and a DTC is stored.

    The DTC associated with multiple cylinder misfire for a type A or type B misfire is DTC P0300. The DTCs associated with an individual cylinder misfire for a type A or type B misfire are DTCs P0301, P0302, P0303, P0304, P0305, P0306, P0307, P0308, P0309, and P0310.

- **Fuel trim monitor.** The PCM continuously monitors short- and long-term fuel trim. Constantly updated adaptive fuel tables are stored in long-term memory (KAM), and used by the PCM for compensation due to wear and aging of the fuel system components. The MIL illuminates when the PCM determines the fuel trim values have reached and stayed at their limits for too long a period of time.

NONCONTINUOUS MONITORS Noncontinuous monitors run (at most) once per vehicle drive cycle. The noncontinuous monitors are as follows:

O2S monitor
O2S heater monitor
Catalyst monitor
EGR monitor
EVAP monitor
Secondary AIR monitor
Transmission monitor
PCV system monitor
Thermostat monitor

Once a noncontinuous monitor has run to completion, it does not run again until the conditions are met during the next vehicle drive cycle. Also, after a noncontinuous monitor has run to completion, the readiness status on your scan tool shows "complete" or "done" for that monitor. Monitors that have not run to completion show up on your scanner as "incomplete."

OBD-II MONITOR INFORMATION

COMPREHENSIVE COMPONENT MONITOR The circuits and components covered by the comprehensive component monitor (CCM) do not include those directly monitored by another monitor.

However, OBD II also requires that inputs from powertrain components to the PCM be tested for **rationality**, and that outputs to powertrain components from the PCM be tested for **functionality**. Both inputs and outputs are to be checked *electrically.* Rationality checks refer to a PCM comparison of input values to values from other sensors to determine if they make sense and are normal (rational).

Example:

TPS	3 V
MAP	18 in. Hg
RPM	700 RPM
PRNDL	Park

NOTE: Comprehensive component monitors are continuous. Therefore, enabling conditions do not apply.

- Monitor runs continuously
- Monitor includes sensors, switches, relays, solenoids, and PCM hardware
- All are checked for opens, shorts-to-ground, and shorts-to-voltage
- Inputs are checked for rationality
- Outputs are checked for functionality
- Most are one-trip DTCs
- Freeze-frame is priority 3
- Three consecutive good trips are used to extinguish the MIL
- Forty warm-up cycles are necessary to self-erase the DTC and freeze-frame
- Two minutes run time without reoccurrence of the fault constitutes a "good trip"

CONTINUOUS RUNNING MONITORS Continuous monitors run continuously and only stop if they fail and include:

- Fuel system: rich/lean
- Misfire: catalyst damaging/FTP (emissions)
- Two-trip faults (except early-generation catalyst damaging misfire)
- MIL, DTC, freeze-frame after two consecutive faults
- Freeze-frame is priority 2 on first trip
- Freeze-frame is priority 4 on maturing trip

- Three consecutive good trips in a similar condition window are used to extinguish the MIL
- Forty warm-up cycles are used to erase DTC and freeze-frame (80 to erase one-trip failure, if similar conditions cannot be met)

ONCE PER TRIP MONITORS

- Monitor runs once per trip, pass or fail
- O_2 response, O_2 heaters, EGR, purge flow EVAP leak, secondary air, catalyst
- Two-trip DTCs
- MIL, DTC, freeze-frame after two consecutive faults
- Freeze-frame is priority 1 on first trip
- Freeze-frame is priority 3 on maturing trip
- Three consecutive good trips are used to extinguish the MIL
- Forty warm-up cycles are used to erase DTC and freeze-frame

EXPONENTIALLY WEIGHTED MOVING AVERAGE (EWMA) MONITORS The **exponentially weighted moving average (EWMA) monitor** is a mathematical method used to determine performance.

This method smooths out any variables in the readings over time and results in a running average. This method is used by some vehicle manufacturers for two monitors.

1. Catalyst monitor
2. EGR monitor

ENABLING CRITERIA

With so many different tests (monitors) to run, the PCM needs an internal director to keep track of when each monitor should run. As mentioned, different manufacturers have different names for this director, such as the diagnostic executive or the task manager. Each monitor has enabling criteria. These criteria are a set of conditions that must be met before the task manager gives the go-ahead for each monitor to run. Most enabling criteria follow simple logic, for example:

- The task manager does not authorize the start of the O2S monitor until the engine has reached operating temperature and the system has entered closed loop.
- The task manager does not authorize the start of the EGR monitor when the engine is at idle, because the EGR is always closed at this time.

Because each monitor is responsible for testing a different part of the system, the enabling criteria can differ greatly from one monitor to the next. The task manager must decide when each monitor should run, and in what order, to avoid confusion.

There may be a conflict if two monitors run at the same time. The results of one monitor might also be tainted if a second monitor runs simultaneously. In such cases, the task manager decides which monitor has a higher priority. Some monitors also depend on the results of other monitors before they can run.

A monitor may be classified as pending if a failed sensor or other system fault is keeping it from running on schedule.

The task manager may suspend a monitor if the conditions are not correct to continue. For example, if the catalyst monitor is running during a road test and the PCM detects a misfire, the catalyst monitor is suspended for the duration of the misfire.

TRIP A trip is defined as a key-on condition that contains the necessary conditions for a particular test to be performed, followed by a key-off. These conditions are called the **enable criteria**. For example, for the EGR test to be performed, the engine must be at normal operating temperature and decelerating for a minimum amount of time. Some tests are performed when the engine is cold, whereas others require that the vehicle be cruising at a steady highway speed.

WARM-UP CYCLE Once a MIL is deactivated, the original code remains in memory until 40 warm-up cycles are completed without the fault reappearing. A warm-up cycle is defined as a trip with an engine temperature increase of at least 40°F and where engine temperature reaches at least 160°F (71°C).

MIL CONDITION: OFF This condition indicates that the PCM has not detected any faults in an emissions-related component or system, or that the MIL circuit is not working.

MIL CONDITION: ON STEADY This condition indicates a fault in an emissions-related component or system that could affect the vehicle emission levels.

MIL CONDITION: FLASHING This condition indicates a misfire or fuel control system fault that could damage the catalytic converter.

NOTE: In a misfire condition with the MIL on steady, if the driver reaches a vehicle speed and load condition with the engine misfiring at a level that could cause catalyst damage, the MIL starts flashing. It continues to flash until engine speed and load conditions cause the level of misfire to subside. Then, the MIL goes back to the on-steady condition. This situation might result in a customer complaint of a MIL with an intermittent flashing condition.

MIL: OFF The PCM turns off the MIL if any of the following actions or conditions occur:

- The codes are cleared with a scan tool.
- Power to the PCM is removed at the battery or with the PCM power fuse for an extended period of time (may be up to several hours or longer).
- A vehicle is driven on three consecutive trips with a warm-up cycle and meets all code set conditions without the PCM detecting any faults.

What is a Drive Cycle?

A drive cycle is a vehicle being driven under specified speed and times that allows all monitors to run. In other words, the PCM is looking at a series of data points representing speed and time and determines from these data points when the conditions are right to perform a monitor or a test of a component. These data points and, therefore, the drive cycle are vehicle-specific and are not the same for each vehicle. Some common conditions for a drive cycle to successfully run all of the monitors include:

1. Cold start with intake air temperature (IAT) and engine coolant temperature (ECT) close to each other, indicating that the engine has cooled to the temperature of the surrounding air temperature.
2. Fuel level within a certain range, usually between 15% and 85%.
3. Vehicle speed within a certain speed range for certain amount of time, usually 4 to 12 minutes.
4. Stop and idle for a certain time.

Each monitor requires its own set of parameters needed to run the test, and sometimes these conditions cannot be met. For example, some evaporate emissions control (EVAP) systems require a temperature that may not be possible in winter months in a cold climatic area.

A typical universal drive cycle that works for many vehicles includes the following steps.

MIL must be off.
No DTCs present.
Fuel fill between 15% and 85%.
Cold start—Preferred = 8-hour soak at 68°F to 86°F.
Alternative = ECT below 86°F.

STEP 1 With the ignition off, connect scan tool.

STEP 2 Start engine and drive between 20 and 30 mph for 22 minutes, allowing speed to vary.

STEP 3 Stop and idle for 40 seconds, gradually accelerate to 55 mph.

STEP 4 Maintain 55 mph for 4 minutes using a steady throttle input.

STEP 5 Stop and idle for 30 seconds, then accelerate to 30 mph.

STEP 6 Maintain 30 mph for 12 minutes.

STEP 7 Repeat steps 4 and 5 four times.

Using scan tool, check readiness. Always check service information for the exact drive cycle conditions for the vehicle being serviced for best results.

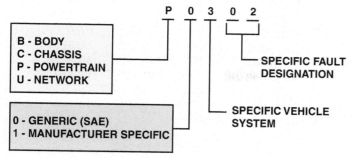

EXAMPLE: P0302 = CYLINDER #2 MISFIRE DETECTED

FIGURE 43–2 OBD-II DTC identification format.

The PCM sets a code if a fault is detected that could cause tailpipe emissions to exceed 1.5 times the FTP standard; however, the PCM does not deactivate the MIL until the vehicle has been driven on three consecutive trips with vehicle conditions similar to actual conditions present when the fault was detected. This is not merely three vehicle start-ups and trips. It means three trips during which certain engine operating conditions are met, so that the OBD-II monitor that found the fault can run again and pass the diagnostic test.

OBD-II DTC NUMBERING DESIGNATION

A scan tool is required to retrieve DTCs from an OBD-II vehicle. Every OBD-II scan tool is able to read all generic **Society of Automotive Engineers (SAE)** DTCs from any vehicle. ● **SEE FIGURE 43–2.** for definitions and explanations of OBD alphanumeric DTCs. The DTCs are grouped into major categories, depending on the location of the fault on the system involved.

Pxxx codes—powertrain DTCs (engine, transmission-related faults)

Bxxx codes—body DTCs (accessories, interior-related faults)

Cxxx codes—chassis DTCs (suspension and steering-related faults)

Uxxx codes—network DTCs (module communication-related faults)

DTC NUMBERING EXPLANATION
The number in the hundredth position indicates the specific vehicle system or subgroup that failed. This position should be consistent for P0xxx and P1xxx type codes. The following numbers and systems were established by SAE:

- P0100—Air metering and fuel system fault
- P0200—Fuel system (fuel injector only) fault
- P0300—Ignition system or misfire fault
- P0400—Emission control system fault
- P0500—Idle speed control, vehicle speed (VS) sensor fault
- P0600—Computer output circuit (relay, solenoid, etc.) fault
- P0700—Transaxle, transmission faults

NOTE: The tens and ones numbers indicate the part of the system at fault.

TYPES OF DTCS Not all OBD-II DTCs are of the same importance for exhaust emissions. Each type of DTC has different requirements for it to set, and the computer only turns on the MIL for emissions-related DTCs.

TYPE A CODES. A type A DTC is emission-related and causes the MIL to be turned on the first trip if the computer has detected a problem. Engine misfire or a very rich or lean air–fuel ratio, for example, causes a type A DTC. These codes alert the driver to an emission problem that may cause damage to the catalytic converter.

TYPE B CODES. A type B code is stored and the MIL is turned on during the second consecutive trip, alerting the driver to the fact that a diagnostic test was performed and failed.

NOTE: Type A and B codes are emission-related codes that cause the lighting of the MIL, usually labeled "check engine" or "service engine soon."

TYPE C AND D CODES. Type C and D codes are for use with non-emission-related diagnostic tests; they cause the lighting of a "service" lamp (if the vehicle is so equipped). Type C codes are also called type C1 codes and D codes are also called type C0 codes.

DIAGNOSTIC TROUBLE CODE PRIORITY CARB has also mandated that all diagnostic trouble codes (DTCs) be stored according to individual priority. DTCs with a higher priority overwrite those with a lower priority. The OBD-II System DTC Priority is listed below.

Priority 0—Non-emission-related codes

Priority 1—One-trip failure of two-trip fault for non-fuel, non-misfire codes

Priority 2—One-trip failure of two-trip fault for fuel or misfire codes

Priority 3—Two-trip failure or matured fault of non-fuel, non-misfire codes

Priority 4—Two-trip failure or matured fault for fuel or misfire codes

OBD-II FREEZE-FRAME

To assist the service technician, OBD II requires the computer to take a "snapshot" or freeze-frame of all data at the instant an emission-related DTC is set. A scan tool is required to retrieve this data.

NOTE: Although OBD II requires that just one freeze-frame of data be stored, the instant an emission-related DTC is set, vehicle manufacturers usually provide expanded data

MONITOR NAME	MONITOR TYPE (HOW OFTEN IT COMPLETES)	NUMBER OF FAULTS ON SEPARATE TRIPS TO SET A PENDING DTC	NUMBER OF SEPARATE CONSECUTIVE TRIPS TO LIGHT MIL, STORE A DTC	NUMBER OF TRIPS WITH NO FAULTS TO ERASE A MATURING DTC	NUMBER OF TRIPS WITH NO FAULT TO TURN THE MIL OFF	NUMBER OF WARM-UP CYCLES TO ERASE DTC AFTER MIL IS TURNED OFF
CCM	Continuous (when trip conditions allow it)	1	2	1–Trip	3–Trips	40
Catalyst	Once per drive cycle	1	3	1–Trip	3–OBD-II drive cycle	40
Misfire Type A	Continuous		1		3–Similar conditions	80
Misfire Type B	Continuous	1	2	1–Trip	3–Similar conditions	80
Fuel System	Continuous	1	2	1–Trip	3–Similar conditions	80
Oxygen Sensor	Once per trip	1	2	1–Trip	3–Trips	40
EGR	Once per trip	1	2	1–Trip	3–Trips	40
EVAP	Once per trip	1	1	1–Trip	3–Trips	40
AIR	Once per trip	1	2	1–Trip	3–Trips	40

CHART 43–1

PCM Determination of faults chart.

about the DTC beyond that required. However, retrieving this enhanced data usually requires the use of the vehicle-specific scan tool.

Freeze-frame items include:

- Calculated load value
- Engine speed (RPM)
- Short-term and long-term fuel trim percent
- Fuel system pressure (on some vehicles)
- Vehicle speed (mph)
- Engine coolant temperature
- Intake manifold pressure
- Closed-open-loop status
- Fault code that triggered the freeze-frame
- If a misfire code is set, identify which cylinder is misfiring

A DTC should not be cleared from the vehicle computer memory unless the fault has been corrected and the technician is so directed by the diagnostic procedure. If the problem that caused the DTC to be set has been corrected, the computer automatically clears the DTC after 40 consecutive warm-up cycles with no further faults detected. It requires 80 warm-up cycles to erase the pending fault if similar conditions cannot be met. The codes can also be erased by using a scan tool. ● **SEE CHART 43–1.**

NOTE: Disconnecting the battery may not erase OBD-II DTCs or freeze-frame data. Most vehicle manufacturers recommend using a scan tool to erase DTCs, rather than disconnecting the battery, because the memory for the radio, seats, and learned engine operating parameters is lost if the battery is disconnected.

 FREQUENTLY ASKED QUESTION

What Are Pending Codes?

Pending codes are set when operating conditions are met and the component or circuit is not within the normal range, yet the conditions have not yet been met to set a DTC. For example, a sensor may require two consecutive faults before a DTC is set. If a scan tool displays a pending code or a failure, a driveability concern could also be present. The pending code can help the technician to determine the root cause before the customer complains of a check engine light indication.

ENABLING CONDITIONS

These are the exact engine operating conditions required for a diagnostic monitor to run.

Example:

Specific RPM
Specific ECT, MAP, run time, etc.

PENDING Under some situations, the PCM does not run a monitor if the MIL is illuminated and a fault is stored from another monitor. In these situations, the PCM postpones monitors pending a resolution of the original fault. The PCM does not run the test until the problem is remedied.

For example, when the MIL is illuminated for an oxygen sensor fault, the PCM does not run the catalyst monitor until the oxygen sensor fault is remedied. Since the catalyst monitor is based on signals from the oxygen sensor, running the test produces inaccurate results.

CONFLICT There are also situations when the PCM does not run a monitor if another monitor is in progress. In these situations, the effects of another monitor running could result in an erroneous failure. If this conflict is present, the monitor is not run until the conflicting condition passes. Most likely, the monitor runs later, after the conflicting monitor has passed.

For example, if the fuel system monitor is in progress, the PCM does not run the EGR monitor. Since both tests monitor changes in air–fuel ratio and adaptive fuel compensation, the monitors conflict with each other.

SUSPEND Occasionally, the PCM may not allow a two-trip fault to mature. The PCM suspends the maturing fault if a condition exists that may induce erroneous failure. This prevents illuminating the MIL for the wrong fault and allows more precise diagnosis.

For example, if the PCM is storing a one-trip fault for the oxygen sensor and the EGR monitor, the PCM may still run the EGR monitor, but suspends the results until the oxygen sensor monitor either passes or fails. At that point, the PCM can determine if the EGR system is actually failing or if an oxygen sensor is failing.

PCM TESTS

RATIONALITY TEST While input signals to the PCM are constantly being monitored for electrical opens and shorts, they are also tested for rationality. This means that the input signal is compared against other inputs and information to see if it makes sense under the current conditions.

PCM sensor inputs that are checked for rationality include:

- MAP sensor
- O_2 sensor
- ECT
- Camshaft position sensor (CMP)
- VS sensor
- Crankshaft position sensor (CKP)
- IAT sensor
- TP sensor
- Ambient air temperature sensor
- Power steering switch
- O_2 sensor heater
- Engine controller
- Brake switch
- P/N switch (range switch)
- Transmission controls

FUNCTIONALITY TEST A functionality test refers to PCM inputs checking the operation of the outputs.

Example

PCM commands the IAC open; expected change in engine RPM is not seen
IAC 60 counts
RPM 700 RPM

PCM outputs that are checked for functionality include:

- EVAP canister purge solenoid
- EVAP purge vent solenoid
- Cooling fan
- Idle air control solenoid
- Ignition control system
- Transmission torque converter clutch solenoid
- Transmission shift solenoids (A, B, 1–2, etc.)

ELECTRICAL TEST Refers to the PCM check of both input and outputs for the following:

- Open
- Shorts
- Ground

Example:

ECT

Shorted high (input to PCM) above capable voltage, i.e., 5-volt sensor with 12-volt input to PCM indicates a short to voltage.

Monitor Type	Conditions to Set DTC and Illuminate MIL	Extinguish MIL	Clear DTC Criteria	Applicable DTC
Continuous 1-trip monitor	(See note below) Input and output failure—rationally, functionally, electrically	3 consecutive pass trips	40 warm-up cycles	P0123

NOTE: The number of times the comprehensive component monitor must detect a fault depends on the vehicle manufacturer. On some vehicles, the comprehensive component monitor activates the MIL as soon as it detects a fault. On other vehicles, the comprehensive component monitor must fail two times in a row.

- Freeze-frame captured on first-trip failure.
- Enabling conditions: Many PCM sensors and output devices are tested at key-on or immediately after engine start-up. However, some devices (ECT, idle speed control) are only tested by the comprehensive component monitor after the engine meets particular engine conditions.

- Pending: No pending condition
- Conflict: No conflict conditions
- Suspend: No suspend conditions

GLOBAL OBD-II

All OBD-II vehicles must be able to display data on a global (also called *generic*) scan tool under nine different modes of operation. These modes include:

Mode One	Current powertrain data (**parameter identification** display or **PID**)
Mode Two	Freeze-frame data
Mode Three	DTCs
Mode Four	Clear and reset DTCs, freeze-frame data, and readiness status monitors for noncontinuous monitors only
Mode Five	Oxygen sensor monitor test results
Mode Six	On-board monitoring of test results for non-continuously monitored systems
Mode Seven	On-board monitoring of test results for continuously monitored systems
Mode Eight	Bidirectional control of on-board systems
Mode Nine	Module identification
Mode 10 ($0A)	Permanent DTCs

The global (generic) data is used by most state emission programs. Global OBD-II displays often use hexadecimal numbers, which use 16 numbers instead of 10. The numbers 0 to 9 (zero counts as a number) make up the first 10 and then capital letters A to F complete the 16 numbers. To help identify the number as being in a hexadecimal format, a dollar sign ($) is used in front of the number or letter. See the conversion chart below:

Decimal Number	Hexadecimal Code
0	$0
1	$1
2	$2
3	$3
4	$4
5	$5
6	$6
7	$7
8	$8
9	$9
10	$A
11	$B
12	$C
13	$D
14	$E
15	$F

Hexadecimal coding is also used to identify tests (**test identification [TID]** and **component identification [CID]**).

DIAGNOSING PROBLEMS USING MODE SIX

Mode six information can be used to diagnose faults by following three steps:

1. Check the monitor status before starting repairs. This step shows how the system failed.
2. Look at the component or parameter that triggered the fault. This step helps pin down the root cause of the failure.
3. Look to the monitor enable criteria, which shows what it takes to fail or pass the monitor.

FREQUENTLY ASKED QUESTION

How Can You Tell Generic from Factory?

When using a scan tool on an OBD-II-equipped vehicle, if the display asks for make, model, and year, then the factory or enhanced part of the PCM is being accessed. If the generic or global part of the PCM is being scanned, then there is no need to know the vehicle identification details.

SUMMARY

1. If the MIL is on, retrieve the DTC and follow the manufacturer's recommended procedure to find the root cause of the problem.
2. All monitors must have the enable criteria achieved before a test is performed.
3. OBD-II vehicles use common generic DTCs.
4. OBD-II includes generic (SAE) as well as vehicle manufacturer- specific DTCs and data display.

1. What does the PCM do during a trip to test emission-related components?
2. What is the difference between a type A and type B OBD-II DTC?
3. What is the difference between a trip and a warm-up cycle?
4. What could cause the MIL to flash?
5. What modes are available using Mode $06?

CHAPTER QUIZ

1. A freeze-frame is generated on an OBD-II vehicle _____.
   a. when a type C or D diagnostic trouble code is set
   b. when a type A or B diagnostic trouble code is set
   c. every other trip
   d. when the PCM detects a problem with the O2S

2. An ignition misfire or fuel mixture problem is an example of what type of DTC?
   a. Type A
   b. Type C
   c. Type B
   d. Type D

3. The comprehensive component monitor checks computer- controlled devices for _____.
   a. opens
   b. shorts-to-ground
   c. rationality
   d. All of the above

4. A freeze-frame is a _____ of all data at the instant an emission-related DTC is set.
   a. comprehensive component monitor
   b. failure record
   c. snapshot
   d. trip

5. Which is a continuous monitor?
   a. Fuel system monitor
   b. EGR monitor
   c. Oxygen sensor monitor
   d. Catalyst monitor

6. DTC P0302 is a _____.
   a. generic DTC
   b. vehicle manufacturer-specific DTC
   c. idle speed-related DTC
   d. transmission/transaxle-related DTC

7. Enable criteria means _____?
   a. the same thing as a trip
   b. conditions for a particular test to be performed
   c. a drive cycle
   d. a warm-up cycle

8. By looking at the way diagnostic trouble codes are formatted, which DTC could indicate that the gas cap is loose or defective?
   a. P0221
   b. P1301
   c. P0442
   d. P1603

9. The computer automatically clears a DTC if there are no additional detected faults after _____.
   a. forty consecutive warm-up cycles
   b. eighty warm-up cycles
   c. two consecutive trips
   d. four key-on/key-off cycles

10. A pending code is set when a fault is detected on _____.
    a. a one-trip fault item
    b. the first fault of a two-trip failure
    c. the catalytic converter efficiency
    d. thermostat problem (too long to closed-loop status)

SCAN TOOLS AND ENGINE PERFORMANCE DIAGNOSIS

After studying this chapter, the reader will be able to:

1. List the steps of the diagnostic process.
2. Discuss the types of scan tools that are used to assess vehicle components.
3. Explain the troubleshooting procedures to follow if no diagnostic trouble code has been set.
4. Explain the troubleshooting procedures to follow if a diagnostic trouble code has been set.
5. Describe the methods that can be used to reprogram (reflash) a vehicle computer.

This chapter will help you prepare for the ASE computerized engine controls diagnosis (A8) certification test content area "E."

KEY TERMS

Data link connector (DLC) 683

Drive cycle 696

Long-term fuel trim (LTFT) 692

Paper test 682

Pending code 682

Short-term fuel trim (STFT) 692

Smoke machine 681

Technical service bulletins (TSBs) 683

Trip 692

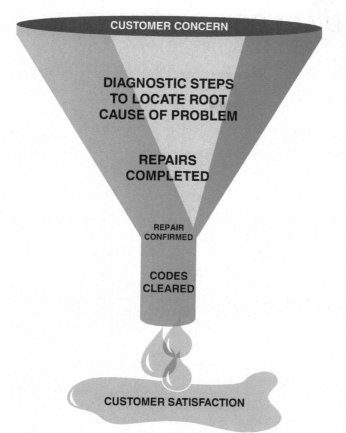

FIGURE 44–1 A funnel is one way to visualize the diagnostic process. The purpose is to narrow the possible causes of a concern until the root cause is determined and corrected.

THE EIGHT-STEP DIAGNOSTIC PROCEDURE

STRATEGY-BASED DIAGNOSIS The diagnostic process is a strategy that eliminates known good components or systems in order to find the root cause of automotive engine performance problems. All vehicle manufacturers recommend a diagnostic procedure, and the plan suggested in this chapter combines most of the features of these plans plus additional steps developed over years of real-world problem solving.

Many different things can cause an engine performance problem or concern. The service technician has to narrow the possibilities to find the cause of the problem and correct it. A funnel is a way of visualizing a diagnostic procedure. ● **SEE FIGURE 44–1**. At the wide top are the symptoms of the problem; the funnel narrows as possible causes are eliminated until the root cause is found and corrected at the bottom of the funnel.

All problem diagnosis deals with symptoms that could be the result of many different causes. The wide range of possible solutions must be narrowed to the most likely and these must eventually be further narrowed to the actual cause. The following section describes eight steps the service technician can take to narrow the possibilities to one cause.

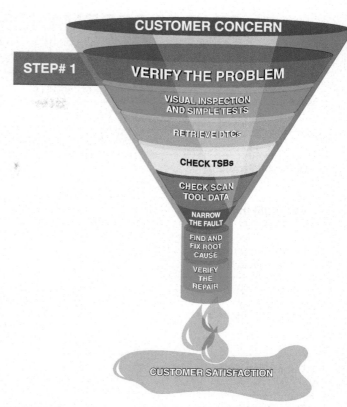

FIGURE 44–2 Step 1 is to verify the customer concern or problem. If the problem cannot be verified, then the repair cannot be performed.

STEP 1 VERIFY THE PROBLEM (CONCERN) Before a minute is spent on diagnosis, be certain that a problem exists. If the problem cannot be verified, it cannot be solved or tested to verify that the repair was complete. ● **SEE FIGURE 44–2**.

The driver of the vehicle knows much about the vehicle and how it is driven. *Before* diagnosis, always ask the following questions:

- Is the malfunction indicator light (check engine) on?
- What was the temperature outside?
- Was the engine warm or cold?
- Was the problem during starting, acceleration, cruise, or some other condition?
- How far had the vehicle been driven?
- Were any dash warning lights on? If so, which one(s)?
- Has there been any service or repair work performed on the vehicle lately?

NOTE: This last question is very important. Many engine performance faults are often the result of something being knocked loose or a hose falling off during repair work. Knowing that the vehicle was just serviced before the problem began may be an indicator as to where to look for the solution to a problem.

After the nature and scope of the problem are determined, the complaint should be verified before further diagnostic tests are performed. A sample form that customers could fill out with details of the problem is shown in ● **FIGURE 44–3**.

ENGINE PERFORMANCE DIAGNOSIS WORKSHEET
(To Be Filled Out By the Vehicle Owner)

Name: _____ Mileage: _____ Date: _____

Make: _____ Model: _____ Year: _____ Engine: _____

(Please Circle All That Apply in All Categories)	
Describe Problem:	
When Did the Problem First Occur?	• Just Started • Last Week • Last Month • Other _____
List Previous Repairs in the Last 6 Months:	
Starting Problems	• Will Not Crank • Cranks, but Will Not Start • Starts, but Takes a Long Time
Engine Quits or Stalls	• Right after Starting • When Put into Gear • During Steady Speed Driving • Right after Vehicle Comes to a Stop • While Idling • During Acceleration • When Parking
Poor Idling Conditions	• Is Too Slow at All Times • Is Too Fast • Intermittently Too Fast or Too Slow • Is Rough or Uneven • Fluctuates Up and Down
Poor Running Conditions	• Runs Rough • Lacks Power • Bucks and Jerks • Poor Fuel Economy • Hesitates or Stumbles on Acceleration • Backfires • Misfires or Cuts Out • Engine Knocks, Pings, Rattles • Surges • Dieseling or Run-On
Auto. Transmission Problems	• Improper Shifting (Early/Late) • Changes Gear Incorrectly • Vehicle Does Not Move when in Gear • Jerks or Bucks
Usually Occurs	• Morning • Afternoon • Anytime
Engine Temperature	• Cold • Warm • Hot
Driving Conditions During Occurrence	• Short—Less Than 2 Miles • 2–10 Miles • Long—More Than 10 Miles • Stop and Go • While Turning • While Braking • At Gear Engagement • With A/C Operating • With Headlights On • During Acceleration • During Deceleration • Mostly Downhill • Mostly Uphill • Mostly Level • Mostly Curvy • Rough Road
Driving Habits	• Mostly City Driving • Highway • Park Vehicle Inside • Park Vehicle Outside **Drive Per Day:** • Less Than 10 Miles • 10–50 • More Than 50
Gasoline Used	**Fuel Octane:** • 87 • 89 • 91 • More Than 91 **Brand:** _____
Temperature when Problem Occurs	• 32–55° F • Below Freezing (32° F) • Above 55° F
Check Engine Light/ Dash Warning Light	• Light on Sometimes • Light on Always • Light Never On
Smells	• "Hot" • Gasoline • Oil Burning • Electrical
Noises	• Rattle • Knock • Squeak • Other

FIGURE 44–3 A form that the customer should fill out if there is a driveability concern to help the service technician more quickly find the root cause.

NOTE: Because drivers differ, it is sometimes the best policy to take the customer on the test-drive to verify the concern.

STEP 2 PERFORM A THOROUGH VISUAL INSPECTION AND BASIC TESTS

The visual inspection is the most important aspect of diagnosis! Most experts agree that between 10% and 30% of all engine performance, problems can be found simply by performing a *thorough* visual inspection. The inspection should include the following:

- **Check for obvious problems (basics, basics, basics).**

  Fuel leaks

  Vacuum hoses that are disconnected or split

  Corroded connectors

  Unusual noises, smoke, or smell

  Check the air cleaner and air duct (squirrels and other small animals can build nests or store dog food in them). ● **SEE FIGURE 44–4.**

- **Check everything that does and does not work.** This step involves turning things on and observing that everything is working properly.

- **Look for evidence of previous repairs.** Any time work is performed on a vehicle, there is always a risk that something will be disturbed, knocked off, or left disconnected.

- **Check oil level and condition.** Another area for visual inspection is oil level and condition.

  Oil level. Oil should be to the proper level.

  Oil condition. Using a match or lighter, try to light the oil on the dipstick; if the oil flames up, gasoline is present in the engine oil. Drip some engine oil from the dipstick

FIGURE 44–4 This is what was found when removing an air filter from a vehicle that had a lack-of-power concern. Obviously, the nuts were deposited by squirrels or some other animal, blocking a lot of the airflow into the engine.

onto the hot exhaust manifold. If the oil bubbles or boils, coolant (water) is present in the oil. Check for grittiness by rubbing the oil between your fingers.

NOTE: **Gasoline in the oil will cause the engine to run rich by drawing fuel through the positive crankcase ventilation (PCV) system.**

- **Check coolant level and condition.** Many mechanical engine problems are caused by overheating. The proper operation of the cooling system is critical to the life of any engine.

NOTE: **Check the coolant level in the radiator only if the radiator is cool. If the radiator is hot and the radiator cap is removed, the drop in pressure above the coolant will cause the coolant to boil immediately, which can cause severe burns because the coolant expands explosively upward and outward from the radiator opening.**

TECH TIP

"Original Equipment" Is Not a Four-Letter Word

To many service technicians, an original-equipment part is considered to be only marginal, and to get the really "good stuff" an aftermarket (renewal market) part has to be purchased. However, many problems can be traced to the use of an aftermarket part that has failed early in its service life. Technicians who work at dealerships usually go immediately to an aftermarket part that is observed during a visual inspection. It has been their experience that simply replacing the aftermarket part with the factory original-equipment (OE) part often solves the problem.

Original equipment parts are *required* to pass quality and durability standards and tests at a level not required of aftermarket parts. The technician should be aware that the presence of a new part does not necessarily mean that the part is good.

TECH TIP

Smoke Machine Testing

Vacuum (air) leaks can cause a variety of driveability problems and are often difficult to locate. One good method is to use a machine that generates a stream of smoke. Connecting the outlet of the **smoke machine** to the hose that was removed from the vacuum brake booster allows smoke to enter the intake manifold. Any vacuum leaks will be spotted by observing smoke coming out of the leak. ● **SEE FIGURE 44–5.**

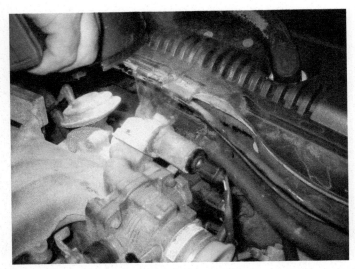

FIGURE 44–5 Using a bright light makes seeing where the smoke is coming from easier. In this case, smoke was added to the intake manifold with the inlet blocked with a yellow plastic cap and smoke was seen escaping past a gasket at the idle air control.

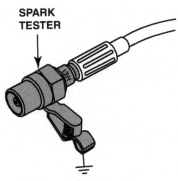

FIGURE 44–6 A spark tester connected to a spark plug wire or coil output. A typical spark tester will fire only if at least 25,000 volts is available from the coil, making a spark tester a useful tool. Do not use one that just lights when a spark is present, because it does not require more than about 2,000 volts to light.

- **Use the paper test.** A soundly running engine should produce even and steady exhaust at the tailpipe. For the **paper test**, hold a piece of paper (even a dollar bill works) or a 3-by-5 inch card within 1 inch (2.5 cm) of the tailpipe with the engine running at idle. The paper should blow evenly away from the end of the tailpipe without "puffing" or being drawn inward toward the end of the tailpipe. If the paper is at times drawn *toward* the tailpipe, the valves in one or more cylinders could be burned. Other reasons why the paper might be drawn toward the tailpipe include the following:
  1. The engine could be misfiring because of a lean condition that could occur normally when the engine is cold.
  2. Pulsing of the paper toward the tailpipe could also be caused by a hole in the exhaust system. If exhaust escapes through a hole in the exhaust system, air could be drawn—in the intervals between the exhaust puffs—from the tailpipe to the hole in the exhaust, causing the paper to be drawn toward the tailpipe.

- **Ensure adequate fuel level.** Make certain that the fuel tank is at least one-fourth to one-half full; if the fuel level is low, it is possible that any water or alcohol at the bottom of the fuel tank is more concentrated and can be drawn into the fuel system.

- **Check the battery voltage.** The voltage of the battery should be at least 12.4 volts and the charging voltage (engine running) should be 13.5 to 15.0 volts at 2000 RPM. Low battery voltage can cause a variety of problems including reduced fuel economy and incorrect (usually too high) idle speed. Higher-than-normal battery voltage can also cause the PCM problems and could cause damage to electronic modules.

- **Check the spark using a spark tester.** Remove one spark plug wire and attach the removed plug wire to the spark tester. Attach the grounding clip of the spark tester to a good clean engine ground, start or crank the engine, and observe the spark tester. ● **SEE FIGURE 44–6**. The spark at the spark tester should be steady and consistent. If an intermittent spark occurs, then this condition should be treated as a no-spark condition. If this test does not show satisfactory spark, carefully inspect and test all components of the primary and secondary ignition systems.

NOTE: Do not use a standard spark plug to check for proper ignition system voltage. An electronic ignition spark tester is designed to force the spark to jump about 0.75 inch (19 mm). This amount of gap requires between 25,000 and 30,000 volts (25 to 30 kV) at atmospheric pressure, which is enough voltage to ensure that a spark can occur under compression inside an engine.

- **Check the fuel-pump pressure.** Checking the fuel-pump pressure is relatively easy on many port fuel-injected engines. Often the cause of intermittent engine performance is due to a weak electric fuel pump or clogged fuel filter. Checking fuel pump pressure early in the diagnostic process eliminates low fuel pressure as a possibility.

STEP 3 RETRIEVE THE DIAGNOSTIC TROUBLE CODES (DTCs)
If a diagnostic trouble code (DTC) is present in the computer memory, it may be signaled by illuminating a malfunction indicator lamp (MIL), commonly labeled "check engine" or "service engine soon." ● **SEE FIGURE 44–7**. Any code(s) that is displayed when the MIL is *not* on is called a **pending code**. Because the MIL is not on, this indicates that the fault has not repeated to cause the PCM to turn on the MIL. Although this pending code is helpful to the technician to know that a fault has, in the past, been detected, further testing will be needed to find the root cause of the problem.

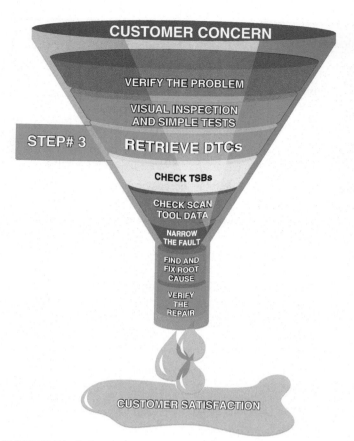

FIGURE 44–7 Step 3 in the diagnostic process is to retrieve any stored diagnostic trouble codes.

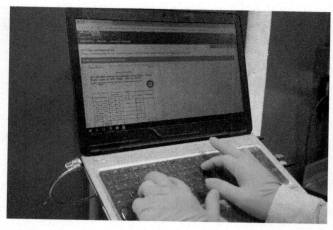

FIGURE 44–8 After checking for stored diagnostic trouble codes (DTCs), the wise technician checks service information for any technical service bulletins that may relate to the vehicle being serviced.

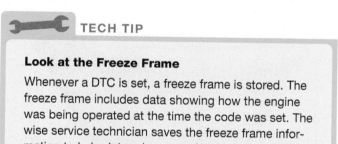

🔧 TECH TIP

Look at the Freeze Frame

Whenever a DTC is set, a freeze frame is stored. The freeze frame includes data showing how the engine was being operated at the time the code was set. The wise service technician saves the freeze frame information to help determine not only what might have caused the code to set but also to allow the technician to drive the vehicle under similar conditions to verify that the problem has been corrected.

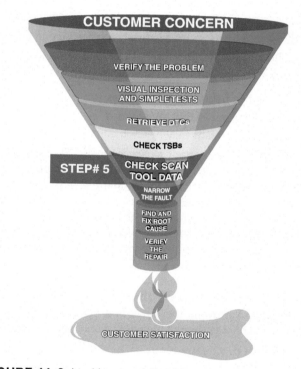

FIGURE 44–9 Looking carefully at the scan tool data is very helpful in locating the source of a problem.

STEP 4 CHECK FOR TECHNICAL SERVICE BULLETINS (TSBs) Check for corrections in **technical service bulletins (TSBs)** that match the symptoms. ● SEE FIGURE 44–8. According to studies performed by automobile manufacturers, as many as 30% of vehicles can be repaired following the information, suggestions, or replacement parts found in a service bulletin. DTCs must be known before searching for service bulletins, because bulletins often include information on solving problems that involve a stored diagnostic trouble code.

STEP 5 LOOK CAREFULLY AT SCAN TOOL DATA
Vehicle manufacturers have been giving the technician more and more data on a scan tool connected to the **data link connector (DLC)**. ● SEE FIGURE 44–9. Beginning technicians are often observed scrolling through scan data without a real clue about what they are looking for. When asked, they usually reply that they are looking for something unusual, as if the screen will flash a big message "LOOK HERE—THIS IS NOT CORRECT." That statement does not appear on scan tool displays. The best way to look at scan data is in a definite sequence and with specific,

Rich/Lean Air-Fuel Ratio				
Total Fuel Trim (LTFT+STFT) at Idle	2,500 RPM Fuel Trim	Loaded Fuel Trim	Drivability Symptoms	Possible Causes
0–5%	0–5%	0–5%	No issues	Preferred fuel trim values
6–10%	6–10%	6–10%	No issues	Acceptable fuel trim valves
−10+%	−10+%	−10+%	Poor fuel economy	PCM is reducing fuel do to faults in the fuel system over-fueling the engine
+10%+	+10%+	+10%+	Low power, possible hesitation on acceleration	PCM is increasing fuel delivery do to faults in the air induction system

CHART 44–1

Normal short term fuel trim (STFT and long term fuel trim (LTFT) are considered to be less than +/- 10%.

selected bits of data that can tell the most about the operation of the engine, such as the following:

- Engine coolant temperature (ECT) is the same as intake air temperature (IAT) after the vehicle sits for several hours.
- Idle air control (IAC) valve is being commanded to an acceptable range.
- Oxygen sensor (O2S) is operating properly:

  1. Readings below 200 mV at times
  2. Readings above 800 mV at times
  3. Rapid transitions between rich and lean

The oxygen sensor data is used by the PCM to make any necessary adjustments to the fuel delivery to ensure that the catalytic converter is receiving an air—fuel ratio that can be most efficient not only for driveability but also for the lowest possible exhaust emissions. The correction is called fuel trim, and this represents the percentage of fuel either added or subtracted from the amount that was programmed as being the required.
● **SEE CHART 44–1.**

STEP 6 NARROW THE PROBLEM TO A SYSTEM OR CYLINDER
Narrowing the focus to a system or individual cylinder is the hardest part of the entire diagnostic process.

- Perform a cylinder power balance test.
- If a weak cylinder is detected, perform a compression and a cylinder leakage test to determine the probable cause.

STEP 7 REPAIR THE PROBLEM AND DETERMINE THE ROOT CAUSE
The repair or part replacement must be performed following vehicle manufacturer's recommendations and be certain that the root cause of the problem has been found. Also follow the manufacturer's recommended repair procedures and methods.

STEP 8 VERIFY THE REPAIR AND CLEAR ANY STORED DTCS
● **SEE FIGURE 44–10.**

- Test-drive to verify that the original problem (concern) is fixed.
- Verify that no additional problems have occurred during the repair process.

- Check for and then clear all diagnostic trouble codes. (This step ensures that the computer will not make any changes based on a stored DTC, but should not be performed if the vehicle is going to be tested for emissions because all of the monitors will need to be run and pass.)
- Return the vehicle to the customer and double-check the following:

  1. The vehicle is clean.
  2. The radio is turned off.
  3. The clock is set to the right time and the radio stations have been restored if the battery was disconnected during the repair procedure.

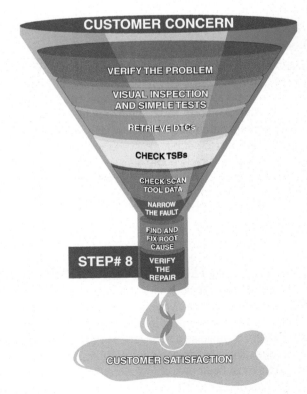

FIGURE 44–10 Step 8 is very important. Be sure that the customer's concern has been corrected.

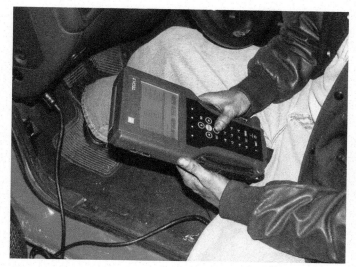

FIGURE 44–11 A TECH 2 scan tool is the factory scan tool used on General Motors vehicles.

FIGURE 44–12 A Bluetooth adapter that plugs into the DLC and transmits global OBD II information to a smart phone that has a scan tool app installed.

TECH TIP

One Test Is Worth 1,000 "Expert" Opinions

Whenever any vehicle has an engine performance or driveability concern, certain people always say:

"Sounds like it's a bad injector."

"I'll bet you it's a bad computer."

"I had a problem just like yours yesterday and it was a bad EGR valve."

Regardless of the skills and talents of those people, it is still more accurate to perform tests on the vehicle than to rely on feelings or opinions of others who have not even seen the vehicle. Even your own opinion should not sway your thinking. Follow a plan, perform tests, and the test results will lead to the root cause.

SCAN TOOLS

Scan tools are the workhorse for any diagnostic work on all vehicles. Scan tools can be divided into two basic groups:

1. **Factory scan tools.** These are the scan tools required by all dealers that sell and service the brand of vehicle. Examples of factory scan tools include:
   - **General Motors**—Tech 2 or MDI (Multiple Diagnostic Interface). ● **SEE FIGURE 44–11**.
   - **Ford**—New Generation Star (NGS) or IDS (Integrated Diagnostic System)
   - **Chrysler**—DRB-III, Star Scan, or wiTECH.
   - **Honda**—HDS or Master Tech
   - **Toyota**—Master Tech

All factory scan tools are designed to provide bidirectional capability that allows the service technician the

opportunity to operate components using the scan tool thereby confirming that the component is able to work when commanded. Also all factory scan tools are capable of displaying all factory parameters.

2. **Aftermarket scan tools.** These scan tools are designed to function on more than one brand of vehicle. Examples of aftermarket scan tools include:
   - **Snap-on** (various models including the MT2500 and Modis)
   - **OTC** (various models including Genisys and Task Master)
   - **AutoEnginuity** and other programs that use a laptop or handheld computer for the display

While many aftermarket scan tools can display most if not all of the parameters of the factory scan tool, there can be a difference when trying to troubleshoot some faults. ● **SEE FIGURE 44–12**.

RETRIEVAL OF DIAGNOSTIC INFORMATION

To retrieve diagnostic information from the Powertrain Control Module (PCM), a scan tool is needed. If a factory or factory-level scan tool is used, then all of the data can be retrieved. If a global (generic) only type scan tool is used, only the emissions-related data can be retrieved. To retrieve diagnostic information from the PCM, use the following steps:

STEP 1 Locate and gain access to the data link connector (DLC).

STEP 2 Connect the scan tool to the DLC and establish communication.

NOTE: If no communication is established, follow the vehicle manufacturer's specified instructions.

Parameter Identification (PID)

Scan Tool Parameter	Units Displayed	Typical Data Value
Engine Idling/Radiator Hose Hot/Closed Throttle/ Park or Neutral/Closed Loop/Accessories Off/ Brake Pedal Released		
3X Crank Sensor	RPM	Varies
24X Crank Sensor	RPM	Varies
Actual EGR Position	Percent	0
BARO	kPa/Volts	65–110 kPa/ 3.5–4.5 volts
CMP Sensor Signal Present	Yes/No	Yes
Commanded Fuel Pump	On/Off	On
Cycles of Misfire Data	Counts	0–99
Desired EGR Position	Percent	0
ECT	°C/°F	Varies
EGR Duty Cycle	Percent	0
Engine Run Time	Hr: Min: Sec	Varies
EVAP Canister Purge	Percent	Low and Varying
EVAP Fault History	No Fault/ Excess Vacuum/ Purge Valve Leak/ Small Leak/ Weak Vacuum	No Fault
Fuel Tank Pressure	Inches of H_2O/ Volts	Varies
HO2S Sensor 1	Ready/ Not Ready	Ready
HO2S Sensor 1	Millivolts	0–1,000 and Varying
HO2S Sensor 2	Millivolts	0–1,000 and Varying
HO2S X Counts	Counts	Varies
IAC Position	Counts	15–25 preferred
IAT	°C/°F	Varies
Knock Retard	Degrees	0
Long-Term FT	Percent	0–10
MAF	Grams per second	3–7
MAF Frequency	Hz	1,200–3,000 (depends on altitude and engine load)
MAP	kPa/Volts	20–48 kPa/0.75–2 Volts (depends on altitude)
Misfire Current Cyl. 1–10	Counts	0

(CONTINUED)

Scan Tool Parameter	Units Displayed	Typical Data Value
Misfire History Cyl. 1–10	Counts	0
Short-Term FT	Percent	0–10
Start-Up ECT	°C/°F	Varies
Start-Up IAT	°C/°F	Varies
Total Misfire Current Count	Counts	0
Total Misfire Failures	Counts	0
Total Misfire Passes	Counts	0
TP Angle	Percent	0
TP Sensor	Volts	0.20–0.74
Vehicle Speed	Mph/Km/h	0

Note: Viewing the PID screen on the scanner is useful in determining if a problem is occurring at the present time.

STEP 3 Follow the on-screen instructions of the scan tool to correctly identify the vehicle.

STEP 4 Observe the scan data, as well as any diagnostic trouble codes.

STEP 5 Follow vehicle manufacturer's instructions if any DTCs are stored. If no DTCs are stored, compare all sensor values with a factory acceptable range chart to see if any sensor values are out of range.

TROUBLESHOOTING USING DIAGNOSTIC TROUBLE CODES

Pinning down causes of the actual problem can be accomplished by trying to set the opposite code. For example, if a code indicates an open throttle position (TP) sensor (high resistance), clear the code and create a shorted (low-resistance) condition. This can be accomplished by using a jumper wire and connecting the signal terminal to the 5-volt reference terminal. This should set a diagnostic trouble code.

- **If the opposite code sets,** this indicates that the wiring and connector for the sensor is okay and the sensor itself is defective (open).

- **If the same code sets,** this indicates that the wiring or electrical connection is open (has high resistance) and is the cause of the setting of the DTC.

METHODS FOR CLEARING DIAGNOSTIC TROUBLE CODES
Clearing diagnostic trouble codes from a vehicle computer sometimes needs to be performed. There are three methods that can be used to clear stored diagnostic trouble codes.

CAUTION: Clearing diagnostic trouble codes (DTCs) also will clear all of the noncontinuous monitors.

- **Clearing codes—Method 1.** The preferred method of clearing codes is by using a scan tool. This is the method recommended by most vehicle manufacturers if the procedure can be performed on the vehicle. The computer of some vehicles cannot be cleared with a scan tool.

- **Clearing codes—Method 2.** If a scan tool is not available or a scan tool cannot be used on the vehicle being serviced, the power to the computer can be disconnected.

  1. Disconnect the fusible link (if so equipped) that feeds the computer.
  2. Disconnect the fuse or fuses that feed the PCM.

  NOTE: The fuse may not be labeled as a PCM fuse. For example, many Toyotas can be cleared by disconnecting the fuel-injection fuse. Some vehicles require that two fuses be disconnected to clear any stored codes.

- **Clearing codes—Method 3.** If the other two methods cannot be used, the negative (−) battery cable can be disconnected to clear stored diagnostic trouble codes.

NOTE: Because of the adaptive learning capacity of the PCM, a vehicle may fail an exhaust emissions test if the vehicle is not driven enough to allow the computer to run all of the monitors.

CAUTION: By disconnecting the battery, the radio presets and clock information will be lost. They should be reset before returning the vehicle to the customer. If the radio has a security code, the code must be entered before the radio will function. Before disconnecting the battery, always check with the vehicle owner to be sure that the code is available.

RETRIEVING CODES PRIOR TO 1996

FLASH CODES Most vehicles from the early 1980s through 1995 used some method to retrieve diagnostic trouble codes. For example, General Motors diagnostic trouble codes could be retrieved by using a metal tool and contacting terminals A and B of the 12-pin DLC. ● **SEE FIGURE 44–13.**

This method is called flash code retrieval because the MIL will flash to indicate diagnostic trouble codes. The steps of the method are as follows:

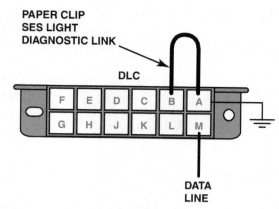

FIGURE 44–13 To retrieve flash codes from an OBD-I General Motors vehicle, connect terminals A and B with the ignition on–engine off. The M terminal is used to retrieve data from the sensors to a scan tool.

 **TECH TIP**

Quick and Easy Chrysler Code Retrieval

Most Chrysler-made vehicles (Dodge, Ram, and Chrysler) can display the diagnostic trouble code on the dash by turning the ignition switch on and then off and then on three times with the last time being on. This makes it easy for anyone to see if there are any stored trouble codes without having to use a scan tool. This works on vehicles built after 1996 too. ● **SEE FIGURE 44–14.**

 **TECH TIP**

Do Not Lie to a Scan Tool!

Because computer calibration may vary from year to year, using the incorrect year for the vehicle while using a scan tool can cause the data retrieved to be incorrect or inaccurate.

1. Turn the ignition switch to on (engine off). The "check engine" light or "service engine soon" light should be on. If the amber malfunction indicator light (MIL) is not on, a problem exists within the light circuit.

2. Connect terminals A and B at the DLC.

3. Observe the MIL. A code 12 (one flash, then a pause, then two flashes) reveals that there is no engine speed indication to the computer. Because the engine is not running, this simply indicates that the computer diagnostic system is working correctly.

FIGURE 44-14 Diagnostic trouble codes (DTCs) from Chrysler and Dodge vehicles can be retrieved by turning the ignition switch to on and then off three times.

RETRIEVAL METHODS Check service information for the exact procedure to follow to retrieve diagnostic trouble codes. Depending on the exact make, model, and year of manufacture, the procedure can include the use of one or more of the following:

- Scan tool
- Special tester
- Fused jumper wire
- Test light

DLC LOCATIONS

The data link connector (DLC) is a standardized 16-cavity connector to which a scan tool can be connected to retrieve diagnostic information from the vehicle's computers. The normal location is under the dash on the driver's side of the vehicle. It can be covered; and if it is, then it should be easy to remove the cover without the use of any tool, such as when located underneath the ash tray. ● **SEE FIGURE 44-15**.

OBD-II DIAGNOSIS

Starting with the 1996 model year, all vehicles sold in the United States must use the same type of 16-pin data link connector (DLC) and must monitor emissions-related components. ● **SEE FIGURE 44-16**.

RETRIEVING OBD-II CODES A scan tool is required to retrieve diagnostic trouble codes from most OBD-II vehicles. Every OBD-II scan tool will be able to read all generic Society of Automotive Engineers (SAE) DTCs from any vehicle.

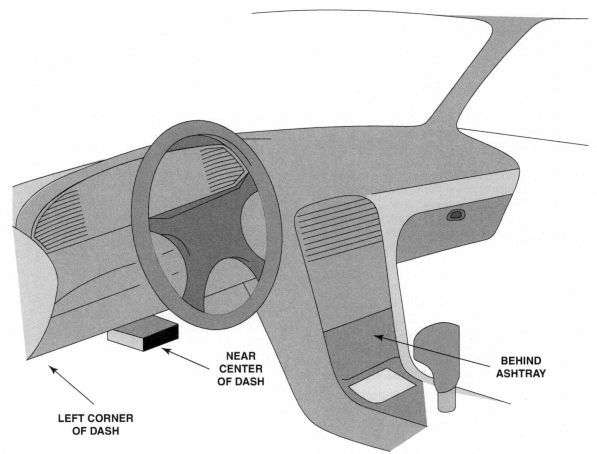

NEAR
CENTER
OF DASH

BEHIND
ASHTRAY

LEFT CORNER
OF DASH

FIGURE 44–15 The data link connector (DLC) can be located in various locations.

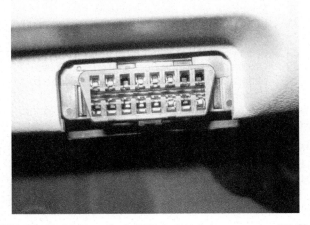

FIGURE 44–16 A typical OBD-II data link connector (DLC). The location varies with make and model and may even be covered, but a tool is not needed to gain access. Check service information for the exact location if needed.

Fuel and Air Metering System

P0100	Mass or Volume Airflow Circuit Problem
P0101	Mass or Volume Airflow Circuit Range or Performance Problem
P0102	Mass or Volume Airflow Circuit Low Input
P0103	Mass or Volume Airflow Circuit High Input
P0105	Manifold Absolute Pressure or Barometric Pressure Circuit Problem
P0106	Manifold Absolute Pressure or Barometric Pressure Circuit Range or Performance Problem
P0107	Manifold Absolute Pressure or Barometric Pressure Circuit Low Input
P0108	Manifold Absolute Pressure or Barometric Pressure Circuit High Input
P0110	Intake Air Temperature Circuit Problem
P0111	Intake Air Temperature Circuit Range or Performance Problem
P0112	Intake Air Temperature Circuit Low Input
P0113	Intake Air Temperature Circuit High Input
P0115	Engine Coolant Temperature Circuit Problem
P0116	Engine Coolant Temperature Circuit Range or Performance Problem
P0117	Engine Coolant Temperature Circuit Low Input
P0118	Engine Coolant Temperature Circuit High Input
P0120	Throttle Position Circuit Problem
P0121	Throttle Position Circuit Range or Performance Problem
P0122	Throttle Position Circuit Low Input
P0123	Throttle Position Circuit High Input
P0125	Excessive Time to Enter Closed-Loop Fuel Control
P0128	Coolant Temperature Below Thermostat Regulating Temperature
P0130	O2 Sensor Circuit Problem (Bank 1* Sensor 1)
P0131	O2 Sensor Circuit Low Voltage (Bank 1* Sensor 1)
P0132	O2 Sensor Circuit High Voltage (Bank 1* Sensor 1)

Fuel and Air Metering System—Continued

P0133   O2 Sensor Circuit Slow Response (Bank 1* Sensor 1)
P0134   O2 Sensor Circuit No Activity Detected (Bank 1* Sensor 1)
P0135   O2 Sensor Heater Circuit Problem (Bank 1* Sensor 1)
P0136   O2 Sensor Circuit Problem (Bank 1* Sensor 2)
P0137   O2 Sensor Circuit Low Voltage (Bank 1* Sensor 2)
P0138   O2 Sensor Circuit High Voltage (Bank 1* Sensor 2)
P0139   O2 Sensor Circuit Slow Response (Bank 1* Sensor 2)
P0140   O2 Sensor Circuit No Activity Detected (Bank 1* Sensor 2)
P0141   O2 Sensor Heater Circuit Problem (Bank 1* Sensor 2)
P0142   O2 Sensor Circuit Problem (Bank 1* Sensor 3)
P0143   O2 Sensor Circuit Low Voltage (Bank 1* Sensor 3)
P0144   O2 Sensor Circuit High Voltage (Bank 1* Sensor 3)
P0145   O2 Sensor Circuit Slow Response (Bank 1* Sensor 3)
P0146   O2 Sensor Circuit No Activity Detected (Bank 1* Sensor 3)
P0147   O2 Sensor Heater Circuit Problem (Bank 1* Sensor 3)
P0150   O2 Sensor Circuit Problem (Bank 2 Sensor 1)
P0151   O2 Sensor Circuit Low Voltage (Bank 2 Sensor 1)
P0152   O2 Sensor Circuit High Voltage (Bank 2 Sensor 1)
P0153   O2 Sensor Circuit Slow Response (Bank 2 Sensor 1)
P0154   O2 Sensor Circuit No Activity Detected (Bank 2 Sensor 1)
P0155   O2 Sensor Heater Circuit Problem (Bank 2 Sensor 1)
P0156   O2 Sensor Circuit Problem (Bank 2 Sensor 2)
P0157   O2 Sensor Circuit Low Voltage (Bank 2 Sensor 2)
P0158   O2 Sensor Circuit High Voltage (Bank 2 Sensor 2)
P0159   O2 Sensor Circuit Slow Response (Bank 2 Sensor 2)
P0160   O2 Sensor Circuit No Activity Detected (Bank 2 Sensor 2)
P0161   O2 Sensor Heater Circuit Problem (Bank 2 Sensor 2)
P0162   O2 Sensor Circuit Problem (Bank 2 Sensor 3)
P0163   O2 Sensor Circuit Low Voltage (Bank 2 Sensor 3)
P0164   O2 Sensor Circuit High Voltage (Bank 2 Sensor 3)
P0165   O2 Sensor Circuit Slow Response (Bank 2 Sensor 3)
P0166   O2 Sensor Circuit No Activity Detected (Bank 2 Sensor 3)
P0167   O2 Sensor Heater Circuit Problem (Bank 2 Sensor 3)
P0170   Fuel Trim Problem (Bank 1*)
P0171   System Too Lean (Bank 1*)
P0172   System Too Rich (Bank 1*)
P0173   Fuel Trim Problem (Bank 2)
P0174   System Too Lean (Bank 2)
P0175   System Too Rich (Bank 2)
P0176   Fuel Composition Sensor Circuit Problem
P0177   Fuel Composition Sensor Circuit Range or Performance
P0178   Fuel Composition Sensor Circuit Low Input
P0179   Fuel Composition Sensor Circuit High Input
P0180   Fuel Temperature Sensor Problem
P0181   Fuel Temperature Sensor Circuit Range or Performance
P0182   Fuel Temperature Sensor Circuit Low Input
P0183   Fuel Temperature Sensor Circuit High Input

Fuel and Air Metering (Injector Circuit)

P0201   Injector Circuit Problem—Cylinder 1
P0202   Injector Circuit Problem—Cylinder 2
P0203   Injector Circuit Problem—Cylinder 3
P0204   Injector Circuit Problem—Cylinder 4
P0205   Injector Circuit Problem—Cylinder 5

P0206   Injector Circuit Problem—Cylinder 6
P0207   Injector Circuit Problem—Cylinder 7
P0208   Injector Circuit Problem—Cylinder 8
P0209   Injector Circuit Problem—Cylinder 9
P0210   Injector Circuit Problem—Cylinder 10
P0211   Injector Circuit Problem—Cylinder 11
P0212   Injector Circuit Problem—Cylinder 12
P0213   Cold Start Injector 1 Problem
P0214   Cold Start Injector 2 Problem

Ignition System or Misfire

P0300   Random Misfire Detected
P0301   Cylinder 1 Misfire Detected
P0302   Cylinder 2 Misfire Detected
P0303   Cylinder 3 Misfire Detected
P0304   Cylinder 4 Misfire Detected
P0305   Cylinder 5 Misfire Detected
P0306   Cylinder 6 Misfire Detected
P0307   Cylinder 7 Misfire Detected
P0308   Cylinder 8 Misfire Detected
P0309   Cylinder 9 Misfire Detected
P0310   Cylinder 10 Misfire Detected
P0311   Cylinder 11 Misfire Detected
P0312   Cylinder 12 Misfire Detected
P0320   Ignition or Distributor Engine Speed Input Circuit Problem
P0321   Ignition or Distributor Engine Speed Input Circuit Range or Performance
P0322   Ignition or Distributor Engine Speed Input Circuit No Signal
P0325   Knock Sensor 1 Circuit Problem
P0326   Knock Sensor 1 Circuit Range or Performance
P0327   Knock Sensor 1 Circuit Low Input
P0328   Knock Sensor 1 Circuit High Input
P0330   Knock Sensor 2 Circuit Problem
P0331   Knock Sensor 2 Circuit Range or Performance
P0332   Knock Sensor 2 Circuit Low Input
P0333   Knock Sensor 2 Circuit High Input
P0335   Crankshaft Position Sensor Circuit Problem
P0336   Crankshaft Position Sensor Circuit Range or Performance
P0337   Crankshaft Position Sensor Circuit Low Input
P0338   Crankshaft Position Sensor Circuit High Input

Auxiliary Emissions Control

P0400   Exhaust Gas Recirculation Flow Problem
P0401   Exhaust Gas Recirculation Flow Insufficient Detected
P0402   Exhaust Gas Recirculation Flow Excessive Detected
P0405   Air Conditioner Refrigerant Charge Loss
P0410   Secondary Air Injection System Problem
P0411   Secondary Air Injection System Insufficient Flow Detected
P0412   Secondary Air Injection System Switching Valve or Circuit Problem
P0413   Secondary Air Injection System Switching Valve or Circuit Open
P0414   Secondary Air Injection System Switching Valve or Circuit Shorted
P0420   Catalyst System Efficiency below Threshold (Bank 1*)
P0421   Warm Up Catalyst Efficiency below Threshold (Bank 1*)

Auxiliary Emissions Control—Continued

P0422   Main Catalyst Efficiency below Threshold (Bank 1*)
P0423   Heated Catalyst Efficiency below Threshold (Bank 1*)
P0424   Heated Catalyst Temperature below Threshold (Bank 1*)
P0430   Catalyst System Efficiency below Threshold (Bank 2)
P0431   Warm Up Catalyst Efficiency below Threshold (Bank 2)
P0432   Main Catalyst Efficiency below Threshold (Bank 2)
P0433   Heated Catalyst Efficiency below Threshold (Bank 2)
P0434   Heated Catalyst Temperature below Threshold (Bank 2)
P0440   Evaporative Emission Control System Problem
P0441   Evaporative Emission Control System Insufficient Purge Flow
P0442   Evaporative Emission Control System Leak Detected
P0443   Evaporative Emission Control System Purge Control Valve Circuit Problem
P0444   Evaporative Emission Control System Purge Control Valve Circuit Open
P0445   Evaporative Emission Control System Purge Control Valve Circuit Shorted
P0446   Evaporative Emission Control System Vent Control Problem
P0447   Evaporative Emission Control System Vent Control Open
P0448   Evaporative Emission Control System Vent Control Shorted
P0450   Evaporative Emission Control System Pressure Sensor Problem
P0451   Evaporative Emission Control System Pressure Sensor Range or Performance
P0452   Evaporative Emission Control System Pressure Sensor Low Input
P0453   Evaporative Emission Control System Pressure Sensor High Input

Vehicle Speed Control and Idle Control

P0500   Vehicle Speed Sensor Problem
P0501   Vehicle Speed Sensor Range or Performance
P0502   Vehicle Speed Sensor Low Input
P0505   Idle Control System Problem
P0506   Idle Control System RPM Lower Than Expected
P0507   Idle Control System RPM Higher Than Expected
P0510   Closed Throttle Position Switch Problem

Computer Output Circuit

P0600   Serial Communication Link Problem
P0605   Internal Control Module (Module Identification Defined by J1979)

Transmission

P0703   Brake Switch Input Problem
P0705   Transmission Range Sensor Circuit Problem (PRNDL Input)
P0706   Transmission Range Sensor Circuit Range or Performance
P0707   Transmission Range Sensor Circuit Low Input

P0708   Transmission Range Sensor Circuit High Input
P0710   Transmission Fluid Temperature Sensor Problem
P0711   Transmission Fluid Temperature Sensor Range or Performance
P0712   Transmission Fluid Temperature Sensor Low Input
P0713   Transmission Fluid Temperature Sensor High Input
P0715   Input or Turbine Speed Sensor Circuit Problem
P0716   Input or Turbine Speed Sensor Circuit Range or Performance
P0717   Input or Turbine Speed Sensor Circuit No Signal
P0720   Output Speed Sensor Circuit Problem
P0721   Output Speed Sensor Circuit Range or Performance
P0722   Output Speed Sensor Circuit No Signal
P0725   Engine Speed Input Circuit Problem
P0726   Engine Speed Input Circuit Range or Performance
P0727   Engine Speed Input Circuit No Signal
P0730   Incorrect Gear Ratio
P0731   Gear 1 Incorrect Ratio
P0732   Gear 2 Incorrect Ratio
P0733   Gear 3 Incorrect Ratio
P0734   Gear 4 Incorrect Ratio
P0735   Gear 5 Incorrect Ratio
P0736   Reverse Incorrect Ratio
P0740   Torque Converter Clutch System Problem
P0741   Torque Converter Clutch System Performance or Stuck Off
P0742   Torque Converter Clutch System Stuck On
P0743   Torque Converter Clutch System Electrical
P0745   Pressure Control Solenoid Problem
P0746   Pressure Control Solenoid Performance or Stuck Off
P0747   Pressure Control Solenoid Stuck On
P0748   Pressure Control Solenoid Electrical
P0750   Shift Solenoid A Problem
P0751   Shift Solenoid A Performance or Stuck Off
P0752   Shift Solenoid A Stuck On
P0753   Shift Solenoid A Electrical
P0755   Shift Solenoid B Problem
P0756   Shift Solenoid B Performance or Stuck Off
P0757   Shift Solenoid B Stuck On
P0758   Shift Solenoid B Electrical
P0760   Shift Solenoid C Problem
P0761   Shift Solenoid C Performance or Stuck Off
P0762   Shift Solenoid C Stuck On
P0763   Shift Solenoid C Electrical
P0765   Shift Solenoid D Problem
P0766   Shift Solenoid D Performance or Stuck Off
P0767   Shift Solenoid D Stuck On
P0768   Shift Solenoid D Electrical
P0770   Shift Solenoid E Problem
P0771   Shift Solenoid E Performance or Stuck Off
P0772   Shift Solenoid E Stuck On
P0773   Shift Solenoid E Electrical

* The side of the engine where number one cylinder is located.

OBD-II ACTIVE TESTS

The vehicle computer must run tests on the various emission-related components and turn on the malfunction indicator lamp (MIL) if faults are detected. OBD II is an *active* computer analysis system because it actually tests the operation of the oxygen sensors, exhaust gas recirculation system, and so forth whenever conditions permit. It is the purpose and function of the Powertrain Control Module (PCM) to monitor these components and perform these active tests.

For example, the PCM may open the EGR valve momentarily to check its operation while the vehicle is decelerating. A change in the manifold absolute pressure (MAP) sensor signal will indicate to the computer that the exhaust gas is, in fact, being introduced into the engine. Because these tests are active and certain conditions must be present before these tests can be run, the computer uses its internal diagnostic program to keep track of all the various conditions and to schedule active tests so that they will not interfere with each other.

OBD-II DRIVE CYCLE The vehicle must be driven under a variety of operating conditions for all active tests to be performed. A **trip** is defined as an engine-operating drive cycle that contains the necessary conditions for a particular test to be performed. For example, for the EGR test to be performed, the engine has to be at normal operating temperature and decelerating for a minimum amount of time. Some tests are performed when the engine is cold, whereas others require that the vehicle be cruising at a steady highway speed.

TYPES OF OBD-II CODES Not all OBD-II diagnostic trouble codes are of the same importance for exhaust emissions. Each type of DTC has different requirements for it to set, and the computer will only turn on the MIL for emissions-related DTCs.

TYPE A CODES. A type A diagnostic trouble code is emissions-related and will cause the MIL to be turned on at the *first trip* if the computer has detected a problem. Engine misfire or a very rich or lean air–fuel ratio, for example, would cause a type A diagnostic trouble code. These codes alert the driver to an emissions problem that may cause damage to the catalytic converter.

TYPE B CODES. A type B code will be stored and the MIL will be turned on during the *second consecutive trip*, alerting the driver to the fact that a diagnostic test was performed and failed.

NOTE: Type A and Type B codes are emissions-related and will cause the lighting of the malfunction indicator lamp, usually labeled "check engine" or "service engine soon."

TYPE C AND D CODES. Type C and type D codes are for use with nonemissions-related diagnostic tests. They will cause the lighting of a "service" lamp (if the vehicle is so equipped).

OBD-II FREEZE-FRAME To assist the service technician, OBD II requires the computer to take a "snapshot" or freeze-frame of all data at the instant an emissions-related DTC is set. A scan tool is required to retrieve this data. CARB and EPA regulations require that the controller store specific freeze-frame (engine-related) data when the first emissions-related fault is detected. The data stored in freeze-frame can only be replaced by data from a trouble code with a higher priority such as a trouble related to a fuel system or misfire monitor fault.

NOTE: Although OBD II requires that just one freeze-frame of data be stored, the instant an emissions-related DTC is set, vehicle manufacturers usually provide expanded data about the DTC beyond that required. However, retrieving enhanced data usually requires the use of the vehicle-specific scan tool.

The freeze-frame has to contain data values that occurred at the time the code was set (these values are provided in standard units of measurement). Freeze-frame data is recorded during the first trip on a two-trip fault. As a result, OBD-II systems record the data present at the time an emissions-related code is recorded and the MIL activated. This data can be accessed and displayed on a scan tool. Freeze-frame data is one frame or one instant in time. Freeze-frame data is not updated (refreshed) if the same monitor test fails a second time.

REQUIRED FREEZE-FRAME DATA ITEMS.

- Code that triggered the freeze-frame
- A/F ratio, airflow rate, and calculated engine load
- Base fuel-injector pulse width
- ECT, IAT, MAF, MAP, TP, and VS sensor data
- Engine speed and amount of ignition spark advance
- Open- or closed-loop status
- Short- and long-term fuel trim values
- For misfire codes—identify the cylinder that misfired

NOTE: All freeze-frame data will be lost if the battery is disconnected, power to the PCM is removed, or the scan tool is used to erase or clear trouble codes.

DIAGNOSING INTERMITTENT MALFUNCTIONS
Of all the different types of conditions that you will see, the hardest to accurately diagnose and repair are intermittent malfunctions. These conditions may be temperature related (only occur when the vehicle is hot or cold), or humidity related (only occur when it is raining). Regardless of the conditions that will cause the malfunction to occur, you must diagnose and correct the condition.

When dealing with an intermittent concern, you should determine the conditions when the malfunction occurs, and then try to duplicate those conditions. If a cause is not readily apparent to you, ask the customer when the symptom occurs. Ask if there are any conditions that seem to be related to, or cause the concern.

Another consideration when working on an OBD-II-equipped vehicle is whether a concern is intermittent, or if it only occurs when a specific diagnostic test is performed by the PCM. Since OBD-II systems conduct diagnostic tests only under very precise conditions, some tests may only be run once during an ignition cycle. Additionally, if the requirements needed to perform the test are not met, the test will not run during an ignition cycle. This type of onboard diagnostics could be mistaken as "intermittent" when, in fact, the tests are only infrequent (depending on how the vehicle is driven). Examples of this type of diagnostic test are HO2S heaters, evaporative canister purge, catalyst efficiency, and EGR flow. When diagnosing intermittent concerns on an OBD-II-equipped vehicle, a logical diagnostic strategy is essential. The use of stored freeze-frame information can also be very useful when diagnosing an intermittent malfunction if a code has been stored.

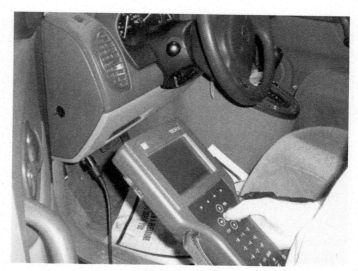

FIGURE 44–17 The first step in the reprogramming procedure is to determine the current software installed using a scan tool. Not all scan tools can be used. In most cases using the factory scan tool is needed for reprogramming unless the scan tool is equipped to handle reprogramming.

SERVICE/FLASH PROGRAMMING

Designing a program that allows an engine to meet strict air quality and fuel economy standards while providing excellent performance is no small feat. However, this is only part of the challenge facing engineers assigned with the task of developing OBD-II software. The reason for this is the countless variables involved with running the diagnostic monitors. Although programmers do their best to factor in any and all operating conditions when writing this complex code, periodic revisions are often required.

Reprogramming consists of downloading new calibration files from a scan tool, personal computer, or modem into the PCM's electronically erasable programmable read-only memory (EEPROM). This can be done on or off the vehicle using the appropriate equipment. Since reprogramming is not an OBD-II requirement however, many vehicles will need a new PCM in the event software changes become necessary. Physically removing and replacing the PROM chip is no longer possible.

The following are three industry-standard methods used to reprogram the EEPROM:

- Remote programming
- Direct programming
- Off-board programming

REMOTE PROGRAMMING. Remote programming uses the scan tool to transfer data from the manufacturer's shop PC to the vehicle's PCM. This is accomplished by performing the following steps:

- Connect the scan tool to the vehicle's DLC. ● **SEE FIGURE 44–17**.
- Enter the vehicle information into the scan tool through the programming application software incorporated in the scan tool. ● **SEE FIGURE 44–18**.

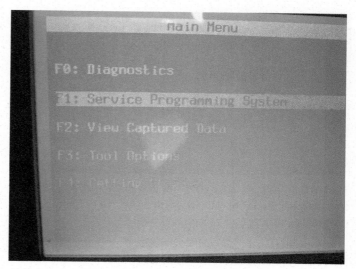

FIGURE 44–18 Follow the on-screen instructions.

- Download VIN and current EEPROM calibration using a scan tool.
- Disconnect the scan tool from the DLC and connect the tool to the shop PC.
- Download the new calibration from the PC to the scan tool. ● **SEE FIGURE 44–19**.
- Reconnect the scan tool to the vehicle's DLC and download the new calibration into the PCM.

CAUTION: Before programming, the vehicle's battery must be between 11 and 14 volts. Do not attempt to program while charging the battery unless using a special

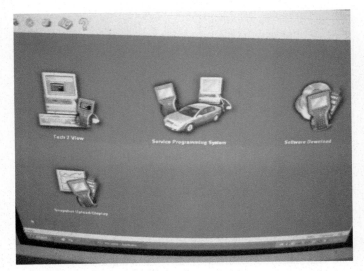

FIGURE 44-19 An Internet connection is usually needed to perform updates although some vehicle manufacturers use CDs which are updated regularly at a cost to the shop.

FIGURE 44-21 Connecting cables and a computer to perform off-board programming.

FIGURE 44-20 A battery charger that does not introduce any alternating current (AC) when charging the battery is extremely important when programming a PCM.

battery charger that does not produce excessive ripple voltage such as the Midtronics PSC-300 (30 amp) or PSC-550 (55 amp), or similar as specified by the vehicle manufacturer ● SEE FIGURE 44-20.

DIRECT PROGRAMMING. Direct programming does utilize a connection between the shop PC and the vehicle DLC.

OFF-BOARD PROGRAMMING. Off-board programming is used if the PCM must be programmed away from the vehicle. This is performed using the off-board programming adapter. ● SEE FIGURE 44-21.

J2534 REPROGRAMMING
Legislation has mandated that vehicle manufacturers meet the SAE J2534 standards for all emissions-related systems on all new vehicles starting with model year 2004. This standard enables independent service repair operators to program or reprogram emissions-related

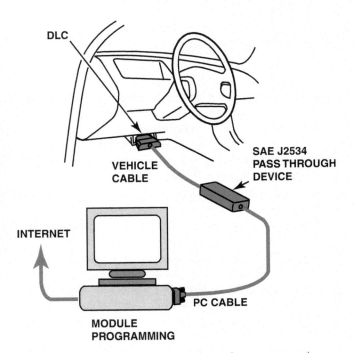

FIGURE 44-22 The J2534 pass-through reprogramming system does not need a scan tool to reflash the PCM on most 2004 and newer vehicles.

ECMs from a wide variety of vehicle manufacturers with a single tool. ● SEE FIGURE 44-22. A J2534 compliant pass-through system is a standardized programming and diagnostic system. It uses a personal computer (PC) plus a standard interface to a software device driver, and a hardware vehicle communication interface. The interface connects to a PC, and to a programmable ECM on a vehicle through the J1962 data link connector (DLC). This system allows programming of all vehicle manufacturer ECMs using a single set of programming hardware. Programming software made available by the vehicle manufacturer must be functional with a J2534 compliant pass-through system.

FIGURE 44–23 A typical J2534 universal reprogrammer that uses the J2534 standards.

The software for a typical pass-through application consists of two major components:

- The part delivered by the company that furnishes the hardware for J2534 enables the pass-through vehicle communication interface to communicate with the PC and provides for all Vehicle Communication Protocols as required by SAE J2534. It also provides for the software interface to work with the software applications as provided for by the vehicle manufacturers. ● **SEE FIGURE 44–23**.

- The second part of the pass-through enabling software is provided for by the vehicle manufacturers. This is normally a subset of the software used with their original equipment manufacturer (OEM) tools and their website will indicate how to obtain this software and under what conditions it can be used. Refer to the National Automotive Service Task Force (NASTF) website for the addresses for all vehicle manufacturers' service information and cost, *www.NASTF.org.*

Since the majority of vehicle manufacturers make this software available in downloadable form, having an Internet browser (Explorer/Netscape) and connection is a must.

MANUFACTURER'S DIAGNOSTIC ROUTINES

Each vehicle manufacturer has established their own diagnostic routines and they should be followed. Most include the following steps:

STEP 1 Retrieve diagnostic trouble codes.

STEP 2 Check for all technical service bulletins that could be related to the stored DTC.

STEP 3 If there are multiple DTCs, the diagnostic routine may include checking different components or systems instead of when only one DTC was stored.

STEP 4 Perform system checks.

STEP 5 Perform a road test matching the parameters recorded in the freeze-frame to check that the repair has corrected the malfunction.

STEP 6 Repeat the road test to cause the MIL to be extinguished.

NOTE: Do not clear codes (DTCs) unless instructed by the service information.

Following the vehicle manufacturer's specific diagnostic routines will ensure that the root cause is found and the repair verified. This is important for customer satisfaction.

COMPLETING SYSTEM REPAIRS

After the repair has been successfully completed, the vehicle should be driven under similar conditions that caused the original concern. Verify that the problem has been corrected. To perform this test-drive, it is helpful to have a copy of the freeze-frame parameters that were present when the DTC was set. By driving under similar conditions, the PCM may perform a test of the system and automatically extinguish the MIL. This is the method preferred by most vehicle manufacturers. The DTC can be cleared using a scan tool, but then that means that monitors will have to be run and the vehicle may fail an emissions inspection if driven directly to the testing station.

PROCEDURES FOR RESETTING THE PCM

The PCM can be reset or cleared of previously set DTCs and freeze-frame data in the following ways:

1. **Driving the Vehicle.** Drive the vehicle under similar conditions that were present when the fault occurred. If the conditions are similar and the PCM performed the noncontinuous monitor test and it passed three times, then the PCM will extinguish the MIL. This is the method preferred by most vehicle manufacturers; however, this method could be time consuming. If three passes cannot be achieved, the owner of the vehicle will have to be told that even though the check engine light (MIL) is on, the problem has been corrected and the MIL should go out in a few days of normal driving.

2. **Clear DTCs Using a Scan Tool.** A scan tool can be used to clear the diagnostic trouble code (DTC), which will also delete all of the freeze-frame data. The advantage of using a scan tool is that the check engine (MIL) will be out and the customer will be happy that the problem (MIL on) has been corrected. Do not use a scan tool to clear a DTC if the vehicle is going to be checked soon at a test station for state-mandated emissions tests.

3. **Battery Disconnect.** Disconnecting the negative battery cable will clear the DTCs and freeze-frame on many vehicles but not all. Besides clearing the DTCs, disconnecting the battery for about 20 minutes will also erase radio station presets and other memory items in many cases. Most vehicle manufacturers do not recommend that the battery be disconnected to clear DTCs and it may not work on some vehicles.

ROAD TEST (DRIVE CYCLE)

Use the freeze-frame data and test-drive the vehicle so that the vehicle is driven to match the conditions displayed on the freeze-frame. If the battery has been disconnected, then the vehicle may have to be driven under conditions that allow the PCM to conduct monitor tests. This drive pattern is called a **drive cycle**. The drive cycle is different for each vehicle manufacturer but a universal drive cycle may work in many cases. In many cases, performing a universal drive cycle will reset most monitors in most vehicles.

UNIVERSAL DRIVE CYCLE
PRECONDITIONING: PHASE 1.

MIL must be off.

No DTCs present.

Fuel fill between 15% and 85%.

Cold start—Preferred = eight-hour soak at 68°F to 86°F.

Alternative = ECT below 86°F.

1. With the ignition off, connect scan tool.
2. Start engine and drive between 20 and 30 mph for 22 minutes, allowing speed to vary.
3. Stop and idle for 40 seconds, gradually accelerate to 55 mph.
4. Maintain 55 mph for 4 minutes using a steady throttle input.
5. Stop and idle for 30 seconds, then accelerate to 30 mph.
6. Maintain 30 mph for 12 minutes.
7. Repeat steps 4 and 5 four times.

The Brake Pedal Trick

If the vehicle manufacturer recommends that battery power be disconnected, first disconnect the negative battery cable and then depress the brake pedal. Because the brake lights are connected to battery power, depressing the brake pedal causes all of the capacitors in the electrical system and computer(s) to discharge through the brake lights.

Using scan tool, check readiness. If insufficient readiness set, continue to universal drive trace phase II.

Important: (Do not shut off engine between phases).
Phase II:

1. Bring vehicle to a stop and idle for 45 seconds, then accelerate to 30 mph.
2. Maintain 30 mph for 22 minutes.
3. Repeat steps 1 and 2 three times.
4. Bring vehicle to a stop and idle for 45 seconds, then accelerate to 35 mph.
5. Maintain speed between 30 and 35 mph for 4 minutes.
6. Bring vehicle to a stop and idle for 45 seconds, then accelerate to 30 mph.
7. Maintain 30 mph for 22 minutes.
8. Repeat steps 6 and 7 five times.
9. Using scan tool, check readiness.

TECH TIP

Drive the Light Out

If working on a vehicle that is subject to state emissions testing, it is best to not clear codes. When diagnostic trouble codes are cleared, all of the monitors have to be rerun and this can be a time-consuming job. Instead of clearing the code, simply drive the vehicle until the PCM clears the code. This will likely take less time compared to trying to drive the vehicle under varying conditions to run all of the monitors.

SUMMARY

1. Funnel diagnostics is a visual approach to a diagnostic procedure and involves the following steps:

Step 1 Verify the problem (concern)

Step 2 Perform a thorough visual inspection and basic tests

Step 3 Retrieve the diagnostic trouble codes (DTCs)

Step 4 Check for technical service bulletins (TSBs)

Step 5 Look carefully at scan tool data

Step 6 Narrow the problem to a system or cylinder

Step 7 Repair the problem and determine the root cause
Step 8 Verify the repair and check for any stored DTCs

2. Care should be taken to not induce high voltage or current around any computer or computer-controlled circuit or sensor.

3. A thorough visual inspection is important during the diagnosis and troubleshooting of any engine performance problem or electrical malfunction.

4. If the MIL is on, retrieve the DTC and follow the manufacturer's recommended procedure to find the root cause of the problem.

5. OBD-II vehicles use a 16-pin DLC and common DTCs.

REVIEW QUESTIONS

1. Explain the procedure to follow when diagnosing a vehicle with stored DTCs using a scan tool.

2. Discuss what the PCM does during a drive cycle to test emissions-related components.

3. Explain the difference between a type A and type B OBD-II diagnostic trouble code.

4. List three things that should be checked as part of a thorough visual inspection.

5. Explain why a bulletin search should be performed after stored DTCs are retrieved.

CHAPTER QUIZ

1. Technician A says that the first step in the diagnostic process is to verify the problem (concern). Technician B says the second step is to perform a thorough visual inspection. Which technician is correct?
   a. Technician A only
   b. Technician B only
   c. Both Technicians A and B
   d. Neither Technician A nor B

2. Which item is *not* important to know before starting the diagnosis of an engine performance problem?
   a. List of previous repairs
   b. The brand of engine oil used
   c. The type of gasoline used
   d. The temperature of the engine when the problem occurs

3. A paper test can be used to check for a possible problem with _____.
   a. the ignition system (bad spark plug wire)
   b. a faulty injector on a multiport engine
   c. a burned valve
   d. All of the above

4. Which step should be performed *last* when diagnosing an engine performance problem?
   a. Checking for any stored diagnostic trouble codes
   b. Checking for any technical service bulletins (TSBs)
   c. Performing a thorough visual inspection
   d. Verifying the repair

5. Technician A says that if the opposite DTC can be set, the problem is the component itself. Technician B says if the opposite DTC cannot be set, the problem is with the wiring or grounds. Which technician is correct?
   a. Technician A only
   b. Technician B only
   c. Both Technicians A and B
   d. Neither Technician A nor B

6. The preferred method to clear diagnostic trouble codes (DTCs) is to _____.
   a. disconnect the negative battery cable for 10 seconds
   b. use a scan tool
   c. remove the computer (PCM) power feed fuse
   d. cycle the ignition key on and off 40 times

7. Which is the factory scan tool for Chrysler brand vehicles equipped with CAN?
   a. Star Scan   c. NGS
   b. Tech 2   d. Master Tech

8. Technician A says that reprogramming a PCM using the J2534 system requires a factory scan tool, while Technician B says it requires Internet access. Which technician is correct?
   a. Technician A only
   b. Technician B only
   c. Both Technicians A and B
   d. Neither Technician A nor B

9. Technician A says that knowing if there are any stored diagnostic trouble codes (DTCs) may be helpful when checking for related technical service bulletins (TSBs). Technician B says that only a factory scan tool should be used to retrieve DTCs. Which technician is correct?
   a. Technician A only
   b. Technician B only
   c. Both Technicians A and B
   d. Neither Technician A nor B

10. Which method can be used to reprogram a PCM?
    a. Remote   c. Off-board
    b. Direct   d. All of the above

chapter 45

HYBRID SAFETY AND SERVICE PROCEDURES

After studying this chapter, the reader will be able to:

1. Safely depower a hybrid electric vehicle.
2. Safely perform high-voltage disconnects.
3. Understand the unique service issues related to HEV high-voltage systems.
4. Correctly use appropriate personal protective equipment (PPE).
5. Perform routine vehicle service procedure on a hybrid electric vehicle.
6. Explain hazards while driving, moving, and hoisting a hybrid electric vehicle.

KEY TERMS

ANSI 699
ASTM 699
CAT III 700
DMM 700
Floating ground 703
HV 699
HV cables 699

IEC 700
Lineman's gloves 699
Loss of insulation/
  isolation (LOI) 701
NiMH 706
OSHA 699
Service plug 705

HIGH-VOLTAGE SAFETY

NEED FOR CAUTION There have been electrical systems on vehicles for over 100 years. Technicians have been repairing vehicle electrical systems without fear of serious injury or electrocution. However, when working with hybrid electric vehicles, this is no longer true. It is now possible to be seriously injured or electrocuted (killed) if proper safety procedures are not followed.

Hybrid electric vehicles and all electric vehicles use **high-voltage (HV)** circuits that if touched with an unprotected hand could cause serious burns or even death.

IDENTIFYING HIGH-VOLTAGE CIRCUITS **High-voltage cables** are identified by color of the plastic conduit and include:

- **Blue or yellow.** 42 volts (not a shock hazard but an arc will be maintained if a circuit is opened)
- **Orange.** 144 to 600 volts or higher

 WARNING

> Touching circuits or wires containing high voltage can cause severe burns or death.

HIGH-VOLTAGE SAFETY EQUIPMENT

RUBBER GLOVES Before working on the high-voltage system of a hybrid electric vehicle, be sure that high-voltage **lineman's gloves** are available. Be sure that the gloves are rated at least 1,000 volts and class "0" by ANSI/ASTM. The **American National Standards Institute (ANSI)** is a private, nonprofit organization that administers and coordinates the U.S. voluntary standardization and conformity assessment system. ASTM International, originally known as the **American Society for Testing and Materials (ASTM)**, was formed over a century ago, to address the need for component testing in industry. The **Occupational Safety and Health Administration (OSHA)** requirements specify that the HV gloves get inspected every six months by a qualified glove inspection laboratory. Use an outer leather glove to protect the HV rubber gloves. Inspect the gloves carefully before each use. High voltage and current (amperes) in combination is fatal. ● **SEE FIGURES 45–1 AND 45–2.**

NOTE: **The high-voltage insulated safety gloves must be recertified every six months to remain within Occupational Safety and Health Administration (OSHA) guidelines.**

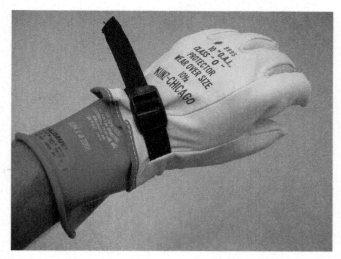

FIGURE 45–1 Appropriate personal protective equipment (PPE) must be worn whenever working on or around a hybrid vehicle high-voltage system, including high-voltage gloves with protective leather gloves to protect the rubber from being cut or pierced.

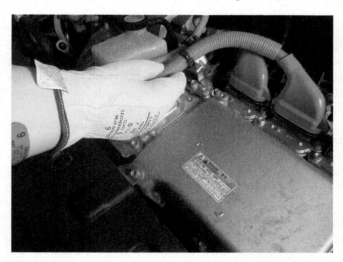

FIGURE 45–2 Whenever working around the high-voltage circuit, it is recommended that one hand be kept in a pocket to prevent the possibility of a high-voltage shock passing through the body.

Before using the rubber gloves, they should be tested for leaks using the following procedure:

1. Roll the glove up from the open end until the lower portion of the glove begins to balloon from the resulting air pressure. Be sure to "lean" into the sealed glove to raise the internal air pressure. If the glove leaks any air, discard the gloves. ● **SEE FIGURE 45–3.**
2. The gloves should not be used if they show any signs of wear and tear.

 WARNING

> Cables and wiring are orange in color. High-voltage insulated safety gloves and a face shield must be worn when carrying out any diagnostics involving the high-voltage systems or components.

FIGURE 45-3 Checking rubber lineman's gloves for pinhole leaks.

FIGURE 45-4 Be sure to only use a meter that is CAT III-rated when taking electrical voltage measurements on a hybrid electric or electric vehicle.

CAT III-RATED DIGITAL MULTIMETER Hybrid electric vehicles are equipped with electrical systems whose voltages can exceed 600 volts DC. A CAT III-certified **digital multimeter (DMM)** is required for making measurements on these high-voltage systems.

The **International Electrotechnical Commission (IEC)** has several categories of voltage standards for meter and meter leads. These categories are ratings for over-voltage protection and are rated CAT I, CAT II, CAT III, and CAT IV. The higher the category (CAT) rating, the greater the protection to the technician when measuring high-energy voltage. Under each category there are various voltage ratings.

CAT I Typically a CAT I meter is used for low-voltage measurements, such as voltage measurements at wall outlets in the home. Meters with a CAT I rating are usually rated at 300 to 800 volts. CAT I is for relatively low-energy levels, and while the voltage level has to be high enough for use when working on a hybrid electric vehicle, the protective energy level is lower than what is needed.

CAT II A higher-rated meter that would be typically used for checking voltages at the circuit-breaker panel in the home. Meters with a CAT II rating are usually rated at 300 to 600 volts. CAT II-rated meters have similar voltage ratings as the other CAT ratings, but the energy level of protection is higher with a CAT II compared to a CAT I.

CAT III **CAT III** is the minimum-rated meter that should be used for hybrid vehicles. Meters with a CAT III rating are usually rated at 600 to 1,000 volts and the highest energy level which is needed to protect the service technician.

CAT IV CAT IV meters are for clamp-on meters only. A clamp-on meter is used to measure current (amperes) in a

FIGURE 45-5 The meter leads should also be CAT III-rated when checking voltages on a hybrid electric vehicle.

? FREQUENTLY ASKED QUESTION

Is It the Voltage Rating That Determines the CAT Rating?

Yes and no. The voltages stated for the various CAT ratings are important, but the potential harm to a technician due to the energy level is what is most important. For example, some CAT II-rated meters may have a stated voltage higher than a meter that has a CAT III rating. Always use a meter that has a CAT III rating when working on a hybrid electric vehicle. ● **SEE FIGURES 45-4 AND 45-5.**

circuit by placing the clamp around the wire carrying the current. If a clamp-on meter also has meter leads for voltage measurements, that part of the meter will be rated as CAT III.

FIGURE 45–6 The HV disconnect plug has two small terminals used to signal the HV controller that the safety/service plug has been removed.

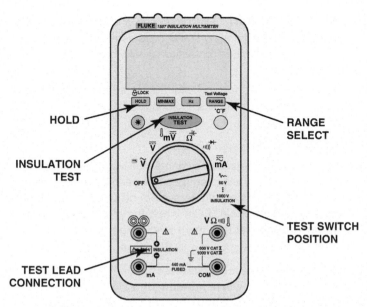

FIGURE 45–7 An insulation tester showing where the meter leads should be attached and where to select the voltage level to be used to test the insulation (usually 1,000 V). The resistance between the insulated HV circuit and ground should be higher than one million ohms (1.0 to 2.2 MΩ).

SAFETY INTERLOCK SYSTEM

PURPOSE AND FUNCTION The high-voltage system uses conductors or switches to detect opens in the high-voltage circuits. This is a safety system that keeps the power relays from closing with an open high-voltage circuit. The manual safety disconnect switch protects the high-voltage battery pack, and it includes a safety interlock switch that uses two small terminals. ● **SEE FIGURE 45–6**.

With an open detected, the hybrid controller does the following to keep the vehicle safe.

- ■ If the engine is running, it will detect a fault and set a diagnostic trouble code (DTC). It also opens the power relays, turning off the "ready" light.

- ■ If the vehicle is moving, it will allow it to continue until a stop, then it will disable the ICE.

- ■ If the vehicle is not moving, it will disable the ICE immediately.

LOCAL INTERLOCK A local interlock uses separate switches to detect when there has been an open in high-voltage circuits or components. The local interlock detects covers removed from modules that have high-voltage circuits. If an open has been detected, the controller (ECM) signals the hybrid controller to open the power relays and discharge the capacitors.

LOSS OF INSULATION TEST

PURPOSE The high-voltage (HV) circuits do not use a common ground. The circuit starts at the positive side of the HV battery pack and returns to the negative side of the pack in a loop. When the ground fault system detects high voltage leaking to ground, it sets a diagnostic trouble code that includes the location of the fault. This type of fault is called a **loss of insulation/isolation (LOI)**.

TEST PROCEDURE An electrical insulation tester, such as the Fluke 1587, is used to test for electrical continuity between the high-voltage wires or components and the body of the vehicle. Test the circuit with a high-voltage ohmmeter that measures megaohms, and perform the following steps:

STEP 1 Disable the HV system by removing the safety switch, and allow time for the capacitors to discharge, usually 10 to 20 minutes. Measure the high voltage with a voltmeter to check that the capacitor voltage is zero.

STEP 2 Use diagnostic trouble codes and use a vehicle-specific electrical schematic to identify the problem area.

STEP 3 To test the power cables from the battery pack to the inverter/converter assembly, for example, disconnect both ends of the cable.

STEP 4 The insulation tester applies a high voltage to test the insulation value. Select the 1,000-volt scale. Press and hold the "insulation test" button for 2 seconds to perform the test and the meter will display the measured resistance. ● **SEE FIGURE 45–7**.

EYE PROTECTION Eye protection should be worn when testing for high voltage, which is considered by many experts to be over 60 volts. Eye protection should include the following features:

1. Plastic frames (avoid metal frames as these are conductive and could cause a shock hazard)
2. Side shields
3. Meet the standard ANSI Z87.1

Most hybrid electric systems use voltages higher than this threshold. If the system has not been powered down or has not had the high-voltage system disabled, a shock hazard is always possible. Even when the high-voltage system has been disconnected, there is still high voltage in the HV battery box.

NOTE: Some vehicle manufacturers specify that full face shields be worn instead of safety glasses when working with high-voltage circuits or components.

SAFETY CONES Ford requires that cones be placed at the four corners of any hybrid electric vehicle when service work on the high-voltage system is being performed. They are used to establish a safety zone around the vehicles so that other technicians will know that a possible shock hazard may be present.

FIBERGLASS POLE Ford requires that a 10-foot insulated fiberglass pole be available outside the safety zone to be used to pull a technician away from the vehicle in the unlikely event of an accident where the technician is shocked or electrocuted.

FIGURE 45–8 The Ford Escape Hybrid instrument panel showing the vehicle in park and the tachometer on "EV" instead of 0 RPM. This means the gasoline engine could start at any time depending on the state of charge of the high-voltage batteries and other factors.

ELECTRIC SHOCK POTENTIAL

LOCATIONS WHERE SHOCKS CAN OCCUR Accidental and unprotected contact with any electrically charged ("hot" or "live") high-voltage component can cause serious injury or death. However, receiving an electric shock from a hybrid vehicle is highly unlikely because of the following:

1. Contact with the battery module or other components inside the battery box can occur only if the box is damaged and the contents are exposed, or the box is opened without following proper precautions.
2. Contact with the electric motor can occur only after one or more components are removed.
3. The high-voltage cables can be easily identified by their distinctive orange color, and contact with them can be avoided.
4. The system main relays (SMRs) disconnect power from the cables the moment the ignition is turned off.

 TECH TIP

Silence Is NOT Golden

Never assume the vehicle is shut off just because the engine is off. When working with a Toyota or Lexus hybrid electric vehicle, always look for the **READY** indicator status on the dash display. The vehicle is shut off when the **READY** indicator is off.

The vehicle may be powered by:

1. The electric motor only.
2. The gasoline engine only.
3. A combination of both the electric motor and the gasoline engine.

The vehicle computer determines the mode in which the vehicle operates to improve fuel economy and reduce emissions. The driver cannot manually select the mode. ● **SEE FIGURE 45–8.**

☠ **WARNING**

Power remains in the high-voltage electrical system for up to 10 minutes after the HV battery pack is shut off. Never touch, cut, or open any orange high-voltage power cable or high-voltage component without confirming that the high voltage has been completely discharged.

TECH TIP

High Voltage Is Insulated From the Vehicle Body

Both positive and negative high-voltage power cables are isolated from the metal chassis, so there is no possibility of shock by touching the metal chassis. This design is called a **floating ground**.

A ground fault monitor continuously monitors for high-voltage leakage to the metal chassis while the vehicle is running. If a malfunction is detected, the vehicle computer will illuminate the master warning light in the instrument cluster and the hybrid warning light in the LCD display. The HV battery pack relays will automatically open to stop electricity flow in a collision sufficient to activate the SRS airbags.

FREQUENTLY ASKED QUESTION

How Do You Keep the Engine Running on a Hybrid?

There are times when the service technician or a vehicle inspector needs to bypass the idle stop feature and to keep the engine running such as:

- Checking the air-conditioning pressures on a unit that has an engine-driven A/C compressor
- Attempting to get the engine (ICE) up to operating temperature in order to check for proper operation of the cooling system
- Safety inspection of the exhaust system

The mode to keep the ICE running can often be done using a scan tool such as the Snap-on Solus Ultra being used on a Lexus RX 450h hybrid. ● **SEE FIGURE 45–9**.

This mode is called the

- Service mode
- Maintenance mode
- Inspection mode

Most vehicle manufacturers warn to not drive the vehicle while in this mode because many of the torque limiting factors are also disabled, which could cause damage to the powertrain components if driven aggressively. ● **SEE CHART 45–1** for the method to use to keep the ICE operating and to prevent the idle stop mode without using a scan tool.

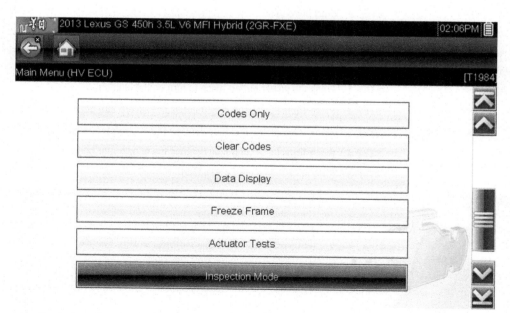

FIGURE 45–9 To enter the inspection mode, select this feature on a scan tool and follow the on-screen procedure.

VEHICLE MAKE	ENGINE START PROCEDURE
Toyota/Lexus	**STEP 1** Turn the ignition on (NOT READY)
	STEP 2 While in Park, press accelerator 2 times
	STEP 3 Press and hold brake pedal, shift to Neutral
	STEP 4 While in Neutral, press accelerator pedal 2 times
	STEP 5 Shift to Park, while in Park, depress accelerator pedal 2 times
	STEP 6 Turn READY-ON
Ford/Lincoln/Mercury	**STEP 1** Apply parking brake and place gear selector in Park
	STEP 2 Switch ignition to on
	STEP 3 Within 5 seconds, fully depress accelerator pedal and hold for 10 seconds
	STEP 4 Within 5 seconds, release accelerator pedal and shift to the Drive position and fully depress accelerator pedal
	STEP 5 Hold accelerator pedal down for 10 seconds
	STEP 6 Release accelerator pedal and shift into the Park position
	STEP 7 The amber "wrench" lamp will flash if procedure was successful
	STEP 8 ICE can now be started
	STEP 9 Exit by: 1—Shift into any other gear or, 2—Turn the ignition off
Honda/Acura	**STEP 1** Set parking brake
	STEP 2 Turn the ignition off
	STEP 3 Turn the ignition on two times with foot off the brake pedal
	STEP 4 With the shift lever in Park, depress the accelerator pedal two times to the floor
	STEP 5 Depress the brake pedal and move the gear selector to Neutral
	STEP 6 Depress the accelerator pedal to the floor two times
	STEP 7 Move the shift lever to Park
	STEP 8 Depress the accelerator pedal to the floor two times
	STEP 9 Depress the brake pedal and push the start button. The engine will start in the maintenance mode. To exit the maintenance mode, turn off the engine
Chevrolet/GMC Truck (PHT or 2-Mode)	**STEP 1** Open the hood
	STEP 2 Start the engine
	The engine will remain running until it is turned off as long as the hood is open.
Buick, Chevrolet (BAS system)	Allow the ICE to idle when the engine is in normal operating temperature for 2 minutes. Idle stop is disabled.
Nissan Altima	**STEP 1** Press the power button twice to turn on the ignition
	STEP 2 Place Trans in "P" and fully depress the accelerator pedal twice
	STEP 3 Place Trans in "N" and fully depress the accelerator pedal twice
	STEP 4 Place Trans in "P" and fully depress the accelerator pedal twice
	STEP 5 Start engine. Idle stop is disabled

CHART 45–1

Hybrid engine service mode chart. This procedure is needed to be followed if the technician or safety inspector requires that the internal combustion engine (ICE) needs to be kept running and prevented from entering stop/ start (idle stop) operation.

DEPOWER THE HIGH-VOLTAGE SYSTEM

THE NEED TO DEPOWER THE HV SYSTEM During routine vehicle service work, there is no need to go through any procedures needed to depower or to shut off the high-voltage circuits. However, if work is going to be performed on any of the following components, service information procedures must be followed to prevent possible electrical shock and personal injury.

- The high-voltage (HV) battery pack
- Any of the electronic controllers that use orange cables, such as the inverter and converters
- The air-conditioning compressor if electrically driven and has orange cables attached

To safely depower the vehicle, always follow the instructions found in service information for the exact vehicle being serviced. The steps usually include:

STEP 1 Turn the ignition off and remove the key (if equipped) from the ignition.

CAUTION: If a push-button start is used, remove the key fob at least 15 feet (5 m) from the vehicle to prevent the vehicle from being powered up.

STEP 2 Remove the 12-volt power source to the HV controller. This step could involve:

- Removing a fuse or a relay
- Disconnecting the negative battery cable from the auxiliary 12-volt battery

STEP 3 Remove the high-voltage fuse or **service plug** or switch.

> ☠ **WARNING**
>
> Even if all of the above steps are followed, there is still a risk for electrical shock at the high-voltage batteries. Always follow the vehicle manufacturer's instructions exactly and wear high-voltage gloves and other specified personal protective equipment (PPE).

COLLISION AND REPAIR INDUSTRY ISSUES

JUMP STARTING The 12-volt auxiliary battery may be jump started if the vehicle does not start. The 12-volt auxiliary battery is located under the hood or in the cargo (trunk) area

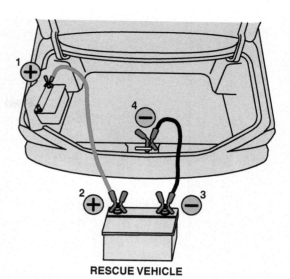

RESCUE VEHICLE

FIGURE 45–10 Jump starting a Toyota Prius using a 12-volt supply to boost the 12-volt auxiliary battery in the trunk.

> **?** **FREQUENTLY ASKED QUESTION**
>
> **When Do I Need to depower the High-Voltage System?**
>
> During routine service work, there is no need for a technician to depower the high-voltage system. The only time when this process is needed is if service repairs or testing are being performed on any circuit that has an orange cable attached. These include:
>
> - AC compressor if electrically powered
> - High-voltage battery pack or electronic controllers
>
> The electric power steering system usually operates on 12 volts or 42 volts and neither is a shock hazard. However, an arc will be maintained if a 42-volt circuit is opened. Always refer to service information if servicing the electric power steering system or any other system that may contain high voltage.

of some HEVs. Using a jump box or jumper cable from another vehicle, make the connections to the positive and negative battery terminals. ● **SEE FIGURE 45–10**.

On 2004 Toyota Prius vehicles, there is a stud located under the hood that can be used to jump start the auxiliary battery, which is located in the truck. ● **SEE FIGURE 45–11**.

NOTE: The high-voltage (HV) battery pack cannot be jump started on most HEVs. One exception is the Ford Escape/Mercury Mariner hybrids that use a special "jump-start" button located behind the left kick panel. When this button is pushed, the auxiliary battery is used to boost the HV battery through a DC–DC converter.

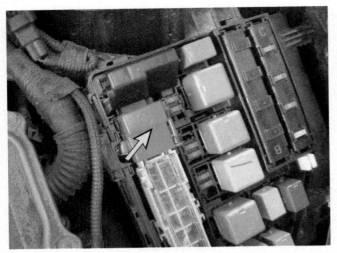

FIGURE 45–11 The underhood 12-volt jump-start terminal on this **2004** Toyota Prius has a red plastic cover with a "+" sign. The positive booster cable clamp will attach directly to the vertical metal bracket.

FIGURE 45–12 Using a warning cover over the steering wheel helps others realize that work is being performed on the high-voltage system and that no one is to attempt to start or move the vehicle.

 FREQUENTLY ASKED QUESTION

Will the Heat from Paint Ovens Hurt the High-Voltage Batteries?

Nickel-metal hydride (NiMH) batteries may be damaged if exposed to high temperatures, such as in a paint oven. The warning labels on hybrid vehicles specify that the battery temperature not exceed 150° F (66° C). Therefore, be sure to check the temperature of any paint oven before allowing a hybrid electric vehicle into one that may be hotter than specified. Check service information for details on the vehicle being repaired.

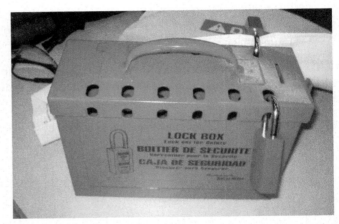

FIGURE 45–13 A lock box is a safe location to keep the ignition keys of a hybrid electric vehicle while it is being serviced.

MOVING THE HYBRID VEHICLE IN THE SHOP After an HEV has been serviced, it may be necessary to push the vehicle to another part of the shop or outside as parts are ordered. Make sure to tape any orange cable ends that were disconnected during the repair procedure. Permanent magnets are used in all the drive motors and generators and it is possible that a high-voltage arc could occur as the wheels turn and produce voltage. Another way to prevent this is to use wheel dollies. A sign that says "HIGH VOLTAGE—DO NOT TOUCH" could also be added to the roof of the vehicle. Remove the keys from the vehicle and keep in a safe location. ● **SEE FIGURES 45–12 AND 45–13**.

MOVING AND TOWING A HYBRID

TOWING If a disabled vehicle needs to be moved a short distance (to the side of the road, for example) and the vehicle can still roll on the ground, the easiest way is to shift the transmission into neutral and manually push the vehicle. To transport a vehicle away from an emergency location, a flatbed truck should be used if the vehicle might be repaired. If a flatbed is not available, the vehicle should be towed by wheel-lift equipment with the front wheels off the ground (FWD hybrid electric vehicles only). Do not use sling-type towing equipment. In the case of 4WD HEVs, such as the Toyota Highlander, only a flatbed vehicle should be used.

REMOVING THE HIGH-VOLTAGE BATTERIES

PRECAUTIONS The HV battery box should always be removed as an assembly, placed on a rubber-covered work bench, and handled carefully. Every other part, especially the capacitors,

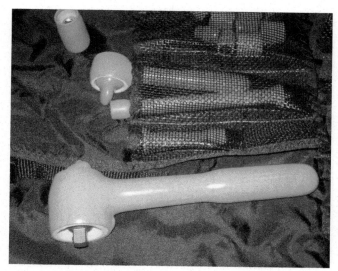

FIGURE 45–14 Insulated tools, such as this socket set, would provide an additional margin of safety to the service technician when working around high-voltage components and systems.

FIGURE 19–15 The high-voltage wiring on this Honda hybrid is colored orange for easy identification.

TECH TIP

High-Voltage Battery SOC Considerations

NiMH batteries do not store well for long lengths of time. After a repair job, or when the HV system has been powered down by a technician and powered up again, do not be surprised if a warning lamp lights, diagnostic trouble codes are set, and the malfunction indicator lamp (MIL) is illuminated. If everything was done correctly, a couple road tests may be all that is required to reset the MIL. The HV battery indicator on the dash may also read zero charge level. After a road test, the HV battery level indicator will most likely display the proper voltage level.

should be checked for voltage reading while wearing HV rubber gloves. Always check for voltage as the components become accessible before proceeding. When removing high-voltage components, it is wise to use insulated tools. ● **SEE FIGURE 45–14.**

STORING THE HIGH-VOLTAGE BATTERIES

If a hybrid is to be stored for any length of time, the state of charge of the HV batteries must be maintained. If possible, start the vehicle every month and run it for at least 30 minutes to help recharge the HV batteries. This is necessary because NiMH batteries suffer from self-discharge over time. High-voltage battery chargers are expensive and may be hard to find. If the HV battery SOC was over 60% when it was put into storage, the batteries may be stored for about a month without a problem. If, however, the SOC is less than 60%, a problem with a discharged HV battery may result.

HOISTING A HYBRID VEHICLE

When hoisting or using a floor jack, pay attention to the lift points. Orange cables run under the vehicle just inside the frame rails on most hybrids. ● **SEE FIGURE 45–15.**

Some Honda hybrid vehicles use an aluminum pipe painted orange that includes three HV cables for the starter/generator and also three more cables for the HV air-conditioning compressor. If any damage occurs to any high-voltage cables, the MIL will light up and a no-start will result if the PCM senses a fault. The cables are not repairable and are expensive. The cables can be identified by an orange outer casing, but in some cases, the orange casing is not exposed until a black plastic underbelly shield is removed first.

HV BATTERY DISPOSAL

The hybrid electric vehicle manufacturers are set up to ship NiMH battery packs to a recycling center. There is an 800 number located under the hood or on the HV battery pack that can be used to gain information on how to recycle these batteries.

Always follow the proper safety procedures, and then minor service to hybrid vehicles can be done with a reasonable level of safety.

ROUTINE SERVICE PROCEDURES

DIAGNOSIS PROCEDURES

Hybrid electric vehicles should be diagnosed the same as any other type of vehicle. This means following a diagnostic routine, which usually includes the following steps:

STEP 1 Verify the customer concern.

STEP 2 Check for diagnostic trouble codes (DTCs). An enhanced or factory level scan tool may be needed to get access to codes and sub codes.

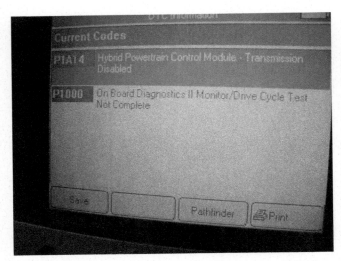

FIGURE 19–16 A scan tool display showing two hybrid-related faults in this Ford Escape hybrid.

FIGURE 45–17 Always use the specified viscosity of oil in a hybrid electric vehicle not only for best fuel economy, but also because of the need for fast lubrication because of the engine (idle) stop feature.

STEP 3 Perform a thorough visual inspection. If a DTC is stored, carefully inspect those areas that might be the cause of the trouble code.

STEP 4 Check for technical service bulletins (TSBs) that may relate to the customer concern.

STEP 5 Follow service information specified steps and procedures. This could include checking scan tool data for sensors or values that are not within normal range.

STEP 6 Determine and repair the root cause of the problem.

STEP 7 Verify the repair and clear any stored diagnostic trouble codes unless in an emission testing area. If in an emission test area, drive the vehicle until the powertrain control module (PCM) passes the fault and turns off the malfunction indicator lamp, thereby allowing the vehicle to pass the inspection.

STEP 8 Complete the work order and record the "three Cs" (complaint, cause, and correction). ● **SEE FIGURE 45–16**.

OIL CHANGE Performing an oil change is similar to changing oil in any vehicle equipped with an internal combustion engine. However, there are several items to know when changing oil in a hybrid electric vehicle including:

■ **Use vehicle manufacturer's recommended hoisting locations.** Use caution when hoisting a hybrid electric vehicle and avoid placing the pads on or close to the orange high-voltage cables that are usually located under the vehicle.

■ **Always use the specified oil viscosity.** Most hybrid electric vehicles require:

SAE 0W-16

SAE 0W-20

SAE 5W-20

Using the specified oil viscosity is important because the engine stops and starts many times and using the incorrect viscosity not only can cause a

decrease in fuel economy but also could cause engine damage. ● **SEE FIGURE 45–17**.

■ **Always follow the specified procedures.** Be sure that the internal combustion engine is off and that the "READY" lamp is off. If there is a smart key or the vehicle has a push-button start, be sure that the key fob is at least 15 feet (5 m) away from the vehicle to help prevent the engine from starting accidentally.

COOLING SYSTEM SERVICE Performing cooling system service is similar to performing this service in any vehicle equipped with an internal combustion engine. However, there are several items to know when servicing the cooling system on a hybrid electric vehicle including:

■ **Always check service information for the exact procedure to follow.** The procedure will include the following:

1. **The specified coolant.** Most vehicle manufacturers will recommend using premixed coolant because using water (half of the coolant) that has minerals could cause corrosion issues.

2. **The specified coolant replacement interval.** While this may be similar to the coolant replacement interval for a conventional vehicle, always check to be sure that this service is being performed at the specified time or mileage interval.

3. **The specified precautions.** Some Toyota Prius HEVs use a coolant storage bottle that keeps the coolant hot for up to three days. Opening a coolant hose could cause the release of this hot coolant and can cause serious burns to the technician.

4. Always read, understand, and follow all of the service information instructions when servicing the cooling system on a hybrid electric vehicle.

A Bad Day Changing Oil

A shop owner was asked by a regular customer who had just bought a Prius if the oil could be changed there. The owner opened the hood, made sure the filter was in stock (it is a standard Toyota filter used on other models), and said yes. A technician with no prior knowledge of hybrids drove the warmed-up vehicle into the service bay. The internal combustion engine never started, as it was in electric (stealth) mode at the time. Not hearing the engine running, the technician hoisted the vehicle into the air, removed the drain bolt, and drained the oil into the oil drain unit. When the filter was removed, oil started to fly around the shop. The engine was in "standby" mode during the first part of the oil change. When the voltage level dropped, the onboard computer started the engine so that the HV battery could recharge. The technician should have removed the key to keep this from happening. Be sure that the "ready" light is off before changing the oil or doing any other service work that may cause personal harm or harm to the vehicle if the engine starts.

Summary:

- **Complaint**—A technician was not aware that the hybrid vehicle was not off when changing the oil.
- **Cause**—The "ready" light was still on when the technician started to change the oil.
- **Correction**—The technician learned that all hybrids need to be shut off because just because the engine is not running does not mean that the vehicle itself has been turned off.

AIR FILTER SERVICE

Performing air filter service is similar to performing this service in any vehicle equipped with an internal combustion engine. However, there are several items to know when servicing the air filter on a hybrid electric vehicle including:

1. Always follow the service information recommended air filter replacement interval.

2. For best results use the factory type and quality air filter.

3. Double-check that all of the air ducts are securely fastened after checking or replacing the air filter.

AIR-CONDITIONING SERVICE

Performing air-conditioning system service is similar to performing this service in any vehicle equipped with an internal combustion engine. However, there are several items to know when servicing the air-conditioning system on a hybrid electric vehicle including:

1. Many hybrid electric vehicles use an air-conditioning compressor that uses high voltage from the high-voltage battery pack to operate the compressor either all of the time, such as many Toyota/Lexus models, or during idle stop periods, such as on Honda hybrids.

2. If the system is electrically driven, special refrigerant oil is used that is nonconductive. This means a separate recovery machine should be used to avoid the possibility of mixing regular refrigerant oils with the oil used in hybrids.

3. Always read, understand, and follow all of the service information instructions when servicing the air-conditioning system on a hybrid electric vehicle.

STEERING SYSTEM SERVICE

Performing steering system service is similar to performing this service in any vehicle equipped with an internal combustion engine. However, there are several items to know when servicing the steering system on a hybrid electric vehicle including:

1. Check service information for any precautions that are specified to be followed when servicing the steering system on a hybrid electric vehicle.

2. Most hybrid electric vehicles use an electric power steering system. These can be powered by one of two voltages:

   - **12 volts**—These systems can be identified by the red or black wiring conduit and often use an inverter that increases the voltage to operate the actuator motor (usually to 42 V). While this higher voltage is contained in the controller and should not create a shock hazard, always follow the specified safety precautions and wear protective high-voltage gloves as needed.

   - **42 volts**—These systems use a yellow or blue plastic conduit over the wires to help identify the possible hazards from this voltage level. This voltage level is not a shock hazard, but can maintain an arc if a circuit carrying 42 volts is opened.

BRAKING SYSTEM SERVICE

Performing braking system service is similar to performing this service in any vehicle equipped with an internal combustion engine. However, there are several items to know when servicing the braking system on a hybrid electric vehicle including:

1. Check service information for any precautions that are specified to be followed when servicing the braking system on a hybrid electric vehicle.

2. All hybrid electric vehicles use a regenerative braking system, which captures the kinetic energy of the moving vehicle, converts it to electrical energy, and is sent to the high-voltage battery pack. The amount of current produced during hard braking can exceed 100 amperes. This current is stored in the high-voltage battery pack and is used as needed to help power the vehicle.

3. The base brakes used on hybrid electric vehicles are the same as any other conventional vehicle except for the master cylinder and related control systems. There are no high-voltage circuits associated with the braking

FIGURE 45–18 The radiation emitted from a hybrid electric vehicle is very low, as shown being measured in units of milligauss.

FIGURE 45–19 This 12-volt battery under the hood on a Ford Fusion hybrid is a flooded-cell-type auxiliary battery.

 FREQUENTLY ASKED QUESTION

Is the Radiation From a Hybrid Dangerous?

No. While there is a changing magnetic field surrounding any wire carrying an electrical current, the amount of electromagnetic radiation is very low. ● **SEE FIGURE 45–18.**

system as the regeneration occurs inside the electric drive (traction) motors and is controlled by the motor controller.

4. The base brakes on many hybrid vehicles are often found to be stuck or not functioning correctly because the brakes are not doing much work and can rust.

NOTE: Always check the base brakes whenever there is a poor fuel economy complaint heard from an owner of a hybrid vehicle. Often when a disc brake caliper sticks, the brakes drag but the driver is not aware of any performance problems, but the fuel economy drops.

TIRES Performing tire-related service is similar to performing this service in any vehicle equipped with an internal combustion engine. However, there are several items to know when servicing tires on a hybrid electric vehicle including:

1. Tire pressure is very important, not only to the fuel economy, but also on the life of the tire. Lower inflation pressure increases rolling resistance and reduces load-carrying capacity and tire life. Always inflate the tires to the pressure indicated on the door jamb sticker or found in service information or the owner's manual.

2. All tires create less rolling resistance as they wear. This means even if the same identical tire is used as a replacement, the owner may experience a drop in fuel economy.

3. Tires can have a big effect on fuel economy. It is best to warn the owner that replacement of the tires can and often will cause a drop in fuel economy, even if low rolling resistance tires are selected.

4. Try to avoid using tires that are larger than used from the factory. The larger the tire, the heavier it is and it takes more energy to rotate, resulting in a decrease in fuel economy.

5. Follow normal tire inspections and tire rotation intervals as specified by the vehicle manufacturer.

AUXILIARY BATTERY TESTING AND SERVICE

Performing auxiliary battery service is similar to performing this service in any vehicle equipped with an internal combustion engine. However, there are several items to know when servicing the auxiliary battery on a hybrid electric vehicle including:

1. Auxiliary 12-volt batteries used in hybrid electric vehicles are located in one of two general locations.

   ■ **Under the hood**—If the 12-volt auxiliary battery is under the hood, it is generally a flooded-type lead–acid battery and should be serviced the same as any conventional battery. ● **SEE FIGURE 45–19.**

   ■ **In the passenger or trunk area**—If the battery is located in the passenger or trunk area of the vehicle, it is usually of the absorbed glass mat design. This type of battery requires that a special battery charger that limits the charging voltage be used.

2. The auxiliary 12-volt battery is usually smaller than a battery used in a conventional vehicle because it is not used to actually start the engine unless under extreme conditions on Honda hybrids only.

3. The 12-volt auxiliary battery can be tested and serviced the same as any battery used in a conventional vehicle.

4. Always read, understand, and follow all of the service information instructions when servicing the auxiliary battery on a hybrid electric vehicle.

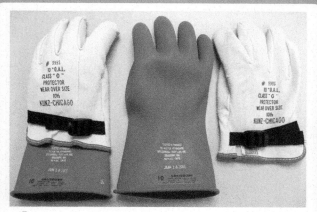

1 The cuff of the rubber glove should extend at least 1/2 inch beyond the cuff of the leather protector.

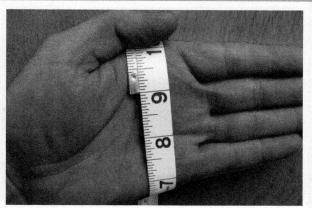

2 To determine correct glove size, use a soft tape to measure around the palm of the hand. A measurement of 9 inches would correspond with a glove size of 9.

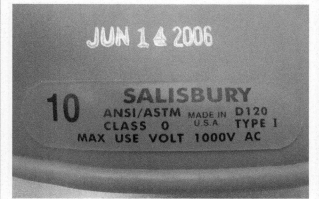

3 The glove rating and the date of the last test should be stamped on the glove cuff.

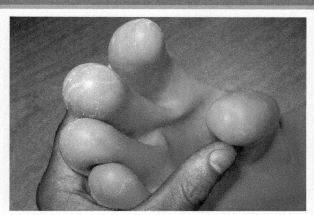

4 Start with a visual inspection of the glove fingertips, making sure that no cuts or other damage is present.

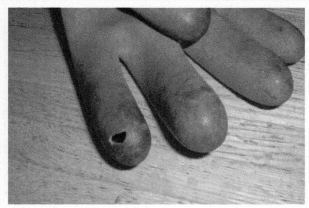

5 The damage on this glove was easily detected with a simple visual inspection. Note that the rubber glove material can be damaged by petroleum products, detergents, certain hand soaps, and talcum powder.

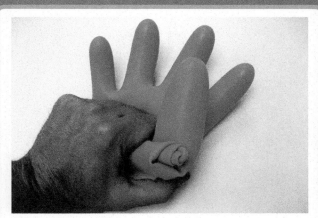

6 Manually inflate the glove to inspect for pinhole leaks. Starting at the cuff, roll up the glove and trap air at the finger end. Listen and watch carefully for deflation of the glove. If a leak is detected, the glove must be discarded.

CONTINUED ▶

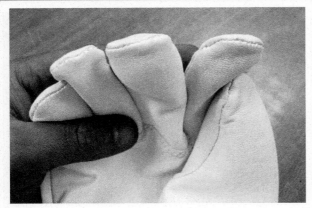

7 Petroleum on the leather protector's surfaces will damage the rubber glove underneath.

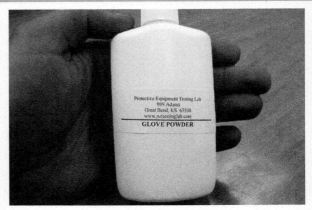

8 Glove powder (glove dust) should be used to absorb moisture and reduce friction.

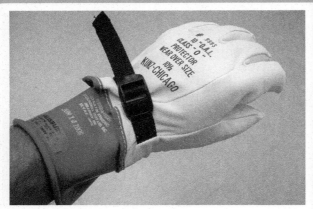

9 Put on the gloves and tighten the straps on the back of the leather protectors.

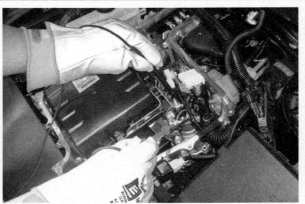

10 Technicians MUST wear HV gloves and leather protectors whenever working around the high-voltage areas of a hybrid electric vehicle.

11 HV gloves and leather protectors should be placed in a canvas storage bag when not in use. Note the ventilation hole at the bottom of this bag.

12 Make sure that the rubber gloves are not folded when placed in the canvas bag. Folding increases mechanical stress on the rubber and can lead to premature failure of the glove material.

1. Personal protective equipment (PPE) for work on hybrid electric vehicles includes the wearing of high-voltage rubber gloves rated at 1,000 volts or more worn with outer leather gloves to help protect the rubber gloves.

2. A digital meter that meets CAT III standards should be used when working around the high-voltage section of a hybrid electric vehicle.

3. Safety glasses and a face shield should be worn whenever working around the high-voltage circuits of a hybrid electric vehicle.

4. The high-voltage system can be shut off at the battery pack by simply being certain that the ignition is off. Disconnecting the 12-volt battery is additional security that the high-voltage circuits are depowered.

5. When servicing a hybrid electric vehicle, always observe safety procedures.

REVIEW QUESTIONS

1. What are the recommended items that should be used when working with the high-voltage circuits of a hybrid electric vehicle?

2. What actions are needed to disable the high-voltage (HV) circuit?

3. What are the precautions that service technicians should adhere to when servicing hybrid electric vehicles?

4. How should high-voltage gloves be tested before use?

5. How will the ICE keep running if this is needed to perform some service inspections or service operations?

CHAPTER QUIZ

1. Rubber gloves should be worn whenever working on or near the high-voltage circuits or components of a hybrid electric vehicle. Technician A says that the rubber gloves should be rated at 1,000 volts or higher. Technician B says that leather gloves should be worn over the high-voltage rubber gloves. Which technician is correct?
   a. Technician A only
   b. Technician B only
   c. Both Technicians A and B
   d. Neither Technician A nor B

2. A CAT III-certified DMM should be used whenever measuring high-voltage circuits or components. The CAT III rating relates to _____.
   a. high voltage
   b. high energy
   c. high electrical resistance
   d. both a and b

3. All of the following will shut off the high voltage to components and circuits, except _____.
   a. opening the driver's door
   b. turning the ignition off
   c. disconnecting the 12-volt auxiliary battery
   d. removing the main fuse, relay, or HV plug

4. If the engine is not running, Technician A says that the high-voltage circuits are depowered. Technician B says that all high-voltage wiring is orange-colored. Which technician is correct?
   a. Technician A only
   b. Technician B only
   c. Both Technicians A and B
   d. Neither Technician A nor B

5. Which statement is false about high-voltage wiring?
   a. Connects the battery pack to the electric controller
   b. Connects the controller to the motor/generator
   c. Is electrically grounded to the frame (body) of the vehicle
   d. Is controlled by a relay that opens if the ignition is off

6. What routine service procedure could result in lower fuel economy, which the owner may discover?
   a. Using the wrong viscosity engine oil
   b. Replacing tires
   c. Replacing the air filter
   d. Either a or b

7. Two technicians are discussing jump starting a hybrid electric vehicle. Technician A says that the high-voltage batteries can be jumped on some HEV models. Technician B says that the 12-volt auxiliary battery can be jumped using a conventional jump box or jumper. Which technician is correct?
   a. Technician A only
   b. Technician B only
   c. Both Technicians A and B
   d. Neither Technician A nor B

8. What can occur if a hybrid electric vehicle is pushed in the shop?
   a. The HV battery pack can be damaged
   b. The tires will be locked unless the ignition is on
   c. Damage to the electronic controller can occur
   d. High voltage will be generated by the motor/generator

9. Nickel-metal hydride (NiMH) batteries can be damaged if exposed to temperatures higher than about _____.
   a. 150°F (66°C)
   b. 175°F (79°C)
   c. 200°F (93°C)
   d. 225°F (107°C)

10. How should nickel-metal hydride batteries be disposed?
    a. In regular trash
    b. Call an 800 number shown under the hood of the vehicle for information
    c. Submerged in water and disposed of in regular trash
    d. Burned at an EPA-certified plant

chapter 46

FUEL CELLS AND ADVANCED TECHNOLOGIES

FIGURE 46–1 Ford Motor Company has produced a number of demonstration fuel-cell vehicles based on the Ford Focus.

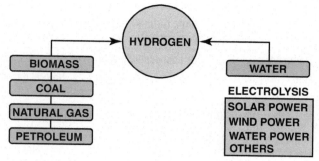

FIGURE 46–2 Hydrogen does not exist by itself in nature. Energy must be expended to separate it from other, more complex materials.

FUEL-CELL TECHNOLOGY

WHAT IS A FUEL CELL? A **fuel cell** is an electrochemical device in which the chemical energy of hydrogen and oxygen is converted into electrical energy. The principle of the fuel cell was first discovered in 1839 by Sir William Grove, a Welsh physician. In the 1950s, NASA put this principle to work in building devices for powering space exploration vehicles. In the present day, fuel cells are being developed to power homes and vehicles while producing low or zero emissions. ● **SEE FIGURE 46–1**.

The chemical reaction in a fuel cell is the opposite of **electrolysis**. Electrolysis is the process in which electrical current is passed through water in order to break it into its components, hydrogen and oxygen. While energy is required to bring about electrolysis, this same energy can be retrieved by allowing hydrogen and oxygen to reunite in a fuel cell. It is important to note that while hydrogen can be used as a fuel, it is **not** an energy source. Instead, hydrogen is only an **energy carrier,** as energy must be expended to generate the hydrogen and store it so it can be used as a fuel.

In simple terms, a fuel cell is a hydrogen-powered battery. Hydrogen is an excellent fuel because it has a very high **specific energy** when compared to an equivalent amount of fossil fuel. One kilogram (kg) of hydrogen has three times the energy content as 1 kilogram of gasoline. Hydrogen is the most abundant element on earth, but it does not exist by itself in nature. This is because its natural tendency is to react with oxygen in the atmosphere to form water (H_2O). Hydrogen is also found in many other compounds, most notably hydrocarbons, such as natural gas or crude oil. In order to store hydrogen for use as a fuel, processes must be undertaken to separate it from these materials. ● **SEE FIGURE 46–2**.

BENEFITS OF A FUEL CELL A fuel cell can be used to move a vehicle by generating electricity to power electric drive motors as well as powering the remainder of the vehicle's electrical system. Since they are powered by hydrogen and oxygen, fuel cells by themselves do not generate carbon emissions such as CO_2. Instead, their only emissions are water vapor and heat, and this makes the fuel cell an ideal candidate for a zero-emission vehicle (ZEV).

FIGURE 46–3 The Mercedes-Benz B-Class fuel-cell car was introduced in 2005.

A fuel cell is also much more energy efficient than a typical internal combustion engine. While a vehicle powered by an internal combustion engine (ICE) is anywhere from 15% to 20% efficient, a fuel-cell vehicle can achieve efficiencies upward of 40%. Another major benefit of fuel cells is that they have very few moving parts and have the potential to be very reliable. A number of OEMs have spent many years and millions of dollars in order to develop a low-cost, durable, and compact fuel cell that will operate satisfactorily under all driving conditions. ● **SEE FIGURE 46–3**.

A **fuel-cell vehicle (FCV)** uses the fuel cell as its only source of power, whereas a **fuel-cell hybrid vehicle (FCHV)** would also have an electrical storage device that can be used to power the vehicle. Most new designs of fuel-cell vehicles are now based on a hybrid configuration because of the significant increase in efficiency and driveability that can be achieved with this approach. ● **SEE FIGURE 46–4**.

FUEL-CELL CHALLENGES While major automobile manufacturers continue to build demonstration vehicles and work on improving fuel-cell system design, no vehicle powered by a fuel cell has been placed into mass production. There are a number of reasons for this, including the following:

- High cost
- Lack of refueling infrastructure
- Safety perception

	PAFC (PHOSPHORIC ACID FUEL CELL)	PEM (POLYMER ELECTROLYTE MEMBRANE)	MCFC (MOLTEN CARBONATE FUEL CELL)	SOFC (SOLID OXIDE FUEL CELL)
Electrolyte	Orthophosphoric acid	Sulfonic acid in polymer	Li and K carbonates	Yttrium-stabilized zirconia
Fuel	Natural gas, hydrogen	Natural gas, hydrogen, methanol	Natural gas, synthetic gas	Natural gas, synthetic gas
Operating Temp (F) (C)	360–410°F	176–212°F	1,100–1,300°F	1,200–3,300°F
	180–210°C	80–100°C	600–700°C	650–1,800°C
Electric Efficiency	40%	30%–40%	43%–44%	50%–60%
Manufacturers	ONSI Corp.	Avista, Ballard, Energy Partners, H-Power, International, Plug Power	Fuel Cell Energy, IHI, Hitachi, Siemens	Honeywell, Siemens-Westinghouse, Ceramic
Applications	Stationary power	Vehicles, portable power, small stationary power	Industrial and institutional power	Stationary power, military vehicles

CHART 46–1

Fuel cell types and their operating temperature range.

FIGURE 46–4 The Toyota FCHV is based on the Highlander platform and uses much of Toyota's Hybrid Synergy Drive (HSD) technology in its design.

- Insufficient vehicle range
- Lack of durability
- Freeze starting problems
- Insufficient power density

All of these problems are being actively addressed by researchers, and significant improvements are being made. Once cost and performance levels meet that of current vehicles, fuel cells will be adopted as a mainstream technology. ● SEE CHART 46–1.

TYPES OF FUEL CELLS There are a number of different types of fuel cells, and these are differentiated by the type of **electrolyte** that is used in their design. Some electrolytes operate best at room temperature, whereas others are made to operate at up to 1,800°F. See the accompanying chart showing the various fuel-cell types and applications.

The fuel-cell design that is best suited for automotive applications is the **proton exchange membrane (PEM)**. A PEM fuel cell must have hydrogen for it to operate, and this may be stored on the vehicle or generated as needed from another type of fuel.

PEM FUEL CELLS

DESCRIPTION AND OPERATION The Proton Exchange Membrane fuel cell is also known as a **polymer electrolyte fuel cell (PEFC)**. The PEM fuel cell is known for its lightweight and compact design as well as its ability to operate at ambient temperatures. This means that a PEM fuel cell can start quickly and produce full power without an extensive warm-up period. The PEM is a simple design based on a membrane that is coated on both sides with a catalyst such as platinum or palladium. There are two electrodes, one located on each side of the membrane. These are responsible for distributing hydrogen and oxygen over the membrane surface, removing waste heat, and providing a path for electrical current flow. The part of the PEM fuel cell that contains the membrane, catalyst coatings, and electrodes is known as the **membrane electrode assembly (MEA)**.

The negative electrode (anode) has hydrogen gas directed to it, while oxygen is sent to the positive electrode (cathode). Hydrogen is sent to the negative electrode as H2 molecules, which break apart into H^+ ions (protons) in the presence of the catalyst. The electrons (e^-) from the hydrogen atoms are sent through the external circuit, generating electricity that can be utilized to perform work. These same electrons are then sent to

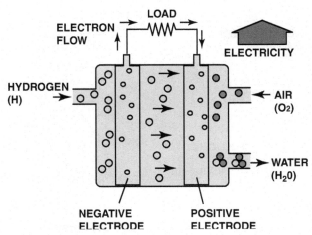

FIGURE 46–5 The polymer electrolyte membrane allows only H$^+$ ions (protons) to pass through it. This means that electrons must follow the external circuit and pass through the load to perform work.

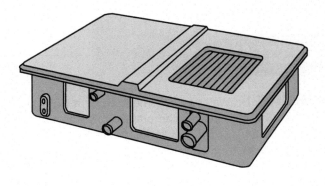

FIGURE 46–6 A fuel-cell stack is made up of hundreds of individual cells connected in series.

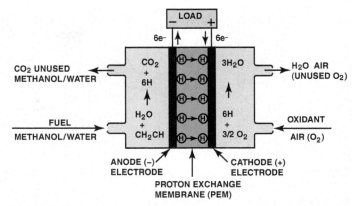

FIGURE 46–7 A direct methanol fuel cell uses a methanol/water solution for fuel instead of hydrogen gas.

🔧 **TECH TIP**

CO Poisons the PEM Fuel-Cell Catalyst

Purity of the fuel gas is critical with PEM fuel cells. If more than 10 parts per million (ppm) of carbon monoxide is present in the hydrogen stream being fed to the PEM anode, the catalyst will be gradually poisoned, and the fuel cell will eventually be disabled. This means that the purity must be "five nines" (99.999% pure). This is a major concern in vehicles where hydrogen is generated by reforming hydrocarbons such as gasoline because it is difficult to remove all CO from the hydrogen during the reforming process. In these applications, some means of hydrogen purification must be used to prevent CO poisoning of the catalyst.

the positive electrode, where they rejoin the H1 ions that have passed through the membrane and have reacted with oxygen in the presence of the catalyst. This creates H$_2$O and waste heat, which are the only emissions from a PEM fuel cell. ● **SEE FIGURE 46–5**.

NOTE: It is important to remember that a fuel cell generates direct current (DC) electricity as electrons flow in only one direction (from the anode to the cathode).

FUEL-CELL STACKS A single fuel cell by itself is not particularly useful, as it will generate less than 1 volt of electrical potential. It is more common for hundreds of fuel cells to be built together in a **fuel-cell stack**. In this arrangement, the fuel cells are connected in series so that total voltage of the stack is the sum of the individual cell voltages. The fuel cells are placed end to end in the stack, much like slices in a loaf of bread. Automotive fuel-cell stacks contain more than 400 cells in their construction. ● **SEE FIGURE 46–6**.

The total voltage of the fuel-cell stack is determined by the number of individual cells incorporated into the assembly. The current-producing ability of the stack, however, is dependent on the surface area of the electrodes. Since output of the fuel-cell stack is related to both voltage and current (voltage × current = power), increasing the number of cells or increasing the surface area of the cells will increase power output. Some fuel-cell vehicles will use more than one stack, depending on power output requirements and space limitations.

DIRECT METHANOL FUEL CELLS High-pressure cylinders are one method of storing hydrogen onboard a vehicle for use in a fuel cell. This is a simple and lightweight storage method but often does not provide sufficient vehicle driving range. Another approach has been to fuel a modified PEM fuel cell with liquid methanol instead of hydrogen gas. ● **SEE FIGURE 46–7** .

Methanol is most often produced from natural gas and has a chemical symbol of CH$_3$OH. It has a higher **energy density**

FIGURE 46–8 A direct methanol fuel cell can be refueled similar to a gasoline-powered vehicle.

FREQUENTLY ASKED QUESTION

What Is the Role of the Humidifier in a PEM Fuel Cell?

The polymer electrolyte membrane assembly in a PEM fuel cell acts as conductor of positive ions and as a gas separator. However, it can perform these functions effectively only if it is kept moist. A fuel-cell vehicle uses an air compressor to supply air to the positive electrodes of each cell, and this air is sometimes sent through a humidifier first to increase its moisture content. The humid air then comes in contact with the membrane assembly and keeps the electrolyte damp and functioning correctly.

than gaseous hydrogen because it exists in a liquid state at normal temperatures and is easier to handle since no compressors or other high-pressure equipment is needed. This means that a fuel-cell vehicle can be refueled with a liquid instead of high-pressure gas, which makes the refueling process simpler and produces a greater vehicle driving range. ● **SEE FIGURE 46–8**.

Unfortunately, direct methanol fuel cells suffer from a number of problems, not the least of which is the corrosive nature of methanol itself. This means that methanol cannot be stored in existing tanks and thus requires a separate infrastructure for handling and storage. Another problem is "fuel crossover," in which methanol makes its way across the membrane assembly and diminishes performance of the cell. Direct methanol fuel cells also require much greater amounts of catalyst in their construction, which leads to higher costs. These challenges are leading researchers to look for alternative electrolyte materials and catalysts to lower cost and improve cell performance.

NOTE: Direct methanol fuel cells are not likely to see service in automotive applications. However, they are well suited for low-power applications, such as cell phones or laptop computers.

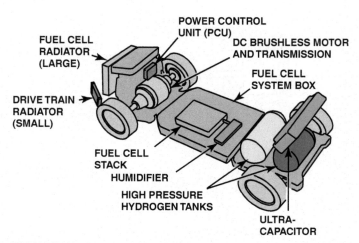

FIGURE 46–9 Powertrain layout in a Honda FCX fuel-cell vehicle. Note the use of a humidifier behind the fuel-cell stack to maintain moisture levels in the membrane electrode assemblies.

FUEL-CELL VEHICLE SYSTEMS

HUMIDIFIERS Water management inside a PEM fuel cell is critical. Too much water can prevent oxygen from making contact with the positive electrode; too little water can allow the electrolyte to dry out and lower its conductivity. The amount of water and where it resides in the fuel cell is also critical in determining at how low a temperature the fuel cell will start because water freezing in the fuel cell can prevent it from starting. The role of the humidifier is to achieve a balance where it is providing sufficient moisture to the fuel cell by recycling water that is evaporating at the cathode. The humidifier is located in the air line leading to the cathode of the fuel-cell stack. ● **SEE FIGURE 46–9**.

Some newer PEM designs manage the water in the cells in such a way that there is no need to prehumidify the incoming reactant gases. This eliminates the need for the humidifier assembly and makes the system simpler overall.

FUEL-CELL COOLING SYSTEMS Heat is generated by the fuel cell during normal operation. Excess heat can lead to a breakdown of the polymer electrolyte membrane, so a liquid cooling system must be utilized to remove waste heat from the fuel-cell stack. One of the major challenges for engineers in this regard is the fact that the heat generated by the fuel cell is classified as **low-grade heat**. This means that there is only a small difference between the temperature of the coolant and that of the ambient air. Heat transfers very slowly under these conditions, so heat exchangers with a much larger surface area must be utilized. ● **SEE FIGURE 46–10**.

In some cases, heat exchangers may be placed in other areas of the vehicle when available space at the front of the engine compartment is insufficient. In the case of the Toyota

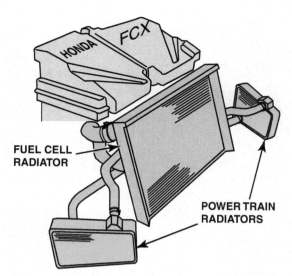

FIGURE 46–10 The Honda FCX uses one large radiator for cooling the fuel cell and two smaller ones on either side for cooling drivetrain components.

FIGURE 46–11 Space is limited at the front of the Toyota FCHV engine compartment, so an auxiliary heat exchanger is located under the vehicle to help cool the fuel-cell stack.

FCHV, an auxiliary heat exchanger is located underneath the vehicle to increase the cooling system heat-rejection capacity. ● SEE FIGURE 46–11.

An electric water pump and a fan drive motor are used to enable operation of the fuel cell's cooling system. These and other support devices use electrical power that is generated by the fuel cell and therefore tend to decrease the overall efficiency of the vehicle.

AIR SUPPLY PUMPS
Air must be supplied to the fuel-cell stack at the proper pressure and flow rate to enable proper performance under all driving conditions. This function is performed by an onboard air supply pump that compresses atmospheric air and supplies it to the fuel cell's positive electrode (cathode). This pump is often driven by a high-voltage electric drive motor.

FUEL-CELL HYBRID VEHICLES
Hybridization tends to increase efficiency in vehicles with conventional drivetrains, as energy that was once lost during braking and otherwise normal operation is instead stored for later use in a high-voltage battery or **ultracapacitor**. This same advantage can be gained by applying the hybrid design concept to fuel-cell vehicles. Whereas the fuel cell is the only power source in a fuel-cell vehicle, the fuel-cell hybrid vehicle (FCHV) relies on both the fuel cell and an electrical storage device for motive power. Driveability is also enhanced with this design, as the electrical storage device is able to supply energy immediately to the drive motors and overcome any "throttle lag" on the part of the fuel cell.

SECONDARY BATTERIES
All hybrid vehicle designs require a means of storing electrical energy that is generated during regenerative braking and other applications. In most FCHV designs, a high-voltage nickel-metal hydride (NiMH) battery pack is used as a secondary battery. This is most often located near the back of the vehicle, either under or behind the rear passenger seat. ● SEE FIGURE 46–12. The secondary battery is built similar to a fuel-cell stack because it is made up of many low-voltage cells connected in series to build a high-voltage battery.

ULTRACAPACITORS
An alternative to storing electrical energy in batteries is to use ultracapacitors. A capacitor is best known as an electrical device that will block DC current but allow AC to pass. However, a capacitor can also be used to store electrical energy, and it is able to do this without a chemical reaction. Instead, a capacitor stores electrical energy using the principle of electrostatic attraction between positive and negative charges.

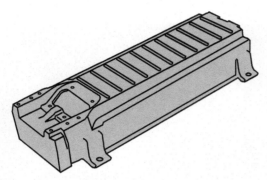

FIGURE 46–12 The secondary battery in a fuel-cell hybrid vehicle is made up of many individual cells connected in series, much like a fuel-cell stack.

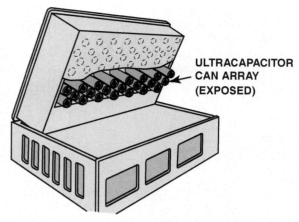

ULTRACAPACITOR CAN ARRAY (EXPOSED)

FIGURE 46–14 An ultracapacitor can be used in place of a high-voltage battery in a hybrid electric vehicle. This example is from the Honda FCX fuel-cell hybrid vehicle.

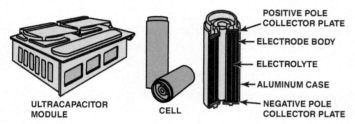

ULTRACAPACITOR MODULE

CELL

POSITIVE POLE COLLECTOR PLATE
ELECTRODE BODY
ELECTROLYTE
ALUMINUM CASE
NEGATIVE POLE COLLECTOR PLATE

FIGURE 46–13 The Honda ultracapacitor module and construction of the individual cells.

Ultracapacitors are built very different from conventional capacitors. Ultracapacitor cells are based on **double-layer technology**, in which two activated-carbon electrodes are immersed in an organic electrolyte. The electrodes have a very large surface area and are separated by a membrane that allows ions to migrate but prevents the electrodes from touching. ● **SEE FIGURE 46–13**. Charging and discharging occur as ions move within the electrolyte, but no chemical reaction takes place. Ultracapacitors can charge and discharge quickly and efficiently, making them especially suited for electric assist applications in fuel-cell hybrid vehicles.

Ultracapacitors that are used in fuel-cell hybrid vehicles are made up of multiple cylindrical cells connected in parallel. ● **SEE FIGURE 46–14**. This results in the total capacitance being the sum of the values of each individual cell. For example, ten 1.0-**farad** capacitors connected in parallel will have a total capacitance of 10.0 farads. Greater capacitance means greater electrical storage ability, and this contributes to greater assist for the electric motors in a fuel-cell hybrid vehicle.

Ultracapacitors have excellent cycle life, meaning that they can be fully charged and discharged many times without degrading their performance. They are also able to operate over a wide temperature range and are not affected by low temperatures to the same degree as many battery technologies. The one major downside of ultracapacitors is a lack of specific energy, which means that they are best suited for sudden bursts of energy as opposed to prolonged discharge cycles. Research is being conducted to improve this and other aspects of ultracapacitor performance.

FIGURE 46–15 Drive motors in fuel-cell hybrid vehicles often use stator assemblies similar to ones found in Toyota hybrid electric vehicles. The rotor turns inside the stator and has permanent magnets on its outer circumference.

FUEL-CELL TRACTION MOTORS Much of the technology behind the electric drive motors being used in fuel-cell vehicles was developed during the early days of the California ZEV mandate. This was a period when battery-powered electric vehicles were being built by the major vehicle manufacturers in an effort to meet a legislated quota in the state of California. The ZEV mandate rules were eventually relaxed to allow other types of vehicles to be substituted for credit, but the technology that had been developed for pure electric vehicles was now put to work in these other vehicle designs.

The electric traction motors used in fuel-cell hybrid vehicles are very similar to those being used in current hybrid electric vehicles. The typical drive motor is based on an AC synchronous design, which is sometimes referred to as a DC brushless motor. This design is very reliable, as it does not use a commutator or brushes but instead has a three-phase stator and a permanent magnet rotor. ● **SEE FIGURE 46–15**.

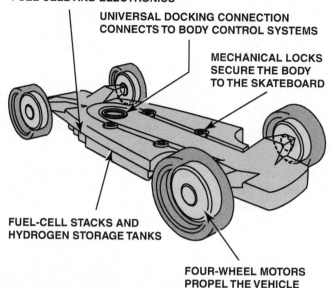

HEAT VENTS TO DISSIPATE
HEAT GENERATED BY THE
FUEL CELL AND ELECTRONICS

UNIVERSAL DOCKING CONNECTION
CONNECTS TO BODY CONTROL SYSTEMS

MECHANICAL LOCKS
SECURE THE BODY
TO THE SKATEBOARD

FUEL-CELL STACKS AND
HYDROGEN STORAGE TANKS

FOUR-WHEEL MOTORS
PROPEL THE VEHICLE

FIGURE 46–16 The General Motors "Skateboard" concept uses a fuel-cell propulsion system with wheel motors at all four corners.

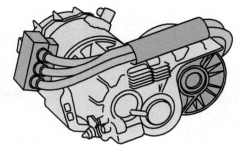

FIGURE 46–17 The electric drive motor and transaxle assembly from a Toyota FCHV. Note the three orange cables, indicating that this motor is powered by high-voltage three-phase alternating current.

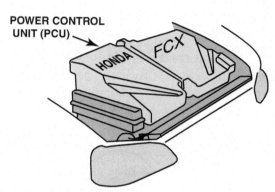

POWER CONTROL
UNIT (PCU)

FIGURE 46–18 The power control unit (PCU) on a Honda FCX fuel-cell hybrid vehicle is located under the hood.

An electronic controller (inverter) is used to generate the three-phase high-voltage AC current required by the motor. While the motor itself is very simple, the electronics required to power and control it are complex.

Some fuel-cell hybrid vehicles use a single electric drive motor and a transaxle to direct power to the vehicle's wheels. It is also possible to use **wheel motors** to drive individual wheels. While this approach adds a significant amount of unsprung weight to the chassis, it allows for greater control of the torque being applied to each individual wheel. ● **SEE FIGURE 46–16.**

TRANSAXLES Aside from the hydrogen fueling system, fuel-cell hybrid vehicles are effectively pure electric vehicles in that their drivetrain is electrically driven. Electric motors work very well for automotive applications because they produce high torque at low rpms and are able to maintain a consistent power output throughout their entire rpm range. This is in contrast to vehicles powered by internal combustion engines, which produce very little torque at low rpms and have a narrow range where significant horsepower is produced.

ICE-powered vehicles require complex transmissions with multiple speed ranges in order to accelerate the vehicle quickly and maximize the efficiency of the ICE. Fuel-cell hybrid vehicles use electric drive motors that require only a simple reduction in their final drive and a differential to send power to the drive wheels. No gear shifting is required, and mechanisms such as torque converters and clutches are done away with completely. A reverse gear is not required either, as the electric drive motor is simply powered in the opposite direction. The transaxles used in fuel-cell hybrid vehicles are extremely simple with few moving parts, making them extremely durable, quiet, and reliable. ● **SEE FIGURE 46–17.**

POWER CONTROL UNITS The drivetrain of a fuel-cell hybrid vehicle is controlled by a power control unit (PCU), which controls fuel-cell output and directs the flow of electricity between the various components. One of the functions of the PCU is to act as an **inverter**, which changes direct current from the fuel-cell stack into three-phase alternating current for use in the vehicle drive motor(s). ● **SEE FIGURE 46–18.**

Power to and from the secondary battery is directed through the power control unit, which is also responsible for maintaining the battery pack's state of charge and for controlling and directing the output of the fuel-cell stack. ● **SEE FIGURE 46–19.**

During regenerative braking, the electric drive motor acts as a generator and converts kinetic (moving) energy of the vehicle into electricity for recharging the high-voltage battery pack. The PCU must take the three-phase power from the motor (generator) and convert (or *rectify*) this into DC voltage to be sent to the battery. DC power from the fuel cell will also be processed through the PCU for recharging the battery pack.

A DC-to-DC converter is used in hybrid-electric vehicles for converting the high voltage from the secondary battery pack into the 12 volts required for the remainder of the vehicle's electrical system. Depending on the vehicle, there may also be 42 volts required to operate accessories such as the electric-assist power steering. In fuel-cell hybrid vehicles, the DC-to-DC converter function may be built into the power control unit, giving it full responsibility for the vehicle's power distribution.

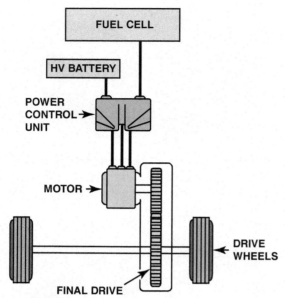

FIGURE 46–19 Toyota's FCHV uses a power control unit that directs electrical energy flow between the fuel cell, battery, and drive motor.

FIGURE 46–20 This GM fuel-cell vehicle uses compressed hydrogen in three high-pressure storage tanks.

HYDROGEN STORAGE One of the pivotal design issues with fuel-cell hybrid vehicles is how to store sufficient hydrogen onboard to allow for reasonable vehicle range. Modern drivers have grown accustomed to having a minimum of 300 miles between refueling stops, a goal that is extremely difficult to achieve when fueling the vehicle with hydrogen. Hydrogen has a very high energy content on a pound-for-pound basis, but its energy density is less than that of conventional liquid fuels. This is because gaseous hydrogen, even at high pressure, has a very low physical density (mass per unit volume). ● SEE FIGURE 46–20.

A number of methods of hydrogen storage are being considered for use in fuel-cell hybrid vehicles. These include high-pressure compressed gas, liquefied hydrogen, and solid storage in metal hydrides. Efficient hydrogen storage is one of the technical issues that must be solved in order for fuel cells to be adopted for vehicle applications. Much research is being conducted to solve the issue of onboard hydrogen storage.

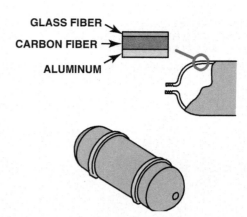

FIGURE 46–21 The Toyota FCHV uses high-pressure storage tanks that are rated at 350 bar. This is the equivalent of 5,000 pounds per square inch.

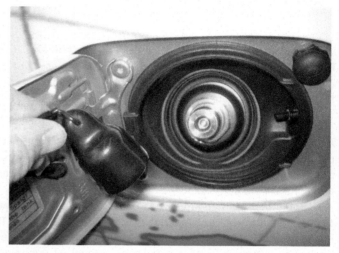

FIGURE 46–22 The high-pressure fitting used to refuel a fuel-cell hybrid vehicle.

HIGH-PRESSURE COMPRESSED GAS Most current fuel-cell hybrid vehicles use compressed hydrogen that is stored in tanks as a high-pressure gas. This approach is the least complex of all the storage possibilities but also has the least energy density. Multiple small storage tanks are often used rather than one large one in order to fit them into unused areas of the vehicle. One drawback with this approach is that only cylinders can be used to store gases at the required pressures. This creates a good deal of unused space around the outside of the cylinders and leads to further reductions in hydrogen storage capacity. It is common for a pressure of 5,000 PSI (350 bar) to be used, but technology is available to store hydrogen at up to 10,000 PSI (700 bar). ● SEE FIGURE 46–21.

The tanks used for compressed hydrogen storage are typically made with an aluminum liner wrapped in several layers of carbon fiber and an external coating of fiberglass. In order to refuel the compressed hydrogen storage tanks, a special high-pressure fitting is installed in place of the filler neck used for conventional vehicles. ● SEE FIGURE 46–22. There is also a special electrical connector that is used to enable

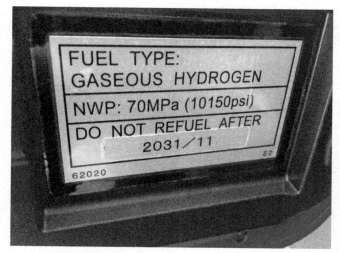

FIGURE 46–23 Note that high-pressure hydrogen storage tanks must be replaced in 2031.

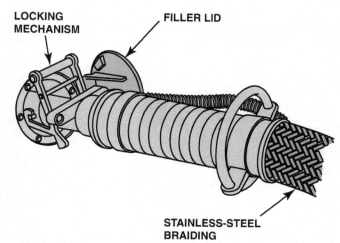

LOCKING MECHANISM

FILLER LID

STAINLESS-STEEL BRAIDING

FIGURE 46–25 Refueling a vehicle with liquid hydrogen.

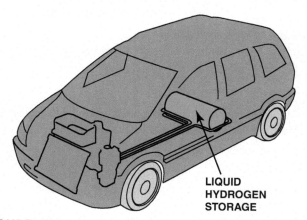

LIQUID HYDROGEN STORAGE

FIGURE 46–24 GM's Hydrogen3 has a range of 249 miles when using liquid hydrogen.

FIGURE 46–26 Carbon deposits, such as these, are created by incomplete combustion of a hydrocarbon fuel.

communication between the vehicle and the filling station during the refueling process. ● SEE FIGURE 46–23.

The filling station utilizes a special coupler to connect to the vehicle's high-pressure refueling fitting. The coupler is placed on the vehicle fitting, and a lever on the coupler is rotated to seal and lock it into place.

LIQUID HYDROGEN Hydrogen can be liquefied in an effort to increase its energy density, but this requires that it be stored in cryogenic tanks at −423°F (−253°C). This increases vehicle range but impacts overall efficiency, as a great deal of energy is required to liquefy the hydrogen, and a certain amount of the liquid hydrogen will "boil off" while in storage.

One liter of liquid hydrogen only has one-fourth the energy content of 1 liter of gasoline. ● SEE FIGURES 46–24 AND 46–25.

SOLID STORAGE OF HYDROGEN One method discovered to store hydrogen in solid form is as a metal hydride, similar to how a nickel-metal hydride (NiMH) battery works.

A demonstration vehicle features a lightweight fiber-wrapped storage tank under the body that stores 3 kilogram

TECH TIP

Hydrogen Fuel = No Carbon

Most fuels contain hydrocarbons or molecules that contain both hydrogen and carbon. During combustion, the first element that is burned is the hydrogen. If combustion is complete, then all of the carbon is converted to carbon dioxide gas and exits the engine in the exhaust. However, if combustion is not complete, carbon monoxide is formed, leaving some unburned carbon to accumulate in the combustion chamber. ● SEE FIGURE 46–26.

(about 6.6 lbs) of hydrogen as a metal hydride at low pressure. The vehicle can travel almost 200 miles with this amount of fuel. One kilogram of hydrogen is equal to 1 gallon of gasoline. Three gallons of water will generate 1 kilogram of hydrogen.

A metal hydride is formed when gaseous hydrogen molecules disassociate into individual hydrogen atoms and bond with the metal atoms in the storage tank. This process uses powdered metallic alloys capable of rapidly absorbing hydrogen to make this occur.

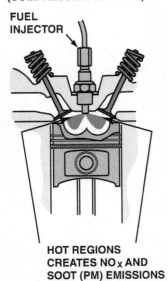

DIESEL ENGINE
(COMPRESSION IGNITION)

FUEL
INJECTOR

HOT REGIONS
CREATES NO$_X$ AND
SOOT (PM) EMISSIONS

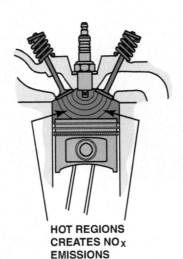

GASOLINE ENGINE
(SPARK IGNITED)

HOT REGIONS
CREATES NO$_X$
EMISSIONS

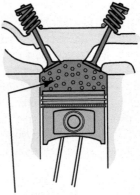

HCCI ENGINE
(HOMOGENEOUS CHARGE
COMPRESSION IGNITION)

LOW-TEMPERATURE
COMBUSTION RESULTS
IN REDUCED EMISSIONS

FIGURE 46–27 Both diesel and conventional gasoline engines create exhaust emissions due to high peak temperatures created in the combustion chamber. The lower combustion temperatures during HCCI operation result in high efficiency with reduced emissions.

HYDRAULIC HYBRID STORAGE SYSTEM

Ford Motor Co. is experimenting with a system it calls **hydraulic power assist (HPA)**. This system converts kinetic energy to hydraulic pressure and then uses that pressure to help accelerate the vehicle. It is currently being tested on a four-wheel-drive (4WD) Lincoln Navigator with a 4.0-L V-8 engine in place of the standard 5.4-L engine.

A variable-displacement hydraulic pump/motor is mounted on the transfer case and connected to the output shaft that powers the front driveshaft. The HPA system works with or without 4WD engaged. A valve block mounted on the pump contains solenoid valves to control the flow of hydraulic fluid. A 14-gallon, high-pressure accumulator is mounted behind the rear axle, with a low-pressure accumulator right behind it to store hydraulic fluid. The master cylinder has a "deadband," meaning the first few fractions of an inch of travel do not pressurize the brake system. When the driver depresses the brake pedal, a pedal movement sensor signals the control unit, which then operates solenoid valves to send hydraulic fluid from the low-pressure reservoir to the pump. The pumping action slows the vehicle, similar to engine compression braking, and the fluid is pumped into the high-pressure reservoir. Releasing the brake and pressing on the accelerator signal the control unit to send that high-pressure fluid back to the pump, which then acts as a hydraulic motor and adds torque to the driveline. The system can be used to launch the vehicle from a stop and/or add torque for accelerating from any speed.

While the concept is simple, the system itself is very complicated. Additional components include the following:

- Pulse suppressors
- Filters
- An electric circulator pump for cooling the main pump/motor

Potential problems with this system include leakage problems with seals and valves, getting air out of the hydraulic fluid system, and noise. In prototype stages the system demands different driving techniques. Still, this system was built to prove the concept, and engineers believe that these problems can be solved and that a control system can be developed that will make HPA transparent to the driver. A 23% improvement in fuel economy and improvements in emissions reduction were achieved using a dynamometer set for a 7,000-pound vehicle. While the HPA system could be developed for any type of vehicle with any type of drivetrain, it does add weight and complexity, which would add to the cost.

HCCI

Homogeneous charge compression ignition (HCCI) is a combustion process. HCCI is the combustion of a very lean gasoline air–fuel mixture without the use of a spark ignition. It is a low-temperature, chemically controlled (flameless) combustion process. ● **SEE FIGURE 46–27.**

HCCI combustion is difficult to control and extremely sensitive to changes in temperature, pressure, and fuel type. While the challenges of HCCI are difficult, the advantages include having a gasoline engine being able to deliver 80% of diesel efficiency (a 20% increase in fuel economy) for 50% of the cost. A diesel engine using HCCI can deliver gasoline-like emissions. Spark and injection timing are no longer a factor as they are in a conventional port-fuel injection system.

While much research and development needs to be performed using this combustion process, it has been shown to give excellent performance from idle to midload and from ambient to warm operating temperatures as well as cold-start and run capability. Because an engine only operates in HCCI mode at light throttle settings, such as during cruise conditions at highway speeds, engineers need to improve the transition in and out of the HCCI mode. Work is also being done on piston and combustion chamber shape to reduce combustion noise and vibration that is created during operation in the HCCI operating mode.

Ongoing research is focusing on improving fuel economy under real-world operating conditions as well as controlling costs.

PLUG-IN HYBRID ELECTRIC VEHICLES

PRINCIPLES A **plug-in hybrid electric vehicle (PHEV)** is a vehicle that is designed to be plugged into an electrical outlet at night to charge the batteries. By charging the batteries in the vehicle, it can operate using electric power alone (stealth mode) for a longer time, thereby reducing the use of the internal combustion engine (ICE). The less the ICE is operating, the less fuel is consumed and the lower the emissions.

PHEV BATTERY CAPACITY The size or capacity of the battery pack used determines how far that the vehicle can travel without using the ICE, commonly called the electric vehicle or EV range.

- A lower kilowatt-hour (kWh)-rated battery weighs less and is less expensive but the range that the vehicle can travel on battery power alone is limited.
- A higher kWh rating battery means that the battery is capable of propelling the vehicle for a greater distance before the ICE is used. This reduces the fuel used but the larger battery weighs and costs more.
- Therefore, a plug-in vehicle is a compromise between cost and weight of the battery.

PHEV EXAMPLES A standard Toyota Prius has a 1.3 kWh battery pack, whereas the plug-in version has a larger 4.4 kWh battery, allowing electric-only travel of about 10 miles before the ICE is used. When the battery pack SOC has been depleted, the vehicle operates as a standard HEV with the ICE and the electric motor, both used to propel the vehicle.

A Chevrolet Volt has a larger 16 kWh battery pack and, as a result, can travel over 30 miles on electric power alone,

without using the ICE until the battery has been discharged to about 25% to 35%. At this stage, the ICE is operated to keep the battery pack at a level high enough to keep propelling the vehicle. ● **SEE FIGURE 46–28.**

CHARGING A PHEV After the battery pack has been discharged propelling the vehicle, the ICE is used to keep the battery charged enough to propel the vehicle, but it does not fully recharge the battery pack. To fully charge the high-voltage battery pack in a plug-in hybrid electric vehicle requires that it be plugged into either a 120-volt or a 240-volt outlet. ● **SEE FIGURE 46–29.**

ELECTRIC VEHICLES

PRINCIPLES **Electric vehicles (EV)** use a high-voltage battery pack to supply electrical energy to an electric motor(s) to propel the vehicle under all driving conditions. The capacity of the battery pack in kilowatt-hours (kWh) determines the range of the vehicle and has to be plugged in to recharge the battery before it can be driven further.

COLD WEATHER CONCERNS Past models of electric vehicles, such as the General Motors electric vehicle (EV1), were restricted to locations such as Arizona and southern California that had a warm climate. Cold weather is a major disadvantage to the use of electric vehicles for the following reasons:

- Cold temperatures reduce battery efficiency.
- Additional electrical power from the batteries is needed to heat the batteries themselves to be able to achieve reasonable performance.
- Passenger compartment heating is a concern for an electric vehicle because it requires the use of resistance units or other technology that reduces the range of the vehicle.

HOT WEATHER CONCERNS Batteries do not function well at high temperatures, and therefore, some type of battery cooling system must be added to the vehicle to allow for maximum battery performance. This results in a reduction of vehicle range due to the use of battery power needed just to keep the batteries working properly. Besides, the batteries also have to supply the power needed to keep the interior and the other accessories of the vehicle cool. These combined electrical loads represent a huge battery drain and reduce the range of the vehicle.

RANGE How far an electric vehicle can travel on a full battery charge is called its **range**. The range of an electric vehicle depends on many factors, including:

- Battery energy storage capacity
- Vehicle weight
- Outside temperature
- Terrain (driving in hilly or mountainous areas requires more energy from the battery)
- Use of air-conditioning and other electrical devices

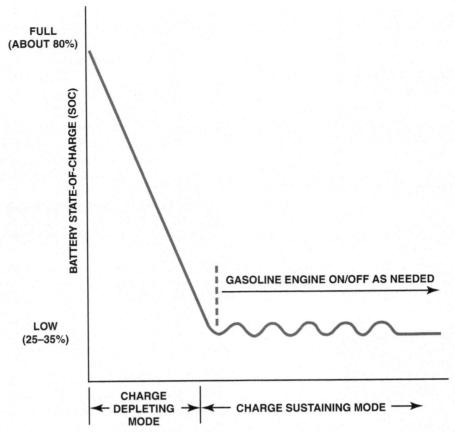

FIGURE 46-28 After the Chevrolet Volt has been charged, it uses the electrical power stored in the high-voltage battery to propel the vehicle and provide heating and cooling for 25 to 50 miles (40 to 80 km). Then the gasoline engine starts and maintains the SOC between 25% and 35%. The gasoline engine cannot fully charge the high-voltage batteries but rather the vehicle has to be plugged in to provide a higher SOC level.

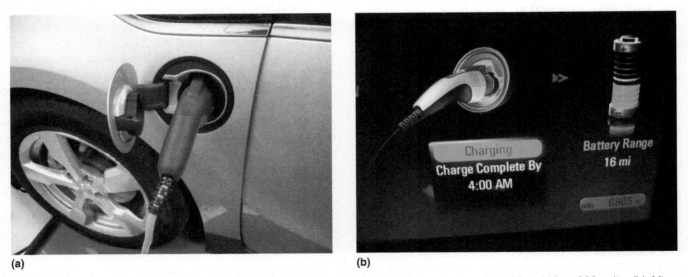

FIGURE 46-29 (a) The Chevrolet Volt is charged using a standard SAE 1772 connector using either 110 or 220 volts. (b) After connecting the charging plug, a light on the top of the dash turns green and the dash display shows the estimated time when the high-voltage battery will be fully charged and the estimated current range using battery power alone.

Batteries Like the Same Temperature Range as Humans

Batteries work best when they are kept within a temperature range that is also the most comfortable for humans. Most people are comfortable when the temperature is between 68°F and 78°F (20°C and 26°C).

- Below 68°F (20°C), most people want heat.
- Above 78°F (26°C), most people want cooling.

Batteries perform best when they too are exposed to the same temperature range. Therefore, a proper heating and cooling system must be used to keep the batteries within this fairly narrow temperature range for best performance.

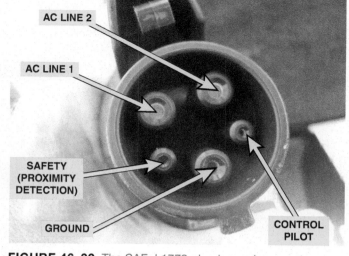

FIGURE 46–30 The SAE J 1772 plug is used on most electric and plug-in hybrid electric vehicles and is designed to work with Level 1 (110 to 120 V) and Level 2 (220 to 240 V) charging.

BATTERY CAPACITY AND RANGE EXAMPLES ●SEE

CHART 46–2 for some examples of the battery capacity and the range of selected electric vehicles:

VEHICLE	BATTERY CAPACITY IN kWh	RANGE (Miles/km)
Nissan Leaf	24	84/135
Ford Focus EV	23	76/122
Chevrolet Spark Electric	21	82/132
Fiat 500 EV	24	87/140
Honda Fit EV	20	82/132
Mitsubishi i-MiEV	16	62/100
Tesla	60	208/335
	85	265/426

CHART 46–2

Selected electric vehicles and their battery capacity and published range.

SAE STANDARD CHARGER PLUG

Most electric vehicles and plug-in hybrid electric vehicles, such as the Chevrolet Volt and Toyota Prius, use a standard charger plug. The standard charger plug meets the specification as designated by SAE standard J1772 (updated in 2009). ● **SEE FIGURE 46–30.**

Because electric vehicles have a relatively short range, charging stations must be made available in areas where these vehicles are driven. For example, when the state of California mandated the sale of zero-emission vehicles (ZEV), charging stations were set up in many areas, usually in parking lots of businesses and schools. The parking spaces near the charging

stations are designated for electric vehicles only and can be used for free to recharge electric vehicles.

CHARGING LEVELS

There are three levels of chargers that can be used to charge a plug-in hybrid electric vehicle (PHEV) or electric vehicle (EV). They are:

- **Level 1** Level 1 uses 110- to 120-volt standard electric outlets and is capable of charging a Chevrolet Volt extended range electric vehicle in 10 hours or more. The advantage is that there is little if any installation cost as most houses are equipped with 110-volt outlets and can charge up to 16 amperes.

- **Level 2** Level 2 chargers use 220 to 240 volts to charge the same vehicle in about 4 hours. Level 2 chargers can be added to most houses, making recharging faster (up to 80 amperes) when at home, and are the most commonly used charging stations available at stores and colleges. Adding a Level 2 charging outlet to the garage or parking location can cost $2,000 or more depending on the location and the wiring of the house or apartment.

- **Level 3** Level 3 charging stations use 440 volts and can charge most electric vehicles to 80% charge in less than 30 minutes. This high-charge rate may be harmful to battery life. Always follow the charging instructions and recommendations as stated in the owner's manual of the vehicle being charged. Level 3 chargers charge the vehicle using direct current (DC) at a rate up to 125 amperes. A Level 3 charger station can cost $50,000 or more, making this type of charger most suitable where facilities will be selling the service of rapidly charging the vehicle. The Tesla "superchargers" are Level 3 chargers and are free to use by Tesla owners.

CHAdeMO LEVEL 3 CONNECTOR | SAE J1772 LEVEL 1 AND LEVEL 2 CONNECTOR

FIGURE 46–31 A Nissan Leaf electric vehicle charging ports located at the front of the vehicle under a hinged door for easy access.

FIGURE 46–32 A typical wind generator that is used to generate electricity.

 FREQUENTLY ASKED QUESTION

What Is a "CHAdeMO" Connector?

CHAdeMO is a Japanese trade name of a quick charging method for Level 3 charging using DC electricity at a high rate. "CHAdeMO" is an abbreviation of "CHArge de Move," which can be translated to mean "charge for moving." ● **SEE FIGURE 46–31.**

WIND POWER

Wind power is used to help supplement electric power generation in many parts of the country. Because AC electricity cannot be stored, this energy source is best used to reduce the use of natural gas and coal to help reduce CO_2 emissions. Wind power is most economical if the windmills are located where the wind blows consistently above 8 miles per hour (13 km/h). Locations include the eastern slope of mountain ranges, such as the Rocky Mountains, or on high ground in many states. Often, wind power is used as supplemental power in the evenings when it is most needed and is allowed to stop rotating in daylight hours when the power is not needed. Windmills are usually grouped together to form **wind farms**, where the product is electrical energy. Energy from wind farms can be used to charge plug-in hybrid vehicles as well as for domestic lighting and power needs. ● **SEE FIGURE 46–32.**

FIGURE 46–33 The Hoover Dam in Nevada/Arizona is used to create electricity for use in the southwestern United States.

HYDROELECTRIC POWER

Hydroelectric power is limited to locations where there are dammed rivers and hydroelectric plants. However, electricity can and is transmitted long distances—so that electricity generated at the Hoover Dam can be used in California and other remote locations. Electrical power from hydroelectric sources can be used to charge plug-in hybrid electric vehicles, thereby reducing emissions that would normally be created by burning coal or natural gas to create electricity. However, hydroelectric plants are limited as to the amount of power they can produce, and constructing new plants is extremely expensive. ● **SEE FIGURE 46–33.**

1. The chemical reaction inside a fuel cell is the opposite of electrolysis in that electricity is created when hydrogen and oxygen are allowed to combine in the fuel cell.

2. A fuel cell produces electricity and releases heat and water as the only by-products.

3. The major disadvantages of fuel cells include the following:
   - High cost
   - Lack of hydrogen refueling stations
   - Short range
   - Freezing-temperature starting problems

4. Types of fuel cells include PEM (the most commonly used), PAFC, MCFC, and SOFC.

5. Ultracapacitors are an alternative to batteries for the storage of electrical energy.

6. A gasoline-powered engine can be more efficient if it uses a homogeneous charge compression ignition (HCCI) combustion process.

7. Plug-in hybrid electric vehicles could expand the range of hybrid vehicles by operating on battery power alone.

8. Wind power and hydroelectric power are being used to recharge plug-in hybrids and provide electrical power for all uses, without harmful emissions.

REVIEW QUESTIONS

1. How does a fuel cell work?

2. What are the advantages and disadvantages of fuel cells?

3. What are the uses of the various types of fuel cells?

4. How does an ultracapacitor work?

5. What are the advantages and disadvantages of using hydrogen?

CHAPTER QUIZ

1. A fuel cell produces electricity from _____ and _____.
   - **a.** gasoline/oxygen
   - **b.** nitrogen/hydrogen
   - **c.** hydrogen/oxygen
   - **d.** water/oxygen

2. What are the by-products (emissions) from a fuel cell?
   - **a.** Water
   - **b.** CO_2
   - **c.** CO
   - **d.** Nonmethane hydrocarbon

3. Which type of fuel cell is the most likely to be used to power vehicles?
   - **a.** PAFC
   - **b.** PEM
   - **c.** MCFC
   - **d.** SOFC

4. Which liquid fuel could be used to directly power a fuel cell?
   - **a.** Methanol
   - **b.** Ethanol
   - **c.** Biodiesel
   - **d.** Unleaded gasoline

5. Which is *not* a function of an ultracapacitor?
   - **a.** Can pass AC current
   - **b.** Can be charged with DC current
   - **c.** Discharges DC current
   - **d.** Can pass DC current

6. Hydrogen is commonly stored at what pressure?
   - **a.** 100,000 PSI
   - **b.** 50,000 PSI
   - **c.** 5,000 PSI
   - **d.** 1,000 PSI

7. Hydrogen storage tanks are usually constructed from _____.
   - **a.** steel
   - **b.** aluminum
   - **c.** carbon fiber
   - **d.** Both b and c

8. HCCI is a process that eliminates what parts or components in a gasoline engine?
   - **a.** Fuel tank
   - **b.** Battery
   - **c.** Fuel injectors
   - **d.** Ignition system

9. A plug-in hybrid is different from a conventional hybrid electric vehicle because it has _____.
   - **a.** a built-in battery charger
   - **b.** Li Ox batteries
   - **c.** more batteries
   - **d.** bigger motor/generator

10. Which energy source(s) is (are) currently being used to help reduce the use of fossil fuels?
    - **a.** Hydrogen
    - **b.** Wind power
    - **c.** Hydroelectric power
    - **d.** Both b and c

appendix 1
ELECTRICAL/ELECTRONIC SYSTEMS (A6) SAMPLE ASE-TYPE CERTIFICATION TEST AND ANSWERS

CONTENT AREA	QUESTIONS IN TEST	PERCENTAGE OF TEST
A. General Electrical/Electronic System Diagnosis	13	26%
B. Battery and Starting System Diagnosis and Repair	9	18%
C. Charging System Diagnosis and Repair	5	10%
D. Lighting Systems Diagnosis and Repair	6	12%
E. Instrument Cluster and Driver Information Systems Diagnosis and Repair	6	12%
F. Body Electrical Systems Diagnosis and Repair	11	22%
TOTAL	50	100%

1. Copper wiring resistance _____ as the temperature increases.
   a. Increases
   b. Decreases

2. A voltage spike is created whenever any component containing a coil is shut off.
   a. True
   b. False

3. A corroded light socket could most likely cause _____.
   a. A fuse to blow in the circuit
   b. The light to be dim as a result of reduced current flow
   c. A feedback to occur to another circuit
   d. Damage to occur to the bulb as a result of decreased voltage

4. A fuse keeps blowing. Technician A says that a test light can be used in place of the fuse to help find the problem. Technician B says that a circuit breaker can be used in the place of the fuse. Which technician is correct?
   a. Technician A only
   b. Technician B only
   c. Both Technicians A and B
   d. Neither Technician A nor B

5. Technician A says that a low or zero reading on an ohmmeter indicates continuity. Technician B says that a meter reading indicating infinity means no continuity. Which technician is correct?
   a. Technician A only
   b. Technician B only
   c. Both Technicians A and B
   d. Neither Technician A nor B

6. What makes a meter a high-impedance tester?
   a. The effective resistance of the meter circuit
   b. The amount of current the meter can safely carry
   c. The maximum voltage that can be measured
   d. The maximum resistance that can be measured

7. The wire at the output terminal of a generator (alternator) connects to _____.
   a. The ignition switch input terminal
   b. The starter at the S terminal
   c. The battery positive terminal
   d. The fuse panel

8. When the parking lamps are on and the turn signal is flashing, the side-marker lamp alternates flashes with the turn signal. The reason for this is that _____.
   a. There are opposing voltages at the marker light filament
   b. The marker lamp ground path goes through the turn signal lamp

c. The marker lamp feed comes from the parking lamp circuit

   d. All of the above

9. The headlamp on the right side is dim and yellow when turned on. The left headlamp is bright and normal in color. Which statement is false?

   a. The left side has more current.

   b. The left side is normal.

   c. The right side has more resistance.

   d. The right side has a bad sealed beam.

10. A meter reads OL. This means that the component or circuit being measured _____.

   a. Is open

   b. Is shorted

   c. Is grounded

   d. Has low resistance

11. A starter motor is drawing too many amperes (current). Technician A says that this could be due to low battery voltage. Technician B says that it could be due to a defective starter motor. Which technician is correct?

   a. Technician A only

   b. Technician B only

   c. Both Technicians A and B

   d. Neither Technician A nor B

12. All of the following could be a cause of excessive starter ampere draw except _____.

   a. A misadjusted starter pinion gear

   b. A loose starter housing

   c. Armature wires separated from the commutator

   d. A bent armature

13. The starter motor armature has been rubbing on the pole shoes. The probable cause is _____.

   a. A bent starter shaft

   b. A worn commutator on the armature

   c. Worn starter bushing(s)

   d. Both a and c

14. A starter cranks for a while, then whines. Technician A says that the starter solenoid may be bad. Technician B says that the starter drive may be bad. Which technician is correct?

   a. Technician A only

   b. Technician B only

   c. Both Technicians A and B

   d. Neither Technician A nor B

15. Airbag wiring is _____.

   a. Red

   b. Orange

   c. Yellow

   d. Blue

16. A blower motor stopped working on all speeds. A technician tested the motor by touching a jumper wire from the battery positive terminal to the motor power terminal, and the motor did run. Technician A says that the motor should be checked using a fused jumper lead or ammeter to test for excessive current draw. Technician B says that

the resistor pack and/or the relay are/is likely to be defective. Which technician is correct?

   a. Technician A only

   b. Technician B only

   c. Both Technicians A and B

   d. Neither Technician A nor B

17. A technician is checking the charging system for low output. A voltage drop of 1.67 volts is found between the generator (alternator) output terminal and the battery positive terminal. Technician A says that a corroded connector could be the cause. Technician B says that a defective rectifier diode could be the cause. Which technician is correct?

   a. Technician A only

   b. Technician B only

   c. Both Technicians A and B

   d. Neither Technician A nor B

18. An ohmmeter on the 30-K scale reads 1.93 on a digital face. How many ohms of resistance is being measured?

   a. 193

   b. 19,300

   c. 1930

   d. 19.30

19. In a parallel 12-volt circuit with three bulbs (each 10 ohms in resistance), which statement below would be correct if one of the bulbs burned out (had an open)?

   a. The total resistance would be the same.

   b. The total resistance would be lower.

   c. The current would increase in the circuit.

   d. The current would decrease in the circuit.

20. Technician A says that high resistance in the cables or connections can cause rapid clicking of the solenoid. Technician B says that a battery must be 75% charged for accurate testing of the starting and charging systems. Which technician is correct?

   a. Technician A only

   b. Technician B only

   c. Both Technicians A and B

   d. Neither Technician A nor B

21. On a negative ground battery system _____.

   a. Disconnect the ground cable first and reconnect the positive cable first

   b. Disconnect the ground cable first and reconnect the positive cable last

   c. Disconnect the positive cable first and reconnect the ground cable first

   d. Disconnect the positive cable first and reconnect the ground cable last

22. A starter motor is drawing too many amperes (current) and the starter motor is not working. Technician A says that this could be due to low battery voltage. Technician B says that it could be due to a defective (grounded) starter motor. Which technician is correct?

   a. Technician A only

   b. Technician B only

c. Both Technicians A and B
d. Neither Technician A nor B

23. On a single-headlight system, the right-side high beam does not work. The probable cause is _____.
    a. A bad dimmer switch
    b. A bad headlight
    c. A bad headlight ground
    d. A discharged battery

24. A driver turns the ignition switch to "start" and nothing happens (the dome light remains bright). Technician A says that dirty battery connections or a defective or discharged battery could be the cause. Technician B says that an *open* control circuit such as a defective neutral safety switch could be the cause. Which technician is correct?
    a. Technician A only
    b. Technician B only
    c. Both Technicians A and B
    d. Neither Technician A nor B

25. Normal battery drain (parasitic drain) on a vehicle with many computer and electronic circuits is _____.
    a. 20 to 30 milliamperes
    b. 2 to 3 amperes
    c. 150 to 300 milliamperes
    d. 0.3 to 0.4 amperes

26. Whenever jump starting _____.
    a. The last connection should be the positive post of the dead battery
    b. The last connection should be the engine block of the dead vehicle
    c. The generator (alternator) must be disconnected on both vehicles
    d. The bumpers should touch to provide a good ground between the vehicles

27. A charge light is on, but dim. The most likely cause is _____.
    a. A defective rectifier bridge
    b. A defective diode trio
    c. A defective rotor
    d. Worn brushes

28. An electric motor is drawing more current (amperes) than specified. Technician A says that a corroded connector at the motor could be the cause. Technician B says that a corroded ground connection could be the cause. Which technician is correct?
    a. Technician A only
    b. Technician B only
    c. Both Technicians A and B
    d. Neither Technician A nor B

29. Technician A says that many wiper motors use a three-brush, two-speed motor. Technician B says that if the low speed does not work, then the wiper will also not operate on pulse (delay). Which technician is correct?
    a. Technician A only
    b. Technician B only

c. Both Technicians A and B
d. Neither Technician A nor B

30. Two technicians are discussing jump starting a computer-equipped vehicle with another computer-equipped vehicle. Technician A says that the ignition of both vehicles should be in the off position while making the jumper cable connections. Technician B says that the computer-equipped vehicles should not be jump started. Which technician is correct?
    a. Technician A only
    b. Technician B only
    c. Both Technicians A and B
    d. Neither Technician A nor B

31. Technician A says not to touch a halogen bulb with your fingers. Technician B says to handle a halogen bulb with care because it has high-pressure gas in it. Which technician is correct?
    a. Technician A only
    b. Technician B only
    c. Both Technicians A and B
    d. Neither Technician A nor B

32. Which of the following is the correct range for charging voltage measured across the battery terminals?
    a. 9.5 to 12 volts
    b. 13 to 15 volts
    c. 14 to 16.5 volts
    d. 15.2 to 18.5 volts

33. Battery voltage reads 11.85 volts on a DMM during cranking. Technician A says that the battery could be weak. Technician B says the starter may be defective. Which technician is correct?
    a. Technician A only
    b. Technician B only
    c. Both Technicians A and B
    d. Neither Technician A nor B

34. A technician is checking a headlight door motor with an ammeter. It shows excessive current draw. The most likely cause is a _____.
    a. Bad ground
    b. Binding headlight door
    c. Loose connection
    d. Blown fuse

35. The charge light does not come on when the key is turned to the "run" position. This could be caused by _____.
    a. An open circuit to the sending unit
    b. A burned-out bulb
    c. A bad diode
    d. A short inside the generator (alternator)

36. When the key is turned to the "start" position, the solenoid chatters and the interior lights flicker. The most likely cause is _____.
    a. Low battery voltage
    b. Defective pull-in winding

    c. Defective hold-in winding
    d. Defective starter motor

37. A vehicle being checked for parasitic draw shows a reading of 300 mA. The specification for the vehicle is 0.02 A. Technician A says this reading is satisfactory. Technician B says this reading needs to be taken with the key on. Which technician is correct?
    a. Technician A only
    b. Technician B only
    c. Both Technicians A and B
    d. Neither Technician A nor B

38. A blower is running slow on all speeds. The most likely cause is _____.
    a. A blown resistor
    b. Worn/dry bearings in the motor
    c. A bad fan switch
    d. Open ignition switch

39. A rebuilt starter turns but will not disengage the flywheel. The most likely cause is _____.
    a. A missing solenoid return spring
    b. A defective starter drive
    c. The shifting fork installed backward
    d. The solenoid contact installed backward

40. Technician A says a high-scale ammeter can be used to test the current draw of a starting circuit. Technician B says a high-scale voltmeter can be used to test the current draw of a starting circuit. Which technician is correct?
    a. Technician A only
    b. Technician B only
    c. Both Technicians A and B
    d. Neither Technician A nor B

41. The left-turn signal indicator on the instrument panel stays on and does not flash. The right-side signal functions properly. What is the most likely cause?
    a. A defective flasher
    b. A bad bulb
    c. A defective turn signal switch
    d. A low battery voltage

42. A fusible link between the battery and generator (alternator) is hot to the touch. The charging system voltage is 9.8 volts. This could indicate _____.
    a. Overcharging
    b. Undercharging
    c. High resistance in the fusible link
    d. A poor connection

43. A vehicle comes in with a nonfunctioning gas gauge. When the sending unit wire is grounded, the gauge reading goes to "full." Technician A says this proves that the gauge is OK. Technician B says this proves that the sending unit is bad. Which technician is correct?
    a. Technician A only
    b. Technician B only

    c. Both Technicians A and B
    d. Neither Technician A nor B

44. A vehicle's reverse lights are always on, even in "drive." The most likely cause is _____.
    a. A misadjusted neutral safety switch
    b. An open neutral safety switch
    c. A bulb installed backward
    d. A wrong bulb installed for the reverse lights

45. A vehicle cannot hold a steady speed in cruise control over bumpy roads. The most likely cause is _____.
    a. A misadjusted brake switch
    b. A vacuum leak to the servo
    c. A loose ground connection at the servo unit
    d. A defective fuse

46. Technician A says that disconnecting a battery can cause driveability problems after the battery has been reconnected. Technician B says that disconnecting a battery can cause radio station presets to be lost. Which technician is correct?
    a. Technician A only
    b. Technician B only
    c. Both Technicians A and B
    d. Neither Technician A nor B

47. When do you remove a battery surface charge?
    a. Before load testing
    b. After load testing
    c. Anytime you are testing the battery, starter, or generator (alternator)
    d. Before starting the engine to avoid damage to the generator (alternator)

48. A customer comes in complaining of radio static. Technician A says to check the antenna. Technician B says to check the speakers and radio ground. Which technician is correct?
    a. Technician A only
    b. Technician B only
    c. Both Technicians A and B
    d. Neither Technician A nor B

49. A customer arrives at a shop and his vehicle's battery voltage is measured to be 13.6 volts with the engine off. This indicates _____.
    a. Overcharging
    b. Undercharging
    c. Normal surface charge
    d. Sulfated battery

50. When the parking lights are turned on, the left light is dim while the right light is a normal brightness. When the brake is applied, the left light totally goes out, while the right side works properly. What is the problem?
    a. A bad ground at the left bulb
    b. A shorted left bulb
    c. A bad switch
    d. A shorted right bulb

ANSWERS

1.	a	14.	b	27.	b	40.	a
2.	a	15.	c	28.	d	41.	b
3.	b	16.	c	29.	b	42.	c
4.	c	17.	a	30.	a	43.	a
5.	c	18.	c	31.	c	44.	a
6.	a	19.	d	32.	b	45.	a
7.	c	20.	c	33.	d	46.	c
8.	d	21.	a	34.	b	47.	a
9.	d	22.	b	35.	b	48.	c
10.	a	23.	c	36.	a	49.	c
11.	c	24.	b	37.	d	50.	a
12.	c	25.	a	38.	b		
13.	d	26.	b	39.	c		

appendix 2
SAMPLE ASE-TYPE CERTIFICATION ENGINE PERFORMANCE (A8) TEST

CONTENT AREA	QUESTIONS IN TEST	PERCENTAGE OF TEST
A. General Engine Diagnosis	12	24%
B. Ignition System Diagnosis and Repair	8	16%
C. Fuel, Air Induction, and Exhaust Systems Diagnosis and Repair	9	18%
D. Emissions Control Systems Diagnosis and Repair 1. Positive Crankcase Ventilation (1) 2. Exhaust Gas Recirculation (2) 3. Secondary Air Injection (AIR) and Catalytic Converter (2) 4. Evaporative Emissions Controls (3)	8	16%
E. Computerized Engine Controls Diagnosis and Repair(Including OBD II)	13	26%
TOTAL	50	100%

A. GENERAL ENGINE DIAGNOSIS

1. A blown head gasket is suspected on a 5-year-old vehicle. The service technician should perform which of the following tests to confirm the problem?
   a. Running compression test, vacuum test
   b. Leak-down test, compression test
   c. Oil pressure test, leak-down test
   d. Check for DTCs, Check for TSBs

2. Two technicians are discussing oil leaks. Technician A says that an oil leak can be found using a fluorescent dye in the oil with a black light to check for leaks. Technician B says that a white spray powder can be used to locate oil leaks. Which technician is correct?
   a. Technician A only
   b. Technician B only
   c. Both Technicians A and B
   d. Neither Technician A nor B

3. A smoothly operating engine depends on _____.
   a. High compression on most cylinders
   b. Equal compression among cylinders
   c. Cylinder compression levels above 100 PSI (700 kPa) and within 70 PSI (500 kPa) of each other
   d. Compression levels below 100 PSI (700 kPa) on most cylinders

4. A good reading for a cylinder leakage test would be _____.
   a. Within 20% among cylinders
   b. All cylinders below 20% leakage
   c. All cylinders above 20% leakage
   d. All cylinders above 70% leakage and within 7% of each other

5. Technician A says that during a power balance test, the cylinder that causes the biggest RPM drop is the weak cylinder. Technician B says that if one spark plug wire is grounded out and the engine speed does not drop, a weak or dead cylinder is indicated. Which technician is correct?
   a. Technician A only
   b. Technician B only
   c. Both Technicians A and B
   d. Neither Technician A nor B

6. White exhaust can be caused by _____
   a. Coolant entering the combustion chamber
   b. Engine oil getting past the piston rings
   c. A vacuum leak at the intake manifold gasket
   d. Any of the above

7. An engine is misfiring. A power balance test indicates that when the spark to cylinder #4 is grounded, there is no change in the engine speed. Technician A says that a burned valve is a possible cause. Technician B says that a defective cylinder #4 injector or spark plug wire could be the cause. Which technician is correct?
   a. Technician A only
   b. Technician B only
   c. Both Technicians A and B
   d. Neither Technician A nor B

8. Two technicians are discussing an engine vibration during acceleration. Technician A says that a defective (collapsed) mount can cause an engine or driveline vibration. Technician B says that the some mounts are fluid filled and should be checked for leakage. Which technician is correct?
   a. Technician A only
   b. Technician B only
   c. Both Technicians A and B
   d. Neither Technician A nor B

9. An engine uses an excessive amount of oil and the exhaust is blue but only at first engine start in the morning. What is the most likely cause?
   a. Leaking fuel injector
   b. Worn valve stem seals
   c. Leaking valve (cylinder head) cover
   d. Overfilled oil level

10. Two technicians are discussing the diagnosis of a lack-of-power problem. Technician A says that a clogged catalytic converter could be the cause. Technician B says that a restricted or clogged muffler could be the cause. Which technician is correct?
    a. Technician A only
    b. Technician B only
    c. Both Technicians A and B
    d. Neither Technician A nor B

11. A compression test gave the following results:

    cylinder #1 = 155, cylinder #2 = 140, cylinder #3 = 110, cylinder #4 = 105

    Technician A says that a defective (burned) valve is the most likely cause. Technician B says that a leaking head gasket could be the cause. Which technician is correct?
    a. Technician A only
    b. Technician B only
    c. Both Technicians A and B
    d. Neither Technician A nor B

12. Two technicians are discussing a compression test. Technician A says that the engine should be cranked over with the pressure gauge installed for "4 puffs." Technician B says that the maximum difference between the highest-reading cylinder and the lowest-reading cylinder should be 20%. Which technician is correct?
    a. Technician A only
    b. Technician B only
    c. Both Technicians A and B
    d. Neither Technician A nor B

B. IGNITION SYSTEM DIAGNOSIS AND REPAIR

13. How should a service technician test for spark?
    a. Hold the plug wire ¼ inch from the block
    b. Use a spark tester
    c. Pull the spark plug wire away from the plug ½ in.
    d. Measure the output with a meter set to kV

14. An engine will not start and a check of the ignition system output indicates no spark to any of the spark plugs. Technician A says that a defective crankshaft position sensor (CKP) could be the cause. Technician B says a defective ignition switch could be the cause. Which technician is correct?
    a. Technician A only
    b. Technician B only
    c. Both Technicians A and B
    d. Neither Technician A nor B

15. A spark plug wire is 2.5 feet long. If it is okay, its resistance should be less than _____.
    a. 25 k ohms
    b. 200,000 ohms
    c. 250,000 ohms
    d. 2.50 k ohms

16. A P0300 (random misfire detected) diagnostic trouble code (DTC) was being diagnosed and a defective (open) spark plug wire was found on a waste-spark-type ignition system. Technician A says that the companion cylinder spark plug wire should also be carefully inspected and replaced if necessary. Technician B says that the ignition coil should be replaced because the bad wire could have caused the coil to become damaged (tracked) internally. Which technician is correct?
    a. Technician A only
    b. Technician B only
    c. Both Technicians A and B
    d. Neither Technician A nor B

17. What can be adjusted to set the ignition timing on a waste-spark or coil-on-plug-type ignition system?
    a. Crankshaft position (CKP) sensor
    b. Camshaft position (CMP) sensor
    c. Either a or b depending on make and model
    d. None of the above

18. An engine produces less than normal power and is slow to accelerate when the throttle is opened. Technician A says that the exhaust system could be restricted. Technician B says the valve timing may be retarded. Which technician is correct?
    a. Technician A only
    b. Technician B only
    c. Both Technicians A and B
    d. Neither Technician A nor B

19. Which is the *least likely* to cause a weak spark at the spark plug?
    a. A partially shorted primary winding in the ignition coil
    b. A 12.2-volt battery voltage
    c. A high resistance spark plug wire(s)
    d. A voltage drop across the ignition switch

20. Which is *most likely* to cause an engine miss on one cylinder?
    a. An open spark plug wire
    b. A high resistance spark plug wire
    c. Excessive rotor gap
    d. A clogged fuel filter

C. FUEL, AIR INDUCTION, AND EXHAUST SYSTEMS DIAGNOSIS AND REPAIR

21. An engine equipped with a turbocharger is burning oil (blue exhaust smoke all the time). Technician A says that a defective wastegate could be the cause. Technician

B says that a clogged PCV system could be the cause. Which technician is correct?
a. Technician A only
b. Technician B only
c. Both Technicians A and B
d. Neither Technician A nor B

22. A vehicle equipped with a mass airflow sensor as shown will stumble or stall when in "drive" but operate normally when driven in reverse. What is the most likely cause?
a. A split or crack in the air intake hose
b. A clogged fuel filter
c. A restricted air filter
d. A leaking fuel injector

23. A poor fuel economy concern is being discussed. Technician A says that a pinched fuel return line could be the cause. Technician B says that a partially clogged fuel filter could be the cause. Which technician is correct?
a. Technician A only
b. Technician B only
c. Both Technicians A and B
d. Neither Technician A nor B

24. An engine equipped with return–type electronic port fuel injection is hard to start and emits black exhaust smoke when being started when hot. What is the most likely cause?
a. A defective fuel pressure regulator
b. A shorted fuel injector
c. A clogged fuel filter
d. A clogged air filter

25. A vehicle fails an enhanced emission test for excessive carbon monoxide (CO) emission. Which is the most likely cause?
a. Clogged fuel injector(s)
b. A stuck open fuel pressure regulator
c. A stuck idle air control (IAC)
d. A clogged fuel return line

26. Technician A says that the exhaust system can be checked for restriction by using a vacuum gauge attached to manifold vacuum and operating the engine at idle speed. Technician B says the exhaust is restricted if the vacuum increases at 2000 RPM. Which technician is correct?
a. Technician A only
b. Technician B only
c. Both Technicians A and B
d. Neither Technician A nor B

27. A fuel pump should be tested for all of the following except:
a. Pressure
b. Volume
c. Current draw
d. Resistance

28. An engine idles roughly and stalls occasionally when hot. This can be caused by _____.
a. A partially clogged air filter
b. A partially clogged fuel filter
c. Using winter-blended gasoline in warm weather
d. A loose gas cap

29. Technician A says that black exhaust smoke is an indication of excessive oil consumption. Technician B says that blue smoke is an indication of excessive amount

of fuel being burned in the engine. Which technician is correct?
a. Technician A only
b. Technician B only
c. Both Technicians A and B
d. Neither Technician A nor B

D. EMISSIONS CONTROL SYSTEMS DIAGNOSIS AND REPAIR

30. Two technicians are discussing positive crankcase ventilation (PCV) valves. Technician A says that if the valve rattles, it is good. Technician B says the PCV valve may still require replacement even if it rattles. Which technician is correct?
a. Technician A only
b. Technician B only
c. Both Technicians A and B
d. Neither Technician A nor B

31. Technician A says that a defective one-way exhaust check valve could cause the air pump to fail. Technician B says that the airflow to the exhaust manifold when the engine is warm can cause a drivability problem. Which technician is correct?
a. Technician A only
b. Technician B only
c. Both Technicians A and B
d. Neither Technician A nor B

32. A vehicle is running rich. Technician A says that overfilling the fuel tank can cause the carbon canister to become saturated with gasoline, which can cause a rich running condition. Technician B says that an exhaust leak upstream from the O2S could be the cause. Which technician is correct?
a. Technician A only
b. Technician B only
c. Both Technicians A and B
d. Neither Technician A nor B

33. Technician A says that a partially clogged EGR passage can cause the vehicle to fail due to excessive NOx emissions. Technician B says the vehicle could fail for excessive CO if the EGR passage were clogged. Which technician is correct?
a. Technician A only
b. Technician B only
c. Both Technicians A and B
d. Neither Technician A nor B

34. Technician A says the catalytic converter must be replaced if it rattles when tapped. Technician B says a catalytic converter can be defective and not be working yet not be clogged. Which technician is correct?
a. Technician A only
b. Technician B only
c. Both Technicians A and B
d. Neither Technician A nor B

35. Used catalytic converters must be kept for possible inspection by the EPA for how long?
a. 30 days
b. 60 days
c. 90 days
d. 6 months

36. A vehicle fails an emission test for excessive NOx. Which exhaust control device has the greatest effect on the amount of NOx produced by the engine?
   a. PCV
   b. Air pump
   c. Carbon (charcoal) canister
   d. EGR

37. The oxygen sensor of a vehicle has a constant voltage output of about 750 mV. Which exhaust emission control device could be damaged if the vehicle is not repaired to operate correctly?
   a. PCV
   b. Carbon (charcoal) canister
   c. Catalytic converter
   d. EGR

38. Two technicians are discussing the evaporative control system. Technician A says that the carbon (charcoal) canister should be replaced regularly as part of routine maintenance. Technician B says the carbon (charcoal) inside of the EVAP canister can dissolve in gasoline and leave a yellow deposit in the engine when burned. Which technician is correct?
   a. Technician A only
   b. Technician B only
   c. Both Technicians A and B
   d. Neither Technician A nor B

39. An EGR valve is stuck partially open. What is the most likely result?
   a. Pinging (spark knock)
   b. Rough idle—runs normally at highway speeds
   c. Fast idle
   d. Lack of power at highway speeds

E. COMPUTERIZED ENGINE CONTROLS DIAGNOSIS AND REPAIR (INCLUDING OBD II)

40. An oxygen sensor (O2S) is being tested and the O2S voltage is fluctuating between 800 millivolts and 200 millivolts. Technician A says the engine is operating too lean. Technician B says the engine is operating too rich. Which technician is correct?
   a. Technician A only
   b. Technician B only
   c. Both Technicians A and B
   d. Neither Technician A nor B

41. An oxygen sensor in a fuel-injected engine is slow to react to changes in air–fuel mixture. Technician A says that the O2S may need to be replaced. Technician B says that driving the vehicle at highway speeds may restore proper operation of the O2S. Which technician is correct?
   a. Technician A only
   b. Technician B only
   c. Both Technicians A and B
   d. Neither Technician A nor B

42. Technician A says that OBD II SAE (generic) codes are the same for all OBD II vehicles. Technician B says that the DLC is located under the hood on all OBD II vehicles. Which technician is correct?
   a. Technician A only
   b. Technician B only

   c. Both Technicians A and B
   d. Neither Technician A nor B

43. The IAC counts are zero. Technician A says that the engine may have a vacuum leak or a stuck throttle cable. Technician B says the throttle plate(s) may be dirty or partially clogged. Which technician is correct?
   a. Technician A only
   b. Technician B only
   c. Both Technicians A and B
   d. Neither Technician A nor B

44. An engine is operating at idle speed with all accessories off and the gear selector in Park. Technician A says that a scan tool should display injector pulse width between 1.5 and 3.5 milliseconds. Technician B says that the oxygen sensor activity as displayed on a scan tool should indicate over 800 millivolts and less than 200 millivolts. Which technician is correct?
   a. Technician A only
   b. Technician B only
   c. Both Technicians A and B
   d. Neither Technician A nor B

45. Two technicians are discussing fuel trim. Technician A says that oxygen sensor activity determines short-term fuel trim numbers. Technician B says that a positive (+) long-term fuel trim means that the computer is adding fuel to compensate for a lean exhaust. Which technician is correct?
   a. Technician A only
   b. Technician B only
   c. Both Technicians A and B
   d. Neither Technician A nor B

46. An engine will not go into closed loop. Which sensor is the most likely to be at fault?
   a. Oxygen sensor (O2S)
   b. Intake air temperature (IAT)
   c. MAP sensor
   d. BARO sensor

47. A technician is looking at scan data with the engine at idle speed and in Park and notices that the MAP sensor voltage reading is about 1.0 volt (18 in. Hg). Technician A says that the reading is normal. Technician B says that the reading indicates a possible MAP sensor fault. Which technician is correct?
   a. Technician A only
   b. Technician B only
   c. Both Technicians A and B
   d. Neither Technician A nor B

48. The voltage output of a zirconia oxygen sensor is low (close to zero volts). Technician A says the engine is operating too lean. Technician B says the engine is operating too rich. Which technician is correct?
   a. Technician A only
   b. Technician B only
   c. Both Technicians A and B
   d. Neither Technician A nor B

49. A typical TP sensor used in electronic throttle control (ETC) systems includes _____.
   a. One standard three-wire TP sensor
   b. Two TP sensors in one with one producing an increase in voltage as the other one produces a

decreasing voltage as the throttle plate moves toward wide open.

c. Three TP sensors in one with two producing an increase in voltage as the other one produces a decreasing voltage as the throttle plate moves toward wide open.

d. Either b or c

50. Which of the following describes acceptable oxygen sensor activity as measured with a multimeter set to read DC volts?

a. 0.350 to 0.550 volts
b. 0.150 to 0.950 volts
c. 0.450 to 0.850 volts
d. 0.450 volts and steady

ANSWERS TO SAMPLE A8 ASE-TYPE CERTIFICATION TEST

1.	b	14.	c	27.	d	40.	d
2.	c	15.	a	28.	c	41.	c
3.	b	16.	c	29.	d	42.	a
4.	b	17.	d	30.	c	43.	a
5.	b	18.	c	31.	c	44.	c
6.	a	19.	b	32.	c	45.	c
7.	c	20.	a	33.	a	46.	a
8.	c	21.	b	34.	c	47.	a
9.	b	22.	a	35.	b	48.	a
10.	c	23.	a	36.	d	49.	b
11.	b	24.	a	37.	c	50.	b
12.	c	25.	d	38.	d		
13.	b	26.	a	39.	b		

appendix 3
2017 ASE CORRELATION CHART

MLR—Maintenance & Light Repair
AST—Auto Service Technology (Includes MLR)
MAST—Master Auto Service Technology (Includes MLR and AST)

TASK	PRIORITY	MLR	AST	MAST	TEXT PAGE #	TASK PAGE #
		Electrical/Electronic (A6)				
A. GENERAL: ELECTRICAL SYSTEMS DIAGNOSIS						
1. Research vehicle service information including vehicle service history, service precautions, and technical service bulletins.	P-1	✓	✓	✓	2–4	4–9, 34, 42, 51, 57
2. Demonstrate knowledge of electrical/electronic series, parallel, and series-parallel circuits using principles of electricity (Ohm's Law).	P-1	✓	✓	✓	64–69; 72–81	16–24
3. Demonstrate proper use of a digital multimeter (DMM) when measuring source voltage, voltage drop (including grounds), current flow and resistance.	P-1	✓	✓	✓	87–103	25
4. Demonstrate knowledge of the causes and effects from shorts, grounds, opens, and resistance problems in electrical/electronic circuits.	P-1	✓	✓	✓	118–103	36
5. Demonstrate proper use of a test light on an electrical circuit.	P-1	(P-2)	✓	✓	85–86	26
6. Use fused jumper wires to check operation of electrical circuits.	P-1	(P-2)	✓	✓	85	27
7. Use wiring diagrams during the diagnosis (troubleshooting) of electrical/electronic circuit problems.	P-1			✓	131–147	35
8. Diagnose the cause(s) of excessive key-off battery drain (parasitic draw); determine needed action.	P-1	✓	✓	✓	241–243	43
9. Inspect and test fusible links, circuit breakers, and fuses; determine needed action.	P-1	✓	✓	✓	118–123	29
10. Inspect, test, repair, and/or replace components, connectors, terminals, harnesses, and wiring in electrical/electronic systems (including solder repairs).	P-1		✓	✓	123–128	30–33
11. Check electrical/electronic circuit waveforms; interpret readings and determine needed repairs.	P-2			✓	106–112	28
12. Repair data bus wiring harness.	P-1			✓	123–128	33

TASK	PRIORITY	MLR	AST	MAST	TEXT PAGE #	TASK PAGE #
B. BATTERY DIAGNOSIS AND SERVICE						
1. Perform battery state-of-charge test; determine needed action.	P-1	✓	✓	✓	234–235	44
2. Confirm proper battery capacity for vehicle application; perform battery capacity and load test; determine needed action.	P-1	✓	✓	✓	235–237	44
3. Maintain or restore electronic memory functions.	P-1	✓	✓	✓	243–244	45
4. Inspect and clean battery; fill battery cells; check battery cables, connectors, clamps, and hold-downs.	P-1	✓	✓	✓	233	46
5. Perform slow/fast battery charge according to manufacturer's recommendations.	P-1	✓	✓	✓	238–239	47
6. Jump-start vehicle using jumper cables and a booster battery or an auxiliary power supply.	P-1	✓	✓	✓	240	48
7. Identify safety precautions for high voltage systems on hybrid electric, hybrid electric, and diesel vehicles.	P-2	✓	✓	✓	699–705	10, 11, 130–132
8. Identify electrical/electronic modules, security systems, radios, and other accessories that require reinitialization or code entry after reconnecting vehicle battery.	P-1	✓	✓	✓	342–343	49
9. Identify hybrid vehicle auxiliary (12v) battery service, repair, and test procedures.	P-3	✓	✓	✓	705	50
C. STARTING SYSTEM DIAGNOSIS AND REPAIR						
1. Perform starter current draw tests; determine needed action.	P-1	✓	✓	✓	266–267	54
2. Perform starter circuit voltage drop tests; determine needed action.	P-1	✓	✓	✓	264–265	54
3. Inspect and test starter relays and solenoids; determine needed action.	P-2	✓	✓	✓	266–267	55
4. Remove and install starter in a vehicle.	P-1	✓	✓	✓	267, 270	56
5. Inspect and test switches, connectors, and wires of starter control circuits; determine needed action.	P-2	✓	✓	✓	263, 266	55
6. Differentiate between electrical and engine mechanical problems that cause a slow-crank or a no-crank condition.	P-2		✓	✓	266–267	54
7. Demonstrate knowledge of an automatic idle-stop/start-stop system.	P-2	✓	✓	✓	258–260	-
D. CHARGING SYSTEM DIAGNOSIS AND REPAIR						
1. Perform charging system output test; determine needed action.	P-1	✓	✓	✓	298	62
2. Diagnose (troubleshoot) charging system for causes of undercharge, no-charge, or overcharge conditions.	P-1		✓	✓	292–298	63

TASK	PRIORITY	MLR	AST	MAST	TEXT PAGE #	TASK PAGE #
3. Inspect, adjust, and/or replace generator (alternator) drive belts; check pulleys and tensioners for wear; check pulley and belt alignment.	P-1	✓	✓	✓	293–296, 299, 304	64
4. Remove, inspect, and/or replace generator (alternator).	P-1	(P-2)	✓	✓	299; 304	64
5. Perform charging circuit voltage drop tests; determine needed action.	P-1	✓	✓	✓	296–297	65

E. LIGHTING SYSTEMS DIAGNOSIS AND REPAIR

TASK	PRIORITY	MLR	AST	MAST	TEXT PAGE #	TASK PAGE #
1. Diagnose (troubleshoot) the causes of brighter-than-normal, intermittent, dim, or no light operation; determine needed action.	P-1	✓	✓	✓	314–327	66
2. Inspect interior and exterior lamps and sockets including headlights and auxiliary lights (fog lights/driving lights); replace as needed.	P-1		✓	✓	326; 328–330	38, 66
3. Aim headlights.	P-2	✓	✓	✓	328	68
4. Identify system voltage and safety precautions associated with high-intensity discharge headlights.	P-2	✓	✓	✓	322–324	67

F. INSTRUMENT CLUSTER AND DRIVER INFORMATION SYSTEMS DIAGNOSIS AND REPAIR

TASK	PRIORITY	MLR	AST	MAST	TEXT PAGE #	TASK PAGE #
1. Inspect and test gauges and gauge sending units for causes of abnormal readings; determine needed action.	P-2		✓	✓	337–338; 344	69
2. Diagnose (troubleshoot) the causes of incorrect operation of warning devices and other driver information systems; determine needed action.	P-2		✓	✓	335–336; 343–344	70
3. Reset maintenance indicators as required.	P-2	✓	✓	✓	337	71

G. REPAIR BODY ELECTRICAL SYSTEMS DIAGNOSIS AND REPAIR

TASK	PRIORITY	MLR	AST	MAST	TEXT PAGE #	TASK PAGE #
1. Diagnose operation of comfort and convenience accessories and related circuits (such as: power window, power seats, pedal height, power locks, truck locks, remote start, moon roof, sun roof, sun shade, remote keyless entry, voice activation, steering wheel controls, back-up camera, park assist, cruise control, and auto dimming headlamps); determine needed repairs.	P-2		✓	✓	336; 344–345; 365–378	37, 75, 79
2. Diagnose operation of security/anti-theft systems and related circuits (such as: theft deterrent, door locks, remote keyless entry, remote start, and starter/fuel disable); determine needed repairs.	P-2		✓	✓	375–379; 395–402	81
3. Diagnose operation of entertainment and related circuits (such as: radio, DVD, remote CD changer, navigation, amplifiers, speakers, antennas, and voice-activated accessories); determine needed repairs.	P-3		✓	✓	336; 346–348; 421–436	84

TASK	PRIORITY	MLR	AST	MAST	TEXT PAGE #	TASK PAGE #
4. Diagnose operation of safety systems and related circuits (such as: horn, airbags, seat belt pretensioners, occupancy classification, wipers, washers, speed control/collision avoidance, heads-up display, park assist, and back-up camera); determine needed repairs.	P-1		✓	✓	338; 344; 353–365	72–74
5. Diagnose body electronic systems circuits using a scan tool; check for module communication errors (data bus systems); determine needed action.	P-2		✓	✓	400–402	76
6. Describe the process for software transfer, software updates, or reprogramming of electronic modules.	P-2		✓	✓	693–696	76

appendix 4
2017 ASE CORRELATION CHART

MLR—Maintenance & Light Repair
AST—Auto Service Technology (Includes MLR)
MAST—Master Auto Service Technology (Includes MLR and AST)

TASK	PRIORITY	MLR	AST	MAST	TEXT PAGE #	TASK PAGE #
Engine Performance (A8)						
A. GENERAL: ENGINE DIAGNOSIS						
1. Identify and interpret engine performance concerns; determine needed action.	P-1		✓	✓	679–691	114
2. Research vehicle service information including, vehicle service history, service precautions, and technical service bulletins.	P-1	✓	✓	✓	679–683	85–87, 89, 106, 107, 125, 128
3. Diagnose abnormal engine noises or vibration concerns; determine needed action.	P-3		✓	✓	681–682	-
4. Diagnose the cause of excessive oil consumption, coolant consumption, unusual exhaust color, odor, and sound; determine needed action.	P-2		✓	✓	681–682	-
5. Perform engine absolute manifold pressure tests (vacuum/boost); determine needed action.	P-1		✓	✓	523–525	116
6. Perform cylinder power balance test; determine needed action.	P-1		✓	✓	-	-
7. Perform cylinder cranking and running compression tests; determine needed action.	P-1		✓	✓	-	-
8. Perform cylinder leakage test; determine needed action.	P-1		✓	✓	-	-
9. Diagnose engine mechanical, electrical, electronic, fuel, and ignition concerns; determine needed action.	P-2		✓	✓	679–685	-
10. Verify engine operating temperature; determine needed action.	P-1		✓	✓	504–508	-
11. Verify correct camshaft timing including engines equipped with variable valve timing systems (WT).	P-1	✓	✓	✓	-	-
B. COMPUTERIZED CONTROLS DIAGNOSIS AND REPAIR						
1. Retrieve and record diagnostic trouble codes (DTC), OBD monitor status, and freeze frame data; clear codes when applicable.	P-1		✓	✓	682–683	108, 127
2. Access and use service information to perform step-by-step (troubleshooting) diagnosis.	P-1		✓	✓	679–684; 695–696	129

TASK	PRIORITY	MLR	AST	MAST	TEXT PAGE #	TASK PAGE #
3. Perform active tests of actuators using a scan tool; determine needed action.	P-1		✓	✓	685	40, 129
4. Describe the use of OBD monitors for repair verification	P-1	✓	✓	✓	695–696	127
5. Diagnose the causes of emissions or drivability concerns with stored or active diagnostic trouble codes (DTC); obtain, graph, and interpret scan tool data.	P-1		✓	✓	682–683	115
6. Diagnose emissions or drivability concerns without stored diagnostic trouble codes; determine needed action.	P-1			✓	692–693	109
7. Inspect and test computerized engine control system sensors, powertrain/engine control module (PCM/ECM), actuators, and circuits using a graphing multimeter (GMM)/digital storage oscilloscope (DSO); perform needed action.	P-2			✓	508; 518; 537; 548–549; 554; 616–617	28, 41, 91–101
8. Diagnose drivability and emissions problems resulting from malfunctions of interrelated systems (cruise control, security alarms, suspension controls, traction controls, HVAC, automatic transmissions, non-OEM installed accessories, or similar systems); determine needed action.	P-2			✓	395	126

C. IGNITION SYSTEM DIAGNOSIS AND REPAIR

TASK	PRIORITY	MLR	AST	MAST	TEXT PAGE #	TASK PAGE #
1. Diagnose (troubleshoot) ignition system-related problems such as no-starting, hard starting, engine misfire, poor drivability, spark knock, power loss, poor mileage, and emissions concerns; determine needed action.	P-2		✓	✓	482–500	90–92
2. Inspect and test crankshaft and camshaft position sensor(s); determine needed action.	P-1		✓	✓	483–485	95
3. Inspect, test, and/or replace ignition control module, powertrain/engine control module; reprogram/initialize as needed.	P-3		✓	✓	483	-
4. Remove and replace spark plugs; inspect secondary ignition components for wear and damage.	P-1	✓	✓	✓	490–492	93, 94

D. FUEL, AIR INDUCTION, AND EXHAUST SYSTEMS DIAGNOSIS AND REPAIR

TASK	PRIORITY	MLR	AST	MAST	TEXT PAGE #	TASK PAGE #
1. Diagnose (troubleshoot) hot or cold no-starting, hard starting, poor drivability, incorrect idle speed, poor idle, flooding, hesitation, surging, engine misfire, power loss, stalling, poor mileage, dieseling, and emissions problems; determine needed action.	P-2			✓	609–622	110
2. Check fuel for contaminants; determine needed action.	P-2		✓	✓	445–446	88
3. Inspect and test fuel pumps and pump control systems for pressure, regulation, and volume; perform needed action.	P-1		✓	✓	609–611	102, 103
4. Replace fuel filter(s) where applicable.	P-2	✓	✓	✓	567	104

TASK	PRIORITY	MLR	AST	MAST	TEXT PAGE #	TASK PAGE #
5. Inspect, service, or replace air filters, filter housings, and intake duct work.	P-1	✓	✓	✓	535; 608	103
6. Inspect throttle body, air induction system, intake manifold and gaskets for vacuum leaks and/or unmetered air.	P-2		✓	✓	609–610; 617–618	103
7. Inspect test and/or replace fuel injectors.	P-2		✓	✓	613–618	111–113
8. Verify idle control operation.	P-1		✓	✓	620	103
9. Inspect integrity of the exhaust manifold, exhaust pipes, muffler(s), catalytic converter(s), resonator(s), tail pipe(s), and heat shields; perform needed action.	P-1	✓	✓	✓	654–657	-
10. Inspect condition of exhaust system hangers, brackets, clamps, and heat shields; determine needed action.	P-1	✓	✓	✓	-	-
11. Perform exhaust system back-pressure test; determine needed action.	P-2			✓	655	-
12. Check and refill diesel exhaust fluid (DEF).	P-2	✓	✓	✓	-	-
13. Test the operation of turbocharger/supercharger systems; determine needed action.	P-2			✓	-	-

E. EMISSIONS CONTROL SYSTEMS DIAGNOSIS AND REPAIR

TASK	PRIORITY	MLR	AST	MAST	TEXT PAGE #	TASK PAGE #
1. Diagnose oil leaks, emissions, and drivability concerns caused by the positive crankcase ventilation (PCV) system; determine needed action.	P-3		✓	✓	647	117
2. Inspect, test, service and/or replace positive crankcase ventilation (PCV) filter/breather, valve, tubes, orifices, and hoses; perform needed action.	P-2	✓	✓	✓	647–650	117
3. Diagnose emissions and drivability concerns caused by the exhaust gas recirculation (EGR) system; inspect, and test, service and/or replace electrical/electronic sensors, controls, and wiring of exhaust gas recirculation (EGR) systems tubing, exhaust passages, vacuum/pressure controls, filters and hoses of exhaust gas recirculation (EGR) systems; determine needed action.	P-2		✓	✓	640–646	118–120
4. Diagnose emissions and drivability concerns caused by the components and circuits of air injection systems; inspect, test, repair, and/or replace electrical/electronically-operated components and circuits of secondary air injection systems; determine needed action.	P-2		✓	✓	650–652	122
5. Diagnose emissions and drivability concerns caused by the evaporative emissions control (EVAP) system; determine needed action.	P-2			✓	658–665	123

TASK	PRIORITY	MLR	AST	MAST	TEXT PAGE #	TASK PAGE #
6. Diagnose emission and drivability concerns caused by catalytic converter system; determine needed action.	P-2			✓	654–657	121
7. Interpret diagnostic trouble codes (DTCs) and scan tool data related to the emissions control systems; determine needed action.	P-3		✓	✓	646; 650; 652; 658; 665	115

GLOSSARY

AC coupling A signal that passes the AC signal component to the meter, but blocks the DC component. Useful to observe an AC signal that is normally riding on a DC signal; for example, a charging ripple.

AC/DC clamp-on DMM A type of meter with a clamp placed around the wire to measure current.

Accumulator A temporary location for fluid under pressure.

Active crossover A type of crossover that uses electronic components to block certain frequencies.

Actuator An electromechanical device that performs mechanical movement as commanded by a controller.

Adhesive-lined heat shrink tubing A type of heat shrink tubing that shrinks to one-third of its original diameter and has glue inside.

AFS Active front headlight system. A name for the system that causes the headlights to turn when cornering.

AGM Absorbed glass mat. AGM batteries are lead-acid batteries, but use an absorbent material between the plates to hold the electrolyte. AGM batteries are classified as valve-regulated lead acid (VRLA) batteries.

AGST Aboveground storage tank, used to store used oil.

AIR Air injection reaction.

Airbag An inflatable fabric bag that deploys in the event of a collision severe enough to cause personal injury.

Alternator An electric generator that produces alternating current; also called an AC generator.

Alternator whine A noise made by an alternator with a defective diode(s).

AM Amplitude modulation.

American wire gauge A method used to measure wire diameter.

Ammeter An electrical test instrument used to measure amperes (unit of the amount of current flow).

Ampere The unit that measures the amount of current flow. Named for André Ampère (1775–1836).

Ampere-turns The unit of measurement for electrical magnetic field strength.

Analog-to-digital (AD) converter An electronic circuit that converts analog signals into digital signals that can then be used by a computer.

Anode The positive electrode; the electrode toward which electrons flow.

ANSI American National Standards Institute, an organization that publishes safety standards for safety glasses and other personal protective equipment.

Armature The rotating unit inside a DC generator or starter, consisting of a series of coils of insulating wire wound around a laminated iron core.

Arming sensor A sensor used in an airbag circuit that is most sensitive and completes the circuit; first of two sensors that are needed to deploy an airbag.

Asbestosis A health condition in which asbestos causes scar tissue to form in the lungs, causing shortness of breath.

ASD Automatic shutdown relay.

ASM Acceleration simulation mode.

ASTM American Society for Testing Materials.

Auto link A type of automotive fuse.

Baffle A plate or shield used to direct the flow of a liquid or gas.

BARO sensor Barometric pressure sensor.

Base The name for the section of a transistor that controls the current flow through the transistor.

Battery cables Cables that attach to the positive and negative terminals of the battery.

Battery electrical drain test A test to determine if a component or circuit is draining the battery.

Baud rate The speed at which bits of computer information are transmitted on a serial data stream. Measured in bits per second (bps).

BCI Battery Council International.

Bench testing Testing a component such as a starter before installing it in the vehicle.

Bias voltage In electrical terms, bias is the voltage applied to a device or component to establish the reference point for operation.

Binary system A computer system that uses a series of zeros and ones to represent the information.

Bipolar transistor A type of transistor that has a base, emitter, and collector.

Bluetooth A short range wireless communication standard named after a Danish king that had a blue tooth.

BMAP Barometric manifold absolute pressure.

BNC connector Coaxial-type input connector. Named for its inventor, Neil Councilman.

BOB Break out box.

Bound electrons Electrons that are close to the nucleus of the atom.

Braided ground straps Ground wires that are not insulated and braided to help increase flexibility and reduce RFI.

Branches Electrical parts of a parallel circuit.

Breaker bar A handle used to rotate a socket; also called a flex handle.

Brush-end housing The end of a starter or generator (alternator) where the brushes are located.

Brushes A copper or carbon conductor used to transfer electrical current from, or to, a revolving electrical part such as that used in an electrical motor or generator.

Bump cap A hat that is hard and plastic to protect the head from bumps.

Burn-in A process of operating an electronic device for a period from several hours to several days.

BUS A term used to describe a communication network.

CAA Clean Air Act. Federal legislation passed in 1970 that established national air quality standards.

Calibration codes Codes used on many powertrain control modules.

California Air Resources Board A state of California agency that regulates the air quality standards for the state.

Campaign A recall where vehicle owners are contacted to return a vehicle to a dealer for corrective action.

CAN Controller area network. A type of serial data transmission.

Candlepower Measures the amount of light produced by a bulb.

Capacitance A term used to measure or describe how much charge can be stored in a capacitor (condenser) for a given voltage potential difference. Capacitance is measured in farads or smaller increments of farads such as microfarads.

Casting number An identification code cast into an engine block or other large cast part of a vehicle.

CAT III An electrical measurement equipment rating created by the International Electrotechnical Commission (IEC). CAT III indicates the lowest level of instrument protection that should be in place when performing electrical measurements on hybrid electric vehicles.

Catalytic converter An emission control device located in the exhaust system that changes HC and CO into harmless H_2O and CO_2. If a three-way catalyst, NO_x is also divided into harmless separate nitrogen (N_2) and Oxygen (O_2).

Cathode The negative electrode.

CCA Cold cranking amps. A rating of a battery tested at zero degrees F.

CCM Comprehensive component monitor.

Cells A group of negative and positive plates that form a cell capable of producing 2.1 V.

CEMF Counter electromotive force.

CFR Code of Federal Regulations.

Charging voltage test Using a voltmeter and an ammeter to test the condition of the charging circuit.

Cheater bar A pipe or other object used to lengthen the handle of a ratchet or breaker bar. Not recommended as the extra force can cause the socket or ratchet to break.

CHMSL Centre high-mounted stop-light; the third brake light.

CHT Cylinder head temperature.

Circuit A circuit is the path that electrons travel from a power source, through a resistance, and back to the power source.

Circuit breaker A mechanical unit that opens an electrical circuit in the event of excessive flow.

Clamping diode A diode installed in a circuit with the cathode toward the positive. The diode becomes forward biased when the circuit is turned off, thereby reducing the high-voltage surge created by the current flowing through a coil.

Class 2 A type of BUS communication used in General Motors vehicles.

Claw poles The magnetic points of a generator (alternator) rotor.

Clock generator A crystal that determines the speed of computer circuits.

Clockspring A flat ribbon of wire used under the steering wire to transfer airbag electrical signals. May also carry horn and steering wheel control circuits depending on the make and model of vehicle.

Coil-on-plug ignition system An ignition system without a distributor, where each spark plug is integrated with an ignition coil.

Cold solder joint A type of solder joint that was not heated to high enough temperature to create a good electrical connection. Often has a dull gray appearance rather than being shiny for a good solder connection.

Collector The name of one section of a transistor.

Color shift A term used to describe the change in the color of an HID arc tube assembly over time.

Combination circuit Another name for a series-parallel electrical circuit.

Commutator-end housing The end of a starter motor that contains the commutator and brushes. Also called the brush-end housing.

Complete circuit A type of electrical circuit that has continuity; current would flow if connected to power and ground.

Composite headlight A type of headlight that uses a separate, replaceable bulb.

Compound circuit Another name for a series-parallel electrical circuit.

Compression spring A spring that is part of a starter drive and acts on the starter pinion gear.

Condenser An A/C system component located in front of the radiator in most vehicles that removes heat from the refrigerant and causes it to change from a gas to a liquid.

Conductor A material that conducts electricity and heat. A metal that contains fewer than four electrons in its atom's outer shell.

Continuity Instrument setup to check wiring, circuits, connectors, or switches for breaks (open circuit) or short circuits (closed circuit).

Continuity light A test light that has a battery; it lights if there is continuity (electrical connection) between the two points that are connected to the tester.

Controller A term that usually refers to a computer or an electronic control unit (ECU).

Conventional theory The theory that electricity flows from positive (1) to negative (2).

Coulomb A measurement of electrons. A coulomb is 6.28 101 (6.28 billion) electrons.

Courtesy lights General term used to describe all interior lights.

CPA Connector position assurance. A clip used to help hold the two parts of an electrical connector together.

CPU Central processor unit.

Crimp-and-seal connectors A type of electrical connector that has glue inside which provides a weather-proof seal after it is heated.

Crossover An electronic circuit that separates frequencies in a sound (audio) system.

CRT Cathode ray tube.

Cruise control A system that maintains the desired vehicle speed. Also called speed control.

Darlington pair Two transistors electrically connected to form an amplifier. This permits a very small current flow to control a large current flow. Named for Sidney Darlington, a physicist at Bell Laboratories from 1929 to 1971.

dB Decibels.

DC coupling A signal transmission that passes both AC and DC signal components to the meter. See also AC coupling.

DDS Demand delivery system.

Deceleration sensor A sensor mounted to the body or frame of a vehicle that detects and measures the deceleration of the vehicle. Used to control the activation of the airbags and vehicle stability systems.

Deep cycling The full discharge, and then the full recharge, of a battery.

Despiking diode Another name for a clamping diode.

Detonation A violent explosion in the combustion chamber created by uncontrolled burning of the air–fuel mixture; often causes a loud, audible knock. Also known as spark knock or ping.

Dielectric Resistance to electrical penetration.

Digital computer A computer that uses on and off signals only. Uses an A to D converter to change analog signals to digital before processing.

Diode An electrical device that allows current to flow in one direction only.

DIS Distributorless ignition system.

Division A specific segment of a waveform, as defined by the grid on the display.

DLC Data link connector.

DMM Digital multimeter. A digital multimeter is capable of measuring electrical current, resistance, and voltage.

Doping The adding of impurities to pure silicon or germanium to form either P- or N-type material.

Double-layer technology Technology used to build ultracapacitors. Involves the use of two carbon electrodes separated by a membrane.

DPDT Double-pole, double-throw switch.

DPFE Delta pressure feedback EGR.

DPST Double-pole, single-throw switch.

Drive size The size in fractions of an inch of the square drive for sockets.

Drive-end (DE) housing The end of a starter motor that has the drive pinion gear.

DRL Daytime running lights. Lights that are located in the front of the vehicle and come on whenever the ignition is on. Some vehicles have to be moving before they come on. Used as a safety device on many vehicles and required in many countries such as Canada since 1990.

DSO Digital storage oscilloscope.

Dual inline pins A type of electronic chip that has two parallel lines of pins.

Dual-stage airbags Airbags that can deploy with minimum force, full force, or both together based on the information sent to the airbag controller regarding the forces involved in the collision.

Duty cycle Refers to the percentage of on-time of the signal during one complete cycle.

DVOM Digital volt-ohm-meter.

Dwell The amount of time, recorded on a dwell meter in degrees, that voltage passes through a closed switch.

Dynamic voltage Voltage measured with the circuit energized and current flowing through the circuit.

E & C Entertainment and comfort.

EAC Electronic air control.

ECA Electronic control module. The name Ford used to describe the computer that controlled spark and fuel on older model vehicles.

ECM Electronic control module on a vehicle.

ECT Engine coolant temperature.

ECU Electronic control unit on a vehicle.

EDR Event data recorder. The hardware and software used to record vehicle information before, during, and after an airbag deployment.

EEPROM Electronically erasable programmable read-only memory.

EI Electronic ignition.

EIS Electronic ignition system.

Electrical load Applying a load to a component such as a battery to measure its performance.

Electrical potential Another term to describe voltage.

Electricity The movement of free electrons from one atom to another.

Electrochemistry The chemical reaction that occurs inside a battery to produce electricity.

Electrolysis The process in which electric current is passed through water in order to break it into hydrogen and oxygen gas.

Electrolyte Any substance which, in solution, is separated into ions and is made capable of conducting an electric current. The acid solution of a lead-acid battery.

Electromotive force The force (pressure) that can move electrons through a conductor.

Electron theory The theory that electricity flows from negative (+) to positive (−).

Element Any substance that cannot be separated into different substances.

EMI Electromagnetic interference. An undesirable electronic signal. It is caused by a magnetic field building up and collapsing, creating unwanted electrical interference on a nearby circuit.

Emitter The name of one section of a transistor. The arrow used on a symbol for a transistor is on the emitter and the arrow points toward the negative section of the transistor.

Energy carrier Any medium that is utilized to store or transport energy. Hydrogen is an energy carrier because energy is used to generate hydrogen gas that is used as a fuel.

Energy density A measure of the amount of energy that can be stored in a battery relative to the volume of the battery container. Energy density is measured in terms of Watt-hours per liter (Wh/L).

Engine mapping A computer program that uses engine test data to determine the best fuel–air ratio and spark advance to use at each speed of the engine for best performance.

EPA Environmental Protection Agency.

EPM Electrical power management. A General Motors term used to describe a charging system control sensor and the control of the generator (alternator) output based on the needs of the vehicle.

ERFS Electronic returnless fuel system. A fuel delivery system that does not return fuel to the tank.

ESD Electrostatic discharge. Another term for ESD is static electricity.

EST Electronic spark timing.

ETC Electronic throttle control. The intake system throttle plate is controlled by a servo motor instead of a mechanical linkage. Also known as drive-by wire.

EV Electric vehicle. A term used to describe battery-powered vehicles.

EVP EGR valve position.

EVRV Electronic vacuum regulator valve.

Extension A socket wrench tool used between a ratchet or breaker bar and a socket.

External trigger Using an oscilloscope to trigger or start another scope measuring a circuit.

Eye wash station A water fountain designed to rinse the eyes with a large volume of water.

Farad A unit of capacitance named for Michael Faraday (1791–1867), an English physicist. A farad is the capacity to store 1 coulomb of electrons at 1 volt of potential difference.

FCHV Fuel cell hybrid vehicle.

FCV Fuel cell vehicle.

FET Field effect transistor.

Field coils Coils of wire wound around metal pole shoes to form the electromagnetic field inside an electric motor.

Field housing The part of a starter that supports the field coils.

Field poles The magnets used as field coils in a starter motor.

Fire blanket A fire-proof wool blanket used to cover a person who is on fire and smother the fire.

Fire extinguisher classes The types of fire extinguishers designed for specific types of fires.

Floating ground An electrical system where neither the power nor ground circuits are connected to a chassis or body ground.

Flux density The density of the magnetic lines of force around a magnet or other object.

FM Frequency modulation.

Forward bias Current flow in normal direction.

Free electrons The outer electrons in an atom that has fewer than four electrons in its outer orbit.

Frequency The number of times a waveform repeats in one second, measured in Hertz (Hz), frequency band.

FTP Federal test procedure.

Fuel cell An electrochemical device that converts the energy stored in hydrogen gas into electricity, water, and heat.

Fuel trim A computer function that adjusts fuel delivery during closed-loop operation to bring the air–fuel mixture to as close to 14.7:1 as possible.

Fuel-cell stack A collection of individual fuel cells, which are stacked end-to-end into one compact package.

Fuse link A safety device used on a solvent washer that melts and causes the lid to close in the event of a fire. A type of fuse used to control the maximum current in a circuit.

Fusible link A type of fuse that will melt and open the protected circuit in the event of a short circuit, which could cause excessive current flow through the fusible link. Most fusible links are actually wires that are four gauge sizes smaller than the wire of the circuits being protected.

Gassing The release of hydrogen and oxygen gas from the plates of a battery during charging or discharging.

GAWR Gross axle weight rating. A rating of the load capacity of a vehicle; included on placards on the vehicle and in the owner's manual.

GDI A fuel injection system design in which gasoline is injected directly into the combustion chamber.

Gel Battery A lead-acid battery with silica added to the electrolyte to make it leak proof and spill proof.

Germanium A semiconductor material.

GMLAN GM local area network. A type of serial data transmission by General Motors.

GMM Graphing multimeter.

Grade The strength rating of a bolt.

Graticule The series of squares on the face of a scope. Usually 8 by 10 on a screen.

Grid The lead-alloy framework (support) for the active materials of an automotive battery.

Ground brushes The brushes in a starter motor that carry current to the housing of the starter or ground.

Ground plane A part of an antenna that is metal and usually the body of the vehicle.

Growler Electrical tester designed to test the starter and DC generator armatures.

GVWR Gross vehicle weight rating. The total weight of the vehicle including the maximum cargo.

Hall-effect switch A semiconductor moving relative to a magnetic field, creating a variable voltage output. Used to determine position. A type of electromagnetic sensor used in electronic ignition and other systems. Named for Edwin H. Hall, who discovered the Hall effect in 1879.

Hazard warning A sticker or decal warning that a hazard is close.

Heat sink Usually, a metallic-finned unit used to keep electronic components cool.

HEPA vacuum High-efficiency particulate air filter vacuum used to clean brake dust.

Hertz A unit of measurement of frequency. One Hertz is one cycle per second, abbreviated Hz. Named for Heinrich R. Hertz, a 19th-century German physicist.

HEV Hybrid electric vehicle. Describes any vehicle that uses more than one source of propulsion, such as an internal combustion engine (ICE) and electric motor(s).

HID High-intensity discharge. A type of headlight that uses high voltage to create an arc inside the arc tube assembly, which then produces a blue-white light.

High-pass filter A filter in an audio system that blocks low frequencies and only allows high frequencies to pass through to the speakers.

HO2S1 Heated oxygen sensor.

Hold-in winding One of two electromagnetic windings inside a solenoid; used to hold the movable core into the solenoid.

Hole theory A theory that states that as an electron flows from negative (−) to positive (+), it leaves behind a hole. According to the hole theory, the hole would move from positive (+) to negative (−).

Horn An electromechanical device that creates a loud sound when activated.

HV High voltage. Applies to any voltage above 50 volts.

HV cables Vehicle cables that carry high voltage.

Hydraulic power assist A hybrid vehicle configuration that utilizes hydraulic pumps and accumulators for energy regeneration.

Hydrometer An instrument used to measure the specific gravity of a liquid. A battery hydrometer is calibrated to read the expected specific gravity of battery electrolyte.

IAC Idle air control.

ICE Internal combustion engine.

ICM Ignition control module.

IEC International Electrotechnical Commission.

Ignition coil An electrical device consisting of two separate coils of wire: a primary and a secondary winding. The purpose of an ignition is to produce a high-voltage (20,000 to 40,000 V), low-amperage (about 80 mA) current necessary for spark ignition.

Ignition timing The exact point of ignition in relation to piston position.

Impedance The resistance of a coil of wire, measured in ohms.

Impurities Doping elements.

Inductive ammeter A type of ammeter used as a Hall-effect sensor in a clamp that is used around a conductor carrying a current.

Inductive reactance An opposing current created in a conductor whenever there is a charging current flow in a conductor.

Input Information on data from sensors to an electronic controller is called input. Sensors and switches provide the input signals.

Input conditioning What the computer does to the input signals to make them useful; usually includes an analog-to-digital converter and other electronic circuits that eliminate electrical noise.

Insulated brushes Brushes used in a starter motor that connect to battery power through the solenoid.

Insulated path The power side of an electrical circuit.

Insulators Thin strips of plastic or hard rubber used to separate the leaves of a leaf spring.

Integral sensor A term used to describe a crash sensor that is built into the airbag control module.

Integrated circuit An electronic circuit that contains many circuits all in one chip.

Inverter An electronic device used to convert DC (direct current) into AC (alternating current).

IOD Ignition off draw. A Chrysler term used to describe battery electrical drain or parasitic draw.

Ion An atom with an excess or deficiency of electrons forming either a negative or a positive charged particle.

Ion-sensing ignition An electronic ignition system that uses the spark plug as a sensor to determine camshaft position, misfire, and knock.

ISC Idle speed control.

Jumper cables Heavy-gauge (4 to 2/0) electrical cables with large clamps, used to connect a vehicle that has a discharged battery to a vehicle that has a good battery.

Junction The point where two types of materials join.

KAM Keep-alive memory.

Kelvin A temperature scale where absolute zero is zero degrees. Nothing is colder than absolute zero.

Key fob A decorative unit attached to keys. Often includes a remote control to unlock/lock vehicles.

Keyword A type of network communication used in many General Motors vehicles.

Kilo Means 1,000; abbreviated k or K.

Kirchhoff's current law A law that states: "The current flowing into any junction of an electrical circuit is equal to the current flowing out of that junction."

Kirchhoff's voltage law A law about electrical circuits that states: "The voltage around any closed circuit is equal to the sum (total) of the resistances."

Knock sensor A sensor that can detect engine spark knock.

KOEO Key-on–engine off test.

KOER Key-on–engine running test.

LDP Leak detection pump.

LED Light-emitting diode. A high-efficiency light source that uses very little electricity and produces very little heat.

Left-hand rule A method of determining the direction of magnetic lines of force around a conductor. The left-hand rule is used with the electron flow theory (+ flowing to +).

Legs Another name for the branches of a parallel circuit.

Lenz's law The relative motion between a conductor and a magnetic field is opposed by the magnetic field of the current it has induced.

Leyden jar A device first used to store an electrical charge. The first type of capacitor.

Lineman's gloves Type of gloves worn by technicians when working around high-voltage circuits. Usually includes a rubber inner glove rated at 1,000 volts and a protective leather outer glove used for hybrid electric vehicle service.

Load A term used to describe a device an electrical current is flowing through.

Load test A type of battery test where an electrical load is applied to the battery and the voltage is monitored to determine the condition of a battery.

LOC Light-off converter.

Lock tang A mechanical tab that is used to secure a terminal into a connector. This lock tang must be depressed to be able to remove the terminal from the connector.

Lockout switch A lock placed on the circuit breaker box to ensure that no one turns on the electrical circuit while repairs are being made.

Logic probe A type of tester that can detect either power or ground. Most testers can detect voltage but most of the others cannot detect if a ground is present without further testing.

Low-grade heat Cooling system temperatures that are very close to the temperature of the ambient air, resulting in lowered heat transfer efficiency.

Low-pass filter A device in an audio system that blocks high frequencies and only allows low frequencies to pass to the speakers.

Low-water loss battery A type of battery that uses little water in normal service. Most batteries used in cars and light trucks use this type of battery.

LSD Low-side drivers.

Lumbar The lower section of the back.

MAF Mass airflow sensor.

Magnetic flux The lines of force produced in a magnetic field.

Magnetic induction The transfer of the magnetic lines of force to another nearby metal object or coil of wire.

Magnetism A form of energy that is recognized by the attraction it exerts on other materials.

Maintenance-free battery A type of battery that does not require routine adding of water to the cells. Most batteries used in cars and light trucks are maintenance-free design.

Malfunction indicator lamp This amber dashboard warning light may be labeled check engine or service engine soon.

MAP Manifold absolute pressure.

Mega Million. Used when writing larger numbers or measuring large amounts of resistance.

Membrane electrode assembly The part of the PEM fuel cell that contains the membrane, catalyst coatings, and electrodes.

Mercury A heavy metal.

Mesh spring A spring used behind the starter pinion on a starter drive to force the drive pinion into mesh with the ring gear on the engine.

Meter accuracy The accuracy of a meter measured in percent.

Meter resolution The specification of meter that indicates how small or fine a measurement the meter can detect and display.

Metric bolts Bolts manufactured and sized in the metric system of measurement.

Metric wire gauge The metric method for measuring wire size in square millimeters. This is the measure of the core of the wire and does not include the insulation.

Milli One-thousandth of a volt or ampere.

MNHC Non-methane hydrocarbon.

Modulation The combination of these two frequencies is referred to as modulation.

Momentary switch A type of switch that toggles between on and off.

MOSFET Metal oxide semiconductor field-effect transistor. A type of transistor.

MRFS A returnless fuel delivery system design that uses a mechanical pressure regulator located in the fuel tank.

MSDS Material safety data sheets.

Multiplexing A process of sending multiple signals of information at the same time over a signal wire.

Mutual induction The generation of an electric current due to a changing magnetic field of an adjacent coil.

N.C. Normally closed.

N.O. Normally open.

Network A communications system used to link multiple computers or modules.

Neutral charge An atom that has the same number of electrons as protons.

Neutral safety switch A switch connected in series in the starter control circuit that allows operation of the starter motor to occur only when the gear selector is in neutral (N) or park (P).

NiMH Nickel-metal hydride. A battery design used for the high voltage batteries in most hybrid electric vehicles.

Node A module and computer that is part of a communications network.

NPN transistor A type of transistor that uses the P-type material in the base and the N-type material for the emitter and collector.

NTC Negative temperature coefficient. Usually used in reference to a temperature sensor (coolant or air temperature). As the temperature increases, the resistance of the sensor decreases.

N-type material Silicon or germanium doped with phosphorus, arsenic, or antimony.

O₂ sensor Oxygen sensor.

OAD Override alternator dampener.

OAP Override alternator pulley.

OBD On-board diagnosis.

Occupant detection systems An airbag system with a sensor in the passenger seat to detect whether or not a passenger is seated in the passenger side and, if so, the weight range of that passenger.

Ohm The unit of electrical resistance. Named for Georg Simon Ohm (1787–1854).

Ohmmeter An electrical test instrument used to measure ohms (unit of electrical resistance).

Ohm's law An electrical law that requires 1 volt to push 1 ampere through 1 ohm of resistance.

OL Overload or over limit.

OP-amps Used in circuits to control and simplify digital signals.

Open circuit Any circuit that is not complete and in which no current flows.

Open circuit voltage Voltage measured without the circuit in operation.

Open-end wrench A type of wrench that allows access to the flats of a bolt or nut from the side.

Open-loop operation A phase of computer-controlled engine operation where the air–fuel mixture is calculated in the absence of oxygen sensor signals. During open loop, calculations are based primarily on throttle position, engine RPM, and engine coolant temperature.

ORVR Onboard refueling vapor recovery.

OSC Oxygen storage capacity.

Oscilloscope A visual display of electrical waves on a fluorescent screen or cathode ray tube.

OSHA Occupational Safety and Health Administration. OSHA is the main federal agency responsible for enforcement of workplace safety and health legislation.

Overrunning alternator dampener An alternator (generator) drive pulley that has a one-way clutch and a dampener spring used to smooth the operation of the alternator and reduce the stress on the drive belt.

Overrunning alternator pulley An alternator (generator) drive pulley that has a one-way clutch used to smooth the operation of the alternator and reduce the stress on the drive belt.

Overrunning clutch A mechanical coupling device that allows torque to be transmitted in one direction of rotation, but freewheels when turned in the opposite direction. Also known as a one-way clutch.

Ozone Oxygen rich (O₃) gas created by sunlight reaction with unburned hydrocarbons (HC) and oxides of nitrogen (NOₓ); also called smog.

Pacific fuse element A type of automotive fuse.

Parallel circuit An electrical circuit with more than one path from the power side to the ground side. Has more than one branch or leg.

Parasitic load test An electrical test that measures how much current (amperes) is draining from the battery with the ignition off and all electrical loads off.

Partitions Separations between the cells of a battery. Partitions are made of the same material as that used on the outside case of the battery.

Passenger presence system An airbag system with a sensor in the passenger seat to detect whether or not a passenger is seated in the passenger side and, if so, the weight range of that passenger.

PATS Passive anti-theft system. A type of anti-theft system used in Ford, Lincoln, and Mercury vehicles.

PCM Powertrain control module.

PCV Pressure control valve.

PEFC Polymer electrolyte fuel cell.

Peltier effect A French scientist, Peltier found that electrons moving through a solid can carry heat from one side of the material to the other side. This effect is called the Peltier effect.

PEM Proton exchange membrane fuel cell. A low-temperature fuel cell known for fast starts and relatively simple construction.

Permeability The measure of how well a material conducts magnetic lines of force.

PFE Pressure feedback EGR.

PHEV Plug-in hybrid electric vehicle.

Photodiodes A type of diode used as a sun-load sensor. Connected in reverse bias, the current flow is proportional to the sun load.

Photoelectricity When certain metals are exposed to light, some of the light energy is transferred to the free electrons of the metal. This excess energy breaks the electrons loose from the surface of the metal. They can then be collected and made to flow in a conductor, which is called photoelectricity.

Photons Light is emitted from an LED by the release of energy in the form of photons.

Photoresistor A semiconductor that changes in resistance with the presence or absence of light. Dark is high resistance and light is low resistance.

Phototransistor An electronic device that can detect light and turn on or off. Used in some suspension height sensors.

PID Parameter identification.

Pinch weld seam A strong section under a vehicle where two body panels are welded together.

Ping Secondary rapid burning of the last 3% to 5% of the air–fuel mixture in the combustion chamber. This causes a second flame front that collides with the first flame front, causing a knock noise. Also called detonation or spark knock.

Pitch The pitch of a threaded fastener refers to the number of threads per inch.

PIV Peak inverse voltage. A rating for a diode.

PNP transistor A type of transistor that used N-type material for the base and P-type material for the emitter and collector.

Polarity The condition of being positive or negative in relation to a magnetic pole.

Pole The point where magnetic lines of force enter or leave a magnet.

Pole shoes The metal part of the field coils in a starter motor.

Potentiometer A three-terminal variable resistor that varies the voltage drop in a circuit.

Porous lead Lead with many small holes to make a surface porous for use in battery negative plates; the chemical symbol for lead is Pb.

Power assist mode A phase of hybrid vehicle operation in which the ICE is assisted by the electric motor(s) to propel the vehicle.

Power source In electrical terms, the battery or generator (alternator).

Powertrain control module The on-board computer that controls both the engine management and transmission functions of the vehicle.

PPE Personal protective equipment, which can include gloves, safety glasses, and other items.

Pressure differential A difference in pressure from one brake circuit to another.

Pretensioners An explosive device used to remove the slack from a safety belt when an airbag is deployed.

Prevailing torque nut A special design of nut fastener that is deformed slightly or has other properties that permit the nut to remain attached to the fastener without loosening.

Primary wire Wire used for low voltage automotive circuits, typically 12 volts.

Programmable controller interface A type of network communications protocol used in Chrysler brand vehicles.

PROM Programmable read-only memory.

PRV See PIV.

P-type material Silicon or germanium doped with boron or indium.

Pull-in winding One of two electromagnetic windings inside a solenoid used to move a movable core.

Pulse train A DC voltage that turns on and off in a series of pulses.

Pulse width The amount of "on" time of an electronic fuel injector.

Pulse wipers Windshield wipers that operate intermittently. Also called delay wipers.

PVV A valve located in the fuel tank to prevent overpressure due to the thermal expansion of the fuel.

PWM Pulse-width modulation. The control of a device by varying the on-time of the current flowing through the device.

Radio choke A small coil of wire installed in the power lead, leading to a pulsing unit such as an IVR to prevent radio interference.

Radio frequency A high-frequency type of EMI that is in the radio frequency band.

RAM Random access memory.

Range The distance a vehicle can travel on a full charge or full-fuel tank without recharging or refueling. Range is measured in miles or kilometers.

RCRA Resource Conservation and Recovery Act.

Recall A notification to the owner of a vehicle that a safety issue needs to be corrected.

Rectifier bridge A group of six diodes, three positive (+) and three negative (−), commonly used in alternators.

Relay An electromagnetic switch that uses a movable arm.

Reluctance The resistance to the movement of magnetic lines of force.

Reserve capacity The number of minutes a battery can produce 25 A and still maintain a battery voltage of 1.75 V per cell (10.5 V for a 12 V battery).

Residual magnetism Magnetism remaining after the magnetizing force is removed.

Resistance The opposition to current flow measured in ohms.

Reverse bias Current flow in the opposite direction from normal.

Rheostat A two-terminal variable resistor.

Right-to-know laws Laws that state that employees have a right to know when the materials they use at work are hazardous.

Ripple voltage Excessive AC voltage produced by a generator (alternator), usually caused by a defective diode.

RMS Root-mean-square.

ROM Read-only memory.

Rosin-core solder A type of solder for use in electrical repairs. Inside the center of the solder is a rosin that acts as a flux to clean and help the solder flow.

Rotor The rotating part of a generator where the magnetic field is created.

RVS Remote vehicle start. A General Motors term for the system that allows the driver to start the engine using a remote control.

SAE Society of Automotive Engineers.

SAI Secondary air injection.

Saturation The point of maximum magnetic field strength of a coil.

Sediment chamber A space below the cell plates of some batteries to permit the accumulation of sediment deposits flaking from the battery plates. A sediment chamber keeps the sediment from shorting the battery plates.

Self-induction The generation of an electric current in the wires of a coil created when the current is first connected or disconnected.

Semiconductor A material that is neither a conductor nor an insulator; it has exactly four electrons in the atom's outer shell.

Serial communication interface A type of serial data transmission used by Chrysler.

Serial data Data that is transmitted by a series of rapidly changing voltage signals.

Series circuit An electrical circuit that provides only one path for current to flow.

Series circuit laws Laws that were developed by Kirchhoff which pertain to series circuits.

Series-parallel circuits Any type of circuit containing resistances in both series and parallel in one circuit.

Series-parallel hybrid A hybrid vehicle design that can operate as a series hybrid, a parallel hybrid, or both series and parallel at the same time.

Series-wound field A typical starter motor circuit where the current through the field windings is connected in series with the armature before going to ground. Also called a series-wound starter.

SFI A fuel injection system in which injectors are pulsed individually in sequence with the firing order.

SHED Sealed housing for evaporative determination test.

Shims A thin metal spacer.

Short circuit A circuit in which current flows, but bypasses some or all the resistance in the circuit. A connection that results in a "copper-to-copper" connection.

Short to ground A short circuit in which the current bypasses some or all the resistance of the circuit and flows to ground. Because ground is usually steel in automotive electricity, a short to ground (grounded) is a "copper-to-steel" connection.

Short to voltage A circuit in which current flows, but bypasses some or all the resistance in the circuit. A connection that results in a "copper-to-copper" connection.

Shunt A device used to divert or bypass part of the current from the main circuit.

Silicon A semiconductor material.

SIP State implementation plan.

SIR Supplemental inflatable restraints. Another term for airbags.

SLA Abbreviation for short/long arm suspension.

SLI The battery that is responsible for starting, charging, and lighting in a vehicle's electrical system.

Slip-ring-end (SRE) housing The end of a generator (alternator) that has the brushes and the slip rings.

Socket A tool that fits over the head of a bolt or nut and is rotated by a ratchet or breaker bar.

Socket adapter An adapter that allows the use of one size of driver (ratchet or breaker bar) to rotate another drive size of socket.

Solvent Usually colorless liquids that are used to remove grease and oil.

Spark knock Secondary rapid burning of the last 3% to 5% of the air–fuel mixture in the combustion chamber. Causes a second flame front that collides with the first flame front, causing a knock noise.

SPDT Single pole, double throw. A type of electrical switch.

Speakers A device consisting of a magnet, coil of wire, and a cone which reproduces sounds from the electrical signals sent to the speakers from a radio or amplifier.

Specific energy The energy content of a battery relative to the mass of the battery. Specific energy is measured in Watt-hours per kilogram (Wh/kg).

Specific gravity The ratio of the weight of a given volume of a liquid divided by the weight of an equal volume of water.

Spike protection resistor A resistor, usually between 300 and 500 ohms, that is connected in a circuit in parallel with the load. It helps reduce a voltage spike caused when a current following through a coil is turned off.

Splice pack A central point where many serial data lines jam together, often abbreviated SP.

Sponge lead Lead with many small holes used to make a surface porous or sponge-like for use in battery negative plates; the chemical symbol for lead is Pb.

Spontaneous combustion A condition that can cause some materials, such as oily rags, to catch fire without a source of ignition.

SPOUT Spark output.

SPST Single pole, single throw. A type of electrical switch.

Squib The heating element of an inflator module; it starts the chemical reaction to create the gas which inflates an airbag.

SRS Supplemental restraint system. Another term for an airbag system.

SST Special service tools.

Standard corporate protocol A type of serial data transmission used by Ford.

STAR Self-test automatic readout.

Starter drive A term used to describe the starter motor drive pinion gear with overrunning clutch.

Starter solenoid A type of starter motor that uses a solenoid to activate the starter drive.

State of health A signal sent by modules to all of the other modules in the network indicating that it is well and able to transmit.

Static electricity An electrical charge that builds up in insulators and then discharges to conductors.

Stator A name for three interconnected windings inside an alternator. A rotating rotor provides a moving magnetic field and induces a current in the windings of the stator.

Stiffening capacitor See powerline capacitor.

Stud A short rod with threads on both ends.

Subwoofer A type of speaker that is used to reproduce low frequency sounds.

Suppression diode A diode installed in the reverse bias direction. It is used to reduce the voltage spike created when a circuit that contains a coil is opened and the coil discharges.

SVR Sealed valve-regulated. A term used to describe a type of battery that is valve regulated lead acid or sealed lead acid.

SWCAN An abbreviation for single wire CAN (controller area network).

TBI Throttle-body injection.

Tensile strength The maximum stress used under tension (lengthwise force) without causing failure.

Terminal The metal end of a wire which fits into a plastic connector and is the electrical connection part of a junction.

Terminating resistors Resistors placed at the end of a high-speed serial data circuit to help reduce electromagnetic interference.

Test light A light used to test for voltage. Contains a light bulb with a ground wire at one end and a pointed tip at the other end.

TFT Transmission fluid temperature.

THD Total harmonic distortion. A rating for an amplifier used in a sound system.

Thermistor A resistor that changes resistance with temperature. A positive-coefficient thermistor has increased resistance with an increase in temperature. A negative coefficient thermistor has decreased resistance with an increase in temperature.

Thermocouple Two dissimilar metals that, when connected and heated, create a voltage. Used for measuring temperature.

Thermoelectricity The production of current flow created by heating the connection of two dissimilar metals.

Threshold voltage Another name for barrier voltage or the voltage difference needed to forward bias a diode.

Through bolts The bolts used to hold the parts of a starter motor together. The long bolts go through field housing and into the drive-end housing.

Throws The term used to describe the number of output circuits in a switch.

TID Test identification.

Time base The setting of the amount of time per division when adjusting a scope.

Tone generator tester A type of tester used to find a shorted circuit that uses a tone generator. Headphones are used along with a probe to locate where the tone stops, which indicates where in the circuit the fault is located.

Total circuit resistance The total resistance in a circuit.

TP Throttle position.

Transistor A semiconductor device that can operate as an amplifier or an electrical switch.

Trigger level The voltage level that a waveform must reach to start display.

Trigger slope The voltage direction that a waveform must have to start display. A positive slope requires the voltage to be increasing as it crosses the trigger level; a negative slope requires the voltage to be decreasing.

TSB Technical service bulletin.

Turns ratio The ratio between the number of turns used in the primary winding of the coil to the number of turns used in the secondary winding. In a typical ignition coil the ratio is 100:1.

TWC Three-way catalytic converter.

Tweeter A type of speaker used in an audio system that is designed to transmit high-frequency sounds.

Twisted pair A pair of wires that are twisted together from 9 to 16 turns per foot of length. Most are twisted once every inch (12 per foot) to help reduce electromagnetic inference from being induced in the wires as one wire would tend to cancel out any interference pickup up by the other wire.

UART Universal asynchronous receive/transmit, a type of serial data transmission.

UBP UART-based protocol.

Ultracapacitor A specialized capacitor technology with increased storage capacity for a given volume.

UNC Unified national coarse.

UNF Unified national fine.

Universal joint A joint in a steering or drive shaft that allows torque to be transmitted at an angle.

Used oil Any petroleum-based or synthetic oil that has been used.

UST Underground storage tank.

Vacuum Any pressure less than atmospheric pressure (14.7 PSI).

VAF Vane airflow sensor.

Valence ring The outermost ring or orbit of electrons around a nucleus of an atom.

Vapor lock A lean condition caused by vaporized fuel in the fuel system.

VATS Vehicle antitheft system. A system used on some General Motors vehicles.

VECI Vehicle emission control information. This sticker is located under the hood on all vehicles and includes emission-related information that is important to the service technician.

VIN Vehicle identification number.

VOC Volatile organic compounds. These compounds include gases emitted from paints, solvents, glass, and many other products.

Voice recognition A system which uses a microphone and a speaker connected to an electronic module which can control the operation of electronic devices in a vehicle.

Voltage drop Voltage loss across a wire, connector, or any other conductor. Voltage drop equals resistance in ohms times current in amperes (Ohm's law).

Voltmeter An electrical test instrument used to measure volts (unit of electrical pressure). A voltmeter is connected in parallel with the unit or circuit being tested.

VRLA Valve-regulated lead-acid battery. A sealed battery that is both spillproof and leakproof. AGM and gelled electrolyte are both examples of VRLA batteries.

Watt An electrical unit of power; 1 watt equals current (amperes) voltage (1/746 hp). Named after James Watt, a Scottish inventor.

Watt's law The formula for Watts is the voltage times the amperes in the circuit, which represents the electrical power in the circuit.

Wheel motors An electric motor that is mounted directly on the vehicle's wheel, eliminating the connecting drive shaft.

WHMIS Workplace hazardous materials information systems.

Wide-band oxygen sensor An oxygen sensor design that is capable of detecting actual air–fuel ratios. This is in contrast to a conventional oxygen sensor that only changes voltage when a stoichiometric air–fuel ratio has been achieved.

Wind farms An area of land that is populated with wind-generating plants.

Wiring schematic A drawing showing the wires and the components in a circuit using symbols to represent the components.

Wrench A hand tool used to grasp and rotate a threaded fastener.

Zener diode A specially constructed (heavily doped) diode designed to operate with a reverse-bias current after a certain voltage has been reached. Named for Clarence Melvin Zener.

INDEX